For Reference

Not to be taken from this room

The College Blue Book®

35th Edition

Distance Learning Programs

The College Blue Book®

35th Edition

Distance Learning Programs

MACMILLAN REFERENCE USA
An imprint of Thomson Gale, a part of The Thomson Corporation

THOMSON
★
GALE

Detroit • New York • San Francisco • New Haven, Conn. • Waterville, Maine • London

THOMSON ™
GALE

The College Blue Book, 35th Edition
Volume 6

Project Editor
Bohdan Romaniuk

Editorial Support Services
Wayne Fong

Imaging and Multimedia
Lezlie Light

Rights and Acquisitions
Vernon English, Sue Rudolph, Sara Teller

Composition and Electronic Prepress
Gary Leach, Evi Seoud

Manufacturing
Rita Wimberley

Product Management
David Forman

ISBN-13:
978-0-02-866013-4 (set)
978-0-02-866019-6 (vol. 6)

ISBN-10:
0-02-866013-7 (set)
0-02-866019-6 (vol. 6)

ISSN 1556-0570

This book is also available as an e-book
ISBN 13: 978-0-02-866113-1 (set)   ISBN 10: 0-02-866113-3 (set)
Contact your Thomson Gale sales representative for ordering information.

Printed in the United States of America
10 9 8 7 6 5 4 3 2 1

TABLE OF CONTENTS

HOW TO USE THIS GUIDE

INSTITUTION PROFILES AND SPECIAL MESSAGES

Here, in alphabetical order, you'll find more than 800 institutions offering postsecondary education at a distance. Each profile covers such items as accreditation information, availability of financial aid, degrees and awards offered, course subject areas offered outside of degree programs, and the person or office to contact for program information. In addition, there are **Special Messages** from institutions about new programs or special events.

For each institution, specific degrees and award programs are listed, followed by a list of subjects for which individual courses (undergraduate, graduate, and non-credit) are offered.

INSTITUTIONAL INFORMATION

The sections here describe overall characteristics of an institution and its distance learning offerings, featuring key facts and figures about the institutions, including:

- institution Web site,
- background information on the institution,
- the type of accreditation held by the institution,
- when distance learning courses were first offered at the institution,
- the number of students enrolled in distance learning courses in fall 2006,
- the availability of financial aid,
- services available to distance learners, and
- the person or office to contact for more information about the institution's distance learning courses.

DEGREES AND AWARDS

This part of the profile lists each program leading to a degree or certificate that can be completed entirely at a distance. Programs are grouped by the level of award: associate degrees, baccalaureate degrees, graduate degrees, undergraduate certificates, and graduate certificates.

COURSE SUBJECT AREAS OFFERED OUTSIDE OF DEGREE PROGRAMS

Listed here are the general subject areas in which the institution offers courses at a distance. Subjects are divided into those offered for undergraduate credit and for graduate credit and those that are non-credit. Note that this is not a listing of course titles; you will need to contact the institution for a detailed list of courses offered.

IN-DEPTH DESCRIPTIONS OF DISTANCE LEARNING PROGRAMS

Additional details on distance learning offerings are provided by participating institutions and consortia. Each two-page entry provides details on delivery media, programs of study, special programs, credit options, faculty, students, admission, tuition and fees, financial aid, and applying.

An institution's absence from this section does not constitute an editorial decision on the part of Peterson's. Rather, this section is an open forum for institutions to expand upon information provided in the **Institution Profiles and Special Messages** section of the book. The descriptions are arranged alphabetically by institution name.

IN-DEPTH DESCRIPTIONS OF DISTANCE LEARNING CONSORTIA

The organizations listed in this section represent consortia of institutions offering distance learning programs. Each consortium has been formed so that an expanded set of distance learning options can be offered beyond the resources available through any single member institution. These consortia do not have a central application process and/or do not directly award credits and degrees. Applications are processed, and credits and conferred degrees are awarded, through one of the member institutions. Further, consortia generally are not directly granted accreditations; rather, credits and degrees reflect the accreditation of the awarding institution. The reader should obtain specific information directly from the consortium.

APPENDIX

The **Appendix** lists resources that can give you more information on subjects presented in previous sections of this guide.

GLOSSARY

With the **Glossary**, you'll be able to learn all the pertinent terms from A to Z.

INDEXES

If you are interested in locating a certificate or degree program in a specific field of study, refer to the index of **Institutions Offering Degree and Certificate Programs.** Here you'll find institutions offering everything from accounting to theological and ministerial studies.

If it is individual courses you're looking for, the index of **Non-Degree-Related Course Subject Areas** will guide you to institutions offering credit and noncredit courses at either the undergraduate or graduate level.

The **Geographical Listing of Distance Learning Programs** lets you find programs that are offered by institutions that are located near you. Keep in mind that most institutions' offerings are available nationally, and sometimes internationally. See individual listings for details.

DATA COLLECTION PROCEDURES

The information provided in these profiles was collected during the summer of 2007 by way of a survey posted online for colleges and universities. With minor exceptions, all data included in this edition have been submitted by officials at the schools themselves. In addition, many of the institutions that submitted data were contacted directly by the Peterson's research staff to verify unusual figures, resolve discrepancies, and obtain additional data. All usable information received in time for publication has been included. The omission of any particular item from an index or profile listing signifies that the item is either not applicable to that institution or that data were not available. Although Peterson's has every reason to believe that the information presented in this guide is accurate, students should check with each college or university to verify such figures as tuition and fees, which may have changed since the publication of this guide.

CRITERIA FOR INCLUSION IN THIS BOOK

In the research for this guide, the following definition of distance learning was used: a planned teaching/learning experience in which teacher and students are separated by physical distance and use any of a wide spectrum of media. This definition is based on the one developed by the University of Wisconsin Extension.

The College Blue Book: Distance Learning Programs profiles more than 800 institutions of higher education currently offering courses or entire programs at a distance. To be included, all U.S. institutions must have full accreditation or candidate-for-accreditation (preaccreditation) status granted by an institutional or specialized accrediting body recognized by the U.S. Department of Education or the Council for Higher Education Accreditation. The six U.S. regional accrediting associations are: the New England Association of Schools and Colleges, Middle States Association of Colleges and Schools, North Central Association of Colleges and Schools, Northwest Commission on Colleges and Universities, Southern Association of Colleges and Schools, and Western Association of Schools and Colleges. Approval by state educational agencies is conferred separately on some distance education courses. Canadian institutions must be chartered and authorized to grant degrees by the provincial government, be affiliated with a chartered institution, or be accredited by a recognized U.S. accrediting body.

WHAT IS DISTANCE LEARNING?

One student is a busy professional who needs to update work-related skills by taking a couple of computer applications courses in his spare time. Another student, a working mother, never finished her bachelor's degree and would love to have that diploma and get a better job. A third student attends a local community college, but what he'd really like is a degree offered by a four-year institution halfway across the country—without moving. Another would-be student is employed full-time in a field in which a master's degree, perhaps even a doctorate, would really give her career a boost. What all these diverse people have in common is an already full life. For them, disrupting family and work by commuting to sometimes distant on-campus classes on a rigid schedule is simply not a workable option. Instead, students like these are turning to distance learning in order to pursue their educational goals. For many people, and perhaps you, distance learning is a blessing—it means you can get the education you need, which might otherwise be difficult or impossible to obtain in the traditional manner.

What, exactly, is distance learning (also called distance education)? Broadly defined, distance learning is the delivery of educational programs to students who are off site. In a distance learning course, the instructor is not in the same place as the student; the students may be widely separated by geography and time; and the instructor and students communicate with each other using various means, from the U.S. mail to the Internet. Students that take a distance education course are called distance learners, whether they live 300 miles from the university or right across the street.

Distance learning makes use of many technologies, and courses are structured in many different ways. Adding to the variety of distance learning programs provided by traditional institutions of higher education are programs offered by new types of institutions, many worthy, others known as diploma mills, that help to fuel the growth in distance education. With so many technologies, courses, programs, and institutions involved in distance education, your distance learning options can be confusing at first. However, it's critical that you understand what distance education involves and which institutions offer a solid education *before* you enroll. That way you'll be sure that you spend your effort, time, and money wisely on a reputable education.

In this section, we'll give you an overview of distance learning; in "Is Distance Learning Right for You?", we'll help you determine whether or not distance education is right for you; and then in later sections we'll give you enough background and guidance so you can make an informed choice when selecting a program. We'll also provide suggestions for handling the application process, paying for your education, and making the most of your distance learning experience.

A BRIEF HISTORY OF DISTANCE EDUCATION

In the last five to ten years, distance education has mushroomed, so it's easy to think of it as a completely recent phenomenon. However, today's distance education, based primarily on video and Internet technologies, has its roots in the correspondence courses that arose in the late 1800s. Instructors would send print materials to students by mail, and students would do their assignments and return them by mail. Correspondence courses were asynchronous; that is, the student was not tied to the instructor's timetable. He or she would do the work when it was convenient. Correspondence courses still exist, mostly for single courses, but they have lost ground over the last seventy years to more modern technologies. The first generation of technology that began to supplant correspondence courses was radio in the 1930s, followed by broadcast television in the 1950s and 1960s. Radio and television courses provided one-way communication, and so they were most suitable for delivering information from the faculty to the students. Typically, there was only minimal interaction between instructor and students, and no interaction at all among students. Another constraint on radio and television courses was time. Broadcast courses are synchronous; students had to be listening to the radio or watching television when the course was broadcast, or they would miss the class.

By about 1960, the advent of cable television, audiocassette recorders, and videocassette recorders solved the time problem posed by the earlier broadcast courses. Courses could be broadcast over cable channels several times so students could watch at their convenience. With a VCR or tape recorder, a student could record a lecture or class session when it was broadcast and view or hear it at any time. In fact, recorders made broadcasting unnecessary. The content of a course could be recorded on an audiocassette or videotape and sent to students, who could listen or view it when they had time. Although recording technology provided convenience for students, because courses are asynchronous, it did not solve the major drawback of broadcast courses—the lack of interaction among faculty members and students.

Beginning in the 1980s, the personal computer, two-way audio and videoconferencing, and the Internet greatly expanded the scope of distance education. With these new technologies, much more information could be conveyed from the faculty to students. More important, two-way communication became possible, using interactive video technology or e-mail, newsgroups, bulletin boards, and chat rooms on the Internet. Today, distance education makes use of a wide range of technologies.

INSTRUCTIONAL TECHNOLOGIES IN DISTANCE LEARNING

Today's distance learning courses can be divided into several main categories according to the primary technologies they use to deliver instruction: print-based courses, audio-based courses, video-based courses, and Internet-based courses. The audio, video, and Internet courses all have variations that are synchronous—classes take place at specific times only—and asynchronous—classes that occur at flexible times that may be more convenient for the student.

PRINT-BASED COURSES

Correspondence courses use print materials as the medium of instruction. Students receive the materials by mail at the start of the course and return completed assignments by mail. Sometimes fax machines are used to speed up the delivery of assignments, and the telephone can be used if communication between instructor and student is necessary. Patti Iversen, who lives in Montana, completed part of her Bachelor of Science in Nursing degree from the University of Mary in North Dakota by correspondence course. "The correspondence courses offered no direct contact with the instructor or other students," she recalls. "I purchased a syllabus and book and was otherwise on my own." In addition to the lack of interaction between instructor and students, correspondence courses have the disadvantage of being slow. The low-tech nature of a print-based course means lots of delay between assignments and feedback. Of course, the low-tech nature of the course is an advantage, too. Students don't have to invest in expensive technology and can do their work anywhere. Even though print materials continue to play a very important role in distance learning, they are now usually supplemented by more modern instructional technologies.

AUDIO-BASED COURSES

Audio-based courses may involve two-way communication, as in audio or phone conferencing; or they may involve one-way communication, including radio broadcast and prerecorded audiotapes sent to students. Fritz J. Messere, associate professor and coordinator of broadcasting at the State University of New York at Oswego, recalls the first time, in 1981, he was involved in teaching a course that used phone conferencing. Once a week, faculty members and students from ten universities as well as representatives from the Federal Communications Commission "met" for a class. "The first three weeks were chaotic," recalls Messere. "We didn't know who was talking." However, they worked out a plan in which a different faculty member moderated the session each week by asking questions. At midsession there was a break, followed by a round-robin discussion, in which each site participated in a predetermined sequence.

According to the National Center for Education Statistics of the U.S. Department of Education, audio-based technologies are not widely used today, with only about 12 percent of institutions of higher learning reporting their use as the primary means of delivering a course. Instead, audio technologies may be used to supplement the main technology used in the course. For example, in an Internet-based distance education course, students and professors may call one another periodically.

VIDEO-BASED COURSES

Video-based technologies include two-way interactive video conferencing, one-way video with two-way audio, one-way live video, and one-way prerecorded videotapes provided to students. Of these, two-way interactive video and prerecorded videotapes are the most popular. Of the institutions of higher learning surveyed by the U.S. Department of Education, 54 percent used two-way interactive video and 47 percent used prerecorded videotapes as the primary mode of instructional delivery in their distance education courses.

Two-Way Interactive Video

A course taught by means of two-way interactive video takes place simultaneously in two or more sites. The instructor is located in the home site with a group of students, and other students are located in satellite sites, often with a facilitator to help out. Each site has TV monitors or large screens on which the instructor and students can be viewed. One student in a biology of horticulture course at the University of Cincinnati described the technology used in her course: "Both [home and satellite] classrooms are set up with cameras and two video screens each, which show what is going on in both classrooms. There is a technical assistant present in each location, one on the main campus to set things up and work with the camera, etc., and another in the remote location to set equipment up and to adjust settings should there be any problems." The course itself was conducted as a lecture: "For the most part, the instructor lectures, with students occasionally asking or answering questions. When any student speaks in class, they press a button on a little apparatus on the desk in front of them, which makes the camera point to them as they speak and allows their voice to be transmitted to the other location." Quizzes and exams are faxed to the satellite site and faxed back or mailed by an assistant when they are completed. Like the best classroom teaching, two-way interactive video works well when the instructor is comfortable with "performing" on camera. "You have to keep students at all sites involved with you by making the lecture as entertaining as possible," says Dr. Larry Anthony, coordinator of the addiction studies baccalaureate program based at the University of Cincinnati. "I've had to adapt my teaching to the medium. For example, instead of using overheads as I might in a regular classroom, I'm more inclined to use a series of PowerPoint slides because they're more entertaining."

Two-way interactive video bridges geographical distances but not time. Students must be in a particular place at a particular time to take the course.

Prerecorded Video

A far less sophisticated, though almost as popular, means of instruction is prerecorded videotape. Each course session is videotaped and mailed to off-site students. To supplement this, the course may have a Web site where notes and assignments are posted, or these may be mailed to the off-site students along with the tapes. If students have any questions, they can call or e-mail the instructor after they view the tape. For many students, the lack of interactivity is made up for by the benefit of "attending" class at their own convenience. Nicole DeRaleau, who is studying for a Master of Engineering degree at Worcester Polytechnic Institute in Massachusetts, says, "Watching the videotaped class is really not very different from sitting in class, except that I can't raise my hand and ask questions." On the other hand, she points out that the asynchronous nature of prerecorded video is an advantage: "I can watch half a class at one sitting, and the other half at a later time. I often work late, and I don't have to worry about missing class."

The time and place dimensions of various distance learning instructional technologies.

	Specific place	Any place
Any time (asynchronous)		◆ Online courses (newsgroups, bulletin boards, websites, e-mail) ◆ CD ROMs, DVDs ◆ Videotapes ◆ Audiotapes ◆ Correspondence courses
Specific time (synchronous)	◆ Two-way interactive videoconferencing ◆ Two-way interactive audioconferencing ◆ Traditional on-campus classes	◆ Online course (interactive computer conferencing, chat rooms, MUDs, MOOs) ◆ Radio broadcasts ◆ TV broadcasts, satellite, and cable

INTERNET-BASED COURSES

Today many distance learning courses, called online courses or e-learning, are offered over the Internet. Some online courses use synchronous, "real-time" instruction based primarily on interactive computer conferencing or chat rooms. However, most Internet-based courses use asynchronous instruction, making use of online course management systems, Web sites, e-mail, electronic mailing lists, newsgroups, bulletin boards, and messaging programs.

In asynchronous online courses, instructors post instructional material and assignments, including text, images, video, audio, and even interactive simulations, on the course Web site. Using messaging systems, newsgroups, or bulletin boards, they can start online discussions by posting a comment or question; students can log on using a password and join the discussion at their convenience. In some courses there may be periodic "real-time" interaction in chat rooms or interactive environments like MUDS (multiple-user dungeons) and MOOs (multiple-object orientations). Feedback and guidance to individual students can be done by e-mail or telephone. Note that most of the interaction in an online course is text-based; instructors and students communicate primarily through the keyboarded word. Joanne Simon, who is earning a Master of Business Administration degree from the University of Phoenix Online, describes the setup of her courses: "We use newsgroup folders—the main classroom, a chat room, a course material folder, an assignment folder, and four study group folders. We post a minimum of three messages per day to the main folder in which that week's readings are discussed. In those messages we encourage other students to share ideas, experiences, and opinions on various topics . . . ." Besides this seminar-style interaction, there are many assignments, according to Simon. "We also submit weekly summaries, one graded group assignment, and two personal assignments weekly." Needless to say, students must have a computer with the appropriate software and Internet access in order to take an Internet-based course. The cost of technology aside, online distance learning programs have considerable advantages. Because the course material stays on line for a period of time, students can log on at their own convenience. "There are time stamps on everything they submit," says Michael S. Ameigh, Assistant Provost for Distance Learning and Information Resources and Associate Professor of Communication Studies at the State University of New York at Oswego. "I can see that students are often working in the middle of the night." This flexibility is one of the main attractions of online courses for students, but it can also be its main disadvantage. "It's a common misperception that online courses can be dropped into and out of," says Claudine SchWeber, Assistant Vice President for Distance Education and Lifelong Learning at the University of Maryland University College. Without class sessions to attend at scheduled times, the impetus to log on and do course work must come from within, which requires a great deal of self-discipline.

To help ensure that students keep up, many instructors structure the learning environment by setting weekly deadlines for reading lectures and completing assignments, requiring group projects, and making participation in online discussions mandatory. "I personally contact students who do not participate," says Fritz Messere, who has been teaching broadcasting and business courses online for several years. "Students must interact with me in order to pass the course." At the University of Phoenix Online, students are required to log on to a course and post messages five days out of seven as one of the requirements for passing. In online courses with participation requirements, the amount of interaction between the faculty and students is far greater than in a large lecture class held on campus. There's no lying low in the back of the classroom in a well-run online course.

MIXING THE TECHNOLOGIES

Many courses use a combination of technologies as well as print materials. For example, at Southwest Texas State University, a course in geography for elementary and high school teachers begins with a videoconference, with the instructor introducing himself or herself and outlining the course requirements. A printed study guide with all assigned readings and activities is distributed to all participants at the first session. Teachers who cannot get to a videoconferencing site are sent a videocassette of the first session along with the study guide. After the first session, the course moves on line. Using chat rooms, threaded discussions, and e-mail, participants do their assignments and group projects and interact on line. Assignments are snail-mailed to the faculty member. Finally, the class concludes with another synchronous videoconference or recorded videotape.

This course may be unusual in that it combines two of the major distance learning technologies, but it is not unusual to find courses that use one of the major technologies and supplement it with another. For example, e-mail is used for individual student-instructor communication in most courses, even if the course is conducted by two-way interactive videotape or prerecorded video.

FUTURE TRENDS

Today, online instruction, two-way interactive video, and one-way prerecorded video are the most popular instructional technologies in distance education. According to the Department of Education's National Center for Education Statistics, colleges and universities are planning to increase their use of Internet-based instruction and two-way interactive video. Prerecorded video is likely to decrease in popularity. The explosive growth in distance learning in the last five years has come primarily from online courses, and that is likely to continue. With better databases and other sources of information continuing to appear on the Internet, ease of access to reliable data will increase. As high bandwidth connections to the Internet start to replace phone connections, the capacity to quickly transmit large amounts of data will increase dramatically. For example, with a high-speed modem and phone connection, it can take several minutes to download a video snippet. Thus, most online courses today use text, images, and perhaps some animation, but they are limited in their video capabilities. Eventually, high bandwidth technologies will make individualized, customized, and live video interactions possible, with lengthy video programming available. Online distance learning is also causing a shift to a more collaborative learning model. "Because of the nature of online resources and communication, the faculty is no longer the one authoritative voice," explains Claudine SchWeber of the University of Maryland University College. An undergraduate there agrees. "Students learn from each other as well as from the instructor and course materials," she commented. "Instructors who are comfortable with online technology . . . create a classroom environment that is interactive, inviting, stimulating, motivating, and lively." Another interesting trend to note is the incorporation of the new instructional technologies in conventional, classroom-based courses. "What we are finding is that our distance technology is having an impact on the way we teach on-campus courses to undergraduate and graduate students," comments McRae C. Banks, head of the department of management and professor of entrepreneurship at Worcester Polytechnic Institute in Massachusetts. "As one

example, some faculty members have students take online quizzes before each class period . . . . Before the professor goes into class, he or she knows what areas the students understand and what areas are troubling them. Now more time can be spent where the students are having difficulty." Other professors hold office hours or help sessions in chat rooms when they are at home or out of town at conferences. Still others require students to respond to each class lecture by posting a comment to a discussion group. "For us, the bottom line is finding ways to enhance the educational experience for students," says Banks.

WHAT CAN YOU LEARN VIA DISTANCE EDUCATION?

The short answer is almost anything. You can take a single course in almost any field, or earn a certificate or degree in many fields, by distance education. Next, we'll give you an overview of what's available, and in "What Can You Study via Distance Learning" we'll discuss these programs in more detail.

COURSE OFFERINGS

According to the National Center for Education Statistics, an estimated 54,470 different distance education courses were offered in academic year 1997–1998, the last year for which reliable figures are available. That number has undoubtedly increased considerably since then. As you can see in Figure 1-1, most of these courses were college-level, credit-granting courses at the undergraduate level, and about one quarter were at the graduate/first professional level. Fewer than one tenth were noncredit-granting courses.

According to Figure 1-2, of the courses offered, the greatest number can be found in fields that are part of a general undergraduate education, such as English, humanities, and the social and behavioral sciences; physical and life sciences; and mathematics. However, in the fields of education, engineering, and library and information sciences, more courses are offered at the graduate/first-professional level than at the undergraduate level. According to the Department of Education, there are three likely reasons for this: the emphasis on graduate education in these fields, the suitability of course content for distance education, and the likelihood that groups of students would be located in particular places, such as a school district or engineering firm, to receive broadcast or interactive video courses.

DEGREE AND CERTIFICATE PROGRAMS

Many institutions of higher learning simply offer a smorgasbord of distance education courses that can be taken for credit. An increasing number of institutions, however, have taken distance education to the next step; they have begun to offer undergraduate and graduate certificate and degree programs that can be completed entirely by distance education. For example, a student with an associate's degree from a local community college can go on to earn a baccalaureate degree from a four-year institution by distance learning, without relocating. Or a working professional can earn a master's degree or professional certificate on a part-time basis through distance learning. According to the National Center on Education Statistics, in 1997–1998, there were an estimated 1,230 degree programs available through distance learning.

**Figure 1–1: Distance Education Course Offerings
in 1997–1998 (by level)**

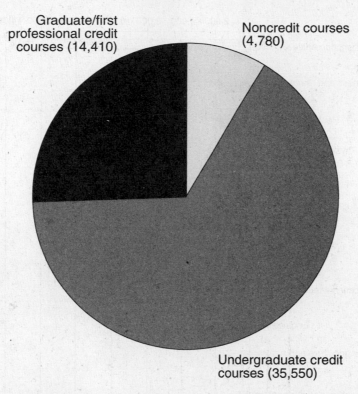

Graduate/first
professional credit
courses (14,410)

Noncredit courses
(4,780)

Undergraduate credit
courses (35,550)

Source: Data from U.S. Department of Education, National Center for Education
Statistics, Postsecondary Education Quick Information System, *Survey on
Distance Education at Postsecondary Education Institutions*, 1998-1999,
p. 19.

Peterson's *Guide to Distance Learning Programs 2003* lists about 3,000 degree and certificate programs, so you can see there was a phenomenal increase within a few years. Unlike individual course offerings, degree and certificate programs are more likely to be offered at the graduate and first-professional level than at the undergraduate level, as you can see in Figure 1-3. Most degree and certificate programs are in the fields of liberal/general studies, business and management, health professions, education, and engineering.

WHO OFFERS DISTANCE LEARNING?

The better question might be, "Who doesn't?" With lifelong learning becoming commonplace and communications technologies improving rapidly, the demand for distance education has grown dramatically, and with it the number and variety of providers. The first group of providers consists of the traditional colleges, universities, graduate schools, community colleges, technical schools, and vocational schools. These providers range from schools only their neighbors have heard of to household names like Stanford, Virginia Tech, and the University of California, to name just a few. The challenges posed by distance education have forced colleges and universities to be creative in their approaches. Some schools have formed partnerships with cable companies, public broadcasting services, satellite broadcasters, and online education companies to deliver high-quality

distance education. Colleges and universities also partner with corporations to deliver courses and degree programs to employees. For example, the University of Cincinnati's College of Pharmacy offers courses and a master's degree program via distance learning to employees of Procter & Gamble Pharmaceuticals Norwich, New York, location as well as other P&G sites.

Many schools have formed consortia, or collaborative groups, within a state or region or even internationally, which enables students to take courses as needed from all the participating institutions. An example of a consortium is the University of Texas (UT) TeleCampus, which does not confer degrees but supports the participating University of Texas campuses, which do award degrees.

A few colleges and universities are virtual, meaning they don't have a campus. These schools offer most or all of their instruction by means of distance education, providing complete degree programs. The University of Phoenix Online and Walden University are two well-known examples.

Finally, there are many online purveyors of noncredit distance education courses on subjects that range from candlemaking and beauty secrets to C++ programming and Spanish. These courses may be fun and even instructive, but they won't contribute to your formal educational credentials.

We'll discuss the providers of distance education more fully in "Who Offers Distance Education?"

Figure 1–2: Distance Education Course Offerings by Field of Study, 1997–1998

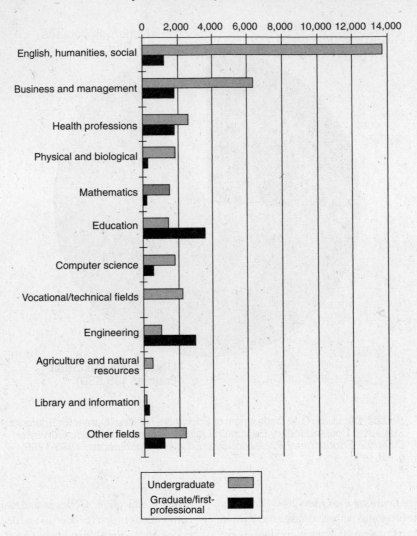

Source: Data from U.S. Department of Education, National Center for Education Statistics, Postsecondary Education Quick Information System, *Survey on Distance Education at Postsecondary Education Institutions*, 1998-1999, p. 25.

HOW EFFECTIVE IS DISTANCE LEARNING?

There is a great deal of interest in the effectiveness of distance learning. Research into this subject is largely anecdotal and much of it is out-of-date, given the rapid development of instructional technology in the last few years. However, Thomas L. Russell, in a widely quoted report entitled *The No Significant Difference Phenomenon*, concluded from a review of 355 research studies and summaries published between 1928 and 1999 that the learning outcomes (test scores and course grades) of distance learning and traditional students are similar. In addition, Russell found that distance learners themselves have positive attitudes toward distance education and are generally satisfied with it. There are a number of questions regarding the effectiveness of distance education that have not yet been answered by the research. For example, how do the different learning styles of students relate to the use of particular technologies? How do individual differences among students affect their ability to learn by distance education? Why do more students drop out of distance education courses than drop out of traditional courses? What types of content are most suitable for distance learning? Common sense suggests that distance education is more effective for some people than for others, the different instructional technologies are more effective with different types of learners, and some subjects are more suitable for distance education than other subjects.

Some educators are not fans of distance education, believing that technology, no matter how sophisticated, cannot substitute the face-to-face interactions of a community of teachers and learners. Even proponents of distance learning concede that students who have the time and money for a traditional on-campus education should go for it. "Technology can't provide the intangible experiences of campus life, especially on the undergraduate level," comments Robert V. Steiner, who directs the distance learning project at Columbia University's Teachers College. "However, distance education is extremely helpful for adult learners who need to get their education in a flexible manner."

Barbara Lockee, Virginia Tech's distance learning program developer and an assistant professor of instructional technology,

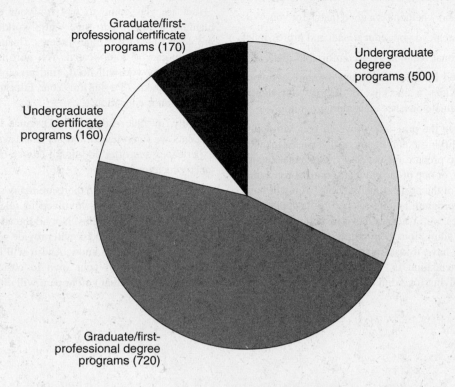

**Figure 1–3: Distance Education Degree
and Certificate Programs, 1997–1998**

Graduate/first-
professional certificate
programs (170)

Undergraduate
degree
programs (500)

Undergraduate
certificate
programs (160)

Graduate/first-
professional degree
programs (720)

Source: Data from U.S. Department of Education, National Center for Education
Statistics, Postsecondary Education Quick Information System, *Survey on
Distance Education at Postsecondary Education Institutions*, 1998-1999,
p. 34.

agrees. "Distance education has the increased potential to reach new audiences that haven't had access to higher education," says Lockee. "Because of the changing needs of our work force, people who are employed need on-going, lifelong education. So new higher-ed participants are in their 30s and beyond, and many probably have their undergraduate degree but need skills to be successful in the information age."

Distance education may have benefits beyond accessibility, flexibility, and convenience. For example, when asked to compare the experiences of teaching a course to a single classroom of students and by two-way interactive video, Larry Anthony indicated that the students in the distance learning course had the richer experience. "We were hearing from people in different parts of the country," he explained. "In addiction studies, there are different cultural issues and problems in different places. In terms of diversity, the distance learning class was great." Kevin Ruthen, who earned a Master of Science degree in information resource management from Syracuse University, also thought that distance education had added to the value of his degree: "The students and professors . . . were all different ages, from many professional fields, and from many regions of the world," he recalls. "I learned a tremendous amount and gained many different perspectives due to this diversity as opposed to what would be, in my opinion, a less diverse class environment in an on-campus class."

PURSUING YOUR EDUCATION BY DISTANCE LEARNING

Still interested in distance learning? Then the next question is: What's involved in finding a reputable distance education program and getting in? A lot. The first, and perhaps the most important part of this process, is a combination of introspection and research. You are going to have to assess yourself and what's out there to find a good match. You'll have to answer questions like: What are my professional goals? What are my interests and abilities? Which courses or certificate or degree programs will help me achieve my goals? Am I prepared for higher education in this field? What must I do to improve my qualifications? Do I have the motivation, personal characteristics, and skills that will enable me to learn at a distance? In "Is Distance Learning Right for You?", we will help you assess the advantages and disadvantages of distance learning as well as your strengths and weaknesses; this will enable you to decide whether or not distance education is for you. Then in "What Can You Study via Distance Learning?", we'll describe the different degree and certificate programs that are available, what's involved in transferring credits, and how you may be able to earn credits for prior learning and life experience. In "Who Offers Distance Education?", we'll describe the various types of distance learning providers. We'll give you suggestions on how to find out more about programs and institutions.

Once you've done your research on distance education programs, on what basis should you evaluate them? In addition to finding out the all-important accreditation status of the programs in which you are interested, you'll have to find out what each program is really like and whether it's a good match for you. Will the program help you achieve your educational and professional goals? Is the instructional technology a comfortable match for you? "Selecting a Good Distance Learning Program" discusses these issues and provides a checklist of factors you should consider when you evaluate distance education programs.

Once you've identified the programs to which you will apply, what standardized qualifying exams, if any, will you need to take? What should you do to prepare for the SAT*, Graduate Record Examinations (GRE®), or one of the graduate admissions examinations used by many of the professional schools? You will have to find out what each program requires as part of its application and what the deadlines are. You may have to write a personal statement so that the admissions committee can evaluate your background. You will have to ask instructors or colleagues to write letters of recommendation. In "Taking Standardized Admissions Tests" and "Applying for Admission to Degree Programs"

we will describe the process in more detail and give you suggestions on how to prepare applications that will gain you admission.

How are you going to pay for your education? If you are planning to attend part-time while working, that may not be a problem. But for full-time students, financing a distance degree program can be complicated. You will have to figure out how much money you will need, find possible sources of aid, and apply for them. "Paying for Your Education" covers financing your distance education.

Finally, in "Succeeding as a Distance Learner," some of the students we interviewed and surveyed will share more of their experiences and offer additional advice on succeeding in a distance education program.

In the pages that follow, there are many suggestions for accomplishing all of the tasks involved in selecting and applying to distance learning programs. Not all the advice will be applicable to everyone. Still, this book will provide you with an overview of what you will need to know. And it will indicate what you will need to find out on your own to ensure that your distance education does all that you hope it will do.

---

*SAT is a registered trademark of the College Board, which was not involved in the production of, and does not endorse, this book.

GRE® is a registered trademark of Educational Testing Service (ETS). This book is not endorsed or approved by ETS.

IS DISTANCE LEARNING RIGHT FOR YOU?

Distance learning can satisfy a wide range of needs for many people in diverse circumstances, but it's not for everyone. Some students don't have the study skills or self-discipline to succeed as a distance learner. Others are interested in a field of study or a degree that is not offered via distance learning. Still, for most people distance learning has the potential to open up new possibilities in higher education. For many adult students, the advantages of distance learning far outweigh the disadvantages. In this section, we'll discuss the pros and cons of distance learning and help you assess whether or not distance learning is right for you.

THE ADVANTAGES OF DISTANCE LEARNING

Distance learning has many benefits. That's why distance-learning programs meet the needs of so many different people of all ages, genders, professions, and educational backgrounds.

As you read the following list of distance learning benefits, ask yourself if any of them provide a way to overcome an obstacle that is standing in your way when you think about going back to school. Do any of these advantages make continuing your education a real possibility right now, rather than a vague goal for sometime in the future?

Here are the benefits of distance learning in general:

- **Distance learning breaks down time barriers.** In most distance learning programs, you don't have to be at a certain place at a certain time. You can learn when it's convenient for you, so you can fit your education into a busy work and home life. You only take as many courses as you can handle at a time, and sometimes you can start whenever you like instead of at the beginning of a semester.

- **Distance learning breaks down geographical barriers.** Whether you are logging on to a course from your own computer at home or traveling a short distance to a satellite classroom, distance education makes your geographical distance from a college or university irrelevant. Students who live in remote areas, who don't have time to commute to a campus, and who travel a lot on business benefit from this aspect of distance education.

- **Distance learning goes at your own pace.** Distance learning is ideal for students who like to set their own pace and who learn best on their own. As you work through course material, you can spend more time on difficult concepts and less time on easier ones. Although you are likely to have weekly or other periodic deadlines, as long as you make them, you can approach the work at a pace that suits your schedule.

- **Distance learning can save money.** Although the tuition and fees for distance learning courses are usually comparable to those charged for on-campus courses, you can save money on child care, gas, parking, and other commuting costs. In addition, you generally don't have to take time off from work to attend class.

- **Distance learning fits individual needs.** You can often tailor a program to fit your particular educational and professional goals and take courses from various institutions if necessary.

- **Distance learning provides freedom of choice.** Since you are not confined to schools within easy commuting distance, you are able to consider distance learning programs at reputable colleges and universities around the country and the world.

- **Distance learning teaches more than just the course material.** Depending on the type of program you take, distance learning can improve your computer, Internet, reading, writing, and oral communication skills, which benefits you no matter what kind of career you pursue.

- **Distance learning broadens your perspective.** Often, your classmates will be from diverse backgrounds and places. You will interact with a more diverse group of people than you would normally find on most campuses.

Refer to Figure 2-1 for the specific advantages of each of the major distance learning instructional technologies.

THE DISADVANTAGES OF DISTANCE LEARNING

Lest you think that distance learning is the solution to all problems of access to education, it does have its drawbacks. Consider whether or not any of the following general disadvantages would cause you to eliminate distance learning from your education plans. For disadvantages specific to a particular instructional technology, refer to Figure 2-1.

- **Distance learning requires a high degree of discipline and self-motivation.** Dropout rates are higher for distance learning programs than for campus-based programs. No doubt, some dropouts are students who did not realize that distance learning requires as much, if not more, time than a traditional on-campus class. For older distance education students, it's easy for work or family needs to take priority over education. Many distance learners drop out because the distance course is the easiest thing to let go of when things get too hectic.

- **Distance learning can be lonely.** Some people need the face-to-face interaction that a traditional classroom provides. Even though instructors may try to overcome social isolation in distance learning courses, for some students there is simply not enough social contact to keep them enthusiastic and motivated.

- **Distance learning can take longer.** Because distance learning is self-motivated, it's easier to give in to other demands on your time and postpone taking courses, increasing the time it takes to complete a degree program.

- **Distance learning students may get poor student services.** On-campus students have convenient access to the library,

**Figure 2-1: Specific Advantages and Disadvantages of the
Major Distance Learning Technologies**

Distance Learning Technology	Advantages	Disadvantages
Online	▲Course work can be done at any time of day or night. ▲Any computer with Internet access can be used. ▲Courses can easily be taken from more than one school. ▲Computer skills are developed. ▲There are no commuting costs.	▼Lots of self-discipline and motivation are needed. ▼A computer with Internet access is needed—a significant cost. ▼Social interaction is on line only.
Two-way interactive videoconferencing	▲There is access to courses at distant campuses. ▲Social interaction is most similar to that of a traditional classroom. ▲There is no cost to the student for technology.	▼Classes are held at particular times and places.
Videotapes of class sessions	▲Course work can be done at any time of day or night. ▲Any TV and VCR can be used. ▲There are no commuting costs.	▼Lots of self-discipline and motivation are needed. ▼Social interaction is minimal. ▼Distance learners are several days behind on-campus class.

academic advisers, job placement services, tutoring, and student centers. Many distance learning programs offer student services such as online library access and registration, but in most schools the services still can't compare to those available to on-campus students.

- **Distance learning students miss the college experience.** College campuses offer a lot more than classes, with cultural and sports activities, dorm life, faculty-student interaction, and the opportunity to form lifelong friendships. Although this is not an important consideration for most older distance learners, younger students that pursue an undergraduate education may find the on-campus experience too valuable to pass up.

- **A traditional college degree is a better choice to meet some future goals.** Although distance learning is becoming more mainstream and is usually accepted by employers, as long as it is from a reputable institution, it is still regarded by some in the traditional academic community as inferior. Thus, a traditional degree may be more valuable if you are considering applying in the future to the more prestigious graduate and professional programs, including law school and medical school.

ASSESSING YOURSELF

With the advantages and disadvantages of distance learning in mind, you should take some time to honestly answer the following questions. Consider your own goals, circumstances, personality, skills, social support, and comfort with technology to determine whether or not you are a good candidate for distance learning.

GOALS

What are your educational and professional goals?

First you must determine your educational and professional goals. Ask yourself what you would like to be doing in five or ten years, and then determine what courses or degree programs will help you achieve your goals. Do you need a course to update your skills, a certificate to provide professional credentials, or a degree to solidify or advance your professional standing?

For example, when Head Start announced that an associate's degree in early childhood education would soon be a requirement for its teachers, Angela Butcher had a problem. Butcher, who teaches at Jackson-Vinton Community Action Head Start in Ohio, just had a high school diploma. "I was so scared of losing my job. Going to a college campus (the closest is 45 minutes away) after working 8 hours a day and finding a sitter for my two children because my husband works second shift—it was just impossible to even think about doing it. Then my director received a brochure about the distance learning program at the University of Cincinnati and asked if I would like to give college a shot that way." Butcher continues, "I felt this was a true gift to help me to [keep] the profession that is dear to me."

For Butcher, the goal was crystal clear and the means of achieving that goal fell into place quite nicely. However, for any student, it's important to know what you hope to accomplish by undertaking any degree program. "Make sure you have your goals defined," advises Scott Garrod, a Master of Business candidate at Syracuse University. "Then the decision between a distance or traditional [program] will be easy." Keep in mind that in some fields a distance education degree is not as acceptable as it is in others. Although most business employers don't make any distinctions between distance and on-campus degrees, as long as they are from reputable institutions, in academia and some professions employers may not be so accommodating. Be sure you understand what academic credentials will carry weight in the field in which you are interested.

Why are you considering distance education?

Do you have a busy schedule full of commitments to work, family, and community? If so, your top reason for enrolling in a distance education course or program may be the flexibility it offers. The ability to do course work at your own convenience is the key consideration for most distance learners.

"My schedule does not permit consistent attendance in a traditional classroom," comments one 46-year-old undergraduate. "As a consultant, I may be required to spend up to 60 hours at a client site . . . . As a parent, I have many commitments that would take priority over my attending class." She continues, "The online program at the University of Maryland University College offers me maximum flexibility in which to pursue my educational goals without interfering with the rest of my crazy schedule." Another student, Kimberly Foreman, who is studying for a Master of Healthcare Administration from Seton Hall University's online program in New Jersey, investigated several programs. "Traditional on-campus evening classes interfered with work and family obligations. The weekend programs still required that I be at a certain place at a certain time, and this was also inconvenient," she explains. "I wanted flexibility and a program that allowed me to be self-directed but still have interaction with faculty members and classmates." The online program she found at Seton Hall met her needs.

Some students need the flexibility of distance education because their work involves a great deal of travel. "With my job, travel is a requirement . . . sometimes unpredictable travel," says Scott Garrod of Syracuse University. "So a distance learning program that was not classroom-dependent was a great alternative." Another student, Paul Nashawaty, explains, "My profession has me traveling around and moving from place to place." Nashawaty, who is earning a Master of Business Administration from Worcester Polytechnic Institute in Massachusetts, concluded, "It would be very difficult for me to transfer from school to school."

Other students enroll in distance education courses and programs because they live too far from the institutions of higher learning that offer the education they need. These are students for whom the word "distance" in distance learning has a literal meaning. "My husband is a farmer, so my family is not mobile," explains Patti Iversen, a nurse who lives in Montana and is working on a Master of Science in Nursing degree (family nurse practitioner) from Gonzaga University in Spokane, Washington. "I live in a rural community and the closest colleges and universities are 250 to 300 miles from my home. I did not want to leave my family for extended periods of time in order to meet my educational and career objectives." For Iversen, distance learning was the only way to achieve her goals.

"I wanted a degree from a respected and vigorous program but didn't want to move my family or quit my job," says Lara Hollenczer, a marketing manager who lives in Maryland and is pursuing a master's degree in communications management from Syracuse University in New York. Distance learning provided Hollenczer the means to earn the degree she wanted without disrupting her work and family life. So, when you consider taking a course or enrolling in a degree program, ask yourself whether flexibility of time and place is critical for you. If flexibility is one of your top needs, distance learning may be the right choice for you.

PERSONAL ATTITUDES AND SKILLS

Are you prepared to do as much work as you would have to do in a traditional course, and perhaps more?

Many people believe that distance learning is an easier or faster way to earn a degree. This is because in recent years many fraudulent distance-learning schools have sprung up, promising degrees in little or no time for little or no work. These diploma mills have given rise to the false perception that distance learning degrees are somehow easier to earn than degrees earned the traditional way. However, distance learning courses and degree programs offered by reputable schools require just as much time and effort as their on-campus counterparts.

"Some students think that an online course is cybersurfing for credit," says Michael S. Ameigh, Assistant Provost for Distance Learning and Information Resources and Associate Professor of Communication Studies at the State University of New York at Oswego. "But an online course is actually more work than if students took the course in the classroom." That's because online instructors often require a certain amount of participation from students in order to pass the course, whereas most classroom instructors do not demand participation from students beyond completing the assignments and exams. So, at the beginning of each course, Ameigh tries to weed out students who think that online learning is easier than conventional courses. He provides a six-minute "welcome document," a streaming media PowerPoint presentation with narration that gives an overview of what the course covers and what he expects of students. In courses taken by distance learners and on-campus students, instructors make no distinctions between distance learners and traditional students when it comes to the course work that they must do. For example, in Gonzaga University's undergraduate and graduate nursing programs, "Course requirements for students at a distance are identical to those for their on-campus colleagues," according to Dale Ann Abendroth, Assistant Professor of Nursing.

From the student's perspective, a high-quality distance education course is as rigorous as a traditional course. "Certainly the expectations of the instructor and the volume of readings and assignments were as stringent, or even more so, than on-site courses I have taken," comments a high school librarian of her Rutgers University postgraduate course in critical issues for the wired classroom. "Be prepared for a great deal of work. It seems to me that more work is assigned than in a 'regular' class, so students shouldn't perceive distance learning as an easy way out. It isn't!"

Do you have the time-management skills necessary to juggle work, home, and school responsibilities?

As we have seen, a distance learning course or program takes as much time as a traditional one, and sometimes more. So ask yourself, do you have enough time to take a distance learning course or courses? Will you be able to juggle your course work, professional work, family obligations, and community activities to make time for all your responsibilities? "I've seen students register for four or five classes in a semester and try to work full-time," says Patti Wolf, Assistant Academic Director and Assistant Professor of Computer Science at the University of Maryland University College. "Many of these students have underestimated the time required for their online courses and ended up doing poorly." Wolf adds, "You should expect to spend as much time on line (or otherwise preparing for class) as you would in a traditional classroom." Distance learner Patti Iversen advises students to "be realistic about the amount of time that will be needed for study and travel, if required [for programs with residency periods]."

In addition to having enough time to do the course work, students have to be able to plan their time, make a schedule, and stick to it. "The biggest problem I see among my students is an inability to budget their time," says Wolf. "They get to the third week of class and realize that it's Saturday night and they haven't done their homework."

Iversen agrees. "Failure to adequately anticipate and plan for the rigors of independent learning leads to frustration and poor outcomes," she warns. Even though many courses, like Wolf's, are set up in weekly blocks to help students pace themselves, it's still up to the student to make time to log on or watch the videotape and do the assignments.

Do you have the discipline and self-motivation to work regularly if you don't have to show up for class at a given time and place?

When we asked students and faculty members what personal qualities a distance learner needs, most people mentioned discipline and self-motivation as the keys to success. "Success as a distance learner requires more self-discipline and greater ability to learn autonomously than site-based learning," claims distance learner Patti Iversen. M.B.A. candidate Paul Nashawaty echoes her remarks, "You must keep on top of the workload and try not to slack off," he says. "Discipline is my number-one factor for success in this program." A University of Maryland University College undergraduate agrees, "Students [must] have the discipline to complete course work studies and assignments on time and independently without the in-person reminders that come with regularly scheduled class meetings." When you are considering distance education, ask yourself whether or not you have the qualities needed to see it through. According to Denise Petrosino, a certified public accountant working on a master's in organizational management from the University of Phoenix Online, "As long as you are goal-oriented and self-motivated, you can do it."

Do you have the initiative and assertiveness needed to succeed in a distance learning environment?

Initiative and assertiveness are qualities needed for success in distance learning. Students need to take the initiative to ask questions and resolve problems that the instructor may not be able to perceive.

In addition, students in distance learning courses need to be assertive in order to make themselves known to the instructor and to other students. For example, in an online course, a student who never participates in threaded discussions tends to "disappear." "In the online environment, students have to be assertive," says Michael S. Ameigh of the State University of New York at Oswego. "Otherwise we don't know who they are." Similarly, in a prerecorded video course, a student who never contacts the instructor has little presence in the instructor's mind. Of course, initiative and assertiveness are pluses for traditional on-campus students, too. The student who speaks up in class is more likely to have a good learning experience and succeed in a course than the student who sits silently in the back of the room. For many adults, maturity brings assertiveness. "My students are a professional group," says Dale Ann Abendroth, Assistant Professor of Nursing at Gonzaga University. "It's rare that I have a wallflower in a course."

YOUR ACADEMIC AND PROFESSIONAL SKILLS

Do you have sound study skills, including reading, researching, writing papers, and taking exams?

Good study skills are a necessary prerequisite for distance learning. In fact, many institutions that offer distance learning courses and degree programs require that students have taken at least some college-level courses before they enroll in a distance education degree program. For example, some distance education bachelor's programs prefer students with an associate's degree from a community college or a certain minimum number of undergraduate credit hours. In this way, they ensure that students are ready to tackle course work via distance learning without needing much help with basic study skills.

For graduate programs, it is simply assumed that students have the necessary study skills and are ready to undertake graduate-level work. Laurie Noe, a doctoral candidate in management of children and youth programs at Nova Southeastern University, explains, "You are required to produce papers, take tests, conduct research, and formulate and state your opinions just as if you were in a traditional setting."

Do you have good communication skills? Can you present yourself well in writing? Can you speak up on camera?

Good communication skills—reading, writing, listening, and speaking—are necessary to succeed in all types of distance learning courses and programs. However, different distance learning technologies emphasize different communication skills.

"Online students have to be reasonably articulate in the written mode of communication," explains Claudine SchWeber, Assistant Vice President for Distance Education and Lifelong Learning at the University of Maryland University College. That's because virtually all communication in an online course takes place through the written word, therefore you must be comfortable with reading messages and responding in writing.

For some people, this is ideal. "Students who are petrified to talk in class often find it easy to communicate in writing on line. They can make well-reasoned, thought-out responses to the discussion," explains Patti Wolf of the University of Maryland University College. "One of the things that happens on line is that people who talk little in the classroom feel more comfortable and tend to communicate well on line," says Karen Novick, Director of Professional Development Studies at Rutgers University in New Jersey. Robert V. Steiner, who directs the distance learning project at Teachers College, Columbia University, also agrees. "For some students, online learning may provide a more comfortable environment in which to express themselves. Students can reflect on what they want to say before they post a message." On the other hand, some students are simply more visual and more oriented to getting information via television rather than the written word. For them, two-way interactive video is a more comfortable way to communicate. It's easier for these students to speak up and communicate with people they can see and hear rather than to write messages to unseen students and instructors. "Once students get used to being on camera, they react fairly normally," says Larry Anthony, Director of the Addiction Studies Program at the University of Cincinnati. Of course, students who take courses via video still need written communication skills because most of their assignments and exams are in writing.

If you are pursuing a degree or certificate to improve your professional standing, do you have the background that may be required?

Many graduate-level professional programs require that students have worked in the field for several years before they apply. For example, many programs that offer a Master in Business Administration prefer students who have demonstrated their professional capabilities through several years of work. Graduate-level work in other fields, such as nursing, social work, and education, often requires related work experience. Be sure you have the necessary professional background for the programs you are considering.

SOCIAL FACTORS

Do you have the support of your family and employers?

As you have realized by now, a distance learning course or program can be challenging. Taking such a course or program means that you will be working harder than ever, so having the backing of your family and employer can be very helpful. "It's important to have a good support group behind you," says Barbara Rosenbaum, who is working on a master's degree in communications management from Syracuse University. "My husband, friends, family, and colleagues helped me keep my energy and focus up." Distance learner Patti Iversen agrees. "A local support network is a valuable asset in helping to overcome the occasional slump in motivation that occurs over time."

Are you comfortable with the social interaction that is characteristic of distance learning? Can you overcome or accept the social isolation that often occurs?

The issue of social interaction and isolation is complex because different factors, including instructional technology, personality, and life circumstances, influence how each person reacts to the social element of distance learning.

Instructional technology. As we saw when we discussed communication skills, each distance learning technology draws on particular skills. Similarly, each distance learning technology offers a different type of social interaction. Let's look at each major distance learning technology to get a better idea of how it affects the social elements of distance education.

The technology that offers a social experience most similar to that of the conventional classroom is two-way interactive video.

Even though the students may be geographically distant from one another, communication is in real time, people can see one another, and the feeling of social isolation is minimized. Kenneth Wachter, Professor of Demography at the University of California at Berkeley, offered an advanced postgraduate course in mathematical demography via two-way interactive video to students at Berkeley and the University of California at Los Angeles. He was delighted by how the two groups of students were brought together. "The thing that works best is the human back and forth," says Wachter.

Online courses can also offer social interaction, but in a new and, to some, unfamiliar form. "At first it is strange e-mailing someone you don't know. However, you get to know the person via e-mail just as you would talking or writing a letter," explains an undergraduate at the University of Maryland University College. "In the cybercafes that are provided for classmates, we talk about class work, movies, music, time management, and sports. It helps bring the class together socially." Denise Petrosino, who is enrolled in a master's program in organizational management at the University of Phoenix Online, agrees. "If you have a fear of limited interaction with the teacher and students, you can put that aside because I believe that we learn more about our teacher and classmates in the online program than in the live classroom," says Petrosino. "The reason I say this is because you get to read all correspondence between students and teacher."

In courses in which class videotapes are mailed to off-site students, the sense of social isolation is the most pronounced. That's because these courses often do not provide a means for ongoing discussion between off-site students, on-site students, and instructors. "The professors do not know much about the distance students' personalities, or even what they look like," explains Nicole DeRaleau, who lives in Connecticut and is a Master of Engineering student at Worcester Polytechnic Institute in Massachusetts. "Their interaction with us is minimal, and the closest form of personal interaction may be a telephone call, which is almost always initiated by the student." Note that some courses that rely on videotapes for instructional delivery are now moving on line as well, establishing class bulletin boards on which discussions can take place, thus improving the social interaction of the off-site students.

Personality. The second factor that influences how social interaction and social isolation are perceived is an individual's personality—one person's social isolation is another person's cherished privacy. For some people, the type of interaction that characterizes distance learning is not enough to overcome a sense of social isolation. "Eye contact, vocal inflection, body language—all these elements of communication are missing [online]," explains Robert V. Steiner, who directs the distance learning project at Teachers College, Columbia University. "For some people, the sense of isolation can be significant." Joanne Simon, a student at the University of Phoenix Online who actually prefers online classes to traditional classes, admits, "I like to talk, so for me, the social interaction is lacking." Another distance learner thinks that people who are "social butterflies" will find the social interactions of distance learning unfulfilling.

On the other hand, people who are not especially extroverted may find distance learning suits them. They can participate, especially in online courses, without risking too much personal revelation.

Personal circumstances. How important is social interaction? Clearly, there must be enough interaction to facilitate learning. But for many adult students, the lack of social interaction is simply not a problem.

"For the most part, I feel detached from the class itself, and that is okay," says Brigit Dolan, a nurse who lives in Boise, Idaho, and is enrolled in Gonzaga University's Master of Science in Nursing program in Spokane, Washington. In this program, students are required to attend classes three times per semester. The remaining classes are mailed to them on videotape. "I feel okay to share my ideas and experiences when I'm there, but I'm fulfilled enough in other areas of my life that I don't yearn for that much interaction from my school life . . . . I just do my work, communicate with my professors and classmates occasionally, and that's about it." Like Brigit Dolan, most adult students are not looking for the social life and collegiality that are characteristics of the on-campus under-graduate experience. A librarian taking a postgraduate course at Rutgers University explains, "I don't think social interaction is a high priority in the kind of postgrad courses I take; we all have jobs and personal lives, and time is precious." Carla Gentry, a nurse enrolled in a distance learning master's program, agrees. "At my stage in life, I am not going to school for the social benefits."

How well do you work with others?

After the discussion of social interaction and social isolation, you may wonder why working well with others is important in the distance learning environment. The reason is that many instructors try to overcome the potential social isolation of the distance education course by assigning group work, thus forcing people to interact with each other.

Doing a group project in a distance learning class is challenging. The first challenge is to coordinate the activities of a group of people who are extremely busy, geographically distant from one another, and doing their work at different hours of the day and night. The second challenge is to get a group of distance learners to work together. "Since distance learners are so independent and self-motivated, they also like to do things their own way," says Brigit Dolan, who finds group projects the most challenging aspect of distance education. Trust, cooperation, and flexibility are key.

TECHNOLOGY ISSUES

Do you have the technical skills, or the willingness to acquire these skills, that may be required of a distance learning program?

Those of you who see yourselves as technologically challenged may have been dismayed by the discussion in "What Is Distance Learning?" of the technology involved in many distance learning courses. Don't be. Remember that the technology is just a tool, a means to an end, and it can be learned.

In fact, some distance learning technology is not particularly advanced from the user's point of view. For example, in two-way interactive video courses, all you have to do is learn to activate the microphone (some even activate automatically when you speak) and watch the video monitors. For prerecorded video, you just pop the videocassette into the VCR and turn on the TV. Online courses do involve a little more technological savvy. However,

consider the experience of one librarian who was taking a traditional on-campus postgraduate course at Rutgers University. "My first online course was thrust upon me," she recalls. The instructor, who developed a serious health problem that prevented her from coming in to class, gave students the option of con-tinuing online. "I, on my own, would never have chosen this mode; I was too computer-illiterate at that time. However, I quickly found that the technical skills required were really not onerous at all and that I could master them easily . . . . If I can succeed—no spring chicken with little technology experience—anyone can." Denise Petrosino agrees. "You do not have to be a technical genius to go to school on line. If you have a computer, can log onto the Web, and know how to use e-mail, you are set."

Do you have or are you willing to gain access to the necessary equipment, which may include a computer, VCR, television, or fax machine?

Most people own a television and VCR, so these are not usually items that a new distance learner needs to purchase. However, investing in the proper computer hardware and software for a distance education program can be costly. Even if you already own a computer with Internet access, you may have to upgrade your hardware or Internet browser or purchase additional software in order to meet the minimum technical requirements of a course.

Can you tolerate dealing with technology problems?

Technology sometimes fails, and distance learners have to learn how to cope when it does. Many schools offer technical support for distance learners, and sometimes problems can be solved quickly. But if your computer system crashes for a week, you'll have to find other alternatives until you can fix the problem. "Students should be comfortable with the technology triad—fax, phone, and computer," says Claudine SchWeber of the University of Maryland University College. "Then if one goes down, they have other channels of communication."

A MINI SELF-ASSESSMENT

If you do an Internet search using the phrase "distance learning self-assessment," you will find dozens of brief quizzes designed to evaluate whether or not distance learning suits your personality, skills, and learning style. Most are posted on the Web sites of colleges and universities that offer distance education courses. For example, the University of Texas at Brownsville's distance learning self-assessment can be found at http://pubs.utb.edu/semester_courses/spring2001/distance_learnself_assessment.htm, and St. Louis Community College offers its self-assessment at http://www.stlcc.cc.mo.us/distance/assessment.

For your convenience, we've provided a brief self-assessment. Although most of the online quizzes focus on Internet-based courses, this assessment is broader. Take it and see how you do!

DISTANCE LEARNING SELF-ASSESSMENT

1. When I think about how I learn, I think:
   (A) I learn best independently. I am self-motivated and like to work at my own pace. I don't need a lot of handholding.

  (B) I like to work independently, but I like to get some feedback once in a while on how I'm doing. I don't need a lot of support, just a little help every once in a while.

  (C) I can work independently, but I want to know where I stand. I like to be in an interactive situation where I get regular feedback on how I am doing.

  (D) I need lots of interaction with my teachers and peers. I like the give and take of the classroom setting. It keeps me engaged in my classes.

2. When I think about learning through different media, such as the Internet or videoconferencing, I think:

  (A) It would be exciting to be able to do my work through a different medium. The idea of sitting in a classroom does nothing for me.

  (B) I am open to the idea of trying something different, like an Internet class. I would like to see how it would work for me.

  (C) I'm not sure that I would be ready to work that independently. When I think of furthering my education, I see myself in a more traditional setting.

  (D) I absolutely want a traditional learning experience. I want to be in a classroom setting and experience all that school has to offer.

3. When I think about interacting with my teachers, I think:

  (A) I don't really care whether or not I have any face-to-face contact with my teachers. As long as I'm getting the kind of information I need to be successful in my classes, I can be satisfied as a student.

  (B) I don't need a great deal of direct contact with my teachers. I'm a good, independent worker. I do want to be able to ask for help and direction when I need it.

  (C) I don't need to be in a situation where I have daily conversations with my teachers, but I do like to know that they are there if I need them. I find a good teacher really helps me get excited about a topic.

  (D) I really value my contacts with my teachers. I like to be able to engage in a dialogue in the classroom. A good teacher helps me connect to the subject.

4. When I think about trying to do schoolwork at home, I think:

  (A) I have a great setup at home, which is conducive to studying. I like the idea of being able to work in my own "space" and at my own pace.

  (B) I can work fairly well at home, I just have to make sure that I don't get too distracted by what is going on around me.

  (C) I could work at home, but I really don't see that as an ideal situation. There is too much going on and I would be able to concentrate better in a classroom or library setting.

  (D) There is no way I want to learn from home. I want to get out of the house and be in a classroom with other students.

5. When it comes to setting my schedule for learning and studying, I think:

  (A) I need as much flexibility as I can get. I've got a lot of other things going on in my life and I'd really like to be able to work at my own pace.

  (B) I would like to have some flexibility in scheduling my classes, but I don't want to drag it out either. I want to get through my education as quickly as possible.

  (C) I like the idea of having my time fairly structured. If I don't have someone pushing me along, it may take me longer than I want to get through school.

  (D) I need to have a structured schedule to keep me on task.

6. When I think about the traditional education experience, I think:

  (A) Campus or classroom life doesn't really appeal to me at this stage in my life. I don't need or want the experience, for example, of living in a dorm or sitting in a classroom. I want to find an alternative way of earning my degree or certificate.

  (B) I'm not sure if I want to commit to the classroom experience. It may work for me, but I'm willing to look at other ways of earning a degree.

  (C) I think I would be happier if I were on a campus somewhere. I think I'd probably regret missing out on the learning experience. I wouldn't rule out the notion of being a commuter, though.

  (D) I really want a traditional learning experience where I can get away from home. I'm at a point in my life where that seems to be the logical next step for me.

To evaluate your readiness for distance education, count the number of (A)s, (B)s, (C)s, and (D)s among your responses. If most of your answers were

- (A)—you should carefully investigate distance education as an option for continuing your education.

- (B)—you should investigate whether distance learning programs are suitable for meeting at least part of your educational needs. For example, you may want to complete a significant portion of your academic work through a distance learning program but still allow yourself time for some of your work to be completed in a traditional classroom setting.

- (C)—you're probably better-suited for a traditional campus-based college experience than a distance learning environment. However, some course work through a distance learning program may be a great way to supplement your on-campus course work. You should probably look for a program that will provide you with faculty or mentor feedback on a regular basis.

- (D)—you are clearly suited for a traditional classroom setting where you can have more immediate interaction with your teachers and peers. This is not to say that you may not find distance learning programs useful at some point in the future, but it sounds like you need something more hands-on so you can get immediate feedback in the classroom while enjoying the other benefits of college life.

CONCLUSION

 As you have seen in this section, distance learning is not for those who lack motivation or need other people to keep them on task. On the other hand, it is perfectly suited for those who have definite educational and professional goals, are committed to getting an education, are focused and organized, can persevere when things get tough, and need the flexibility that distance education offers.

Finding the time in a busy schedule to successfully complete distance learning courses is a challenge for most adults. It's easy for work and family obligations to take precedence over getting an education. Still, distance learning makes it possible for many adults who cannot regularly attend on-campus classes to get a high-quality education. As one undergraduate distance learner commented, "For working adults (and particularly working parents), distance learning may provide the best means for obtaining an undergraduate or graduate degree from a highly respected university without interfering with life's other commitments."

WHAT CAN YOU STUDY VIA DISTANCE LEARNING?

If you are interested in pursuing your education by distance learning, you are not limited to a few specialized courses or degree programs. Actually, almost every course, certificate, and degree program that you can take on campus is also available in a distance learning format. There are exceptions, of course. Degree programs in subjects that require laboratory work or performance, for example, cannot usually be done completely at a distance. Still, distance education spans a wide range of offerings, from accredited graduate-level degree programs to self-help and hobby courses. Although some programs and courses are limited to residents of certain states or regions, many are available nationwide and internationally.

In this section we will focus on programs and courses offered by institutions of higher education, including technical institutes, community colleges, four-year colleges, and universities. Figure 3-1 shows how higher education is structured in the United States, and how distance learning programs and courses are available at most levels of postsecondary education. The exceptions are some professional degrees, such as doctor of medicine, and postdoctoral study and research. Another partial exception is the law degree (LL.B., J.D.). Although you can acquire a law degree via distance learning, at the time this book was published, no distance learning law program has been accredited by the American Bar Association. Thus, a person with a law degree from an unaccredited distance learning program will not be able to take the bar exam in most states. The accreditation issue is important in many fields besides law, and we will examine it more closely in "Selecting a Good Distance Learning Program." In this section we'll simply give you an overview of the degrees, certificates, and courses that are available via distance learning and guidance on how to find programs and courses of interest to you.

UNDERGRADUATE DEGREE PROGRAMS

Today you can earn an associate or bachelor's degree entirely by distance learning. You may also be able to shorten the time it takes to earn a degree if you transfer college credits from other institutions of higher learning, earn credits through equivalency exams, or present a portfolio of your accomplishments. For adults, earning credits for past academic and other work can cut a year or more off the time it takes to earn an undergraduate degree. So don't be shy about negotiating for credits with the school in which you plan to enroll—the time and money you save may be considerable.

ASSOCIATE DEGREE

The degree conferred by community colleges is the associate degree. Students enrolled full-time can earn an associate degree in two years, but part-time students may take much longer to earn the 60 to 64 credits required. The two most common associate degrees are the Associate of Arts (A.A.) and the Associate of Science (A.S.), although there are many other titles that range from Associate of Business Administration (A.B.A.) to Associate of General Studies (A.G.S.). Distance learning associate degrees are offered in a wide range of fields, including liberal arts, business, computer science, and health professions. Many students who have earned an associate degree go on to apply those credits toward a bachelor's degree.

BACHELOR'S DEGREE

The bachelor's degree is recognized worldwide as the first university degree a student earns. In the United States, the bachelor's degree is conferred by four-year colleges, universities, and technical institutes. Although students enrolled full-time can earn the degree in four years, many actually take up to six years. Part-time students take longer, of course, to earn the 120 to 128 credits required for the bachelor's degree.

In most colleges and universities, the course of study that leads to a bachelor's degree consists of concentrated work in a "major" such as psychology or business and wide-ranging work in a variety of subjects—the liberal arts—to give students a broad foundation of knowledge. However, some bachelor's degree programs focus on intensive study in a particular field without the broad liberal arts background.

The most common bachelor's degrees are the Bachelor of Arts (B.A.) and the Bachelor of Science (B.S.), although there are scores of other titles in use as well. Distance learning bachelor's degrees are offered in many fields, including business, engineering, computer science, economics, English, history, nursing, psychology, and telecommunications. Some colleges and universities offer interdisciplinary degrees, such as environmental studies or arts management, and some permit students to design their own interdisciplinary program.

TRANSFERRING CREDITS

Adult students who have earned some college credits during the course of their career can decrease the time it takes to earn an undergraduate degree by transferring the credits they've earned to a degree program. Many institutions of higher learning will accept transfer credits toward a degree. *Since each school's requirements vary, it's important to check before you enroll.* The school may have rules regarding the maximum number of transfer credits and the types of courses for which credit will be granted. Consult the academic advising office before you register.

EARNING CREDITS BY TAKING EXAMS

It's also possible to earn credit for prior learning if you take examinations to assess your knowledge and skills. For example, if you have worked in the human resources department of a large organization for years, you may know a lot about human resource management. If you take and pass a college-level exam in human

Figure 3–1: The Structure of Higher Education in the U.S.

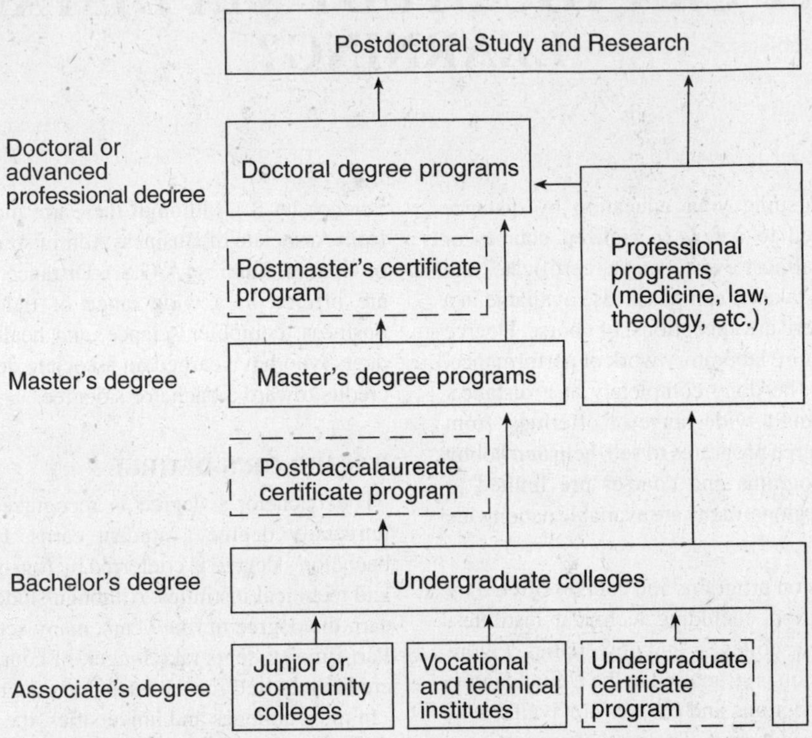

Structure of higher education in the United States. Note that the arrows indicate common pathways of students, but not the only possible pathway. *Source:* Adapted from U.S. Department of Education, National Center for Educational Statistics.

resource management, you can earn 3 credits toward your degree—without taking a course or paying tuition. Although some schools have developed their own equivalency exams, most schools accept the results of examinations taken through national programs.

CLEP Exams. The most well-known of the national equivalency exam programs is the College-Level Examination Program (CLEP), which is administered by the College Entrance Examination Board and recognized by about 2,900 colleges and universities. Most of the CLEP tests are multiple-choice exams, and some are multiple-choice and essay. There are five general exams: social sciences and history, English composition, humanities, college mathematics, and natural sciences. In addition, there are about thirty specific subject area tests, including American government, Spanish, principles of management, and introductory sociology. A good score on an exam is worth between 3 and 12 credits, it depends on the exam and the credits accepted by your school.

Earning credits by scoring well on equivalency exams can save you both time and tuition money. If you'd like more information about the CLEP exams, visit the College Board Web site at www.collegeboard.org/clep, e-mail them at clep@info.collegeboard.org, or call 609-771-7865.

Excelsior College Examinations. The Excelsior College Examination series, formerly the Regents College Examination series, is similar to the CLEP exams. The series consists of about forty subject area equivalency examinations that are 3 or 4 hours long.

Subjects include anatomy and physiology, auditing, organizational behavior, and educational psychology; and the exams are recognized by almost 1,000 colleges and universities. For more information, visit the Excelsior College Web site at www.excelsior.edu, e-mail them at testadmn@excelsior.edu, or call 888-647-2388 (toll-free).

DANTES Subject Standardized Tests. Another series of equivalency exams are the DANTES Subject Standardized Tests, or DSSTs. The DSSTs are examinations offered by The Chauncey Group International, a subsidiary of the Educational Testing Service, in trust for the United States Department of Defense as part of the military's Defense Activity for Nontraditional Education Support (DANTES). These tests were originally developed for military personnel but are now available for civilians as well. The tests are similar to the CLEP exams, but there are some subject areas not offered by CLEP, such as geography, criminal justice, marketing, technical writing, and ethics in America.

For more information about the DSSTs, you can check the Chauncey Group Web site at www.chauncey.com/dantes.html, e-mail them at dantes@chauncey.com, or call 609-720-6740. If you are on active duty in the military, you can get further information about the exams from the DANTES Web site at www.voled.doded.mil/dantes/exam or e-mail them at exams@voled.doded.mil.

Graduate Record Examinations Subject Tests. The GRE Subject Tests, administered by the Educational Testing Service (ETS), assess knowledge that would ordinarily be acquired during the course of majoring in a subject as an undergraduate. Although they are usually used as entrance exams for graduate schools, some colleges and universities will award undergraduate credit if you get a good score. The subjects include biochemistry, cell and molecular biology; biology; chemistry; computer science; literature in English; mathematics; physics; and psychology.

For more information about the GRE Subject Tests, visit the GRE Online site at www.gre.org, send an e-mail to gre-info@ets.org, or call 609-771-7670.

EARNING CREDITS FOR LIFE EXPERIENCE

Many undergraduate degree programs, especially those designed for adults, give credit for knowledge and skills you've gained through life experience. Although the knowledge usually comes through paid employment, it can also be acquired through volunteer work, company or military training courses, travel, recreational activities and hobbies, and reading.

There is a catch, of course—you must document the specifics of what you have learned. It's simply not enough to say that you learned about marketing while selling widgets for XYZ Company. Instead, you must demonstrate what you have learned about pricing, promotion, and product mix; for example, showing plans for a marketing campaign. Thus, to earn credit for life experience, you should assemble a file, or portfolio, of information about your work and other accomplishments. The file may include writing samples, awards, taped presentations or performances, copies of speeches, newspaper articles, official job descriptions, military records, works of art, designs, blueprints, films, or photographs. Your portfolio is then evaluated by an institution's faculty. A student can earn as many as 30 credits—one quarter the number needed for a bachelor's degree—as the result of a good portfolio review. For example, through a portfolio evaluation, a senior marketing executive in her forties earned 30 credits, mostly in marketing and communications, toward her distance learning bachelor's degree from University of Maryland University College. For more information about assessment opportunities for adult learners, check the Web site of the Council for Adult and Experiential Learning (CAEL) at www.cael.org or call 312-499-2600.

Credit for Work Training. Since 1974, thousands of employees have been earning college credit for selected educational programs sponsored by businesses, industry, professional associations, labor unions, and government agencies. The American Council on Education's College Credit Recommendation Service evaluates such programs according to established college-level criteria and recommends college credit for those programs that measure up to these standards. You can check their Web site at www.acenet.edu, e-mail them at credit@ace.nche.edu, or call 202-939-9475.

Credit for Military Training. Service in the military, specialized training, and occupational experience have the potential to earn you college credit. Many military programs have already been evaluated in terms of their equivalency to college credit. The institutions that belong to Servicemembers Opportunities Colleges (SOC) have agreed to assess students' prior learning and accept each other's credits in transfer. To find out more, check the SOC Web site at www.soc.aascu.org, e-mail them at socmail@aascu.org, or call 800-368-5622 (toll-free).

GRADUATE DEGREE PROGRAMS

MASTER'S DEGREE

The master's degree is the first academic or professional degree earned after the bachelor's degree. A traditional, full-time master's degree student may take a year or two to earn the required 30 credits. Part-time students usually take longer, it depends on the design of the degree program. In some master's degree programs, students are simply expected to take advanced-level courses and perhaps pass a culminating exam. In others, original research and a thesis are also required. Some distance learning master's degree programs have a brief residency requirement. Students usually earn a Master of Arts (M.A.), a Master of Science (M.S.), or a Master of Business Administration (M.B.A.) degree.

At the time this book was published, distance learning master's degree programs outnumbered other distance learning degree programs by a considerable margin. Most of these degree programs are professional in nature and are designed for working adults with experience in the field. If you are interested in a master's degree in library science, business, or education, you are in luck. These are fields in which there are many distance master's degree programs from which to choose.

However, if you are looking for a distance learning master's degree program in an academic field, such as English language and literature, chemistry, or ethnic and cultural studies, your choices are far more limited. That's because most master's programs in academic fields are campus based. Still, *Peterson's Guide to Distance Learning Programs* lists at least one distance master's degree program in each of these academic subject areas.

Another type of master's degree that is offered via distance learning is the interdisciplinary degree. Some are offered in liberal studies or humanities and are granted for advanced study and a culminating project or thesis. Others combine academic and professional areas of study. Still others are offered in broad subject areas like environmental studies, in which students are expected to design their own course of study based on their particular interests.

In the future, the number of distance academic and interdisciplinary master's degree programs is likely to increase, but far slower than the number of professional degree programs, for which the demand is much greater.

DOCTORAL DEGREE

The doctoral degree, the highest degree awarded, is earned after an advanced course of study that usually culminates in original research and a dissertation, an extended written work. The traditional on-campus doctoral student takes four to ten years to complete the degree, but many distance learning doctoral programs are structured to streamline the process. Thus, some doctoral degrees can be earned in as little as three years. Most distance learning doctoral programs, even those offered by virtual universities like the University of Phoenix Online, have a brief residency requirement. The Doctor of Philosophy (Ph.D.) is the most common doctoral degree; it is awarded in fields that range from philosophy to geology to communication. Other frequently awarded doctoral degrees include the Doctor of Education (Ed.D.), Doctor of Business Administration (D.B.A.), Doctor of Engineering (Eng.D.), and Doctor of Psychology (Psy.D.). There are far fewer distance learning doctoral programs than master's programs. However, you can find programs in a wide range of fields, although the number of programs within each field may be limited. You can earn a distance learning doctoral degree in fields as diverse as business, engineering, computer science, counseling psychology, instructional technology, education, human services, library science, English literature, management, pharmacy, and public policy. As with distance learning master's degrees, distance learning doctoral degrees tend to be professional rather than academic in orientation. Many of these degree programs are designed with the professional working adult in mind.

EARNING GRADUATE-LEVEL CREDIT FOR KNOWLEDGE AND EXPERIENCE

There is disagreement among institutions of higher education about whether or not to award graduate-level credit for knowledge acquired outside academia. At present, many graduate schools do not offer credit to students for knowledge and experience acquired before enrollment in the program, no matter how deep or extensive that knowledge and experience may be. However, other less conservative institutions are more open to granting graduate credit for life experience. Check with the schools and programs in which you are interested to see what their policies are.

CERTIFICATE PROGRAMS

Distance learning certificate programs can train you for a new career or give you a foundation in a new subject even if you've already earned a college degree in an entirely different field. A certificate program usually consists of around six to ten courses, all focused on a single profession or subject, and it can be earned at the undergraduate or graduate level. Some schools now offer a portion of a master's or other degree as a certificate. This allows you to take part of the full degree curriculum and either stop at the certification level or proceed through for the entire degree. If this is an option that interests you, be sure to consider the admissions requirements carefully. If you think you may matriculate through to the entire degree, be sure you understand the admissions requirements for each program because they may differ.

PROFESSIONAL CERTIFICATE PROGRAMS

To give you just a few examples of professional certificate programs offered via distance learning, within the engineering profession there are certificates in computer-integrated manufacturing, systems engineering, and fire-protection engineering. In business, there are distance learning certificate programs in information technology and health services management. In education, distance learning certificates include early reading instruction, children's literature, and English as a second language. In health care, certificates include medical assisting, home health nursing, and health-care administration. In law, distance learning certificates are offered in paralegal/legal assistant studies and legal issues for business professionals.

Professional certificate programs are often designed with the help of professional associations and licensing boards, and thus encompass real-world, practical knowledge. Many are designed to prepare students for professional certification or licensure. At the end of the program, the student sits for an exam and earns a state-recognized certificate from a certifying agency or licensing

board. *If this is your goal, you should make sure that the certification program you want to take meets the certifying agency or licensing board's requirements.* That way, you won't waste your time or money completing a program that won't help you meet your ultimate professional goals.

CERTIFICATE PROGRAMS IN ACADEMIC SUBJECTS

Less common, but still available via distance learning, are undergraduate and graduate certificate programs in many academic subjects. At the undergraduate level, you can earn a certificate in areas such as American studies, Chinese language and literature, English composition, creative writing, ethnic and cultural studies, general studies, humanities, and liberal arts and sciences. If you later enroll in an undergraduate degree program, you may be able to apply the credits earned in a certificate program toward your degree.

At the graduate level, you can earn a certificate via distance learning in subjects like biology, English language and literature, geography, physiological psychology, religious studies, and statistics.

INDIVIDUAL COURSES

If you are seeking to update your professional skills, acquire specialized knowledge, earn a few credits toward a degree, or simply take a class for your own pleasure, individual distance learning courses may be for you. Many institutions of higher education venture into distance learning by offering a few classes scattered throughout various departments. As their experience with distance education increases, they begin to offer complete programs of study. Thus, if you are interested in just taking a few courses, you have the widest range of choices. You can find individual courses in subjects that range from accounting to animal sciences and from art history to aviation—and that's just a random sample beginning with the letter *A*.

There are several options that may be open to you when you take an individual course, such as taking the course for credit, taking it without earning credit, or earning Continuing Education Units (CEUs). The option you select depends on your purpose for taking the course.

TAKING A COURSE FOR CREDIT

If you are enrolled in a degree program and need a few credits, taking a distance learning course may help you satisfy your degree requirements. Your own college or university may offer courses via distance learning. In fact, students enrolled in conventional on-campus degree programs sometimes take distance learning courses from their schools when they go home for the summer. For example, Iowa's Drake University offers online summer courses to its students.

If your own institution does not offer suitable distance learning courses, you may be able to take a distance education course from any regionally accredited college or university and get credit for it. You may even be able to save some tuition money if you select a course at a community college or a less expensive four-year college or university. The credits you earn will probably be transferable to the institution in which you are enrolled. *But before you enroll in a course at another college or university, be sure to check with your own school to make sure it will accept the credits.* Many colleges and universities require that you obtain a minimum number of credits from core courses and courses in your major in order to earn their degree. To avoid losing time and money on a course that won't be recognized by your school, it's wise to check with your academic adviser and work out a degree plan before you take courses from other institutions. If you are not currently enrolled in a degree program but think you may be in the future, taking a couple of distance education courses for credit is a good way to see whether or not a distance education degree program is for you. Later you may be able to apply the credits toward your degree.

NONCREDIT COURSES

If learning for the sake of learning or acquiring specific professional knowledge is your goal, taking a distance education course on a noncredit basis may be the way to go. Such courses may help you prepare for a new career or study for professional licensure and certification.

Just as you can audit an on-campus course for a lesser charge than if you were taking the course for credit, you can audit a distance learning course as well. Students who audit a course don't receive a grade, so they are not usually required to turn in assignments or take exams. Still, many do so in order to maximize the learning experience.

CONTINUING EDUCATION UNITS

Distance learning is a good option for working adults whose professions require continuing education, even after they've earned their degree, certificate, or license. Many states mandate continuing education for people in professions such as teaching, nursing, and accounting. For example, New Jersey requires teachers to complete 100 hours of professional development work every five years. Professionals in engineering, business, and computer science may also opt to keep up with developments in their field through distance learning. If you take a distance learning course for professional enhancement, you don't necessarily have to earn regular college credits for it. Instead, you may be able to earn Continuing Education Units. The CEU system is a nationally recognized program that provides a standardized measure for accumulating, transferring, and recognizing participation in continuing education programs. One CEU is defined as 10 contact hours of participation in an organized continuing education experience under responsible sponsorship, capable direction, and qualified instruction. Some institutions will permit you to take courses for continuing education credits rather than for regular credit or no credit. It is still important to take the

courses from a properly accredited program, however, so that employers and professional agencies will recognize them.

FINDING PROGRAMS AND COURSES

THE INTERNET

The Internet is an excellent place to start your search for information about distance learning courses and programs. Perhaps the most comprehensive database of distance learning offerings is the one maintained by Peterson's at www.petersons.com/dlearn. Peterson's, an education information provider and publisher of college directories and other education-related material (including this book), provides online access to current information about distance learning programs and courses. You can search the Peterson's distance learning database in a number of ways: by institution, degree program, or field of study. Once you have found courses or programs that match your search criteria, there are links to further information about them. Peterson's distance learning database is especially good for locating degree programs, including undergraduate and graduate certificates, associate degrees, bachelor's degrees, master's degrees, and doctoral degrees.

Another Internet database is the International Distance Learning Course Finder, provided by International Where and How. When you search for a course, you can specify course subject, course name, country, or institution; and you can narrow the search by language of instruction, mode of instructional technology, and type of credit you are seeking. The Course Finder seemed to work well for locating individual courses, but it seemed less efficient when asked to locate degree programs.

If you have particular institutions in mind, you can log on to their Web sites to find out about their distance learning courses and degrees. Some of these sites provide distance learning self-assessments and explanations of course delivery systems as well as academic information about courses and programs.

PRINT DIRECTORIES

Print directories are another excellent source of information about distance education courses and degree programs, although one should adhere to this word of caution about using the print directories: There are many directories still in libraries and bookstores that were published just a year or two ago but that are already quite out of date. So many new distance learning courses and degree programs are being offered each year that you must make sure you consult the most recent directories. Otherwise, you may miss the ideal course or program for you.

WHO OFFERS DISTANCE EDUCATION?

As communication technologies have improved and the need for continuous lifelong learning has increased, the nature of postsecondary education has begun to change. Traditional colleges and universities, which used to be the sole purveyors of higher education, now find themselves competing with a range of unconventional providers, including corporate universities, for-profit virtual universities, and unaffiliated distance learning providers. From the student's point of view, the array of institutions that offer distance learning can be confusing. What difference does it make to you whether you take a distance learning course or program from a traditional college, through a consortium of institutions of higher education, from one of the new virtual universities, or from an unaffiliated online provider?

Whether or not the institution matters depends on your purpose. If you just take a few courses for professional development or for your own pleasure and never plan to seek certification or college credit, then your choice of institution is not critical. You can just choose the distance learning provider that seems to have the courses that best suit your informal needs. However, if you plan to earn college credit, professional certification, or a degree, your choice of provider becomes much more important. You must choose an institution whose courses and degrees are widely recognized and accepted in your field. That may mean sticking to the accredited bricks-and-mortar colleges for distance learning programs, or it may mean enrolling in an innovative degree program from a virtual university only a few years old. In this section, we'll describe some of the institutions and partnerships that offer distance learning in order to acquaint you with the variety of providers that exists. In the next section, we will explain some criteria that you can use to evaluate distance education offerings.

TRADITIONAL COLLEGES AND UNIVERSITIES

The most familiar group of distance education providers consists of the traditional colleges, universities, graduate schools, community colleges, technical schools, and vocational schools. In these institutions, distance education arose as individual administrators and faculty members took the initiative to use new technologies to deliver off-campus instruction to students. As the number of courses grew, many institutions developed whole degree programs as the next step.

Among the traditional colleges and universities, public institutions are more likely to offer distance education courses and degree programs than private institutions. In addition, larger institutions are more likely to have distance learning offerings than smaller institutions.

The greatest advantage that most traditional colleges and universities bring to the distance education field is that they are established, well-known institutions with reputable faculty members

and lots of experience in education. In other words, they enter the distance learning market with solid educational credentials. If they fall short, it is likely to be in the areas of instructional and information technology. Because a lot of distance education courses are developed ad hoc, the quality of the instructional technology may vary considerably, even from one course to another within the same school. In addition, traditional colleges and universities may fall short in information technology support for faculty members and students. For example, the Gartner Group, an information technology research organization, recommends that organizations have one information technology staff person for every 50 to 75 users. In contrast, colleges and universities report an average of one technical support person for every 150 to 800 users. Recognizing this shortcoming, many colleges and universities have established policies and procedures to set up instructional technology standards and consistency, and they have increased their technical resources and training efforts to support faculty members and students. In addition, because developing quality distance education courses and programs is time-consuming and expensive, colleges and universities have begun to form partnerships to pool their resources. These partnerships, called consortia, have quickly developed into major players in the world of distance higher education.

CONSORTIA

Distance learning consortia are associations or partnerships of higher education institutions that have agreed to cooperate to provide distance learning courses and resources. Most consortia are designed to provide students with a greater selection of both courses and faculty expertise than is available at a single institution. Some consortia also offer centralized student and faculty support services. Just as there are many variations on the basic on-campus program, there are many distance education consortium models too.

It's important to remember that most distance learning consortia are not degree-granting institutions to which the student applies. Though there are exceptions to this, as in the case of Western Governors University and National Technological University (discussed later in the section), students normally apply directly to at least one school in the consortium as a means of accessing the resources of other member institutions.

Almost without exception, accredited universities in consortia have roughly the same application procedures and admissions requirements for distance degree programs as for traditional campus-based programs. In general, minimum grade point averages, standardized test scores of a certain percentile, and letters of recommendation or intent are required for both bachelor's and master's degree programs. The exception is the competency-based program that waives academic credentials and previous schooling and instead uses workplace experience and learned skill-based assessments to place students. So why do you need to know about consortia if you probably will never apply to one? The answer is that by enrolling in a college or university degree program, you may find yourself in a consortium without even realizing it, especially if you attend a state university.

TYPES OF CONSORTIA

Over the last few years, several types of consortia have emerged as the most successful and most popular distance education models. Among them are statewide consortia of public universities and colleges, statewide consortia of public and private institutions, regional consortia, consortia of peer institutions of higher education, and specialized consortia.

Statewide Consortia of Public Colleges and Universities. On the tightly focused side of the spectrum, a consortium may consist of the campuses of a single state university system. Students access the distance learning offerings of the various state colleges through a portal sometimes referred to as a virtual university.

A good example of a public statewide consortium is the University of Texas TeleCampus collaboration, which consists of fifteen UT campuses (www.telecampus.utsystem.edu). In collaborative degree plans offered via the TeleCampus, you may apply to one school, take courses from several partner institutions, use centralized support services, and receive a fully accredited degree from the "home" campus to which you originally applied. The TeleCampus serves as both a portal to distance education offerings in the Texas system and as a centralized point of service.

Many other states operate or develop consortia of their public colleges and universities, including Connecticut, Illinois, Kansas, Massachusetts, Michigan, New Jersey, New York, Ohio, Oklahoma, Oregon, South Dakota, and Tennessee. All have arrangements in place whereby students can take some transferable credits on line from more than one institution and apply them to a degree at their home institution.

Statewide Consortia of Public and Private Colleges and Universities. Broadening the scope a bit is the statewide consortium that includes both public and private institutions of higher education. Students in the state can use a single Web site to select distance education courses offered by member colleges and universities. If you are enrolled in a degree program at one member institution, you have access to distance learning courses given by other member institutions. Although the consortia members typically work together to maximize the transferability of credits from one college or university to another, it is still usually up to you to ensure that credits earned elsewhere can be applied to your home institution's degree.

For example, Kentucky Commonwealth Virtual University (KCVU) encompasses more than fifty institutions in the state of Kentucky, ranging from universities to technical colleges (www.kcvu.org). Each member institution charges its own tuition rates for in-state and out-of-state students. In addition to maintaining a centralized Internet directory of all distance learning courses offered in Kentucky, KCVU offers exceptional student support services. For example, you can fill out a common form to apply on line to any of the fifty member institutions. Once you are admitted to the KCVU system, you have centralized online access to every library book in the system as well as online access to the full text

of 5,000 journals. If you wish to check out a book, it will be sent to the nearest public library, where you can pick it up free of charge. If there is no library nearby, the book will be sent by courier to your home or office. Your academic records will be maintained by each institution at which you take a course, but also by KCVU, which will keep your complete records from all institutions.

Regional Consortia. Regional consortia include institutions of higher education from more than one state. Such consortia may involve public institutions, private institutions, or a mix of both. The Southern Regional Education Board (SREB) launched the Southern Regional Electronic Campus (SREC) in 1998 and now offers more than 3,200 courses from 262 colleges and universities in sixteen states (www.electroniccampus.org). SREC attempts to guarantee a standard of quality in the courses it lists by reviewing them to make sure they are well set up and supported by adequate services. It does not judge curriculum (it leaves that to member institutions) nor does it list courses in their first year of instruction.

From the Electronic Campus Web site, you can identify distance learning programs and courses that are available from all member institutions. For more detailed information, you can search the site by college or university, discipline, level, and state, including course descriptions and how the programs and courses are delivered. You can also connect directly to a particular college or university to learn about registration, enrollment, and cost. To improve its student services, the Electronic Campus has formed a partnership with the University System of Georgia to create a new Web site known as Ways In (www.waysin.org). From that site, students are able to apply for admission, register for classes, get information about and apply for financial aid, make payments, purchase textbooks, and use new online library services.

The SREC system is administratively decentralized. The acceptance of transfer credits and the use of credits for program requirements are determined by the college or university in which the student is enrolled. Likewise, all institutions set their own levels for in-state and out-of-state tuition, maintain individual student records, and determine policy with respect to access to their own student services. Therefore, if you take three classes from three different institutions you might have to be admitted to all three, pay three different tuition rates, and contact all three institutions for your academic records. A unique model of regional distance education collaboration, consisting of members from nineteen states, is Western Governors University (www.wgu.edu). Unlike most other virtual universities that serve as the hub of a consortium, WGU enrolls its own students and grants its own degrees by assessing students' knowledge through competency-based examinations. WGU does not teach its own courses, but it provides its students with access to courses from member institutions.

Other regional consortia include the National Universities Degree Consortium, a collaboration of ten accredited universities from across the United States (www.nudc.org); and the Canadian Virtual University, which includes seven universities across Canada (www.cvu-uvc.ca). Today, students can even choose to participate in a global consortium like CREAD, the Inter-American network of institutions throughout North, Central, and South America.

Consortia of Peer Institutions of Higher Education. Groups of institutions sometimes form consortia because they have a common orientation or complementary strengths from which students might benefit.

For example, the Jesuit Distance Education Network of the Association of Jesuit Colleges and Universities seeks to expand the array of learning options for students on its twenty-four campuses in nineteen states (www.jesuitnet.com). Administrators hope to develop the JesuitNET system so that a student enrolled at any member institution will be able to take fully transferable online courses at any other member institution. Tuition rates will be set by individual colleges and universities. Through its Web site, JesuitNET promotes these schools' online degree and certificate programs as well as individual courses.

Another, more recent private college and university consortium uses a "team teaching" approach to deliver courses to students on multiple campuses. Thirteen institutions in the Associated Colleges of the South have created a "virtual classics department," (www.sunoikisis.org). In this case, students must all log on at the same time in order to tune in to an online audio broadcast of a lecture. During the lecture students may pose questions and make comments in a live chat room. Classes are "team taught" in the sense that professors from several campuses may take responsibility for course material and all log on together with the students.

Specialized Consortia. Some consortia are formed by institutions that focus on a particular field. For example, National Technological University (NTU) is one of the oldest technology-based consortia (www.ntu.edu). A global university, NTU, arranges for its member colleges and universities across the country to deliver advanced technical education and training, usually to employees of corporate clients. Currently, more than 1,200 courses are available through NTU's participating universities, which provides fourteen master's degree programs. An unusual aspect of the NTU consortium is that the consortium itself, rather than the member institutions, is the degree-granting body.

NTU's focus is on technical education and training that is ready to use in the workforce. Its corporate customers typically have purchased the equipment necessary to receive the courses. Though students who are not employed by an NTU corporate client may take courses, they must pay an extra fee to have tapes or CD-ROMs of courses sent to them. NTU has also partnered with the Public Broadcasting System (PBS) to create the Business and Technology Network, a series of more than seventy-five engineering programs per year delivered directly to organizations via satellite.

PROS AND CONS OF CONSORTIA LEARNING MODELS

One obvious advantage of consortia is the pooling of resources. More university partners translates to more choices in curriculum, and often a shared expense in developing instructional design and technology. Consortia can offer a centralized database or course schedule that allows you to find members' courses easily rather than having to search many institutions' materials and Web sites for what you need. You may also have the chance to choose from among a group of respected faculty members from within the consortia, which allows you to find the teachers with expertise most closely suited to your academic and professional interests.

This large sampling of faculty members tends to offer a more diverse worldview in the classroom. And, a consortium can often provide essential student services on a scale not fiscally achievable by a single university. For example, a dozen universities can pool resources for a much broader digital library than any single school could supply on its own.

However, from the student's point of view, consortia can have problems, many of which can be attributed to their relative newness. The most critical of these for students are problems with transferring credits. Other drawbacks may include large class sizes and problems in communication.

Problems with Transferring Credits. One problem that sometimes comes up for students trying to earn an entire degree, or part of a degree, on line is that their home institution may require a minimum number of "home" credits, yet it may not offer enough courses via distance learning for a student to meet that minimum. "I am concerned because [my home campus] offers a limited number of online classes," says Andrea Bessel, who is working toward a bachelor's degree in business administration with a concentration in finance. Bessel, who works full time and prefers the convenience of online to on-campus courses, has been taking classes from several institutions in the State University of New York (SUNY) Learning Network (www.sln.suny.edu). "It is great that other SUNY campuses offer more courses," continues Bessel, "but I am concerned about accumulating too many transfer credits—you are only allowed so many."

In the future, this problem is likely to arise less often for several reasons. First, as distance education degree programs become more common and well known, students are likely to search them out and apply directly to the institution that offers them. In contrast, like many other students, Bessel applied to her local state college campus and only later discovered that taking online courses within the statewide system was much more convenient than traveling to class. Second, individual institutions will continue to add to their distance education offerings, broadening the course choices for their "home" students. And third, some state systems and other consortia may eventually decide to liberalize their rules on transfer credit maximums within the consortium as the demand for distance degrees increases.

Indeed, some consortia have already succeeded in solving credit transfer problems, and others are addressing the challenge of reconciling differing credit transfer policies and logistics. *However, to ensure that any courses you take will successfully transfer from one institution to another (and ultimately toward your degree), you should secure an academic adviser at the start of your program and investigate the transferrability of credits before you register for courses at other institutions within the consortium.* Serving as your own adviser brings the risk that some courses may ultimately not transfer toward your degree.

Large Class Size. Because so many students have access to courses in a consortium, online classes may reach an unmanageable size if limits are not placed on the student-to-teacher ratio. Many schools now adopt a ceiling on the number of students allowed in an online class, with teaching assistants or subsections of the course added for each additional set of students. This is vital to the processing of information and interaction required in the successful online course. Faculty members often find that a class of 25 students is quite manageable, but more may become problematic.

Miscommunication. Communication may be difficult in a consortium. The larger the consortium, the more likely that many universities or university systems are involved, and therefore you may need to communicate with several institutions that have differing policies and procedures. Additional communication snags can arise when you try to move your student records from one campus to the next. Some consortia have spent considerable time, effort, and money to make this tedious and laborious process appear seamless to you as a student. For those that have not, you should be prepared to take a proactive stance in helping to see that your records are successfully moved from one department, college, or university to another.

COMPARING THE SINGLE UNIVERSITY TO THE CONSORTIUM

A student who is looking for a learning community with school pride and a great deal of local loyalty may find the multicampus environment of a consortium less desirable than the collegiality of the single university environment. In today's workplace and economy, however, many students opt for the flexibility and increased curriculum choices of a consortium over an individual school. Many consortia have succeeded in creating a sense of community for learners, and many more are attempting to do so. The high level of dialogue in the online environment can often build friendships, connections, and communities not achieved in a traditional environment. A single university can offer you the chance to immerse yourself in one department (of your major, for example), but a consortium can offer a wider variety of choices in mentors and philosophies. As a student, you should think about which you'd prefer.

VIRTUAL UNIVERSITIES

In recent years, the development of communication technology has led to a new type of institution called a virtual university. It's a school without a campus that delivers instruction and degree programs exclusively via technology and usually for a profit. The University of Phoenix Online, Walden University, the United States Open University, and Jones International University are all examples of virtual universities. Some of these institutions have years of experience in distance learning and have evolved as the technologies have changed. For example, Walden University is more than thirty years old, and the University of Phoenix Online was established in 1989 as an offshoot of the University of Phoenix, which was founded in 1976. Others, like the United States Open University, are newly established with a much shorter track record. What most of these institutions have in common is a focus on education for adults. Their course offerings, degree

programs, and student services are all geared toward the busy working adult who needs the flexibility of distance education. For example, courses at the University of Phoenix Online are delivered via the Internet. Students take one 5-week course at a time, which allows them to focus their effort intensively on one subject. Student services can be accessed via the university Web site. "We are customer-service oriented," says Russell Paden, regional executive director of academic affairs at the University of Phoenix Online. "We make things easy and convenient for the student." Virtual universities have a mixed reputation in the world of higher education. Although their degrees are accepted by many employers, they are often looked down upon by traditional academics. A few are regionally accredited, some are too new to be accredited, and some are modern versions of the old diploma mills (see "Selecting a Good Distance Learning Program" for more on accreditation).

From a student's point of view, then, the biggest disadvantage of a virtual university may be its less-than-stellar educational reputation, whether deserved or not. A great advantage of the best of these institutions, however, is that they tend to be sophisticated in terms of instructional technology and design and technical support. To the student, this can mean ease, convenience, and flexibility.

THE NEW ONLINE PROVIDERS

The growth of the distance learning market in higher education, continuing education, and training has attracted investors and educators who are eager to provide courses to adults, primarily via the Internet. There are many of these startup ventures, and they take many forms. A few examples to illustrate:

- UNext.com is working with faculty members from prestigious schools like Columbia and Stanford to develop online business courses for the corporate market. At present, it is piloting courses with groups of employees from large corporations. Eventually it hopes to offer a complete M.B.A. program as well as other degrees through its subsidiary, Cardean University.
- The Global Education Network (GEN) plans to offer distance education courses from some of the top colleges in the United States, including Brown, Wellesley, and Williams.
- Harcourt Higher Education, an online college, a division of Thomson Learning.
- KaplanCollege.com is planning to offer graduate courses for teachers through the John F. Kennedy University.

All of these ventures are so new that it's impossible to guess which will still exist in five years' time. In the next few years, the new online providers will begin to sort themselves out as some models succeed and some fail. If you are taking courses through your employer or for personal reasons, you may find that one of these companies has courses that meet your needs. If, however, you are looking for a degree program, you are better off sticking with well-established institutions of higher education, at least at present.

SELECTING A GOOD DISTANCE LEARNING PROGRAM

As a prospective distance learning student, you should begin to evaluate programs in which you are interested as much as you would any campus-based, traditional program. The first question, of course, is: Does the curriculum meet your educational and professional goals? If it doesn't, there's not much point in looking into that program any further, however flexible and convenient it seems. If the program does seem to meet your educational needs, then the real work of evaluating it must begin.

Distance education students need to be especially concerned about the quality of the programs they are considering for two main reasons. First, there are a lot of diploma mills out there. As we've seen, there has been a proliferation of distance learning degree programs spurred by the Internet. Many are legitimate, but some are not. As one distance bachelor's degree student put it, "Admission to some online programs consists of nothing more than your name, date of birth, and a check." In fact, to demonstrate how easy it is to set up an online "university" that looks authentic, Emir Mohammed created a Web site for Oxford Open University, a fictitious virtual university, complete with a list of imaginary faculty members with degrees from bogus institutions. So if you run across a school that promises you a degree for little time, effort, or money, be cautious. If it sounds too good to be true, it probably is.

The second reason distance learning students must be especially careful about quality is that in many quarters, distance degrees are still considered the poor relations of degrees earned on campus. "One area of confusion for working adult students is the reaction to distance learning from traditional academia," says Russell Paden, regional executive director of academic affairs for the University of Phoenix Online. "Although attitudes are changing, some in the traditional academic world still think their way is the only way." Robert V. Steiner, who directs the distance learning project at Teachers College, Columbia University, agrees. "For better or worse, justly or not," he says, "there continues to be a perception that distance education degree programs are inferior to traditional programs." Fritz J. Messere, associate professor of broadcasting at the State University of New York at Oswego, thinks that in five or six years, that attitude will change. "When we see what the people with distance degrees actually accomplish in the future, our reluctance to acknowledge that these are real degrees and meaningful educational experiences will disappear."

However, in the meantime you need to evaluate each distance education program that looks promising to ensure that its certificate or degree will be of value to you in the future. What can you do to ensure that a distance credential will be recognized in the academic, professional, and/or business communities? What can you do to assess whether or not the program and the university are of high quality? Basically, you must do a lot of research. You must gather information from the program, university, accrediting agencies, professional associations, faculty, current and former

students, and colleagues. Only then can you make an informed decision about whether a program is good as well as right for you.

To guide you in this task, this section describes some of the criteria you should keep in mind as you evaluate each distance education program. *Pay particular attention to the sections on reputation and accreditation.* More than any other factors, a school and program's reputation and accreditation status can serve as benchmarks of quality that will affect the value of your degree.

REPUTATION

"Look for a brand name—a recognized university," suggests Fritz J. Messere of SUNY Oswego. For many students, the reputation of the school is the paramount factor in selecting a program. Sonja Cole, a middle-school media specialist who is enrolled in a continuing professional education program at Rutgers University in New Jersey, explains, "I know that Rutgers has an excellent reputation for academic rigor, so I assumed that their online courses would be just as challenging and stimulating." She continues, "The most important factor to me was the reputation of the school, because distance learning programs are not always taken seriously by administrators and business people . . . . If you can say you took distance courses at a very reputable school, they will be more likely to give you credit." Not only should you consider the reputation of a university in general, you should consider the reputation of a distance degree from a university *in your field.* For example, if you plan to earn a bachelor's degree at a distance to prepare for graduate work, find out whether or not graduate programs in your field will accept an undergraduate distance degree, even from a reputable institution.

"If you are in doubt about the validity of a distance degree in your chosen field, ask around," advises Patti Wolf, assistant professor of computer science at University of Maryland University College. When Wolf was looking for a doctoral program for herself, almost all of her colleagues advised her that a distance degree would not be as well accepted in her chosen career as a traditional degree. Another doctoral student, who is earning an Ed.D. from a relatively new virtual university, regrets that "the one thing I didn't do [was] speak to administrators in local universities to review the reputation of the school I finally chose. Even though the program is still exactly what I wanted and the convenience, schedule, and costs meet my needs, the public perception of this program is not wonderful." Carla Gentry, who is earning a distance master's degree in nursing (nurse practitioner) at Gonzaga University in Washington, puts the importance of reputation succinctly: "You wouldn't want to spend all that time and money and then find out that the degree isn't worth anything."

ACCREDITATION

The accreditation status of a college, university, or program can give you an indication of its general quality and reputation. But just what does accreditation mean, and how does it affect distance learners?

WHAT IS ACCREDITATION?

In the United States, authority over postsecondary educational institutions is decentralized. The states, not the federal government, have the authority to regulate educational institutions within their borders, and as a consequence, standards and quality vary considerably for "state-approved" schools. You will find many state-approved schools that are not accredited, and many that are.

In order to ensure a basic level of quality, the practice of accrediting institutions arose. Private, nongovernmental educational agencies with a regional or national scope have adopted standards to evaluate whether or not colleges and universities provide educational programs at basic levels of quality. Institutions that seek accreditation conduct an in-depth self-study to measure their performance against the standards. The accrediting agency then conducts an on-site evaluation and either awards accreditation or preaccreditation status—or denies accreditation. Periodically the agency reevaluates each institution to make sure its continued accreditation is warranted. So accreditation is not a one-shot deal—an institution must maintain high standards or it runs the risk of jeopardizing its accreditation status as a result of one of the periodic evaluations.

Seeking accreditation is entirely voluntary on the part of the institution of higher education. The initial accreditation process takes a long time—as much as five or ten years—and it costs money. You can see that a very new school will not have been in operation long enough to be accredited.

INSTITUTIONAL AND SPECIALIZED ACCREDITATION

There are two basic types of accreditation: institutional accreditation and specialized accreditation. Institutional accreditation is awarded to an institution by one of six regional accrediting agencies and many national accrediting agencies, such as the Distance Education and Training Council. The regional accrediting agencies play the largest role in institutional accreditation (see the Appendix for a list of the regional accrediting agencies). If a college or university is regionally accredited, that means that the institution as a whole has met the accrediting agency's standards. Within the institution, particular programs and departments contribute to the institution's objectives at varying levels of quality. There are several benefits of enrolling in a program at a regionally accredited college or university:

- You are assured of a basic level of quality education and services.
- Any credits you earn are more likely to be transferable to other regionally accredited institutions, although we've seen that each institution makes its own decisions on transfer credits on a case-by-case basis.
- Any certificate or degree you earn is more likely to be recognized by other colleges and universities and by employers as a legitimate credential.

- You may qualify for federal loans and grants because regionally accredited institutions are eligible to participate in Title IV financial aid programs (see "Paying for Your Education" for more on financial aid).

In contrast to institutional accreditation, specialized accreditation usually applies to a single department, program, or school that is part of a larger institution of higher education. The accredited unit may be as big as a college within a university or as small as a curriculum within a field of study. Most specialized accrediting agencies review units within institutions that are regionally accredited, although some also accredit freestanding institutions. There are specialized accrediting agencies in almost fifty fields, including allied health, art and design, Bible college education, business, engineering, law, marriage and family therapy, nursing, psychology, and theology. Specialized accreditation may or may not be a consideration for you when you evaluate distance education programs. That's because the role of specialized accreditation varies considerably depending on the field of study. In some professional fields, you must have a degree or certificate from a program with specialized accreditation in order to take qualifying exams or practice the profession. In other fields, specialized accreditation has little or no effect on your ability to work. Thus, it's especially important that you find out what role accreditation plays in your field since it may affect your professional future as well as the quality of your education.

CHECKING ON A SCHOOL AND ITS ACCREDITORS

Since accreditation is awarded by private organizations, any group can hang out a shingle and proclaim itself an accrediting agency. Some diploma mills, for example, have been known to create their own accrediting agency and then proclaim themselves "accredited." So how can you tell (1) if the school or college in which you are interested is regionally accredited, (2) if the program has the specialized accreditation you need, and (3) if the agencies that have accredited the school and program are legitimate? Of course, you can simply ask the school or program, but since accreditation is so important, it's probably a lot wiser to check elsewhere.

First, check with the regional accrediting agency that covers the state in which the school is located. Then check with any specialized accrediting agency that may assess the particular program in which you are interested.

To find out if an accrediting agency is legitimate and nationally recognized, you can consult the Council for Higher Education Accreditation (CHEA), a private agency that accredits the accreditors (www.chea.org). Or you can check with the U.S. Department of Education. Their Web site has a complete list of institutional and specialized accrediting agencies recognized by the federal government (www.ed.gov/offices/OPE/accreditation/natlagencies.html). This Web site will also tell you whether or not accreditation by a particular agency makes the school eligible to participate in federal financial aid programs. A list of regional and specialized accrediting agencies, with contact information, is also provided in the Appendix.

CHECKING ON CANADIAN INSTITUTIONS OF HIGHER EDUCATION

In Canada, as in the United States, there is no centralized governmental accrediting agency. Instead, the provincial governments evaluate the quality of university programs in each province, with a few nationwide agencies evaluating professional programs. To check on a Canadian university, you can contact the appropriate provincial department of education. To get general information about accreditation in Canada, visit the Web site of the Council of Ministers of Education at www.cmec.ca. Their Web site also has contact information and links to the provincial departments of education.

CHECKING ON AN UNACCREDITED INSTITUTION

As we've seen, seeking accreditation is a voluntary process, and some legitimate schools choose not to undertake it. In addition, the newer virtual universities may not have been around long enough to be accredited. So what can you do to make sure a school is legitimate if it is not accredited?

First, you can call the state agency with jurisdiction over higher education in the state in which the school is located. The agency can at least tell you whether or not the school is operating with a legitimate charter, and it may be able to tell you if any complaints have been lodged or legal action taken against it. Second, you can call the school and ask why it is not accredited and whether the school has plans to seek accreditation. If the school tells you it has applied for accreditation, double-check its status with the agency it names. Third, you can consult with people in your field about the school's reputation and the value of its degree. Remember, in some fields, a degree from an unaccredited school or program will bar you from professional licensure and practice. So keep in mind that enrolling in an unaccredited school or program can be risky. If you can avoid it, do so.

ACCREDITATION ISSUES RELATING TO DISTANCE EDUCATION

In the United States during the 1990s, controversy arose over the accreditation of online programs within traditional universities and the accreditation of completely virtual universities. On the one hand, many felt that online degree programs should be evaluated using the same criteria as other degree programs within institutions of higher education. Others thought that new standards were needed to properly evaluate distance education.

Although this issue has not yet been settled, the six regional accrediting agencies have proposed uniform guidelines for evaluating distance education. The impetus for this move is the fact that many distance education programs cross regional borders; the agencies want to ensure that similar standards are adopted across the country. Among the proposed criteria specific to accrediting distance education are faculty control of course content, technical and program support for both faculty members and students, and evaluation and assessment methods for measuring student learning. However, until these or other guidelines are accepted, distance education programs will continue to be evaluated using the same criteria as on-campus programs.

PROGRAM QUALITY

The reputation of a college or university and its accreditation status can give you a broad idea of its standing in the academic and professional world. If you are pursuing a graduate degree or know your field of interest as an undergraduate, it's important to separate the reputation of the program or department in which you are interested from the reputation of the university to which it belongs. Granted, in many cases, both the program and the university will have similar reputations. But in some cases, you may find a below average program at an excellent university or an above average program at a university with a lesser reputation.

Keep in mind that you should be looking for a high-quality curriculum and good faculty; the fact that the program is taught at a distance should be secondary. "I chose this program because it would have been one of my top three choices if I had decided to pursue a full-time [on-campus] master's program," explains Lara Hollenczer, who is earning a distance master's degree in communications management at Syracuse University. Hollenczer suggests talking to professors and current students to get a better idea of a program in which you are interested.

ACADEMIC QUALITY

One way to assess the quality of a program, as we have seen, is to find out whether or not it is accredited by a specialized agency—if that applies in your field. But there are other ways to assess a program's academic quality. First, look at the curriculum. Does it cover what you need to learn? Is the syllabus up to date? For one master's degree student in nursing (family nurse practitioner studies), the quality of the curriculum was the factor that led her to choose Gonzaga University. "I definitely wanted to know that when I graduated I would have a good education and know what I was doing," she explains.

Next, check some of the program's student data. For example, what percentage of students who enroll actually complete the degree? What percentage of students is employed in a field relating to their studies? What are some of the program's graduates doing today? A program with a high completion rate and successful graduates is preferable to one with a high dropout rate.

FACULTY

Second, check out the faculty members. What are their credentials? What are their areas of expertise? Are they well regarded in their field? If the program is professional in nature, look for faculty members with a blend of academic background and professional experience. If the program is academic, you should find out whether tenure-track professors with Ph.D.'s teach both the on-campus and distance courses or if distance courses are relegated to part-time adjunct faculty members and/or assistants. Finally, evaluate whether or not the faculty is experienced both with the course content and with the instructional medium. If a program looks interesting to you, get in touch with a couple of faculty members to discuss it. You can tell a lot about a program by whether or not the faculty members are willing to take some time to talk to prospective students.

EXPERIENCE WITH ADULT LEARNERS

A third area of concern is the program's experience with adult learners. If you're an adult learner and choose to enroll in a college oriented to young undergraduates, you may find yourself struggling to cope. "My concern would be that in some programs the adult learner is an afterthought," says Claudine SchWeber, assistant vice president for distance education and lifelong learning at University of Maryland University College. "Adults are more critical consumers, and that won't fly these days." Working adult students have different needs than full-time on-campus students, and assessing the degree to which a program takes those needs into account can help you decide whether or not a program is a good match for you.

For Robin Barnes, who is pursuing a distance master's degree in nursing (family nurse practitioner studies) at Gonzaga University, the flexibility of the faculty in dealing with adult students was extremely important. "We were adult learners who had lives and jobs outside of school. If we needed more time for a paper due to work schedules or a family crisis, the instructors were very understanding." Carla Gentry, in the same program, agrees. "The most important factor to me is the flexibility of the program and the staff's willingness to work with my schedule."

INSTRUCTIONAL DESIGN AND TECHNOLOGY

There are several areas that fall under the broad category of instructional design and technology that you should assess for each program you consider.

IS THE INSTRUCTIONAL TECHNOLOGY A GOOD MATCH FOR THE CONTENT?

Your first concern in the area of instructional design and technology should be whether or not the delivery system and the content are a good match. "How can you evaluate whether the technology and content mesh?" asks Robert V. Steiner of Teacher's College, Columbia University. "Online courses are more suitable for knowledge-intensive fields like business and engineering," he points out. "Subjects involving skills development and human interaction are more difficult to convey on line." So, for example, in many behavioral sciences courses that involve clinical components, you need to be able to watch human interaction. In many science courses, you need to be able to do lab work. Such courses are more suited to two-way interactive video or on-campus formats than to the online format.

IS THE INSTRUCTIONAL TECHNOLOGY A GOOD MATCH FOR YOU?

Your second consideration is whether or not the instructional technology is a good match for your skills, personality, and learning style. In "Is Distance Learning Right for You?", we covered the pros and cons of the various technologies and described the skills and temperaments best suited to each.

If you are uncertain about your ability to adapt to a program's instructional technology, there are several things you can do. "If possible, take a tour of the technology being used before you enroll," advises Patti Wolf of University of Maryland University College. Many institutional Web sites offer short demos, previews, or tutorials so you can get an idea of what the instructional technology will be like. For example, if you are interested in a distance program at Penn State, you can take a sample course on its World Campus Web site. If the programs in which you are interested do not offer such amenities, ask previous students how the instructional technology worked and what level of expertise is necessary. If technology is an area of particular concern for you, you might even consider a trial run. "I would recommend taking one course before deciding to apply to a school, to see if the style works for the individual," suggests Nicole DeRaleau, an environmental engineering master's degree candidate at Worcester Poly-

technic Institute. "If it doesn't work, then perhaps the credits can be transferred and there is no major loss."

HOW RELIABLE IS THE TECHNOLOGY?

On a related note, because distance students depend on technology, it's important that it be reliable. Not only will you depend on your own computer, VCR, or television, but you will depend on the institution's technology, too. Ask current students what their experiences have been. Does the server often go down? Are there frequent problems with camera equipment or satellite transmissions?

If the program is newly formatted for distance education, be prepared for some technological bugs to be worked out on your watch. If the prospect of participating in a maiden voyage is too anxiety-provoking, look for programs that have been running for at least a year.

Last, find out what technical support is offered to students. The best setup is free technical support accessed via an 800-number 24 hours a day, seven days a week.

HOW DO THE FACULTY AND STUDENTS INTERACT?

You should also investigate how the communication and social issues involved in distance learning are dealt with in the programs in which you are interested. (For a review of these issues, see "Is Distance Learning Right for You?") For example, how do students and faculty members communicate? Will you be expected to log on to an online course at specific times or at your convenience? Will you be expected to participate in online discussions a certain number of times during the course? For example, at the University of Phoenix Online, students are expected to log on and participate five days out of seven. At other schools, participation requirements may be program-wide or set by individual instructors.

Another question to ask is: What is done to overcome the distance learner's social isolation? Some programs do little; others rely on group work to forge a community of learning; and still others use a cohort format, in which a group of students enrolls in a program at the same time and proceeds through it together at the same pace.

Pay particular attention to the faculty-to-student ratio in online courses. If there are more than 25 to 30 students per instructor, you're not likely to get much individual attention.

ADVISING AND OTHER SERVICES

Academic advising is one of the most important student services for distance learners, especially if you are seeking to transfer credits or earn credits through examinations or from life experience to apply to a degree. Check what advising services are offered to distance learners, and see how easy they are to access. "I tested academic advising services," reports a distance learning undergraduate at University of Maryland University College. "That was important to me because I've been out of college for such a long time and I needed some help in selecting courses to complete requirements." Advising is also of particular interest to students in a consortium. If you are interested in a program that is part of a consortium, find out if the consortium offers advising or mentoring to help you navigate among institutions and to guide your overall progress.

Other support services that are important to distance education students are libraries, bookstores, administrative support, record keeping, and technical support (discussed above). Many institutions and consortia offer online and telephone access to these services for distance students. In particular, access to an online library is extremely important, especially if you don't live near a good college or university library. Find out what type of access is offered, what the library's resources are, how materials are delivered, and if training on how to use an online library is offered.

If the program in which you are interested is part of a consortium, be sure you understand how each of these student services is handled. In some cases you will have access only to your home institution's services; in other cases you will have access to the services of all member institutions.

Another thing to watch out for is the extent to which the institution as a whole has kept up with an innovative degree program. For example, at many universities, distance learning courses and programs originate in a couple of departments eager to pursue new ways of educating. However, the university's centralized academic and administrative services may lag behind, leaving distance students to struggle with a system not designed for their needs.

As you investigate a program and its services, keep in mind that the way you are treated as a prospective student can tell you something about what you will encounter once enrolled. "Look at the responsiveness of the institution," advises Robert V. Steiner of Teacher's College, Columbia University, "and ask yourself, 'How client-centered is that program?'"

RESIDENCY REQUIREMENT

Some programs, especially doctoral programs, have a residency requirement for distance learning students. The requirement may be several campus visits during the course of a semester, or a brief on-site meeting at the start of a semester. Some residency periods may last up to a week or two. In addition, you may have to travel to campus to take exams, or you may be able to take them locally with a proctor. Be sure you understand what the on-site requirements of a program are, and whether or not you can fulfill them.

TIME FRAMES

Check to see how much time you have to complete a certificate or degree program, and decide whether or not the time frame meets your needs. Some programs have a generous upper limit on the number of years you may take to complete a degree, which allows you to proceed at your own pace. Other programs may be structured on an accelerated or cohort model, with a timetable and lots of interim deadlines. If that's the case, make sure your own schedule can accommodate this. For example, if a program goes year-round and you are usually at a cabin in the woods without Internet access every summer, the program is not a good match for

your lifestyle. In addition, if you are considering an accelerated or cohort degree program, make sure you have the support of your family, who may not get much attention from you during this period.

COST

The cost of a distance education degree or certificate program is often the same for on-campus and distance students. However, there are some things you should look out for:

- If you enroll in a consortium, member institutions may charge tuition at different rates.
- If you enroll in a public university, you will probably be charged out-of-state tuition if you are not a state resident.
- Some institutions charge an extra technology fee to cover the costs associated with distance education.
- If there is a residency period, you should plan on spending money for travel, accommodations, and meals.
- If you enroll in an online program, you need to budget for hardware, software, and Internet access as well as books.
- If you are interested in receiving federal financial aid, you must be enrolled in an institution accredited by one of the regional accrediting agencies or certain of the specialized agencies approved by the U.S. Department of Education (check their Website at www.ed.gov/offices/OPE/accreditation/natlagencies.html).

YOUR PERSONAL CHECKLIST

This section discusses many factors that you can consider when evaluating a distance education program. Here is a checklist to sum up the criteria you should keep in mind:

- ✔ The institution's reputation
- ✔ Institutional (regional) accreditation
- ✔ Specialized accreditation, if applicable
- ✔ The program's quality: curriculum, faculty, and responsiveness to adult learners
- ✔ A good match between instructional technology and content
- ✔ A good match between instructional technology and your skills, personality, and learning style
- ✔ Interaction among students and faculty members
- ✔ Reliability of technology and good technical support
- ✔ Academic advising services
- ✔ Other support services: library, bookstore, administrative support, and record keeping
- ✔ Residency requirements, if any
- ✔ Time frame for completing certificate or degree
- ✔ Cost

Although we have described many factors, in the end there may be only three or four aspects of a program that really concern you. You may be more interested in a program's reputation than in any other factor. Or accreditation may be the most important issue for you. Perhaps you are concerned about finding a good match between your personality and learning style and the instructional design of a program. That is why the self-assessment you did while reading "Is Distance Learning Right for You?" is so crucial, since you can now focus on what's important to you when you evaluate distance programs.

So remember, keep your own educational, professional, and personal needs in the forefront during the selection process. Choosing a good program not only means choosing a high-quality program; it also means choosing a program that's a good match for you.

TAKING STANDARDIZED ADMISSIONS TESTS

For some people, the prospect of taking one of the standardized admissions tests is enough to make them put aside the idea of earning a degree indefinitely. You may be anxious about taking the SAT, Graduate Record Examinations (GRE), or one of the professional exams, but if you have chosen to apply to a program that requires an admissions test, there is no way of avoiding the experience. Many undergraduate programs require the SAT or ACT. Graduate programs often require the GRE or a professional examination, and some require a subject area test and writing assessment as well. Finally, if you are not a native speaker of English, you may need to pass a test of English language proficiency. So unless you've chosen to apply to programs that do not require an examination, you are going to have to take at least one exam—and do well on it.

Note that community colleges and many programs designed specifically for adult learners, including some distance learning programs, do not require a standardized admissions test as part of the application process. Therefore, the first thing you should do is to determine which exam(s), if any, you are expected to take. This information should appear in the packet that accompanies the program's application form. If you do not yet have this material, you should simply call the admissions office or program and ask or check the program's Web site. Once you know which exam you must take, contact the testing service that gives the exam and request registration materials or register on line. Information on contacting the testing services appears in the Appendix.

Before we go into detail about the tests, it might be helpful to discuss how an admissions committee might use your score. The role played by the SAT or ACT on the undergraduate level is similar to the GRE or GMAT on the graduate level. These tests provide a benchmark. Essentially, your test score is one of the few objective bits of information in your application that can be used to gauge where you fall in the range of applicants. A few programs, especially the top professional programs that receive many more applicants than they can admit, may use the score as a means of reducing the applicant pool. If your score is below their cutoff, they will not even look at the rest of your application. But most programs are much more flexible in the way they evaluate scores. If your score is low, you may still be considered for admission, especially if your grade point average is high, your work experience is relevant, or your application is otherwise strong. Others will index your exam score and your grade point average to arrive at a more balanced number. Some programs offer a conditional admission when a standardized exam score is low. In order to earn an unconditional admission, you may have to retake the exam to boost your score or achieve a certain GPA in the first courses you take.

Basically, you should regard taking a standardized admissions test as an opportunity to improve your application. And that means you must take the test with plenty of time left to meet application deadlines (see "Taking Standardized Admissions Tests" and "Applying for Admission to Degree Programs" for more information on applying). That way, if you take the test early and are disappointed with the results, you will have time to retake it. Note that test registration deadlines precede test dates by about six weeks and that you must also allow a few weeks after the testing date for score reporting.

You must also prepare. Thorough preparation, including taking practice tests, can add points to your score by refreshing your memory and giving you experience with test taking. Preparation is especially important if you have been out of school for a long time. As one student who had been out of school for twenty years put it, "Logarithms?! Geometry rules?!" If this sounds like you, you may need to do a quick recap of high school mathematics to do well on the mathematics portion of the SAT, ACT, GRE, or GMAT. And you may have forgotten what test taking is like, but if you study and practice it will help you overcome any weaknesses you may have. We'll discuss ways to prepare for the exams later in this section after we describe the various tests.

UNDERGRADUATE ADMISSIONS TESTS

Bachelor's degree programs that require a standardized admissions test will usually accept either the SAT or the ACT. Some programs will also require SAT Subject Tests in specific subjects.

THE SAT: A TEST OF REASONING

The SAT, which is administered by the Educational Testing Service (ETS) for the College Board, tests your critical reading, writing, and math reasoning skills. These are analytical skills developed over time both in school and at work; the test does not assess your knowledge of specific content areas.

The SAT is a 3-hour-and-45-minute paper test divided into nine sections: three critical reading sections, three math sections, and three writing sections. The 25-minute essay will always be the first section of the test.

Critical Reading Sections. The critical reading sections of the SAT test your ability to understand and analyze what you read, see relationships between the parts of a sentence, and understand word meaning in context. In other words, they test your language skills. The critical reading sections last 25 minutes, and there are three types of questions:

- Reading comprehension questions measure your ability to read, understand, and think analytically about a single reading passage or a pair of passages. Reading passages range from 500 to 800 words.

- Paragraph-length critical reading questions are based on paragraphs of about 100 words, followed by questions that are similar to those accompanying the longer reading passages.

- Sentence completion questions assess your ability to understand the meaning of words and to recognize correct grammatical patterns.

Math Sections. The math sections of the SAT assess your ability to solve arithmetic, algebra I, algebra II, and geometry problems. The test does not include trigonometry or calculus. Each section lasts 20 or 25 minutes and has three main types of questions:

- 44 multiple-choice questions with five choices test your ability to solve math problems.
- 10 questions require a student-generated answer.

Writing Sections. The writing sections include multiple-choice questions and a 25-minute essay. The multiple-choice questions assess your ability to improve sentences and paragraphs and to identify grammatical errors. The short essay assesses your ability to organize and express your ideas clearly. The multiple-choice sections last 35 minutes and has three main types of questions:

- Improving sentences
- Improving paragraphs
- Identifying errors

Note that you are permitted to bring, in the College Board's words, "almost any four-function, scientific, or graphing calculator" to use on the math sections. According to the College Board, students who use a calculator do slightly better because they do not make computational errors.

Tips for Taking the SAT. It pays to familiarize yourself with the test directions and typical question format beforehand so you don't waste precious testing time trying to figure out what to do (see the section below on test preparation). Because the sections appear in a paper booklet, you can do the questions in a section in any order. For that reason, it makes sense to answer the easy questions first and place a check mark beside the hard questions. Later, if you have time, you can return to the hard questions.

The way the SAT is scored should also influence your approach. First, you are awarded one point for each correct answer. But you lose a fraction of a point for each incorrect answer, except on the student-response questions in the math section. On those questions, you do not lose points for an incorrect answer. If you omit a question, you are not penalized. This means that guessing is only worth it if you can eliminate one or two choices as clearly wrong, improving your odds of picking the correct answer. So if a question and its choices are truly mysterious to you, skip it. The test booklet can be used for computations and notes. Don't make any extra marks on the answer sheet, because it's read by a machine that cannot tell the difference between an answer and a doodle.

THE SAT SUBJECT TESTS

The SAT Subject Tests are 1-hour subject area tests that assess your knowledge of a particular content area taught in high school. The questions are primarily multiple-choice. The subject areas include literature in English, U.S. history, world history, two mathematics tests, biology, chemistry, and physics. There are reading-only language tests in French, German, modern Hebrew, Italian, Latin, and Spanish. Finally, there are reading and listening language tests in Chinese, French, German, Japanese, Korean, Spanish, and English Language Proficiency.

THE ACT

The ACT is an admissions exam consisting of four tests: English, reading, mathematics, science reasoning, and an optional writing test. The examination takes about 3½ to 4 hours, and it includes 215 multiple-choice questions with either four or five answer choices, as well as an optional 30-minute essay. Since you are not penalized for an incorrect answer on the ACT, you should answer all the questions even if you have to guess.

Unlike the SAT, the ACT is not an aptitude test. Instead, it is based on the high school English, math, and science curriculum. The questions are directly related to what you learned in high school.

GRADUATE ADMISSIONS TESTS

If you apply to graduate school, you may need to take one of the graduate admissions tests. There are two types of Graduate Record Examinations: the General Test, which is usually referred to as the GRE, and the Subject Tests. Each of these tests has a different purpose, and you may need to take more than one of them. If so, try not to schedule two tests on the same day. The experience may be more arduous than you anticipate. Another general admissions test that is sometimes required instead of the GRE is the Miller Analogies Test. In addition, there are specialized exams required for admission to various professional programs.

THE GENERAL TEST (GRE)

According to ETS, the GRE "measures verbal, quantitative, and analytical reasoning skills that have been developed over a long period of time and are not necessarily related to any field of study." Like the SAT, the GRE is a test designed to assess whether or not you have the aptitude for higher-level study. Even though the GRE may not have subject area relevance, it can indicate that you are capable of doing the difficult reading, synthesizing, and writing demanded of most graduate students.

The test is divided into three separately timed parts, and all the questions are multiple choice: (1) a 30-minute verbal section with 30 questions, (2) a 45-minute quantitative section with 28 questions, and (3) an analytical section with two questions: an issue task (45 minutes) and an argument task (30 minutes). The parts may be presented in any order. In addition, an unidentified verbal, quantitative, or analytical section that doesn't count in your score may be included. You won't have any way to tell which of the duplicated sections is the "real" one, so you should complete all sections carefully. Finally, another section, on which ETS is still doing research, may also appear. This section will be identified as such and will not count toward your score. ETS tells test takers to plan to spend 2½ to 4 hours at the testing site.

In addition, beginning in November 2007, test takers may encounter a new type of question in both the verbal and quantitative sections. These are part of the first phase of improvements endorsed by graduate school educators to test validity, provide faculty with better information regarding applicants' performance, address security concerns, increase worldwide access to the test, and make better use of advances in technology and psychometric design.

Verbal Section. The thirty questions in the verbal section of the GRE test your ability to recognize relationships between words and concepts, analyze sentences, and analyze and evaluate written material. In other words, they test your vocabulary and your reading and thinking skills. At present there are four main types of questions in this section:

- In sentence completion questions, sentences are presented with missing word(s). You are asked to select the words that best complete the sentences. Answering correctly involves figuring out the meanings of the missing words from their context in the sentence.

- Analogy questions present a pair of words or phrases that are related to one another. Your task is to figure out the relationship between the two words or phrases. Then you must select the pair of words or phrases whose relationship is most similar to that of the given pair.

- Reading comprehension questions test your ability to understand a reading passage and synthesize information on the basis of what you've read.

The words and reading material on which you are tested in this section come from a wide range of subjects, from daily life to the sciences and humanities.

Quantitative Section. This section of the GRE tests your basic mathematical skills and your understanding of elementary mathematical concepts. You will be tested on your ability to reason quantitatively and solve quantitative problems. At present there are three main types of questions in this section:

- Quantitative comparison questions require that you determine which of two quantities is the larger, if possible. If such a determination is not possible, then you must so indicate.

- Data analysis questions provide you with a graph or a table on which to base your solution to a problem.

- Problem-solving questions test a variety of mathematical concepts. They may be word problems or symbolic problems.

The quantitative questions test your knowledge of arithmetic and high school algebra, geometry, and data analysis. They do not cover trigonometry or calculus.

Analytical Writing Section. This section of the GRE tests your critical thinking and analytical writing skills, assesses your ability to articulate and support complex ideas, analyze an argument, and sustain a focused and coherent discussion. It is not meant to assess specific knowledge. There are two separately timed analytical writing tasks:

- The 45-minute "Present Your Perspective on an Issue" prompt asks you to take a position on a topic of general interest and then develop your opinion from any perspective that you choose.

- The 30-minute "Analyze an Argument" topic requires you to critique an argument by assessing the reasonableness of its assumptions, the validity of its logic, and the reliability of its conclusion.

Changes to the analytical writing section may eventually include new, more focused prompts that reduce the possibility of reliance on memorized materials. No changes for the analytical section are planned for fall 2007. Analytical writing scores are reported on a 0–6 score scale, in half-point increments.

Tips for Taking the GRE. The GRE is now given only in computer format except in areas of the world where computer-based testing is not available. The test is somewhat different from the old paper-and-pencil test. At the start of each section, you are given questions of moderate difficulty. The computer uses your responses to each question and its knowledge of the test's structure to decide which question to give you next. If your responses continue to be correct, the computer "rewards" you by giving you a harder question. On the other hand, if you answer incorrectly, the next question will typically be easier. In short, the computer uses a cumulative assessment of your performance along with information about the test's design to decide which question you get next.

One result of this format is that you cannot skip a question. The computer needs your answer to a question before it can give you the next one. So you have no choice. You must answer or you get a "no score." In addition, this format means you cannot go back to a previous question to change your answer. The computer has already taken your answer and used it to give you subsequent questions. No backtracking is possible once you've entered and confirmed your answer. What this also means is that each person's test is different. Even if two people start with the same item set in the basic test section, once they differ on an answer, the subsequent portion of the test will branch differently.

According to ETS, even though people take different tests, their scores are comparable. This is because the characteristics of the questions answered correctly and incorrectly, including their difficulty levels, are taken into account in the calculation of the score. In addition, ETS claims that the computer-based test scores are also comparable to the old paper-and-pencil test scores.

One benefit of the computer-based format is that when you finish you can cancel the test results—before seeing them—if you feel you've done poorly. If you do decide to keep the test, then you can see your unofficial scores right away. In addition, official score reporting is relatively fast—ten to fifteen days.

A drawback of the format, besides the fact that you cannot skip around, is that some of the readings, graphs, and questions are too large to appear on the screen in their entirety. You have to scroll up and down to see the whole item. Likewise, referring to a passage or graph while answering a question means that you must scroll up. In addition, you can't underline sentences in a passage or make marks in the margin as you could on the paper test. To make up for this, ETS provides scratch paper that you can use to make notes and do calculations.

To help test takers accustom themselves to the computerized format, ETS provides a tutorial that you complete before starting on the actual test. The tutorial familiarizes you with the use of a mouse, the conventions of pointing, clicking, and scrolling and the format of the test. If you are familiar with computers, the tutorial will take you less than half an hour. If you are not, you are permitted to spend more time on it. According to ETS, the system is easy to use, even for a person with no previous computer experience. However, if you are not accustomed to computers, you would be far better off if you practice your basic skills before you get to the testing site. Although in theory a mouse is easy to use, novices often have trouble getting the cursor to go where they want it to go. The last thing you want to deal with while taking the GRE is a wild mouse and accidental clicking on the wrong answers. If it's any consolation, no knowledge of the keyboard is required—everything is accomplished by pointing and clicking.

GRE SUBJECT AREA TESTS

The subject area tests are achievement tests, and they test your content knowledge of a particular subject. There are eight subject area tests, and they are given in paper-and-pencil format only. The subjects include biochemistry, cell and molecular biology; biology; chemistry; computer science; literature in English; mathematics; physics; and psychology. The subject area tests assume a level of knowledge consistent with majoring in a subject or at least having an extensive background in it. ETS suggests allowing about 3½ hours at the testing site when taking a subject area test.

Unlike the General Test, which is given many times year round, the subject tests are given only three times a year. Keep in mind that because the tests are paper-based, it takes four to six weeks for your scores to be mailed to your designated institutions. Because the tests are given infrequently and score reporting is slow, be sure you plan ahead carefully so your test results will arrive before your deadlines.

MILLER ANALOGIES TEST

The Miller Analogies Test (MAT), which is run by Harcourt Assessment, is accepted by over 2,300 graduate school programs. It is a test of mental ability given entirely in the form of analogies. For example, the analogies may tap your knowledge of fine arts, literature, mathematics, natural science, and social science.

On the MAT, you have 60 minutes to solve 120 problems. The test is given on an as-needed basis at more than 500 test centers in the United States, Canada, and overseas.

PROFESSIONAL SCHOOL EXAMS

Professional graduate programs are likely to require you to take the appropriate graduate admissions test. The major tests are the Graduate Management Admissions Test (GMAT) for business school applicants; the Law School Admissions Test (LSAT) for law school applicants; and the Medical College Admissions Test (MCAT) for medical school applicants. However, there are also specialized graduate admissions tests in the fields of dentistry, veterinary science, pharmacy, optometry, and education.

Graduate Management Admissions Test. The test most likely to be taken by prospective distance learning students is the GMAT. It is run by the Graduate Management Admissions Council and administered by Pearson VUE. Like the GRE, the GMAT is a computer-based test. It is designed to help schools of business assess applicants' aptitude for graduate level programs in business and management.

The GMAT tests verbal, quantitative, and analytic writing skills:

- In the Verbal section, you will be asked to understand and evaluate written English. There are 41 multiple-choice questions of three basic types: reading comprehension, critical reasoning, and sentence correction. You have 75 minutes to complete this section.

- The Quantitative section tests your basic math skills, understanding of elementary mathematical concepts, and ability to solve quantitative problems. There are 37 multiple-choice questions of two basic types: data sufficiency (is there enough information to answer the question?) and problem solving. You have 75 minutes to complete this section.

- The Analytical Writing Assessment measures your ability to think critically and communicate in writing. There are two essay topics, and you are allowed 30 minutes to respond to each. You must analyze an issue and an argument in this section of the test.

TESTS OF ENGLISH LANGUAGE PROFICIENCY

Regardless of whether you're applying to an undergraduate or graduate program, if your native language is not English, you may be required to take the Test of English as a Foreign Language (TOEFL) or Test of Spoken English (TSE) in order to determine your readiness to take courses in English. Both tests are administered by ETS.

The TOEFL is given in computer-based form throughout most of the world. Like the computer-based GRE, the TOEFL does not require previous computer experience. You are given the opportunity to practice on the computer before the test begins. The TOEFL has four sections—listening, reading, structure, and writing—and it lasts about 4 hours.

The TSE evaluates your ability to speak English. During the test, which takes about a half an hour, you answer questions that are presented in written and recorded form. Your responses are recorded; there is no writing required on this test. The TSE is not given in as many locations as the TOEFL, so you may have to travel a considerable distance to take it.

PREPARING FOR A STANDARDIZED TEST

You can improve your scores and reduce your test anxiety by preparing for the exams you need to take. At the very least, preparation will mean that you are familiar with the test instructions and the types of questions you will be asked. If your computer skills need improvement, adequate preparation will mean that you focus on the questions rather than struggle with the mouse when you take the computer-based tests. For achievement tests such as the subject area tests, you will actually need to study content. There are many ways you can prepare for the tests, but whichever method you choose, start early.

- **Practice by taking old tests.** You can check the Web sites of the various tests to download or request practice tests, or you can buy practice test books at a bookstore. You'll find free sample test questions on many other Web sites, including Peterson's (http://www.petersons.com).

- **Use test-preparation workbooks.** These books give information and test taking strategies, as well as practice items. There are many workbooks on the market, some with CD-ROMs, that will help you prepare for an admissions test. You'll find a long list of titles to choose from in Peterson's online bookstore at http://www.petersons.com.

- **Use test-preparation software.** Test preparation software is becoming more popular as more of the tests shift to computerized format. You can purchase the software in just about any computer software store. You can also take practice tests online at http://www.petersons.com/testprep.

- **Take a test-preparation course.** If you don't trust yourself to stick with a self-study program using practice tests, workbooks, or software, sign up for a review course such as those given by Kaplan. Although the courses are much more expensive than the do-it-yourself approach, they may be worth it if they make you study.

- **If your math is rusty, study math content.** According to the College Board, people who study math boost their scores more than people who focus only on test taking skills.

For a list of test preparation resources, see the Appendix.

REDUCING TEST ANXIETY

The best way to reduce test anxiety is to be thoroughly prepared. If you are well-acquainted with the format, directions, and types of questions you will encounter, you will not need to waste precious testing time puzzling over these aspects of the exam. In addition to thorough preparation, here are some suggestions to reduce the stress of taking the exam.

- Get a good night's rest and don't tank up on caffeinated beverages—they will only make you feel more stressed.

- Make sure you've got all the things you will need, including your admission ticket and proper identification; pencils and erasers if you are taking a paper based test; and a calculator, if one is permitted.
- Dress in layers so you will be prepared for a range of room temperatures.
- Get to the testing site at least a half an hour early. Make sure you know the way and leave yourself plenty of time to get there.
- Pace yourself during the exam. Know how the exam is scored so you can plan your approach.

Last, try to keep things in perspective. Remember, the exam score is just one item on your application. We'll discuss the remaining parts of an application in the next section.

APPLYING FOR ADMISSION TO DEGREE PROGRAMS

Now that you have narrowed your selection of programs and ascertained whether or not you need to take a standardized admissions test, it's time to prepare and assemble your applications. If you have not already done so, request an application and information packet from each program to which you plan to apply, download these items from their Web sites, or review them on line.

When you look over these materials, you will see that there may be a lot of work involved in applying to a degree program. It may take you a few months to register for and take standardized tests and to assemble and submit all the necessary information, especially if you're an international student or you've been out of school for a few years. Because the process can be complicated and time consuming, you should start well ahead of time. Even if you apply to a certificate program or an associate's degree program at a community college, a process that is typically less complicated, you should still make sure to start in time.

DEADLINES

For programs at traditional colleges and universities, application deadlines for fall admission may range from August (one full year prior to your planned enrollment) to late spring or summer for programs with rolling admissions. However, most programs require that you submit your application between January and March of the year in which you wish to start. For certificate programs and at community colleges, the deadlines may be later.

At some of the online universities, students can start their studies at any time of year. For example, at Walden University you can start on the first of any month. At Walden, the deadline for application materials is the first of the month two months prior to the month of enrollment.

Different programs have different deadlines. So be careful when you check the deadlines in the application materials from your various programs. And remember, the deadlines are not suggestions. One student applying to a traditional university who mistook a March deadline for May recalls that "not only would they not consider my application, but they wouldn't refund my application fee, either. I had to reapply the next year and pay again to be considered for their program." So don't be careless about dates— double-check them. Make a checklist like Figure 7-1 to help you keep track of things and stay on top of deadlines.

Application Checklist. Keep track of your applications by inserting a check mark or a completion date in the appropriate column or row. Note that the last four items are financial aid documents, which will be discussed in "Paying for Your Education."

PARTS OF AN APPLICATION

For each program to which you apply, you will have to submit a number of items to make your application complete. For most bachelor's and graduate degree programs, these include:

- Standardized admissions test scores (see "Taking Standardized Admissions Tests")
- An application form
- Your high school, undergraduate, or other transcripts
- Letters of recommendation
- Personal essay(s)

In addition, if you are seeking credit for life experience, an assessment portfolio will be required (see "What Can You Study via Distance Learning?"). A personal interview may be required for some programs, although for most, an interview is optional. A program may require additional items, such as a resume or arts portfolio.

For most associate degree programs at community colleges, the application is much simpler. Typically, it consists of just an application form; you may not even need to submit high school transcripts. For certificate programs, the application may consist of an application form and one or two other items.

Because requirements vary so widely, be sure you read the admissions information thoroughly so you understand what each program expects of you. Since each program may require a slightly different set of items, be sure your checklist reflects this in order to keep track of what you'll need to do.

We'll discuss the main elements of an application below; we'll cover financial aid applications in the next section.

THE APPLICATION FORM

On the application form, you provide basic information such as the program or department to which you are applying; your name, date of birth, social security number, address, and contact information; your citizenship status; your demographic background (usually optional); your current employer and position; your educational background; names of people who are providing references (ask them first!); and admissions test dates. Sometimes the application form also includes a section for applying for financial aid. However, a separate application form for financial aid may be necessary. Be sure you understand what forms you need to submit and to whom if you are applying for aid.

If you use a paper application, you should type the information on the form. If a typewriter is not available, then print your entries neatly. Be sure you do not accidentally omit information, and double-check that there are no spelling errors. "Photocopy the application and fill the copy out," suggests Nicole DeRaleau, a

Figure 7–1: Application Checklist

Item	Program 1		Program 2		Program 3	
	Date Due/Date Completed		Date Due/Date Completed		Date Due/Date Completed	
Application form						
Test scores requested						
Transcripts requested						
Letters of recommendation solicited						
Letters of recommendation follow up						
Personal essay(s)						
Application fee						
Other items required (specify)						
Application submitted						
Application follow up						
FAFSA						
Other financial aid forms						
Financial aid supporting documents						
Financial aid application follow up						

graduate student in engineering at Worcester Polytechnic Institute. "Make sure it is clear and concise, and then copy it onto the actual form."

If you decide to apply on line, don't just sit at the computer and dash off the application. Download the application form, fill it in, then proofread it carefully. Only then should you transmit it, being sure to keep a copy. Note that if you apply to an online degree program and the school does not offer an online application, you should think twice about applying. The lack of an online application is probably indicative of the low level of online student services you can expect once you are enrolled.

Many undergraduate colleges accept a common application form in place of their own. This means that most of the fields you will need to fill in will be the same for all of the schools that accept the common application. You may have to fill out a supplementary form for a college if you use one of these standardized forms. Using a standardized application form lets you concentrate on being organized and writing good essays.

TRANSCRIPTS

As proof of your academic background, you will need to submit official transcripts from each high school (for undergraduate programs), college, and university you have attended, even if you have taken just one course from that institution. To request official transcripts, contact your high school's guidance office or the registrars of your undergraduate college and other institutions you have attended. Be sure to allow two or three months for your request to be processed. It will save time if you call ahead to find out what the fee for each transcript is and what information they need to pull your file and send the transcript to the proper recipient. Then you can enclose a check for that amount with your written request.

Since many schools will send the transcripts directly to the admissions offices of the programs to which you are applying, you may also want to request an unofficial copy of your transcript. You can use this copy for your own reference during the application process.

When you review your transcripts, look for weaknesses that may need explaining, even if they occurred years ago. For example, a low GPA one semester, a very poor grade in a course, or even a below-average overall GPA may hurt your chances of acceptance unless you have a good reason for them. You can explain any shortfalls in your transcripts in your personal essay, cover letter, or addendum to the application.

LETTERS OF RECOMMENDATION

You will probably have to provide letters of recommendation for each program to which you apply. These letters are important, because like the personal essay, they give the members of the admissions committee a more personal view of you than is possible from your grades and test scores. Good letters of recommendation can tremendously increase your chances of admission, and lukewarm letters can harm your application. So it's important to approach the task of choosing and preparing your letter writers in a thoughtful and timely fashion.

In fact, it's a good idea to start asking for references a few months before your application deadline. Professionals and professors are extremely busy people, and the more time that you can give them to work on your recommendation, the better it will reflect who you are. Starting early will also give you an opportunity to follow up with your recommenders well before the application deadlines.

CHOOSING PEOPLE TO WRITE RECOMMENDATIONS

If possible, at least one of your recommendations should be from a teacher or professor, because (1) they are in the best position to judge you as a potential student and (2) members of the admissions committee will consider them peers and so be more inclined to trust their judgment of you.

If you cannot make up the full complement of letters from faculty members or if you are applying to professional programs, you can ask employers or people who know you in a professional capacity to write references for you. In fact, if you are applying to professional programs, having letters of recommendation from those already practicing in the field is a plus.

When you are trying to decide whom to ask for recommendations, keep these criteria in mind. The people you ask should

- have a high opinion of you.
- know you well, preferably in more than one context.
- be familiar with your field.
- be familiar with the programs to which you apply.
- have taught a large number of students (or have managed a large number of employees) so they have a good basis upon which to compare you (favorably!) to your peers.
- be known by the admissions committee as someone whose opinion can be trusted.
- have good writing skills.
- be reliable enough to write and mail the letter on time.

A tall order? Yes. It's likely that no one person you choose will meet all these criteria, but try to find people who come close to this ideal.

APPROACHING YOUR LETTER WRITERS

Once you've decided whom you plan to ask for references, be diplomatic. Don't simply show up in their offices, ask them to write a letter, and give them the letter of recommendation forms. Plan your approach so that you leave the potential recommender, as well as yourself, a graceful "out" in case the recommender reacts less than enthusiastically.

On your first approach, you should remind the person about who you are (if necessary) and then ask if they think they can write you a good letter of recommendation. This gives the person a chance to say no. If the person agrees, but hesitates or seems to be lukewarm, you can thank them for agreeing to help you. Later, you can write them a note saying that you won't need a letter of recommendation after all. On the other hand, if the person seems genuinely pleased to help you, you can then make an appointment to give them the letter of recommendation forms and the other information they will need.

WAIVING YOUR RIGHT TO SEE A LETTER

The letter of recommendation forms in your application packets contain a waiver. If you sign the waiver, you give up your right to see the letter of recommendation. Before you decide whether or not to sign it, discuss the waiver with each person who is writing you a reference. Some people will write you a reference only if you agree to sign the waiver and they can be sure the letter is confidential. This does not necessarily mean they intend to write a negative letter; instead, it means that they think a confidential letter will carry more weight with the admissions committee. In fact, they are right. A confidential letter usually has more validity in the eyes of the admissions committee. From the committee's point of view, an "open" letter may be less than candid because the letter writer knew you were going to read it. So, in general, it's better for you to waive your right to see a letter. If this makes you anxious in regard to a particular recommender, then do not choose that person to write a letter.

HELPING YOUR LETTER WRITERS

Once a faculty member or employer has agreed to write a letter of recommendation for you, he or she wants to write something positive on your behalf. No matter how great you are, this won't be possible if the letter writer cannot remember you and your accomplishments very well.

So when you meet with your letter writers to give them the letter of recommendation forms, use this opportunity to provide them with information about yourself. Bring a resume that highlights your academic, professional, and personal accomplishments. List the course or courses you took with them, the grades you got, and any significant work you did, such as a big research paper or presentation. The resume can be the basis of a conversation you have with the letter writer that amplifies your notable accomplishments.

What should you do if the letter writer asks *you* to draft the letter? Accept gracefully. Then pretend you are the writer, and craft a letter extolling your virtues and accomplishments in detail. Remember, if the letter writer does not like what you've written, he or she is free to change it in the final draft.

You can help your letter writers by filling in as much of the information as you can on the letter of recommendation forms. It's also a nice gesture to provide stamped, addressed envelopes for the letters if they are to be mailed directly to the programs or to you for inclusion in your application. Be sure your letter writers understand what their deadlines are. In other words, do everything you can to expedite the process, especially since you may be approaching people who are already extremely busy.

Last, send thank-you notes to professors and employers who have come through for you with letters of recommendation. Cementing good relationships now can only help you in the future.

IF YOU'VE BEEN OUT OF SCHOOL FOR YEARS

What should you do if you have been out of school for years and have lost touch with your teachers and professors? There are several things you can do to overcome the problems associated with the passage of time.

First, if a teacher or professor is still at your alma mater, you can get in touch by mail or e-mail, remind the person of who you are, describe what you've done since they taught you and what your plans for school are, and include a resume. Tell the instructor what you remember most about the courses you took with him or her. Most people keep their course records for at least a few years and can look up your grades. If you are still near your high school or undergraduate institution, you can make your approach in person. Once you've made this initial approach, you can then call and ask if the person thinks he or she can write a strong recommendation for you.

Another strategy if you've been out of school for a while is to obtain letters of recommendation from faculty members teaching in the programs to which you plan to apply. In order to obtain such a letter, you may have to take a course in the program before you enroll so that the faculty member gets to know you. Members of an admissions committee will hesitate to reject a candidate who has been strongly recommended by one of their colleagues.

Finally, if you are having trouble recruiting teachers and professors to recommend you, call the programs to which you are applying and ask what their policy is for applicants in your situation. Many programs designed for adult learners, especially the professional programs, allow you to use letters from employers. But remember, if you apply to an academic rather than a professional program, letters from employers will not carry as much weight as letters from faculty members.

THE PERSONAL ESSAY

The application to a degree program is not all numbers and outside evaluations. Schools are also interested in finding out about you as an individual and in more intangible qualities, like your ability to write a good essay. Thus, the personal essay is the part of the application in which you can take control and demonstrate who you are and why you deserve to be admitted. Other parts of your application—test scores, grade point average, and transcripts—may reflect your academic ability, but not much else. The letters of recommendation are beyond your control once you've chosen the writers. But a good personal essay can make you stand out. It can show the qualities that will make you an excellent student and professional. In other words, the essay is your showcase and you should make the most of it. Even if you can write superb prose in your sleep, you still need to know *what* to write. In this section, you'll get a step-by-step guide to preparing the personal essay.

REQUIREMENTS VARY

The essays required of applicants vary widely. For some programs, you may just have to explain in one or two paragraphs why you want to go to that school. For others, you may have to write on a more creative topic, such as the person who influenced you the most. Still for others, such as graduate business programs, the application may call for two, three, or even more essays on different topics. Business schools and programs pay a lot of attention to the personal essay because professional experience is an important criterion for admission, and this is best reflected in the essays.

The admissions committee gleans a lot of information from *what* you write. But they can also tell a lot from *how* you write. If your writing is clear and conveys your ideas effectively, you are demonstrating your ability to communicate. If your writing is free of grammatical and spelling errors, you are demonstrating your attention to detail. Good writing skills are essential for a student in any field, so a poorly written essay can hurt an application. A well-written statement, on the other hand, will help your case.

THINK BEFORE YOU WRITE

Do you remember the self-assessment you did in "Is Distance Learning Right for You?" You answered many difficult questions about your goals, interests, strengths, and weaknesses in order to decide if pursuing an education through distance learning was right for you. If you did an honest and thorough job of assessing yourself then, you will have already thought through many of the issues you will now need to address when you write your personal essay.

Things to Think About. Your self-assessment should make it easier for you to get a handle on issues such as:

- your personal and professional goals and their relationship to your education
- how you came to be interested in a particular field and why you think you are well suited for it
- aspects of your life that make you uniquely qualified to pursue study in this field
- experiences or qualities that distinguish you from other applicants
- unusual hardships or obstacles that you've had to overcome
- unusual accomplishments, whether personal, professional, or academic
- professional experiences that have contributed to your personal growth
- how your skills and personal characteristics would contribute to your success in a distance learning degree program

In addition, when you researched and evaluated programs to which you would apply, you learned a lot about the programs that were good matches for you. In your essay, you may also have to address issues like

- what appeals to you about a particular program.
- how your interests and strengths match their needs.

Be Yourself . . . The most common piece of advice from most admissions directors about writing the personal essay is to be yourself. **Remember, you are seeking to be accepted by a program that is a good match for you. If you disguise who you really are in an effort to impress an admissions committee,**

you are doing yourself—and the school—a disservice. So, be honest. If you demonstrate self-knowledge by presenting your strengths as well as your limitations, your essay will be a true reflection of who you are.

. . . But Be Diplomatic. Honesty is important, but so is diplomacy. Try not to reveal weaknesses in your personality such as laziness, dishonesty, or selfishness. Don't say you want to enroll in a program just because it's on line or you know you can get in. Even though these things may be true, they are not reasons with which the admissions committee will necessarily be sympathetic. Instead, frame your points in a positive light: you can fulfill the admission requirements because you have the proper prerequisites, and you know of its reputation for quality online teaching.

WRITE A STRONG OPENING

When you write your essay, put yourself in the position of an admissions committee member who may be reading fifty essays a day. By the end of all this reading, this poor individual may be bored to tears and would be pleased by any essay that simply engages his or her interest. How are you going to accomplish this? By writing an opening that grabs the reader's attention.

Describe an Important Experience. Instead of beginning with, "I want to go to school because . . ." try to engage the reader with something significant. For example, was there an experience that led you to make the decision to pursue your education? If so, describe it.

The opening is also the place where you can set forth any unusual experience you have had that contributed significantly to the person you are today. The experience may be growing up poor, being an Olympic athlete, or moving to the United States at the age of fourteen. Whatever the experience is, show how it has formed your character and life and how it relates to the education you want to pursue now.

Be Specific. What if you have not had a defining moment or experience that sparked your interest in further education? Then write an opening that is specific enough to have some real interest. The key is to remember that specific details are usually more interesting than general statements. Use concrete examples of your successes and action verbs to describe events. Be specific and you'll have a better chance of connecting with your readers.

TELL HOW YOUR STORY INTERSECTS WITH THEIRS

If you apply to several programs, you will be tempted to write a boilerplate essay. Resist the temptation. Admissions committees grow adept at picking out the generic personal statements.

Remember that when you were evaluating programs you were looking for a good match for you. The personal essay is the place where you can explain to the admissions committee why you are a good match for that school. The story of your intellectual and professional development and your goals should culminate in your reasons for choosing this particular program. Your reasons should reflect a knowledge of the program.

Use the Brochure or Catalog as a Resource. You can use the knowledge you've gained from researching the program if you don't know it firsthand to explain why you want to enroll in a program. In particular, the program brochure or catalog can be a good resource when you write this section of the essay. It's important to know what a school has to offer before you write the essay. The admissions committee members will be looking for a good fit for their program.

In addition to identifying the tangible characteristics of a program, you can also get a sense of its philosophy and values from the brochure or catalog.

DESCRIBE YOUR GOALS

In most essays, you will have to explain how a degree will help you achieve your goals. Even if you are not exactly sure what you want to do professionally, describe what you might be interested in doing once you receive the degree. Indicating that you have a purpose in obtaining a degree shows that you are focused and motivated and have a real sense of the possibilities.

EXPLAIN SHORTCOMINGS IN YOUR BACKGROUND

There is a difference of opinion on whether or not the personal essay is the place to explain any weaknesses in your academic or professional preparation if you are not directly asked to do so. Some people think that the essay should concentrate on a positive presentation of your qualifications. They feel that an explanation of poor standardized test scores, for example, belongs in an addendum or cover letter. Others think that the essay is the place to address your application's weaknesses.

Perhaps a good rule of thumb is to address any weaknesses or shortcomings that are directly relevant to your proposed studies in the essay. On the other hand, if the weak spot in your application is not directly related to your field of study, you may prefer to address it in an addendum or cover letter. For example, if when you were a college freshman you had a poor GPA, you can explain this separately. Try to put a positive spin on it, too. Explain, for example, how your GPA in your major was much higher, or how your GPA improved as you matured. Essentially, your decision as to where to address your weaknesses will depend on their importance and relevance to your pursuit of a degree.

EDIT YOUR DRAFTS

Follow the Instructions. When you sit down to draft your essay, the first thing you should make sure is that you are *answering the question posed on the application*. Be sure you read the instructions for each program's personal statement carefully. Small differences in wording can affect how you approach writing the essay.

Don't Write Too Much or Too Little. The second thing you should keep in mind as you begin your draft is the length of the essay. Often, the length is specified. What should you do if length is not specified? Write one to two typed pages. An essay that is shorter than one page does not allow room for you to develop your ideas, and an essay that is longer than two pages becomes a chore for the admissions committee to read. Don't play with font size, either, in order to get the statement to come out the right length. Admissions officers don't really want to read eight-point type. Stick with a basic font, such as Times New Roman, and keep the size between 10 and 12 points. If the essay asks for a specific word count, follow it to the letter. If you come in over or under by 10 words or so, don't worry too much about it. But if you're 100 or more words short or long, you'll have some adding or cutting to do.

Finally, when you write your first draft, do not waste space by repeating information that the admissions committee can get from other parts of your application like your transcript or resume. Use the essay to provide new information or to highlight particular accomplishments.

Review the First Draft. Once you have drafted your essay, read the question again. Has your draft answered the question fully? If the essay is incomplete, go back and fill in the missing material. Then ask people for feedback. Although your spouse and friends may be helpful, you may get more valuable suggestions from faculty members or colleagues who know you and who also know what a personal essay should be like. Ask whether you've included things you should leave out or should add things you've forgotten. Is the tone right? Have you achieved the right balance between boasting and being too modest? Are there any problems with organization, clarity, grammar, or spelling?

Prepare the Final Draft. Once you've revised the essay, set it aside for a couple of days. Then proofread it with a fresh eye. If you are satisfied with your final draft, ask someone else to proofread it for you. The final draft should be absolutely free of grammar and spelling errors, so do not rely on grammar or spellcheckers to find all the errors. Once you are done, be sure to keep backup files as well as a hard copy. Although you won't be able to use the whole essay for all your applications, you may be able to use parts of it. If you do work this way, be absolutely sure when you submit the final essays to different programs that you have not made any embarrassing cutting and pasting mistakes.

Finally, if you submit the statement on separate sheets of paper rather than on the application form itself, put your name, social security number, and the question at the top of the essay and type "see attached essay" on the application form.

MAKE IT YOURS

If after reading this section you are still daunted by the prospect of writing your personal statement, just put the whole task aside for a few days. You will find that the ideas and suggestions you've just read will trigger some mental activity and that soon you will have some ideas of your own to jot down.

Remember, also, that it's not necessary to have an exotic background or a dramatic event to recount in order to write a good essay and gain admission to a program. Admissions committees look for diversity—in gender, race, ethnicity, nationality, and socioeconomic status—to name some obvious characteristics. But they are also look for people with diverse life experiences to add richness to their student body. Your background, which may seem perfectly ordinary to you, nevertheless has unique and relevant elements that can be assets to the program you choose. Your task is to identify and build upon these elements to persuade the admissions committee that you should be selected.

INTERVIEWS

Interviews are rarely a requirement of the distance education application process. However, if you think you do well in interviews, you can call each program and ask for an interview. A good interview may be an opportunity to sway the admissions committee in your favor. Human nature being what it is, an excellent half-hour interview may loom larger than years of average grades in the minds of those who evaluate your application.

Most interviewers are interested in the way you approach problems, think, and articulate your ideas, and so they will concentrate on questions that will reveal these aspects of your character and not on questions that test your technical knowledge. They may ask you controversial questions or give you hypothetical problems to solve. Or they may ask about your professional goals, motivation for study, and areas of interest—much the same material that is in a typical personal essay. Remember that interviewers are interested more in how you think than in what you think.

When you prepare for an interview, it would be helpful if you have already written your personal essay, because the thought processes involved in preparing the essay will help you articulate many of the issues that are likely to come up in an interview. It is also helpful to do your homework on the program, so if the opportunity arises for you to ask questions, you can do so intelligently. Last, be sure you are dressed properly. That means dress as if you are going to a professional job interview.

SUBMITTING YOUR APPLICATION

As we mentioned at the beginning of this section, you should submit your completed applications well before they are due. *Be sure to keep a copy of everything.* That way, you won't lose hours of work if the application gets lost. You can either mail the application to the admissions office or file portions of it on line through the programs' Web sites. Remember, however, that some elements of the application, such as the fee and official transcripts, will still need to be mailed in paper form. Note also that most schools that accept online applications simply print them and process them as if they had come in by regular mail.

Try to submit all of your materials at once, which simplifies the task of compiling and tracking your application at the admissions office. If that's impossible, as it is for many students, keep track of missing items and forward them as soon as possible. Remember that if items are missing, your application is likely just to sit in the admissions office.

FOLLOWING UP

It's important that you check up on the status of your applications, especially if you don't receive acknowledgment that an application is complete. Give the admissions office a couple of weeks to process your application, and then call or send an e-mail to find out whether or not it's complete. For some schools, you can check the status of your application on line through their Web sites. Usually the missing items are transcripts or letters of recommendation.

IN SUMMARY

Preparing a thorough, focused, and well-written application is one of the most important tasks you will ever undertake. A good application can gain you admission to a program that can help you achieve your goals. "The application process is just one of those hoops you have to jump through to get where you want to go," advises a distance learning student at Gonzaga University. With your destination in mind, work on your applications as if they are the most important things you can possibly be doing, because they are.

PAYING FOR YOUR EDUCATION

ursuing a certificate or degree can cost a lot of money, but it is usually money well spent. On average, people with undergraduate nd graduate degrees make more money than those who do not ave these credentials. Still, the question remains: How are you oing to pay for school and support yourself (and perhaps your amily) at the same time?

Most adult distance learning students solve the problem of aying for their education by continuing to work full-time and ttending school part time. As one student put it, "I work and I pay s I go." Although attending part-time does not cut the total cost f your certificate or degree, it does have the advantage of preading your costs over a longer period and enables you to pay or your education out of your current income. Note, however, at attending school less than half-time will disqualify you from ost forms of financial aid.

In this section, we'll discuss ways to pay for your education, oth by looking for low-cost alternatives and by finding financial id. We'll discuss types and sources of aid, where you can find nformation about financial aid, and the application process. inally, we'll describe some of the tax issues that may be relevant o students pursuing higher education.

OOKING FOR LOW-COST ALTERNATIVES

There are ways you can cut the cost of your education, even efore you look for sources of financial aid. These include ttending a community college rather than a four-year college and ttending a public institution of higher education rather than a rivate one.

OMMUNITY COLLEGE VERSUS FOUR-YEAR OLLEGE

If you are an undergraduate pursuing a bachelor's degree, you ould consider enrolling at a community college for your first two ears of study. Most community colleges charge less tuition than our-year colleges do. Toward the end of your second year of udy, you can apply to a four-year college as a transfer student nd complete your bachelor's degree there.

UBLIC VERSUS PRIVATE COLLEGE OR NIVERSITY

Since four-year public colleges and universities get most of their upport from government funding, they are less expensive than rivate colleges and universities. Public colleges and universities sually have two scales for tuition and fees—one for out-of-state esidents and a much less expensive scale for state residents. With so much money at stake, and if moving is an option for you, is definitely worthwhile to find out how you can establish esidency in the state in which you plan to get your degree. You ay simply have to reside in the state for a year—your first year

of school—in order to be considered a legal resident. But being a resident while a student may not count, and you may have to move to the state a year before you plan to enroll. The legal residency requirements of each state vary, so be sure you have the right information if you decide to pursue this strategy.

TYPES OF FINANCIAL AID

Before we get into a discussion of the various sources of financial aid, it would be helpful to understand some basics. For example, financial aid can be classified in a few ways. First, it can be categorized by type of aid:

- **Grants, scholarships,** and **fellowships** are gifts that do not have to be repaid. These words are used somewhat interchangeably; there is no real difference among them, except that scholarships are usually awarded to undergraduates and fellowships are awarded to graduate students.

- **Loans** are awards that do have to be repaid, with interest, either while you are in school or after you leave school, it depends on the terms of the loan. If you consider loans, note that financial aid counselors recommend that your total student debt payment should not exceed 8 to 15 percent of your projected monthly income after you receive your degree.

- **Work-study awards** are amounts you earn through part-time work in a federal aid program.

- **Reimbursements**, generally from employers, repay you for amounts you've already spent on tuition.

You can also classify financial aid according to the reason the student is awarded the aid:

- **Need-based aid** is financial aid awarded on the basis of your financial need. It may take the form of grants, loans, or work-study.

- **Merit-based aid** is funding awarded on the basis of academic merit, regardless of financial need.

A subset of merit-based aid is student profile-based aid—financial aid to students because of their identities. For example, some scholarships are targeted for veterans, minorities, or women; and others are targeted for people with very specific qualifications that the philanthropist wants to reward, such as an Eagle Scout studying labor relations.

A third way to classify financial aid is by its source. The major sources of aid for students are as follows:

- The **federal government**, by far the largest disburser of financial aid—over $50 billion to more than 8.5 million students each year

- **State governments**, some of which have large financial aid programs

- **Private sources of aid**, which include colleges and universities, employers, foundations, service organizations, national scholarship and fellowship programs, home equity loans, and private loan programs

THE LANGUAGE OF FINANCIAL AID

There's some financial aid jargon that you'll have to master in order to understand need-based financial aid programs. Some terms that you'll see frequently include the following:

- **Enrollment status**—Whether you are enrolled full-time, three-quarter time, half-time, or less than half-time in a degree or certificate program. Your status affects your eligibility for most types of aid.

- **Expected Family Contribution (EFC)**—The amount you and your family are expected to contribute to the cost of your education per academic year. If you are a dependent, *family* means you and your parents; if you are independent, this means you and your spouse, if you are married. The formula was established by the U.S. Congress to help estimate federal aid amounts for eligible students, and it is used by college financial aid offices as well as the U.S. Department of Education.

- **Cost of attendance**—The total cost—tuition, fees, living expenses, books, supplies, and miscellaneous expenses—of attending a particular school for an academic year. Each school estimates its own cost of attendance, and you can find out what it is if you check your admissions information packet or call the financial aid office. Distance learners should make sure that technology costs are included in the school's cost of attendance and in their own budgets. The cost of transportation, hotels, and meals during residency periods, if any, should also be accounted for in the cost of attendance.

- **Financial need**—The amount of money you need to be given or loaned or that you will earn through work-study in order to attend your school. It is calculated by subtracting your Estimated Family Contribution from your cost of attendance:

> Cost of Attendance
> – Expected Family Contribution
> = Financial Need

Note that your financial need will differ from program to program. That's because the cost of attendance will vary from school to school, but your Expected Family Contribution will remain the same, whether you attend the local community college or an expensive private university.

FEDERAL FINANCIAL AID

As we've mentioned, the U.S. government is the largest player in the financial aid arena, and most of your financial aid is likely to come from this source. The federal government provides need-based aid in the form of grants, work-study programs, and loans. Up-to-date information about federal financial aid programs can be found at the U.S. Department of Education's Web site, www.ed.gov/studentaid, or by calling 800-4-FEDAID (toll-free). Eligibility issues relevant to distance learners and some of the basics of federal aid are discussed below. Note that some of these eligibility criteria may change in the future as distance

degrees become more common and financial aid programs are modified to reflect the new realities.

ARE YOU ELIGIBLE FOR FEDERAL FINANCIAL AID?

Your financial need is just one criterion used to determine whether or not you are eligible to receive aid from the federal government. In addition, you must

- have a high school diploma or GED or pass a test approved by the Department of Education.
- be enrolled in a degree or certificate program.
- be enrolled in an eligible institution (see below).
- be a U.S. citizen or eligible noncitizen.
- have a Social Security number.
- register with the Selective Service if required.
- maintain satisfactory academic progress once you are in school.

If you have been convicted under federal or state laws of the sale or possession of illegal drugs, you may not be eligible to participate in federal financial aid programs. Call the Federal Student Aid Information Center at 800-4-FEDAID (toll-free) for further information.

If you are not sure if you qualify as an eligible noncitizen, call the financial aid office of the school you plan to attend.

INSTITUTIONAL ELIGIBILITY: AN ISSUE PERTINENT TO DISTANCE LEARNERS

In order to participate in federal financial aid programs, an institution of higher learning must fulfill the criteria established by Congress for the disbursement of Title IV funds, as federal student aid is officially known. There are many complex regulations that establish institutional eligibility. Of these, several may apply to institutions that offer certificates or degrees at a distance. For example, in order to be eligible to participate in federal financial aid programs, an institution must be accredited by an agency—other than the Distance Education and Training Council (DETC)—recognized by the U.S. Department of Education. The reason that schools accredited only by the DETC are not eligible is that they are classified as "correspondence schools," and schools that teach primarily by correspondence are ineligible according to the law. In order to qualify to disburse Title IV aid, an institution must teach at least 50.1 percent of its classes in the traditional classroom or must be classified as an independent study institution rather than a correspondence school. Other requirements for participation in federal financial aid programs involve the academic schedule; for example, there must be a thirty-week academic year, a template that doesn't fit some of the new virtual universities.

The Distance Education Demonstration Program. The rules governing federal aid were originally promulgated to prevent fraud and to assure that funds would be provided to students at schools that met certain standards. However, with the growth of distance education, these regulations are increasingly becoming obstacles to provide aid to students at legitimate but innovative institutions. Recognizing this, Congress established the Distance Education Demonstration Program under the direction of the Department of Education. "The purpose of the Distance Education Demonstration Program is to collect data that will provide some understanding of what constitutes quality in distance education," explains Marianne R. Phelps, former special assistant to the assistant secretary for postsecondary education. "Congress needs information in order to become comfortable with the risks involved in funding distance education." Under this program, the department is permitted to waive some of the Title IV regulations, if necessary, for the fifteen participating institutions of higher education. Eventually, the experiences and data generated by the Distance Education Demonstration Program may provide a basis for a review of current rules and regulations.

Determining the Eligibility Status of an Institution or Program.

In the meantime, what can you do to make sure that the school and program in which you are interested are eligible to participate in federal financial aid programs? The simple answer, of course, is call them and ask. However, you can also do some double-checking on your own to confirm what the school tells you.

If you plan to enroll in a regionally accredited traditional college or university, you can safely assume that the institution as a whole is eligible to participate in federal aid programs—since distance certificates and degrees are likely to be a very small proportion of its overall offerings (see "Selecting a Good Distance Learning Program" for a discussion of accreditation). However, because institutions have the discretion to exclude specific programs, you should double-check to see if the school disperses federal aid to students enrolled in programs that interest you. Call the financial aid office and ask. If you are not sure of the accreditation status, and therefore the Title IV status, of the school in which you are interested, first check with the school to find out which agencies, if any, have accredited it. Then visit the Department of Education's Web site to check on the accrediting agencies. The department lists the accrediting agencies of which it approves, and in its short description of each agency, it indicates whether or not the institutions it accredits qualify for Title IV funding. You can then call the accrediting agency to make sure it has indeed accredited the school or program in which you are interested.

FEDERAL AID PROGRAMS

Once you've established the eligibility of the institution and program in which you are interested, you may want to check the federal aid programs in which they participate. Not all schools participate in all the available programs.

Among the federal aid programs are Pell Grants, Federal Supplemental Educational Opportunity Grants, work-study, Federal Family Education Loans (FFEL) and William D. Ford Direct Loans (commonly called Stafford loans), and Perkins Loans.

Pell Grants. Pell Grants, which do not have to be repaid, are awarded to undergraduate students on the basis of need, even if they are enrolled less than half time. In some cases, a student enrolled in a postbaccalaureate teacher certification program may be awarded a Pell Grant. There are no Pell Grants for other graduate students.

The maximum amount of the Pell Grant changes each year and depends on annual funding allocations by Congress. The maximum award for the school year 2006–07 was $4,310. The amount of an award depends on a combination of your financial need, your costs to attend school, your enrollment status as a full-time or part-time student, and whether or not you plan to study for a full academic year or less.

If you are awarded a Pell Grant, the money can be applied directly to your school costs or be paid to you directly or some combination of these methods. Your school must inform you on how it will be disbursing your grant. Disbursements must occur at least once per term or a minimum of twice a year.

Federal Supplemental Educational Opportunity Grants. Federal Supplemental Educational Opportunity Grants (FSEOGs) are awards to undergraduates with exceptional financial need, even if they are enrolled less than half time. These grants generally go to Pell Grant recipients with the lowest Estimated Family Contributions. The amount of an FSEOG ranges from $100 to $4,000 per year.

Unlike the Pell Grant program, which provides funds to each eligible student, the FSEOG program is campus-based. This means that the federal government awards each participating institution a certain amount of money, and the school's financial aid office decides how to allocate it. When the school uses up its funding for the year, there are no more FSEOGs awarded. Check with your school to see whether or not it participates in this program.

Federal Work-Study Program. Some colleges and universities participate in the federal work-study program, which provides part-time jobs in public and private nonprofit organizations to both undergraduate and graduate students who demonstrate financial need. The government pays up to 75 percent of your wages, and your employer pays the balance. The value of a work-study job depends on your need, the other elements in your financial aid package, and the amount of money the school has to offer. Not all universities have work-study funds, and some that do have the funds limit their use to undergraduates.

If you receive work-study funds, you may be able to use them in a job that is related to your field. You will have to check with the financial aid office to find out what jobs are available, whether or not you can use the funds in a job you find elsewhere, and what bureaucratic requirements you will have to satisfy.

Stafford Loan Programs (FFEL and Direct Loans). The Federal Family Education Loan (FFEL) program and the William D. Ford Direct Loan Program, commonly called Stafford loans, are two loan programs sponsored by the federal government. Schools generally participate in one of the two programs. The terms and conditions of these loans are similar; the major differences are the source of the funds and some repayment provisions. If you get a FFEL, your funds will come from a bank, credit union, or other participating lender. If you get a Direct Loan, the money comes directly from the federal government.

You are eligible to borrow under these loan programs if you are enrolled at least half time and have financial need remaining after your Estimated Family Contribution, Pell Grant eligibility, and aid from other sources are subtracted from your annual cost of attendance. Depending on your need, you may be eligible for a subsidized loan in which the government pays the interest that accrues while you are enrolled at least half time. If you cannot demonstrate sufficient financial need according to government criteria, you may still be able to borrow, but your Stafford loan will be unsubsidized. This means that interest will accrue on the loan while you are still in school unless you arrange to pay it during this period.

In both types of Stafford loans, repayment of the principal as well as future interest begins six months after you are last enrolled on at least a half-time basis. Undergraduates may borrow a maximum of $3,500 to $10,500 per year. Graduate students may borrow up to $18,500 per year up to a maximum of $138,500, which includes any undergraduate loans you may still have. The interest rate varies annually and is set each July. Right now it is capped at 8.25 percent.

Perkins Loan Program. Another source of federal funds is the Perkins Loan program. The Perkins Loan is available to both undergraduate and graduate students who demonstrate exceptional financial need, whether enrolled full-time or part-time, and it is administered by each individual college or university. In some cases, schools reserve Perkins Loans for undergraduates. If you are an undergraduate eligible for a Perkins Loan, you may be able to borrow up to $4,000 per year with a $20,000 maximum. An eligible graduate student may be able to borrow up to $6,000 per year with a $40,000 maximum including undergraduate and graduate Perkins borrowing.

At present, the interest rate is 5 percent, and no interest accrues while you are enrolled in school at least half-time. You must start repaying the loan nine months after you are last enrolled on a half-time basis. This loan is the best deal offered by the government.

REPAYING YOUR FEDERAL LOANS

After you graduate, leave school, or drop below half-time status, you will have a grace period of either six or nine months before loan payments start. During the grace period, you will be sent information about payment plans and your first payment due date. You can repay the loan over a maximum of 10 years with a $50 minimum monthly payment, with a graduated plan in which the payments start out low and gradually increase, or with a plan that bases your payments on your income level.

You can also consolidate all your outstanding federal loans into one loan. Having one loan to repay will minimize the chances of administrative error and allow you to write one check per month rather than several.

If you have trouble repaying your federal loans, you may qualify for a deferment or forbearance on your loan. During a deferment, payments are suspended, and if the loan is subsidized, interest does not accrue. During forbearance, payments are postponed or reduced. Repayment assistance may be available if you serve in the military.

STATE AID PROGRAMS

Some states offer financial aid to state residents that attend school in-state, some offer aid to state residents that attend school in-state or elsewhere, and some offer aid to students that attend school in their state regardless of their residency status. Some states, like California, New York, Michigan, Oklahoma, and Texas, have large aid programs. Other states may have little or nothing to offer. Contact your state scholarship office directly to find out what's available and whether you are eligible to apply. Telephone numbers are listed in the Appendix.

PRIVATE SOURCES OF FINANCIAL AID

In addition to the federal government, other organizations provide financial aid to students. These include your school, national and local organizations, private lenders, employers, internships, and cooperative education programs.

THE COLLEGE OR UNIVERSITY

Second only to the federal government in the amount of financial aid disbursed yearly are colleges and universities. Many of these institutions award both need-based and merit-based aid to deserving students. To find out more about the types of aid that the school you are interested in disburses, contact the financial aid office.

NATIONAL AND LOCAL ORGANIZATIONS

Foundations, nonprofit organizations, churches, service and fraternal organizations, professional associations, corporations, unions, and many other national and local organizations award grants to students of higher education. Many of these awards go to students who fit a certain profile, but many of them are open to anyone who applies. The drawback of this type of aid is that you have to locate it and apply on your own.

PRIVATE LENDERS

Many students borrow from private lenders, whether through alternative loan programs, home equity loans, or other types of loans.

Alternative Loan Programs. In addition to the federal loan programs, there are many private alternative loan programs designed to help students. Most private loan programs disburse funds based on your creditworthiness rather than your financial need. Some loan programs target all types of students; others are designed specifically for graduate or professional students. In addition, you can use other types of private loans not specifically designed for education to help finance your degree. For more information, check with your bank and your school's financial aid office.

Home Equity Loans. For students who own their own homes, a home equity loan or line of credit can be an attractive financing alternative to private loan programs. Some of these loans are offered at low rates and allow you to defer payment of the principal for years. In addition, if you use the loan to pay for educational expenses, the interest on the loan is tax deductible.

Credit Cards. Whatever you do, do not use your credit cards to borrow money for school on a long-term basis. The interest rates and finance charges will be high, and the balance will grow astronomically. Credit cards are useful to pay tuition and fees if you (1) can pay the balance in full, (2) expect a student loan to come through shortly, (3) expect your employer to reimburse your costs. Otherwise, avoid them.

INTERNSHIPS AND COOPERATIVE EDUCATION PROGRAMS

In addition to the federal work-study program, there are other employment opportunities that may help you finance your education. Internships with organizations outside the university can provide money as well as practical experience in your field. As an intern, you are usually paid by the outside organization, and you may or may not get credit for the work you do. Although they have been common in the professional programs, such as design and business, for years, lately internships have been growing in popularity in academic programs as well.

In cooperative education programs, you usually alternate periods of full-time work in your field with periods of full-time study. You are paid for the work you do, and you may or may not get academic credit for it as well.

Internship and cooperative education programs may be administered in your department or by a separate office, so you will have to ask to find out.

EMPLOYER REIMBURSEMENT

If you work full-time and attend school part-time, you may be reimbursed for part or all of your tuition by your employer. Many employers require that you receive a minimum grade in order to qualify for reimbursement. Keep in mind, however, that your employer will withhold taxes and other deductions when it reimburses you, and you will have to make up the difference. Check with your employer before you enroll; some employers reimburse tuition only for job-related courses. Others will not reimburse employees for distance learning courses.

Some large corporations that consider job-related certificate and degrees as forms of employee training may underwrite the entire cost of a program. For example, AT&T pays Denise Petrosino's tuition directly to the University of Phoenix Online. "As long as I maintain a B average, I have 100 percent coverage," explains Petrosino, who is earning a master's degree in organizational management.

LOCATING INFORMATION ABOUT FINANCIAL AID

Finding information about financial aid can be a challenge. There is no one central clearinghouse for information about financial aid for undergraduate and graduate study. You are going to have to check a number of different sources to get the full picture on possible sources of aid that is available for you. We'll discuss a few of them here, but for a list of financial aid resources, see the Appendix.

THE GOVERNMENT

The best source of information on federal aid for students is the U.S. government itself. The federal aid programs are administered by the U.S. Department of Education. You can contact them through their Web site, by telephone, or by mail. (See the Appendix for specifics.) Remember, however, that not all colleges and universities participate in each federal program, so if a particular federal aid program interests you, you will have to contact your school's financial aid office to make sure it's available.

If you are a graduate student, you should note that many agencies of the federal government offer fellowships to graduate students in related fields. Contact the agencies that are relevant to your field of study for further information.

For information on state aid, contact your state agency of higher education (see the Appendix).

THE COLLEGE OR UNIVERSITY

At a small college, the financial aid office is usually the source of all financial aid information. However, at a university, there is more than one office involved with student aid, and thus more than one source of information about it. Each university has a different administrative structure, so you will have to figure out the offices you will most likely need to contact. These may include:

- **The financial aid office.** The university-wide financial aid office is generally the best source of information about federal and private loan programs as well as university-based grants and federal work-study assistance. They may also be able to steer you to other sources of information.

- **The college or school's administrative office.** The next place to check is the administrative office of the college or school to which you are applying. For example, you may be applying for a master's degree in special education. This department may be under the jurisdiction of the College of Education. That office may or may not administer grants to the students of the college. Call to find out.

- **The office of the graduate school.** If you are a graduate student, it pays to check this administrative office; it may or may not have funding to award. If it does, the fellowships or grants are likely to be awarded on a university-wide, competitive basis.

- **The specific program or department to which you are applying.** Often a program brochure describes the types of aid that the department awards its students. If you cannot find this information in the materials you have, then call the program and ask. You'll be able to find out about program aid from this source.

It's important to check with all these offices to see what's available. It's also important to be proactive and call the financial aid office as well as other offices to find out your chances of receiving aid.

THE INTERNET

The Internet is an excellent source of information about all types of financial aid. One of the best places to start your Internet search for financial aid is the Financial Aid Information Page at www.finaid.org. This site has a great deal of information about the different types of financial aid and provides links to other relevant sites as well. It provides a good overview of the financial aid situation. In addition, the site offers several calculators that enable you to estimate many useful figures, including your Estimated Family Contribution, projected costs of attendance, and future student loan payments. There are also a number of searchable databases of national scholarships and fellowships on the Internet. One searchable database of financial aid resources can be found on Peterson's Web site (www.petersons.com/finaid), which lists millions of sources of aid totaling billions of dollars. Another scholarship database is FastWeb at www.fastweb.com. On each of these sites, you'll need to answer a questionnaire about your educational background, field of study, and personal characteristics. When you are done, the database is searched to match your data with eligibility requirements of several hundred thousand fellowships and scholarships. You are then given a list of possible fellowships and scholarships to pursue on your own. There is no cost for either of these services.

There are a few things you should beware of when using Internet search services. First, a searchable database is only as good as its index, so you may find yourself getting some odd matches. In addition, most searchable databases of scholarships and fellowships are designed primarily for undergraduates, so the number of potential matches for a graduate student is far fewer than the several hundred thousand sources of aid that a database may contain. Finally, some of these Internet search services charge a fee. Given the amount of free information that's available, both on the Internet and in libraries, it's not necessary to pay for this type of research.

PRINT DIRECTORIES

Although the searchable databases on the Internet are easy to use, it's still a good idea to check print directories of national scholarships, grants, and fellowships. These directories have indexes that make locating potential sources of funds easy. Scholarships, grants, and fellowships are indexed by field of study as well as by type of student. So, for example, you can search for all funding related to the study of Latin America or electrical engineering. Or you can search for funding that is targeted to Hispanic students, disabled students, or adult students. It's a good idea just to browse, too, in case something catches your eye.

There are quite a few directories that you can consult. For undergraduates, Peterson's *Scholarships, Grants, & Prizes* lists many private sources of aid, and Peterson's *College Money Handbook* covers college and university sources of financial aid. For graduate students, the *Annual Register of Grant Support: A Directory of Funding Sources*, published by the National Register Publishing Company, is a comprehensive guide to awards from the government, foundations, and business and professional organizations.

APPLYING FOR FINANCIAL AID

Depending on your personal situation and the requirements of the school, you may have to submit just one or a number of applications for financial aid. If you apply for need-based aid, university merit aid, national scholarships and fellowships, or private loan programs, you will have several application forms to deal with. However many applications you must submit, start the process early.

DEADLINES

"I cannot overemphasize the importance of applying early," says Emerelle McNair, director of scholarships and financial aid at Southern Polytechnic State University in Georgia. "Most awards are made in spring for the following academic year." Be sure you've picked the correct deadlines from your program application information packet. *Students applying for financial aid often have an earlier deadline for the entire application.* If you look for sources of aid outside the program and university, such as national scholarships and fellowships, then it is even more important to start your research early—a full year or more before you plan to enroll.

Remember, it can easily take months to fill out applications and assemble all the supporting data for a financial aid request. You may need to submit income tax forms, untaxed income verifi- cation, asset verification, and documents that support any special circumstances you are claiming. For private scholarship applications, you may need to write an essay and provide letters of recommendation. So give yourself plenty of time to submit the initial application. Later, if you are asked to provide additional information or supporting documents, do so as quickly as possible.

THE FAFSA

The Free Application for Federal Student Aid (FAFSA) is the only form you will need to apply for most federal need-based aid programs and state aid programs as well. FAFSA is used by both undergraduate and graduate students. The FAFSA form is issued annually by the Department of Education at the end of each calendar year (see www.fafsa.ed.gov), and it is available both in paper and on line. You use it to report financial data from the previous year in order to be considered for aid in the school year that starts the following fall. It's much easier to fill out the FAFSA if you have already done your federal income tax forms for the year, but since most schools require you to file the FAFSA in January or February, that may be difficult. If your federal income tax return is not done, use estimates so you can file the FAFSA on time. You can amend it later if necessary. Because the FAFSA is designed for undergraduate students who are dependent on their parents, if you are a working adult student you may find you are having difficulty interpreting some of the questions or that the questions do not cover all your circumstances. If there is information about your financial situation that is not elicited by the FAFSA but that you feel is germane to your application, then explain the circumstances in a separate letter to the financial aid office of the schools to which you apply. Suppose, for example, that you have been working full-time for a few years but you are planning to quit your job and attend school full-time. You would complete the FAFSA using the previous year's full-time income figures, but this would not be an accurate reflection of your financial situation during the following school year because your income will drop precipitously. In such a case, you would notify the financial aid office so that it can make a professional judgment as to whether or not your need should be revised upward.

After you submit the FAFSA, you will receive a Student Aid Report (SAR), an acknowledgment that includes a summary of the data you have sent them. Check to make sure the information is accurate and that the schools you have chosen to have the data sent to are correctly listed. If there are errors, make corrections right away. The SAR will also show your Expected Family Contribution, the amount you and your spouse (or parents if you are still a dependent) will be expected to contribute. This information is used by each school to calculate your financial need (cost of attendance minus Expected Family Contribution) and to award need-based aid.

SCHOOL'S FINANCIAL AID APPLICATION FORM OR CSS PROFILE

A school may require that you submit a separate financial aid application in addition to the program application and the FAFSA. If you do not see such a form in the program application packet, call the admissions office to find out whether or not you need to obtain it from another office.

Some schools do not have their own financial aid application form. Instead, they require you to submit a standardized form, the College Scholarship Service's (CSS) Financial Aid PROFILE. This form is similar to the FAFSA, but it is used to award university aid.

THE PROGRAM APPLICATION

For many schools, the program application is the main application for university-based aid. Much of the nonfederal university-based aid for incoming students is determined by the admissions committee's assessment of the merit of program applications. So a strong program application, submitted on time, will improve your chances of getting aid from the program or university. Since you cannot predict which elements of your application will be weighted most heavily by a given admissions committee, do your best on all of them.

NATIONAL AND PRIVATE SCHOLARSHIP AND FELLOWSHIP APPLICATIONS

If you apply for national and/or private scholarships and fellowships, you will have to submit separate applications for each one to the awarding organizations. Follow instructions carefully, making sure you meet all deadlines. Some scholarship applications can be as elaborate as program applications, with letters of recommendation and essays, so allow yourself a lot of time to complete them.

FOLLOWING UP

Just as you do with your program application, follow up with your financial aid applications as well. If you do not receive the SAR, an acknowledgment that your FAFSA form was received, within a few weeks of filing the FAFSA, check on its status. In addition, call the university offices with which you are dealing to make sure everything is proceeding smoothly.

TAX BENEFITS FOR STUDENTS

Whether or not you receive financial aid, there are many recently enacted tax benefits for adults who want to return to school (as well as for parents who send or plan to send their children to college). In effect, these tax cuts make the first two years of college universally available, and they give many more working adults the financial means to go back to school. About 12.9 million students benefit—5.8 million under the HOPE Scholarship tax credit and 7.1 million under the Lifetime Learning tax credit. Countless others benefit from new rules concerning Individual Retirement Accounts (IRAs) and state tuition savings plans as well as from deductions on student loan interest and employer reimbursements for education expenses.

THE HOPE SCHOLARSHIP TAX CREDIT

The HOPE Scholarship tax credit helps make the first two years of college or career school more affordable. Students whose adjusted gross income falls within certain limits receive a 100 percent tax credit for the first $1,000 of tuition and required fees and a 50 percent credit on the second $1,000. This credit is available for tuition and required fees less grants, scholarships, and other tax-free educational assistance. The credit is phased out for joint filers whose adjusted gross income is between $80,000 and $100,000 and for single filers whose adjusted gross income is between $40,000 and $50,000.

The HOPE Scholarship tax credit can be claimed for students who are in their first two years of college or career school and who are enrolled on at least a half-time basis in a degree or certificate program for any portion of the year. The taxpayer can claim a credit for his own tuition expense or for the expenses of his or her spouse or dependent children.

THE LIFETIME LEARNING TAX CREDIT

The Lifetime Learning tax credit is targeted toward adults who want to go back to school, change careers, or take a course or two to upgrade their skills as well as to college juniors, seniors, and graduate and professional degree students. A family may receive a 20 percent tax credit for the first $5,000 of tuition and required fees paid each year through 2002, and for the first $10,000 thereafter.

Just like the HOPE Scholarship tax credit, the Lifetime Learning tax credit is available for tuition and required fees less grants, scholarships, and other tax-free educational assistance. The maximum credit is determined on a per-taxpayer (family) basis, regardless of the number of postsecondary students in the family, and it is phased out at the same income levels as the HOPE Scholarship tax credit. Families can claim the Lifetime Learning tax credit for some members of their family and the HOPE Scholarship tax credit for others who qualify in the same year.

INDIVIDUAL RETIREMENT ACCOUNTS

Since January 1, 1998, taxpayers have been able to withdraw funds from an IRA, without penalty, for their own higher education expenses or those of their spouse, child, or even grandchild. However, you do have to pay income taxes on the amount you withdraw.

In addition, for each child under age 18, families may deposit $500 per year into an education IRA in the child's name. Earnings in the education IRA accumulate tax-free, and no taxes are due upon withdrawal if the money is used to pay for postsecondary tuition and required fees (less grants, scholarships, and other tax-free educational assistance), books, equipment, and eligible room and board expenses. Once the child reaches age 30, his or her education IRA must be closed or transferred to a younger member of the family.

A taxpayer's ability to contribute to an education IRA is phased out when the taxpayer is a joint filer with an adjusted gross income between $150,000 and $160,000, or a single filer with an adjusted gross income between $95,000 and $110,000. There are a few restrictions. For example, a student who receives the tax-free distributions from an education IRA may not, in the same year, benefit from the HOPE Scholarship or Lifetime Learning tax credits.

STATE TUITION PLANS

When a family uses a qualified state-sponsored tuition plan to save for college, no tax is due in connection with the plan until the time of withdrawal. Families can now use these plans to save not only for tuition but also for certain room and board expenses for students who attend college on at least a half-time basis. Tuition and required fees paid with withdrawals from a qualified state tuition plan are eligible for the HOPE Scholarship tax credit and Lifetime Learning tax credit.

TAX-DEDUCTIBLE STUDENT LOAN INTEREST

For many graduates, one of the first financial obligations is to repay their student loans. The new student loan interest deduction reduces the burden of the repayment obligation by allowing students or their families to take a tax deduction for interest paid in the first 60 months of repayment on student loans. The deduction is available even if an individual does not itemize other deductions.

The maximum deduction of $2,000 in 2000 rose to $2,500 in 2001 and beyond. It is phased out for joint filers with adjusted gross income between $60,000 and $75,000, and for single filers with adjusted gross income between $40,000 and $55,000.

TAX-DEDUCTIBLE EMPLOYER REIMBURSEMENTS

If you take undergraduate courses and your employer reimburses you for education-related expenses, you may be able to exclude up to $5,250 of employer-provided education benefits from your income. Reimbursement for graduate and professional courses is not eligible for this exclusion and is counted as taxable income.

COMMUNITY SERVICE LOAN FORGIVENESS

This provision excludes from your income any student loan amounts forgiven by nonprofit, tax-exempt charitable, or educa-tional institutions for borrowers who take community-service jobs that address unmet community needs. For example, a recent graduate who takes a low-paying job in a rural school will not owe any additional income tax if in recognition of this service her college or another charity forgives a loan it made to her to help pay her college costs. This provision applies to loans forgiven after August 5, 1997.

FOR ADDITIONAL INFORMATION

The tax issues relating to higher education are discussed in more detail in Internal Revenue Service Publication 970, *Tax Benefits for Higher Education.* To obtain a copy, visit the Internal Revenue Service Web site at www.irs.gov or call 800-829-3676 (toll-free).

PAYING FOR SCHOOL IS POSSIBLE

You can see that it *is* possible to find the financial aid that will help you pay for school. You will have to be persistent in your search for funds. You may have to spend time working on financial aid research and applications. You may have to borrow money. And once you enter a program, you may have to simplify your lifestyle in order to cut your expenses.

But if you really want to earn a degree or certificate, you can find the financial help that will make it possible. Be realistic about your needs, leave yourself enough time to complete all the paperwork, and do your homework. Now is a good time to look back on all the reasons why you want to continue your education—to remind yourself why it's worth it.

SUCCEEDING AS A DISTANCE LEARNER

Congratulations! You have weathered the selection and application process and you are about to embark on a new phase of your education. As you will soon find out for yourself, taking courses at a distance is not like going to class on campus. Distance learners often have the convenience of setting their own hours and pacing themselves in their studies. As we have seen in previous sections, the instructional technology lends itself to innovative approaches to teaching and learning, including more student participation and collaboration, especially in online courses. You'll find that because you work at a distance you will have more time to reflect about and respond to what you learn as well as to take part in discussions. You may be surprised at the ways in which the community of learning develops in a well-run distance course.

Of course, distance learners face a few challenges unique to the instructional design of distance courses. As a distance learner, you'll be expected to organize your time, work independently as well as collaboratively, take the initiative in your studies, and monitor your own progress, all while mastering the technology and using it as a valuable tool for learning.

So, in addition to the basic study skills you would need to earn any degree—reading, writing, analytical thinking, and test-taking skills—you will need other skills and strategies to succeed at distance learning. In this section we'll give you some suggestions and tips from successful distance learners that will help you become a more effective and successful student yourself.

MASTERING THE TECHNOLOGY

We'll start with technology, because success in distance learning depends first upon reliable technology that you understand how to use. Once you've mastered the technology, it will recede into the background and become something you simply use and even take for granted.

HAVING THE RIGHT EQUIPMENT

Before you start a course, make sure you have the technological tools you will need to participate in discussions and complete assignments. Most programs provide a list of technical requirements ahead of time. If your course is on line, get a list of the hardware and software required, and make sure the computer you plan to use is properly equipped and that you have a reliable Internet service provider. If you take a course via broadcast or videotapes, learn how to use your VCR. If you have to buy equipment, don't skimp on specifications to save a few dollars now. The money you spend now to make sure you have the appropriate hardware and software is money well spent, because you'll find it much easier to get your work done properly if you are not struggling with inadequate machinery.

IMPROVING YOUR TECHNOLOGY SKILLS

If you have the proper equipment but think you may not be up to speed technologically, try to improve your technology skills before courses start. As we discussed in "Selecting a Good Distance Learning Program," many colleges offer online tutorials or sample minicourses that you can take if you feel you need some practice with the technology before you actually take your first course. "I am a computer novice and never realized the extent of the computer's online capabilities until I had to learn about it through trial and error," reports a language arts literacy teacher who took a graduate course on line from Rutgers University. "This was very frustrating." So if you have the opportunity for a sample course or practice session before courses begin, take it.

TIPS FOR SUCCEEDING WITH TECHNOLOGY

To master the technology involved in your distance courses:

- Make sure you have the appropriate hardware and software for your courses, and don't skimp on the specifications if you need to purchase any items.
- Take a tutorial or sample minicourse ahead of time to familiarize yourself with the instructional technology.
- Allow yourself extra time at the beginning of the course to navigate the technology.
- Keep copies of your assignments and back up your computer files.
- Ask for help when you need it. Well-run distance programs have technological support via telephone seven days a week, 24 hours a day.

Remember, the technology involved in distance learning is a tool that anyone can master—it just may take some effort.

LEARNING ABOUT LIBRARY RESOURCES

Once you've got the technology working for you, the next resource you need to familiarize yourself with is the library. Understanding how to use a library is important to any student's success, but it is especially important for distance students who may not be able to get to a good bricks-and-mortar university library to get the materials they need.

TAKING AN ORIENTATION PROGRAM

One of the first things you should check before courses begin is whether or not a library services orientation program designed for distance students is available. If it is, sign up to take the orientation right away. "An early orientation to library resources, particularly interlibrary loans, is needed for those who can't physically access a library," recommends Kurt Krause, a hotel manager who took an online hospitality management course from

Virginia Tech. Learning about library services through an orientation program will save you time later on when you actually need to do research for a course.

LEARNING WHAT'S AVAILABLE ON LINE

Although the Internet has revolutionized the way we look for and store information, don't make the mistake of thinking that all the information you will need is available on the Internet. True, many journals, databases, catalogs, and newspapers are instantaneously available on line, and you can access them directly or through the university library if a subscription is needed. However, the material that's available on line is only a fraction of the total resources of a library. Books, for example, are still primarily in print form. Many academic journals provide only abstracts (not full-text articles) on line, and a few are not on line at all. Reference services may be available only face-to-face or by telephone. And reserve collections may or may not be available on line. So one of the first tasks you face is to learn just what you can access on line via the university library or directly on the Internet and what you must access in paper, microform, or other physical media.

PLANNING AHEAD TO GET THE MATERIALS YOU NEED

The reason you will need to know what your research resources are fairly early in the game is that you will have to plan ahead if you need to access nondigitized (paper) information at a distance, especially if the material needs to be secured via interlibrary loan. "Because I did not have physical access to a medical library in my community, I had to organize my data collection for assigned papers early in the semester," explains Patti Iversen. "The biggest handicap was the time delay in ordering and receiving full-text articles. A time lapse of three weeks from time of request to delivery of articles was common." You can see the need to plan ahead under these circumstances.

TIPS FOR SUCCEEDING WITH LIBRARY RESOURCES

In order to be prepared for course work, early in the term or, even better, before the term starts:

- **Take a library orientation if one is available.** If there is no formal distance orientation, call the library and ask for an informal orientation.
- **Check your local public and university libraries.** Find out what resources they have and whether or not you can arrange access.
- **Check each course syllabus very early in the term.** Determine whether you can obtain everything you will need on line or whether you will have to make other arrangements for some items.
- **Use the reference services of your university library.** Ask for help. Reference librarians are there to help you, even if it's by e-mail or over the phone.

MANAGING YOUR TIME

"If you are a student at any college, there is one thing you just don't have enough of....TIME! Everything is about time," says Cena Barber, an undergraduate who has taken online courses toward her degree in political science and history at Drake University in Iowa. For students who have family and work responsibilities as well, lack of time is a particularly acute problem. "With life's challenges, kids, family, job—it's hard to keep your studies a high priority," explains Scott Garrod, who is earning a master's degree in business from Syracuse University. "When your four-year-old wants a story read, do you have to study your accounting? That's an easy choice, but it means making up the accounting at a later time."

GENERAL TIPS FOR MANAGING YOUR TIME

Not having enough time is a common problem. Distance learners can approach this problem in several ways:

- **Be realistic about how many courses you can handle.** If you work and/or have a family, you will have relatively little time to spend on schoolwork. Start out with one or two courses at a time, and then if you feel you can increase your courseload, do so. This is especially important if you take a distance course for the first time and don't know exactly what to expect.
- **Set up a regular time to study, but expect to be interrupted.** If you have a study schedule, you are more likely to get your schoolwork done, but be sure to leave some extra time. Unless you live alone, you'll need time for your family commitments. Young kids, especially, don't much care what you are doing when they need a parent, so if possible try to schedule study time when they are not around.
- **Set up a regular place to study.** Although it may be difficult if you are doing schoolwork at home, try to establish a study area that's yours alone to use. If possible, the area should be quiet and free of distractions. "Since you are doing the work at home you can be easily distracted," explains Andrea Bessel, who is earning a bachelor's degree in business administration from the State University of New York at Oswego. "A lot of times something comes up and I end up setting my homework aside, which is not a good habit to get into." So if necessary, do schoolwork at your local public library or from work if your employer permits it.
- **Set priorities on what you have to do.** Make judgments about what you need to do, and then spend your time on activities that are the most important and must be done first. Get used to the fact that you may have to postpone some tasks.
- **Set deadlines.** Distance learning can be very unstructured, so you probably will have to be your own taskmaster. "I have learned that I have to set deadlines for myself," says Brigit Dolan, who is earning a master's degree from Gonzaga University in Washington, "or I will never get anything done."
- **Don't procrastinate.** "Procrastination is your worst enemy," claims Robin Barnes, who earned a master's degree in nursing (family nurse-practitioner) from Gonzaga University.
- **Use time-management tools to help you schedule your time.** Planners, whether paper or electronic, can help you allocate time and keep track of deadlines. "To do" lists can help you manage your short-term commitments.

MANAGING TIME IN ONLINE COURSES

In addition to the lack of time that all students contend with, online distance learners face unique challenges associated with time, namely, managing the flexibility of the online format and dealing with lag time when communicating with students and faculty members.

MANAGING THE FLEXIBILITY OF ONLINE COURSES

Flexibility is a unique advantage that attracts people to asynchronous courses, especially online courses. But flexibility can have a downside as well. "The best thing about distance learning is the freedom to set one's own hours for study and learning. The worst thing about distance learning is the freedom to set one's own hours for study and learning!" exclaims a middle school language arts literacy teacher taking an online graduate course from Rutgers. "Although it hasn't happened to me, it is easy to put aside work and projects for the course when one is not locked into a regular schedule. I can see how one could easily fall behind through a lack of discipline." So you can see that you'll have to use your time-management skills to take advantage of the flexibility and not let it take advantage of you.

MANAGING THE AMOUNT OF TIME SPENT ON LINE

Not only does the flexibility of online courses mean that you need discipline to log on regularly, but once you are connected you have, in theory, as much time as you want to spend on the course. Cena Barber points out, "There is no time limit as to how long the class lasts. It could be five minutes one day and five hours the next." Unless you are careful, it's easy to spend more time than you really have on an online course, so before you log on, decide how much time you have to spend during that session.

GETTING ACCUSTOMED TO THE PACE

Another difference between online and traditional courses that comes as a surprise to many students is the pace at which discussions proceed. In an online course, there is a time interval between when you post a message and when you get a response—in an asynchronous discussion group—or when you send an e-mail and get a reply. Hours, even days, may elapse between exchanges on a topic, and it can take a while to get used to the slow progress of communication.

The time delay sometimes becomes a problem when students work on a group project with deadlines. "Given the time lag, it took ever so much more time to get anything done if you had to collaborate with anyone," explains a library media specialist taking an online postgraduate course from Rutgers. "When would they open the discussion thread? When would they respond? These were frustrations that I hadn't counted on and found difficult to deal with." To solve these problems, groups working on projects often communicate by telephone or in real-time chat rooms.

TIPS FOR MANAGING TIME IN ONLINE COURSES

Given the asynchronous nature of online courses, you will not be able to completely solve the time problems they pose. However, you can minimize or avoid them to some degree.

- **Set a schedule for logging on.** Even though no one may have given you a daily class schedule, you will benefit if you work one out for yourself. "You should become accustomed to getting on line on a regular basis," advises Vania McBean, a computer studies major at University of Maryland University College. "I log on each day to see what is new."
- **Limit the amount of time you will spend on line at one session.** The limit might be 1 hour, for example. On some days that will be too much time, and on others, too little, but at least you will have a benchmark to aim for.
- **Don't fret about the time delays in asynchronous discussions.** Before you know it, you will have become used to this method of communication and it will no longer seem odd.
- **Use a chat room or the telephone when asynchronous communication becomes too slow.** You can make an appointment to meet in a chat room or have a teleconference if group work needs to be accomplished more efficiently. If e-mailing a fellow student or the instructor takes too long, try telephoning.

MANAGING TIME IN VIDEOTAPED COURSES

Students that take courses in which on-campus lectures are videotaped and mailed to them face a different set of time-management challenges. First, the weekly videotapes may take a considerable amount of time to watch. And second, the taping, duplicating, and delivery time means that distance students lag behind on-campus students in the same course.

SCHEDULING TIME TO WATCH THE VIDEOS

Depending on the course load, students that take videotaped courses may find themselves with 3 to 12 hours or more of videotape to watch each week on top of their assignments. Essentially, the amount of time is the same as it would be if they had to attend classes. Since they don't have to attend classes, inexperienced students may put off watching the videos, thinking they can catch up at a later date. "In the first semester, the learning curve is steep," comments Dale Ann Abendroth, assistant professor of nursing at Gonzaga University. "So I set up my assignments to force students into a pattern of watching the videotapes." If you have a savvy instructor, the assignments will put you on a schedule. If the instructor doesn't take a structured approach, you will need to plan a regular schedule to watch the videos in order to keep up with the course work.

MANAGING THE DELAY BETWEEN DISTANCE AND ON-CAMPUS STUDENTS

In videotaped courses, the distance students are a half-week to a week behind the on-campus students. "It can get a little confusing when reading topics don't correspond with lecture topics because the tapes arrive one week later than the class," explains Carla Gentry, who is earning a Master of Science in Nursing (family nurse practitioner) from Gonzaga University. If the course also has a Web-based component, the distance students have to cope with joining the Web-based discussion group and receiving the readings before the videotaped lectures arrive.

Schools do try to solve this time-delay problem, with mixed success. "Throughout the semester, we have a one-week lag on assignment due dates (in comparison to the students who are actually in class on campus)," explains Nicole DeRaleau, who is earning a master's degree in engineering from Worcester Polytechnic Institute in Massachusetts. "At the end of the semester, however, we have a one-week disadvantage because the whole class has to turn in final assignments, projects, and finals on the same date in order to get grades done on time," says DeRaleau. "This can be *very* stressful." In contrast, at Gonzaga University's nursing program, distance students are permitted to take their final exams in their local communities a few days later than the on-campus students. "These are logistical problems that both the faculty and students become accustomed to solving," explains Abendroth.

TIPS FOR MANAGING TIME IN VIDEOTAPED COURSES

There are a couple of things you can do to manage your time if you take videotaped courses:

- **Set a schedule for watching the videotapes.** Even though you don't have to show up for class, you still need to put in classroom time in front of your own TV. If you're good at multitasking, you can follow Brigit Dolan's lead. "Sometimes I'm able to pick up my house while listening and taking in the information," explains the graduate student.
- **Keep up with your course work.** Since at times you may need to complete assignments or take exams with less lead time than on-campus students have, it's imperative that you keep up with the work on a regular basis. You may face an end-of-term time crunch, so study regularly throughout the course to minimize its effect.

COMMUNICATING WITH FACULTY

When you are a distance learner you can't just raise your hand and ask a question or stay after class to talk with the instructor. Even in two-way interactive video classes, which are more similar to traditional classes than other distance learning formats, there can be difficulties in communicating with an instructor at a remote location. "It can be a little more inconvenient to speak with your instructor if you need to ask about something you wouldn't ask in front of the whole class," reports a horticulture student taking a two-way interactive video course from the University of Cincinnati.

For students in online and videotaped courses, communicating with an instructor can be slow. "Sometimes you do more self-teaching because you cannot just drop into the instructor's office," explains Robin Barnes. "You may have to wait a day or two for an answer to a question. Have patience and be kind to yourself." However, you can use technology to your advantage in communicating with faculty members. E-mail, for example, is an excellent way to contact a faculty member to find out what his or her expectations are, to clarify assignments, or simply to ask a question. You may not get a response immediately, but most faculty members will answer their e-mail within a day or two. In fact, you should make a point of communicating with your instructor in distance courses. "Be sure to communicate regularly with your professor because [the course] can seem pretty far removed if you are not getting feedback every week or so," advises Sonja Cole, a middle school media specialist taking online courses from Rutgers.

TIPS FOR COMMUNICATING WITH FACULTY MEMBERS

To ensure you get the input an instructor can provide and to make yourself known, here are some strategies for communicating with faculty members:

- **Participate in online discussion groups.** Although your instructor may not comment all the time, he or she is following the class's discussions and will get to know you there.
- **Participate in class discussions in two-way interactive video courses.** It's easy to "hide in the back of the class" if you attend a course in a remote location, but you'll get more out of the class if you respond to the instructor and the class discussion.
- **Be assertive in communicating with your instructors.** "You have to take the initiative," advises a distance learning student. "If you do not make sure that you get the best learning opportunity that you can, no one is going to do that for you." Remember, most faculty members are more than happy to help their students.
- **Use e-mail or the telephone.** If you need to communicate with the instructor privately, use e-mail or the telephone. Most faculty members will respond within a day or two.

REACHING OUT TO YOUR FELLOW STUDENTS

Just as you should take the initiative in communicating with your instructors, you should also be proactive in communicating with fellow students. Communicating with your peers has two benefits: it helps you feel connected to the learning community and it enables you to learn from your fellow students. In addition, establishing good communication with fellow students is key to successful collaborative efforts.

MAKING CONNECTIONS WITH THE LEARNING COMMUNITY

"I have made a conscious effort to build relationships with other students and to keep e-mail contact with them," explains Patti Iversen, a graduate student who lives in Montana and takes distance courses from Gonzaga University in Washington. "This allows each of us the opportunity to get feedback and commiserate." Another student, who is earning a bachelor's degree in information systems management from University of Maryland University College, reports, "My experience with fellow classmates in the online classroom has been very positive. I have found that establishing relationships, despite the fact that they are short-lived, has aided me." During periods when your motivation flags, this connection with others in your courses can help energize you and put you back on track.

TAKING ADVANTAGE OF WHAT YOUR PEERS HAVE TO OFFER

Second, your fellow students can be resources for you. Many distance students are adults with considerable life and professional experience, so they can contribute as much as they learn from the interactions in a course. According to Michael Olsen, who teaches distance courses on the hospitality industry at Virginia Tech, students in his courses "are mature, industry-experienced professionals who come extremely well prepared. They are good contributors and they are not afraid to interact." Scott Garrod, who is pursuing a master's degree in business from Syracuse University, likes the broad range of people he meets through his distance courses. "You do not develop deep relationships," he explains, "but in a distance program you meet a wider range of individuals across multiple countries and careers."

Since all this knowledge and experience is within easy reach, you should take advantage of it. "You need to read through the responses that others post on the Web, so that you actually gain something from the forum discussion," explains Beth Grote, a Drake University student who took a course on line. Some students do more than simply participate in class and in online discussion groups—they form study groups of their own. "You just have to make it a point to form an Internet study group," suggests Robin Barnes. "We would try to converse once a week, more often if we were working on a project."

WORKING ON GROUP PROJECTS

Since instructors often assign group projects in distance courses to help forge a community of learners, you will probably find yourself working with others much more frequently than you did in your past on-campus classes. According to several distance students we surveyed, doing group projects well is one of the most challenging aspects of distance learning. Often the logistics of getting a group of busy working adults in different time zones to meet at an appointed time in a chat room or be available for a conference call can be daunting. In some online courses, separate discussion groups are formed so group members can communicate asynchronously. "You need to have lots of patience and dedication," warns Kevin Ruthen, who earned a master's degree in information resource management from Syracuse University. "Interaction in an online environment can often be more time-consuming than an on-campus meeting."

And the problems of interaction are not limited to time factors. In the online environment, it's sometimes difficult for a group to coalesce and assign roles and tasks to its members. "In one of my courses, members tiptoed around each other, no one wanting to seem overbearing and declare themselves the leader, boss, facilitator, whatever. But we really needed one," explains a library media specialist taking online courses from Rutgers. "It took quite a while for a shakedown to occur so that some work could be accomplished." She continues, "Another problem was what to do about members of the team who were unproductive. It's very hard to prod people over the Internet. On the other hand, since you don't have the opportunity for meandering, off-topic conversations that start in onsite classes, things move swiftly, on schedule."

TIPS FOR COMMUNICATING WELL WITH YOUR PEERS

To make the most of your interactions with your fellow students, you can use these suggestions:

- **Participate.** You should participate in discussions, whether they are in class in two-way interactive video courses or are on line. You will get a lot more out of your courses if you take an active part. In addition, you will get to know the other students and they will get to know you.

- **Share your knowledge and experiences.** Don't assume you have nothing to offer. Most adults have plenty of experience and knowledge that can be of value to others.

- **If you need support from other students, ask for it.** Everyone runs into occasional problems in a course, even if the problem is simply feeling overwhelmed by the amount of work you have to do. Communicating with other students can help you solve

problems and get back on track, or it can simply make you feel better because you've let off some steam.

- **Use various forms of communication as needed.** Don't feel limited to class time or discussion groups. You can e-mail or call people with whom you'd like to converse in private. Remember, other distance students may feel somewhat disconnected from the group, too, and they will probably welcome an overture from you.

- **Be assertive.** When you work in a group, be assertive about what you can contribute. If the group is not making progress, try to use some of your leadership skills to get things moving.

ENLISTING YOUR FAMILY'S SUPPORT

One of the main benefits of most distance learning courses is that you can take the course from home. But unless you live alone, that means that you are working from a shared space in the presence of your family. Not only do they have to cope with the fact that you have less time for them, but they have to watch you be inaccessible—not an easy task. Therefore you should make sure you enlist the support and cooperation of your family; having their support will make your life—and theirs—much easier.

One distance student has made her education something of a family enterprise. "I work full-time, and I am blessed with a wonderful, supportive husband and the two greatest children one could ever dream of," says LaVonne Johnson, who is earning a master's degree in nursing from Gonzaga University. "We are in this together, everyone helping on some level," she continues. "My husband cooks, cleans, does laundry, and will proof papers if he is the last resort. My thirteen-year-old daughter is a great help around the house and my sixteen-year-old son is always helping with Power Point projects, statistical analyses, and Excel graphs. Needless to say, in return I try really hard not to impact my family any more than they already are, and we get by."

IN CONCLUSION

Distance learning is challenging, but with motivation, self-discipline, and the support of family, coworkers, and fellow students, you can succeed in your courses and earn a certificate or degree if that's your goal. Perhaps the best summation of distance education we encountered from the scores of students we surveyed came from Patti Iversen:

Distance learning isn't for the faint of heart or those who require considerable reinforcement to remain on task. It is sometimes difficult for others to recognize the challenges of the distance learner, as job, family, and community activities all continue as before. Finding a way to carve out of a busy schedule the time necessary to successfully complete courses that seem relatively invisible is a big challenge. At the same time, there is absolutely no way that I could have hoped to accomplish the goal that I have set for myself except as a distance learner. I am able to stretch and grow, professionally and personally, while continuing to live a lifestyle that I value immensely. It isn't always an easy task—it is often rigorous and sometimes frustrating—but distance learning has opened a gate of opportunity for me that previously was inaccessible.

Distance learning can provide that opportunity for you as well.

APPENDIX

WHAT IS DISTANCE LEARNING?

You can find countless sources of information about distance learning by doing an Internet search. One Web site that lists links to distance learning resources is dmoz.org/Reference/Education/Distance_Learning. Some other good sources of information include the following:

The Chronicle of Higher Education
1255 23rd Street, NW
Washington, DC 20037
Telephone: 202-466-1000
E-mail: circulation@chronicle.com
Web site: http://chronicle.com

Distance Learning in Higher Education. Council for Higher Education Accreditation, CHEA Update No. 3, June 2000. Available at www.chea.org/Commentary/distance-learning-3.cfm.

Russell, Thomas L. *The No Significant Difference Phenomenon*. Available at teleeducation.nb.ca/nosignificantdifference/.

Survey on Distance Education at Postsecondary Education Institutions, 1997–1998. NCES 2000-13, by Laurie Lewis, Kyle Snow, Elizabeth Farris, Douglas Levin. Bernie Green, project officer. U.S. Department of Education, National Center for Education Statistics, Washington, DC, 1999. Available online at http://nces.ed.gov.

U.S. Distance Learning Association
140 Gould Street
Needham, MA 02494-2397
Telephone: 800-275-5162 (toll-free)
Web site: www.usdla.org

IS DISTANCE LEARNING RIGHT FOR YOU?

Sometimes it helps to have some objective help when you are assessing your goals, aptitudes, strengths, and weaknesses:

National Board for Certified Counselors
3 Terrace Way, Suite D
Greensboro, NC 27403-3660
Telephone: 800-398-5389 (toll-free)
E-mail: nbcc@nbcc.org
Web site: www.nbcc.org

WHAT CAN YOU STUDY VIA DISTANCE LEARNING?

Internet Databases

Peterson's: www.petersons.com/distancelearning

Print Directories

Guide to Distance Learning Programs in Canada 2001. Education International, 2001.

Peterson's *MBA Distance Learning Programs 2000*. Princeton, NJ: Peterson's, 1999.

Equivalency Examinations

College Level Examination Program (CLEP)
P.O. Box 6600
Princeton, NJ 08541-6600
Telephone: 609-771-7865
E-mail: clep@info.collegeboard.org
Web site: www.collegeboard.org/clep

CLEP Success. Lawrenceville, NJ: Peterson's, 2007. Lieberman, Leo, et al.

DANTES Subject Standardized Tests (DSSTs)
Telephone: 609-720-6740
E-mail: dantes@chauncey.com *or* exams@voled.doded.mil
Web site: www.chauncey.com/dantes *or* www.voled.doded.mil/dantes/exam

Excelsior College Examination Program (formerly Regents College Examinations)
Test Administration Office
Excelsior College
7 Columbia Circle
Albany, NY 12203-5159
Telephone: 888-647–2388 (toll-free)
E-mail: testadmn@excelsior.edu
Web site: www.excelsior.edu/100.htm

GRE Subject Area Tests
GRE-ETS
P.O. Box 6000
Princeton, NJ 08541-6000
Telephone: 609-771-7670
E-mail: gre-info@ets.org
Web site: www.gre.org

Assessment for Life Experience

Council for Adult and Experiential Learning (CAEL)
55 East Monroe Street, Suite 1930
Chicago, IL 60603
Telephone: 312-499-2600
Web site: www.cael.org

Credit for Work Training

American Council on Education
Center for Adult Learning Educational Credentials
One Dupont Circle NW
Washington, DC 20036

Telephone: 202-939-9475
E-mail: credit@ace.nche.edu
Web site: www.acenet.edu

Credit for Military Training

Servicemembers Opportunities Colleges
1307 New York Avenue NW, fifth floor
Washington, DC 20005-4701
Telephone: 800-368-5622 (toll-free)
E-mail: socmail@aascu.org
Web site: www.soc.aascu.org

SELECTING A GOOD DISTANCE LEARNING PROGRAM

The names and contact information of all agencies recognized by the U.S. Department of Education (www.ed.gov/offices/OPE/accreditation/natlagencies.html) and the Council for Higher Education Accreditation (www.chea.org) are listed below.

Institutional Accrediting Agencies—Regional

Middle States Association of Colleges and Schools

Accredits institutions in Delaware, District of Columbia, Maryland, New Jersey, New York, Pennsylvania, Puerto Rico, and the Virgin Islands.

Jean Avnet Morse, Executive Director
Commission on Higher Education
3624 Market Street
Philadelphia, PA 19104-2680
Telephone: 267-284-5000
Fax: 215-662-5501
E-mail: info@msache.org
Web site: www.msache.org

New England Association of Schools and Colleges

Accredits institutions in Connecticut, Maine, Massachusetts, New Hampshire, Rhode Island, and Vermont.

Jacob Ludes III, Executive Director
Commission on Institutions of Higher Education
209 Burlington Road
Bedford, MA 01730-1433
Telephone: 781-271-0022
Fax: 781-271-0950
E-mail: ccook@neasc.org
Web site: www.neasc.org

North Central Association of Colleges and Schools

Accredits institutions in Arizona, Arkansas, Colorado, Illinois, Indiana, Iowa, Kansas, Michigan, Minnesota, Missouri, Nebraska, New Mexico, North Dakota, Ohio, Oklahoma, South Dakota, West Virginia, Wisconsin, and Wyoming.

Steve Crow, Executive Director
The Higher Learning Commission
30 North LaSalle Street, Suite 2400
Chicago, IL 60602-2504
Telephone: 800-621-7440
Fax: 312-263-7462
E-mail: scrow@hlcommission.org
Web site: www.ncahigherlearningcommission.org

Northwest Commission on Colleges and Universities

Accredits institutions in Alaska, Idaho, Montana, Nevada, Oregon, Utah, and Washington.

Sandra E. Elman, Executive Director
Commission on Colleges
8060 165th Avenue, NE, Ste 100
Redmond, WA 98052
Telephone: 425-558-4224
Fax: 425-376-0596
E-mail: selman@nwccu.org
Web site: www.nwccu.org

Southern Association of Colleges and Schools

Accredits institutions in Alabama, Florida, Georgia, Kentucky, Louisiana, Mississippi, North Carolina, South Carolina, Tennessee, Texas, and Virginia.

Belle Wheelan, President
Commission on Colleges
1866 Southern Lane
Decatur, GA 30033-4097
Telephone: 404-679-4500
Fax: 404-679-4528
E-mail: bwheelan@sacscoc.org
Web site: www.sacscoc.org

Western Association of Schools and Colleges

Accredits institutions in California, Guam, and Hawaii.

Ralph A. Wolff, Executive Director
Accrediting Commission for Senior Colleges and Universities
985 Atlantic Avenue, Suite 100
Alameda, CA 94501
Telephone: 510-748-9001
Fax: 510-748-9797
E-mail: rwolff@wascsenior.org
Web site: www.wascweb.org

Institutional Accrediting Agencies—Other

Accrediting Council for Independent Colleges and Schools

Stephen A. Eggland, Executive Director
750 First Street, NE, Suite 980
Washington, DC 20002-4241
Telephone: 202-336-6780
Fax: 202-842-2593
E-mail: steve@acics.org
Web site: www.acics.org

Distance Education and Training Council

Michael P. Lambert, Executive Secretary
1601 Eighteenth Street, NW
Washington, DC 20009-2529
Telephone: 202-234-5100
Fax: 202-332-1386
E-mail: detc@detc.org
Web site: www.detc.org

Specialized Accrediting Agencies

Acupuncture

Dort S. Bigg, Executive Director
Accreditation Commission for Acupuncture and Oriental Medicine

1010 Wayne Avenue, Suite 1270
Silver Spring, MD 20910
Telephone: 301-608-9680
Fax: 301-608-9576
E-mail: ccaom@compuserve.com
Web site: www.ccaom.org

Art and Design

Samuel Hope, Executive Director
National Association of Schools of Art and Design
11250 Roger Bacon Drive, Suite 21
Reston, VA 20190
Telephone: 703-437-0700
Fax: 703-437-6312
E-mail: info@arts-accredit.org
Web site: www.arts-accredit.org

Chiropractic

Paul D. Walker, Executive Director
The Council on Chiropractic Education
8049 North 85th Way
Scottsdale, AZ 85258-4321
Telephone: 480-443-8877
Fax: 480-483-7333
E-mail: cce@cce-usa.org
Web site: www.cce-usa.org

Clinical Laboratory Science

Betty Craft, Chairman
National Accrediting Agency for Clinical Laboratory Sciences
8410 West Bryn Mawr Avenue, Suite 670
Chicago, IL 60631
Telephone: 312-714-8880
Fax: 312-714-8886
E-mail: naaclsinfo@naacls.org
Web site: www.naacls.org

Dance

Samuel Hope, Executive Director
National Association of Schools of Dance
11250 Roger Bacon Drive, Suite 21
Reston, VA 20190
Telephone: 703-437-0700
Fax: 703-437-6312
E-mail: info@arts-accredit.org
Web site: www.arts-accredit.org

Dentistry

Laura M. Neumann, D.D.S., M.P.H., Associate Executive
  Director, Education
American Dental Association
211 East Chicago Avenue, 18th Floor
Chicago, IL 60611
Telephone: 312-440-2500
Fax: 312-440-2800
E-mail: education@ada.org
Web site: www.ada.org

Education

Arthur Wise, President
National Council for Accreditation of Teacher Education
2010 Massachusetts Avenue, NW
Washington, DC 20036-1023

Telephone: 202-466-7496
Fax: 202-296-6620
E-mail: info@ncate.org
Web site: www.ncate.org

Engineering

George D. Peterson, Executive Director
Accreditation Board for Engineering and Technology, Inc.
111 Market Place, Suite 1050
Baltimore, MD 21202
Telephone: 410-347-7700
Fax: 410-625-2238
E-mail: accreditation@abet.org
Web site: www.abet.org

Environment

National Environmental Health Science and Protection
  Accreditation Council
720 South Colorado Boulevard, Suite 970-S
Denver, CO 80246-1925
Telephone: 303-756-9090
Fax: 303-691-9490
E-mail: staff@neha.org
Web site: www.neha.org/AccredCouncil.html

Forestry

Michele Harvey, Director, Science and Education
Committee on Education
Society of American Foresters
5400 Grosvenor Lane
Bethesda, MD 20814-2198
Telephone: 301-897-8720 Ext. 119
Fax: 301-897-3690
E-mail: harveym@safnet.org
Web site: www.safnet.org

Health Services Administration

Andrea Barone-Wodjouatt, Executive Director
Accrediting Commission on Education for Health Services
  Administration
730 11th Street, NW, Fourth Floor
Washington, DC 20001-4510
Telephone: 202-638-5131
Fax: 202-638-3429
E-mail: accredcom@aol.com
Web site: monkey.hmi.missouri.edu/acehsa

Interior Design

Kayem Dunn, Director
Foundation for Interior Design Education Research
60 Monroe Center, NW, Suite 300
Grand Rapids, MI 49503-2920
Telephone: 616-458-0400
Fax: 616-458-0460
E-mail: fider@fider.org
Web site: www.fider.org

Journalism and Mass Communications

Susanne Shaw, Executive Director
Accrediting Council on Education in Journalism and Mass
  Communications
School of Journalism
Stauffer-Flint Hall

University of Kansas
Lawrence, KS 66045
Telephone: 785-864-3986
Fax: 785-864-5225
E-mail: sshaw@kuhub.cc.ukans.edu
Web site: www.ukans.edu/P5acejmc

Landscape Architecture

Ronald C. Leighton, Accreditation Manager
Landscape Architectural Accreditation Board
American Society of Landscape Architects
636 Eye Street, NW
Washington, DC 20001-3736
Telephone: 202-898-2444
Fax: 202-898-1185
E-mail: rleighton@asla.org
Web site: www.asla.org/asla/

Law

Carl Monk, Executive Vice President and Executive Director
Accreditation Committee
Association of American Law Schools
1201 Connecticut Avenue, NW, Suite 800
Washington, DC 20036-2605
Telephone: 202-296-8851
Fax: 202-296-8869
E-mail: cmonk@aals.org
Web site: www.aals.org

John A. Sebert, Consultant on Legal Education
American Bar Association
750 North Lake Shore Drive
Chicago, IL 60611
Telephone: 312-988-6746
E-mail: legaled@abanet.org
Web site: www.abanet.org/legaled

Library

Mary Taylor, Assistant Director
Committee on Accreditation
American Library Association
50 East Huron Street
Chicago, IL 60611
Telephone: 800-545-2433 (toll-free)
Fax: 312-280-2433
E-mail: mtaylor@ala.org
Web site: www.ala.org/accreditation

Marriage and Family Therapy

Michael Bowers, Executive Director
American Association for Marriage and Family Therapy
1133 15th Street, NW, Suite 300
Washington, DC 20005-2710
Telephone: 202-452-0109
Fax: 202-232-2329
E-mail: COAMFTE@aamft.org
Web site: www.aamft.org

Medical Illustration

William C. Andrea, Chair
Accreditation Review Committee for the Medical Illustrator
St. Luke's Hospital
Instructional Resources

232 South Woods Mill Road
Chesterfield, MO 63017
Telephone: 314-205-6158
Fax: 314-205-6144
E-mail: andrwc@stlo.smhs.com
Web site: www.caahep.org/accreditation/mi/mi-accreditation.htm

Medicine

Liaison Committee on Medical Education
The LCME is administered in even-numbered years, beginning
  each July 1, by:
David P. Stevens, M.D., Secretary
Association of American Medical Colleges
2450 N Street, NW
Washington, DC 20037
Telephone: 202-828-0596
Fax: 202-828-1125
E-mail: dstevens@aamc.org
Web site: www.aamc.org
The LCME is administered in odd-numbered years, beginning
  each July 1, by:
Frank Simon, M.D., Secretary
American Medical Association
515 North State Street
Chicago, IL 60610
Telephone: 312-464-4657
Fax: 312-464-5830
E-mail: frank_simon@ama-assn.org
Web site: www.ama-assn.org

Music

Samuel Hope, Executive Director
National Association of Schools of Music
11250 Roger Bacon Drive, Suite 21
Reston, VA 20190
Telephone: 703-437-0700
Fax: 703-437-6312
E-mail: info@arts-accredit.org
Web site: www.arts-accredit.org

Naturopathic Medicine

Robert Lofft, Executive Director
Council on Naturopathic Medical Education
P.O. Box 11426
Eugene, OR 97440-3626
Telephone: 541-484-6028
E-mail: dir@cnme.org
Web site: www.cnme.org

Nurse Anesthesia

Betty J. Horton, Director of Accreditation
Council on Accreditation of Nurse Anesthesia Educational
  Programs
222 South Prospect Avenue, Suite 304
Park Ridge, IL 60068-4010
Telephone: 847-692-7050
Fax: 847-693-7137
E-mail: cwargin@compuserve.com
Web site: www.aana.com/coa

Nurse Midwifery

Betty Watts Carrington, Chair
Division of Accreditation

American College of Nurse-Midwives
818 Connecticut Avenue, NW, Suite 900
Washington, DC 20006
Telephone: 202-728-9877
Fax: 202-728-9897
E-mail: educatio@acnm.org
Web site: www.midwife.org/educ

Nursing

Geraldene Felton, Executive Director
National League for Nursing
61 Broadway, 33rd Floor
New York, NY 10006
Telephone: 800-669-1656 (toll-free)
Fax: 212-812-0393
E-mail: gfelton@nlnac.org
Web site: www.nln.org

Occupational Therapy

Doris Gordon, Director of Accreditation
American Occupational Therapy Association
4720 Montgomery Lane
P.O. Box 31220
Bethesda, MD 20824-1220
Telephone: 301-652-2682
Fax: 301-652-7711
E-mail: accred@aota.org
Web site: www.aota.org

Optometry

Joyce Urbeck, Administrative Director
Council on Optometric Education
American Optometric Association
243 North Lindbergh Boulevard
St. Louis, MO 63141
Telephone: 314-991-4100
Fax: 314-991-4101
E-mail: coe@theaoa.org
Web site: www.aoanet.org

Osteopathic Medicine

John B. Crosby, Executive Director
Bureau of Professional Education, Council on Predoctoral Education
American Osteopathic Association
142 East Ontario Street
Chicago, IL 60611
Telephone: 800-621-1773 (toll-free)
Fax: 312-202-8200
E-mail: ssweet@aoa-net.org
Web site: www.aoa-net.org

Pastoral Education

Reverend Teresa E. Snorton, Executive Director
Accreditation Commission
Association for Clinical Pastoral Education, Inc.
1549 Clairmont Road, Suite 103
Decatur, GA 30033-4611
Telephone: 404-320-1472
Fax: 404-320-0849
E-mail: teresa@acpe.edu
Web site: www.acpe.edu

Pharmacy

Peter H. Vlasses, Executive Director
American Council on Pharmaceutical Education
311 West Superior Street
Chicago, IL 60610
Telephone: 312-664-3575
Fax: 312-664-4652
E-mail: csinfo@acpe-accredit.org
Web site: www.acpe-accredit.org

Physical Therapy

Mary Jane Harris, Director
Department of Accreditation
American Physical Therapy Association
1111 North Fairfax Street
Alexandria, VA 22314-1488
Telephone: 800-999-2782 (toll-free) *or* 703-684-2782
Fax: 703-684-7343
E-mail: accreditation@apta.org
Web site: www.apta.org

Planning

Beatrice Clupper, Director
American Institute of Certified Planners/Association of Collegiate Schools of Planning
Merle Hay Tower, Suite 302
3800 Merle Hay Road
Des Moines, IA 50310
Telephone: 515-252-0729
Fax: 515-252-7404
E-mail: fi_pab@netins.net
Web site: http://netins.net/web/pab_fi66

Podiatric Medicine

Alan R. Tinkleman, Director
Council on Podiatric Medical Education
American Podiatric Medical Association
9312 Old Georgetown Road
Bethesda, MD 20814-1698
Telephone: 301-571-9200
Fax: 301-530-2752
E-mail: sbsaylor@apma.org
Web site: www.apm.org/cpme

Psychology and Counseling

Susan F. Zlotlow, Director
Committee on Accreditation
American Psychological Association
750 First Street, NE
Washington, DC 20002-4242
Telephone: 202-336-5979
Fax: 202-336-5978
E-mail: apaaccred@apa.org
Web site: www.apa.org/ed/accred.html

Carol L. Bobby, Executive Director
Council for Accreditation of Counseling and Related Educational Programs
American Counseling Association
5999 Stevenson Avenue, Fourth Floor
Alexandria, VA 22304
Telephone: 800-347-6647 Ext. 301 (toll-free)

Fax: 703-823-1581
E-mail: cacrep@aol.com
Web site: www.counseling.org/CACREP

Public Affairs and Administration

Michael A. Brintnall, Executive Director
Commission on Peer Review and Accreditation
National Association of Schools of Public Affairs and Administration
1120 G Street, NW, Suite 730
Washington, DC 20005
Telephone: 202-628-8965
Fax: 202-626-4978
E-mail: naspaa@naspaa.org
Web site: www.naspaa.org

Public Health

Patricia Evans, Executive Director
Council on Education for Public Health
800 I Street, NW, Suite 202
Washington, DC 20001-3710
Telephone: 202-789-1050
Fax: 202-789-1895
E-mail: patevans@ceph.org
Web site: www.ceph.org

Rabbinical and Talmudic Education

Bernard Fryshman, Executive Vice President
Association of Advanced Rabbinical and Talmudic Schools
175 Fifth Avenue, Suite 711
New York, NY 10010
Telephone: 212-477-0950
Fax: 212-533-5335

Rehabilitation Education

Jeanne Patterson, Executive Director
Council on Rehabilitation Education
Commission on Standards and Accreditation
1835 Rohlwing Road, Suite E
Rolling Meadows, IL 60008
Telephone: 847-394-1785
Fax: 847-394-2108
E-mail: patters@polaris.net
Web site: www.core-rehab.org

Social Work

Nancy Randolph, Director
Council on Social Work Education
1725 Duke Street, Suite 500
Alexandria, VA 22314
Telephone: 703-683-8080
Fax: 703-683-8099
E-mail: accred@cswe.org
Web site: www.cswe.org

Speech-Language Pathology and Audiology

Sharon Goldsmith, Director
American Speech-Language-Hearing Association
10801 Rockville Pike
Rockville, MD 20852
Telephone: 301-897-5700
Fax: 301-571-0457
E-mail: accreditation@asha.org

Web site: www.asha.org

Theater

Samuel Hope, Executive Director
National Association of Schools of Theatre
11250 Roger Bacon Drive, Suite 21
Reston, VA 20190
Telephone: 703-437-0700
Fax: 703-437-6312
E-mail: info@arts-accredit.org
Web site: www.arts-accredit.org

Theology

Daniel O. Aleshire, Executive Director
Association of Theological Schools in the United States and Canada
10 Summit Park Drive
Pittsburgh, PA 15275-1103
Telephone: 412-788-6505
Fax: 412-788-6510
E-mail: ats@ats.edu
Web site: www.ats.edu

Veterinary Medicine

Donald G. Simmons, Director of Education and Research Division
American Veterinary Medical Association
1931 North Meacham Road, Suite 100
Schaumburg, IL 60173
Telephone: 847-925-8070
Fax: 847-925-1329
E-mail: dsimmons@avma.org
Web site: www.avma.org

Accreditation in Canada

To get general information about accreditation in Canada, visit the Web site of the Council of Ministers of Education. Their Web site also has contact information and links to the provincial departments of education.

Council of Ministers of Education, Canada
95 St. Clair Avenue West, Suite 1106
Toronto, Ontario
Canada M4V 1N6
Telephone: 416-962-8100
Fax: 416-962-2800
E-mail: cmec@cmec.ca
Web site: www.cmec.ca

Other Resources for Evaluating Programs

Bear, Mariah P., John Bear, and John B. Bear. *Bear's Guide to Earning Degrees Nontraditionally, 13th ed.*

Ten Speed Press, 1999.

Quality on the Line: Benchmarks for Success in Internet-Based Distance Education. Washington, DC: The Institute for Higher Education Policy, March 2000. Available at www.ihep.com/qualityonline.pdf.

TAKING STANDARDIZED ADMISSIONS TESTS

SAT

For information about the SAT, contact the College Board:

SAT Program

The College Board
P.O. Box 025505
Miami, FL 33102
Telephone: 866-756-7346 (in the U.S.);
   212-713-7789 (international)
E-mail: sat@info.collegeboard.org
Web site: www.collegeboard.org

The College Board offers free preparation advice and practice tests. The Web site also offers other test-preparation materials, including books, videos, and software, for a charge. Order at www.collegeboard.org or call 609-771-7243:

The Official SAT Study Guide. 889 pp. 2004.

Real SAT Subject Tests. 740 pp. 2005.

Other test-preparation resources:

Carris, Joan. *Panic Plan for the SAT.* Lawrenceville, NJ: Peterson's, 2004.

Ultimate SAT Toolkit. Lawrenceville, NJ: Peterson's, 2005.

ACT

ACT Registration
P.O. Box 414
Iowa City, IA 52243-0414
Telephone: 319-337-1270
Web site: www.act.org/aap

The Web site offers test-preparation strategies, sample questions, and information about other ACT resources.

ACT Inc., *The Real ACT Prep Guide.* Lawrenceville, NJ: Peterson's, 2005.

GRE

For information about the GRE, contact the Educational Testing Service:

GRE-ETS
P.O. Box 6000
Princeton, NJ 08541-6000
Telephone: (609) 771-7670
E-mail: gre-info@ets.org
Web site (GRE Online): www.gre.org

The Web site offers a lot of material that can be downloaded: information bulletins, practice tests, descriptions of the subject area tests, and preparation software. Order from ETS at www.gre.org:

GRE Big Book

GRE Powerprep Software. Includes test preparation for both the General Test and the Writing Assessment.

GRE Practicing to Take the General Test

Practice Books for Subject Area Tests

Other resources:

Ultimate GRE Toolkit. Lawrenceville, NJ: Peterson's, 2004.

MAT

Harcourt Assessment
19500 Bulverde Rd.
San Antonio, TX 78259

Telephone: (800) 211-8378 (toll-free)
Web site: www.milleranalogies.com

Bader, William, and Daniel S. Burt. *Master the Miller Analogies Test.* Lawrenceville, NJ: Peterson's, 2006.

GMAT

GMAT
Distribution and Receiving Center
225 Phillips Boulevard
Ewing, NJ 08628-7435
Telephone: 609-771-7330
E-mail: gmat@ets.org
Web site (MBA Explorer): www.gmac.com

Ultimate GMAT Toolkit. Lawrenceville, NJ: Peterson's, 2004.

TOEFL

Information on the TOEFL can be obtained from the Educational Testing Service:

TOEFL
P.O. Box 6151
Princeton, NJ 08541-6151
Telephone: 609-771-7100
E-mail: toefl@ets.org
Web site: www.toefl.org

Master TOEFL Writing Skills, Master TOEFL Reading Skills, Master TOEFL Vocabulary. Lawrenceville, NJ: Peterson's, 2007.

APPLYING FOR ADMISSION TO DEGREE PROGRAMS

Davidson, Wilma, and Susan McCloskey. *Writing a Winning College Application Essay.* Lawrenceville, NJ: Peterson's, 2002.

Hayden, Thomas C. *Insider's Guide to College Admissions.* Lawrenceville, NJ: Peterson's, 2000.

Stelzer, Richard J. *How to Write a Winning Personal Statement for Graduate and Professional School, 3rd ed.* Princeton, NJ: Peterson's, 1997. Lots of suggestions, both from the author and admissions representatives of graduate and professional schools, along with many sample essays.

PAYING FOR YOUR EDUCATION

General Information

Financial Aid Information Page (www.finaid.org). The best place to start an Internet search for financial aid information.

National Association of Student Financial Aid Administrators (www.nasfaa.org). Lots of essays explain various aspects of financial aid, including educational tax credits.

State Residency

Todd, Daryl F., Jr. *How to Cut Tuition: The Complete Guide to In-State Tuition.* Linwood, NJ: Atlantic Educational Publishing, 1997.

Federal Aid

Federal Student Aid Information Center
P.O. Box 84
Washington, DC 20044-0084
Telephone: 800-4-FED-AID (toll-free) (general information, assistance, and publications)
Web sites:
General information and home page: www.ed.gov/studentaid

For a copy of *Financial Aid: The Student Guide:* www.ed.gov/prog_info/SFA/StudentGuide.

For the FAFSA, go to FAFSA Online: www.fafsa.ed.gov.

For more on the Distance Education Demonstration Program: www.ed.gov/offices/OPE/PPI/DistEd/proginfo.html.

State Agencies of Higher Education

Alabama: 334-242-2274
Alaska: 907-465-6741
Arizona: 602-229-2591
Arkansas: 800-547-8839 (toll-free)
California: 916-526-7590
Colorado: 303-866-2723
Connecticut: 860-947-1855
Delaware: 800-292-7935 (toll-free)
District of Columbia: 202-698-2400
Florida: 888-827-2004 (toll-free)
Georgia: 770-724-9030 or 404-656-5969
Hawaii: 808-956-8213
Idaho: 208-334-2270
Illinois: 800-899-4722 (toll-free)
Indiana: 317-232-2350
Iowa: 515-242-3344
Kansas: 785-296-3517
Kentucky: 800-928-8926 (toll-free)
Louisiana: 800-259-5626 (toll-free)
Maine: 800-228-3734 (toll-free)
Maryland: 410-260-4565
Massachusetts: 617-727-9420
Michigan: 877-323-2287 (toll-free)
Minnesota: 800-657-3866 (toll-free)
Mississippi: 601-432-6997
Missouri: 800-473-6757 (toll-free)
Montana: 800-537-7508 (toll-free)
Nebraska: 402-471-2847
Nevada: 775-687-9228
New Hampshire: 603-271-2555
New Jersey: 800-792-8670 (toll-free)
New Mexico: 800-279-9777 (toll-free)
New York: 800-642-6234 (toll-free)
North Carolina: 800-600-3453 (toll-free)
North Dakota: 701-328-4114
Ohio: 888-833-1133 (toll-free)
Oklahoma: 800-858-1840 (toll-free)
Oregon: 800-452-8807 (toll-free)
Pennsylvania: 800-692-7392 or 7435(toll-free)
Rhode Island: 800-922-9855 (toll-free)
South Carolina: 803-737-2260
South Dakota: 605-773-3134

Tennessee: 800-342-1663 (toll-free)
Texas: 800-242-3062 (toll-free)
Utah: 800-418-8757 (toll-free)
Vermont: 800-642-3177 (toll-free)
Virginia: 804-786-1690
Washington: 360-753-7850
West Virginia: 888-825-5707 (toll-free)
Wisconsin: 608-267-2206
Wyoming: 307-777-7763
Guam: 671-475-0457
Northern Marianas: 670-234-6128
Puerto Rico: 787-724-7100
Republic of Palau: 680-488-2471
Virgin Islands: 340-774-4546

CSS Financial Aid Profile

Contact the College Scholarship Service at www.collegeboard.org or 305-829-9793.

Grants, Fellowships, and Scholarships

AJR Newslink (www.newslink.org). Awards, grants, and scholarships for journalism students.

Annual Register of Grant Support: A Directory of Funding Sources. Wilmette, IL.: National Register Publishing Company.

College Money Handbook 2008. Lawrenceville, NJ: Peterson's, 2007.

Corporate Foundation Profiles. New York: Foundation Center, 1999 (http://fdncenter.org or 212-620-4230).

FastWeb (http://fastweb.com). Online searchable database of scholarships and fellowships.

Petersons.com. Online searchable database of scholarships and fellowships.

Getting Money for Graduate School. Lawrenceville, NJ: Peterson's, 2002.

Scholarships, Grants, & Prizes 2008. Lawrenceville, NJ: Peterson's, 2007.

Cooperative Education

Re, Joseph M. *Earn and Learn.* Octameron Associates, 1997.

Credit Reporting Agencies

It's a good idea to check your credit rating before you apply for any loans. Call first to find out if there is a fee.

Experian
P.O. Box 9530
Allen, TX 75013
Telephone: 888-397-3742 (toll-free)

Equifax
P.O. Box 105873
Atlanta, GA 30348
Telephone: 800-685-1111 (toll-free)

CSC Credit Services
Consumer Assistance Center
P.O. Box 674402
Houston, TX 77267-4402
Telephone: 800-759-5979 (toll-free)

Trans Union Corporation
P.O. Box 390
Springfield, PA 19064-0390
Telephone: 800-888-4213 (toll-free)

Tax Issues

Educational Expenses, IRS Publication 508.

Tax Benefits for Higher Education. IRS Publication 970.

To get a copy of these publications, visit the Internal Revenue Service Web site at www.irs.ustreas.gov/prod/forms_pubs/pubs or call 800-829-3676 (toll-free).

Women, Minority Students, Disabled Students, and Veterans

Bruce-Young, Doris M., and William C. Young. *Higher Education Money Book for Women and Minorities.* Young Enterprises International, 1997.

Minority and Women's Complete Scholarship Book; plus Scholarships for Religious Affiliations and People with Disabilities. Sourcebooks, 1998.

Olson, Elizabeth A. *Dollars for College (Women).* Garrett Park Press, 1995.

Saludos Web Education Center (www.saludos.com). Internships and scholarships targeted to Hispanic Americans as well as those not considering race or ethnicity.

Schlachter, Gail Ann, and R. David Weber. *Financial Aid for African Americans.* Reference Service Press, 1997.

Schlachter, Gail Ann, and R. David Weber. *Financial Aid for the Disabled and Their Families.* Reference Service Press, 1998.

Schlachter, Gail Ann, and R. David Weber. *Financial Aid for Veterans, Military Personnel, and Their Dependents.* Reference Service Press, 1996.

Schlachter, Gail Ann. *Directory of Financial Aid for Women.* Reference Service Press, 1997.

International Students

Funding for U.S. Study—A Guide for International Students and Professionals and *Financial Resources for International Study.* New York: Institute of International Education (www.iiebooks.org).

SUCCEEDING AS A DISTANCE LEARNER

Bruno, Frank J. *Going Back to School: College Survival Strategies for Adult Students.* New York, Arco, 1998.

GLOSSARY

accreditation—in the United States, the process by which private, nongovernmental educational agencies with regional or national scope certify that colleges and universities provide educational programs at basic levels of quality

ACT—a standardized undergraduate admissions test that is based on the typical high school curriculum

associate degree—a degree awarded upon the successful completion of a prebaccalaureate-level program, usually consisting of two years of full-time study at the college level

asynchronous—not simultaneous or concurrent; for example, discussion groups in online courses are asynchronous because students can log on and post messages at any time

audioconferencing—electronic meeting in which participants in remote locations can communicate with one another using phones

bachelor's degree—a degree awarded upon the successful completion of about four years of full-time study at the college level

bandwidth—the width of frequencies required to transmit a communications signal without too much distortion; video, animation, and sound require more bandwidth than text

broadband—a high-speed, high-capacity transmission channel carried on coaxial or fiber-optic cable; it has a higher *bandwidth* than telephone lines and so can transmit more data more quickly than telephone lines

broadcast radio and television—radio and television programs sent out over the airwaves; one of the earliest distance learning technologies still used today

browser—a computer program used to view, download, upload, or otherwise access documents (sites) on the World Wide Web

bulletin board—a site on the Internet where people can post messages

cable television—television programming transmitted over optical fiber, coaxial, or twisted pair (telephone) cables

CD-ROM—compact disc, read-only memory; an optical storage technology that allows you to store and play back data

certificate—an educational credential awarded upon completion of a structured curriculum, typically including several courses but lasting for a period of time less than that required for a degree

certification—the awarding of a credential, usually by a professional or industry group, usually after a course of study and the passing of an exam

chat room—a site on the Internet in which people can communicate synchronously by typing messages to one another

CLEP—the College Level Examination Program, administered by the College Board, that tests students' subject knowledge in order to award college-level credit for noncollegiate learning

common application form—a standardized basic admissions application form, available online, that is used by many colleges

consortium—a group of colleges and universities that pool resources to enable students to take courses as needed from all participating institutions

continuing education unit—10 contact hours of participation in an organized continuing education program; a nationwide, standardized measure of continuing education courses

correspondence course—individual or self-guided study by mail from a college or university for which credit is typically granted through written assignments and proctored examinations; also referred to as *independent study*

correspondence school—a school whose primary means of delivering instruction is via *correspondence courses*

cost of attendance—the total cost, including tuition, fees, living expenses, books, supplies, and miscellaneous expenses, of attending a particular school for an academic year

DANTES Subject Standardized Tests—a series of equivalency examinations used primarily by the U.S. Department of Defense but available to civilians as well

distance learning—the delivery of educational programs to students who are off site; also called *distance education*

doctoral degree—the highest degree awarded upon demonstrated mastery of a subject, including the ability to do scholarly research

DVD—digital video disc; an optical storage technology that allows you to store and retrieve audio and video data

e-learning—distance learning via the Internet; sometimes called *online learning*

e-mail—text or other messages sent over the Internet

enrollment status—whether a student is enrolled full-time, three-quarter-time, half-time, or less than half-time in a degree or certificate program

equivalency examination—an examination similar to the final exam of a college-level course; if you pass, you may be awarded college-level credit; for example, the CLEP and DANTES exams

Excelsior College Examinations—a series of equivalency examinations administered by Excelsior College; formerly the Regents College Examinations

Expected Family Contribution (EFC)—the amount a student and his or her family are expected to contribute to the cost of the student's education per academic year

FAFSA—the Free Application for Federal Student Aid; needed to apply for federal aid programs

fax machine—a telecopying device that transmits written or graphic material over telephone lines to produce a hard copy at a remote location

Federal Supplemental Educational Opportunity Grant (FSEOG)—a federal grant awarded to students that demonstrate the greatest financial need

Federal Work-Study Program—provides part-time jobs in public and private nonprofit organizations to both undergraduate and graduate students who demonstrate financial need; the government pays up to 75 percent of the student's wages, and the employer pays the balance

fellowship—monies to be used for a student's education that does not have to be repaid; also called a *grant* or *scholarship*

financial need—the amount of money a student needs to be given or loaned or earn through work-study, in order to attend school for one year, calculated by subtracting Expected Family Contribution (EFC) from cost of attendance

first-professional degree—a degree awarded upon the successful completion of a program of study (for which a bachelor's degree is normally the prerequisite) that prepares a student for a specific profession

GMAT—the Graduate Management Admissions Test, a standardized test used by many graduate programs in business

graduate degree—a degree awarded upon the successful completion of a program of study at the postbaccalaureate level; usually a master's or doctoral degree

grant—monies to be used for a student's education that do not have to be repaid; also called a *scholarship* or *fellowship*

GRE General Test—the Graduate Record Examinations General Test, which tests verbal, quantitative, and analytical skills; usually taken by prospective graduate students

GRE Subject Area Tests—examinations that assess knowledge usually acquired in college-level courses

instructional design—the way course content is organized for the learner; it varies from one distance technology to another

Internet—the global computer network of networks that allows for the transmission of words, images, and sound to anyone with an Internet connection; one of the major instructional delivery systems for distance learning

Internet service provider (ISP)—a company such as AOL or Earthlink that serves as a gateway to the Internet; by subscribing to its service, an individual can connect to the Internet

life experience—a basis for earning college credit, usually demonstrated by means of a portfolio

LSAT—the Law School Admissions Test, taken by law school applicants

master's degree—a degree awarded upon the successful completion of a program of study beyond the baccalaureate level that typically requires one or two years of full-time study

MAT—the Miller Analogies Test, a standardized admissions test used by some graduate programs

MCAT—the Medical College Admissions Test, taken by medical school applicants

merit-based aid—funding awarded on the basis of academic merit, regardless of financial need

modem—MOdulator DEModulator; a device that allows a computer to connect with other computers (and therefore the Internet) over telephone lines; the faster the modem speed, the faster data is transmitted

need-based aid—financial aid awarded on the basis of financial need; it may take the form of grants, loans, or work-study

online course—a course offered primarily over the Internet

online learning—distance learning via the Internet; sometimes called *e-learning*

Pell Grant—a federal grant that is awarded to students on the basis of financial need

Perkins Loan—a loan offered by the federal government to students with exceptional financial need

PowerPoint—a software program that enables the user to prepare slides with text, graphics, and sound; often used by instructors in their class presentations

PROFILE®—the financial aid application service of the College Board is a standardized financial aid application form used by many colleges and universities

SAT—a standardized undergraduate admissions test

SAT Subject Tests—subject area tests that assess high school–level knowledge; used by some schools for undergraduate admissions

satellite television—programming beamed to an orbiting satellite, then retrieved by one or more ground-based satellite dishes

scholarship—monies to be used for a student's education that do not have to be repaid; also called a *grant* or *fellowship*

Stafford Loan—a subsidized or unsubsidized loan that is offered by the federal government

streaming video—high *bandwidth* video data transmission

synchronous—occurring simultaneously, in real time

Title IV funds—federal money disbursed to eligible students through eligible, accredited institutions of higher learning or directly from the government

TOEFL—the Test of English as a Foreign Language, taken by students who are not native speakers of English

two-way interactive video—two-way communication of video and audio signals so that people in remote locations can see and hear one another

videoconferencing—one-way video and two-way audio transmission, or two-way video transmission conducted via satellite; instructors and students can communicate between remote locations

videotaped lecture—recording of an on-campus lecture or class session; usually mailed to distance learners enrolled in the course

virtual university—a college or university that offers most or all of its instruction exclusively via technology and usually for a profit

whiteboard—a program that allows multiple users at their own computers to draw and write comments on the same document

work-study award—an amount a student earns through part-time work as part of the Federal Work-Study Program

Institution Profiles

This section contains factual profiles of institutions, with a focus on their Distance Learning programs. Each profile covers such items as accreditation information, availability of financial aid, degree and certificate programs offered, non-degree-related course topics offered, and whom to contact for program information.

The profile information presented here was collected during the summer of 2007 via an online survey for Distance Learning Programs and is arranged alphabetically.

ABILENE CHRISTIAN UNIVERSITY
Abilene, Texas
Instructional Technology
http://www.acu.edu/distanceeducation

Abilene Christian University was founded in 1906. It is accredited by Southern Association of Colleges and Schools. It first offered distance learning courses in 1996. In fall 2006, there were 450 students enrolled in distance learning courses. Institutionally administered financial aid is available to distance learners.

Services Distance learners have accessibility to academic advising, bookstore, campus computer network, career placement assistance, e-mail services, library services, tutoring.

Contact Mr. William Horn, Director of Graduate Recruiting, Abilene Christian University, ACU Box 29000, Admissions and Recruiting, Abilene, TX 79699-9201. Telephone: 325-674-2656. Fax: 325-674-2130. E-mail: hornw@acu.edu.

DEGREES AND AWARDS

Certificate Conflict Resolution and Reconciliation

Technical Certificate Applied Studies

MA Conflict Resolution and Reconciliation

MEd Leadership of Learning

COURSE SUBJECT AREAS OFFERED OUTSIDE OF DEGREE PROGRAMS

Undergraduate—biblical and other theological languages and literatures; biblical studies; business/corporate communications; communication and media; economics; education; English.

Graduate—biblical studies; education; human development, family studies, and related services.

ACADEMY OF ART UNIVERSITY
San Francisco, California

Academy of Art University was founded in 1929. It is accredited by Accrediting Council for Independent Colleges and Schools. It first offered distance learning courses in 2002. In fall 2006, there were 4,246 students enrolled in distance learning courses. Institutionally administered financial aid is available to distance learners.

Services Distance learners have accessibility to academic advising, bookstore, campus computer network, career placement assistance, e-mail services, tutoring.

Contact Admissions, Academy of Art University, 79 New Montgomery Street, San Francisco, CA 94105. Telephone: 800-544-2787. E-mail: info@academyart.edu.

DEGREES AND AWARDS

AA Advertising; Animation and Visual Effects; Computer Arts/New Media; Fashion; Fine Art; Graphic Design; Illustration; Industrial Design; Interior Architecture and Design; Motion Pictures and Television; Photography

BA Advertising; Animation and Visual Effects; Computer Arts/New Media; Fashion; Fine Art; Graphic Design; Illustration; Industrial Design; Interior Architecture and Design; Motion Pictures and Television; Photography

MFA Advertising; Animation and Visual Effects; Computer Arts/New Media; Fashion; Fine Art; Graphic Design; Illustration; Industrial Design; Interior Architecture and Design; Motion Pictures and Television; Photography

COURSE SUBJECT AREAS OFFERED OUTSIDE OF DEGREE PROGRAMS

Undergraduate—apparel and textiles; design and applied arts; film/video and photographic arts; fine and studio art; graphic communications; interior architecture; visual and performing arts.

Graduate—apparel and textiles; design and applied arts; film/video and photographic arts; fine and studio art; graphic communications; interior architecture; visual and performing arts.

ACADIA UNIVERSITY
Wolfville, Nova Scotia, Canada
Division of Continuing and Distance Education
http://conted.acadiau.ca

Acadia University was founded in 1838. It is provincially chartered. It first offered distance learning courses in 1968. In fall 2006, there were 1,000 students enrolled in distance learning courses. Institutionally administered financial aid is available to distance learners.

Services Distance learners have accessibility to academic advising, bookstore, campus computer network, e-mail services, library services, tutoring.

Contact Ms. Brenda Harris, Student Services Representative, Acadia University, Division of Continuing and Distance Education, 38 Crowell Drive, Wolfville, NS B4P 2R6, Canada. Telephone: 800-565-6568. Fax: 902-585-1068. E-mail: continuing.education@acadiau.ca.

DEGREES AND AWARDS
Programs offered do not lead to a degree or other formal award.

COURSE SUBJECT AREAS OFFERED OUTSIDE OF DEGREE PROGRAMS

Undergraduate—biology; business administration, management and operations; business/commerce; business/corporate communications; business, management, and marketing related; chemistry; computer programming; computer science; economics; education; educational/instructional media design; education related; English; English composition; English language and literature related; experimental psychology; fine and studio art; foods, nutrition, and related services; geological and earth sciences/geosciences; gerontology; health psychology; history; languages (foreign languages related); liberal arts and sciences, general studies and humanities; linguistic, comparative, and related language studies; marketing; microbiological sciences and immunology; multi-/interdisciplinary studies related; nutrition sciences; philosophy; physics; political science and government; psychology; social sciences; sociology; special education.

Graduate—educational assessment, evaluation, and research; educational/instructional media design; education related.

Non-credit—English as a second language.

ADAMS STATE COLLEGE
Alamosa, Colorado
Extended Studies
http://exstudies.adams.edu

Adams State College was founded in 1921. It is accredited by North Central Association of Colleges and Schools. It first offered distance learning courses in 1978. In fall 2006, there were 590 students enrolled in distance learning courses. Institutionally administered financial aid is available to distance learners.

Services Distance learners have accessibility to academic advising, bookstore, e-mail services, library services.

Contact Mr. Walter Roybal, Student Advisor, Adams State College, Extended Studies, 208 Edgemont Boulevard, Alamosa, CO 81102. Telephone: 800-548-6679. Fax: 719-587-7974. E-mail: ascadvisor@adams.edu.

DEGREES AND AWARDS

AA General Education requirements
AS General Education requirements
BA Business Administration; Interdisciplinary Studies; Sociology
BS Business Administration

COURSE SUBJECT AREAS OFFERED OUTSIDE OF DEGREE PROGRAMS

Undergraduate—business/commerce; business/corporate communications; business, management, and marketing related; business/managerial economics; criminal justice and corrections; criminology; English composition; English language and literature related; finance and financial management services; history; human resources management; legal studies (non-professional general, undergraduate); legal support services; medieval and Renaissance studies; sociology.

Graduate—biology; education; educational/instructional media design; education (specific subject areas); technology education/industrial arts.
Non-credit—accounting and related services; business/commerce; computer software and media applications; creative writing; data processing; entrepreneurial and small business operations; gerontology; linguistic, comparative, and related language studies; sales, merchandising, and related marketing operations (general); sales, merchandising, and related marketing operations (specialized).
See full description on page 306.

ADELPHI UNIVERSITY
Garden City, New York
Distance Education Program
http://www.adelphi.edu/
Adelphi University was founded in 1896. It is accredited by Middle States Association of Colleges and Schools. It first offered distance learning courses in 1998. Institutionally administered financial aid is available to distance learners.
Services Distance learners have accessibility to academic advising, bookstore, campus computer network, e-mail services, library services.
Contact Audrey Blumberg, Senior Provost of Academic Affairs, Adelphi University, School of Management and Business, Room 327, 1 South Avenue, Garden City, NY 11530. Telephone: 516-877-3159. Fax: 516-877-4571. E-mail: blumberg@adelphi.edu.

DEGREES AND AWARDS
Programs offered do not lead to a degree or other formal award.

COURSE SUBJECT AREAS OFFERED OUTSIDE OF DEGREE PROGRAMS
Undergraduate—astronomy and astrophysics; business administration, management and operations; health and physical education/fitness; nursing.
Graduate—accounting and related services; education (specific subject areas); social work.
Non-credit—social work.

ALASKA PACIFIC UNIVERSITY
Anchorage, Alaska
RANA (Rural Alaska Native Adult) Program
http://rana.alaskapacific.edu
Alaska Pacific University was founded in 1959. It is accredited by Northwest Commission on Colleges and Universities. It first offered distance learning courses in 1999. In fall 2006, there were 46 students enrolled in distance learning courses. Institutionally administered financial aid is available to distance learners.
Services Distance learners have accessibility to academic advising, bookstore, campus computer network, career placement assistance, e-mail services, library services.
Contact Ms. Rebecca Prieto, Admissions Counselor, Alaska Pacific University, 4101 University Drive, Anchorage, AK 99508. Telephone: 907-564-8222. Fax: 907-564-8317. E-mail: rprieto@alaskapacific.edu.

DEGREES AND AWARDS
AA Education (K-8)
BA Business Administration and Management–Nonprofit emphasis; Business Administration and Management; Education (K-8); Health Services Administration; Human Services

ALLEN COLLEGE
Waterloo, Iowa
http://www.allencollege.edu/
Allen College was founded in 1989. It is accredited by North Central Association of Colleges and Schools. It first offered distance learning courses in 2000. In fall 2006, there were 450 students enrolled in distance learning courses. Institutionally administered financial aid is available to distance learners.
Services Distance learners have accessibility to academic advising, bookstore, campus computer network, career placement assistance, e-mail services, library services, tutoring.

Contact Ms. Lisa Doreen Brodersen, Associate Professor of Nursing, Internet Learning Coordinator, Allen College, 1825 Logan Avenue, Waterloo, IA 50703. Telephone: 319-226-2034. Fax: 319-226-2075. E-mail: broderld@ihs.org.

DEGREES AND AWARDS
MSN Nursing; Nursing

COURSE SUBJECT AREAS OFFERED OUTSIDE OF DEGREE PROGRAMS
Undergraduate—area, ethnic, cultural, and gender studies related; creative writing; nursing; nutrition sciences.
Graduate—nursing.
Non-credit—nursing.

ALPENA COMMUNITY COLLEGE
Alpena, Michigan
http://www.alpenacc.edu
Alpena Community College was founded in 1952. It is accredited by North Central Association of Colleges and Schools. It first offered distance learning courses in 1997. In fall 2006, there were 140 students enrolled in distance learning courses. Institutionally administered financial aid is available to distance learners.
Services Distance learners have accessibility to academic advising, bookstore, e-mail services, library services, tutoring.
Contact Dr. Mark Curtis, Vice President of Instruction, Alpena Community College, 666 Johnson Street, Alpena, MI 49707. Telephone: 989-358-7443. Fax: 989-358-7561. E-mail: curtisr@alpenacc.edu.

DEGREES AND AWARDS
Certificate Corrections Officer Academic program

COURSE SUBJECT AREAS OFFERED OUTSIDE OF DEGREE PROGRAMS
Undergraduate—computer/information technology administration and management; computer systems networking and telecommunications; construction trades related; criminal justice and corrections; electrical and electronic engineering technologies; English composition; fine and studio art; health and medical administrative services; philosophy; political science and government; psychology; sociology.
Non-credit—construction trades related; work and family studies.

ALVIN COMMUNITY COLLEGE
Alvin, Texas
Instructional Services
http://www.alvincollege.edu/de
Alvin Community College was founded in 1949. It is accredited by Southern Association of Colleges and Schools. It first offered distance learning courses in 1995. In fall 2006, there were 1,100 students enrolled in distance learning courses. Institutionally administered financial aid is available to distance learners.
Services Distance learners have accessibility to academic advising, bookstore, career placement assistance, e-mail services, library services, tutoring.
Contact Mrs. Dena L. Faust, Coordinator of Distance Education, Alvin Community College, 3110 Mustang Road, Alvin, TX 77511. Telephone: 281-756-3728. Fax: 281-756-3880. E-mail: dfaust@alvincollege.edu.

DEGREES AND AWARDS
Programs offered do not lead to a degree or other formal award.

COURSE SUBJECT AREAS OFFERED OUTSIDE OF DEGREE PROGRAMS
Undergraduate—American literature (United States and Canadian); anthropology; applied mathematics; archeology; biology; business administration, management and operations; business operations support and assistant services; computer and information sciences; computer/information technology administration and management; computer programming; computer science; computer software and media applications;

creative writing; curriculum and instruction; economics; English; English composition; geography and cartography; geological and earth sciences/geosciences; history; liberal arts and sciences, general studies and humanities; mathematics; mathematics and computer science; mathematics and statistics related; psychology; psychology related.
Non-credit—business operations support and assistant services; computer and information sciences; computer and information sciences and support services related.

AMBERTON UNIVERSITY
Garland, Texas
http://www.amberton.edu/
Amberton University was founded in 1971. It is accredited by Southern Association of Colleges and Schools. It first offered distance learning courses in 1992. In fall 2006, there were 800 students enrolled in distance learning courses. Institutionally administered financial aid is available to distance learners.
Services Distance learners have accessibility to academic advising, bookstore, library services.
Contact Dr. Jo Lynn Loyd, Vice President, Strategic Services, Amberton University, 1700 Eastgate Drive, Garland, TX 75041. Telephone: 972-279-6511 Ext. 126. Fax: 972-279-9773. E-mail: jloyd@amberton.edu.

DEGREES AND AWARDS
BA Professional Development
BBA Management
MA Professional Development
MBA Management
MS Human Relations and Business

COURSE SUBJECT AREAS OFFERED OUTSIDE OF DEGREE PROGRAMS
Undergraduate—accounting and related services; business administration, management and operations.
Graduate—business administration, management and operations; counseling psychology.

THE AMERICAN COLLEGE
Bryn Mawr, Pennsylvania
http://www.amercoll.edu/
The American College was founded in 1927. It is accredited by Middle States Association of Colleges and Schools. It first offered distance learning courses in 1997. In fall 2006, there were 30,000 students enrolled in distance learning courses. Institutionally administered financial aid is available to distance learners.
Services Distance learners have accessibility to academic advising, bookstore, library services.
Contact Office of Student Services, The American College, 270 South Bryn Mawr Avenue, Bryn Mawr, PA 19010. Telephone: 888-263-7265. Fax: 610-526-1465. E-mail: studentservices@theamericancollege.edu.

DEGREES AND AWARDS
Certificate CFP(r) Certification Curriculum; Pensions and Executive Compensation
Diploma Chartered Advisor for Senior Living (CASL) Designation; Chartered Financial Consultant (ChFC(r)) Designation; Chartered Leadership Fellow(r) (CLF(r)) Designation; Chartered Life Underwriter (CLU(r)) Designation; LUTC Fellow Designation; Registered Employee Benefits Consultant(r) (REBC(r)) Designation; Registered Health Underwriter(r) (RHU(r)) Designation
Advanced Graduate Diploma Chartered Advisor in Philanthropy(r)(CAP) Designation
Graduate Certificate Asset Management; Business Succession Planning; Charitable Planning; Estate Planning and Taxation; Financial Planning–Graduate Financial Planning track
MSFS Financial Services
MSM Leadership

COURSE SUBJECT AREAS OFFERED OUTSIDE OF DEGREE PROGRAMS
Undergraduate—business administration, management and operations; business/commerce; finance and financial management services; gerontology; human resources management; insurance; sales, merchandising, and related marketing operations (specialized); social psychology.
Graduate—business administration, management and operations; business/commerce; finance and financial management services; human resources management; insurance.

AMERICAN GRADUATE UNIVERSITY
Covina, California
http://www.agu.edu/
American Graduate University was founded in 1969. It is accredited by Distance Education and Training Council. It first offered distance learning courses in 1975. In fall 2006, there were 956 students enrolled in distance learning courses. Institutionally administered financial aid is available to distance learners.
Services Distance learners have accessibility to academic advising, bookstore, library services.
Contact Ms. Marie J. Sirney, Executive Vice President, American Graduate University, 733 North Dodsworth Avenue, Covina, CA 91724. Telephone: 626-966-4576 Ext. 1003. Fax: 626-915-1709. E-mail: mariesirney@agu.edu.

DEGREES AND AWARDS
MA Acquisition Management–Master of Acquisition Management; Contract Management–Master of Contract Management; Project Management–Master of Project Management
MBA Acquisition and Contracting concentration or Project Management concentration

COURSE SUBJECT AREAS OFFERED OUTSIDE OF DEGREE PROGRAMS
Graduate—accounting and related services; business administration, management and operations; business/corporate communications; business/managerial economics.

AMERICAN INTERCONTINENTAL UNIVERSITY ONLINE
Hoffman Estates, Illinois
http://www.aiuonline.edu
American InterContinental University Online was founded in 1970. It is accredited by Southern Association of Colleges and Schools. It first offered distance learning courses in 2001. Institutionally administered financial aid is available to distance learners.
Services Distance learners have accessibility to academic advising, bookstore, career placement assistance, e-mail services, library services.
Contact Robyn Palmersheim, Vice President of Admissions, American InterContinental University Online, 5550 Prairie Stone Parkway, Suite 400, Hoffman Estates, IL 60192. Telephone: 877-701-3800. Fax: 866-647-9403. E-mail: info@aiuonline.edu.

DEGREES AND AWARDS
AAB Business concentration; Completion Program; Criminal Justice Administration concentration; Healthcare Administration concentration; Human Resources concentration; Information Systems concentration; Medical Coding and Billing concentration; Visual Communication concentration
BA Visual Communication–Digital Design concentration (completion program); Visual Communication–Web Design concentration (completion program)
BBA Accounting and Finance concentration (completion program); Healthcare Management concentration (completion program); Human Resource Management concentration (completion program); International Business concentration (completion program); Management concentration (completion program); Marketing concentration (completion program); Operations Management concentration (completion program);

Organizational Psychology and Development concentration (completion program); Project Management concentration (completion program)

BS Criminal Justice, Special Populations concentration

BST Information Technology and Bachelor of Information Technology (BIT), Computer Forensics concentration (completion program); Information Technology and Bachelor of Information Technology (BIT), Internet Security concentration (completion program); Information Technology–Bachelor of Information Technology (BIT)–Computer Systems concentration (completion program); Information Technology–Bachelor of Information Technology (BIT)–Network Administration concentration (completion program); Information Technology–Bachelor of Information Technology (BIT)–Programming concentration (completion program)

MBA Accounting and Finance concentration (10-month program); Healthcare Management concentration (10-month program); Human Resource Management concentration (10-month program); International Business concentration (10-month program); Management concentration (10-month program); Marketing concentration (10-month program); Operations Management concentration (10-month program); Organizational Psychology and Development concentration (10-month program); Project Management concentration (10-month program)

MEd Curriculum and Instruction concentration (10-month program); Educational Assessment and Evaluation concentration (10-month program); Instructional Technology concentration (10-month program); Leadership of Educational Organizations concentration (10-month program)

MIT IT Project Management concentration (10 month program); Internet Security concentration (10-month program)

See full description on page 308.

AMERICAN PUBLIC UNIVERSITY SYSTEM
Charles Town, West Virginia
http://www.apus.edu/

American Public University System was founded in 1991. It is accredited by Distance Education and Training Council. It first offered distance learning courses in 1993. In fall 2006, there were 16,700 students enrolled in distance learning courses. Institutionally administered financial aid is available to distance learners.

Services Distance learners have accessibility to academic advising, bookstore, campus computer network, e-mail services, library services, tutoring.

Contact Ms. Terry Grant, Director, Enrollment Management and Retention, American Public University System, 111 West Congress Street, Charles Town, WV 25414. Telephone: 877-468-6268 Ext. 3720. E-mail: tgrant@apus.edu.

DEGREES AND AWARDS

AA General Studies

BA Criminal Justice; Emergency and Disaster Management; English; Family Development; Fire Science Management; History; Homeland Security; Hospitality Management; International Relations; Legal Studies; Management; Marketing; Military History, Military Management, Intelligence Studies; Philosophy; Political Science; Psychology; Religion; Security Management; Sociology; Transportation and Logistics Management

BBA Business Administration

BS Environmental Studies; Information Technology Management; Middle Eastern Studies; Public Health; Space Studies; Sports and Health Sciences

MA Criminal Justice; Emergency and Disaster Management; History; Homeland Security; Humanities; International Relations and Conflict Resolution; Military Studies; National Security Studies; Political Science; Security Management; Sports Management; Strategic Intelligence; Transportation and Logistics Management

MAM Management

MBA Business Administration

MPA Public Administration

MS Environmental Policy and Management; Space Studies

MS/MPH Public Health

COURSE SUBJECT AREAS OFFERED OUTSIDE OF DEGREE PROGRAMS

Undergraduate—area studies; business administration, management and operations; computer/information technology administration and management; criminal justice and corrections; English; English composition; health and medical administrative services; history; human development, family studies, and related services; human resources management; international business; international relations and affairs; liberal arts and sciences, general studies and humanities; management information systems; military studies; military technologies; philosophy; philosophy and religious studies related; political science and government; psychology; public administration; public policy analysis.

Graduate—business/commerce; criminal justice and corrections; ethnic, cultural minority, and gender studies; history; international relations and affairs; military studies; military technologies; public administration and social service professions related; transportation and materials moving related.

See full description on page 310.

ANDERSON UNIVERSITY
Anderson, Indiana
http://www.anderson.edu/

Anderson University was founded in 1917. It is accredited by North Central Association of Colleges and Schools. It first offered distance learning courses in 1999. In fall 2006, there were 40 students enrolled in distance learning courses. Institutionally administered financial aid is available to distance learners.

Services Distance learners have accessibility to academic advising, bookstore, campus computer network, e-mail services, library services.

Contact Dr. John H. Aukerman, Director of Distance Education, Anderson University, 1100 East 5th Street, Anderson, IN 46012. Telephone: 765-641-4530. Fax: 765-641-3005. E-mail: jhaukerman@anderson.edu.

DEGREES AND AWARDS

MA Christian Ministries

ANDOVER NEWTON THEOLOGICAL SCHOOL
Newton Centre, Massachusetts

Andover Newton Theological School was founded in 1807. It is accredited by New England Association of Schools and Colleges. It first offered distance learning courses in 1999. In fall 2006, there were 175 students enrolled in distance learning courses. Institutionally administered financial aid is available to distance learners.

Services Distance learners have accessibility to academic advising, bookstore, e-mail services, library services.

Contact Dr. Jeffrey Jones, Director of Distance Learning, Andover Newton Theological School, 210 Herrick Road, Newton Centre, MA 02459. Telephone: 617-964-1100 Ext. 291. E-mail: jjones@ants.edu.

DEGREES AND AWARDS
Programs offered do not lead to a degree or other formal award.

COURSE SUBJECT AREAS OFFERED OUTSIDE OF DEGREE PROGRAMS
Graduate—biblical studies; history; pastoral counseling and specialized ministries; religious education; religious studies; theological and ministerial studies; theology and religious vocations related.
Non-credit—biblical studies; religious education; religious studies.

ANDREW JACKSON UNIVERSITY
Birmingham, Alabama
http://www.aju.edu/

Andrew Jackson University was founded in 1994. It is accredited by Distance Education and Training Council. It first offered distance learning courses in 1994. In fall 2006, there were 350 students enrolled in distance learning courses. Institutionally administered financial aid is available to distance learners.

Services Distance learners have accessibility to academic advising, bookstore, library services.

Contact Ms. Betty J. Howell, Vice President, Andrew Jackson University, 2919 John Hawkins Parkway, Birmingham, AL 35244. Telephone: 800-429-9300 Ext. 1. Fax: 205-871-9294. E-mail: admissions@aju.edu.

DEGREES AND AWARDS

AS Business; Communication; Criminal Justice
BA Communications
BS Business–Entrepreneurship; Business–General Business concentration; Business–Management/Leadership concentration; Business–Sales Management; Business–Sales concentration; Criminal Justice
MBA Entrepreneurship concentration; Finance concentration; Health Services Management concentration; Human Resource Management concentration; Management Concentration; Marketing concentration; Sales Management concentration; Strategic Leadership concentration
MPA Public Administration
MS Criminal Justice

COURSE SUBJECT AREAS OFFERED OUTSIDE OF DEGREE PROGRAMS

Undergraduate—business administration, management and operations; communication and media; criminal justice and corrections; entrepreneurial and small business operations.
Graduate—business administration, management and operations; criminal justice and corrections; entrepreneurial and small business operations; finance and financial management services; human resources management; public administration; sales, merchandising, and related marketing operations (specialized).

ANDREWS UNIVERSITY
Berrien Springs, Michigan
http://www.andrews.edu/dlit

Andrews University was founded in 1874. It is accredited by North Central Association of Colleges and Schools. It first offered distance learning courses in 1997. In fall 2006, there were 78 students enrolled in distance learning courses. Institutionally administered financial aid is available to distance learners.
Services Distance learners have accessibility to academic advising, campus computer network, e-mail services, library services, tutoring.
Contact Mrs. Marsha Jean Beal, Director of the Center for Distance Learning and Instructional Technology, Andrews University, Room #304, James White Library, Berrien Springs, MI 49104-0074. Telephone: 269-471-6200. Fax: 269-471-6166. E-mail: bealmj@andrews.edu.

DEGREES AND AWARDS

AA Liberal Arts, General Studies, Humanities
BA Liberal Arts, General Studies, Humanities; Theological Studies
BS Liberal Arts, General Studies, Humanities
MA Educational Administration
MS Nursing Education

COURSE SUBJECT AREAS OFFERED OUTSIDE OF DEGREE PROGRAMS

Undergraduate—area studies; astronomy and astrophysics; biblical studies; developmental and child psychology; English composition; geography and cartography; history; languages (Romance languages); mathematics and statistics related; religious studies; social psychology; sociology.
Graduate—education; religious studies.

ANNE ARUNDEL COMMUNITY COLLEGE
Arnold, Maryland
Distance Learning Center
http://www.aacc.edu/diseduc

Anne Arundel Community College was founded in 1961. It is accredited by Middle States Association of Colleges and Schools. It first offered distance learning courses in 1981. In fall 2006, there were 3,384 students enrolled in distance learning courses. Institutionally administered financial aid is available to distance learners.
Services Distance learners have accessibility to academic advising, bookstore, campus computer network, career placement assistance, e-mail services, library services, tutoring.

Contact Mrs. Patty McCarthy-O'Neill, Distance Learning Center Coordinator, Anne Arundel Community College, Distance Learning Center, 101 College Parkway, Arnold, MD 21012-1895. Telephone: 410-777-2514. Fax: 410-777-2691. E-mail: pmmccarthyoneill@aacc.edu.

DEGREES AND AWARDS

AA General Studies; Transfer Studies
AAS Business Management
AS Business Administration Transfer

COURSE SUBJECT AREAS OFFERED OUTSIDE OF DEGREE PROGRAMS

Undergraduate—accounting and related services; allied health and medical assisting services; applied mathematics; behavioral sciences; biological and physical sciences; business administration, management and operations; business, management, and marketing related; business/managerial economics; chemistry; communication and media; computer and information sciences; computer science; criminal justice and corrections; developmental and child psychology; economics; English composition; finance and financial management services; geography and cartography; health and physical education/fitness; history; hospitality administration; intercultural/multicultural and diversity studies; legal studies (non-professional general, undergraduate); legal support services; marketing; mathematics and statistics related; philosophy; political science and government; social psychology; social sciences related; sociology; statistics.

ANTIOCH UNIVERSITY MCGREGOR
Yellow Springs, Ohio
http://www.mcgregor.edu

Antioch University McGregor was founded in 1988. It is accredited by North Central Association of Colleges and Schools. It first offered distance learning courses in 1988. In fall 2006, there were 178 students enrolled in distance learning courses. Institutionally administered financial aid is available to distance learners.
Services Distance learners have accessibility to academic advising, bookstore, campus computer network, e-mail services, library services.
Contact Mr. Seth Gordon, Enrollment Services Manager, Antioch University McGregor, 800 Livermore Street, Yellow Springs, OH 45387. Telephone: 937-769-1825. Fax: 937-769-1804. E-mail: sgordon@mcgregor.edu.

DEGREES AND AWARDS

MA Community Change and Civic Leadership; Community College Management; Conflict Resolution; Individualized Liberal and Professional Studies (various self-designed topics); Intercultural Conflict Management

COURSE SUBJECT AREAS OFFERED OUTSIDE OF DEGREE PROGRAMS

Undergraduate—business administration, management and operations; education; ethnic, cultural minority, and gender studies; human resources management; human services.
Graduate—business administration, management and operations; education.

APPALACHIAN STATE UNIVERSITY
Boone, North Carolina
http://www.appstate.edu/

Appalachian State University was founded in 1899. It is accredited by Southern Association of Colleges and Schools. It first offered distance learning courses in 1960. In fall 2006, there were 1,400 students enrolled in distance learning courses.
Services Distance learners have accessibility to academic advising, bookstore, campus computer network, career placement assistance, e-mail services, library services.
Contact Ms. Cynthia Weaver, Interim Director, Office of Extension and Distance Education, Appalachian State University, Office of Extension

and Distance Education, PO Box 32054, Boone, NC 28607. Telephone: 800-355 4084. E-mail: weraverch@appstate.edu.

DEGREES AND AWARDS
MA Educational Media, New Media and Global Education

ARAPAHOE COMMUNITY COLLEGE
Littleton, Colorado
Educational Technology
http://www.arapahoe.edu

Arapahoe Community College was founded in 1965. It is accredited by North Central Association of Colleges and Schools. It first offered distance learning courses in 1985. In fall 2006, there were 1,856 students enrolled in distance learning courses. Institutionally administered financial aid is available to distance learners.

Services Distance learners have accessibility to academic advising, bookstore, campus computer network, e-mail services, library services.
Contact Lee Christopher, eLearning Manager, Arapahoe Community College, 5900 South Santa Fe Drive, Littleton, CO 80160. Telephone: 303-797-5965. Fax: 303-797-5700 Ext. 6700. E-mail: lee.christopher@arapahoe.edu.

DEGREES AND AWARDS
Programs offered do not lead to a degree or other formal award.

COURSE SUBJECT AREAS OFFERED OUTSIDE OF DEGREE PROGRAMS

Undergraduate—accounting and computer science; accounting and related services; allied health and medical assisting services; allied health diagnostic, intervention, and treatment professions; alternative and complementary medical support services; alternative and complementary medicine and medical systems; American literature (United States and Canadian); American Sign Language (ASL); anthropology; apparel and textiles; applied mathematics; architecture related; area, ethnic, cultural, and gender studies related; astronomy and astrophysics; audiovisual communications technologies; behavioral sciences; biochemistry, biophysics and molecular biology; bioethics/medical ethics; biology; business administration, management and operations; business/corporate communications; business, management, and marketing related; chemistry; clinical child psychology; clinical/medical laboratory science and allied professions; clinical psychology; cognitive psychology and psycholinguistics; cognitive science; communication and journalism related; communication and media; communications technology; comparative literature; computer and information sciences; computer and information sciences and support services related; computer/information technology administration and management; computer programming; computer science; computer software and media applications; computer systems analysis; computer systems networking and telecommunications; criminal justice and corrections; economics; education; educational administration and supervision; educational assessment, evaluation, and research; educational/instructional media design; educational psychology; education related; education (specific levels and methods); education (specific subject areas); electrical and electronic engineering technologies; engineering technologies related; English; English as a second language; English composition; English language and literature related; English literature (British and Commonwealth); entrepreneurial and small business operations; ethnic, cultural minority, and gender studies; family psychology; film/video and photographic arts; finance and financial management services; funeral service and mortuary science; geography and cartography; geological and earth sciences/geosciences; geological/geophysical engineering; graphic communications; ground transportation; health aides/attendants/orderlies; health and medical administrative services; health and physical education/fitness; health/medical preparatory programs; health professions related; health psychology; health services/allied health/health sciences; history; hospitality administration; human development, family studies, and related services; information science/studies; journalism; languages (Romance languages); languages (South Asian); legal professions and studies related; legal research and advanced professional studies; legal studies (non-professional general, undergraduate); legal support services; liberal arts and sciences, general studies and humanities; management information systems; marketing; mathematics; mathematics and computer science; mathematics and statistics related; medical basic sciences; medical clinical sciences/graduate medical studies; medical illustration and informatics; mental and social health services and allied professions; music; nursing; personality psychology; pharmacology and toxicology; pharmacy, pharmaceutical sciences, and administration; philosophy; physics; political science and government; psychology; public health; public relations, advertising, and applied communication related; publishing; real estate; sales, merchandising, and related marketing operations (general); sales, merchandising, and related marketing operations (specialized); security and protective services related; social and philosophical foundations of education; sociology; special education; speech and rhetoric; teaching assistants/aides; technical and business writing; vehicle maintenance and repair technologies; visual and performing arts.

ARGOSY UNIVERSITY, CHICAGO CAMPUS
Chicago, Illinois
http://online.argosyu.edu

Argosy University, Chicago Campus was founded in 1999. It is accredited by North Central Association of Colleges and Schools. It first offered distance learning courses in 2000. In fall 2006, there were 1,400 students enrolled in distance learning courses. Institutionally administered financial aid is available to distance learners.

Services Distance learners have accessibility to bookstore, campus computer network, e-mail services, library services.
Contact Mr. Jamal Scott, Director of Admissions, Argosy University, Chicago Campus, 350 North Orleans, Chicago, IL 60654. Telephone: 312-777-7600. Fax: 312-777-7750. E-mail: jscott@argosy.edu.

DEGREES AND AWARDS
Programs offered do not lead to a degree or other formal award.

COURSE SUBJECT AREAS OFFERED OUTSIDE OF DEGREE PROGRAMS

Undergraduate—business/commerce; education; English; English composition; mathematics; psychology; sociology.

Graduate—business administration, management and operations; business/commerce; educational administration and supervision; educational/instructional media design; educational psychology; education related; psychology.

ARIZONA WESTERN COLLEGE
Yuma, Arizona
http://www.azwestern.edu

Arizona Western College was founded in 1962. It is accredited by North Central Association of Colleges and Schools. It first offered distance learning courses in 1992. In fall 2006, there were 2,573 students enrolled in distance learning courses. Institutionally administered financial aid is available to distance learners.

Services Distance learners have accessibility to academic advising, bookstore, campus computer network, e-mail services, library services.
Contact Bryan Doak, Dean of Enrollment, Arizona Western College, PO Box 929, Yuma, AZ 85366-0929. Telephone: 928-317-6100. Fax: 928-344-7543. E-mail: bryan.doak@azwestern.edu.

DEGREES AND AWARDS
AD Administration of Justice; Business Administration; Education

COURSE SUBJECT AREAS OFFERED OUTSIDE OF DEGREE PROGRAMS

Undergraduate—accounting and related services; business/commerce; computer and information sciences; criminal justice and corrections; English; fire protection; liberal arts and sciences, general studies and humanities.

ARKANSAS STATE UNIVERSITY–BEEBE
Beebe, Arkansas
http://www.asub.edu

Arkansas State University–Beebe was founded in 1927. It is accredited by North Central Association of Colleges and Schools. It first offered distance learning courses in 1999. In fall 2006, there were 814 students enrolled in distance learning courses. Institutionally administered financial aid is available to distance learners.

Services Distance learners have accessibility to academic advising, bookstore, career placement assistance, e-mail services, library services, tutoring.

Contact Chris Boyett, Director of Distance Learning, Arkansas State University–Beebe, PO Box 1000, Beebe, AR 72012. Telephone: 501-882-4442. Fax: 501-882-4412. E-mail: jcboyett@asub.edu.

DEGREES AND AWARDS
AA Liberal Arts–Associate of Arts in Liberal Arts

COURSE SUBJECT AREAS OFFERED OUTSIDE OF DEGREE PROGRAMS

Undergraduate—accounting and related services; agricultural business and management; biological and physical sciences; biology; business administration, management and operations; business/corporate communications; business, management, and marketing related; chemistry; communication and media; computer and information sciences; computer programming; computer systems networking and telecommunications; creative writing; criminal justice and corrections; data entry/microcomputer applications; developmental and child psychology; ecology, evolution, and population biology; economics; English; English composition; geography and cartography; geological and earth sciences/geosciences; history; mathematics; microbiological sciences and immunology; music; philosophy; physical sciences; political science and government; psychology; sociology; statistics; visual and performing arts.

ARKANSAS STATE UNIVERSITY–MOUNTAIN HOME
Mountain Home, Arkansas
http://www.asumh.edu

Arkansas State University–Mountain Home was founded in 2000. It is accredited by North Central Association of Colleges and Schools. It first offered distance learning courses in 2000. In fall 2006, there were 203 students enrolled in distance learning courses. Institutionally administered financial aid is available to distance learners.

Services Distance learners have accessibility to academic advising, bookstore, campus computer network, e-mail services, library services, tutoring.

Contact Mr. Scott Raney, Director of Student Services, Arkansas State University–Mountain Home, 1600 South College Street, Mountain Home, AR 72653. Telephone: 870-508-6168. Fax: 870-508-6284. E-mail: sraney@asumh.edu.

DEGREES AND AWARDS
AAS Opticianry

COURSE SUBJECT AREAS OFFERED OUTSIDE OF DEGREE PROGRAMS
Undergraduate—biology; computer science; dramatic/theater arts and stagecraft; economics; English composition; health professions related; mathematics.

ARKANSAS TECH UNIVERSITY
Russellville, Arkansas
Virtual Learning Center
http://ccc.atu.edu

Arkansas Tech University was founded in 1909. It is accredited by North Central Association of Colleges and Schools. It first offered distance learning courses in 1996. In fall 2006, there were 1,199 students enrolled in distance learning courses. Institutionally administered financial aid is available to distance learners.

Services Distance learners have accessibility to academic advising, bookstore, campus computer network, career placement assistance, e-mail services, library services.

Contact Admissions Office, Arkansas Tech University, Russellville, AR 72801. Telephone: 479-968-0343. E-mail: tech.enroll@atu.edu.

DEGREES AND AWARDS
AS Early Childhood Education
BS Early Childhood Education; Emergency Administration and Management
MS College Student Personnel

COURSE SUBJECT AREAS OFFERED OUTSIDE OF DEGREE PROGRAMS

Undergraduate—agricultural business and management; biology; business administration, management and operations; computer and information sciences; educational/instructional media design; education related; education (specific levels and methods); education (specific subject areas); electrical, electronics and communications engineering; English language and literature related; health and medical administrative services; history; hospitality administration; journalism; marketing; mathematics; mechanic and repair technologies related; music; nursing; physical sciences; political science and government; psychology; rehabilitation and therapeutic professions; security and protective services related.
Graduate—educational administration and supervision; educational/instructional media design; education related; education (specific subject areas); journalism.

ARLINGTON BAPTIST COLLEGE
Arlington, Texas
Distance Education Department
http://www.abconline.edu/

Arlington Baptist College was founded in 1939. It is accredited by Association for Biblical Higher Education. It first offered distance learning courses in 1994. In fall 2006, there were 26 students enrolled in distance learning courses. Institutionally administered financial aid is available to distance learners.

Services Distance learners have accessibility to academic advising, bookstore, campus computer network, e-mail services, library services.

Contact Janie Taylor, Registrar, Arlington Baptist College, 3001 West Division, Arlington, TX 76012. Telephone: 817-461-8741 Ext. 105. Fax: 817-274-1138. E-mail: jhall@abconline.org.

DEGREES AND AWARDS
Programs offered do not lead to a degree or other formal award.

COURSE SUBJECT AREAS OFFERED OUTSIDE OF DEGREE PROGRAMS

Undergraduate—biblical studies; education related; pastoral counseling and specialized ministries; philosophy and religious studies related; theological and ministerial studies.
Non-credit—biblical studies; theological and ministerial studies.

ASHFORD UNIVERSITY
Clinton, Iowa
http://www.tfu.edu

Ashford University was founded in 1918. It is accredited by North Central Association of Colleges and Schools. It first offered distance learning courses in 2002. In fall 2006, there were 3,422 students enrolled in distance learning courses. Institutionally administered financial aid is available to distance learners.

Services Distance learners have accessibility to academic advising, bookstore, e-mail services, library services, tutoring.

Contact Mr. Ross Woodard, Vice President of Marketing, Ashford University, 400 North Bluff Boulevard, PO Box 2967, Clinton, IA 52733-2967. Telephone: 858-513-9240 Ext. 2251. Fax: 866-385-6093. E-mail: admissions@ashford.edu.

DEGREES AND AWARDS
AAB Business
BA Organizational Management; Psychology; Social Science; Social and Criminal Justice

MA Teach and Learning with Technology
MAT Teaching
MBA Business Administrations

COURSE SUBJECT AREAS OFFERED OUTSIDE OF DEGREE PROGRAMS

Undergraduate—accounting and related services; American literature (United States and Canadian); business administration, management and operations; business/commerce; business/corporate communications; business, management, and marketing related; business/managerial economics; business operations support and assistant services; communication and media; comparative literature; criminal justice and corrections; curriculum and instruction; economics; education; educational administration and supervision; educational assessment, evaluation, and research; educational/instructional media design; English; English composition; English language and literature related; history; liberal arts and sciences, general studies and humanities; mathematics; mathematics and statistics related; philosophy; philosophy and religious studies related; physical sciences; physical sciences related; psychology; psychology related; religious studies; social sciences; social sciences related; statistics.

Graduate—accounting and computer science; accounting and related services; business/commerce; business/corporate communications; business, management, and marketing related; business/managerial economics; business operations support and assistant services; curriculum and instruction; education; educational administration and supervision; educational assessment, evaluation, and research; education related.

ASSEMBLIES OF GOD THEOLOGICAL SEMINARY
Springfield, Missouri
Office of Continuing Education
http://www.agts.edu
Assemblies of God Theological Seminary was founded in 1972. It is accredited by North Central Association of Colleges and Schools. It first offered distance learning courses in 1980. In fall 2006, there were 5 students enrolled in distance learning courses. Institutionally administered financial aid is available to distance learners.
Services Distance learners have accessibility to academic advising, bookstore, campus computer network, e-mail services, library services, tutoring.
Contact Rev. Joel Triska, Distance Learning Specialist, Assemblies of God Theological Seminary, 1435 North Glenstone Avenue, Springfield, MO 65802. Telephone: 800-467-2487 Ext. 1046. Fax: 417-268-1009. E-mail: jtriska@agts.edu.

DEGREES AND AWARDS
Programs offered do not lead to a degree or other formal award.

COURSE SUBJECT AREAS OFFERED OUTSIDE OF DEGREE PROGRAMS

Graduate—biblical and other theological languages and literatures; biblical studies; history; missionary studies and missiology; pastoral counseling and specialized ministries; philosophy and religious studies related; religious studies; theological and ministerial studies; theology and religious vocations related.

ATHABASCA UNIVERSITY
Athabasca, Alberta, Canada
http://www.athabascau.ca
Athabasca University was founded in 1970. It is provincially chartered. It first offered distance learning courses in 1972. In fall 2006, there were 37,000 students enrolled in distance learning courses. Institutionally administered financial aid is available to distance learners.
Services Distance learners have accessibility to academic advising, bookstore, campus computer network, e-mail services, library services, tutoring.
Contact Information Centre, Athabasca University, 1 University Drive, Athabasca, AB T9S 3A3, Canada. Telephone: 800-788-9041. Fax: 780-675-6437. E-mail: inquire@athabascau.ca.

DEGREES AND AWARDS

BA Anthropology (3 year); Anthropology (4 year); Canadian Studies (3 year); Canadian Studies (4 year); English (3 year); English (4 year); French (3 year); French (4 year); History (3 year); History (4 year); Human Resources Management/Marketing (3 year); Human Resources Management/Marketing (4 year); Human Resources and Labour Relations; Humanities (3 year); Humanities (4 year); Information Systems (3 year); Information Systems (4 year); Labour Studies (3 year); Labour Studies (4 year); Management Post-Diploma (3 year); Management Post-Diploma (4 year); Political Economy (3 year); Political Economy (4 year); Psychology (3 year); Psychology (4 year); Sociology (3 year); Sociology (4 year); Women's Studies (3 year); Women's Studies (4 year)
BComm Accounting; E-Commerce
BGS Applied Studies; Arts and Science
BN Nursing–Post-LPN; Nursing–Post-RN
BPA Communication Studies; Criminal Justice; Governance, Law, and Management; Human Services
BS Computing and Information Systems–Post-Diploma; Computing and Information Systems; Health Administration Post-Diploma; Health Administration; Human Science–Post-Diploma; Human Science
Certificate Accounting; Accounting, advanced; Administration; Career Development; Computers and Management Information Systems; Computing and Information Systems; Counseling Women; English Language Studies; French Language Proficiency; Health Development Administration; Human Resources and Labour Relations; Labour Studies; Public Administration
Diploma Arts; Inclusive Education
Advanced Graduate Diploma Distance Education (Technology); Management; Nursing–Nursing Practice, advanced; Project Management
MA Integrated Studies
MBA Business Administration; Energy Elective; MBA–Policing Elective; Project Management
MCDCC Counseling
MCH Health Studies–Master of Health Studies
MDE Distance Education
MN Nursing
MSIS Information Systems

COURSE SUBJECT AREAS OFFERED OUTSIDE OF DEGREE PROGRAMS

Undergraduate—accounting and related services; anthropology; astronomy and astrophysics; biological and biomedical sciences related; biological and physical sciences; biology; business administration, management and operations; business/commerce; business/corporate communications; business, management, and marketing related; business/managerial economics; chemistry; communication and journalism related; communication and media; communication disorders sciences and services; communications technology; community health services; community organization and advocacy; community psychology; comparative literature; computer and information sciences; computer and information sciences and support services related; computer/information technology administration and management; computer programming; computer science; computer software and media applications; computer systems analysis; computer systems networking and telecommunications; counseling psychology; creative writing; criminal justice and corrections; criminology; data processing; demography and population; developmental and child psychology; economics; educational assessment, evaluation, and research; English; English as a second language; English composition; environmental control technologies; finance and financial management services; fine and studio art; foods, nutrition, and related services; geography and cartography; geological and earth sciences/geosciences; health and medical administrative services; health/medical preparatory programs; health professions related; history; human development, family studies, and related services; human resources management; human services; industrial and organizational psychology; international relations and affairs; journalism; legal studies (nonprofessional general, undergraduate); linguistic, comparative, and related language studies; management information systems; marketing; mathematics; mathematics and computer science; mental and social health services and allied professions; music; natural resources conservation and research; natural resources management and policy; nursing; philosophy; philosophy and religious studies related; physical sciences; physiological psychology/psychobiology; plant sciences; political science and government; psychology; psychology related; public administration; public health; public policy analysis; public relations, advertising, and applied communication related; sales, merchandising, and related marketing operations (general); social sciences; sociology; statistics.

Graduate—accounting and related services; agricultural business and management; business administration, management and operations; business/corporate communications; business, management, and marketing related; business/managerial economics; community health services; community organization and advocacy; community psychology; computer and information sciences; computer and information sciences and support services related; computer/information technology administration and management; computer science; computer systems analysis; counseling psychology; curriculum and instruction; developmental and child psychology; economics; educational administration and supervision; educational assessment, evaluation, and research; educational psychology; education related; health/medical preparatory programs; health professions related; history; human development, family studies, and related services; human resources management; human services; industrial and organizational psychology; information science/studies; international business; international relations and affairs; management information systems; management sciences and quantitative methods; marketing; mathematics and computer science; mental and social health services and allied professions; nursing; philosophy; political science and government; psychology; public administration; public administration and social service professions related; public health; public policy analysis; public relations, advertising, and applied communication related; sales, merchandising, and related marketing operations (general); sales, merchandising, and related marketing operations (specialized); social sciences; social sciences related; social work; sociology; special education; taxation.

Non-credit—accounting and related services; anthropology; astronomy and astrophysics; biology; building/construction finishing, management, and inspection; business administration, management and operations; business/commerce; business/corporate communications; business, management, and marketing related; business/managerial economics; business operations support and assistant services; chemistry; city/urban, community and regional planning; clinical psychology; communication and media; communication disorders sciences and services; communications technology; community health services; community organization and advocacy; community psychology; computer and information sciences; computer/information technology administration and management; computer programming; computer science; computer software and media applications; computer systems analysis; counseling psychology; criminal justice and corrections; criminology; data entry/microcomputer applications; data processing; developmental and child psychology; economics; educational administration and supervision; educational assessment, evaluation, and research; educational/instructional media design; educational psychology; education related; English; English as a second/foreign language (teaching); English as a second language; English composition; environmental control technologies; ethnic, cultural minority, and gender studies; finance and financial management services; fine and studio art; foods, nutrition, and related services; geological and earth sciences/geosciences; gerontology; health professions related; history; human development, family studies, and related services; human resources management; human services; industrial and organizational psychology; international business; international relations and affairs; journalism; liberal arts and sciences, general studies and humanities; linguistic, comparative, and related language studies; management information systems; management sciences and quantitative methods; marketing; mathematics; mathematics and computer science; medical basic sciences; mental and social health services and allied professions; music; nursing; philosophy; philosophy and religious studies related; physical sciences; political science and government; psychology; public administration; public administration and social service professions related; public health; public policy analysis; public relations, advertising, and applied communication related; radio, television, and digital communication; sales, merchandising, and related marketing operations (general); sales, merchandising, and related marketing operations (specialized); school psychology; science technologies related; science, technology and society;

social and philosophical foundations of education; social psychology; social sciences; social sciences related; social work; sociology; statistics; taxation.

See full description on page 312.

ATLANTIC SCHOOL OF THEOLOGY
Halifax, Nova Scotia, Canada
http://www.astheology.ns.ca/
Atlantic School of Theology was founded in 1971. It is provincially chartered. It first offered distance learning courses in 1999. In fall 2006, there were 48 students enrolled in distance learning courses. Institutionally administered financial aid is available to distance learners.
Services Distance learners have accessibility to academic advising, bookstore, e-mail services, library services.
Contact Dr. Thomas McIllwraith, Director of Distributed Education, Atlantic School of Theology, 660 Francklyn Street, Halifax, NS B3H 3B5, Canada. Telephone: 902-496-7945. Fax: 902-492-4048. E-mail: tmcillwraith@astheology.ns.ca.

DEGREES AND AWARDS
Programs offered do not lead to a degree or other formal award.

COURSE SUBJECT AREAS OFFERED OUTSIDE OF DEGREE PROGRAMS

Graduate—biblical studies; religious education; religious/sacred music; religious studies; theological and ministerial studies; theology and religious vocations related.

Non-credit—biblical studies; religious education; religious studies; theological and ministerial studies; theology and religious vocations related.

ATLANTIC UNIVERSITY
Virginia Beach, Virginia
http://www.atlanticuniv.edu/
Atlantic University was founded in 1930. It is accredited by Distance Education and Training Council. It first offered distance learning courses in 1985. In fall 2006, there were 175 students enrolled in distance learning courses. Institutionally administered financial aid is available to distance learners.
Services Distance learners have accessibility to academic advising, e-mail services, library services.
Contact Mr. Gregory Deming, Director of Admissions, Atlantic University, 215 67th Street, Virginia Beach, VA 23451. Telephone: 757-631-8101 Ext. 7173. Fax: 757-631-8096. E-mail: admissions@atlanticuniv.edu.

DEGREES AND AWARDS
MA Transpersonal Studies

COURSE SUBJECT AREAS OFFERED OUTSIDE OF DEGREE PROGRAMS

Graduate—alternative and complementary medical support services; alternative and complementary medicine and medical systems; biblical studies; counseling psychology; creative writing; education related; fine and studio art; movement and mind-body therapies; peace studies and conflict resolution; philosophy and religious studies related; psychology related; religious studies; visual and performing arts.

Non-credit—alternative and complementary medical support services; alternative and complementary medicine and medical systems; biblical studies; counseling psychology; creative writing; education related; fine and studio art; movement and mind-body therapies; peace studies and conflict resolution; philosophy and religious studies related; psychology related; religious studies; visual and performing arts.

AUBURN UNIVERSITY
Auburn University, Alabama
Distance Learning/Outreach Technology
http://www.auburn.edu/auonline

Auburn University was founded in 1856. It is accredited by Southern Association of Colleges and Schools. It first offered distance learning courses in 1975. In fall 2006, there were 1,000 students enrolled in distance learning courses. Institutionally administered financial aid is available to distance learners.

Services Distance learners have accessibility to academic advising, bookstore, campus computer network, career placement assistance, e-mail services, library services.

Contact Distance Learning, Auburn University, 305 O.D. Smith Hall, Auburn University, AL 36849. Telephone: 334-844-3103. Fax: 334-844-3118.

DEGREES AND AWARDS
Certificate Dietary Management
EMBA Business Administration; Physicians Executive MBA
MA Early Childhood Intervention
MAE Aerospace Engineering; Foreign Language
MBA Business Administration
MBA/M Acc Accountancy
MBA/MSMIS Management Information Systems
MCE Chemical Engineering; Civil Engineering
MCSE Computer Science and Engineering
MEd Collaborative Teacher and Early Childhood Education; Music; Rehabilitation Counseling
MISE Industrial and Systems Engineering
MME Materials Engineering; Mechanical Engineering
MS Hotel and Restaurant Management
PharmD Pharmacy

COURSE SUBJECT AREAS OFFERED OUTSIDE OF DEGREE PROGRAMS
Undergraduate—agriculture; animal sciences; communication and media; communication disorders sciences and services; computer science; film/video and photographic arts; geography and cartography; health and physical education/fitness; political science and government; speech and rhetoric.

Graduate—accounting and related services; aerospace, aeronautical and astronautical engineering; business administration, management and operations; civil engineering; civil engineering technology; computer science; education; education related; education (specific levels and methods); education (specific subject areas); engineering-related fields; engineering science; foods, nutrition, and related services; pharmacy, pharmaceutical sciences, and administration; special education.

Non-credit—animal sciences; computer/information technology administration and management; construction management; data processing; dietetics and clinical nutrition services; engineering; foods, nutrition, and related services; veterinary biomedical and clinical sciences.

See full description on page 314.

AUSTIN PEAY STATE UNIVERSITY
Clarksville, Tennessee
http://www.apsu.edu/

Austin Peay State University was founded in 1927. It is accredited by Southern Association of Colleges and Schools. It first offered distance learning courses in 1996. In fall 2006, there were 5,032 students enrolled in distance learning courses. Institutionally administered financial aid is available to distance learners.

Services Distance learners have accessibility to academic advising, bookstore, campus computer network, e-mail services, library services, tutoring.

Contact Ms. Julia McGee, Director of Extended Education, Austin Peay State University, PO Box 4678, Clarksville, TN 37044. Telephone: 931-221-7743. Fax: 931-221-7748. E-mail: mcgeej@apsu.edu.

DEGREES AND AWARDS
AS Law Enforcement Administration; Liberal Arts
BA Communication Arts (BA or BS)
BN Nursing–Registered Nurse to Bachelor of Science in Nursing
BPS Regents Online degree program
BS Computer Science–Information Systems; Criminal Justice–Homeland Security; Criminal Justice–Homeland Security; Criminal Justice–Homeland Security; Political Science; Professional Studies
MA Corporate Communication; Military History; Psychology–Industrial/Organizational Psychology
MS Health Service Administration
MSM Management

COURSE SUBJECT AREAS OFFERED OUTSIDE OF DEGREE PROGRAMS
Undergraduate—astronomy and astrophysics; health and physical education/fitness; mathematics and computer science; psychology; public administration; sociology; speech and rhetoric.

Graduate—communication and journalism related; health and physical education/fitness.

AZUSA PACIFIC UNIVERSITY
Azusa, California
http://online.apu.edu/

Azusa Pacific University was founded in 1899. It is accredited by Western Association of Schools and Colleges. It first offered distance learning courses in 1999. In fall 2006, there were 1,000 students enrolled in distance learning courses. Institutionally administered financial aid is available to distance learners.

Services Distance learners have accessibility to bookstore, e-mail services, library services.

Contact Dr. Bruce Simmerok, Director of Distance Learning and Continuing Education, Azusa Pacific University, 901 East Alosta Avenue, Azusa, CA 91702-7000. Telephone: 626-815-5038. E-mail: bsimmerok@apu.edu.

DEGREES AND AWARDS
Certificate Library Media Teaching
MA Educational Technology
MAE Library Science–School Librarianship

COURSE SUBJECT AREAS OFFERED OUTSIDE OF DEGREE PROGRAMS
Undergraduate—computer science; history; religious studies.

Graduate—computer science; educational administration and supervision; educational assessment, evaluation, and research; educational/instructional media design; education (specific subject areas); nursing; theological and ministerial studies.

BAINBRIDGE COLLEGE
Bainbridge, Georgia
http://www.bainbridge.edu

Bainbridge College was founded in 1972. It is accredited by Southern Association of Colleges and Schools. It first offered distance learning courses in 2000. In fall 2006, there were 250 students enrolled in distance learning courses. Institutionally administered financial aid is available to distance learners.

Services Distance learners have accessibility to academic advising, bookstore, career placement assistance, e-mail services, library services, tutoring.

Contact Ms. Connie B. Snyder, Director of Admissions and Records, Bainbridge College, 2500 East Shotwell Street, PO Box 990, Bainbridge, GA 39818-0990. Telephone: 229-248-2504. Fax: 229-248-2623. E-mail: csnyder@bainbridge.edu.

DEGREES AND AWARDS
Programs offered do not lead to a degree or other formal award.

COURSE SUBJECT AREAS OFFERED OUTSIDE OF DEGREE PROGRAMS

Undergraduate—accounting and related services; applied mathematics; business/commerce; business operations support and assistant services; computer and information sciences; liberal arts and sciences, general studies and humanities; speech and rhetoric.

Non-credit—allied health and medical assisting services; business administration, management and operations; communication and media; computer software and media applications; computer systems networking and telecommunications; linguistic, comparative, and related language studies; real estate.

BAKER COLLEGE OF FLINT
Flint, Michigan
Baker College OnLine
http://online.baker.edu

Baker College of Flint was founded in 1911. It is accredited by North Central Association of Colleges and Schools. It first offered distance learning courses in 1994. In fall 2006, there were 15,021 students enrolled in distance learning courses. Institutionally administered financial aid is available to distance learners.

Services Distance learners have accessibility to academic advising, bookstore, campus computer network, career placement assistance, e-mail services, library services, tutoring.

Contact Mr. Chuck J. Gurden, Vice President of Graduate and Online Admissions, Baker College of Flint, 1116 West Bristol Road, Flint, MI 48507. Telephone: 800-469-3165. Fax: 810-766-2051. E-mail: cgurde01@baker.edu.

DEGREES AND AWARDS

ABA Business Administration
BBA Business Administration
MBA Business Administration

COURSE SUBJECT AREAS OFFERED OUTSIDE OF DEGREE PROGRAMS

Undergraduate—business administration, management and operations; computer/information technology administration and management.

See full description on page 316.

BAKKE GRADUATE UNIVERSITY OF MINISTRY
Seattle, Washington

Bakke Graduate University of Ministry was founded in 1990. It is accredited by Transnational Association of Christian Colleges and Schools. It first offered distance learning courses in 1995. In fall 2006, there were 6 students enrolled in distance learning courses. Institutionally administered financial aid is available to distance learners.

Services Distance learners have accessibility to academic advising, e-mail services, library services.

Contact Mrs. Judi Melton, Registrar, Bakke Graduate University of Ministry, 1013 Eighth Avenue, Seattle, WA 98104. Telephone: 206-264-9100 Ext. 14. Fax: 206-264-8828. E-mail: judim@bgu.edu.

DEGREES AND AWARDS

Programs offered do not lead to a degree or other formal award.

COURSE SUBJECT AREAS OFFERED OUTSIDE OF DEGREE PROGRAMS

Graduate—biblical studies; religious studies; theological and ministerial studies; theology and religious vocations related; urban studies/affairs.

BALL STATE UNIVERSITY
Muncie, Indiana
School of Continuing Education and Public Service
http://www.bsu.edu/distance

Ball State University was founded in 1918. It is accredited by North Central Association of Colleges and Schools. It first offered distance learning courses in 1984. In fall 2006, there were 3,315 students enrolled in distance learning courses. Institutionally administered financial aid is available to distance learners.

Services Distance learners have accessibility to academic advising, bookstore, campus computer network, career placement assistance, e-mail services, library services.

Contact Ms. Diane K. Watters, Marketing Manager, Ball State University, School of Extended Education, Carmichael Hall, Room 200, Muncie, IN 47306. Telephone: 765-285-9042. Fax: 765-285-7161. E-mail: dbuck@bsu.edu.

DEGREES AND AWARDS

AA General Program
AS Business Administration Management
BGS General Studies
BSN Nursing
MA Career and Technical Education; Physical Education–Coaching specialization; Technology Education
MAE Educational Administration and Supervision; Elementary Education
MBA Business Administration
MSN Nursing

COURSE SUBJECT AREAS OFFERED OUTSIDE OF DEGREE PROGRAMS

Undergraduate—geography and cartography; health services/allied health/health sciences; political science and government; real estate.
Graduate—English as a second/foreign language (teaching); special education.

BALTIMORE HEBREW UNIVERSITY
Baltimore, Maryland
http://www.bhu.edu/

Baltimore Hebrew University was founded in 1919. It is accredited by Middle States Association of Colleges and Schools. It first offered distance learning courses in 2005. In fall 2006, there were 25 students enrolled in distance learning courses. Institutionally administered financial aid is available to distance learners.

Services Distance learners have accessibility to library services.

Contact Dr. Barbara G. Zirkin, Dean/ Chief Academic Officer, Baltimore Hebrew University, 5800 Park Heights Avenue, Baltimore, MD 21215. Telephone: 410-578-6917. Fax: 410-578-6940. E-mail: bzirkin@bhu.edu.

DEGREES AND AWARDS

Programs offered do not lead to a degree or other formal award.

COURSE SUBJECT AREAS OFFERED OUTSIDE OF DEGREE PROGRAMS

Graduate—education (specific subject areas); history.

THE BAPTIST COLLEGE OF FLORIDA
Graceville, Florida
Division of Distance Learning
http://www.baptistcollege.edu

The Baptist College of Florida was founded in 1943. It is accredited by Southern Association of Colleges and Schools. It first offered distance learning courses in 1999. In fall 2006, there were 100 students enrolled in distance learning courses. Institutionally administered financial aid is available to distance learners.

Services Distance learners have accessibility to academic advising, bookstore, campus computer network, career placement assistance, e-mail services, library services, tutoring.

Contact Dr. David Coggins, Director of Distance Learning, The Baptist College of Florida, 5400 College Drive, Graceville, FL 32440. Telephone: 850-263-3261 Ext. 482. Fax: 850-263-7506. E-mail: jdcoggins @baptistcollege.edu.

DEGREES AND AWARDS

AD Divinity
BS Biblical Studies

COURSE SUBJECT AREAS OFFERED OUTSIDE OF DEGREE PROGRAMS

Undergraduate—biblical studies; counseling psychology; philosophy and religious studies related.

BAPTIST MISSIONARY ASSOCIATION THEOLOGICAL SEMINARY
Jacksonville, Texas
http://bmats.edu

Baptist Missionary Association Theological Seminary was founded in 1955. It is accredited by Southern Association of Colleges and Schools. It first offered distance learning courses in 2000. In fall 2006, there were 25 students enrolled in distance learning courses. Institutionally administered financial aid is available to distance learners.
Services Distance learners have accessibility to academic advising, bookstore, library services.
Contact Dr. Philip W. Attebery, Dean/Registrar, Baptist Missionary Association Theological Seminary, 1530 East Pine Street, Jacksonville, TX 75766. Telephone: 903-586-2501. Fax: 903-586-0378. E-mail: bmatsem@bmats.edu.

DEGREES AND AWARDS

Programs offered do not lead to a degree or other formal award.

COURSE SUBJECT AREAS OFFERED OUTSIDE OF DEGREE PROGRAMS

Undergraduate—religious education; religious studies; theological and ministerial studies; theology and religious vocations related.
Graduate—religious education; religious studies; theological and ministerial studies; theology and religious vocations related.
Non-credit—theological and ministerial studies; theology and religious vocations related.

BARCLAY COLLEGE
Haviland, Kansas
Home College Program
http://www.barclaycollege.edu

Barclay College was founded in 1917. It is accredited by Association for Biblical Higher Education. It first offered distance learning courses in 1993. In fall 2006, there were 19 students enrolled in distance learning courses. Institutionally administered financial aid is available to distance learners.
Services Distance learners have accessibility to academic advising, bookstore, e-mail services, library services.
Contact Dr. Glenn Leppert, Registrar, Barclay College, 607 North Kingman, Haviland, KS 67059-0288. Telephone: 620-862-5252 Ext. 46. Fax: 620-862-5242. E-mail: registrar@barclaycollege.edu.

DEGREES AND AWARDS

Programs offered do not lead to a degree or other formal award.

COURSE SUBJECT AREAS OFFERED OUTSIDE OF DEGREE PROGRAMS

Undergraduate—behavioral sciences; biblical studies; education related; English; English composition; mathematics; missionary studies and missiology; physical sciences; psychology; religious/sacred music; sociology; theological and ministerial studies.

BEAUFORT COUNTY COMMUNITY COLLEGE
Washington, North Carolina
Distance Education Center
http://www.beaufort.cc.nc.us/

Beaufort County Community College was founded in 1967. It is accredited by Southern Association of Colleges and Schools. It first offered distance learning courses in 1995. In fall 2006, there were 500 students enrolled in distance learning courses. Institutionally administered financial aid is available to distance learners.
Services Distance learners have accessibility to academic advising, bookstore, campus computer network, career placement assistance, e-mail services, library services, tutoring.
Contact Penny Sermons, Director of Learning Resources Center, Beaufort County Community College, PO Box 1069, Washington, NC 27889. Telephone: 252-940-6243. Fax: 252-946-9575. E-mail: pennys@email. beaufort.cc.nc.us.

DEGREES AND AWARDS

Programs offered do not lead to a degree or other formal award.

COURSE SUBJECT AREAS OFFERED OUTSIDE OF DEGREE PROGRAMS

Undergraduate—accounting and related services; business administration, management and operations; computer and information sciences; English; liberal arts and sciences, general studies and humanities; management information systems; psychology; social psychology; sociology.
Non-credit—accounting and related services; business/corporate communications; computer and information sciences; computer software and media applications.

BELLEVUE COMMUNITY COLLEGE
Bellevue, Washington
Telecommunications Program–Distance Learning Department
http://distance-ed.bcc.ctc.edu

Bellevue Community College was founded in 1966. It is accredited by Northwest Commission on Colleges and Universities. It first offered distance learning courses in 1980. In fall 2006, there were 3,100 students enrolled in distance learning courses. Institutionally administered financial aid is available to distance learners.
Services Distance learners have accessibility to academic advising, bookstore, campus computer network, e-mail services, library services, tutoring.
Contact Liz Anderson, Director of Distance Education, Bellevue Community College, 3000 Landerholm Circle SE, Bellevue, WA 98007-6484. Telephone: 425-564-2438. Fax: 425-564-5564. E-mail: landerso@bcc. ctc.edu.

DEGREES AND AWARDS

AA General Studies
AAS Transfer degree for Business Students; Transfer degree
Certificate of Achievement Business Intelligence Developer
Certificate Bookkeeping–Paraprofessional Accounting program; Business Intelligence Analyst; Business Software Specialist–Business Technology Systems; Introductory C++ Programming

COURSE SUBJECT AREAS OFFERED OUTSIDE OF DEGREE PROGRAMS

Undergraduate—accounting and related services; American literature (United States and Canadian); anthropology; archeology; astronomy and astrophysics; atmospheric sciences and meteorology; biology; botany/ plant biology; business administration, management and operations; business/commerce; business/corporate communications; business, management, and marketing related; business operations support and assistant services; chemistry; communication and media; comparative literature; computer and information sciences; computer and information sciences and support services related; computer programming; computer science; computer software and media applications; creative writing; criminology; developmental and child psychology; ecology, evolution, and population biology; economics; education; English; English composition; English language and literature related; English literature (British and Commonwealth); entrepreneurial and small business operations; fire protection; geography and cartography; geological and earth sciences/geosciences; health professions related; history; liberal arts and sciences, general studies and humanities; management information systems; marketing; mathematics; mathematics and statistics related; medieval and Renaissance studies; music; natural sciences; nutrition sciences; philosophy; physical sciences; physical sciences related; plant sciences; political science and government; psychology; psychology related; social psychology; social sciences; social sciences related; sociology; speech and rhetoric.

BELLEVUE UNIVERSITY
Bellevue, Nebraska
Online Programs
http://www.bellevue.edu
Bellevue University was founded in 1965. It is accredited by North Central Association of Colleges and Schools. It first offered distance learning courses in 1996. In fall 2006, there were 3,000 students enrolled in distance learning courses. Institutionally administered financial aid is available to distance learners.

Services Distance learners have accessibility to academic advising, campus computer network, e-mail services, library services.

Contact Roberta Mersch, Online Admissions, Bellevue University, 1000 Galvin Road South, Bellevue, NE 68005. Telephone: 800-756-7920. Fax: 402-293-3730. E-mail: mm@bellevue.edu.

DEGREES AND AWARDS

BA Leadership

BS Business Administration of Technical Studies; Business Information Systems; Correctional Administration and Management; Criminal Justice Administration; E-Business; Global Business Management; Health Care Administration; Internet Systems and Software Technology; Management Information Systems; Management of Human Resources; Management; Marketing Management

BSBA Business Administration

MA Leadership; Management

MBA Business Administration

MS Computer Information Systems; Health Care Administration

COURSE SUBJECT AREAS OFFERED OUTSIDE OF DEGREE PROGRAMS

Undergraduate—American literature (United States and Canadian); biological and physical sciences; business administration, management and operations; business/commerce; business, management, and marketing related; business/managerial economics; communication and media; comparative literature; computer and information sciences; computer and information sciences and support services related; computer/information technology administration and management; computer programming; computer software and media applications; computer systems analysis; computer systems networking and telecommunications; English; English literature (British and Commonwealth); finance and financial management services; fine and studio art; health and medical administrative services; human resources management; human services; management information systems; management sciences and quantitative methods; marketing; sales, merchandising, and related marketing operations (specialized).

Graduate—business administration, management and operations; business/commerce; business/corporate communications; business, management, and marketing related; business/managerial economics; health and medical administrative services; management information systems; management sciences and quantitative methods; sales, merchandising, and related marketing operations (specialized).

See full description on page 318.

BELMONT TECHNICAL COLLEGE
St. Clairsville, Ohio
http://www.belmont.cc.oh.us/
Belmont Technical College was founded in 1971. It is accredited by North Central Association of Colleges and Schools. It first offered distance learning courses in 1999. In fall 2006, there were 187 students enrolled in distance learning courses. Institutionally administered financial aid is available to distance learners.

Services Distance learners have accessibility to academic advising, bookstore, career placement assistance, e-mail services, library services, tutoring.

Contact Catherine L. Bennett, Associate Dean of Learning, Information Services, and Technology, Belmont Technical College, 120 Fox Shannon Place, St. Clairsville, OH 43950. Telephone: 740-695-9500 Ext. 1088. Fax: 740-695-2247. E-mail: cbennett@btc.edu.

DEGREES AND AWARDS

AAS Information Technology and Information Services Library Paraprofessional

COURSE SUBJECT AREAS OFFERED OUTSIDE OF DEGREE PROGRAMS

Undergraduate—accounting and computer science; accounting and related services; computer and information sciences; computer and information sciences and support services related; computer programming; computer science; computer software and media applications; English; English composition; English language and literature related; health services/allied health/health sciences; information science/studies; library assistant; library science related; philosophy; physical sciences; psychology; sociology; statistics; technical and business writing.

BEMIDJI STATE UNIVERSITY
Bemidji, Minnesota
Center for Extended Learning
http://www.bemidjistate.edu
Bemidji State University was founded in 1919. It is accredited by North Central Association of Colleges and Schools. It first offered distance learning courses in 1977. In fall 2006, there were 1,500 students enrolled in distance learning courses. Institutionally administered financial aid is available to distance learners.

Services Distance learners have accessibility to academic advising, bookstore, career placement assistance, e-mail services, library services, tutoring.

Contact Robert J. Griggs, JD, Dean of Distance Learning and Summer Session, Bemidji State University, 1500 Birchmont Drive NE, #4, Bemidji, MN 56601-2699. Telephone: 218-755-2068. Fax: 218-755-4604. E-mail: rgriggs@bemidjistate.edu.

DEGREES AND AWARDS

AS Criminal Justice

BS Business Administration; Criminal Justice; Elementary Education

MS Industrial Technology

MSE Education

COURSE SUBJECT AREAS OFFERED OUTSIDE OF DEGREE PROGRAMS

Undergraduate—anthropology; business administration, management and operations; criminal justice and corrections; criminology; economics; education (specific levels and methods); education (specific subject areas); English composition; geography and cartography; health and physical education/fitness; history; industrial production technologies; philosophy; psychology; social work; sociology.

Graduate—education; educational/instructional media design; industrial production technologies.

BERGEN COMMUNITY COLLEGE
Paramus, New Jersey
Center for Distance Learning
http://www.bergen.edu/

Bergen Community College was founded in 1965. It is accredited by Middle States Association of Colleges and Schools. It first offered distance learning courses in 1974. In fall 2006, there were 2,031 students enrolled in distance learning courses. Institutionally administered financial aid is available to distance learners.

Services Distance learners have accessibility to academic advising, bookstore, e-mail services, library services, tutoring.

Contact Ms. Kathy Morley, Distance Learning Supervisor, Bergen Community College, 400 Paramus Road, Paramus, NJ 07652. Telephone: 201-612-5288. Fax: 201-612-8225. E-mail: kmorley@bergen.edu.

DEGREES AND AWARDS
Programs offered do not lead to a degree or other formal award.

COURSE SUBJECT AREAS OFFERED OUTSIDE OF DEGREE PROGRAMS

Undergraduate—accounting and related services; American literature (United States and Canadian); anthropology; business administration, management and operations; computer programming; computer science; criminal justice and corrections; developmental and child psychology; dramatic/theater arts and stagecraft; education; educational psychology; English composition; finance and financial management services; foods, nutrition, and related services; geological and earth sciences/geosciences; history; journalism; philosophy; philosophy and religious studies related; political science and government; psychology; religious studies; social psychology; social sciences; sociology; speech and rhetoric; visual and performing arts.

BERKELEY COLLEGE
West Paterson, New Jersey
http://www.berkeleycollege.edu/

Berkeley College was founded in 1931. It is accredited by Middle States Association of Colleges and Schools. It first offered distance learning courses in 2001. In fall 2006, there were 477 students enrolled in distance learning courses. Institutionally administered financial aid is available to distance learners.

Services Distance learners have accessibility to academic advising, bookstore, campus computer network, career placement assistance, e-mail services, library services, tutoring.

Contact Mr. David Bertone, Senior Director, Enrollment, Berkeley College, 44 Rifle Camp Road, West Paterson, NJ 07424. Telephone: 800-446-5400. Fax: 973-278-2431. E-mail: online@berkeleycollege. edu.

DEGREES AND AWARDS
AAS Business Administration; Financial Services; Health Services Administration–Medical Insurance, Billing, and Coding; Health Services Administration; International Business; Justice Studies–Criminal Justice
BS Business Administration; Justice Studies–Criminal Justice; Management

COURSE SUBJECT AREAS OFFERED OUTSIDE OF DEGREE PROGRAMS

Undergraduate—accounting and related services; American literature (United States and Canadian); anthropology; area, ethnic, cultural, and gender studies related; biological and physical sciences; business administration, management and operations; business/commerce; business, management, and marketing related; business/managerial economics; communication and media; computer software and media applications; criminal justice and corrections; criminology; data entry/microcomputer applications; economics; English composition; English language and literature related; entrepreneurial and small business operations; ethnic, cultural minority, and gender studies; finance and financial management services; health and medical administrative services; history; human resources management; industrial and organizational psychology; intercultural/multicultural and diversity studies; international business; legal studies

(non-professional general, undergraduate); liberal arts and sciences, general studies and humanities; management sciences and quantitative methods; marketing; mathematics and statistics related; multi-/interdisciplinary studies related; philosophy; philosophy and religious studies related; physical sciences related; political science and government; psychology; public relations, advertising, and applied communication related; sales, merchandising, and related marketing operations (general); sales, merchandising, and related marketing operations (specialized); security and protective services related; social sciences related; sociology; statistics.

BERKELEY COLLEGE-NEW YORK CITY CAMPUS
New York, New York
http://www.berkeleycollege.edu/

Berkeley College-New York City Campus was founded in 1936. It is accredited by Middle States Association of Colleges and Schools. It first offered distance learning courses in 1998. In fall 2006, there were 299 students enrolled in distance learning courses. Institutionally administered financial aid is available to distance learners.

Services Distance learners have accessibility to academic advising, bookstore, campus computer network, career placement assistance, e-mail services, library services, tutoring.

Contact Mr. David Bertone, Senior Director, Enrollment, Berkeley College-New York City Campus, 3 East 43rd Street, New York, NY 10017. Telephone: 800-446-5400. Fax: 212-818-1079. E-mail: online@ berkeleycollege.edu.

DEGREES AND AWARDS
AAS Business Administration–Information Systems Management; Business Administration–Management; Business Administration–Marketing; Health Services Administration–Medical Insurance, Billing, and Coding; Health Services Administration; International Business
BBA Business Administration–Information Systems Management; Business Administration–Management; Business Administration–Marketing; Business, general; Health Services Administration; International Business

COURSE SUBJECT AREAS OFFERED OUTSIDE OF DEGREE PROGRAMS

Undergraduate—accounting and related services; American literature (United States and Canadian); anthropology; area, ethnic, cultural, and gender studies related; biological and physical sciences; business administration, management and operations; business/commerce; business, management, and marketing related; business/managerial economics; communication and media; computer software and media applications; criminology; data entry/microcomputer applications; economics; English composition; English language and literature related; entrepreneurial and small business operations; ethnic, cultural minority, and gender studies; finance and financial management services; health and medical administrative services; history; human resources management; industrial and organizational psychology; intercultural/multicultural and diversity studies; international business; legal studies (non-professional general, undergraduate); liberal arts and sciences, general studies and humanities; management sciences and quantitative methods; marketing; mathematics and statistics related; multi-/interdisciplinary studies related; philosophy; philosophy and religious studies related; physical sciences related; political science and government; psychology; public relations, advertising, and applied communication related; sales, merchandising, and related marketing operations (general); sales, merchandising, and related marketing operations (specialized); security and protective services related; social sciences related; sociology; statistics.

BERKELEY COLLEGE-WESTCHESTER CAMPUS
White Plains, New York
http://www.berkeleycollege.edu/

Berkeley College-Westchester Campus was founded in 1945. It is accredited by Middle States Association of Colleges and Schools. It first offered distance learning courses in 1998. In fall 2006, there were 89 students enrolled in distance learning courses. Institutionally administered financial aid is available to distance learners.

Services Distance learners have accessibility to academic advising, bookstore, campus computer network, career placement assistance, e-mail services, library services, tutoring.

Contact Mr. David Bertone, Senior Director, Enrollment, Berkeley College-Westchester Campus, 44 Rifle Camp Road, West Paterson, NJ 07424. Telephone: 800-446-5400. Fax: 973-278-2431. E-mail: online@ berkeleycollege.edu.

DEGREES AND AWARDS

AAS Business Administration–Information Systems Management; Business Administration–Management; Business Administration–Marketing; Health Services Administration–Medical Insurance, Billing, and Coding; Health Services Administration; International Business

BBA Business Administration–Information Systems Management; Business Administration–Management; Business Administration–Marketing; Business, general; Health Services Management; International Business

COURSE SUBJECT AREAS OFFERED OUTSIDE OF DEGREE PROGRAMS

Undergraduate—accounting and related services; American literature (United States and Canadian); anthropology; area, ethnic, cultural, and gender studies related; biological and physical sciences; business administration, management and operations; business/commerce; business, management, and marketing related; business/managerial economics; communication and media; computer software and media applications; criminology; data entry/microcomputer applications; economics; English composition; English language and literature related; entrepreneurial and small business operations; ethnic, cultural minority, and gender studies; finance and financial management services; health and medical administrative services; history; human resources management; industrial and organizational psychology; intercultural/multicultural and diversity studies; international business; legal studies (non-professional general, undergraduate); liberal arts and sciences, general studies and humanities; management sciences and quantitative methods; marketing; mathematics and statistics related; multi-/interdisciplinary studies related; philosophy; philosophy and religious studies related; physical sciences related; political science and government; psychology; public relations, advertising, and applied communication related; sales, merchandising, and related marketing operations (general); sales, merchandising, and related marketing operations (specialized); security and protective services related; social sciences related; sociology; statistics.

BERKLEE COLLEGE OF MUSIC
Boston, Massachusetts
Berkleemusic
http://www.berklee.edu/
Berklee College of Music was founded in 1945. It is accredited by New England Association of Schools and Colleges. It first offered distance learning courses in 2002. In fall 2006, there were 1,500 students enrolled in distance learning courses. Institutionally administered financial aid is available to distance learners.
Services Distance learners have accessibility to academic advising, bookstore, library services.
Contact Dorothy Lannon, Continuing Education Registrar, Berklee College of Music, 1140 Boylston Street, MS-855, Boston, MA 02215. Telephone: 617-747-2146. Fax: 617-747-2149. E-mail: registrar@ berkleemusic.com.

DEGREES AND AWARDS
Programs offered do not lead to a degree or other formal award.

COURSE SUBJECT AREAS OFFERED OUTSIDE OF DEGREE PROGRAMS
Undergraduate—business/commerce; music; visual and performing arts.
Non-credit—business/commerce; music; visual and performing arts.

BIG BEND COMMUNITY COLLEGE
Moses Lake, Washington
http://www.bbcc.ctc.edu/
Big Bend Community College was founded in 1962. It is accredited by Northwest Commission on Colleges and Universities. It first offered distance learning courses in 2000. In fall 2006, there were 373 students enrolled in distance learning courses. Institutionally administered financial aid is available to distance learners.
Services Distance learners have accessibility to academic advising, bookstore, campus computer network, e-mail services, library services.

Contact Dean Rachel Anderson, PhD, Dean of Arts and Sciences, Big Bend Community College, 7662 Chanute Street NE, Moses Lake, WA 98837. Telephone: 509-793-2051. Fax: 509-762-6279. E-mail: rachela @bigbend.edu.

DEGREES AND AWARDS
Programs offered do not lead to a degree or other formal award.

COURSE SUBJECT AREAS OFFERED OUTSIDE OF DEGREE PROGRAMS
Undergraduate—accounting and related services; allied health and medical assisting services; anthropology; behavioral sciences; business/ commerce; chemistry; communication and journalism related; crafts, folk art and artisanry; dietetics and clinical nutrition services; economics; English; English composition; English language and literature related; geological and earth sciences/geosciences; history; library science; mathematics; music; natural sciences; philosophy and religious studies related; physical sciences.

BISMARCK STATE COLLEGE
Bismarck, North Dakota
http://www.bismarckstate.edu
Bismarck State College was founded in 1939. It is accredited by North Central Association of Colleges and Schools. It first offered distance learning courses in 1991. In fall 2006, there were 1,400 students enrolled in distance learning courses. Institutionally administered financial aid is available to distance learners.
Services Distance learners have accessibility to academic advising, bookstore, career placement assistance, e-mail services, library services, tutoring.
Contact Mr. Lane Huber, Director of Distance Education, Bismarck State College, PO Box 5587, Bismarck, ND 58506. Telephone: 701-224-5714. Fax: 701-224-5719. E-mail: lane.huber@bsc.nodak.edu.

DEGREES AND AWARDS
AA Criminal Justice
AAS Criminal Justice; Electric Power Technology; Electric Transmission System Technology; Human Services; Nuclear Power Technology; Power Plant Technology; Process Plant Technology; Web Page Development and Design
Certificate of Completion Electric Power Technology; Electric Transmission System Technology; Information Processing Specialist; Power Plant Technology; Process Plant Technology

COURSE SUBJECT AREAS OFFERED OUTSIDE OF DEGREE PROGRAMS
Undergraduate—accounting and computer science; accounting and related services; agriculture; area, ethnic, cultural, and gender studies related; biology; business/commerce; business, management, and marketing related; communication and journalism related; computer science; computer software and media applications; criminal justice and corrections; criminology; economics; English; English composition; history; human services; information science/studies; marketing; mathematics; nuclear and industrial radiologic technologies; philosophy; philosophy and religious studies related; physical sciences related; psychology; sales, merchandising, and related marketing operations (general); social sciences; sociology; technical and business writing.
Non-credit—electrical and electronic engineering technologies; heavy/ industrial equipment maintenance technologies; industrial production technologies; nuclear and industrial radiologic technologies; nuclear engineering; plant sciences.

BLACKHAWK TECHNICAL COLLEGE
Janesville, Wisconsin
http://www.blackhawk.edu
Blackhawk Technical College was founded in 1968. It is accredited by North Central Association of Colleges and Schools. It first offered distance learning courses in 2000. In fall 2006, there were 250 students enrolled in distance learning courses. Institutionally administered financial aid is available to distance learners.
Services Distance learners have accessibility to academic advising, bookstore, career placement assistance, e-mail services, library services.

Contact Ms. Linda Brown, High School Community Relations Specialist, Blackhawk Technical College, PO Box 5009, Janesville, WI 53547. Telephone: 608-757-7670. E-mail: lbrown@blackhawk.edu.

DEGREES AND AWARDS

AS Accounting

COURSE SUBJECT AREAS OFFERED OUTSIDE OF DEGREE PROGRAMS

Undergraduate—accounting and related services; allied health and medical assisting services; business administration, management and operations; business, management, and marketing related; business operations support and assistant services; computer and information sciences and support services related; computer programming; computer systems networking and telecommunications; criminal justice and corrections; culinary arts and related services; dental support services and allied professions; education (specific levels and methods); electromechanical and instrumentation and maintenance technologies; fire protection; health and medical administrative services; heating, air conditioning, ventilation and refrigeration maintenance technology; legal support services; marketing; mechanical engineering related technologies; nursing.
Non-credit—apparel and textiles; business operations support and assistant services; computer software and media applications; crafts, folk art and artisanry; creative writing; criminal justice and corrections; drafting/design engineering technologies; English as a second language; film/video and photographic arts; fire protection; foods, nutrition, and related services; human development, family studies, and related services; languages (foreign languages related); leatherworking and upholstery; real estate; sales, merchandising, and related marketing operations (specialized); woodworking.

BLACK HILLS STATE UNIVERSITY
Spearfish, South Dakota
Extended Services and Instructional Technology
http://www.bhsu.edu/academics/distlrn/
Black Hills State University was founded in 1883. It is accredited by North Central Association of Colleges and Schools. It first offered distance learning courses in 1994. In fall 2006, there were 758 students enrolled in distance learning courses. Institutionally administered financial aid is available to distance learners.
Services Distance learners have accessibility to academic advising, bookstore, campus computer network, career placement assistance, e-mail services, library services.
Contact Sheila R. Aaker, Extended Services Director, Black Hills State University, Extended Services, 1200 University Street, Unit 9508, Spearfish, SD 57799-9508. Telephone: 605-642-6258. Fax: 605-642-6031. E-mail: sheilaaaker@bhsu.edu.

DEGREES AND AWARDS

AA General Studies
Advanced Graduate Diploma Curriculum and Instruction

COURSE SUBJECT AREAS OFFERED OUTSIDE OF DEGREE PROGRAMS

Undergraduate—accounting and computer science; biblical and other theological languages and literatures; business administration, management and operations; business/commerce; business, management, and marketing related; developmental and child psychology; economics; educational psychology; education related; English; English composition; finance and financial management services; fine and studio art; geography and cartography; human resources management; international business; languages (foreign languages related); library science related; marketing; mathematics; psychology; psychology related; social sciences; sociology; technical and business writing.
Graduate—business, management, and marketing related; developmental and child psychology; education; educational assessment, evaluation, and research; educational/instructional media design; education related; hospitality administration.

BLOOMFIELD COLLEGE
Bloomfield, New Jersey
http://www.bloomfield.edu/
Bloomfield College was founded in 1868. It is accredited by Middle States Association of Colleges and Schools. It first offered distance learning courses in 1997. In fall 2006, there were 234 students enrolled in distance learning courses. Institutionally administered financial aid is available to distance learners.
Services Distance learners have accessibility to campus computer network, e-mail services, library services.
Contact Dr. Marion Terenzio, Vice President for Academic Affairs, Bloomfield College, 467 Franklin Street, Bloomfield, NJ 07003. Telephone: 973-748-9000 Ext. 226. Fax: 973-743-3998. E-mail: marion_terenzio@bloomfield.edu.

DEGREES AND AWARDS

Programs offered do not lead to a degree or other formal award.

COURSE SUBJECT AREAS OFFERED OUTSIDE OF DEGREE PROGRAMS

Undergraduate—business administration, management and operations; computer/information technology administration and management; economics; English; history; nursing; psychology; sociology.

BLOOMSBURG UNIVERSITY OF PENNSYLVANIA
Bloomsburg, Pennsylvania
School of Graduate Studies
http://www.bloomu.edu
Bloomsburg University of Pennsylvania was founded in 1839. It is accredited by Middle States Association of Colleges and Schools. It first offered distance learning courses in 1983. In fall 2006, there were 125 students enrolled in distance learning courses. Institutionally administered financial aid is available to distance learners.
Services Distance learners have accessibility to academic advising, bookstore, campus computer network, career placement assistance, e-mail services, library services.
Contact Dr. James Matta, Dean, Bloomsburg University of Pennsylvania, 400 East 2nd Street, Bloomsburg, PA 17815-1301. Telephone: 570-389-4015. Fax: 570-389-3054. E-mail: jmatta@bloomu.edu.

DEGREES AND AWARDS

MS Instructional Technology Education Specialist; Radiologist Assistant

COURSE SUBJECT AREAS OFFERED OUTSIDE OF DEGREE PROGRAMS

Undergraduate—business, management, and marketing related; nursing.
Graduate—business, management, and marketing related; curriculum and instruction; educational/instructional media design.

BOISE STATE UNIVERSITY
Boise, Idaho
Division of Extended Studies
http://www.boisestate.edu/distance
Boise State University was founded in 1932. It is accredited by Northwest Commission on Colleges and Universities. It first offered distance learning courses in 1980. In fall 2006, there were 4,690 students enrolled in distance learning courses. Institutionally administered financial aid is available to distance learners.
Services Distance learners have accessibility to academic advising, bookstore, campus computer network, career placement assistance, e-mail services, library services, tutoring.
Contact Ms. Betty Miller, Distance Education Coordinator, Boise State University, 1910 University Drive, Distance Education Department, Boise, ID 83725-1120. Telephone: 208-426-5622. Fax: 208-426-3467. E-mail: distanceed@boisestate.edu.

DEGREES AND AWARDS

Programs offered do not lead to a degree or other formal award.

COURSE SUBJECT AREAS OFFERED OUTSIDE OF DEGREE PROGRAMS

Undergraduate—accounting and related services; anthropology; behavioral sciences; biological and physical sciences; business, management, and marketing related; chemistry; computer and information sciences and support services related; criminal justice and corrections; curriculum and instruction; economics; education; educational/instructional media design; electrical and electronic engineering technologies; English composition; geological and earth sciences/geosciences; health and medical administrative services; history; human resources management; languages (foreign languages related); languages (Romance languages); mathematics; music; nursing; philosophy; physics; psychology; social work; sociology; technical and business writing; visual and performing arts related.

Graduate—educational/instructional media design; education related; health and medical administrative services; human resources management; management sciences and quantitative methods.

BOISE STATE UNIVERSITY
Boise, Idaho
Department of Educational Technology
http://education.boisestate.edu/edtech2

Boise State University was founded in 1932. It is accredited by Northwest Commission on Colleges and Universities. It first offered distance learning courses in 1999. In fall 2006, there were 220 students enrolled in distance learning courses. Institutionally administered financial aid is available to distance learners.

Services Distance learners have accessibility to academic advising, bookstore, campus computer network, career placement assistance, e-mail services, library services, tutoring.

Contact Jerry Foster, Associate Program Developer, Boise State University, Department of Educational Technology, E-304, 1910 University Drive, Boise, ID 83725-1747. Telephone: 208-426-1966. Fax: 208-426-1451. E-mail: edtech@boisestate.edu.

DEGREES AND AWARDS

Graduate Certificate School Technology Coordination; Teaching–Online Teaching; Technology Integration
MEd Educational Technology–Master of Educational Technology
MS Educational Technology

COURSE SUBJECT AREAS OFFERED OUTSIDE OF DEGREE PROGRAMS

Graduate—computer software and media applications; educational/instructional media design; education related; education (specific subject areas).

BOISE STATE UNIVERSITY
Boise, Idaho
Department of Instructional and Performance Technology
http://ipt.boisestate.edu

Boise State University was founded in 1932. It is accredited by Northwest Commission on Colleges and Universities. It first offered distance learning courses in 1989. In fall 2006, there were 155 students enrolled in distance learning courses. Institutionally administered financial aid is available to distance learners.

Services Distance learners have accessibility to academic advising, bookstore, campus computer network, career placement assistance, e-mail services, library services, tutoring.

Contact Ms. Jo Ann Fenner, Associate Program Developer, Boise State University, Instructional and Performance Technology, 1910 University Drive, ET-327, Boise, ID 83725-2070. Telephone: 208-424-5135. Fax: 208-426-1970. E-mail: bsuipt@boisestate.edu.

DEGREES AND AWARDS

MS Instructional and Performance Technology

COURSE SUBJECT AREAS OFFERED OUTSIDE OF DEGREE PROGRAMS

Graduate—computer software and media applications; curriculum and instruction; educational assessment, evaluation, and research; educational/instructional media design; human resources management.

BOSTON ARCHITECTURAL COLLEGE
Boston, Massachusetts
http://www.the-bac.edu/

Boston Architectural College was founded in 1889. It is accredited by New England Association of Schools and Colleges. It first offered distance learning courses in 2000. In fall 2006, there were 96 students enrolled in distance learning courses. Institutionally administered financial aid is available to distance learners.

Services Distance learners have accessibility to academic advising, e-mail services, library services.

Contact Ms. Maia Brindley-Nilsson, Director of Continuing Education, Boston Architectural College, 320 Newbury Street, Boston, MA 02115. Telephone: 617-585-0101. Fax: 617-585-0121. E-mail: ce@the-bac.edu.

DEGREES AND AWARDS

Programs offered do not lead to a degree or other formal award.

COURSE SUBJECT AREAS OFFERED OUTSIDE OF DEGREE PROGRAMS

Undergraduate—architectural engineering; architectural engineering technology; architectural technology; architecture; architecture related; ecology, evolution, and population biology; environmental design; heating, air conditioning, ventilation and refrigeration maintenance technology; interior architecture.

Graduate—architectural engineering; architectural engineering technology; architectural technology; architecture; architecture related; ecology, evolution, and population biology; environmental design; heating, air conditioning, ventilation and refrigeration maintenance technology; interior architecture.

Non-credit—architectural engineering; architectural engineering technology; architectural technology; architecture; architecture related; ecology, evolution, and population biology; environmental design; heating, air conditioning, ventilation and refrigeration maintenance technology; interior architecture.

BOSTON UNIVERSITY
Boston, Massachusetts
Department of Manufacturing Engineering
http://www.bu.edu/mfg/dlp

Boston University was founded in 1839. It is accredited by New England Association of Schools and Colleges. It first offered distance learning courses in 1989. In fall 2006, there were 20 students enrolled in distance learning courses. Institutionally administered financial aid is available to distance learners.

Services Distance learners have accessibility to academic advising, bookstore, campus computer network, e-mail services, library services, tutoring.

Contact Ms. Sarah Cowen, Distance Learning Administrator, Boston University, Department of Manufacturing Engineering, 15 St. Mary's Street, Brookline, MA 02446. Telephone: 617-353-2943. Fax: 617-353-5548. E-mail: scowen@bu.edu.

DEGREES AND AWARDS

MS Manufacturing Engineering

COURSE SUBJECT AREAS OFFERED OUTSIDE OF DEGREE PROGRAMS

Graduate—electrical, electronics and communications engineering; engineering design; industrial production technologies; management information systems; manufacturing engineering; materials engineering; mechanical engineering related technologies; operations research; systems engineering.

BOWLING GREEN STATE UNIVERSITY
Bowling Green, Ohio
http://ideal.bgsu.edu
Bowling Green State University was founded in 1910. It is accredited by North Central Association of Colleges and Schools. It first offered distance learning courses in 1998. In fall 2006, there were 1,130 students enrolled in distance learning courses. Institutionally administered financial aid is available to distance learners.

Services Distance learners have accessibility to academic advising, bookstore, campus computer network, career placement assistance, e-mail services, library services, tutoring.

Contact Connie Molnar, Director of Distance Learning, Bowling Green State University, 14 College Park, CEE/IDEAL, Bowling Green, OH 43403. Telephone: 419-372-8181. Fax: 419-372-8667. E-mail: cmolnar @bgnet.bgsu.edu.

DEGREES AND AWARDS

BLS Liberal Studies–Bachelor of Liberal Studies Online Degree program

BS Technological Education, advanced

BSN Nursing–RN-to-BSN completion

Graduate Certificate Food and Nutrition; Gifted Education Endorsement; International Scientific and Technical Communication; Ohio Reading Endorsement program; Quality Systems

MBA Executive Master of Organization Development

MEd Assistive Technology specialization

PhD Technology Management

COURSE SUBJECT AREAS OFFERED OUTSIDE OF DEGREE PROGRAMS

Undergraduate—American literature (United States and Canadian); applied mathematics; biology; business/commerce; business, management, and marketing related; communication and media; computer and information sciences; computer programming; computer science; computer software and media applications; computer systems networking and telecommunications; creative writing; educational administration and supervision; educational/instructional media design; educational psychology; English; English composition; English literature (British and Commonwealth); environmental control technologies; environmental/environmental health engineering; ethnic, cultural minority, and gender studies; film/video and photographic arts; foods, nutrition, and related services; geography and cartography; geological and earth sciences/geosciences; health and medical administrative services; history; human development, family studies, and related services; information science/studies; international/global studies; liberal arts and sciences, general studies and humanities; library science related; mathematics; music; nursing; philosophy; philosophy and religious studies related; political science and government; psychology; public health; public relations, advertising, and applied communication related; social sciences; social work; sociology; technical and business writing; technology education/industrial arts.

Graduate—American literature (United States and Canadian); building/construction finishing, management, and inspection; computer software and media applications; construction engineering technology; creative writing; educational assessment, evaluation, and research; English; English literature (British and Commonwealth); foods, nutrition, and related services; gerontology; languages (Romance languages); mathematics; psychology; special education; speech and rhetoric; technical and business writing; technology education/industrial arts.

Non-credit—business/commerce; computer and information sciences and support services related; computer software and media applications; construction trades related; health professions related.

BRADLEY UNIVERSITY
Peoria, Illinois
Division of Continuing Education and Professional Development
http://www.bradley.edu/continue
Bradley University was founded in 1897. It is accredited by North Central Association of Colleges and Schools. It first offered distance learning courses in 1985. In fall 2006, there were 256 students enrolled in distance learning courses. Institutionally administered financial aid is available to distance learners.

Services Distance learners have accessibility to academic advising, bookstore, campus computer network, career placement assistance, e-mail services, library services.

Contact Andy Kindler, Associate Registrar, Bradley University, 1501 West Bradley Avenue, Peoria, IL 61625. Telephone: 309-677-3106. Fax: 309-677-2715. E-mail: akindler@bradley.edu.

DEGREES AND AWARDS
Programs offered do not lead to a degree or other formal award.

COURSE SUBJECT AREAS OFFERED OUTSIDE OF DEGREE PROGRAMS

Undergraduate—business, management, and marketing related; communication and media; computer and information sciences; education; English; family and consumer sciences/human sciences; international business; nursing; psychology; social work; sociology; theological and ministerial studies.

Graduate—education; electrical and electronic engineering technologies; nursing; political science and government.

BRAZOSPORT COLLEGE
Lake Jackson, Texas
http://www.brazosport.edu/
Brazosport College was founded in 1968. It is accredited by Southern Association of Colleges and Schools. It first offered distance learning courses in 1997. In fall 2006, there were 600 students enrolled in distance learning courses. Institutionally administered financial aid is available to distance learners.

Services Distance learners have accessibility to academic advising, bookstore, e-mail services, library services.

Contact Mr. Terry Comingore, Director, Learning Assistance, Distance Learning, and Instructional Media, Brazosport College, 500 College Drive, Lake Jackson, TX 77566. Telephone: 979-230-3318. Fax: 979-230-3443. E-mail: terry.comingore@brazosport.edu.

DEGREES AND AWARDS
Programs offered do not lead to a degree or other formal award.

COURSE SUBJECT AREAS OFFERED OUTSIDE OF DEGREE PROGRAMS

Undergraduate—accounting and related services; chemistry; computer and information sciences; economics; English composition; fine and studio art; geography and cartography; history; mathematics; nutrition sciences; political science and government; psychology.

BRENAU UNIVERSITY
Gainesville, Georgia
Department of Distance Learning
http://online.brenau.edu
Brenau University was founded in 1878. It is accredited by Southern Association of Colleges and Schools. It first offered distance learning courses in 1998. In fall 2006, there were 338 students enrolled in distance learning courses. Institutionally administered financial aid is available to distance learners.

Services Distance learners have accessibility to academic advising, bookstore, career placement assistance, e-mail services, library services, tutoring.

Contact Dr. Heather Snow Gibbons, Director of the Online College, Brenau University, 500 Washington Street, SE, Gainesville, GA 30501. Telephone: 770-718-5327. Fax: 770-718-5329. E-mail: hgibbons@brenau.edu.

DEGREES AND AWARDS

BA Criminal Justice
BBA Management; Marketing
BS Criminal Justice
BSN Nursing–RN to BSN
MBA Accounting; Healthcare Management; Leadership Development; Management Studies, advanced
MEd Early Childhood Education; Middle Grades Education

COURSE SUBJECT AREAS OFFERED OUTSIDE OF DEGREE PROGRAMS

Undergraduate—accounting and related services; allied health and medical assisting services; American literature (United States and Canadian); anthropology; astronomy and astrophysics; business administration, management and operations; business/commerce; business/corporate communications; business, management, and marketing related; business/managerial economics; communication and media; community health services; computer and information sciences; criminal justice and corrections; criminology; curriculum and instruction; design and applied arts; developmental and child psychology; economics; education; educational administration and supervision; educational assessment, evaluation, and research; educational/instructional media design; educational psychology; education related; education (specific levels and methods); education (specific subject areas); English; English composition; English language and literature related; geography and cartography; health/medical preparatory programs; health professions related; history; human development, family studies, and related services; human resources management; information science/studies; international business; journalism; legal studies (non-professional general, undergraduate); liberal arts and sciences, general studies and humanities; linguistic, comparative, and related language studies; management information systems; management sciences and quantitative methods; marketing; mathematics; mathematics and statistics related; museum studies; music; nursing; peace studies and conflict resolution; pharmacology and toxicology; philosophy; political science and government; psychology; psychology related; public administration; public administration and social service professions related; public relations, advertising, and applied communication related; sales, merchandising, and related marketing operations (specialized); social and philosophical foundations of education; social sciences; sociology; special education; statistics; taxation; technical and business writing; visual and performing arts related.

Graduate—accounting and related services; allied health diagnostic, intervention, and treatment professions; business administration, management and operations; business/commerce; business/corporate communications; business, management, and marketing related; business/managerial economics; computer and information sciences; economics; education; educational administration and supervision; educational assessment, evaluation, and research; educational psychology; education related; finance and financial management services; health and medical administrative services; health professions related; international business; management information systems; management sciences and quantitative methods; marketing; nursing; rehabilitation and therapeutic professions; sales, merchandising, and related marketing operations (general); sales, merchandising, and related marketing operations (specialized); taxation.

See full description on page 320.

BRIDGEWATER STATE COLLEGE
Bridgewater, Massachusetts
Distance Learning and Technology Programs
http://www.bridgew.edu/distance

Bridgewater State College was founded in 1840. It is accredited by New England Association of Schools and Colleges. It first offered distance learning courses in 1996. In fall 2006, there were 800 students enrolled in distance learning courses. Institutionally administered financial aid is available to distance learners.

Services Distance learners have accessibility to bookstore, campus computer network, e-mail services, library services.

Contact Dr. Mary W. Fuller, EdD, Director of Continuing and Distance Education, Bridgewater State College, John Joseph Moakley Center for Technological Applications, Burrill Avenue, Bridgewater, MA 02325. Telephone: 508-531-6145. Fax: 508-531-6121. E-mail: mfuller@bridgew.edu.

DEGREES AND AWARDS

Programs offered do not lead to a degree or other formal award.

COURSE SUBJECT AREAS OFFERED OUTSIDE OF DEGREE PROGRAMS

Undergraduate—anthropology; business/corporate communications; business/managerial economics; communication and media; communication disorders sciences and services; computer/information technology administration and management; criminology; curriculum and instruction; education; educational administration and supervision; educational assessment, evaluation, and research; English composition; entrepreneurial and small business operations; ethnic, cultural minority, and gender studies; geography and cartography; geological and earth sciences/geosciences; history; music; political science and government; psychology; sociology; special education; technical and business writing.

Graduate—communication and media; economics; educational administration and supervision; linguistic, comparative, and related language studies; psychology; special education.

Non-credit—accounting and related services; allied health and medical assisting services; business administration, management and operations; business/commerce; business, management, and marketing related; business/managerial economics; business operations support and assistant services; communication and media; computer systems analysis; creative writing; finance and financial management services; health and medical administrative services; information science/studies; sales, merchandising, and related marketing operations (specialized).

BRIERCREST DISTANCE LEARNING
Caronport, Saskatchewan, Canada
http://www.briercrest.ca/bdl/

Briercrest Distance Learning was founded in 1980. It is provincially chartered. It first offered distance learning courses in 1981. In fall 2006, there were 648 students enrolled in distance learning courses. Institutionally administered financial aid is available to distance learners.

Services Distance learners have accessibility to academic advising, bookstore, career placement assistance, library services, tutoring.

Contact Kevin Weeks, Admissions Coordinator, Briercrest Distance Learning, 510 College Drive, Caronport, SK S0H 0S0, Canada. Telephone: 800-667-5199. Fax: 800-667-2329. E-mail: distanceinfo@briercrest.ca.

DEGREES AND AWARDS

AA Christian Studies
BA Christian Studies
Certificate Bible; Seminary

COURSE SUBJECT AREAS OFFERED OUTSIDE OF DEGREE PROGRAMS

Undergraduate—biblical and other theological languages and literatures; biblical studies; counseling psychology; creative writing; English language and literature related; ethnic, cultural minority, and gender studies; history; liberal arts and sciences, general studies and humanities; missionary studies and missiology; pastoral counseling and specialized ministries; religious education; religious studies; theological and ministerial studies; theology and religious vocations related.

Graduate—biblical and other theological languages and literatures; biblical studies; history; religious education; religious studies; theological and ministerial studies; theology and religious vocations related.

Non-credit—biblical studies; history; religious studies.

BRISTOL COMMUNITY COLLEGE
Fall River, Massachusetts
Distance Learning
http://dl.mass.edu

Bristol Community College was founded in 1965. It is accredited by New England Association of Schools and Colleges. It first offered distance learning courses in 1990. In fall 2006, there were 850 students enrolled in distance learning courses. Institutionally administered financial aid is available to distance learners.

Services Distance learners have accessibility to academic advising, bookstore, campus computer network, e-mail services, library services, tutoring.

Contact April Bellafiore, Director of Distance Learning, Bristol Community College, 777 Elsbree Street, Fall River, MA 02720. Telephone: 508-678-2811 Ext. 2387. E-mail: abellafi@bristol.mass.edu.

DEGREES AND AWARDS

AS Computer Information Systems/Computer Programming; Computer Information Systems/Multimedia and Internet

Certificate Computer Programming; Desktop Publishing Technology; Information Technology Fluency; Multimedia Communications; Web Page Development, basic

COURSE SUBJECT AREAS OFFERED OUTSIDE OF DEGREE PROGRAMS

Undergraduate—accounting and related services; business/commerce; computer and information sciences; computer and information sciences and support services related; computer/information technology administration and management; computer programming; computer science; computer software and media applications; computer systems analysis; computer systems networking and telecommunications; data entry/microcomputer applications; data processing; English composition; English literature (British and Commonwealth); geography and cartography; history; information science/studies; management information systems; mathematics; mathematics and statistics related; psychology; psychology related; social sciences related; sociology; statistics; technical and business writing.

Non-credit—accounting and related services; business administration, management and operations; business/commerce; business/corporate communications; business, management, and marketing related; business operations support and assistant services; communication and journalism related; communication and media; computer and information sciences; computer and information sciences and support services related; computer engineering; computer/information technology administration and management; computer programming; computer science; computer software and media applications; computer systems analysis; computer systems networking and telecommunications; data entry/microcomputer applications; data processing; electrical and electronic engineering technologies; electrical and power transmission installation; electrical, electronics and communications engineering; electrical/electronics maintenance and repair technology; electromechanical and instrumentation and maintenance technologies; engineering/industrial management; engineering-related technologies; engineering technologies related; ground transportation; human resources management; information science/studies; management information systems; management sciences and quantitative methods; marketing; mathematics; mechanical engineering related technologies; mechanic and repair technologies related; precision production related; sales, merchandising, and related marketing operations (general); sales, merchandising, and related marketing operations (specialized); systems engineering; technology education/industrial arts; vehicle maintenance and repair technologies.

BROCK UNIVERSITY
St. Catharines, Ontario, Canada
Centre for Adult Studies and Distance Learning, Faculty of Education
http://adult.ed.brocku.ca

Brock University was founded in 1964. It is provincially chartered. It first offered distance learning courses in 1993. In fall 2006, there were 500 students enrolled in distance learning courses. Institutionally administered financial aid is available to distance learners.

Services Distance learners have accessibility to academic advising, bookstore, campus computer network, career placement assistance, e-mail services, library services, tutoring.

Contact Sandra Plavinskis, Coordinator of B.Ed. in Adult Education Degree and Certificate Programs, Brock University, Centre for Adult Education and Community Outreach, Faculty of Education, St. Catharines, ON L2S 3A1, Canada. Telephone: 905-688-5550 Ext. 4308. Fax: 905-984-4842. E-mail: adulted@brocku.ca.

DEGREES AND AWARDS

BEd Adult Education (BEd in Adult Education)
Certificate Adult Education

COURSE SUBJECT AREAS OFFERED OUTSIDE OF DEGREE PROGRAMS

Undergraduate—education; education related.

BROOKDALE COMMUNITY COLLEGE
Lincroft, New Jersey
Telecourse Program–Division of Arts and Communication
http://www.brookdalecc.edu

Brookdale Community College was founded in 1967. It is accredited by Middle States Association of Colleges and Schools. It first offered distance learning courses in 1974. In fall 2006, there were 1,000 students enrolled in distance learning courses. Institutionally administered financial aid is available to distance learners.

Services Distance learners have accessibility to bookstore, campus computer network, e-mail services, library services, tutoring.

Contact Norah Kerr-McCurry, Director, Brookdale Community College, Distance Education Applications, 765 Newman Springs Road, Lincroft, NJ 07738. Telephone: 732-224-2089. Fax: 732-224-2001. E-mail: nmccurry@brookdalecc.edu.

DEGREES AND AWARDS

AA Business Administration; Liberal Arts; Psychology; Social Sciences

COURSE SUBJECT AREAS OFFERED OUTSIDE OF DEGREE PROGRAMS

Undergraduate—accounting and related services; American literature (United States and Canadian); anthropology; biology; business administration, management and operations; chemistry; creative writing; developmental and child psychology; dramatic/theater arts and stagecraft; English; English composition; marketing; mathematics; philosophy and religious studies related; social psychology; social sciences related; sociology.

BROOME COMMUNITY COLLEGE
Binghamton, New York
http://www.sunybroome.edu/

Broome Community College was founded in 1946. It is accredited by Middle States Association of Colleges and Schools. It first offered distance learning courses in 1998. In fall 2006, there were 936 students enrolled in distance learning courses. Institutionally administered financial aid is available to distance learners.

Services Distance learners have accessibility to academic advising, bookstore, campus computer network, career placement assistance, e-mail services, library services, tutoring.

Contact Martin J. Guzzi, Registrar, Broome Community College, PO Box 1017, Binghamton, NY 13902. Telephone: 607-778-5527. Fax: 607-778-5294. E-mail: guzzi_m@sunybroome.edu.

DEGREES AND AWARDS

AAS Computer Technology; Early Childhood; Medical Lab Technology
AS Human Services; Liberal Arts–General Studies

COURSE SUBJECT AREAS OFFERED OUTSIDE OF DEGREE PROGRAMS

Undergraduate—anthropology; biology; business/commerce; computer science; English composition; health professions related; history; nursing; physical sciences; psychology; social sciences; sociology.

BRYANT AND STRATTON ONLINE
Lackawanna, New York
http://www.bryantstratton.edu

Bryant and Stratton Online is accredited by Middle States Association of Colleges and Schools. It first offered distance learning courses in 1997. In fall 2006, there were 750 students enrolled in distance learning courses. Institutionally administered financial aid is available to distance learners.
Services Distance learners have accessibility to academic advising, bookstore, e-mail services, library services, tutoring.
Contact Admissions, Bryant and Stratton Online, Sterling Park, 200 Redtail, Orchard Park, NY 14127. Telephone: 716-677-8800 Ext. 241. Fax: 716-677-8899. E-mail: online@bryantstratton.edu.

DEGREES AND AWARDS

AD Accounting Online; Business Online; Information Technology Online; Paralegal Online

COURSE SUBJECT AREAS OFFERED OUTSIDE OF DEGREE PROGRAMS

Undergraduate—accounting and related services; business administration, management and operations; business/commerce; business/corporate communications; computer/information technology administration and management; computer programming; computer software and media applications; computer systems networking and telecommunications; legal support services.

BUENA VISTA UNIVERSITY
Storm Lake, Iowa
Centers
http://centers.bvu.edu

Buena Vista University was founded in 1891. It is accredited by North Central Association of Colleges and Schools. It first offered distance learning courses in 1975. In fall 2006, there were 1,378 students enrolled in distance learning courses. Institutionally administered financial aid is available to distance learners.
Services Distance learners have accessibility to academic advising, bookstore, campus computer network, career placement assistance, e-mail services, library services.
Contact Marge Welch, Associate Dean for Centers Programs, Buena Vista University, 610 West 4th Street, Storm Lake, IA 50588. Telephone: 712-749-2250. Fax: 712-749-1470. E-mail: welchm@bvu.edu.

DEGREES AND AWARDS

BA Business; Elementary Education; English; History; Information Management; Political Science–Criminal Justice; Social Sciences
Certification Education–Middle School Education; Education–Secondary Education; Special Education–Instructional Specialist I
MSE Guidance and Counseling–School Guidance and Counseling

COURSE SUBJECT AREAS OFFERED OUTSIDE OF DEGREE PROGRAMS

Undergraduate—accounting and related services; business administration, management and operations; business/commerce; business, management, and marketing related; criminal justice and corrections; criminology; education; education related; education (specific levels and methods); education (specific subject areas); English; entrepreneurial and small business operations; finance and financial management services; health and medical administrative services; history; human services;

management information systems; political science and government; psychology; psychology related; social sciences; social sciences related; sociology; special education.
Graduate—education related.

BUENA VISTA UNIVERSITY
Storm Lake, Iowa
Master of Education
http://www.bvu.edu/

Buena Vista University was founded in 1891. It is accredited by North Central Association of Colleges and Schools. It first offered distance learning courses in 2004. In fall 2006, there were 196 students enrolled in distance learning courses. Institutionally administered financial aid is available to distance learners.
Services Distance learners have accessibility to academic advising, bookstore, campus computer network, career placement assistance, e-mail services, library services, tutoring.
Contact Laura Harris, BVU Online, Buena Vista University, 610 West 4th Street, Storm Lake, IA 50588. Telephone: 712-749-1893. Fax: 712-749-1241. E-mail: harrisl@bvu.edu.

DEGREES AND AWARDS

MEd Curriculum and Instruction–Effective Teaching and Instructional Leadership emphasis; Curriculum and Instruction–Teaching English as a Second Language emphasis

COURSE SUBJECT AREAS OFFERED OUTSIDE OF DEGREE PROGRAMS

Undergraduate—accounting and related services; business administration, management and operations; business/commerce; business/corporate communications; business, management, and marketing related; business/managerial economics; communication and journalism related; communication and media; criminal justice and corrections; curriculum and instruction; education; English; English composition; finance and financial management services; marketing; political science and government; psychology.
Graduate—curriculum and instruction; education; English as a second/foreign language (teaching).

BUFFALO STATE COLLEGE, STATE UNIVERSITY OF NEW YORK
Buffalo, New York
http://www.buffalostate.edu/offices/elearning

Buffalo State College, State University of New York was founded in 1867. It is accredited by Middle States Association of Colleges and Schools. It first offered distance learning courses in 1998. In fall 2006, there were 224 students enrolled in distance learning courses. Institutionally administered financial aid is available to distance learners.
Services Distance learners have accessibility to academic advising, bookstore, career placement assistance, e-mail services, library services.
Contact Meghan Pereira, Instructional Technology Specialist, Buffalo State College, State University of New York, 1300 Elmwood Avenue, BC 113, Buffalo, NY 14222. Telephone: 716-878-3877. Fax: 716-878-3131. E-mail: pereirme@buffalostate.edu.

DEGREES AND AWARDS

CAGS Adult Education; Creative Studies; Human Resource Development
MS Adult Education; Creative Studies

COURSE SUBJECT AREAS OFFERED OUTSIDE OF DEGREE PROGRAMS

Undergraduate—business, management, and marketing related; communication and media; computer science; education; education related; history; political science and government.
Graduate—education related.

BURLINGTON COUNTY COLLEGE
Pemberton, New Jersey
Distance Learning Office
http://www.bcc.edu/

Burlington County College was founded in 1966. It is accredited by Middle States Association of Colleges and Schools. It first offered distance learning courses in 1978. In fall 2006, there were 1,550 students enrolled in distance learning courses. Institutionally administered financial aid is available to distance learners.

Services Distance learners have accessibility to academic advising, bookstore, e-mail services, library services, tutoring.

Contact Kathleen Devone, Coordinator of Distance Learning, Burlington County College, 601 Pemberton-Browns Mills Road, Pemberton, NJ 08068. Telephone: 609-894-9311 Ext. 1790. Fax: 609-894-4189. E-mail: kdevone@bcc.edu.

DEGREES AND AWARDS

AA Liberal Arts

AAS Liberal Arts and Sciences

AS Business Management

COURSE SUBJECT AREAS OFFERED OUTSIDE OF DEGREE PROGRAMS

Undergraduate—anthropology; biology; developmental and child psychology; ecology, evolution, and population biology; English composition; film/video and photographic arts; fine and studio art; history; languages (Romance languages); marketing; sociology; statistics.

BUTLER COMMUNITY COLLEGE
El Dorado, Kansas
http://www.butlercc.edu/

Butler Community College was founded in 1927. It is accredited by North Central Association of Colleges and Schools. It first offered distance learning courses in 1998. In fall 2006, there were 1,800 students enrolled in distance learning courses. Institutionally administered financial aid is available to distance learners.

Services Distance learners have accessibility to academic advising, bookstore, e-mail services, library services, tutoring.

Contact Ms. Meg McGranaghan, Director, Instructional Technology, Butler Community College, 901 South Haverhill Road, El Dorado, KS 67042. Telephone: 316-322-3345. Fax: 316-322-3315. E-mail: megmcg@butlercc.edu.

DEGREES AND AWARDS

AA History; Liberal Arts; Philosophy and Religion

AAS Marketing and Management

AGS Liberal Arts

AS History; Liberal Arts; Software Development

COURSE SUBJECT AREAS OFFERED OUTSIDE OF DEGREE PROGRAMS

Undergraduate—accounting and related services; allied health and medical assisting services; applied mathematics; astronomy and astrophysics; behavioral sciences; business, management, and marketing related; chemistry; computer programming; criminal justice and corrections; criminology; data entry/microcomputer applications; developmental and child psychology; drafting/design engineering technologies; economics; English composition; fine and studio art; gerontology; health and physical education/fitness; health professions related; history; human development, family studies, and related services; human resources management; marketing; mathematics; mathematics and statistics related; music; nursing; nutrition sciences; philosophy; philosophy and religious studies related; physical sciences; physical sciences related; physics; political science and government; psychology; social sciences; social sciences related; sociology; speech and rhetoric.

Non-credit—nursing.

BUTLER COUNTY COMMUNITY COLLEGE
Butler, Pennsylvania
http://www.bc3.edu/distlearn

Butler County Community College was founded in 1965. It is accredited by Middle States Association of Colleges and Schools. It first offered distance learning courses in 1998. In fall 2006, there were 600 students enrolled in distance learning courses. Institutionally administered financial aid is available to distance learners.

Services Distance learners have accessibility to academic advising, bookstore, career placement assistance, e-mail services, library services, tutoring.

Contact Deborah Ayers, Dean of Educational Technology, Butler County Community College, PO Box 1203, Butler, PA 16003. Telephone: 888-826-2829 Ext. 8279. E-mail: deborah.ayers@bc3.edu.

DEGREES AND AWARDS

AA General Studies

COURSE SUBJECT AREAS OFFERED OUTSIDE OF DEGREE PROGRAMS

Undergraduate—accounting and related services; allied health and medical assisting services; applied mathematics; biology; botany/plant biology; business administration, management and operations; business, management, and marketing related; chemistry; communication and media; computer programming; computer science; computer systems networking and telecommunications; creative writing; criminology; data entry/microcomputer applications; economics; education; educational psychology; English composition; finance and financial management services; fire protection; foods, nutrition, and related services; health and physical education/fitness; history; human resources management; marketing; mathematics; music; philosophy; philosophy and religious studies related; political science and government; psychology; sociology; technical and business writing.

CABRILLO COLLEGE
Aptos, California
Instruction, Transfer and Distance Education
http://www.cabrillo.edu/

Cabrillo College was founded in 1959. It is accredited by Western Association of Schools and Colleges. It first offered distance learning courses in 1994. In fall 2006, there were 3,232 students enrolled in distance learning courses. Institutionally administered financial aid is available to distance learners.

Services Distance learners have accessibility to academic advising, bookstore, career placement assistance, e-mail services, library services, tutoring.

Contact Francine Van Meter, Director, Teaching and Learning Center, Cabrillo College, 6500 Soquel Drive, Aptos, CA 95003. Telephone: 831-479-6191. Fax: 831-479-5721. E-mail: frvanmet@cabrillo.edu.

DEGREES AND AWARDS
Programs offered do not lead to a degree or other formal award.

COURSE SUBJECT AREAS OFFERED OUTSIDE OF DEGREE PROGRAMS

Undergraduate—accounting and computer science; accounting and related services; allied health and medical assisting services; anthropology; biological and biomedical sciences related; biological and physical sciences; business/commerce; cell biology and anatomical sciences; communication and journalism related; computer and information sciences; computer science; criminal justice and corrections; culinary arts and related services; English; English composition; film/video and photographic arts; fire protection; foods, nutrition, and related services; geography and cartography; geological and earth sciences/geosciences; health professions related; history; journalism; languages (Romance languages); legal studies (non-professional general, undergraduate); library science related; mathematics; music; philosophy; philosophy and religious studies related; physical sciences; real estate; sociology; visual and performing arts related.

CALDWELL COMMUNITY COLLEGE AND TECHNICAL INSTITUTE
Hudson, North Carolina
http://www.cccti.edu

Caldwell Community College and Technical Institute was founded in 1964. It is accredited by Southern Association of Colleges and Schools. It first offered distance learning courses in 1989. In fall 2006, there were 1,200 students enrolled in distance learning courses. Institutionally administered financial aid is available to distance learners.

Services Distance learners have accessibility to academic advising, bookstore, career placement assistance, e-mail services, library services, tutoring.

Contact Jennifer S. Sime, Director, Distance Learning, Caldwell Community College and Technical Institute, 2855 Hickory Boulevard, Hudson, NC 28638-2397. Telephone: 828-726-2707. Fax: 828-759-4632. E-mail: jsime@cccti.edu.

DEGREES AND AWARDS
Programs offered do not lead to a degree or other formal award.

COURSE SUBJECT AREAS OFFERED OUTSIDE OF DEGREE PROGRAMS
Undergraduate—accounting and related services; biological and biomedical sciences related; biological and physical sciences; biology; business administration, management and operations; business/commerce; business/corporate communications; business operations support and assistant services; communication and media; computer and information sciences; educational psychology; English; English composition; fine and studio art; fire protection; history; human development, family studies, and related services; liberal arts and sciences, general studies and humanities; marketing; mathematics; music; physical sciences; psychology; social sciences; sociology; technical and business writing.
Non-credit—accounting and related services; business administration, management and operations; business/corporate communications; business/managerial economics; business operations support and assistant services; computer and information sciences and support services related; computer/information technology administration and management; computer software and media applications; creative writing; criminal justice and corrections; finance and financial management services; health/medical preparatory programs; linguistic, comparative, and related language studies; peace studies and conflict resolution; sales, merchandising, and related marketing operations (specialized); technical and business writing.

CALIFORNIA INSTITUTE OF INTEGRAL STUDIES
San Francisco, California
Transformative Studies
http://www.ciis.edu

California Institute of Integral Studies was founded in 1968. It is accredited by Western Association of Schools and Colleges. It first offered distance learning courses in 1993. In fall 2006, there were 150 students enrolled in distance learning courses. Institutionally administered financial aid is available to distance learners.

Services Distance learners have accessibility to academic advising, bookstore, campus computer network, e-mail services, library services.

Contact Ms. Allyson Werner, Admissions Counselor for the School of Consciousness and Transformation, California Institute of Integral Studies, 1453 Mission Street, San Francisco, CA 94103. Telephone: 415-575-6155. Fax: 415-575-1268. E-mail: awerner@ciis.edu.

DEGREES AND AWARDS
MA Transformative Leadership
PhD Transformative Studies

COURSE SUBJECT AREAS OFFERED OUTSIDE OF DEGREE PROGRAMS
Graduate—area studies; community organization and advocacy; ecology, evolution, and population biology; ethnic, cultural minority, and gender studies; philosophy and religious studies related; religious studies; sociology.

Non-credit—area studies; community organization and advocacy; ecology, evolution, and population biology; ethnic, cultural minority, and gender studies; philosophy and religious studies related; religious studies; sociology.

See full description on page 322.

CALIFORNIA STATE UNIVERSITY, CHICO
Chico, California
Center for Regional and Continuing Education
http://rce.csuchico.edu/online

California State University, Chico was founded in 1887. It is accredited by Western Association of Schools and Colleges. It first offered distance learning courses in 1975. In fall 2006, there were 850 students enrolled in distance learning courses. Institutionally administered financial aid is available to distance learners.

Services Distance learners have accessibility to academic advising, bookstore, campus computer network, e-mail services, library services, tutoring.

Contact Mr. Jeffrey S. Layne, Program Director, California State University, Chico, Chico, CA 95929-0250. Telephone: 530-898-6105. Fax: 530-898-4020. E-mail: jlayne@csuchico.edu.

DEGREES AND AWARDS
BA Liberal Studies; Social Science
BS Computer Science
BSN Nursing
MN Nursing
MS Computer Science

COURSE SUBJECT AREAS OFFERED OUTSIDE OF DEGREE PROGRAMS
Undergraduate—agriculture; area, ethnic, cultural, and gender studies related; behavioral sciences; community health services; curriculum and instruction; dance; education; English; ethnic, cultural minority, and gender studies; geography and cartography; health and medical administrative services; history; human development, family studies, and related services; legal professions and studies related; legal studies (non-professional general, undergraduate); liberal arts and sciences, general studies and humanities; neuroscience; nursing; psychology; religious studies; social sciences; sociology.
Graduate—computer science; nursing.

CALIFORNIA STATE UNIVERSITY, DOMINGUEZ HILLS
Carson, California
Distance Learning
http://dominguezonline.csudh.edu

California State University, Dominguez Hills was founded in 1960. It is accredited by Western Association of Schools and Colleges. It first offered distance learning courses in 1974. In fall 2006, there were 4,000 students enrolled in distance learning courses. Institutionally administered financial aid is available to distance learners.

Services Distance learners have accessibility to academic advising, bookstore, campus computer network, e-mail services, library services, tutoring.

Contact Registration Department, California State University, Dominguez Hills, College of Extended and International Education, 1000 East Victoria Street, Carson, CA 90747. Telephone: 877-GO-HILLS. Fax: 310-516-3971. E-mail: eeinfo@csudh.edu.

DEGREES AND AWARDS
BS Applied Studies; Nursing Completion program; Quality Assurance
Certificate of Completion Quality Assurance
Certificate Assistive Technology; Community College Teaching; Production and Inventory Control; Purchasing
CCCPE Administrative Medical Specialist with Medical Billing and coding certificate; Advanced Coding for the Physician's Office Certificate; Advanced Hospital Coding and CCS Prep; Medical Billing and

Coding certificate; Medical Transcription certificate; Paralegal Certificate; Technical Writing certificate
MA Humanities; Negotiation, Conflict Resolution and Peacebuilding
MBA Business Administration
MPA Master of Public Administration
MS Nursing; Quality Assurance
MSEM Master of Science Engineering Management

COURSE SUBJECT AREAS OFFERED OUTSIDE OF DEGREE PROGRAMS

Undergraduate—biology; education; educational administration and supervision; education related; landscape architecture; music; physics.
Non-credit—accounting and related services; alternative and complementary medicine and medical systems; business/corporate communications; business, management, and marketing related; communication and journalism related; computer and information sciences; computer/ information technology administration and management; design and applied arts; dietetics and clinical nutrition services; education; educational administration and supervision; film/video and photographic arts; finance and financial management services; fine and studio art; gerontology; graphic communications; health and medical administrative services; history; human resources management; mathematics; museum studies; music; personal and culinary services related; psychology related; quality control and safety technologies; sales, merchandising, and related marketing operations (general); sales, merchandising, and related marketing operations (specialized).

See full description on page 324.

CALIFORNIA STATE UNIVERSITY, EAST BAY
Hayward, California
Division of Continuing and International Education
http://www.online.csuhayward.edu

California State University, East Bay was founded in 1957. It is accredited by Western Association of Schools and Colleges. It first offered distance learning courses in 1998. In fall 2006, there were 200 students enrolled in distance learning courses. Institutionally administered financial aid is available to distance learners.
Services Distance learners have accessibility to academic advising, bookstore, campus computer network, e-mail services, library services.
Contact Dr. Nan Chico, Graduate Coordinator, MS Ed. (Option Online Teaching and Learning), California State University, East Bay, College of Education and Allied Studies, Interdisciplinary Education, Hayward, CA 94542. Telephone: 510-885-4384. Fax: 510-885-4498. E-mail: nan. chico@csueastbay.edu.

DEGREES AND AWARDS
Certificate Teaching and Learning–Online Teaching and Learning
MSE Online Teaching and Learning; Teaching and Learning–Option in Online Teaching and Learning

COURSE SUBJECT AREAS OFFERED OUTSIDE OF DEGREE PROGRAMS
Undergraduate—biomedical/medical engineering; computer software and media applications; engineering/industrial management; fine and studio art; hospitality administration; human development, family studies, and related services.
Graduate—biomathematics and bioinformatics; education related.

CALIFORNIA STATE UNIVERSITY, MONTEREY BAY
Seaside, California
http://csumb.edu/online

California State University, Monterey Bay was founded in 1994. It is accredited by Western Association of Schools and Colleges. It first offered distance learning courses in 2000. In fall 2006, there were 625 students enrolled in distance learning courses. Institutionally administered financial aid is available to distance learners.
Services Distance learners have accessibility to academic advising, bookstore, campus computer network, e-mail services, library services, tutoring.

Contact Monique Rutland, Administrative Assistant to the Provost, California State University, Monterey Bay, Office of the Provost, Seaside, CA 93955. Telephone: 831-582-4401. E-mail: monique_rutland@ csumb.edu.

DEGREES AND AWARDS
BA Liberal Studies degree completion

COURSE SUBJECT AREAS OFFERED OUTSIDE OF DEGREE PROGRAMS
Undergraduate—business administration, management and operations; computer and information sciences; computer software and media applications; education; educational/instructional media design; entrepreneurial and small business operations; ethnic, cultural, minority, and gender studies; geological and earth sciences/geosciences; international business; linguistic, comparative, and related language studies; marketing; sales, merchandising, and related marketing operations (general); social and philosophical foundations of education; special education.
Non-credit—computer and information sciences and support services related.

CALIFORNIA STATE UNIVERSITY, SACRAMENTO
Sacramento, California
College of Business Administration

California State University, Sacramento was founded in 1947. It is accredited by Western Association of Schools and Colleges. It first offered distance learning courses in 2004. In fall 2006, there were 80 students enrolled in distance learning courses. Institutionally administered financial aid is available to distance learners.
Services Distance learners have accessibility to academic advising, bookstore, campus computer network, career placement assistance, e-mail services, library services.
Contact Nancy J. Thompson, Director, California State University, Sacramento, Tahoe Hall 1039, Sacramento, CA 95819-6088. Telephone: 916-278-2894. Fax: 916-278-4233. E-mail: thompsonn@csus.edu.

DEGREES AND AWARDS
M Tax MSBA/Taxation
MS Accountancy
See full description on page 326.

CALIFORNIA STATE UNIVERSITY, SAN BERNARDINO
San Bernardino, California
http://www.csusb.edu/

California State University, San Bernardino was founded in 1965. It is accredited by Western Association of Schools and Colleges. It first offered distance learning courses in 1988. In fall 2006, there were 7,000 students enrolled in distance learning courses. Institutionally administered financial aid is available to distance learners.
Services Distance learners have accessibility to academic advising, bookstore, e-mail services, library services.
Contact Dr. James Michael Monaghan, Director, Office of Distributed Learning, California State University, San Bernardino, 5500 University Parkway, San Bernardino, CA 92407. Telephone: 909-537-7439. Fax: 909-537-7637. E-mail: monaghan@csusb.edu.

DEGREES AND AWARDS
BSN Nursing–Online RN to BSN program
MPA MPA Online

COURSE SUBJECT AREAS OFFERED OUTSIDE OF DEGREE PROGRAMS
Undergraduate—accounting and computer science; accounting and related services; Air Force J.R.O.T.C/R.O.T.C; allied health and medical assisting services; American literature (United States and Canadian); area, ethnic, cultural, and gender studies related; astronomy and astrophysics; bilingual, multilingual, and multicultural education; business administration, management and operations; business, management, and

marketing related; clinical child psychology; cognitive psychology and psycholinguistics; communication and journalism related; communication and media; communications technology; community health services; criminal justice and corrections; economics; education; educational/instructional media design; education related; education (specific subject areas); English; ethnic, cultural minority, and gender studies; finance and financial management services; languages (foreign languages related); liberal arts and sciences, general studies and humanities; mathematics; multi-/interdisciplinary studies related; nursing; political science and government; psychology; social work; visual and performing arts.
Graduate—allied health diagnostic, intervention, and treatment professions; communication and media; communications technology; criminal justice and corrections; education; educational/instructional media design; education (specific subject areas); public administration.
Non-credit—education related.

CALIFORNIA STATE UNIVERSITY, SAN MARCOS
San Marcos, California
Extended Studies
http://www.csusm.edu/es
California State University, San Marcos was founded in 1990. It is accredited by Western Association of Schools and Colleges. It first offered distance learning courses in 1997. In fall 2006, there were 250 students enrolled in distance learning courses. Institutionally administered financial aid is available to distance learners.
Services Distance learners have accessibility to academic advising, bookstore, campus computer network, career placement assistance, e-mail services, library services, tutoring.
Contact Ms. Veronica Martinelli, Credit Programs Coordinator, California State University, San Marcos, 333 South Twin Oaks Valley Road, San Marcos, CA 92096. Telephone: 760-750-8717. Fax: 760-750-3138. E-mail: vmartine@csusm.edu.

DEGREES AND AWARDS
BSN Accelerated Program
Certificate Biotechnology Laboratory Technician; Construction Supervision; Paralegal Studies; Preparation for Clinical Nurse Faculty certificate

COURSE SUBJECT AREAS OFFERED OUTSIDE OF DEGREE PROGRAMS
Undergraduate—accounting and computer science; allied health and medical assisting services; applied mathematics; business administration, management and operations; business operations support and assistant services; computer and information sciences and support services related; computer programming; education (specific subject areas); mathematics; social work.
Graduate—education related; education (specific subject areas).
Non-credit—accounting and computer science; business/commerce; communication and journalism related; community health services; comparative literature; computer and information sciences; dramatic/theater arts and stagecraft; English as a second language; family and consumer economics; fine and studio art; health/medical preparatory programs; health services/allied health/health sciences; languages (foreign languages related); mathematics; nursing; philosophy; psychology related; work and family studies.

CALIFORNIA UNIVERSITY OF PENNSYLVANIA
California, Pennsylvania
http://www.cup.edu/graduate
California University of Pennsylvania was founded in 1852. It is accredited by Middle States Association of Colleges and Schools. It first offered distance learning courses in 2004. In fall 2006, there were 1,100 students enrolled in distance learning courses. Institutionally administered financial aid is available to distance learners.
Services Distance learners have accessibility to academic advising, bookstore, campus computer network, career placement assistance, e-mail services, library services.

Contact Ms. Millie Rodriguez, Director, Office of Web Based Programs, California University of Pennsylvania, School of Graduate Studies and Research, 250 University Avenue, California, PA 15419. Telephone: 724-938-5958. Fax: 724-938-4270. E-mail: rodriguez@cup.edu.

DEGREES AND AWARDS
BS Science and Technology Legal Studies option; Sport Management Studies–Wellness and Fitness track
Certification Administrative Principals program; Superintendent's Letter of Eligibility
MA Tourism Planning and Development
MAT Secondary Education, advanced studies
MEd Administrative Principal program
MS Exercise Science and Health Promotion–Performance Enhancement and Injury Prevention; Exercise Science and Health Promotion–Rehabilitation Sciences; Exercise Science and Health Promotion–Sports Psychology; Exercise Science and Health Promotion–Wellness and Fitness; Legal Studies–Homeland Security; Legal Studies–Law and Public Policy; Sport Management Studies

COURSE SUBJECT AREAS OFFERED OUTSIDE OF DEGREE PROGRAMS
Undergraduate—applied mathematics; business administration, management and operations; criminal justice and corrections; dramatic/theater arts and stagecraft; education; geological and earth sciences/geosciences; health and physical education/fitness; industrial production technologies; music; philosophy; philosophy and religious studies related; psychology; sociology; technology education/industrial arts.
Graduate—criminal justice and corrections; educational administration and supervision; health and physical education/fitness; health professions related; legal research and advanced professional studies; public administration.

CAMPBELLSVILLE UNIVERSITY
Campbellsville, Kentucky
http://www.campbellsville.edu/
Campbellsville University was founded in 1906. It is accredited by Southern Association of Colleges and Schools. It first offered distance learning courses in 1999. In fall 2006, there were 188 students enrolled in distance learning courses. Institutionally administered financial aid is available to distance learners.
Services Distance learners have accessibility to academic advising, bookstore, campus computer network, career placement assistance, e-mail services, library services.
Contact Ms. Karla Deaton, Coordinator of Academic Outreach, Campbellsville University, 1 University Drive, Campbellsville, KY 42718-2799. Telephone: 270-789-5078. Fax: 270-789-5550. E-mail: krdeaton @campbellsville.edu.

DEGREES AND AWARDS
MSE Special Education

COURSE SUBJECT AREAS OFFERED OUTSIDE OF DEGREE PROGRAMS
Undergraduate—religious studies; social work.
Graduate—educational administration and supervision; religious studies; social work.

CAMPBELL UNIVERSITY
Buies Creek, North Carolina
http://www.campbell.edu
Campbell University was founded in 1887. It is accredited by Southern Association of Colleges and Schools. It first offered distance learning courses in 2000. In fall 2006, there were 1,200 students enrolled in distance learning courses. Institutionally administered financial aid is available to distance learners.
Services Distance learners have accessibility to academic advising, bookstore, campus computer network, e-mail services, library services.

Contact Mr. Frank Signorile, Jr., Director, Distance Education, Campbell University, PO Box 264, Buies Creek, NC 27506. Telephone: 910-814-4739. Fax: 910-814-4736. E-mail: signorile@campbell.edu.

DEGREES AND AWARDS
Programs offered do not lead to a degree or other formal award.

COURSE SUBJECT AREAS OFFERED OUTSIDE OF DEGREE PROGRAMS

Undergraduate—accounting and related services; American literature (United States and Canadian); biblical studies; business administration, management and operations; business/corporate communications; English composition; fine and studio art; geography and cartography; history; mathematics and computer science; political science and government; psychology; sociology; statistics.

CAPE BRETON UNIVERSITY
Sydney, Nova Scotia, Canada
http://www.uccb.ca/distance

Cape Breton University was founded in 1974. It is provincially chartered. It first offered distance learning courses in 1997. In fall 2006, there were 1,000 students enrolled in distance learning courses. Institutionally administered financial aid is available to distance learners.

Services Distance learners have accessibility to academic advising, bookstore, career placement assistance, e-mail services, library services, tutoring.

Contact Jennifer Pino, Coordinator of Distance Education, Cape Breton University, PO Box 5300, Sydney, NS B1P 6L2, Canada. Telephone: 902-563-1806. Fax: 902-539-9451. E-mail: distance_ed@cbu.ca.

DEGREES AND AWARDS

BA Community Studies
BES Bachelor of Technology–Environmental Studies
BHS Bachelor of Technology–Public Health
BST Bachelor of Technology–Emergency Management; Bachelor of Technology–Manufacturing
BTHM Bachelor of Hospitality & Tourism Management
Certificate Crime Prevention through Social Development; Public Administration
Diploma Public Administration
MEd Educational Technology; Educational counseling, curriculum, or technology

COURSE SUBJECT AREAS OFFERED OUTSIDE OF DEGREE PROGRAMS

Undergraduate—accounting and related services; creative writing; developmental and child psychology; environmental/environmental health engineering; international business; marketing; social psychology; statistics.
Graduate—education.
Non-credit—business, management, and marketing related; computer/information technology administration and management; computer programming; computer software and media applications.

CAPE COD COMMUNITY COLLEGE
West Barnstable, Massachusetts
Distance and Learning Technology
http://learning.capecod.mass.edu

Cape Cod Community College was founded in 1961. It is accredited by New England Association of Schools and Colleges. It first offered distance learning courses in 1993. In fall 2006, there were 500 students enrolled in distance learning courses. Institutionally administered financial aid is available to distance learners.

Services Distance learners have accessibility to academic advising, bookstore, campus computer network, career placement assistance, e-mail services, library services, tutoring.

Contact Greg Masterson, Director of Distance Learning, Cape Cod Community College, 2240 Iyanough Road, West Barnstable, MA 02668. Telephone: 508-375-4040 Ext. 4345. Fax: 508-375-4041. E-mail: gmasters@capecod.edu.

DEGREES AND AWARDS
Programs offered do not lead to a degree or other formal award.

COURSE SUBJECT AREAS OFFERED OUTSIDE OF DEGREE PROGRAMS

Undergraduate—business administration, management and operations; computer software and media applications; developmental and child psychology; economics; English composition; fine and studio art; history; marketing; mathematics; natural sciences; nursing; psychology; psychology related; social sciences; sociology.
Non-credit—dental support services and allied professions.

CAPELLA UNIVERSITY
Minneapolis, Minnesota
http://www.capellauniversity.edu/

Capella University was founded in 1993. It is accredited by North Central Association of Colleges and Schools. It first offered distance learning courses in 1993. In fall 2006, there were 17,203 students enrolled in distance learning courses. Institutionally administered financial aid is available to distance learners.

Services Distance learners have accessibility to academic advising, bookstore, career placement assistance, library services, tutoring.

Contact Enrollment Services, Capella University, 225 South Sixth St, 9th Floor, Minneapolis, MN 55402. Telephone: 888-227-3552 Ext. 3. Fax: 612-977-5060. E-mail: info@capella.edu.

DEGREES AND AWARDS

BS Business; Information Technology; Public Safety
MBA Business
MS Education; Human Services; Information Technology; Organization and Management; Psychology; Public Safety
PhD Education; Human Services; Information Technology; Organization and Management; Psychology; Public Safety
Psy D Psychology

COURSE SUBJECT AREAS OFFERED OUTSIDE OF DEGREE PROGRAMS

Graduate—business administration, management and operations; business/corporate communications; business, management, and marketing related; clinical psychology; computer/information technology administration and management; computer systems networking and telecommunications; counseling psychology; criminal justice and corrections; education; educational administration and supervision; educational/instructional media design; educational psychology; human resources management; human services; industrial and organizational psychology; international business; marketing; psychology; sales, merchandising, and related marketing operations (general); school psychology.

See full description on page 328.

CAPITOL COLLEGE
Laurel, Maryland
http://www.capitol-college.edu/academicprograms/
graduateprograms/index.shtml

Capitol College was founded in 1964. It is accredited by Middle States Association of Colleges and Schools. It first offered distance learning courses in 1998. In fall 2006, there were 400 students enrolled in distance learning courses. Institutionally administered financial aid is available to distance learners.

Services Distance learners have accessibility to academic advising, bookstore, career placement assistance, e-mail services, library services.

Contact Mr. Darnell Edwards, Director of Admissions, Capitol College, Office of Admissions, 11301 Springfield Road, Laurel, MD 20708. Telephone: 301-369-2800 Ext. 3033. Fax: 301-953-3876. E-mail: gradadmit@capitol-college.edu.

DEGREES AND AWARDS

MBA Business Administration

MS Computer Science; Electrical Engineering; Information Assurance; Information and Telecommunication Systems Management; Internet Engineering; Network Security

COURSE SUBJECT AREAS OFFERED OUTSIDE OF DEGREE PROGRAMS

Graduate—computer and information sciences; computer and information sciences and support services related; computer engineering technologies; computer/information technology administration and management; computer science; computer software and media applications; computer systems networking and telecommunications; engineering; information science/studies; management information systems; management sciences and quantitative methods; systems engineering; systems science and theory.

CARDINAL STRITCH UNIVERSITY
Milwaukee, Wisconsin
College of Education
http://www.stritch.edu/
Cardinal Stritch University was founded in 1937. It is accredited by North Central Association of Colleges and Schools. It first offered distance learning courses in 1995. In fall 2006, there were 30 students enrolled in distance learning courses. Institutionally administered financial aid is available to distance learners.
Services Distance learners have accessibility to bookstore, campus computer network, career placement assistance, e-mail services, library services.
Contact Judy Wendorf, Director of University Outreach–Professional Development, Cardinal Stritch University, 6801 North Yates Road, Milwaukee, WI 53217-3985. Telephone: 414-410-4428. E-mail: jawendorf@stritch.edu.

DEGREES AND AWARDS

BS Public Safety Management
MEd Education

COURSE SUBJECT AREAS OFFERED OUTSIDE OF DEGREE PROGRAMS

Undergraduate—management information systems; management sciences and quantitative methods; public administration and social service professions related.
Graduate—education; educational administration and supervision.
Non-credit—business administration, management and operations; computer software and media applications; creative writing; family and consumer sciences/human sciences business services.

CARL ALBERT STATE COLLEGE
Poteau, Oklahoma
http://www.carlalbert.edu
Carl Albert State College was founded in 1934. It is accredited by North Central Association of Colleges and Schools. It first offered distance learning courses in 1996. In fall 2006, there were 1,035 students enrolled in distance learning courses. Institutionally administered financial aid is available to distance learners.
Services Distance learners have accessibility to academic advising, bookstore, library services.
Contact Ms. Kathy A. Harrell, Vice President of Academic Affairs, Carl Albert State College, 1507 South McKenna, Poteau, OK 74953. Telephone: 918-647-1230. Fax: 918-647-1201. E-mail: kharrell@carlalbert.edu.

DEGREES AND AWARDS

AA Business Administration; Psychology/Sociology; Social Sciences

COURSE SUBJECT AREAS OFFERED OUTSIDE OF DEGREE PROGRAMS

Undergraduate—accounting and related services; biological and physical sciences; business administration, management and operations; computer and information sciences; computer systems networking and telecommunications; data entry/microcomputer applications; economics; English composition; health and physical education/fitness; history; mathematics; political science and government; psychology.

CARLOW UNIVERSITY
Pittsburgh, Pennsylvania
http://www.carlow.edu/
Carlow University was founded in 1929. It is accredited by Middle States Association of Colleges and Schools. It first offered distance learning courses in 1995. In fall 2006, there were 2,134 students enrolled in distance learning courses. Institutionally administered financial aid is available to distance learners.
Services Distance learners have accessibility to academic advising, bookstore, campus computer network, career placement assistance, e-mail services, library services, tutoring.
Contact Nola Coulson, Coordinator, Instructional Technology, Carlow University, 3333 Fifth Avenue, Pittsburgh, PA 15213. Telephone: 412-578-6338. Fax: 412-578-6595. E-mail: coulsonna@carlow.edu.

DEGREES AND AWARDS

Programs offered do not lead to a degree or other formal award.

COURSE SUBJECT AREAS OFFERED OUTSIDE OF DEGREE PROGRAMS

Undergraduate—accounting and computer science; biology; business, management, and marketing related; chemistry; computer science; education; English; information science/studies; management information systems; mathematics; nursing; philosophy; political science and government; psychology; social psychology; social work; sociology; special education.
Graduate—business, management, and marketing related; counseling psychology; education; nursing; special education.

CARROLL COLLEGE
Waukesha, Wisconsin
http://www.cc.edu/
Carroll College was founded in 1846. It is accredited by North Central Association of Colleges and Schools. It first offered distance learning courses in 1995. In fall 2006, there were 228 students enrolled in distance learning courses. Institutionally administered financial aid is available to distance learners.
Services Distance learners have accessibility to academic advising, bookstore, campus computer network, career placement assistance, e-mail services, library services, tutoring.
Contact Ms. Tina Wood, Director of Admissions, Carroll College, 100 North East Avenue, Waukesha, WI 53186. Telephone: 262-524-7518. Fax: 262-650-4851. E-mail: twood@cc.edu.

DEGREES AND AWARDS

Programs offered do not lead to a degree or other formal award.

COURSE SUBJECT AREAS OFFERED OUTSIDE OF DEGREE PROGRAMS

Undergraduate—accounting and computer science; business, management, and marketing related; computer science; economics; English; finance and financial management services; history; philosophy; religious education.
Graduate—computer science; computer software and media applications; education (specific subject areas).

CARROLL COMMUNITY COLLEGE
Westminster, Maryland
http://www.carrollcc.edu
Carroll Community College was founded in 1993. It is accredited by Middle States Association of Colleges and Schools. It first offered distance learning courses in 1993. In fall 2006, there were 395 students enrolled in distance learning courses. Institutionally administered financial aid is available to distance learners.
Services Distance learners have accessibility to academic advising, bookstore, library services.
Contact Ms. Janenne Corcoran, Director of Advising, Counseling, and Admissions, Carroll Community College, 1601 Washington Road, Westminster, MD 21157. Telephone: 410-386-8405. Fax: 410-386-8446. E-mail: jcorcoran@carrollcc.edu.

DEGREES AND AWARDS
Programs offered do not lead to a degree or other formal award.

COURSE SUBJECT AREAS OFFERED OUTSIDE OF DEGREE PROGRAMS
Undergraduate—accounting and related services; atmospheric sciences and meteorology; business administration, management and operations; business/corporate communications; business, management, and marketing related; computer and information sciences; computer/information technology administration and management; computer programming; computer systems networking and telecommunications; criminal justice and corrections; economics; education related; English composition; health and physical education/fitness; history; legal studies (non-professional general, undergraduate); legal support services; management information systems; marketing; mathematics; nutrition sciences; philosophy; psychology; social psychology; statistics; taxation; technical and business writing.
Non-credit—accounting and related services; business administration, management and operations; business/commerce; business, management, and marketing related; business operations support and assistant services; computer programming; computer software and media applications; computer systems networking and telecommunications; creative writing; family and consumer economics; finance and financial management services; gerontology; graphic communications; health and medical administrative services; languages (Romance languages); legal studies (non-professional general, undergraduate); legal support services; technical and business writing; veterinary biomedical and clinical sciences.

CASCADIA COMMUNITY COLLEGE
Bothell, Washington
http://www.cascadia.ctc.edu/
Cascadia Community College was founded in 1999. It is accredited by Northwest Commission on Colleges and Universities. It first offered distance learning courses in 2001. In fall 2006, there were 500 students enrolled in distance learning courses. Institutionally administered financial aid is available to distance learners.
Services Distance learners have accessibility to academic advising, bookstore, campus computer network, e-mail services, library services, tutoring.
Contact Norm Wright, Distance Advising, Cascadia Community College, 18345 Campus Way NE, Bothell, WA 98011. Telephone: 425-352-8147. E-mail: nwright@cascadia.ctc.edu.

DEGREES AND AWARDS
AA Integrated Studies–Associate in Integrated Studies (DTA); Integrated Studies–Associate in Integrated Studies (DTA); Integrated Studies–Associate in Integrated Studies (DTA)

COURSE SUBJECT AREAS OFFERED OUTSIDE OF DEGREE PROGRAMS
Undergraduate—accounting and related services; astronomy and astrophysics; biological and physical sciences; business administration, management and operations; chemistry; communication and journalism related; comparative literature; computer and information sciences and support services related; computer software and media applications; ecology,

evolution, and population biology; economics; English composition; geological and earth sciences/geosciences; history; mathematics; political science and government; psychology; sociology.

CASPER COLLEGE
Casper, Wyoming
http://www.caspercollege.edu/
Casper College was founded in 1945. It is accredited by North Central Association of Colleges and Schools. It first offered distance learning courses in 1986. In fall 2006, there were 1,000 students enrolled in distance learning courses. Institutionally administered financial aid is available to distance learners.
Services Distance learners have accessibility to academic advising, bookstore, career placement assistance, e-mail services, library services, tutoring.
Contact Michael Woodhead, Director of Distance Learning, Casper College, 125 College Drive, Casper, WY 82601-4699. Telephone: 307-268-2590. Fax: 307-268-2224. E-mail: mwoodhead@caspercollege.edu.

DEGREES AND AWARDS
AD General Studies
AS Early Childhood Education; Education; Fire Science

COURSE SUBJECT AREAS OFFERED OUTSIDE OF DEGREE PROGRAMS
Undergraduate—accounting and related services; anthropology; astronomy and astrophysics; biological and biomedical sciences related; biological and physical sciences; biology; business administration, management and operations; business/commerce; business, management, and marketing related; chemistry; computer and information sciences; computer programming; computer science; computer software and media applications; creative writing; economics; education; educational psychology; education related; engineering; engineering science; English composition; fine and studio art; geography and cartography; mathematics; music; psychology; sociology; special education; statistics; teaching assistants/aides; zoology/animal biology.

THE CATHOLIC DISTANCE UNIVERSITY
Hamilton, Virginia
http://www.cdu.edu/
The Catholic Distance University was founded in 1983. It is accredited by Distance Education and Training Council. It first offered distance learning courses in 1983. In fall 2006, there were 1,000 students enrolled in distance learning courses. Institutionally administered financial aid is available to distance learners.
Services Distance learners have accessibility to academic advising, bookstore, campus computer network, e-mail services, library services.
Contact Ms. Carol Ciullo, Director of Admissions, The Catholic Distance University, 120 East Colonial Highway, Hamilton, VA 20158. Telephone: 888-254-4238 Ext. 700. Fax: 540-338-4788. E-mail: cciullo@cdu.edu.

DEGREES AND AWARDS
BA Theology
Certification Advanced Catechist Certificate
Diploma Catechetical Diploma
MA Theology

COURSE SUBJECT AREAS OFFERED OUTSIDE OF DEGREE PROGRAMS
Undergraduate—religious education; religious studies; theology and religious vocations related.
Graduate—religious education; religious studies; theology and religious vocations related.
Non-credit—religious education; religious studies; theological and ministerial studies; theology and religious vocations related.

CAYUGA COUNTY COMMUNITY COLLEGE
Auburn, New York
http://www.cayuga-cc.edu/

Cayuga County Community College was founded in 1953. It is accredited by Middle States Association of Colleges and Schools. It first offered distance learning courses in 1998. In fall 2006, there were 800 students enrolled in distance learning courses. Institutionally administered financial aid is available to distance learners.

Services Distance learners have accessibility to academic advising, bookstore, career placement assistance, e-mail services, library services, tutoring.

Contact Ed Kowalski, Director of Online Programs, Cayuga County Community College, 197 Franklin Street, Auburn, NY 13021. Telephone: 315-255-1743. Fax: 315-255-2117. E-mail: kowalskie@cayuga-cc.edu.

DEGREES AND AWARDS

AA Liberal Arts and Humanities
AAS Business Administration; Criminal Justice–Police
AS Business Administration; Liberal Arts and Sciences/Mathematics and Sciences

COURSE SUBJECT AREAS OFFERED OUTSIDE OF DEGREE PROGRAMS

Undergraduate—accounting and related services; anthropology; biological and physical sciences; biology; business administration, management and operations; business/commerce; computer science; computer systems networking and telecommunications; economics; English; health and physical education/fitness; history; mathematics; political science and government; psychology; social psychology; social sciences; social sciences related; statistics.

CEDAR CREST COLLEGE
Allentown, Pennsylvania
http://www.cedarcrest.edu/

Cedar Crest College was founded in 1867. It is accredited by Middle States Association of Colleges and Schools. It first offered distance learning courses in 2000. In fall 2006, there were 143 students enrolled in distance learning courses. Institutionally administered financial aid is available to distance learners.

Services Distance learners have accessibility to academic advising, bookstore, campus computer network, e-mail services, library services.

Contact Ms. Nancy L. Hollinger, Director of Center for Lifelong Learning, Cedar Crest College, 100 College Drive, Allentown, PA 18104. Telephone: 610-740-3770. Fax: 610-740-3786. E-mail: nlhollin@cedarcrest.edu.

DEGREES AND AWARDS

Programs offered do not lead to a degree or other formal award.

COURSE SUBJECT AREAS OFFERED OUTSIDE OF DEGREE PROGRAMS

Undergraduate—accounting and related services; business/commerce; computer and information sciences; education; health and medical administrative services; information science/studies; languages (foreign languages related); nursing; nutrition sciences; psychology related.
Graduate—education.

CEDARVILLE UNIVERSITY
Cedarville, Ohio
http://www.cedarville.edu/

Cedarville University was founded in 1887. It is accredited by North Central Association of Colleges and Schools. It first offered distance learning courses in 1999. In fall 2006, there were 275 students enrolled in distance learning courses. Institutionally administered financial aid is available to distance learners.

Services Distance learners have accessibility to academic advising, bookstore, campus computer network, career placement assistance, e-mail services, library services.

Contact Chuck Allport, Assistant to the Academic Vice President, Cedarville University, 251 North Main Street, Cedarville, OH 45314. Telephone: 937-766-7681. Fax: 937-766-3217. E-mail: chuckallport@cedarville.edu.

DEGREES AND AWARDS

Programs offered do not lead to a degree or other formal award.

COURSE SUBJECT AREAS OFFERED OUTSIDE OF DEGREE PROGRAMS

Undergraduate—anthropology; biology; business/corporate communications; English; English language and literature related; history; mathematics; social sciences; social work; sociology; soil sciences; special education.

CENTRAL CAROLINA COMMUNITY COLLEGE
Sanford, North Carolina
http://www.cccc.edu

Central Carolina Community College was founded in 1962. It is accredited by Southern Association of Colleges and Schools. It first offered distance learning courses in 1997. In fall 2006, there were 1,300 students enrolled in distance learning courses. Institutionally administered financial aid is available to distance learners.

Services Distance learners have accessibility to academic advising, bookstore, campus computer network, career placement assistance, e-mail services, library services, tutoring.

Contact Mr. Brian S. Merritt, Distance Education Counselor, Central Carolina Community College, 1105 Kelly Drive, Sanford, NC 27330. Telephone: 919-718-7511. Fax: 919-718-7380. E-mail: bmerritt@cccc.edu.

DEGREES AND AWARDS

AA Associate of Arts–General Studies
AAS Applied Science–Diploma in Applied Science and Associate in Applied Science; Applied Science–Diploma in Applied Science and Associate in Applied Science
AS Associate in Science–General Studies
Certificate Various Subjects–BioQuality, Entrepreneur, Human Resources Management; Various Subjects–Income Tax Preparer, Library Services, Manager Trainee; Various Subjects–Medical Transcription, Networking, News Writing; Various Subjects–Payroll Accounting, Photo Journalism, Small Business Financial Advisor I and II

COURSE SUBJECT AREAS OFFERED OUTSIDE OF DEGREE PROGRAMS

Undergraduate—accounting and related services; agriculture; American literature (United States and Canadian); biblical studies; biological and physical sciences; biomedical/medical engineering; biotechnology; business/commerce; business operations support and assistant services; computer programming; computer science; criminal justice and corrections; economics; education; electrical and electronic engineering technologies; English; health and physical education/fitness; history; journalism; languages (foreign languages related); library science related; marketing; mathematics; sociology.
Non-credit—clinical/medical laboratory science and allied professions; computer and information sciences; criminal justice and corrections; English as a second language; management information systems.

CENTRAL GEORGIA TECHNICAL COLLEGE
Macon, Georgia
http://www.macon.tec.ga.us/

Central Georgia Technical College was founded in 1966. It is accredited by Council on Occupational Education. It first offered distance learning courses in 1997. In fall 2006, there were 1,500 students enrolled in distance learning courses. Institutionally administered financial aid is available to distance learners.

Services Distance learners have accessibility to academic advising, bookstore, campus computer network, career placement assistance, e-mail services, library services, tutoring.

Contact Gardner Long, Director of Curriculum, Central Georgia Technical College, 3300 Macon Tech Drive, Macon, GA 31206. Telephone: 478-757-3498. Fax: 912-757-3534. E-mail: gardner@cgtcollege.org.

DEGREES AND AWARDS

AAS Accounting; Administrative Office Technology; Administrative Office Technology; Banking and Finance
Certificate Computer Science–AutoCAD Operator; Computer Science–CISCO Specialist; Computer Science–Microsoft User Specialist; Computer Software Application Specialist; Construction Worker–Certified Construction Worker; Insurance Specialist; Residential Drawing Technician

COURSE SUBJECT AREAS OFFERED OUTSIDE OF DEGREE PROGRAMS

Undergraduate—accounting and related services; allied health and medical assisting services; applied mathematics; behavioral sciences; building/construction finishing, management, and inspection; business administration, management and operations; business operations support and assistant services; carpentry; chemistry; computer/information technology administration and management; computer programming; computer software and media applications; computer systems networking and telecommunications; cosmetology and related personal grooming services; criminal justice and corrections; data entry/microcomputer applications; data processing; design and applied arts; drafting/design engineering technologies; economics; electrical and electronic engineering technologies; English; English composition; entrepreneurial and small business operations; finance and financial management services; health and medical administrative services; health services/allied health/health sciences; insurance; legal support services; mathematics; nursing; psychology; technical and business writing.

CENTRAL MICHIGAN UNIVERSITY
Mount Pleasant, Michigan
Distance/Distributed Learning
http://DDLcampus.cmich.edu
Central Michigan University was founded in 1892. It is accredited by North Central Association of Colleges and Schools. It first offered distance learning courses in 1971. In fall 2006, there were 8,000 students enrolled in distance learning courses. Institutionally administered financial aid is available to distance learners.
Services Distance learners have accessibility to academic advising, bookstore, campus computer network, career placement assistance, e-mail services, library services, tutoring.
Contact Ms. Marnie Roestel, Coordinator of Recruitment Services, Central Michigan University, 802 Industrial Drive, Mount Pleasant, MI 48858. Telephone: 800-950-1144 Ext. 3937. E-mail: roest1m@cmich.edu.

DEGREES AND AWARDS

BS Administration–Building Code Administration; Administration–Organizational Administration; Community Development, Community Services major; Community Development, Health Sciences major; Community Development, Public Administration major
MAE Education; Educational Leadership, Charter School Administration emphasis
MBA MIS concentration and SAP emphasis
MS Administration–General Administration concentration; Administration–Health Services Administration concentration; Administration–Human Resource Administration; Administration–Information Resource Management concentration; Administration–Leadership concentration; Administration–Public Administration concentration; Nutrition and Dietetics
DH Sc Healthcare Administration

COURSE SUBJECT AREAS OFFERED OUTSIDE OF DEGREE PROGRAMS

Undergraduate—accounting and computer science; allied health and medical assisting services; architecture related; behavioral sciences; building/construction finishing, management, and inspection; business administration, management and operations; business/commerce; business/corporate communications; business, management, and marketing related;

business/managerial economics; business operations support and assistant services; community health services; community organization and advocacy; construction management; construction trades; economics; family and consumer sciences/human sciences; family and consumer sciences/human sciences related; health and medical administrative services; health and physical education/fitness; health professions related; health services/allied health/health sciences; human development, family studies, and related services; human resources management; human services; industrial and organizational psychology; marketing; multi-/interdisciplinary studies related; political science and government; psychology; psychology related; public administration; public administration and social service professions related; public policy analysis; work and family studies.
Graduate—accounting and computer science; behavioral sciences; business administration, management and operations; business/commerce; business/corporate communications; business, management, and marketing related; business/managerial economics; communication and journalism related; communications technology; computer and information sciences; computer and information sciences and support services related; computer systems analysis; curriculum and instruction; dietetics and clinical nutrition services; economics; education (specific levels and methods); education (specific subject areas); entrepreneurial and small business operations; finance and financial management services; food science and technology; foods, nutrition, and related services; health and medical administrative services; health professions related; hospitality administration; human resources management; management information systems; management sciences and quantitative methods; marketing; multi-/interdisciplinary studies related; nutrition sciences; political science and government; public administration; public administration and social service professions related; public policy analysis; public relations, advertising, and applied communication related; sales, merchandising, and related marketing operations (general).

See full description on page 330.

CENTRAL NEW MEXICO COMMUNITY COLLEGE
Albuquerque, New Mexico
http://planet.tvi.edu/distancelearn
Central New Mexico Community College was founded in 1965. It is accredited by North Central Association of Colleges and Schools. It first offered distance learning courses in 1997. In fall 2006, there were 1,686 students enrolled in distance learning courses. Institutionally administered financial aid is available to distance learners.
Services Distance learners have accessibility to academic advising, bookstore, campus computer network, career placement assistance, e-mail services, library services, tutoring.
Contact Mr. Brian Ditmer, Distance Learning Specialist, Central New Mexico Community College, Distance Learning Office, 525 Buena Vista SE, Albuquerque, NM 87106. Telephone: 505-224-3318. Fax: 505-224-3321. E-mail: bditmer@cnm.edu.

DEGREES AND AWARDS

AAS Business Administration; Office Administration

COURSE SUBJECT AREAS OFFERED OUTSIDE OF DEGREE PROGRAMS

Undergraduate—accounting and related services; biology; building/construction finishing, management, and inspection; business administration, management and operations; business/commerce; business, management, and marketing related; business/managerial economics; business operations support and assistant services; clinical/medical laboratory science and allied professions; communication and media; computer and information sciences; computer programming; creative writing; criminal justice and corrections; culinary arts and related services; data processing; economics; English; English composition; entrepreneurial and small business operations; fire protection; foods, nutrition, and related services; information science/studies; international business; legal studies (non-professional general, undergraduate); mathematics; microbiological sciences and immunology; nursing; philosophy; psychology; real estate; sales, merchandising, and related marketing operations (general); sociology; speech and rhetoric.

CENTRAL OREGON COMMUNITY COLLEGE
Bend, Oregon
Open Campus Distance Learning Program
http://www.cocc.edu/opencampus
Central Oregon Community College was founded in 1949. It is accredited by Northwest Commission on Colleges and Universities. It first offered distance learning courses in 1996. In fall 2006, there were 260 students enrolled in distance learning courses. Institutionally administered financial aid is available to distance learners.

Services Distance learners have accessibility to academic advising, bookstore, campus computer network, e-mail services, library services, tutoring.

Contact Barbara Klett, Instructional Technology Coordinator, Central Oregon Community College, 2600 NW College Way, Bend, OR 97701. Telephone: 541-383-7785. E-mail: bklett@cocc.edu.

DEGREES AND AWARDS
Programs offered do not lead to a degree or other formal award.

COURSE SUBJECT AREAS OFFERED OUTSIDE OF DEGREE PROGRAMS
Undergraduate—allied health and medical assisting services; business administration, management and operations; computer and information sciences; English composition; English literature (British and Commonwealth); geological and earth sciences/geosciences; health and physical education/fitness; health services/allied health/health sciences; history; liberal arts and sciences, general studies and humanities; library science; mathematics; nursing.

CENTRAL TEXAS COLLEGE
Killeen, Texas
Distance Education and Educational Technology
http://online.ctcd.edu
Central Texas College was founded in 1967. It is accredited by Southern Association of Colleges and Schools. It first offered distance learning courses in 1972. In fall 2006, there were 12,240 students enrolled in distance learning courses. Institutionally administered financial aid is available to distance learners.

Services Distance learners have accessibility to academic advising, bookstore, career placement assistance, library services, tutoring.

Contact Mrs. Angela Dawn Reese, Coordinator, Recruiting and Retention, Central Texas College, PO Box 1800, Killeen, TX 76540. Telephone: 254-526-1104. Fax: 254-526-1751. E-mail: angela.reese@ctcd.edu.

DEGREES AND AWARDS
AAS Applied Management with Computer Applications (non-Texas students only); Applied Management; Applied Technology; At-Risk Youth Specialization; Business Management Marketing and Sales Management; Business Management; Chemical Dependency specialization; Computer Science–Information Technology; Criminal Justice Corrections specialization; Criminal Justice; Hospitality Management–Food and Beverage Management; Hospitality Management; Interdisciplinary Studies; Office Management; Social Science; Social Work
AGS General Studies
Certificate At Risk Youth Specialization; Business Management Marketing and Sales; Business Management; Chemical Dependency specialization; Criminal Justice Corrections specialization; Criminal Justice Studies specialization; Hospitality Management–Food and Beverage Management; Hospitality Management–Property Management Advanced; Hospitality Management–Rooms Division; Information Center Specialist; Medical Transcription; Office Assistant; Office Management Levels 1&2; Software Applications Specialist

COURSE SUBJECT AREAS OFFERED OUTSIDE OF DEGREE PROGRAMS
Undergraduate—accounting and related services; allied health and medical assisting services; American literature (United States and Canadian); anthropology; applied mathematics; area, ethnic, cultural, and gender studies related; business administration, management and operations; business/corporate communications; business, management, and marketing related; business operations support and assistant services; communication and media; community psychology; computer and information sciences; computer and information sciences and support services related; computer programming; computer science; computer software and media applications; computer systems analysis; computer systems networking and telecommunications; counseling psychology; criminal justice and corrections; criminology; culinary arts and related services; developmental and child psychology; economics; English; English composition; English language and literature related; English literature (British and Commonwealth); entrepreneurial and small business operations; ethnic, cultural minority, and gender studies; fine and studio art; fire protection; foods, nutrition, and related services; geography and cartography; health and physical education/fitness; history; hospitality administration; human resources management; legal studies (non-professional general, undergraduate); management information systems; marketing; mathematics; mathematics and statistics related; mental and social health services and allied professions; military studies; multi-/interdisciplinary studies related; music; nursing; philosophy; philosophy and religious studies related; political science and government; psychology; psychology related; real estate; sales, merchandising, and related marketing operations (specialized); social sciences; social sciences related; social work; sociology; statistics; technical and business writing.

CENTRAL VIRGINIA COMMUNITY COLLEGE
Lynchburg, Virginia
Learning Resources
http://www.cvcc.vccs.edu
Central Virginia Community College was founded in 1966. It is accredited by Southern Association of Colleges and Schools. It first offered distance learning courses in 1984. In fall 2006, there were 1,563 students enrolled in distance learning courses. Institutionally administered financial aid is available to distance learners.

Services Distance learners have accessibility to academic advising, bookstore, campus computer network, e-mail services, library services, tutoring.

Contact Susan S. Beasley, Distance Education Coordinator, Central Virginia Community College, 3506 Wards Road, Lynchburg, VA 24502. Telephone: 434-832-7742. Fax: 434-832-7880. E-mail: beasleys@cvcc.vccs.edu.

DEGREES AND AWARDS
AAS Medical Laboratory Technology

COURSE SUBJECT AREAS OFFERED OUTSIDE OF DEGREE PROGRAMS
Undergraduate—accounting and related services; applied mathematics; astronomy and astrophysics; biology; business operations support and assistant services; chemistry; computer and information sciences; economics; education related; English; English composition; health professions related; history; information science/studies; library science related; marketing; music; philosophy; political science and government; psychology; religious studies; sociology; speech and rhetoric; technical and business writing; visual and performing arts related.

CENTRAL WASHINGTON UNIVERSITY
Ellensburg, Washington
Center for Learning Technologies
http://www.cwu.edu/~media/
Central Washington University was founded in 1891. It is accredited by Northwest Commission on Colleges and Universities. It first offered distance learning courses in 1996. In fall 2006, there were 1,415 students enrolled in distance learning courses. Institutionally administered financial aid is available to distance learners.

Services Distance learners have accessibility to academic advising, bookstore, campus computer network, career placement assistance, e-mail services, library services.

Contact Tracy Terrell, Registrar, Central Washington University, Mitchell Hall, 400 East University Way, Ellensburg, WA 98926-7465. Telephone: 509-963-3076. Fax: 509-963-3022. E-mail: reg@cwu.edu.

DEGREES AND AWARDS

MS Physical Education, Health, and Leisure Studies

COURSE SUBJECT AREAS OFFERED OUTSIDE OF DEGREE PROGRAMS

Undergraduate—accounting and related services; business administration, management and operations; business/commerce; chemistry; computer/information technology administration and management; criminal justice and corrections; education; family and consumer sciences/human sciences related; history; human resources management; management information systems; marketing; nutrition sciences; philosophy and religious studies related; psychology; sociology.

Graduate—accounting and related services; business administration, management and operations; education; health and physical education/fitness.

Non-credit—education.

CENTRAL WYOMING COLLEGE
Riverton, Wyoming
Distance Education and Extended Studies
http://www.cwc.edu

Central Wyoming College was founded in 1966. It is accredited by North Central Association of Colleges and Schools. It first offered distance learning courses in 1983. In fall 2006, there were 630 students enrolled in distance learning courses. Institutionally administered financial aid is available to distance learners.

Services Distance learners have accessibility to academic advising, bookstore, campus computer network, e-mail services, library services, tutoring.

Contact Ms. Judy Hubbard, Workforce and Community Education Assistant, Central Wyoming College, 2660 Peck Avenue, Riverton, WY 82501. Telephone: 307-855-2181. Fax: 307-855-2041. E-mail: jhubbard @cwc.edu.

DEGREES AND AWARDS

Programs offered do not lead to a degree or other formal award.

COURSE SUBJECT AREAS OFFERED OUTSIDE OF DEGREE PROGRAMS

Undergraduate—accounting and related services; anthropology; area, ethnic, cultural, and gender studies related; atmospheric sciences and meteorology; biology; chemistry; communication and media; computer and information sciences; computer science; data entry/microcomputer applications; economics; education (specific subject areas); English composition; fine and studio art; geography and cartography; health and physical education/fitness; languages (American Indian/Native American); library science; mathematics; mechanics and repair; music; nursing; political science and government; psychology; religious studies; social sciences; sociology; vehicle maintenance and repair technologies; zoology/animal biology.

Non-credit—agricultural and domestic animal services; air transportation; animal sciences; applied horticulture/horticultural business services; area, ethnic, cultural, and gender studies related; botany/plant biology; business operations support and assistant services; computer software and media applications; culinary arts and related services; dance; data entry/microcomputer applications; design and applied arts; dramatic/theater arts and stagecraft; electrical and power transmission installation; electrical/electronics maintenance and repair technology; English composition; film/video and photographic arts; finance and financial management services; fine and studio art; food science and technology; foods, nutrition, and related services; graphic communications; health and physical education/fitness; health professions related; health services/allied health/health sciences; history; landscape architecture; languages (foreign languages related); mechanics and repair; medical basic sciences; mental and social health services and allied professions; movement and mind-body therapies; music; neuroscience; nutrition sciences; personal and culinary services related; precision metal working; psychology; vehicle maintenance and repair technologies; vet-

erinary biomedical and clinical sciences; visual and performing arts; visual and performing arts related; wildlife and wildlands science and management; woodworking.

CERRITOS COLLEGE
Norwalk, California
Distributed Education Program
http://www.cerritos.edu/de

Cerritos College was founded in 1956. It is accredited by Western Association of Schools and Colleges. It first offered distance learning courses in 1985. In fall 2006, there were 9,000 students enrolled in distance learning courses. Institutionally administered financial aid is available to distance learners.

Services Distance learners have accessibility to academic advising, bookstore, e-mail services, library services.

Contact Yvette Juarez, Program Assistant, Distance Education, Cerritos College, 11110 Alondra Boulevard, Norwalk, CA 90650. Telephone: 562-860-2451 Ext. 2405. Fax: 562-467-5091. E-mail: yjuarez@cerritos. edu.

DEGREES AND AWARDS

Programs offered do not lead to a degree or other formal award.

COURSE SUBJECT AREAS OFFERED OUTSIDE OF DEGREE PROGRAMS

Undergraduate—anthropology; business/commerce; business operations support and assistant services; curriculum and instruction; data entry/microcomputer applications; English composition; history; journalism; legal studies (non-professional general, undergraduate); management information systems; radio, television, and digital communication; sociology; woodworking; zoology/animal biology.

CERRO COSO COMMUNITY COLLEGE
Ridgecrest, California
Cerro Coso Online
http://cconline.cerrocoso.edu

Cerro Coso Community College was founded in 1973. It is accredited by Western Association of Schools and Colleges. It first offered distance learning courses in 1997. In fall 2006, there were 2,400 students enrolled in distance learning courses. Institutionally administered financial aid is available to distance learners.

Services Distance learners have accessibility to academic advising, bookstore, career placement assistance, library services, tutoring.

Contact Matt Hightower, Director, Cerro Coso Community College, PO Box 1865, 100 College Parkway, Mammoth Lakes, CA 93546. Telephone: 888-537-6932. Fax: 760-924-1613. E-mail: mhightow@ cerrocoso.edu.

DEGREES AND AWARDS

AA Business; Humanities; Liberal Arts; Media Arts; Social Sciences
AS Administration of Justice; Business Administration; Business Management; Computer Information Systems
Certificate Teaching–Online Teaching

COURSE SUBJECT AREAS OFFERED OUTSIDE OF DEGREE PROGRAMS

Undergraduate—anthropology; computer programming; criminal justice and corrections; English; human development, family studies, and related services; mathematics; music; sales, merchandising, and related marketing operations (general); speech and rhetoric.

CHADRON STATE COLLEGE
Chadron, Nebraska
Extended Campus Programs
http://www.csc.edu

Chadron State College was founded in 1911. It is accredited by North Central Association of Colleges and Schools. It first offered distance learning courses in 1991. In fall 2006, there were 700 students enrolled in distance learning courses. Institutionally administered financial aid is available to distance learners.

Services Distance learners have accessibility to academic advising, bookstore, campus computer network, career placement assistance, e-mail services, library services, tutoring.

Contact Ms. Jodi Banzhaf, Distance Learning Coordinator, Chadron State College, 1000 Main Street, Chadron, NE 69337. Telephone: 800-600-4099. Fax: 308-432-6473. E-mail: dlrep@csc.edu.

DEGREES AND AWARDS

BA Business Administration/Management Information Systems; Business Administration/Management; Business Administration/Marketing; Business, general; Library Information Management; Psychology
BS Math
MAE Math
MBA Business Administration
MEd Educational Technology; Math
MS Organizational Management, Human Services option

COURSE SUBJECT AREAS OFFERED OUTSIDE OF DEGREE PROGRAMS

Undergraduate—accounting and computer science; accounting and related services; applied mathematics; biological and physical sciences; business administration, management and operations; business/commerce; business/corporate communications; business, management, and marketing related; business/managerial economics; computer and information sciences; criminology; developmental and child psychology; economics; education; educational administration and supervision; educational assessment, evaluation, and research; educational/instructional media design; educational psychology; education related; education (specific levels and methods); education (specific subject areas); English composition; English literature (British and Commonwealth); family and consumer sciences/human sciences; family and consumer sciences/human sciences related; geography and cartography; history; housing and human environments; human development, family studies, and related services; human resources management; human services; industrial and organizational psychology; information science/studies; legal professions and studies related; legal studies (non-professional general, undergraduate); liberal arts and sciences, general studies and humanities; library science; library science related; management information systems; management sciences and quantitative methods; marketing; mathematics; mathematics and computer science; mathematics and statistics related; philosophy; philosophy and religious studies related; physical sciences; physical sciences related; physiological psychology/psychobiology; psychology; psychology related; real estate; sales, merchandising, and related marketing operations (general); sales, merchandising, and related marketing operations (specialized); social sciences; social sciences related; social work; sociology; special education; statistics; technical and business writing.
Graduate—accounting and computer science; accounting and related services; business administration, management and operations; business/commerce; business, management, and marketing related; business/managerial economics; counseling psychology; curriculum and instruction; economics; education; educational administration and supervision; educational assessment, evaluation, and research; educational/instructional media design; educational psychology; education related; education (specific levels and methods); education (specific subject areas); English; history; human resources management; industrial and organizational psychology; management information systems; management sciences and quantitative methods; marketing; mathematics; mathematics and computer science; mathematics and statistics related; psychology; psychology related; sales, merchandising, and related marketing operations (general); sales, merchandising, and related marketing operations (specialized); school psychology; special education; statistics; technology education/industrial arts.
Non-credit—education related.

CHAMINADE UNIVERSITY OF HONOLULU
Honolulu, Hawaii
http://www.chaminade.edu/

Chaminade University of Honolulu was founded in 1955. It is accredited by Western Association of Schools and Colleges. It first offered distance learning courses in 1997. In fall 2006, there were 762 students enrolled in distance learning courses. Institutionally administered financial aid is available to distance learners.
Services Distance learners have accessibility to academic advising, bookstore, campus computer network, e-mail services, library services.

Contact Skip Lee, Director of Accelerated Undergraduate Program, Chaminade University of Honolulu, 3140 Waialae Avenue, Honolulu, HI 96816-1578. Telephone: 808-735-4851. Fax: 808-735-4766. E-mail: slee@chaminade.edu.

DEGREES AND AWARDS
Programs offered do not lead to a degree or other formal award.

COURSE SUBJECT AREAS OFFERED OUTSIDE OF DEGREE PROGRAMS

Undergraduate—accounting and related services; anthropology; business administration, management and operations; criminal justice and corrections; dramatic/theater arts and stagecraft; economics; education; English; English composition; finance and financial management services; history; mathematics; music; philosophy; philosophy and religious studies related; physics; political science and government; psychology; religious studies; sociology.
Graduate—criminal justice and corrections; education; religious studies.

CHARTER OAK STATE COLLEGE
New Britain, Connecticut
http://www.charteroak.edu/

Charter Oak State College was founded in 1973. It is accredited by New England Association of Schools and Colleges. It first offered distance learning courses in 1992. In fall 2006, there were 884 students enrolled in distance learning courses. Institutionally administered financial aid is available to distance learners.
Services Distance learners have accessibility to academic advising, bookstore, library services, tutoring.
Contact Peggy Intravia, Associate, Academic Affairs, Charter Oak State College, 55 Paul J. Manafort Drive, New Britain, CT 06053-2150. Telephone: 860-832-3837. Fax: 860-832-3999. E-mail: mintravia@charteroak.edu.

DEGREES AND AWARDS
AA General Studies
AS General Studies
BA General Studies
BS General Studies

COURSE SUBJECT AREAS OFFERED OUTSIDE OF DEGREE PROGRAMS

Undergraduate—accounting and related services; American literature (United States and Canadian); behavioral sciences; biology/biotechnology laboratory technician; business administration, management and operations; business, management, and marketing related; cognitive psychology and psycholinguistics; communication and media; computer and information sciences; computer systems networking and telecommunications; criminology; educational administration and supervision; educational/instructional media design; English language and literature related; finance and financial management services; foods, nutrition, and related services; forensic psychology; genetics; geological and earth sciences/geosciences; health services/allied health/health sciences; management information systems; marketing; mathematics; mathematics and statistics related; philosophy and religious studies related; psychology; psychology related; public administration; public administration and social service professions related; social sciences related; sociology; speech and rhetoric; statistics.
Non-credit—nursing; pharmacy, pharmaceutical sciences, and administration.

See full description on page 332.

CHATHAM UNIVERSITY
Pittsburgh, Pennsylvania

Chatham University was founded in 1869. It is accredited by Middle States Association of Colleges and Schools. It first offered distance learning courses in 2005.
Services Distance learners have accessibility to academic advising, bookstore, campus computer network, career placement assistance, e-mail services, library services.

Contact Sarah Wojdylak, Admissions Support Specialist, College for Continuing and Professional Studies, Chatham University, Chatham University College for Continuing and Professional Studies, Woodland Road, Pittsburgh, PA 15232. Telephone: 412-365-1148. Fax: 412-365-1720. E-mail: sce@chatham.edu.

DEGREES AND AWARDS

BSN Nursing–RN-BSN—RN to Bachelor of Science in Nursing
MEd Health
MHS Health Sciences–Master of Health Sciences
MSE Education; Education
OTD Professional Doctor of Occupational Therapy

CHATTANOOGA STATE TECHNICAL COMMUNITY COLLEGE
Chattanooga, Tennessee
Distance Learning Program
http://www.chattanoogastate.edu/cde/
Chattanooga State Technical Community College was founded in 1965. It is accredited by Southern Association of Colleges and Schools. It first offered distance learning courses in 1985. In fall 2006, there were 1,500 students enrolled in distance learning courses. Institutionally administered financial aid is available to distance learners.
Services Distance learners have accessibility to academic advising, bookstore, campus computer network, career placement assistance, e-mail services, library services, tutoring.
Contact Tim Dills, Assistant Director, Center for Distributed Education, Chattanooga State Technical Community College, 4501 Amnicola Highway, Chattanooga, TN 37406-1097. Telephone: 423-697-2592. Fax: 423-697-4479. E-mail: tim.dills@chattanoogastate.edu.

DEGREES AND AWARDS
Programs offered do not lead to a degree or other formal award.

COURSE SUBJECT AREAS OFFERED OUTSIDE OF DEGREE PROGRAMS
Undergraduate—accounting and computer science; accounting and related services; allied health and medical assisting services; American literature (United States and Canadian); American Sign Language (ASL); behavioral sciences; biblical studies; biology; building/construction finishing, management, and inspection; business administration, management and operations; business/commerce; business, management, and marketing related; chemistry; communication and media; computer and information sciences; computer science; dental support services and allied professions; developmental and child psychology; economics; education; educational psychology; English; English composition; English literature (British and Commonwealth); finance and financial management services; fire protection; geography and cartography; health and medical administrative services; health/medical preparatory programs; health professions related; history; liberal arts and sciences, general studies and humanities; marketing; mathematics; mathematics and statistics related; music; philosophy; philosophy and religious studies related; physics; political science and government; psychology; religious studies; sociology; speech and rhetoric; statistics; technical and business writing.

CHEMEKETA COMMUNITY COLLEGE
Salem, Oregon
Chemeketa Online
http://online.chemeketa.edu
Chemeketa Community College was founded in 1955. It is accredited by Northwest Commission on Colleges and Universities. It first offered distance learning courses in 1979. In fall 2006, there were 8,229 students enrolled in distance learning courses. Institutionally administered financial aid is available to distance learners.
Services Distance learners have accessibility to academic advising, bookstore, e-mail services, library services, tutoring.
Contact Department Reception Desk, Secretary, Chemeketa Community College, 4000 Lancaster Drive NE, PO Box 14007, Salem, OR 97309-7070. Telephone: 503-399-7873. E-mail: col@chemeketa.edu.

DEGREES AND AWARDS
AA Oregon Transfer
AAS Fire Protection Technology–Fire Prevention; Fire Protection Technology–Fire Suppression; Hospitality Management; Speech/Language Pathology Assistant; Tourism and Travel Management
AGS General Studies
AS Business
Certificate of Completion Computer Assisted Drafting (CAD); Oregon Transfer Module
Certificate Business Software; Hospitality Management; Speech/ Language Pathology Assistant; Tourism and Travel Management

COURSE SUBJECT AREAS OFFERED OUTSIDE OF DEGREE PROGRAMS
Undergraduate—accounting and related services; allied health and medical assisting services; American literature (United States and Canadian); anthropology; applied mathematics; archeology; area, ethnic, cultural, and gender studies related; astronomy and astrophysics; biological and biomedical sciences related; biological and physical sciences; biology; business administration, management and operations; business/commerce; business/corporate communications; business, management, and marketing related; business operations support and assistant services; chemistry; computer and information sciences; computer and information sciences and support services related; computer programming; computer science; computer software and media applications; computer systems networking and telecommunications; creative writing; criminal justice and corrections; criminology; curriculum and instruction; data entry/microcomputer applications; developmental and child psychology; drafting/design engineering technologies; economics; education; education related; English composition; ethnic, cultural minority, and gender studies; fine and studio art; fire protection; foods, nutrition, and related services; geography and cartography; geological and earth sciences/geosciences; health and physical education/fitness; health professions related; history; hospitality administration; human development, family studies, and related services; information science/studies; liberal arts and sciences, general studies and humanities; management information systems; mathematics; mathematics and computer science; mathematics and statistics related; music; philosophy; philosophy and religious studies related; physical sciences; physical sciences related; political science and government; psychology; psychology related; religious studies; sales, merchandising, and related marketing operations (general); sales, merchandising, and related marketing operations (specialized); social sciences; social sciences related; sociology; speech and rhetoric; statistics; technical and business writing.

CHESAPEAKE COLLEGE
Wye Mills, Maryland
http://www.chesapeake.edu/distance
Chesapeake College was founded in 1965. It is accredited by Middle States Association of Colleges and Schools. It first offered distance learning courses in 1994. In fall 2006, there were 1,000 students enrolled in distance learning courses. Institutionally administered financial aid is available to distance learners.
Services Distance learners have accessibility to academic advising, bookstore, campus computer network, e-mail services, library services, tutoring.
Contact Mary Celeste Alexander, Director, Chesapeake College, 1000 College Circle, Wye Mills, MD 21679. Telephone: 410-822-5400 Ext. 263. Fax: 410-827-5875. E-mail: mcalexander@chesapeake.edu.

DEGREES AND AWARDS
Programs offered do not lead to a degree or other formal award.

COURSE SUBJECT AREAS OFFERED OUTSIDE OF DEGREE PROGRAMS
Undergraduate—accounting and computer science; allied health and medical assisting services; American literature (United States and Canadian); behavioral sciences; biological and physical sciences; business, management, and marketing related; communication and media; computer and information sciences and support services related; criminal

justice and corrections; education; English; English as a second language; liberal arts and sciences, general studies and humanities; mathematics and computer science; nursing.

CINCINNATI CHRISTIAN UNIVERSITY
Cincinnati, Ohio
Correspondence Department
http://www.cincybible.edu/eagleonline

Cincinnati Christian University was founded in 1924. It is accredited by Association for Biblical Higher Education. It first offered distance learning courses in 1980. In fall 2006, there were 237 students enrolled in distance learning courses. Institutionally administered financial aid is available to distance learners.

Services Distance learners have accessibility to academic advising, bookstore, campus computer network, e-mail services, library services, tutoring.

Contact Ms. Suzanne Faber, Administrative Assistant to the Dean of Distance Education and Institutional Research, Cincinnati Christian University, 2700 Glenway Avenue, Cincinnati, OH 45204-3200. Telephone: 513-244-8475. Fax: 513-244-8123. E-mail: suzanne.faber@ ccuniversity.edu.

DEGREES AND AWARDS
Programs offered do not lead to a degree or other formal award.

COURSE SUBJECT AREAS OFFERED OUTSIDE OF DEGREE PROGRAMS

Undergraduate—biblical and other theological languages and literatures; biblical studies; education; history.
Graduate—biblical and other theological languages and literatures; biblical studies; counseling psychology; education; history; religious studies.

CINCINNATI STATE TECHNICAL AND COMMUNITY COLLEGE
Cincinnati, Ohio
http://www.cincinnatistate.edu

Cincinnati State Technical and Community College was founded in 1966. It is accredited by North Central Association of Colleges and Schools. It first offered distance learning courses in 1994. In fall 2006, there were 1,156 students enrolled in distance learning courses. Institutionally administered financial aid is available to distance learners.

Services Distance learners have accessibility to academic advising, bookstore, campus computer network, e-mail services, library services.

Contact Ms. Gaby Boeckermann, Director of Admissions, Cincinnati State Technical and Community College, 3520 Central Parkway, Cincinnati, OH 45223. Telephone: 513-569-1550. E-mail: gaby. boeckermann@cincinnatistate.edu.

DEGREES AND AWARDS
Programs offered do not lead to a degree or other formal award.

COURSE SUBJECT AREAS OFFERED OUTSIDE OF DEGREE PROGRAMS

Undergraduate—accounting and related services; allied health and medical assisting services; applied horticulture/horticultural business services; business administration, management and operations; business/ commerce; business operations support and assistant services; civil engineering technology; communication and media; computer and information sciences; computer/information technology administration and management; computer software and media applications; computer systems networking and telecommunications; data processing; engineering technologies related; health and medical administrative services; health professions related; history; information science/studies; management information systems; mechanical engineering related technologies; sociology.

CITY UNIVERSITY
Bellevue, Washington
Distance Learning Option
http://www.cityu.edu

City University was founded in 1973. It is accredited by Northwest Commission on Colleges and Universities. It first offered distance learning courses in 1985. In fall 2006, there were 600 students enrolled in distance learning courses. Institutionally administered financial aid is available to distance learners.

Services Distance learners have accessibility to academic advising, bookstore, e-mail services, library services, tutoring.

Contact Office of Admissions, City University, 11900 NE First Street, Bellevue, WA 98005. Telephone: 800-422-4898. Fax: 425-709-5361. E-mail: info@cityu.edu.

DEGREES AND AWARDS
AS General Studies
BA Psychology–Applied Psychology
BS Accounting; Business Administration (Information Systems/ Technology emphasis); Business Administration (Marketing emphasis); Business Administration (Project Management emphasis); Business Administration–E-Commerce emphasis (Bulgaria); Business Administration–General Management emphasis; Business Administration–Human Resource emphasis; Business Administration–Individualized Study emphasis; Computer Systems (Networking/Telecommunications emphasis); Computer Systems (Programming in C++ emphasis); Computer Systems (Web Design emphasis); Computer Systems–Database Technology emphasis; Computer Systems–Individualized Study emphasis; Computer Systems–Information Technology Security emphasis; Computer Systems–Web Languages emphasis; General Studies
Certificate Accounting; Marketing; Networking/Telecommunications; Programming in C++; Project Management; Web Design; Web Languages
Graduate Certificate Computer Programming–C++ Programming; Financial Management; General Management; Information Systems; Marketing; Personal Financial Planning; Project Management; Technology Management; Web Development; Web Programming in E-Commerce
MA Management–General Management emphasis
MBA Personal Financial Planning
MS Computer Systems–C++ Programming emphasis; Computer Systems–Individualized Study emphasis; Computer Systems–Technology Management emphasis; Computer Systems–Web Development emphasis; Computer Systems–Web Programming in E-Commerce emphasis; Project Management

See full description on page 334.

CLACKAMAS COMMUNITY COLLEGE
Oregon City, Oregon
Learning Resources
http://dl.clackamas.edu

Clackamas Community College was founded in 1966. It is accredited by Northwest Commission on Colleges and Universities. It first offered distance learning courses in 1997. In fall 2006, there were 9,422 students enrolled in distance learning courses. Institutionally administered financial aid is available to distance learners.

Services Distance learners have accessibility to academic advising, bookstore, campus computer network, career placement assistance, e-mail services, library services, tutoring.

Contact Debra Carino, Director of Distance Learning, Clackamas Community College, 19600 South Molalla Avenue, Oregon City, OR 97045. Telephone: 503-657-6958 Ext. 5198. E-mail: debrac@clackamas.edu.

DEGREES AND AWARDS
Programs offered do not lead to a degree or other formal award.

COURSE SUBJECT AREAS OFFERED OUTSIDE OF DEGREE PROGRAMS

Undergraduate—accounting and computer science; accounting and related services; allied health and medical assisting services; astronomy and astrophysics; biology; building/construction finishing, management, and inspection; business administration, management and operations; business, management, and marketing related; chemistry; computer science; criminal justice and corrections; education; English composition; English literature (British and Commonwealth); environmental/ environmental health engineering; human development, family studies, and related services; legal professions and studies related; mathematics; music; physics; speech and rhetoric; technical and business writing.

CLARION UNIVERSITY OF PENNSYLVANIA
Clarion, Pennsylvania
Extended Studies and Distance Learning Department
http://www.clarion.edu/academic/distance/index.shtml
Clarion University of Pennsylvania was founded in 1867. It is accredited by Middle States Association of Colleges and Schools. It first offered distance learning courses in 1996. In fall 2006, there were 1,929 students enrolled in distance learning courses. Institutionally administered financial aid is available to distance learners.
Services Distance learners have accessibility to academic advising, bookstore, campus computer network, e-mail services, library services.
Contact Ms. Lynne M. Lander Fleisher, Associate Director, Clarion University of Pennsylvania, Office of Extended Programs, 840 Wood Street, Clarion, PA 16214. Telephone: 814-393-2778. Fax: 814-393-2779. E-mail: lfleisher@clarion.edu.

DEGREES AND AWARDS
AA Arts and Sciences
AD Early Childhood Education
BS Liberal Studies, Library Science concentration
BSN Nursing
Certification Education–Graduate PA Secondary Teacher certification program; Instructional Technology Specialist
MA Rehabilitative Science
MBA Business Administration; Business Administration
MLS Library Science
MSN Nursing–Family Nurse Practitioner

COURSE SUBJECT AREAS OFFERED OUTSIDE OF DEGREE PROGRAMS
Undergraduate—atmospheric sciences and meteorology; biology; chemistry; communication and media; computer science; economics; education related; English composition; health and physical education/ fitness; languages (foreign languages related); legal professions and studies related; library science; music; nursing; philosophy; psychology; real estate; visual and performing arts related.
Graduate—business administration, management and operations; education; library science; nursing; rehabilitation and therapeutic professions.
Non-credit—real estate.

CLARKSON COLLEGE
Omaha, Nebraska
Office of Distance Education
http://www.clarksoncollege.edu
Clarkson College was founded in 1888. It is accredited by North Central Association of Colleges and Schools. It first offered distance learning courses in 1986. In fall 2006, there were 426 students enrolled in distance learning courses. Institutionally administered financial aid is available to distance learners.
Services Distance learners have accessibility to academic advising, bookstore, campus computer network, career placement assistance, e-mail services, library services, tutoring.
Contact Admissions, Clarkson College, 101 South 42nd Street, Omaha, NE 68131. Telephone: 800-647-5500. Fax: 402-552-6057. E-mail: admiss@clarksoncollege.edu.

DEGREES AND AWARDS
AD Health Information Management

BS Health Care Business–Health Information Management major; Health Care Business–Informatics major; Health Care Business–Management major; Medical Imaging
BSN Nursing–RN to BSN
Certificate Health Information Management–Foundations; Health Information Management–HIM; PACS Administrator; PACS Manager
MS Health Care Business Leadership
MSN Adult Nurse Practitioner; Family Nurse Practitioner; Nursing Education; Nursing Health Care Leadership

CLARK STATE COMMUNITY COLLEGE
Springfield, Ohio
Alternative Methods of Instructional Delivery
http://www.clarkstate.edu/
Clark State Community College was founded in 1962. It is accredited by North Central Association of Colleges and Schools. It first offered distance learning courses in 1996. In fall 2006, there were 2,000 students enrolled in distance learning courses. Institutionally administered financial aid is available to distance learners.
Services Distance learners have accessibility to academic advising, bookstore, campus computer network, career placement assistance, e-mail services, library services, tutoring.
Contact Amy Sues, Coordinator of Advising, Clark State Community College, PO Box 570, Springfield, OH 45501-0570. Telephone: 937-328-3867. Fax: 937-328-3853. E-mail: suesa@clarkstate.edu.

DEGREES AND AWARDS
AA University Transfer
AAS Medical Laboratory Technology; Nursing–Registered Nursing; Physical Therapist Assistant

COURSE SUBJECT AREAS OFFERED OUTSIDE OF DEGREE PROGRAMS
Undergraduate—accounting and computer science; agricultural business and management; allied health and medical assisting services; applied horticulture/horticultural business services; behavioral sciences; biological and biomedical sciences related; biological and physical sciences; biology; biology/biotechnology laboratory technician; business administration, management and operations; business/commerce; business, management, and marketing related; cell biology and anatomical sciences; chemistry; communication and media; computer and information sciences and support services related; computer software and media applications; creative writing; English; English composition; geological and earth sciences/geosciences; health professions related; history; nursing; psychology; psychology related; sociology; technical and business writing.
Non-credit—transportation and materials moving related.

CLATSOP COMMUNITY COLLEGE
Astoria, Oregon
http://www.clatsopcc.edu
Clatsop Community College was founded in 1958. It is accredited by Northwest Commission on Colleges and Universities. It first offered distance learning courses in 1986. In fall 2006, there were 215 students enrolled in distance learning courses. Institutionally administered financial aid is available to distance learners.
Services Distance learners have accessibility to bookstore, e-mail services, library services.
Contact Kirsten Horning, Distance Education Coordinator, Clatsop Community College, 1680 Lexington, Astoria, OR 97103. Telephone: 503-338-2341. Fax: 503-325-5738. E-mail: khorning@clatsopcc.edu.

DEGREES AND AWARDS
Programs offered do not lead to a degree or other formal award.

COURSE SUBJECT AREAS OFFERED OUTSIDE OF DEGREE PROGRAMS
Undergraduate—accounting and related services; anthropology; business administration, management and operations; business/commerce; business management, and marketing related; computer and information sciences

creative writing; criminology; developmental and child psychology; English; English composition; foods, nutrition, and related services; health and physical education/fitness; history; human development, family studies, and related services; marketing; mathematics; nursing; political science and government; psychology; sociology; statistics.

CLEAR CREEK BAPTIST BIBLE COLLEGE
Pineville, Kentucky
http://www.ccbbc.edu/OnlineClasses/default.asp
Clear Creek Baptist Bible College was founded in 1926. It is accredited by Association for Biblical Higher Education. It first offered distance learning courses in 2002. In fall 2006, there were 75 students enrolled in distance learning courses. Institutionally administered financial aid is available to distance learners.
Services Distance learners have accessibility to academic advising, bookstore, career placement assistance, e-mail services, library services.
Contact Rev. Billy Howell, Director of Admissions, Clear Creek Baptist Bible College, 300 Clear Creek Road, Pineville, KY 40977. Telephone: 606-337-3196 Ext. 103. Fax: 606-337-2372. E-mail: bhowell@ccbbc.edu.

DEGREES AND AWARDS
Programs offered do not lead to a degree or other formal award.

COURSE SUBJECT AREAS OFFERED OUTSIDE OF DEGREE PROGRAMS
Undergraduate—biblical studies; theological and ministerial studies; theology and religious vocations related.

CLEMSON UNIVERSITY
Clemson, South Carolina
Distance Education, Educational Technology Services
http://www.ets.clemson.edu/
Clemson University was founded in 1889. It is accredited by Southern Association of Colleges and Schools. It first offered distance learning courses in 1988. In fall 2006, there were 1,842 students enrolled in distance learning courses. Institutionally administered financial aid is available to distance learners.
Services Distance learners have accessibility to academic advising, bookstore, campus computer network, career placement assistance, e-mail services, library services.
Contact Kathy Hoellen, Director, Teaching and Learning Technologies, Clemson University, 439 Brackett Hall, PO Box 342803, Clemson, SC 29634-2803. Telephone: 864-653-0379. Fax: 864-656-0750. E-mail: hoellen@clemson.edu.

DEGREES AND AWARDS
BS Nursing
MCSM Construction Science and Management
MEngr Electrical Engineering
MS Human Resource Development; Nursing; Youth Development
PhD Educational Leadership

COURSE SUBJECT AREAS OFFERED OUTSIDE OF DEGREE PROGRAMS
Undergraduate—astronomy and astrophysics; business/commerce; communication and media; construction management; economics; electrical and electronic engineering technologies; English composition; marketing; mathematics; music; nutrition sciences; parks, recreation and leisure; physics; sociology.
Graduate—agriculture; animal sciences; business administration, management and operations; communication and media; construction management; electrical and electronic engineering technologies; English; history; human resources management; nutrition sciences; statistics.
Non-credit—accounting and related services; allied health and medical assisting services; building/construction finishing, management, and inspection; business/commerce; business, management, and marketing related; business operations support and assistant services; communication and media; computer and information sciences; computer pro-

gramming; computer software and media applications; computer systems networking and telecommunications; construction engineering technology; creative writing; data entry/microcomputer applications; data processing; English composition; languages (Romance languages); legal professions and studies related; mathematics; publishing; teaching assistants/aides; technical and business writing.

CLEVELAND INSTITUTE OF ELECTRONICS
Cleveland, Ohio
http://www.cie-wc.edu/WorldCollege/Main.html
Cleveland Institute of Electronics was founded in 1934. It is accredited by Distance Education and Training Council. It first offered distance learning courses in 1941.
Services Distance learners have accessibility to academic advising, bookstore, library services, tutoring.
Contact Guidance Counselor, Cleveland Institute of Electronics, 1776 East 17th Street, Cleveland, OH 44114. Telephone: 216-781-9400. Fax: 216-781-0331. E-mail: instruct@cie-wc.edu.

DEGREES AND AWARDS
AAS Computer Information Technology and Systems Management; Electronic Engineering Technology
Diploma A+ Certification and Computer Technology; Broadcast Engineering; Computer Programming with Java and C#; Electronics Engineering; Electronics Technology and Advanced Troubleshooting; Electronics Technology with Digital Microprocessor Lab; Electronics Technology with FCC License Preparation; Electronics Technology with Laboratory; Industrial Electronics with PLC Technology; Network+ Certification and Computer Technology; Wireless and Electronic Communications
Specialized diploma Introduction to Home Automation Installation

COURSE SUBJECT AREAS OFFERED OUTSIDE OF DEGREE PROGRAMS
Undergraduate—communication and media; computer engineering; electrical and electronic engineering technologies; engineering; social sciences related.
Non-credit—accounting and computer science; building/construction finishing, management, and inspection; business administration, management and operations; business/commerce; business/corporate communications; carpentry; computer/information technology administration and management; computer programming; computer science; computer software and media applications; construction engineering; construction trades; counseling psychology; crafts, folk art and artisanry; creative writing; data entry/microcomputer applications; drafting/design engineering technologies; electrical and power transmission installation; electrical/electronics maintenance and repair technology; engineering design; engineering/industrial management; film/video and photographic arts; marketing; mathematics; mathematics and computer science; mechanical engineering related technologies; mechanic and repair technologies related; mechanics and repair; woodworking.

CLEVELAND INSTITUTE OF MUSIC
Cleveland, Ohio
Cleveland Institute of Music was founded in 1920. It is accredited by North Central Association of Colleges and Schools. It first offered distance learning courses in 1997. In fall 2006, there were 10,000 students enrolled in distance learning courses. Institutionally administered financial aid is available to distance learners.
Contact Mr. Adam Phillips, Manager of Distance Learning Programs, Cleveland Institute of Music, 11021 East Boulevard, Cleveland, OH 44106. Telephone: 216-707-4516. E-mail: axp99@case.edu.

DEGREES AND AWARDS
Programs offered do not lead to a degree or other formal award.

COURSE SUBJECT AREAS OFFERED OUTSIDE OF DEGREE PROGRAMS
Undergraduate—music.
Graduate—music.
Non-credit—music.

CLEVELAND STATE UNIVERSITY
Cleveland, Ohio
Off-Campus Academic Programs
http://www.csuohio.edu/offcampus

Cleveland State University was founded in 1964. It is accredited by North Central Association of Colleges and Schools. It first offered distance learning courses in 1994. In fall 2006, there were 1,105 students enrolled in distance learning courses. Institutionally administered financial aid is available to distance learners.

Services Distance learners have accessibility to academic advising, bookstore, campus computer network, career placement assistance, e-mail services, library services, tutoring.

Contact Mr. Paul E. Bowers, Director of eLearning, Cleveland State University, Rhodes Tower 203, 2121 Euclid Avenue, Cleveland, OH 44115. Telephone: 216-875-9624. Fax: 216-687-9733. E-mail: p.bowers@csuohio.edu.

DEGREES AND AWARDS

Certificate Bioethics
Endorsement Computer/Technology
Graduate Certificate Adult Learning and Development; Bioethics; Research Administration
MEd Adult Learning and Development; Educational Technology
MS Health Science
MSN Forensic Nursing
MSW Social Work

COURSE SUBJECT AREAS OFFERED OUTSIDE OF DEGREE PROGRAMS

Undergraduate—accounting and computer science; accounting and related services; area, ethnic, cultural, and gender studies related; bioethics/medical ethics; biological and biomedical sciences related; biology; chemistry; city/urban, community and regional planning; civil engineering; communication and journalism related; communication and media; computer and information sciences; computer engineering; computer programming; computer science; computer software and media applications; education; electrical and electronic engineering technologies; engineering; engineering-related fields; engineering technology; English; geography and cartography; geological and earth sciences/geosciences; history; linguistic, comparative, and related language studies; nursing; pharmacy, pharmaceutical sciences, and administration; philosophy; public administration; public administration and social service professions related; social work; special education; urban studies/affairs.

Graduate—accounting and related services; area, ethnic, cultural, and gender studies related; bioethics/medical ethics; chemical engineering; city/urban, community and regional planning; civil engineering; computer engineering; crafts, folk art and artisanry; curriculum and instruction; education; educational assessment, evaluation, and research; education related; education (specific levels and methods); education (specific subject areas); electrical, electronics and communications engineering; engineering; engineering/industrial management; engineering related; engineering-related fields; engineering-related technologies; environmental/environmental health engineering; health and medical administrative services; health/medical preparatory programs; health professions related; health services/allied health/health sciences; industrial engineering; linguistic, comparative, and related language studies; manufacturing engineering; mechanical engineering; mechanical engineering related technologies; nursing; philosophy; philosophy and religious studies related; public administration; public administration and social service professions related; social work; special education; student counseling and personnel services; technology education/industrial arts; urban studies/affairs.

Non-credit—accounting and related services; business administration, management and operations; business/commerce; business/corporate communications; computer software and media applications; computer systems networking and telecommunications; data entry/microcomputer applications; education related; entrepreneurial and small business operations; family and consumer economics; film/video and photographic arts; foods, nutrition, and related services; health and physical education/fitness; health professions related; human development, family studies, and related services; journalism; languages (foreign languages related); legal support services; management information systems; public health; sales, merchandising, and related marketing operations (specialized); technology education/industrial arts.

CLINTON COMMUNITY COLLEGE
Plattsburgh, New York
http://clinton.edu

Clinton Community College was founded in 1969. It is accredited by Middle States Association of Colleges and Schools. It first offered distance learning courses in 2000. In fall 2006, there were 300 students enrolled in distance learning courses. Institutionally administered financial aid is available to distance learners.

Services Distance learners have accessibility to academic advising, bookstore, campus computer network, career placement assistance, e-mail services, library services, tutoring.

Contact Prof. Vicky Sloan, Distance Learning Coordinator, Clinton Community College, 136 Clinton Point Drive, Plattsburgh, NY 12901. Telephone: 518-562-4281. E-mail: vicky.sloan@clinton.edu.

DEGREES AND AWARDS

AA Liberal Arts/Humanities and Social Science
AAS Business
AS Business Administration and Liberal Arts; Humanities and Social Science

COURSE SUBJECT AREAS OFFERED OUTSIDE OF DEGREE PROGRAMS

Undergraduate—accounting and related services; applied mathematics; biological and physical sciences; business administration, management and operations; business/corporate communications; clinical/medical laboratory science and allied professions; computer and information sciences; computer programming; criminal justice and corrections; economics; English; English composition; history; human development, family studies, and related services; human services; liberal arts and sciences, general studies and humanities; music; political science and government; psychology; sociology; statistics.

CLOUD COUNTY COMMUNITY COLLEGE
Concordia, Kansas

Cloud County Community College was founded in 1965. It is accredited by North Central Association of Colleges and Schools. It first offered distance learning courses in 2000. In fall 2006, there were 600 students enrolled in distance learning courses. Institutionally administered financial aid is available to distance learners.

Services Distance learners have accessibility to academic advising, bookstore, career placement assistance, library services, tutoring.

Contact Holly Andrews, Coordinator of Outreach Instruction, Cloud County Community College, 2221 Campus Drive, Concordia, KS 66901. Telephone: 785-243-0435 Ext. 371. Fax: 785-243-1640. E-mail: handrews@cloud.edu.

DEGREES AND AWARDS

Programs offered do not lead to a degree or other formal award.

COURSE SUBJECT AREAS OFFERED OUTSIDE OF DEGREE PROGRAMS

Undergraduate—accounting and computer science; accounting and related services; allied health and medical assisting services; behavioral sciences; computer science; criminal justice and corrections; economics; English; history; legal professions and studies related; mathematics; nutrition sciences; psychology; sociology.

Non-credit—accounting and computer science; computer and information sciences.

CLOVIS COMMUNITY COLLEGE
Clovis, New Mexico
http://www.clovis.edu/

Clovis Community College was founded in 1990. It is accredited by North Central Association of Colleges and Schools. It first offered distance learning courses in 1990. In fall 2006, there were 700 students enrolled in distance learning courses. Institutionally administered financial aid is available to distance learners.

Services Distance learners have accessibility to academic advising, bookstore, e-mail services, library services, tutoring.

Contact Mrs. Susan M. Fulgham, Educational Technologist, Clovis Community College, 417 Schepps Boulevard, Clovis, NM 88101. Telephone: 505-769-4903. Fax: 505-769-4190. E-mail: susan.fulgham@ clovis.edu.

DEGREES AND AWARDS
AAS Criminal Justice

COURSE SUBJECT AREAS OFFERED OUTSIDE OF DEGREE PROGRAMS
Undergraduate—biblical studies; biology; business administration, management and operations; communication and media; computer and information sciences; criminal justice and corrections; developmental and child psychology; economics; English composition; fine and studio art; history; languages (Romance languages); mathematics; mathematics and statistics related; sociology.

COGSWELL POLYTECHNICAL COLLEGE
Sunnyvale, California
http://www.cogswell.edu/

Cogswell Polytechnical College was founded in 1887. It is accredited by Western Association of Schools and Colleges. It first offered distance learning courses in 1981. In fall 2006, there were 74 students enrolled in distance learning courses. Institutionally administered financial aid is available to distance learners.

Services Distance learners have accessibility to academic advising, e-mail services, library services.

Contact Ms. Milla Zlatanov, Data Manager, Cogswell Polytechnical College, 1175 Bordeaux Drive, Sunnyvale, CA 94089. Telephone: 408-541-0100 Ext. 133. Fax: 408-747-0764. E-mail: mzlatanov@cogswell.edu.

DEGREES AND AWARDS
BS Fire Science

COLLEGE OF DUPAGE
Glen Ellyn, Illinois
Alternative Learning Division
http://www.cod.edu/cil

College of DuPage was founded in 1967. It is accredited by North Central Association of Colleges and Schools. It first offered distance learning courses in 1980. In fall 2006, there were 6,000 students enrolled in distance learning courses. Institutionally administered financial aid is available to distance learners.

Services Distance learners have accessibility to academic advising, bookstore, campus computer network, e-mail services, library services, tutoring.

Contact Ron Schiesz, Counselor, Alternative Learning Program, College of DuPage, Center for Independent Learning, 425 Fawell Street, Glen Ellyn, IL 60137-6599. Telephone: 630-942-3326 Ext. 3326. Fax: 630-942-3764. E-mail: schiesz@cdnet.cod.edu.

DEGREES AND AWARDS
Programs offered do not lead to a degree or other formal award.

COURSE SUBJECT AREAS OFFERED OUTSIDE OF DEGREE PROGRAMS
Undergraduate—accounting and related services; anthropology; biology; business administration, management and operations; chemistry; communication and media; computer programming; computer software and media applications; computer systems networking and telecommunications; criminal justice and corrections; developmental and child psychology; economics; English as a second language; English composition; history; human services; journalism; languages (Romance languages); liberal arts and sciences, general studies and humanities; library assistant; library science; mathematics; music; philosophy and religious studies related; physics; psychology; religious studies; sales, merchandising, and related marketing operations (general); social psychology; social sciences; social sciences related; sociology.

COLLEGE OF EMMANUEL AND ST. CHAD
Saskatoon, Saskatchewan, Canada

College of Emmanuel and St. Chad was founded in 1879. It is provincially chartered. It first offered distance learning courses in 1995. In fall 2006, there were 5 students enrolled in distance learning courses. Institutionally administered financial aid is available to distance learners.

Services Distance learners have accessibility to academic advising, bookstore, campus computer network, library services.

Contact Ms. Colleen Walker, Registrar, College of Emmanuel and St. Chad, 114 Seminary Crescent, Saskatoon, SK S7N 0X3, Canada. Telephone: 306-975-1558. Fax: 306-934-2683. E-mail: colleen.walker@ usask.ca.

DEGREES AND AWARDS
Programs offered do not lead to a degree or other formal award.

COURSE SUBJECT AREAS OFFERED OUTSIDE OF DEGREE PROGRAMS
Graduate—biblical and other theological languages and literatures; biblical studies; theological and ministerial studies; theology and religious vocations related.

COLLEGE OF MOUNT ST. JOSEPH
Cincinnati, Ohio
http://www.msj.edu/

College of Mount St. Joseph was founded in 1920. It is accredited by North Central Association of Colleges and Schools. It first offered distance learning courses in 1997. In fall 2006, there were 85 students enrolled in distance learning courses. Institutionally administered financial aid is available to distance learners.

Services Distance learners have accessibility to academic advising, bookstore, campus computer network, career placement assistance, e-mail services, library services, tutoring.

Contact Ms. Peggy Minnich, Director of Admissions, College of Mount St. Joseph, 5701 Delhi Road, Cincinnati, OH 45233. Telephone: 513-244-4814. E-mail: peggy_minnich@mail.msj.edu.

DEGREES AND AWARDS
Programs offered do not lead to a degree or other formal award.

COURSE SUBJECT AREAS OFFERED OUTSIDE OF DEGREE PROGRAMS
Undergraduate—biology; business administration, management and operations; computer and information sciences; education; legal support services; music; political science and government; religious studies; social psychology.
Graduate—business administration, management and operations; education; religious studies.

THE COLLEGE OF ST. SCHOLASTICA
Duluth, Minnesota
Graduate Studies
http://grad.css.edu

The College of St. Scholastica was founded in 1912. It is accredited by North Central Association of Colleges and Schools. It first offered distance learning courses in 1986. In fall 2006, there were 137 students enrolled in distance learning courses. Institutionally administered financial aid is available to distance learners.

Services Distance learners have accessibility to academic advising, bookstore, campus computer network, career placement assistance, e-mail services, library services, tutoring.

Contact Tonya J. Roth, Graduate Recruitment Counselor, The College of St. Scholastica, 1200 Kenwood Avenue, Duluth, MN 55811. Telephone: 218-723-6285. Fax: 218-733-2275. E-mail: gradstudies@css.edu.

DEGREES AND AWARDS

BA Health Information Management Degree completion; Nursing–RN to BA completion
Certificate Computer Information Systems; Graduate Teaching Licensure; Healthcare Informatics
MA Computer Information Systems; Health Information Management
MEd Curriculum and Instruction; Educational Media and Technology; Graduate Teaching Licensure

COURSE SUBJECT AREAS OFFERED OUTSIDE OF DEGREE PROGRAMS

Undergraduate—biology; computer and information sciences; economics; gerontology; health and medical administrative services; music; nursing; psychology.
Graduate—biology; curriculum and instruction; health and medical administrative services; library science related; music; nursing.

COLLEGE OF SAN MATEO
San Mateo, California
http://www.collegeofsanmateo.edu

College of San Mateo was founded in 1922. It is accredited by Western Association of Schools and Colleges. It first offered distance learning courses in 1977. In fall 2006, there were 1,325 students enrolled in distance learning courses. Institutionally administered financial aid is available to distance learners.
Services Distance learners have accessibility to academic advising, bookstore, campus computer network, career placement assistance, e-mail services, library services, tutoring.
Contact Betty Fleming, Distance Learning Coordinator, College of San Mateo, 1700 West Hillsdale Boulevard, San Mateo, CA 94402-3784. Telephone: 650-524-6933. Fax: 650-574-6345. E-mail: fleming@smccd.edu.

DEGREES AND AWARDS

Programs offered do not lead to a degree or other formal award.

COURSE SUBJECT AREAS OFFERED OUTSIDE OF DEGREE PROGRAMS

Undergraduate—accounting and related services; anthropology; astronomy and astrophysics; business/commerce; business/corporate communications; chemistry; computer programming; English composition; film/video and photographic arts; health and physical education/fitness; languages (Romance languages); legal studies (non-professional general, undergraduate); marketing; mathematics; philosophy; political science and government; psychology; sociology.

COLLEGE OF SOUTHERN MARYLAND
La Plata, Maryland
Distance Learning Department
http://www.csmd.edu

College of Southern Maryland was founded in 1958. It is accredited by Middle States Association of Colleges and Schools. It first offered distance learning courses in 1980. In fall 2006, there were 2,083 students enrolled in distance learning courses. Institutionally administered financial aid is available to distance learners.
Services Distance learners have accessibility to academic advising, bookstore, campus computer network, career placement assistance, e-mail services, library services, tutoring.
Contact Paul Toscano, Distance Learning Coordinator, College of Southern Maryland, 8730 Mitchell Road, PO Box 910, La Plata, MD 20646-0910. Telephone: 301-934-7615. Fax: 301-934-7699. E-mail: pault@csmd.edu.

DEGREES AND AWARDS

AA Arts and Sciences–Applied Science and Technology; Arts and Sciences–Arts and Humanities; Arts and Sciences–Social Sciences; Arts and Sciences; General Studies
AAS Computer Programming; Information Services Technology–Web Developer; Information Services Technology; Management Development
AS Business Administration–Technical Management; Business Administration
Certificate Accounting, advanced; Accounting, basic; Computer Skills for Managers; General Studies; Information Services Technology; Management Development–Marketing; Management Development; Web Developer

COURSE SUBJECT AREAS OFFERED OUTSIDE OF DEGREE PROGRAMS

Undergraduate—accounting and related services; astronomy and astrophysics; biology; business/commerce; business/corporate communications; communication and media; computer systems analysis; computer systems networking and telecommunications; creative writing; criminal justice and corrections; economics; educational psychology; education related; English composition; fine and studio art; geography and cartography; health and physical education/fitness; history; human development, family studies, and related services; human resources management; information science/studies; international business; languages (Romance languages); legal studies (non-professional general, undergraduate); marketing; mathematics; mathematics and statistics related; philosophy; philosophy and religious studies related; physics; political science and government; psychology; sociology; statistics; technical and business writing.
Non-credit—computer/information technology administration and management; education; health professions related; nursing.

COLLEGE OF THE ALBEMARLE
Elizabeth City, North Carolina
Distance Education
http://www.albemarle.edu

College of The Albemarle was founded in 1960. It is accredited by Southern Association of Colleges and Schools. It first offered distance learning courses in 1993. In fall 2006, there were 1,000 students enrolled in distance learning courses. Institutionally administered financial aid is available to distance learners.
Services Distance learners have accessibility to academic advising, bookstore, career placement assistance, e-mail services, library services, tutoring.
Contact Jerry Oliver, Distance Education Coordinator, College of The Albemarle, PO Box 2327, Elizabeth City, NC 27906-2327. Telephone: 252-335-0821 Ext. 2313. Fax: 252-337-6710. E-mail: joliver@albemarle.edu.

DEGREES AND AWARDS

AAS Business Administration; Criminal Justice

COURSE SUBJECT AREAS OFFERED OUTSIDE OF DEGREE PROGRAMS

Undergraduate—accounting and related services; biology; business administration, management and operations; business/commerce; business/corporate communications; computer and information sciences; computer science; economics; education related; electrical and electronic engineering technologies; English composition; English literature (British and Commonwealth); fine and studio art; health and physical education/fitness; history; human development, family studies, and related services; legal studies (non-professional general, undergraduate); marketing; mathematics and statistics related; psychology; sociology.
Non-credit—accounting and related services; business administration, management and operations; business/commerce; business/corporate communications; business, management, and marketing related; business operations support and assistant services; communication and media; computer and information sciences; computer engineering; computer/information technology administration and management; computer pro-

gramming; computer science; computer software and media applications; computer systems networking and telecommunications; data entry/microcomputer applications; data processing; educational administration and supervision; English; English composition; gerontology; human services; information science/studies; management information systems; mental and social health services and allied professions; public administration; public administration and social service professions related; sales, merchandising, and related marketing operations (specialized); technical and business writing.

COLLEGE OF THE SISKIYOUS
Weed, California
Distance Learning
http://www.siskiyous.edu/distancelearning/
College of the Siskiyous was founded in 1957. It is accredited by Western Association of Schools and Colleges. It first offered distance learning courses in 1975. In fall 2006, there were 549 students enrolled in distance learning courses. Institutionally administered financial aid is available to distance learners.
Services Distance learners have accessibility to academic advising, bookstore, career placement assistance, e-mail services, library services, tutoring.
Contact Nancy Shepard, Telecommunications Specialist, College of the Siskiyous, 800 College Avenue, Weed, CA 96094. Telephone: 530-938-5520. E-mail: shepard@siskiyous.edu.

DEGREES AND AWARDS
Programs offered do not lead to a degree or other formal award.

COURSE SUBJECT AREAS OFFERED OUTSIDE OF DEGREE PROGRAMS
Undergraduate—accounting and related services; business/commerce; business/corporate communications; computer science; English composition; English language and literature related; English literature (British and Commonwealth); family and consumer economics; family psychology; health and physical education/fitness; history; liberal arts and sciences, general studies and humanities; mathematics; nursing; nutrition sciences; political science and government; psychology; social sciences; student counseling and personnel services; teaching assistants/aides. **Non-credit**—creative writing.

COLLEGE OF THE SOUTHWEST
Hobbs, New Mexico
http://www.csw.edu/
College of the Southwest was founded in 1962. It is accredited by North Central Association of Colleges and Schools. It first offered distance learning courses in 1994. In fall 2006, there were 300 students enrolled in distance learning courses. Institutionally administered financial aid is available to distance learners.
Services Distance learners have accessibility to academic advising, bookstore, campus computer network, e-mail services, library services, tutoring.
Contact Renee M. Stark, Registrar, College of the Southwest, 6610 Lovington Highway, Hobbs, NM 88240. Telephone: 505-392-6561 Ext. 1008. Fax: 505-392-6006. E-mail: rstark@csw.edu.

DEGREES AND AWARDS
BS Criminal Justice
MSE Educational Administration and Counseling; Educational Diagnostician

COURSE SUBJECT AREAS OFFERED OUTSIDE OF DEGREE PROGRAMS
Undergraduate—accounting and related services; biology; business administration, management and operations; computer science; creative writing; criminal justice and corrections; developmental and child psychology; economics; education; English as a second language; English composition; history; industrial and organizational psychology; marketing; psychology; religious studies; social psychology; sociology.

Graduate—counseling psychology; curriculum and instruction; educational administration and supervision; educational assessment, evaluation, and research.

COLORADO MOUNTAIN COLLEGE DISTRICT SYSTEM
Glenwood Springs, Colorado
Educational Technology
http://www.coloradomtn.edu/distlearn/
Colorado Mountain College District System first offered distance learning courses in 1985. In fall 2006, there were 800 students enrolled in distance learning courses. Institutionally administered financial aid is available to distance learners.
Services Distance learners have accessibility to bookstore, e-mail services, library services.
Contact Mr. Daryl D. Yarrow, Distance Learning Coordinator, Colorado Mountain College District System, 831 Grand Avenue, Glenwood Springs, CO 81601. Telephone: 800-621-8559 Ext. 8336. Fax: 970-947-8307. E-mail: distance@coloradomtn.edu.

DEGREES AND AWARDS
Programs offered do not lead to a degree or other formal award.

COURSE SUBJECT AREAS OFFERED OUTSIDE OF DEGREE PROGRAMS
Undergraduate—accounting and related services; anthropology; astronomy and astrophysics; biology; business/commerce; business/corporate communications; chemistry; computer science; computer software and media applications; developmental and child psychology; economics; education related; English composition; fine and studio art; geography and cartography; health professions related; history; hospitality administration; languages (foreign languages related); library science related; mathematics and statistics related; philosophy; physics; psychology; social psychology; sociology; statistics.

COLORADO STATE UNIVERSITY
Fort Collins, Colorado
College of Business
http://www.csumba.com
Colorado State University was founded in 1870. It is accredited by North Central Association of Colleges and Schools. It first offered distance learning courses in 1967. In fall 2006, there were 525 students enrolled in distance learning courses. Institutionally administered financial aid is available to distance learners.
Services Distance learners have accessibility to academic advising, bookstore, campus computer network, career placement assistance, e-mail services, library services.
Contact Ms. Rachel Stoll, Graduate Admissions Coordinator, Colorado State University, College of Business, 1270 Campus Delivery, 164 Rockwell Hall, Fort Collins, CO 80523-1270. Telephone: 800-491-4622 Ext. 1. Fax: 970-491-3481. E-mail: rachel.stoll@colostate.edu.

DEGREES AND AWARDS
MBA Business Administration–Distance MBA program; Distance MBA Program

COURSE SUBJECT AREAS OFFERED OUTSIDE OF DEGREE PROGRAMS
Graduate—accounting and related services; business administration, management and operations; business/commerce; business/corporate communications; business, management, and marketing related; business/managerial economics; computer and information sciences; management information systems; management sciences and quantitative methods; marketing; statistics.

See full description on page 336.

COLORADO STATE UNIVERSITY
Fort Collins, Colorado
Division of Continuing Education
http://www.learn.colostate.edu

Colorado State University was founded in 1870. It is accredited by North Central Association of Colleges and Schools. It first offered distance learning courses in 1967. In fall 2006, there were 1,949 students enrolled in distance learning courses. Institutionally administered financial aid is available to distance learners.

Services Distance learners have accessibility to academic advising, bookstore, library services.

Contact Ms. Frances Betts, Program Coordinator, Colorado State University, Continuing Education, 1040 Campus Delivery, Fort Collins, CO 80523-1040. Telephone: 970-491-0675. Fax: 970-491-7885. E-mail: frances.betts@colostate.edu.

DEGREES AND AWARDS

BA Liberal Arts

BS Fire and Emergency Services Administration; Human Development and Family Studies

Certificate of Completion Teaching with Technology and Distance Learning certificate; Veterinary Medicine Online

Certificate Apparel and Merchandising (Graduate); Apparel and Merchandising; Apparel and Merchandising; Applied Statistics and Data Analysis; Business; Child Care Administration Training; Community-Based Development; Ergonomics (Basic); Fire and Emergency Services Administration (FESA); Information Science and Technology; Mediation; Natural Resources and the Environment; Postsecondary Teaching; School/Community Safety; Seed Analysis Training; Six Sigma eBlack Belt (20 weeks); Six Sigma eGreen Belt (12 weeks); Statistical Theory and Method

EMBA Business Administration

MAg Agricultural Extension Education

MBA Business Administration

MCS Computer Science

ME Civil Engineering; Electrical and Computer Engineering (Telecommunications); Mechanical Engineering (Engineering Management program); Mechanical Engineering (Ind Engg and Operations Res program); Mechanical Engineering (Materials Engineering)

MEd Education and Human Resource Studies (Adult Education and Training–AET); Education and Human Resource Studies (Organizational Performance and Change–OPC); Education and Human Resource Studies (Organizational Performance and Change–OPC)

MS Apparel and Merchandising; Mechanical Engineering (Engineering Management program); Mechanical Engineering (Ind Engg and Operations Res program); Mechanical Engineering (Materials Engineering); Rangeland Ecosystem Science; Statistics

MSW Social Work–Advanced Standing; Social Work

PhD Mechanical Engineering (Ind Engg and Operations Res program)

COURSE SUBJECT AREAS OFFERED OUTSIDE OF DEGREE PROGRAMS

Undergraduate—accounting and computer science; agricultural production; agriculture; animal sciences; anthropology; biology; business/commerce; computer science; construction management; design and applied arts; developmental and child psychology; economics; education; engineering; engineering technologies related; English; English composition; ethnic, cultural minority, and gender studies; finance and financial management services; fine and studio art; fishing and fisheries sciences and management; foods, nutrition, and related services; geography and cartography; health and physical education/fitness; landscape architecture; marketing; mathematics; music; natural resources conservation and research; plant sciences; psychology; social sciences; sociology; speech and rhetoric; statistics; wildlife and wildlands science and management.

Graduate—agriculture; business administration, management and operations; civil engineering; computer science; drafting/design engineering technologies; education; education related; fishing and fisheries sciences and management; human resources management; human services; math-

ematics; mechanical engineering; natural resources management and policy; social work; statistics; wildlife and wildlands science and management.

Non-credit—accounting and computer science; animal sciences; business, management, and marketing related; community health services; community organization and advocacy; community psychology; education; health and physical education/fitness; information science/studies; legal support services; management sciences and quantitative methods; veterinary biomedical and clinical sciences.

See full description on page 338.

COLORADO STATE UNIVERSITY-PUEBLO
Pueblo, Colorado
Division of Continuing Education
http://coned.colostate-pueblo.edu

Colorado State University-Pueblo was founded in 1933. It is accredited by North Central Association of Colleges and Schools. It first offered distance learning courses in 1970. In fall 2006, there were 1,500 students enrolled in distance learning courses. Institutionally administered financial aid is available to distance learners.

Services Distance learners have accessibility to academic advising, bookstore, library services.

Contact Ms. Angela Healy, Program Manager, Colorado State University-Pueblo, 2200 Bonforte Boulevard, Pueblo, CO 81001-4901. Telephone: 800-388-6154. Fax: 719-549-2438. E-mail: coned@colostate-pueblo.edu.

DEGREES AND AWARDS

BS Social Sciences; Sociology; Sociology/Criminology
Certificate Paralegal Studies

COURSE SUBJECT AREAS OFFERED OUTSIDE OF DEGREE PROGRAMS

Undergraduate—anthropology; biology; business administration, management and operations; business/commerce; chemistry; economics; education; English; English composition; geography and cartography; geological and earth sciences/geosciences; history; liberal arts and sciences, general studies and humanities; marketing; mathematics; nursing; political science and government; psychology; sociology.

Graduate—education.

Non-credit—business administration, management and operations; business operations support and assistant services; computer software and media applications; data entry/microcomputer applications; entrepreneurial and small business operations; health and medical administrative services; management information systems; pharmacy, pharmaceutical sciences, and administration; sales, merchandising, and related marketing operations (specialized).

COLORADO TECHNICAL UNIVERSITY
Colorado Springs, Colorado
http://www.ctuonline.edu

Colorado Technical University was founded in 1965. It is accredited by North Central Association of Colleges and Schools. It first offered distance learning courses in 2003. Institutionally administered financial aid is available to distance learners.

Services Distance learners have accessibility to academic advising, bookstore, campus computer network, career placement assistance, e-mail services, library services.

Contact Admissions Department, Colorado Technical University, 4435 North Chestnut Street, Suite E, Colorado Springs, CO 80907. Telephone: 800-416-8904. E-mail: info@ctuonline.edu.

DEGREES AND AWARDS

AS Accounting; Business Administration; Criminal Justice; Information Technology; Medical Billing and Coding

BS Accounting; Criminal Justice; Information Technology, Network Management concentration; Information Technology, Security concentration; Information Technology, Software Systems Engineering concentration

BSBA Finance concentration; Health Care Management concentration; Human Resource Management concentration; Information Technology concentration; International Business concentration; Management concentration; Marketing concentration; Project Management concentration
EMBA Executive Master of Business Administration
MBA Accounting concentration; Finance concentration; Health Care Management concentration; Human Resource Management concentration; Marketing concentration
MSM Business Management concentration; Information Systems Security concentration; Information Technology Management concentration; Project Management concentration

COURSE SUBJECT AREAS OFFERED OUTSIDE OF DEGREE PROGRAMS

Undergraduate—accounting and computer science; accounting and related services; business administration, management and operations; business/commerce; business, management, and marketing related; computer and information sciences; computer/information technology administration and management; computer science; criminal justice and corrections; criminology; finance and financial management services; health and medical administrative services; human resources management; legal professions and studies related; management sciences and quantitative methods; marketing; sales, merchandising, and related marketing operations (general); systems engineering.
Graduate—business administration, management and operations; business/commerce; business, management, and marketing related; computer/information technology administration and management; health and medical administrative services; human resources management; management sciences and quantitative methods; systems engineering.
See full description on page 340.

COLUMBIA COLLEGE
Columbia, Missouri
http://www.ccis.edu/online
Columbia College was founded in 1851. It is accredited by North Central Association of Colleges and Schools. It first offered distance learning courses in 2000. In fall 2006, there were 6,100 students enrolled in distance learning courses. Institutionally administered financial aid is available to distance learners.
Services Distance learners have accessibility to academic advising, bookstore, campus computer network, career placement assistance, e-mail services, library services.
Contact Ms. Marilyn Whitehead, Assistant Director for Online Campus, Columbia College, 1001 Rogers Street, Attention: Online Campus,. Columbia, MO 65216. Telephone: 573-875-7459. Fax: 573-875-7445. E-mail: mawhitehead@ccis.edu.

DEGREES AND AWARDS
AA General Studies
AGS General Studies
AS Business Administration; Criminal Justice; Environmental Studies; Fire Science Administration; Human Services
BA American Studies; Business Administration; Criminal Justice; General Studies; History; Interdisciplinary Studies; Psychology; Sociology
BS Business Administration
MBA Business Administration

COURSE SUBJECT AREAS OFFERED OUTSIDE OF DEGREE PROGRAMS

Undergraduate—accounting and related services; American literature (United States and Canadian); anthropology; area, ethnic, cultural, and gender studies related; astronomy and astrophysics; behavioral sciences; biological and biomedical sciences related; business administration, management and operations; business/commerce; business, management, and marketing related; chemistry; computer and information sciences; criminal justice and corrections; curriculum and instruction; education; English literature (British and Commonwealth); entrepreneurial and small business operations; history; mathematics; mathematics and computer science; multi-/interdisciplinary studies related; philosophy and religious studies related; political science and government; psychology; sales, merchandising, and related marketing operations (general); social sciences related; social work; sociology.
Graduate—business administration, management and operations; business, management, and marketing related; business/managerial economics.

COLUMBIA INTERNATIONAL UNIVERSITY
Columbia, South Carolina
Distance Education Center
http://www.ciuextension.com
Columbia International University was founded in 1923. It is accredited by Association for Biblical Higher Education. It first offered distance learning courses in 1978. In fall 2006, there were 900 students enrolled in distance learning courses. Institutionally administered financial aid is available to distance learners.
Services Distance learners have accessibility to academic advising, bookstore, campus computer network, career placement assistance, e-mail services, library services.
Contact Mrs. Alisa Fulton, Assessment and Student Services Coordinator, Columbia International University, 7435 Monticello Road, Columbia, SC 29203. Telephone: 803-807-5731 Ext. 3710. Fax: 803-223-2502. E-mail: distance@ciu.edu.

DEGREES AND AWARDS
Programs offered do not lead to a degree or other formal award.

COURSE SUBJECT AREAS OFFERED OUTSIDE OF DEGREE PROGRAMS

Undergraduate—biblical studies; missionary studies and missiology; religious studies; theological and ministerial studies; theology and religious vocations related.
Graduate—anthropology; biblical and other theological languages and literatures; biblical studies; curriculum and instruction; education; educational administration and supervision; education related; history; languages (classics and classical); linguistic, comparative, and related language studies; missionary studies and missiology; religious studies; theological and ministerial studies; theology and religious vocations related.
Non-credit—anthropology; biblical studies; education; educational psychology; languages (classics and classical); missionary studies and missiology; religious studies; theological and ministerial studies; theology and religious vocations related.

COLUMBIA UNIVERSITY
New York, New York
Columbia Video Network
http://www.cvn.columbia.edu
Columbia University was founded in 1754. It is accredited by Middle States Association of Colleges and Schools. It first offered distance learning courses in 1986. In fall 2006, there were 475 students enrolled in distance learning courses. Institutionally administered financial aid is available to distance learners.
Services Distance learners have accessibility to academic advising, bookstore, campus computer network, career placement assistance, e-mail services, library services.
Contact Online Recruiter, Columbia University, 530 Mudd Building, MC 4719, 500 West 120th Street, New York, NY 10027. Telephone: 212-854-6447. Fax: 212-854-2325. E-mail: info@cvn.columbia.edu.

DEGREES AND AWARDS
Certificate of Achievement Business and Technology; Civil Engineering; Financial Engineering; Industrial Engineering; Information Systems; Intelligent Systems; Manufacturing Engineering; Materials Science and Engineering; Mathematics–Applied Mathematics; Multimedia Networking; Nanotechnology; Networking and Systems; New Media Engineering; Operations Research; Telecommunications; Wireless and Mobile Communications
MS Biomedical Engineering; Chemical Engineering; Civil Engineering–Construction Engineering and Management; Civil Engineering; Computer Science; Earth and Environmental Engineering; Engineering and

Management Systems; Finance–Methods in Finance; Materials Science and Engineering; Mathematics–Applied Mathematics

MSEE Electrical Engineering

MSME Mechanical Engineering

PMC Computer Science; Electrical Engineering; Industrial Engineering and Operations Research; Mechanical Engineering

COURSE SUBJECT AREAS OFFERED OUTSIDE OF DEGREE PROGRAMS

Undergraduate—computer science; electrical and electronic engineering technologies; materials science.

Graduate—applied mathematics; biomedical/medical engineering; chemical engineering; civil engineering; computer science; electrical, electronics and communications engineering; engineering/industrial management; environmental/environmental health engineering; finance and financial management services; materials science; mechanical engineering.

Non-credit—applied mathematics; business/commerce; chemical engineering; civil engineering; computer science; engineering; engineering/industrial management; environmental/environmental health engineering; finance and financial management services; mechanical engineering.

COLUMBUS STATE COMMUNITY COLLEGE
Columbus, Ohio
Global Campus
http://www.cscc.edu

Columbus State Community College was founded in 1963. It is accredited by North Central Association of Colleges and Schools. It first offered distance learning courses in 1980. In fall 2006, there were 8,000 students enrolled in distance learning courses. Institutionally administered financial aid is available to distance learners.

Services Distance learners have accessibility to academic advising, bookstore, campus computer network, career placement assistance, e-mail services, library services, tutoring.

Contact Dr. Leslie King, Administrator for Instructional Technologies and Distance Learning, Columbus State Community College, Box 1609, Columbus, OH 43216-1609. Telephone: 614-287-2589. Fax: 614-287-5123. E-mail: lking01@cscc.edu.

DEGREES AND AWARDS

AA General Studies

AAS Business Management; Marketing

CCCPE E-Commerce; Geographic Information Systems

COURSE SUBJECT AREAS OFFERED OUTSIDE OF DEGREE PROGRAMS

Undergraduate—accounting and related services; allied health and medical assisting services; allied health diagnostic, intervention, and treatment professions; American literature (United States and Canadian); anthropology; biological and biomedical sciences related; business administration, management and operations; business/corporate communications; chemistry; communication and journalism related; comparative literature; computer and information sciences; computer programming; computer software and media applications; construction management; counseling psychology; creative writing; culinary arts and related services; developmental and child psychology; drafting/design engineering technologies; dramatic/theater arts and stagecraft; economics; engineering mechanics; engineering technologies related; English; English composition; English language and literature related; English literature (British and Commonwealth); environmental control technologies; ethnic, cultural minority, and gender studies; finance and financial management services; foods, nutrition, and related services; geography and cartography; graphic communications; health and medical administrative services; health and physical education/fitness; health professions related; history; hospitality administration; human resources management; languages (Romance languages); legal studies (non-professional general, undergraduate); legal support services; marketing; mathematics; mechanical engineering related technologies; mental and social health services and allied professions; natural sciences; nursing; nutrition sciences; philosophy; philosophy and religious studies related; political science and government; psychology; public relations, advertising, and applied communication related; quality control and safety technologies; sales, merchandising, and related marketing operations (general); science technologies related; social sciences related; sociology; speech and rhetoric; technical and business writing; vehicle maintenance and repair technologies; visual and performing arts related.

THE COMMUNITY COLLEGE OF BALTIMORE COUNTY
Baltimore, Maryland
Office of Distance/Extended Learning
http://www.ccbcmd.edu/distance/index.html

The Community College of Baltimore County was founded in 1957. It is accredited by Middle States Association of Colleges and Schools. It first offered distance learning courses in 1997. In fall 2006, there were 2,700 students enrolled in distance learning courses. Institutionally administered financial aid is available to distance learners.

Services Distance learners have accessibility to academic advising, bookstore, campus computer network, e-mail services, library services, tutoring.

Contact Tinnie A. Ward, PhD, Senior Director of Distance/Extended Learning, The Community College of Baltimore County, 7201 Rossville Boulevard, Baltimore, MD 21237. Telephone: 410-780-6504. Fax: 410-780-6144. E-mail: tward@ccbcmd.edu.

DEGREES AND AWARDS

AA Business Administration

AAS Criminal Justice; E-Business Management; E-Business Management; E-Business Technology; E-Business Technology; Information Technology, general

AGS General Studies

COURSE SUBJECT AREAS OFFERED OUTSIDE OF DEGREE PROGRAMS

Undergraduate—accounting and related services; applied mathematics; astronomy and astrophysics; biology; business administration, management and operations; business/commerce; business/corporate communications; business operations support and assistant services; cell biology and anatomical sciences; communication and media; computer and information sciences; computer/information technology administration and management; computer programming; computer science; computer systems analysis; computer systems networking and telecommunications; criminal justice and corrections; criminology; data processing; economics; English composition; entrepreneurial and small business operations; geography and cartography; history; human resources management; legal studies (non-professional general, undergraduate); marketing; mathematics; parks, recreation and leisure; parks, recreation, and leisure related; physical sciences; political science and government; psychology; sociology; statistics; technical and business writing.

Non-credit—computer and information sciences; computer and information sciences and support services related; computer programming; computer software and media applications.

COMMUNITY COLLEGE OF BEAVER COUNTY
Monaca, Pennsylvania
http://www.ccbc.cc.pa.us/

Community College of Beaver County was founded in 1966. It is accredited by Middle States Association of Colleges and Schools. It first offered distance learning courses in 1998. In fall 2006, there were 500 students enrolled in distance learning courses. Institutionally administered financial aid is available to distance learners.

Services Distance learners have accessibility to academic advising, bookstore, campus computer network, e-mail services, library services, tutoring.

Contact Registrar, Community College of Beaver County, One Campus Drive, Registrar's Office, Building 1, Monaca, PA 15061-2588. Telephone: 724-775-8561 Ext. 253. Fax: 724-775-4687. E-mail: dan.slater@ccbc.edu.

DEGREES AND AWARDS

Programs offered do not lead to a degree or other formal award.

COURSE SUBJECT AREAS OFFERED OUTSIDE OF DEGREE PROGRAMS

Undergraduate—accounting and computer science; air transportation; American literature (United States and Canadian); behavioral sciences; business administration, management and operations; business, management, and marketing related; business/managerial economics; cognitive psychology and psycholinguistics; computer and information sciences; computer programming; computer science; computer software and media applications; criminal justice and corrections; developmental and child psychology; economics; education; English; English composition; English literature (British and Commonwealth); fine and studio art; history; liberal arts and sciences, general studies and humanities; mathematics; nursing; nutrition sciences; philosophy; psychology; psychology related; social psychology; social sciences; social sciences related; sociology; statistics; technical and business writing.

Non-credit—accounting and computer science; business administration, management and operations; business/commerce; business/corporate communications; business, management, and marketing related; business/managerial economics; business operations support and assistant services; computer and information sciences; computer science; computer software and media applications; entrepreneurial and small business operations; graphic communications.

COMMUNITY COLLEGE OF DENVER
Denver, Colorado
Distance Learning
http://www.ccd.edu/OnlineLearning/index.html
Community College of Denver was founded in 1970. It is accredited by North Central Association of Colleges and Schools. It first offered distance learning courses in 1986. In fall 2006, there were 2,000 students enrolled in distance learning courses. Institutionally administered financial aid is available to distance learners.
Services Distance learners have accessibility to academic advising, bookstore, e-mail services, library services, tutoring.
Contact Jeanne Stroh, Director for Online Learning, Community College of Denver, Campus Box 900, PO Box 173363, Denver, CO 80217-3363. Telephone: 303-352-3302. Fax: 303-556-6319. E-mail: jeanne.stroh@ccd.edu.

DEGREES AND AWARDS
AA Business Administration; Economics; English/Literature emphasis; History emphasis; Humanities/Philosophy emphasis; Sociology emphasis
AAS Business Administration–Management emphasis; Business Generalist emphasis; Management emphasis, General Management; Marketing emphasis; Veterinary Technology
AGS Elementary Education; Generalist
AS Generalist
Certificate Business Administration; Business Administration, Entrepreneurship; Business Administration, International Business; Early Childhood Education, Group/Leader/Child Development Associate–Infant/Toddler; Early Childhood Education, Group/Leader/Child Development Associate–Preschool; Teacher Education, Paraeducator
Diploma Business Administration

COURSE SUBJECT AREAS OFFERED OUTSIDE OF DEGREE PROGRAMS
Undergraduate—accounting and related services; anthropology; astronomy and astrophysics; biology; business administration, management and operations; business/corporate communications; business, management, and marketing related; chemistry; comparative literature; computer/information technology administration and management; computer software and media applications; creative writing; economics; education (specific levels and methods); education (specific subject areas); English; English composition; entrepreneurial and small business operations; fine and studio art; geography and cartography; geological and earth sciences/geosciences; health/medical preparatory programs; history; human development, family studies, and related services; liberal arts and sciences, general studies and humanities; mathematics; microbiological sciences and immunology; nursing; philosophy; philosophy and religious studies related; physics; political science and government; psychology; religious

studies; sales, merchandising, and related marketing operations (general); sociology; speech and rhetoric; teaching assistants/aides; technical and business writing; veterinary biomedical and clinical sciences.

CONCORDIA COLLEGE–NEW YORK
Bronxville, New York
CUENET (Concordia University Education Network)
http://www.concordia-ny.edu
Concordia College–New York was founded in 1881. It is accredited by Middle States Association of Colleges and Schools. It first offered distance learning courses in 1995. In fall 2006, there were 12 students enrolled in distance learning courses. Institutionally administered financial aid is available to distance learners.
Contact Prof. Sherry Fraser, Academic Dean, Concordia College–New York, 171 White Plains Road, Bronxville, NY 10708. Telephone: 914-337-9300 Ext. 2211. Fax: 914-395-4500. E-mail: sjf@concordia-ny.edu.

DEGREES AND AWARDS
Programs offered do not lead to a degree or other formal award.

COURSE SUBJECT AREAS OFFERED OUTSIDE OF DEGREE PROGRAMS
Undergraduate—biblical studies; education; religious studies; social work.

CONCORDIA UNIVERSITY
Portland, Oregon
Concordia University was founded in 1905. It is accredited by Northwest Commission on Colleges and Universities. It first offered distance learning courses in 1998. In fall 2006, there were 250 students enrolled in distance learning courses. Institutionally administered financial aid is available to distance learners.
Services Distance learners have accessibility to academic advising, bookstore, campus computer network, career placement assistance, e-mail services, library services.
Contact Ms. Bobi Swan, Dean of Admissions, Concordia University, 2811 NE Holman Street, Portland, OR 97211. Telephone: 503-280-8501. E-mail: bswan@cu-portland.edu.

DEGREES AND AWARDS
MEd Education Leadership

COURSE SUBJECT AREAS OFFERED OUTSIDE OF DEGREE PROGRAMS
Undergraduate—English; environmental design; geography and cartography; history; psychology; sociology.
Graduate—educational administration and supervision; educational/instructional media design; education (specific levels and methods).

CONCORDIA UNIVERSITY, ST. PAUL
St. Paul, Minnesota
Concordia University, St. Paul was founded in 1893. It is accredited by North Central Association of Colleges and Schools. It first offered distance learning courses in 1998. In fall 2006, there were 670 students enrolled in distance learning courses. Institutionally administered financial aid is available to distance learners.
Services Distance learners have accessibility to academic advising, bookstore, campus computer network, e-mail services, library services, tutoring.
Contact Ms. Kimberly Craig, Director of Graduate and Degree Completion Admissions, Concordia University, St. Paul, 275 Syndicate Street North, Saint Paul, MN 55104-5494. Telephone: 800-333-4705. Fax: 651-603-6320. E-mail: craig@csp.edu.

DEGREES AND AWARDS
BA Child Development; Criminal Justice; Family Life Education; Human Resource Management; Information Technology Management; Marketing Management; Organizational Managment and Leadership

MA Christian Outreach; Human Services–Criminal Justice Leadership emphasis; Human Services–Family Life Education emphasis; Organizational Management–Human Resources emphasis; Organizational Management
MAE Differentiated Instruction; Early Childhood
MBA Business Administration

COURSE SUBJECT AREAS OFFERED OUTSIDE OF DEGREE PROGRAMS

Undergraduate—business/commerce; developmental and child psychology; education; human development, family studies, and related services; sociology.
Graduate—business/commerce; developmental and child psychology; education; human development, family studies, and related services; sociology.
Non-credit—business/commerce; communication and media; fine and studio art; mathematics and computer science; social sciences.

CONCORDIA UNIVERSITY WISCONSIN
Mequon, Wisconsin
Continuing Education Division
http://www.cuw.edu
Concordia University Wisconsin was founded in 1881. It is accredited by North Central Association of Colleges and Schools. It first offered distance learning courses in 1994. In fall 2006, there were 800 students enrolled in distance learning courses. Institutionally administered financial aid is available to distance learners.
Services Distance learners have accessibility to academic advising, bookstore, campus computer network, career placement assistance, e-mail services, library services, tutoring.
Contact Sarah Weaver Pecor, Director, Concordia University Wisconsin, 12800 North Lake Shore Drive, Mequon, WI 53097. Telephone: 262-243-4257. Fax: 262-243-4459. E-mail: sarah.weaver@cuw.edu.

DEGREES AND AWARDS
BA Business Management
BSN Nursing–BSN completion for RN's
MBA Business Administration
MS Curriculum and Instruction; Education Administration; Education Counseling; Reading; Rehabilitation Science
MSN Nursing

COURSE SUBJECT AREAS OFFERED OUTSIDE OF DEGREE PROGRAMS

Undergraduate—accounting and related services; business, management, and marketing related; computer science; economics; finance and financial management services; history; management sciences and quantitative methods; marketing; nursing.
Graduate—business administration, management and operations; curriculum and instruction; educational administration and supervision; educational psychology; education related; nursing.

CONNECTICUT STATE UNIVERSITY SYSTEM
Hartford, Connecticut
OnlineCSU
http://www.onlinecsu.net
Connecticut State University System is accredited by New England Association of Schools and Colleges. It first offered distance learning courses in 1998. In fall 2006, there were 1,000 students enrolled in distance learning courses. Institutionally administered financial aid is available to distance learners.
Services Distance learners have accessibility to academic advising, bookstore, career placement assistance, e-mail services, library services, tutoring.
Contact Ms. Rebecca L. Putt, Marketing and Planning Manager, Connecticut State University System, 39 Woodland Street, Hartford, CT 06105-2337. Telephone: 860-493-0039. E-mail: puttr@so.ct.edu.

DEGREES AND AWARDS
BSN Nursing–RN to BSN Bachelors completion program
MLS Library Science
MS Data Mining; Educational Technology

COURSE SUBJECT AREAS OFFERED OUTSIDE OF DEGREE PROGRAMS

Undergraduate—accounting and related services; anthropology; area studies; communication and media; computer science; criminal justice and corrections; curriculum and instruction; economics; education (specific levels and methods); English composition; geography and cartography; information science/studies; management information systems; marketing; mechanical engineering; nursing; philosophy; sociology; statistics.
Graduate—accounting and related services; anthropology; area studies; computer systems networking and telecommunications; curriculum and instruction; educational/instructional media design; education (specific levels and methods); English composition; management information systems; marketing; mechanical engineering; social work; sociology; statistics.
Non-credit—statistics.

CORBAN COLLEGE
Salem, Oregon
Management and Communication Online Program/Family Studies Online Program
http://www.wbc.edu
Corban College was founded in 1935. It is accredited by Northwest Commission on Colleges and Universities. It first offered distance learning courses in 1994. In fall 2006, there were 130 students enrolled in distance learning courses. Institutionally administered financial aid is available to distance learners.
Services Distance learners have accessibility to academic advising, bookstore, campus computer network, e-mail services, library services, tutoring.
Contact Ms. Nancy L. Martyn, Dean of Adult Studies, Corban College, Adult Studies, 5000 Deer Park Drive SE, Salem, OR 97301. Telephone: 503-375-7590. Fax: 503-375-7583. E-mail: nmartyn@corban.edu.

DEGREES AND AWARDS
BS Business, Management, and Communication; Psychology/Family Studies

COURSE SUBJECT AREAS OFFERED OUTSIDE OF DEGREE PROGRAMS

Undergraduate—biblical studies; business administration, management and operations; counseling psychology; history; human development, family studies, and related services; marketing; physical sciences; psychology related; religious studies; theological and ministerial studies.
See full description on page 342.

COUNTY COLLEGE OF MORRIS
Randolph, New Jersey
Professional Programs and Distance Education
http://www.ccm.edu
County College of Morris was founded in 1966. It is accredited by Middle States Association of Colleges and Schools. It first offered distance learning courses in 1979. In fall 2006, there were 1,800 students enrolled in distance learning courses. Institutionally administered financial aid is available to distance learners.
Services Distance learners have accessibility to academic advising, bookstore, campus computer network, e-mail services, library services.
Contact Ms. Sheri Ventura, Coordinator of Distance Learning Services, County College of Morris, 214 Center Grove Road, Randolph, NJ 07869-2086. Telephone: 973-328-5184. Fax: 973-328-5082. E-mail: sventura@ccm.edu.

DEGREES AND AWARDS
AA Humanities
AS Business Administration

COURSE SUBJECT AREAS OFFERED OUTSIDE OF DEGREE PROGRAMS
Undergraduate—agriculture; applied horticulture/horticultural business services; applied mathematics; biological and biomedical sciences related; biology; business/commerce; cell biology and anatomical sciences; comparative psychology; computer science; creative writing; culinary arts and related services; developmental and child psychology; economics; educational psychology; engineering; English; English as a second language; English composition; health and physical education/fitness; history; marketing; mathematics; mathematics and statistics related; microbiological sciences and immunology; philosophy; plant sciences; psychology; sociology; statistics.

COVENANT THEOLOGICAL SEMINARY
St. Louis, Missouri
External Studies Office
http://access.covenantseminary.edu
Covenant Theological Seminary was founded in 1956. It is accredited by North Central Association of Colleges and Schools. It first offered distance learning courses in 1989. In fall 2006, there were 130 students enrolled in distance learning courses. Institutionally administered financial aid is available to distance learners.
Services Distance learners have accessibility to academic advising, bookstore, campus computer network, e-mail services, library services, tutoring.
Contact Rev. Brad Anderson, Director of Admissions, Covenant Theological Seminary, 12330 Conway Road, St. Louis, MO 63141. Telephone: 800-264-8064. Fax: 314-434-4819. E-mail: admissions@covenantseminary.edu.

DEGREES AND AWARDS
Graduate Certificate Biblical and Theological Studies
MA Theological Studies

COURSE SUBJECT AREAS OFFERED OUTSIDE OF DEGREE PROGRAMS
Graduate—biblical studies; missionary studies and missiology; religious education; religious studies; theological and ministerial studies; theology and religious vocations related.
Non-credit—biblical studies; missionary studies and missiology; religious education; religious studies; theological and ministerial studies; theology and religious vocations related.

CULVER-STOCKTON COLLEGE
Canton, Missouri
http://www.culver.edu/
Culver-Stockton College was founded in 1853. It is accredited by North Central Association of Colleges and Schools. It first offered distance learning courses in 2002. In fall 2006, there were 43 students enrolled in distance learning courses. Institutionally administered financial aid is available to distance learners.
Services Distance learners have accessibility to academic advising, bookstore, campus computer network, career placement assistance, e-mail services, library services, tutoring.
Contact Dr. R. Joseph Dieker, Dean of Academic Affairs, Culver-Stockton College, One College Hill, Canton, MO 63435. Telephone: 573-288-6325. Fax: 573-288-6616. E-mail: jdieker@culver.edu.

DEGREES AND AWARDS
BS Business Administration; Management Information Systems

COURSE SUBJECT AREAS OFFERED OUTSIDE OF DEGREE PROGRAMS
Undergraduate—astronomy and astrophysics; biology; business administration, management and operations; computer and information sciences; management information systems; nursing.

CUMBERLAND COUNTY COLLEGE
Vineland, New Jersey
Multimedia and Distance Learning Services
http://www.cccnj.edu
Cumberland County College was founded in 1963. It is accredited by Middle States Association of Colleges and Schools. It first offered distance learning courses in 1990. In fall 2006, there were 107 students enrolled in distance learning courses. Institutionally administered financial aid is available to distance learners.
Services Distance learners have accessibility to academic advising, bookstore, campus computer network, career placement assistance, e-mail services, library services, tutoring.
Contact Michael R. Farinelli, Senior Manager, Multimedia Support Services, Cumberland County College, College Drive, PO Box 1500, Vineland, NJ 08362-0517. Telephone: 856-691-8600 Ext. 303. Fax: 856-691-9489. E-mail: mfarinelli@cccnj.edu.

DEGREES AND AWARDS
Programs offered do not lead to a degree or other formal award.

COURSE SUBJECT AREAS OFFERED OUTSIDE OF DEGREE PROGRAMS
Undergraduate—anthropology; business administration, management and operations; clinical child psychology; economics; English composition; history; languages (foreign languages related); psychology; sociology; speech and rhetoric.

DAEMEN COLLEGE
Amherst, New York
http://distance.daemen.edu
Daemen College was founded in 1947. It is accredited by Middle States Association of Colleges and Schools. It first offered distance learning courses in 1999. In fall 2006, there were 1,200 students enrolled in distance learning courses. Institutionally administered financial aid is available to distance learners.
Services Distance learners have accessibility to academic advising, bookstore, campus computer network, e-mail services, library services.
Contact Ms. Cheryl Littlejohn, Distance Learning Coordinator, Daemen College, 4380 Main Street, BC211A, Amherst, NY 14226. Telephone: 716-839 8532. Fax: 716-839 8261. E-mail: clittlej@daemen.edu.

DEGREES AND AWARDS
Programs offered do not lead to a degree or other formal award.

COURSE SUBJECT AREAS OFFERED OUTSIDE OF DEGREE PROGRAMS
Undergraduate—business/commerce; education; English composition; entrepreneurial and small business operations; health and medical administrative services; health/medical preparatory programs; health professions related; linguistic, comparative, and related language studies; nursing.
Graduate—medical clinical sciences/graduate medical studies; nursing.

DAKOTA STATE UNIVERSITY
Madison, South Dakota
Extended Programs
http://www.departments.dsu.edu/disted/
Dakota State University was founded in 1881. It is accredited by North Central Association of Colleges and Schools. It first offered distance learning courses in 1991. In fall 2006, there were 732 students enrolled in distance learning courses. Institutionally administered financial aid is available to distance learners.
Services Distance learners have accessibility to academic advising, bookstore, campus computer network, career placement assistance, e-mail services, library services, tutoring.
Contact Ms. Susan Eykamp, E-Education Services, Dakota State University, 820 North Washington Avenue, Technology Classroom Building, Madison, SD 57042-1799. Telephone: 800-641-4309. Fax: 605-256-5095. E-mail: dsuinfo@dsu.edu.

DEGREES AND AWARDS

AA General Studies
AS Health Information Technology
BBA Management Information Systems
BS Health Information Administration
MS Educational Technology; Information Assurance and Computer Security
MSIS Information Systems

COURSE SUBJECT AREAS OFFERED OUTSIDE OF DEGREE PROGRAMS

Undergraduate—accounting and related services; communications technology; computer and information sciences; computer and information sciences and support services related; computer/information technology administration and management; computer programming; computer science; computer systems analysis; education related; English; English composition; English language and literature related; fine and studio art; health and medical administrative services; health and physical education/fitness; human resources management; information science/studies; mathematics; music; psychology; sociology; special education; speech and rhetoric.
Graduate—computer and information sciences; computer and information sciences and support services related; educational/instructional media design; education related; information science/studies.

DALLAS BAPTIST UNIVERSITY
Dallas, Texas
Dallas Baptist University Online (DBU Online)
http://online.dbu.edu

Dallas Baptist University was founded in 1965. It is accredited by Southern Association of Colleges and Schools. It first offered distance learning courses in 1998. In fall 2006, there were 1,300 students enrolled in distance learning courses. Institutionally administered financial aid is available to distance learners.
Services Distance learners have accessibility to academic advising, bookstore, campus computer network, career placement assistance, e-mail services, library services, tutoring.
Contact Mrs. Julia Smith, Online Student Coordinator, Dallas Baptist University, Online Education, 3000 Mountain Creek Parkway, Dallas, TX 75211-9299. Telephone: 800-460-8188. Fax: 214-333-5373. E-mail: online@dbu.edu.

DEGREES AND AWARDS

BA Biblical Studies; Christian Ministries; Communication; Health Care Management; Psychology; Sociology
BBA Management Information Systems; Management
BS Business Administration; Management Information Systems; Management
Certificate E-Business
MACE Christian Education
MAM Human Resource Management; Management, general
MBA E-Business; Finance; International Business; Management Information Systems; Management; Marketing
MEd Educational Leadership; Higher Education

COURSE SUBJECT AREAS OFFERED OUTSIDE OF DEGREE PROGRAMS

Undergraduate—accounting and related services; American literature (United States and Canadian); atmospheric sciences and meteorology; biblical studies; biological and physical sciences; biology; business administration, management and operations; business/corporate communications; business, management, and marketing related; business/managerial economics; communication and journalism related; communication and media; communications technologies and support services related; communications technology; community health services; computer and information sciences; computer science; computer software and media applications; computer systems analysis; computer systems networking and telecommunications; creative writing; criminal justice and corrections; criminology; economics; education; education related; English; English composition; English language and literature related;

family psychology; finance and financial management services; fine and studio art; geological and earth sciences/geosciences; graphic communications; health and physical education/fitness; health professions related; history; human resources management; international agriculture; liberal arts and sciences, general studies and humanities; management information systems; marketing; mathematics; mathematics and statistics related; missionary studies and missiology; natural sciences; personality psychology; philosophy; philosophy and religious studies related; political science and government; psychology; psychology related; public health; religious education; religious studies; sales, merchandising, and related marketing operations (general); social psychology; social sciences; social sciences related; sociology; speech and rhetoric; statistics; theological and ministerial studies.
Graduate—accounting and related services; business administration, management and operations; business/commerce; business/corporate communications; business, management, and marketing related; business/managerial economics; computer and information sciences; computer/information technology administration and management; computer software and media applications; computer systems analysis; computer systems networking and telecommunications; criminal justice and corrections; criminology; curriculum and instruction; economics; education; educational administration and supervision; educational assessment, evaluation, and research; educational/instructional media design; education related; English as a second/foreign language (teaching); entrepreneurial and small business operations; finance and financial management services; human resources management; information science/studies; international business; liberal arts and sciences, general studies and humanities; management information systems; management sciences and quantitative methods; marketing; missionary studies and missiology; philosophy and religious studies related; religious education; religious studies; sales, merchandising, and related marketing operations (general); statistics; theological and ministerial studies.

DANVILLE COMMUNITY COLLEGE
Danville, Virginia
Learning Resource Center
http://www.dcc.vccs.edu

Danville Community College was founded in 1967. It is accredited by Southern Association of Colleges and Schools. It first offered distance learning courses in 1990. In fall 2006, there were 750 students enrolled in distance learning courses. Institutionally administered financial aid is available to distance learners.
Services Distance learners have accessibility to academic advising, bookstore, career placement assistance, e-mail services, library services.
Contact Dr. Chris Ezell, Vice President of Instruction and Student Services, Danville Community College, 1008 South Main Street, Danville, VA 24541. Telephone: 434-797-8410. Fax: 434-797-8514. E-mail: cezell@dcc.vccs.edu.

DEGREES AND AWARDS
Programs offered do not lead to a degree or other formal award.

COURSE SUBJECT AREAS OFFERED OUTSIDE OF DEGREE PROGRAMS

Undergraduate—accounting and related services; allied health and medical assisting services; allied health diagnostic, intervention, and treatment professions; behavioral sciences; biological and biomedical sciences related; biology; business administration, management and operations; business/commerce; business, management, and marketing related; business operations support and assistant services; communication and media; community health services; computer programming; computer science; computer software and media applications; criminal justice and corrections; criminology; dental support services and allied professions; dentistry and oral sciences (advanced/graduate); design and applied arts; developmental and child psychology; drafting/design engineering technologies; education; educational/instructional media design; education (specific levels and methods); English; English composition; English language and literature related; English literature (British and Commonwealth); foods, nutrition, and related services; geography and cartography; graphic communications; health and physical education/fitness; health professions related; history; human development, family studies, and related services; marketing; mathematics; mathematics and computer science; music; natural sciences; nursing; nutrition sciences; political science and government; psychology; social psychology; social sciences; sociology; theological and ministerial studies.

DARTON COLLEGE
Albany, Georgia
Office of Distance Learning
http://www.darton.edu

Darton College was founded in 1965. It is accredited by Southern Association of Colleges and Schools. It first offered distance learning courses in 1993. In fall 2006, there were 2,758 students enrolled in distance learning courses. Institutionally administered financial aid is available to distance learners.

Services Distance learners have accessibility to academic advising, bookstore, campus computer network, career placement assistance, e-mail services, library services, tutoring.

Contact Ms. Tarrah N. Mirus, Technology Coordinator, Darton College, 2400 Gillionville Road, Albany, GA 31707. Telephone: 229-317-6838. Fax: 229-317-6682. E-mail: tarrah.mirus@darton.edu.

DEGREES AND AWARDS

AA Art; English; Foreign Language; History; Journalism and Mass Communication; Music; Philosophy; Speech; Theater

AAS Accounting; Business Computer Specialist option; Governmental Services; Histologic Technology; Management; Office Administration (Administrative Support)

AS Anthropology; Biological Science; Business Administration; Business Education; Computer Information Systems; Criminal Justice; Dentistry–Pre-Dentistry; Diagnostic Medical Sonography; Economics; Forensic Science; General Studies; Health Information Management; Health Information Technology; Health and Physical Education (Exercise Science); Health and Physical Education (Recreation); Health and Physical Education (Sports Management); Health and Physical Education (Teacher Ed option); Law–Pre-Law; Medical Laboratory Technology; Medical Technology; Nuclear Medicine Technology; Nursing; Occupational Therapy; Office Administration (Secretarial Science); Optometry–Pre-Optometry; Pharmacy–Pre-Pharmacy; Physical Therapy Assistant; Physical Therapy; Political Science; Pre-Medicine; Pre-Physician's Assistant; Psychology; Respiratory Therapy; Social Work; Sociology; Teacher Education (Early Childhood); Teacher Education (Middle Grades); Teacher Education (Secondary Education); Teacher Education (Special Education); Teacher Education (Trade and Industrial Education); Trade and Industrial Education; Veterinary Science–Pre-Veterinary Science

Certificate Histology; Medical Coding

COURSE SUBJECT AREAS OFFERED OUTSIDE OF DEGREE PROGRAMS

Undergraduate—accounting and computer science; accounting and related services; allied health and medical assisting services; allied health diagnostic, intervention, and treatment professions; American literature (United States and Canadian); applied mathematics; biological and biomedical sciences related; business administration, management and operations; business/commerce; cell biology and anatomical sciences; clinical/medical laboratory science and allied professions; communication and media; computer software and media applications; computer systems networking and telecommunications; criminal justice and corrections; economics; education; education related; education (specific levels and methods); education (specific subject areas); English; English composition; English literature (British and Commonwealth); finance and financial management services; health and medical administrative services; health and physical education/fitness; health/medical preparatory programs; health professions related; health services/allied health/health sciences; history; languages (East Asian); languages (foreign languages related); languages (Germanic); languages (Romance languages); liberal arts and sciences, general studies and humanities; linguistic, comparative, and related language studies; mathematics; mathematics and computer science; mathematics and statistics related; music; philosophy; philosophy and religious studies related; physical sciences;

physiology, pathology and related sciences; political science and government; psychology; social work; sociology; speech and rhetoric; statistics.

Non-credit—business administration, management and operations; business/corporate communications; business, management, and marketing related; computer software and media applications; creative writing; finance and financial management services; real estate; sales, merchandising, and related marketing operations (specialized); technical and business writing.

DAWSON COMMUNITY COLLEGE
Glendive, Montana
Continuing and Extension Education Department
http://www.dawson.edu

Dawson Community College was founded in 1940. It is accredited by Northwest Commission on Colleges and Universities. It first offered distance learning courses in 1990. In fall 2006, there were 20 students enrolled in distance learning courses. Institutionally administered financial aid is available to distance learners.

Services Distance learners have accessibility to academic advising, bookstore, career placement assistance, library services.

Contact Jolene Myers, Director of Admissions, Dawson Community College, 300 College Drive, Glendive, MT 59330. Telephone: 406-377-9410. Fax: 406-377-8132. E-mail: myers@dawson.edu.

DEGREES AND AWARDS

AA General Studies

AAS Business Management; Human Services; Law Enforcement

COURSE SUBJECT AREAS OFFERED OUTSIDE OF DEGREE PROGRAMS

Undergraduate—agricultural business and management; agriculture; American literature (United States and Canadian); anthropology; biology; business administration, management and operations; communication and media; computer software and media applications; creative writing; criminal justice and corrections; developmental and child psychology; English composition; fine and studio art; human services; psychology; sociology.

DAYMAR COLLEGE
Owensboro, Kentucky
http://online.daymarcollege.edu

Daymar College was founded in 1963. It is accredited by Accrediting Council for Independent Colleges and Schools. It first offered distance learning courses in 1999. In fall 2006, there were 36 students enrolled in distance learning courses. Institutionally administered financial aid is available to distance learners.

Services Distance learners have accessibility to academic advising, campus computer network, career placement assistance, library services.

Contact Jim Weber, Director of eLearning, Daymar College, 5030 Back Square Drive, Owensboro, KY 42301. Telephone: 270-926-1188. Fax: 270-686-8912. E-mail: jweber@daymarcollege.edu.

DEGREES AND AWARDS

Programs offered do not lead to a degree or other formal award.

COURSE SUBJECT AREAS OFFERED OUTSIDE OF DEGREE PROGRAMS

Undergraduate—accounting and computer science; accounting and related services; business administration, management and operations; business operations support and assistant services; computer software and media applications; medical basic sciences.

DE ANZA COLLEGE
Cupertino, California
Distance Learning Center
http://distance.deanza.fhda.edu

De Anza College was founded in 1967. It is accredited by Western Association of Schools and Colleges. It first offered distance learning courses in 1974. In fall 2006, there were 2,900 students enrolled in distance learning courses. Institutionally administered financial aid is available to distance learners.

Services Distance learners have accessibility to academic advising, bookstore, campus computer network, career placement assistance, e-mail services, library services, tutoring.

Contact Ann Leever, Instructional Associate, De Anza College, 21250 Stevens Creek Boulevard, Cupertino, CA 95014. Telephone: 408-864-8969. Fax: 408-864-8245. E-mail: information@dadistance.fhda.edu.

DEGREES AND AWARDS

AA Liberal Arts

Certificate Business Administration

COURSE SUBJECT AREAS OFFERED OUTSIDE OF DEGREE PROGRAMS

Undergraduate—accounting and related services; allied health and medical assisting services; anthropology; area studies; biology; business administration, management and operations; computer programming; computer software and media applications; computer systems networking and telecommunications; data entry/microcomputer applications; developmental and child psychology; economics; English composition; environmental control technologies; ethnic, cultural minority, and gender studies; graphic communications; history; human development, family studies, and related services; journalism; legal studies (non-professional general, undergraduate); marketing; mathematics and statistics related; music; philosophy and religious studies related; political science and government; psychology; real estate; social psychology; sociology; statistics; visual and performing arts.

DEFIANCE COLLEGE
Defiance, Ohio
Design for Leadership
http://www.defiance.edu/pages/design_leadership.html

Defiance College was founded in 1850. It is accredited by North Central Association of Colleges and Schools. It first offered distance learning courses in 1971. In fall 2006, there were 35 students enrolled in distance learning courses. Institutionally administered financial aid is available to distance learners.

Services Distance learners have accessibility to academic advising, campus computer network, career placement assistance, e-mail services, library services, tutoring.

Contact Dr. Marian R. Plant, Coordinator, Design for Leadership, Defiance College, 701 North Clinton Street, Defiance, OH 43512. Telephone: 419-783-2465. Fax: 419-784-0426. E-mail: design@defiance.edu.

DEGREES AND AWARDS

AA Religious Education

BA Religious Education

Certificate African American Ministry Leadership module; Church Education; Youth Ministry Leadership Module

COURSE SUBJECT AREAS OFFERED OUTSIDE OF DEGREE PROGRAMS

Undergraduate—biblical studies; religious education.

DELAWARE COUNTY COMMUNITY COLLEGE
Media, Pennsylvania
Distance Learning
http://www.dccc.edu/dl

Delaware County Community College was founded in 1967. It is accredited by Middle States Association of Colleges and Schools. It first offered distance learning courses in 1980. In fall 2006, there were 2,000 students enrolled in distance learning courses. Institutionally administered financial aid is available to distance learners.

Services Distance learners have accessibility to academic advising, bookstore, campus computer network, e-mail services, library services, tutoring.

Contact Alexander Plachuta, Director of Distance Learning, Delaware County Community College, 901 South Media Line Road, Media, PA 19063. Telephone: 610-359-5158. E-mail: distance@dccc.edu.

DEGREES AND AWARDS

AA General Studies

AAB Business Administration

COURSE SUBJECT AREAS OFFERED OUTSIDE OF DEGREE PROGRAMS

Undergraduate—accounting and related services; American literature (United States and Canadian); anthropology; area, ethnic, cultural, and gender studies related; area studies; astronomy and astrophysics; atmospheric sciences and meteorology; biological and physical sciences; biology; business administration, management and operations; business/commerce; business/corporate communications; business, management, and marketing related; business/managerial economics; business operations support and assistant services; clinical psychology; community psychology; comparative literature; computer and information sciences; computer and information sciences and support services related; computer engineering; computer/information technology administration and management; computer programming; computer science; computer software and media applications; computer systems networking and telecommunications; construction engineering technology; construction trades related; counseling psychology; creative writing; criminal justice and corrections; data entry/microcomputer applications; data processing; demography and population; developmental and child psychology; economics; educational psychology; English; English composition; ethnic, cultural minority, and gender studies; family and consumer sciences/human sciences; finance and financial management services; food science and technology; geography and cartography; history; human development, family studies, and related services; human resources management; information science/studies; journalism; legal studies (non-professional general, undergraduate); liberal arts and sciences, general studies and humanities; management information systems; management sciences and quantitative methods; marketing; mathematics; mathematics and computer science; nursing; pharmacy, pharmaceutical sciences, and administration; philosophy; philosophy and religious studies related; physics; psychology; psychology related; public relations, advertising, and applied communication related; religious studies; sales, merchandising, and related marketing operations (general); sales, merchandising, and related marketing operations (specialized); science technologies related; science, technology and society; social psychology; social sciences; social sciences related; sociology.

Non-credit—computer and information sciences; computer and information sciences and support services related; computer engineering; computer programming; computer science; computer software and media applications; computer systems analysis; computer systems networking and telecommunications.

DELTA COLLEGE
University Center, Michigan
Distance Learning Office and Telelearning
http://www.delta.edu/distancelearning

Delta College was founded in 1961. It is accredited by North Central Association of Colleges and Schools. It first offered distance learning courses in 1982. In fall 2006, there were 1,500 students enrolled in distance learning courses. Institutionally administered financial aid is available to distance learners.

Services Distance learners have accessibility to academic advising, bookstore, campus computer network, career placement assistance, e-mail services, library services, tutoring.

Contact Ms. Jane M. Knochel, eLearning Coordinator, Delta College, 1961 Delta Road, University Center, MI 48710. Telephone: 989-686-9088. E-mail: janeknochel@delta.edu.

DEGREES AND AWARDS
AA General Studies

COURSE SUBJECT AREAS OFFERED OUTSIDE OF DEGREE PROGRAMS

Undergraduate—accounting and computer science; American literature (United States and Canadian); biology; biology/biotechnology laboratory technician; business/corporate communications; computer and information sciences; computer programming; computer software and media applications; criminal justice and corrections; developmental and child psychology; economics; engineering/industrial management; English; English composition; film/video and photographic arts; fine and studio art; health and physical education/fitness; history; industrial production technologies; languages (Romance languages); legal studies (non-professional general, undergraduate); marketing; materials engineering; mathematics; mathematics and statistics related; metallurgical engineering; microbiological sciences and immunology; philosophy; political science and government; psychology; sociology; speech and rhetoric; statistics; technical and business writing; visual and performing arts.

DENVER SEMINARY
Denver, Colorado
http://www.denverseminary.edu

Denver Seminary was founded in 1950. It is accredited by North Central Association of Colleges and Schools. It first offered distance learning courses in 1988. In fall 2006, there were 133 students enrolled in distance learning courses. Institutionally administered financial aid is available to distance learners.

Services Distance learners have accessibility to academic advising, bookstore, career placement assistance, library services.

Contact Dr. Venita Doughty, Director of Educational Technology, Denver Seminary, 6399 South Santa Fe Drive, Littleton, CO 80120. Telephone: 303-762-6933. Fax: 303-761-8060. E-mail: venita.doughty@denverseminary.edu.

DEGREES AND AWARDS
Programs offered do not lead to a degree or other formal award.

COURSE SUBJECT AREAS OFFERED OUTSIDE OF DEGREE PROGRAMS

Graduate—biblical and other theological languages and literatures; biblical studies; history; philosophy and religious studies related; religious education; religious studies; theological and ministerial studies.

DEPAUL UNIVERSITY
Chicago, Illinois
Office of Distance Learning
http://www.lifelearn.depaul.edu/dl

DePaul University was founded in 1898. It is accredited by North Central Association of Colleges and Schools. It first offered distance learning courses in 1996. In fall 2006, there were 1,000 students enrolled in distance learning courses. Institutionally administered financial aid is available to distance learners.

Services Distance learners have accessibility to academic advising, bookstore, campus computer network, e-mail services, library services.

Contact Admissions, DePaul University, One East Jackson Boulevard, Chicago, IL 60604-2287. Telephone: 312-362-8300. E-mail: admission@depaul.edu.

DEGREES AND AWARDS
BA Liberal Arts, general
Certificate Prior Learning Assessment; Professional in Human Resources
MS Computer Science; Computer, Information, and Network Security; Distributed Systems; Telecommunication Systems

COURSE SUBJECT AREAS OFFERED OUTSIDE OF DEGREE PROGRAMS

Undergraduate—computer science; information science/studies.
Graduate—computer programming; computer science; computer systems networking and telecommunications; information science/studies; nursing.
Non-credit—alternative and complementary medical support services; finance and financial management services; human resources management; management sciences and quantitative methods.

DEPAUL UNIVERSITY
Chicago, Illinois
School for New Learning
http://www.snlonline.net

DePaul University was founded in 1898. It is accredited by North Central Association of Colleges and Schools. It first offered distance learning courses in 1996. In fall 2006, there were 800 students enrolled in distance learning courses. Institutionally administered financial aid is available to distance learners.

Services Distance learners have accessibility to academic advising, bookstore, campus computer network, career placement assistance, e-mail services, library services, tutoring.

Contact Academic Advisor, DePaul University, School for New Learning, 25 East Jackson Boulevard, 2nd Floor, Chicago, IL 60604. Telephone: 866-765-3678. Fax: 312-362-8809. E-mail: snladvising@depaul.edu.

DEGREES AND AWARDS
BA Individually designed focus area

COURSE SUBJECT AREAS OFFERED OUTSIDE OF DEGREE PROGRAMS

Undergraduate—liberal arts and sciences, general studies and humanities; science, technology and society; social sciences related.

See full description on page 344.

DEPAUL UNIVERSITY
Chicago, Illinois
School of Computer Science, Telecommunications, and Information Systems
http://www.cti.depaul.edu/admissions

DePaul University was founded in 1898. It is accredited by North Central Association of Colleges and Schools. It first offered distance learning courses in 1995. In fall 2006, there were 900 students enrolled in distance learning courses. Institutionally administered financial aid is available to distance learners.

Services Distance learners have accessibility to academic advising, bookstore, campus computer network, career placement assistance, e-mail services, library services, tutoring.

Contact Maureen Garvey, Executive Director of Admissions, DePaul University, DePaul CTI, 243 South Wabash Avenue, Chicago, IL 60604. Telephone: 312-362-8714. Fax: 312-362-5179. E-mail: ctiadmissions@cti.depaul.edu.

DEGREES AND AWARDS
MA Information Technology
MS Computer Science; Computer, Information, and Network Security; E-Commerce Technology; Information Systems; Information Technology Project Management; Instructional Technology Systems; Software Engineering; Telecommunication Systems

COURSE SUBJECT AREAS OFFERED OUTSIDE OF DEGREE PROGRAMS

Undergraduate—computer and information sciences; computer programming; computer science; computer systems networking and telecommunications.

Graduate—cognitive science; communications technology; computer and information sciences; computer and information sciences and support services related; computer/information technology administration and management; computer programming; computer science; computer software and media applications; computer systems analysis; computer systems networking and telecommunications; educational/instructional media design; information science/studies; systems engineering.

See full description on page 346.

DES MOINES AREA COMMUNITY COLLEGE
Ankeny, Iowa
Distance Learning/Continuing Education
http://www.dmacc.edu/online

Des Moines Area Community College was founded in 1966. It is accredited by North Central Association of Colleges and Schools. It first offered distance learning courses in 1970. In fall 2006, there were 3,800 students enrolled in distance learning courses. Institutionally administered financial aid is available to distance learners.

Services Distance learners have accessibility to academic advising, bookstore, career placement assistance, e-mail services, library services, tutoring.

Contact Pat Thieben, Director of Distance Learning, Des Moines Area Community College, 2006 South Ankeny Boulevard, Ankeny, IA 50023. Telephone: 515-965-7086. Fax: 515-965-6002. E-mail: pathieben@dmacc.edu.

DEGREES AND AWARDS

AAS Business Administration
Certification Management

COURSE SUBJECT AREAS OFFERED OUTSIDE OF DEGREE PROGRAMS

Undergraduate—accounting and computer science; accounting and related services; American literature (United States and Canadian); anthropology; applied mathematics; behavioral sciences; biblical and other theological languages and literatures; biological and physical sciences; biology; business administration, management and operations; business/commerce; business/corporate communications; business, management, and marketing related; business/managerial economics; business operations support and assistant services; chemistry; communication and media; comparative literature; computer and information sciences; computer and information sciences and support services related; computer programming; computer science; creative writing; criminal justice and corrections; criminology; data entry/microcomputer applications; data processing; developmental and child psychology; ecology, evolution, and population biology; economics; educational psychology; education related; English; English composition; English language and literature related; English literature (British and Commonwealth); entrepreneurial and small business operations; finance and financial management services; fire protection; foods, nutrition, and related services; funeral service and mortuary science; geography and cartography; gerontology; health and medical administrative services; history; hospitality administration; human development, family studies, and related services; human resources management; human services; international business; international/global studies; journalism; library science related; management information systems; management sciences and quantitative methods; marketing; mathematics; mathematics and statistics related; music; natural sciences; nursing; personality psychology; philosophy; philosophy and religious studies related; physical sciences; psychology; psychology related; religious education; religious studies; sales, merchandising, and related marketing operations (specialized); social psychology; social sciences; social sciences related; sociology; statistics; technical and business writing.

Non-credit—computer software and media applications.

DEVRY UNIVERSITY ONLINE
Oakbrook Terrace, Illinois
http://www.devry.edu/online

DeVry University Online was founded in 2000. It is accredited by North Central Association of Colleges and Schools. In fall 2006, there were 8,828 students enrolled in distance learning courses. Institutionally administered financial aid is available to distance learners.

Services Distance learners have accessibility to academic advising, bookstore, career placement assistance, e-mail services, library services.

Contact Diane Stegmeyer, DeVry University Online, 1200 East Diehl Road, Naperville, IL 60563. Telephone: 877-496-9050. Fax: 630-382-2939. E-mail: dstegmeyer@devry.com.

DEGREES AND AWARDS

AAS Accounting; Health Information Technology; Network Systems Administration
BS Business Administration; Computer Information Systems; Game and Simulation Programming; Network and Communications Management; Technical Management
MAFM Accounting and Financial Management
MBA Business Administration
MHRM Human Resource Management
MISM Information Systems Management
MPA Public Administration
MPM Project Management
MTM Network and Communications Management

COURSE SUBJECT AREAS OFFERED OUTSIDE OF DEGREE PROGRAMS

Undergraduate—accounting and related services; area, ethnic, cultural, and gender studies related; biological and biomedical sciences related; business/commerce; communication and media; computer and information sciences; creative writing; economics; English composition; legal studies (non-professional general, undergraduate); liberal arts and sciences, general studies and humanities; marketing; mathematics; taxation; technical and business writing.

Graduate—accounting and related services; business/commerce; communication and media; communications technology; computer and information sciences; computer systems networking and telecommunications; economics; entrepreneurial and small business operations; finance and financial management services; health professions related; human resources management; marketing; mathematics; public administration; taxation.

See full description on page 348.

DICKINSON STATE UNIVERSITY
Dickinson, North Dakota
http://www.dsu.nodak.edu/

Dickinson State University was founded in 1918. It is accredited by North Central Association of Colleges and Schools. It first offered distance learning courses in 1998. In fall 2006, there were 570 students enrolled in distance learning courses. Institutionally administered financial aid is available to distance learners.

Services Distance learners have accessibility to academic advising, bookstore, campus computer network, career placement assistance, e-mail services, library services, tutoring.

Contact Ms. Marty Odermann-Gardner, Director, Dickinson State University, 291 Campus Drive, CB 183, Dickinson, ND 58601. Telephone: 701-483-2166. Fax: 701-483-2028. E-mail: marty.odermann.gardner@dsu.nodak.edu.

DEGREES AND AWARDS

AA General Program
AS Agricultural Sales and Services–Equine option
BS Accounting; Business Administration; Computer Science; Computer Technology Management; Education-Elementary Education; Human Resource Management; Secondary Education–Math; Secondary Education; Secondary Education
BSAST Applied Science in Technology (BAST)
BUS University Studies

COURSE SUBJECT AREAS OFFERED OUTSIDE OF DEGREE PROGRAMS

Undergraduate—accounting and related services; agricultural business and management; American literature (United States and Canadian); business administration, management and operations; business/commerce; business/corporate communications; computer science; educational psychology; English; entrepreneurial and small business operations; geography and cartography; history; human resources management; liberal arts and sciences, general studies and humanities; marketing; mathematics and statistics related; nursing; psychology; social sciences.

DODGE CITY COMMUNITY COLLEGE
Dodge City, Kansas

Dodge City Community College was founded in 1935. It is accredited by North Central Association of Colleges and Schools. In fall 2006, there were 1,500 students enrolled in distance learning courses. Institutionally administered financial aid is available to distance learners.

Services Distance learners have accessibility to academic advising.

Contact Stephanie Lanning, Registrar, Dodge City Community College, 2501 North 14th Avenue, Dodge City, KS 67801. Telephone: 620-227-9409. E-mail: slg@dc3.edu.

DEGREES AND AWARDS
Programs offered do not lead to a degree or other formal award.

COURSE SUBJECT AREAS OFFERED OUTSIDE OF DEGREE PROGRAMS

Undergraduate—biology; economics; English; languages (foreign languages related); mathematics; music; psychology; sociology; speech and rhetoric.

DRAKE UNIVERSITY
Des Moines, Iowa
Distance Learning Program
http://www.onlinelearning.drake.edu/summer/

Drake University was founded in 1881. It is accredited by North Central Association of Colleges and Schools. It first offered distance learning courses in 1997. In fall 2006, there were 9,000 students enrolled in distance learning courses. Institutionally administered financial aid is available to distance learners.

Services Distance learners have accessibility to academic advising, bookstore, campus computer network, e-mail services, library services.

Contact Mr. Charles Sengstock, Director of Extension Education, Drake University, School of Education, 3206 University Avenue, Des Moines, IA 50311. Telephone: 515-271-2184. E-mail: charles.sengstrock@drake.edu.

DEGREES AND AWARDS
Programs offered do not lead to a degree or other formal award.

COURSE SUBJECT AREAS OFFERED OUTSIDE OF DEGREE PROGRAMS

Undergraduate—accounting and related services; biochemistry, biophysics and molecular biology; business administration, management and operations; business/commerce; business/managerial economics; communication and journalism related; communication and media; computer and information sciences; creative writing; economics; education; education related; English; fine and studio art; health professions related; history; human resources management; information science/studies; international relations and affairs; journalism; legal research and advanced professional studies; liberal arts and sciences, general studies and humanities; management information systems; management sciences and quantitative methods; marketing; mathematics and computer science; peace studies and conflict resolution; pharmacy, pharmaceutical sciences, and administration; political science and government; psychology; psychology related; public relations, advertising, and applied communication related; social sciences related; special education; visual and performing arts related.

Graduate—accounting and computer science; business administration, management and operations; business/commerce; economics; education; finance and financial management services; health professions related; health services/allied health/health sciences; history; human resources management; information science/studies; insurance; journalism; music; peace studies and conflict resolution; pharmacy, pharmaceutical sciences, and administration; political science and government; psychology; public administration; public administration and social service professions related; public health; public relations, advertising, and applied communication related; rehabilitation and therapeutic professions.

DREW UNIVERSITY
Madison, New Jersey

Drew University was founded in 1867. It is accredited by Middle States Association of Colleges and Schools. It first offered distance learning courses in 1998. In fall 2006, there were 70 students enrolled in distance learning courses. Institutionally administered financial aid is available to distance learners.

Services Distance learners have accessibility to academic advising, bookstore, campus computer network, e-mail services, library services.

Contact Dr. Carl Savage, Associate Director, Doctor of Ministry Program, Drew University, 36 Madison Avenue, Madison, NJ 07940. Telephone: 973-408-3586. Fax: 973-408-3178. E-mail: csavage@drew.edu.

DEGREES AND AWARDS
Programs offered do not lead to a degree or other formal award.

COURSE SUBJECT AREAS OFFERED OUTSIDE OF DEGREE PROGRAMS

Graduate—theological and ministerial studies.
Non-credit—theological and ministerial studies.

DREXEL UNIVERSITY
Philadelphia, Pennsylvania
E-Learning
http://www.drexel.com

Drexel University was founded in 1891. It is accredited by Middle States Association of Colleges and Schools. It first offered distance learning courses in 1997. In fall 2006, there were 3,000 students enrolled in distance learning courses. Institutionally administered financial aid is available to distance learners.

Services Distance learners have accessibility to academic advising, bookstore, career placement assistance, e-mail services, library services, tutoring.

Contact Drexel eLearning, Drexel University, One Drexel Plaza, 3001 Market Street, Suite 300, Philadelphia, PA 19104. Telephone: 866-440-1949. Fax: 215-895-0525. E-mail: info@drexel.com.

DEGREES AND AWARDS
BS Communication; Communications and Applied Technology; Computing and Security Technology; Education; General Studies–Individualized Studies; General Studies, Business minor; Health Services Administration; Psychology
BSN Nursing–RN to BSN
Certificate Clinical Trials Research; Complementary and Integrative Therapies; Contemporary Nursing Faculty; Education–Graduate Intern Teaching Certificate; Education–Post-Bachelor's Teaching Certificate; Epidemiology and Biostatistics; Healthcare Informatics; Innovation and Intra/Entrepreneurship in Advanced Nursing Practice; Instructional Technology Specialist; Medical Billing and Coding; Nursing Leadership in Health Systems Management; Principal's Certification; Retail Leadership; Teaching English as a Second Language (TESL); Toxicology and Industrial Hygiene
CAGS Information Science and Technology
Graduate Certificate Engineering Management
MBA Business Administration
MHS Physicians Assistant Studies
MS Clinical Research Organization and Management; Computer Science; Educational Administration–Collaborative Leadership; Electrical Engineering; Engineering Management; Global and International Education;

Higher Education; Information Systems; Library and Information Science; Science of Instruction; Software Engineering; Teaching, Learning, and Curriculum

MSN Acute Care Nurse Practitioner; Adult Psychiatric Mental Health Nurse Practitioner; Clinical Trials Research; Contemporary Nursing Faculty; Innovation and Intra/Entrepreneurship in Advanced Nursing Practice; Nursing Leadership in Health Systems Management; Women's Health Nurse Practitioner; Women's Health completion program for Nurse Practitioners

COURSE SUBJECT AREAS OFFERED OUTSIDE OF DEGREE PROGRAMS

Undergraduate—apparel and textiles; business administration, management and operations; business/commerce; business, management, and marketing related; communications technologies and support services related; computer and information sciences; computer science; finance and financial management services; health professions related; health services/allied health/health sciences; marketing; nursing; psychology; sales, merchandising, and related marketing operations (general).

Graduate—alternative and complementary medical support services; alternative and complementary medicine and medical systems; business administration, management and operations; business/commerce; business/corporate communications; business, management, and marketing related; clinical/medical laboratory science and allied professions; computer and information sciences; computer and information sciences and support services related; computer engineering; computer engineering technologies; computer science; curriculum and instruction; education; educational administration and supervision; educational assessment, evaluation, and research; educational/instructional media design; education related; education (specific levels and methods); education (specific subject areas); electrical and electronic engineering technologies; electrical, electronics and communications engineering; engineering; engineering/industrial management; engineering related; engineering-related fields; engineering-related technologies; engineering science; engineering technologies related; engineering technology; English as a second/foreign language (teaching); English as a second language; entrepreneurial and small business operations; finance and financial management services; health professions related; information science/studies; international and comparative education; international/global studies; library science; library science related; management information systems; marketing; nursing; pharmacology and toxicology; public health; sales, merchandising, and related marketing operations (general); sales, merchandising, and related marketing operations (specialized); science technologies related; statistics; teaching assistants/aides.

See full description on page 350.

DREXEL UNIVERSITY
Philadelphia, Pennsylvania
LeBow College of Business
http://mbaonline.lebow.drexel.edu
Drexel University was founded in 1891. It is accredited by Middle States Association of Colleges and Schools. It first offered distance learning courses in 1998. In fall 2006, there were 293 students enrolled in distance learning courses. Institutionally administered financial aid is available to distance learners.
Services Distance learners have accessibility to academic advising, bookstore, campus computer network, career placement assistance, e-mail services, library services.
Contact Ms. Anna Serefeas, Director, Graduate Admissions, Drexel University, LeBow College of Business, 207 Matheson Hall, 3141 Chestnut Street, Philadelphia, PA 19104. Telephone: 215-895-0562. Fax: 215-895-1012. E-mail: mba@drexel.edu.

DEGREES AND AWARDS
MBA Business; Pharmaceutical Management

COURSE SUBJECT AREAS OFFERED OUTSIDE OF DEGREE PROGRAMS
Undergraduate—accounting and related services; business administration, management and operations; business/commerce; business/

corporate communications; business/managerial economics; management sciences and quantitative methods; marketing; sales, merchandising, and related marketing operations (general); taxation.
Graduate—accounting and related services; business administration, management and operations; business, management, and marketing related; business/managerial economics; computer/information technology administration and management; management sciences and quantitative methods; marketing; sales, merchandising, and related marketing operations (general).

DUKE UNIVERSITY
Durham, North Carolina
Nicholas School of the Environment and Earth Sciences
http://www.nicholas.duke.edu/del
Duke University was founded in 1838. It is accredited by Southern Association of Colleges and Schools. It first offered distance learning courses in 2004. In fall 2006, there were 20 students enrolled in distance learning courses. Institutionally administered financial aid is available to distance learners.
Services Distance learners have accessibility to academic advising, bookstore, campus computer network, career placement assistance, e-mail services, library services.
Contact Sara Ashenburg, Director, Duke Environmental Leadership Program, Duke University, Nicholas School of the Environment and Earth Sciences, Box 90328, Durham, NC 27708-0328. Telephone: 919-613-8082. Fax: 919-613-9002. E-mail: del@nicholas.duke.edu.

DEGREES AND AWARDS
MEM Duke Environmental Leadership Master of Environmental Management

DUQUESNE UNIVERSITY
Pittsburgh, Pennsylvania
Center for Distance Learning
http://www.distancelearning.duq.edu
Duquesne University was founded in 1878. It is accredited by Middle States Association of Colleges and Schools. It first offered distance learning courses in 1996. In fall 2006, there were 2,105 students enrolled in distance learning courses. Institutionally administered financial aid is available to distance learners.
Services Distance learners have accessibility to academic advising, bookstore, campus computer network, career placement assistance, e-mail services, library services, tutoring.
Contact Ruth Newberry, Director, Educational Technology, Duquesne University, Rockwell Hall, 600 Forbes Avenue, Pittsburgh, PA 15282. Telephone: 412-396-1813. Fax: 412-396-5144. E-mail: edtech@duq.edu.

DEGREES AND AWARDS
BS Degree Completion; Humane Leadership
BSN Nursing–RN to BSN/MSN
Certificate Nursing–Post-BSN
Graduate Certificate Nursing–Post-Masters; Organizational Leadership in Animal Advocacy
MA Leadership and Liberal Studies
MEM Environmental Science and Management
MS Community Leadership; Leadership and Business Ethics; Leadership and Information Technology–Masters of Leadership and Information Technology; Music Education–Masters in Music Education; Sports Leadership
MSN Nursing
EdD Instructional Technology
PhD Nursing

COURSE SUBJECT AREAS OFFERED OUTSIDE OF DEGREE PROGRAMS
Undergraduate—accounting and computer science; business administration, management and operations; business, management, and marketing related; communication and media; computer and information

sciences; fine and studio art; philosophy; philosophy and religious studies related; theological and ministerial studies; theology and religious vocations related.

Graduate—accounting and computer science; business administration, management and operations; communication and media; community health services; community organization and advocacy; computer and information sciences and support services related; computer/information technology administration and management; computer software and media applications; curriculum and instruction; education; educational/instructional media design; management information systems; music; nursing; pastoral counseling and specialized ministries; philosophy and religious studies related; public administration; public policy analysis; technology education/industrial arts.

Non-credit—animal sciences; computer and information sciences; legal support services.

D'YOUVILLE COLLEGE
Buffalo, New York
Distance Learning
http://ddl.dyc.edu

D'Youville College was founded in 1908. It is accredited by Middle States Association of Colleges and Schools. It first offered distance learning courses in 1996. In fall 2006, there were 2,000 students enrolled in distance learning courses. Institutionally administered financial aid is available to distance learners.

Services Distance learners have accessibility to academic advising, bookstore, campus computer network, e-mail services, library services.
Contact Dr. John T. Murphy, Director of Instructional Support Services and Distance Education, D'Youville College, 320 Porter Avenue, Buffalo, NY 14201. Telephone: 716-829-8147. Fax: 716-829-7760. E-mail: murphyj@dyc.edu.

DEGREES AND AWARDS
Programs offered do not lead to a degree or other formal award.

COURSE SUBJECT AREAS OFFERED OUTSIDE OF DEGREE PROGRAMS
Undergraduate—American literature (United States and Canadian); biological and physical sciences; business administration, management and operations; business, management, and marketing related; clinical/medical laboratory science and allied professions; comparative literature; computer and information sciences; computer/information technology administration and management; economics; education; education (specific subject areas); English literature (British and Commonwealth); health professions related; history; human resources management; international business; international/global studies; natural sciences; physics; political science and government; social sciences; special education; statistics.
Graduate—biological and biomedical sciences related; biological and physical sciences; business/commerce; business/managerial economics; cognitive science; creative writing; education; health and medical administrative services; information science/studies; international business; medical clinical sciences/graduate medical studies; nursing; nutrition sciences; social and philosophical foundations of education; special education; statistics.

EARLHAM SCHOOL OF RELIGION
Richmond, Indiana
http://esr.earlham.edu

Earlham School of Religion was founded in 1960. It first offered distance learning courses in 2001. In fall 2006, there were 50 students enrolled in distance learning courses. Institutionally administered financial aid is available to distance learners.
Services Distance learners have accessibility to academic advising, bookstore, campus computer network, e-mail services, library services.
Contact Ms. Susan G. Axtell, Director of Recruitment and Admissions, Earlham School of Religion, 228 College Avenue, Richmond, IN 47374. Telephone: 800-432-1377. Fax: 765-983-1688. E-mail: axtelsu@earlham.edu.

DEGREES AND AWARDS
MA ESR Access
MDiv ESR Access

COURSE SUBJECT AREAS OFFERED OUTSIDE OF DEGREE PROGRAMS
Graduate—biblical and other theological languages and literatures; biblical studies; creative writing; pastoral counseling and specialized ministries; peace studies and conflict resolution; religious studies; theological and ministerial studies; theology and religious vocations related.

EAST ARKANSAS COMMUNITY COLLEGE
Forrest City, Arkansas
http://www.eacc.edu

East Arkansas Community College was founded in 1974. It is accredited by North Central Association of Colleges and Schools. It first offered distance learning courses in 2000. In fall 2006, there were 240 students enrolled in distance learning courses. Institutionally administered financial aid is available to distance learners.
Services Distance learners have accessibility to academic advising, bookstore, campus computer network, career placement assistance, e-mail services, library services, tutoring.
Contact Jacqueline Perkins, Director of Distance Learning, East Arkansas Community College, 1700 Newcastle Road, Forrest City, AR 72335. Telephone: 870-699-4480 Ext. 362. Fax: 870-633-7222. E-mail: jperkins@eacc.edu.

DEGREES AND AWARDS
Programs offered do not lead to a degree or other formal award.

COURSE SUBJECT AREAS OFFERED OUTSIDE OF DEGREE PROGRAMS
Undergraduate—business/managerial economics; education (specific levels and methods); English composition; English literature (British and Commonwealth); environmental/environmental health engineering; health and physical education/fitness; health services/allied health/health sciences; history; hospitality administration; languages (Romance languages); legal professions and studies related; mathematics; mathematics and statistics related.

EAST CAROLINA UNIVERSITY
Greenville, North Carolina
Division of Continuing Studies
http://www.options.ecu.edu

East Carolina University was founded in 1907. It is accredited by Southern Association of Colleges and Schools. It first offered distance learning courses in 1947. In fall 2006, there were 5,644 students enrolled in distance learning courses. Institutionally administered financial aid is available to distance learners.
Services Distance learners have accessibility to academic advising, bookstore, campus computer network, e-mail services, library services.
Contact Melinda Doty, Student Services Coordinator, East Carolina University, Self Help Center, Greenville, NC 27858. Telephone: 800-398-9275. E-mail: options@ecu.edu.

DEGREES AND AWARDS
BS Communication/Public Relations/Journalism concentration; Education–Birth-Kindergarten Education; Health Information Management; Health Services Management; Hospitality Management; Hospitality Management; Industrial Technology–Bioprocess Manufacturing; Industrial Technology–Industrial Distribution and Logistics; Industrial Technology–Industrial Supervision; Industrial Technology–Information and Computer Technology; Industrial Technology–Manufacturing Systems; Information Technologies
BSBA Business Administration
BSN Nursing–RN to BSN

Graduate Certificate Assistive Technology; Communication–Professional Communication; Community College Teaching; Computer Network Professional; Distance Learning; Health Care Management; Information Assurance; Lean Six Sigma; Multicultural Literature; Performance Improvement; Security Studies; Substance Abuse/Addiction Counseling; Technology Facilitator; Virtual Reality in Education and Training; Website Developer

MA English–Professional and Technical Communication concentration; Health Education; Multicultural and Transnational Literatures emphasis; Psychology, general

MAE Art Education; Business Education; Health/Teacher Education; Science Teacher Education; Special Education

MBA Business Administration

MCM Construction Management

MLS Library Science

MS Criminal Justice; Instructional Technology; Nutrition and Dietetics; Occupational Safety; Software Engineering; Speech Language and Auditory Pathology; Technology Systems–Computer Networking Management; Technology Systems–Digital Communications; Technology Systems–Distribution and Logistics; Technology Systems–Information Security; Technology Systems–Manufacturing; Technology Systems–Performance Improvement; Technology Systems–Quality Systems; Vocational Education–Information Technologies

MSE Instructional Technology; Music Education

MSN Adult Nurse Practitioner; Clinical Nurse Specialist; Neonatal Nurse Practitioner; Nurse Midwifery; Nursing Education; Nursing Leadership; Nursing–Family Nurse Practitioner

COURSE SUBJECT AREAS OFFERED OUTSIDE OF DEGREE PROGRAMS

Undergraduate—bilingual, multilingual, and multicultural education; biology; business administration, management and operations; business/commerce; business/corporate communications; business, management, and marketing related; business operations support and assistant services; chemistry; communication and journalism related; communication and media; computer and information sciences; computer and information sciences and support services related; computer/information technology administration and management; curriculum and instruction; data entry/microcomputer applications; data processing; education; educational assessment, evaluation, and research; educational psychology; education (specific subject areas); engineering technology; hospitality administration; human development, family studies, and related services; industrial production technologies; information science/studies; journalism; management information systems; manufacturing engineering; nursing; philosophy; philosophy and religious studies related; sales, merchandising, and related marketing operations (specialized); technology education/industrial arts.

Graduate—accounting and related services; building/construction finishing, management, and inspection; business administration, management and operations; business/commerce; business, management, and marketing related; communication disorders sciences and services; computer and information sciences; computer/information technology administration and management; computer science; computer software and media applications; computer systems networking and telecommunications; construction management; criminal justice and corrections; criminology; data processing; education; educational assessment, evaluation, and research; educational/instructional media design; educational psychology; engineering technologies related; English; fine and studio art; foods, nutrition, and related services; industrial production technologies; library science; nursing; nutrition sciences; psychology; psychology related; quality control and safety technologies; rehabilitation and therapeutic professions; special education; technical and business writing; technology education/industrial arts.

See full description on page 352.

EAST CENTRAL COMMUNITY COLLEGE
Decatur, Mississippi
Adult and Continuing Education
http://www.eccc.cc.ms.us/

East Central Community College was founded in 1928. It is accredited by Southern Association of Colleges and Schools. It first offered distance learning courses in 2000. In fall 2006, there were 450 students enrolled in distance learning courses. Institutionally administered financial aid is available to distance learners.

Services Distance learners have accessibility to academic advising, bookstore, campus computer network, e-mail services, library services, tutoring.

Contact Dr. Chris C. Jenkins, Dean of Distance Learning Education, East Central Community College, PO Box 129, Decatur, MS 39327. Telephone: 601-635-6322. Fax: 601-635-4011. E-mail: cjenkins@eccc.edu.

DEGREES AND AWARDS
Programs offered do not lead to a degree or other formal award.

COURSE SUBJECT AREAS OFFERED OUTSIDE OF DEGREE PROGRAMS

Undergraduate—accounting and computer science; allied health and medical assisting services; American literature (United States and Canadian); biblical studies; biological and physical sciences; business administration, management and operations; chemistry; computer and information sciences; developmental and child psychology; economics; education; English; English composition; history; mathematics; music; nursing; physical sciences; psychology; sociology.

EASTERN IOWA COMMUNITY COLLEGE DISTRICT
Davenport, Iowa
http://www.eicc.edu

Eastern Iowa Community College District is accredited by North Central Association of Colleges and Schools. It first offered distance learning courses in 2000. In fall 2006, there were 1,798 students enrolled in distance learning courses. Institutionally administered financial aid is available to distance learners.

Services Distance learners have accessibility to academic advising, bookstore, career placement assistance, library services, tutoring.

Contact Ms. Heidi Hilbert, HSET Distance Learning Coordinator, Eastern Iowa Community College District, 500 Belmont Road, Bettendorf, IA 52722. Telephone: 563-441-4092. Fax: 563-441-4081. E-mail: hhilbert@eicc.edu.

DEGREES AND AWARDS
AA Liberal Arts
AAS Health, Safety, and Environmental Technology
AS Liberal Arts

COURSE SUBJECT AREAS OFFERED OUTSIDE OF DEGREE PROGRAMS

Non-credit—accounting and computer science; communications technology; computer and information sciences; computer and information sciences and support services related; computer/information technology administration and management; computer programming; computer science; computer software and media applications; computer systems networking and telecommunications; data entry/microcomputer applications; mathematics; mathematics and computer science.

EASTERN KENTUCKY UNIVERSITY
Richmond, Kentucky
Continuing Education and Outreach
http://www.eku.edu/onlinelearning/

Eastern Kentucky University was founded in 1906. It is accredited by Southern Association of Colleges and Schools. It first offered distance learning courses in 1995. In fall 2006, there were 6,000 students enrolled in distance learning courses. Institutionally administered financial aid is available to distance learners.

Services Distance learners have accessibility to academic advising, bookstore, campus computer network, career placement assistance, e-mail services, library services, tutoring.

Contact William St. Pierre, Director of Distance Education, Eastern Kentucky University, 202 Perkins Building, 521 Lancaster Avenue, Richmond, KY 40475. Telephone: 859-622-8342. Fax: 859-622-6205. E-mail: bill.stpierre@eku.edu.

DEGREES AND AWARDS

BS Fire and Safety Engineering Technology
MS Loss Prevention and Safety

COURSE SUBJECT AREAS OFFERED OUTSIDE OF DEGREE PROGRAMS

Undergraduate—anthropology; biology; curriculum and instruction; English composition; fine and studio art; geography and cartography; health professions related; history; journalism; marketing; mathematics and statistics related; philosophy and religious studies related; political science and government; radio, television, and digital communication; social work; sociology.
Graduate—allied health diagnostic, intervention, and treatment professions; computer science; counseling psychology; criminal justice and corrections; curriculum and instruction; educational administration and supervision; library science; nursing; special education.

EASTERN MICHIGAN UNIVERSITY
Ypsilanti, Michigan
Distance Education
http://www.ce.emich.edu

Eastern Michigan University was founded in 1849. It is accredited by North Central Association of Colleges and Schools. It first offered distance learning courses in 1997. In fall 2006, there were 2,818 students enrolled in distance learning courses. Institutionally administered financial aid is available to distance learners.
Services Distance learners have accessibility to academic advising, bookstore, campus computer network, career placement assistance, e-mail services, library services, tutoring.
Contact Jody Cebina, Assistant Director, Distance Education, Eastern Michigan University, Continuing Education, 101 Boone Hall, Ypsilanti, MI 48197. Telephone: 734-487-1081. Fax: 734-487-6695. E-mail: distance.education@emich.edu.

DEGREES AND AWARDS

BS Dietetics; Technology Management (degree completion)
Graduate Certificate Educational Media and Technology; Geographic Information Systems; Human Resource Management
MS Earth Science Education; Educational Media and Technology; Engineering; Human Nutrition; Integrated Marketing Communications; Quality

COURSE SUBJECT AREAS OFFERED OUTSIDE OF DEGREE PROGRAMS

Undergraduate—applied mathematics; Army J.R.O.T.C/R.O.T.C; biological and physical sciences; biology; biotechnology; business administration, management and operations; business/commerce; business/corporate communications; business, management, and marketing related; cell biology and anatomical sciences; chemistry; communication and journalism related; communication and media; computer systems networking and telecommunications; dietetics and clinical nutrition services; dramatic/theater arts and stagecraft; education; educational administration and supervision; educational assessment, evaluation, and research; education (specific subject areas); English; English composition; entrepreneurial and small business operations; ethnic, cultural minority, and gender studies; finance and financial management services; fine and studio art; food science and technology; foods, nutrition, and related services; genetics; geography and cartography; history; hospitality administration; human resources management; legal professions and studies related; legal research and advanced professional studies; legal studies (non-professional general, undergraduate); legal support services; liberal arts and sciences, general studies and humanities; marketing; mathematics; military studies; nursing; nutrition sciences; philosophy; philosophy and religious studies related; political science and government; psychology; sales, merchandising, and related marketing

operations (general); sales, merchandising, and related marketing operations (specialized); social sciences; sociology; special education; technology education/industrial arts.
Graduate—accounting and computer science; accounting and related services; biomathematics and bioinformatics; business administration, management and operations; business/commerce; business/corporate communications; business, management, and marketing related; computer software and media applications; dietetics and clinical nutrition services; education; educational administration and supervision; educational assessment, evaluation, and research; educational/instructional media design; educational psychology; education related; education (specific levels and methods); education (specific subject areas); engineering; engineering/industrial management; engineering related; engineering science; engineering technologies related; ethnic, cultural minority, and gender studies; food science and technology; foods, nutrition, and related services; geography and cartography; geological and earth sciences/geosciences; human resources management; languages (Germanic); legal research and advanced professional studies; marketing; mathematics; mathematics and statistics related; nursing; psychology related; quality control and safety technologies; sales, merchandising, and related marketing operations (general); school psychology; statistics; technology education/industrial arts.
Non-credit—accounting and related services; education; education related; human resources management.

See full description on page 354.

EASTERN OKLAHOMA STATE COLLEGE
Wilburton, Oklahoma
http://www.eosc.edu

Eastern Oklahoma State College was founded in 1908. It is accredited by North Central Association of Colleges and Schools. It first offered distance learning courses in 1994. In fall 2006, there were 569 students enrolled in distance learning courses. Institutionally administered financial aid is available to distance learners.
Services Distance learners have accessibility to academic advising, campus computer network, career placement assistance, e-mail services, library services, tutoring.
Contact MaryEdith Butler, Assistant Vice President, IR, Eastern Oklahoma State College, 1301 West Main Street, Wilburton, OK 74578. Telephone: 918-465-1779. Fax: 918-465-0112. E-mail: mebutler@eosc.edu.

DEGREES AND AWARDS
Programs offered do not lead to a degree or other formal award.

COURSE SUBJECT AREAS OFFERED OUTSIDE OF DEGREE PROGRAMS

Undergraduate—business administration, management and operations; computer software and media applications; criminal justice and corrections; English composition; family and consumer economics; geography and cartography; history; mathematics and statistics related; nursing; political science and government; psychology; social psychology.

EASTERN OREGON UNIVERSITY
La Grande, Oregon
Division of Distance Education
http://www.eou.edu/dde/

Eastern Oregon University was founded in 1929. It is accredited by Northwest Commission on Colleges and Universities. It first offered distance learning courses in 1978. In fall 2006, there were 1,800 students enrolled in distance learning courses. Institutionally administered financial aid is available to distance learners.
Services Distance learners have accessibility to academic advising, bookstore, campus computer network, career placement assistance, e-mail services, library services, tutoring.
Contact Meghan Counsell, Inquiry Coordinator, Eastern Oregon University, Division of Distance Education, One University Boulevard, La Grande, OR 97850-2899. Telephone: 800-544-2195. Fax: 541-962-3627. E-mail: dde@eou.edu.

DEGREES AND AWARDS

BA English Literature; Philosophy, Politics, and Economics; Physical Activity and Health; Psychology

BS Business Administration; Business and Economics; Fire Services Administration; Liberal Studies; Physical Activity and Health; Psychology

COURSE SUBJECT AREAS OFFERED OUTSIDE OF DEGREE PROGRAMS

Undergraduate—accounting and related services; agricultural business and management; anthropology; biology; botany/plant biology; business/commerce; chemistry; computer science; criminology; dramatic/theater arts and stagecraft; economics; English; English language and literature related; geography and cartography; health and physical education/fitness; music; philosophy; physics; political science and government; psychology.

EASTERN WASHINGTON UNIVERSITY

Cheney, Washington

Division for International and Educational Outreach

http://www.deo.ewu.edu

Eastern Washington University was founded in 1882. It is accredited by Northwest Commission on Colleges and Universities. It first offered distance learning courses in 1970. In fall 2006, there were 600 students enrolled in distance learning courses. Institutionally administered financial aid is available to distance learners.

Services Distance learners have accessibility to academic advising, bookstore, campus computer network, e-mail services, library services.

Contact Michele Opsal, Program Coordinator, Eastern Washington University, 300 Senior Hall, Cheney, WA 99004-2442. Telephone: 509-359-2268. Fax: 509-359-6257. E-mail: gothedistance@mail.ewu.edu.

DEGREES AND AWARDS

Programs offered do not lead to a degree or other formal award.

COURSE SUBJECT AREAS OFFERED OUTSIDE OF DEGREE PROGRAMS

Undergraduate—accounting and related services; business/commerce; communication and media; creative writing; education; English; ethnic, cultural minority, and gender studies; fine and studio art; foods, nutrition, and related services; geography and cartography; health and physical education/fitness; history; human resources management; languages (Germanic); philosophy; psychology related; social psychology; social work; sociology.

Graduate—social work.

Non-credit—allied health diagnostic, intervention, and treatment professions; business administration, management and operations; business/commerce; business/corporate communications; business, management, and marketing related; education; health and physical education/fitness; human resources management; international business; languages (foreign languages related); social work; technical and business writing.

EASTERN WEST VIRGINIA COMMUNITY AND TECHNICAL COLLEGE

Moorefield, West Virginia

Eastern West Virginia Community and Technical College was founded in 1999. It is accredited by North Central Association of Colleges and Schools. It first offered distance learning courses in 2001. In fall 2006, there were 200 students enrolled in distance learning courses. Institutionally administered financial aid is available to distance learners.

Services Distance learners have accessibility to academic advising, bookstore, library services, tutoring.

Contact Monica See, Academic Services Program Coordinator, Eastern West Virginia Community and Technical College, 1929 State Road 55, Moorefield, WV 26836. Telephone: 304-434-8000. Fax: 304-434-7000. E-mail: msee1@eastern.wvnet.edu.

DEGREES AND AWARDS

Programs offered do not lead to a degree or other formal award.

COURSE SUBJECT AREAS OFFERED OUTSIDE OF DEGREE PROGRAMS

Undergraduate—accounting and computer science; business, management, and marketing related; business operations support and assistant services; computer and information sciences; economics; English; history; music; political science and government; psychology; sociology.

EASTERN WYOMING COLLEGE

Torrington, Wyoming

Outreach

http://ewc.wy.edu

Eastern Wyoming College was founded in 1948. It is accredited by North Central Association of Colleges and Schools. It first offered distance learning courses in 1990. In fall 2006, there were 250 students enrolled in distance learning courses. Institutionally administered financial aid is available to distance learners.

Services Distance learners have accessibility to academic advising, bookstore, library services, tutoring.

Contact Dee Ludwig, Dean of Instruction–Outreach and Lifelong Learning, Eastern Wyoming College, 3200 West C Street, Torrington, WY 82240. Telephone: 307-532-8221. Fax: 307-532-8222. E-mail: dludwig@ewc.wy.edu.

DEGREES AND AWARDS

AA Criminal Justice; Interdisciplinary Studies

AAS Business Administration

AS Interdisciplinary Studies

COURSE SUBJECT AREAS OFFERED OUTSIDE OF DEGREE PROGRAMS

Undergraduate—accounting and related services; biology; business administration, management and operations; business/commerce; computer and information sciences; computer software and media applications; criminal justice and corrections; economics; English; English composition; geological and earth sciences/geosciences; health and physical education/fitness; physiological psychology/psychobiology; political science and government; sociology; zoology/animal biology.

EAST LOS ANGELES COLLEGE

Monterey Park, California

http://www.elac.edu

East Los Angeles College was founded in 1945. It is accredited by Western Association of Schools and Colleges. It first offered distance learning courses in 1998. In fall 2006, there were 1,400 students enrolled in distance learning courses. Institutionally administered financial aid is available to distance learners.

Services Distance learners have accessibility to academic advising, bookstore, e-mail services, library services.

Contact Dr. Wendy Bass, Distance Education Coordinator, East Los Angeles College, 1301 Avenida Cesar Chavez, Monterey Park, CA 91754. Telephone: 323-415-5313. E-mail: basskew@elac.edu.

DEGREES AND AWARDS

Programs offered do not lead to a degree or other formal award.

COURSE SUBJECT AREAS OFFERED OUTSIDE OF DEGREE PROGRAMS

Undergraduate—accounting and related services; business operations support and assistant services; computer and information sciences; family and consumer economics; fine and studio art; foods, nutrition, and related services; health and physical education/fitness; history; liberal arts and sciences, general studies and humanities; management information systems; mathematics; philosophy; psychology; speech and rhetoric; visual and performing arts.

EAST TENNESSEE STATE UNIVERSITY
Johnson City, Tennessee
Office of Distance Education
http://online.etsu.edu

East Tennessee State University was founded in 1911. It is accredited by Southern Association of Colleges and Schools. It first offered distance learning courses in 1990. In fall 2006, there were 4,700 students enrolled in distance learning courses. Institutionally administered financial aid is available to distance learners.

Services Distance learners have accessibility to academic advising, bookstore, campus computer network, career placement assistance, e-mail services, library services, tutoring.

Contact Pat Westington, Internet Program Support Coordinator, East Tennessee State University, Box 70427, Johnson City, TN 37614-0427. Telephone: 423-439-7058. Fax: 423-439-8564. E-mail: westingt@etsu. edu.

DEGREES AND AWARDS
BGS General Studies–Bachelor of General Studies
BS Allied Health Leadership–BS completion program; Applied Science–Bachelor of Applied Science; Dental Hygiene–BS completion program
MA Liberal Studies

COURSE SUBJECT AREAS OFFERED OUTSIDE OF DEGREE PROGRAMS
Undergraduate—accounting and related services; allied health diagnostic, intervention, and treatment professions; communications technology; comparative literature; criminal justice and corrections; curriculum and instruction; developmental and child psychology; education; educational psychology; education related; English; English composition; geography and cartography; history; liberal arts and sciences, general studies and humanities; psychology; sales, merchandising, and related marketing operations (general); special education; statistics; technical and business writing.
Graduate—business administration, management and operations; city/urban, community and regional planning; curriculum and instruction; education; educational assessment, evaluation, and research; educational/instructional media design; education related; liberal arts and sciences, general studies and humanities; museum studies; public health; religious studies.
Non-credit—allied health and medical assisting services; alternative and complementary medical support services; behavioral sciences; business administration, management and operations; business, management, and marketing related; communication and journalism related; computer and information sciences; computer and information sciences and support services related; computer programming; computer software and media applications; computer systems analysis; computer systems networking and telecommunications; creative writing; culinary arts and related services; entrepreneurial and small business operations; legal support services; liberal arts and sciences, general studies and humanities; marketing; sales, merchandising, and related marketing operations (general).

EDGECOMBE COMMUNITY COLLEGE
Tarboro, North Carolina
http://www.edgecombe.edu

Edgecombe Community College was founded in 1968. It is accredited by Southern Association of Colleges and Schools. It first offered distance learning courses in 1991. In fall 2006, there were 705 students enrolled in distance learning courses. Institutionally administered financial aid is available to distance learners.

Services Distance learners have accessibility to academic advising, bookstore, campus computer network, career placement assistance, e-mail services, library services, tutoring.

Contact Mr. Richard Greene, Distance Learning Director, Edgecombe Community College, 225 Tarboro Street, Rocky Mount, NC 27801. Telephone: 252-823-5166 Ext. 340. Fax: 252-985-2212. E-mail: greener@edgecombe.edu.

DEGREES AND AWARDS
AAS Health Information Technology

COURSE SUBJECT AREAS OFFERED OUTSIDE OF DEGREE PROGRAMS
Undergraduate—accounting and related services; business administration, management and operations; business/commerce; business/corporate communications; business, management, and marketing related; computer and information sciences; computer and information sciences and support services related; computer/information technology administration and management; computer programming; computer software and media applications; computer systems analysis; computer systems networking and telecommunications; data entry/microcomputer applications; education (specific subject areas); English composition; ethnic, cultural minority, and gender studies; health and medical administrative services; health/medical preparatory programs; history; human development, family studies, and related services; management information systems; psychology; sociology; technical and business writing.
Non-credit—accounting and related services; area, ethnic, cultural, and gender studies related; business administration, management and operations; business/commerce; business/corporate communications; business, management, and marketing related; business/managerial economics; business operations support and assistant services; communication and media; community health services; computer and information sciences; computer and information sciences and support services related; computer/information technology administration and management; computer programming; computer science; computer software and media applications; data entry/microcomputer applications; English; English as a second language; health and medical administrative services; management information systems; sales, merchandising, and related marketing operations (specialized).

EDISON COLLEGE
Fort Myers, Florida
Distance Learning
http://www.edison.edu

Edison College was founded in 1962. It is accredited by Southern Association of Colleges and Schools. It first offered distance learning courses in 1993. In fall 2006, there were 1,197 students enrolled in distance learning courses. Institutionally administered financial aid is available to distance learners.

Services Distance learners have accessibility to academic advising, bookstore, campus computer network, e-mail services, library services.

Contact Dr. Roger P. Bober, District Director, Baccalaureate and University Programs, Edison College, 8099 College Parkway SW, Building Q, University Center, Fort Myers, FL 33919. Telephone: 239-489-9295. Fax: 239-489-9250. E-mail: rbober@edison.edu.

DEGREES AND AWARDS
Programs offered do not lead to a degree or other formal award.

COURSE SUBJECT AREAS OFFERED OUTSIDE OF DEGREE PROGRAMS
Undergraduate—business, management, and marketing related; computer programming; computer science; criminal justice and corrections; economics; English composition; health services/allied health/health sciences; human development, family studies, and related services; mathematics; nutrition sciences; physics; psychology; sociology; statistics; taxation.

EDISON STATE COMMUNITY COLLEGE
Piqua, Ohio
http://www.edisonohio.edu/

Edison State Community College was founded in 1973. It is accredited by North Central Association of Colleges and Schools. It first offered distance learning courses in 1987. In fall 2006, there were 500 students enrolled in distance learning courses. Institutionally administered financial aid is available to distance learners.

Services Distance learners have accessibility to academic advising, bookstore, career placement assistance, library services, tutoring.

Contact David Gansz, Dean for Learning Support and Information Literacy, Edison State Community College, 1973 Edison Drive, Piqua, OH 45356. Telephone: 937-778-7951. E-mail: gansz@edisonohio.edu.

DEGREES AND AWARDS

AAB Medical Office Assistant

COURSE SUBJECT AREAS OFFERED OUTSIDE OF DEGREE PROGRAMS

Undergraduate—accounting and related services; anthropology; biology; business administration, management and operations; business/commerce; business/corporate communications; business operations support and assistant services; cell biology and anatomical sciences; chemistry; computer and information sciences; computer engineering; computer/information technology administration and management; computer programming; computer science; computer software and media applications; computer systems analysis; computer systems networking and telecommunications; design and applied arts; dramatic/theater arts and stagecraft; ecology, evolution, and population biology; economics; engineering design; engineering/industrial management; English composition; fine and studio art; human development, family studies, and related services; human resources management; industrial production technologies; management information systems; marketing; mathematics; mathematics and computer science; nursing; philosophy; philosophy and religious studies related; physics; public relations, advertising, and applied communication related; sociology; statistics.
Non-credit—accounting and related services; business administration, management and operations; business/commerce; business operations support and assistant services; computer and information sciences; computer/information technology administration and management; computer software and media applications; human resources management.

EDMONDS COMMUNITY COLLEGE
Lynnwood, Washington
Continuing Education
http://online.edcc.edu
Edmonds Community College was founded in 1967. It is accredited by Northwest Commission on Colleges and Universities. It first offered distance learning courses in 1995. In fall 2006, there were 2,500 students enrolled in distance learning courses. Institutionally administered financial aid is available to distance learners.
Services Distance learners have accessibility to academic advising, bookstore, campus computer network, career placement assistance, library services, tutoring.
Contact Tina Torres, Distance Learning Program Assistant, Edmonds Community College, 20000 68th Avenue West, Lynnwood, WA 98036-5999. Telephone: 425-640-1098. Fax: 425-640-1704. E-mail: ttorres@edcc.edu.

DEGREES AND AWARDS

AA Business Administration; Business Education; Business Information Technology; Business Management; Family Support Studies/Human Development; Social Sciences
Certificate Computer Game Development

COURSE SUBJECT AREAS OFFERED OUTSIDE OF DEGREE PROGRAMS

Undergraduate—accounting and related services; business administration, management and operations; computer programming; developmental and child psychology; English; mathematics.

EDUKAN
Great Bend, Kansas
http://www.edukan.org/
EduKan was founded in 1999. It is accredited by North Central Association of Colleges and Schools. It first offered distance learning courses in 1999. In fall 2006, there were 800 students enrolled in distance learning courses. Institutionally administered financial aid is available to distance learners.
Services Distance learners have accessibility to academic advising, bookstore, campus computer network, career placement assistance, e-mail services, library services, tutoring.

Contact Dr. Dennis L. Franz, Executive Director, EduKan, 245 NE 30th Road, Great Bend, KS 67530. Telephone: 620-792-9204. Fax: 620-792-5624. E-mail: franzd@bartonccc.edu.

DEGREES AND AWARDS

AA Business–Associate in Arts
AGS General Studies
AS Accounting

COURSE SUBJECT AREAS OFFERED OUTSIDE OF DEGREE PROGRAMS

Undergraduate—accounting and related services; anthropology; astronomy and astrophysics; biological and biomedical sciences related; biological and physical sciences; biology; business/commerce; chemistry; communication and media; computer and information sciences; economics; education (specific subject areas); English composition; ethnic, cultural minority, and gender studies; geography and cartography; linguistic, comparative, and related language studies; mathematics; music; physical sciences; psychology; social sciences; sociology; speech and rhetoric.

ELGIN COMMUNITY COLLEGE
Elgin, Illinois
http://www.elgin.edu
Elgin Community College was founded in 1949. It is accredited by North Central Association of Colleges and Schools. It first offered distance learning courses in 1980. In fall 2006, there were 1,500 students enrolled in distance learning courses. Institutionally administered financial aid is available to distance learners.
Services Distance learners have accessibility to academic advising, bookstore, e-mail services, library services, tutoring.
Contact Billie B. Barnett, Distance Learning Operations Coordinator, Elgin Community College, 1700 Spartan Drive, Elgin, IL 60123. Telephone: 847-214-7945. Fax: 847-608-5479. E-mail: bbarnett@elgin.edu.

DEGREES AND AWARDS

Programs offered do not lead to a degree or other formal award.

COURSE SUBJECT AREAS OFFERED OUTSIDE OF DEGREE PROGRAMS

Undergraduate—accounting and related services; allied health and medical assisting services; anthropology; business, management, and marketing related; computer and information sciences; computer/information technology administration and management; education related; English; English composition; legal studies (non-professional general, undergraduate); liberal arts and sciences, general studies and humanities; marketing; mathematics; music; psychology.

ELIZABETH CITY STATE UNIVERSITY
Elizabeth City, North Carolina
http://www.ecsu.edu
Elizabeth City State University was founded in 1891. It is accredited by Southern Association of Colleges and Schools. It first offered distance learning courses in 1998. In fall 2006, there were 275 students enrolled in distance learning courses. Institutionally administered financial aid is available to distance learners.
Services Distance learners have accessibility to academic advising, bookstore, campus computer network, career placement assistance, e-mail services, library services, tutoring.
Contact Mrs. Kimberley N. Stevenson, Director of the Office of Distance Education, Elizabeth City State University, 1704 Weeksville Road, 208 Information Technology Center, Elizabeth City, NC 27909. Telephone: 252-335-3699. Fax: 252-335-3426. E-mail: knstevenson@mail.ecsu.edu.

DEGREES AND AWARDS

Programs offered do not lead to a degree or other formal award.

COURSE SUBJECT AREAS OFFERED OUTSIDE OF DEGREE PROGRAMS

Undergraduate—accounting and related services; air transportation; biology; business administration, management and operations; business/commerce; business/corporate communications; business, management, and marketing related; business/managerial economics; criminal justice and corrections; education; educational/instructional media design; educational psychology; education (specific subject areas); English composition; health and physical education/fitness; history; human development, family studies, and related services; human resources management; management sciences and quantitative methods; music; psychology; public administration; public policy analysis; sales, merchandising, and related marketing operations (general); sociology; special education; statistics; taxation.

Graduate—education; educational administration and supervision.

ELIZABETHTOWN COLLEGE
Elizabethtown, Pennsylvania
Center for Continuing Education and Distance Learning
http://www.etown.edu/cce

Elizabethtown College was founded in 1899. It is accredited by Middle States Association of Colleges and Schools. It first offered distance learning courses in 2001. In fall 2006, there were 150 students enrolled in distance learning courses. Institutionally administered financial aid is available to distance learners.

Services Distance learners have accessibility to academic advising, bookstore, campus computer network, e-mail services, library services.

Contact Dr. John Kokolus, Dean of Continuing Education and Distance Learning, Elizabethtown College, 1 Alpha Drive, Elizabethtown, PA 17022. Telephone: 717-361-1291. Fax: 717-361-1466. E-mail: kokolusj @etown.edu.

DEGREES AND AWARDS

Programs offered do not lead to a degree or other formal award.

COURSE SUBJECT AREAS OFFERED OUTSIDE OF DEGREE PROGRAMS

Undergraduate—accounting and computer science; accounting and related services; American literature (United States and Canadian); area, ethnic, cultural, and gender studies related; business administration, management and operations; business/commerce; business/corporate communications; communication and journalism related; communication and media; English; history; human resources management; medieval and Renaissance studies.

EMBRY-RIDDLE AERONAUTICAL UNIVERSITY
Daytona Beach, Florida
Distance Learning
http://www.erau.edu/db/degrees/ma-mbaaonline.html

Embry-Riddle Aeronautical University was founded in 1926. It is accredited by Southern Association of Colleges and Schools. It first offered distance learning courses in 2003. In fall 2006, there were 65 students enrolled in distance learning courses. Institutionally administered financial aid is available to distance learners.

Services Distance learners have accessibility to academic advising, bookstore, career placement assistance, e-mail services, library services.

Contact Mr. Tom Shea, Director of International and Graduate Admissions, Embry-Riddle Aeronautical University, 600 South Clyde Morris Boulevard, Daytona Beach, FL 32114. Telephone: 386-226-7178. Fax: 386-226-7070. E-mail: graduate.admissions@erau.edu.

DEGREES AND AWARDS

MBA Business Administration in Aviation

COURSE SUBJECT AREAS OFFERED OUTSIDE OF DEGREE PROGRAMS

Undergraduate—aerospace, aeronautical and astronautical engineering; business administration, management and operations; business/managerial economics; English composition; finance and financial management services; legal studies (non-professional general, undergraduate); management sciences and quantitative methods; marketing; mathematics and statistics related; statistics.

Graduate—business administration, management and operations; management information systems; management sciences and quantitative methods.

Non-credit—air transportation.

EMBRY-RIDDLE AERONAUTICAL UNIVERSITY
Daytona Beach, Florida
Worldwide Online
http://www.erau.edu/ec/dleo/index.html

Embry-Riddle Aeronautical University was founded in 1926. It is accredited by Southern Association of Colleges and Schools. It first offered distance learning courses in 1983. In fall 2006, there were 2,199 students enrolled in distance learning courses. Institutionally administered financial aid is available to distance learners.

Services Distance learners have accessibility to academic advising, bookstore, career placement assistance, library services.

Contact Mrs. Linda Dammer, Director, Advising, Enrollment, and Recruitment Online, Embry-Riddle Aeronautical University, 600 South Clyde Morris Boulevard, Daytona Beach, FL 32114-3900. Telephone: 386-226-6397. Fax: 386-226-7627. E-mail: dleo.student.recruiter@ erau.edu.

DEGREES AND AWARDS

AS Aircraft Maintenance; Professional Aeronautics; Technical Management

BS Aviation Maintenance Management; Professional Aeronautics; Technical Management

MAS Aeronautical Science

MS Management

COURSE SUBJECT AREAS OFFERED OUTSIDE OF DEGREE PROGRAMS

Undergraduate—applied mathematics; business/commerce; computer science; economics; English; legal studies (non-professional general, undergraduate); social sciences; statistics; technical and business writing.

Graduate—air transportation; business administration, management and operations; business/commerce; psychology.

Non-credit—air transportation.

EMORY UNIVERSITY
Atlanta, Georgia
Rollins School of Public Health
http://www.sph.emory.edu/CMPH

Emory University was founded in 1836. It is accredited by Southern Association of Colleges and Schools. It first offered distance learning courses in 1997. In fall 2006, there were 150 students enrolled in distance learning courses. Institutionally administered financial aid is available to distance learners.

Services Distance learners have accessibility to academic advising, bookstore, campus computer network, career placement assistance, e-mail services, library services.

Contact Ms. Robie Freeman-Burks, Assistant Director of Academic Programs, Emory University, 1518 Clifton Road, RSPH, Office 148, Atlanta, GA 30322. Telephone: 404-727-8739. Fax: 404-727-3996. E-mail: rfreem2@sph.emory.edu.

DEGREES AND AWARDS

MPH Public Health–Career Master of Public Health program

COURSE SUBJECT AREAS OFFERED OUTSIDE OF DEGREE PROGRAMS

Graduate—public health.

EMPORIA STATE UNIVERSITY
Emporia, Kansas
Office of Lifelong Learning
http://lifelong.emporia.edu

Emporia State University was founded in 1863. It is accredited by North Central Association of Colleges and Schools. It first offered distance learning courses in 1970. In fall 2006, there were 2,376 students enrolled in distance learning courses. Institutionally administered financial aid is available to distance learners.

Services Distance learners have accessibility to academic advising, bookstore, campus computer network, career placement assistance, e-mail services, library services.

Contact Brad Goebel, Director of Lifelong Learning, Emporia State University, 1200 Commercial Street, Emporia, KS 66801-5087. Telephone: 877-332-4249. Fax: 620-341-5744. E-mail: tgoebel@emporia.edu.

DEGREES AND AWARDS
BEd Elementary Education
BGS Integrated Studies
BS Recreation
BSBA Business
MA Teaching English to Speakers of Other Languages
MBE Business Education
MLS Library and Information Science
MS Counseling–School Counseling (K-12); Curriculum and Instruction; Educational Administration; Instructional Design and Technology; Physical Education; Physical Sciences (Earth Science emphasis); Special Education
MSE Early Childhood Education; Master Teacher Elementary

ENDICOTT COLLEGE
Beverly, Massachusetts
http://www.endicott.edu/

Endicott College was founded in 1939. It is accredited by New England Association of Schools and Colleges. It first offered distance learning courses in 2003. In fall 2006, there were 300 students enrolled in distance learning courses. Institutionally administered financial aid is available to distance learners.

Services Distance learners have accessibility to academic advising, bookstore, campus computer network, career placement assistance, e-mail services, library services.

Contact Dr. Mary Huegel, Dean of School of Graduate and Professional Studies, Endicott College, 376 Hale Street, Beverly, MA 01915. Telephone: 978-232-2084. Fax: 978-232-3000. E-mail: mhuegel@endicott.edu.

DEGREES AND AWARDS
Programs offered do not lead to a degree or other formal award.

COURSE SUBJECT AREAS OFFERED OUTSIDE OF DEGREE PROGRAMS
Undergraduate—business/commerce; education.
Graduate—business/commerce; education.
Non-credit—business/commerce.

ERIE COMMUNITY COLLEGE
Buffalo, New York
http://www.ecc.edu/

Erie Community College was founded in 1971. It is accredited by Middle States Association of Colleges and Schools. It first offered distance learning courses in 1992. In fall 2006, there were 2,726 students enrolled in distance learning courses. Institutionally administered financial aid is available to distance learners.

Services Distance learners have accessibility to academic advising, bookstore, campus computer network, career placement assistance, e-mail services, library services, tutoring.

Contact Ms. Martha Dixon, Assistant Academic Dean, Distance Learning, Erie Community College, 4041 Southwestern Boulevard, Orchard Park, NY 14127. Telephone: 716-851-1939. Fax: 716-851-1629. E-mail: dixon@ecc.edu.

DEGREES AND AWARDS
AA Liberal Arts and Science/Humanities and Social Science
AAS Business–Business Administration; Business–Office Management; Telecommunications Technology–Verizon
AS Business–Business Administration (Transfer option)
Certificate Computer Applications for the Office

COURSE SUBJECT AREAS OFFERED OUTSIDE OF DEGREE PROGRAMS
Undergraduate—accounting and related services; American Sign Language (ASL); anthropology; biological and biomedical sciences related; business/commerce; business/corporate communications; clinical/medical laboratory science and allied professions; computer science; computer software and media applications; computer systems analysis; creative writing; criminal justice and corrections; culinary arts and related services; data entry/microcomputer applications; developmental and child psychology; dietetics and clinical nutrition services; dramatic/theater arts and stagecraft; economics; education; electrical and electronic engineering technologies; English; English composition; English language and literature related; finance and financial management services; fine and studio art; geography and cartography; health and medical administrative services; health and physical education/fitness; history; hospitality administration; human resources management; international relations and affairs; legal professions and studies related; legal support services; marketing; mathematics; music; natural resources conservation and research; nutrition sciences; philosophy; political science and government; psychology; religious studies; sales, merchandising, and related marketing operations (general); science, technology and society; social psychology; social sciences related; sociology; statistics; technical and business writing.

ERIKSON INSTITUTE
Chicago, Illinois

Erikson Institute was founded in 1966. It is accredited by North Central Association of Colleges and Schools. It first offered distance learning courses in 2001. In fall 2006, there were 15 students enrolled in distance learning courses. Institutionally administered financial aid is available to distance learners.

Services Distance learners have accessibility to academic advising, bookstore, campus computer network, e-mail services, library services.

Contact Ms. Valerie Williams, Associate Director, Admissions and Multicultural Student Affairs, Erikson Institute, 420 North Wabash Avenue, 6th Floor, Chicago, IL 60611. Telephone: 312-893-7142. Fax: 312-755-0928. E-mail: vwilliams@erikson.edu.

DEGREES AND AWARDS
Programs offered do not lead to a degree or other formal award.

COURSE SUBJECT AREAS OFFERED OUTSIDE OF DEGREE PROGRAMS
Non-credit—human development, family studies, and related services.

EUGENE BIBLE COLLEGE
Eugene, Oregon
External Studies Department
http://www.ebc.edu

Eugene Bible College was founded in 1925. It is accredited by Association for Biblical Higher Education. It first offered distance learning courses in 1987. In fall 2006, there were 21 students enrolled in distance learning courses. Institutionally administered financial aid is available to distance learners.

Services Distance learners have accessibility to academic advising, bookstore, e-mail services.

Contact Mrs. Bettie S. Delury, Director of External Studies, Eugene Bible College, 2155 Bailey Hill Road, Eugene, OR 97405. Telephone: 541-485-1780 Ext. 3200. Fax: 541-762-2301. E-mail: distance-ed@ebc.edu.

DEGREES AND AWARDS
Programs offered do not lead to a degree or other formal award.

COURSE SUBJECT AREAS OFFERED OUTSIDE OF DEGREE PROGRAMS
Undergraduate—applied mathematics; biblical and other theological languages and literatures; biblical studies; biological and physical sciences; biology; education; educational psychology; English literature (British and Commonwealth); history; intercultural/multicultural and diversity studies; languages (Modern Greek); mathematics; missionary studies and missiology; music; pastoral counseling and specialized ministries; physical sciences; religious education; religious/sacred music; religious studies; school psychology; sociology; theological and ministerial studies.

EVEREST COLLEGE
Springfield, Missouri
Everest College was founded in 1976. It is accredited by Accrediting Council for Independent Colleges and Schools. It first offered distance learning courses in 2000. In fall 2006, there were 200 students enrolled in distance learning courses. Institutionally administered financial aid is available to distance learners.
Services Distance learners have accessibility to academic advising, bookstore, campus computer network, career placement assistance, library services, tutoring.
Contact Mr. Steve Marshall, Registrar/Online Coordinator, Everest College, 1010 West Sunshine Street, Springfield, MO 65807. Telephone: 417-864-7220 Ext. 118. Fax: 417-864-5697. E-mail: smarshall@cci.edu.

DEGREES AND AWARDS
Programs offered do not lead to a degree or other formal award.

COURSE SUBJECT AREAS OFFERED OUTSIDE OF DEGREE PROGRAMS
Undergraduate—accounting and computer science; accounting and related services; allied health and medical assisting services; business administration, management and operations; computer and information sciences; computer programming; English; English composition; legal professions and studies related; marketing; mathematics; psychology; sociology; statistics.

EVERETT COMMUNITY COLLEGE
Everett, Washington
Library/Media/Arts and Distance Learning
http://www.everettcc.edu/distance
Everett Community College was founded in 1941. It is accredited by Northwest Commission on Colleges and Universities. It first offered distance learning courses in 1997. In fall 2006, there were 1,200 students enrolled in distance learning courses. Institutionally administered financial aid is available to distance learners.
Services Distance learners have accessibility to academic advising, bookstore, e-mail services, library services, tutoring.
Contact Sara J. Frizelle, Director of Distance Learning, Everett Community College, 2000 Tower Street, Everett, WA 98201. Telephone: 425-388-9585. Fax: 425-259-8257. E-mail: distance@everettcc.edu.

DEGREES AND AWARDS
AAS Direct Transfer
AGS General Studies

COURSE SUBJECT AREAS OFFERED OUTSIDE OF DEGREE PROGRAMS
Undergraduate—accounting and related services; allied health and medical assisting services; American literature (United States and Canadian); anthropology; applied mathematics; area, ethnic, cultural, and gender studies related; biology; business administration, management and operations; business/commerce; communication and journalism related; computer and information sciences; criminal justice and corrections; criminology; economics; English composition; film/video and photographic arts; geography and cartography; graphic communications; health professions related; history; human development, family studies, and related services; journalism; liberal arts and sciences, general studies and humanities; library science related; mathematics; music; nutrition sciences; philosophy; physical sciences; psychology; psychology related; science technologies related; science, technology and society; social sciences; sociology; visual and performing arts.

EXCELSIOR COLLEGE
Albany, New York
Learning Services
http://www.excelsior.edu
Excelsior College was founded in 1970. It is accredited by Middle States Association of Colleges and Schools. It first offered distance learning courses in 1970. In fall 2006, there were 32,110 students enrolled in distance learning courses. Institutionally administered financial aid is available to distance learners.
Services Distance learners have accessibility to academic advising, bookstore, library services, tutoring.
Contact Dana Offerman, PhD, Provost and Chief Academic Officer, Excelsior College, 7 Columbia Circle, Albany, NY 12203. Telephone: 518-464-8500. Fax: 518-464-8700. E-mail: dofferman@excelsior.edu.

DEGREES AND AWARDS
AA Liberal Arts
AAS Administrative/Management Studies; Aviation Studies; Nursing; Technical Studies
AD Occupational Studies in Aviation Studies
AS Business; Computer Software; Electronics Technology; Liberal Arts; Nuclear Technology; Nursing; Science; Technology
BA Liberal Arts; Liberal Studies
BS Accounting NYS CPA Track; Accounting; Business, general; Computer Technology; Criminal Justice; Electronics Engineering Technology; Finance; Global Business; Health Sciences; Hospitality Management; Information Technology; Management Information Systems; Management of Human Resources; Marketing; Nuclear Engineering Technology; Operations Management; Risk Management and Insurance; Science
BSN Nursing
BST Technology
MA Liberal Studies
MBA Business
MS Nursing
See full description on page 356.

FAIRFIELD UNIVERSITY
Fairfield, Connecticut
http://www.fairfield.edu/
Fairfield University was founded in 1942. It is accredited by New England Association of Schools and Colleges. It first offered distance learning courses in 2002. In fall 2006, there were 137 students enrolled in distance learning courses. Institutionally administered financial aid is available to distance learners.
Services Distance learners have accessibility to academic advising, bookstore, campus computer network, e-mail services, library services, tutoring.
Contact Neil Landino, Assistant Dean Advising, Fairfield University, University College, North Benson Road, Fairfield, CT 06824. Telephone: 203-254-4000 Ext. 2622. Fax: 203-254-4106. E-mail: nlandino@mail.fairfield.edu.

DEGREES AND AWARDS
AA Associate of Arts
BA Professional Studies

FAIRMONT STATE UNIVERSITY
Fairmont, West Virginia
http://www.fscwv.edu/

Fairmont State University was founded in 1865. It is accredited by North Central Association of Colleges and Schools. It first offered distance learning courses in 1974. In fall 2006, there were 3,180 students enrolled in distance learning courses. Institutionally administered financial aid is available to distance learners.

Services Distance learners have accessibility to academic advising, bookstore, campus computer network, career placement assistance, e-mail services, library services, tutoring.

Contact Roxann Humbert, Director of Learning Technologies, Fairmont State University, 1201 Locust Avenue, Fairmont, WV 26554. Telephone: 304-367-4160. Fax: 304-367-4599. E-mail: roxann.humbert@fairmontstate.edu.

DEGREES AND AWARDS

AA General Studies

AAS Technical Studies in Information Systems

COURSE SUBJECT AREAS OFFERED OUTSIDE OF DEGREE PROGRAMS

Undergraduate—business/commerce; business/corporate communications; computer software and media applications; economics; education; education related; education (specific levels and methods); English composition; foods, nutrition, and related services; geography and cartography; history; information science/studies; liberal arts and sciences, general studies and humanities; multi-/interdisciplinary studies related; sociology.

Graduate—education; educational administration and supervision; educational assessment, evaluation, and research; educational/instructional media design; educational psychology; education related.

Non-credit—computer/information technology administration and management; computer systems networking and telecommunications.

FAYETTEVILLE STATE UNIVERSITY
Fayetteville, North Carolina
http://www.uncfsu.edu/conted

Fayetteville State University was founded in 1867. It is accredited by Southern Association of Colleges and Schools. It first offered distance learning courses in 1999. In fall 2006, there were 2,000 students enrolled in distance learning courses. Institutionally administered financial aid is available to distance learners.

Services Distance learners have accessibility to academic advising, bookstore, campus computer network, career placement assistance, e-mail services, library services, tutoring.

Contact Ms. Melissa Wells, Administrative Assistant, Extended Learning, Fayetteville State University, Continuing Education Building, 1200 Murchison Road, Fayetteville, NC 28301. Telephone: 910-672-1228. Fax: 910-672-1491. E-mail: mwells@uncfsu.edu.

DEGREES AND AWARDS

Programs offered do not lead to a degree or other formal award.

COURSE SUBJECT AREAS OFFERED OUTSIDE OF DEGREE PROGRAMS

Undergraduate—business/commerce; computer science; criminal justice and corrections; education (specific levels and methods); nursing; psychology; sociology; special education.

Graduate—business administration, management and operations; criminal justice and corrections; education; history; social work; special education.

FEATHER RIVER COLLEGE
Quincy, California
http://www.frc.edu

Feather River College was founded in 1968. It is accredited by Western Association of Schools and Colleges. It first offered distance learning courses in 2002. In fall 2006, there were 300 students enrolled in distance learning courses. Institutionally administered financial aid is available to distance learners.

Services Distance learners have accessibility to academic advising, bookstore, campus computer network, career placement assistance, e-mail services, library services, tutoring.

Contact Dr. Michael Norman Bagley, Dean of Instruction, Feather River College, 570 Golden Eagle Avenue, Quincy, CA 95971. Telephone: 530-283-0202 Ext. 342. Fax: 530-283-3757. E-mail: mbagley@frc.edu.

DEGREES AND AWARDS

Programs offered do not lead to a degree or other formal award.

COURSE SUBJECT AREAS OFFERED OUTSIDE OF DEGREE PROGRAMS

Undergraduate—allied health and medical assisting services; anthropology; biological and biomedical sciences related; business operations support and assistant services; creative writing; criminal justice and corrections; data processing; English composition; health and physical education/fitness; history; insurance; mathematics; psychology; psychology related; sociology.

Non-credit—family and consumer sciences/human sciences; film/video and photographic arts; finance and financial management services; foods, nutrition, and related services; gerontology; health and medical administrative services; historic preservation and conservation; history; human development, family studies, and related services; human resources management; journalism; languages (East Asian); languages (Middle/Near Eastern and Semitic); languages (Slavic, Baltic and Albanian); linguistic, comparative, and related language studies; management information systems; museum studies; music; philosophy; philosophy and religious studies related; psychology; public administration; radio, television, and digital communication; real estate; sales, merchandising, and related marketing operations (general); sales, merchandising, and related marketing operations (specialized); technical and business writing.

FERRIS STATE UNIVERSITY
Big Rapids, Michigan
http://www.ferris.edu/

Ferris State University was founded in 1884. It is accredited by North Central Association of Colleges and Schools. It first offered distance learning courses in 1991. In fall 2006, there were 60 students enrolled in distance learning courses. Institutionally administered financial aid is available to distance learners.

Services Distance learners have accessibility to academic advising, bookstore, campus computer network, career placement assistance, e-mail services, library services, tutoring.

Contact Mr. Steve Cox, Producer and Director, Ferris State University, 1010 Campus Drive, FLITE 460C, Big Rapids, MI 49307. Telephone: 231-591-2721. Fax: 231-591-2785. E-mail: coxs@ferris.edu.

DEGREES AND AWARDS

Programs offered do not lead to a degree or other formal award.

COURSE SUBJECT AREAS OFFERED OUTSIDE OF DEGREE PROGRAMS

Graduate—ophthalmic and optometric support services and allied professions.

FIELDING GRADUATE UNIVERSITY
Santa Barbara, California
http://www.fielding.edu/

Fielding Graduate University was founded in 1974. It is accredited by Western Association of Schools and Colleges. It first offered distance learning courses in 1974. In fall 2006, there were 1,450 students enrolled in distance learning courses. Institutionally administered financial aid is available to distance learners

Services Distance learners have accessibility to academic advising, bookstore, e-mail services, library services.

Contact Kathy Wells, Admissions Assistant, Fielding Graduate University, 2112 Santa Barbara Street, Santa Barbara, CA 93105-3538. Telephone: 800-340-1099. Fax: 805-687-9793. E-mail: admissions@ fielding.edu.

DEGREES AND AWARDS

Certificate Neuropsychology
Certification Integral Studies; Organization Development and Organizational Management; Respecialization in Clinical Psychology; Teaching in the Virtual Classroom
MA Collaborative Educational Leadership; Organizational Management/ Organizational Development
EdD Educational Leadership and Change
PhD Clinical Psychology; Human and Organizational Development; Media Psychology

FINGER LAKES COMMUNITY COLLEGE
Canandaigua, New York
http://www.flcc.edu

Finger Lakes Community College was founded in 1965. It is accredited by Middle States Association of Colleges and Schools. It first offered distance learning courses in 1970. In fall 2006, there were 105 students enrolled in distance learning courses. Institutionally administered financial aid is available to distance learners.

Services Distance learners have accessibility to academic advising, bookstore, campus computer network, career placement assistance, e-mail services, library services.

Contact Ms. Bonnie Ritts, Director of Admissions, Finger Lakes Community College, 4355 Lake Shore Drive, Canandaigua, NY 14424. Telephone: 585-394-3500 Ext. 7278. Fax: 585-394-5005. E-mail: admissions@flcc.edu.

DEGREES AND AWARDS

Programs offered do not lead to a degree or other formal award.

COURSE SUBJECT AREAS OFFERED OUTSIDE OF DEGREE PROGRAMS

Undergraduate—accounting and computer science; biology; business/ commerce; business/corporate communications; computer and information sciences; economics; education; legal studies (non-professional general, undergraduate); marketing; nursing; philosophy; psychology; sales, merchandising, and related marketing operations (specialized); sociology.
Non-credit—computer software and media applications.

FLATHEAD VALLEY COMMUNITY COLLEGE
Kalispell, Montana
Education Services
http://www.fvcc.edu

Flathead Valley Community College was founded in 1967. It is accredited by Northwest Commission on Colleges and Universities. It first offered distance learning courses in 1992. In fall 2006, there were 245 students enrolled in distance learning courses. Institutionally administered financial aid is available to distance learners.

Services Distance learners have accessibility to academic advising, bookstore, e-mail services, library services.

Contact Faith Hodges, Director of Enrollment Planning and Research, Flathead Valley Community College, 777 Grandview Drive, Kalispell, MT 59901. Telephone: 406-756-3812. Fax: 406-756-3815. E-mail: fhodges@fvcc.edu.

DEGREES AND AWARDS

Programs offered do not lead to a degree or other formal award.

COURSE SUBJECT AREAS OFFERED OUTSIDE OF DEGREE PROGRAMS

Undergraduate—accounting and related services; allied health and medical assisting services; anthropology; biological and physical sciences; business administration, management and operations; computer software and media applications; curriculum and instruction; education (specific subject areas); English; English composition; film/video and photographic arts; geological and earth sciences/geosciences; gerontology; heating, air conditioning, ventilation and refrigeration maintenance technology; human services; languages (foreign languages related); political science and government; psychology; real estate; sociology.
Non-credit—accounting and computer science; business/commerce; computer/information technology administration and management; computer programming; computer software and media applications; entrepreneurial and small business operations; film/video and photographic arts; legal studies (non-professional general, undergraduate).

FLORIDA INSTITUTE OF TECHNOLOGY
Melbourne, Florida
School of Extended Studies–Virtual Campus
http://www.ec.fit.edu

Florida Institute of Technology was founded in 1958. It is accredited by Southern Association of Colleges and Schools. It first offered distance learning courses in 1995. In fall 2006, there were 637 students enrolled in distance learning courses. Institutionally administered financial aid is available to distance learners.

Services Distance learners have accessibility to academic advising, bookstore, career placement assistance, e-mail services, library services.

Contact Penny Vassar, Senior Resident Administrator, Florida Institute of Technology, PO Box 3753, Anderson, SC 29622. E-mail: vgc@fit. edu.

DEGREES AND AWARDS

MPA Public Administration
MS Acquisition and Contract Management; Human Resources Management; Information Technology; Logistics Management; Material Acquisition Management; Operations Research; Project Management; Systems Management
MSM Management
PMBA Business Administration–Professional Master of Business Administration

COURSE SUBJECT AREAS OFFERED OUTSIDE OF DEGREE PROGRAMS

Graduate—accounting and related services; business administration, management and operations; business/commerce; business/managerial economics; engineering/industrial management; human resources management; information science/studies; management sciences and quantitative methods; marketing; systems engineering; systems science and theory.
Non-credit—behavioral sciences; psychology related.

See full description on page 358.

FLORIDA STATE UNIVERSITY
Tallahassee, Florida
Office for Distributed and Distance Learning
http://online.fsu.edu

Florida State University was founded in 1851. It is accredited by Southern Association of Colleges and Schools. It first offered distance learning courses in 1987. In fall 2006, there were 1,800 students enrolled in distance learning courses. Institutionally administered financial aid is available to distance learners.

Services Distance learners have accessibility to academic advising, bookstore, campus computer network, career placement assistance, e-mail services, library services, tutoring.

Contact Student Support Services, Florida State University, Academic & Professional Program Services, C3500 University Center, Tallahassee, FL 32306-2550. Telephone: 877-357-8283. Fax: 850-644-5803. E-mail: inquiries@campus.fsu.edu.

DEGREES AND AWARDS

BS Interdisciplinary Social Science; Software Engineering
BSN Nursing–RN to BSN
MBA Business Administration

MS Criminology, Criminal Justice Studies major; Educational Leadership/Administration; Information Studies; Instructional Systems; Instructional Systems; Management Information Systems; Mathematics Education; Physical Education; Risk Management/Insurance; Science Education; Special Education
MSN Nurse Educator
MSW Social Work

COURSE SUBJECT AREAS OFFERED OUTSIDE OF DEGREE PROGRAMS

Undergraduate—classical and ancient studies; economics; music; political science and government; public administration; sociology; urban studies/affairs.
Graduate—educational/instructional media design; human resources management; information science/studies; special education.
Non-credit—computer software and media applications; finance and financial management services.

FONTBONNE UNIVERSITY
St. Louis, Missouri
http://www.fontbonne.edu/

Fontbonne University was founded in 1917. It is accredited by North Central Association of Colleges and Schools. It first offered distance learning courses in 2000. In fall 2006, there were 650 students enrolled in distance learning courses. Institutionally administered financial aid is available to distance learners.
Services Distance learners have accessibility to academic advising, bookstore, campus computer network, e-mail services, library services, tutoring.
Contact Dr. Tony Teoli, Distance Learning Coordinator, Fontbonne University, 6800 Wydown Boulevard, St. Louis, MO 63105-3098. Telephone: 314-889-1499. E-mail: tteoli@fontbonne.edu.

DEGREES AND AWARDS
Programs offered do not lead to a degree or other formal award.

COURSE SUBJECT AREAS OFFERED OUTSIDE OF DEGREE PROGRAMS

Undergraduate—business administration, management and operations; communication and media; computer software and media applications; economics; English composition; housing and human environments; mathematics; philosophy; psychology; religious studies.
Graduate—communication disorders sciences and services; computer software and media applications.

FORT HAYS STATE UNIVERSITY
Hays, Kansas
Virtual College
http://www.fhsu.edu/virtualcollege

Fort Hays State University was founded in 1902. It is accredited by North Central Association of Colleges and Schools. It first offered distance learning courses in 1987. In fall 2006, there were 4,700 students enrolled in distance learning courses. Institutionally administered financial aid is available to distance learners.
Services Distance learners have accessibility to academic advising, bookstore, campus computer network, career placement assistance, e-mail services, library services, tutoring.
Contact Kevin Splichal, Student Success Coordinator, Fort Hays State University, 600 Park Street, Hays, KS 67601-4099. Telephone: 800-628-FHSU. Fax: 785-628-4037. E-mail: klsplichal@fhsu.edu.

DEGREES AND AWARDS
AGS General Studies
BA Sociology
BBA Management
BGS General Studies; Military specialties
BS Elementary Education; Information Networking and Telecommunications (Computer Networking and Telecommunications concentration);

Information Networking and Telecommunications (Web Development concentration); Justice Studies; Organizational Leadership; Technology Leadership
BSN Nursing–RN to BSN
Certificate Community Development; E-Commerce Web Development; Geographic Information Systems (GIS); Grant Proposal Writing and Program Evaluation; Human Resource Management; Leadership; Life Issues; Management; Post-Masters Nursing Administration; Post-Masters Nursing Education; Sociology–Applied Sociology; Web Development
Certification Computer Science–Cisco Certified Network Associate Preparation, Military; Computer Science–Cisco Certified Network Associate Preparation, accelerated
MBA Leadership
MLS Liberal Studies
MS Education; Educational Administration; Health and Human Performance; Instructional Technology; Special Education
MSN Nursing Administration; Nursing Education

COURSE SUBJECT AREAS OFFERED OUTSIDE OF DEGREE PROGRAMS

Undergraduate—accounting and computer science; biological and physical sciences; business administration, management and operations; communication and journalism related; communication disorders sciences and services; computer and information sciences; criminal justice and corrections; economics; educational administration and supervision; education related; English; geological and earth sciences/geosciences; health and physical education/fitness; history; information science/studies; languages (foreign languages related); liberal arts and sciences, general studies and humanities; marketing; mathematics and computer science; multi-/interdisciplinary studies related; music; nursing; philosophy; physics; political science and government; psychology; sociology; special education; technology education/industrial arts.
Graduate—education related; education (specific subject areas); health and physical education/fitness; liberal arts and sciences, general studies and humanities; multi-/interdisciplinary studies related; nursing; special education.
Non-credit—accounting and computer science; accounting and related services; business administration, management and operations; communication and journalism related; economics; family psychology; management information systems; sales, merchandising, and related marketing operations (general).

FRANCISCAN UNIVERSITY OF STEUBENVILLE
Steubenville, Ohio
Distance Learning
http://www.franciscan.edu/distancelearning

Franciscan University of Steubenville was founded in 1946. It is accredited by North Central Association of Colleges and Schools. It first offered distance learning courses in 1995. In fall 2006, there were 300 students enrolled in distance learning courses. Institutionally administered financial aid is available to distance learners.
Services Distance learners have accessibility to academic advising, bookstore, library services.
Contact Ms. Virginia Garrison, Coordinator, Franciscan University of Steubenville, Distance Learning, 1235 University Boulevard, Steubenville, OH 43952. Telephone: 800-466-8336. Fax: 740-284-7037. E-mail: distance@franciscan.edu.

DEGREES AND AWARDS
MA Theology

COURSE SUBJECT AREAS OFFERED OUTSIDE OF DEGREE PROGRAMS

Undergraduate—philosophy; theological and ministerial studies.
Graduate—theological and ministerial studies.
Non-credit—philosophy; theological and ministerial studies.

FRANKLIN PIERCE UNIVERSITY
Rindge, New Hampshire
http://www.fpc.edu/

Franklin Pierce University was founded in 1962. It is accredited by New England Association of Schools and Colleges. It first offered distance learning courses in 2004. In fall 2006, there were 600 students enrolled in distance learning courses. Institutionally administered financial aid is available to distance learners.

Services Distance learners have accessibility to academic advising, bookstore, campus computer network, career placement assistance, e-mail services, library services, tutoring.

Contact Brian Ego, Director, Online Programs, Franklin Pierce University, 670 North Commercial Street, Manchester, NH 03101. Telephone: 603-899-4344. E-mail: egob@fpc.edu.

DEGREES AND AWARDS

AA Criminal Justice; General Studies; Human Services; Management; Marketing

BA Criminal Justice

BS Computer Information Technology; General Studies; Human Services; Management; Marketing

Certificate Accounting; Human Services; Management; Marketing; Paralegal

Graduate Certificate Emerging Network Technologies; Health Practice Management; Human Resource Management; eCommerce

MBA Leadership

MS Information Technology Management

COURSE SUBJECT AREAS OFFERED OUTSIDE OF DEGREE PROGRAMS

Undergraduate—accounting and related services; business administration, management and operations; business/managerial economics; computer and information sciences; computer/information technology administration and management; criminal justice and corrections; economics; finance and financial management services; liberal arts and sciences, general studies and humanities.

Graduate—business/commerce; computer/information technology administration and management; entrepreneurial and small business operations; health professions related; management information systems.

FRANKLIN UNIVERSITY
Columbus, Ohio
Technical and Non-Campus-Based Programs
http://www.franklin.edu

Franklin University was founded in 1902. It is accredited by North Central Association of Colleges and Schools. It first offered distance learning courses in 1996. In fall 2006, there were 4,203 students enrolled in distance learning courses. Institutionally administered financial aid is available to distance learners.

Services Distance learners have accessibility to academic advising, bookstore, campus computer network, career placement assistance, e-mail services, library services, tutoring.

Contact Admissions, Franklin University, 201 South Grant Avenue, Columbus, OH 43215. Telephone: 614-797-4700. Fax: 614-797-4799. E-mail: info@franklin.edu.

DEGREES AND AWARDS

AS Accounting; Business Administration; Computer Science; Information Technology

BS Accounting; Applied Management; Business Administration; Computer Science; Digital Communication; Health Care Management; Information Technology; Management Information Sciences; Management; Public Safety Management

MBA Business Administration–Online MBA

COURSE SUBJECT AREAS OFFERED OUTSIDE OF DEGREE PROGRAMS

Undergraduate—accounting and related services; business administration, management and operations; communication and media; computer science; economics; finance and financial management services;

health and medical administrative services; human resources management; information science/studies; marketing; mathematics and computer science; statistics.

Graduate—business administration, management and operations.

See full description on page 360.

FULLERTON COLLEGE
Fullerton, California
Distance Education–Media Production Center
http://www.media.fullcoll.edu

Fullerton College was founded in 1913. It is accredited by Western Association of Schools and Colleges. It first offered distance learning courses in 1984. In fall 2006, there were 3,088 students enrolled in distance learning courses. Institutionally administered financial aid is available to distance learners.

Services Distance learners have accessibility to academic advising, bookstore, campus computer network, e-mail services, library services, tutoring.

Contact Carol Mattson, Dean, Fullerton College, 321 East Chapman Avenue, Fullerton, CA 92632. Telephone: 714-992-7024. Fax: 714-526-6651. E-mail: cmattson@fullcoll.edu.

DEGREES AND AWARDS

Programs offered do not lead to a degree or other formal award.

COURSE SUBJECT AREAS OFFERED OUTSIDE OF DEGREE PROGRAMS

Undergraduate—accounting and related services; biological and physical sciences; biology; business administration, management and operations; business/commerce; business, management, and marketing related; chemistry; computer science; computer software and media applications; developmental and child psychology; English; English as a second language; film/video and photographic arts; fine and studio art; geography and cartography; health and physical education/fitness; health psychology; history; international business; journalism; linguistic, comparative, and related language studies; management information systems; marketing; mathematics; music; political science and government; psychology; sociology.

FULTON-MONTGOMERY COMMUNITY COLLEGE
Johnstown, New York
http://fmcc.suny.edu/

Fulton-Montgomery Community College was founded in 1964. It is accredited by Middle States Association of Colleges and Schools. It first offered distance learning courses in 2002. In fall 2006, there were 54 students enrolled in distance learning courses. Institutionally administered financial aid is available to distance learners.

Contact Mr. Reid J. Smalley, Director of Workforce Development, Fulton-Montgomery Community College, 2805 State Highway 67, Johnstown, NY 12095. Telephone: 518-762-4651 Ext. 8102. Fax: 518-762-4334. E-mail: reid.smalley@fmcc.suny.edu.

DEGREES AND AWARDS

Programs offered do not lead to a degree or other formal award.

COURSE SUBJECT AREAS OFFERED OUTSIDE OF DEGREE PROGRAMS

Non-credit—accounting and related services; business administration, management and operations; business/commerce; business, management, and marketing related; computer software and media applications; computer systems networking and telecommunications; education related; entrepreneurial and small business operations; health professions related; languages (foreign languages related).

GADSDEN STATE COMMUNITY COLLEGE
Gadsden, Alabama
Distance Learning
http://www.gadsdenstate.edu/dl/

Gadsden State Community College was founded in 1965. It is accredited by Southern Association of Colleges and Schools. It first offered distance learning courses in 1978. In fall 2006, there were 1,109 students enrolled in distance learning courses. Institutionally administered financial aid is available to distance learners.

Services Distance learners have accessibility to academic advising, bookstore, campus computer network, career placement assistance, e-mail services, library services.

Contact Ms. Sara W. Brenizer, Associate Dean, Distance Learning, Gadsden State Community College, PO Box 227, 1001 Wallace Drive, 240 B Inzer Hall, Gadsden, AL 35902. Telephone: 256-439-6833. Fax: 256-549-8466. E-mail: sbrenizer@gadsdenstate.edu.

DEGREES AND AWARDS

AGS General Studies

AS Education, general

COURSE SUBJECT AREAS OFFERED OUTSIDE OF DEGREE PROGRAMS

Undergraduate—accounting and computer science; biology; business administration, management and operations; business/managerial economics; chemistry; civil engineering; computer science; cosmetology and related personal grooming services; economics; education related; English; health and physical education/fitness; history; mathematics; music; nursing; nutrition sciences; philosophy; political science and government; psychology; sociology; speech and rhetoric.

GALVESTON COLLEGE
Galveston, Texas
Distance Education
http://www.gc.edu

Galveston College was founded in 1967. It is accredited by Southern Association of Colleges and Schools. It first offered distance learning courses in 1987. In fall 2006, there were 248 students enrolled in distance learning courses. Institutionally administered financial aid is available to distance learners.

Services Distance learners have accessibility to academic advising, bookstore, career placement assistance, library services, tutoring.

Contact Mrs. Jenni Willis-Opalenik, Distance Education Specialist, Galveston College, 4015 Avenue Q, Galveston, TX 77550. Telephone: 409-944-1243. Fax: 409-944-1501. E-mail: jopaleni@gc.edu.

DEGREES AND AWARDS

Programs offered do not lead to a degree or other formal award.

COURSE SUBJECT AREAS OFFERED OUTSIDE OF DEGREE PROGRAMS

Undergraduate—accounting and computer science; accounting and related services; allied health and medical assisting services; American literature (United States and Canadian); behavioral sciences; biology; business administration, management and operations; chemistry; computer and information sciences; economics; education; English composition; English literature (British and Commonwealth); health professions related; history; information science/studies; nuclear and industrial radiologic technologies; philosophy and religious studies related; political science and government; psychology; social sciences; speech and rhetoric; statistics.

Non-credit—accounting and computer science; accounting and related services; business, management, and marketing related; computer/information technology administration and management; computer programming; family and consumer sciences/human sciences related; legal studies (non-professional general, undergraduate); real estate.

GASTON COLLEGE
Dallas, North Carolina
http://www.gaston.cc.nc.us

Gaston College was founded in 1963. It is accredited by Southern Association of Colleges and Schools. It first offered distance learning courses in 1997. In fall 2006, there were 2,500 students enrolled in distance learning courses. Institutionally administered financial aid is available to distance learners.

Services Distance learners have accessibility to academic advising, bookstore, campus computer network, career placement assistance, library services, tutoring.

Contact Mrs. Kimberly C. Gelsinger, Director of Distance Education, Gaston College, 201 Highway 321 South, Dallas, NC 28034. Telephone: 704-922-6515. Fax: 704-922-6443. E-mail: gelsinger.kim@gaston.cc.nc.us.

DEGREES AND AWARDS

AAS Criminal Justice Technology; Dietetic Technician–Associate in Applied Science degree

AD Education, general

COURSE SUBJECT AREAS OFFERED OUTSIDE OF DEGREE PROGRAMS

Undergraduate—accounting and related services; allied health and medical assisting services; American literature (United States and Canadian); biological and biomedical sciences related; business/commerce; business/corporate communications; business, management, and marketing related; chemistry; communication and media; communications technology; computer and information sciences; computer programming; computer software and media applications; computer systems networking and telecommunications; criminal justice and corrections; criminology; education (specific subject areas); English; English composition; English literature (British and Commonwealth); geography and cartography; geological and earth sciences/geosciences; human development, family studies, and related services; information science/studies; legal studies (non-professional general, undergraduate); liberal arts and sciences, general studies and humanities; management information systems; mathematics; psychology; psychology related; social psychology; sociology.

GATEWAY COMMUNITY COLLEGE
New Haven, Connecticut
http://www.gwcc.commnet.edu/

Gateway Community College was founded in 1992. It is accredited by New England Association of Schools and Colleges. It first offered distance learning courses in 1999. In fall 2006, there were 270 students enrolled in distance learning courses. Institutionally administered financial aid is available to distance learners.

Services Distance learners have accessibility to academic advising, career placement assistance, e-mail services, library services, tutoring.

Contact Ms. Kim Shea, Director of Admissions, Gateway Community College, 60 Sargent Drive, New Haven, CT 06511. Telephone: 203-285-2011. Fax: 203-285-2018. E-mail: kshea@gwcc.commnet.com.

DEGREES AND AWARDS

Programs offered do not lead to a degree or other formal award.

COURSE SUBJECT AREAS OFFERED OUTSIDE OF DEGREE PROGRAMS

Undergraduate—business/commerce; health/medical preparatory programs; microbiological sciences and immunology; philosophy; political science and government; social sciences.

GEORGE C. WALLACE COMMUNITY COLLEGE
Dothan, Alabama
http://wallace.edu

George C. Wallace Community College was founded in 1949. It is accredited by Southern Association of Colleges and Schools. It first offered distance learning courses in 2001. In fall 2006, there were 850 students enrolled in distance learning courses. Institutionally administered financial aid is available to distance learners.

Services Distance learners have accessibility to academic advising, career placement assistance, e-mail services, library services.

Contact Mr. David Cruz-Wells, Distance Education Technology Specialist, George C. Wallace Community College, 1141 Wallace Drive, Dothan, AL 36303. Telephone: 334-556-2255. E-mail: dcruzwells@wallace.edu.

DEGREES AND AWARDS
Programs offered do not lead to a degree or other formal award.

COURSE SUBJECT AREAS OFFERED OUTSIDE OF DEGREE PROGRAMS
Undergraduate—accounting and related services; biological and physical sciences; biology; business administration, management and operations; business/commerce; chemistry; computer and information sciences; data entry/microcomputer applications; economics; English composition; English literature (British and Commonwealth); fine and studio art; history; mathematics; physical sciences; psychology.

GEORGE MASON UNIVERSITY
Fairfax, Virginia
http://www.gmu.edu/

George Mason University was founded in 1957. It is accredited by Southern Association of Colleges and Schools. It first offered distance learning courses in 1990. In fall 2006, there were 695 students enrolled in distance learning courses. Institutionally administered financial aid is available to distance learners.

Services Distance learners have accessibility to academic advising, bookstore, campus computer network, career placement assistance, e-mail services, library services.

Contact Miss Cheryl Choy, Special Assistant for Distance and Technical Education in the Office of the Provost, George Mason University, 4400 University Drive, MSN 1D6, Fairfax, VA 22030. E-mail: cchoy@gmu.edu.

DEGREES AND AWARDS
Graduate Certificate Computer Networking; Nonprofit Management; Quality Improvement and Outcomes Management
MA Transportation Policy, Operations, and Logistics
MSCS Computer Science; Computer Science

COURSE SUBJECT AREAS OFFERED OUTSIDE OF DEGREE PROGRAMS
Undergraduate—computer science; English composition; geography and cartography.
Graduate—biological and biomedical sciences related; business, management, and marketing related; computer science; computer systems networking and telecommunications; health professions related; nursing; public administration and social service professions related.

GEORGIA COLLEGE & STATE UNIVERSITY
Milledgeville, Georgia
http://www.gcsu.edu/

Georgia College & State University was founded in 1889. It is accredited by Southern Association of Colleges and Schools. It first offered distance learning courses in 1995. In fall 2006, there were 203 students enrolled in distance learning courses. Institutionally administered financial aid is available to distance learners.

Services Distance learners have accessibility to campus computer network, career placement assistance, e-mail services, library services.

Contact Rebecca Miles, Coordinator of Graduate Admissions, Georgia College & State University, Campus Box 69, Milledgeville, GA 31061. Telephone: 478-445-1184. Fax: 478-445-1914. E-mail: rebecca.miles@gcsu.edu.

DEGREES AND AWARDS
MBA Web MBA
MMT Music therapy

COURSE SUBJECT AREAS OFFERED OUTSIDE OF DEGREE PROGRAMS
Undergraduate—health professions related.
Graduate—education; health professions related; management information systems; nursing.

GEORGIA HIGHLANDS COLLEGE
Rome, Georgia
Department of Extended Learning
http://www.floyd.edu/extendedlearning/

Georgia Highlands College was founded in 1970. It is accredited by Southern Association of Colleges and Schools. It first offered distance learning courses in 1977. In fall 2006, there were 400 students enrolled in distance learning courses. Institutionally administered financial aid is available to distance learners.

Services Distance learners have accessibility to academic advising, bookstore, campus computer network, e-mail services, library services, tutoring.

Contact Jeff Brown, Director of Extended Learning, Georgia Highlands College, Heritage Hall Campus, 415 East Third Avenue, Rome, GA 30161. Telephone: 706-802-5300. Fax: 706-295-6732. E-mail: jbrown@highlands.edu.

DEGREES AND AWARDS
Programs offered do not lead to a degree or other formal award.

COURSE SUBJECT AREAS OFFERED OUTSIDE OF DEGREE PROGRAMS
Undergraduate—allied health and medical assisting services; biology; developmental and child psychology; economics; English; English composition; English language and literature related; health and physical education/fitness; history; mathematics; nursing; psychology.

GEORGIA INSTITUTE OF TECHNOLOGY
Atlanta, Georgia
Center for Distance Learning
http://www.cdl.gatech.edu

Georgia Institute of Technology was founded in 1885. It is accredited by Southern Association of Colleges and Schools. It first offered distance learning courses in 1977. In fall 2006, there were 1,000 students enrolled in distance learning courses. Institutionally administered financial aid is available to distance learners.

Services Distance learners have accessibility to academic advising, bookstore, campus computer network, e-mail services, library services.

Contact Ms. Tanya Krawiec, Student Support Services Manager, Georgia Institute of Technology, 84 5th Street NW, Room 013, Atlanta, GA 30308-1031. Telephone: 404-894-3378. Fax: 404-894-8924. E-mail: tanya.krawiec@dlpe.gatech.edu.

DEGREES AND AWARDS
MS Aerospace Engineering; Building Construction; Civil Engineering; Electrical Engineering; Environmental Engineering; Industrial and Systems Engineering; Mechanical Engineering; Medical Physics; Operations Research

COURSE SUBJECT AREAS OFFERED OUTSIDE OF DEGREE PROGRAMS
Graduate—aerospace, aeronautical and astronautical engineering; applied mathematics; architectural engineering; architecture related; biomedical/medical engineering; building/construction finishing, management, and inspection; civil engineering; computer engineering; computer engineering technologies; computer science; engineering design; engineering/industrial management; environmental/environmental health engineering; mathematics; mechanical engineering.
Non-credit—aerospace, aeronautical and astronautical engineering; civil engineering; computer engineering; environmental/environmental health engineering; mathematics; mechanical engineering.

See full description on page 362.

GEORGIA PERIMETER COLLEGE
Decatur, Georgia
Georgia Perimeter College was founded in 1964. It is accredited by Southern Association of Colleges and Schools. It first offered distance learning courses in 1980. In fall 2006, there were 3,278 students enrolled in distance learning courses. Institutionally administered financial aid is available to distance learners.

Services Distance learners have accessibility to academic advising, bookstore, library services, tutoring.

Contact Ms. Catherine Binuya, Assistant Director for Distance Learning Student Services, Georgia Perimeter College, Office of Educational Affairs, 3251 Panthersville Road, Decatur, GA 30034. Telephone: 678-891-2805. E-mail: gpcol@gpc.edu.

DEGREES AND AWARDS
Programs offered do not lead to a degree or other formal award.

GLENVILLE STATE COLLEGE
Glenville, West Virginia
http://www.glenville.edu/
Glenville State College was founded in 1872. It is accredited by North Central Association of Colleges and Schools. It first offered distance learning courses in 1997. In fall 2006, there were 178 students enrolled in distance learning courses. Institutionally administered financial aid is available to distance learners.

Services Distance learners have accessibility to bookstore, campus computer network, e-mail services, library services.

Contact Dr. Kathy Butler, Vice President for Academic Affairs, Glenville State College, 200 High Street, Glenville, WV 26351. Telephone: 304-462-4100. Fax: 304-462-8619. E-mail: kathy.butler@glenville.edu.

DEGREES AND AWARDS
Programs offered do not lead to a degree or other formal award.

COURSE SUBJECT AREAS OFFERED OUTSIDE OF DEGREE PROGRAMS
Undergraduate—computer software and media applications; criminal justice and corrections; economics; education (specific subject areas); English; history; multi-/interdisciplinary studies related; nursing; political science and government.

GLOBAL UNIVERSITY OF THE ASSEMBLIES OF GOD
Springfield, Missouri
http://www.globaluniversity.edu/
Global University of the Assemblies of God was founded in 1948. It is accredited by Distance Education and Training Council. It first offered distance learning courses in 1948. In fall 2006, there were 10,350 students enrolled in distance learning courses. Institutionally administered financial aid is available to distance learners.

Services Distance learners have accessibility to academic advising, library services.

Contact Mrs. Jessica Dorn, Director of Enrollment Services/Registrar, Global University of the Assemblies of God, 1211 South Glenstone Avenue, Springfield, MO 65804. Telephone: 417-862-9533. Fax: 417-862-0863. E-mail: jdorn@globaluniversity.edu.

DEGREES AND AWARDS
AA Bible and Theology; Ministerial Studies; Religious Studies
BA Bible and Theology; Bible/Pastoral Ministries; Missions; Religious Education
Diploma Ministry; Theology
MA Biblical Studies; Ministerial Studies
MDiv Divinity

COURSE SUBJECT AREAS OFFERED OUTSIDE OF DEGREE PROGRAMS
Non-credit—biblical and other theological languages and literatures; biblical studies; missionary studies and missiology; pastoral counseling and specialized ministries; philosophy and religious studies related; religious education; religious/sacred music; religious studies; theological and ministerial studies; theology and religious vocations related.

GOD'S BIBLE SCHOOL AND COLLEGE
Cincinnati, Ohio
God's Bible School and College was founded in 1900. It is accredited by Association for Biblical Higher Education. It first offered distance learning courses in 2001. In fall 2006, there were 25 students enrolled in distance learning courses. Institutionally administered financial aid is available to distance learners.

Services Distance learners have accessibility to academic advising, bookstore.

Contact Ms. Betty J. Cochran, Aldersgate Distance Education Program Coordinator, God's Bible School and College, 1810 Young Street, Cincinnati, OH 45202. Telephone: 513-721-7944 Ext. 251. Fax: 513-721-1357. E-mail: bcochran@gbs.edu.

DEGREES AND AWARDS
BA Ministerial Education

COURSE SUBJECT AREAS OFFERED OUTSIDE OF DEGREE PROGRAMS
Undergraduate—biblical and other theological languages and literatures; biblical studies; theological and ministerial studies; theology and religious vocations related.

GOUCHER COLLEGE
Baltimore, Maryland
Center for Graduate and Professional Studies
http://www.goucher.edu
Goucher College was founded in 1885. It is accredited by Middle States Association of Colleges and Schools. It first offered distance learning courses in 1995. In fall 2006, there were 420 students enrolled in distance learning courses. Institutionally administered financial aid is available to distance learners.

Services Distance learners have accessibility to academic advising, bookstore, campus computer network, e-mail services, library services.

Contact Noreen P. Mack, Director for Marketing and Program Development, Goucher College, 1021 Dulaney Valley Road, Baltimore, MD 21204. Telephone: 410-337-6200. Fax: 410-337-6085. E-mail: nmack@goucher.edu.

DEGREES AND AWARDS
Programs offered do not lead to a degree or other formal award.

COURSE SUBJECT AREAS OFFERED OUTSIDE OF DEGREE PROGRAMS
Graduate—creative writing; education; historic preservation and conservation; visual and performing arts related.
Non-credit—historic preservation and conservation.

GOVERNORS STATE UNIVERSITY
University Park, Illinois
Center for Extended Learning and Communications Services
http://www.govst.edu
Governors State University was founded in 1969. It is accredited by North Central Association of Colleges and Schools. It first offered distance learning courses in 1981. In fall 2006, there were 1,221 students enrolled in distance learning courses. Institutionally administered financial aid is available to distance learners.

Services Distance learners have accessibility to academic advising, bookstore, e-mail services, library services, tutoring.

Contact Veronica Williams, Director, Governors State University, 1 University Parkway, University Park, IL 60466. Telephone: 708-534-4099. Fax: 708-534-8458. E-mail: v-williams@govst.edu.

DEGREES AND AWARDS
BA Individualized Studies

COURSE SUBJECT AREAS OFFERED OUTSIDE OF DEGREE PROGRAMS
Undergraduate—accounting and related services; anthropology; communication and media; developmental and child psychology; English composition; fine and studio art; geography and cartography; marketing; psychology; social work; sociology.
Graduate—anthropology; developmental and child psychology; fine and studio art; social work; sociology.

GRACE COLLEGE
Winona Lake, Indiana
http://www.grace.edu/
Grace College was founded in 1948. It is accredited by North Central Association of Colleges and Schools. It first offered distance learning courses in 1999. In fall 2006, there were 56 students enrolled in distance learning courses. Institutionally administered financial aid is available to distance learners.
Services Distance learners have accessibility to bookstore, career placement assistance, e-mail services, library services.
Contact Mrs. Deea N. Breeden, Distance Education, Grace College, 200 Seminary Drive, Winona Lake, IN 46590. Telephone: 800-544-7223 Ext. 6437. Fax: 574-372-5113. E-mail: breededn@grace.edu.

DEGREES AND AWARDS
MA Local Church Ministry

GRACELAND UNIVERSITY
Lamoni, Iowa
Distance Learning
http://www.graceland.edu
Graceland University was founded in 1895. It is accredited by North Central Association of Colleges and Schools. It first offered distance learning courses in 1988. In fall 2006, there were 635 students enrolled in distance learning courses. Institutionally administered financial aid is available to distance learners.
Services Distance learners have accessibility to academic advising, bookstore, campus computer network, e-mail services, library services, tutoring.
Contact Paul Binnicker, Director of Operations, Graceland University, Independence Campus, 1401 West Truman Road, Independence, MO 64050. Telephone: 800-833-0524. Fax: 816-833-2990. E-mail: binnicke@graceland.edu.

DEGREES AND AWARDS
BA Health Care Management
BSN Nursing
MEd Collaborative Learning and Teaching; Quality Schools; Technology Integration
MSN Family Nurse Practitioner; Health Care Administration; Nurse Educator
PMC Family Nurse Practitioner; Health Care Administration; Nurse Educator

COURSE SUBJECT AREAS OFFERED OUTSIDE OF DEGREE PROGRAMS
Undergraduate—accounting and related services; behavioral sciences; biochemistry, biophysics and molecular biology; biology; business administration, management and operations; chemistry; comparative literature; computer and information sciences; developmental and child psychology; dramatic/theater arts and stagecraft; English composition; history; industrial and organizational psychology; information science/studies; marketing; microbiological sciences and immunology; nursing; psychology; sociology; speech and rhetoric; statistics.

GRAND RAPIDS THEOLOGICAL SEMINARY OF CORNERSTONE UNIVERSITY
Grand Rapids, Michigan
http://grbs.cornerstone.edu
Grand Rapids Theological Seminary of Cornerstone University was founded in 1945. It is accredited by North Central Association of Colleges and Schools. It first offered distance learning courses in 1969. Institutionally administered financial aid is available to distance learners.
Services Distance learners have accessibility to academic advising, bookstore, career placement assistance, e-mail services, library services.
Contact Tara Kram, Director of Admissions, Grand Rapids Theological Seminary of Cornerstone University, 1001 East Beltline Avenue NE, Grand Rapids, MI 49525. Telephone: 800-697-1133. Fax: 616-254-1623. E-mail: grts@cornerstone.edu.

DEGREES AND AWARDS
Programs offered do not lead to a degree or other formal award.

COURSE SUBJECT AREAS OFFERED OUTSIDE OF DEGREE PROGRAMS
Graduate—biblical and other theological languages and literatures; biblical studies; religious studies; theological and ministerial studies; theology and religious vocations related.
Non-credit—biblical and other theological languages and literatures; biblical studies; religious studies; theological and ministerial studies; theology and religious vocations related.

GRAND VIEW COLLEGE
Des Moines, Iowa
Camp Dodge Campus
http://www.gvc.edu
Grand View College was founded in 1896. It is accredited by North Central Association of Colleges and Schools. It first offered distance learning courses in 1994. In fall 2006, there were 0 students enrolled in distance learning courses. Institutionally administered financial aid is available to distance learners.
Services Distance learners have accessibility to academic advising, bookstore, campus computer network, career placement assistance, e-mail services, library services.
Contact Ms. Lora Kelly-Benck, Director of Camp Dodge Campus, Grand View College, 1200 Grandview Avenue, Des Moines, IA 50316. Telephone: 515-245-4546. Fax: 515-252-4753. E-mail: lkelly-benck@gvc.edu.

DEGREES AND AWARDS
Programs offered do not lead to a degree or other formal award.

COURSE SUBJECT AREAS OFFERED OUTSIDE OF DEGREE PROGRAMS
Undergraduate—business, management, and marketing related; business/managerial economics; criminal justice and corrections; criminology; English; English composition; history; psychology; social psychology; sociology; speech and rhetoric.

GRANITE STATE COLLEGE
Concord, New Hampshire
http://www.cll.edu
Granite State College was founded in 1972. It is accredited by New England Association of Schools and Colleges. It first offered distance learning courses in 1999. In fall 2006, there were 474 students enrolled in distance learning courses. Institutionally administered financial aid is available to distance learners.
Services Distance learners have accessibility to academic advising, bookstore, e-mail services, library services, tutoring.
Contact Ms. Chris Zerillo, Learner Services Educational Technology Coordinator, Granite State College, 175 Ammon Drive, Unit 210, Manchester, NH 03103-3311. Telephone: 603-627-2010. Fax: 603-627-5103. E-mail: chris.zerillo@granite.edu.

DEGREES AND AWARDS

AA General Studies
AS Behavioral Science; Business
BA Self-Design
BS Applied Technology, option in Allied Health Services; Applied Technology, option in Education and Training; Applied Technology, option in Management; Business Management; Criminal Justice; Criminal Justice, Administration option; Self-Design

COURSE SUBJECT AREAS OFFERED OUTSIDE OF DEGREE PROGRAMS

Undergraduate—behavioral sciences; business administration, management and operations; business, management, and marketing related; communication and media; computer/information technology administration and management; computer programming; criminal justice and corrections; education (specific levels and methods); finance and financial management services; health and medical administrative services; history; human development, family studies, and related services; human resources management; liberal arts and sciences, general studies and humanities; management information systems; management sciences and quantitative methods; mathematics; multi-/interdisciplinary studies related; psychology related; social sciences.
Graduate—education (specific subject areas); special education.
Non-credit—computer software and media applications.

GRANTHAM UNIVERSITY
Kansas City, Missouri
http://www.grantham.edu/

Grantham University was founded in 1951. It is accredited by Distance Education and Training Council. It first offered distance learning courses in 1990. Institutionally administered financial aid is available to distance learners.
Services Distance learners have accessibility to academic advising, bookstore.
Contact Ms. DeAnn Wandler, Director of Admissions, Grantham University, 7200 NW 86th Street, Kansas City, MO 64153. Telephone: 800-955-2527. Fax: 816-595-5757. E-mail: admissions@grantham.edu.

DEGREES AND AWARDS

AS Business Administration; Computer Engineering Technology; Computer Science; Criminal Justice–Computer Science; Criminal Justice–Homeland Security; Criminal Justice; Electronics Engineering Technology; General Studies; Interdisciplinary Studies
BS Business Administration; Computer Engineering Technology; Computer Science; Criminal Justice–Computer Science; Criminal Justice–Homeland Security; Criminal Justice; Electronics Engineering Technology; General Studies; Interdisciplinary Studies
MBA Business Administration; Information Management; Project Management
MS Information Management Technology; Information Management–Project Management; Information Technology

COURSE SUBJECT AREAS OFFERED OUTSIDE OF DEGREE PROGRAMS

Undergraduate—accounting and related services; business administration, management and operations; business/commerce; business, management, and marketing related; business/managerial economics; chemistry; computer and information sciences; computer engineering; computer engineering technologies; computer/information technology administration and management; computer programming; computer science; computer software and media applications; computer systems analysis; computer systems networking and telecommunications; criminal justice and corrections; data entry/microcomputer applications; economics; electrical and electronic engineering technologies; electrical, electronics and communications engineering; engineering; English composition; finance and financial management services; history; human resources management; information science/studies; legal studies (non-professional general, undergraduate); management information systems; marketing; mathematics; mathematics and computer science; mathematics and sta-

tistics related; physics; psychology; psychology related; sales, merchandising, and related marketing operations (general); sociology; technical and business writing.
Graduate—accounting and related services; business/managerial economics; communications technology; finance and financial management services; management information systems; marketing; systems engineering.

See full description on page 364.

GRATZ COLLEGE
Melrose Park, Pennsylvania
http://www.gratz.edu

Gratz College was founded in 1895. It is accredited by Middle States Association of Colleges and Schools. It first offered distance learning courses in 2000. In fall 2006, there were 110 students enrolled in distance learning courses. Institutionally administered financial aid is available to distance learners.
Services Distance learners have accessibility to academic advising, career placement assistance, e-mail services, library services.
Contact Ms. Ronni D. Ticker, Director, Online and Distance Learning, Gratz College, 7605 Old York Road, Melrose Park, PA 19027. Telephone: 215-635-7300 Ext. 115. Fax: 215-635-7399. E-mail: online@gratz.edu.

DEGREES AND AWARDS

BA Jewish Studies
CAGS Holocaust Studies; Jewish Early Childhood Education; Jewish Education; Jewish Music; Jewish Non-Profit Management; Jewish Studies
MA Jewish Studies

GREEN MOUNTAIN COLLEGE
Poultney, Vermont

Green Mountain College was founded in 1834. It is accredited by New England Association of Schools and Colleges. It first offered distance learning courses in 2006. In fall 2006, there were 24 students enrolled in distance learning courses. Institutionally administered financial aid is available to distance learners.
Services Distance learners have accessibility to academic advising, bookstore, campus computer network, career placement assistance, e-mail services, library services, tutoring.
Contact Dr. Sandra Bartholomew, Dean of Enrollment Management, Green Mountain College, Admissions, One College Circle, Poultney, VT 05764. Telephone: 802-287-8220. Fax: 802-287-8099. E-mail: bartholomews@greenmtn.edu.

DEGREES AND AWARDS

MBA Non-Profit Organization Management; Sustainable Business Practices
MS Environmental Studies in Conservation Biology; Self Designed Concentration; Writing and Communictions concentration

GULF COAST COMMUNITY COLLEGE
Panama City, Florida

Gulf Coast Community College was founded in 1957. It is accredited by Southern Association of Colleges and Schools. Institutionally administered financial aid is available to distance learners.
Services Distance learners have accessibility to academic advising, bookstore, campus computer network, e-mail services, library services.
Contact Miss Cindy Lea Mitchell, Administrative Assistant/Distance Education, Gulf Coast Community College, 5230 West U.S. Highway 98, Panama City, FL 32401. Telephone: 850-769-1551 Ext. 5807. Fax: 850-872-3861. E-mail: vcampus@gulfcoast.edu.

DEGREES AND AWARDS

AA General Studies

COURSE SUBJECT AREAS OFFERED OUTSIDE OF DEGREE PROGRAMS

Undergraduate—biological and physical sciences; chemistry; dental support services and allied professions; developmental and child psychology; economics; English composition; fire protection; health/medical preparatory programs; history; mathematics; music; nursing; physical sciences; psychology; social sciences; sociology; statistics.

HAGERSTOWN COMMUNITY COLLEGE
Hagerstown, Maryland
http://www.hagerstowncc.edu/
Hagerstown Community College was founded in 1946. It is accredited by Middle States Association of Colleges and Schools. It first offered distance learning courses in 1998. In fall 2006, there were 189 students enrolled in distance learning courses. Institutionally administered financial aid is available to distance learners.
Services Distance learners have accessibility to bookstore, library services.
Contact Angela Kelley, Test Center Administrator, Hagerstown Community College, Continuing Education, 11400 Robinwood Drive, Hagerstown, MD 21742. Telephone: 301-790-2800 Ext. 553. Fax: 301-733-4229. E-mail: kelleya@hagerstowncc.edu.

DEGREES AND AWARDS
Programs offered do not lead to a degree or other formal award.

COURSE SUBJECT AREAS OFFERED OUTSIDE OF DEGREE PROGRAMS

Non-credit—accounting and related services; allied health and medical assisting services; business, management, and marketing related; computer programming; computer software and media applications; computer systems networking and telecommunications; culinary arts and related services; publishing.

HAMLINE UNIVERSITY
St. Paul, Minnesota
http://www.hamline.edu/
Hamline University was founded in 1854. It is accredited by North Central Association of Colleges and Schools. It first offered distance learning courses in 1998. In fall 2006, there were 124 students enrolled in distance learning courses. Institutionally administered financial aid is available to distance learners.
Services Distance learners have accessibility to campus computer network, career placement assistance, e-mail services, library services.
Contact Annette McNamara, Program Administrator, Hamline University, 1536 Hewitt Avenue, A1720, St. Paul, MN 55104-1284. Telephone: 651-523-2175. Fax: 651-523-2489. E-mail: amcnamara@gw.hamline.edu.

DEGREES AND AWARDS
Programs offered do not lead to a degree or other formal award.

COURSE SUBJECT AREAS OFFERED OUTSIDE OF DEGREE PROGRAMS

Undergraduate—history.
Graduate—bilingual, multilingual, and multicultural education; education; educational/instructional media design; education related; education (specific levels and methods); education (specific subject areas); English as a second/foreign language (teaching); English as a second language; mathematics; public administration and social service professions related; special education.
Non-credit—education; educational administration and supervision; educational/instructional media design; education related; education (specific subject areas); English as a second/foreign language (teaching); English as a second language; political science and government; public administration; public administration and social service professions related.

HARFORD COMMUNITY COLLEGE
Bel Air, Maryland
http://www.harford.edu/distlearn/
Harford Community College was founded in 1957. It is accredited by Middle States Association of Colleges and Schools. It first offered distance learning courses in 1999. In fall 2006, there were 1,500 students enrolled in distance learning courses. Institutionally administered financial aid is available to distance learners.
Services Distance learners have accessibility to academic advising, bookstore, campus computer network, career placement assistance, e-mail services, library services, tutoring.
Contact Christel Vonderscheer, Director of Distance Learning, Harford Community College, 401 Thomas Run Road, Bel Air, MD 21015. Telephone: 410-836-4145. Fax: 410-836-4481. E-mail: cvonders@harford.edu.

DEGREES AND AWARDS
AA General Studies
AAS Computer Information Systems
AS Business Administration

COURSE SUBJECT AREAS OFFERED OUTSIDE OF DEGREE PROGRAMS

Undergraduate—biology; educational psychology; English; English composition; English literature (British and Commonwealth); mathematics; psychology; social sciences related.
Non-credit—computer and information sciences; computer programming; computer systems networking and telecommunications; real estate.

HARRISBURG AREA COMMUNITY COLLEGE
Harrisburg, Pennsylvania
Distance Education Office
http://www.hacc.edu/programs/disted/disted.cfm
Harrisburg Area Community College was founded in 1964. It is accredited by Middle States Association of Colleges and Schools. It first offered distance learning courses in 1987. In fall 2006, there were 3,400 students enrolled in distance learning courses. Institutionally administered financial aid is available to distance learners.
Services Distance learners have accessibility to academic advising, bookstore, career placement assistance, library services, tutoring.
Contact Mr. Robert Karas, Counselor, Harrisburg Area Community College, 1 HACC Drive, Harrisburg, PA 17110. Telephone: 717-780-2613. Fax: 717-780-1925. E-mail: rdkaras@hacc.edu.

DEGREES AND AWARDS
AA Business Administration

COURSE SUBJECT AREAS OFFERED OUTSIDE OF DEGREE PROGRAMS

Undergraduate—accounting and related services; allied health and medical assisting services; American literature (United States and Canadian); anthropology; applied mathematics; astronomy and astrophysics; biological and physical sciences; business administration, management and operations; business/commerce; business, management, and marketing related; business/managerial economics; computer programming; computer science; computer software and media applications; criminal justice and corrections; developmental and child psychology; economics; education; engineering; English; English composition; English literature (British and Commonwealth); environmental/environmental health engineering; foods, nutrition, and related services; geography and cartography; geological and earth sciences/geosciences; history; information science/studies; library science related; mathematics; mathematics and computer science; microbiological sciences and immunology; philosophy; physical sciences; psychology; public health; sociology; statistics; technical and business writing.

HARTFORD SEMINARY
Hartford, Connecticut
http://www.hartsem.edu/academic/distance.htm
Hartford Seminary was founded in 1834. It is accredited by New England Association of Schools and Colleges. It first offered distance learning courses in 2002. In fall 2006, there were 45 students enrolled in distance learning courses. Institutionally administered financial aid is available to distance learners.
Services Distance learners have accessibility to academic advising, bookstore, library services, tutoring.
Contact Dr. Scott Thumma, Director of Distance Education, Hartford Seminary, 77 Sherman Street, Hartford, CT 06105. Telephone: 860-509-9571. E-mail: sthumma@hartsem.edu.

DEGREES AND AWARDS
Programs offered do not lead to a degree or other formal award.

COURSE SUBJECT AREAS OFFERED OUTSIDE OF DEGREE PROGRAMS
Graduate—pastoral counseling and specialized ministries; religious studies.
Non-credit—religious studies.

HAYWOOD COMMUNITY COLLEGE
Clyde, North Carolina
http://www.haywood.edu
Haywood Community College was founded in 1964. It is accredited by Southern Association of Colleges and Schools. It first offered distance learning courses in 1992. In fall 2006, there were 900 students enrolled in distance learning courses. Institutionally administered financial aid is available to distance learners.
Services Distance learners have accessibility to academic advising, bookstore, campus computer network, career placement assistance, e-mail services, library services, tutoring.
Contact Debbie Rowland, Coordinator of Admissions, Haywood Community College, 185 Freedlander Drive, Clyde, NC 28716. Telephone: 828-627-4646. Fax: 828-627-4513. E-mail: drowland@haywood.edu.

DEGREES AND AWARDS
AAS Early Childhood Education; Teacher Associate

COURSE SUBJECT AREAS OFFERED OUTSIDE OF DEGREE PROGRAMS
Undergraduate—accounting and related services; anthropology; applied horticulture/horticultural business services; business administration, management and operations; business/commerce; computer and information sciences; computer programming; economics; education; education related; engineering technologies related; English; English composition; fine and studio art; forestry; health and physical education/fitness; history; information science/studies; liberal arts and sciences, general studies and humanities; management information systems; mathematics; mathematics and computer science; political science and government; psychology; religious studies; sociology; teaching assistants/aides; technical and business writing.
Non-credit—computer software and media applications.

HEBREW COLLEGE
Newton Centre, Massachusetts
http://www.hebrewcollege.edu/online
Hebrew College was founded in 1921. It is accredited by New England Association of Schools and Colleges. It first offered distance learning courses in 1995. In fall 2006, there were 150 students enrolled in distance learning courses. Institutionally administered financial aid is available to distance learners.
Services Distance learners have accessibility to academic advising, bookstore, campus computer network, career placement assistance, library services, tutoring.

Contact Nathan Ehrlich, Dean, Hebrew College Online, Hebrew College, 160 Herrick Road, Newton Centre, MA 02459. Telephone: 617-559-8672. Fax: 617-559-8601. E-mail: nathan@hebrewcollege.edu.

DEGREES AND AWARDS
MA Jewish Studies

COURSE SUBJECT AREAS OFFERED OUTSIDE OF DEGREE PROGRAMS
Undergraduate—biblical and other theological languages and literatures; biblical studies; education related; ethnic, cultural minority, and gender studies; languages (Middle/Near Eastern and Semitic); linguistic, comparative, and related language studies; philosophy and religious studies related; religious studies.
Graduate—biblical and other theological languages and literatures; biblical studies; education related; ethnic, cultural minority, and gender studies; languages (Middle/Near Eastern and Semitic); linguistic, comparative, and related language studies; philosophy and religious studies related; religious studies.
Non-credit—biblical and other theological languages and literatures; biblical studies; education related; ethnic, cultural minority, and gender studies; languages (Middle/Near Eastern and Semitic); linguistic, comparative, and related language studies; philosophy and religious studies related; religious studies.

HENRY FORD COMMUNITY COLLEGE
Dearborn, Michigan
http://www.hfcc.edu
Henry Ford Community College was founded in 1938. It is accredited by North Central Association of Colleges and Schools. It first offered distance learning courses in 2004. Institutionally administered financial aid is available to distance learners.
Services Distance learners have accessibility to bookstore, e-mail services, library services.
Contact Dr. Vivian Beaty, Director of Instructional Technology, Henry Ford Community College, Instructional Technology, 5101 Evergreen Road, Dearborn, MI 48128-1495. Telephone: 313-845-9663 Ext. 3. Fax: 313-845-9844. E-mail: vbeaty@hfcc.edu.

DEGREES AND AWARDS
Programs offered do not lead to a degree or other formal award.

COURSE SUBJECT AREAS OFFERED OUTSIDE OF DEGREE PROGRAMS
Undergraduate—anthropology; applied mathematics; astronomy and astrophysics; cell biology and anatomical sciences; computer and information sciences; computer software and media applications; criminal justice and corrections; educational/instructional media design; English; English composition; history; housing and human environments; journalism; languages (Middle/Near Eastern and Semitic); liberal arts and sciences, general studies and humanities; mathematics; mathematics and statistics related; natural sciences; nutrition sciences; political science and government; precision metal working; psychology; religious studies; science, technology and society; social sciences; sociology; statistics; technical and business writing.

HERKIMER COUNTY COMMUNITY COLLEGE
Herkimer, New York
Internet Academy
http://www.hcccia.com
Herkimer County Community College was founded in 1966. It is accredited by Middle States Association of Colleges and Schools. It first offered distance learning courses in 1997. In fall 2006, there were 1,450 students enrolled in distance learning courses. Institutionally administered financial aid is available to distance learners.
Services Distance learners have accessibility to academic advising, bookstore, career placement assistance, e-mail services, library services, tutoring.

Contact Ms. Linda C. Lamb, Associate Dean of Continuing Education/ Internet Academy, Herkimer County Community College, 100 Reservoir Road, Herkimer, NY 13550. Telephone: 315-866-0300 Ext. 8442. Fax: 315-866-0402 Ext. 8442. E-mail: lamblc@herkimer.edu.

DEGREES AND AWARDS

AA Liberal Arts and Sciences–General Studies; Liberal Arts and Sciences– Humanities; Liberal Arts and Sciences–Social Science
AAS Business Administration; Business–Accounting; Business–Health Services Management Technology; Business–Human Resource Management; Business–Marketing; Business–Small Business Management; Criminal Justice; Human Services; Paralegal; Travel and Tourism– Hospitality and Events Management
AS Business Administration; Business–Accounting; Business–Business Administration; Criminal Justice; Criminal Justice–Economic Crime; Health Services Management
Certificate Corrections; Small Business Management; Teaching Assistant Certificate

COURSE SUBJECT AREAS OFFERED OUTSIDE OF DEGREE PROGRAMS

Undergraduate—accounting and related services; biology; business administration, management and operations; business/commerce; business/ corporate communications; computer and information sciences; computer software and media applications; computer systems networking and telecommunications; criminal justice and corrections; developmental and child psychology; English; entrepreneurial and small business operations; human resources management; human services; liberal arts and sciences, general studies and humanities; mathematics and computer science; psychology; sales, merchandising, and related marketing operations (specialized).

HILLSBOROUGH COMMUNITY COLLEGE
Tampa, Florida
Distance Learning Office
http://www.hccfl.edu/eCampus
Hillsborough Community College was founded in 1968. It is accredited by Southern Association of Colleges and Schools. It first offered distance learning courses in 1971. In fall 2006, there were 4,500 students enrolled in distance learning courses. Institutionally administered financial aid is available to distance learners.
Services Distance learners have accessibility to academic advising, bookstore, career placement assistance, e-mail services, library services, tutoring.
Contact Melissa Zucal, Distance Learning Manager, Hillsborough Community College, 39 Columbia, Suite 714, Tampa, FL 33606. Telephone: 813-259-6531. Fax: 813-259-6536. E-mail: mzucal@hccfl.edu.

DEGREES AND AWARDS
AS Opticianry

COURSE SUBJECT AREAS OFFERED OUTSIDE OF DEGREE PROGRAMS

Undergraduate—American literature (United States and Canadian); American Sign Language (ASL); applied mathematics; astronomy and astrophysics; biology; business administration, management and operations; business/commerce; communication and media; computer and information sciences; computer/information technology administration and management; computer programming; computer science; computer software and media applications; creative writing; developmental and child psychology; economics; English; English composition; finance and financial management services; foods, nutrition, and related services; geological and earth sciences/geosciences; geological/geophysical engineering; health professions related; human development, family studies, and related services; legal studies (non-professional general, undergraduate); marketing; nutrition sciences; ophthalmic and optometric support services and allied professions; political science and government; psychology; sociology.
Non-credit—accounting and related services; crafts, folk art and artisanry; languages (Romance languages).

HOCKING COLLEGE
Nelsonville, Ohio
Instructional Development
http://www.hocking.edu/what_we_offer.htm
Hocking College was founded in 1968. It is accredited by North Central Association of Colleges and Schools. It first offered distance learning courses in 1995. In fall 2006, there were 560 students enrolled in distance learning courses. Institutionally administered financial aid is available to distance learners.
Services Distance learners have accessibility to academic advising, campus computer network, e-mail services, library services.
Contact Mrs. Joni Tornwall, Online Learning Coordinator, Hocking College, JL 256, 3301 Hocking Parkway, Nelsonville, OH 45764. Telephone: 740-753-7116. E-mail: tornwall_j@hocking.edu.

DEGREES AND AWARDS
Programs offered do not lead to a degree or other formal award.

COURSE SUBJECT AREAS OFFERED OUTSIDE OF DEGREE PROGRAMS

Undergraduate—accounting and computer science; allied health and medical assisting services; cell biology and anatomical sciences; communication and media; creative writing; economics; English; English composition; health/medical preparatory programs; hospitality administration; liberal arts and sciences, general studies and humanities; mathematics; psychology; social sciences; speech and rhetoric; technical and business writing; visual and performing arts related.

HODGES UNIVERSITY
Naples, Florida
Hodges University was founded in 1990. It is accredited by Southern Association of Colleges and Schools. It first offered distance learning courses in 1995. In fall 2006, there were 96 students enrolled in distance learning courses. Institutionally administered financial aid is available to distance learners.
Services Distance learners have accessibility to academic advising, campus computer network, e-mail services, library services, tutoring.
Contact Ms. Jane Trembath, Director of Distance Admissions, Hodges University, 2655 Northbrooke Drive, Naples, FL 34119. Telephone: 866-684-6689. Fax: 866-684-6064. E-mail: jtrembath@ internationalcollege.edu.

DEGREES AND AWARDS
AS Health Information Technology; Interdisciplinary Studies; Paralegal Studies
BS Information Systems Management; Interdisciplinary Studies; Management
MISM Information Systems Management
MPA Public Administration
MS Criminal Justice
MSM Management

HOLY APOSTLES COLLEGE AND SEMINARY
Cromwell, Connecticut
http://www.holyapostles.edu
Holy Apostles College and Seminary was founded in 1956. It is accredited by New England Association of Schools and Colleges. It first offered distance learning courses in 1998. In fall 2006, there were 110 students enrolled in distance learning courses. Institutionally administered financial aid is available to distance learners.
Services Distance learners have accessibility to academic advising, library services, tutoring.
Contact Mr. Robert Mish, Distance Learning Coordinator, Holy Apostles College and Seminary, 33 Prospect Hill Road, Cromwell, CT 06416. Telephone: 860-632-3015. Fax: 860-632-3075. E-mail: distancelearn@ holyapostles.edu.

DEGREES AND AWARDS
MA Philosophy; Theology

COURSE SUBJECT AREAS OFFERED OUTSIDE OF DEGREE PROGRAMS

Graduate—philosophy and religious studies related.

HOLYOKE COMMUNITY COLLEGE
Holyoke, Massachusetts

Holyoke Community College was founded in 1946. It is accredited by New England Association of Schools and Colleges. It first offered distance learning courses in 1999. In fall 2006, there were 1,150 students enrolled in distance learning courses. Institutionally administered financial aid is available to distance learners.

Services Distance learners have accessibility to academic advising, bookstore, e-mail services, library services, tutoring.

Contact Dean Gloria A. DeFillipo, Dean of Distance Education, Holyoke Community College, 303 Homestead Avenue, Holyoke, MA 01040. Telephone: 413-552-2236. Fax: 413-552-2045. E-mail: gdefillipo@hcc.mass.edu.

DEGREES AND AWARDS

Programs offered do not lead to a degree or other formal award.

COURSE SUBJECT AREAS OFFERED OUTSIDE OF DEGREE PROGRAMS

Undergraduate—accounting and computer science; business administration, management and operations; business, management, and marketing related; communication and media; computer science; creative writing; criminal justice and corrections; data entry/microcomputer applications; economics; English language and literature related; history; human resources management; human services; mathematics; political science and government; psychology; sociology.

HONOLULU COMMUNITY COLLEGE
Honolulu, Hawaii
Distance Learning
http://honolulu.hawaii.edu/distance

Honolulu Community College was founded in 1920. It is accredited by Western Association of Schools and Colleges. It first offered distance learning courses in 1991. In fall 2006, there were 700 students enrolled in distance learning courses. Institutionally administered financial aid is available to distance learners.

Services Distance learners have accessibility to academic advising, bookstore, campus computer network, career placement assistance, e-mail services, library services.

Contact Janice T. Petersen, Distance Learning Coordinator, Honolulu Community College, 874 Dillingham Boulevard, Honolulu, HI 96817. Telephone: 808-845-9437. Fax: 808-847-9679. E-mail: janp@hcc.hawaii.edu.

DEGREES AND AWARDS

Programs offered do not lead to a degree or other formal award.

COURSE SUBJECT AREAS OFFERED OUTSIDE OF DEGREE PROGRAMS

Undergraduate—anthropology; architectural engineering technology; astronomy and astrophysics; chemistry; English; English composition; fire protection; foods, nutrition, and related services; geological and earth sciences/geosciences; history; liberal arts and sciences, general studies and humanities; microbiological sciences and immunology; philosophy; philosophy and religious studies related; political science and government; psychology; social sciences related; speech and rhetoric.

HOPE INTERNATIONAL UNIVERSITY
Fullerton, California
Distance Learning Department
http://www.hiu.edu

Hope International University was founded in 1928. It is accredited by Western Association of Schools and Colleges. It first offered distance learning courses in 1994. In fall 2006, there were 260 students enrolled in distance learning courses. Institutionally administered financial aid is available to distance learners.

Services Distance learners have accessibility to academic advising, bookstore, career placement assistance, e-mail services, library services.

Contact Wende J. Holtzen, Distance Learning Assistant, Hope International University, 2500 East Nutwood Avenue, Fullerton, CA 92831. Telephone: 714-879-3901 Ext. 1246. Fax: 714-681-7230. E-mail: wholtzen@hiu.edu.

DEGREES AND AWARDS

AA Biblical Studies; Christian Ministry
BS Business Administration and Management; Christian Ministry; Human Development
Certificate Biblical Studies; Christian Ministry
MBA International Development; Management; Nonprofit Management
MSM International Development

COURSE SUBJECT AREAS OFFERED OUTSIDE OF DEGREE PROGRAMS

Undergraduate—biblical studies; history; psychology; religious studies.
Graduate—biblical studies; ethnic, cultural minority, and gender studies; psychology; religious studies.
Non-credit—biblical studies; ethnic, cultural minority, and gender studies; history; psychology; religious studies.

HOPKINSVILLE COMMUNITY COLLEGE
Hopkinsville, Kentucky
http://www.hopkinsville.kctcs.edu

Hopkinsville Community College was founded in 1965. It is accredited by Southern Association of Colleges and Schools. It first offered distance learning courses in 2000. In fall 2006, there were 654 students enrolled in distance learning courses. Institutionally administered financial aid is available to distance learners.

Services Distance learners have accessibility to academic advising, bookstore, campus computer network, career placement assistance, e-mail services, library services, tutoring.

Contact Dr. Lance Roland Angell, Dean, Institutional Effectiveness, Hopkinsville Community College, ADM 212, 720 North Drive, PO Box 2100, Hopkinsville, KY 42241-2100. Telephone: 270-707-3709. Fax: 270-885-5755. E-mail: langell0002@kctcs.edu.

DEGREES AND AWARDS

Programs offered do not lead to a degree or other formal award.

COURSE SUBJECT AREAS OFFERED OUTSIDE OF DEGREE PROGRAMS

Undergraduate—accounting and computer science; architecture related; biology; business, management, and marketing related; communication and journalism related; computer science; drafting/design engineering technologies; engineering technology; English language and literature related; philosophy and religious studies related; quality control and safety technologies.

HORIZON COLLEGE & SEMINARY
Saskatoon, Saskatchewan, Canada

Horizon College & Seminary was founded in 1930. It is provincially chartered. It first offered distance learning courses in 1995. In fall 2006, there were 27 students enrolled in distance learning courses. Institutionally administered financial aid is available to distance learners.

Services Distance learners have accessibility to academic advising, bookstore, campus computer network, e-mail services, tutoring.

Contact Judy Heyer, Assistant Registrar, Horizon College & Seminary, 1303 Jackson Avenue, Saskatoon, SK S7H 2M9, Canada. Telephone: 306-374-6655. Fax: 306-373-6968. E-mail: admissions@cpc-paoc.edu.

DEGREES AND AWARDS

Programs offered do not lead to a degree or other formal award.

COURSE SUBJECT AREAS OFFERED OUTSIDE OF DEGREE PROGRAMS

Undergraduate—biblical and other theological languages and literatures; biblical studies; education; psychology; theological and ministerial studies.

HOUSTON COMMUNITY COLLEGE SYSTEM
Houston, Texas
Distance Education Department
http://www.distance.hccs.edu

Houston Community College System was founded in 1971. It is accredited by Southern Association of Colleges and Schools. It first offered distance learning courses in 1985. In fall 2006, there were 7,166 students enrolled in distance learning courses. Institutionally administered financial aid is available to distance learners.

Services Distance learners have accessibility to academic advising, bookstore, e-mail services, library services, tutoring.

Contact Eva Gonzalez, Distance Education Associate, Houston Community College System, 3100 Main Street, MC 1740, Houston, TX 77002. Telephone: 713-718-5152. Fax: 713-718-5388. E-mail: eva. gonzalez@hccs.edu.

DEGREES AND AWARDS
Programs offered do not lead to a degree or other formal award.

COURSE SUBJECT AREAS OFFERED OUTSIDE OF DEGREE PROGRAMS

Undergraduate—accounting and related services; American literature (United States and Canadian); anthropology; astronomy and astrophysics; biology; business administration, management and operations; chemistry; community health services; computer/information technology administration and management; computer science; criminology; developmental and child psychology; economics; English composition; English literature (British and Commonwealth); film/video and photographic arts; fine and studio art; fire protection; foods, nutrition, and related services; geography and cartography; history; human development, family studies, and related services; human resources management; human services; languages (Romance languages); management information systems; marketing; mathematics; mathematics and statistics related; philosophy; physical sciences; political science and government; psychology; real estate; social psychology; sociology.

ILISAGVIK COLLEGE
Barrow, Alaska
http://www.ilisagvik.cc

Ilisagvik College was founded in 1995. It is accredited by Northwest Commission on Colleges and Universities. It first offered distance learning courses in 2001. In fall 2006, there were 85 students enrolled in distance learning courses. Institutionally administered financial aid is available to distance learners.

Services Distance learners have accessibility to academic advising, bookstore, campus computer network, career placement assistance, e-mail services, library services, tutoring.

Contact Mr. Rob Carrillo, Distance Education Coordinator, Ilisagvik College, PO Box 749, Barrow, AK 99723. Telephone: 907-852-1706. Fax: 907-852-1739. E-mail: rob.carrillo@ilisagvik.cc.

DEGREES AND AWARDS
Programs offered do not lead to a degree or other formal award.

COURSE SUBJECT AREAS OFFERED OUTSIDE OF DEGREE PROGRAMS

Undergraduate—allied health and medical assisting services; business administration, management and operations; computer software and media applications; English composition; science, technology and society.

ILLINOIS EASTERN COMMUNITY COLLEGES, FRONTIER COMMUNITY COLLEGE
Fairfield, Illinois
http://www.iecc.cc.il.us./fcc

Illinois Eastern Community Colleges, Frontier Community College was founded in 1976. It is accredited by North Central Association of Colleges and Schools. It first offered distance learning courses in 1994. In fall 2006, there were 108 students enrolled in distance learning courses. Institutionally administered financial aid is available to distance learners.

Services Distance learners have accessibility to academic advising, bookstore, campus computer network, career placement assistance, e-mail services, library services, tutoring.

Contact Ms. Blenda Demaret, Assistant to the Dean, Illinois Eastern Community Colleges, Frontier Community College, 2 Frontier Drive, Fairfield, IL 62837. Telephone: 618-842-3711 Ext. 4007. Fax: 618-842-6340. E-mail: demaretb@iecc.edu.

DEGREES AND AWARDS
Programs offered do not lead to a degree or other formal award.

COURSE SUBJECT AREAS OFFERED OUTSIDE OF DEGREE PROGRAMS

Undergraduate—business/commerce; foods, nutrition, and related services; health and physical education/fitness; marketing; nutrition sciences.

ILLINOIS EASTERN COMMUNITY COLLEGES, LINCOLN TRAIL COLLEGE
Robinson, Illinois
http://www.iecc.cc.il.us/ltc

Illinois Eastern Community Colleges, Lincoln Trail College was founded in 1969. It is accredited by North Central Association of Colleges and Schools. It first offered distance learning courses in 1994. In fall 2006, there were 239 students enrolled in distance learning courses. Institutionally administered financial aid is available to distance learners.

Services Distance learners have accessibility to academic advising, bookstore, campus computer network, career placement assistance, e-mail services, library services, tutoring.

Contact Ms. Penny Quinn, Dean of Instruction, Illinois Eastern Community Colleges, Lincoln Trail College, 11220 State Highway 1, Robinson, IL 62454. Telephone: 618-544-8657 Ext. 1144. Fax: 618-544-7423. E-mail: quinnp@iecc.edu.

DEGREES AND AWARDS
Programs offered do not lead to a degree or other formal award.

COURSE SUBJECT AREAS OFFERED OUTSIDE OF DEGREE PROGRAMS

Undergraduate—accounting and computer science; astronomy and astrophysics; business/commerce; computer software and media applications; computer systems networking and telecommunications; English composition; geography and cartography; health professions related; mathematics; psychology; psychology related.

ILLINOIS EASTERN COMMUNITY COLLEGES, OLNEY CENTRAL COLLEGE
Olney, Illinois
http://www.iecc.cc.il.us/occ/

Illinois Eastern Community Colleges, Olney Central College was founded in 1962. It is accredited by North Central Association of Colleges and Schools. It first offered distance learning courses in 1994. In fall 2006, there were 449 students enrolled in distance learning courses. Institutionally administered financial aid is available to distance learners.

Services Distance learners have accessibility to academic advising, bookstore, campus computer network, career placement assistance, e-mail services, library services, tutoring.

Contact Ms. Lisa Benson, Dean of Instruction, Illinois Eastern Community Colleges, Olney Central College, 305 North West Street, Olney, IL 62450. Telephone: 618-395-7777 Ext. 2002. Fax: 618-395-5212. E-mail: bensonl@iecc.edu.

DEGREES AND AWARDS
Programs offered do not lead to a degree or other formal award.

COURSE SUBJECT AREAS OFFERED OUTSIDE OF DEGREE PROGRAMS

Undergraduate—accounting and related services; business/commerce; communication and media; computer and information sciences; economics; English composition; liberal arts and sciences, general studies and humanities; mathematics; psychology; social sciences.

ILLINOIS EASTERN COMMUNITY COLLEGES, WABASH VALLEY COLLEGE
Mount Carmel, Illinois
http://www.iecc.cc.il.us/wvc

Illinois Eastern Community Colleges, Wabash Valley College was founded in 1960. It is accredited by North Central Association of Colleges and Schools. It first offered distance learning courses in 1994. In fall 2006, there were 183 students enrolled in distance learning courses. Institutionally administered financial aid is available to distance learners.

Services Distance learners have accessibility to academic advising, bookstore, campus computer network, career placement assistance, e-mail services, library services, tutoring.

Contact Mr. Matt Fowler, Dean of Instruction, Illinois Eastern Community Colleges, Wabash Valley College, 2200 College Drive, Mt. Carmel, IL 62863. Telephone: 618-262-8641 Ext. 3213. Fax: 618-262-5614. E-mail: fowlerm@iecc.edu.

DEGREES AND AWARDS

Programs offered do not lead to a degree or other formal award.

COURSE SUBJECT AREAS OFFERED OUTSIDE OF DEGREE PROGRAMS

Undergraduate—accounting and related services; business/commerce; chemistry; history; human resources management; liberal arts and sciences, general studies and humanities; mathematics; mathematics and statistics related; psychology; statistics.

IMMACULATA UNIVERSITY
Immaculata, Pennsylvania
http://www.immaculata.edu/

Immaculata University was founded in 1920. It is accredited by Middle States Association of Colleges and Schools. It first offered distance learning courses in 1999. In fall 2006, there were 2,100 students enrolled in distance learning courses. Institutionally administered financial aid is available to distance learners.

Services Distance learners have accessibility to academic advising, bookstore, campus computer network, career placement assistance, e-mail services, library services, tutoring.

Contact Dr. Elke Franke, Dean of College of LifeLong Learning, Immaculata University, Box 300, Immaculata, PA 19345-0300. Telephone: 610-647-4400 Ext. 3235. Fax: 610-647-0215. E-mail: efranke@immaculata.edu.

DEGREES AND AWARDS

BA Organization Dynamics; Organization Dynamics; Organization Dynamics

COURSE SUBJECT AREAS OFFERED OUTSIDE OF DEGREE PROGRAMS

Undergraduate—biblical and other theological languages and literatures; biological and biomedical sciences related; biological and physical sciences; biology; business administration, management and operations; business/managerial economics; computer and information sciences; computer and information sciences and support services related; computer/information technology administration and management; computer science; computer software and media applications; computer systems analysis; English composition; family and consumer economics; family and consumer sciences/human sciences; foods, nutrition, and related services; history; human resources management; psychology; religious studies; sociology.

Graduate—counseling psychology; education related; human development, family studies, and related services; statistics.

INDIANA STATE UNIVERSITY
Terre Haute, Indiana
Office of Distance Support Services
http://indstate.edu/distance

Indiana State University was founded in 1865. It is accredited by North Central Association of Colleges and Schools. It first offered distance learning courses in 1969. In fall 2006, there were 2,000 students enrolled in distance learning courses. Institutionally administered financial aid is available to distance learners.

Services Distance learners have accessibility to academic advising, bookstore, campus computer network, career placement assistance, e-mail services, library services.

Contact Distance Support Services, Indiana State University, Erickson Hall, Room 122, Terre Haute, IN 47809. Telephone: 888-237-8080. Fax: 812-237-8540. E-mail: studentservices@indstate.edu.

DEGREES AND AWARDS

AS General Aviation Flight Technology

BS Business Administration; Career and Technical Education; Community Health Promotion; Criminology and Criminal Justice; Electronics Technology; Human Resource Development; Industrial Technology Management; Insurance and Risk Management; Mechanical Engineering Technology; Nursing (LPN-BS); Nursing (RN-BS)

Certificate Corrections; Law Enforcement; Private Security and Loss Prevention

License Driver Education Instructor; Middle/Secondary Teaching; School Administration; Visual Impairment; Vocational Business Education

Graduate Certificate Public Administration; Public Personnel Administration; School Library Media Services; Teaching English as a Second or Foreign Language

MA Criminology

MS Criminology and Criminal Justice; Electronics and Computer Technology; Health and Safety (Occupational Safety Management specialization); Human Resource Development; Nursing (Family Nurse Practitioner specialization); Nursing (Nursing Administration specialization); Nursing (Nursing Education specialization); Student Affairs and Higher Education

PhD Technology Management

COURSE SUBJECT AREAS OFFERED OUTSIDE OF DEGREE PROGRAMS

Undergraduate—accounting and computer science; accounting and related services; aerospace, aeronautical and astronautical engineering; biological and physical sciences; biology; botany/plant biology; business administration, management and operations; business/commerce; business, management, and marketing related; business operations support and assistant services; chemistry; community health services; computer programming; computer science; construction engineering technology; construction management; criminal justice and corrections; criminology; curriculum and instruction; drafting/design engineering technologies; economics; education; education related; electrical and electronic engineering technologies; engineering-related technologies; English; English composition; finance and financial management services; geography and cartography; health and physical education/fitness; history; human resources management; human services; insurance; library science related; management information systems; marketing; mathematics; mathematics and computer science; mathematics and statistics related; mechanical engineering related technologies; music; nursing; personality psychology; psychology; sociology; technical and business writing; technology education/industrial arts.

Graduate—bilingual, multilingual, and multicultural education; counseling psychology; criminal justice and corrections; criminology; curriculum and instruction; developmental and child psychology; education; educational administration and supervision; educational assessment, evaluation, and research; educational/instructional media design; educational psychology; education related; education (specific levels and methods); education (specific subject areas); electrical and electronic engineering technologies; electrical, electronics and communications engineering; electromechanical and instrumentation and maintenance technologies; English as a second/foreign language (teaching); English as a second language; finance and financial management services; human resources management; industrial and organizational psychology; library science related; nursing; public administration; public administration and social service professions related; school psychology; special education; student counseling and personnel services.

See full description on page 366.

INDIANA TECH
Fort Wayne, Indiana
Independent Study
http://www.indianatech.edu

Indiana Tech was founded in 1930. It is accredited by North Central Association of Colleges and Schools. It first offered distance learning courses in 1982. In fall 2006, there were 142 students enrolled in distance learning courses. Institutionally administered financial aid is available to distance learners.

Services Distance learners have accessibility to academic advising, bookstore, campus computer network, e-mail services.

Contact Mrs. Michelle R. Wood, Director of Independent Study, Indiana Tech, 65 Airport Parkway, Suite 100, Greenwood, IN 46143. Telephone: 800-288-1766 Ext. 5300. Fax: 317-807-0377. E-mail: mrwood@indianatech.edu.

DEGREES AND AWARDS

AS Business Administration; General Studies
BS Business Administration
BSBA Human Resources; Management; Marketing

COURSE SUBJECT AREAS OFFERED OUTSIDE OF DEGREE PROGRAMS

Undergraduate—accounting and related services; business administration, management and operations; business/commerce; computer and information sciences; English composition; psychology; social sciences.

INDIANA UNIVERSITY OF PENNSYLVANIA
Indiana, Pennsylvania
School of Continuing Education
http://www.iup.edu/continuing-ed/

Indiana University of Pennsylvania was founded in 1875. It is accredited by Middle States Association of Colleges and Schools. It first offered distance learning courses in 1990. In fall 2006, there were 872 students enrolled in distance learning courses. Institutionally administered financial aid is available to distance learners.

Services Distance learners have accessibility to academic advising, bookstore, campus computer network, career placement assistance, e-mail services, library services.

Contact Mr. George Rogers, Assistant Dean, College of Continuing Education, Indiana University of Pennsylvania, 104 Keith Hall, 390 Pratt Drive, Indiana, PA 15705. Telephone: 724-357-2292. Fax: 724-357-7597. E-mail: grogers@iup.edu.

DEGREES AND AWARDS

Programs offered do not lead to a degree or other formal award.

COURSE SUBJECT AREAS OFFERED OUTSIDE OF DEGREE PROGRAMS

Undergraduate—accounting and related services; anthropology; business, management, and marketing related; finance and financial management services; foods, nutrition, and related services; hospitality administration; information science/studies; management information systems; marketing; mathematics; physics; political science and government; psychology.

Graduate—business, management, and marketing related; engineering-related fields; foods, nutrition, and related services; liberal arts and sciences, general studies and humanities; political science and government.

INDIANA UNIVERSITY–PURDUE UNIVERSITY FORT WAYNE
Fort Wayne, Indiana
http://www.ipfw.edu/dlearning

Indiana University–Purdue University Fort Wayne was founded in 1917. It is accredited by North Central Association of Colleges and Schools. It first offered distance learning courses in 1996. In fall 2006, there were 3,289 students enrolled in distance learning courses. Institutionally administered financial aid is available to distance learners.

Services Distance learners have accessibility to bookstore, campus computer network, e-mail services, library services.

Contact Deborah Hein, Program Assistant, Indiana University–Purdue University Fort Wayne, 2101 East Coliseum Boulevard, Fort Wayne, IN 46805. Telephone: 260-481-6111. Fax: 260-481-6949. E-mail: dlearn@ipfw.edu.

DEGREES AND AWARDS

BGS Associate of Arts and Bachelor of General Studies

COURSE SUBJECT AREAS OFFERED OUTSIDE OF DEGREE PROGRAMS

Undergraduate—accounting and related services; biology; business/commerce; communication and media; comparative literature; computer science; economics; education; engineering/industrial management; English composition; history; journalism; mathematics; nursing; philosophy; political science and government; psychology; sociology.

Graduate—business administration, management and operations; educational administration and supervision; nursing.

Non-credit—business/corporate communications; business, management, and marketing related; business operations support and assistant services; computer software and media applications; computer systems networking and telecommunications.

INDIANA UNIVERSITY SYSTEM
Bloomington, Indiana
School of Continuing Studies
http://scs.indiana.edu

Indiana University System is accredited by North Central Association of Colleges and Schools. It first offered distance learning courses in 1995. In fall 2006, there were 4,000 students enrolled in distance learning courses. Institutionally administered financial aid is available to distance learners.

Services Distance learners have accessibility to academic advising, bookstore, campus computer network, e-mail services, library services.

Contact Peer Advisor, Indiana University System, Owen Hall 001, 790 East Kirkwood Avenue, Bloomington, IN 47405-7101. Telephone: 800-334-1011. Fax: 812-855-8680. E-mail: scs@indiana.edu.

DEGREES AND AWARDS

AA General Studies

BGS General Studies Degree program

Certificate Accounting–Healthcare Accounting and Financial Management; Distance Education

MS Adult Education

COURSE SUBJECT AREAS OFFERED OUTSIDE OF DEGREE PROGRAMS

Undergraduate—liberal arts and sciences, general studies and humanities.

Graduate—education related.

Non-credit—accounting and related services; education (specific levels and methods); taxation.

See full description on page 368.

INDIANA WESLEYAN UNIVERSITY
Marion, Indiana
Center for Distributed Learning
http://www.IWUonline.com

Indiana Wesleyan University was founded in 1920. It is accredited by North Central Association of Colleges and Schools. It first offered distance learning courses in 1996. In fall 2006, there were 3,475 students enrolled in distance learning courses. Institutionally administered financial aid is available to distance learners.

Services Distance learners have accessibility to academic advising, bookstore, library services, tutoring.

Contact Mr. Dennis Zuber, Online Enrollment Services, Indiana Wesleyan University, 1900 West 50th Street, Marion, IN 46953. Telephone: 888-IWU-2day. Fax: 765-677-2601. E-mail: info@iwuonline.com.

DEGREES AND AWARDS

AS Accounting; Business; Criminal Justice; General Studies

BS Accounting (Bachelor completion); Business Information Systems (Bachelor completion); Criminal Justice (Bachelor completion); General Studies; Management (Bachelor completion); Nursing (RN to BS completion)

BSBA Business Administration (Bachelor completion)

Certificate Communications; Criminal Justice; Human Services; Religious Studies

License Exceptional Needs with Mild Interventions (Special Ed)

MA Ministry (Ministerial Leadership and Youth Ministry concentrations)

MBA Business Administration

MEd Education

MSM Management

MSN Nursing Education and Nursing Administration majors

COURSE SUBJECT AREAS OFFERED OUTSIDE OF DEGREE PROGRAMS

Undergraduate—biblical and other theological languages and literatures; biblical studies; communication and media; computer and information sciences; computer software and media applications; criminal justice and corrections; English composition; fine and studio art; history; liberal arts and sciences, general studies and humanities; mathematics; music; philosophy and religious studies related; psychology.

Graduate—educational psychology.

INSTITUTE FOR CHRISTIAN STUDIES
Toronto, Ontario, Canada
http://www.icscanada.edu

Institute for Christian Studies was founded in 1967. It is provincially chartered. It first offered distance learning courses in 1990. In fall 2006, there were 19 students enrolled in distance learning courses. Institutionally administered financial aid is available to distance learners.

Services Distance learners have accessibility to academic advising, bookstore, e-mail services, library services.

Contact Ms. Robbin Burry, Registrar, Academic and Student Services Officer, Institute for Christian Studies, 229 College Street, 2nd floor, Toronto, ON M5T 1R4, Canada. Telephone: 888-326-5347 Ext. 234. Fax: 416-979-2331 Ext. 234. E-mail: registrar@icscanada.edu.

DEGREES AND AWARDS

M Phil Master of Worldview Studies in Education

COURSE SUBJECT AREAS OFFERED OUTSIDE OF DEGREE PROGRAMS

Graduate—education related; philosophy; philosophy and religious studies related; political science and government; theological and ministerial studies.

IONA COLLEGE
New Rochelle, New York

Iona College was founded in 1940. It is accredited by Middle States Association of Colleges and Schools. It first offered distance learning courses in 1999. In fall 2006, there were 254 students enrolled in distance learning courses. Institutionally administered financial aid is available to distance learners.

Services Distance learners have accessibility to academic advising, bookstore, campus computer network, career placement assistance, e-mail services, library services, tutoring.

Contact Mr. Kevin Cavanagh, Assistant Vice President for College Admissions, Iona College, Admissions, 715 North Avenue, New Rochelle, NY 10801. Telephone: 914-633-2502. Fax: 914-633-2642. E-mail: kcavanagh@iona.edu.

DEGREES AND AWARDS
Programs offered do not lead to a degree or other formal award.

COURSE SUBJECT AREAS OFFERED OUTSIDE OF DEGREE PROGRAMS

Undergraduate—business administration, management and operations; business/corporate communications; business, management, and marketing related; business operations support and assistant services; cognitive psychology and psycholinguistics; communication and journalism related; communication and media; computer and information sciences and support services related; computer programming; computer software and media applications; economics; entrepreneurial and small business operations; family psychology; finance and financial management services; health and medical administrative services; health professions related; health services/allied health/health sciences; international business; liberal arts and sciences, general studies and humanities; management information systems; marketing; philosophy; philosophy and religious studies related; psychology; science, technology and society; social work.

Graduate—business administration, management and operations; business/commerce; business/corporate communications; business, management, and marketing related; communication and journalism related; communications technologies and support services related; computer systems analysis; computer systems networking and telecommunications; education; educational administration and supervision; educational assessment, evaluation, and research; educational/instructional media design; education (specific levels and methods); education (specific subject areas); finance and financial management services; health and medical administrative services; health professions related; health services/allied health/health sciences; human resources management; international business; journalism; legal professions and studies related; management information systems; marketing; psychology; public relations, advertising, and applied communication related.

IOWA STATE UNIVERSITY OF SCIENCE AND TECHNOLOGY
Ames, Iowa
Continuing Education and Conference Services
http://www.lifelearner.iastate.edu

Iowa State University of Science and Technology was founded in 1858. It is accredited by North Central Association of Colleges and Schools. It first offered distance learning courses in 1969. In fall 2006, there were 1,601 students enrolled in distance learning courses. Institutionally administered financial aid is available to distance learners.

Services Distance learners have accessibility to academic advising, bookstore, campus computer network, career placement assistance, e-mail services, library services, tutoring.

Contact Karen Smidt, Program Assistant, Continuing and Distance Education, Iowa State University of Science and Technology, 102 Scheman Building, Ames, IA 50011. Telephone: 515-294-7201. Fax: 515-294-6223. E-mail: ksmidt@iastate.edu.

DEGREES AND AWARDS
Certificate Power Systems Engineering
CAGS Information Assurance

Graduate Certificate Environmental Engineering; Family Financial Planning; Gerontology; Systems Engineering
MAg Agriculture
MCP Community and Regional Planning
ME Systems Engineering
MS Agronomy; Computer Engineering; Electrical Engineering; Family and Consumer Sciences; Industrial Engineering; Interdisciplinary Studies, Community Development specialization; Mechanical Engineering; Seed Technology and Business; Statistics
PhD Food Service and Lodging Management

COURSE SUBJECT AREAS OFFERED OUTSIDE OF DEGREE PROGRAMS

Undergraduate—agriculture; atmospheric sciences and meteorology; biochemistry, biophysics and molecular biology; biology; criminal justice and corrections; economics; food science and technology; human development, family studies, and related services; mathematics and computer science; sociology.
Graduate—agricultural business and management; atmospheric sciences and meteorology; biochemistry, biophysics and molecular biology; civil engineering; family and consumer economics; food science and technology; foods, nutrition, and related services.

ITAWAMBA COMMUNITY COLLEGE
Fulton, Mississippi

Itawamba Community College was founded in 1947. It is accredited by Southern Association of Colleges and Schools. It first offered distance learning courses in 2000. In fall 2006, there were 2,400 students enrolled in distance learning courses. Institutionally administered financial aid is available to distance learners.
Services Distance learners have accessibility to academic advising, bookstore, e-mail services, library services.
Contact Dr. Ellene McCrimon, Dean of Distance Learning, Itawamba Community College, 2176 South Eason Boulevard, Tupelo, MS 38804. Telephone: 662-620-5350. Fax: 662-620-5354. E-mail: emmccrimon@iccms.edu.

DEGREES AND AWARDS
Programs offered do not lead to a degree or other formal award.

COURSE SUBJECT AREAS OFFERED OUTSIDE OF DEGREE PROGRAMS

Undergraduate—accounting and computer science; accounting and related services; agriculture; allied health and medical assisting services; American literature (United States and Canadian); applied mathematics; business administration, management and operations; chemistry; communication and media; communications technology; computer programming; computer science; criminology; developmental and child psychology; economics; English composition; English language and literature related; English literature (British and Commonwealth); gerontology; health services/allied health/health sciences; history; languages (foreign languages related); legal professions and studies related; legal research and advanced professional studies; management information systems; marketing; mathematics; mathematics and computer science; mathematics and statistics related; music; natural sciences; nursing; nutrition sciences; philosophy; physical sciences; physical sciences related; physics; psychology; psychology related; religious studies; social sciences; social sciences related; social work; sociology; statistics; technology education/industrial arts; theology and religious vocations related; visual and performing arts; visual and performing arts related.

IVY TECH COMMUNITY COLLEGE–BLOOMINGTON
Bloomington, Indiana
http://www.ivytech.edu/bloomington/

Ivy Tech Community College–Bloomington was founded in 2001. It is accredited by North Central Association of Colleges and Schools. In fall 2006, there were 1,204 students enrolled in distance learning courses. Institutionally administered financial aid is available to distance learners.
Services Distance learners have accessibility to academic advising, bookstore, campus computer network, career placement assistance, e-mail services, library services.

Contact Lori Handy, Director of Enrollment Services, Ivy Tech Community College–Bloomington, 200 Daniels Way, Bloomington, IN 47404-0393. Telephone: 812-330-6023. Fax: 812-330-6200. E-mail: lahndy1@ivytech.edu.

DEGREES AND AWARDS
AAS Computer Information Systems; Early Childhood Education; Human Services; Office Administration; Paralegal
AS Computer Information Systems; Criminal Justice; General Studies; Human Services; Library Assistant; Paralegal

COURSE SUBJECT AREAS OFFERED OUTSIDE OF DEGREE PROGRAMS

Undergraduate—business administration, management and operations; business operations support and assistant services; criminal justice and corrections; mathematics.

IVY TECH COMMUNITY COLLEGE–CENTRAL INDIANA
Indianapolis, Indiana
http://www.ivytech.edu/indianapolis/

Ivy Tech Community College–Central Indiana was founded in 1963. It is accredited by North Central Association of Colleges and Schools. It first offered distance learning courses in 1995. In fall 2006, there were 2,170 students enrolled in distance learning courses. Institutionally administered financial aid is available to distance learners.
Services Distance learners have accessibility to academic advising, bookstore, campus computer network, career placement assistance, e-mail services, library services.
Contact Tracy Funk, Director of Admissions, Ivy Tech Community College–Central Indiana, 50 West Fall Creek Parkway North Drive, Indianapolis, IN 46208-4777. Telephone: 317-921-4371. Fax: 317-921-4753. E-mail: tfunk@ivytech.edu.

DEGREES AND AWARDS
AAS Computer Information Systems; Early Childhood Education; Human Services; Office Administration; Paralegal
AS Computer Information Systems; Criminal Justice; General Studies; Human Services; Library Assistant; Paralegal

COURSE SUBJECT AREAS OFFERED OUTSIDE OF DEGREE PROGRAMS

Undergraduate—business operations support and assistant services; criminal justice and corrections; mathematics.

IVY TECH COMMUNITY COLLEGE–COLUMBUS
Columbus, Indiana
http://www.ivytech.edu/columbus/

Ivy Tech Community College–Columbus was founded in 1963. It is accredited by North Central Association of Colleges and Schools. It first offered distance learning courses in 1995. In fall 2006, there were 791 students enrolled in distance learning courses. Institutionally administered financial aid is available to distance learners.
Services Distance learners have accessibility to academic advising, bookstore, campus computer network, career placement assistance, e-mail services, library services.
Contact Neil S. Bagadiong, Director of Admissions/Assistant to the Dean of Student Affairs, Ivy Tech Community College–Columbus, 4475 Central Avenue, Columbus, IN 47203-1868. Telephone: 812-374-5129 Ext.. Fax: 812-372-0311. E-mail: nbagadio@ivytech.edu.

DEGREES AND AWARDS
AAS Computer Information Systems; Early Childhood Education; Human Services; Office Administration; Paralegal
AS Computer Information Systems; Criminal Justice; General Studies; Human Services; Library Assistant; Paralegal

COURSE SUBJECT AREAS OFFERED OUTSIDE OF DEGREE PROGRAMS

Undergraduate—business administration, management and operations; business operations support and assistant services; mathematics.

IVY TECH COMMUNITY COLLEGE–EAST CENTRAL
Muncie, Indiana
http://www.ivytech.edu/muncie/

Ivy Tech Community College–East Central was founded in 1968. It is accredited by North Central Association of Colleges and Schools. It first offered distance learning courses in 1995. In fall 2006, there were 1,502 students enrolled in distance learning courses. Institutionally administered financial aid is available to distance learners.

Services Distance learners have accessibility to academic advising, bookstore, campus computer network, career placement assistance, e-mail services, library services.

Contact Corey A. Sharp, Admissions Advisor, Ivy Tech Community College–East Central, 4301 South Cowan Road, Muncie, IN 47302-9448. Telephone: 765-289-2291. Fax: 765-289-2292. E-mail: csharp@ivytech.edu.

DEGREES AND AWARDS

AAS Computer Information Systems; Early Childhood Education; Human Services; Office Administration; Paralegal Studies
AS Computer Information Systems; Criminal Justice; General Studies; Human Services; Library Technical Assistant; Paralegal Studies

COURSE SUBJECT AREAS OFFERED OUTSIDE OF DEGREE PROGRAMS

Undergraduate—business administration, management and operations; business operations support and assistant services; criminal justice and corrections; mathematics; psychology.

IVY TECH COMMUNITY COLLEGE–KOKOMO
Kokomo, Indiana
http://www.ivytech.edu/kokomo/

Ivy Tech Community College–Kokomo was founded in 1968. It is accredited by North Central Association of Colleges and Schools. It first offered distance learning courses in 1995. In fall 2006, there were 457 students enrolled in distance learning courses. Institutionally administered financial aid is available to distance learners.

Services Distance learners have accessibility to academic advising, bookstore, campus computer network, career placement assistance, e-mail services, library services.

Contact Suzanne Dillman, Director of Admissions, Ivy Tech Community College–Kokomo, 1815 East Morgan Street, Kokomo, IN 46903-1373. Telephone: 765-459-0561 Ext. 318. Fax: 765-454-5111. E-mail: sdillman@ivytech.edu.

DEGREES AND AWARDS

AAS Computer Information Systems; Early Childhood Education; Human Services; Office Administration; Paralegal Studies
AS Computer Information Systems; Criminal Justice; General Studies; Human Services; Library Technical Assistant; Paralegal

COURSE SUBJECT AREAS OFFERED OUTSIDE OF DEGREE PROGRAMS

Undergraduate—criminal justice and corrections; English composition; history; quality control and safety technologies.

IVY TECH COMMUNITY COLLEGE–LAFAYETTE
Lafayette, Indiana
http://www.ivytech.edu/lafayette/

Ivy Tech Community College–Lafayette was founded in 1968. It is accredited by North Central Association of Colleges and Schools. It first offered distance learning courses in 1995. In fall 2006, there were 839 students enrolled in distance learning courses. Institutionally administered financial aid is available to distance learners.

Services Distance learners have accessibility to academic advising, bookstore, campus computer network, career placement assistance, e-mail services, library services.

Contact Ivan Hernandez, Director of Admissions, Ivy Tech Community College–Lafayette, 3101 South Creasy Lane, Lafayette, IN 47903. Telephone: 765-269-5253. E-mail: ihernand@ivytech.edu.

DEGREES AND AWARDS

AAS Computer Information Systems; Early Childhood Education; Human Services; Office Administration; Paralegal Studies
AS Computer Information Systems; Criminal Justice; General Studies; Human Services; Library Technical Assistant; Paralegal Studies

IVY TECH COMMUNITY COLLEGE–NORTH CENTRAL
South Bend, Indiana
Instructional Technology
http://www.ivytech.edu/southbend/

Ivy Tech Community College–North Central was founded in 1968. It is accredited by North Central Association of Colleges and Schools. It first offered distance learning courses in 1989. In fall 2006, there were 1,179 students enrolled in distance learning courses. Institutionally administered financial aid is available to distance learners.

Services Distance learners have accessibility to academic advising, bookstore, campus computer network, career placement assistance, e-mail services, library services.

Contact Pam Decker, Director of Admissions, Ivy Tech Community College–North Central, 220 Dean Johnson Boulevard, South Bend, IN 46601. Telephone: 574-289-7001. Fax: 574-236-7177. E-mail: pdecker@ivytech.edu.

DEGREES AND AWARDS

AAS Computer Information Systems; Early Childhood Education; Human Services; Office Administration; Paralegal Studies
AS Computer Information Systems; Criminal Justice; General Studies; Human Services; Library Technical Assistant; Paralegal Studies

COURSE SUBJECT AREAS OFFERED OUTSIDE OF DEGREE PROGRAMS

Undergraduate—biology; economics; English composition; philosophy; political science and government; psychology; sales, merchandising, and related marketing operations (general); sociology; visual and performing arts related.

IVY TECH COMMUNITY COLLEGE–NORTHEAST
Fort Wayne, Indiana
http://www.ivytech.edu/fortwayne/

Ivy Tech Community College–Northeast was founded in 1969. It is accredited by North Central Association of Colleges and Schools. It first offered distance learning courses in 1995. In fall 2006, there were 1,068 students enrolled in distance learning courses. Institutionally administered financial aid is available to distance learners.

Services Distance learners have accessibility to academic advising, bookstore, campus computer network, career placement assistance, e-mail services, library services.

Contact Steve Scheer, Director of Admissions, Ivy Tech Community College–Northeast, 3800 North Anthony Boulevard, Fort Wayne, IN 46805-1489. Telephone: 260-480-4221. Fax: 260-480-4177. E-mail: sscheer@ivytech.edu.

DEGREES AND AWARDS

AAS Computer Information Systems; Early Childhood Education; Human Services; Office Administration; Paralegal Studies
AS Computer Information Systems; Criminal Justice; General Studies; General Studies; Human Services; Library Technical Assistant; Paralegal Studies

COURSE SUBJECT AREAS OFFERED OUTSIDE OF DEGREE PROGRAMS

Undergraduate—construction engineering technology; fire protection.

IVY TECH COMMUNITY COLLEGE–NORTHWEST
Gary, Indiana
http://www.ivytech.edu/gary

Ivy Tech Community College–Northwest was founded in 1963. It is accredited by North Central Association of Colleges and Schools. It first offered distance learning courses in 1995. In fall 2006, there were 1,008 students enrolled in distance learning courses. Institutionally administered financial aid is available to distance learners.

Services Distance learners have accessibility to academic advising, bookstore, campus computer network, career placement assistance, e-mail services, library services.

Contact Twilla Lewis, Associate Dean of Student Affairs, Ivy Tech Community College–Northwest, 1440 East 35th Avenue, Gary, IN 46409-1499. Telephone: 219-981-1111 Ext. 273. Fax: 219-981-4415. E-mail: tlewis@ivytech.edu.

DEGREES AND AWARDS

AAS Computer Information Systems; Early Childhood Education; Human Services; Office Administration; Paralegal Studies
AS Computer Information Systems; Criminal Justice; General Studies; Human Services; Library Technical Assistant; Paralegal Studies

COURSE SUBJECT AREAS OFFERED OUTSIDE OF DEGREE PROGRAMS

Undergraduate—accounting and related services; business administration, management and operations; business operations support and assistant services; economics; English composition; fire protection; history; hospitality administration; marketing; mathematics; nursing; physical sciences; psychology; sociology.

IVY TECH COMMUNITY COLLEGE–SOUTHEAST
Madison, Indiana
http://www.ivytech.edu/madison/

Ivy Tech Community College–Southeast was founded in 1963. It is accredited by North Central Association of Colleges and Schools. It first offered distance learning courses in 1995. In fall 2006, there were 719 students enrolled in distance learning courses. Institutionally administered financial aid is available to distance learners.

Services Distance learners have accessibility to academic advising, bookstore, campus computer network, career placement assistance, e-mail services, library services.

Contact Cindy Hutcherson, Assistant Director of Admissions and Career Counselor, Ivy Tech Community College–Southeast, 590 Ivy Tech Drive, Madison, IN 47250-1881. Telephone: 812-265-2580. Fax: 812-265-4028. E-mail: chutcher@ivytech.edu.

DEGREES AND AWARDS

AAS Computer Information Systems; Early Childhood Education; Human Services; Office Administration; Paralegal
AS Computer Information Systems; Criminal Justice; General Studies; Human Services; Library Assistant; Paralegal

COURSE SUBJECT AREAS OFFERED OUTSIDE OF DEGREE PROGRAMS

Undergraduate—business administration, management and operations; business operations support and assistant services; criminal justice and corrections.

IVY TECH COMMUNITY COLLEGE–SOUTHERN INDIANA
Sellersburg, Indiana
http://www.ivytech.edu/sellersburg/

Ivy Tech Community College–Southern Indiana was founded in 1968. It is accredited by North Central Association of Colleges and Schools. It first offered distance learning courses in 1995. In fall 2006, there were 712 students enrolled in distance learning courses. Institutionally administered financial aid is available to distance learners.

Services Distance learners have accessibility to academic advising, bookstore, campus computer network, career placement assistance, e-mail services, library services.

Contact Mindy Steinberg, Director of Admissions, Ivy Tech Community College–Southern Indiana, 8204 Highway 311, Sellersburg, IN 47172-1897. Telephone: 812-246-3301. Fax: 812-246-9905. E-mail: msteinberg@ivytech.edu.

DEGREES AND AWARDS

AAS Computer Information Systems; Early Childhood Education; Human Services; Office Administration; Paralegal
AS Computer Information Systems; Criminal Justice; General Studies; Human Services; Library Assistant; Paralegal

COURSE SUBJECT AREAS OFFERED OUTSIDE OF DEGREE PROGRAMS

Undergraduate—business administration, management and operations; business operations support and assistant services; criminal justice and corrections; mathematics; sociology.

IVY TECH COMMUNITY COLLEGE–SOUTHWEST
Evansville, Indiana
http://www.ivytech.edu/evansville/

Ivy Tech Community College–Southwest was founded in 1963. It is accredited by North Central Association of Colleges and Schools. It first offered distance learning courses in 1995. In fall 2006, there were 737 students enrolled in distance learning courses. Institutionally administered financial aid is available to distance learners.

Services Distance learners have accessibility to academic advising, bookstore, campus computer network, career placement assistance, e-mail services, library services.

Contact Denise Johnson-Kincade, Director of Admissions, Ivy Tech Community College–Southwest, 3501 First Avenue, Evansville, IN 47710-3398. Telephone: 812-429-1430. Fax: 812-246-9905 Ext.. E-mail: ajohnson@ivytech.edu.

DEGREES AND AWARDS

AAS Computer Information Systems; Early Childhood Education; Human Services; Office Administration; Paralegal
AS Computer Information Systems; Criminal Justice; General Studies; Human Services; Library Assistant; Paralegal

COURSE SUBJECT AREAS OFFERED OUTSIDE OF DEGREE PROGRAMS

Undergraduate—business administration, management and operations; business operations support and assistant services; criminal justice and corrections; mathematics.

IVY TECH COMMUNITY COLLEGE–WABASH VALLEY
Terre Haute, Indiana
http://www.ivytech.edu/terrehaute/

Ivy Tech Community College–Wabash Valley was founded in 1966. It is accredited by North Central Association of Colleges and Schools. It first offered distance learning courses in 1995. In fall 2006, there were 1,647 students enrolled in distance learning courses. Institutionally administered financial aid is available to distance learners.

Services Distance learners have accessibility to academic advising, bookstore, campus computer network, career placement assistance, e-mail services, library services.

Contact Michael Fisher, Director of Admissions, Ivy Tech Community College–Wabash Valley, 7999 US Highway 41, Terre Haute, IN 47802-4898. Telephone: 812-298-2300. Fax: 812-299-5723. E-mail: mfisher@ivytech.edu.

DEGREES AND AWARDS

AAS Computer Information Systems; Early Childhood Education; Human Services; Office Administration; Paralegal
AS Computer Information Systems; Criminal Justice; General Studies; Human Services; Library Assistant; Paralegal

COURSE SUBJECT AREAS OFFERED OUTSIDE OF DEGREE PROGRAMS

Undergraduate—biology; business administration, management and operations; business operations support and assistant services; mathematics; psychology.

IVY TECH COMMUNITY COLLEGE–WHITEWATER
Richmond, Indiana
http://www.ivytech.edu/richmond/

Ivy Tech Community College–Whitewater was founded in 1963. It is accredited by North Central Association of Colleges and Schools. It first offered distance learning courses in 1995. In fall 2006, there were 1,051 students enrolled in distance learning courses. Institutionally administered financial aid is available to distance learners.

Services Distance learners have accessibility to academic advising, bookstore, career placement assistance, e-mail services, library services, tutoring.

Contact Jeff Plasterer, Director of Admissions, Ivy Tech Community College–Whitewater, 2325 Chester Boulevard, Richmond, IN 47374-1298. Telephone: 765-966-2656 Ext. 1212. Fax: 765-962-8741. E-mail: jplaster@ivytech.edu.

DEGREES AND AWARDS

AAS Computer Information Systems; Early Childhood Education; Human Services; Office Administration; Paralegal
AS Computer Information Systems; Criminal Justice; General Studies; Human Services; Library Assistant; Paralegal

COURSE SUBJECT AREAS OFFERED OUTSIDE OF DEGREE PROGRAMS

Undergraduate—business administration, management and operations; business operations support and assistant services; criminal justice and corrections; mathematics; psychology.

JACKSONVILLE STATE UNIVERSITY
Jacksonville, Alabama
Department of Distance Education
http://distance.jsu.edu

Jacksonville State University was founded in 1883. It is accredited by Southern Association of Colleges and Schools. It first offered distance learning courses in 1994. In fall 2006, there were 2,385 students enrolled in distance learning courses. Institutionally administered financial aid is available to distance learners.

Services Distance learners have accessibility to academic advising, bookstore, career placement assistance, e-mail services, library services.

Contact Ms. Gina Glass, Secretary to the Associate Vice President of Distance Education, Jacksonville State University, Office of Distance Education, 700 Pelham Road North, Jacksonville, AL 36265-1602. Telephone: 256-782-8172. Fax: 256-782-8128. E-mail: gglass@jsu.edu.

DEGREES AND AWARDS

BS Emergency Management (Homeland Security minor); Emergency Management (Public Safety Communications minor)
BSN Nursing (STEP Nursing program)
Certificate Spatial Analysis and Management
Graduate Certificate Emergency Management
MBA Business Administration
MEd Physical Education
MPA Business Administration; Emergency Management; Political Science; Spatial Analysis and Management concentration
MS Emergency Management; Manufacturing Systems Technology
MSN Nursing

COURSE SUBJECT AREAS OFFERED OUTSIDE OF DEGREE PROGRAMS

Undergraduate—accounting and computer science; accounting and related services; American literature (United States and Canadian); anthropology; applied mathematics; atmospheric sciences and meteorology; behavioral sciences; biological and biomedical sciences related; biological and physical sciences; biology; business administration, management and operations; business/commerce; business, management, and marketing related; business/managerial economics; chemistry; clinical psychology; community health services; computer and information sciences; computer and information sciences and support services related; computer/information technology administration and management; computer programming; computer science; computer software and media applications; computer systems analysis; computer systems networking and telecommunications; criminal justice and corrections; criminology; curriculum and instruction; data processing; developmental and child psychology; economics; education; educational administration and supervision; educational assessment, evaluation, and research; educational/instructional media design; educational psychology; education related; education (specific levels and methods); education (specific subject areas); engineering; English; English composition; English language and literature related; English literature (British and Commonwealth); environmental control technologies; family and consumer sciences/human sciences; family and consumer sciences/human sciences business services; family and consumer sciences/human sciences related; finance and financial management services; foods, nutrition, and related services; geography and cartography; geological and earth sciences/geosciences; health and physical education/fitness; health professions related; history; human development, family studies, and related services; information science/studies; liberal arts and sciences, general studies and humanities; management information systems; management sciences and quantitative methods; marketing; mathematics; mathematics and computer science; mathematics and statistics related; medical basic sciences; music; neuroscience; nursing; nutrition sciences; physical sciences; physics; political science and government; psychology; psychology related; psychopharmacology; public administration; public administration and social service professions related; quality control and safety technologies; sales, merchandising, and related marketing operations (general); sales, merchandising, and related marketing operations (specialized); school psychology; security and protective services related; social sciences; social work; sociology; special education; statistics; student counseling and personnel services; technology education/industrial arts.

Graduate—accounting and related services; biology; business administration, management and operations; business/commerce; business/corporate communications; business, management, and marketing related; business/managerial economics; chemistry; clinical psychology; computer and information sciences; computer and information sciences and support services related; computer engineering; computer/information technology administration and management; computer programming; computer science; computer software and media applications; computer systems analysis; computer systems networking and telecommunications; criminal justice and corrections; criminology; curriculum and instruction; developmental and child psychology; economics; education; educational administration and supervision; educational assessment, evaluation, and research; educational/instructional media design; educational psychology; education related; education (specific subject areas); environmental control technologies; family and consumer sciences/human sciences related; finance and financial management services; fire protection; geography and cartography; geological and earth sciences/geosciences; health and physical education/fitness; health professions related; human development, family studies, and related services; human resources management; information science/studies; liberal arts and sciences, general studies and humanities; management information systems; management sciences and quantitative methods; marketing; mathematics and computer science; medical basic sciences; nursing; physical sciences; political science and government; psychopharmacology; public administration; public administration and social service professions related; quality control and safety technologies; sales, merchandising, and related marketing operations (general); sales, merchandising, and related marketing operations (specialized); school psychology; security and protective services related; social sciences; social work; sociology; special education; statistics.

JAMES MADISON UNIVERSITY
Harrisonburg, Virginia
Distance Learning Center, Office of Continuing Education
http://jmuonline.jmu.edu

James Madison University was founded in 1908. It is accredited by Southern Association of Colleges and Schools. It first offered distance learning courses in 1996. In fall 2006, there were 445 students enrolled in distance learning courses. Institutionally administered financial aid is available to distance learners.

Services Distance learners have accessibility to academic advising, bookstore, campus computer network, career placement assistance, e-mail services, library services.

Contact Dr. Jim Mazoue, Distance Learning Coordinator, Distributed and Distance Learning, James Madison University, 7D Carrier Library, MSC 1702, Harrisonburg, VA 22807. Telephone: 540-568-2591. Fax: 540-568-6734. E-mail: mazouejg@jmu.edu.

DEGREES AND AWARDS

MBA Information Security
MCC Information Security

COURSE SUBJECT AREAS OFFERED OUTSIDE OF DEGREE PROGRAMS

Undergraduate—accounting and related services; biology; business/commerce; communication and media; communications technology; education (specific levels and methods); English; English composition; health and physical education/fitness; health professions related; history; human resources management; linguistic, comparative, and related language studies; nutrition sciences; philosophy; psychology; sociology; statistics; technical and business writing.

Graduate—business administration, management and operations; computer science; special education.

Non-credit—allied health diagnostic, intervention, and treatment professions; American literature (United States and Canadian); applied mathematics; archeology; architecture; astronomy and astrophysics; biological and biomedical sciences related; biological and physical sciences; building/construction finishing, management, and inspection; business/commerce; business/corporate communications; business, management, and marketing related; communication and journalism related; communication disorders sciences and services; computer programming; computer science; computer systems networking and telecommunications; construction engineering technology; construction trades related; cosmetology and related personal grooming services; counseling psychology; crafts, folk art and artisanry; creative writing; criminal justice and corrections; culinary arts and related services; data entry/microcomputer applications; education; education (specific levels and methods); English; English as a second language; English composition; entrepreneurial and small business operations; family and consumer sciences/human sciences; film/video and photographic arts; fine and studio art; fire protection; foods, nutrition, and related services; forestry; geography and cartography; geological and earth sciences/geosciences; health aides/attendants/orderlies; health and physical education/fitness; health/medical preparatory programs; history; human resources management; human services; information science/studies; international business; journalism; landscape architecture; languages (Germanic); languages (Romance languages); liberal arts and sciences, general studies and humanities; library assistant; linguistic, comparative, and related language studies; management sciences and quantitative methods; marketing; mathematics and computer science; museum studies; music; natural resources and conservation related; nursing; parks, recreation, and leisure related; physical sciences; physical sciences related; physics; plant sciences; political science and government; precision systems maintenance and repair technologies; public administration; public health; public relations, advertising, and applied communication related; quality control and safety technologies; radio, television, and digital communication; real estate; sales, merchandising, and related marketing operations (general); sales, merchandising, and related marketing operations (specialized); social sciences; special education; speech and rhetoric; student counseling and personnel services; systems engineering; taxation; transportation and materials moving related; urban studies/affairs; visual and performing arts.

JAMES SPRUNT COMMUNITY COLLEGE
Kenansville, North Carolina
James Sprunt Community College Distance Learning
http://www.sprunt.com

James Sprunt Community College was founded in 1964. It is accredited by Southern Association of Colleges and Schools. It first offered distance learning courses in 1999. In fall 2006, there were 225 students enrolled in distance learning courses. Institutionally administered financial aid is available to distance learners.

Services Distance learners have accessibility to academic advising, bookstore, library services.

Contact Mrs. Heather Lanier, Distance Learning Coordinator, James Sprunt Community College, 221 James Sprunt Circle, PO Box 398, Kenansville, NC 28349. Telephone: 910-296-1334. Fax: 910-296-0731. E-mail: hlanier@jamessprunt.edu.

DEGREES AND AWARDS
Programs offered do not lead to a degree or other formal award.

COURSE SUBJECT AREAS OFFERED OUTSIDE OF DEGREE PROGRAMS

Undergraduate—accounting and computer science; accounting and related services; agricultural business and management; agriculture and agriculture operations related; allied health and medical assisting services; allied health diagnostic, intervention, and treatment professions; animal sciences; business administration, management and operations; business/corporate communications; business, management, and marketing related; business operations support and assistant services; communication and journalism related; computer software and media applications; criminal justice and corrections; data processing; English; English composition; English language and literature related; English literature (British and Commonwealth); health and medical administrative services; history; linguistic, comparative, and related language studies; marketing; mathematics; psychology; religious studies; sociology.

JAMESTOWN COMMUNITY COLLEGE
Jamestown, New York
Distance Education
http://www.sunyjcc.edu/online

Jamestown Community College was founded in 1950. It is accredited by Middle States Association of Colleges and Schools. It first offered distance learning courses in 1995. In fall 2006, there were 500 students enrolled in distance learning courses. Institutionally administered financial aid is available to distance learners.

Services Distance learners have accessibility to academic advising, bookstore, campus computer network, career placement assistance, e-mail services, library services, tutoring.

Contact Admissions Office, Jamestown Community College, 525 Falconer Street, PO Box 20, Jamestown, NY 14702-0020. Telephone: 800-388-8557 Ext. 1001. Fax: 716-338-1450. E-mail: admissions@mail.sunyjcc.edu.

DEGREES AND AWARDS
AA Individual Studies
AAS Computer Information Systems; Individual Studies; Information Technology
AS Computer Science; Individual Studies
CCCPE Individual Studies; Information Technology; Psychology of the Workplace

COURSE SUBJECT AREAS OFFERED OUTSIDE OF DEGREE PROGRAMS

Non-credit—accounting and related services; business administration, management and operations; business/commerce; business/corporate communications; business, management, and marketing related; business operations support and assistant services; communication and media; computer and information sciences; computer and information sciences and support services related; computer software and media applications; computer systems networking and telecommunications; creative writing;

English composition; entrepreneurial and small business operations; finance and financial management services; food science and technology; health and medical administrative services; human resources management; human services; journalism; liberal arts and sciences, general studies and humanities; linguistic, comparative, and related language studies; marketing; psychology related; real estate; sociology.

JEFFERSON COLLEGE OF HEALTH SCIENCES
Roanoke, Virginia
http://www.jchs.edu/
Jefferson College of Health Sciences was founded in 1982. It is accredited by Southern Association of Colleges and Schools. It first offered distance learning courses in 1999. In fall 2006, there were 400 students enrolled in distance learning courses. Institutionally administered financial aid is available to distance learners.
Services Distance learners have accessibility to academic advising, bookstore, e-mail services, library services.
Contact Elizabeth Claybrook, Educational Resource Associate, Jefferson College of Health Sciences, PO Box 13186, Roanoke, VA 24031. Telephone: 540-985-6971. Fax: 540-985-8512. E-mail: eclaybrook@jchs.edu.

DEGREES AND AWARDS
Programs offered do not lead to a degree or other formal award.

COURSE SUBJECT AREAS OFFERED OUTSIDE OF DEGREE PROGRAMS
Undergraduate—allied health diagnostic, intervention, and treatment professions; business administration, management and operations; community health services; computer software and media applications; English composition; foods, nutrition, and related services; gerontology; health and medical administrative services; health and physical education/fitness; health/medical preparatory programs; health professions related; human resources management; nursing; philosophy; psychology; public health; rehabilitation and therapeutic professions; sociology; statistics; technical and business writing.
Graduate—nursing; philosophy.
Non-credit—allied health diagnostic, intervention, and treatment professions; nursing.

JEFFERSON COMMUNITY AND TECHNICAL COLLEGE
Louisville, Kentucky
http://www.jcc.uky.edu/
Jefferson Community and Technical College was founded in 1968. It is accredited by Southern Association of Colleges and Schools. It first offered distance learning courses in 1990. In fall 2006, there were 2,729 students enrolled in distance learning courses. Institutionally administered financial aid is available to distance learners.
Services Distance learners have accessibility to academic advising, bookstore, campus computer network, career placement assistance, e-mail services, library services, tutoring.
Contact Mr. Joshua J. Smith, Kentucky Virtual University Enrollment Coordinator, Jefferson Community and Technical College, 1000 Community College Drive, Louisville, KY 40272. Telephone: 502-213-7100. E-mail: joshuaj.smith@kctcs.edu.

DEGREES AND AWARDS
AAS Administrative Assistant; Financial Assistant; Medical Transcriptionist; Office Assistant
Certificate A+ Certification; Accounting Trainee I; Accounting Trainee II; Business Administration, advanced; Business Administration, basic; Business Transfer; Business, general; Child Care Assistant; Data Entry Operator; Early Childhood Administrator; Financial Assistant Clerk; Financial Assistant Trainee; Financial Record Keeper; Integrated Office Skills; Kentucky Child Care Provider; Leadership; Medicaid Nurse Aide; Microsoft Networking MCSA; Small Business Management; Supervisory Management

COURSE SUBJECT AREAS OFFERED OUTSIDE OF DEGREE PROGRAMS
Undergraduate—accounting and computer science; allied health diagnostic, intervention, and treatment professions; area, ethnic, cultural, and gender studies related; behavioral sciences; biblical studies; biology; business administration, management and operations; communication and journalism related; computer and information sciences; computer engineering technologies; computer/information technology administration and management; creative writing; criminal justice and corrections; data entry/microcomputer applications; dramatic/theater arts and stagecraft; economics; educational administration and supervision; education (specific levels and methods); English as a second language; English composition; English language and literature related; fine and studio art; history; languages (Germanic); languages (Romance languages); mathematics; music; nursing; philosophy; political science and government; psychology; technical and business writing; visual and performing arts.

JEFFERSON COMMUNITY COLLEGE
Watertown, New York
Division of Continuing Education
http://www.sunyjefferson.edu
Jefferson Community College was founded in 1961. It is accredited by Middle States Association of Colleges and Schools. It first offered distance learning courses in 1995. In fall 2006, there were 1,000 students enrolled in distance learning courses. Institutionally administered financial aid is available to distance learners.
Services Distance learners have accessibility to academic advising, bookstore, career placement assistance, e-mail services, library services, tutoring.
Contact MaKeever Clarke, Distance Learning Coordinator, Jefferson Community College, 1220 Coffeen Street, Watertown, NY 13601. Telephone: 315-786-6527. Fax: 315-786-0158. E-mail: mclarke@sunyjefferson.edu.

DEGREES AND AWARDS
AA Individual Studies; Liberal Arts–Humanities and Social Science
AAS Individual Studies
AS Business Administration; Criminal Justice; Individual Studies

COURSE SUBJECT AREAS OFFERED OUTSIDE OF DEGREE PROGRAMS
Undergraduate—business administration, management and operations; business, management, and marketing related; economics; English composition; history; mathematics and statistics related; psychology; sociology; technical and business writing.

JEFFERSON COMMUNITY COLLEGE
Steubenville, Ohio
Jefferson Community College was founded in 1966. It is accredited by North Central Association of Colleges and Schools. It first offered distance learning courses in 2001. In fall 2006, there were 400 students enrolled in distance learning courses. Institutionally administered financial aid is available to distance learners.
Services Distance learners have accessibility to academic advising, library services.
Contact Ms. Kimberly Jean Patterson, Assistant to the Dean of Humanities and Social Sciences, Jefferson Community College, 4000 Sunset Boulevard, Steubenville, OH 43952. Telephone: 740-264-5591 Ext. 112. Fax: 740-266-3195. E-mail: kpatterson@jcc.edu.

DEGREES AND AWARDS
Programs offered do not lead to a degree or other formal award.

COURSE SUBJECT AREAS OFFERED OUTSIDE OF DEGREE PROGRAMS
Undergraduate—accounting and related services; American literature (United States and Canadian); behavioral sciences; biology; business administration, management and operations; business/commerce; business/

corporate communications; business, management, and marketing related; communication and journalism related; communication and media; comparative literature; computer and information sciences; creative writing; criminal justice and corrections; criminology; developmental and child psychology; dramatic/theater arts and stagecraft; economics; education; educational psychology; English; English composition; English language and literature related; English literature (British and Commonwealth); foods, nutrition, and related services; geography and cartography; health services/allied health/health sciences; history; human resources management; journalism; marketing; mathematics; mathematics and statistics related; personality psychology; philosophy; political science and government; psychology; social psychology; social sciences; sociology; statistics.

JOHN A. LOGAN COLLEGE
Carterville, Illinois
Learning Resources
http://www.jalc.edu

John A. Logan College was founded in 1967. It is accredited by North Central Association of Colleges and Schools. It first offered distance learning courses in 1979. In fall 2006, there were 835 students enrolled in distance learning courses. Institutionally administered financial aid is available to distance learners.

Services Distance learners have accessibility to academic advising, campus computer network, career placement assistance, library services, tutoring.

Contact Robert Fester, Advisor and Counselor, John A. Logan College, 700 Logan College Road, Carterville, IL 62918. Telephone: 618-985-2828 Ext. 8385. E-mail: bobfester@jalc.edu.

DEGREES AND AWARDS
Programs offered do not lead to a degree or other formal award.

COURSE SUBJECT AREAS OFFERED OUTSIDE OF DEGREE PROGRAMS

Undergraduate—accounting and computer science; accounting and related services; allied health diagnostic, intervention, and treatment professions; American Sign Language (ASL); biology; business administration, management and operations; business/commerce; business, management, and marketing related; computer and information sciences; creative writing; data processing; dental support services and allied professions; design and applied arts; dramatic/theater arts and stagecraft; education; English; English composition; English language and literature related; film/video and photographic arts; fine and studio art; history; hospitality administration; liberal arts and sciences, general studies and humanities; marketing; mathematics; mathematics and computer science; physics; political science and government; psychology; psychology related; religious studies; speech and rhetoric; technology education/industrial arts; visual and performing arts.

JOHN JAY COLLEGE OF CRIMINAL JUSTICE OF THE CITY UNIVERSITY OF NEW YORK
New York, New York
http://www.jjay.cuny.edu

John Jay College of Criminal Justice of the City University of New York was founded in 1964. It is accredited by Middle States Association of Colleges and Schools. It first offered distance learning courses in 1999. In fall 2006, there were 6,000 students enrolled in distance learning courses. Institutionally administered financial aid is available to distance learners.

Services Distance learners have accessibility to bookstore, campus computer network, e-mail services, library services, tutoring.

Contact Prof. Robert James Hong, Director of Educational Technology, John Jay College of Criminal Justice of the City University of New York, 445 West 59th Street, Room 3410, North Hall, New York, NY 10019-1107. Telephone: 212-237-8849. Fax: 212-237-8919. E-mail: rhong@jjay.cuny.edu.

DEGREES AND AWARDS
Programs offered do not lead to a degree or other formal award.

COURSE SUBJECT AREAS OFFERED OUTSIDE OF DEGREE PROGRAMS

Undergraduate—American literature (United States and Canadian); anthropology; computer/information technology administration and management; criminal justice and corrections; economics; fire protection; health and physical education/fitness; languages (Romance languages); legal studies (non-professional general, undergraduate); political science and government; psychology; public administration; public administration and social service professions related; security and protective services related; technical and business writing.

Graduate—public administration; security and protective services related.

JOHNSON BIBLE COLLEGE
Knoxville, Tennessee
Distance Learning Office
http://www.jbc.edu/mastersnt/

Johnson Bible College was founded in 1893. It is accredited by Association for Biblical Higher Education. It first offered distance learning courses in 1988. In fall 2006, there were 79 students enrolled in distance learning courses. Institutionally administered financial aid is available to distance learners.

Services Distance learners have accessibility to academic advising, bookstore, campus computer network, e-mail services, library services.

Contact Dr. John C. Ketchen, Director of Distance Learning, Johnson Bible College, 7900 Johnson Drive, Knoxville, TN 37998. Telephone: 865-251-2254. Fax: 865-251-2285. E-mail: mketchen@jbc.edu.

DEGREES AND AWARDS
MA New Testament

COURSE SUBJECT AREAS OFFERED OUTSIDE OF DEGREE PROGRAMS

Undergraduate—biblical studies.
Graduate—biblical studies.

JOHN TYLER COMMUNITY COLLEGE
Chester, Virginia
http://www.jtcc.edu/DistanceEd

John Tyler Community College was founded in 1967. It is accredited by Southern Association of Colleges and Schools. It first offered distance learning courses in 1997. In fall 2006, there were 1,243 students enrolled in distance learning courses. Institutionally administered financial aid is available to distance learners.

Services Distance learners have accessibility to bookstore, e-mail services, library services.

Contact Ms. Angela Clarke, Instructional Center Technician, John Tyler Community College, 800 Charter Colony Parkway, Midlothian, VA 23114-4383. Telephone: 804-594-1625. Fax: 804-594-1591. E-mail: distanceed@jtcc.edu.

DEGREES AND AWARDS

AAS Arts and Sciences Degree for transfer; Nursing–Online ADN Nursing program

COURSE SUBJECT AREAS OFFERED OUTSIDE OF DEGREE PROGRAMS

Undergraduate—accounting and related services; American literature (United States and Canadian); biology; business administration, management and operations; chemistry; computer and information sciences; creative writing; criminal justice and corrections; economics; English composition; English literature (British and Commonwealth); funeral service and mortuary science; health services/allied health/health sciences; history; human resources management; mathematics; nursing; philosophy; psychology; religious studies; sociology.

JOHN WOOD COMMUNITY COLLEGE
Quincy, Illinois
Alternative and Distance Learning Center
http://www.jwcc.edu/instruct/

John Wood Community College was founded in 1974. It is accredited by North Central Association of Colleges and Schools. It first offered distance learning courses in 1987. In fall 2006, there were 800 students enrolled in distance learning courses. Institutionally administered financial aid is available to distance learners.

Services Distance learners have accessibility to academic advising, bookstore, campus computer network, career placement assistance, e-mail services, library services, tutoring.

Contact Ms. Bonnie Scranton, Dean of Enrollment Services, John Wood Community College, 1301 South 48th Street, Quincy, IL 62305. Telephone: 217-224-6500 Ext. 4336. Fax: 217-224-4208. E-mail: bscranton @jwcc.edu.

DEGREES AND AWARDS
Programs offered do not lead to a degree or other formal award.

COURSE SUBJECT AREAS OFFERED OUTSIDE OF DEGREE PROGRAMS

Undergraduate—accounting and related services; anthropology; Army J.R.O.T.C/R.O.T.C; astronomy and astrophysics; business administration, management and operations; business/commerce; cell biology and anatomical sciences; computer and information sciences; computer software and media applications; criminal justice and corrections; data entry/microcomputer applications; developmental and child psychology; economics; English composition; fine and studio art; health and physical education/fitness; history; liberal arts and sciences, general studies and humanities; mathematics; military studies; music; philosophy; philosophy and religious studies related; physical sciences; physics; plant sciences; political science and government; psychology; religious studies; security and protective services related; social psychology; social sciences; sociology; special education; statistics.
Non-credit—computer and information sciences; insurance.

JONES COLLEGE
Jacksonville, Florida
http://www.jones.edu/

Jones College was founded in 1918. It is accredited by Accrediting Council for Independent Colleges and Schools. It first offered distance learning courses in 1998. In fall 2006, there were 400 students enrolled in distance learning courses. Institutionally administered financial aid is available to distance learners.

Services Distance learners have accessibility to academic advising, bookstore, campus computer network, career placement assistance, e-mail services, library services, tutoring.

Contact Mr. Thomas A. Clift, Vice President of Academic Affairs, Dean of Distance Learning, Jones College, 5353 Arlington Expressway, Jacksonville, FL 32211-5588. Telephone: 904-743-1122 Ext. 134. Fax: 904-743-4446. E-mail: tclift@jones.edu.

DEGREES AND AWARDS
AS Business Administration; Computer Information Systems; Legal Assistant
BS Business Administration; Computer Information Systems; Interdisciplinary Studies; Paralegal

COURSE SUBJECT AREAS OFFERED OUTSIDE OF DEGREE PROGRAMS

Undergraduate—accounting and related services; allied health and medical assisting services; business administration, management and operations; business/commerce; business/corporate communications; business/managerial economics; communication and media; community psychology; computer and information sciences; computer and information sciences and support services related; computer programming; computer software and media applications; computer systems analysis; data processing; economics; English; English composition; English language and literature related; information science/studies; international

business; international relations and affairs; legal studies (non-professional general, undergraduate); liberal arts and sciences, general studies and humanities; management information systems; mathematics; mathematics and statistics related; sales, merchandising, and related marketing operations (general); social sciences; social sciences related; sociology; taxation; technical and business writing.
Non-credit—English; mathematics.

JONES COUNTY JUNIOR COLLEGE
Ellisville, Mississippi
http://www.jcjc.cc.ms.us/

Jones County Junior College was founded in 1928. It is accredited by Southern Association of Colleges and Schools. It first offered distance learning courses in 2001. In fall 2006, there were 450 students enrolled in distance learning courses. Institutionally administered financial aid is available to distance learners.

Services Distance learners have accessibility to bookstore, campus computer network, e-mail services, library services.

Contact Ms. Jennifer Powell, Distance Learning Coordinator, Jones County Junior College, 900 South Court Street, Ellisville, MS 39437. Telephone: 601-477-5454. E-mail: jennifer.powell@jcjc.edu.

DEGREES AND AWARDS
Programs offered do not lead to a degree or other formal award.

COURSE SUBJECT AREAS OFFERED OUTSIDE OF DEGREE PROGRAMS

Undergraduate—accounting and related services; American literature (United States and Canadian); business/corporate communications; creative writing; criminal justice and corrections; economics; English composition; English literature (British and Commonwealth); history; mathematics; nutrition sciences; philosophy and religious studies related; psychology; sociology.

JONES INTERNATIONAL UNIVERSITY
Centennial, Colorado
http://www.jonesinternational.edu/

Jones International University was founded in 1995. It is accredited by North Central Association of Colleges and Schools. It first offered distance learning courses in 1995. In fall 2006, there were 1,050 students enrolled in distance learning courses. Institutionally administered financial aid is available to distance learners.

Services Distance learners have accessibility to academic advising, bookstore, library services.

Contact Ms. Candice Morrissey, Associate Director of Admissions, Jones International University, 9697 East Mineral Avenue, Englewood, CO 80112. Telephone: 800-811-5663. Fax: 303-799-0966. E-mail: admissions@jonesinternational.edu.

DEGREES AND AWARDS
BA Business Communication
BBA Business Administration
BS Information Technology
MA Business Communication
MBA Business Administration
MEd E-Learning; K-12 Educators and Administration

J. SARGEANT REYNOLDS COMMUNITY COLLEGE
Richmond, Virginia
Division of Instructional Technologies and Distance Education
http://www.jsr.vccs.edu

J. Sargeant Reynolds Community College was founded in 1972. It is accredited by Southern Association of Colleges and Schools. It first offered distance learning courses in 1980. In fall 2006, there were 7,203 students enrolled in distance learning courses. Institutionally administered financial aid is available to distance learners.

Services Distance learners have accessibility to academic advising, bookstore, campus computer network, e-mail services, library services, tutoring.

Contact M.R. Macbeth, Coordinator of Center for Distance Learning, J. Sargeant Reynolds Community College, Center for Distance Learning, PO Box 85622, Richmond, VA 23285-5622. Telephone: 804-523-5612. Fax: 804-371-3822. E-mail: distance-ed@reynolds.edu.

DEGREES AND AWARDS

AAS Early Childhood Development; Marketing; Respiratory Therapy

COURSE SUBJECT AREAS OFFERED OUTSIDE OF DEGREE PROGRAMS

Undergraduate—accounting and related services; American literature (United States and Canadian); biology; business administration, management and operations; business, management, and marketing related; business operations support and assistant services; chemistry; computer science; computer software and media applications; criminal justice and corrections; developmental and child psychology; economics; education; English composition; food science and technology; health and physical education/fitness; history; human development, family studies, and related services; information science/studies; linguistic, comparative, and related language studies; marketing; mathematics; nursing; philosophy; political science and government; psychology; social sciences related; sociology; speech and rhetoric.

JUDSON COLLEGE
Marion, Alabama
Distance Learning Program
http://www.judson.edu

Judson College was founded in 1838. It is accredited by Southern Association of Colleges and Schools. It first offered distance learning courses in 1976. In fall 2006, there were 100 students enrolled in distance learning courses. Institutionally administered financial aid is available to distance learners.

Services Distance learners have accessibility to academic advising, bookstore, campus computer network, career placement assistance, e-mail services, library services.

Contact Angie M. Teague, Director of Distance Learning, Judson College, 302 Bibb Street, Marion, AL 36756. Telephone: 800-447-9472 Ext. 169. Fax: 334-683-5282. E-mail: ateague@judson.edu.

DEGREES AND AWARDS

BA Business; Criminal Justice; Education–Secondary Education; English; History; Music; Psychology; Religious Studies
BMin Ministry Studies
BS Business; Criminal Justice; Education; Psychology

COURSE SUBJECT AREAS OFFERED OUTSIDE OF DEGREE PROGRAMS

Undergraduate—behavioral sciences; biblical studies; bioethics/medical ethics; biological and physical sciences; business administration, management and operations; creative writing; criminal justice and corrections; developmental and child psychology; ecology, evolution, and population biology; economics; education; education (specific levels and methods); education (specific subject areas); English; English composition; English literature (British and Commonwealth); history; music; philosophy and religious studies related; political science and government; psychology; social sciences; sociology.

JUDSON COLLEGE
Elgin, Illinois
Division of Continuing Education
http://www.judsoncollege.edu

Judson College was founded in 1963. It is accredited by North Central Association of Colleges and Schools. It first offered distance learning courses in 1998. In fall 2006, there were 230 students enrolled in distance learning courses. Institutionally administered financial aid is available to distance learners.

Services Distance learners have accessibility to academic advising, bookstore, campus computer network, career placement assistance, e-mail services, library services, tutoring.

Contact Robert Lindahl, Student Specialist for Customized Learning Center, Judson College, 1151 North State Street, Elgin, IL 60123. Telephone: 847-628-1547. Fax: 847-628-1007. E-mail: rlindahl@judsoncollege.edu.

DEGREES AND AWARDS

BA Management and Leadership

COURSE SUBJECT AREAS OFFERED OUTSIDE OF DEGREE PROGRAMS

Undergraduate—astronomy and astrophysics; biblical studies; communication and media; computer software and media applications; criminal justice and corrections; English; English composition; environmental control technologies; fine and studio art; history; liberal arts and sciences, general studies and humanities; mathematics; political science and government; psychology; public relations, advertising, and applied communication related; sociology; technical and business writing.

KANSAS CITY KANSAS COMMUNITY COLLEGE
Kansas City, Kansas
Distance Education
http://www.kckcc.edu

Kansas City Kansas Community College was founded in 1923. It is accredited by North Central Association of Colleges and Schools. It first offered distance learning courses in 1989. In fall 2006, there were 2,000 students enrolled in distance learning courses. Institutionally administered financial aid is available to distance learners.

Services Distance learners have accessibility to academic advising, bookstore, campus computer network, e-mail services, library services.

Contact Tamara Miller, Director of Adult Support Services, Kansas City Kansas Community College, 7250 State Avenue, Kansas City, KS 66112. Telephone: 913-573-3191. E-mail: tmiller@toto.net.

DEGREES AND AWARDS

Programs offered do not lead to a degree or other formal award.

COURSE SUBJECT AREAS OFFERED OUTSIDE OF DEGREE PROGRAMS

Undergraduate—accounting and related services; American literature (United States and Canadian); anthropology; area, ethnic, cultural, and gender studies related; biological and physical sciences; biology; business administration, management and operations; business/commerce; business, management, and marketing related; business operations support and assistant services; computer and information sciences; computer and information sciences and support services related; computer science; computer software and media applications; computer systems networking and telecommunications; criminal justice and corrections; data entry/microcomputer applications; economics; English; English composition; fire protection; funeral service and mortuary science; health professions related; history; human development, family studies, and related services; human resources management; intercultural/multicultural and diversity studies; legal professions and studies related; liberal arts and sciences, general studies and humanities; mathematics; personal and culinary services related; philosophy; physical sciences; psychology; sales, merchandising, and related marketing operations (general); social sciences; sociology.

Non-credit—building/construction finishing, management, and inspection; computer systems networking and telecommunications; creative writing; entrepreneurial and small business operations.

KANSAS STATE UNIVERSITY
Manhattan, Kansas
Division of Continuing Education, Continuing Learning
http://www.dce.ksu.edu/distance

Kansas State University was founded in 1863. It is accredited by North Central Association of Colleges and Schools. It first offered distance learning courses in 1971. In fall 2006, there were 7,000 students enrolled in distance learning courses. Institutionally administered financial aid is available to distance learners.

Services Distance learners have accessibility to academic advising, bookstore, campus computer network, career placement assistance, e-mail services, library services.

Contact Daniel Butcher, Bachelor Degree Completion Program Coordinator, Kansas State University, Division of Continuing Education, 13 College Court Building, Manhattan, KS 66506. Telephone: 785-532-5575. Fax: 785-532-5637. E-mail: informationdce@ksu.edu.

DEGREES AND AWARDS

BS Animal Science and Industry; Business, general; Dietetics; Early Childhood Education; Elementary Education; Food Science and Industry; Interdisciplinary Social Sciences; Technology Management

Certificate of Completion Early Childhood Education Administration Credential; Family Development Credential

Certificate Classroom Technology Specialty; Food Science; Occupational Health Psychology; Personal Financial Planning

Endorsement ESL Endorsement in Elementary and Secondary Education; Early Childhood Education

CAGS Business Administration

CCCPE Conflict Resolution; Conflict Resolution

Graduate Certificate Academic Advising; Applied Statistics; Food Science; Gerontology; Organizational Leadership; Public Administration; Youth Development

MS Adult and Continuing Education; Agribusiness; Chemical Engineering; Civil Engineering; Community Development; Educational Administration; Electrical Engineering; Engineering Management; Food Science and Industry; Gerontology; Industrial/Organizational Psychology; Mechanical Engineering; Merchandising; Personal Financial Planning; Software Engineering; Youth Development

COURSE SUBJECT AREAS OFFERED OUTSIDE OF DEGREE PROGRAMS

Undergraduate—accounting and computer science; accounting and related services; agricultural and domestic animal services; agricultural and food products processing; agricultural business and management; agricultural production; agriculture; agriculture and agriculture operations related; animal sciences; applied horticulture/horticultural business services; area, ethnic, cultural, and gender studies related; behavioral sciences; biochemistry, biophysics and molecular biology; biological and physical sciences; business administration, management and operations; business/commerce; business, management, and marketing related; chemistry; computer and information sciences; developmental and child psychology; dietetics and clinical nutrition services; English; ethnic, cultural minority, and gender studies; family and consumer sciences/human sciences; family and consumer sciences/human sciences related; finance and financial management services; food science and technology; foods, nutrition, and related services; geography and cartography; history; human development, family studies, and related services; information science/studies; management information systems; marketing; music; natural resources and conservation related; natural resources conservation and research; natural resources management and policy; natural sciences; nutrition sciences; physical sciences; physical sciences related; political science and government; psychology; social psychology; social sciences; social sciences related; sociology; statistics.

Graduate—agricultural and food products processing; agricultural business and management; agricultural public services; agriculture; agriculture and agriculture operations related; animal sciences; apparel and textiles; chemical engineering; civil engineering; community health services; community organization and advocacy; community psychology; computer engineering; computer science; computer software and media applications; electrical, electronics and communications engineering; engineering; engineering/industrial management; engineering related; engineering science; family and consumer sciences/human sciences; family and consumer sciences/human sciences related; family psychology; finance and financial management services; gerontology; human resources management; industrial and organizational psychology; mechanical engineering; mechanical engineering related technologies; plant sciences; psychology; quality control and safety technologies.

Non-credit—agricultural and food products processing; agriculture; education; educational administration and supervision; educational assessment, evaluation, and research; educational psychology; education related; education (specific levels and methods); education (specific subject areas); family and consumer economics; family and consumer sciences/human sciences; family and consumer sciences/human sciences related; family psychology; finance and financial management services; food

science and technology; foods, nutrition, and related services; social sciences related; work and family studies.

See full description on page 370.

KAPLAN UNIVERSITY
Davenport, Iowa
Kaplan University Online
http://www.kaplancollegeia.com/

Kaplan University was founded in 1937. It is accredited by North Central Association of Colleges and Schools. It first offered distance learning courses in 1999. In fall 2006, there were 25,122 students enrolled in distance learning courses. Institutionally administered financial aid is available to distance learners.

Services Distance learners have accessibility to academic advising, bookstore, e-mail services, library services, tutoring.

Contact Information, Kaplan University, 6301 Kaplan University Ave, Fort Lauderdale, FL 33309. Telephone: 866-527-5268. E-mail: infoku @kaplan.edu.

DEGREES AND AWARDS

AAS Business Administration/Accounting; Business Administration/Management; Computer Information Systems; Computer Information Systems/Java; Computer Information Systems/Networking; Computer Information Systems/Programming; Computer Information Systems/Web Development; Computer Information Systems/Wireless Networking; Criminal Justice; Criminal Justice/Corrections; Criminal Justice/Law Enforcement; Criminal Justice/Private Security

AS Interdisciplinary Studies; Interdisciplinary Studies/Educational Paraprofessional (Teacher's Aide)

BS Business Security and Assurance; Business; Business/Accounting; Business/Finance; Business/Management of Information Systems; Criminal Justice; Criminal Justice/Corrections; Criminal Justice/Crime Analysis; Criminal Justice/Crime Scene Investigation; Criminal Justice/Forensic Psychology; Criminal Justice/Fraud Examination and Investigation; Criminal Justice/Law Enforcement; Criminal Justice/Private Security; IT/Database; IT/Multimedia and Animation; IT/Networking; IT/Programming; IT/Web Development; Information Technology; Management; Management/E-Business; Management/Health Care Management; Management/Human Resources Management; Management/Sales and Marketing; Paralegal Studies; Paralegal Studies/Alternative Dispute Resolution; Paralegal Studies/Office Management; Paralegal Studies/Personal Injury

BSN Nursing–RN to BSN Completion

Certificate Case Management; Executive Coaching; Financial Planning; Geriatric Care Management; Information Technology Pathway Certificate; Internet and Website Development; Introduction to Computer Programming Language; Iowa Teacher Intern certificate; Legal Nurse Consulting; Life Care Planning; Nursing–Forensic Nursing; Private Security; Professional Development for Teachers; Project Management; Project Management; Risk Management

MA Teaching and Learning

MAT Teaching Literacy and Language–Grades 6-12; Teaching Literacy and Language–Grades K-6; Teaching Mathematics–Grades 6-8; Teaching Mathematics–Grades 9-12; Teaching Mathematics–Grades K-5; Teaching Science–Grades 6-12; Teaching Students with Special Needs; Teaching With Technology

MBA Business Administration; Entrepreneurship; Finance; Human Resources Management; Information Technology; Management, Communication and Quality; Marketing

MEd Secondary Education

MS Criminal Justice; Criminal Justice/Global Issues in Criminal Justice; Criminal Justice/Law; Criminal Justice/Leadership and Executive Management; Criminal Justice/Policing

COURSE SUBJECT AREAS OFFERED OUTSIDE OF DEGREE PROGRAMS

Non-credit—business administration, management and operations; business/corporate communications; business/managerial economics; finance and financial management services; gerontology; health professions related.

See full description on page 372.

KASKASKIA COLLEGE
Centralia, Illinois
http://www.kaskaskia.edu

Kaskaskia College was founded in 1966. It is accredited by North Central Association of Colleges and Schools. It first offered distance learning courses in 1993. In fall 2006, there were 897 students enrolled in distance learning courses. Institutionally administered financial aid is available to distance learners.

Services Distance learners have accessibility to academic advising, bookstore, campus computer network, career placement assistance, e-mail services, library services, tutoring.

Contact Ms. Joyce Pryor, Online Student Support Specialist, Kaskaskia College, 27210 College Road, Centralia, IL 62801. Telephone: 618-545-3240. Fax: 618-532-1990. E-mail: jpryor@kaskaskia.edu.

DEGREES AND AWARDS
Programs offered do not lead to a degree or other formal award.

COURSE SUBJECT AREAS OFFERED OUTSIDE OF DEGREE PROGRAMS

Undergraduate—accounting and related services; biological and physical sciences; business administration, management and operations; business operations support and assistant services; computer and information sciences; computer software and media applications; developmental and child psychology; dramatic/theater arts and stagecraft; English; English composition; fine and studio art; geography and cartography; history; mathematics; music; psychology; speech and rhetoric; statistics.

KAUAI COMMUNITY COLLEGE
Lihue, Hawaii
University Center-Kauai
http://www.kauaicc.hawaii.edu

Kauai Community College was founded in 1965. It is accredited by Western Association of Schools and Colleges. It first offered distance learning courses in 1988. In fall 2006, there were 145 students enrolled in distance learning courses. Institutionally administered financial aid is available to distance learners.

Services Distance learners have accessibility to academic advising, bookstore, e-mail services, library services.

Contact Ms. Alison Shigematsu, Educational Specialist, Kauai Community College, 3-1901 Kaumualii Highway, Lihue, HI 96766-9500. Telephone: 808-245-8330. Fax: 808-245-8232. E-mail: ashigema@hawaii.edu.

DEGREES AND AWARDS
Programs offered do not lead to a degree or other formal award.

COURSE SUBJECT AREAS OFFERED OUTSIDE OF DEGREE PROGRAMS

Undergraduate—computer and information sciences; English composition; journalism; languages (Romance languages); linguistic, comparative, and related language studies.

KEAN UNIVERSITY
Union, New Jersey
http://www.kean.edu/

Kean University was founded in 1855. It is accredited by Middle States Association of Colleges and Schools. It first offered distance learning courses in 1998. In fall 2006, there were 747 students enrolled in distance learning courses. Institutionally administered financial aid is available to distance learners.

Services Distance learners have accessibility to bookstore, campus computer network, e-mail services, library services.

Contact Dr. Michael Searson, Executive Director, Center for External Education and Development, Kean University, 1000 Morris Avenue, Union, NJ 07083. Telephone: 908-737-7147. Fax: 908-737-7007. E-mail: msearson@kean.edu.

DEGREES AND AWARDS
Programs offered do not lead to a degree or other formal award.

COURSE SUBJECT AREAS OFFERED OUTSIDE OF DEGREE PROGRAMS

Undergraduate—accounting and related services; allied health diagnostic, intervention, and treatment professions; criminal justice and corrections; economics; education (specific levels and methods); education (specific subject areas); finance and financial management services; fine and studio art; health and medical administrative services; history; liberal arts and sciences, general studies and humanities; marketing; mathematics; parks, recreation and leisure facilities management; philosophy and religious studies related; political science and government; psychology; sociology.

Graduate—accounting and related services; educational administration and supervision; education (specific levels and methods); special education.

Non-credit—accounting and related services; business administration, management and operations; business, management, and marketing related; communication and journalism related; computer and information sciences; computer programming; computer software and media applications; creative writing; education; English as a second language; family and consumer sciences/human sciences; film/video and photographic arts; finance and financial management services; fine and studio art; health and physical education/fitness; health professions related; languages (Romance languages); legal professions and studies related; mathematics; parks, recreation and leisure; personal and culinary services related; philosophy; technical and business writing; work and family studies.

KEISER UNIVERSITY
Fort Lauderdale, Florida
http://online.keisercollege.edu

Keiser University was founded in 1977. It is accredited by Accrediting Bureau of Health Education Schools. It first offered distance learning courses in 1999. In fall 2006, there were 2,500 students enrolled in distance learning courses. Institutionally administered financial aid is available to distance learners.

Services Distance learners have accessibility to academic advising, bookstore, campus computer network, career placement assistance, e-mail services, library services, tutoring.

Contact Admissions Counselor, Keiser University, 1900 W. Commercial Blvd., Fort Lauderdale, FL 33309. Telephone: 888-453-4737. Fax: 954-351-4040. E-mail: admissions@keiseruniversity.edu.

DEGREES AND AWARDS

AA Accounting; Business; Criminal Justice; Health Service Administration; Homeland Security; Paralegal Studies

AS Computer Networking and Security Management; Medical Assisting

BA Business Administration–offered in the Spanish language; Business Administration; Criminal Justice; Health Services Administration

BS Health Sciences; Information Technology Management; Management of Information Systems

BSN Nursing–RN to Bachelor of Science in Nursing

See full description on page 374.

KELLOGG COMMUNITY COLLEGE
Battle Creek, Michigan
Distributed Learning
http://www.kellogg.edu

Kellogg Community College was founded in 1956. It is accredited by North Central Association of Colleges and Schools. It first offered distance learning courses in 1988. In fall 2006, there were 1,239 students enrolled in distance learning courses. Institutionally administered financial aid is available to distance learners.

Services Distance learners have accessibility to academic advising, bookstore, e-mail services, library services.

Contact Linda Amstutz, Secretary, Distance Learning, Kellogg Community College, 450 North Avenue, Battle Creek, MI 49017. Telephone: 269-965-3931 Ext. 2383. Fax: 269-965.4133. E-mail: amstutzl@kellogg.edu.

DEGREES AND AWARDS
Programs offered do not lead to a degree or other formal award.

COURSE SUBJECT AREAS OFFERED OUTSIDE OF DEGREE PROGRAMS
Undergraduate—accounting and related services; anthropology; biological and physical sciences; business/commerce; business/corporate communications; business/managerial economics; computer and information sciences; computer software and media applications; economics; education (specific levels and methods); English composition; entrepreneurial and small business operations; history; human services; legal studies (non-professional general, undergraduate); marketing; mathematics and statistics related; philosophy and religious studies related; sociology.

KENT STATE UNIVERSITY
Kent, Ohio
Master of Public Administration Program
http://www.kent.edu/mpa
Kent State University was founded in 1910. It is accredited by North Central Association of Colleges and Schools. It first offered distance learning courses in 2001. In fall 2006, there were 40 students enrolled in distance learning courses. Institutionally administered financial aid is available to distance learners.
Services Distance learners have accessibility to academic advising, bookstore, campus computer network, e-mail services, library services, tutoring.
Contact Prof. Joseph Drew, PhD, Coordinator, Kent-MPA Program, Kent State University, Political Science, Kent, OH 44242-0001. Telephone: 330-672-3239. Fax: 330-672-3239. E-mail: jdrew@kent.edu.

DEGREES AND AWARDS
MPA Public Administration

COURSE SUBJECT AREAS OFFERED OUTSIDE OF DEGREE PROGRAMS
Undergraduate—nursing.
Graduate—finance and financial management services; nursing; public administration; public administration and social service professions related; public health.

KETTERING UNIVERSITY
Flint, Michigan
Graduate School
http://graduate.kettering.edu
Kettering University was founded in 1919. It is accredited by North Central Association of Colleges and Schools. It first offered distance learning courses in 1982. In fall 2006, there were 700 students enrolled in distance learning courses. Institutionally administered financial aid is available to distance learners.
Services Distance learners have accessibility to academic advising, bookstore, campus computer network, e-mail services, library services.
Contact Joanne Allen, Publications Coordinator, Kettering University, 1700 West Third Avenue, Flint, MI 48504-4898. Telephone: 866-584-7237 Ext. 5. Fax: 810-762-9935. E-mail: gradoff@kettering.edu.

DEGREES AND AWARDS
MBA General Concentration; I.T. Concentration; Manufacturing Engineering (Industrial and Manufacturing Engineering concentration); Mechanical Design (ME concentration); Power Electronics and Machine Drives (EE Concentration); Systems Engineering (Industrial and Manufacturing Engineering concentration); Wireless Communications (EE Concentration)

MS Information Technology; Manufacturing Management; Manufacturing Operations; Operations Management
MSE Engineering–Electrical and Computer Engineering concentration; Engineering–Manufacturing Engineering concentration; Engineering–Mechanical Design concentration
MSEM Engineering Management

COURSE SUBJECT AREAS OFFERED OUTSIDE OF DEGREE PROGRAMS
Non-credit—business administration, management and operations; business, management, and marketing related; computer/information technology administration and management; electrical, electronics and communications engineering; engineering; engineering design; engineering related; engineering-related fields; industrial engineering; management information systems; management sciences and quantitative methods; manufacturing engineering; mathematics and statistics related; mechanical engineering; quality control and safety technologies.
See full description on page 376.

KIRKWOOD COMMUNITY COLLEGE
Cedar Rapids, Iowa
http://www.kirkwood.edu
Kirkwood Community College was founded in 1966. It is accredited by North Central Association of Colleges and Schools. It first offered distance learning courses in 1980. In fall 2006, there were 4,000 students enrolled in distance learning courses. Institutionally administered financial aid is available to distance learners.
Services Distance learners have accessibility to academic advising, bookstore, campus computer network, career placement assistance, e-mail services, library services, tutoring.
Contact Alan Peterka, Anytime/Anywhere Department Coordinator, Kirkwood Community College, 6301 Kirkwood Boulevard SW, 214 Linn Hall, Cedar Rapids, IA 52406. Telephone: 319-398-1248. Fax: 319-398-5492. E-mail: alan.peterka@kirkwood.edu.

DEGREES AND AWARDS
AA Liberal Arts

COURSE SUBJECT AREAS OFFERED OUTSIDE OF DEGREE PROGRAMS
Undergraduate—accounting and related services; anthropology; business administration, management and operations; business operations support and assistant services; computer software and media applications; criminal justice and corrections; criminology; economics; education (specific subject areas); English composition; family psychology; health/medical preparatory programs; history; human services; journalism; management information systems; social psychology; sociology; statistics.
Non-credit—business/commerce; computer and information sciences; computer software and media applications; computer systems analysis; computer systems networking and telecommunications; data entry/microcomputer applications; data processing.

KNOWLEDGE SYSTEMS INSTITUTE
Skokie, Illinois
http://distancelearning.ksi.edu/
Knowledge Systems Institute was founded in 1978. It is accredited by North Central Association of Colleges and Schools. It first offered distance learning courses in 2007. In fall 2006, there were 20 students enrolled in distance learning courses. Institutionally administered financial aid is available to distance learners.
Services Distance learners have accessibility to academic advising, bookstore, campus computer network, career placement assistance, e-mail services, tutoring.
Contact Ms. Beverly Crockett, Office Manager, Knowledge Systems Institute, 3420 Main Street, Skokie, IL 60076. Telephone: 847-679-3135. Fax: 847-679-3166. E-mail: office@ksi.edu.

DEGREES AND AWARDS
MS Computer and Information Sciences

COURSE SUBJECT AREAS OFFERED OUTSIDE OF DEGREE PROGRAMS

Non-credit—computer and information sciences; computer programming; computer software and media applications.

LABETTE COMMUNITY COLLEGE
Parsons, Kansas
http://www.labette.cc.ks.us/

Labette Community College was founded in 1923. It is accredited by North Central Association of Colleges and Schools. It first offered distance learning courses in 1985. In fall 2006, there were 1,147 students enrolled in distance learning courses. Institutionally administered financial aid is available to distance learners.

Services Distance learners have accessibility to academic advising, bookstore, campus computer network, library services, tutoring.

Contact Ms. Elizabeth Ann Walker, Outreach Director, Labette Community College, 200 South 14th Street, Parsons, KS 67357. Telephone: 620-820-1221. Fax: 620-421-4481. E-mail: elizabethw@labette.edu.

DEGREES AND AWARDS

AAS Financial Services

COURSE SUBJECT AREAS OFFERED OUTSIDE OF DEGREE PROGRAMS

Undergraduate—allied health diagnostic, intervention, and treatment professions; business/managerial economics; communication and media; computer programming; computer science; computer software and media applications; computer systems networking and telecommunications; criminology; developmental and child psychology; English composition; finance and financial management services; fine and studio art; genetics; geography and cartography; health and physical education/fitness; health/medical preparatory programs; history; human resources management; liberal arts and sciences, general studies and humanities; management information systems; mathematics; mathematics and statistics related; music; physical sciences; political science and government; psychology; sociology; speech and rhetoric.

LACKAWANNA COLLEGE
Scranton, Pennsylvania
Distance Learning Center
http://www.lackawanna.edu

Lackawanna College was founded in 1894. It is accredited by Middle States Association of Colleges and Schools. It first offered distance learning courses in 1994. In fall 2006, there were 0 students enrolled in distance learning courses. Institutionally administered financial aid is available to distance learners.

Services Distance learners have accessibility to academic advising, bookstore, career placement assistance, library services.

Contact Mr. Griffith R. Lewis, Senior Director, MIS, Lackawanna College, 501 Vine Street, Scranton, PA 18509. Telephone: 570-961-7853. Fax: 570-961-7877. E-mail: lewisg@lackawanna.edu.

DEGREES AND AWARDS

Programs offered do not lead to a degree or other formal award.

COURSE SUBJECT AREAS OFFERED OUTSIDE OF DEGREE PROGRAMS

Undergraduate—business administration, management and operations.

LAKELAND COLLEGE
Sheboygan, Wisconsin
Lakeland College Online
http://www.lakeland.edu/online

Lakeland College was founded in 1862. It is accredited by North Central Association of Colleges and Schools. It first offered distance learning courses in 1997. In fall 2006, there were 800 students enrolled in distance learning courses. Institutionally administered financial aid is available to distance learners.

Services Distance learners have accessibility to academic advising, bookstore, campus computer network, e-mail services, library services, tutoring.

Contact Carol Butzen, Academic Counselor, Lakeland College, PO Box 359, Sheboygan, WI 53082-0359. Telephone: 800-569-1293. Fax: 920-565-1341. E-mail: butzencl@lakeland.edu.

DEGREES AND AWARDS

BA Accounting; Business Administration; Computer Science; Criminal Justice; Marketing
MBA Business Administration

COURSE SUBJECT AREAS OFFERED OUTSIDE OF DEGREE PROGRAMS

Undergraduate—accounting and related services; business/commerce; computer science; sales, merchandising, and related marketing operations (general).
Graduate—business administration, management and operations.

LAKE SUPERIOR COLLEGE
Duluth, Minnesota
http://www.lsc.mnscu.edu/online/

Lake Superior College was founded in 1995. It is accredited by North Central Association of Colleges and Schools. It first offered distance learning courses in 1997. In fall 2006, there were 1,800 students enrolled in distance learning courses. Institutionally administered financial aid is available to distance learners.

Services Distance learners have accessibility to academic advising, bookstore, campus computer network, career placement assistance, e-mail services, library services, tutoring.

Contact Melissa Leno, Enrollment Services Specialist, Lake Superior College, 2101 Trinity Road, Duluth, MN 55811. Telephone: 218-733-5903. E-mail: m.leno@lsc.edu.

DEGREES AND AWARDS

AA Liberal Education
AAS Accountant; Paralegal Studies
AS Accountant; Business Administration; Paralegal Studies
Certificate Bookkeeping–Professional Bookkeeper; Hemodialysis Patient Care Technician; Microcomputer Office Specialist

COURSE SUBJECT AREAS OFFERED OUTSIDE OF DEGREE PROGRAMS

Undergraduate—accounting and related services; anthropology; astronomy and astrophysics; biological and physical sciences; business/commerce; business/corporate communications; business operations support and assistant services; communication and media; computer and information sciences; computer software and media applications; economics; English composition; fine and studio art; geography and cartography; geological and earth sciences/geosciences; health/medical preparatory programs; health professions related; history; liberal arts and sciences, general studies and humanities; mathematics; philosophy and religious studies related; physical sciences; political science and government; psychology; sociology; technical and business writing.

LAMAR STATE COLLEGE–PORT ARTHUR
Port Arthur, Texas
Academic Division
http://www.pa.lamar.edu/

Lamar State College–Port Arthur was founded in 1909. It is accredited by Southern Association of Colleges and Schools. It first offered distance learning courses in 1996. In fall 2006, there were 600 students enrolled in distance learning courses. Institutionally administered financial aid is available to distance learners.

Services Distance learners have accessibility to academic advising, campus computer network, e-mail services, library services.

Contact Dr. Charles Gongre, Dean of Academic Programs, Lamar State College–Port Arthur, PO Box 310, Port Arthur, TX 77641. Telephone: 409-984-6229. Fax: 409-984-6000. E-mail: charles.gongre@lamarpa.edu.

DEGREES AND AWARDS

Programs offered do not lead to a degree or other formal award.

COURSE SUBJECT AREAS OFFERED OUTSIDE OF DEGREE PROGRAMS

Undergraduate—astronomy and astrophysics; biblical and other theological languages and literatures; business administration, management and operations; computer and information sciences; computer programming; computer science; computer software and media applications; computer systems networking and telecommunications; data entry/microcomputer applications; economics; English composition; foods, nutrition, and related services; health professions related; mathematics; philosophy; philosophy and religious studies related; psychology.

Non-credit—allied health and medical assisting services; allied health diagnostic, intervention, and treatment professions; alternative and complementary medical support services; alternative and complementary medicine and medical systems; American literature (United States and Canadian); business administration, management and operations; business/commerce; business, management, and marketing related; business/managerial economics; business operations support and assistant services; computer and information sciences; computer/information technology administration and management; computer programming; computer science; computer software and media applications; computer systems analysis; computer systems networking and telecommunications; creative writing; data entry/microcomputer applications; data processing; entrepreneurial and small business operations; finance and financial management services; health aides/attendants/orderlies; human resources management; information science/studies; management information systems; marketing; public relations, advertising, and applied communication related; sales, merchandising, and related marketing operations (general); sales, merchandising, and related marketing operations (specialized); technical and business writing.

LANSING COMMUNITY COLLEGE
Lansing, Michigan
Virtual College
http://www.lcc.edu/online/

Lansing Community College was founded in 1957. It is accredited by North Central Association of Colleges and Schools. It first offered distance learning courses in 1979. In fall 2006, there were 3,029 students enrolled in distance learning courses. Institutionally administered financial aid is available to distance learners.

Services Distance learners have accessibility to academic advising, bookstore, campus computer network, e-mail services, library services, tutoring.

Contact Ms. Michelle Detering, Learning Support Coordinator–Help Services, Lansing Community College, 9000 Strategic Learning Partnerships Division, PO Box 40010, Lansing, MI 48901-7210. Telephone: 517-483-5324. Fax: 517-483-1758. E-mail: deterim@lcc.edu.

DEGREES AND AWARDS

AD Business; Computer Database Specialist; Computer Programmer/Analyst; Criminal Justice, Law Enforcement; E-Business; General Studies; International Business

Certificate of Achievement Computer Database Specialist–Certificate of Achievement; E-Business; Internet for Business–Certificate of Achievement

Certificate of Completion Computer Programmer/Analyst; Correctional Officer; Information Technology Basics; Internet for Business–Certificate of Completion; Microsoft Office Specialist Certification Preparation

COURSE SUBJECT AREAS OFFERED OUTSIDE OF DEGREE PROGRAMS

Undergraduate—accounting and related services; architecture; astronomy and astrophysics; biology; chemistry; computer and information sciences; computer programming; creative writing; design and applied arts; English composition; geography and cartography; history; languages (Romance languages); legal studies (non-professional general, undergraduate); linguistic, comparative, and related language studies; mathematics; mathematics and statistics related; music; natural resources

conservation and research; psychology; sales, merchandising, and related marketing operations (general); social psychology; sociology; speech and rhetoric.

LAURENTIAN UNIVERSITY
Sudbury, Ontario, Canada
Centre for Continuing Education
http://cce.laurentian.ca

Laurentian University was founded in 1960. It is provincially chartered. It first offered distance learning courses in 1972. In fall 2006, there were 8,000 students enrolled in distance learning courses. Institutionally administered financial aid is available to distance learners.

Services Distance learners have accessibility to academic advising, bookstore, campus computer network, career placement assistance, e-mail services, library services, tutoring.

Contact Ms. Ruby Gervais, Senior Program Manager/Academic Advisor, Laurentian University, 935 Ramsey Lake Road, Sudbury, ON P3E 2C6, Canada. Telephone: 705-675-1151 Ext. 3942. Fax: 705-675-4897. E-mail: rgervais@laurentian.ca.

DEGREES AND AWARDS

BA Folklore et Ethnologie de l'amerique Francaise; Gerontology; History (in development); Law and Justice; Native Studies (Honours); Native Studies; Psychologie; Psychology; Religious Studies; Sciences Religieuses; Sociology; Women's Studies; Études franþaises (en développement)

BS Liberal Science

BSN Nursing–BSN for Registered Nurses

BSW Service Social (en franþais); Social Work–Native Human Services

Certificate Family Life Studies and Human Sexuality; Folklore et Ethnologie de l'amerique Francaise; Gerontology; Law and Justice; Women's Studies

LAWRENCE TECHNOLOGICAL UNIVERSITY
Southfield, Michigan
http://www.ltu.edu/

Lawrence Technological University was founded in 1932. It is accredited by North Central Association of Colleges and Schools. It first offered distance learning courses in 1998. In fall 2006, there were 394 students enrolled in distance learning courses. Institutionally administered financial aid is available to distance learners.

Services Distance learners have accessibility to academic advising, campus computer network, career placement assistance, e-mail services, library services, tutoring.

Contact Dr. Pam Lowry, Director of Veraldi Instructional Tech Resource Center, Lawrence Technological University, 21000 West Ten Mile Road, Southfield, MI 48075. Telephone: 248-204-3653. Fax: 248-204-3755. E-mail: lowry@ltu.edu.

DEGREES AND AWARDS

Programs offered do not lead to a degree or other formal award.

COURSE SUBJECT AREAS OFFERED OUTSIDE OF DEGREE PROGRAMS

Undergraduate—architecture related; business administration, management and operations; chemistry; civil engineering technology; computer/information technology administration and management; computer systems analysis; engineering; marketing.

Graduate—business administration, management and operations; cell biology and anatomical sciences; education (specific levels and methods); engineering; geological and earth sciences/geosciences; human resources management; information science/studies; international business; management information systems; marketing.

LEHIGH CARBON COMMUNITY COLLEGE
Schnecksville, Pennsylvania
Office of Distance Learning
http://www.lccc.edu/distancelearning.html

Lehigh Carbon Community College was founded in 1967. It is accredited by Middle States Association of Colleges and Schools. It first offered distance learning courses in 1995. In fall 2006, there were 2,600 students enrolled in distance learning courses. Institutionally administered financial aid is available to distance learners.

Services Distance learners have accessibility to academic advising, bookstore, e-mail services, library services, tutoring.

Contact Beverly J. Benfer, Director of Distance Learning and Instructional Technology, Lehigh Carbon Community College, 4750 Orchard Road, Schnecksville, PA 18078. Telephone: 610-799-1591. Fax: 610-799-1159. E-mail: bbenfer@lccc.edu.

DEGREES AND AWARDS

AA Business Administration; Education; Liberal Arts
AAS Business Management; Early Childhood Education
Certification Business Management
Specialized diploma Business Management; Early Childhood Education; Health Care Coding

COURSE SUBJECT AREAS OFFERED OUTSIDE OF DEGREE PROGRAMS

Undergraduate—accounting and related services; American literature (United States and Canadian); astronomy and astrophysics; biology; business administration, management and operations; business, management, and marketing related; business operations support and assistant services; computer and information sciences; computer science; criminal justice and corrections; curriculum and instruction; developmental and child psychology; economics; education; educational administration and supervision; educational psychology; education related; education (specific levels and methods); education (specific subject areas); English; English as a second/foreign language (teaching); English composition; English language and literature related; English literature (British and Commonwealth); finance and financial management services; geography and cartography; health and medical administrative services; health and physical education/fitness; health professions related; history; human development, family studies, and related services; human resources management; industrial and organizational psychology; liberal arts and sciences, general studies and humanities; marketing; mathematics; mathematics and statistics related; multi-/interdisciplinary studies related; music; philosophy; physics; political science and government; psychology; psychology related; school psychology; social sciences; social sciences related; sociology; special education; speech and rhetoric; statistics; technical and business writing.

LEHIGH UNIVERSITY
Bethlehem, Pennsylvania
Office of Distance Learning
http://www.distance.lehigh.edu

Lehigh University was founded in 1865. It is accredited by Middle States Association of Colleges and Schools. It first offered distance learning courses in 1992. In fall 2006, there were 700 students enrolled in distance learning courses. Institutionally administered financial aid is available to distance learners.

Services Distance learners have accessibility to academic advising, bookstore, campus computer network, career placement assistance, e-mail services, library services, tutoring.

Contact Lisa Moughan, Marketing Coordinator, Lehigh University, 436 Brodhead Avenue, Bethlehem, PA 18015. Telephone: 610-758-4372. Fax: 610-758-4190. E-mail: lim2@lehigh.edu.

DEGREES AND AWARDS

Certificate Project Management; Supply Chain Management
Graduate Certificate Regulatory Affairs
MBA Business Administration
ME Chemical Engineering; Polymer Science and Engineering
MME Mechanical Engineering (MS or MEng)

MS Chemistry; Manufacturing Systems Engineering; Molecular Biology; Polymer Science and Engineering; Quality Engineering
MSIS Information and Systems Engineering (MS or MEng)

COURSE SUBJECT AREAS OFFERED OUTSIDE OF DEGREE PROGRAMS

Graduate—biological and physical sciences; business administration, management and operations; cell biology and anatomical sciences; chemical engineering; chemistry; polymer/plastics engineering.
Non-credit—business administration, management and operations; business/corporate communications; chemical engineering; chemistry; engineering/industrial management; polymer/plastics engineering.

LESLEY UNIVERSITY
Cambridge, Massachusetts
http://www.lesley.edu/online_learning/tie/index.html

Lesley University was founded in 1909. It is accredited by New England Association of Schools and Colleges. It first offered distance learning courses in 1996. In fall 2006, there were 450 students enrolled in distance learning courses. Institutionally administered financial aid is available to distance learners.

Services Distance learners have accessibility to academic advising, bookstore, campus computer network, career placement assistance, e-mail services, library services, tutoring.

Contact Ms. Sara Violante, Associate Director of Online Student Recruitment and Admissions, Lesley University, National Programs, 29 Everett Street, Cambridge, MA 02138. Telephone: 617-349-8301. Fax: 617-349-8391. E-mail: online@lesley.edu.

DEGREES AND AWARDS

MEd Mathematics Education (K-8); Science in Education; Technology in Education
MS Ecological Teaching and Learning
PhD Educational Studies, Adult Learning specialization

COURSE SUBJECT AREAS OFFERED OUTSIDE OF DEGREE PROGRAMS

Graduate—curriculum and instruction; education; educational administration and supervision; educational/instructional media design; education related; education (specific levels and methods); education (specific subject areas); mathematics; special education.

See full description on page 378.

LETOURNEAU UNIVERSITY
Longview, Texas
Graduate and Adult Continuing Studies
http://www.letu.edu/

LeTourneau University was founded in 1946. It is accredited by Southern Association of Colleges and Schools. It first offered distance learning courses in 1999. In fall 2006, there were 1,162 students enrolled in distance learning courses. Institutionally administered financial aid is available to distance learners.

Services Distance learners have accessibility to academic advising, bookstore, campus computer network, career placement assistance, e-mail services, library services, tutoring.

Contact Chris Fonatine, Assistant Vice President for Enrollment Management and Market Research, LeTourneau University, PO Box 7668, Longview, TX 75607-7668. Telephone: 903-233-3250 Ext. 3254. Fax: 903-233-3227. E-mail: chrisfontaine@letu.edu.

DEGREES AND AWARDS

BBA Business Administration–Accelerated Online Bachelors of Business Administration
MBA Business Administration; Educational Leadership

COURSE SUBJECT AREAS OFFERED OUTSIDE OF DEGREE PROGRAMS

Undergraduate—biblical studies; biology; communication and media; computer science; education; English; English composition; history; psychology.

Graduate—business, management, and marketing related; educational administration and supervision.

LEWIS AND CLARK COMMUNITY COLLEGE
Godfrey, Illinois
http://www.lc.edu

Lewis and Clark Community College was founded in 1970. It is accredited by North Central Association of Colleges and Schools. It first offered distance learning courses in 1980. In fall 2006, there were 2,800 students enrolled in distance learning courses. Institutionally administered financial aid is available to distance learners.

Services Distance learners have accessibility to academic advising, bookstore, career placement assistance, e-mail services, library services, tutoring.

Contact Mrs. Mary C. Hales, Dean of Business, Continuing Education, and Workforce Development, Lewis and Clark Community College, 5800 Godfrey Road, Godfrey, IL 62035. Telephone: 618-468-4900. Fax: 618-468-7171. E-mail: mhales@lc.edu.

DEGREES AND AWARDS
Certificate of Completion Case Management for Aging Clients

COURSE SUBJECT AREAS OFFERED OUTSIDE OF DEGREE PROGRAMS
Undergraduate—accounting and related services; astronomy and astrophysics; biological and biomedical sciences related; biology; business administration, management and operations; business/managerial economics; business operations support and assistant services; communication and media; computer and information sciences; criminal justice and corrections; criminology; data entry/microcomputer applications; data processing; developmental and child psychology; economics; fine and studio art; history; marketing; mathematics; music; psychology; speech and rhetoric; teaching assistants/aides.

Non-credit—business/commerce; computer software and media applications; crafts, folk art and artisanry; creative writing; curriculum and instruction; finance and financial management services; health professions related; human services.

LEWIS-CLARK STATE COLLEGE
Lewiston, Idaho
Center for Individualized Programs
http://www.lcsc.edu/dl

Lewis-Clark State College was founded in 1893. It is accredited by Northwest Commission on Colleges and Universities. It first offered distance learning courses in 1995. In fall 2006, there were 1,020 students enrolled in distance learning courses. Institutionally administered financial aid is available to distance learners.

Services Distance learners have accessibility to academic advising, bookstore, campus computer network, career placement assistance, e-mail services, library services.

Contact Ms. Kristy A. Roberts, Director, Distance Learning, Lewis-Clark State College, 500 Eighth Avenue, Lewiston, ID 83501. Telephone: 208-792-2239. Fax: 208-792-2444. E-mail: kroberts@lcsc.edu.

DEGREES AND AWARDS
Programs offered do not lead to a degree or other formal award.

COURSE SUBJECT AREAS OFFERED OUTSIDE OF DEGREE PROGRAMS
Undergraduate—accounting and computer science; business administration, management and operations; business operations support and assistant services; communication and media; computer and information sciences; economics; education; English composition; history; human development, family studies, and related services; liberal arts and sciences, general studies and humanities; management information systems; mathematics and statistics related; natural sciences; nursing; philosophy; political science and government; psychology; social sciences.

LIBERTY UNIVERSITY
Lynchburg, Virginia
Distance Learning Program
http://www.liberty.edu

Liberty University was founded in 1971. It is accredited by Southern Association of Colleges and Schools. It first offered distance learning courses in 1985. In fall 2006, there were 18,000 students enrolled in distance learning courses. Institutionally administered financial aid is available to distance learners.

Services Distance learners have accessibility to academic advising, bookstore, campus computer network, career placement assistance, e-mail services, library services, tutoring.

Contact Mrs. Wendy Morales, Director of Admissions, Liberty University, 1971 University Boulevard, Lynchburg, VA 24502-2269. Telephone: 800-424-9595. Fax: 800-628-7977. E-mail: dlpadmissions@liberty.edu.

DEGREES AND AWARDS
AA Accounting; Business; Criminal Justice; General Studies; Management Information Systems; Psychology; Religion
BS Accounting; Business; Criminal Justice; Management Information Systems; Multidisciplinary Studies–Education concentration; Multidisciplinary Studies; Psychology; Religion
BSN Nursing–RN to BSN
MA Christian Leadership; Evangelism and Church Planting; Human Services; Marriage and Family Therapy; Pastoral Counseling; Professional Counseling; Theological Studies; Worship Studies
MAR Religion
MBA Business Administration
MDiv Divinity
MEd Education
MS Accounting
MSM Management
MSN Nursing
DMin Ministry
EdD Education
PhD Counseling

COURSE SUBJECT AREAS OFFERED OUTSIDE OF DEGREE PROGRAMS
Undergraduate—accounting and related services; biblical and other theological languages and literatures; biblical studies; biology; business/commerce; business/corporate communications; business, management, and marketing related; business/managerial economics; clinical child psychology; communication and media; computer/information technology administration and management; criminal justice and corrections; developmental and child psychology; economics; education; educational psychology; English composition; gerontology; history; marketing; philosophy; psychology; religious studies; social psychology; social sciences; taxation; theology and religious vocations related.
Graduate—accounting and related services; biblical studies; business administration, management and operations; business, management, and marketing related; counseling psychology; curriculum and instruction; educational administration and supervision; educational assessment, evaluation, and research; educational/instructional media design; educational psychology; education related; education (specific levels and methods); education (specific subject areas); English; family and consumer sciences/human sciences; psychology; religious studies; school psychology; special education; theological and ministerial studies; theology and religious vocations related.

LIFE PACIFIC COLLEGE
San Dimas, California
School of Distance Learning
http://www.lifepacific.edu/distance

Life Pacific College was founded in 1923. It is accredited by Association for Biblical Higher Education. It first offered distance learning courses in 1941. In fall 2006, there were 400 students enrolled in distance learning courses. Institutionally administered financial aid is available to distance learners.

Services Distance learners have accessibility to academic advising, bookstore, career placement assistance, library services.

Contact Brian Tomhave, Director, Life Pacific College, 1100 West Covina Boulevard, San Dimas, CA 91773. Telephone: 877-851-0900. Fax: 909-706-3099. E-mail: distance@lifepacific.edu.

DEGREES AND AWARDS

AA Biblical Studies
BA Ministry and Leadership degree completion program

COURSE SUBJECT AREAS OFFERED OUTSIDE OF DEGREE PROGRAMS

Undergraduate—biblical studies; philosophy and religious studies related; theological and ministerial studies.
Non-credit—biblical and other theological languages and literatures; biblical studies; religious studies.

LIMESTONE COLLEGE
Gaffney, South Carolina
The Block Program
http://www.limestonevirtualcampus.net
Limestone College was founded in 1845. It is accredited by Southern Association of Colleges and Schools. It first offered distance learning courses in 1997. In fall 2006, there were 1,590 students enrolled in distance learning courses. Institutionally administered financial aid is available to distance learners.
Services Distance learners have accessibility to academic advising, bookstore, campus computer network, career placement assistance, e-mail services, library services.
Contact Mrs. Iuliana Watson, Internet Academic Advisor/WebCT Trainer, Limestone College, Extended Campus, 1115 College Drive, Gaffney, SC 29340-3799. Telephone: 864-488-4539. Fax: 864-488-4595. E-mail: iwatson@limestone.edu.

DEGREES AND AWARDS

AA Business Administration; Computer Science Internet Management; Computer Science Management Information Systems; Computer Science Programming; Liberal Studies
BA Criminal Justice; Human Resource Development; Liberal Studies; Psychology
BS Business Administration–Accounting; Business Administration–Computer Programming; Business Administration–Computer Software Applications; Business Administration–General Business; Business Administration–Management; Computer Science Information Technology; Computer Science Internet Management–Database; Computer Science Internet Management–E-commerce; Computer Science Internet Management–Operations Management; Computer Science Internet Management–Web Development; Computer Science Internet Management, general; Computer Science Programming; Computer Science, Computer and Information Systems Security; Liberal Studies

COURSE SUBJECT AREAS OFFERED OUTSIDE OF DEGREE PROGRAMS

Undergraduate—accounting and related services; American literature (United States and Canadian); astronomy and astrophysics; biblical studies; biology; business administration, management and operations; business/commerce; business/corporate communications; comparative literature; computer and information sciences; computer and information sciences and support services related; computer/information technology administration and management; computer programming; computer science; computer software and media applications; computer systems analysis; computer systems networking and telecommunications; creative writing; criminal justice and corrections; data entry/microcomputer applications; data processing; dramatic/theater arts and stagecraft; economics; education (specific levels and methods); English; English composition; English language and literature related; finance and financial management services; geography and cartography; gerontology; history; human resources management; human services; information science/studies; international business; legal studies (non-professional general, undergraduate); management information systems; management sciences and quantitative methods; marketing; mathematics; music; philosophy; political science and government; psychology; psychology related; reli-gious studies; sales, merchandising, and related marketing operations (general); social psychology; social work; sociology; statistics; technical and business writing.

LINCOLN CHRISTIAN COLLEGE
Lincoln, Illinois
Distance Learning
http://www.lccs.edu
Lincoln Christian College was founded in 1944. It is accredited by Association for Biblical Higher Education. It first offered distance learning courses in 1993. In fall 2006, there were 350 students enrolled in distance learning courses. Institutionally administered financial aid is available to distance learners.
Services Distance learners have accessibility to academic advising, bookstore, campus computer network, e-mail services, library services.
Contact Admissions, Lincoln Christian College, 100 Campus View Drive, Lincoln, IL 62656. Telephone: 217-732-3168 Ext. 2315. E-mail: coladmis@lccs.edu.

DEGREES AND AWARDS
Programs offered do not lead to a degree or other formal award.

COURSE SUBJECT AREAS OFFERED OUTSIDE OF DEGREE PROGRAMS

Undergraduate—biblical and other theological languages and literatures; biblical studies; education (specific levels and methods); English as a second/foreign language (teaching); languages (Middle/Near Eastern and Semitic); religious studies; theological and ministerial studies; theology and religious vocations related.
Graduate—biblical and other theological languages and literatures; biblical studies; English as a second/foreign language (teaching); languages (Middle/Near Eastern and Semitic); religious studies; theological and ministerial studies.
Non-credit—biblical and other theological languages and literatures; biblical studies; education (specific levels and methods); languages (Middle/Near Eastern and Semitic); religious studies; theological and ministerial studies.

LINN-BENTON COMMUNITY COLLEGE
Albany, Oregon
Media Services
http://www.linnbenton.edu
Linn-Benton Community College was founded in 1966. It is accredited by Northwest Commission on Colleges and Universities. It first offered distance learning courses in 1979. In fall 2006, there were 706 students enrolled in distance learning courses. Institutionally administered financial aid is available to distance learners.
Services Distance learners have accessibility to academic advising, bookstore, career placement assistance, e-mail services, library services.
Contact Christine Baker, Outreach Coordinator, Linn-Benton Community College, Admissions and Records, 6500 Pacific Boulevard SW, Albany, OR 97321. Telephone: 541-917-4811. Fax: 541-917-4868. E-mail: admissions@linnbenton.edu.

DEGREES AND AWARDS
Programs offered do not lead to a degree or other formal award.

COURSE SUBJECT AREAS OFFERED OUTSIDE OF DEGREE PROGRAMS

Undergraduate—American literature (United States and Canadian); applied mathematics; business administration, management and operations; business/commerce; business/managerial economics; computer software and media applications; creative writing; criminal justice and corrections; economics; English; health and medical administrative services; health and physical education/fitness; human development, family studies, and related services; journalism; liberal arts and sciences, general studies and humanities; mathematics; public relations, advertising, and applied communication related; technical and business writing.

Non-credit—English as a second language; mathematics; personal and culinary services related.

LIPSCOMB UNIVERSITY
Nashville, Tennessee
http://www.lipscomb.edu/

Lipscomb University was founded in 1891. It is accredited by Southern Association of Colleges and Schools. It first offered distance learning courses in 1999. In fall 2006, there were 80 students enrolled in distance learning courses. Institutionally administered financial aid is available to distance learners.

Services Distance learners have accessibility to bookstore, campus computer network, career placement assistance, e-mail services, library services.

Contact Mr. Al Austelle, Director of the Center for Instructional Technology, Lipscomb University, 3901 Granny White Pike, Nashville, TN 37204-3951. Telephone: 615-966-5703. Fax: 615-966-6559. E-mail: al.austelle@lipscomb.edu.

DEGREES AND AWARDS
Programs offered do not lead to a degree or other formal award.

COURSE SUBJECT AREAS OFFERED OUTSIDE OF DEGREE PROGRAMS
Undergraduate—biblical studies; English.
Graduate—biblical studies; business administration, management and operations.

LOCK HAVEN UNIVERSITY OF PENNSYLVANIA
Lock Haven, Pennsylvania
http://www.lhup.edu/cde

Lock Haven University of Pennsylvania was founded in 1870. It is accredited by Middle States Association of Colleges and Schools. It first offered distance learning courses in 1995. In fall 2006, there were 491 students enrolled in distance learning courses. Institutionally administered financial aid is available to distance learners.

Services Distance learners have accessibility to academic advising, bookstore, campus computer network, e-mail services, library services.
Contact Dr. Ellen P. O'Hara-Mays, Executive Director of eCampus, Lock Haven University of Pennsylvania, Court House Annex 311, Lock Haven, PA 17745. Telephone: 570-484-2072. Fax: 570-484-2638. E-mail: poharama@lhup.edu.

DEGREES AND AWARDS
AA Criminal Justice
AS Nursing; Surgical Technology
MEd Alternative Education; Teaching and Learning
MHS Physician Assistant
MLA Liberal Arts

COURSE SUBJECT AREAS OFFERED OUTSIDE OF DEGREE PROGRAMS
Undergraduate—applied mathematics; bioethics/medical ethics; comparative literature; computer programming; criminology; English composition; fine and studio art; history; music; sociology.
Graduate—education; health professions related; liberal arts and sciences, general studies and humanities.
Non-credit—allied health and medical assisting services; business/commerce; computer and information sciences and support services related; construction trades; education; legal professions and studies related.

See full description on page 380.

LONG BEACH CITY COLLEGE
Long Beach, California
http://de.lbcc.edu

Long Beach City College was founded in 1927. It is accredited by Western Association of Schools and Colleges. It first offered distance learning courses in 1980. In fall 2006, there were 3,485 students enrolled in distance learning courses. Institutionally administered financial aid is available to distance learners.
Services Distance learners have accessibility to academic advising, bookstore, career placement assistance, library services, tutoring.

Contact Ms. Wendi Lopez, Distance Learning Program Specialist, Long Beach City College, 4901 East Carson Street, Long Beach, CA 90808. Telephone: 562-938-4025. Fax: 562-938-4814. E-mail: wlopez@lbcc.edu.

DEGREES AND AWARDS
Programs offered do not lead to a degree or other formal award.

COURSE SUBJECT AREAS OFFERED OUTSIDE OF DEGREE PROGRAMS
Undergraduate—accounting and related services; anthropology; astronomy and astrophysics; biology; business administration, management and operations; computer and information sciences; computer programming; computer science; computer software and media applications; computer systems networking and telecommunications; creative writing; economics; English; English composition; film/video and photographic arts; foods, nutrition, and related services; geography and cartography; history; human development, family studies, and related services; international business; liberal arts and sciences, general studies and humanities; library science; marketing; mathematics; mathematics and statistics related; music; nursing; pharmacy, pharmaceutical sciences, and administration; philosophy; political science and government; psychology; radio, television, and digital communication; real estate; social psychology; social sciences; sociology; statistics.

LONGWOOD UNIVERSITY
Farmville, Virginia
http://www.lwc.edu/

Longwood University was founded in 1839. It is accredited by Southern Association of Colleges and Schools. It first offered distance learning courses in 2004. In fall 2006, there were 300 students enrolled in distance learning courses. Institutionally administered financial aid is available to distance learners.
Services Distance learners have accessibility to academic advising, bookstore, campus computer network, e-mail services, library services, tutoring.
Contact Ms. Charlene Gaines Cook, Administrative Assistant, Longwood University, 201 High Street, Farmville, VA 23909. Telephone: 434-395-2904. Fax: 434-395-2750. E-mail: slponline@longwood.edu.

DEGREES AND AWARDS
CCCPE Speech-Language Pathology Masters Prerequisite program
MAE Literacy and Culture
MS Communication Sciences and Disorders

COURSE SUBJECT AREAS OFFERED OUTSIDE OF DEGREE PROGRAMS
Undergraduate—American literature (United States and Canadian); business, management, and marketing related; communication and media; communication disorders sciences and services; curriculum and instruction; education; English literature (British and Commonwealth); health and physical education/fitness; history; languages (foreign languages related); liberal arts and sciences, general studies and humanities; management information systems; mathematics; music; psychology; social and philosophical foundations of education; sociology; technical and business writing.

Graduate—communication disorders sciences and services; criminal justice and corrections; education; educational administration and supervision; education (specific levels and methods); English as a second/foreign language (teaching); English literature (British and Commonwealth).

Non-credit—allied health and medical assisting services; business administration, management and operations; business/corporate communications; computer programming; construction trades related; education; English composition; family and consumer economics; health professions related; human resources management; languages (foreign languages related); quality control and safety technologies; technical and business writing.

LOS ANGELES HARBOR COLLEGE
Wilmington, California
Distance Education Programs
http://www.lahc.cc.ca.us/acad.htm#onlinecourses
Los Angeles Harbor College was founded in 1949. It is accredited by Western Association of Schools and Colleges. It first offered distance learning courses in 1996. In fall 2006, there were 1,200 students enrolled in distance learning courses. Institutionally administered financial aid is available to distance learners.
Services Distance learners have accessibility to bookstore, campus computer network, e-mail services, library services.
Contact Dr. Robert Richards, Associate Dean, Research and Planning, Los Angeles Harbor College, 1111 Figueroa Place, Wilmington, CA 90744. Telephone: 310-233-4044. Fax: 310-233-4661. E-mail: richarr@lahc.edu.

DEGREES AND AWARDS
Programs offered do not lead to a degree or other formal award.

COURSE SUBJECT AREAS OFFERED OUTSIDE OF DEGREE PROGRAMS
Undergraduate—accounting and related services; business/commerce; computer and information sciences; computer programming; criminal justice and corrections; criminology; economics; English; English composition; English language and literature related; nursing; political science and government; psychology; sociology.

LOUISIANA STATE UNIVERSITY AND AGRICULTURAL AND MECHANICAL COLLEGE
Baton Rouge, Louisiana
Independent Study
http://www.is.lsu.edu
Louisiana State University and Agricultural and Mechanical College was founded in 1860. It is accredited by Southern Association of Colleges and Schools. It first offered distance learning courses in 1941. In fall 2006, there were 9,000 students enrolled in distance learning courses. Institutionally administered financial aid is available to distance learners.
Services Distance learners have accessibility to bookstore, e-mail services, library services.
Contact Student Services Coordinator, Louisiana State University and Agricultural and Mechanical College, Office of Independent Study, 1225 Pleasant Hall, Baton Rouge, LA 70803. Telephone: 800-234-5046. Fax: 225-578-3090. E-mail: iservices@doce.lsu.edu.

DEGREES AND AWARDS
Programs offered do not lead to a degree or other formal award.

COURSE SUBJECT AREAS OFFERED OUTSIDE OF DEGREE PROGRAMS
Undergraduate—accounting and related services; anthropology; biology; business administration, management and operations; cell biology and anatomical sciences; communication and media; community health services; comparative literature; criminology; curriculum and instruction; developmental and child psychology; dramatic/theater arts and stagecraft; ecology, evolution, and population biology; economics; educational assessment, evaluation, and research; educational psychology; education (specific levels and methods); English; English composition; English language and literature related; English literature (British and Commonwealth); ethnic, cultural minority, and gender studies; finance and financial management services; fine and studio art; geography and cartography; geological and earth sciences/geosciences; health and physical education/fitness; history; journalism; languages (classics and classical); languages (Germanic); languages (Romance languages); legal studies (non-professional general, undergraduate); library science related; linguistic, comparative, and related language studies; management information systems; management sciences and quantitative methods; marketing; mathematics; mathematics and statistics related; mechanical engineering; military studies; music; philosophy; philosophy and religious studies related; physical sciences; physics; physiology, pathology and related sciences; political science and government; psychology;

psychology related; school psychology; social sciences; social sciences related; sociology; speech and rhetoric; statistics; technical and business writing.
Graduate—human services.
Non-credit—biology; English composition; mathematics.

LOUISIANA TECH UNIVERSITY
Ruston, Louisiana
Center for Instructional Technology and Distance Learning
http://www.latech.edu/citdl
Louisiana Tech University was founded in 1894. It is accredited by Southern Association of Colleges and Schools. It first offered distance learning courses in 1998. In fall 2006, there were 816 students enrolled in distance learning courses. Institutionally administered financial aid is available to distance learners.
Services Distance learners have accessibility to academic advising, bookstore, campus computer network, e-mail services, library services.
Contact Mr. David R. Cargill, Director of Center for Instructional Technology and Distance Learning, Louisiana Tech University, PO Box 10167, 100 Railroad Avenue, PML 1014, Ruston, LA 71272. Telephone: 318-257-2912. Fax: 318-257-2731. E-mail: david@latech.edu.

DEGREES AND AWARDS
MHSA Health Information–Master of Health Information (MHIM); Health Information–Master of Health Information (MHIM)

COURSE SUBJECT AREAS OFFERED OUTSIDE OF DEGREE PROGRAMS
Undergraduate—architecture; biological and biomedical sciences related; economics; educational administration and supervision; forestry; health professions related; journalism; mathematics; political science and government; technical and business writing.
Graduate—biomedical/medical engineering; educational administration and supervision; English; foods, nutrition, and related services; history; human development, family studies, and related services.

LURLEEN B. WALLACE COMMUNITY COLLEGE
Andalusia, Alabama
Lurleen B. Wallace Community College was founded in 1969. It is accredited by Southern Association of Colleges and Schools. It first offered distance learning courses in 2001. In fall 2006, there were 150 students enrolled in distance learning courses. Institutionally administered financial aid is available to distance learners.
Services Distance learners have accessibility to academic advising, bookstore, campus computer network, career placement assistance, library services, tutoring.
Contact Mr. James G. Aplin, Assistant Dean of Instructional and Information Technology, Lurleen B. Wallace Community College, PO Box 1418, Andalusia, AL 36420. Telephone: 334-881-2227. Fax: 334-881-2300. E-mail: jgaplin@lbwcc.edu.

DEGREES AND AWARDS
Programs offered do not lead to a degree or other formal award.

COURSE SUBJECT AREAS OFFERED OUTSIDE OF DEGREE PROGRAMS
Undergraduate—accounting and computer science; biology; business, management, and marketing related; computer software and media applications; economics; English; fine and studio art; history; mathematics; music; physical sciences; psychology; sociology.

LUZERNE COUNTY COMMUNITY COLLEGE
Nanticoke, Pennsylvania
Telecollege
http://www.luzerne.edu/
Luzerne County Community College was founded in 1966. It is accredited by Middle States Association of Colleges and Schools. It first offered distance learning courses in 1981. In fall 2006, there were 900 students enrolled in distance learning courses. Institutionally administered financial aid is available to distance learners.
Services Distance learners have accessibility to bookstore, career placement assistance, e-mail services, library services.

Contact Mr. Barry E. Cipala, Director of the Distance Learning Center, Luzerne County Community College, 1333 South Prospect Street, Nanticoke, PA 18634. Telephone: 570-740-0559 Ext. 559. Fax: 570-740-0295. E-mail: bcipala@luzerne.edu.

DEGREES AND AWARDS
AS General Studies

COURSE SUBJECT AREAS OFFERED OUTSIDE OF DEGREE PROGRAMS
Undergraduate—accounting and related services; business/commerce; computer software and media applications.

LYNN UNIVERSITY
Boca Raton, Florida
The Institute for Distance Learning
http://www.lynn.edu/distancelearning
Lynn University was founded in 1962. It is accredited by Southern Association of Colleges and Schools. It first offered distance learning courses in 1998. In fall 2006, there were 1,000 students enrolled in distance learning courses. Institutionally administered financial aid is available to distance learners.
Services Distance learners have accessibility to academic advising, bookstore, campus computer network, career placement assistance, e-mail services, library services, tutoring.
Contact Dr. Larissa Baia, Director of Admissions, Lynn University, 3601 North Military Trail, Boca Raton, FL 33431. Telephone: 561-237-7916. Fax: 561-237-7100. E-mail: lbaia@lynn.edu.

DEGREES AND AWARDS
BS Business Administration; Criminal Justice; Psychology
Graduate Certificate Emergency Planning and Administration; Emergency and Disaster Management
MBA Aviation Management; Financial Valuation and Investment Management; Hospitality Management; International Business; Marketing; Mass Communication and Media Management; Sports and Athletics Administration
MEd Educational Leadership, Higher Education Administration specialization; Educational Leadership, School Administration specialization; Educational Leadership, School Administration with ESOL endorsement specialization
MS Criminal Justice Administration; Emergency Planning and Administration
PhD Global Leadership, Corporate and Organizational Management specialization
See full description on page 382.

MADISON AREA TECHNICAL COLLEGE
Madison, Wisconsin
Instructional Media/Distance Education Department
http://www.matcmadison.edu
Madison Area Technical College was founded in 1911. It is accredited by North Central Association of Colleges and Schools. It first offered distance learning courses in 1994. In fall 2006, there were 6,700 students enrolled in distance learning courses. Institutionally administered financial aid is available to distance learners.
Services Distance learners have accessibility to bookstore, e-mail services, library services.
Contact Lisa Franklin, Administrative Assistant for Distance Learning, Madison Area Technical College, 3550 Anderson Street, Madison, WI 53704. Telephone: 608-246-6288. Fax: 608-246-6287. E-mail: lfranklin @matcmadison.edu.

DEGREES AND AWARDS
AD Accounting
AS Administrative Assistant
ASM Supervisory Management/Leadership Development
Certificate Quality Management
Diploma Business Software Applications Specialist

Specialized diploma Optometric Technician

COURSE SUBJECT AREAS OFFERED OUTSIDE OF DEGREE PROGRAMS
Undergraduate—business administration, management and operations; business operations support and assistant services; computer and information sciences; computer/information technology administration and management; computer programming; computer software and media applications; computer systems networking and telecommunications; criminal justice and corrections; drafting/design engineering technologies; English composition; human development, family studies, and related services; liberal arts and sciences, general studies and humanities; management information systems; marketing; mathematics and statistics related; ophthalmic and optometric support services and allied professions; parks, recreation and leisure; real estate; sales, merchandising, and related marketing operations (general); sales, merchandising, and related marketing operations (specialized); statistics.

MALONE COLLEGE
Canton, Ohio
Malone College Online Learning
http://www.malone-online.org
Malone College was founded in 1892. It is accredited by North Central Association of Colleges and Schools. It first offered distance learning courses in 1999. In fall 2006, there were 350 students enrolled in distance learning courses. Institutionally administered financial aid is available to distance learners.
Services Distance learners have accessibility to academic advising, bookstore, career placement assistance, e-mail services, library services.
Contact Sharon Purvis, Online Coordinator, Malone College, 515 25th Street NW, Canton, OH 44709. Telephone: 330-471-8423. Fax: 330-471-8570. E-mail: distancelearning@malone.edu.

DEGREES AND AWARDS
BA Business Management

COURSE SUBJECT AREAS OFFERED OUTSIDE OF DEGREE PROGRAMS
Undergraduate—biblical studies; biology; business administration, management and operations; business/commerce; communication and journalism related; communication and media; developmental and child psychology; educational/instructional media design; English composition; English literature (British and Commonwealth); fine and studio art; health and physical education/fitness; history; human development, family studies, and related services; liberal arts and sciences, general studies and humanities; philosophy; political science and government; psychology; social sciences related; sociology.
Graduate—biblical studies; counseling psychology.

MANATEE COMMUNITY COLLEGE
Bradenton, Florida
Distance Education
http://www.mccfl.edu/
Manatee Community College was founded in 1957. It is accredited by Southern Association of Colleges and Schools. It first offered distance learning courses in 1973. In fall 2006, there were 1,100 students enrolled in distance learning courses. Institutionally administered financial aid is available to distance learners.
Services Distance learners have accessibility to bookstore, campus computer network, e-mail services, library services.
Contact Ms. Nancy H. Edwards, Director of Instructional Technology and Distance Learning, Manatee Community College, 5840 26th Street West, Bradenton, FL 34207. Telephone: 941-752-5645. Fax: 941-727-2058. E-mail: edwardn@mccfl.edu.

DEGREES AND AWARDS
Programs offered do not lead to a degree or other formal award.

COURSE SUBJECT AREAS OFFERED OUTSIDE OF DEGREE PROGRAMS

Undergraduate—accounting and related services; American literature (United States and Canadian); anthropology; applied mathematics; biology; business administration, management and operations; business/commerce; business, management, and marketing related; business/managerial economics; computer and information sciences; developmental and child psychology; English composition; history; legal support services; management information systems; marketing; mathematics and statistics related; philosophy and religious studies related; sales, merchandising, and related marketing operations (specialized); sociology.

MANHATTAN SCHOOL OF MUSIC
New York, New York
Manhattan School of Music was founded in 1917. It is accredited by Middle States Association of Colleges and Schools. It first offered distance learning courses in 1996. In fall 2006, there were 1,700 students enrolled in distance learning courses. Institutionally administered financial aid is available to distance learners.
Contact Ms. Jessica Kepler, Program Coordinator, Recording, and Distance Learning Department, Manhattan School of Music, 120 Claremont Avenue, New York, NY 10027. Telephone: 212-749-2802 Ext. 4488. Fax: 212-749-5471. E-mail: jkepler@msmnyc.edu.

DEGREES AND AWARDS
Programs offered do not lead to a degree or other formal award.

COURSE SUBJECT AREAS OFFERED OUTSIDE OF DEGREE PROGRAMS
Undergraduate—education related; music; visual and performing arts.
Graduate—education related; music; visual and performing arts.
Non-credit—music; visual and performing arts.

MANSFIELD UNIVERSITY OF PENNSYLVANIA
Mansfield, Pennsylvania
Center for Lifelong Learning
http://cll.mansfield.edu
Mansfield University of Pennsylvania was founded in 1857. It is accredited by Middle States Association of Colleges and Schools. It first offered distance learning courses in 1995. In fall 2006, there were 276 students enrolled in distance learning courses. Institutionally administered financial aid is available to distance learners.
Services Distance learners have accessibility to academic advising, bookstore, campus computer network, career placement assistance, e-mail services, library services, tutoring.
Contact Brian Barden, Director of Enrollment Management, Mansfield University of Pennsylvania, Alumni Hall, Mansfield, PA 16933. Telephone: 570-662-4813. Fax: 570-662-4121. E-mail: bbarden@mansfield.edu.

DEGREES AND AWARDS
BA Art History
BSN Nursing–RN to BSN
MEd Art Education
MSE Library and Information Technologies–School Library and Information Technologies
MSN Nursing Education

COURSE SUBJECT AREAS OFFERED OUTSIDE OF DEGREE PROGRAMS
Undergraduate—accounting and related services; business administration, management and operations; communication and journalism related; computer and information sciences; criminal justice and corrections; economics; education; English; English language and literature related; history; mathematics; music; nursing; nutrition sciences; psychology; sociology.
Graduate—education; library science; nursing.

MARANATHA BAPTIST BIBLE COLLEGE
Watertown, Wisconsin
http://www.mbbc.edu/
Maranatha Baptist Bible College was founded in 1968. It is accredited by North Central Association of Colleges and Schools. It first offered distance learning courses in 2001. In fall 2006, there were 50 students enrolled in distance learning courses. Institutionally administered financial aid is available to distance learners.
Services Distance learners have accessibility to academic advising, campus computer network, e-mail services.
Contact Mr. Steven D. Carlson, Assistant Registrar, Maranatha Baptist Bible College, 745 West Main Street, Watertown, WI 53094. Telephone: 920-206-2344. Fax: 920-261-9109. E-mail: scarlson@mbbc.edu.

DEGREES AND AWARDS
Programs offered do not lead to a degree or other formal award.

COURSE SUBJECT AREAS OFFERED OUTSIDE OF DEGREE PROGRAMS
Undergraduate—American literature (United States and Canadian); biblical studies; educational/instructional media design.
Graduate—biblical studies; pastoral counseling and specialized ministries; religious studies.

MARIAN COLLEGE OF FOND DU LAC
Fond du Lac, Wisconsin
http://www.mariancollege.edu/
Marian College of Fond du Lac was founded in 1936. It is accredited by North Central Association of Colleges and Schools. It first offered distance learning courses in 2000. In fall 2006, there were 373 students enrolled in distance learning courses. Institutionally administered financial aid is available to distance learners.
Services Distance learners have accessibility to academic advising, bookstore, campus computer network, career placement assistance, e-mail services, library services.
Contact Ms. Cheryl Teichmiller, Registrar, Marian College of Fond du Lac, 45 South National Avenue, Fond du Lac, WI 54935. Telephone: 800-262-7426 Ext. 7618. Fax: 920-926-6708. E-mail: cteichmiller@mariancollege.edu.

DEGREES AND AWARDS
Programs offered do not lead to a degree or other formal award.

COURSE SUBJECT AREAS OFFERED OUTSIDE OF DEGREE PROGRAMS
Undergraduate—business administration, management and operations; criminal justice and corrections; education; history; languages (Germanic); languages (Romance languages); philosophy.
Graduate—education; history.

MARIST COLLEGE
Poughkeepsie, New York
School of Management
http://www.marist.edu/management
Marist College was founded in 1929. It is accredited by Middle States Association of Colleges and Schools. It first offered distance learning courses in 1998. In fall 2006, there were 250 students enrolled in distance learning courses. Institutionally administered financial aid is available to distance learners.
Services Distance learners have accessibility to academic advising, bookstore, campus computer network, career placement assistance, e-mail services, library services.
Contact Ms. Anu Ailawadhi, Director of Graduate Admissions, Marist College, School of Graduate and Continuing Education, Poughkeepsie, NY 12601. Telephone: 845-575-3800. Fax: 845-575-3166. E-mail: anu.ailawadhi@marist.edu.

DEGREES AND AWARDS

MBA Business Administration
MPA Public Administration

COURSE SUBJECT AREAS OFFERED OUTSIDE OF DEGREE PROGRAMS

Undergraduate—accounting and related services; business, management, and marketing related; economics; finance and financial management services; legal studies (non-professional general, undergraduate); statistics.

Graduate—accounting and related services; business administration, management and operations; business, management, and marketing related; business/managerial economics; finance and financial management services; international business; management sciences and quantitative methods; marketing.

MARLBORO COLLEGE
Marlboro, Vermont
Graduate Center
http://www.persons.marlboro.edu/

Marlboro College was founded in 1946. It is accredited by New England Association of Schools and Colleges. It first offered distance learning courses in 1997. In fall 2006, there were 40 students enrolled in distance learning courses. Institutionally administered financial aid is available to distance learners.

Services Distance learners have accessibility to academic advising, career placement assistance, e-mail services, library services, tutoring.

Contact Bethany Catron, Associate Director of Admissions, Marlboro College, 28 Vernon Street, Brattleboro, VT 05301. Telephone: 802-258-9209. Fax: 802-258-9201. E-mail: bcatron@gradcenter.marlboro.edu.

DEGREES AND AWARDS

Programs offered do not lead to a degree or other formal award.

COURSE SUBJECT AREAS OFFERED OUTSIDE OF DEGREE PROGRAMS

Undergraduate—accounting and computer science; business administration, management and operations; business/corporate communications; business, management, and marketing related; computer and information sciences; computer/information technology administration and management; computer programming; computer science; computer software and media applications; computer systems analysis; computer systems networking and telecommunications; entrepreneurial and small business operations; finance and financial management services; information science/studies; management information systems; marketing; technical and business writing.

Graduate—accounting and computer science; business administration, management and operations; business/commerce; business, management, and marketing related; business/managerial economics; business operations support and assistant services; communications technologies and support services related; communications technology; computer and information sciences; computer and information sciences and support services related; computer engineering; computer engineering technologies; computer/information technology administration and management; computer programming; computer science; computer software and media applications; computer systems analysis; computer systems networking and telecommunications; data entry/microcomputer applications; data processing; economics; education; educational administration and supervision; educational assessment, evaluation, and research; educational/instructional media design; education related.

MARSHALL UNIVERSITY
Huntington, West Virginia
Distributed Education Technology
http://www.marshall.edu/muonline

Marshall University was founded in 1837. It is accredited by North Central Association of Colleges and Schools. It first offered distance learning courses in 1986. In fall 2006, there were 5,626 students enrolled in distance learning courses. Institutionally administered financial aid is available to distance learners.

Services Distance learners have accessibility to academic advising, bookstore, campus computer network, e-mail services, library services, tutoring.

Contact Crystal Stewart, Program Specialist, Marshall University, One John Marshall Drive, CB 216, Huntington, WV 25755-2140. Telephone: 304-696-2970. Fax: 304-696-2973. E-mail: stewar14@marshall.edu.

DEGREES AND AWARDS

AGS General Studies
BA Regents Bachelor of Arts degree
Certification Public Library Technology (PLT)
MEd Elementary or Secondary Education

COURSE SUBJECT AREAS OFFERED OUTSIDE OF DEGREE PROGRAMS

Undergraduate—accounting and related services; business administration, management and operations; business/managerial economics; chemistry; communication and journalism related; communication and media; computer and information sciences; computer and information sciences and support services related; computer engineering; developmental and child psychology; economics; English composition; geography and cartography; history; journalism; management information systems; marketing; mathematics; mathematics and computer science; mathematics and statistics related; nursing; philosophy; psychology; social work; sociology; statistics; visual and performing arts.

Graduate—accounting and related services; computer and information sciences; marketing; social work; sociology; technology education/industrial arts; visual and performing arts.

MARYMOUNT UNIVERSITY
Arlington, Virginia
http://www.marymounte.edu

Marymount University was founded in 1950. It is accredited by Southern Association of Colleges and Schools. It first offered distance learning courses in 1999. Institutionally administered financial aid is available to distance learners.

Services Distance learners have accessibility to academic advising, bookstore, campus computer network, career placement assistance, e-mail services, library services, tutoring.

Contact Ms. Francesca Reed, Director, Graduate Admissions, Marymount University, 2807 North Glebe Road, Arlington, VA 22207. Telephone: 703-284-5901. Fax: 703-527-3815. E-mail: francesca.reed@marymount.edu.

DEGREES AND AWARDS

BSN Nursing–RN-BSN; Nursing–RN-BSN
MEd Catholic School Leadership

COURSE SUBJECT AREAS OFFERED OUTSIDE OF DEGREE PROGRAMS

Undergraduate—nursing.
Graduate—business administration, management and operations; business/commerce; business, management, and marketing related; computer science; education; information science/studies.

MARYVILLE UNIVERSITY OF SAINT LOUIS
St. Louis, Missouri
http://www.maryville.edu/

Maryville University of Saint Louis was founded in 1872. It is accredited by North Central Association of Colleges and Schools. It first offered distance learning courses in 2000. In fall 2006, there were 300 students enrolled in distance learning courses. Institutionally administered financial aid is available to distance learners.

Services Distance learners have accessibility to bookstore, campus computer network, e-mail services.

Contact Ms. Chris Bretz, Coordinator, CEDL, Maryville University of Saint Louis, 650 Maryville University Drive, St. Louis, MO 63141. Telephone: 314-529-9488. Fax: 314-529-9908. E-mail: cbretz@ maryville.edu.

DEGREES AND AWARDS
Programs offered do not lead to a degree or other formal award.

COURSE SUBJECT AREAS OFFERED OUTSIDE OF DEGREE PROGRAMS
Undergraduate—accounting and computer science; data processing; information science/studies.

Non-credit—accounting and related services; business administration, management and operations; business/corporate communications; communications technology; computer and information sciences; computer software and media applications; computer systems analysis; computer systems networking and telecommunications; creative writing; data entry/microcomputer applications; data processing; entrepreneurial and small business operations; human development, family studies, and related services; human resources management; information science/studies; journalism; management information systems; marketing; public relations, advertising, and applied communication related; publishing.

MASSASOIT COMMUNITY COLLEGE
Brockton, Massachusetts
http://www.massasoit.mass.edu/acad_depts/dist_learn/dist_learn.htm

Massasoit Community College was founded in 1966. It is accredited by New England Association of Schools and Colleges. It first offered distance learning courses in 1998. In fall 2006, there were 485 students enrolled in distance learning courses. Institutionally administered financial aid is available to distance learners.

Services Distance learners have accessibility to bookstore, campus computer network, e-mail services, library services, tutoring.

Contact Candy Center, Dean of e-Learning and Non-Traditional Programs, Massasoit Community College, 1 Massasoit Boulevard, Brockton, MA 02302. Telephone: 508-588-9100 Ext. 1615. Fax: 508-427-1250. E-mail: ccenter@massasoit.mass.edu.

DEGREES AND AWARDS
Programs offered do not lead to a degree or other formal award.

COURSE SUBJECT AREAS OFFERED OUTSIDE OF DEGREE PROGRAMS
Undergraduate—accounting and related services; anthropology; biological and physical sciences; business administration, management and operations; business/commerce; business/corporate communications; chemistry; computer and information sciences; computer software and media applications; film/video and photographic arts; geography and cartography; history; human development, family studies, and related services; international business; mathematics; music; philosophy; physical sciences; psychology; psychology related; sales, merchandising, and related marketing operations (specialized); sociology; speech and rhetoric; statistics.

Non-credit—business/commerce; communication and media; computer and information sciences; computer software and media applications; creative writing; gerontology; health professions related; human resources management; journalism; peace studies and conflict resolution; precision systems maintenance and repair technologies; sales, merchandising, and related marketing operations (general); sales, merchandising, and related marketing operations (specialized); social sciences; taxation.

MASTER'S COLLEGE AND SEMINARY
Toronto, Ontario, Canada
http://www.mcs.edu/

Master's College and Seminary was founded in 1939. It is provincially chartered. It first offered distance learning courses in 1996. In fall 2006, there were 250 students enrolled in distance learning courses. Institutionally administered financial aid is available to distance learners.

Services Distance learners have accessibility to academic advising, bookstore, e-mail services, library services.

Contact Rev. Luc Lombardi, Dean of College Operations, Master's College and Seminary, 3080 Yonge Street, Box 70, Suite 3040, Toronto, ON M4N 3N1, Canada. Telephone: 800-295-6368 Ext. 224. E-mail: luciano.lombardi@mcs.edu.

DEGREES AND AWARDS
Programs offered do not lead to a degree or other formal award.

COURSE SUBJECT AREAS OFFERED OUTSIDE OF DEGREE PROGRAMS
Undergraduate—biblical and other theological languages and literatures; biblical studies; counseling psychology; ethnic, cultural minority, and gender studies; missionary studies and missiology; pastoral counseling and specialized ministries; philosophy and religious studies related; psychology related; religious education; religious studies; theological and ministerial studies; theology and religious vocations related.

MAYVILLE STATE UNIVERSITY
Mayville, North Dakota
Enrollment Services Office
http://www.mayvillestate.edu

Mayville State University was founded in 1889. It is accredited by North Central Association of Colleges and Schools. It first offered distance learning courses in 1999. In fall 2006, there were 253 students enrolled in distance learning courses. Institutionally administered financial aid is available to distance learners.

Services Distance learners have accessibility to academic advising, bookstore, campus computer network, career placement assistance, e-mail services, library services.

Contact Mr. Robert Bertsch, Coordinator of Office of Worldwide Learning, Mayville State University, 330 Third Street NE, Mayville, ND 58257. Telephone: 701-788-4631. Fax: 701-788-4748. E-mail: r_bertsch@ mayvillestate.edu.

DEGREES AND AWARDS
AA Early Childhood Education Associate
BA Early Childhood Education
BEd Elementary Education
BS Business Administration (Bachelor of Applied Science); Business Administration; Computer Information Systems (Bachelor of Applied Science)

COURSE SUBJECT AREAS OFFERED OUTSIDE OF DEGREE PROGRAMS
Undergraduate—accounting and related services; biology; business administration, management and operations; chemistry; education; English composition; human development, family studies, and related services; library science.

MCMURRY UNIVERSITY
Abilene, Texas

McMurry University was founded in 1923. It is accredited by Southern Association of Colleges and Schools. It first offered distance learning courses in 2000. In fall 2006, there were 225 students enrolled in distance learning courses. Institutionally administered financial aid is available to distance learners.

Services Distance learners have accessibility to academic advising, bookstore, e-mail services, library services.

Contact Dr. Alicia T. Wyatt, Associate Professor, McMurry University, Box 218, McMurry Station, Abilene, TX 79697. E-mail: awyatt@mcm.edu.

DEGREES AND AWARDS
Programs offered do not lead to a degree or other formal award.

COURSE SUBJECT AREAS OFFERED OUTSIDE OF DEGREE PROGRAMS
Undergraduate—biblical studies; business administration, management and operations; curriculum and instruction; education (specific levels and methods); religious studies.

MEDICAL COLLEGE OF WISCONSIN
Milwaukee, Wisconsin
Master of Public Health Degree Programs
http://instruct.mcw.edu/prevmed
Medical College of Wisconsin was founded in 1913. It is accredited by North Central Association of Colleges and Schools. It first offered distance learning courses in 1986. In fall 2006, there were 137 students enrolled in distance learning courses. Institutionally administered financial aid is available to distance learners.
Services Distance learners have accessibility to academic advising, bookstore, campus computer network, career placement assistance, e-mail services, library services.
Contact Beverly Carlson, Program Coordinator, MPH Degree Program, Medical College of Wisconsin, Department of Population Health, 8701 Watertown Plank Road, Milwaukee, WI 53226. Telephone: 414-456-4510. Fax: 414-456-6520. E-mail: mph@mcw.edu.

DEGREES AND AWARDS
MPH Occupational Medicine; Public Health

COURSE SUBJECT AREAS OFFERED OUTSIDE OF DEGREE PROGRAMS
Graduate—environmental/environmental health engineering; health/medical preparatory programs; health professions related; public health.

MEMORIAL UNIVERSITY OF NEWFOUNDLAND
St. John's, Newfoundland and Labrador, Canada
Distance Education and Learning Technologies
http://www.distance.mun.ca
Memorial University of Newfoundland was founded in 1925. It is provincially chartered. It first offered distance learning courses in 1969. In fall 2006, there were 2,960 students enrolled in distance learning courses. Institutionally administered financial aid is available to distance learners.
Services Distance learners have accessibility to academic advising, bookstore, e-mail services, library services.
Contact Renee Elliott, Manager, Client Relations, Memorial University of Newfoundland, G. A. Hickman Building, ED-2000, St. John's, NF A1B 3X8, Canada. Telephone: 709-737-8700. Fax: 709-737-4070. E-mail: distance@mun.ca.

DEGREES AND AWARDS
BBA Business Administration
BN Nursing–Post-RN
BS Maritime Studies–Bachelor of Maritime Studies (BMS); Technology–Bachelor Technology (BTech)
Certificate Business Administration; Career Development; Criminology; Library Studies; Newfoundland Studies; Public Administration
Diploma Business Administration
MEd Counseling Psychology; Curriculum Teaching and Learning Studies; Educational Leadership Studies; Information Technology; Postsecondary Studies
MN Nursing
MSW Social Work

COURSE SUBJECT AREAS OFFERED OUTSIDE OF DEGREE PROGRAMS
Undergraduate—anthropology; biology; business administration, management and operations; computer science; economics; education; education related; engineering; English; library science; mathematics; nursing; philosophy; political science and government; psychology; religious studies; social work; sociology; statistics.
Graduate—criminology; education related; library science; nursing; social work.

MERCY COLLEGE
Dobbs Ferry, New York
Mercy Online
http://merlin.mercy.edu
Mercy College was founded in 1951. It is accredited by Middle States Association of Colleges and Schools. It first offered distance learning courses in 1990. In fall 2006, there were 2,250 students enrolled in distance learning courses. Institutionally administered financial aid is available to distance learners.
Services Distance learners have accessibility to academic advising, bookstore, campus computer network, career placement assistance, e-mail services, library services, tutoring.
Contact Mr. John DiElsi, Dean, Mercy Online, Mercy College, 555 Broadway, Dobbs Ferry, NY 10522. Telephone: 914-674-7527. Fax: 914-674-7240. E-mail: jdielsi@mercy.edu.

DEGREES AND AWARDS
AA Liberal Arts and Sciences
AAS Business
AS Accounting; Liberal Arts and Sciences
BA Behavioral Science; English; History; Psychology
BS Behavioral Science; Business Administration; Computer Information Systems; Computer Science; Corporate Communications; Criminal Justice; English; Health Science; History; Mathematics; Nursing; Organizational Management; Psychology; Spanish
MA English Literature
MBA Business Administration
MHRM Human Resource Management
MNE Nursing Education
MPA Health Services Management
MS Counseling; Direct Marketing; Health Services Management; Internet Business Systems; Organizational Leadership
MSN Nursing Administration

COURSE SUBJECT AREAS OFFERED OUTSIDE OF DEGREE PROGRAMS
Undergraduate—accounting and related services; area, ethnic, cultural, and gender studies related; biology; business administration, management and operations; business/commerce; communications technology; community organization and advocacy; comparative literature; computer and information sciences; computer science; creative writing; criminal justice and corrections; developmental and child psychology; educational administration and supervision; educational psychology; English; English composition; English literature (British and Commonwealth); environmental/environmental health engineering; fine and studio art; health professions related; health services/allied health/health sciences; history; human services; international business; languages (foreign languages related); legal studies (non-professional general, undergraduate); liberal arts and sciences, general studies and humanities; management information systems; management sciences and quantitative methods; marketing; mathematics and statistics related; nursing; public administration and social service professions related; public health; social psychology; sociology; statistics.
Graduate—American literature (United States and Canadian); business administration, management and operations; business/commerce; business/corporate communications; business, management, and marketing related; business/managerial economics; community health services; comparative literature; computer and information sciences; computer and information sciences and support services related; computer/information technology administration and management; computer science; computer software

and media applications; computer systems analysis; counseling psychology; English; English language and literature related; English literature (British and Commonwealth); health services/allied health/health sciences; human services; management information systems; management sciences and quantitative methods; marketing; peace studies and conflict resolution; psychology; psychology related; sales, merchandising, and related marketing operations (specialized); social sciences related.

MESA COMMUNITY COLLEGE
Mesa, Arizona
http://www.mc.maricopa.edu/other/distance/

Mesa Community College was founded in 1965. It is accredited by North Central Association of Colleges and Schools. It first offered distance learning courses in 1996. In fall 2006, there were 2,400 students enrolled in distance learning courses. Institutionally administered financial aid is available to distance learners.

Services Distance learners have accessibility to academic advising, bookstore, campus computer network, e-mail services, library services, tutoring.

Contact Distance Learning Advisor, Mesa Community College, 1833 West Southern Avenue, Mesa, AZ 85233. E-mail: mcconline@mcmail.maricopa.edu.

DEGREES AND AWARDS
Programs offered do not lead to a degree or other formal award.

COURSE SUBJECT AREAS OFFERED OUTSIDE OF DEGREE PROGRAMS

Undergraduate—biology; business administration, management and operations; communication and media; computer/information technology administration and management; computer programming; computer science; computer software and media applications; creative writing; criminal justice and corrections; economics; English; English composition; family and consumer sciences/human sciences related; foods, nutrition, and related services; health/medical preparatory programs; health professions related; history; linguistic, comparative, and related language studies; mathematics; nursing; physiological psychology/psychobiology; political science and government; religious studies; school psychology; technical and business writing.

MESALANDS COMMUNITY COLLEGE
Tucumcari, New Mexico
http://www.mesalands.edu

Mesalands Community College was founded in 1979. It is accredited by North Central Association of Colleges and Schools. It first offered distance learning courses in 1997. In fall 2006, there were 157 students enrolled in distance learning courses. Institutionally administered financial aid is available to distance learners.

Services Distance learners have accessibility to academic advising, bookstore, campus computer network, library services, tutoring.

Contact Ms. Christine A. Dougherty, Director of Instructional Services, Mesalands Community College, 911 South Tenth Street, Tucumcari, NM 88401. Telephone: 505-461-4413 Ext. 176. Fax: 505-461-1901. E-mail: christined@mesalands.edu.

DEGREES AND AWARDS
Programs offered do not lead to a degree or other formal award.

COURSE SUBJECT AREAS OFFERED OUTSIDE OF DEGREE PROGRAMS

Undergraduate—accounting and related services; agricultural business and management; allied health and medical assisting services; animal sciences; business/commerce; computer and information sciences; computer science; economics; education; English; geography and cartography; geological and earth sciences/geosciences; history; human resources management; marketing; mathematics; music; physical sciences; sociology; teaching assistants/aides.

MESA STATE COLLEGE
Grand Junction, Colorado
Continuing Education Center
http://www2.mesastate.edu

Mesa State College was founded in 1925. It is accredited by North Central Association of Colleges and Schools. It first offered distance learning courses in 1996. In fall 2006, there were 409 students enrolled in distance learning courses. Institutionally administered financial aid is available to distance learners.

Services Distance learners have accessibility to academic advising, bookstore, campus computer network, career placement assistance, e-mail services, library services, tutoring.

Contact Rance Larsen, Director of Admissions, Mesa State College, 1100 North Avenue, Grand Junction, CO 81501. Telephone: 800-982-6372. Fax: 970-248-1464. E-mail: admissions@mesastate.edu.

DEGREES AND AWARDS
Programs offered do not lead to a degree or other formal award.

COURSE SUBJECT AREAS OFFERED OUTSIDE OF DEGREE PROGRAMS

Undergraduate—accounting and computer science; biology; education; electrical, electronics and communications engineering; English; history; management sciences and quantitative methods; mathematics; nursing; parks, recreation and leisure; political science and government; psychology; visual and performing arts.

METROPOLITAN STATE UNIVERSITY
St. Paul, Minnesota
http://www.metrostate.edu

Metropolitan State University was founded in 1971. It is accredited by North Central Association of Colleges and Schools. It first offered distance learning courses in 1994. In fall 2006, there were 1,018 students enrolled in distance learning courses. Institutionally administered financial aid is available to distance learners.

Services Distance learners have accessibility to academic advising, bookstore, career placement assistance, e-mail services, library services, tutoring.

Contact Ms. Monir Johnson, Director of Admissions, Metropolitan State University, 700 East 7th Street, St. Paul, MN 55106. Telephone: 651-793-1303. Fax: 651-793-1310. E-mail: monir.johnson@metrostate.edu.

DEGREES AND AWARDS
BA Individualized Studies
BS Business Administration; Management; Marketing; Organizational Administration
Certificate Nursing–Continence Care Nurse; Nursing–Ostomy Care Nurse; Nursing–Wound Care Nurse; Nursing–Wound Ostomy Continence Nurse
MS Public and Non-Profit Management–Master of Public and Non-Profit Management
MSN Nursing

COURSE SUBJECT AREAS OFFERED OUTSIDE OF DEGREE PROGRAMS

Undergraduate—accounting and related services; anthropology; business administration, management and operations; communication and journalism related; criminal justice and corrections; dramatic/theater arts and stagecraft; economics; English composition; English language and literature related; finance and financial management services; history; hospitality administration; human resources management; human services; information science/studies; international business; legal studies (non-professional general, undergraduate); management information systems; marketing; mathematics; multi-/interdisciplinary studies related; music; nursing; philosophy; physics; political science and government; psychology; public administration; statistics.
Graduate—business administration, management and operations; criminal justice and corrections; economics; management information systems; marketing; nursing; public administration.

MGH INSTITUTE OF HEALTH PROFESSIONS
Boston, Massachusetts
http://www.mghihp.edu
MGH Institute of Health Professions was founded in 1977. It is accredited by New England Association of Schools and Colleges. It first offered distance learning courses in 2000. In fall 2006, there were 280 students enrolled in distance learning courses. Institutionally administered financial aid is available to distance learners.

Services Distance learners have accessibility to academic advising, bookstore, campus computer network, e-mail services, library services, tutoring.

Contact Ms. Maureen R. Judd, Director of Admissions, MGH Institute of Health Professions, 36 1st Avenue, Boston, MA 02129-4557. Telephone: 617-726-6069. Fax: 617-726-8010. E-mail: mjudd@mghihp.edu.

DEGREES AND AWARDS
Certificate Medical Imaging Post-Baccalaureate certificate
Graduate Certificate Clinical Investigation
MS Clinical Investigations
DPT Physical Therapy–Transitional Doctor of Physical Therapy

COURSE SUBJECT AREAS OFFERED OUTSIDE OF DEGREE PROGRAMS
Graduate—communication disorders sciences and services; health professions related; nursing.

MIAMI DADE COLLEGE
Miami, Florida
Virtual College
http://www.mdc.edu/vcollege/
Miami Dade College was founded in 1960. It is accredited by Southern Association of Colleges and Schools. It first offered distance learning courses in 1997. In fall 2006, there were 4,471 students enrolled in distance learning courses. Institutionally administered financial aid is available to distance learners.

Services Distance learners have accessibility to academic advising, bookstore, library services.

Contact Lloyd Hollingsworth, Student Services Coordinator, Miami Dade College, 300 NE 2nd Avenue, Miami, FL 33132-2297. Telephone: 305-237-3873. Fax: 305-237-3863. E-mail: lholling@mdc.edu.

DEGREES AND AWARDS
AA Pre-Bachelor of Arts
AS Business Administration

COURSE SUBJECT AREAS OFFERED OUTSIDE OF DEGREE PROGRAMS
Undergraduate—accounting and related services; American literature (United States and Canadian); atmospheric sciences and meteorology; biblical studies; biological and biomedical sciences related; biological and physical sciences; biology; business administration, management and operations; computer and information sciences; economics; education; English; English composition; health and medical administrative services; human development, family studies, and related services; international relations and affairs; liberal arts and sciences, general studies and humanities; library science related; management sciences and quantitative methods; marketing; mathematics; nursing; philosophy and religious studies related; physical sciences related; political science and government; psychology; religious studies; social sciences; speech and rhetoric; statistics; taxation.
Non-credit—health professions related.

MIAMI UNIVERSITY–MIDDLETOWN CAMPUS
Middletown, Ohio
http://www.mid.muohio.edu/
Miami University–Middletown Campus was founded in 1966. It is accredited by North Central Association of Colleges and Schools. It first offered distance learning courses in 1996. In fall 2006, there were 160 students enrolled in distance learning courses. Institutionally administered financial aid is available to distance learners.

Services Distance learners have accessibility to academic advising, bookstore, campus computer network, career placement assistance, e-mail services, library services.

Contact Sandra Sandlin, Administrative Assistant to the Center of Online Learning, Miami University–Middletown Campus, 4200 East University Boulevard, Middletown, OH 45042. Telephone: 513-217-4029. Fax: 513-727-3367. E-mail: sandlisl@muohio.edu.

DEGREES AND AWARDS
Programs offered do not lead to a degree or other formal award.

COURSE SUBJECT AREAS OFFERED OUTSIDE OF DEGREE PROGRAMS
Undergraduate—business administration, management and operations; chemistry; electrical and electronic engineering technologies; electromechanical and instrumentation and maintenance technologies; engineering technologies related; nursing; physics; psychology; statistics.

MICHIGAN STATE UNIVERSITY COLLEGE OF LAW
East Lansing, Michigan
Michigan State University College of Law was founded in 1891. It is accredited by Association of American Law Schools. It first offered distance learning courses in 1999. In fall 2006, there were 20 students enrolled in distance learning courses. Institutionally administered financial aid is available to distance learners.

Services Distance learners have accessibility to academic advising, career placement assistance, e-mail services, library services.

Contact Theresa Allen, Michigan State University College of Law, 230 Law College Building, East Lansing, MI 48824. Telephone: 517-432-6827. E-mail: allenthe@law.msu.edu.

DEGREES AND AWARDS
Programs offered do not lead to a degree or other formal award.

COURSE SUBJECT AREAS OFFERED OUTSIDE OF DEGREE PROGRAMS
Graduate—legal professions and studies related; legal research and advanced professional studies; legal support services.
Non-credit—legal professions and studies related; legal research and advanced professional studies; legal studies (non-professional general, undergraduate); legal support services.

MICHIGAN TECHNOLOGICAL UNIVERSITY
Houghton, Michigan
Sponsored Educational Programs
http://www.admin.mtu.edu/sep
Michigan Technological University was founded in 1885. It is accredited by North Central Association of Colleges and Schools. It first offered distance learning courses in 1984. In fall 2006, there were 275 students enrolled in distance learning courses. Institutionally administered financial aid is available to distance learners.

Services Distance learners have accessibility to academic advising, bookstore, campus computer network, career placement assistance, e-mail services, library services, tutoring.

Contact Ms. Patricia A. Lins, Director, Educational Technology/Online Learning, Michigan Technological University, Educational Technology/Online Learning, 1400 Townsend Drive, Houghton, MI 49931. Telephone: 906-487-2925. Fax: 906-487-2787. E-mail: plins@mtu.edu.

DEGREES AND AWARDS
AAS Engineering Technology
BS Engineering
Certificate Engineering Design
MS Electrical Engineering; Mechanical Engineering
PhD Electrical Engineering; Mechanical Engineering

COURSE SUBJECT AREAS OFFERED OUTSIDE OF DEGREE PROGRAMS
Undergraduate—astronomy and astrophysics; engineering mechanics; engineering technologies related; mathematics; mechanical engineering.
Graduate—electrical, electronics and communications engineering; mechanical engineering.

Non-credit—astronomy and astrophysics; engineering mechanics; engineering technologies related; mathematics; mechanical engineering.

MIDDLESEX COMMUNITY COLLEGE
Middletown, Connecticut
http://www.mxctc.commnet.edu/

Middlesex Community College was founded in 1966. It is accredited by New England Association of Schools and Colleges. It first offered distance learning courses in 1999. In fall 2006, there were 244 students enrolled in distance learning courses. Institutionally administered financial aid is available to distance learners.

Services Distance learners have accessibility to academic advising, bookstore, campus computer network, e-mail services, library services, tutoring.

Contact Dr. Yi Guan-Raczkowski, Director of Distance Learning, Middlesex Community College, 100 Training Hill Road, Middletown, CT 06457. Telephone: 860-343-5783. E-mail: yguan@mxcc.commnet.edu.

DEGREES AND AWARDS
Programs offered do not lead to a degree or other formal award.

COURSE SUBJECT AREAS OFFERED OUTSIDE OF DEGREE PROGRAMS

Undergraduate—accounting and computer science; biology; business administration, management and operations; communication and media; computer and information sciences; economics; education; psychology; sociology.

MIDDLESEX COMMUNITY COLLEGE
Bedford, Massachusetts
http://online.middlesex.mass.edu

Middlesex Community College was founded in 1970. It is accredited by New England Association of Schools and Colleges. It first offered distance learning courses in 1996. In fall 2006, there were 1,800 students enrolled in distance learning courses. Institutionally administered financial aid is available to distance learners.

Services Distance learners have accessibility to academic advising, bookstore, campus computer network, e-mail services, library services, tutoring.

Contact Sanford A. Arbogast, Instructional Technology Analyst, Middlesex Community College, Academic Resources Building, Springs Road, Bedford, MA 01730. Telephone: 781-280-3739. Fax: 781-280-3771. E-mail: arbogasts@middlesex.mass.edu.

DEGREES AND AWARDS
AA Liberal Arts and Sciences
AAS Liberal Studies
ABA Accounting; Business Administration Career; Hospitality Management; Small Business Administration
AS Business Administration Transfer; Criminal Justice–Administration option; Criminal Justice–Law Enforcement option; Fire Protection
Certificate Liberal Studies; Small Business Management; Web Publishing

COURSE SUBJECT AREAS OFFERED OUTSIDE OF DEGREE PROGRAMS

Undergraduate—accounting and related services; anthropology; area, ethnic, cultural, and gender studies related; behavioral sciences; biological and biomedical sciences related; biological and physical sciences; biology; business administration, management and operations; business/commerce; business/corporate communications; business, management, and marketing related; business/managerial economics; clinical child psychology; communication and journalism related; communication and media; communications technology; community health services; community psychology; comparative literature; computer and information sciences; computer and information sciences and support services related; computer programming; computer science; computer software and media applications; creative writing; criminal justice and corrections; crimi-

nology; data entry/microcomputer applications; dental support services and allied professions; developmental and child psychology; economics; education; educational psychology; English; English composition; English language and literature related; English literature (British and Commonwealth); ethnic, cultural minority, and gender studies; family psychology; fine and studio art; fire protection; foods, nutrition, and related services; geography and cartography; history; hospitality administration; human resources management; human services; journalism; languages (foreign languages related); legal professions and studies related; legal studies (non-professional general, undergraduate); liberal arts and sciences, general studies and humanities; linguistic, comparative, and related language studies; marketing; mathematics; mathematics and computer science; mathematics and statistics related; museum studies; natural sciences; philosophy; philosophy and religious studies related; physical sciences; political science and government; psychology; psychology related; public health; public relations, advertising, and applied communication related; publishing; radio, television, and digital communication; social psychology; social sciences; social sciences related; sociology; statistics; taxation; technical and business writing.

Non-credit—business administration, management and operations; business/commerce; computer software and media applications; computer systems analysis; creative writing; finance and financial management services; fine and studio art; gerontology; technical and business writing.

MIDDLE TENNESSEE STATE UNIVERSITY
Murfreesboro, Tennessee
College of Continuing Education and Distance Learning
http://www.mtsu.edu/learn

Middle Tennessee State University was founded in 1911. It is accredited by Southern Association of Colleges and Schools. It first offered distance learning courses in 1994. In fall 2006, there were 5,021 students enrolled in distance learning courses. Institutionally administered financial aid is available to distance learners.

Services Distance learners have accessibility to academic advising, bookstore, campus computer network, e-mail services, library services, tutoring.

Contact Dr. Dianna Rust, Director, Academic Outreach and Distance Learning, Middle Tennessee State University, 1301 East Main Street, MTSU Box X109, Murfreesboro, TN 37132. Telephone: 615-898-5611. Fax: 615-896-7925. E-mail: drust@mtsu.edu.

DEGREES AND AWARDS
BS Liberal Studies; Professional Studies, Information Technology concentration; Professional Studies, Organizational Leadership concentration
BSN Nursing
MEd Teaching and Learning, advanced studies
MPS Professional Studies, Strategic Leadership concentration
MSN Nursing

COURSE SUBJECT AREAS OFFERED OUTSIDE OF DEGREE PROGRAMS

Undergraduate—accounting and related services; aerospace, aeronautical and astronautical engineering; agricultural business and management; American literature (United States and Canadian); area, ethnic, cultural, and gender studies related; astronomy and astrophysics; business administration, management and operations; business/corporate communications; communication and media; criminal justice and corrections; economics; education; educational psychology; English; English composition; food science and technology; geological and earth sciences/geosciences; health and physical education/fitness; human resources management; journalism; liberal arts and sciences, general studies and humanities; mathematics; nursing; political science and government; radio, television, and digital communication; sales, merchandising, and related marketing operations (general); social sciences; social work; sociology.

Graduate—aerospace, aeronautical and astronautical engineering; economics; educational assessment, evaluation, and research; marketing; mathematics; nursing.

Non-credit—allied health and medical assisting services; area, ethnic, cultural, and gender studies related; bilingual, multilingual, and multicultural education; business administration, management and operations; business/commerce; business/corporate communications; business, management, and marketing related; business/managerial economics; city/urban, community and regional planning; computer and information sciences; computer/information technology administration and management; computer programming; computer science; computer software and media applications; computer systems networking and telecommunications; crafts, folk art and artisanry; culinary arts and related services; dance; dramatic/theater arts and stagecraft; engineering/industrial management; English as a second language; fine and studio art; human resources management; industrial and organizational psychology; linguistic, comparative, and related language studies; management information systems; nursing; real estate; sales, merchandising, and related marketing operations (specialized); wildlife and wildlands science and management.

MIDSTATE COLLEGE
Peoria, Illinois
http://www.midstate.edu/
Midstate College was founded in 1888. It is accredited by North Central Association of Colleges and Schools. It first offered distance learning courses in 1999. In fall 2006, there were 232 students enrolled in distance learning courses. Institutionally administered financial aid is available to distance learners.
Services Distance learners have accessibility to academic advising, bookstore, career placement assistance, e-mail services, library services, tutoring.
Contact Ms. Jessica Hancock, Director of Admissions, Midstate College, 411 West Northmoor Road, Peoria, IL 61614. Telephone: 309-692-4092 Ext. 1090. Fax: 309-692-3893. E-mail: admissions@midstate.edu.

DEGREES AND AWARDS
BBA Business Administration

COURSE SUBJECT AREAS OFFERED OUTSIDE OF DEGREE PROGRAMS
Undergraduate—accounting and related services; allied health and medical assisting services; applied mathematics; business, management, and marketing related; computer and information sciences; computer software and media applications; English composition; psychology.

MID-STATE TECHNICAL COLLEGE
Wisconsin Rapids, Wisconsin
Information Services
http://www.mstc.edu/academics/distance/cbt.htm
Mid-State Technical College was founded in 1917. It is accredited by North Central Association of Colleges and Schools. It first offered distance learning courses in 1996. In fall 2006, there were 300 students enrolled in distance learning courses. Institutionally administered financial aid is available to distance learners.
Services Distance learners have accessibility to academic advising, bookstore, e-mail services, library services.
Contact Dr. John Higgs, Dean, Business Division, Mid-State Technical College, 500 32nd Street North, Wisconsin Rapids, WI 54494. Telephone: 715-422-5356. Fax: 715-422-5609. E-mail: john.higgs@mstc.edu.

DEGREES AND AWARDS
AD Supervisory Management

COURSE SUBJECT AREAS OFFERED OUTSIDE OF DEGREE PROGRAMS
Undergraduate—business administration, management and operations; civil engineering technology; computer and information sciences; computer and information sciences and support services related; nursing; sociology; systems engineering.

MIDWAY COLLEGE
Midway, Kentucky
http://www.midway.edu/
Midway College was founded in 1847. It is accredited by Southern Association of Colleges and Schools. It first offered distance learning courses in 2003. In fall 2006, there were 328 students enrolled in distance learning courses. Institutionally administered financial aid is available to distance learners.
Services Distance learners have accessibility to academic advising, bookstore, e-mail services.
Contact Patti Kirk, Admissions Counselor/Recruiter, Midway College, 512 East Stephens Street, Midway, KY 40347. Telephone: 800-952-4122. E-mail: midwayonlinecollege@midway.edu.

DEGREES AND AWARDS
Programs offered do not lead to a degree or other formal award.

COURSE SUBJECT AREAS OFFERED OUTSIDE OF DEGREE PROGRAMS
Undergraduate—accounting and related services; biological and physical sciences; computer science; economics; education related; finance and financial management services; geography and cartography; mathematics; music; psychology; religious studies.

MIDWESTERN STATE UNIVERSITY
Wichita Falls, Texas
http://www.mwsu.edu/
Midwestern State University was founded in 1922. It is accredited by Southern Association of Colleges and Schools. It first offered distance learning courses in 1972. In fall 2006, there were 750 students enrolled in distance learning courses. Institutionally administered financial aid is available to distance learners.
Services Distance learners have accessibility to academic advising, bookstore, campus computer network, career placement assistance, e-mail services, library services.
Contact Dr. Pamela Morgan, Director of Extended Education, Midwestern State University, 3410 Taft Boulevard, Wichita Falls, TX 76308-2099. Telephone: 940-397-4785. Fax: 940-397-4868. E-mail: pamela.morgan@mwsu.edu.

DEGREES AND AWARDS
BAA Arts and Science–Applied Arts and Sciences
BSRS Radiologic Sciences
MAE Educational Leadership
MS Radiologic Sciences (Education or Administration major)

COURSE SUBJECT AREAS OFFERED OUTSIDE OF DEGREE PROGRAMS
Undergraduate—business/commerce; business/corporate communications; communication and media; computer and information sciences; criminal justice and corrections; education; geography and cartography; health professions related; liberal arts and sciences, general studies and humanities; political science and government; psychology related; public administration; sociology.
Graduate—education related; health professions related; nursing.

MILLERSVILLE UNIVERSITY OF PENNSYLVANIA
Millersville, Pennsylvania
MU Online
http://muweb.millersville.edu/~muonline
Millersville University of Pennsylvania was founded in 1855. It is accredited by Middle States Association of Colleges and Schools. It first offered distance learning courses in 1998. In fall 2006, there were 1,007 students enrolled in distance learning courses. Institutionally administered financial aid is available to distance learners.
Services Distance learners have accessibility to academic advising, bookstore, campus computer network, career placement assistance, e-mail services, library services.

Contact Ms. Loreal L. Maguire, Assistant Director, Professional Training and Education, Millersville University of Pennsylvania, PO Box 1002, Millersville, PA 17551. Telephone: 717-872-3030. Fax: 717-871-2022. E-mail: loreal.maguire@millersville.edu.

DEGREES AND AWARDS
MS Emergency Management

COURSE SUBJECT AREAS OFFERED OUTSIDE OF DEGREE PROGRAMS
Undergraduate—atmospheric sciences and meteorology; business administration, management and operations; chemistry; communication and media; economics; education; education (specific subject areas); English composition; health and physical education/fitness; linguistic, comparative, and related language studies; music; nursing; psychology; sociology; special education.
Graduate—business administration, management and operations; education; education (specific subject areas); English composition; health and physical education/fitness; linguistic, comparative, and related language studies; nursing; special education; technology education/industrial arts.

See full description on page 384.

MILLERSVILLE UNIVERSITY OF PENNSYLVANIA
Millersville, Pennsylvania
MS in Nursing Education
http://www.millersville.edu/
Millersville University of Pennsylvania was founded in 1855. It is accredited by Middle States Association of Colleges and Schools. It first offered distance learning courses in 2002. In fall 2006, there were 992 students enrolled in distance learning courses. Institutionally administered financial aid is available to distance learners.
Services Distance learners have accessibility to e-mail services, library services, tutoring.
Contact Dr. Victor DeSantis, Dean, Graduate Studies, Millersville University of Pennsylvania, PO Box 1002, Millersville, PA 17551. Telephone: 717-872-3099. Fax: 717-872-3453. E-mail: victor.desantis@millersville.edu.

DEGREES AND AWARDS
MSN Education

COURSE SUBJECT AREAS OFFERED OUTSIDE OF DEGREE PROGRAMS
Undergraduate—communication and media.
Graduate—business, management, and marketing related.

See full description on page 386.

MILWAUKEE SCHOOL OF ENGINEERING
Milwaukee, Wisconsin
MSOE-TV
http://www.msoe.edu/admiss
Milwaukee School of Engineering was founded in 1903. It is accredited by North Central Association of Colleges and Schools. It first offered distance learning courses in 1989. In fall 2006, there were 157 students enrolled in distance learning courses. Institutionally administered financial aid is available to distance learners.
Services Distance learners have accessibility to academic advising, bookstore, campus computer network, career placement assistance, e-mail services, library services.
Contact Ms. Mary Nielsen, Registrar, Milwaukee School of Engineering, 1025 North Broadway, Milwaukee, WI 53202-3109. Telephone: 414-277-7216. Fax: 414-277-6914. E-mail: nielsen@msoe.edu.

DEGREES AND AWARDS
Programs offered do not lead to a degree or other formal award.

COURSE SUBJECT AREAS OFFERED OUTSIDE OF DEGREE PROGRAMS
Undergraduate—business, management, and marketing related; computer and information sciences; management information systems.
Graduate—business administration, management and operations.

MINNEAPOLIS COLLEGE OF ART AND DESIGN
Minneapolis, Minnesota
MCAD Distance Learning
http://online.mcad.edu
Minneapolis College of Art and Design was founded in 1886. It is accredited by North Central Association of Colleges and Schools. It first offered distance learning courses in 1995. In fall 2006, there were 150 students enrolled in distance learning courses. Institutionally administered financial aid is available to distance learners.
Services Distance learners have accessibility to bookstore, campus computer network, e-mail services, library services, tutoring.
Contact Rebecca J. Alm, Director of Distance Learning, Minneapolis College of Art and Design, 2501 Stevens Avenue, Minneapolis, MN 55404. Telephone: 612-874-3658. Fax: 612-874-3704. E-mail: rebecca_alm@mcad.edu.

DEGREES AND AWARDS
Programs offered do not lead to a degree or other formal award.

COURSE SUBJECT AREAS OFFERED OUTSIDE OF DEGREE PROGRAMS
Undergraduate—design and applied arts; film/video and photographic arts; fine and studio art; visual and performing arts; visual and performing arts related.
Graduate—design and applied arts; film/video and photographic arts; fine and studio art; visual and performing arts; visual and performing arts related.
Non-credit—design and applied arts; film/video and photographic arts; fine and studio art; visual and performing arts; visual and performing arts related.

MINNESOTA SCHOOL OF BUSINESS–RICHFIELD
Richfield, Minnesota
http://www.msbcollege.edu
Minnesota School of Business–Richfield was founded in 1877. It is accredited by Accrediting Council for Independent Colleges and Schools. It first offered distance learning courses in 2000. In fall 2006, there were 990 students enrolled in distance learning courses. Institutionally administered financial aid is available to distance learners.
Services Distance learners have accessibility to academic advising, campus computer network, career placement assistance, e-mail services, library services, tutoring.
Contact Jeff Myhre, Director, Minnesota School of Business–Richfield, 1401 West 76th Street, Suite 500, Richfield, MN 55423. Telephone: 612-861-2000. Fax: 800-752-4223. E-mail: jmyhre@msbcollege.edu.

DEGREES AND AWARDS
AAS Accounting and Tax Specialist; Business Administration; Cosmetology Business; Information Technology; Management Accounting; Paralegal; Transportation Business
BS Accounting; Business Administration; Health Care Management; Information Technology; Paralegal
MBA Business Administration

COURSE SUBJECT AREAS OFFERED OUTSIDE OF DEGREE PROGRAMS
Undergraduate—accounting and related services; animal sciences; biology; business administration, management and operations; communication and media; computer science; entrepreneurial and small business operations; health and medical administrative services; international business; legal professions and studies related; legal studies (nonprofessional general, undergraduate); liberal arts and sciences, general

studies and humanities; mathematics; taxation; technical and business writing; veterinary biomedical and clinical sciences.
Graduate—business administration, management and operations.

MINNESOTA STATE COMMUNITY AND TECHNICAL COLLEGE–FERGUS FALLS
Fergus Falls, Minnesota
http://www.ff.cc.mn.us/

Minnesota State Community and Technical College–Fergus Falls was founded in 1960. It is accredited by North Central Association of Colleges and Schools. It first offered distance learning courses in 1995. In fall 2006, there were 1,000 students enrolled in distance learning courses. Institutionally administered financial aid is available to distance learners.
Services Distance learners have accessibility to tutoring.
Contact Minnesota Online Support Center, Minnesota State Community and Technical College–Fergus Falls, 150 2nd Avenue SW, Suite B, Box 209, Perham, MN 56573. Telephone: 800-456-8519. Fax: 218-347-6214. E-mail: mnonline@custhelp.com.

DEGREES AND AWARDS
AA Transfer degree
AAS Computer Programming; Computer and Network Technology; Health Information Technology; Human Resources; Legal Administrative Assistant; Medical Administrative Assistant; Paralegal; Pharmacy Technology; Radiologic Technology
AS Human Resources

MINNESOTA STATE UNIVERSITY MOORHEAD
Moorhead, Minnesota
http://www.mnstate.edu/continue/

Minnesota State University Moorhead was founded in 1885. It is accredited by North Central Association of Colleges and Schools. It first offered distance learning courses in 1970. In fall 2006, there were 500 students enrolled in distance learning courses. Institutionally administered financial aid is available to distance learners.
Services Distance learners have accessibility to academic advising, bookstore, campus computer network, e-mail services, library services.
Contact Ms. Jan A. Flack, Director of Continuing Studies, Minnesota State University Moorhead, 1104 7th Avenue South, PO Box 82, Moorhead, MN 56563. Telephone: 218-477-2182. Fax: 218-477-5030. E-mail: flackjan@mnstate.edu.

DEGREES AND AWARDS
BSN Nursing–Bachelor of Science
CCCPE Teaching and Learning with Technology (Grad and Undergrad)
MS Educational Administration–Educational Technology emphasis
MSN Nursing

COURSE SUBJECT AREAS OFFERED OUTSIDE OF DEGREE PROGRAMS
Undergraduate—accounting and related services; anthropology; business/commerce; community health services; creative writing; ethnic, cultural minority, and gender studies; history; mathematics; psychology; public health; sociology; technology education/industrial arts.
Graduate—educational administration and supervision; educational assessment, evaluation, and research; educational/instructional media design; nursing; special education.

MINOT STATE UNIVERSITY
Minot, North Dakota
Continuing Education
http://online.minotstateu.edu

Minot State University was founded in 1913. It is accredited by North Central Association of Colleges and Schools. It first offered distance learning courses in 1991. In fall 2006, there were 2,173 students enrolled in distance learning courses. Institutionally administered financial aid is available to distance learners.
Services Distance learners have accessibility to academic advising, bookstore, campus computer network, career placement assistance, e-mail services, library services, tutoring.

Contact Jolina Miller, Online Program Coordinator, Minot State University, Center for Extended Learning, 500 University Avenue West, Minot, ND 58707. Telephone: 701-858-3430. Fax: 701-858-4343. E-mail: online@minotstateu.edu.

DEGREES AND AWARDS
AS Developmental Disabilities
BGS General Studies
BS Management Information Systems; Management; Virtual Business
BSAST Business Information Technology; Management
BSN Nursing for Registered Nurses
Certificate Developmental Disabilities
CAGS Knowledge Management
CCCPE Application Software Specialist; Web and Desktop Publishing
MS Information Systems; Management

COURSE SUBJECT AREAS OFFERED OUTSIDE OF DEGREE PROGRAMS
Undergraduate—accounting and related services; American literature (United States and Canadian); anthropology; computer science; creative writing; criminal justice and corrections; economics; education; education (specific levels and methods); English; English composition; history; management information systems; mathematics; nursing; philosophy; psychology; sociology; special education; technical and business writing.
Graduate—business administration, management and operations; management information systems; special education.

MINOT STATE UNIVERSITY–BOTTINEAU CAMPUS
Bottineau, North Dakota
http://www.misu-b.nodak.edu

Minot State University–Bottineau Campus was founded in 1906. It is accredited by North Central Association of Colleges and Schools. It first offered distance learning courses in 2000. In fall 2006, there were 179 students enrolled in distance learning courses. Institutionally administered financial aid is available to distance learners.
Services Distance learners have accessibility to academic advising, bookstore, library services.
Contact Kayla O'Toole, Training Coordinator, Minot State University–Bottineau Campus, 105 Simrall Boulevard, Bottineau, ND 58318. Telephone: 888-918-5623. E-mail: kayle.otoole@misu.nodak.edu.

DEGREES AND AWARDS
AA Liberal Arts
AAS Accounting Technician; Administrative Assistant; Medical Assistant; Medical Secretary; Paraeducation; Recreation Management
Certificate of Completion Grounds Worker Skills, basic; Medical Coding; Medical Transcription; Recreation Management
Diploma Bookkeeping; Greenhouse Technology; Landscape Technician; Medical Assistant; Medical Coding; Medical Transcription; Reception Services; Urban Forestry Technology

COURSE SUBJECT AREAS OFFERED OUTSIDE OF DEGREE PROGRAMS
Undergraduate—allied health and medical assisting services; applied horticulture/horticultural business services; biological and biomedical sciences related; business, management, and marketing related; business operations support and assistant services; health and medical administrative services; liberal arts and sciences, general studies and humanities; medical basic sciences; teaching assistants/aides.

MISSISSIPPI STATE UNIVERSITY
Mississippi State, Mississippi
Division of Continuing Education
http://www.distance.msstate.edu

Mississippi State University was founded in 1878. It is accredited by Southern Association of Colleges and Schools. It first offered distance learning courses in 1987. In fall 2006, there were 1,700 students enrolled in distance learning courses. Institutionally administered financial aid is available to distance learners.
Services Distance learners have accessibility to academic advising, bookstore, campus computer network, career placement assistance, e-mail services, library services.

Contact Dr. Laura A. Crittenden, Manager, Office of Academic Outreach, Mississippi State University, Division of Academic Outreach and Continuing Education, 1 Barr Avenue, PO Box 5247, Mississippi State, MS 39762-5247. Telephone: 662-325-2677. Fax: 662-325-0930. E-mail: lcrittenden@aoce.msstate.edu.

DEGREES AND AWARDS

BS Elementary Education; Geosciences; Interdisciplinary Studies

Certificate Geosciences, Broadcast Meteorology; Geosciences, Operational Meteorology

MAT Community College Leadership

MBA Business Administration

MS Food Science, Nutrition, and Health Promotion; Geosciences, Teachers in Geoscience; Industrial Engineering; Master of Engineering; Public Policy Administration; Workforce Education Leadership

PhD PhD Community College Leadership; PhD Engineering, Concentration Industrial Engineering

COURSE SUBJECT AREAS OFFERED OUTSIDE OF DEGREE PROGRAMS

Undergraduate—accounting and computer science; accounting and related services; biological and physical sciences; biology; communication and journalism related; communication and media; computer and information sciences; computer science; counseling psychology; curriculum and instruction; developmental and child psychology; educational/instructional media design; educational psychology; education related; education (specific levels and methods); education (specific subject areas); fine and studio art; forestry; geological and earth sciences/geosciences; human development, family studies, and related services; insurance; landscape architecture; mathematics; multi-/interdisciplinary studies related; physical sciences related; physics; special education; statistics; technology education/industrial arts; zoology/animal biology.

Graduate—agriculture; business administration, management and operations; business/commerce; business/managerial economics; chemical engineering; civil engineering; computer engineering; computer science; counseling psychology; curriculum and instruction; educational administration and supervision; educational assessment, evaluation, and research; educational/instructional media design; educational psychology; education (specific subject areas); electrical, electronics and communications engineering; engineering; engineering technologies related; health professions related; public administration.

MISSISSIPPI UNIVERSITY FOR WOMEN
Columbus, Mississippi
Continuing Education
http://www.muw.edu/

Mississippi University for Women was founded in 1884. It is accredited by Southern Association of Colleges and Schools. It first offered distance learning courses in 1994. In fall 2006, there were 20 students enrolled in distance learning courses. Institutionally administered financial aid is available to distance learners.

Services Distance learners have accessibility to academic advising, bookstore, career placement assistance, e-mail services, library services.

Contact Kathy McShane, Coordinator, Mississippi University for Women, Advanced Placement Option, 1918 Briar Ridge Road, Tupelo, MS 38804. Telephone: 662-844-0284. Fax: 662-844-1927. E-mail: kmshane@muw.edu.

DEGREES AND AWARDS

BSN Nursing

COURSE SUBJECT AREAS OFFERED OUTSIDE OF DEGREE PROGRAMS

Undergraduate—American literature (United States and Canadian); nursing.

MISSOURI SOUTHERN STATE UNIVERSITY
Joplin, Missouri
Continuing Education
http://www.mssu.edu/lifelonglearning

Missouri Southern State University was founded in 1937. It is accredited by North Central Association of Colleges and Schools. It first offered distance learning courses in 1986. In fall 2006, there were 790 students enrolled in distance learning courses. Institutionally administered financial aid is available to distance learners.

Services Distance learners have accessibility to academic advising, bookstore, campus computer network, career placement assistance, e-mail services, library services, tutoring.

Contact Dr. Jerry Williams, Director of Continuing Education, Missouri Southern State University, 3950 East Newman Road, Joplin, MO 64801. Telephone: 417-625-9384. Fax: 417-625-3024. E-mail: williams-j@mssu.edu.

DEGREES AND AWARDS

AA General Studies; Paralegal Studies
AS Business, general; Law Enforcement
BA General Studies
BS Criminal Justice
BSBA Business
BSN Nursing–for Prelicensure and Licensed; Nursing–for Registered Nurses

COURSE SUBJECT AREAS OFFERED OUTSIDE OF DEGREE PROGRAMS

Undergraduate—accounting and related services; biological and physical sciences; biology; cell biology and anatomical sciences; communication and media; computer science; criminal justice and corrections; dental support services and allied professions; developmental and child psychology; education; history; mathematics; nursing; physics; political science and government; psychology; social psychology; sociology.

Non-credit—American Sign Language (ASL); business/commerce; entrepreneurial and small business operations; industrial production technologies; legal research and advanced professional studies; work and family studies.

MISSOURI STATE UNIVERSITY
Springfield, Missouri
College of Continuing Education and the Extended University
http://ce.smsu.edu

Missouri State University was founded in 1905. It is accredited by North Central Association of Colleges and Schools. It first offered distance learning courses in 1974. In fall 2006, there were 3,000 students enrolled in distance learning courses. Institutionally administered financial aid is available to distance learners.

Services Distance learners have accessibility to academic advising, bookstore, campus computer network, career placement assistance, e-mail services, library services.

Contact Dr. Diana Garland, EdD, Associate Director, Academic Outreach and Distance Learning, Missouri State University, The Extended Campus, Academic Outreach and Distance Learning, 901 South National, Springfield, MO 65897. Telephone: 877-678-2005. Fax: 417-836-6016. E-mail: dianagarland@missouristate.edu.

DEGREES AND AWARDS

BA Bachelor of Applied Science in Technology Management (two-year completion)
BS Elementary Education; General Business (completion degree)
BSN Nursing
Certificate Manufacturing Management
Certification Education–Missouri Visual Impairment Certification Training program
Graduate Certificate Instructional Technology Specialist; Project Management; Sports Management
MBA Business Administration Foundation courses; Business Administration

MS Administrative Studies; Computer Information Systems; Elementary Education

MSW Social Work

PMC Nurse Educator

COURSE SUBJECT AREAS OFFERED OUTSIDE OF DEGREE PROGRAMS

Undergraduate—accounting and related services; agricultural and domestic animal services; agricultural business and management; anthropology; apparel and textiles; astronomy and astrophysics; chemistry; communication and journalism related; computer and information sciences; creative writing; developmental and child psychology; economics; English language and literature related; film/video and photographic arts; finance and financial management services; health and physical education/fitness; history; human development, family studies, and related services; industrial production technologies; marketing; mathematics and statistics related; music; nursing; physics; political science and government; religious studies; social work; sociology; special education.

Graduate—accounting and related services; agricultural and domestic animal services; communication and media; computer and information sciences; counseling psychology; criminal justice and corrections; curriculum and instruction; economics; education; educational administration and supervision; education (specific levels and methods); education (specific subject areas); finance and financial management services; health and physical education/fitness; history; industrial production technologies; legal research and advanced professional studies; library science; marketing; nursing; political science and government; psychology; religious studies; sales, merchandising, and related marketing operations (specialized); social work; taxation.

Non-credit—information science/studies; management information systems; mental and social health services and allied professions.

MITCHELL TECHNICAL INSTITUTE
Mitchell, South Dakota
http://mti.tec.sd.us/

Mitchell Technical Institute was founded in 1968. It is accredited by North Central Association of Colleges and Schools. It first offered distance learning courses in 1994. In fall 2006, there were 200 students enrolled in distance learning courses. Institutionally administered financial aid is available to distance learners.

Services Distance learners have accessibility to academic advising, career placement assistance, e-mail services.

Contact John J. Heemstra, Telecommunications Coordinator, Mitchell Technical Institute, 821 North Capital, Mitchell, SD 57301. Telephone: 605-995-3065. Fax: 605-995-3067. E-mail: john.heemstra@mitchelltech.edu.

DEGREES AND AWARDS

Programs offered do not lead to a degree or other formal award.

COURSE SUBJECT AREAS OFFERED OUTSIDE OF DEGREE PROGRAMS

Undergraduate—accounting and computer science; business, management, and marketing related; computer and information sciences; computer software and media applications; culinary arts and related services; curriculum and instruction; engineering-related technologies; health services/allied health/health sciences.

Non-credit—business, management, and marketing related; business operations support and assistant services; computer and information sciences; computer software and media applications; data entry/microcomputer applications; entrepreneurial and small business operations; health professions related; heating, air conditioning, ventilation and refrigeration maintenance technology; quality control and safety technologies.

MOBERLY AREA COMMUNITY COLLEGE
Moberly, Missouri
http://www.macc.edu/

Moberly Area Community College was founded in 1927. It is accredited by North Central Association of Colleges and Schools. It first offered distance learning courses in 1995. In fall 2006, there were 442 students enrolled in distance learning courses. Institutionally administered financial aid is available to distance learners.

Services Distance learners have accessibility to academic advising, bookstore, campus computer network, career placement assistance, e-mail services, library services.

Contact Dr. James Grant, Dean of Student Services, Moberly Area Community College, 101 College Avenue, Moberly, MO 65270. Telephone: 660-263-4110 Ext. 239. Fax: 660-263-2406. E-mail: jamesg@macc.edu.

DEGREES AND AWARDS

AAS Computer Information Systems

COURSE SUBJECT AREAS OFFERED OUTSIDE OF DEGREE PROGRAMS

Undergraduate—accounting and related services; biology; business administration, management and operations; computer science; electrical and electronic engineering technologies; English; fine and studio art; geography and cartography; history; human development, family studies, and related services; mathematics; psychology; social sciences related; sociology; speech and rhetoric.

MODESTO JUNIOR COLLEGE
Modesto, California
Instruction
http://www.gomjc.org

Modesto Junior College was founded in 1921. It is accredited by Western Association of Schools and Colleges. It first offered distance learning courses in 1989. In fall 2006, there were 6,258 students enrolled in distance learning courses. Institutionally administered financial aid is available to distance learners.

Services Distance learners have accessibility to academic advising, bookstore, campus computer network, career placement assistance, library services.

Contact Kathy Haskin, Support Staff III, Modesto Junior College, MJC Telecourse Office, 435 College Avenue, Modesto, CA 95350. Telephone: 209-575-6236. Fax: 209-575-6669. E-mail: haskink@mjc.edu.

DEGREES AND AWARDS

Programs offered do not lead to a degree or other formal award.

COURSE SUBJECT AREAS OFFERED OUTSIDE OF DEGREE PROGRAMS

Undergraduate—anthropology; behavioral sciences; cognitive psychology and psycholinguistics; community health services; comparative psychology; ethnic, cultural minority, and gender studies; family psychology; health and physical education/fitness; history; human development, family studies, and related services; intercultural/multicultural and diversity studies; languages (Romance languages); personality psychology; philosophy; psychology; psychology related; social psychology; sociology; work and family studies.

Non-credit—student counseling and personnel services.

MONMOUTH UNIVERSITY
West Long Branch, New Jersey
http://www.monmouth.edu/

Monmouth University was founded in 1933. It is accredited by Middle States Association of Colleges and Schools. It first offered distance learning courses in 1998. In fall 2006, there were 122 students enrolled in distance learning courses. Institutionally administered financial aid is available to distance learners.

Services Distance learners have accessibility to academic advising, bookstore, campus computer network, career placement assistance, e-mail services, library services.

Contact Robert D. McCaig, EdD, Vice President for Enrollment Management, Monmouth University, 400 Cedar Avenue, West Long Branch, NJ 07764-1898. Telephone: 732-571-3413. Fax: 732-263-5101. E-mail: rmccaig@monmouth.edu.

DEGREES AND AWARDS
Programs offered do not lead to a degree or other formal award.

COURSE SUBJECT AREAS OFFERED OUTSIDE OF DEGREE PROGRAMS
Undergraduate—education.
Graduate—criminal justice and corrections; education; nursing; social work.

MONROE COMMUNITY COLLEGE
Rochester, New York
http://www.monroecc.edu/
Monroe Community College was founded in 1961. It is accredited by Middle States Association of Colleges and Schools. It first offered distance learning courses in 1997. In fall 2006, there were 2,120 students enrolled in distance learning courses. Institutionally administered financial aid is available to distance learners.
Services Distance learners have accessibility to academic advising, campus computer network, career placement assistance, e-mail services, library services.
Contact Online Learning, Monroe Community College, 1000 East Henrietta Road, Rochester, NY 14623-5780. E-mail: registration@monroecc.edu.

DEGREES AND AWARDS
AAS Criminal Justice
AS Business Administration; Liberal Arts; Physical Education Studies
Certificate of Completion Coaching–New York State Coaching certification
Certificate Dental Assisting

COURSE SUBJECT AREAS OFFERED OUTSIDE OF DEGREE PROGRAMS
Undergraduate—accounting and related services; American literature (United States and Canadian); biology; business/commerce; communication and media; criminal justice and corrections; dental support services and allied professions; English composition; liberal arts and sciences, general studies and humanities; mathematics; psychology; public relations, advertising, and applied communication related; social sciences.

MONTANA STATE UNIVERSITY
Bozeman, Montana
Extended University/Burns Technology Center
http://www.montana.edu/distance
Montana State University was founded in 1893. It is accredited by Northwest Commission on Colleges and Universities. It first offered distance learning courses in 1992. In fall 2006, there were 1,000 students enrolled in distance learning courses. Institutionally administered financial aid is available to distance learners.
Services Distance learners have accessibility to academic advising, bookstore, campus computer network, e-mail services, library services.
Contact Kelly Boyce, Program Manager, Montana State University, EPS 128, Bozeman, MT 59717. Telephone: 406-994-6812. Fax: 406-994-7856. E-mail: kboyce@montana.edu.

DEGREES AND AWARDS
Certification Library Media Certification
MN Nursing
MS Family and Financial Planning; Mathematics; Science Education

COURSE SUBJECT AREAS OFFERED OUTSIDE OF DEGREE PROGRAMS
Graduate—astronomy and astrophysics; biological and physical sciences; biology; education (specific subject areas); finance and financial management services; foods, nutrition, and related services; health and physical education/fitness; library science related; mathematics; mathematics and statistics related; microbiological sciences and immunology; physics; soil sciences; statistics.

MONTANA STATE UNIVERSITY–BILLINGS
Billings, Montana
http://www.msubonline.org
Montana State University–Billings was founded in 1927. It is accredited by Northwest Commission on Colleges and Universities. It first offered distance learning courses in 1998. In fall 2006, there were 1,700 students enrolled in distance learning courses. Institutionally administered financial aid is available to distance learners.
Services Distance learners have accessibility to academic advising, bookstore, career placement assistance, e-mail services, library services, tutoring.
Contact Mr. Kurt Laudicina, Admissions Counselor for MSU-B Online University, Montana State University–Billings, McMullen Hall 100, 1500 North 30th Street, Billings, MT 59101. Telephone: 406-896-5911. Fax: 406-657-2302. E-mail: inquiry@msubonline.org.

DEGREES AND AWARDS
AAS Accounting Technology
BA Business Administration; Communication/Organizational Communications/Mass Communication/Public Relations
BS Liberal Studies–Management and Communication concentration; Public Relations
MHA Health Administration
MS Public Relations

COURSE SUBJECT AREAS OFFERED OUTSIDE OF DEGREE PROGRAMS
Undergraduate—accounting and related services; biology; business administration, management and operations; business/commerce; business/corporate communications; communication and media; communications technology; curriculum and instruction; dramatic/theater arts and stagecraft; economics; education; English composition; fine and studio art; geography and cartography; history; human resources management; industrial and organizational psychology; liberal arts and sciences, general studies and humanities; marketing; mathematics; physics; psychology; public relations, advertising, and applied communication related; special education; statistics.
Graduate—communication and media; counseling psychology; curriculum and instruction; education; health and medical administrative services; public relations, advertising, and applied communication related; rehabilitation and therapeutic professions.

See full description on page 388.

MONTANA TECH OF THE UNIVERSITY OF MONTANA
Butte, Montana
Office of Extended Studies
http://www.mtech.edu
Montana Tech of The University of Montana was founded in 1895. It is accredited by Northwest Commission on Colleges and Universities. It first offered distance learning courses in 1996. In fall 2006, there were 495 students enrolled in distance learning courses. Institutionally administered financial aid is available to distance learners.
Services Distance learners have accessibility to academic advising, bookstore, campus computer network, career placement assistance, e-mail services, library services.
Contact Ms. Laura Riddle, Inquiry Processing Specialist, Montana Tech of The University of Montana, 1300 West Park Street, Butte, MT 59701-8997. Telephone: 406-496-4791. Fax: 406-496-4710. E-mail: lriddle@mtech.edu.

DEGREES AND AWARDS
MPM Project Engineering and Management
MS Industrial Hygiene

COURSE SUBJECT AREAS OFFERED OUTSIDE OF DEGREE PROGRAMS

Undergraduate—business/commerce; computer software and media applications; English composition; health professions related; mathematics; nursing; philosophy; psychology; sociology; technical and business writing.
Graduate—engineering/industrial management; health professions related; public health.

MONTEREY PENINSULA COLLEGE
Monterey, California
http://www.mpc.edu/

Monterey Peninsula College was founded in 1947. It is accredited by Western Association of Schools and Colleges. It first offered distance learning courses in 2000. In fall 2006, there were 222 students enrolled in distance learning courses. Institutionally administered financial aid is available to distance learners.
Services Distance learners have accessibility to academic advising, bookstore, campus computer network, career placement assistance, e-mail services, library services, tutoring.
Contact Mr. Bruce Wilder, Instructional Technology Specialist, Monterey Peninsula College, 980 Fremont Street, Monterey, CA 93940. Telephone: 831-646-3074. E-mail: bwilder@mpc.edu.

DEGREES AND AWARDS
Programs offered do not lead to a degree or other formal award.

COURSE SUBJECT AREAS OFFERED OUTSIDE OF DEGREE PROGRAMS

Undergraduate—American literature (United States and Canadian); biological and physical sciences; business, management, and marketing related; developmental and child psychology; English as a second language; English composition; international business; mathematics; psychology.

MONTGOMERY COMMUNITY COLLEGE
Troy, North Carolina
http://www.montgomery.cc.nc.us/

Montgomery Community College was founded in 1967. It is accredited by Southern Association of Colleges and Schools. It first offered distance learning courses in 2000. In fall 2006, there were 350 students enrolled in distance learning courses. Institutionally administered financial aid is available to distance learners.
Services Distance learners have accessibility to academic advising, bookstore, campus computer network, career placement assistance, library services, tutoring.
Contact Dean Thomas M. Sargent, Dean of Education Technology, Montgomery Community College, 1011 Page Street, Troy, NC 27371. Telephone: 910-576-6222 Ext. 217. Fax: 910-576-2176. E-mail: sargentt@montgomery.edu.

DEGREES AND AWARDS
AAB Business Administration
AAS Criminal Justice

COURSE SUBJECT AREAS OFFERED OUTSIDE OF DEGREE PROGRAMS

Undergraduate—American literature (United States and Canadian); business administration, management and operations; business/commerce; business operations support and assistant services; computer and information sciences; computer software and media applications; criminal justice and corrections; English; English composition; human resources management; liberal arts and sciences, general studies and humanities; medical basic sciences; psychology; religious education; sociology; technical and business writing.
Non-credit—allied health and medical assisting services; biblical studies; business administration, management and operations; business/corporate communications; computer and information sciences; computer software and media applications; English; English composition.

MONTGOMERY COUNTY COMMUNITY COLLEGE
Blue Bell, Pennsylvania
Learning Resources Unit
http://www.mc3.edu/aa/DISTLRN/DISTLRN.htm

Montgomery County Community College was founded in 1964. It is accredited by Middle States Association of Colleges and Schools. It first offered distance learning courses in 1992. In fall 2006, there were 1,721 students enrolled in distance learning courses. Institutionally administered financial aid is available to distance learners.
Services Distance learners have accessibility to academic advising, bookstore, campus computer network, career placement assistance, e-mail services, library services, tutoring.
Contact Mr. Richard D. Greenwood, Director of Distance Learning, Montgomery County Community College, 340 DeKalb Pike, Blue Bell, PA 19422. Telephone: 215-641-6325. Fax: 215-619-7182. E-mail: rdgreenw@mc3.edu.

DEGREES AND AWARDS

AA Elementary Education; Secondary Education; Social Science
AGS General Studies
AS Accounting; Business Administration–International option; Business Administration; Liberal Studies
Certificate International Studies

COURSE SUBJECT AREAS OFFERED OUTSIDE OF DEGREE PROGRAMS

Undergraduate—accounting and related services; anthropology; astronomy and astrophysics; biology; business administration, management and operations; business/commerce; computer and information sciences; computer programming; computer science; computer software and media applications; criminology; dental support services and allied professions; developmental and child psychology; economics; education; English composition; English literature (British and Commonwealth); geography and cartography; geological and earth sciences/geosciences; health professions related; history; liberal arts and sciences, general studies and humanities; marketing; mathematics; nursing; nutrition sciences; philosophy; psychology; social psychology; sociology; statistics; technical and business writing.

MOTLOW STATE COMMUNITY COLLEGE
Tullahoma, Tennessee
Academic Affairs
http://www.mscc.edu

Motlow State Community College was founded in 1969. It is accredited by Southern Association of Colleges and Schools. It first offered distance learning courses in 1996. In fall 2006, there were 594 students enrolled in distance learning courses. Institutionally administered financial aid is available to distance learners.
Services Distance learners have accessibility to academic advising, bookstore, campus computer network, career placement assistance, e-mail services, library services, tutoring.
Contact Dr. Mary McLemore, Vice President for Academic Affairs, Motlow State Community College, PO Box 8500, Lynchburg, TN 37352. Telephone: 931-393-1696. Fax: 931-393-1681. E-mail: mmclemore@mscc.edu.

DEGREES AND AWARDS

AAS Business Technology

COURSE SUBJECT AREAS OFFERED OUTSIDE OF DEGREE PROGRAMS

Undergraduate—computer and information sciences; management information systems; mathematics; statistics.

MOUNTAIN EMPIRE COMMUNITY COLLEGE
Big Stone Gap, Virginia
Office of Continuing and Distance Education
http://www.me.vccs.edu/distance/index.html
Mountain Empire Community College was founded in 1972. It is accredited by Southern Association of Colleges and Schools. It first offered distance learning courses in 1979. In fall 2006, there were 900 students enrolled in distance learning courses. Institutionally administered financial aid is available to distance learners.
Services Distance learners have accessibility to academic advising, bookstore, campus computer network, career placement assistance, e-mail services, library services, tutoring.
Contact Susan Kennedy, Coordinator of Distance Education, Mountain Empire Community College, 3441 Mountain Empire Road, Big Stone Gap, VA 24219. Telephone: 276-523-7488. Fax: 276-523-7486. E-mail: skennedy@me.vccs.edu.

DEGREES AND AWARDS
AAS Accounting; Administrative Support Technology Medical Office Specialist; Administrative Support Technology; Business Administration; Correctional Services; General Studies; Liberal Arts; Water/Wastewater specialization
Certificate Career Studies Certificate–Accounting; Career Studies Certificate–Child Development; Career Studies Certificate–Computer Software Specialist; Career Studies Certificate–Geographical Information Systems; Career Studies Certificate–Health Information Technology; Career Studies Certificate–Legal Office Assisting; Career Studies Certificate–Medical Records Clerk; Career Studies Certificate–Medical Transcriptionist; Career Studies Certificate–Office Automation Specialist; Career Studies Certificate–Personal Computing for Home and Office; Career Studies Certificate–Polysomnography; Career Studies Certificate–Wastewater Plant Operator; Career Studies Certificate–Water Plant Operator; Career Studies Certificate–Word Processing; Clerical Assistant

COURSE SUBJECT AREAS OFFERED OUTSIDE OF DEGREE PROGRAMS
Undergraduate—accounting and related services; astronomy and astrophysics; atmospheric sciences and meteorology; biology; business/commerce; communication and media; computer and information sciences; criminal justice and corrections; criminology; developmental and child psychology; economics; English composition; fine and studio art; geological and earth sciences/geosciences; health and physical education/fitness; history; human development, family studies, and related services; languages (Romance languages); legal studies (non-professional general, undergraduate); linguistic, comparative, and related language studies; marketing; mathematics; music; psychology; religious studies; sociology; speech and rhetoric.

MOUNTAIN VIEW COLLEGE
Dallas, Texas
http://www.mvc.dcccd.edu/
Mountain View College was founded in 1970. It is accredited by Southern Association of Colleges and Schools. It first offered distance learning courses in 1972. In fall 2006, there were 1,000 students enrolled in distance learning courses. Institutionally administered financial aid is available to distance learners.
Services Distance learners have accessibility to bookstore, e-mail services, library services.
Contact Dean Glenda Hall, Registrar, Mountain View College, Dallas, TX 75211. E-mail: ghall@dcccd.edu.

DEGREES AND AWARDS
AA Arts and Sciences

COURSE SUBJECT AREAS OFFERED OUTSIDE OF DEGREE PROGRAMS
Undergraduate—accounting and related services; computer and information sciences and support services related.

Non-credit—computer and information sciences and support services related.

MOUNT ALLISON UNIVERSITY
Sackville, New Brunswick, Canada
Continuing and Distance Education
http://www.mta.ca/conted/index.html
Mount Allison University was founded in 1839. It is provincially chartered. It first offered distance learning courses in 1965. In fall 2006, there were 400 students enrolled in distance learning courses. Institutionally administered financial aid is available to distance learners.
Services Distance learners have accessibility to academic advising, bookstore, campus computer network, e-mail services, library services.
Contact Ms. Heather Patterson, Director, Mount Allison University, Continuous Learning, 65 York Street, Sackville, NB E4L 1E4, Canada. Telephone: 506-364-2266. Fax: 506-364-2272. E-mail: hpatters@mta.ca.

DEGREES AND AWARDS
Programs offered do not lead to a degree or other formal award.

COURSE SUBJECT AREAS OFFERED OUTSIDE OF DEGREE PROGRAMS
Undergraduate—American literature (United States and Canadian); anthropology; economics; English; English language and literature related; English literature (British and Commonwealth); history; mathematics and statistics related; political science and government; psychology; religious education; religious studies; statistics.
Non-credit—creative writing; languages (foreign languages related).

MOUNT SAINT VINCENT UNIVERSITY
Halifax, Nova Scotia, Canada
Distance Learning and Continuing Education
http://www.msvu.ca/distance
Mount Saint Vincent University was founded in 1873. It is provincially chartered. It first offered distance learning courses in 1980. In fall 2006, there were 3,000 students enrolled in distance learning courses. Institutionally administered financial aid is available to distance learners.
Services Distance learners have accessibility to academic advising, bookstore, campus computer network, e-mail services, library services.
Contact Receptionist, Mount Saint Vincent University, 166 Bedford Highway, Halifax, NS B3M 2J6, Canada. Telephone: 902-457-6511. Fax: 902-443-2135. E-mail: distance@msvu.ca.

DEGREES AND AWARDS
BA Liberal Arts and General Studies
BBA Business Administration; Marketing
BTHM Tourism and Hospitality Management
Certificate Accounting; Gerontology; Information Technology Management
MEd Education

COURSE SUBJECT AREAS OFFERED OUTSIDE OF DEGREE PROGRAMS
Undergraduate—accounting and computer science; accounting and related services; behavioral sciences; business, management, and marketing related; communication and media; computer and information sciences; data entry/microcomputer applications; dietetics and clinical nutrition services; economics; education; education (specific subject areas); English; English literature (British and Commonwealth); entrepreneurial and small business operations; family and consumer sciences/human sciences related; finance and financial management services; foods, nutrition, and related services; gerontology; hospitality administration; international business; languages (foreign languages related); legal studies (non-professional general, undergraduate); marketing; mathematics; nutrition sciences; peace studies and conflict resolution; physiological psychology/psychobiology; psychology related; public relations, advertising, and applied communication related; religious education.
Graduate—education; educational psychology; education related.

Non-credit—creative writing; mathematics.

MT. SAN ANTONIO COLLEGE
Walnut, California
Distance Learning
http://vclass.mtsac.edu

Mt. San Antonio College was founded in 1946. It is accredited by Western Association of Schools and Colleges. It first offered distance learning courses in 1993. In fall 2006, there were 1,877 students enrolled in distance learning courses. Institutionally administered financial aid is available to distance learners.

Services Distance learners have accessibility to academic advising, bookstore, campus computer network, e-mail services, library services, tutoring.

Contact Kerry C. Stern, Dean, Mt. San Antonio College, Learning Resources, 1100 North Grand Avenue, Walnut, CA 91789. Telephone: 909-594-5611 Ext. 5658. Fax: 909-468-3992. E-mail: kstern@mtsac.edu.

DEGREES AND AWARDS
Programs offered do not lead to a degree or other formal award.

COURSE SUBJECT AREAS OFFERED OUTSIDE OF DEGREE PROGRAMS
Undergraduate—accounting and related services; anthropology; biology; business administration, management and operations; chemistry; computer and information sciences; creative writing; economics; English as a second language; English composition; family and consumer sciences/human sciences; hospitality administration; journalism; legal studies (non-professional general, undergraduate); philosophy; psychology; real estate; religious studies; sales, merchandising, and related marketing operations (specialized); sociology.
Non-credit—computer software and media applications.

MOUNT WACHUSETT COMMUNITY COLLEGE
Gardner, Massachusetts
Division of Continuing Education
http://www.mwcc.edu

Mount Wachusett Community College was founded in 1963. It is accredited by New England Association of Schools and Colleges. It first offered distance learning courses in 1994. In fall 2006, there were 1,150 students enrolled in distance learning courses. Institutionally administered financial aid is available to distance learners.

Services Distance learners have accessibility to academic advising, bookstore, campus computer network, career placement assistance, e-mail services, library services, tutoring.

Contact Ms. Debora Brennan, Distance Learning Administrative Assistant, Mount Wachusett Community College, 444 Green Street, Gardner, MA 01440. Telephone: 978-630-9275. Fax: 978-630-9537. E-mail: dbrennan@mwcc.mass.edu.

DEGREES AND AWARDS
AS Business Administration; Computer Information Systems; General Studies; Human Services; Paralegal Studies

COURSE SUBJECT AREAS OFFERED OUTSIDE OF DEGREE PROGRAMS
Undergraduate—biology; business administration, management and operations; communication and journalism related; computer programming; computer software and media applications; criminal justice and corrections; criminology; economics; English composition; film/video and photographic arts; history; human development, family studies, and related services; human resources management; human services; journalism; legal professions and studies related; management information systems; marketing; mathematics; mathematics and statistics related; mental and social health services and allied professions; nursing; political science and government; psychology; social sciences; sociology; statistics.

Non-credit—business operations support and assistant services; computer software and media applications; forestry.

MURRAY STATE UNIVERSITY
Murray, Kentucky
Continuing Education
http://ceao.murraystate.edu

Murray State University was founded in 1922. It is accredited by Southern Association of Colleges and Schools. It first offered distance learning courses in 1990. In fall 2006, there were 3,714 students enrolled in distance learning courses. Institutionally administered financial aid is available to distance learners.

Services Distance learners have accessibility to academic advising, bookstore, campus computer network, e-mail services, library services.

Contact Crystal Riley, Coordinator of Distance Learning, Murray State University, 303 Sparks Hall, CEAO, Murray, KY 42071-0009. Telephone: 800-669-7654. Fax: 270-809-3593. E-mail: crystal.riley@murraystate.edu.

DEGREES AND AWARDS
BBA Business–Bachelor of Science in Business
BGS Independent Studies–Bachelor of Independent Studies/General Studies
BS Telecommunications Systems Management
Endorsement English as a Second Language; Gifted and Talented

COURSE SUBJECT AREAS OFFERED OUTSIDE OF DEGREE PROGRAMS
Undergraduate—agricultural business and management; agriculture; agriculture and agriculture operations related; animal sciences; anthropology; business administration, management and operations; business/commerce; communication disorders sciences and services; computer and information sciences; computer programming; computer science; computer systems networking and telecommunications; education; English composition; geography and cartography; geological and earth sciences/geosciences; graphic communications; history; human development, family studies, and related services; journalism; legal studies (non-professional general, undergraduate); mathematics and statistics related; music; nursing; philosophy; philosophy and religious studies related; public relations, advertising, and applied communication related; radio, television, and digital communication; social sciences; social sciences related; social work; sociology.
Graduate—bilingual, multilingual, and multicultural education; communication disorders sciences and services; computer systems networking and telecommunications; educational administration and supervision; English as a second/foreign language (teaching); English as a second language; human services; marketing; nursing; quality control and safety technologies; special education.

MYERS UNIVERSITY
Cleveland, Ohio
COOL Program (College Options On-Line)
http://www.dnmyers.edu/online

Myers University was founded in 1848. It is accredited by North Central Association of Colleges and Schools. It first offered distance learning courses in 1976. In fall 2006, there were 414 students enrolled in distance learning courses. Institutionally administered financial aid is available to distance learners.

Services Distance learners have accessibility to academic advising, bookstore, campus computer network, career placement assistance, e-mail services, library services, tutoring.

Contact Ms. Brooke A. Scharlott, Associate Dean, Online Learning Center, Myers University, 3921 Chester Avenue, Cleveland, OH 44114. Telephone: 866-388-1578. Fax: 585-388-1518. E-mail: bscharlott@myers.edu.

DEGREES AND AWARDS
BS Criminal Justice Administration; Health Services Management; Information Technology

BSBA Accounting; Corporate Management; Finance; Forensic Accounting; Human Resource Management; Industrial Management; Management Information Systems; Marketing; Small Business Entrepreneurship

COURSE SUBJECT AREAS OFFERED OUTSIDE OF DEGREE PROGRAMS

Undergraduate—accounting and related services; American literature (United States and Canadian); applied mathematics; business administration, management and operations; business/commerce; business/corporate communications; business, management, and marketing related; business/managerial economics; communication and media; computer and information sciences; computer and information sciences and support services related; computer engineering; computer/information technology administration and management; computer programming; computer science; computer software and media applications; computer systems analysis; computer systems networking and telecommunications; criminal justice and corrections; criminology; data entry/microcomputer applications; economics; English composition; entrepreneurial and small business operations; finance and financial management services; geography and cartography; history; human resources management; information science/studies; international business; legal studies (non-professional general, undergraduate); management information systems; management sciences and quantitative methods; marketing; mathematics; military studies; political science and government; psychology; public administration; public relations, advertising, and applied communication related; sales, merchandising, and related marketing operations (specialized); sociology.

Graduate—business administration, management and operations; business/commerce.

NAROPA UNIVERSITY
Boulder, Colorado
Outreach Office
http://www.naropa.edu/distance

Naropa University was founded in 1974. It is accredited by North Central Association of Colleges and Schools. It first offered distance learning courses in 1999. In fall 2006, there were 168 students enrolled in distance learning courses. Institutionally administered financial aid is available to distance learners.

Services Distance learners have accessibility to academic advising, bookstore, career placement assistance, e-mail services, library services.

Contact Jirka Hladis, Director of Distance Learning Curriculum Development, Naropa University, 2130 Arapahoe Avenue, Boulder, CO 80302. Telephone: 303-245-4702. E-mail: jirka@naropa.edu.

DEGREES AND AWARDS

MA Contemplative Education; Transpersonal Psychology with Ecopsychology concentration; Transpersonal Psychology
MFA Creative Writing

COURSE SUBJECT AREAS OFFERED OUTSIDE OF DEGREE PROGRAMS

Undergraduate—area, ethnic, cultural, and gender studies related; clinical psychology; community psychology; comparative literature; counseling psychology; creative writing; developmental and child psychology; ethnic, cultural minority, and gender studies; experimental psychology; liberal arts and sciences, general studies and humanities; multi-/interdisciplinary studies related; philosophy and religious studies related; psychology; religious studies.

Graduate—area, ethnic, cultural, and gender studies related; education; English; languages (East Asian); liberal arts and sciences, general studies and humanities; multi-/interdisciplinary studies related; psychology related; religious education.

Non-credit—area, ethnic, cultural, and gender studies related; area studies; creative writing; education; educational psychology; education related; ethnic, cultural minority, and gender studies; human development, family studies, and related services; philosophy; philosophy and religious studies related; psychology; psychology related; religious education; religious/sacred music; religious studies; theological and ministerial studies; theology and religious vocations related.

See full description on page 390.

NASHVILLE STATE TECHNICAL COMMUNITY COLLEGE
Nashville, Tennessee

Nashville State Technical Community College was founded in 1970. It is accredited by Southern Association of Colleges and Schools. It first offered distance learning courses in 1998. In fall 2006, there were 3,800 students enrolled in distance learning courses. Institutionally administered financial aid is available to distance learners.

Services Distance learners have accessibility to academic advising, bookstore, career placement assistance, library services, tutoring.

Contact Doug Jameson, Coordinator of Distance Education, Nashville State Technical Community College, 120 White Bridge Road, Nashville, TN 37209. Telephone: 615-353-3461. Fax: 615-353-3774. E-mail: doug.jameson@nscc.edu.

DEGREES AND AWARDS

AAS Applied Science; Associate of Arts

COURSE SUBJECT AREAS OFFERED OUTSIDE OF DEGREE PROGRAMS

Undergraduate—accounting and computer science; architectural engineering technology; biology/biotechnology laboratory technician; business, management, and marketing related; computer and information sciences.

Non-credit—business operations support and assistant services.

NASSAU COMMUNITY COLLEGE
Garden City, New York
College of the Air
http://www.ncc.edu

Nassau Community College was founded in 1959. It is accredited by Middle States Association of Colleges and Schools. It first offered distance learning courses in 1991. In fall 2006, there were 1,800 students enrolled in distance learning courses. Institutionally administered financial aid is available to distance learners.

Services Distance learners have accessibility to academic advising, bookstore, campus computer network, e-mail services, library services.

Contact Prof. Arthur L. Friedman, EdD, Coordinator, Distance Education, Nassau Community College, 1 Education Drive, Garden City, NY 11530-6793. Telephone: 516-572-7883. Fax: 516-572-0690. E-mail: friedma@ncc.edu.

DEGREES AND AWARDS

Programs offered do not lead to a degree or other formal award.

COURSE SUBJECT AREAS OFFERED OUTSIDE OF DEGREE PROGRAMS

Undergraduate—accounting and related services; anthropology; apparel and textiles; astronomy and astrophysics; atmospheric sciences and meteorology; biology; business administration, management and operations; business/commerce; computer and information sciences; developmental and child psychology; economics; English composition; English language and literature related; entrepreneurial and small business operations; geological and earth sciences/geosciences; health and physical education/fitness; history; languages (Romance languages); legal studies (non-professional general, undergraduate); marketing; mathematics; mathematics and statistics related; music; nutrition sciences; physical sciences related; psychology; psychology related; sociology; statistics.

Non-credit—mathematics.

NATIONAL UNIVERSITY
La Jolla, California
NU Online
http://www.online.nu.edu
National University was founded in 1971. It is accredited by Western Association of Schools and Colleges. It first offered distance learning courses in 1994. In fall 2006, there were 16,122 students enrolled in distance learning courses. Institutionally administered financial aid is available to distance learners.

Services Distance learners have accessibility to academic advising, bookstore, campus computer network, career placement assistance, e-mail services, library services, tutoring.

Contact Mr. James Wilson, Associate Regional Dean, Online, National University, 4121 Camino del Rio South, San Diego, CA 92108. Telephone: 800-NAT-UNIV Ext. 7288. Fax: 858-563 7211. E-mail: jwilson @nu.edu.

DEGREES AND AWARDS

AA General Studies–Associate of Arts

BA Early Childhood Development; English–Single Subject Preparation in English; English; Global Studies; History; Management; Marketing; Psychology

BBA Business Administration

BS Accountancy; Allied Health; Computer Science; Construction Engineering; Criminal Justice Administration; Financial Management; Information Systems; Information Technology Management; Nursing; Organizational Behavior; Software Engineering

Certificate Early Childhood Special Education

Certification Administrative Services Certificate; Education–Level I Education Specialist Credential: Mild/Mod; Education–TED Multiple or Single Subject Teaching Credential

EMBA Executive Master of Business Administration (Spanish Version)

Graduate Certificate Supply Chain Management

MA English; Human Behavior; Human Resource Management and Organizational Development; Management

MAT Teaching

MBA Business Administration; Business Administration

MBA/MHA Master of Health Care Administration

MEd Cross Cultural Teaching

MFA Creative Writing; Digital Cinema

MPA Public Administration

MS Computer Science; Educational Administration and Administrative Services; Educational Technology; Educational and Instructional Technology; Electronic Business; Engineering Management; Forensic Sciences–Master of Forensic Sciences; Homeland Security and Safety Engineering; Information Systems; Organizational Leadership; Special Education and Level I Specialist Credential Mild/Moderate; Technology Management

COURSE SUBJECT AREAS OFFERED OUTSIDE OF DEGREE PROGRAMS

Undergraduate—accounting and related services; allied health and medical assisting services; biological and physical sciences; building/construction finishing, management, and inspection; business administration, management and operations; business/commerce; communications technology; computer software and media applications; construction engineering technology; counseling psychology; criminal justice and corrections; developmental and child psychology; education; English; history; information science/studies; international/global studies; management sciences and quantitative methods; nursing; psychology; public administration.

Graduate—accounting and related services; business administration, management and operations; business/commerce; computer and information sciences; computer programming; computer science; computer software and media applications; computer systems analysis; counseling psychology; creative writing; criminology; education; educational administration and supervision; educational/instructional media design; education (specific subject areas); human resources management; public administration; special education; technology education/industrial arts.

NAUGATUCK VALLEY COMMUNITY COLLEGE
Waterbury, Connecticut
http://www.nvcc.commnet.edu
Naugatuck Valley Community College was founded in 1992. It is accredited by New England Association of Schools and Colleges. It first offered distance learning courses in 2003. In fall 2006, there were 250 students enrolled in distance learning courses. Institutionally administered financial aid is available to distance learners.

Services Distance learners have accessibility to academic advising, campus computer network, e-mail services, library services.

Contact Ms. Stacey L. Williams, Director of Distance Learning, Naugatuck Valley Community College, 750 Chase Parkway, Waterbury, CT 06708. Telephone: 203-575-8182. E-mail: swilliams@nvcc.commnet.edu.

DEGREES AND AWARDS
Programs offered do not lead to a degree or other formal award.

COURSE SUBJECT AREAS OFFERED OUTSIDE OF DEGREE PROGRAMS

Undergraduate—accounting and related services; business administration, management and operations; business operations support and assistant services; computer and information sciences; criminal justice and corrections; culinary arts and related services; fine and studio art; health professions related; human development, family studies, and related services; liberal arts and sciences, general studies and humanities; music; nursing; sales, merchandising, and related marketing operations (specialized); social work; vehicle maintenance and repair technologies; visual and performing arts related.

Non-credit—accounting and related services; crafts, folk art and artisanry; dance; data entry/microcomputer applications; data processing; English as a second language; health and physical education/fitness; health/medical preparatory programs; real estate.

NEUMANN COLLEGE
Aston, Pennsylvania
neumannonline.org
http://www.neumann.edu/
Neumann College was founded in 1965. It is accredited by Middle States Association of Colleges and Schools. It first offered distance learning courses in 1998. In fall 2006, there were 300 students enrolled in distance learning courses. Institutionally administered financial aid is available to distance learners.

Services Distance learners have accessibility to academic advising, bookstore, campus computer network, career placement assistance, e-mail services, library services, tutoring.

Contact Dr. Patricia Szymurski, Dean, Division of Continuing Adult and Professional Studies, Neumann College, One Neumann Drive, Aston, PA 19014-1298. Telephone: 610-558-5530. Fax: 610-361-5490. E-mail: szymurst@neumann.edu.

DEGREES AND AWARDS
AA Liberal Studies
MS Management Science

COURSE SUBJECT AREAS OFFERED OUTSIDE OF DEGREE PROGRAMS

Undergraduate—criminology; English; English literature (British and Commonwealth); human resources management; mathematics and statistics related; psychology; religious studies; technical and business writing.

Graduate—management information systems; management sciences and quantitative methods; nursing.

NEW ENGLAND COLLEGE
Henniker, New Hampshire
New England College was founded in 1946. It is accredited by New England Association of Schools and Colleges. It first offered distance learning courses in 2004. Institutionally administered financial aid is available to distance learners.

Contact Dean Richard Keating, PhD, Dean, School of Graduate and Professional Studies, New England College, School of Graduate and

Professional Studies, 24 Bridge Street, Henniker, NH 03242. Telephone: 603-428-2479. Fax: 603-428-8123. E-mail: rkeating@nec.edu.

DEGREES AND AWARDS

BS Healthcare Administration

NEW ENGLAND COLLEGE OF FINANCE
Boston, Massachusetts
http://www.finance.edu/

New England College of Finance was founded in 1909. It is accredited by New England Association of Schools and Colleges. It first offered distance learning courses in 2002. In fall 2006, there were 350 students enrolled in distance learning courses. Institutionally administered financial aid is available to distance learners.

Services Distance learners have accessibility to academic advising, bookstore, library services.

Contact Carrie Newell, Enrollment Advisor, New England College of Finance, 10 High Street, Suite 204, Boston, MA 02110. Telephone: 617-951-2350 Ext. 233. Fax: 617-951-2533. E-mail: carrie.newell@ finance.edu.

DEGREES AND AWARDS

AS Business Administration

CCCPE Accounting and Finance; Banking Studies; Branch Management; Commercial Lending; Financial Services Studies; Forensic Accounting; Mutual Funds and Investments

COURSE SUBJECT AREAS OFFERED OUTSIDE OF DEGREE PROGRAMS

Undergraduate—accounting and related services; American literature (United States and Canadian); business administration, management and operations; business, management, and marketing related; business operations support and assistant services; computer and information sciences; economics; English; finance and financial management services; history; insurance; mathematics and statistics related; personality psychology; statistics.

Non-credit—accounting and related services; business administration, management and operations; business/commerce; business, management, and marketing related; business/managerial economics; business operations support and assistant services; finance and financial management services.

NEW ENGLAND INSTITUTE OF TECHNOLOGY
Warwick, Rhode Island
http://blackboard.neit.edu

New England Institute of Technology was founded in 1940. It is accredited by New England Association of Schools and Colleges. It first offered distance learning courses in 1996. In fall 2006, there were 138 students enrolled in distance learning courses. Institutionally administered financial aid is available to distance learners.

Services Distance learners have accessibility to academic advising, e-mail services, library services.

Contact Mr. Michael Caruso, Admissions Officer, New England Institute of Technology, 2500 Post Road, Warwick, RI 02886. Telephone: 401-739-5000 Ext. 3411. E-mail: mcaruso@neit.edu.

DEGREES AND AWARDS

Programs offered do not lead to a degree or other formal award.

COURSE SUBJECT AREAS OFFERED OUTSIDE OF DEGREE PROGRAMS

Undergraduate—English composition; mathematics; physics; physiology, pathology and related sciences; psychology; sociology.

NEW JERSEY CITY UNIVERSITY
Jersey City, New Jersey
Continuing Education
http://newlearning.njcu.edu

New Jersey City University was founded in 1927. It is accredited by Middle States Association of Colleges and Schools. It first offered distance learning courses in 1997. In fall 2006, there were 1,713 students enrolled in distance learning courses. Institutionally administered financial aid is available to distance learners.

Services Distance learners have accessibility to e-mail services, library services.

Contact Marie A. Fosello, Director of Online Learning, New Jersey City University, 2039 Kennedy Boulevard, Jersey City, NJ 07305-1597. Telephone: 201-200-3449. Fax: 201-200-2188. E-mail: conted@njcu. edu.

DEGREES AND AWARDS

MA Educational Technology
MS Finance

COURSE SUBJECT AREAS OFFERED OUTSIDE OF DEGREE PROGRAMS

Undergraduate—accounting and related services; business/commerce; criminal justice and corrections; economics; international relations and affairs; mathematics; physics; political science and government; public health.

Graduate—accounting and related services; business administration, management and operations; criminology; educational administration and supervision; educational/instructional media design; public health; special education.

NEW JERSEY INSTITUTE OF TECHNOLOGY
Newark, New Jersey
Continuing Professional Education
http://cpe.njit.edu/

New Jersey Institute of Technology was founded in 1881. It is accredited by Middle States Association of Colleges and Schools. It first offered distance learning courses in 1985. In fall 2006, there were 900 students enrolled in distance learning courses. Institutionally administered financial aid is available to distance learners.

Services Distance learners have accessibility to academic advising, bookstore, campus computer network, career placement assistance, e-mail services, library services, tutoring.

Contact Ellen Schreihoffer, Director of Extended Learning Delivery, New Jersey Institute of Technology, University Heights, Newark, NJ 07102. Telephone: 973-596-6093. Fax: 973-596-3288. E-mail: el@njit. edu.

DEGREES AND AWARDS

Graduate Certificate Data Mining; Emergency Management; Enterprise Systems Architecture; Information Management for Managers; Information Systems Implementation; Information Systems Implementation; Internet Systems Engineering; Management Essentials; Management of Technology; Network Security and Information Assurance; Object-Oriented Design; Pharmaceutical Managment; Practice of Technical Communications; Programming Environment Tools; Project Management; Telecommunications Networking; User Centered Design
MS Engineering Management; Professional and Technical Communications

COURSE SUBJECT AREAS OFFERED OUTSIDE OF DEGREE PROGRAMS

Undergraduate—accounting and computer science; computer and information sciences; computer science; computer systems networking and telecommunications; engineering; information science/studies; management information systems; technical and business writing.

Graduate—accounting and computer science; business administration, management and operations; business, management, and marketing related; communication and journalism related; computer/information technology administration and management; computer science; computer systems networking and telecommunications; engineering technologies related; information science/studies; technical and business writing.

NEWMAN THEOLOGICAL COLLEGE
Edmonton, Alberta, Canada
http://www.newman.edu

Newman Theological College was founded in 1969. It is provincially chartered. It first offered distance learning courses in 1987. In fall 2006, there were 76 students enrolled in distance learning courses.
Services Distance learners have accessibility to bookstore, campus computer network, library services.
Contact Carol Anne Seed, Registrar, Newman Theological College, 15611 St. Albert Trail, Edmonton, AB T6V 1H3, Canada. Telephone: 780-447-2993. Fax: 780-447-2685. E-mail: registrar@newman.edu.

DEGREES AND AWARDS
Certificate Theological Studies
Advanced Graduate Diploma Religious Education

COURSE SUBJECT AREAS OFFERED OUTSIDE OF DEGREE PROGRAMS
Undergraduate—theological and ministerial studies.
Graduate—religious education.

NEW MEXICO INSTITUTE OF MINING AND TECHNOLOGY
Socorro, New Mexico
Distance Education Department
http://www.nmt.edu/~eodi

New Mexico Institute of Mining and Technology was founded in 1889. It is accredited by North Central Association of Colleges and Schools. It first offered distance learning courses in 2000. In fall 2006, there were 130 students enrolled in distance learning courses. Institutionally administered financial aid is available to distance learners.
Services Distance learners have accessibility to academic advising, bookstore, campus computer network, career placement assistance, e-mail services, library services, tutoring.
Contact Mrs. Wendi Rae Carrillo, Student and Faculty Support Specialist, New Mexico Institute of Mining and Technology, 801 Leroy Place, Socorro, NM 87801. Telephone: 505-835-6908. Fax: 505-835-5541. E-mail: wcarrillo@admin.nmt.edu.

DEGREES AND AWARDS
Programs offered do not lead to a degree or other formal award.

COURSE SUBJECT AREAS OFFERED OUTSIDE OF DEGREE PROGRAMS
Undergraduate—aerospace, aeronautical and astronautical engineering; management information systems.
Graduate—aerospace, aeronautical and astronautical engineering; computer science; education (specific subject areas); engineering mechanics; environmental/environmental health engineering; management sciences and quantitative methods; materials engineering; mathematics; mechanical engineering; petroleum engineering.

NEW MEXICO JUNIOR COLLEGE
Hobbs, New Mexico
http://www.nmjc.edu

New Mexico Junior College was founded in 1965. It is accredited by North Central Association of Colleges and Schools. It first offered distance learning courses in 2001. In fall 2006, there were 1,000 students enrolled in distance learning courses. Institutionally administered financial aid is available to distance learners.
Services Distance learners have accessibility to academic advising, bookstore, campus computer network, career placement assistance, e-mail services, library services, tutoring.

Contact Mrs. Lisa Hardison, Dean, New Mexico Junior College, 5317 Lovington Highway, Hobbs, NM 88240. Telephone: 505-492-2641. Fax: 505-392-5757. E-mail: lhardison@nmjc.edu.

DEGREES AND AWARDS
AA Criminal Justice

COURSE SUBJECT AREAS OFFERED OUTSIDE OF DEGREE PROGRAMS
Undergraduate—accounting and computer science; agricultural/biological engineering and bioengineering; allied health and medical assisting services; American literature (United States and Canadian); biblical and other theological languages and literatures; biology; business administration, management and operations; communication and journalism related; communication and media; computer software and media applications; criminal justice and corrections; design and applied arts; economics; education related; English composition; geological and earth sciences/geosciences; history; mathematics; mathematics and statistics related.

NEW MEXICO STATE UNIVERSITY
Las Cruces, New Mexico
Office of Distance Education and Weekend College
http://www.nmsu.edu/distance

New Mexico State University was founded in 1888. It is accredited by North Central Association of Colleges and Schools. It first offered distance learning courses in 1989. In fall 2006, there were 2,612 students enrolled in distance learning courses. Institutionally administered financial aid is available to distance learners.
Services Distance learners have accessibility to academic advising, bookstore, campus computer network, career placement assistance, e-mail services, library services.
Contact Dr. Roberta Derlin, Associate Vice Provost for Distance Education, New Mexico State University, Box 3WEC, Las Cruces, NM 88003. Telephone: 505-646-5095. Fax: 505-646-2044. E-mail: rderlin@nmsu.edu.

DEGREES AND AWARDS
BA Human and Community Services–Bachelor of Human and Community Services; Sociology
BBA Business Administration
BS Elementary Education; Hotel, Restaurant and Tourism Management; Information and Communication Technology–Bachelor of Information and Communication Technology
BSN Nursing
Certificate Teaching and Learning–Online Teaching and Learning
Endorsement Information Technology Coordinator; Reading
License Educational Administrative Licensure; Elementary Licensure (Post BA); School Counseling Licensure; Special Education Alternative Licensure
MA Agricultural and Extension Educator; Education; Educational Administration
MAT Teaching–Master of Arts in Teaching
MCJ Criminal Justice
MS Industrial Engineering–Master of Science in Industrial Engineering; Industrial Engineering
MSN Psychiatric-Mental Health
MSW Social Work
EdD Educational Administration (Educational Leadership)
PhD Curriculum and Instruction–Learning Technologies emphasis

COURSE SUBJECT AREAS OFFERED OUTSIDE OF DEGREE PROGRAMS
Undergraduate—business administration, management and operations; business/commerce; community health services; human services; sociology.
Graduate—criminal justice and corrections; education related; industrial engineering; manufacturing engineering, mechanical engineering.

THE NEW SCHOOL: A UNIVERSITY
New York, New York
The New School Online–Bachelor's Program
http://www.newschool.edu/

The New School: A University was founded in 1919. It is accredited by Middle States Association of Colleges and Schools. It first offered distance learning courses in 1994. Institutionally administered financial aid is available to distance learners.

Services Distance learners have accessibility to academic advising, bookstore, campus computer network, e-mail services, library services.
Contact Ms. Gerianne Brusati, Associate Dean of Admissions, The New School: A University, 66 West 12th Street, Room 401, New York, NY 10011. Telephone: 212-229-5630. Fax: 212-989-3887. E-mail: brusatig @newschool.edu.

DEGREES AND AWARDS
BA Liberal Arts

COURSE SUBJECT AREAS OFFERED OUTSIDE OF DEGREE PROGRAMS
Undergraduate—communication and journalism related; communication and media; creative writing; liberal arts and sciences, general studies and humanities.
Non-credit—communication and journalism related; communication and media; creative writing; liberal arts and sciences, general studies and humanities.

See full description on page 392.

THE NEW SCHOOL: A UNIVERSITY
New York, New York
The New School Online–Media Management Program
http://www.dialnsa.edu

The New School: A University was founded in 1919. It is accredited by Middle States Association of Colleges and Schools. It first offered distance learning courses in 1994. Institutionally administered financial aid is available to distance learners.
Services Distance learners have accessibility to academic advising, bookstore, campus computer network, e-mail services, library services.
Contact Ms. Gerianne Brusati, Associate Dean for Admissions, The New School: A University, 66 West 12th Street, Room 401, New York, NY 10011. Telephone: 212-229-5630. Fax: 212-989-3887. E-mail: brusatig @newschool.edu.

DEGREES AND AWARDS
Graduate Certificate Media Management
MA Media Studies
See full description on page 394.

THE NEW SCHOOL: A UNIVERSITY
New York, New York
The New School Online–Teaching ESL
http://www.newschool.edu/

The New School: A University was founded in 1919. It is accredited by Middle States Association of Colleges and Schools. It first offered distance learning courses in 1994. Institutionally administered financial aid is available to distance learners.
Services Distance learners have accessibility to academic advising, bookstore, campus computer network, e-mail services, library services.
Contact Ms. Gerianne Brusati, Associate Dean of Admissions, The New School: A University, 66 West 12th Street, Room 401, New York, NY 10011. Telephone: 212-229-5630. Fax: 212-989-3887. E-mail: brusatig @newschool.edu.

DEGREES AND AWARDS
MA Teaching English to Speakers of Other Languages
See full description on page 396.

NEW YORK INSTITUTE OF TECHNOLOGY
Old Westbury, New York
On-Line Campus
http://www.nyit.edu

New York Institute of Technology was founded in 1955. It is accredited by Middle States Association of Colleges and Schools. It first offered distance learning courses in 1984. In fall 2006, there were 2,878 students enrolled in distance learning courses. Institutionally administered financial aid is available to distance learners.
Services Distance learners have accessibility to academic advising, bookstore, campus computer network, career placement assistance, e-mail services, library services.
Contact Ms. Kathleen Lyons, Assistant Director of Admissions, New York Institute of Technology, Carleton Avenue, PO Box 9029, Central Islip, NY 11729-9029. Telephone: 631-348-3200. Fax: 631-348-0912. E-mail: klyons@nyit.edu.

DEGREES AND AWARDS
BA Interdisciplinary Studies
BPS Hospitality Management; Interdisciplinary Studies
BS Business Administration; Community Mental Health; Criminal Justice; Interdisciplinary Studies; Psychology; Sociology
MBA Business
MS Energy Management

COURSE SUBJECT AREAS OFFERED OUTSIDE OF DEGREE PROGRAMS
Undergraduate—accounting and related services; anthropology; biology; business administration, management and operations; business, management, and marketing related; communication and media; creative writing; criminal justice and corrections; design and applied arts; economics; English; English composition; English language and literature related; environmental control technologies; finance and financial management services; journalism; legal studies (non-professional general, undergraduate); marketing; mechanical engineering; philosophy; philosophy and religious studies related; political science and government; social psychology; social work; sociology; speech and rhetoric; statistics.
Graduate—accounting and related services; business administration, management and operations; educational/instructional media design; management information systems; marketing.
Non-credit—computer and information sciences; computer and information sciences and support services related; computer/information technology administration and management; computer software and media applications; culinary arts and related services.

NORTH ARKANSAS COLLEGE
Harrison, Arkansas
Articulated Programs and Distance Learning
http://pioneer.northark.net/

North Arkansas College was founded in 1974. It is accredited by North Central Association of Colleges and Schools. It first offered distance learning courses in 1988. In fall 2006, there were 600 students enrolled in distance learning courses. Institutionally administered financial aid is available to distance learners.
Services Distance learners have accessibility to bookstore, campus computer network, e-mail services, library services.
Contact Mr. John P. Walsh, Director of Distance Education, North Arkansas College, 1515 Pioneer Drive, Harrison, AR 72601. Telephone: 870-391-3308. Fax: 870-391-3250. E-mail: jwalsh@northark.edu.

DEGREES AND AWARDS
Programs offered do not lead to a degree or other formal award.

COURSE SUBJECT AREAS OFFERED OUTSIDE OF DEGREE PROGRAMS
Undergraduate—accounting and related services; agricultural business and management; agricultural production; anthropology; biological and physical sciences; business/corporate communications; computer/information technology administration and management; economics; education related; English composition; fine and studio art; history;

human resources management; management information systems; mathematics; nursing; psychology; social sciences related; technical and business writing.

Non-credit—computer and information sciences and support services related; computer/information technology administration and management; computer software and media applications.

NORTH CAROLINA STATE UNIVERSITY
Raleigh, North Carolina
Distance Education
http://distance.ncsu.edu

North Carolina State University was founded in 1887. It is accredited by Southern Association of Colleges and Schools. It first offered distance learning courses in 1976. In fall 2006, there were 4,113 students enrolled in distance learning courses. Institutionally administered financial aid is available to distance learners.

Services Distance learners have accessibility to academic advising, bookstore, campus computer network, career placement assistance, e-mail services, library services, tutoring.

Contact Sharon Ferguson-Broere, Distance Education Registration Coordinator, North Carolina State University, Campus Box 7113, DELTA, Venture III, Raleigh, NC 27695-7113. Telephone: 919-515-9030. Fax: 919-515-6668. E-mail: sharon_broere@ncsu.edu.

DEGREES AND AWARDS

BA Leadership in the Public Sector

Certificate Computer Programming; HACCP/Food Safety Managers

Graduate Certificate Biological and Agricultural Engineering; Community College Teaching; Geographic Information Systems; Horticulture Science

MBAE Biological and Agricultural Engineering

MCE Chemical Engineering; Civil Engineering

MCS Computer Science

ME Engineering Online

MEd Curriculum and Instruction; Training and Development

MS Wood and Paper Science

MSAE Aerospace Engineering

MSE Agricultural Teacher Education

MSME Mechanical Engineering

MT Textiles Off-Campus programs (TOP)

COURSE SUBJECT AREAS OFFERED OUTSIDE OF DEGREE PROGRAMS

Undergraduate—accounting and related services; agricultural and domestic animal services; agricultural and food products processing; agricultural production; agriculture; American literature (United States and Canadian); animal sciences; anthropology; apparel and textiles; biological and physical sciences; business/commerce; business, management, and marketing related; chemistry; computer programming; educational psychology; education (specific subject areas); English; English as a second/foreign language (teaching); English composition; forestry; genetics; health and physical education/fitness; history; languages (Modern Greek); languages (Romance languages); languages (South Asian); mathematics; multi-/interdisciplinary studies related; music; nutrition sciences; parks, recreation and leisure facilities management; philosophy; physics; political science and government; psychology; soil sciences; technical and business writing; textile sciences and engineering; zoology/animal biology.

Graduate—agricultural and food products processing; agriculture; agriculture and agriculture operations related; biological and physical sciences; chemical engineering; civil engineering; computer engineering; curriculum and instruction; educational administration and supervision; education (specific subject areas); engineering; information science/studies; textile sciences and engineering.

NORTH CENTRAL STATE COLLEGE
Mansfield, Ohio
http://www.ncstate.tec.oh.us/

North Central State College was founded in 1961. It is accredited by North Central Association of Colleges and Schools. It first offered distance learning courses in 1994. In fall 2006, there were 329 students enrolled in distance learning courses. Institutionally administered financial aid is available to distance learners.

Services Distance learners have accessibility to academic advising, bookstore, campus computer network, e-mail services, library services.

Contact Gina Kamwithi, Chair, Community Education Department, North Central State College, Community Education Department, 2441 Kenwood Cirlce, Mansfield, OH 44901. Telephone: 419-755-4711. Fax: 419-755-5674. E-mail: dl@ncstatcollege.edu.

DEGREES AND AWARDS

Programs offered do not lead to a degree or other formal award.

COURSE SUBJECT AREAS OFFERED OUTSIDE OF DEGREE PROGRAMS

Undergraduate—accounting and computer science; allied health and medical assisting services; behavioral sciences; biological and physical sciences; business administration, management and operations; business/corporate communications; counseling psychology; English composition; English literature (British and Commonwealth); international business; physiological psychology/psychobiology; soil sciences.

NORTH DAKOTA STATE COLLEGE OF SCIENCE
Wahpeton, North Dakota
http://www.ndscs.edu/

North Dakota State College of Science was founded in 1903. It is accredited by North Central Association of Colleges and Schools. It first offered distance learning courses in 1968. In fall 2006, there were 531 students enrolled in distance learning courses. Institutionally administered financial aid is available to distance learners.

Services Distance learners have accessibility to academic advising, bookstore, career placement assistance, e-mail services, library services, tutoring.

Contact Ms. Margaret Wall, Distance Education Director, North Dakota State College of Science, 800 Sixth Street North, Wahpeton, ND 58076-0002. Telephone: 701-671-2430. Fax: 701-671-2416. E-mail: margaret.wall@ndscs.nodak.edu.

DEGREES AND AWARDS

AAS Administrative Assistant; Architectural Drafting and Estimating Technology; Business Management–eBusiness emphasis; Health Information Technician; Pharmacy Technician

AS Nursing–Practical Nursing

Certificate Computer Information Systems–Web Design; HIT–Medical Coding; Medical Transcription

COURSE SUBJECT AREAS OFFERED OUTSIDE OF DEGREE PROGRAMS

Undergraduate—accounting and related services; allied health and medical assisting services; applied mathematics; biology; business administration, management and operations; business, management, and marketing related; chemistry; computer and information sciences; computer and information sciences and support services related; computer/information technology administration and management; computer programming; developmental and child psychology; drafting/design engineering technologies; economics; English; English composition; foods, nutrition, and related services; health and medical administrative services; health and physical education/fitness; health professions related; history; marketing; mathematics; microbiological sciences and immunology; psychology; psychology related; social sciences; sociology; technical and business writing.

NORTH DAKOTA STATE UNIVERSITY
Fargo, North Dakota
Division of Distance and Continuing Education
http://www.ndsu.edu/dce

North Dakota State University was founded in 1890. It is accredited by North Central Association of Colleges and Schools. It first offered distance learning courses in 1998. Institutionally administered financial aid is available to distance learners.

Services Distance learners have accessibility to academic advising, bookstore, career placement assistance, e-mail services, library services, tutoring.

Contact Karen Murie, Distance Learning Coordinator, North Dakota State University, PO Box 5819, University Station, Fargo, ND 58105. Telephone: 701-231-7015. Fax: 701-231-7016. E-mail: karen.murie@ndsu.edu.

DEGREES AND AWARDS

CAGS Family Financial Planning; Food Protection; Gerontology; Merchandising; Software Engineering

MS Communication; Family Financial Planning; Family and Consumer Science Education; Gerontology; Merchandising

COURSE SUBJECT AREAS OFFERED OUTSIDE OF DEGREE PROGRAMS

Undergraduate—applied mathematics; clinical psychology; communication and media; computer and information sciences; data entry/microcomputer applications; developmental and child psychology; education; foods, nutrition, and related services; hospitality administration; human development, family studies, and related services; mathematics.

Graduate—clinical psychology; communication and media; computer engineering; curriculum and instruction; education; educational administration and supervision; educational/instructional media design; education (specific levels and methods); family and consumer economics; human development, family studies, and related services; psychology; special education.

Non-credit—aerospace, aeronautical and astronautical engineering; allied health and medical assisting services; business/commerce; business operations support and assistant services; clinical psychology; computer and information sciences; computer programming; computer science; computer software and media applications; data entry/microcomputer applications; human development, family studies, and related services.

NORTHEAST ALABAMA COMMUNITY COLLEGE
Rainsville, Alabama

Northeast Alabama Community College was founded in 1963. It is accredited by Southern Association of Colleges and Schools. It first offered distance learning courses in 2000. In fall 2006, there were 853 students enrolled in distance learning courses. Institutionally administered financial aid is available to distance learners.

Services Distance learners have accessibility to academic advising, bookstore, campus computer network, career placement assistance, e-mail services, library services, tutoring.

Contact Dr. Joe Burke, Vice President/Dean of Instruction, Northeast Alabama Community College, PO Box 159, Rainsville, AL 35986. Telephone: 256-228-6001 Ext. 320. Fax: 256-228-6558. E-mail: burkej@nacc.edu.

DEGREES AND AWARDS
Programs offered do not lead to a degree or other formal award.

COURSE SUBJECT AREAS OFFERED OUTSIDE OF DEGREE PROGRAMS

Undergraduate—accounting and computer science; American literature (United States and Canadian); behavioral sciences; biology; business administration, management and operations; chemistry; computer science; criminal justice and corrections; data processing; economics; English composition; English literature (British and Commonwealth); mathematics; music; psychology; sociology.

NORTHEASTERN ILLINOIS UNIVERSITY
Chicago, Illinois
http://www.neiu.edu/

Northeastern Illinois University was founded in 1961. It is accredited by North Central Association of Colleges and Schools. Institutionally administered financial aid is available to distance learners.

Services Distance learners have accessibility to campus computer network, e-mail services, library services.

Contact Bradley F. Baker, Dean of Libraries/Learning Resources, Northeastern Illinois University, 5500 North St. Louis Avenue, Chcago, IL 60625-4699. Telephone: 773-442-4466. Fax: 773-442-4531. E-mail: b-baker@neiu.edu.

DEGREES AND AWARDS

Programs offered do not lead to a degree or other formal award.

COURSE SUBJECT AREAS OFFERED OUTSIDE OF DEGREE PROGRAMS

Undergraduate—business administration, management and operations; educational/instructional media design; fine and studio art; geological and earth sciences/geosciences; music; psychology; social work.

Graduate—educational administration and supervision; education (specific subject areas); gerontology.

NORTHEASTERN UNIVERSITY
Boston, Massachusetts
Distance Learning Center
http://www.nuol.edu

Northeastern University was founded in 1898. It is accredited by New England Association of Schools and Colleges. It first offered distance learning courses in 1984. In fall 2006, there were 1,000 students enrolled in distance learning courses. Institutionally administered financial aid is available to distance learners.

Services Distance learners have accessibility to academic advising, bookstore, campus computer network, career placement assistance, e-mail services, library services.

Contact Denise Weir, Director, Distance Learning, Northeastern University, 360 Huntington Avenue, 266 RY, Boston, MA 02115. Telephone: 617-373-5622. Fax: 617-373-5625. E-mail: d.weir@neu.edu.

DEGREES AND AWARDS

AS Accounting; Arts and Sciences; Business Administration; Finance; Human Resources Management; Management Information Systems; Marketing; Marketing; Paralegal Studies; Supply Chain Management

BS English; Finance and Accounting Management; History; Human Services; Information Technology; Leadership; Liberal Arts with Business minor; Liberal Studies; Management; Operations Technology; Organizational Communications; Political Science; Psychology; Public Affairs; Sociology; Technical Communications

Certification Business English

Graduate Certificate Forensic Accounting; Higher Education Administration; Information Security Management; International Regulatory Affairs; Interpreter Education Master Mentor; Leadership; Network Security Management; Nonprofit Management; Pharmacogenetics Essentials; Project Management; Vaccines–Technologies, Trends, and Bioterrorism

MEd K-12 Specialization

MPS Informatics

MS Leadership; Regulatory Affairs for Drugs, Biologics, and Medical Devices; Respiratory Care Leadership

MSEE Electrical and Computer Engineering

MSIS Information Systems

NORTHEAST STATE TECHNICAL COMMUNITY COLLEGE
Blountville, Tennessee
Evening and Distance Education
http://northeaststate.edu

Northeast State Technical Community College was founded in 1966. It is accredited by Southern Association of Colleges and Schools. It first offered distance learning courses in 1996. In fall 2006, there were 3,100 students enrolled in distance learning courses. Institutionally administered financial aid is available to distance learners.

Services Distance learners have accessibility to academic advising, bookstore, campus computer network, career placement assistance, e-mail services, library services.

Contact Ms. Tammy B. Bartlett, Coordinator of Distance Education Programs and Services, Northeast State Technical Community College, PO Box 246, Blountville, TN 37617. Telephone: 423-354-2497. Fax: 423-323-0224. E-mail: tdbartlett@northeaststate.edu.

DEGREES AND AWARDS
Programs offered do not lead to a degree or other formal award.

COURSE SUBJECT AREAS OFFERED OUTSIDE OF DEGREE PROGRAMS
Undergraduate—accounting and related services; astronomy and astrophysics; biological and physical sciences; business administration, management and operations; chemistry; computer and information sciences; economics; education; English; English composition; history; mathematics; music; political science and government; psychology; social sciences; speech and rhetoric.

NORTHERN ARIZONA UNIVERSITY
Flagstaff, Arizona
NAU Distance Learning
http://www.distance.nau.edu

Northern Arizona University was founded in 1899. It is accredited by North Central Association of Colleges and Schools. It first offered distance learning courses in 1977. In fall 2006, there were 5,950 students enrolled in distance learning courses. Institutionally administered financial aid is available to distance learners.

Services Distance learners have accessibility to academic advising, bookstore, campus computer network, career placement assistance, e-mail services, library services, tutoring.

Contact Distance Learning Service Center, Northern Arizona University, PO Box 4117, Flagstaff, AZ 86011-4117. Telephone: 800-426-8315. Fax: 928-523-1169. E-mail: distance.programs@nau.edu.

DEGREES AND AWARDS
BA Psychology; Spanish
BEd Career and Technical Education (BS Ed.); Elementary Education (BS Ed.); Secondary Education (BS Ed.); Special and Elementary Education (BS Ed.)
BLS BAILS Arts and Letters; BAILS Criminal Justice; BAILS Enterprise in Society; BAILS Learning and Pedagogy; BAILS Mathematics/Statistics; BAILS Organizational Communication; BAILS Parks and Recreation Management; BAILS Psychology; BAILS Sociology; Environmental Sciences
BS BAILS Environmental Sciences; Criminal Justice; Dental Hygiene Completion Program; Health Promotion; Hotel and Restaurant Management; Interior Design; Management (BSBA); Nursing–Accelerated Option; Nursing; Parks and Recreation Management
BSAST Computer Technology (BAS); Early Childhood (BAS); Health Promotion (BAS); Justice Systems and Policy Planning (BAS); Public Agency Services (BAS)
BSN Nursing–RN to BSN
BSW Social Work
Certificate Educational Technology; Elementary Education Postdegree; International Tourism Management; Parks and Recreation Management; Restaurant Management; Secondary Education Postdegree; Special Education Postdegree

Certification Principalship; Professional Writing; Superintendency; Supervisory
Endorsement Bilingual Education Endorsement; English as a Second Language; Gifted Education; Middle School Education; Reading
Graduate Certificate Public Management
MA Applied Communication; Counseling; English
MAT Mathematics; Teaching English as a Second Language
MEd Bilingual/Multicultural Education; Career and Technical Education; Counseling/Human Relations; Counseling/School Counseling; Early Childhood Education; Educational Leadership; Educational Technology; Elementary Education; Secondary Education with Certification Emphasis; Secondary Education; Special Education
MEngr Engineering
MS Nursing
EdD Educational Leadership

COURSE SUBJECT AREAS OFFERED OUTSIDE OF DEGREE PROGRAMS
Undergraduate—art history, criticism and conservation; curriculum and instruction; environmental/environmental health engineering; marketing/marketing management; social work; sociology.
Graduate—curriculum and instruction; physical therapy.

See full description on page 398.

NORTHERN KENTUCKY UNIVERSITY
Highland Heights, Kentucky
Educational Outreach
http://dl.nku.edu

Northern Kentucky University was founded in 1968. It is accredited by Southern Association of Colleges and Schools. It first offered distance learning courses in 1983. In fall 2006, there were 1,000 students enrolled in distance learning courses. Institutionally administered financial aid is available to distance learners.

Services Distance learners have accessibility to academic advising, bookstore, campus computer network, career placement assistance, e-mail services, library services, tutoring.

Contact Debbie Poweleit, Associate Director of Educational Outreach, Northern Kentucky University, Educational Outreach, FH 305A, Highland Heights, KY 41099-5700. Telephone: 859-572-1500. Fax: 859-572-5174. E-mail: dl@nku.edu.

DEGREES AND AWARDS
BA Organizational Leadership
BS Construction Management–Surveying
BSN Nursing–RN-BSN
Certificate Entrepreneurship; Nurse Practitioner Advancement
Endorsement Gifted and Talented Education
MAE Instructional Leadership; MAEd
MSN Nursing

COURSE SUBJECT AREAS OFFERED OUTSIDE OF DEGREE PROGRAMS
Undergraduate—entrepreneurial and small business operations; liberal arts and sciences, general studies and humanities.
Graduate—education related; engineering technologies related.

NORTHERN STATE UNIVERSITY
Aberdeen, South Dakota
Continuing Education
http://www.northern.edu

Northern State University was founded in 1901. It is accredited by North Central Association of Colleges and Schools. It first offered distance learning courses in 1994. In fall 2006, there were 208 students enrolled in distance learning courses. Institutionally administered financial aid is available to distance learners.

Services Distance learners have accessibility to academic advising, bookstore, campus computer network, career placement assistance, e-mail services, library services, tutoring.

Contact Peggy Hallstrom, Registrar, Northern State University, 1200 South Jay Street, Aberdeen, SD 57401-7198. Telephone: 605-626-2012. Fax: 605-626-2587. E-mail: hallstrp@northern.edu.

DEGREES AND AWARDS
Programs offered do not lead to a degree or other formal award.

COURSE SUBJECT AREAS OFFERED OUTSIDE OF DEGREE PROGRAMS

Undergraduate—biological and physical sciences; business/commerce; computer and information sciences; criminology; dramatic/theater arts and stagecraft; economics; educational psychology; English; English composition; health and physical education/fitness; languages (Germanic); library science; linguistic, comparative, and related language studies; mathematics; mathematics and statistics related; music; sociology.
Graduate—education; educational psychology.

NORTHERN VIRGINIA COMMUNITY COLLEGE
Annandale, Virginia
Extended Learning Institute
http://eli.nvcc.edu
Northern Virginia Community College was founded in 1965. It is accredited by Southern Association of Colleges and Schools. It first offered distance learning courses in 1975. In fall 2006, there were 6,000 students enrolled in distance learning courses. Institutionally administered financial aid is available to distance learners.
Services Distance learners have accessibility to academic advising, bookstore, campus computer network, e-mail services, library services, tutoring.
Contact Jayne Townend, Admissions and Records, Northern Virginia Community College, 8333 Little River Turnpike, Annandale, VA 22003-3796. Telephone: 703-323-3368. Fax: 703-323-3392. E-mail: jtownend @nvcc.edu.

DEGREES AND AWARDS
AA Liberal Arts
AAS Business Management–Public Management specialization; Business Management
AS Business Administration; General Studies
Specialized diploma Information Systems Technology

COURSE SUBJECT AREAS OFFERED OUTSIDE OF DEGREE PROGRAMS

Undergraduate—accounting and related services; biology; creative writing; developmental and child psychology; dramatic/theater arts and stagecraft; English composition; film/video and photographic arts; finance and financial management services; fine and studio art; geography and cartography; history; journalism; languages (Romance languages); legal studies (non-professional general, undergraduate); management information systems; marketing; mathematics and statistics related; mechanical engineering; philosophy and religious studies related; sociology; statistics.

NORTH HARRIS MONTGOMERY COMMUNITY COLLEGE DISTRICT
Houston, Texas
The Center for Teaching and Distance Learning
http://www.nhmccd.edu
North Harris Montgomery Community College District was founded in 1972. It first offered distance learning courses in 1993. In fall 2006, there were 10,000 students enrolled in distance learning courses. Institutionally administered financial aid is available to distance learners.
Services Distance learners have accessibility to academic advising, bookstore, campus computer network, career placement assistance, e-mail services, library services, tutoring.
Contact Hilton Lasalle, Director, Center for Teaching and Distance Learning, North Harris Montgomery Community College District, 5000

Research Forest Drive, The Woodlands, TX 77381-4399. Telephone: 832-813-6752. Fax: 832-813-6753. E-mail: hilton.j.lasalle@nhmccd.edu.

DEGREES AND AWARDS
AA General Studies
AAS Legal Office; Management; Medical Office
AS General Studies

COURSE SUBJECT AREAS OFFERED OUTSIDE OF DEGREE PROGRAMS

Undergraduate—accounting and related services; behavioral sciences; biology; business administration, management and operations; business, management, and marketing related; business operations support and assistant services; communication and media; computer and information sciences; computer programming; computer software and media applications; computer systems networking and telecommunications; creative writing; data entry/microcomputer applications; English; English composition; geography and cartography; graphic communications; history; human resources management; legal support services; marketing; mathematics; music; nutrition sciences; philosophy; social psychology; sociology; technical and business writing; visual and performing arts; visual and performing arts related.

NORTH IDAHO COLLEGE
Coeur d'Alene, Idaho
http://www.nic.edu
North Idaho College was founded in 1933. It is accredited by Northwest Commission on Colleges and Universities. It first offered distance learning courses in 1997. In fall 2006, there were 600 students enrolled in distance learning courses. Institutionally administered financial aid is available to distance learners.
Services Distance learners have accessibility to academic advising, bookstore, campus computer network, career placement assistance, e-mail services, library services, tutoring.
Contact Dr. Candace Wheeler, Director of Distance Education, North Idaho College, 1000 West Garden Avenue, Coeur d'Alene, ID 83814. Telephone: 208-769-3436. Fax: 208-769-7728. E-mail: candace_wheeler@nic.edu.

DEGREES AND AWARDS
AS General Program

COURSE SUBJECT AREAS OFFERED OUTSIDE OF DEGREE PROGRAMS

Undergraduate—accounting and related services; allied health and medical assisting services; American literature (United States and Canadian); anthropology; area, ethnic, cultural, and gender studies related; biology; business/commerce; communication and media; English composition; fine and studio art; human development, family studies, and related services; mathematics; philosophy; political science and government; psychology; sociology.
Non-credit—accounting and computer science; accounting and related services; allied health and medical assisting services; allied health diagnostic, intervention, and treatment professions; alternative and complementary medicine and medical systems; American literature (United States and Canadian); applied mathematics; behavioral sciences; business administration, management and operations; business/commerce; communication and journalism related; communication and media; communications technologies and support services related; computer and information sciences; computer and information sciences and support services related; computer/information technology administration and management; computer programming; computer software and media applications; computer systems networking and telecommunications; creative writing; entrepreneurial and small business operations; film/video and photographic arts; languages (classics and classical); publishing; technical and business writing.

NORTHLAND COMMUNITY AND TECHNICAL COLLEGE–THIEF RIVER FALLS
Thief River Falls, Minnesota
http://www.northland.cc.mn.us/

Northland Community and Technical College–Thief River Falls was founded in 1965. It is accredited by North Central Association of Colleges and Schools. It first offered distance learning courses in 1996. In fall 2006, there were 150 students enrolled in distance learning courses. Institutionally administered financial aid is available to distance learners.
Services Distance learners have accessibility to academic advising, bookstore, career placement assistance, e-mail services, library services, tutoring.
Contact Minnesota Online Support Center, Northland Community and Technical College–Thief River Falls, 150 2nd Avenue SW, Suite B, Box 309, Perham, MN 56573. Telephone: 800-456-8519. Fax: 218-347-6217. E-mail: mnonline@custhellp.com.

DEGREES AND AWARDS
Programs offered do not lead to a degree or other formal award.

COURSE SUBJECT AREAS OFFERED OUTSIDE OF DEGREE PROGRAMS
Undergraduate—accounting and related services; biology; business administration, management and operations; business/commerce; business operations support and assistant services; communication and media; computer and information sciences; mathematics; nursing.

NORTH SEATTLE COMMUNITY COLLEGE
Seattle, Washington
Distance Learning Office
http://www.virtualcollege.org

North Seattle Community College was founded in 1970. It is accredited by Northwest Commission on Colleges and Universities. It first offered distance learning courses in 1994. In fall 2006, there were 875 students enrolled in distance learning courses. Institutionally administered financial aid is available to distance learners.
Services Distance learners have accessibility to academic advising, bookstore, campus computer network, career placement assistance, e-mail services, library services, tutoring.
Contact Carol Howe, Program Coordinator, North Seattle Community College, 9600 College Way North, LB2237, Seattle, WA 98103. Telephone: 206-527-3738. Fax: 206-985-3984. E-mail: chowe@sccd.ctc.edu.

DEGREES AND AWARDS
AA General Studies

COURSE SUBJECT AREAS OFFERED OUTSIDE OF DEGREE PROGRAMS
Undergraduate—accounting and related services; anthropology; astronomy and astrophysics; biological and physical sciences; business/commerce; communication and media; computer programming; computer software and media applications; computer systems networking and telecommunications; economics; English composition; film/video and photographic arts; geological and earth sciences/geosciences; human development, family studies, and related services; journalism; library science related; mathematics; music; philosophy; psychology.

NORTHWEST ARKANSAS COMMUNITY COLLEGE
Bentonville, Arkansas
Northwest Arkansas Distance Education
http://www.nwacc.edu/disted

NorthWest Arkansas Community College was founded in 1989. It is accredited by North Central Association of Colleges and Schools. It first offered distance learning courses in 1997. In fall 2006, there were 926 students enrolled in distance learning courses. Institutionally administered financial aid is available to distance learners.
Services Distance learners have accessibility to academic advising, bookstore, e-mail services, library services, tutoring.

Contact Mr. Clint Brooks, Director of Distance Learning, NorthWest Arkansas Community College, BH 2413, One College Drive, Bentonville, AR 72712. Telephone: 479-619-4382. Fax: 479-619-4383. E-mail: cbrooks@nwacc.edu.

DEGREES AND AWARDS
AA Transfer degree
AGS General Studies

COURSE SUBJECT AREAS OFFERED OUTSIDE OF DEGREE PROGRAMS
Undergraduate—accounting and related services; agricultural and food products processing; agriculture; allied health diagnostic, intervention, and treatment professions; apparel and textiles; applied mathematics; behavioral sciences; biology; business administration, management and operations; business/corporate communications; business, management, and marketing related; chemistry; communication and media; computer and information sciences; computer and information sciences and support services related; computer programming; computer software and media applications; computer systems networking and telecommunications; criminal justice and corrections; developmental and child psychology; economics; English; English composition; English language and literature related; fine and studio art; fire protection; foods, nutrition, and related services; health and physical education/fitness; health services/allied health/health sciences; history; hospitality administration; liberal arts and sciences, general studies and humanities; mathematics; medical basic sciences; music; nutrition sciences; philosophy; political science and government; psychology; psychology related; social sciences; social sciences related; sociology; speech and rhetoric.
Non-credit—English composition; mathematics.

NORTHWEST CHRISTIAN COLLEGE
Eugene, Oregon
http://www.nwcc.edu/

Northwest Christian College was founded in 1895. It is accredited by Northwest Commission on Colleges and Universities. It first offered distance learning courses in 1999. In fall 2006, there were 19 students enrolled in distance learning courses. Institutionally administered financial aid is available to distance learners.
Services Distance learners have accessibility to academic advising, bookstore, career placement assistance, e-mail services, library services.
Contact Ms. Kathy Sweetman, Director of Undergraduate Admissions, Northwest Christian College, 828 East 11th Avenue, Eugene, OR 97401. Telephone: 541-684-7201. Fax: 541-684-7317. E-mail: admissions@nwcc.edu.

DEGREES AND AWARDS
Programs offered do not lead to a degree or other formal award.

COURSE SUBJECT AREAS OFFERED OUTSIDE OF DEGREE PROGRAMS
Undergraduate—biblical studies; education (specific levels and methods); English language and literature related.

NORTHWESTERN COLLEGE
St. Paul, Minnesota
Center for Distance Education
http://distance.nwc.edu

Northwestern College was founded in 1902. It is accredited by North Central Association of Colleges and Schools. It first offered distance learning courses in 1994. In fall 2006, there were 800 students enrolled in distance learning courses. Institutionally administered financial aid is available to distance learners.
Services Distance learners have accessibility to academic advising, bookstore, campus computer network, career placement assistance, e-mail services, library services, tutoring.
Contact Betty Piper, Assistant Director, Northwestern College, 3003 Snelling Avenue North, St. Paul, MN 55113. Telephone: 800-308-5495. Fax: 651-631-5133. E-mail: distance@nwc.edu.

DEGREES AND AWARDS

AA Biblical Studies
BA Biblical Studies; Intercultural Ministries degree completion
Certificate Bible

COURSE SUBJECT AREAS OFFERED OUTSIDE OF DEGREE PROGRAMS

Undergraduate—archeology; astronomy and astrophysics; biblical studies; chemistry; communication and media; computer software and media applications; ethnic, cultural minority, and gender studies; history; languages (Modern Greek); liberal arts and sciences, general studies and humanities; mathematics; missionary studies and missiology; philosophy and religious studies related; psychology; religious/sacred music; religious studies; speech and rhetoric; theological and ministerial studies; theology and religious vocations related.

See full description on page 400.

NORTHWESTERN CONNECTICUT COMMUNITY COLLEGE

Winsted, Connecticut
http://www.commnet.edu/nwctc

Northwestern Connecticut Community College was founded in 1965. It is accredited by New England Association of Schools and Colleges. It first offered distance learning courses in 1997. In fall 2006, there were 279 students enrolled in distance learning courses. Institutionally administered financial aid is available to distance learners.

Services Distance learners have accessibility to academic advising, bookstore, e-mail services, library services, tutoring.

Contact Beverly J. King, Education Technology Specialist, Northwestern Connecticut Community College, Park Place East, Winsted, CT 06098. Telephone: 860-738-6323. E-mail: bking@nwcc.commnet.edu.

DEGREES AND AWARDS

AS Educational Technology

COURSE SUBJECT AREAS OFFERED OUTSIDE OF DEGREE PROGRAMS

Undergraduate—allied health and medical assisting services; biological and physical sciences; computer and information sciences; English as a second/foreign language (teaching); English composition; geography and cartography; history; mathematics; philosophy; psychology; science, technology and society; sociology.
Non-credit—computer and information sciences; computer software and media applications; technical and business writing.

NORTHWESTERN OKLAHOMA STATE UNIVERSITY

Alva, Oklahoma
http://www.nwalva.edu/

Northwestern Oklahoma State University was founded in 1897. It is accredited by North Central Association of Colleges and Schools. It first offered distance learning courses in 2004. In fall 2006, there were 923 students enrolled in distance learning courses. Institutionally administered financial aid is available to distance learners.

Services Distance learners have accessibility to bookstore, campus computer network, e-mail services, library services.

Contact Dr. Nancy J. Knous, Coordinator of Distance Learning, Northwestern Oklahoma State University, 709 Oklahoma Boulevard, Alva, OK 73717. Telephone: 580-327-8443. Fax: 580-327-8431. E-mail: njknous @nwosu.edu.

DEGREES AND AWARDS

Programs offered do not lead to a degree or other formal award.

COURSE SUBJECT AREAS OFFERED OUTSIDE OF DEGREE PROGRAMS

Undergraduate—accounting and computer science; accounting and related services; business administration, management and operations; business/commerce; business/corporate communications; criminal justice and corrections; curriculum and instruction; education; English; English

literature (British and Commonwealth); public relations, advertising, and applied communication related; social psychology; sociology.
Graduate—bilingual, multilingual, and multicultural education; business administration, management and operations; educational administration and supervision; education related.

NORTHWESTERN UNIVERSITY

Evanston, Illinois
Masters in Medical Informatics
http://www.northwestern.edu/

Northwestern University was founded in 1851. It is accredited by North Central Association of Colleges and Schools. It first offered distance learning courses in 2006. In fall 2006, there were 100 students enrolled in distance learning courses. Institutionally administered financial aid is available to distance learners.

Services Distance learners have accessibility to academic advising, bookstore, campus computer network, e-mail services, library services.

Contact Enrollment Advisor, Northwestern University, 5401 S. Kirkman Road, Suite 200, Orlando, FL 32819. Telephone: 877-664-3347. Fax: 321-239-1870.

DEGREES AND AWARDS

MS Medical Informatics

COURSE SUBJECT AREAS OFFERED OUTSIDE OF DEGREE PROGRAMS

Graduate—medical illustration and informatics.
Non-credit—medical illustration and informatics.

See full description on page 402.

NORTHWEST MISSISSIPPI COMMUNITY COLLEGE

Senatobia, Mississippi

Northwest Mississippi Community College was founded in 1927. It is accredited by Southern Association of Colleges and Schools. It first offered distance learning courses in 1990. In fall 2006, there were 890 students enrolled in distance learning courses. Institutionally administered financial aid is available to distance learners.

Services Distance learners have accessibility to campus computer network, e-mail services, library services.

Contact Mrs. Kim Steinman, Distance Learning Secretary, Northwest Mississippi Community College, 4975 Highway 51 North, Box 7042, Senatobia, MS 38668. Telephone: 662-560-5230. Fax: 662-560-5232. E-mail: ksteinman@northwestms.edu.

DEGREES AND AWARDS

AA Administration of Criminal Justice

COURSE SUBJECT AREAS OFFERED OUTSIDE OF DEGREE PROGRAMS

Undergraduate—accounting and computer science; American literature (United States and Canadian); applied mathematics; behavioral sciences; biological and physical sciences; computer software and media applications; criminal justice and corrections; criminology; economics; English; English composition; English language and literature related; foods, nutrition, and related services; geography and cartography; health and physical education/fitness; history; liberal arts and sciences, general studies and humanities; mathematics; music; natural sciences; physical sciences related; psychology; social sciences; social work; sociology.

NORTHWEST MISSOURI STATE UNIVERSITY

Maryville, Missouri
Center for Information Technology in Education
http://www.NorthwestOnline.org

Northwest Missouri State University was founded in 1905. It is accredited by North Central Association of Colleges and Schools. It first offered distance learning courses in 1999. In fall 2006, there were 1,100 students enrolled in distance learning courses. Institutionally administered financial aid is available to distance learners.

Services Distance learners have accessibility to academic advising, bookstore, campus computer network, career placement assistance, e-mail services, library services.

Contact Dr. Roger Von Holzen, Director of Center for Information Technology in Education, Northwest Missouri State University, OL 246, Maryville, MO 64468. Telephone: 660-562-1532. Fax: 660-562-1049. E-mail: rvh@nwmissouri.edu.

DEGREES AND AWARDS

BS Accounting; Business Management; Computer Science; Management Information Systems; Office Information Systems
MS Applied Computer Science; Geographic Information Science
MSE Special Education; Teaching–Instructional Technology

COURSE SUBJECT AREAS OFFERED OUTSIDE OF DEGREE PROGRAMS

Undergraduate—communication and media; computer and information sciences; dramatic/theater arts and stagecraft; geography and cartography; history; linguistic, comparative, and related language studies; mathematics; music; philosophy; political science and government; psychology.
Graduate—computer and information sciences; computer and information sciences and support services related; computer/information technology administration and management; education; educational/instructional media design; geography and cartography; special education.
Non-credit—educational/instructional media design; geography and cartography.

NORTHWEST TECHNICAL COLLEGE
Bemidji, Minnesota

Northwest Technical College was founded in 1993. It is accredited by North Central Association of Colleges and Schools. It first offered distance learning courses in 1995. In fall 2006, there were 1,000 students enrolled in distance learning courses. Institutionally administered financial aid is available to distance learners.
Services Distance learners have accessibility to academic advising, bookstore, career placement assistance, e-mail services, library services, tutoring.
Contact Minnesota Online Support Center, Northwest Technical College, 150 2nd Avenue SW, Suite B, Box 309, Perham, MN 56573. Telephone: 800-456-8519. Fax: 218-347-6214. E-mail: mnonline@custhellp.com.

DEGREES AND AWARDS

AAS Accounting; Administrative Assistant; Individualized Occupational Preparation; Medical Administrative Secretary Technology; Sales, Marketing, and Management; Supervisory Management
AS Nursing

COURSE SUBJECT AREAS OFFERED OUTSIDE OF DEGREE PROGRAMS

Undergraduate—accounting and related services; allied health and medical assisting services; applied mathematics; behavioral sciences; biological and physical sciences; business administration, management and operations; business, management, and marketing related; chemistry; English composition; health and medical administrative services; marketing; nursing.

NORTHWOOD UNIVERSITY
Midland, Michigan
University College
http://www.northwoodonline.org

Northwood University was founded in 1959. It is accredited by North Central Association of Colleges and Schools. It first offered distance learning courses in 1965. In fall 2006, there were 300 students enrolled in distance learning courses. Institutionally administered financial aid is available to distance learners.
Services Distance learners have accessibility to academic advising, bookstore, campus computer network, career placement assistance, e-mail services, library services, tutoring.
Contact Kimberly G. Leach, Program Center Manager, Northwood University, 4000 Whiting Drive, Midland, MI 48640. Telephone: 800-445-5873. Fax: 989-837-4457. E-mail: leachk@northwood.edu.

DEGREES AND AWARDS
Programs offered do not lead to a degree or other formal award.

COURSE SUBJECT AREAS OFFERED OUTSIDE OF DEGREE PROGRAMS

Undergraduate—business, management, and marketing related.

NOVA SCOTIA AGRICULTURAL COLLEGE
Truro, Nova Scotia, Canada
Center for Continuing and Distance Education
http://www.nsac.ns.ca

Nova Scotia Agricultural College was founded in 1905. It is provincially chartered. It first offered distance learning courses in 1996. In fall 2006, there were 45 students enrolled in distance learning courses. Institutionally administered financial aid is available to distance learners.
Services Distance learners have accessibility to academic advising, bookstore, e-mail services, library services.
Contact Mrs. Pamela Doyle, Administrative Assistant, Nova Scotia Agricultural College, PO Box 550, 23 Sheep Hill Lane, Truro, NS B2N 5E3, Canada. Telephone: 902-893-6666. Fax: 902-895-5528. E-mail: cde@nsac.ca.

DEGREES AND AWARDS
Programs offered do not lead to a degree or other formal award.

COURSE SUBJECT AREAS OFFERED OUTSIDE OF DEGREE PROGRAMS

Undergraduate—agricultural business and management; agricultural production; agriculture; animal sciences; plant sciences.
Non-credit—agriculture; animal sciences; plant sciences.

NOVA SOUTHEASTERN UNIVERSITY
Fort Lauderdale, Florida
Masters in Clinical Vision Research
http://www.nova.edu/cvr

Nova Southeastern University was founded in 1964. It is accredited by Southern Association of Colleges and Schools. It first offered distance learning courses in 2002. In fall 2006, there were 7 students enrolled in distance learning courses. Institutionally administered financial aid is available to distance learners.
Services Distance learners have accessibility to academic advising, bookstore, campus computer network, e-mail services, library services.
Contact Josephine Shallo-Hoffmann, Chair of Research and Graduate Programs, Nova Southeastern University, 3200 South University Drive, Fort Lauderdale, FL 33328. Telephone: 954-262-4226. Fax: 954-262-3875. E-mail: shoffman@nova.edu.

DEGREES AND AWARDS
MS Clinical Vision Research

COURSE SUBJECT AREAS OFFERED OUTSIDE OF DEGREE PROGRAMS

Graduate—medical clinical sciences/graduate medical studies.
Non-credit—medical clinical sciences/graduate medical studies.

NOVA SOUTHEASTERN UNIVERSITY
Fort Lauderdale, Florida
Graduate School of Computer and Information Sciences
http://www.scis.nova.edu/

Nova Southeastern University was founded in 1964. It is accredited by Southern Association of Colleges and Schools. It first offered distance learning courses in 1983. In fall 2006, there were 1,200 students enrolled in distance learning courses. Institutionally administered financial aid is available to distance learners.
Services Distance learners have accessibility to academic advising, bookstore, campus computer network, career placement assistance, e-mail services, library services.

Contact Program Counselor, Nova Southeastern University, Recruitment Office, Carl DeSantis Building, 4th Floor, 3301 College Avenue, Fort Lauderdale, FL 33314. Telephone: 800-986-2247. Fax: 954-262-3915. E-mail: scisinfo@nova.edu.

DEGREES AND AWARDS

MS Computer Information Systems; Computer Science; Computing Technology in Education; Information Security; Management Information Systems

PhD Computer Information Systems; Computer Science; Computing Technology in Education; Information Systems

COURSE SUBJECT AREAS OFFERED OUTSIDE OF DEGREE PROGRAMS

Graduate—computer and information sciences; computer and information sciences and support services related; computer/information technology administration and management; computer programming; computer science; computer software and media applications; computer systems analysis; computer systems networking and telecommunications; educational/instructional media design; education related; management information systems; medical illustration and informatics; systems science and theory; technology education/industrial arts.

OAKTON COMMUNITY COLLEGE
Des Plaines, Illinois

Oakton Community College was founded in 1969. It is accredited by North Central Association of Colleges and Schools. It first offered distance learning courses in 1975. In fall 2006, there were 1,500 students enrolled in distance learning courses. Institutionally administered financial aid is available to distance learners.

Services Distance learners have accessibility to academic advising, bookstore, career placement assistance, e-mail services, library services, tutoring.

Contact Ms. Robin Nash, Manager of Alternative Education, Oakton Community College, 1600 East Golf Road, Des Plaines, IL 60016. Telephone: 847-635-1971. Fax: 847-635-1987. E-mail: rnash@oakton.edu.

DEGREES AND AWARDS
Programs offered do not lead to a degree or other formal award.

COURSE SUBJECT AREAS OFFERED OUTSIDE OF DEGREE PROGRAMS

Undergraduate—accounting and related services; American literature (United States and Canadian); anthropology; applied mathematics; area studies; astronomy and astrophysics; behavioral sciences; biological and physical sciences; business/commerce; business/corporate communications; communication and journalism related; communication and media; computer and information sciences; computer science; computer software and media applications; data entry/microcomputer applications; developmental and child psychology; dramatic/theater arts and stagecraft; economics; engineering; English; English composition; film/video and photographic arts; geography and cartography; graphic communications; health and medical administrative services; health professions related; history; human development, family studies, and related services; international business; journalism; languages (Germanic); languages (Romance languages); languages (Southeast Asian and Australasian/Pacific); legal studies (non-professional general, undergraduate); library science related; linguistic, comparative, and related language studies; marketing; mathematics; mechanical engineering; nursing; pharmacy, pharmaceutical sciences, and administration; philosophy; philosophy and religious studies related; physical sciences; political science and government; psychology; radio, television, and digital communication; sales, merchandising, and related marketing operations (general); social sciences; sociology; statistics; technical and business writing.

Non-credit—business/commerce; communication and journalism related; computer and information sciences; culinary arts and related services; data entry/microcomputer applications; family and consumer economics; languages (Romance languages).

ODESSA COLLEGE
Odessa, Texas
Division of Distance Education
http://www.odessa.edu

Odessa College was founded in 1946. It is accredited by Southern Association of Colleges and Schools. It first offered distance learning courses in 1986. In fall 2006, there were 2,673 students enrolled in distance learning courses. Institutionally administered financial aid is available to distance learners.

Services Distance learners have accessibility to academic advising, bookstore, campus computer network, career placement assistance, e-mail services, library services.

Contact Wilma Chastain, Director of Distance Learning, Odessa College, 201 West University, Odessa, TX 79764. Telephone: 432-335-6317. Fax: 432-335-6667. E-mail: wchastain@odessa.edu.

DEGREES AND AWARDS
Programs offered do not lead to a degree or other formal award.

COURSE SUBJECT AREAS OFFERED OUTSIDE OF DEGREE PROGRAMS

Undergraduate—accounting and related services; allied health and medical assisting services; biology; business/commerce; business, management, and marketing related; business operations support and assistant services; communication and journalism related; computer and information sciences; computer and information sciences and support services related; computer science; developmental and child psychology; economics; English; English composition; environmental control technologies; environmental/environmental health engineering; mathematics; mathematics and statistics related; nursing; social psychology; sociology; speech and rhetoric.

Non-credit—business administration, management and operations; business, management, and marketing related; computer software and media applications; creative writing; linguistic, comparative, and related language studies; sales, merchandising, and related marketing operations (specialized).

THE OHIO STATE UNIVERSITY
Columbus, Ohio
Technology Enhanced Learning and Research (TELR)
http://telr.ohio-state.edu

The Ohio State University was founded in 1870. It is accredited by North Central Association of Colleges and Schools. It first offered distance learning courses in 1995. In fall 2006, there were 2,800 students enrolled in distance learning courses. Institutionally administered financial aid is available to distance learners.

Services Distance learners have accessibility to academic advising, bookstore, campus computer network, e-mail services, library services, tutoring.

Contact Dr. Joanne E. Dehoney, EdD, Interim Executive Director for e-Learning, The Ohio State University, Technology Enhanced Learning and Research, 1971 Neil Avenue, BSE 480, Columbus, OH 43210. Telephone: 614-247-6819. Fax: 614-292-7081. E-mail: dehoney.1@osu.edu.

DEGREES AND AWARDS
EMBA Business Administration
MSE Welding Engineering
PharmD NonTraditional PharmD

COURSE SUBJECT AREAS OFFERED OUTSIDE OF DEGREE PROGRAMS

Undergraduate—business/commerce; engineering related; family and consumer economics; forestry; linguistic, comparative, and related language studies; plant sciences; political science and government; social work; visual and performing arts related.

Graduate—business administration, management and operations; educational administration and supervision; education related; engineering related; mechanical engineering; nuclear engineering; nursing; plant sciences; social work.

Non-credit—gerontology; mental and social health services and allied professions; special education.

OKLAHOMA STATE UNIVERSITY
Stillwater, Oklahoma
Distance Learning
http://ueied.ue.okstate.edu/dl/index.htm
Oklahoma State University was founded in 1890. It is accredited by North Central Association of Colleges and Schools. It first offered distance learning courses in 1945. In fall 2006, there were 2,000 students enrolled in distance learning courses. Institutionally administered financial aid is available to distance learners.
Services Distance learners have accessibility to academic advising, bookstore, campus computer network, library services.
Contact Cecilia Boardman, Administrative Support Specialist, Oklahoma State University, 309 Wes Watkins Center, Stillwater, OK 74078. Telephone: 405-744-6390. Fax: 405-744-3420. E-mail: ics-inf@okstate.edu.

DEGREES AND AWARDS
Programs offered do not lead to a degree or other formal award.

COURSE SUBJECT AREAS OFFERED OUTSIDE OF DEGREE PROGRAMS
Undergraduate—accounting and related services; American literature (United States and Canadian); animal sciences; anthropology; applied horticulture/horticultural business services; business administration, management and operations; business/corporate communications; communication disorders sciences and services; counseling psychology; creative writing; economics; education related; electrical and electronic engineering technologies; engineering technologies related; English composition; English literature (British and Commonwealth); finance and financial management services; fire protection; foods, nutrition, and related services; geography and cartography; geological and earth sciences/geosciences; health and physical education/fitness; history; journalism; languages (Germanic); languages (Romance languages); legal studies (non-professional general, undergraduate); management information systems; marketing; mathematics and statistics related; music; political science and government; psychology; sales, merchandising, and related marketing operations (general); sociology; statistics; technical and business writing.
Non-credit—fire protection.

OLD DOMINION UNIVERSITY
Norfolk, Virginia
Office of Distance Learning and Extended Education
http://www.dl.odu.edu
Old Dominion University was founded in 1930. It is accredited by Southern Association of Colleges and Schools. It first offered distance learning courses in 1984. In fall 2006, there were 5,040 students enrolled in distance learning courses. Institutionally administered financial aid is available to distance learners.
Services Distance learners have accessibility to academic advising, bookstore, campus computer network, career placement assistance, e-mail services, library services.
Contact Mrs. Anita Wiggins Bailey, Enrollment Services Specialist, Old Dominion University, Gornto TELETECHNET Center, Norfolk, VA 23529. Telephone: 800-968-2638. Fax: 757-683-5492. E-mail: awiggins@odu.edu.

DEGREES AND AWARDS
BA Criminal Justice
BHS Health Sciences
BS Computer Science; Criminal Justice; Education–Teacher Preparation; Human Services Counseling; Occupational and Technical Studies
BSBA Accounting, Finance, Information Systems, Marketing; Management
BSET Civil Engineering Technology; Electrical Engineering Technology; Engineering Technology, general; Mechanical Engineering Technology

BSN Nursing
MEM Engineering Management
MS Community Health; Education–Pre-K through 6; Occupational and Technical Studies; Special Education
MSN Nursing–Nurse Leader and Nurse Educator options
PhD Community College Leadership; Occupation and Technical Studies

COURSE SUBJECT AREAS OFFERED OUTSIDE OF DEGREE PROGRAMS
Undergraduate—accounting and related services; business/corporate communications; business/managerial economics; communication and media; community health services; computer science; criminal justice and corrections; education related; engineering technologies related; finance and financial management services; industrial and organizational psychology; management information systems; management sciences and quantitative methods; marketing; philosophy; social psychology; sociology.
Graduate—accounting and related services; aerospace, aeronautical and astronautical engineering; education related; environmental/environmental health engineering; finance and financial management services; management information systems; marketing; mechanical engineering.

ORAL ROBERTS UNIVERSITY
Tulsa, Oklahoma
http://www.oru.edu/
Oral Roberts University was founded in 1963. It is accredited by North Central Association of Colleges and Schools. It first offered distance learning courses in 1975. In fall 2006, there were 96 students enrolled in distance learning courses. Institutionally administered financial aid is available to distance learners.
Services Distance learners have accessibility to academic advising, bookstore, campus computer network, career placement assistance, e-mail services, library services, tutoring.
Contact Mr. Gary Brougher, SLLE Representative, Oral Roberts University, School of LifeLong Education, 7777 South Lewis Avenue, Tulsa, OK 74171. Telephone: 800-643-7976. Fax: 918-495-6055. E-mail: gbrougher@oru.edu.

DEGREES AND AWARDS
BS Business Administration; Christian Care and Counseling; Church Ministries; Elementary Education with certification; Liberal Studies
MA Practical Theology
MAE Christian School Administration; Christian School Curriculum; Christian School Postsecondary Administration; Early Childhood Education; Public School Administration; Teaching English as a Second Language (TESL); Teaching with certification
MAM Nonprofit Management
MBA Business Administration
MDiv Divinity
MM Management–Master of Management
DMin Ministry
EdD Christian School Administration (PK–12); Education–Postsecondary School Administration; Public School Administration

COURSE SUBJECT AREAS OFFERED OUTSIDE OF DEGREE PROGRAMS
Undergraduate—biblical studies; biology; English; history; liberal arts and sciences, general studies and humanities; mathematics; political science and government.
Non-credit—biblical studies; theological and ministerial studies.

ORANGEBURG-CALHOUN TECHNICAL COLLEGE
Orangeburg, South Carolina
http://www.octech.org/
Orangeburg-Calhoun Technical College was founded in 1968. It is accredited by Southern Association of Colleges and Schools. It first offered distance learning courses in 1996. In fall 2006, there were 500 students enrolled in distance learning courses. Institutionally administered financial aid is available to distance learners.
Services Distance learners have accessibility to academic advising, bookstore, career placement assistance, library services, tutoring.

Contact Mike Hammond, Dean of Administration, Orangeburg-Calhoun Technical College, 3250 St. Matthews Road, Orangeburg, SC 29118-8299. Telephone: 803-535-1267. Fax: 803-535-1388. E-mail: hammondm@octech.edu.

DEGREES AND AWARDS
Programs offered do not lead to a degree or other formal award.

COURSE SUBJECT AREAS OFFERED OUTSIDE OF DEGREE PROGRAMS
Undergraduate—allied health and medical assisting services; business/commerce; computer/information technology administration and management; computer systems networking and telecommunications; criminal justice and corrections; economics; English composition; English literature (British and Commonwealth); history; legal studies (nonprofessional general, undergraduate); mathematics; psychology; sociology; technical and business writing.

ORANGE COAST COLLEGE
Costa Mesa, California
http://www.orangecoastcollege.com
Orange Coast College was founded in 1947. It is accredited by Western Association of Schools and Colleges. It first offered distance learning courses in 1998. In fall 2006, there were 3,669 students enrolled in distance learning courses. Institutionally administered financial aid is available to distance learners.
Services Distance learners have accessibility to bookstore, library services.
Contact Dr. Nancy Kidder, Administrative Dean of Admissions and Records and International Programs, Orange Coast College, 2701 Fairview Road, Costa Mesa, CA 92626. Telephone: 714-432-0202. E-mail: nkidder@mail.occ.cccd.edu.

DEGREES AND AWARDS
Programs offered do not lead to a degree or other formal award.

COURSE SUBJECT AREAS OFFERED OUTSIDE OF DEGREE PROGRAMS
Undergraduate—accounting and related services; allied health and medical assisting services; anthropology; apparel and textiles; architecture; biology; business, management, and marketing related; business operations support and assistant services; computer and information sciences; computer/information technology administration and management; computer programming; computer software and media applications; construction engineering technology; dance; drafting/design engineering technologies; electrical/electronics maintenance and repair technology; electromechanical and instrumentation and maintenance technologies; English composition; food science and technology; foods, nutrition, and related services; health and medical administrative services; health professions related; heating, air conditioning, ventilation and refrigeration maintenance technology; hospitality administration; human development, family studies, and related services; music; real estate; sales, merchandising, and related marketing operations (specialized).

OREGON HEALTH & SCIENCE UNIVERSITY
Portland, Oregon
School of Nursing
http://www.ohsu.edu/son
Oregon Health & Science University was founded in 1974. It is accredited by Northwest Commission on Colleges and Universities. It first offered distance learning courses in 1992. In fall 2006, there were 200 students enrolled in distance learning courses. Institutionally administered financial aid is available to distance learners.
Services Distance learners have accessibility to academic advising, bookstore, campus computer network, career placement assistance, e-mail services, library services, tutoring.
Contact Tami Buedefeldt, Admissions Counselor, Oregon Health & Science University, OHSU SoN Office of Admissions, Mail Code SN-ADM, 3455 SW US Veterans Hospital Road, Portland, OR 97239-2941. Telephone: 503-494-7725. Fax: 503-494-6433. E-mail: proginfo @ohsu.edu.

DEGREES AND AWARDS
BSN Nursing
MPH Primary Health Care and Health Disparities

OREGON INSTITUTE OF TECHNOLOGY
Klamath Falls, Oregon
http://www.oit.edu/dist
Oregon Institute of Technology was founded in 1947. It is accredited by Northwest Commission on Colleges and Universities. It first offered distance learning courses in 1997. In fall 2006, there were 688 students enrolled in distance learning courses. Institutionally administered financial aid is available to distance learners.
Services Distance learners have accessibility to academic advising, bookstore, campus computer network, career placement assistance, e-mail services, library services, tutoring.
Contact Beth Murphy, Director, Distance Education, Oregon Institute of Technology, 3201 Campus Drive, Klamath Falls, OR 97601. Telephone: 541-885-1141. Fax: 541-885-1139. E-mail: beth.murphy@oit.edu.

DEGREES AND AWARDS
BS Dental Hygiene–degree completion in Dental Hygiene; Information Technology Online; Radiological Science–Radiological Science degree completion; Respiratory Care; Ultrasound–degree completion in Ultrasound, Echocardiography option; Ultrasound–degree completion in Ultrasound, Vascular Technology option
Certificate of Completion Polysomnographic Technology

COURSE SUBJECT AREAS OFFERED OUTSIDE OF DEGREE PROGRAMS
Undergraduate—accounting and related services; allied health diagnostic, intervention, and treatment professions; anthropology; business administration, management and operations; business/commerce; computer and information sciences; computer/information technology administration and management; dental support services and allied professions; economics; engineering/industrial management; human development, family studies, and related services; management information systems; mathematics; psychology; social sciences; technical and business writing.

OREGON STATE UNIVERSITY
Corvallis, Oregon
Extended Campus
http://ecampus.oregonstate.edu
Oregon State University was founded in 1868. It is accredited by Northwest Commission on Colleges and Universities. It first offered distance learning courses in 1986. In fall 2006, there were 2,360 students enrolled in distance learning courses. Institutionally administered financial aid is available to distance learners.
Services Distance learners have accessibility to academic advising, bookstore, campus computer network, career placement assistance, e-mail services, library services, tutoring.
Contact Ecampus Student Services Center, Oregon State University, OSU Extended Campus, 4943 The Valley Library, Corvallis, OR 97331-4504. Telephone: 800-667-1465. Fax: 541-737-2734. E-mail: ecampus @oregonstate.edu.

DEGREES AND AWARDS
BA Liberal Studies
BS Agriculture, general; Environmental Sciences; Liberal Studies; Natural Resources
Certificate of Completion Management and Human Resource Skills for Pharmacists
Certificate Geographic Information Sciences
Endorsement ESOL/Bilingual Education
License Continuing Teaching Licensure

Graduate Certificate Health Management and Policy; Sustainable Natural Resources; Sustainable Natural Resources; Teaching English as a Second Language
MAT Early Childhood/Elementary Education
MEd Adult Education; Education
MHP Radiation Health Physics
MS Radiation Health Physics
EdD Community College Leadership concentration
PhD Community College Leadership concentration; Radiation Health Physics

COURSE SUBJECT AREAS OFFERED OUTSIDE OF DEGREE PROGRAMS

Undergraduate—agricultural business and management; agriculture; agriculture and agriculture operations related; American literature (United States and Canadian); anthropology; area, ethnic, cultural, and gender studies related; atmospheric sciences and meteorology; botany/plant biology; business/commerce; business/corporate communications; chemistry; communication and media; creative writing; ecology, evolution, and population biology; economics; education; education related; English; English composition; ethnic, cultural minority, and gender studies; fishing and fisheries sciences and management; forestry; geological and earth sciences/geosciences; health and medical administrative services; health services/allied health/health sciences; history; liberal arts and sciences, general studies and humanities; mathematics and statistics related; natural resources and conservation related; natural resources conservation and research; natural resources management and policy; philosophy; philosophy and religious studies related; plant sciences; political science and government; psychology; sales, merchandising, and related marketing operations (general); science, technology and society; social sciences related; sociology; soil sciences; statistics; technical and business writing; wildlife and wildlands science and management.
Graduate—education; educational administration and supervision; education related; education (specific levels and methods); education (specific subject areas); English as a second/foreign language (teaching); English as a second language; environmental/environmental health engineering; foods, nutrition, and related services; geography and cartography; geological and earth sciences/geosciences; health and medical administrative services; health professions related; natural resources conservation and research; natural resources management and policy; nuclear and industrial radiologic technologies; public health.
Non-credit—business, management, and marketing related; communication and media; computer software and media applications; English; English as a second language; family and consumer economics; film/video and photographic arts; fine and studio art; health and medical administrative services; human resources management; languages (Romance languages); linguistic, comparative, and related language studies; pharmacology and toxicology; pharmacy, pharmaceutical sciences, and administration; psychology; sales, merchandising, and related marketing operations (specialized).

See full description on page 404.

OUACHITA TECHNICAL COLLEGE
Malvern, Arkansas
http://www.otcweb.edu
Ouachita Technical College was founded in 1972. It is accredited by North Central Association of Colleges and Schools. It first offered distance learning courses in 1998. In fall 2006, there were 300 students enrolled in distance learning courses. Institutionally administered financial aid is available to distance learners.
Services Distance learners have accessibility to academic advising, bookstore, campus computer network, career placement assistance, e-mail services, library services, tutoring.
Contact Mr. Tony Hunnicutt, Distance Learning Coordinator, Ouachita Technical College, One College Circle, Malvern, AR 72104. Telephone: 501-337-5000 Ext. 1106. Fax: 501-337-9382. E-mail: thunnicutt@otcweb.edu.

DEGREES AND AWARDS
AA Education, general
AAS Criminal Justice

COURSE SUBJECT AREAS OFFERED OUTSIDE OF DEGREE PROGRAMS

Undergraduate—behavioral sciences; biological and physical sciences; biology; business administration, management and operations; computer and information sciences; computer software and media applications; computer systems networking and telecommunications; criminal justice and corrections; English composition; history; human resources management; liberal arts and sciences, general studies and humanities; mathematics; philosophy; political science and government; psychology; social sciences; sociology.

OWENSBORO COMMUNITY AND TECHNICAL COLLEGE
Owensboro, Kentucky
http://www.octc.kctcs.edu
Owensboro Community and Technical College was founded in 1986. It is accredited by Council on Occupational Education. It first offered distance learning courses in 1998. In fall 2006, there were 383 students enrolled in distance learning courses. Institutionally administered financial aid is available to distance learners.
Services Distance learners have accessibility to e-mail services, library services.
Contact Ms. Barbara Tipmore, Admissions Counselor, Owensboro Community and Technical College, 4800 New Hartford Road, Owensboro, KY 42303. Telephone: 270-686-4527. Fax: 270-686-4487. E-mail: barb.tipmore@kctcs.edu.

DEGREES AND AWARDS
Programs offered do not lead to a degree or other formal award.

COURSE SUBJECT AREAS OFFERED OUTSIDE OF DEGREE PROGRAMS

Undergraduate—accounting and related services; behavioral sciences; business administration, management and operations; business/commerce; communication and media; computer and information sciences; English; history; human development, family studies, and related services; human services; psychology; psychology related.

PACE UNIVERSITY
New York, New York
Online Pace
http://www.online.pace.edu
Pace University was founded in 1906. It is accredited by Middle States Association of Colleges and Schools. It first offered distance learning courses in 1997. In fall 2006, there were 2,000 students enrolled in distance learning courses. Institutionally administered financial aid is available to distance learners.
Services Distance learners have accessibility to academic advising, bookstore, campus computer network, career placement assistance, e-mail services, library services, tutoring.
Contact Ms. Christine Moloughney, Coordinator of Online Support Services, Pace University, One Pace Plaza, New York, NY 10038. Telephone: 212-346-1471. E-mail: cmoloughney@pace.edu.

DEGREES AND AWARDS
AS Applied Information Technology, Telecommunications Degree
BS Communication Studies–Professional Communication Studies; Professional Technology Studies; Telecommunications
Specialized diploma Computing–Doctor of Professional Studies in Computing
Graduate Certificate Business Aspects of Publishing; Internet Technologies; Internet Technology; Telecommunications
MBA Business Administration–e.MBA
MS Internet Technology for E-Commerce; Publishing

COURSE SUBJECT AREAS OFFERED OUTSIDE OF DEGREE PROGRAMS

Undergraduate—accounting and related services; American literature (United States and Canadian); anthropology; biological and physical

sciences; biology; business administration, management and operations; business/commerce; chemistry; communication and media; computer and information sciences and support services related; computer programming; computer science; computer software and media applications; computer systems networking and telecommunications; criminal justice and corrections; criminology; economics; education; education (specific subject areas); English; English composition; ethnic, cultural minority, and gender studies; finance and financial management services; fine and studio art; history; information science/studies; international business; languages (foreign languages related); legal studies (non-professional general, undergraduate); linguistic, comparative, and related language studies; marketing; mathematics; mathematics and statistics related; nursing; physical sciences; political science and government; psychology; science, technology and society; social sciences; sociology; statistics; visual and performing arts.
Graduate—bilingual, multilingual, and multicultural education; business administration, management and operations; business/commerce; computer and information sciences; computer and information sciences and support services related; computer/information technology administration and management; computer programming; computer software and media applications; computer systems analysis; computer systems networking and telecommunications; curriculum and instruction; education; educational administration and supervision; educational assessment, evaluation, and research; educational/instructional media design; education related; information science/studies; management information systems; marketing; nursing; public administration; publishing.
Non-credit—business/commerce; computer and information sciences; education; liberal arts and sciences, general studies and humanities; nursing; personal and culinary services related.

PACIFIC GRADUATE SCHOOL OF PSYCHOLOGY
Palo Alto, California
Master's Degree (M.S.) in Psychology
http://www.pgsp.edu/distance.htm
Pacific Graduate School of Psychology was founded in 1975. It is accredited by Western Association of Schools and Colleges. It first offered distance learning courses in 1999. In fall 2006, there were 26 students enrolled in distance learning courses. Institutionally administered financial aid is available to distance learners.
Services Distance learners have accessibility to academic advising, e-mail services, library services.
Contact Ms. Elizabeth Hilt, Vice President of Enrollment Management, Pacific Graduate School of Psychology, 935 East Meadow Drive, Palo Alto, CA 94303. Telephone: 800-818-6136. Fax: 650-493-6147. E-mail: ehit@pgsp.edu.

DEGREES AND AWARDS
MS Psychology

COURSE SUBJECT AREAS OFFERED OUTSIDE OF DEGREE PROGRAMS
Graduate—psychology.
See full description on page 406.

PACIFIC OAKS COLLEGE
Pasadena, California
Distance Learning
http://www.pacificoaks.edu
Pacific Oaks College was founded in 1945. It is accredited by Western Association of Schools and Colleges. It first offered distance learning courses in 1996. In fall 2006, there were 202 students enrolled in distance learning courses. Institutionally administered financial aid is available to distance learners.
Services Distance learners have accessibility to academic advising, bookstore, library services.
Contact Betty Jones, Co-Director of Distance Learning, Pacific Oaks College, 5 Westmoreland Place, Pasadena, CA 91103. Telephone: 800-613-0300. Fax: 626-397-1317. E-mail: bjones@pacificoaks.edu.

DEGREES AND AWARDS
BA Human Development
MA Human Development

COURSE SUBJECT AREAS OFFERED OUTSIDE OF DEGREE PROGRAMS
Undergraduate—education (specific levels and methods); human development, family studies, and related services.
Graduate—education (specific levels and methods); family psychology; human development, family studies, and related services.

PACIFIC UNION COLLEGE
Angwin, California
http://www.puc.edu/
Pacific Union College was founded in 1882. It is accredited by Western Association of Schools and Colleges. It first offered distance learning courses in 2001. In fall 2006, there were 32 students enrolled in distance learning courses. Institutionally administered financial aid is available to distance learners.
Services Distance learners have accessibility to academic advising, bookstore, campus computer network, e-mail services, library services, tutoring.
Contact Nancy Lecourt, PhD, Academic Dean, Pacific Union College, One Angwin Avenue, Angwin, CA 94508. Telephone: 707-965-6234. E-mail: nlecourt@puc.edu.

DEGREES AND AWARDS
Programs offered do not lead to a degree or other formal award.

COURSE SUBJECT AREAS OFFERED OUTSIDE OF DEGREE PROGRAMS
Undergraduate—health and physical education/fitness; mathematics; nursing; religious studies.

PALOMAR COLLEGE
San Marcos, California
Educational Television
http://www.palomar.edu
Palomar College was founded in 1946. It is accredited by Western Association of Schools and Colleges. It first offered distance learning courses in 1975. In fall 2006, there were 4,756 students enrolled in distance learning courses. Institutionally administered financial aid is available to distance learners.
Services Distance learners have accessibility to academic advising, bookstore, campus computer network, career placement assistance, e-mail services, library services, tutoring.
Contact Ms. Marlene deLeon, Distance Education Specialist, Palomar College, 1140 West Mission Road, San Marcos, CA 92069. Telephone: 760-744-1150 Ext. 3055. Fax: 760-761-3519. E-mail: mdeleon@palomar.edu.

DEGREES AND AWARDS
Programs offered do not lead to a degree or other formal award.

COURSE SUBJECT AREAS OFFERED OUTSIDE OF DEGREE PROGRAMS
Undergraduate—accounting and related services; American Sign Language (ASL); anthropology; archeology; area, ethnic, cultural, and gender studies related; behavioral sciences; bilingual, multilingual, and multicultural education; biology; botany/plant biology; business administration, management and operations; business/commerce; business, management, and marketing related; business operations support and assistant services; cell biology and anatomical sciences; chemistry; communication and journalism related; communication and media; computer and information sciences; computer and information sciences and support services related; computer programming; computer science; computer software and media applications; counseling psychology; criminal justice and corrections; data entry/microcomputer applications; developmental and child psychology; economics; educational/instructional

media design; English; English composition; ethnic, cultural minority, and gender studies; family and consumer economics; family and consumer sciences/human sciences; family and consumer sciences/human sciences business services; family and consumer sciences/human sciences related; finance and financial management services; fine and studio art; fire protection; foods, nutrition, and related services; geography and cartography; geological and earth sciences/geosciences; graphic communications; health and physical education/fitness; history; human development, family studies, and related services; information science/studies; insurance; international business; journalism; languages (American Indian/Native American); languages (Iranian/Persian); languages (Romance languages); legal professions and studies related; legal research and advanced professional studies; legal studies (non-professional general, undergraduate); legal support services; liberal arts and sciences, general studies and humanities; library assistant; library science; library science related; marketing; music; natural sciences; nutrition sciences; philosophy; philosophy and religious studies related; political science and government; psychology; psychology related; radio, television, and digital communication; real estate; sales, merchandising, and related marketing operations (general); social psychology; social sciences; social sciences related; sociology; statistics.

PAMLICO COMMUNITY COLLEGE
Grantsboro, North Carolina

Pamlico Community College was founded in 1963. It is accredited by Southern Association of Colleges and Schools. It first offered distance learning courses in 1999. In fall 2006, there were 200 students enrolled in distance learning courses. Institutionally administered financial aid is available to distance learners.

Services Distance learners have accessibility to academic advising, campus computer network, career placement assistance, e-mail services, library services.

Contact Ms. Kathleen Mayo, Distance Learning Coordinator, Pamlico Community College, PO Box 185, Grantsboro, NC 28529. Telephone: 252-249-1851 Ext. 3012. Fax: 252-249-2377. E-mail: kmayo@pamlicocc.edu.

DEGREES AND AWARDS

Programs offered do not lead to a degree or other formal award.

COURSE SUBJECT AREAS OFFERED OUTSIDE OF DEGREE PROGRAMS

Undergraduate—accounting and computer science; accounting and related services; allied health and medical assisting services; American literature (United States and Canadian); applied mathematics; behavioral sciences; biological and physical sciences; biology; business administration, management and operations; business/commerce; business, management, and marketing related; business/managerial economics; chemistry; communications technology; computer and information sciences; computer/information technology administration and management; computer programming; computer software and media applications; computer systems networking and telecommunications; cosmetology and related personal grooming services; criminal justice and corrections; criminology; education; education (specific levels and methods); electrical and electronic engineering technologies; English; English as a second language; English composition; English language and literature related; fire protection; health aides/attendants/orderlies; health and medical administrative services; health services/allied health/health sciences; history; masonry; mathematics; mathematics and computer science; mathematics and statistics related; psychology.

PARKLAND COLLEGE
Champaign, Illinois
Distance Education
http://online.parkland.edu

Parkland College was founded in 1967. It is accredited by North Central Association of Colleges and Schools. It first offered distance learning courses in 1988. In fall 2006, there were 1,639 students enrolled in distance learning courses. Institutionally administered financial aid is available to distance learners.

Services Distance learners have accessibility to academic advising, bookstore, campus computer network, career placement assistance, e-mail services, library services, tutoring.

Contact Brett Coup, Director, Distance and Virtual Learning, Parkland College, 2400 West Bradley Avenue, Champaign, IL 61821. Telephone: 217-353-2639. E-mail: bcoup@parkland.edu.

DEGREES AND AWARDS

AA Early Childhood Education, Elementary Education, Secondary Education, Special Education, and Mass Communication (Integrated) concentrations; History, Liberal Arts and Sciences, Mass Communications (Advertising/Public Relations; Journalism), Political Science, and Psychology concentrations
AAS Business Management
AGS General Studies
AS Business Administration and Business Education concentrations
Certificate Independent Business Management

COURSE SUBJECT AREAS OFFERED OUTSIDE OF DEGREE PROGRAMS

Undergraduate—accounting and related services; agricultural business and management; anthropology; astronomy and astrophysics; biology; cell biology and anatomical sciences; chemistry; communication and media; computer and information sciences; computer programming; computer software and media applications; developmental and child psychology; dramatic/theater arts and stagecraft; economics; English composition; fine and studio art; health and physical education/fitness; history; journalism; legal studies (non-professional general, undergraduate); marketing; mathematics and statistics related; music; philosophy; physics; political science and government; psychology; social psychology; social sciences related; sociology; speech and rhetoric; statistics.

PARK UNIVERSITY
Parkville, Missouri
School for Extended Learning
http://www.park.edu/online

Park University was founded in 1875. It is accredited by North Central Association of Colleges and Schools. It first offered distance learning courses in 1996. In fall 2006, there were 5,500 students enrolled in distance learning courses. Institutionally administered financial aid is available to distance learners.

Services Distance learners have accessibility to academic advising, bookstore, career placement assistance, e-mail services, library services, tutoring.

Contact Ms. Nancy Eastman, Enrollment Management, Park University, 8700 NW River Park Drive, Parkville, MO 64152-3795. Telephone: 816-584-6524. Fax: 816-741-5133. E-mail: neastman@park.edu.

DEGREES AND AWARDS

BS Criminal Justice Administration; Management; Management/Computer Information Systems; Management/Human Resources; Management/Marketing; Social Psychology
MBA Business Administration; Health Care/Health Services Management; International Business
MEd Education, general; Law–School Law; Multi-Cultural Education; Teaching At-Risk Students
MPA Disaster and Emergency Management; Government–Business Relations; Nonprofit and Community Services Management; Public Management

COURSE SUBJECT AREAS OFFERED OUTSIDE OF DEGREE PROGRAMS

Undergraduate—accounting and related services; American literature (United States and Canadian); area, ethnic, cultural, and gender studies related; biblical studies; biology; business administration, management and operations; business/commerce; business/corporate communications; business, management, and marketing related; communication and journalism related; communication and media; computer and information sciences; computer programming; creative writing; criminal justice and corrections; criminology; economics; education related; English; English composition; finance and financial management services; geography and cartography; geological and earth sciences/geosciences; health and medical administrative services; history; human resources management; management information systems; marketing; mathematics; philosophy and religious studies related; political science and government; psychology; sales, merchandising, and related marketing operations (general); social psychology; statistics.

Graduate—business administration, management and operations; business, management, and marketing related; computer and information sciences; education; educational administration and supervision; international business; public administration; public administration and social service professions related.

See full description on page 408.

PASCO-HERNANDO COMMUNITY COLLEGE
New Port Richey, Florida
http://www.phcc.edu
Pasco-Hernando Community College was founded in 1972. It is accredited by Southern Association of Colleges and Schools. It first offered distance learning courses in 1993. In fall 2006, there were 3,908 students enrolled in distance learning courses. Institutionally administered financial aid is available to distance learners.
Services Distance learners have accessibility to academic advising, campus computer network, library services.
Contact Adm. Cheryl Sandoe, Assistant Dean of Academic Technology, Pasco-Hernando Community College, 10230 Ridge Road, New Port Richey, FL 34654-5199. Telephone: 727-816-3367. Fax: 727-816-3300. E-mail: sandoec@phcc.edu.

DEGREES AND AWARDS
Programs offered do not lead to a degree or other formal award.

COURSE SUBJECT AREAS OFFERED OUTSIDE OF DEGREE PROGRAMS

Undergraduate—biology; business administration, management and operations; business/commerce; computer programming; computer software and media applications; computer systems networking and telecommunications; education (specific levels and methods); English composition; English literature (British and Commonwealth); health and physical education/fitness; history; legal support services; mathematics; nutrition sciences; physical sciences; political science and government; psychology; religious studies; social sciences related; sociology; speech and rhetoric.

Non-credit—business/corporate communications; computer and information sciences; computer programming; computer software and media applications; education; education related; family and consumer economics; health professions related; insurance; personal and culinary services related; sales, merchandising, and related marketing operations (specialized); technical and business writing.

PASSAIC COUNTY COMMUNITY COLLEGE
Paterson, New Jersey
http://www.pccc.cc.nj.us/
Passaic County Community College was founded in 1968. It is accredited by Middle States Association of Colleges and Schools. It first offered distance learning courses in 1998. In fall 2006, there were 750 students enrolled in distance learning courses. Institutionally administered financial aid is available to distance learners.
Services Distance learners have accessibility to academic advising, bookstore, e-mail services, library services, tutoring.

Contact Mr. Rick Perdew, Coordinator of Instructional Technology, Passaic County Community College, 1 College Boulevard, Paterson, NJ 07505-1179. Telephone: 973-684-5790. Fax: 973-684-5413. E-mail: rperdew@pccc.edu.

DEGREES AND AWARDS
AA Humanities option; Humanities option
AAS Health Information Technology

COURSE SUBJECT AREAS OFFERED OUTSIDE OF DEGREE PROGRAMS

Undergraduate—business/commerce; communication and media; computer and information sciences; criminal justice and corrections; English; fire protection; health professions related; history; mathematics and statistics related; physical sciences; psychology; sociology; statistics.

PATRICK HENRY COLLEGE
Purcellville, Virginia
http://www.phc.edu/distancelearning
Patrick Henry College was founded in 1999. It is accredited by American Academy for Liberal Education. It first offered distance learning courses in 2001. In fall 2006, there were 100 students enrolled in distance learning courses. Institutionally administered financial aid is available to distance learners.
Services Distance learners have accessibility to academic advising, bookstore, library services.
Contact Mr. Daniel Burns, Admissions Counselor for Distance Learning, Patrick Henry College, One Patrick Henry Circle, Purcellville, VA 20132. Telephone: 540-338-1776. Fax: 540-338-9808. E-mail: dpburns@phc.edu.

DEGREES AND AWARDS
Programs offered do not lead to a degree or other formal award.

COURSE SUBJECT AREAS OFFERED OUTSIDE OF DEGREE PROGRAMS

Undergraduate—biblical studies; biology; economics; English composition; history; languages (classics and classical); legal studies (non-professional general, undergraduate); liberal arts and sciences, general studies and humanities; music; philosophy; philosophy and religious studies related; political science and government; public policy analysis.

PATRICK HENRY COMMUNITY COLLEGE
Martinsville, Virginia
Learning Resource Center
http://www.ph.vccs.edu
Patrick Henry Community College was founded in 1962. It is accredited by Southern Association of Colleges and Schools. It first offered distance learning courses in 1981. In fall 2006, there were 1,800 students enrolled in distance learning courses. Institutionally administered financial aid is available to distance learners.
Services Distance learners have accessibility to academic advising, bookstore, campus computer network, career placement assistance, e-mail services, library services, tutoring.
Contact Mark Nelson, Distance Learning Webmaster, Patrick Henry Community College, PO Box 5311, Martinsville, VA 24115. Telephone: 276-656-0275. Fax: 276-656-0353. E-mail: mnelson@ph.vccs.edu.

DEGREES AND AWARDS
AAS General Studies; Information Systems Technology
AS Business Administration
Certificate Career Studies–Allied Health; Career Studies–Management Assistant; Career Studies–Medical Transcriptionist; Career Studies–Office Assisting; Career Studies–Wellness; Clerical Studies

COURSE SUBJECT AREAS OFFERED OUTSIDE OF DEGREE PROGRAMS

Undergraduate—accounting and related services; biological and physical sciences; business administration, management and operations; communication and media; computer/information technology administration and management; computer systems networking and telecommunications; developmental and child psychology; economics; English composition; English literature (British and Commonwealth); fine and studio art; health and physical education/fitness; history; management information systems; mathematics; psychology; religious studies; sociology.

PEIRCE COLLEGE
Philadelphia, Pennsylvania
Peirce College Non-Traditional Education
http://www.peirce.edu

Peirce College was founded in 1865. It is accredited by Middle States Association of Colleges and Schools. It first offered distance learning courses in 1997. In fall 2006, there were 1,799 students enrolled in distance learning courses. Institutionally administered financial aid is available to distance learners.

Services Distance learners have accessibility to academic advising, bookstore, career placement assistance, library services, tutoring.

Contact Ms. Nadine M. Maher, Dean, Enrollment Management, Peirce College, 1420 Pine Street, Philadelphia, PA 19102. Telephone: 888-467-3472 Ext. 9214. Fax: 215-670-9366. E-mail: info@peirce.edu.

DEGREES AND AWARDS

AS Business Administration–Accounting concentration; Business Administration–Business Law concentration; Business Administration–Entrepreneurship/Small Business Management concentration; Business Administration–Human Resource Management concentration; Business Administration–Management concentration; Business Administration–Marketing concentration; Information Technology–Desktop Applications for Business concentration; Information Technology–Network Security concentration; Information Technology–Networking concentration; Information Technology–Programming Application and Development concentration; Information Technology–Technology Management concentration; Paralegal Studies

BS Business Administration–Accounting concentration; Business Administration–Business Law concentration; Business Administration–Entrepreneurship/Small Business Management concentration; Business Administration–Human Resource Management concentration; Business Administration–Management concentration; Business Administration–Marketing concentration; Business Administration–Real Estate Management concentration; Information Technology–Desktop Applications for Business concentration; Information Technology–Information Security concentration; Information Technology–Network Security concentration; Information Technology–Networking concentration; Information Technology–Programming and Application Development concentration; Information Technology–Technology Management concentration; Paralegal Studies

Certificate Business Administration–Business Law concentration; Certified Information Systems Security Professional (CISSP); Information Technology–.NET Technology concentration; Information Technology–Help Desk Technician concentration; Information Technology–Windows Network Operating System concentration; Paralegal Studies

COURSE SUBJECT AREAS OFFERED OUTSIDE OF DEGREE PROGRAMS

Undergraduate—accounting and related services; business administration, management and operations; business/commerce; business, management, and marketing related; computer and information sciences and support services related; computer/information technology administration and management; computer programming; computer software and media applications; computer systems networking and telecommunications; entrepreneurial and small business operations; human resources management; information science/studies; legal studies (non-professional general, undergraduate); management information systems; marketing; real estate; sales, merchandising, and related marketing operations (general); security and protective services related.

See full description on page 410.

PENINSULA COLLEGE
Port Angeles, Washington
http://pc.ctc.edu/

Peninsula College was founded in 1961. It is accredited by Northwest Commission on Colleges and Universities. It first offered distance learning courses in 1994. In fall 2006, there were 1,062 students enrolled in distance learning courses. Institutionally administered financial aid is available to distance learners.

Services Distance learners have accessibility to academic advising, bookstore, career placement assistance, library services, tutoring.

Contact Vicki Sievert, Distance Learning Coordinator, Peninsula College, 1502 East Lauridsen Boulevard, Port Angeles, WA 98362. Telephone: 360-417-6272. Fax: 360-417-6295. E-mail: vickis@pcadmin.ctc.edu.

DEGREES AND AWARDS

AA Liberal Arts
AAS Criminal Justice

COURSE SUBJECT AREAS OFFERED OUTSIDE OF DEGREE PROGRAMS

Undergraduate—accounting and related services; allied health and medical assisting services; American literature (United States and Canadian); anthropology; astronomy and astrophysics; biblical and other theological languages and literatures; biochemistry, biophysics and molecular biology; biological and physical sciences; business administration, management and operations; business/commerce; business, management, and marketing related; chemistry; communication and journalism related; computer and information sciences; computer software and media applications; criminal justice and corrections; dental support services and allied professions; developmental and child psychology; economics; education; English composition; English literature (British and Commonwealth); entrepreneurial and small business operations; family psychology; geological and earth sciences/geosciences; health and physical education/fitness; health professions related; history; human development, family studies, and related services; information science/studies; journalism; liberal arts and sciences, general studies and humanities; mathematics; mathematics and computer science; mathematics and statistics related; music; natural sciences; nursing; nutrition sciences; pharmacology and toxicology; philosophy; physical sciences; political science and government; psychology; social sciences; sociology.

PENN STATE UNIVERSITY PARK
State College, Pennsylvania
Department of Distance Education/World Campus
http://www.worldcampus.psu.edu

Penn State University Park was founded in 1855. It is accredited by Middle States Association of Colleges and Schools. It first offered distance learning courses in 1999. In fall 2006, there were 25,454 students enrolled in distance learning courses. Institutionally administered financial aid is available to distance learners.

Services Distance learners have accessibility to academic advising, bookstore, campus computer network, e-mail services, library services.

Contact Student Services, Penn State University Park, 128 Outreach Building, 100 Innovation Boulevard, University Park, PA 16802. Telephone: 800-252-3592. Fax: 814-865-3290. E-mail: psuwd@psu.edu.

DEGREES AND AWARDS

AA Letters, Arts, and Sciences
AS Business Administration; Dietetic Food Systems Management, Dietetic Technician emphasis; Dietetic Food Systems Management, School Food Service emphasis; Hotel, Restaurant, and Institutional Management; Human Development and Family Studies; Information Sciences and Technology
BA Law and Society; Letters, Arts, and Sciences
BS Criminal Justice; Organizational Leadership; Turfgrass Science
BSN Nursing (RN to BSN)
Certificate Adult Development and Aging Services; Business Management; Children, Youth, and Family Services; Family Literacy; Hospitality Management; Hotel, Restaurant, and Institutional Management; Human Resources; Information Science and Technology; Labor Studies

and Industrial Relations; Organizational Communication; School Food Service Management; Turfgrass Management; Turfgrass Management, advanced; Weather Forecasting; Writing Social Commentary

Certification SNA Level 3 Certification Module

Graduate Certificate Applied Behavior Analysis for Special Education; Applied Statistics; Autism; Bioterrorism Preparedness; Children's Literature; Community and Economic Development; Disaster Readiness; Distance Education; Educational Technology Integration; Family Literacy; Geographic Information Systems; Institutional Research; Project Management; Project Management, advanced; Reading Instruction for Special Education (RISE); Supply Chain and Information Systems

MA Geographic Information Systems

MBA i-MBA

MEd Adult Education; Curriculum and Instruction–Children's Literature; Curriculum and Instruction–Teacher Leadership; Instructional Systems–Educational Technology

MPM Project Management

MS/MPH Homeland Security in Public Health Preparedness

See full description on page 412.

PENNSYLVANIA COLLEGE OF TECHNOLOGY
Williamsport, Pennsylvania
http://www.pct.edu/

Pennsylvania College of Technology was founded in 1965. It is accredited by Middle States Association of Colleges and Schools. It first offered distance learning courses in 1996. In fall 2006, there were 500 students enrolled in distance learning courses. Institutionally administered financial aid is available to distance learners.

Services Distance learners have accessibility to academic advising, bookstore, campus computer network, career placement assistance, e-mail services, library services, tutoring.

Contact Paula Neal, Distance Learning Services Assistant, Pennsylvania College of Technology, One College Avenue, DIF #50, Williamsport, PA 17701. Telephone: 570-320-8019. Fax: 570-321-5559. E-mail: distancelearning@pct.edu.

DEGREES AND AWARDS

BS Applied Health Studies; Automotive Technology Management; Dental Hygiene; Technology Management

BSN Nursing

COURSE SUBJECT AREAS OFFERED OUTSIDE OF DEGREE PROGRAMS

Undergraduate—accounting and related services; architecture; biological and biomedical sciences related; biology; building/construction finishing, management, and inspection; business/commerce; business/corporate communications; chemistry; computer and information sciences; construction engineering technology; dental support services and allied professions; English language and literature related; environmental/environmental health engineering; finance and financial management services; fine and studio art; geological and earth sciences/geosciences; health professions related; history; international business; marketing; mathematics; nursing; philosophy and religious studies related; statistics.

See full description on page 414.

PHILADELPHIA UNIVERSITY
Philadelphia, Pennsylvania
http://www.philau.edu/

Philadelphia University was founded in 1884. It is accredited by Middle States Association of Colleges and Schools. It first offered distance learning courses in 1998. In fall 2006, there were 262 students enrolled in distance learning courses. Institutionally administered financial aid is available to distance learners.

Services Distance learners have accessibility to academic advising, bookstore, campus computer network, career placement assistance, e-mail services, library services, tutoring.

Contact Mr. Jack Klett, Interim Director of Graduate Admissions, Philadelphia University, School House Lane and Henry Avenue, Philadelphia, PA 19144. Telephone: 215-951-2943. E-mail: gradadms@philau.edu.

DEGREES AND AWARDS

Certificate Nurse-Midwifery

MBA Textile and Apparel Marketing

MS Disaster Medicine and Management; Midwifery

COURSE SUBJECT AREAS OFFERED OUTSIDE OF DEGREE PROGRAMS

Undergraduate—accounting and related services; business administration, management and operations; economics; finance and financial management services; legal studies (non-professional general, undergraduate); management information systems; management sciences and quantitative methods; marketing; operations research; statistics.

Graduate—accounting and related services; apparel and textiles; finance and financial management services; international business; management information systems; management sciences and quantitative methods; marketing; statistics.

PIEDMONT TECHNICAL COLLEGE
Greenwood, South Carolina
Division of Instructional Technology
http://www.ptc.edu/dl

Piedmont Technical College was founded in 1966. It is accredited by Southern Association of Colleges and Schools. It first offered distance learning courses in 1995. In fall 2006, there were 2,400 students enrolled in distance learning courses. Institutionally administered financial aid is available to distance learners.

Services Distance learners have accessibility to academic advising, bookstore, campus computer network, career placement assistance, e-mail services, library services, tutoring.

Contact Dr. Daniel D. Koenig, Associate Vice President for Instructional Support and Technology, Piedmont Technical College, 620 North Emerald Road, PO Box 1467, Greenwood, SC 29648. Telephone: 864-941-8446. Fax: 864-941-8703. E-mail: koenig.d@ptc.edu.

DEGREES AND AWARDS

AA Liberal Arts

AD Business–Associate in Business, General Business major; Business–Associate in Business, Office Systems Technology major

COURSE SUBJECT AREAS OFFERED OUTSIDE OF DEGREE PROGRAMS

Undergraduate—American literature (United States and Canadian); biology; business administration, management and operations; business/commerce; cell biology and anatomical sciences; chemistry; communication and media; computer science; design and applied arts; English composition; English literature (British and Commonwealth); fine and studio art; history; languages (Romance languages); legal studies (non-professional general, undergraduate); management information systems; mathematics and statistics related; music; philosophy and religious studies related; plant sciences; political science and government; psychology; sociology; speech and rhetoric; statistics.

PIMA COMMUNITY COLLEGE
Tucson, Arizona
Telecommunications and Production Service
http://www.pimacc.pima.edu

Pima Community College was founded in 1966. It is accredited by North Central Association of Colleges and Schools. It first offered distance learning courses in 1975. In fall 2006, there were 4,000 students enrolled in distance learning courses. Institutionally administered financial aid is available to distance learners.

Services Distance learners have accessibility to academic advising, bookstore, campus computer network, career placement assistance, e-mail services, library services, tutoring.

Contact Mr. Jim Johnson, Dean of Instruction, Pima Community College, Community Campus, 401 North Bonita Avenue, Tucson, AZ 85709-5030. Telephone: 520-206-3996. Fax: 520-206-6409. E-mail: jejohnson @pima.edu.

DEGREES AND AWARDS

AA General Studies
AAS Business and Industry Technology
AD Liberal Arts
Certificate Business and Industrial Technology (Advanced); Business and Industry Technology (Basic); Elementary Education (post-baccalaureate); Human Resources Management; Liberal Arts; Secondary Education (postbaccalaureate)

COURSE SUBJECT AREAS OFFERED OUTSIDE OF DEGREE PROGRAMS

Undergraduate—English composition; sociology.

PITTSBURG STATE UNIVERSITY
Pittsburg, Kansas
http://www.pittstate.edu/
Pittsburg State University was founded in 1903. It is accredited by North Central Association of Colleges and Schools. It first offered distance learning courses in 1994. In fall 2006, there were 423 students enrolled in distance learning courses. Institutionally administered financial aid is available to distance learners.
Services Distance learners have accessibility to bookstore, campus computer network, e-mail services, library services.
Contact Ms. Kathleen M. Flannery, Director, Pittsburg State University, Continuing and Graduate Studies, 1701 South Broadway, Pittsburg, KS 66762. Telephone: 620-235-4181. Fax: 620-235-4219. E-mail: kflanner @pittstate.edu.

DEGREES AND AWARDS

MS Educational Technology; Engineering Technology

COURSE SUBJECT AREAS OFFERED OUTSIDE OF DEGREE PROGRAMS

Undergraduate—accounting and related services; biology; building/construction finishing, management, and inspection; business, management, and marketing related; communication and journalism related; computer and information sciences; construction engineering technology; criminal justice and corrections; curriculum and instruction; design and applied arts; economics; education; engineering technologies related; English; family and consumer sciences/human sciences business services; health and physical education/fitness; history; marketing; mathematics; nursing; philosophy; physiology, pathology and related sciences; psychology; social sciences; technology education/industrial arts.
Graduate—communication and journalism related; curriculum and instruction; design and applied arts; education; educational administration and supervision; education (specific levels and methods); engineering technologies related; history; human resources management; library science related; nursing; psychology; special education; technology education/industrial arts.

PLYMOUTH STATE UNIVERSITY
Plymouth, New Hampshire
Plymouth State University was founded in 1871. It is accredited by New England Association of Schools and Colleges. It first offered distance learning courses in 2000. In fall 2006, there were 185 students enrolled in distance learning courses. Institutionally administered financial aid is available to distance learners.
Services Distance learners have accessibility to academic advising, bookstore, campus computer network, e-mail services, library services, tutoring.
Contact Ms. Stacey L. Curdie, Director of Online Education, Plymouth State University, MSC 61, 17 High Street, Plymouth, NH 03264. Telephone: 603-535-2975. E-mail: scurdie@plymouth.edu.

DEGREES AND AWARDS

Programs offered do not lead to a degree or other formal award.

COURSE SUBJECT AREAS OFFERED OUTSIDE OF DEGREE PROGRAMS

Undergraduate—bilingual, multilingual, and multicultural education; business administration, management and operations; business/corporate communications; communication and media; computer software and media applications; criminal justice and corrections; criminology; English; English as a second/foreign language (teaching); English composition; geography and cartography; human resources management; linguistic, comparative, and related language studies; music; social psychology.
Graduate—business/commerce; business/corporate communications; business, management, and marketing related; computer and information sciences; education; educational assessment, evaluation, and research; special education.
Non-credit—accounting and computer science; allied health and medical assisting services; animal sciences; business administration, management and operations; business/commerce; business/corporate communications; business, management, and marketing related; business operations support and assistant services; computer software and media applications; computer systems analysis; computer systems networking and telecommunications; film/video and photographic arts; finance and financial management services; graphic communications; health professions related; veterinary biomedical and clinical sciences.

PORTLAND COMMUNITY COLLEGE
Portland, Oregon
Distance Learning Department
http://www.distance.pcc.edu
Portland Community College was founded in 1961. It is accredited by Northwest Commission on Colleges and Universities. It first offered distance learning courses in 1981. In fall 2006, there were 5,732 students enrolled in distance learning courses. Institutionally administered financial aid is available to distance learners.
Services Distance learners have accessibility to academic advising, bookstore, career placement assistance, e-mail services, library services.
Contact Dennis Hitchcox, Programming Coordinator, Distance Education, Portland Community College, PO Box 19000, Portland, OR 97280-0990. Telephone: 503-977-4655. Fax: 503-977-4858. E-mail: dhitchco@pcc.edu.

DEGREES AND AWARDS

Programs offered do not lead to a degree or other formal award.

COURSE SUBJECT AREAS OFFERED OUTSIDE OF DEGREE PROGRAMS

Undergraduate—accounting and related services; aerospace, aeronautical and astronautical engineering; allied health and medical assisting services; anthropology; biology; business administration, management and operations; business, management, and marketing related; business operations support and assistant services; computer and information sciences; computer and information sciences and support services related; computer science; computer software and media applications; dental support services and allied professions; developmental and child psychology; economics; education; English composition; fire protection; foods, nutrition, and related services; geography and cartography; health and physical education/fitness; health professions related; history; human development, family studies, and related services; marketing; mathematics; mathematics and statistics related; music; nursing; physical sciences related; psychology; real estate; social sciences; sociology; statistics; technical and business writing.
Non-credit—computer/information technology administration and management; computer programming; computer software and media applications; computer systems networking and telecommunications; creative writing; education related; health professions related; languages (foreign languages related); legal professions and studies related; pharmacy, pharmaceutical sciences, and administration; psychology related.

PORTLAND STATE UNIVERSITY
Portland, Oregon
Independent Study
http://www.istudy.pdx.edu

Portland State University was founded in 1946. It is accredited by Northwest Commission on Colleges and Universities. In fall 2006, there were 3,000 students enrolled in distance learning courses. Institutionally administered financial aid is available to distance learners.

Services Distance learners have accessibility to bookstore, library services.

Contact Alba Scholz, Manager, Portland State University, PO Box 1491, Portland, OR 97207-1491. Telephone: 800-547-8887 Ext. 4865. Fax: 503-725-4880. E-mail: scholza@pdx.edu.

DEGREES AND AWARDS
Programs offered do not lead to a degree or other formal award.

COURSE SUBJECT AREAS OFFERED OUTSIDE OF DEGREE PROGRAMS

Undergraduate—chemistry; criminal justice and corrections; economics; English; English composition; geological and earth sciences/geosciences; history; mathematics and statistics related; psychology; sociology; statistics.

PRESCOTT COLLEGE
Prescott, Arizona
http://www.prescott.edu/

Prescott College was founded in 1966. It is accredited by North Central Association of Colleges and Schools. It first offered distance learning courses in 1978. In fall 2006, there were 600 students enrolled in distance learning courses. Institutionally administered financial aid is available to distance learners.

Services Distance learners have accessibility to academic advising, bookstore, career placement assistance, e-mail services, library services, tutoring.

Contact Melanie Lefever, Assistant Director of Admissions, Prescott College, Admissions, 220 Grove Avenue, Prescott, AZ 86301. Telephone: 877-350-2100 Ext. 2106. Fax: 928-776-5242. E-mail: admissions@prescott.edu.

DEGREES AND AWARDS
BA Adventure Education; Art; Business; Communications; Computer Information Systems; Counseling Psychology/Human Services; Creative Writing; Criminal Justice; Cultural and Regional Studies; Education; Elementary Education; Environmental Studies; History; Humanities; Journalism; Management; Music; Natural Resources and Conservation; Political Science; Special Education; Sustainable Community Development; Theater

Certification Teacher Certification

MA Adventure Education; Alternative Energy Systems; Anthropology; Art History; Art Therapy; Arts Management; Bilingual Education; Counseling and Psychology; Counseling–School Guidance Counseling; Cultural Studies; Ecology; Education; Educational Administration; Environmental Education; Environmental Studies; Equine Assisted Mental Health; Film and Cinema Studies; Fire Science; Foreign Languages; Gay and Lesbian Studies; Gender Studies; Higher Education Administration; Humanities; Land Use Planning; Mental Health Counseling; Museum Studies; Natural Resources and Conservation; Peace Studies; Philosophy; Photography; Playwriting and Screenwriting; Religious Studies; Sustainability Education; Sustainable Community Development; Wetlands Management; Wildlife Management

PhD Education–Sustainability Education

COURSE SUBJECT AREAS OFFERED OUTSIDE OF DEGREE PROGRAMS

Undergraduate—accounting and related services; bilingual, multilingual, and multicultural education; business administration, management and operations; communication and media; community organization and advocacy; counseling psychology; creative writing; education; English; ethnic, cultural minority, and gender studies; history; human development, family studies, and related services; human services; liberal arts and sciences, general studies and humanities; natural resources conservation and research; parks, recreation and leisure; philosophy and religious studies related; psychology; visual and performing arts; wildlife and wildlands science and management.

Graduate—area, ethnic, cultural, and gender studies related; city/urban, community and regional planning; clinical psychology; communication and media; community organization and advocacy; creative writing; education; ethnic, cultural minority, and gender studies; history; human development, family studies, and related services; human services; movement and mind-body therapies; natural resources and conservation related; natural resources management and policy; parks, recreation and leisure facilities management; peace studies and conflict resolution; philosophy and religious studies related; psychology; visual and performing arts; wildlife and wildlands science and management.

See full description on page 416.

PRESENTATION COLLEGE
Aberdeen, South Dakota
http://www.presentation.edu/

Presentation College was founded in 1951. It is accredited by North Central Association of Colleges and Schools. It first offered distance learning courses in 1994. In fall 2006, there were 360 students enrolled in distance learning courses. Institutionally administered financial aid is available to distance learners.

Services Distance learners have accessibility to academic advising, bookstore, campus computer network, career placement assistance, e-mail services, library services, tutoring.

Contact JoEllen Lindner, Vice President for Enrollment and Student Retention Services, Presentation College, 1500 North Main Street, Aberdeen, SD 57401. Telephone: 605-229-8492. Fax: 605-229-8425. E-mail: joellen.lindner@presentation.edu.

DEGREES AND AWARDS
AS Medical Office Administration

BS Business Completion; Nursing–LPN Certificate to BSN Nursing completion; Nursing–RN to BSN Nursing completion; Nursing&AD-LPN to BSN Nursing completion; Radiologic Technology completion program; Social Work Completion

Certificate Medical Transcription

COURSE SUBJECT AREAS OFFERED OUTSIDE OF DEGREE PROGRAMS

Undergraduate—American Sign Language (ASL); English composition; mathematics; psychology; statistics.

PROVIDENCE COLLEGE AND THEOLOGICAL SEMINARY
Otterburne, Manitoba, Canada
Department of Continuing Education
http://www.prov.ca

Providence College and Theological Seminary was founded in 1925. It is provincially chartered. It first offered distance learning courses in 1975. In fall 2006, there were 100 students enrolled in distance learning courses. Institutionally administered financial aid is available to distance learners.

Services Distance learners have accessibility to academic advising, bookstore, campus computer network, career placement assistance, e-mail services, library services.

Contact Ms. Joy Lise, Director of Enrollment, Providence College and Theological Seminary, 10 College Crescent, Otterburne, MB R0A 1G0, Canada. Telephone: 204-433-7488 Ext. 247. Fax: 204-433-7158. E-mail: info@prov.ca.

DEGREES AND AWARDS
Programs offered do not lead to a degree or other formal award.

COURSE SUBJECT AREAS OFFERED OUTSIDE OF DEGREE PROGRAMS

Undergraduate—biblical and other theological languages and literatures; biblical studies; communication and media; theological and ministerial studies; theology and religious vocations related.

Graduate—area, ethnic, cultural, and gender studies related; biblical and other theological languages and literatures; biblical studies; business operations support and assistant services; counseling psychology; education related; missionary studies and missiology; pastoral counseling and specialized ministries; religious studies; theological and ministerial studies; theology and religious vocations related.

Non-credit—area, ethnic, cultural, and gender studies related; biblical and other theological languages and literatures; biblical studies; counseling psychology; education related; human resources management; missionary studies and missiology; pastoral counseling and specialized ministries; religious/sacred music; theological and ministerial studies; theology and religious vocations related.

PULASKI TECHNICAL COLLEGE
North Little Rock, Arkansas
http://www.pulaskitech.edu

Pulaski Technical College was founded in 1945. It is accredited by North Central Association of Colleges and Schools. It first offered distance learning courses in 1999. In fall 2006, there were 2,641 students enrolled in distance learning courses. Institutionally administered financial aid is available to distance learners.

Services Distance learners have accessibility to bookstore, campus computer network, e-mail services, library services, tutoring.

Contact Mr. Mark Burris, Distance Education Director, Pulaski Technical College, 3000 West Scenic Drive, North Little Rock, AR 72118. Telephone: 501-812-2716. Fax: 501-771-2844. E-mail: mburris@pulaskitech.edu.

DEGREES AND AWARDS
AA General Education

COURSE SUBJECT AREAS OFFERED OUTSIDE OF DEGREE PROGRAMS

Undergraduate—accounting and computer science; accounting and related services; allied health and medical assisting services; American literature (United States and Canadian); anthropology; applied mathematics; biology; business/commerce; business operations support and assistant services; computer and information sciences; computer systems networking and telecommunications; education; English composition; health and medical administrative services; history; legal professions and studies related; liberal arts and sciences, general studies and humanities; mathematics; natural sciences; philosophy; physical sciences; political science and government; psychology; religious studies; social sciences.

Non-credit—languages (Romance languages).

QUEEN'S UNIVERSITY AT KINGSTON
Kingston, Ontario, Canada
Continuing and Distance Studies
http://www.queensu.ca/cds

Queen's University at Kingston was founded in 1841. It is provincially chartered. It first offered distance learning courses in 1941. In fall 2006, there were 2,500 students enrolled in distance learning courses. Institutionally administered financial aid is available to distance learners.

Services Distance learners have accessibility to academic advising, bookstore, campus computer network, career placement assistance, e-mail services, library services, tutoring.

Contact Wilma Fernetich, Distance Education Advisor, Queen's University at Kingston, Kingston, ON K7L 2N6, Canada. Telephone: 613-533-6000 Ext. 77770. Fax: 613-533-6805. E-mail: fernetic@post.queensu.ca.

DEGREES AND AWARDS
Programs offered do not lead to a degree or other formal award.

COURSE SUBJECT AREAS OFFERED OUTSIDE OF DEGREE PROGRAMS

Undergraduate—biology; classical and ancient studies; creative writing; dramatic/theater arts and stagecraft; English composition; English literature (British and Commonwealth); ethnic, cultural minority, and gender studies; geography and cartography; history; languages (Germanic); nutrition sciences; pharmacology and toxicology; philosophy; political science and government; psychology; religious studies; social psychology; sociology; statistics.

QUINEBAUG VALLEY COMMUNITY COLLEGE
Danielson, Connecticut
http://www.qvcc.commnet.edu/

Quinebaug Valley Community College was founded in 1971. It is accredited by New England Association of Schools and Colleges. It first offered distance learning courses in 1998. In fall 2006, there were 387 students enrolled in distance learning courses. Institutionally administered financial aid is available to distance learners.

Services Distance learners have accessibility to academic advising, library services, tutoring.

Contact Dr. Toni T. Moumouris, Enrollment and Transition Counselor, Quinebaug Valley Community College, 742 Upper Maple Street, Danielson, CT 06239. Telephone: 860-774-1130 Ext. 318. Fax: 860-779-2998. E-mail: tmoumouris@qvcc.commnet.edu.

DEGREES AND AWARDS
Certificate Health Information Management Technology

COURSE SUBJECT AREAS OFFERED OUTSIDE OF DEGREE PROGRAMS

Undergraduate—anthropology; biological and physical sciences; business, management, and marketing related; education; English language and literature related; health and medical administrative services; history; human services; liberal arts and sciences, general studies and humanities; materials science; nutrition sciences; political science and government; polymer/plastics engineering; sociology.

Non-credit—accounting and computer science; allied health and medical assisting services; building/construction finishing, management, and inspection; computer software and media applications; engineering-related fields; health and medical administrative services; legal professions and studies related; real estate; sales, merchandising, and related marketing operations (general); technology education/industrial arts.

QUINNIPIAC UNIVERSITY
Hamden, Connecticut
http://www.quinnipiac.edu/quonline

Quinnipiac University was founded in 1929. It is accredited by New England Association of Schools and Colleges. It first offered distance learning courses in 2001. In fall 2006, there were 200 students enrolled in distance learning courses. Institutionally administered financial aid is available to distance learners.

Services Distance learners have accessibility to academic advising, bookstore, campus computer network, career placement assistance, e-mail services, library services, tutoring.

Contact Cynthia Gallatin, Associate Vice President for Online Programs, Quinnipiac University, 275 Mount Carmel Avenue, Hamden, CT 06518. Telephone: 203-582-5669. Fax: 203-582-3352. E-mail: quonline@quinnipiac.edu.

DEGREES AND AWARDS
Programs offered do not lead to a degree or other formal award.

COURSE SUBJECT AREAS OFFERED OUTSIDE OF DEGREE PROGRAMS

Undergraduate—accounting and related services; biological and biomedical sciences related; biological and physical sciences; business administration, management and operations; business/commerce; chemistry; communications technology; computer science; computer systems analysis; economics; education; education (specific subject areas); history; journalism; marketing; mathematics; philosophy.

Graduate—accounting and related services; business, management, and marketing related; business/managerial economics; computer science; economics; education; education (specific subject areas); finance and financial management services; journalism; management sciences and quantitative methods; marketing; nursing; sales, merchandising, and related marketing operations (general).

Non-credit—mathematics; nursing.

RADFORD UNIVERSITY
Radford, Virginia
http://www.radford.edu/

Radford University was founded in 1910. It is accredited by Southern Association of Colleges and Schools. It first offered distance learning courses in 1995. In fall 2006, there were 500 students enrolled in distance learning courses. Institutionally administered financial aid is available to distance learners.

Services Distance learners have accessibility to academic advising, bookstore, campus computer network, career placement assistance, e-mail services, library services, tutoring.

Contact Ellen Taylor, Director of Extended Education, Radford University, Office of Extended Education, Radford, VA 24142. Telephone: 540-831-5845. Fax: 540-831-6061. E-mail: eltaylor@radford.edu.

DEGREES AND AWARDS
Programs offered do not lead to a degree or other formal award.

COURSE SUBJECT AREAS OFFERED OUTSIDE OF DEGREE PROGRAMS

Graduate—allied health diagnostic, intervention, and treatment professions; business administration, management and operations; business/commerce; business/corporate communications; business/managerial economics; communication and media; community health services; criminology; curriculum and instruction; educational administration and supervision; education (specific levels and methods); finance and financial management services; health and medical administrative services; health/medical preparatory programs; health professions related; nursing.

Non-credit—accounting and related services; business administration, management and operations; business, management, and marketing related; computer and information sciences; computer and information sciences and support services related; computer software and media applications; nursing; public health; sales, merchandising, and related marketing operations (specialized).

RANDOLPH COMMUNITY COLLEGE
Asheboro, North Carolina
Virtual Campus
http://www.virtualrandolph.org

Randolph Community College was founded in 1962. It is accredited by Southern Association of Colleges and Schools. It first offered distance learning courses in 1998. In fall 2006, there were 1,200 students enrolled in distance learning courses. Institutionally administered financial aid is available to distance learners.

Services Distance learners have accessibility to academic advising, bookstore, e-mail services, library services, tutoring.

Contact Crystal J. Kingrey, Assistant to the Director of Distance Education, Randolph Community College, 629 Industrial Park Avenue, PO Box 1009, Asheboro, NC 27205. Telephone: 336-633-0263. Fax: 336-629-4695. E-mail: cjkingrey@randolph.edu.

DEGREES AND AWARDS
AA College Transfer
AAS Accounting; Business Administration; Criminal Justice; Information Systems; Office Systems Technology

COURSE SUBJECT AREAS OFFERED OUTSIDE OF DEGREE PROGRAMS

Undergraduate—accounting and related services; allied health and medical assisting services; computer and information sciences; computer

software and media applications; criminal justice and corrections; economics; education (specific subject areas); English composition; ethnic, cultural minority, and gender studies; finance and financial management services; history; human development, family studies, and related services; legal studies (non-professional general, undergraduate); marketing; music; philosophy and religious studies related; psychology; sociology.

Non-credit—accounting and related services; allied health and medical assisting services; allied health diagnostic, intervention, and treatment professions; business operations support and assistant services; clinical/medical laboratory science and allied professions; computer software and media applications; gerontology; medical basic sciences; pharmacy, pharmaceutical sciences, and administration.

RAPPAHANNOCK COMMUNITY COLLEGE
Glenns, Virginia
Flexible Learning Opportunities (FLO)
http://www.rcc.vccs.edu

Rappahannock Community College was founded in 1970. It is accredited by Southern Association of Colleges and Schools. It first offered distance learning courses in 1995. In fall 2006, there were 1,200 students enrolled in distance learning courses. Institutionally administered financial aid is available to distance learners.

Services Distance learners have accessibility to academic advising, bookstore, campus computer network, career placement assistance, e-mail services, library services, tutoring.

Contact Kristy Walker, Assistant for Distance Learning and Technology, Rappahannock Community College, 52 Campus Drive, Warsaw, VA 22572. Telephone: 804-333-6786. Fax: 804-333-6784. E-mail: kwalker @rappahannock.edu.

DEGREES AND AWARDS
AAS General Studies
Certificate Administrative Support; Bookkeeping/Accounting

COURSE SUBJECT AREAS OFFERED OUTSIDE OF DEGREE PROGRAMS

Undergraduate—accounting and related services; allied health and medical assisting services; American literature (United States and Canadian); business administration, management and operations; business/corporate communications; community health services; criminal justice and corrections; English composition; fine and studio art; health and physical education/fitness; history; mathematics; psychology; religious studies; sociology.

Non-credit—real estate.

RED ROCKS COMMUNITY COLLEGE
Lakewood, Colorado
Learning and Resource Center
http://www.rrcc.edu/online

Red Rocks Community College was founded in 1969. It is accredited by North Central Association of Colleges and Schools. It first offered distance learning courses in 1980. In fall 2006, there were 1,200 students enrolled in distance learning courses. Institutionally administered financial aid is available to distance learners.

Services Distance learners have accessibility to academic advising, bookstore, library services.

Contact Rebecca Woulfe, Director of eLearning, Red Rocks Community College, 13300 West 6th Avenue, Lakewood, CO 80228. Telephone: 303-914-6444. Fax: 303-914-6716. E-mail: rebecca.woulfe@rrcc.edu.

DEGREES AND AWARDS
AAS Building Code Enforcement; Business; Construction Technology–Construction Electrician emphasis; Construction Technology–Power Technology emphasis; Emergency Management and Planning; Fire Science Management

COURSE SUBJECT AREAS OFFERED OUTSIDE OF DEGREE PROGRAMS

Undergraduate—accounting and related services; anthropology; applied mathematics; building/construction finishing, management, and inspection; computer and information sciences; computer programming; computer science; computer software and media applications; computer systems analysis; computer systems networking and telecommunications; data processing; design and applied arts; developmental and child psychology; education related; English as a second language; English composition; fine and studio art; fire protection; geography and cartography; history; mathematics; music; social psychology; sociology; visual and performing arts related.

REEDLEY COLLEGE
Reedley, California
http://www.reedleycollege.edu

Reedley College was founded in 1926. It is accredited by Western Association of Schools and Colleges. It first offered distance learning courses in 1997. In fall 2006, there were 1,023 students enrolled in distance learning courses. Institutionally administered financial aid is available to distance learners.

Services Distance learners have accessibility to academic advising, bookstore, campus computer network, career placement assistance, e-mail services, library services, tutoring.

Contact Leticia Alvarez, Admissions and Records Manager, Reedley College, 995 North Reed Avenue, Reedley, CA 93654. Telephone: 559-638-3641 Ext. 3624. Fax: 559-638-5040. E-mail: leticia.alvarez@ reedleycollege.edu.

DEGREES AND AWARDS
Programs offered do not lead to a degree or other formal award.

COURSE SUBJECT AREAS OFFERED OUTSIDE OF DEGREE PROGRAMS

Undergraduate—accounting and related services; business administration, management and operations; chemistry; computer programming; creative writing; criminal justice and corrections; economics; education; engineering; English; English composition; foods, nutrition, and related services; health and medical administrative services; information science/ studies; mathematics; music; natural resources conservation and research; psychology; sales, merchandising, and related marketing operations (general); speech and rhetoric.

Non-credit—accounting and related services; business administration, management and operations; chemistry; computer programming; creative writing; economics; engineering; English language and literature related; foods, nutrition, and related services; health and medical administrative services; human development, family studies, and related services; information science/studies; linguistic, comparative, and related language studies; mathematics; music; natural resources conservation and research; psychology; sales, merchandising, and related marketing operations (general); speech and rhetoric.

REGENT UNIVERSITY
Virginia Beach, Virginia
Distance Education
http://www.regent.edu

Regent University was founded in 1977. It is accredited by Southern Association of Colleges and Schools. It first offered distance learning courses in 1989. In fall 2006, there were 2,755 students enrolled in distance learning courses. Institutionally administered financial aid is available to distance learners.

Services Distance learners have accessibility to academic advising, bookstore, campus computer network, career placement assistance, e-mail services, library services, tutoring.

Contact Mr. Jerrod Fishback, Central Enrollment Management, Regent University, 1000 Regent University Drive, SC 218, Virginia Beach, VA 23464. Telephone: 800-373-5504. Fax: 757-226-4381. E-mail: admissions@regent.edu.

DEGREES AND AWARDS

BA Communications; English; Religious Studies

BS Global Business; Interdisciplinary Studies; Organizational Leadership and Management; Political Science; Psychology

Certificate Coaching and Mentoring; Future Studies; Human Resource Studies; Information Systems Technology; International Organizations; Manufacturing; New Business Development; Organizational Communication; Organizational Development Consulting; Philanthropic and Nonprofit Organizations; Public Executive Leadership; Sales Management; TESOL; Virtual Organizations

CAGS Education; Leadership

Graduate Certificate Leadership; Strategic Foresight

MA Biblical Studies; Cinema Arts; Communication Studies; Government; Human Services Counseling; Journalism; Organizational Leadership; Practical Theology; Strategic Foresight; Television Arts; Theater Arts

MBA Business Administration

MDiv Practical Theology

MEd Christian School Program; Cross-Categorical Special Education; Educational Leadership; Individualized Degree program; Student Affairs; TESOL

DMin Ministry–Leadership and Renewal

DSL Strategic Leadership

EdD Education Doctorate

PhD Communication; Counseling Education and Supervision; Organizational Leadership; Renewal Studies

COURSE SUBJECT AREAS OFFERED OUTSIDE OF DEGREE PROGRAMS

Undergraduate—business administration, management and operations; business/commerce; business, management, and marketing related; communication and journalism related; communication and media; communications technology; education; English; film/video and photographic arts; history; international business; mathematics; natural sciences; physical sciences; political science and government; psychology; social sciences; theological and ministerial studies; theology and religious vocations related; visual and performing arts.

Graduate—accounting and related services; biblical studies; business administration, management and operations; business/commerce; business, management, and marketing related; communication and journalism related; communication and media; communications technology; counseling psychology; education; English as a second language; international business; pastoral counseling and specialized ministries; political science and government; psychology; public administration; public policy analysis; theological and ministerial studies; theology and religious vocations related; visual and performing arts.

Non-credit—accounting and related services; business administration, management and operations; business/commerce; business, management, and marketing related; communication and journalism related; education; educational administration and supervision; education related; English as a second language; film/video and photographic arts; human resources management; international business; international/global studies; international relations and affairs; pastoral counseling and specialized ministries; public policy analysis; religious education; religious studies; theology and religious vocations related; visual and performing arts.

REGIONS UNIVERSITY
Montgomery, Alabama
Extended Learning Program
http://www.southernchristian.edu

Regions University was founded in 1967. It is accredited by Southern Association of Colleges and Schools. It first offered distance learning courses in 1993. In fall 2006, there were 725 students enrolled in distance learning courses. Institutionally administered financial aid is available to distance learners.

Services Distance learners have accessibility to academic advising, bookstore, library services, tutoring.

Contact Rick Johnson, Director of Enrollment Management, Regions University, 1200 Taylor Road, Montgomery, AL 36117-3553. Telephone: 800-351-4040 Ext. 7513. Fax: 334-387-3878. E-mail: rickjohnson@ regionsuniversity.edu.

DEGREES AND AWARDS

AA Liberal Studies
BA Biblical Studies
BS Business Administration/General Business; Business Administration/ Information Communication; Business Administration/Information Systems Management; Human Development; Human Resource Leadership; Liberal Studies; Management Communication; Ministry/Bible; Public Safety and Business/Organization Security; Public Safety and Criminal Justice; Public Safety and Homeland Security
MA Behavioral Leadership and Management; Biblical Studies; Marriage and Family Therapy; Practical Theology; Professional Counseling
MDiv Marriage and Family Therapy; Ministerial Leadership; Ministry; Pastoral Counseling; Professional Counseling
MS Leadership and Management; Ministerial Leadership; Pastoral Counseling
DMin Christian Ministry; Family Therapy
PhD Biblical Studies; Family Therapy

COURSE SUBJECT AREAS OFFERED OUTSIDE OF DEGREE PROGRAMS

Undergraduate—human services; liberal arts and sciences, general studies and humanities; missionary studies and missiology; pastoral counseling and specialized ministries; philosophy and religious studies related; religious studies; theological and ministerial studies.
Graduate—human services; missionary studies and missiology; pastoral counseling and specialized ministries; philosophy and religious studies related; religious studies; theological and ministerial studies.
Non-credit—human services; liberal arts and sciences, general studies and humanities; missionary studies and missiology; pastoral counseling and specialized ministries; philosophy and religious studies related; religious studies; theological and ministerial studies.

See full description on page 418.

REGIS UNIVERSITY
Denver, Colorado
School for Professional Studies and Distance Learning
http://www.regisonline.org
Regis University was founded in 1877. It is accredited by North Central Association of Colleges and Schools. It first offered distance learning courses in 1992. In fall 2006, there were 5,328 students enrolled in distance learning courses. Institutionally administered financial aid is available to distance learners.
Services Distance learners have accessibility to academic advising, bookstore, campus computer network, career placement assistance, e-mail services, library services, tutoring.
Contact Denise Copeland, Administrative Coordinator of SPS Distance Learning, Regis University, Adult Learning Center, Mail Code K-18, 3333 Regis Boulevard, Denver, CO 80221. Telephone: 303-964-3651. Fax: 303-964-5436. E-mail: dcopelan@regis.edu.

DEGREES AND AWARDS

BS Business Administration; Computer Information Systems; Computer Networking; Computer Science; Finance; Marketing; Public Administration
BSN Nursing–RN to BSN
Certificate of Completion Computer Networking; Computer Programming–Java Programming; Computer Programming–UNIX (Solaris); Irish Studies; Management Information Systems
Certificate Public Administration
Graduate Certificate Database Technologies (MSCIT); E-Commerce Engineering (MSCIT); Executive International Management (MSM); Executive Leadership (MSM); Humane and Environmental Studies (MNM); Leadership (MNM); Management of Technology (MSCIT); Networking Technologies (MSCIT); Object-Oriented Technologies (MSCIT);

Program Management (MNM); Project Management–Executive Project Management (MSM); Resource Development (MNM); Strategic Business Management (MSM)
MBA Business Administration
MEd Education
MS Computer Information Technology; Nonprofit Management
MSM Management

COURSE SUBJECT AREAS OFFERED OUTSIDE OF DEGREE PROGRAMS

Undergraduate—accounting and related services; business administration, management and operations; business/managerial economics; communication and media; computer/information technology administration and management; computer programming; computer science; computer systems networking and telecommunications; finance and financial management services; history; information science/studies; marketing; philosophy and religious studies related; public administration; religious studies; sales, merchandising, and related marketing operations (general); social psychology; sociology; statistics.
Graduate—accounting and related services; anthropology; business/ corporate communications; business, management, and marketing related; business/managerial economics; computer and information sciences; computer and information sciences and support services related; computer/ information technology administration and management; computer programming; computer science; computer systems networking and telecommunications; curriculum and instruction; educational administration and supervision; education related; education (specific levels and methods); finance and financial management services; international business; management information systems; management sciences and quantitative methods; marketing; philosophy and religious studies related; public administration; public administration and social service professions related.

REND LAKE COLLEGE
Ina, Illinois
Learning Resource Center
http://www.rlc.edu
Rend Lake College was founded in 1967. It is accredited by North Central Association of Colleges and Schools. It first offered distance learning courses in 1995. In fall 2006, there were 900 students enrolled in distance learning courses. Institutionally administered financial aid is available to distance learners.
Services Distance learners have accessibility to academic advising, bookstore, campus computer network, career placement assistance, e-mail services, library services, tutoring.
Contact Karla J. Lewis, Coordinator of Distance Learning and Media Technology, Rend Lake College, 468 North Ken Gray Parkway, Ina, IL 62846. Telephone: 618-437-5321 Ext. 1299. Fax: 618-437-5677. E-mail: lewisk@rlc.edu.

DEGREES AND AWARDS
Programs offered do not lead to a degree or other formal award.

COURSE SUBJECT AREAS OFFERED OUTSIDE OF DEGREE PROGRAMS

Undergraduate—agriculture; anthropology; biology; business/commerce; business/corporate communications; clinical child psychology; computer science; criminal justice and corrections; English; English composition; geological and earth sciences/geosciences; health and physical education/ fitness; health services/allied health/health sciences; history; liberal arts and sciences, general studies and humanities; mathematics; microbiological sciences and immunology; music; nursing; nutrition sciences; philosophy and religious studies related; plant sciences; political science and government; psychology; real estate; religious studies; social sciences; sociology; speech and rhetoric; work and family studies.
Non-credit—accounting and related services; business administration, management and operations; business/commerce; business operations support and assistant services; computer software and media applications; entrepreneurial and small business operations; human resources management; languages (foreign languages related); sales, merchandising, and related marketing operations (general).

THE RICHARD STOCKTON COLLEGE OF NEW JERSEY
Pomona, New Jersey
Office of Distance Education
http://www.stockton.edu

The Richard Stockton College of New Jersey was founded in 1969. It is accredited by Middle States Association of Colleges and Schools. It first offered distance learning courses in 1996. In fall 2006, there were 1,800 students enrolled in distance learning courses. Institutionally administered financial aid is available to distance learners.

Services Distance learners have accessibility to campus computer network, e-mail services, library services.

Contact Dennis Fotia, Distance Education Coordinator, The Richard Stockton College of New Jersey, PO Box 195, Pomona, NJ 08240-0195. Telephone: 609-652-4580. Fax: 609-626-5562. E-mail: dennis.fotia@stockton.edu.

DEGREES AND AWARDS
Programs offered do not lead to a degree or other formal award.

COURSE SUBJECT AREAS OFFERED OUTSIDE OF DEGREE PROGRAMS
Undergraduate—allied health and medical assisting services; anthropology; applied mathematics; business administration, management and operations; English composition; ethnic, cultural minority, and gender studies; film/video and photographic arts; gerontology; health professions related; journalism; liberal arts and sciences, general studies and humanities; marketing; nursing; psychology; sociology.
Graduate—allied health and medical assisting services; business, management, and marketing related; information science/studies; nursing.

RICHLAND COMMUNITY COLLEGE
Decatur, Illinois
Lifelong Learning Division

Richland Community College was founded in 1971. It is accredited by North Central Association of Colleges and Schools. It first offered distance learning courses in 1994. In fall 2006, there were 400 students enrolled in distance learning courses. Institutionally administered financial aid is available to distance learners.

Services Distance learners have accessibility to academic advising, campus computer network, career placement assistance, e-mail services, library services.

Contact Ms. Catherine L. Sebok, Director, Recruitment and Outreach Services, Richland Community College, One College Park, Decatur, IL 62521. Telephone: 217-875-7200 Ext. 558. Fax: 217-875-7783. E-mail: csebok@richland.cc.edu.

DEGREES AND AWARDS
Programs offered do not lead to a degree or other formal award.

COURSE SUBJECT AREAS OFFERED OUTSIDE OF DEGREE PROGRAMS
Undergraduate—accounting and related services; business/corporate communications; computer software and media applications; creative writing; developmental and child psychology; English composition; fine and studio art; history; psychology; social psychology; sociology.

RIO SALADO COLLEGE
Tempe, Arizona
Distance Learning
http://www.rio.maricopa.edu

Rio Salado College was founded in 1978. It is accredited by North Central Association of Colleges and Schools. It first offered distance learning courses in 1978. In fall 2006, there were 35,000 students enrolled in distance learning courses. Institutionally administered financial aid is available to distance learners.

Services Distance learners have accessibility to academic advising, bookstore, e-mail services, library services, tutoring.

Contact Student Enrollment Services, Student Enrollment Services, Rio Salado College, 2323 West 14th Street, Tempe, AZ 85281. Telephone: 480-517-8540. Fax: 480-517-8579. E-mail: student.services@riomail.maricopa.edu.

DEGREES AND AWARDS
AA General Studies
AGS General Studies

RIVERSIDE COMMUNITY COLLEGE DISTRICT
Riverside, California
Open Campus
http://www.opencampus.com

Riverside Community College District was founded in 1916. It is accredited by Western Association of Schools and Colleges. It first offered distance learning courses in 1982. In fall 2006, there were 9,000 students enrolled in distance learning courses. Institutionally administered financial aid is available to distance learners.

Services Distance learners have accessibility to academic advising, bookstore, campus computer network, career placement assistance, e-mail services, library services.

Contact Col. Glen Brady, Director, Distance Education, Riverside Community College District, Open Campus, 4800 Magnolia Avenue, Riverside, CA 92506-1299. Telephone: 951-222-8561. Fax: 951-328-3596. E-mail: glen.brady@rcc.edu.

DEGREES AND AWARDS
Programs offered do not lead to a degree or other formal award.

COURSE SUBJECT AREAS OFFERED OUTSIDE OF DEGREE PROGRAMS
Undergraduate—accounting and related services; anthropology; architecture; astronomy and astrophysics; business administration, management and operations; business/commerce; communication and media; computer and information sciences; computer science; computer systems networking and telecommunications; criminology; economics; English; geography and cartography; graphic communications; history; hospitality administration; languages (foreign languages related); legal support services; linguistic, comparative, and related language studies; marketing; mathematics; music; nursing; nutrition sciences; philosophy; political science and government; psychology; real estate; religious studies; sociology; transportation and materials moving related; visual and performing arts; work and family studies.
Non-credit—business administration, management and operations; computer and information sciences; computer programming; computer software and media applications; creative writing; economics; graphic communications; health professions related; linguistic, comparative, and related language studies.

ROCHESTER INSTITUTE OF TECHNOLOGY
Rochester, New York
Graduate Enrollment Services
http://www.rit.edu/online

Rochester Institute of Technology was founded in 1829. It is accredited by Middle States Association of Colleges and Schools. It first offered distance learning courses in 1979. In fall 2006, there were 1,600 students enrolled in distance learning courses. Institutionally administered financial aid is available to distance learners.

Services Distance learners have accessibility to academic advising, bookstore, campus computer network, e-mail services, library services.

Contact Ms. Diane Ellison, Director, Office of Part-time and Graduate Enrollment Services, Rochester Institute of Technology, Bausch & Lomb Center, 58 Lomb Memorial Drive, Rochester, NY 14623. Telephone: 585-475-2229. Fax: 585-475-7164. E-mail: distance@rit.edu.

DEGREES AND AWARDS
BS Arts and Science–Applied Arts and Science; Electrical/Mechanical Engineering Technology; Safety Technology; Telecommunications Technology

Certificate Disaster and Emergency Management; E-business; Health Systems Administration; Industrial Environmental Management; International Logistics and Transportation Management; Introduction to Programming–NTID; Public Relations Communications–Professional Writing; Quality Implementation; Quality Management, basic; Safety and Health Technology; Structural Design; Technical Communication, basic; Technical Communications, advanced; Telecommunications–Data Communications; Telecommunications–Network Management; Telecommunications–Voice Communications

Graduate Certificate Digital Print and Publishing; Elements of Health Care Leadership; Health Information Resources; Health Systems Finance; Human Resource Development; Learning and Knowledge Management Systems; Project Management; Senior Living Management; Statistical Methods for Product and Process Improvement; Statistical Quality; Technical Information Design

MS Applied Statistics; Cross Disciplinary Professional Studies; Environmental Health and Safety Management; Facility Management; Health Systems Administration; Imaging Science; Information Technology; Learning and Knowledge Management Systems; Microelectronics Manufacturing Engineering; Networking & Systems Administration; Print Media; Software Development and Management; Telecommunications Engineering Technology

COURSE SUBJECT AREAS OFFERED OUTSIDE OF DEGREE PROGRAMS

Undergraduate—anthropology; business administration, management and operations; chemistry; engineering mechanics; English composition; mechanical engineering; political science and government; psychology; sociology.

See full description on page 420.

ROCKLAND COMMUNITY COLLEGE
Suffern, New York
Telecourse and Distance Learning Department
http://www.sunyrockland.edu/virtualrcc
Rockland Community College was founded in 1959. It is accredited by Middle States Association of Colleges and Schools. It first offered distance learning courses in 1985. In fall 2006, there were 800 students enrolled in distance learning courses. Institutionally administered financial aid is available to distance learners.
Services Distance learners have accessibility to academic advising, bookstore, campus computer network, career placement assistance, e-mail services, library services.
Contact Mr. Rick Echevarria, Distance Education Supervisor, Rockland Community College, 145 College Road, Room 8300, Suffern, NY 10901. Telephone: 845-574-4713. E-mail: rechevar@sunyrockland.edu.

DEGREES AND AWARDS
AA Liberal Arts and Sciences

COURSE SUBJECT AREAS OFFERED OUTSIDE OF DEGREE PROGRAMS

Undergraduate—anthropology; biology; business/commerce; chemistry; computer science; economics; English; English composition; finance and financial management services; fine and studio art; geography and cartography; health/medical preparatory programs; health professions related; history; liberal arts and sciences, general studies and humanities; marketing; mathematics; medical basic sciences; nursing; philosophy; physical sciences; political science and government; psychology; social sciences related.
Graduate—economics; statistics.
Non-credit—nursing.

ROGERS STATE UNIVERSITY
Claremore, Oklahoma
Distance Learning
http://www.rsuonline.edu
Rogers State University was founded in 1909. It is accredited by North Central Association of Colleges and Schools. It first offered distance learning courses in 1989. In fall 2006, there were 928 students enrolled in distance learning courses. Institutionally administered financial aid is available to distance learners.
Services Distance learners have accessibility to academic advising, bookstore, career placement assistance, e-mail services, library services.
Contact Chelley Nelson, Online Counselor, Rogers State University, 1701 West Will Rogers Boulevard, Claremore, OK 74017. Telephone: 918-343-7726. Fax: 918-343-7595. E-mail: mnelson@rsu.edu.

DEGREES AND AWARDS
AA Business Administration; Liberal Arts
AAS Applied Technology
AS Computer Science
BA Liberal Arts
BAA Applied Technology
BS Information Technology

COURSE SUBJECT AREAS OFFERED OUTSIDE OF DEGREE PROGRAMS

Undergraduate—business administration, management and operations; computer/information technology administration and management; liberal arts and sciences, general studies and humanities; technology education/industrial arts.

ROGER WILLIAMS UNIVERSITY
Bristol, Rhode Island
School of Continuing Studies
http://www.rwu.edu/Academics/Academic+Programs/
School+of+Continuing+Studies/
Roger Williams University was founded in 1956. It is accredited by New England Association of Schools and Colleges. It first offered distance learning courses in 1974. In fall 2006, there were 234 students enrolled in distance learning courses. Institutionally administered financial aid is available to distance learners.
Services Distance learners have accessibility to academic advising, bookstore, campus computer network, career placement assistance, e-mail services, library services.
Contact John Stout, Dean, School of Continuing Studies, Roger Williams University, 150 Washington Street, Providence, RI 02903. Telephone: 401-254-3530. Fax: 401-254-3560. E-mail: jstout@rwu.edu.

DEGREES AND AWARDS
Programs offered do not lead to a degree or other formal award.

COURSE SUBJECT AREAS OFFERED OUTSIDE OF DEGREE PROGRAMS

Undergraduate—criminal justice and corrections; criminology; finance and financial management services; health and medical administrative services; health services/allied health/health sciences; history; industrial production technologies; legal studies (non-professional general, undergraduate); physical sciences related; public administration; public administration and social service professions related; sociology.

ROOSEVELT UNIVERSITY
Chicago, Illinois
Distance Learning
http://www.roosevelt.edu/ruonline
Roosevelt University was founded in 1945. It is accredited by North Central Association of Colleges and Schools. It first offered distance learning courses in 2001. In fall 2006, there were 1,000 students enrolled in distance learning courses. Institutionally administered financial aid is available to distance learners.
Services Distance learners have accessibility to academic advising, bookstore, campus computer network, career placement assistance, e-mail services, library services.

Contact Dr. Karen S. Gersten, Associate Provost for Academic Programs and Distance Learning, Roosevelt University, Office of the Provost, 430 South Michigan Avenue, Chicago, IL 60605. Telephone: 312-341-2337. Fax: 312-281-3258. E-mail: kgersten@roosevelt.edu.

DEGREES AND AWARDS
BGS Psychology
BPS Criminal Justice Leadership; Organizational Leadership
Certificate Criminal Justice Leadership; Organizational Leadership
Graduate Certificate E-Learning; Instructional Design; Online Teaching; Performance Consulting; Training and Development
MA Teacher Leadership; Training and Development

COURSE SUBJECT AREAS OFFERED OUTSIDE OF DEGREE PROGRAMS
Undergraduate—accounting and related services; business administration, management and operations; business/corporate communications; criminal justice and corrections; curriculum and instruction; education; educational/instructional media design; education related; education (specific levels and methods); education (specific subject areas); English composition; hospitality administration; intercultural/multicultural and diversity studies; legal studies (non-professional general, undergraduate); liberal arts and sciences, general studies and humanities; multi-/interdisciplinary studies related; personality psychology; physical sciences; psychology; social sciences; sociology; statistics.
Graduate—business/corporate communications; communications technology; education; educational administration and supervision; educational/instructional media design; education related; hospitality administration; legal professions and studies related.
Non-credit—legal professions and studies related.

ROSALIND FRANKLIN UNIVERSITY OF MEDICINE AND SCIENCE
North Chicago, Illinois
http://www.rosalindfranklin.edu
Rosalind Franklin University of Medicine and Science was founded in 1912. It is accredited by North Central Association of Colleges and Schools. It first offered distance learning courses in 1993. In fall 2006, there were 146 students enrolled in distance learning courses. Institutionally administered financial aid is available to distance learners.
Services Distance learners have accessibility to academic advising, bookstore, campus computer network, e-mail services, library services, tutoring.
Contact Ms. Laura Nelson, Administrative Assistant, Rosalind Franklin University of Medicine and Science, 3333 Green Bay Road, North Chicago, IL 60064-3095. Telephone: 847-578-3310. Fax: 847-578-8623. E-mail: laura.nelson@rosalindfranklin.edu.

DEGREES AND AWARDS
CAGS Healthcare Management; Women's Health
MS Clinical Laboratory Sciences (advanced and categorical); Clinical Laboratory Sciences (entry-level); Clinical Nutrition/Nutrition Education; Healthcare Management; Women's Health
DPT Physical Therapy–Post-Professional Doctor of Physical Therapy

ROSE STATE COLLEGE
Midwest City, Oklahoma
Academic Affairs
http://www.rose.edu/
Rose State College was founded in 1968. It is accredited by North Central Association of Colleges and Schools. It first offered distance learning courses in 1972. In fall 2006, there were 2,299 students enrolled in distance learning courses. Institutionally administered financial aid is available to distance learners.
Services Distance learners have accessibility to academic advising, bookstore, campus computer network, career placement assistance, e-mail services, library services, tutoring.

Contact Chris Meyer, Director of Distance Learning, Rose State College, Learning Resources Center, 6420 SE 15th Street, Midwest City, OK 73110. Telephone: 405-733-7913. E-mail: cmeyer@rose.edu.

DEGREES AND AWARDS
AA Business; English; History; Liberal Arts; Social Sciences
AAS E-commerce and Webmaster Technology; Library Technical Assistant

COURSE SUBJECT AREAS OFFERED OUTSIDE OF DEGREE PROGRAMS
Undergraduate—accounting and computer science; accounting and related services; allied health and medical assisting services; allied health diagnostic, intervention, and treatment professions; alternative and complementary medical support services; alternative and complementary medicine and medical systems; American literature (United States and Canadian); apparel and textiles; audiovisual communications technologies; biology; business administration, management and operations; business/commerce; business/corporate communications; business, management, and marketing related; business/managerial economics; communication and journalism related; computer/information technology administration and management; computer programming; computer science; computer software and media applications; computer systems analysis; computer systems networking and telecommunications; creative writing; criminal justice and corrections; developmental and child psychology; economics; English; English composition; English language and literature related; English literature (British and Commonwealth); foods, nutrition, and related services; geography and cartography; geological and earth sciences/geosciences; geological/geophysical engineering; graphic communications; health and physical education/fitness; health/medical preparatory programs; health professions related; health services/allied health/health sciences; history; information science/studies; legal professions and studies related; legal research and advanced professional studies; legal studies (non-professional general, undergraduate); liberal arts and sciences, general studies and humanities; library assistant; library science; library science related; marketing; mathematics; nursing; philosophy; philosophy and religious studies related; physical sciences; physical sciences related; political science and government; psychology; psychology related; social psychology; social sciences; social sciences related; sociology.
Non-credit—health and physical education/fitness.

RYERSON UNIVERSITY
Toronto, Ontario, Canada
Distance Education
http://www.ryerson.ca/ce/de
Ryerson University was founded in 1948. It is provincially chartered. It first offered distance learning courses in 1999. In fall 2006, there were 5,311 students enrolled in distance learning courses. Institutionally administered financial aid is available to distance learners.
Services Distance learners have accessibility to academic advising, bookstore, campus computer network, career placement assistance, e-mail services, library services, tutoring.
Contact Sushila Parikh, Acting Manager, Support Services, Ryerson University, G. Raymond Chang School of Continuing Education, Distance Education, 350 Victoria Street, Toronto, ON M5B 2K3, Canada. Telephone: 416-979-5000 Ext. 7874. Fax: 416-979-5196. E-mail: sparikh@ryerson.ca.

DEGREES AND AWARDS
Programs offered do not lead to a degree or other formal award.

COURSE SUBJECT AREAS OFFERED OUTSIDE OF DEGREE PROGRAMS
Undergraduate—accounting and related services; business administration, management and operations; business/commerce; business/corporate communications; business/managerial economics; communication and media; community health services; computer/information technology administration and management; criminal justice and corrections; economics; English; entrepreneurial and small business operations; finance and financial management services; foods, nutrition, and related services; geography and cartography; gerontology; health professions

related; history; hospitality administration; human development, family studies, and related services; human resources management; legal studies (non-professional general, undergraduate); liberal arts and sciences, general studies and humanities; management information systems; management sciences and quantitative methods; marketing; nursing; philosophy; political science and government; psychology; public administration; public administration and social service professions related; public relations, advertising, and applied communication related; publishing; sales, merchandising, and related marketing operations (general); social sciences; sociology.

Non-credit—English composition.

SACRED HEART UNIVERSITY
Fairfield, Connecticut
University College/ Continuing Education
http://onlinelearning.sacredheart.edu

Sacred Heart University was founded in 1963. It is accredited by New England Association of Schools and Colleges. It first offered distance learning courses in 1997. In fall 2006, there were 600 students enrolled in distance learning courses. Institutionally administered financial aid is available to distance learners.

Services Distance learners have accessibility to academic advising, bookstore, campus computer network, career placement assistance, e-mail services, library services, tutoring.

Contact David M. Demers, PhD, Director, Instructional Technology, Sacred Heart University, 5151 Park Avenue, Fairfield, CT 06825. Telephone: 203-365-7613. Fax: 203-365-7695. E-mail: demersd@sacredheart.edu.

DEGREES AND AWARDS
BSN Nursing
MSHA Geriatric Rehabilitation and Wellness
MSN Nursing–Patient Care Services Administration–Family Nurse Practitioner

COURSE SUBJECT AREAS OFFERED OUTSIDE OF DEGREE PROGRAMS
Undergraduate—biological and physical sciences; business administration, management and operations; chemistry; communication and media; computer and information sciences; computer science; English composition; English language and literature related; fine and studio art; health professions related; history; international business; languages (foreign languages related); liberal arts and sciences, general studies and humanities; linguistic, comparative, and related language studies; marketing; music; philosophy; philosophy and religious studies related; physical sciences; political science and government; religious education; religious studies; social sciences related.
Graduate—accounting and related services; business administration, management and operations; computer science; economics; education; finance and financial management services; gerontology; health professions related; marketing; mathematics; nursing.

SADDLEBACK COLLEGE
Mission Viejo, California
Office of Instruction
http://www.saddlebackcollege.edu

Saddleback College was founded in 1967. It is accredited by Western Association of Schools and Colleges. It first offered distance learning courses in 1975. In fall 2006, there were 6,000 students enrolled in distance learning courses. Institutionally administered financial aid is available to distance learners.

Services Distance learners have accessibility to academic advising, bookstore, campus computer network, career placement assistance, e-mail services, library services.

Contact Ms. Sheri L. Nelson, Senior Administrative Assistant, Saddleback College, AGB 117, 28000 Marguerite Parkway, Mission Viejo, CA 92692. Telephone: 949-582-4515. Fax: 949-347-0438. E-mail: snelson@saddleback.edu.

DEGREES AND AWARDS
Programs offered do not lead to a degree or other formal award.

COURSE SUBJECT AREAS OFFERED OUTSIDE OF DEGREE PROGRAMS
Undergraduate—accounting and computer science; accounting and related services; American Sign Language (ASL); anthropology; business, management, and marketing related; business/managerial economics; communication and journalism related; computer science; developmental and child psychology; educational administration and supervision; English; geography and cartography; gerontology; health/medical preparatory programs; history; human development, family studies, and related services; international business; journalism; library science related; management information systems; marketing; mathematics; music; nursing; physics; political science and government; radio, television, and digital communication; real estate; sales, merchandising, and related marketing operations (general); sales, merchandising, and related marketing operations (specialized); social sciences related; sociology.

ST. CLAIR COUNTY COMMUNITY COLLEGE
Port Huron, Michigan
http://www.SC4.edu/

St. Clair County Community College was founded in 1923. It is accredited by North Central Association of Colleges and Schools. It first offered distance learning courses in 2000. In fall 2006, there were 660 students enrolled in distance learning courses. Institutionally administered financial aid is available to distance learners.

Services Distance learners have accessibility to academic advising, bookstore, career placement assistance, e-mail services, library services, tutoring.

Contact Linda Davis, Associate Dean of eLearning and Instructional Technology, St. Clair County Community College, 323 Erie Street, PO Box 5015, Port Huron, MI 48061-5015. Telephone: 810-989-5765. E-mail: ldavis@sc4.edu.

DEGREES AND AWARDS
AA Associate in Arts
AD AAS Nursing, Health Care Provider to RN Articulation; Associate in Business (Transfer Program); General Education

COURSE SUBJECT AREAS OFFERED OUTSIDE OF DEGREE PROGRAMS
Undergraduate—accounting and related services; astronomy and astrophysics; business administration, management and operations; business/corporate communications; chemistry; communication and journalism related; computer and information sciences; creative writing; economics; education (specific levels and methods); electrical and electronic engineering technologies; English composition; geography and cartography; history; mathematics; nursing; political science and government; psychology; social sciences; sociology; speech and rhetoric; statistics.

ST. CLOUD STATE UNIVERSITY
St. Cloud, Minnesota
Center for Continuing Studies
http://www.stcloudstate.edu/~ccs/

St. Cloud State University was founded in 1869. It is accredited by North Central Association of Colleges and Schools. It first offered distance learning courses in 1975. In fall 2006, there were 3,000 students enrolled in distance learning courses. Institutionally administered financial aid is available to distance learners.

Services Distance learners have accessibility to academic advising, bookstore, campus computer network, career placement assistance, e-mail services, library services, tutoring.

Contact Ms. Patricia Aceves, Director of Distributed Learning, St. Cloud State University, 720 4th Avenue South, St. Cloud, MN 56301. Telephone: 320-308-3081. Fax: 320-308-5041. E-mail: paceves@stcloudstate.edu.

DEGREES AND AWARDS

AA Liberal Arts
BA Criminal Justice Studies
BGS Community Psychology; Self-Designed
BS Special Education
BSAST Aviation Maintenance Management
MA Teaching English as a Second Language
MBA Business Administration
MS Behavior Analysis; Criminal Justice Studies; Educational Administration; Environmental and Technological Studies; Information Media

COURSE SUBJECT AREAS OFFERED OUTSIDE OF DEGREE PROGRAMS

Undergraduate—aerospace, aeronautical and astronautical engineering; American literature (United States and Canadian); anthropology; astronomy and astrophysics; biology; botany/plant biology; chemistry; communication and media; counseling psychology; creative writing; criminal justice and corrections; economics; educational administration and supervision; English; English as a second language; English composition; environmental/environmental health engineering; history; management information systems; mathematics; philosophy; physics; psychology; social sciences related; sociology; special education; speech and rhetoric; statistics.
Graduate—behavioral sciences; community psychology; criminal justice and corrections; English as a second language; psychology related; statistics.

SAINT FRANCIS MEDICAL CENTER COLLEGE OF NURSING
Peoria, Illinois

Saint Francis Medical Center College of Nursing was founded in 1986. It is accredited by North Central Association of Colleges and Schools. It first offered distance learning courses in 2000. In fall 2006, there were 77 students enrolled in distance learning courses. Institutionally administered financial aid is available to distance learners.
Services Distance learners have accessibility to academic advising, campus computer network, e-mail services, library services.
Contact Dr. Janice F. Boundy, Associate Dean, Graduate Program/Professor, Saint Francis Medical Center College of Nursing, 511 NE Greenleaf Street, Peoria, IL 61603. Telephone: 309-655-2230. Fax: 309-624-8973. E-mail: janice.f.boundy@osfhealthcare.org.

DEGREES AND AWARDS

MSN Nursing

COURSE SUBJECT AREAS OFFERED OUTSIDE OF DEGREE PROGRAMS

Undergraduate—nursing.
Graduate—nursing.

ST. JOHN'S UNIVERSITY
Queens, New York
The School of Education

St. John's University was founded in 1870. It is accredited by Middle States Association of Colleges and Schools. It first offered distance learning courses in 1994. In fall 2006, there were 742 students enrolled in distance learning courses. Institutionally administered financial aid is available to distance learners.
Services Distance learners have accessibility to academic advising, bookstore, campus computer network, career placement assistance, e-mail services, library services, tutoring.
Contact Kelly K. Ronayne, Assistant Dean, St. John's University, 8000 Utopia Parkway, Sullivan Hall, SB 9, Queens, NY 11439. Telephone: 718-990-2304. Fax: 718-990-2343. E-mail: graded@stjohns.edu.

DEGREES AND AWARDS

MSE School Building Leader in Educational Administration and Supervision
PMC School District Leader Professional Diploma

COURSE SUBJECT AREAS OFFERED OUTSIDE OF DEGREE PROGRAMS

Graduate—education; educational administration and supervision; educational assessment, evaluation, and research; educational/instructional media design; education related; education (specific levels and methods); education (specific subject areas); library science.

ST. JOHN'S UNIVERSITY
Queens, New York
http://www.stjohns.edu/distancelearning

St. John's University was founded in 1870. It is accredited by Middle States Association of Colleges and Schools. It first offered distance learning courses in 1994. In fall 2006, there were 1,150 students enrolled in distance learning courses. Institutionally administered financial aid is available to distance learners.
Services Distance learners have accessibility to academic advising, bookstore, campus computer network, career placement assistance, e-mail services, library services, tutoring.
Contact Dr. Jeffery E. Olson, Associate Vice President, Online Learning and Services, St. John's University, 8000 Utopia Parkway, Queens, NY 11439. Telephone: 718-990-5705. Fax: 718-990-5689. E-mail: distancelearning@stjohns.edu.

DEGREES AND AWARDS

AA Liberal Studies
AS Business; Criminal Justice
BA Liberal Studies
BS Administrative Studies; Criminal Justice
MSE School Building Leader in Educational Administration and Supervision
PMC School District Leader Professional Diploma

COURSE SUBJECT AREAS OFFERED OUTSIDE OF DEGREE PROGRAMS

Undergraduate—business administration, management and operations; communication and journalism related; computer science; criminal justice and corrections; economics; education; English; history; languages (Romance languages); legal studies (non-professional general, undergraduate); marketing; mathematics; pharmacy, pharmaceutical sciences, and administration; physics; political science and government; science technologies related; sociology; theology and religious vocations related.
Graduate—business, management, and marketing related; economics; education; educational administration and supervision; education (specific subject areas); library science.

SAINT JOSEPH'S COLLEGE OF MAINE
Standish, Maine
Graduate & Professional Studies
http://www.sjcme.edu/gps

Saint Joseph's College of Maine was founded in 1912. It is accredited by New England Association of Schools and Colleges. It first offered distance learning courses in 1976. In fall 2006, there were 4,000 students enrolled in distance learning courses. Institutionally administered financial aid is available to distance learners.
Services Distance learners have accessibility to academic advising, bookstore, campus computer network, career placement assistance, e-mail services, library services, tutoring.
Contact Lynne Robinson, Director of Admissions, Saint Joseph's College of Maine, 278 Whites Bridge Road, Standish, ME 04084-5263. Telephone: 800-752-4723. Fax: 207-892-7480. E-mail: info@sjcme.edu.

DEGREES AND AWARDS

AS Adult Education and Training; Business Administration; Criminal Justice; General Studies; Human Services; Information Technology Management; Management; Psychology
BA Adult Religious Education
BLS Christian Tradition
BS General Studies; Health Care Administration; Long-Term Care Administration; Radiological Sciences

BSBA Business Administration
BSN Nursing
BSPA Professional Arts
Certificate Adult Education and Training; Business Administration; Christian Tradition; Health Care Management; Health Care Management, advanced; Information Technology Management; Long-Term Care Administration; Long-Term Care Administration, advanced; Professional Studies
Graduate Certificate Nursing Administration and Leadership; Nursing and Healthcare Education
MBA Quality Leadership
MBA/MSN Health Services Administration and Nursing Dual degree
MHSA Health Services Administration
MSE Education
MSN Nursing

COURSE SUBJECT AREAS OFFERED OUTSIDE OF DEGREE PROGRAMS

Undergraduate—accounting and related services; biblical studies; business administration, management and operations; communication and media; computer/information technology administration and management; criminology; developmental and child psychology; educational assessment, evaluation, and research; education (specific subject areas); English composition; health and medical administrative services; human services; industrial and organizational psychology; marketing; multi-/interdisciplinary studies related; nursing; pastoral counseling and specialized ministries; philosophy and religious studies related; religious education; social psychology; sociology.

Graduate—accounting and related services; business administration, management and operations; business/corporate communications; business, management, and marketing related; business/managerial economics; curriculum and instruction; educational administration and supervision; educational assessment, evaluation, and research; education (specific subject areas); entrepreneurial and small business operations; health and medical administrative services; management sciences and quantitative methods; marketing; nursing; public administration; sales, merchandising, and related marketing operations (specialized).

Non-credit—biblical studies; pastoral counseling and specialized ministries; religious studies.

See full description on page 422.

ST. LOUIS COMMUNITY COLLEGE SYSTEM
St. Louis, Missouri
Telelearning Services
http://stlcc.edu/distance
St. Louis Community College System is accredited by North Central Association of Colleges and Schools. It first offered distance learning courses in 1973. In fall 2006, there were 6,814 students enrolled in distance learning courses. Institutionally administered financial aid is available to distance learners.
Services Distance learners have accessibility to academic advising, bookstore, e-mail services, library services.
Contact Daniel A. Bain, PhD, Director of Telelearning Services, St. Louis Community College System, Telelearning Services Department, 300 South Broadway, St. Louis, MO 63102. Telephone: 314-539-5056. Fax: 314-539-5125. E-mail: dbain@stlcc.edu.

DEGREES AND AWARDS
Programs offered do not lead to a degree or other formal award.

COURSE SUBJECT AREAS OFFERED OUTSIDE OF DEGREE PROGRAMS
Undergraduate—accounting and computer science; American literature (United States and Canadian); biological and physical sciences; communication and journalism related; computer and information sciences; computer and information sciences and support services related; computer software and media applications; data entry/microcomputer applications; funeral service and mortuary science; history; languages (Romance languages); marketing; mathematics; sociology.

Non-credit—business administration, management and operations; business/commerce; business, management, and marketing related; management information systems.

See full description on page 424.

ST. MARY'S UNIVERSITY OF SAN ANTONIO
San Antonio, Texas
Graduate School
http://www.stmarytx.edu
St. Mary's University of San Antonio was founded in 1852. It is accredited by Southern Association of Colleges and Schools. It first offered distance learning courses in 1997. In fall 2006, there were 51 students enrolled in distance learning courses. Institutionally administered financial aid is available to distance learners.
Services Distance learners have accessibility to academic advising, bookstore, campus computer network, career placement assistance, e-mail services, library services.
Contact Dr. Henry Flores, Dean of the Graduate School, St. Mary's University of San Antonio, One Camino Santa Maria, Box 43, San Antonio, TX 78228. Telephone: 210-436-3101. E-mail: hflores@stmarytx.edu.

DEGREES AND AWARDS
MA Community Counseling; International Relations

SAINT PAUL COLLEGE–A COMMUNITY & TECHNICAL COLLEGE
St. Paul, Minnesota
http://www.saintpaul.edu
Saint Paul College–A Community & Technical College was founded in 1919. It is accredited by North Central Association of Colleges and Schools. It first offered distance learning courses in 1999. In fall 2006, there were 600 students enrolled in distance learning courses. Institutionally administered financial aid is available to distance learners.
Services Distance learners have accessibility to academic advising, bookstore, campus computer network, career placement assistance, e-mail services, library services.
Contact Enrollment Services, Saint Paul College–A Community & Technical College, 235 Marshall Avenue, St. Paul, MN 55102. Telephone: 800-227-6029. Fax: 651-846-1555. E-mail: admissions@saintpaul.edu.

DEGREES AND AWARDS
Programs offered do not lead to a degree or other formal award.

COURSE SUBJECT AREAS OFFERED OUTSIDE OF DEGREE PROGRAMS
Undergraduate—business administration, management and operations; business/corporate communications; business operations support and assistant services; computer software and media applications; education; human resources management; management information systems.

ST. PETERSBURG COLLEGE
St. Petersburg, Florida
Electronic Campus
http://e.spcollege.edu
St. Petersburg College was founded in 1927. It is accredited by Southern Association of Colleges and Schools. It first offered distance learning courses in 1970. In fall 2006, there were 20,000 students enrolled in distance learning courses. Institutionally administered financial aid is available to distance learners.
Services Distance learners have accessibility to academic advising, bookstore, career placement assistance, e-mail services, library services, tutoring.
Contact Dr. James Connolly, eCampus Director, St. Petersburg College, PO Box 13489, St. Petersburg, FL 33733. Telephone: 727-394-6006. E-mail: connolly.james@spcollege.edu.

DEGREES AND AWARDS

AA General Program

AS Crime Scene Technology; Emergency Administration and Management; Funeral Services; Medical Laboratory Technology; Veterinary Technology

BA Dental Hygiene; Technology Management

Certificate Computer Related Crime Investigations; Crime Scene Technology; Critical Care (advanced technical certification); Emergency Administration and Management; Fire Inspector I; Fire Inspector II; Fire Investigator I; Fire Investigator II; Fire Officer I; Fire Officer II; Nursing–Perioperative Nursing; Quality Assurance and Software Testing; Veterinary Hospital Management; Veterinary Hospital Manager

COURSE SUBJECT AREAS OFFERED OUTSIDE OF DEGREE PROGRAMS

Undergraduate—accounting and related services; American literature (United States and Canadian); anthropology; archeology; area studies; astronomy and astrophysics; biblical studies; biological and physical sciences; biology; business administration, management and operations; business/commerce; business/corporate communications; chemistry; communication and media; computer science; economics; education; educational assessment, evaluation, and research; educational/instructional media design; educational psychology; English as a second language; entrepreneurial and small business operations; finance and financial management services; fine and studio art; funeral service and mortuary science; geography and cartography; history; liberal arts and sciences, general studies and humanities; linguistic, comparative, and related language studies; mathematics; microbiological sciences and immunology; music; philosophy; political science and government; psychology; social psychology.

SALEM STATE COLLEGE

Salem, Massachusetts

http://www.salemstate.edu/

Salem State College was founded in 1854. It is accredited by New England Association of Schools and Colleges. It first offered distance learning courses in 2005. In fall 2006, there were 45 students enrolled in distance learning courses. Institutionally administered financial aid is available to distance learners.

Services Distance learners have accessibility to bookstore, campus computer network, e-mail services, library services.

Contact Mrs. Connie Nielson, Academic Advisor, Salem State College, Division of Continuing Education, 352 Lafayette Street, Salem, MA 019701. Telephone: 978-542-6935. Fax: 978-542-7215. E-mail: cnielson@salemstate.edu.

DEGREES AND AWARDS

BS Fire Science Administration

COURSE SUBJECT AREAS OFFERED OUTSIDE OF DEGREE PROGRAMS

Undergraduate—computer and information sciences; criminal justice and corrections; economics; English composition; English language and literature related; geography and cartography; history; information science/studies; marketing; mathematics and statistics related; philosophy.

Graduate—education; educational/instructional media design; library science.

SAM HOUSTON STATE UNIVERSITY

Huntsville, Texas

Correspondence Course Division

http://www.shsu.edu/~cor_www

Sam Houston State University was founded in 1879. It is accredited by Southern Association of Colleges and Schools. It first offered distance learning courses in 1953. In fall 2006, there were 1,200 students enrolled in distance learning courses. Institutionally administered financial aid is available to distance learners.

Services Distance learners have accessibility to bookstore, e-mail services, library services.

Contact Gail M. Wright, Correspondence Course Coordinator, Sam Houston State University, Box 2536, Huntsville, TX 77341-2536. Telephone: 936-294-1003. Fax: 936-294-3703. E-mail: cor_gmw@shsu.edu.

DEGREES AND AWARDS

Programs offered do not lead to a degree or other formal award.

COURSE SUBJECT AREAS OFFERED OUTSIDE OF DEGREE PROGRAMS

Undergraduate—agricultural business and management; anthropology; business, management, and marketing related; chemistry; creative writing; economics; English; family and consumer economics; film/video and photographic arts; finance and financial management services; foods, nutrition, and related services; geological and earth sciences/geosciences; gerontology; health professions related; history; legal studies (non-professional general, undergraduate); marketing; mathematics and statistics related; nutrition sciences; philosophy; political science and government; psychology; sociology; statistics.

SAMPSON COMMUNITY COLLEGE

Clinton, North Carolina

http://www.sampson.cc.nc.us/

Sampson Community College was founded in 1965. It is accredited by Southern Association of Colleges and Schools. It first offered distance learning courses in 1999. In fall 2006, there were 400 students enrolled in distance learning courses. Institutionally administered financial aid is available to distance learners.

Services Distance learners have accessibility to academic advising, e-mail services, library services.

Contact Amy Noel Slater, Director of Distance Learning, Sampson Community College, 1801 Sunset Avenue, PO Box 318, Clinton, NC 28329. Telephone: 910-592-8081 Ext. 2044. Fax: 910-592-9864. E-mail: anoel-slater@sampsoncc.edu.

DEGREES AND AWARDS

Programs offered do not lead to a degree or other formal award.

COURSE SUBJECT AREAS OFFERED OUTSIDE OF DEGREE PROGRAMS

Undergraduate—agricultural and food products processing; agricultural production; agriculture and agriculture operations related; animal sciences; behavioral sciences; bilingual, multilingual, and multicultural education; business administration, management and operations; business/managerial economics; computer and information sciences; computer and information sciences and support services related; computer systems networking and telecommunications; criminal justice and corrections; data entry/microcomputer applications; English composition; finance and financial management services; human development, family studies, and related services; sociology.

Non-credit—computer and information sciences.

SAMUEL MERRITT COLLEGE

Oakland, California

Academic Affairs

http://www.samuelmerritt.edu

Samuel Merritt College was founded in 1909. It is accredited by Western Association of Schools and Colleges. It first offered distance learning courses in 2001. In fall 2006, there were 20 students enrolled in distance learning courses. Institutionally administered financial aid is available to distance learners.

Services Distance learners have accessibility to academic advising, bookstore, campus computer network, e-mail services, library services, tutoring.

Contact Mr. John Garten-Shuman, Vice President of Enrollment Services, Samuel Merritt College, Bechtel Hall, 450 30th Street, Oakland, CA 94609. Telephone: 800-607-6377. Fax: 510-869-6525. E-mail: jgartens@samuelmerritt.edu.

DEGREES AND AWARDS
MSN Nursing

COURSE SUBJECT AREAS OFFERED OUTSIDE OF DEGREE PROGRAMS
Graduate—nursing.

SAN FRANCISCO STATE UNIVERSITY
San Francisco, California
Multimedia Studies Program
http://www.sfsu.edu/

San Francisco State University was founded in 1899. It is accredited by Western Association of Schools and Colleges. It first offered distance learning courses in 1999. In fall 2006, there were 38 students enrolled in distance learning courses. Institutionally administered financial aid is available to distance learners.

Services Distance learners have accessibility to academic advising, bookstore.

Contact Richard Sinrich, Online Program Coordinator, MSP/CEL Online, San Francisco State University, MSP/CEL Online, 835 Market Street, Suite 600, San Francisco, CA 94103-1901. Telephone: 415-817-4227. Fax: 415-817-4299. E-mail: rsinrich@sfsu.edu.

DEGREES AND AWARDS
Programs offered do not lead to a degree or other formal award.

COURSE SUBJECT AREAS OFFERED OUTSIDE OF DEGREE PROGRAMS
Non-credit—computer software and media applications; design and applied arts; education (specific levels and methods); information science/studies.

SANTA MONICA COLLEGE
Santa Monica, California
SMC Online
http://smconline.org

Santa Monica College was founded in 1929. It is accredited by Western Association of Schools and Colleges. It first offered distance learning courses in 1999. Institutionally administered financial aid is available to distance learners.

Services Distance learners have accessibility to academic advising, bookstore, library services.

Contact Julie Yarrish, Director of Online Services and Support, Santa Monica College, 1900 Pico Boulevard, Santa Monica, CA 90405. Telephone: 310-434-3762. Fax: 310-434-3769. E-mail: yarrish_julie@smc.edu.

DEGREES AND AWARDS
Programs offered do not lead to a degree or other formal award.

SAUK VALLEY COMMUNITY COLLEGE
Dixon, Illinois
http://www.svcc.edu/

Sauk Valley Community College was founded in 1965. It is accredited by North Central Association of Colleges and Schools. It first offered distance learning courses in 1993. In fall 2006, there were 377 students enrolled in distance learning courses. Institutionally administered financial aid is available to distance learners.

Services Distance learners have accessibility to academic advising, bookstore, career placement assistance, e-mail services, library services, tutoring.

Contact Alan Pfeifer, Dean of Information Services, Sauk Valley Community College, 173 Illinois Route 2, Dixon, IL 61021. Telephone: 815-288-5511 Ext. 218. Fax: 815-288-5958. E-mail: pfeifer@svcc.edu.

DEGREES AND AWARDS
Programs offered do not lead to a degree or other formal award.

COURSE SUBJECT AREAS OFFERED OUTSIDE OF DEGREE PROGRAMS
Undergraduate—accounting and related services; biology; business administration, management and operations; business/commerce; business operations support and assistant services; computer and information sciences; computer and information sciences and support services related; computer/information technology administration and management; computer programming; computer software and media applications; criminal justice and corrections; criminology; economics; English composition; history; international business; mathematics and statistics related; psychology; sociology.
Non-credit—computer and information sciences.

SAVANNAH COLLEGE OF ART AND DESIGN
Savannah, Georgia
http://www.scad.edu

Savannah College of Art and Design was founded in 1978. It is accredited by Southern Association of Colleges and Schools. It first offered distance learning courses in 2003. In fall 2006, there were 369 students enrolled in distance learning courses. Institutionally administered financial aid is available to distance learners.

Services Distance learners have accessibility to academic advising, bookstore, campus computer network, career placement assistance, e-mail services, library services, tutoring.

Contact Ms. Ginger Hansen, Executive Director of Recruitment, Savannah College of Art and Design, PO Box 3146, Savannah, GA 31402-3146. Telephone: 912-525-5100. Fax: 912-525-5986. E-mail: ghunt@scad.edu.

DEGREES AND AWARDS
BA Digital Media; Visual Communication
Certificate Digital Publishing
Graduate Certificate Digital Publishing Management; Historic Preservation; Interactive Design; Typeface Design
MA Broadcast Design and Motion Graphics; Digital Photography; Graphic Design; Historic Preservation; Illustration Design; Interactive Design and Game Development; Interior Design; Interior Design; Painting

COURSE SUBJECT AREAS OFFERED OUTSIDE OF DEGREE PROGRAMS
Undergraduate—English composition; fine and studio art.
Graduate—fine and studio art.

See full description on page 426.

SAYBROOK GRADUATE SCHOOL AND RESEARCH CENTER
San Francisco, California
http://www.saybrook.edu/

Saybrook Graduate School and Research Center was founded in 1970. It is accredited by Western Association of Schools and Colleges. It first offered distance learning courses in 1971. In fall 2006, there were 479 students enrolled in distance learning courses. Institutionally administered financial aid is available to distance learners.

Services Distance learners have accessibility to academic advising, bookstore, campus computer network, library services.

Contact Ms. Kathryn Troy, Marketing, Saybrook Graduate School and Research Center, 747 Front Street, Third Floor, San Francisco, CA 94111. Telephone: 800-825-4480. Fax: 415-403 1206. E-mail: ktroy@saybrook.edu.

DEGREES AND AWARDS
Graduate Certificate Building a Sustainable World; Community Health and Development; Creativity Studies; Dream Studies; Expressive Arts for Healing and Social Change; Leading Organizational Transformation; Organizational Consulting; Peace and Conflict Resolution (International focus); Socially Engaged Spirituality; Violence Prevention and Response
MA Human Science; Marriage and Family Therapy; Organizational Systems; Psychology in Creativity Studies specialization

PhD Doctoral Completion program; Human Science; Organizational Studies; Psychology

COURSE SUBJECT AREAS OFFERED OUTSIDE OF DEGREE PROGRAMS

Graduate—agriculture; allied health diagnostic, intervention, and treatment professions; alternative and complementary medical support services; alternative and complementary medicine and medical systems; business administration, management and operations; clinical child psychology; clinical psychology; cognitive science; community health services; community organization and advocacy; community psychology; counseling psychology; criminal justice and corrections; developmental and child psychology; educational administration and supervision; environmental psychology; ethnic, cultural minority, and gender studies; family and consumer sciences/human sciences; family psychology; gerontology; health psychology; housing and human environments; human development, family studies, and related services; industrial and organizational psychology; intercultural/multicultural and diversity studies; operations research; peace studies and conflict resolution; physiology, pathology and related sciences; psychology; psychology related; public administration and social service professions related; rehabilitation and therapeutic professions; social psychology; social sciences related; somatic bodywork and related therapeutic services; theological and ministerial studies; urban studies/affairs.

Non-credit—business administration, management and operations; educational administration and supervision; industrial and organizational psychology; psychology; psychology related; public administration and social service professions related; theology and religious vocations related.

See full description on page 428.

SCHENECTADY COUNTY COMMUNITY COLLEGE
Schenectady, New York
http://www.sunysccc.edu

Schenectady County Community College was founded in 1969. It is accredited by Middle States Association of Colleges and Schools. It first offered distance learning courses in 1998. In fall 2006, there were 775 students enrolled in distance learning courses. Institutionally administered financial aid is available to distance learners.

Services Distance learners have accessibility to academic advising, bookstore, campus computer network, e-mail services, library services, tutoring.

Contact Shirlee Dufort, Associate for Continuing Education, Schenectady County Community College, 78 Washington Avenue, Schenectady, NY 12305. Telephone: 518-381-1315. E-mail: dufortsa@gw.sunysccc.edu.

DEGREES AND AWARDS
Programs offered do not lead to a degree or other formal award.

COURSE SUBJECT AREAS OFFERED OUTSIDE OF DEGREE PROGRAMS

Undergraduate—accounting and related services; astronomy and astrophysics; biology; business administration, management and operations; computer software and media applications; criminal justice and corrections; culinary arts and related services; English composition; entrepreneurial and small business operations; fire protection; history; hospitality administration; human development, family studies, and related services; legal studies (non-professional general, undergraduate); mathematics; music; nutrition sciences; psychology; sociology; technical and business writing.

SCHILLER INTERNATIONAL UNIVERSITY
Largo, Florida
http://www.schiller.edu/

Schiller International University was founded in 1991. It is accredited by Accrediting Council for Independent Colleges and Schools. It first offered distance learning courses in 1999. In fall 2006, there were 197 students enrolled in distance learning courses. Institutionally administered financial aid is available to distance learners.

Services Distance learners have accessibility to academic advising, bookstore, career placement assistance, e-mail services, library services.

Contact Ms. Susan Russeff, Associate Director of Admissions, Schiller International University, 300 East Bay Drive, Largo, FL 33770. Telephone: 727-736-5082 Ext. 239. Fax: 727-734-0359. E-mail: admissions @schiller.edu.

DEGREES AND AWARDS
AS International Business
BA Interdepartmental Studies; International Relations and Diplomacy
BBA International Business; International Hotel and Tourism Management
MBA Business Administration; Financial Planning; International Hotel and Tourism Management; Management of Information Technology
MBAIB International Business
MIM Master of International Management in International Business

COURSE SUBJECT AREAS OFFERED OUTSIDE OF DEGREE PROGRAMS

Undergraduate—accounting and related services; business administration, management and operations; business/commerce; business/corporate communications; business/managerial economics; English composition; history; hospitality administration; human resources management; information science/studies; international business; international relations and affairs; management information systems; marketing; mathematics; physical sciences; political science and government; psychology; statistics.

Graduate—accounting and related services; business administration, management and operations; business/corporate communications; business/managerial economics; computer/information technology administration and management; finance and financial management services; hospitality administration; human resources management; industrial and organizational psychology; international business; legal research and advanced professional studies; marketing; sales, merchandising, and related marketing operations (specialized); statistics.

See full description on page 430.

SCHOOLCRAFT COLLEGE
Livonia, Michigan
Distance Learning Office
http://www.schoolcraft.edu/distance

Schoolcraft College was founded in 1961. It is accredited by North Central Association of Colleges and Schools. It first offered distance learning courses in 1982. In fall 2006, there were 4,200 students enrolled in distance learning courses. Institutionally administered financial aid is available to distance learners.

Services Distance learners have accessibility to academic advising, bookstore, campus computer network, career placement assistance, library services, tutoring.

Contact Marc R. Robinson, Director, Distance Learning, Schoolcraft College, Distance Learning Department, 18600 Haggerty Road, Livonia, MI 48152-2696. Telephone: 734-462-4573. Fax: 734-462-4589. E-mail: mrobinso@schoolcraft.edu.

DEGREES AND AWARDS
AA Liberal Arts
AAS Aviation Management; Business, general; Homeland Security
AGS Liberal Arts
Certificate Aviation Management

COURSE SUBJECT AREAS OFFERED OUTSIDE OF DEGREE PROGRAMS

Undergraduate—accounting and related services; allied health and medical assisting services; American literature (United States and Canadian); anthropology; astronomy and astrophysics; biological and biomedical sciences related; biological and physical sciences; biology; business/commerce; business, management, and marketing related; business/managerial economics; business operations support and assistant services; communication and journalism related; communication and media; computer and information sciences; computer programming; computer science; computer software and media applications; criminal justice and corrections; culinary arts and related services; developmental and child psychology; economics; engineering; English; English composition; English language and literature related; entrepreneurial and small business operations; fine and studio art; geography and cartography; health professions related; health services/allied health/health sciences; history; journalism; marketing; mathematics; music; philosophy; philosophy and religious studies related; physical sciences; physics; psychology; public relations, advertising, and applied communication related; security and protective services related; social sciences; social sciences related; sociology; speech and rhetoric; technical and business writing. **Non-credit**—community health services; computer programming; computer software and media applications.

SEATTLE CENTRAL COMMUNITY COLLEGE
Seattle, Washington
Distance Learning Program
http://www.seattlecentral.edu/distance
Seattle Central Community College was founded in 1966. It is accredited by Northwest Commission on Colleges and Universities. It first offered distance learning courses in 1990. In fall 2006, there were 700 students enrolled in distance learning courses. Institutionally administered financial aid is available to distance learners.
Services Distance learners have accessibility to academic advising, bookstore, campus computer network, e-mail services, library services.
Contact Ms. Queenie L. Baker, Director, Seattle Central Community College, 1701 Broadway, NP304, Seattle, WA 98122-2400. Telephone: 800-510-1724. Fax: 206-287-5562. E-mail: qbaker@sccd.ctc.edu.

DEGREES AND AWARDS
AA General Program; Liberal Arts

COURSE SUBJECT AREAS OFFERED OUTSIDE OF DEGREE PROGRAMS
Undergraduate—accounting and related services; anthropology; developmental and child psychology; English composition; film/video and photographic arts; geography and cartography; journalism; languages (foreign languages related); mathematics and statistics related; medieval and Renaissance studies; philosophy and religious studies related; sociology; statistics.

SEATTLE PACIFIC UNIVERSITY
Seattle, Washington
School of Education
http://www.spu.edu/connection
Seattle Pacific University was founded in 1891. It is accredited by Northwest Commission on Colleges and Universities. It first offered distance learning courses in 1984. In fall 2006, there were 441 students enrolled in distance learning courses. Institutionally administered financial aid is available to distance learners.
Services Distance learners have accessibility to bookstore, campus computer network, e-mail services, library services.
Contact Megan Bartlett, Distance Learning Program Coordinator, Seattle Pacific University, 3307 Third Avenue West, Suite 215, Seattle, WA 98119-1950. Telephone: 800-482-3848. Fax: 206-281-2271. E-mail: connect@spu.edu.

DEGREES AND AWARDS
Programs offered do not lead to a degree or other formal award.

COURSE SUBJECT AREAS OFFERED OUTSIDE OF DEGREE PROGRAMS
Undergraduate—linguistic, comparative, and related language studies. **Graduate**—astronomy and astrophysics; bilingual, multilingual, and multicultural education; computer software and media applications; curriculum and instruction; education; education (specific levels and methods); education (specific subject areas); English as a second/foreign language (teaching); geography and cartography; history; library science; mathematics; parks, recreation and leisure; special education.

SEMINOLE COMMUNITY COLLEGE
Sanford, Florida
Distance Learning Department
http://www.scc-fl.edu/dl
Seminole Community College was founded in 1966. It is accredited by Southern Association of Colleges and Schools. It first offered distance learning courses in 1970. In fall 2006, there were 3,100 students enrolled in distance learning courses. Institutionally administered financial aid is available to distance learners.
Services Distance learners have accessibility to academic advising, bookstore, campus computer network, career placement assistance, e-mail services, library services.
Contact Mrs. Lillie Gibson, Distance Learning Support Specialist, Seminole Community College, 100 Weldon Boulevard, Sanford, FL 32773. Telephone: 407-328-2424. Fax: 407-328-2233. E-mail: gibsonl@scc-fl.edu.

DEGREES AND AWARDS
AA Accounting; Advertising and Public Relations; Anthropology Pre-Major; Business, general; Economics (Business track); Economics (Liberal Arts track); General Studies; Interpersonal Communications; Journalism; Management Information Systems; Organizational Communication; Psychology; Public Relations and Organizational Communication; Social Work; Sociology

AS Computer Programming and Analysis (C++ Programming specialization); Computer Programming and Analysis Visual Basic Programming specialization; Computer Programming and Analysis; Programming and Analysis (WWW Programming specialization); e-Business Technology (Security specialization); e-Business Technology (Software specialization); e-Business Technology (Technology specialization)

Certificate Computer Programming; Computer Science–Microsoft Certified Systems Administrator

Technical Certificate Accounting Applications; Computer Science–Microsoft Certified Systems Engineer; Office Software Applications; Office Support; e-Business Software (Database track); e-Business Software (Web Design track); e-Business Technology (Microsoft track)

COURSE SUBJECT AREAS OFFERED OUTSIDE OF DEGREE PROGRAMS
Undergraduate—accounting and computer science; accounting and related services; anthropology; applied mathematics; astronomy and astrophysics; atmospheric sciences and meteorology; behavioral sciences; biological and physical sciences; business administration, management and operations; business/commerce; business/corporate communications; business, management, and marketing related; business operations support and assistant services; communication and journalism related; communication and media; community health services; computer and information sciences; computer and information sciences and support services related; computer/information technology administration and management; computer programming; computer science; computer software and media applications; computer systems analysis; computer systems networking and telecommunications; construction engineering; criminal justice and corrections; criminology; data entry/microcomputer applications; data processing; developmental and child psychology; economics; education; education related; education (specific subject areas); English; English composition; family psychology; fire protection; geography and cartography; geological and earth sciences/geosciences; health professions related; history; human development, family studies, and related services; legal research and advanced professional studies; legal support services; liberal arts and sciences, general studies and humanities; library science; library science related; management information systems; marketing; mathematics; mathematics and computer science; mathematics and statistics related; nutrition sciences; physical sciences; physical sciences related; political science and government; psychology; psychology related; public health; social sciences related; sociology; statistics; technical and business writing.

Non-credit—education (specific levels and methods); health and medical administrative services; security and protective services related.

SETON HALL UNIVERSITY
South Orange, New Jersey
MA in Counseling
http://www.shu.edu/

Seton Hall University was founded in 1856. It is accredited by Middle States Association of Colleges and Schools. It first offered distance learning courses in 1998. Institutionally administered financial aid is available to distance learners.

Services Distance learners have accessibility to academic advising, bookstore, campus computer network, career placement assistance, e-mail services, library services.

Contact Ms. Rosalie Maiorella, Program Administrator, Seton Hall University, 400 South Orange Avenue, South Orange, NJ 07079. Telephone: 973-313-6239. E-mail: setonworldwide@shu.edu.

DEGREES AND AWARDS
MA Counseling
See full description on page 432.

SETON HALL UNIVERSITY
South Orange, New Jersey
MA Education Leadership Management and Policy
http://www.shu.edu/

Seton Hall University was founded in 1856. It is accredited by Middle States Association of Colleges and Schools. It first offered distance learning courses in 1998. Institutionally administered financial aid is available to distance learners.

Services Distance learners have accessibility to academic advising, bookstore, campus computer network, career placement assistance, e-mail services, library services.

Contact Ms. Cindy Jimenez, Program Coordinator, Seton Hall University, 400 South Orange Avenue, South Orange, NJ 07079. Telephone: 973-761-9087. Fax: 973-761-9325. E-mail: setonworldwide@shu.edu.

DEGREES AND AWARDS
MA Education Leadership, Management, and Policy (ELMP)
See full description on page 434.

SETON HALL UNIVERSITY
South Orange, New Jersey
MA in Health Administration
http://www.shu.edu/

Seton Hall University was founded in 1856. It is accredited by Middle States Association of Colleges and Schools. It first offered distance learning courses in 1998. Institutionally administered financial aid is available to distance learners.

Contact Ms. Cindy Jimenez, Program Coordinator, Seton Hall University, 400 South Orange Avenue, South Orange, NJ 07079. Telephone: 973-761-9087. Fax: 973-761-9325. E-mail: setonworldwide@shu.edu.

DEGREES AND AWARDS
MHA Healthcare Administration
See full description on page 436.

SETON HALL UNIVERSITY
South Orange, New Jersey
MA in Strategic Communication and Leadership
http://www.shu.edu/

Seton Hall University was founded in 1856. It is accredited by Middle States Association of Colleges and Schools. It first offered distance learning courses in 1998. Institutionally administered financial aid is available to distance learners.

Services Distance learners have accessibility to academic advising, bookstore, campus computer network, career placement assistance, e-mail services, library services.

Contact Ms. Cindy Jimenez, Program Coordinator, Seton Hall University, 400 South Orange Avenue, South Orange, NJ 07079. Telephone: 973-761-9087. Fax: 973-761-9325. E-mail: setonworldwide@shu.edu.

DEGREES AND AWARDS
MA Strategic Communication and Leadership
See full description on page 438.

SETON HALL UNIVERSITY
South Orange, New Jersey
Programs in Nursing
http://www.shu.edu/

Seton Hall University was founded in 1856. It is accredited by Middle States Association of Colleges and Schools. It first offered distance learning courses in 1998. Institutionally administered financial aid is available to distance learners.

Services Distance learners have accessibility to academic advising, bookstore, campus computer network, career placement assistance, e-mail services, library services.

Contact Ms. Cindy Jimenez, Program Coordinator, Seton Hall University, 400 South Orange Avenue, South Orange, NJ 07079. Telephone: 973-761-9087. Fax: 973-761-9325. E-mail: setonworldwide@shu.edu.

DEGREES AND AWARDS
BSN Nursing–RN to BSN
MSN Nursing
See full description on page 440.

SHASTA BIBLE COLLEGE
Redding, California
Individualized Distance Learning
http://www.shasta.edu

Shasta Bible College was founded in 1971. It is accredited by Transnational Association of Christian Colleges and Schools. It first offered distance learning courses in 1999. In fall 2006, there were 30 students enrolled in distance learning courses. Institutionally administered financial aid is available to distance learners.

Services Distance learners have accessibility to academic advising, bookstore, e-mail services, library services.

Contact Mr. Mark Mueller, Registrar and Enrollment Manager, Shasta Bible College, 2951 Goodwater Avenue, Redding, CA 96002. Telephone: 530-221-4275 Ext. 206. Fax: 530-221-6929. E-mail: admissions@shasta.edu.

DEGREES AND AWARDS
BA Christian Professional Studies
MS School and Church Administration

COURSE SUBJECT AREAS OFFERED OUTSIDE OF DEGREE PROGRAMS
Undergraduate—biblical studies; counseling psychology; education related; religious studies.
Graduate—counseling psychology; educational administration and supervision.
Non-credit—biblical studies.

SHAWNEE STATE UNIVERSITY
Portsmouth, Ohio
Department of Nursing
http://www.shawnee.edu/acadamics/hsc/nurs/index.html

Shawnee State University was founded in 1986. It is accredited by North Central Association of Colleges and Schools. It first offered distance learning courses in 1998. In fall 2006, there were 103 students enrolled in distance learning courses. Institutionally administered financial aid is available to distance learners.

Services Distance learners have accessibility to bookstore, e-mail services, library services.

Contact Dr. Mattie Burton, Chair, Nursing, Shawnee State University, 940 Second Street, Health Sciences Building, Room 121, Portsmouth, OH 45662. Telephone: 740-351-3378. E-mail: mburton@shawnee.edu.

DEGREES AND AWARDS
Programs offered do not lead to a degree or other formal award.

COURSE SUBJECT AREAS OFFERED OUTSIDE OF DEGREE PROGRAMS
Undergraduate—health and medical administrative services; nursing.

SHIPPENSBURG UNIVERSITY OF PENNSYLVANIA
Shippensburg, Pennsylvania
Extended Studies
http://www.ship.edu/extended/
Shippensburg University of Pennsylvania was founded in 1871. It is accredited by Middle States Association of Colleges and Schools. It first offered distance learning courses in 1998. In fall 2006, there were 207 students enrolled in distance learning courses. Institutionally administered financial aid is available to distance learners.
Services Distance learners have accessibility to academic advising, bookstore, campus computer network, career placement assistance, e-mail services, library services, tutoring.
Contact Dr. Anthony S. Winter, Interim Dean of Extended Studies, Shippensburg University of Pennsylvania, 1871 Old Main Drive, Shippensburg, PA 17257-2299. Telephone: 717-477-1348. Fax: 717-477-4050. E-mail: extended@ship.edu.

DEGREES AND AWARDS
MBA Business Administration
MSIS Information Systems

COURSE SUBJECT AREAS OFFERED OUTSIDE OF DEGREE PROGRAMS
Undergraduate—accounting and related services; communication and media; computer science; criminal justice and corrections; economics; education; English; finance and financial management services; fine and studio art; geography and cartography; gerontology; history; information science/studies; international business; management information systems; management sciences and quantitative methods; marketing; mathematics; music; philosophy; physics; political science and government; psychology; social work; sociology; speech and rhetoric.
Graduate—accounting and related services; business administration, management and operations; communication and media; criminal justice and corrections; education; English; entrepreneurial and small business operations; gerontology; history; information science/studies; international business; management information systems; political science and government; psychology; social work; sociology.

SILVER LAKE COLLEGE
Manitowoc, Wisconsin
Silver Lake College was founded in 1869. It is accredited by North Central Association of Colleges and Schools. It first offered distance learning courses in 1986. In fall 2006, there were 220 students enrolled in distance learning courses. Institutionally administered financial aid is available to distance learners.
Services Distance learners have accessibility to academic advising, bookstore, campus computer network, career placement assistance, e-mail services, library services.
Contact Dr. George Grinde, Vice President of Academic Affairs, Silver Lake College, 2406 South Alverno Road, Manitowoc, WI 54220. Telephone: 920-686-6125. Fax: 920-684-7082. E-mail: ggrinde@silver.sl.edu.

DEGREES AND AWARDS
Programs offered do not lead to a degree or other formal award.

SIMMONS COLLEGE
Boston, Massachusetts
Simmons College was founded in 1899. It is accredited by New England Association of Schools and Colleges. It first offered distance learning courses in 2001. In fall 2006, there were 250 students enrolled in distance learning courses. Institutionally administered financial aid is available to distance learners.
Services Distance learners have accessibility to academic advising, bookstore, campus computer network, e-mail services, library services, tutoring.
Contact Ms. Yolanda Mendez Rainey, Administrative Assistant, Simmons College, School for Health Studies, 300 The Fenway, Boston, MA 02115-5898. Telephone: 617-521-2652. Fax: 617-521-3137. E-mail: yolanda.rainey@simmons.edu.

DEGREES AND AWARDS
CAGS Clinical Genetics; Health Professions Education; Sports Nutrition
DPT Bridge Doctor of Physical Therapy

COURSE SUBJECT AREAS OFFERED OUTSIDE OF DEGREE PROGRAMS
Non-credit—developmental and child psychology; statistics.

SIMPSON COLLEGE
Indianola, Iowa
Division of Adult Learning
http://www.simpson.edu/dal
Simpson College was founded in 1860. It is accredited by North Central Association of Colleges and Schools. It first offered distance learning courses in 1996. In fall 2006, there were 250 students enrolled in distance learning courses. Institutionally administered financial aid is available to distance learners.
Services Distance learners have accessibility to academic advising, bookstore, campus computer network, career placement assistance, e-mail services, library services.
Contact Walter Pearson, Director, Simpson College, 701 North C Street, Indianola, IA 50125. Telephone: 515-961-1615. Fax: 515-961-1498. E-mail: pearsonw@simpson.edu.

DEGREES AND AWARDS
Programs offered do not lead to a degree or other formal award.

COURSE SUBJECT AREAS OFFERED OUTSIDE OF DEGREE PROGRAMS
Undergraduate—accounting and related services; communication and media; computer science; criminal justice and corrections; English; finance and financial management services; human resources management; journalism; liberal arts and sciences, general studies and humanities; marketing.
Graduate—education (specific subject areas).

SINCLAIR COMMUNITY COLLEGE
Dayton, Ohio
Distance Learning Division
http://www.sinclair.edu/distance
Sinclair Community College was founded in 1887. It is accredited by North Central Association of Colleges and Schools. It first offered distance learning courses in 1979. In fall 2006, there were 5,000 students enrolled in distance learning courses. Institutionally administered financial aid is available to distance learners.
Services Distance learners have accessibility to academic advising, bookstore, e-mail services, library services.
Contact Ms. Linda M. Stowe, Coordinator of Distance Learning Services, Sinclair Community College, Distance Learning and Instructional Support Division, Room 14-223, 444 West Third Street, Dayton, OH 45402. Telephone: 937-512-2694. Fax: 937-512-2891. E-mail: linda.stowe@sinclair.edu.

DEGREES AND AWARDS

AA Liberal Arts and Sciences
AS Business Administration; Liberal Arts and Sciences
Certificate Programmer Analyst–Fast Track—Programmer Analyst Short-Term Certificate; Software Applications for the Professional; Web Programming–Visual Basic or Java Track Short-Term certificate
Certification Human Services Short-Term Certificate; Medical Office Coding Specialist; Radiologic Technology Continuing Education Units (CEUs)

COURSE SUBJECT AREAS OFFERED OUTSIDE OF DEGREE PROGRAMS

Undergraduate—accounting and computer science; architectural engineering; behavioral sciences; business administration, management and operations; business, management, and marketing related; business operations support and assistant services; chemistry; civil engineering technology; communication and media; computer and information sciences; computer programming; computer software and media applications; computer systems networking and telecommunications; creative writing; developmental and child psychology; drafting/design engineering technologies; economics; English composition; entrepreneurial and small business operations; film/video and photographic arts; fine and studio art; history; human services; legal studies (non-professional general, undergraduate); liberal arts and sciences, general studies and humanities; marketing; mathematics; psychology; social psychology; sociology; speech and rhetoric; technical and business writing.
Non-credit—health professions related.

SIOUX FALLS SEMINARY
Sioux Falls, South Dakota
Sioux Falls Seminary was founded in 1858. It is accredited by North Central Association of Colleges and Schools. It first offered distance learning courses in 2000. In fall 2006, there were 16 students enrolled in distance learning courses. Institutionally administered financial aid is available to distance learners.
Services Distance learners have accessibility to academic advising, bookstore, campus computer network, e-mail services, library services.
Contact Mr. Bryce H. Eben, Director of Enrollment Development, Sioux Falls Seminary, 1525 South Grange Avenue, Sioux Falls, SD 57105. Telephone: 605-336-6588 Ext. 706. Fax: 605-335-9090. E-mail: beben @sfseminary.edu.

DEGREES AND AWARDS
Programs offered do not lead to a degree or other formal award.

COURSE SUBJECT AREAS OFFERED OUTSIDE OF DEGREE PROGRAMS

Graduate—education (specific subject areas); religious/sacred music; theological and ministerial studies; theology and religious vocations related.

SKIDMORE COLLEGE
Saratoga Springs, New York
University Without Walls
http://www.skidmore.edu/uww
Skidmore College was founded in 1903. It is accredited by Middle States Association of Colleges and Schools. It first offered distance learning courses in 1971. In fall 2006, there were 200 students enrolled in distance learning courses. Institutionally administered financial aid is available to distance learners.
Services Distance learners have accessibility to academic advising, bookstore, campus computer network, career placement assistance, e-mail services, library services.
Contact Tracy Riley, Administrative Assistant, Skidmore College, University Without Walls, 815 North Broadway, Saratoga Springs, NY 12866. Telephone: 518-580-5450. Fax: 518-580-5449. E-mail: uww@ skidmore.edu.

DEGREES AND AWARDS

BA American Studies; Anthropology; Art History; Asian Studies; Biology; Chemistry; Classics; Computer Science; Economics; English; Environmental Studies; Foreign Languages and Literature; French; German; Government; History; Individualized Studies; International Affairs; Mathematics; Music; Philosophy; Physics; Psychology; Psychology-Sociology; Religious Studies; Sociology; Sociology-Anthropology; Spanish; Theater; Women's Studies
BS Art (studio); Business and Management; Dance; Educational Administration; Exercise Science; Individualized Studies

COURSE SUBJECT AREAS OFFERED OUTSIDE OF DEGREE PROGRAMS

Undergraduate—liberal arts and sciences, general studies and humanities.
See full description on page 442.

SKIDMORE COLLEGE
Saratoga Springs, New York
Graduate Programs
http://www.skidmore.edu/mals
Skidmore College was founded in 1903. It is accredited by Middle States Association of Colleges and Schools. It first offered distance learning courses in 1992. In fall 2006, there were 57 students enrolled in distance learning courses. Institutionally administered financial aid is available to distance learners.
Services Distance learners have accessibility to academic advising, bookstore, campus computer network, e-mail services, library services, tutoring.
Contact Dr. John Anzalone, Director of Master of Arts in Liberal Studies, Skidmore College, 815 North Broadway, Saratoga Springs, NY 12866. Telephone: 518-580-5480. Fax: 518-580-5486. E-mail: janzalon@ skidmore.edu.

DEGREES AND AWARDS
Programs offered do not lead to a degree or other formal award.

COURSE SUBJECT AREAS OFFERED OUTSIDE OF DEGREE PROGRAMS

Graduate—liberal arts and sciences, general studies and humanities.

SNEAD STATE COMMUNITY COLLEGE
Boaz, Alabama
http://www.snead.edu/
Snead State Community College was founded in 1898. It is accredited by Southern Association of Colleges and Schools. It first offered distance learning courses in 1998. In fall 2006, there were 1,200 students enrolled in distance learning courses. Institutionally administered financial aid is available to distance learners.
Services Distance learners have accessibility to academic advising, bookstore, campus computer network, e-mail services, library services.
Contact Dr. Greg D. Chapman, EdD, Dean of Academic Services, Snead State Community College, PO Box 734, Boaz, AL 35957. Telephone: 256-840-4111. Fax: 256-593-7180. E-mail: gchapman@snead.edu.

DEGREES AND AWARDS
AS General Program

COURSE SUBJECT AREAS OFFERED OUTSIDE OF DEGREE PROGRAMS

Undergraduate—accounting and related services; American literature (United States and Canadian); applied mathematics; atmospheric sciences and meteorology; biblical studies; biological and biomedical sciences related; biological and physical sciences; biology; business/commerce; business/corporate communications; chemistry; computer and information sciences; computer science; computer software and media applications; creative writing; criminal justice and corrections; criminology; dramatic/theater arts and stagecraft; economics; English; English composition; English literature (British and Commonwealth); fine and studio art; geography and cartography; health and physical education/fitness; history; human development, family studies, and related services; linguistic, comparative, and related language studies; mathematics; mathematics and computer science; microbiological sciences and immunology; music; nursing; physical sciences; physics; psychology; religious studies; sociology; speech and rhetoric; statistics.

SONOMA STATE UNIVERSITY
Rohnert Park, California
Liberal Studies Special Sessions Degree Programs
http://www.sonoma.edu/exed/Degrees/dindex.html
Sonoma State University was founded in 1960. It is accredited by Western Association of Schools and Colleges. It first offered distance learning courses in 1996. In fall 2006, there were 120 students enrolled in distance learning courses. Institutionally administered financial aid is available to distance learners.
Services Distance learners have accessibility to academic advising, bookstore, campus computer network, career placement assistance, e-mail services, library services.
Contact Beth Warner, Administrative Coordinator, Sonoma State University, 1801 East Cotati Avenue, Rohnert Park, CA 94928-3609. Telephone: 707-664-3977. Fax: 707-664-2613. E-mail: beth.warner@sonoma.edu.

DEGREES AND AWARDS
BA Liberal Studies
MA Interdisciplinary Studies–Action for a Viable Future

COURSE SUBJECT AREAS OFFERED OUTSIDE OF DEGREE PROGRAMS
Undergraduate—educational/instructional media design; environmental design.
Non-credit—business administration, management and operations; business/corporate communications; business, management, and marketing related; computer/information technology administration and management; computer software and media applications; computer systems networking and telecommunications.

SOUTHEAST ARKANSAS COLLEGE
Pine Bluff, Arkansas
http://www.seark.edu/
Southeast Arkansas College was founded in 1991. It is accredited by North Central Association of Colleges and Schools. It first offered distance learning courses in 1995. In fall 2006, there were 719 students enrolled in distance learning courses. Institutionally administered financial aid is available to distance learners.
Services Distance learners have accessibility to e-mail services, library services.
Contact Daytra Demmings, Coordinator of Distance Learning, Southeast Arkansas College, 1900 Hazel Street, Pine Bluff, AR 71603. Telephone: 870-543-5992. Fax: 870-543-5937. E-mail: ddemmings@seark.edu.

DEGREES AND AWARDS
Programs offered do not lead to a degree or other formal award.

COURSE SUBJECT AREAS OFFERED OUTSIDE OF DEGREE PROGRAMS
Undergraduate—anthropology; applied mathematics; business administration, management and operations; business/commerce; business/corporate communications; business, management, and marketing related; business/managerial economics; computer/information technology administration and management; computer programming; computer science; computer software and media applications; computer systems analysis; computer systems networking and telecommunications; criminal justice and corrections; criminology; data entry/microcomputer applications; economics; English; English composition; entrepreneurial and small business operations; fire protection; foods, nutrition, and related services; geography and cartography; health and physical education/fitness; health professions related; history; insurance; international business; marketing;

mathematics; mathematics and computer science; mathematics and statistics related; nursing; psychology; real estate; sociology; statistics.

SOUTHEASTERN COMMUNITY COLLEGE
Whiteville, North Carolina
http://www.sccnc.edu/dislearn/index.htm
Southeastern Community College was founded in 1964. It is accredited by Southern Association of Colleges and Schools. It first offered distance learning courses in 1980. In fall 2006, there were 1,400 students enrolled in distance learning courses. Institutionally administered financial aid is available to distance learners.
Services Distance learners have accessibility to academic advising, bookstore, career placement assistance, library services, tutoring.
Contact Ms. Angela Spears, Distance and e-Learning Technician, Southeastern Community College, PO Box 151, Whiteville, NC 28472. Telephone: 910-642-7141 Ext. 229. Fax: 910-642-5658. E-mail: aspears@sccnc.edu.

DEGREES AND AWARDS
AA Business Administration; College Transfer; Elementary, Middle Grades, and Special Education
AAS Business Administration; Electronic Commerce

COURSE SUBJECT AREAS OFFERED OUTSIDE OF DEGREE PROGRAMS
Undergraduate—accounting and related services; biology; business administration, management and operations; chemistry; computer and information sciences; economics; English; English composition; history; mathematics; music; psychology; social sciences; sociology.

SOUTHEASTERN ILLINOIS COLLEGE
Harrisburg, Illinois
Distance Learning
http://sic.edu/virtual.htm
Southeastern Illinois College was founded in 1960. It is accredited by North Central Association of Colleges and Schools. It first offered distance learning courses in 1988. In fall 2006, there were 300 students enrolled in distance learning courses. Institutionally administered financial aid is available to distance learners.
Services Distance learners have accessibility to academic advising, bookstore, campus computer network, e-mail services, library services.
Contact Mrs. Terry Lucas, Media Specialist, Southeastern Illinois College, 3575 College Road, Harrisburg, IL 62946. Telephone: 618-252-5400 Ext. 2265. Fax: 618-252-2713. E-mail: terry.lucas@sic.edu.

DEGREES AND AWARDS
Programs offered do not lead to a degree or other formal award.

COURSE SUBJECT AREAS OFFERED OUTSIDE OF DEGREE PROGRAMS
Undergraduate—business/commerce; communication and journalism related; English; family and consumer sciences/human sciences related; health professions related; history; mathematics; philosophy; political science and government; psychology; religious studies.

SOUTHERN ILLINOIS UNIVERSITY CARBONDALE
Carbondale, Illinois
Office of Distance Education
http://www.dce.siu.edu/siuconnected
Southern Illinois University Carbondale was founded in 1869. It is accredited by North Central Association of Colleges and Schools. It first offered distance learning courses in 1981. In fall 2006, there were 1,335 students enrolled in distance learning courses. Institutionally administered financial aid is available to distance learners.
Services Distance learners have accessibility to bookstore, campus computer network, e-mail services, library services, tutoring.

Contact Dr. Susan Edgren, Associate Director, Southern Illinois University Carbondale, Washington Square C, Mailcode 6705, Carbondale, IL 62901. Telephone: 618-536-7751. Fax: 618-453-5668. E-mail: sedgren@siu.edu.

DEGREES AND AWARDS
BS Information Systems Technology

COURSE SUBJECT AREAS OFFERED OUTSIDE OF DEGREE PROGRAMS
Undergraduate—agricultural business and management; agricultural mechanization; agriculture; American literature (United States and Canadian); Army J.R.O.T.C/R.O.T.C; biological and biomedical sciences related; biological and physical sciences; biology; business/commerce; business, management, and marketing related; computer and information sciences; computer/information technology administration and management; criminal justice and corrections; criminology; educational administration and supervision; educational psychology; education related; education (specific subject areas); English; finance and financial management services; geography and cartography; health/medical preparatory programs; history; information science/studies; insurance; journalism; landscape architecture; languages (East Asian); languages (Romance languages); management sciences and quantitative methods; marketing; mathematics; mathematics and statistics related; music; philosophy; philosophy and religious studies related; plant sciences; political science and government; quality control and safety technologies; real estate; religious studies; sales, merchandising, and related marketing operations (general); social sciences; sociology.
Graduate—education; rehabilitation and therapeutic professions.
Non-credit—marketing.

SOUTHERN METHODIST UNIVERSITY
Dallas, Texas
School of Engineering–Distance Learning
http://www.engr.smu.edu
Southern Methodist University was founded in 1911. It is accredited by Southern Association of Colleges and Schools. It first offered distance learning courses in 1968. In fall 2006, there were 500 students enrolled in distance learning courses. Institutionally administered financial aid is available to distance learners.
Services Distance learners have accessibility to academic advising, bookstore, campus computer network, career placement assistance, e-mail services, library services.
Contact Ms. Teresa Harvey, Assistant Director of Business Development, Southern Methodist University, PO Box 750335, Dallas, TX 75275-0335. Telephone: 214-768-4661. Fax: 214-768-3778. E-mail: tharvey@engr.smu.edu.

DEGREES AND AWARDS
MS Computer Engineering; Computer Science; Environmental Engineering; Environmental Science (Environmental Systems Management major); Environmental Science (Hazardous and Waste Materials Management major); Environmental Science; Facilities Management; Information Engineering and Management; Manufacturing Systems Management; Operations Research; Packaging of Electronic and Optical Devices; Security Engineering; Software Engineering; Systems Engineering; Telecommunications
MSCE Civil Engineering
MSEE Electrical Engineering
MSEM Engineering Management
MSME Mechanical Engineering

COURSE SUBJECT AREAS OFFERED OUTSIDE OF DEGREE PROGRAMS
Graduate—civil engineering; civil engineering technology; computer and information sciences; computer and information sciences and support services related; computer engineering; computer engineering technologies; computer/information technology administration and management; computer science; computer software and media applications; computer systems networking and telecommunications; construction engineering; electrical and electronic engineering technologies; electrical, electronics and communications engineering; engineering design; engineering/industrial management; engineering mechanics; engineering related; engineering-related fields; engineering-related technologies; engineering science; engineering technologies related; engineering technology; environmental design; environmental/environmental health engineering; industrial engineering; information science/studies; mechanical engineering; mechanical engineering related technologies; systems engineering.

See full description on page 444.

SOUTHERN NEW HAMPSHIRE UNIVERSITY
Manchester, New Hampshire
SNHU Online
http://www.snhu.edu/online
Southern New Hampshire University was founded in 1932. It is accredited by New England Association of Schools and Colleges. It first offered distance learning courses in 1996. In fall 2006, there were 14,000 students enrolled in distance learning courses. Institutionally administered financial aid is available to distance learners.
Services Distance learners have accessibility to academic advising, bookstore, campus computer network, career placement assistance, e-mail services, library services, tutoring.
Contact Ms. Yvonne Simon, CEO—SNHU Online, Southern New Hampshire University, SNHU Online, 2500 North River Road, Manchester, NH 03106-1045. Telephone: 866-860-0449. Fax: 603-645-9706. E-mail: online@snhu.edu.

DEGREES AND AWARDS
AA Liberal Arts
AS Accounting; Business Administration; Information Technology; Marketing
BA Communications; English Language and Literature; Psychology (Child and Adolescent Development concentration); Psychology; Social Science
BS Accounting; Accounting/Finance; Accounting/Information Systems; Business Administration (Human Resource Management concentration); Business Administration (Organizational Leadership concentration); Business Administration (Small Business Management concentration); Business Administration; Business Studies (Accounting concentration); Business Studies (Business Administration concentration); Business Studies (Business Finance concentration); Business Studies (Human Resource Management concentration); Business Studies (Information Technology concentration); Business Studies (International Management concentration); Business Studies (Marketing concentration); Business Studies (Organizational Leadership concentration); Business Studies (Small Business Management concentration); Finance/Economics; Information Technology; International Business; Marketing; Technical Management
Certificate Accounting; Business Information Systems; Human Resource Management
Graduate Certificate Accounting; Human Resource Management; Integrated Marketing Communications; International Business; Marketing; Microfinance Management; Operations Management; Sport Management; Training and Development
MBA Global MBA
MS Accounting/Finance; Business Education; Justice Studies; Marketing; Organizational Leadership; Sport Management

COURSE SUBJECT AREAS OFFERED OUTSIDE OF DEGREE PROGRAMS
Undergraduate—accounting and computer science; accounting and related services; business administration, management and operations; business/commerce; business/corporate communications; business, management, and marketing related; communication and journalism related; communication and media; computer and information sciences; developmental and child psychology; economics; English language and literature related; entrepreneurial and small business operations; finance and financial management services; human resources management; information science/studies; international relations and affairs; liberal arts and sciences, general studies and humanities; marketing; psychology; social sciences.

Graduate—accounting and computer science; accounting and related services; business administration, management and operations; business/commerce; business/corporate communications; business, management, and marketing related; criminal justice and corrections; human resources management; international business; international/global studies; marketing; operations research.

See full description on page 446.

SOUTHERN POLYTECHNIC STATE UNIVERSITY
Marietta, Georgia
http://eu.spsu.edu/DistanceLearning/index.htm
Southern Polytechnic State University was founded in 1948. It is accredited by Southern Association of Colleges and Schools. It first offered distance learning courses in 1995. In fall 2006, there were 300 students enrolled in distance learning courses. Institutionally administered financial aid is available to distance learners.
Services Distance learners have accessibility to academic advising, bookstore, career placement assistance, e-mail services, library services.
Contact Dean Dawn Ramsey, Dean of Extended University, Southern Polytechnic State University, 1100 South Marietta Parkway, Atrium Building, Suite J-330, Marietta, GA 30060-2855. Telephone: 678-915-4287. Fax: 678-915-3576. E-mail: dramsey@spsu.edu.

DEGREES AND AWARDS
BS Information Technology
Certificate Specialty Construction
Graduate Certificate Communications Management; Content Development; Instructional Design; Technical Communication; Visual Communication and Graphics
MS Quality Assurance; Systems Engineering

COURSE SUBJECT AREAS OFFERED OUTSIDE OF DEGREE PROGRAMS
Undergraduate—building/construction finishing, management, and inspection; civil engineering technology; communication and journalism related; computer science; educational/instructional media design; electrical and electronic engineering technologies; engineering design; information science/studies; speech and rhetoric; statistics; textile sciences and engineering.
Graduate—communication and journalism related; computer and information sciences; computer engineering; computer programming; computer science; computer systems analysis; computer systems networking and telecommunications.
Non-credit—computer programming.
See full description on page 448.

SOUTH PIEDMONT COMMUNITY COLLEGE
Polkton, North Carolina
http://www.spcc.edu
South Piedmont Community College was founded in 1962. It is accredited by Southern Association of Colleges and Schools. It first offered distance learning courses in 1982. In fall 2006, there were 900 students enrolled in distance learning courses. Institutionally administered financial aid is available to distance learners.
Services Distance learners have accessibility to academic advising, bookstore, library services.
Contact Ms. Judith A. Smith, Associate Vice President, Distance Learning, South Piedmont Community College, PO Box 126, 680 Highway 74 West, Polkton, NC 28135. Telephone: 704-272-5397. E-mail: j-smith@spcc.edu.

DEGREES AND AWARDS
Programs offered do not lead to a degree or other formal award.

COURSE SUBJECT AREAS OFFERED OUTSIDE OF DEGREE PROGRAMS
Undergraduate—accounting and computer science; accounting and related services; allied health and medical assisting services; allied health diagnostic, intervention, and treatment professions; applied mathematics;

behavioral sciences; biological and biomedical sciences related; biology; business administration, management and operations; business/commerce; business, management, and marketing related; business/managerial economics; carpentry; cell biology and anatomical sciences; chemistry; communication and media; communications technology; computer and information sciences; computer and information sciences and support services related; computer/information technology administration and management; computer programming; computer software and media applications; computer systems networking and telecommunications; criminal justice and corrections; dietetics and clinical nutrition services; economics; education; educational administration and supervision; education related; education (specific levels and methods); education (specific subject areas); electrical/electronics maintenance and repair technology; English; English as a second language; English composition; English language and literature related; entrepreneurial and small business operations; finance and financial management services; foods, nutrition, and related services; geography and cartography; health professions related; health services/allied health/health sciences; heating, air conditioning, ventilation and refrigeration maintenance technology; history; human development, family studies, and related services; human services; intercultural/multicultural and diversity studies; legal professions and studies related; marketing; mathematics; nursing; psychology; psychology related; social sciences; sociology; special education; teaching assistants/aides.
Non-credit—health aides/attendants/orderlies.

SOUTH SUBURBAN COLLEGE
South Holland, Illinois
http://www.ssc.cc.il.us/
South Suburban College was founded in 1927. It is accredited by North Central Association of Colleges and Schools. Institutionally administered financial aid is available to distance learners.
Services Distance learners have accessibility to library services, tutoring.
Contact Student Help Center & Recruitment, South Suburban College, 15800 South State Street, South Holland, IL 60473. Telephone: 708-210-5718. E-mail: newstudentquestions@southsuburbancollege.edu.

DEGREES AND AWARDS
Programs offered do not lead to a degree or other formal award.

COURSE SUBJECT AREAS OFFERED OUTSIDE OF DEGREE PROGRAMS
Undergraduate—air transportation; biology; computer and information sciences; English composition; legal professions and studies related; mathematics; philosophy.

SOUTHWESTERN BAPTIST THEOLOGICAL SEMINARY
Fort Worth, Texas
Department of Continuing Education
http://swbts.edu
Southwestern Baptist Theological Seminary was founded in 1908. It is accredited by Southern Association of Colleges and Schools. It first offered distance learning courses in 1993. In fall 2006, there were 227 students enrolled in distance learning courses. Institutionally administered financial aid is available to distance learners.
Services Distance learners have accessibility to academic advising, bookstore, campus computer network, career placement assistance, e-mail services, library services.
Contact Dr. Jim Wicker, Director of Web-Based Education, Southwestern Baptist Theological Seminary, PO Box 22147, Fort Worth, TX 76122. Telephone: 817-923-1921 Ext. 6805. Fax: 817-921-8760. E-mail: jwicker@swbts.edu.

DEGREES AND AWARDS
Programs offered do not lead to a degree or other formal award.

COURSE SUBJECT AREAS OFFERED OUTSIDE OF DEGREE PROGRAMS

Undergraduate—biblical studies; religious education; religious studies; theological and ministerial studies.

Graduate—biblical and other theological languages and literatures; biblical studies; educational administration and supervision; educational assessment, evaluation, and research; educational/instructional media design; educational psychology; education related; human development, family studies, and related services; linguistic, comparative, and related language studies; pastoral counseling and specialized ministries; philosophy and religious studies related; psychology; psychology related; religious education; religious/sacred music; religious studies; theological and ministerial studies; theology and religious vocations related.

SOUTHWESTERN COLLEGE
Winfield, Kansas
Southwestern College Online
http://www.sckans.edu/online

Southwestern College was founded in 1885. It is accredited by North Central Association of Colleges and Schools. It first offered distance learning courses in 2001. In fall 2006, there were 1,200 students enrolled in distance learning courses. Institutionally administered financial aid is available to distance learners.

Services Distance learners have accessibility to academic advising, bookstore, career placement assistance, library services, tutoring.

Contact Linda Bussman, Director of Enrollment Management, Southwestern College, 2040 South Rock Road, Wichita, KS 67207. Telephone: 888-684-5335 Ext. 214. Fax: 316-688-5218. E-mail: linda.bussman@sckans.edu.

DEGREES AND AWARDS

BA Pastoral Studies
BS Accounting; Business Administration; Business Quality Management; Computer Operations Technology; Computer Programming Technology; Criminal Justice; Human Resource Development; Nursing–RN to BSN; Operations Management; Security Management; Strategic Leadership
MA Specialized Ministries–Youth and Young Adult Ministry
MBA Business Administration
MS Leadership; Management; Security Administration

COURSE SUBJECT AREAS OFFERED OUTSIDE OF DEGREE PROGRAMS

Undergraduate—business/commerce; computer/information technology administration and management; economics; English; English composition; industrial production technologies; liberal arts and sciences, general studies and humanities; nursing; philosophy; social sciences.
Graduate—business administration, management and operations; education.
Non-credit—business, management, and marketing related.

SOUTHWEST GEORGIA TECHNICAL COLLEGE
Thomasville, Georgia

Southwest Georgia Technical College was founded in 1963. It is accredited by Council on Occupational Education. It first offered distance learning courses in 2001. In fall 2006, there were 550 students enrolled in distance learning courses. Institutionally administered financial aid is available to distance learners.

Services Distance learners have accessibility to academic advising, bookstore, career placement assistance, e-mail services, library services, tutoring.

Contact Mrs. Carla W. Barrow, GVTC Coordinator, Southwest Georgia Technical College, 15689 US Highway 19 North, Thomasville, GA 31792. Telephone: 229-227-2680. Fax: 229-225-5289. E-mail: cbarrow@southwestgatech.edu.

DEGREES AND AWARDS

Programs offered do not lead to a degree or other formal award.

COURSE SUBJECT AREAS OFFERED OUTSIDE OF DEGREE PROGRAMS

Undergraduate—accounting and computer science; accounting and related services; applied mathematics; business/commerce; business, management, and marketing related; computer and information sciences; computer/information technology administration and management; computer programming; computer software and media applications; computer systems networking and telecommunications; criminal justice and corrections; criminology; curriculum and instruction; data entry/microcomputer applications; data processing; dietetics and clinical nutrition services; economics; educational/instructional media design; education (specific levels and methods); English; English composition; gerontology; mathematics; psychology; sociology; technical and business writing.
Non-credit—computer software and media applications; real estate.

SOUTHWEST VIRGINIA COMMUNITY COLLEGE
Richlands, Virginia
Audiovisual and Distance Education Services
http://desweb.sw.edu

Southwest Virginia Community College was founded in 1968. It is accredited by Southern Association of Colleges and Schools. It first offered distance learning courses in 1991. In fall 2006, there were 1,800 students enrolled in distance learning courses. Institutionally administered financial aid is available to distance learners.

Services Distance learners have accessibility to academic advising, bookstore, campus computer network, career placement assistance, e-mail services, library services, tutoring.

Contact Thomas A. Cash, Director of Distance and Distributed Learning, Southwest Virginia Community College, PO Box SVCC, Richlands, VA 24641. Telephone: 276-964-7280. Fax: 276-964-7686. E-mail: tom.cash@sw.edu.

DEGREES AND AWARDS

AAS Arts and Science Degree Program; Arts and Science Degree Program
AS General Studies
Certificate Network and Internet Administration

COURSE SUBJECT AREAS OFFERED OUTSIDE OF DEGREE PROGRAMS

Undergraduate—creative writing; developmental and child psychology; English composition; history; languages (Romance languages); mathematics and statistics related; sociology; statistics.
Non-credit—computer and information sciences and support services related.

SOUTHWEST WISCONSIN TECHNICAL COLLEGE
Fennimore, Wisconsin
http://www.swtc.edu/

Southwest Wisconsin Technical College was founded in 1967. It is accredited by North Central Association of Colleges and Schools. It first offered distance learning courses in 1989. In fall 2006, there were 800 students enrolled in distance learning courses. Institutionally administered financial aid is available to distance learners.

Services Distance learners have accessibility to academic advising, bookstore, career placement assistance, e-mail services, library services, tutoring.

Contact Kristal Davenport, Instructional Technology Support Specialist, Southwest Wisconsin Technical College, 1800 Bronson Boulevard, Fennimore, WI 53809. Telephone: 608-822-2426. Fax: 608-822-6019. E-mail: kdavenport@swtc.edu.

DEGREES AND AWARDS

Diploma Medical Transcription
Technical Certificate Medical Coding Specialist

COURSE SUBJECT AREAS OFFERED OUTSIDE OF DEGREE PROGRAMS

Undergraduate—accounting and related services; allied health and medical assisting services; applied mathematics; business/corporate communications; communication and journalism related; communication and media; computer and information sciences; computer programming; computer software and media applications; computer systems networking and telecommunications; cosmetology and related personal grooming services; culinary arts and related services; curriculum and instruction; economics; educational/instructional media design; foods, nutrition, and related services; health/medical preparatory programs; hospitality administration; human resources management; management information systems; mathematics; nursing; psychology; social sciences; sociology; statistics.

SPARTANBURG COMMUNITY COLLEGE
Spartanburg, South Carolina
http://dl.stcsc.edu

Spartanburg Community College was founded in 1961. It is accredited by Southern Association of Colleges and Schools. It first offered distance learning courses in 1997. In fall 2006, there were 815 students enrolled in distance learning courses. Institutionally administered financial aid is available to distance learners.

Services Distance learners have accessibility to academic advising, bookstore, e-mail services, library services, tutoring.

Contact Mr. Mark Roseveare, Director of SCCOnline, Spartanburg Community College, PO Box 4386, Business I-85 and New Cut Road, Spartanburg, SC 29305-4386. Telephone: 864-592-4763. Fax: 864-592-4941. E-mail: rosevearem@sccsc.edu.

DEGREES AND AWARDS

AA Arts

AD Interpreter Training (General Technology–AD in Occupational Technology); Management

COURSE SUBJECT AREAS OFFERED OUTSIDE OF DEGREE PROGRAMS

Undergraduate—accounting and related services; applied mathematics; business administration, management and operations; business/commerce; computer software and media applications; data entry/microcomputer applications; English; English composition; mathematics; music; psychology; sales, merchandising, and related marketing operations (general); sociology; statistics.

SPERTUS INSTITUTE OF JEWISH STUDIES
Chicago, Illinois
http://www.spertus.edu/

Spertus Institute of Jewish Studies was founded in 1924. It is accredited by North Central Association of Colleges and Schools. It first offered distance learning courses in 1994. In fall 2006, there were 250 students enrolled in distance learning courses. Institutionally administered financial aid is available to distance learners.

Services Distance learners have accessibility to academic advising, library services.

Contact Dr. Ellen LeVee, Assistant Dean for Jewish Studies, Spertus Institute of Jewish Studies, 618 South Michigan Avenue, Chicago, IL 60605. Telephone: 888-322-1794. Fax: 312-922-6406. E-mail: college@spertus.edu.

DEGREES AND AWARDS

MS Jewish Education–Master of Science in Jewish Education (MSJE)

MSJS Jewish Studies

DJS Jewish Studies

SPOON RIVER COLLEGE
Canton, Illinois
http://www.spoonrivercollege.edu/

Spoon River College was founded in 1959. It is accredited by North Central Association of Colleges and Schools. It first offered distance learning courses in 1994. In fall 2006, there were 627 students enrolled in distance learning courses. Institutionally administered financial aid is available to distance learners.

Services Distance learners have accessibility to academic advising, bookstore, campus computer network, career placement assistance, e-mail services, library services, tutoring.

Contact Mr. Jim Genandt, Dean of Instruction, Spoon River College, 23235 North County 22, Canton, IL 61520. Telephone: 309-647-4645. Fax: 309-649-6215. E-mail: info@spoonrivercollege.edu.

DEGREES AND AWARDS
Programs offered do not lead to a degree or other formal award.

COURSE SUBJECT AREAS OFFERED OUTSIDE OF DEGREE PROGRAMS

Undergraduate—agricultural and domestic animal services; biology; education; English; English composition; fine and studio art; health professions related; human development, family studies, and related services; philosophy and religious studies related.

Non-credit—computer software and media applications.

SPRING ARBOR UNIVERSITY
Spring Arbor, Michigan
http://www.arboronline.org

Spring Arbor University was founded in 1873. It is accredited by North Central Association of Colleges and Schools. It first offered distance learning courses in 1998. In fall 2006, there were 900 students enrolled in distance learning courses. Institutionally administered financial aid is available to distance learners.

Services Distance learners have accessibility to academic advising, bookstore, campus computer network, e-mail services, library services, tutoring.

Contact Mr. Jim Weidman, Director of SAUonline, Spring Arbor University, 106 East Main Street, ST22, Spring Arbor, MI 49283. Telephone: 517-750-6584. Fax: 517-750-2618. E-mail: jimw@arbor.edu.

DEGREES AND AWARDS

BA Management and Organizational Development

MA Communication; Communication; Spiritual Formation and Leadership

MIM Organizational Management

COURSE SUBJECT AREAS OFFERED OUTSIDE OF DEGREE PROGRAMS

Undergraduate—business administration, management and operations; computer software and media applications; creative writing; criminal justice and corrections; English composition; finance and financial management services; history; hospitality administration; human resources management; marketing; music; philosophy; psychology; sociology.

Graduate—business administration, management and operations; business/corporate communications; business/managerial economics; criminal justice and corrections; finance and financial management services; international business; marketing.

STANFORD UNIVERSITY
Stanford, California
Stanford Center for Professional Development
http://scpd.stanford.edu

Stanford University was founded in 1891. It is accredited by Western Association of Schools and Colleges. It first offered distance learning courses in 1969. In fall 2006, there were 1,500 students enrolled in distance learning courses. Institutionally administered financial aid is available to distance learners.

Services Distance learners have accessibility to academic advising, bookstore, campus computer network, e-mail services, library services.

Contact Valeriana Allende, Customer Service Coordinator, Stanford University, 496 Lomita Mall, Durand Building, Room 300, Stanford, CA 94305-4036. Telephone: 650-725-3000. Fax: 650-725-2868. E-mail: vallende@stanford.edu.

DEGREES AND AWARDS

Graduate Certificate Artificial Intelligence; Biodesign; Bioinformatics; Cardiovascular Bioengineering; Clinical Informatics; Computer Architecture; Computer Hardware and VLSI Design; Computer Languages and Operating Systems; Computer Science–Foundations in Computer Science; Control and System Engineering; Data Mining and Applications (Statistics); Databases; Decision Analysis; Design for Customer Value and Market Success; Digital Communication; Electronic Circuits; Electronic Devices and Technology; Engineering Mechanics–Mathematical Foundations and Applications; Guidance and Control (Aeronautics and Astronautics); International Security; Management Science and Engineering; Nanoscale Materials Science; Networking (Electrical Engineering); Optics, Imaging, and Communications; Product Creation and Innovative Manufacturing; Quantitative Methods in Finance and Risk Management (Statistics); Risk Analysis (Management Science and Engineering); Signal Processing; Software Systems; Software Systems, advanced; Spacecraft Design and Operation proficiency; Telecommunications; Wireless Personal Communication

MS Aeronautics and Astronautics; Biomedical Informatics; Computer Science; Electrical Engineering; Engineering–Computational and Mathematical Engineering; Management Science and Engineering; Mechanical Engineering

COURSE SUBJECT AREAS OFFERED OUTSIDE OF DEGREE PROGRAMS

Non-credit—biomedical/medical engineering; biotechnology; business administration, management and operations; business/managerial economics; civil engineering; computer science; computer systems networking and telecommunications; construction engineering technology; electrical, electronics and communications engineering; engineering/industrial management; entrepreneurial and small business operations; finance and financial management services; management sciences and quantitative methods.

STATE UNIVERSITY OF NEW YORK AT NEW PALTZ
New Paltz, New York
Center for Continuing and Professional Education
http://www.newpaltz.edu

State University of New York at New Paltz was founded in 1828. It is accredited by Middle States Association of Colleges and Schools. It first offered distance learning courses in 1995. In fall 2006, there were 230 students enrolled in distance learning courses. Institutionally administered financial aid is available to distance learners.
Services Distance learners have accessibility to bookstore, campus computer network, e-mail services, library services.
Contact Helise Winters, Director, Extension and Distance Learning, State University of New York at New Paltz, 1 Hawk Drive, Suite 9, New Paltz, NY 12561-2443. Telephone: 845-257-2894. Fax: 845-257-2899. E-mail: edl@newpaltz.edu.

DEGREES AND AWARDS
Programs offered do not lead to a degree or other formal award.

COURSE SUBJECT AREAS OFFERED OUTSIDE OF DEGREE PROGRAMS

Undergraduate—American literature (United States and Canadian); anthropology; communication and media; comparative literature; computer science; curriculum and instruction; developmental and child psychology; economics; English composition; English literature (British and Commonwealth); geography and cartography; geological and earth sciences/geosciences; history; industrial and organizational psychology; philosophy; psychology; public relations, advertising, and applied communication related; social and philosophical foundations of education; sociology.
Graduate—computer science; education.

STATE UNIVERSITY OF NEW YORK AT OSWEGO
Oswego, New York
Office of Distance Learning
http://www.oswego.edu

State University of New York at Oswego was founded in 1861. It is accredited by Middle States Association of Colleges and Schools. It first offered distance learning courses in 1995. In fall 2006, there were 750 students enrolled in distance learning courses. Institutionally administered financial aid is available to distance learners.
Services Distance learners have accessibility to academic advising, bookstore, campus computer network, career placement assistance, e-mail services, library services, tutoring.
Contact Allison Lovallo, Associate Director, State University of New York at Oswego, Continuing Education, 100 Sheldon Hall, Oswego, NY 13126. Telephone: 315-312-2270. Fax: 315-312-3078. E-mail: ced@oswego.edu.

DEGREES AND AWARDS
BA Communications; Public Justice
BS Vocational Teacher Preparation
MS Vocational Teacher Preparation

COURSE SUBJECT AREAS OFFERED OUTSIDE OF DEGREE PROGRAMS

Undergraduate—anthropology; archeology; biology; business administration, management and operations; business/managerial economics; chemistry; communication and journalism related; communication and media; computer and information sciences; computer science; computer systems networking and telecommunications; counseling psychology; criminal justice and corrections; developmental and child psychology; dramatic/theater arts and stagecraft; economics; educational psychology; education (specific subject areas); geological and earth sciences/geosciences; health services/allied health/health sciences; history; information science/studies; journalism; philosophy and religious studies related; psychology; public relations, advertising, and applied communication related; sociology.
Graduate—accounting and related services; anthropology; business administration, management and operations; counseling psychology; curriculum and instruction; economics; education; education (specific subject areas); gerontology; information science/studies; psychology.

See full description on page 450.

STATE UNIVERSITY OF NEW YORK AT PLATTSBURGH
Plattsburgh, New York
Distance Learning Office
http://www.plattsburgh.edu/cll

State University of New York at Plattsburgh was founded in 1889. It is accredited by Middle States Association of Colleges and Schools. It first offered distance learning courses in 1990. In fall 2006, there were 843 students enrolled in distance learning courses. Institutionally administered financial aid is available to distance learners.
Services Distance learners have accessibility to academic advising, bookstore, campus computer network, e-mail services, library services, tutoring.
Contact Mr. Michael J. Bozonie, Associate Dean, Library and Information Services, State University of New York at Plattsburgh, Feinberg Library, 2 Draper Avenue, Plattsburgh, NY 12901. E-mail: michael.bozonie@plattsburgh.edu.

DEGREES AND AWARDS
BS Nursing

COURSE SUBJECT AREAS OFFERED OUTSIDE OF DEGREE PROGRAMS

Undergraduate—anthropology; area, ethnic, cultural, and gender studies related; biochemistry, biophysics and molecular biology; biology; biopsychology; business administration, management and operations; computer and information sciences; education; education related; English; entrepreneurial and small business operations; ethnic, cultural minority, and gender studies; geological and earth sciences/geosciences; health and physical education/fitness; health professions related; history; library science related; marketing; mathematics; music; nursing; political science and government; psychology related; sales, merchandising, and related marketing operations (specialized); social sciences; sociology; statistics. **Graduate**—business administration, management and operations; education; educational administration and supervision; educational/instructional media design; education related; entrepreneurial and small business operations; special education.

STATE UNIVERSITY OF NEW YORK COLLEGE AT POTSDAM
Potsdam, New York
http://www.potsdam.edu/

State University of New York College at Potsdam was founded in 1816. It is accredited by Middle States Association of Colleges and Schools. It first offered distance learning courses in 2002. In fall 2006, there were 55 students enrolled in distance learning courses. Institutionally administered financial aid is available to distance learners.
Services Distance learners have accessibility to academic advising, bookstore, campus computer network, e-mail services, library services.
Contact Ms. Lee Ghostlaw, Staff Assistant, Continuing Education, State University of New York College at Potsdam, 44 Pierrepont Avenue, Potsdam, NY 13676. Telephone: 315-267-2166. Fax: 315-267-3088. E-mail: ghostllk@potsdam.edu.

DEGREES AND AWARDS
Programs offered do not lead to a degree or other formal award.

COURSE SUBJECT AREAS OFFERED OUTSIDE OF DEGREE PROGRAMS

Undergraduate—anthropology; behavioral sciences; biology; business administration, management and operations; business, management, and marketing related; business/managerial economics; communication and journalism related; community health services; data processing; economics; education (specific subject areas); entrepreneurial and small business operations; geography and cartography; geological and earth sciences/geosciences; languages (foreign languages related); management information systems; music; physical sciences; psychology; sociology. **Graduate**—education (specific levels and methods). **Non-credit**—accounting and related services; business administration, management and operations; business/commerce; communication and media; computer and information sciences; computer programming; computer software and media applications; creative writing; culinary arts and related services; data entry/microcomputer applications; entrepreneurial and small business operations; finance and financial management services; languages (Romance languages); linguistic, comparative, and related language studies; sales, merchandising, and related marketing operations (specialized).

STATE UNIVERSITY OF NEW YORK COLLEGE OF AGRICULTURE AND TECHNOLOGY AT MORRISVILLE
Morrisville, New York
http://www.morrisville.edu/

State University of New York College of Agriculture and Technology at Morrisville was founded in 1908. It is accredited by Middle States Association of Colleges and Schools. It first offered distance learning courses in 1997. In fall 2006, there were 139 students enrolled in distance learning courses. Institutionally administered financial aid is available to distance learners.
Services Distance learners have accessibility to academic advising, bookstore, campus computer network, e-mail services, library services.
Contact Office of Admission, State University of New York College of Agriculture and Technology at Morrisville, Morrisville State College, Morrisville, NY 13408. Telephone: 315-684-6046. Fax: 315-684-6427. E-mail: admisions@morrisville.edu.

DEGREES AND AWARDS
Programs offered do not lead to a degree or other formal award.

COURSE SUBJECT AREAS OFFERED OUTSIDE OF DEGREE PROGRAMS

Undergraduate—accounting and related services; agricultural business and management; agriculture; business/commerce; computer/information technology administration and management; computer software and media applications; creative writing; English composition; hospitality administration; management sciences and quantitative methods; mathematics; technical and business writing.

STATE UNIVERSITY OF NEW YORK EMPIRE STATE COLLEGE
Saratoga Springs, New York
Center for Distance Learning
http://www.esc.edu/cdl

State University of New York Empire State College was founded in 1971. It is accredited by Middle States Association of Colleges and Schools. It first offered distance learning courses in 1979. In fall 2006, there were 5,580 students enrolled in distance learning courses. Institutionally administered financial aid is available to distance learners.
Services Distance learners have accessibility to academic advising, bookstore, campus computer network, career placement assistance, e-mail services, library services, tutoring.
Contact Ms. Kathleen Schechner, Outreach Specialist, State University of New York Empire State College, 111 West Avenue, Saratoga Springs, NY 12866. Telephone: 518-587-2100 Ext. 2300. Fax: 518-587-2660. E-mail: kathy.schechner@esc.edu.

DEGREES AND AWARDS

AA Business, Management, and Economics; Community and Human Services; Cultural Studies; Educational Studies; Historical Studies; Human Development; Interdisciplinary Studies; Labor Studies; Science, Math, and Technology; Social Theory, Social Structure, and Change; the Arts
AS Business, Management, and Economics; Community and Human Services; Cultural Studies; Educational Studies; Historical Studies; Human Development; Interdisciplinary Studies; Labor Studies; Science, Math, and Technology; Social Theory, Social Structure, and Change; the Arts
BA Business, Management, and Economics; Community and Human Services; Cultural Studies; Educational Studies; Historical Studies; Human Development; Interdisciplinary Studies; Labor Studies; Science, Math, and Technology; Social Theory, Social Structure, and Change; the Arts
BPS Business, Management, and Economics
BS Business, Management, and Economics; Community and Human Services; Community and Human Services; Cultural Studies; Educational Studies; Historical Studies; Human Development; Interdisciplinary Studies; Labor Studies; Science, Math, and Technology; Social Theory, Social Structure, and Change; the Arts
MA Liberal Studies; Policy Studies
MAT Teaching
MBA Business Administration

COURSE SUBJECT AREAS OFFERED OUTSIDE OF DEGREE PROGRAMS

Undergraduate—accounting and related services; biology; communication and media; computer/information technology administration and management; criminal justice and corrections; education; English composition; finance and financial management services; fire protection; history; human development, family studies, and related services; international business; legal studies (non-professional general, undergraduate); management information systems; mathematics and statistics related; political science and government; social psychology; sociology; statistics.
Graduate—business/commerce; education; political science and government; social sciences.

See full description on page 452.

STEVENS INSTITUTE OF TECHNOLOGY
Hoboken, New Jersey
Graduate School
http://www.webcampus.stevens.edu

Stevens Institute of Technology was founded in 1870. It is accredited by Middle States Association of Colleges and Schools. It first offered distance learning courses in 1999. In fall 2006, there were 1,000 students enrolled in distance learning courses. Institutionally administered financial aid is available to distance learners.

Services Distance learners have accessibility to academic advising, bookstore, campus computer network, career placement assistance, e-mail services, library services.

Contact Robert Zotti, Director, Online Learning, Stevens Institute of Technology, Castle Point on the Hudson, Howe Center, 12th Floor, Hoboken, NJ 07030. Telephone: 201-216-5231. Fax: 201-216-5090. E-mail: webcampus@stevens.edu.

DEGREES AND AWARDS

Graduate Certificate Atmospheric and Environmental Science and Engineering; Communications–Professional Communications; Computer Graphics; Computer Science–Elements of Computer Science; Cyber Security; Database Systems; Digital Signal Processing; Financial Engineering; Human Resources Management; Management Information Systems; Multimedia Technology; Networked Information Systems; Pharmaceutical Manufacturing Practices; Project Management for the Life Sciences Industries; Project Management; Quantitative Software Engineering; Secure Network Systems Design; Technology Management; Telecommunications Management; Wireless Communications

MBA Technology Management

ME Engineering Management; Networked Information Systems

MS Computer Science–CyberSecurity concentration; Computer Science; Information Systems; Management in Computer Science/Telecom with Security Management and Forensics; Management; Microelectronics and Photonics; Pharmaceutical Manufacturing; Project Management; Quantitative Software Engineering; Systems Engineering; Telecommunication Management

COURSE SUBJECT AREAS OFFERED OUTSIDE OF DEGREE PROGRAMS

Undergraduate—engineering/industrial management; mathematics.

Graduate—computer software and media applications; management information systems; management sciences and quantitative methods.

Non-credit—computer science; engineering; technology education/industrial arts.

See full description on page 454.

STONY BROOK UNIVERSITY, STATE UNIVERSITY OF NEW YORK
Stony Brook, New York
Electronic Extension Program
http://www.stonybrook.edu/spd/online/

Stony Brook University, State University of New York was founded in 1957. It is accredited by Middle States Association of Colleges and Schools. It first offered distance learning courses in 1996. In fall 2006, there were 900 students enrolled in distance learning courses. Institutionally administered financial aid is available to distance learners.

Services Distance learners have accessibility to academic advising, bookstore, campus computer network, library services.

Contact Kim Giacalone, Assistant Director, Stony Brook University, State University of New York, School of Professional Development, N 213 SBS Building, Stony Brook, NY 11794-4310. Telephone: 631-632-9484. Fax: 631-632-9046. E-mail: kim.giacalone@stonybrook.edu.

DEGREES AND AWARDS

Graduate Certificate Human Resource Management
MA Liberal Studies

COURSE SUBJECT AREAS OFFERED OUTSIDE OF DEGREE PROGRAMS

Graduate—education; educational administration and supervision; English language and literature related; human resources management; liberal arts and sciences, general studies and humanities.

STRAYER UNIVERSITY
Washington, District of Columbia

Strayer University was founded in 1892. It is accredited by Middle States Association of Colleges and Schools. It first offered distance learning courses in 1997. In fall 2006, there were 31,000 students enrolled in distance learning courses. Institutionally administered financial aid is available to distance learners.

Services Distance learners have accessibility to academic advising, bookstore, campus computer network, e-mail services, library services, tutoring.

Contact Patti Pellicci, Director of Online Operations, Strayer University, PO Box 487, Newington, VA 22122. Telephone: 866-344-3286. Fax: 703-339-4849. E-mail: info@strayer.edu.

DEGREES AND AWARDS

AA Accounting; Acquisition and Contract Management; Business Administration; Economics; General Studies; Information Systems; Marketing

BBA Acquisition and Contract Management; Banking; E-business; Finance; Hospitality and Tourism Management; Human Resource Management; Legal Studies; Management; Marketing; Retail Management

BS Accounting; Economics; Information Systems; International Business

Certificate Accounting; Business Administration; Information Systems

Diploma Accounting; Acquisition and Contract Management; Information Systems

MBA Business Administration

MEd Education

MHSA Health Services Administration

MPA Public Administration

MS Information Systems; Professional Accounting

COURSE SUBJECT AREAS OFFERED OUTSIDE OF DEGREE PROGRAMS

Undergraduate—accounting and related services; area, ethnic, cultural, and gender studies related; business/commerce; economics; English; English composition; finance and financial management services; history; information science/studies; international business; legal studies (non-professional general, undergraduate); linguistic, comparative, and related language studies; mathematics; political science and government; psychology; sales, merchandising, and related marketing operations (specialized); sociology.

Graduate—accounting and related services; business/commerce; economics; information science/studies; legal research and advanced professional studies; mathematics.

See full description on page 456.

SUFFOLK UNIVERSITY
Boston, Massachusetts
Suffolk MBA Online
http://www.suffolk.edu/mbaonline

Suffolk University was founded in 1906. It is accredited by New England Association of Schools and Colleges. It first offered distance learning courses in 1999. In fall 2006, there were 300 students enrolled in distance learning courses. Institutionally administered financial aid is available to distance learners.

Services Distance learners have accessibility to academic advising, bookstore, campus computer network, career placement assistance, e-mail services, library services.

Contact Dr. Lillian M. Hallberg, Assistant Dean of Graduate Programs and Director of MBA Programs, Suffolk University, 8 Ashburton Place, Boston, MA 02108-2770. Telephone: 617-573-8306. Fax: 617-573-8653. E-mail: lhallber@suffolk.edu.

DEGREES AND AWARDS

MBA Business Administration–Accelerated MBA for Attorneys; Business Administration–Accelerated MBA for CPAs; Business Administration

COURSE SUBJECT AREAS OFFERED OUTSIDE OF DEGREE PROGRAMS

Graduate—accounting and related services; business, management, and marketing related; entrepreneurial and small business operations; finance and financial management services; human resources management; international business; management information systems; marketing; taxation.

SUMMIT PACIFIC COLLEGE
Abbotsford, British Columbia, Canada
http://www.summitpacific.ca
Summit Pacific College was founded in 1941. It is provincially chartered. It first offered distance learning courses in 1999. In fall 2006, there were 125 students enrolled in distance learning courses. Institutionally administered financial aid is available to distance learners.
Services Distance learners have accessibility to academic advising, bookstore, career placement assistance, tutoring.
Contact Rev. Robert McIntyre, Director, Distance Education, Summit Pacific College, 35235 Straiton Road, PO Box 1700, Abbotsford, BC V2S 7E7, Canada. Telephone: 604-851-7228. Fax: 604-853-8951. E-mail: distanceed@summitpacific.ca.

DEGREES AND AWARDS
Programs offered do not lead to a degree or other formal award.

COURSE SUBJECT AREAS OFFERED OUTSIDE OF DEGREE PROGRAMS
Undergraduate—biblical studies; pastoral counseling and specialized ministries; religious education; religious studies; theological and ministerial studies.
Non-credit—biblical studies; religious education; religious studies; theological and ministerial studies.

SYRACUSE UNIVERSITY
Syracuse, New York
University College
http://www.suce.syr.edu/distance
Syracuse University was founded in 1870. It is accredited by Middle States Association of Colleges and Schools. It first offered distance learning courses in 1966. In fall 2006, there were 1,000 students enrolled in distance learning courses. Institutionally administered financial aid is available to distance learners.
Services Distance learners have accessibility to academic advising, bookstore, campus computer network, career placement assistance, e-mail services, library services.
Contact Dr. Geraldine de Berly, Associate Dean, University College, Syracuse University, 700 University Avenue, Suite 403, Syracuse, NY 13244-2530. Telephone: 315-443-5753. Fax: 315-443-4410. E-mail: deberly@uc.syr.edu.

DEGREES AND AWARDS
AA Liberal Arts
BA Liberal Studies
BPS Organizational Leadership
Certificate Organizational Leadership
CAGS Digital Libraries; Information Security Management; Information Security Management; Information Systems and Telecommunications Management; School Media
MA Advertising Design; Illustration
MBA iMBA
MS Communications Management; Information Management; Library and Information Science in School Media; Library and Information Science; Social Sciences; Telecommunications and Network Management

COURSE SUBJECT AREAS OFFERED OUTSIDE OF DEGREE PROGRAMS
Undergraduate—biological and physical sciences; business, management, and marketing related; computer and information sciences; English language and literature related; ethnic, cultural minority, and gender studies; liberal arts and sciences, general studies and humanities; science, technology and society; social sciences; speech and rhetoric; statistics; technical and business writing; visual and performing arts related.

Graduate—anthropology; business administration, management and operations; communication and media; computer and information sciences; computer/information technology administration and management; computer systems networking and telecommunications; ethnic, cultural minority, and gender studies; history; information science/studies; library science; library science related; management information systems; psychology; sociology; visual and performing arts related.
See full description on page 458.

SYRACUSE UNIVERSITY
Syracuse, New York
Martin J. Whitman School of Management
http://whitman.syr.edu/imba
Syracuse University was founded in 1870. It is accredited by Middle States Association of Colleges and Schools. It first offered distance learning courses in 1977. In fall 2006, there were 250 students enrolled in distance learning courses. Institutionally administered financial aid is available to distance learners.
Services Distance learners have accessibility to academic advising, bookstore, campus computer network, career placement assistance, e-mail services, library services.
Contact Pamela Suzadail, Assistant Director, External Programs, Syracuse University, 721 University Avenue, Syracuse, NY 13244-2450. Telephone: 315-443-8384. E-mail: pjsuzada@syr.edu.

DEGREES AND AWARDS
MBA iMBA
MS iMS Accounting

COURSE SUBJECT AREAS OFFERED OUTSIDE OF DEGREE PROGRAMS
Graduate—accounting and related services; business administration, management and operations; business/commerce; business/managerial economics; entrepreneurial and small business operations; finance and financial management services; management information systems; management sciences and quantitative methods; marketing; sales, merchandising, and related marketing operations (general).

SYRACUSE UNIVERSITY
Syracuse, New York
School of Information Studies
http://www.ist.syr.edu
Syracuse University was founded in 1870. It is accredited by Middle States Association of Colleges and Schools. It first offered distance learning courses in 1993. In fall 2006, there were 350 students enrolled in distance learning courses. Institutionally administered financial aid is available to distance learners.
Services Distance learners have accessibility to academic advising, bookstore, campus computer network, career placement assistance, e-mail services, library services, tutoring.
Contact Kathryn Allen, Director of Distance Learning, Syracuse University, School of Information Studies, 114 Hinds Hall, Syracuse, NY 13244. Telephone: 315-443-4251. Fax: 315-443-5673. E-mail: kallen02@syr.edu.

DEGREES AND AWARDS
CAGS Digital Libraries; Information Security Management; Information Systems and Telecommunications Management; School Media
MLIS Library and Information Science
MS Information Management
MTM Telecommunications and Network Management

COURSE SUBJECT AREAS OFFERED OUTSIDE OF DEGREE PROGRAMS
Undergraduate—business administration, management and operations; communications technology; computer systems networking and telecommunications; information science/studies; management information systems; science, technology and society; systems science and theory.

Graduate—communications technology; computer and information sciences; computer/information technology administration and management; computer software and media applications; computer systems analysis; computer systems networking and telecommunications; data processing; information science/studies; library assistant; library science; library science related; management information systems; systems science and theory.

TACOMA COMMUNITY COLLEGE
Tacoma, Washington
Distance Learning Program
http://www.tacoma.ctc.edu/inst_dept/distancelearning/
Tacoma Community College was founded in 1965. It is accredited by Northwest Commission on Colleges and Universities. It first offered distance learning courses in 1975. In fall 2006, there were 3,100 students enrolled in distance learning courses. Institutionally administered financial aid is available to distance learners.
Services Distance learners have accessibility to academic advising, bookstore, e-mail services, library services.
Contact Mr. Andy Duckworth, Coordinator, Distance Learning and Multimedia Services, Tacoma Community College, 6501 South 19th Street, Building 7, Tacoma, WA 98466. Telephone: 253-460-3958. Fax: 253-566-5398. E-mail: aduckworth@tacomacc.edu.

DEGREES AND AWARDS
Programs offered do not lead to a degree or other formal award.

COURSE SUBJECT AREAS OFFERED OUTSIDE OF DEGREE PROGRAMS
Undergraduate—accounting and related services; allied health and medical assisting services; allied health diagnostic, intervention, and treatment professions; American literature (United States and Canadian); anthropology; applied mathematics; behavioral sciences; bilingual, multilingual, and multicultural education; biological and physical sciences; biology; botany/plant biology; business/commerce; chemistry; computer and information sciences; computer programming; computer science; creative writing; criminal justice and corrections; data entry/microcomputer applications; design and applied arts; developmental and child psychology; engineering; engineering physics; engineering related; English as a second language; English composition; fine and studio art; geography and cartography; geological and earth sciences/geosciences; health and medical administrative services; health professions related; history; human development, family studies, and related services; human services; information science/studies; legal studies (non-professional general, undergraduate); library science; library science related; linguistic, comparative, and related language studies; mathematics; music; nursing; philosophy; physics; political science and government; psychology; social sciences; social work; sociology; speech and rhetoric.
Non-credit—business administration, management and operations; computer and information sciences; management information systems.

TAYLOR UNIVERSITY
Fort Wayne, Indiana
Center for Lifelong Learning
http://cll.taylor.edu
Taylor University was founded in 1938. It is accredited by North Central Association of Colleges and Schools. It first offered distance learning courses in 1941. In fall 2006, there were 1,300 students enrolled in distance learning courses. Institutionally administered financial aid is available to distance learners.
Services Distance learners have accessibility to academic advising, bookstore, e-mail services, library services.
Contact Kevin J. Mahaffy, Director, Taylor University, Center for Lifelong Learning, 1025 West Rudisill Boulevard, Fort Wayne, IN 46807-2197. Telephone: 260-744-8750. Fax: 260-744-8796. E-mail: info@cll.taylor.edu.

DEGREES AND AWARDS
AA Biblical Studies; Justice Administration — Ministry Concentration; Justice Administration — Public Policy Concentration; Liberal Arts —

History concentration; Liberal Arts — Interdisciplinary concentration; Liberal Arts — Social Science concentration
BBA Business Administration
Certificate Biblical Studies; Biblical and Cultural Leadership; Christian Worker; Justice and Ministry; Leadership Development; Missions Studies; Professional Writing

COURSE SUBJECT AREAS OFFERED OUTSIDE OF DEGREE PROGRAMS
Undergraduate—American literature (United States and Canadian); area, ethnic, cultural, and gender studies related; area studies; behavioral sciences; biblical and other theological languages and literatures; biblical studies; biological and physical sciences; biology; business administration, management and operations; business/commerce; business, management, and marketing related; business/managerial economics; communication and journalism related; computer and information sciences; computer/information technology administration and management; computer science; counseling psychology; creative writing; criminal justice and corrections; developmental and child psychology; economics; education; educational/instructional media design; educational psychology; education related; English; English composition; English literature (British and Commonwealth); fine and studio art; geography and cartography; history; information science/studies; journalism; liberal arts and sciences, general studies and humanities; management information systems; marketing; mathematics; medieval and Renaissance studies; missionary studies and missiology; multi-/interdisciplinary studies related; music; pastoral counseling and specialized ministries; peace studies and conflict resolution; philosophy; philosophy and religious studies related; physical sciences; physical sciences related; political science and government; psychology; psychology related; religious education; religious/sacred music; religious studies; social psychology; social sciences; social sciences related; social work; sociology; speech and rhetoric; theological and ministerial studies; theology and religious vocations related.
Non-credit—accounting and related services; applied mathematics; biblical and other theological languages and literatures; biblical studies; business administration, management and operations; business/commerce; business/corporate communications; business, management, and marketing related; business operations support and assistant services; communication and journalism related; communication and media; computer and information sciences; computer and information sciences and support services related; computer/information technology administration and management; computer programming; computer software and media applications; computer systems networking and telecommunications; creative writing; data entry/microcomputer applications; data processing; English composition; entrepreneurial and small business operations; family and consumer economics; human development, family studies, and related services; human resources management; information science/studies; management information systems; marketing; mathematics and computer science; public relations, advertising, and applied communication related; religious studies; sales, merchandising, and related marketing operations (general); sales, merchandising, and related marketing operations (specialized); technical and business writing; theological and ministerial studies.

See full description on page 460.

TEMPLE BAPTIST SEMINARY
Chattanooga, Tennessee
Distance Education
http://www.templebaptistseminary.edu/
Temple Baptist Seminary was founded in 1948. It is accredited by Transnational Association of Christian Colleges and Schools. It first offered distance learning courses in 1993. In fall 2006, there were 53 students enrolled in distance learning courses. Institutionally administered financial aid is available to distance learners.
Services Distance learners have accessibility to academic advising, bookstore, campus computer network, career placement assistance, e-mail services, library services.
Contact Ms. Rachel Anderson, TBS DE Coordinator, Temple Baptist Seminary, Distance Education Office, 1815 Union Avenue, Chattanooga, TN 37404. Telephone: 423-493-4288. Fax: 423-493-4379. E-mail: tbsde@tntemple.edu.

DEGREES AND AWARDS

Certificate Biblical Studies; Christian Ministries

MABS Biblical Studies–over 20 concentrations available

MACE Christian Education–4 distinct concentrations

MDiv Divinity–Master of Divinity–English Bible Track with over 20 concentrations available

MMin Ministry–Master of Ministry–various concentrations available

DMin Ministry Studies–6 distinct concentrations available

COURSE SUBJECT AREAS OFFERED OUTSIDE OF DEGREE PROGRAMS

Graduate—biblical studies; missionary studies and missiology; pastoral counseling and specialized ministries; philosophy and religious studies related; religious education.

Non-credit—biblical studies; missionary studies and missiology; pastoral counseling and specialized ministries; philosophy and religious studies related; religious studies.

TENNESSEE TECHNOLOGICAL UNIVERSITY
Cookeville, Tennessee
Extended Education
http://www2.tntech.edu/exted/

Tennessee Technological University was founded in 1915. It is accredited by Southern Association of Colleges and Schools. It first offered distance learning courses in 1985. In fall 2006, there were 1,277 students enrolled in distance learning courses. Institutionally administered financial aid is available to distance learners.

Services Distance learners have accessibility to academic advising, bookstore, campus computer network, career placement assistance, e-mail services, library services.

Contact Susan A. Elkins, Dean, School of Interdisciplinary Studies, Tennessee Technological University, School of Interdisciplinary Studies, Box 5073, Cookeville, TN 38505. Telephone: 931-372-3394. Fax: 931-372-3499. E-mail: selkins@tntech.edu.

DEGREES AND AWARDS

BGS Interdisciplinary Studies

BPS Professional Studies

MBA Business Administration

MPS Professional Studies

MSN Nursing

COURSE SUBJECT AREAS OFFERED OUTSIDE OF DEGREE PROGRAMS

Non-credit—accounting and related services; entrepreneurial and small business operations; finance and financial management services; marketing; nursing; technical and business writing.

TEXAS A&M UNIVERSITY–COMMERCE
Commerce, Texas
Instructional Technology and Distance Learning
http://www7.tamu-commerce.edu/itde/

Texas A&M University–Commerce was founded in 1889. It is accredited by Southern Association of Colleges and Schools. It first offered distance learning courses in 1993. In fall 2006, there were 2,560 students enrolled in distance learning courses. Institutionally administered financial aid is available to distance learners.

Services Distance learners have accessibility to academic advising, bookstore, campus computer network, career placement assistance, e-mail services, library services, tutoring.

Contact Dr. Charlotte A. Larkin, Director of Instructional Technology and Distance Education, Texas A&M University–Commerce, PO Box 3011, Commerce, TX 75429. Telephone: 903-886-5511. Fax: 903-886-5991. E-mail: charlotte_larkin@tamu-commerce.edu.

DEGREES AND AWARDS

Programs offered do not lead to a degree or other formal award.

COURSE SUBJECT AREAS OFFERED OUTSIDE OF DEGREE PROGRAMS

Undergraduate—accounting and computer science; agricultural production; animal sciences; biology; botany/plant biology; business administration, management and operations; business/commerce; business, management, and marketing related; business/managerial economics; communication and media; computer and information sciences; computer science; creative writing; criminal justice and corrections; developmental and child psychology; economics; English; English composition; history; industrial engineering; journalism; management information systems; marketing; mathematics; psychology; social work; sociology.

Graduate—accounting and related services; agriculture; business, management, and marketing related; business/managerial economics; computer and information sciences; construction management; curriculum and instruction; economics; education; educational administration and supervision; educational/instructional media design; English composition; finance and financial management services; industrial engineering; library science related; marketing; psychology; radio, television, and digital communication; social work; special education.

Non-credit—economics; finance and financial management services.

TEXAS A&M UNIVERSITY–TEXARKANA
Texarkana, Texas
http://www.tamut.edu/

Texas A&M University–Texarkana was founded in 1971. It is accredited by Southern Association of Colleges and Schools. It first offered distance learning courses in 1995. In fall 2006, there were 579 students enrolled in distance learning courses. Institutionally administered financial aid is available to distance learners.

Services Distance learners have accessibility to academic advising, career placement assistance, e-mail services, library services.

Contact Mrs. Patricia Black, Director of Admissions and Registrar, Texas A&M University–Texarkana, PO Box 5518, Texarkana, TX 75505-5518. Telephone: 903-223-3069. Fax: 903-223-3140. E-mail: pat.black@tamut.edu.

DEGREES AND AWARDS

Programs offered do not lead to a degree or other formal award.

COURSE SUBJECT AREAS OFFERED OUTSIDE OF DEGREE PROGRAMS

Undergraduate—accounting and related services; business administration, management and operations; criminal justice and corrections; education (specific subject areas); English; history; marketing; mathematics; political science and government; psychology; sales, merchandising, and related marketing operations (general); sociology.

Graduate—accounting and related services; business administration, management and operations; economics; educational administration and supervision; educational/instructional media design; education related; education (specific levels and methods); management information systems; marketing.

TEXAS CHRISTIAN UNIVERSITY
Fort Worth, Texas
Cyberlearning
http://www.tcuglobal.edu

Texas Christian University was founded in 1873. It is accredited by Southern Association of Colleges and Schools. It first offered distance learning courses in 1999. In fall 2006, there were 103 students enrolled in distance learning courses. Institutionally administered financial aid is available to distance learners.

Services Distance learners have accessibility to academic advising, bookstore, campus computer network, career placement assistance, e-mail services, library services, tutoring.

Contact Mrs. Romana J. Hughes, Assistant Director of Learning Resources, Texas Christian University, Box 298970, Fort Worth, TX 76129. Telephone: 817-257-7434. Fax: 817-257-7393. E-mail: r.hughes@tcu.edu.

DEGREES AND AWARDS
Advanced Graduate Diploma Liberal Arts–Master of Liberal Arts
MSN Nursing

COURSE SUBJECT AREAS OFFERED OUTSIDE OF DEGREE PROGRAMS
Undergraduate—biology; dramatic/theater arts and stagecraft; fine and studio art; history.

TEXAS STATE TECHNICAL COLLEGE WACO
Waco, Texas
http://www.waco.tstc.edu/
Texas State Technical College Waco was founded in 1965. It is accredited by Southern Association of Colleges and Schools. It first offered distance learning courses in 1995. In fall 2006, there were 1,000 students enrolled in distance learning courses. Institutionally administered financial aid is available to distance learners.
Services Distance learners have accessibility to academic advising, bookstore, campus computer network, career placement assistance, e-mail services, library services, tutoring.
Contact Lance Zimmerman, Director, Distance Education, Texas State Technical College Waco, 3801 Campus Drive, Waco, TX 76705-1696. Telephone: 800-792-8784 Ext. 3257. Fax: 254-867-3470. E-mail: lance. zimmerman@tstc.edu.

DEGREES AND AWARDS
AAS Web Designer; Web Developer

COURSE SUBJECT AREAS OFFERED OUTSIDE OF DEGREE PROGRAMS
Undergraduate—computer programming; computer science; computer software and media applications; computer systems analysis; computer systems networking and telecommunications; data entry/microcomputer applications; English composition; mathematics.
Non-credit—business/commerce; computer programming; computer software and media applications; graphic communications.

TEXAS STATE UNIVERSITY-SAN MARCOS
San Marcos, Texas
Correspondence and Extension Studies
http://www.ideal.swt.edu/correspondence/
Texas State University-San Marcos was founded in 1899. It is accredited by Southern Association of Colleges and Schools. It first offered distance learning courses in 1953. In fall 2006, there were 2,000 students enrolled in distance learning courses. Institutionally administered financial aid is available to distance learners.
Services Distance learners have accessibility to bookstore, campus computer network, e-mail services, library services, tutoring.
Contact Carolyn Bettelheim, Administrative Assistant, Texas State University-San Marcos, Office of Correspondence Studies, 302 ASB North, 601 University Drive, San Marcos, TX 78666. Telephone: 512-245-2322. Fax: 512-245-8934. E-mail: corrstudy@txstate.edu.

DEGREES AND AWARDS
Programs offered do not lead to a degree or other formal award.

COURSE SUBJECT AREAS OFFERED OUTSIDE OF DEGREE PROGRAMS
Undergraduate—allied health and medical assisting services; American literature (United States and Canadian); behavioral sciences; biological and physical sciences; biology; business/commerce; cell biology and anatomical sciences; community psychology; comparative literature; creative writing; criminology; dance; developmental and child psychology; English; English composition; English language and literature related; English literature (British and Commonwealth); family psychology; fine and studio art; health and medical administrative services; health professions related; history; industrial and organizational psychology; journalism; languages (Romance languages); legal professions and studies related; liberal arts and sciences, general studies and humanities;

mathematics; mathematics and computer science; music; philosophy; political science and government; psychology; psychology related; social psychology; social sciences; social sciences related; sociology.
Graduate—mathematics.
Non-credit—health and medical administrative services.

TEXAS TECH UNIVERSITY
Lubbock, Texas
Outreach and Distance Education
http://www.ttu.edu/
Texas Tech University was founded in 1923. It is accredited by Southern Association of Colleges and Schools. It first offered distance learning courses in 1941. In fall 2006, there were 1,918 students enrolled in distance learning courses. Institutionally administered financial aid is available to distance learners.
Services Distance learners have accessibility to academic advising, bookstore, campus computer network, e-mail services, library services.
Contact Mrs. Michele L. Moskos, Marketing Director, Division of Outreach and Extended Studies, Texas Tech University, Box 42191, Lubbock, TX 79409-2191. Telephone: 806-742-7200 Ext. 276. Fax: 806-742-7277. E-mail: dldegrees.oes@ttu.edu.

DEGREES AND AWARDS
BGS General Studies
BS Architecture; Horticulture
Certificate Educational Diagnostician; Master Reading Teacher; Orientation and Mobility; Post-baccalaureate Secondary Teacher; Special Education, generic; Superintendent Professional; Visual Impairment
CAGS Autism; Deaf and Hard of Hearing; Dual Impairments; Gerontology
MA Art Education; Technical Communication
MAg Agriculture
ME Engineering
MEd Educational Leadership and Principal Professional Certification Preparation; Instructional Technology (Distance Education emphasis); Language Literacy Education; Special Education
MS Agricultural Education; Computer Science; Crop Science; Family Studies and Consumer Science Education; Horticulture; Human Development and Family Studies (Gerontology emphasis); Restaurant, Hotel, and Institutional Management; Software Engineering; Systems and Engineering Management
EdD Agricultural Education; Educational Leadership
PhD Computer Science; Systems and Engineering Mangament; Technical Communication and Rhetoric

COURSE SUBJECT AREAS OFFERED OUTSIDE OF DEGREE PROGRAMS
Undergraduate—accounting and related services; agricultural business and management; agriculture; American literature (United States and Canadian); anthropology; applied horticulture/horticultural business services; business administration, management and operations; developmental and child psychology; economics; educational psychology; English composition; English literature (British and Commonwealth); food science and technology; foods, nutrition, and related services; history; journalism; languages (Romance languages); legal studies (non-professional general, undergraduate); liberal arts and sciences, general studies and humanities; marketing; mathematics and statistics related; music; psychology; sales, merchandising, and related marketing operations (specialized); social psychology; sociology; technical and business writing.
Graduate—agriculture; animal sciences; architecture; chemical engineering; civil engineering; computer and information sciences and support services related; computer science; curriculum and instruction; education; educational administration and supervision; educational assessment, evaluation, and research; educational/instructional media design; education related; electrical and electronic engineering technologies; engineering; engineering related; English; English composition; environmental/environmental health engineering; family and consumer economics; gerontology; mathematics; mechanical engineering; music; petroleum engineering; plant sciences; special education; statistics; technical and business writing; textile sciences and engineering; visual and performing arts.

Non-credit—business administration, management and operations; languages (Romance languages).

TEXAS WOMAN'S UNIVERSITY
Denton, Texas
http://www.twuonline.com
Texas Woman's University was founded in 1901. It is accredited by Southern Association of Colleges and Schools. It first offered distance learning courses in 1994. In fall 2006, there were 4,700 students enrolled in distance learning courses. Institutionally administered financial aid is available to distance learners.
Services Distance learners have accessibility to academic advising, bookstore, campus computer network, career placement assistance, e-mail services, library services, tutoring.
Contact Ms. Julie Brown, DE Senior Administrative Assistant, Texas Woman's University, PO Box 425649, Denton, TX 76204. Telephone: 940-898-3409. Fax: 940-898-3416. E-mail: dl@twu.edu.

DEGREES AND AWARDS
BGS General Studies
BS Health Studies
BSN Nursing–RN–BS in Nursing
EMBA Business Administration
MA Occupational Therapy
MAT Teaching
MLS Library Science
MOT COTA to MOT
MS Deaf Education; Family Studies; Health Studies; Institutional Administration (Nutrition); Kinesiology; Speech-Language Pathology
PhD Nursing

COURSE SUBJECT AREAS OFFERED OUTSIDE OF DEGREE PROGRAMS
Undergraduate—business administration, management and operations; communication disorders sciences and services; computer and information sciences; education; English; family and consumer economics; health and physical education/fitness; health services/allied health/health sciences; history; nursing; nutrition sciences; psychology; sociology; visual and performing arts.
Graduate—bilingual, multilingual, and multicultural education; business administration, management and operations; business/commerce; communication disorders sciences and services; computer and information sciences; education; education related; family and consumer economics; health and physical education/fitness; health services/allied health/health sciences; library science; nursing; nutrition sciences; rehabilitation and therapeutic professions; school psychology; sociology; visual and performing arts.

THOMAS COLLEGE
Waterville, Maine
Continuing Education Division
http://www.thomas.edu
Thomas College was founded in 1894. It is accredited by New England Association of Schools and Colleges. It first offered distance learning courses in 1995. In fall 2006, there were 100 students enrolled in distance learning courses. Institutionally administered financial aid is available to distance learners.
Services Distance learners have accessibility to academic advising, bookstore, campus computer network, e-mail services, library services.
Contact Libby LaRochelle, Administrative Assistant, Thomas College, 180 West River Road, Waterville, ME 04901. Telephone: 207-859-1102. Fax: 207-859-1114. E-mail: ced@thomas.edu.

DEGREES AND AWARDS
Programs offered do not lead to a degree or other formal award.

COURSE SUBJECT AREAS OFFERED OUTSIDE OF DEGREE PROGRAMS
Undergraduate—accounting and computer science; business administration, management and operations; business/commerce.
Graduate—business/commerce; business/managerial economics.

THOMAS EDISON STATE COLLEGE
Trenton, New Jersey
DIAL–Distance and Independent Adult Learning
http://www.tesc.edu
Thomas Edison State College was founded in 1972. It is accredited by Middle States Association of Colleges and Schools. It first offered distance learning courses in 1972. In fall 2006, there were 13,173 students enrolled in distance learning courses. Institutionally administered financial aid is available to distance learners.
Services Distance learners have accessibility to academic advising, library services.
Contact Director of Admissions, Thomas Edison State College, 101 West State Street, Trenton, NJ 08608-1176. Telephone: 888-442-8372. Fax: 609-984-8447. E-mail: admissions@tesc.edu.

DEGREES AND AWARDS
AA Liberal Arts/General Studies
AAS Administrative Studies; Applied Computer Studies; Applied Electronic Studies; Applied Health Studies; Mechanics and Maintenance; Occupational Studies
AS Business Administration (ASBA)
ASAST Air Traffic Control; Architectural Design; Aviation Flight Technology; Aviation Maintenance Technology; Biomedical Electronics; Civil and Construction Engineering Technology; Clinical Lab Science; Computer Science Technology; Electrical Technology; Electronic Engineering Technology; Engineering Graphics; Environmental Sciences; Fire Protection Science; Forestry; Horticulture; Laboratory Animal Science; Manufacturing Engineering Technology; Marine Engineering Technology; Mechanical Engineering Technology; Medical Imaging; Nondestructive Testing Technology; Nuclear Engineering Technology; Nuclear Medicine Technology; Radiation Protection; Radiation Therapy; Respiratory Care; Surveying
ASNSM Biology; Computer Science; Mathematics
ASPSS Administration of Justice; Child Development Services; Community Services; Emergency Disaster Services; Fitness and Wellness Services; Gerontology; Legal Services; Recreation Services; Social Services for Special Populations; Social Services
BA Anthropology; Art; Biology; Communications; Computer Science; Criminal Justice; Economics; English; Environmental Studies; Foreign Language; History; Humanities; Journalism; Labor Studies; Liberal Studies; Mathematics; Music; Natural Sciences/Mathematics; Philosophy; Photography; Political Science; Psychology; Religion; Social Sciences; Sociology; Theater
BS Administration of Justice; Child Development Services; Community Services; Emergency Disaster Services; Gerontology; Health Services Administration; Health Services Education; Health Services; Health and Nutrition Counseling; Legal Services; Mental Health and Rehabilitation Services; Recreation Services; Social Services Administration; Social Services for Special Populations; Social Services
BSAST Air Traffic Control; Architectural Design; Aviation Flight Technology; Aviation Maintenance Technology; Biomedical Electronics; Civil Engineering Technology; Clinical Lab Science; Computer Science Technology; Construction; Cytotechnology; Dental Hygiene; Electrical Technology; Electronic Engineering Technology; Energy Utility Technology; Engineering Graphics; Environmental Sciences; Fire Protection Science; Forestry; Horticulture; Laboratory Animal Science; Manufacturing Engineering Technology; Marine Engineering Technology; Mechanical Engineering Technology; Medical Imaging; Nondestructive Testing Technology; Nuclear Engineering Technology; Nuclear Medicine Technology; Perfusion Technology; Radiation Protection; Radiation Therapy; Respiratory Care; Surveying
BSBA Accounting; Computer Information Systems; Entrepreneurship; Finance; Financial Institution Management; General Management; Hospital Health Care Administration; Hospitality Management; Human

Resources Management/Organizational Management; International Business; Marketing; Operations Management; Public Administration; Real Estate

BSN Nursing
MA Liberal Studies
MSHRM Human Resources Management
MSM Management
MSN Nursing
See full description on page 462.

See full description on page 462.

THREE RIVERS COMMUNITY COLLEGE
Norwich, Connecticut
http://www.trcc.commnet.edu/

Three Rivers Community College was founded in 1963. It is accredited by New England Association of Schools and Colleges. It first offered distance learning courses in 2000. In fall 2006, there were 300 students enrolled in distance learning courses. Institutionally administered financial aid is available to distance learners.

Services Distance learners have accessibility to academic advising, bookstore, career placement assistance, library services, tutoring.

Contact Mr. R. Kem Barfield, Director of Distance Learning, Three Rivers Community College, 7 Mahan Drive, Norwich, CT 06360. Telephone: 860-383-5215. E-mail: rbarfield@trcc.commnet.edu.

DEGREES AND AWARDS

AS Computer Support Specialist; General Studies
CCCPE Laser and Fiber Optic Technology

COURSE SUBJECT AREAS OFFERED OUTSIDE OF DEGREE PROGRAMS

Undergraduate—accounting and related services; business administration, management and operations; computer and information sciences; education (specific subject areas); environmental/environmental health engineering; history; mathematics; nutrition sciences; psychology; sociology.

Non-credit—allied health and medical assisting services; computer software and media applications.

THREE RIVERS COMMUNITY COLLEGE
Poplar Bluff, Missouri
http://www.trcc.cc.mo.us/

Three Rivers Community College was founded in 1966. It is accredited by North Central Association of Colleges and Schools. It first offered distance learning courses in 1996. In fall 2006, there were 1,000 students enrolled in distance learning courses. Institutionally administered financial aid is available to distance learners.

Services Distance learners have accessibility to academic advising, bookstore, library services.

Contact Cindy Clark, Registrar, Three Rivers Community College, 2080 Three Rivers Boulevard, Poplar Bluff, MO 63901. Telephone: 573-840-9665. Fax: 573-840-9666. E-mail: cclark@trcc.edu.

DEGREES AND AWARDS

Programs offered do not lead to a degree or other formal award.

COURSE SUBJECT AREAS OFFERED OUTSIDE OF DEGREE PROGRAMS

Undergraduate—accounting and computer science; agriculture; allied health and medical assisting services; American literature (United States and Canadian); biology; business administration, management and operations; computer and information sciences; computer science; creative writing; criminal justice and corrections; developmental and child psychology; English language and literature related; English literature (British and Commonwealth); health and medical administrative services; history; mathematics; nursing; psychology; social work; sociology; speech and rhetoric.

THUNDERBIRD SCHOOL OF GLOBAL MANAGEMENT
Glendale, Arizona
http://www.thunderbird.edu/globalmba/

Thunderbird School of Global Management was founded in 1946. It is accredited by North Central Association of Colleges and Schools. It first offered distance learning courses in 1998. In fall 2006, there were 480 students enrolled in distance learning courses. Institutionally administered financial aid is available to distance learners.

Services Distance learners have accessibility to academic advising, bookstore, campus computer network, career placement assistance, e-mail services, library services, tutoring.

Contact Dr. Bert Valencia, Vice President for Distance Learning and Global MBA Programs, Thunderbird School of Global Management, 15249 North 59th Avenue, Glendale, AZ 85306-6000. Telephone: 800-848-9084. Fax: 602-978-7729. E-mail: admissions@thunderbird.edu.

DEGREES AND AWARDS

GMBA Global Master of Business Administration On-Demand; Global Master of Business Administration for Latin American Managers
MBA/MIM Kelley Direct MBA/M-GM Dual Degree–Thunderbird and Indiana University
MIM Post-MBA Masters–Global Management On-Demand

COURSE SUBJECT AREAS OFFERED OUTSIDE OF DEGREE PROGRAMS

Graduate—accounting and related services; business administration, management and operations; business/corporate communications; business, management, and marketing related; international business; management information systems; sales, merchandising, and related marketing operations (specialized).

Non-credit—business administration, management and operations; business/commerce; business/corporate communications; business, management, and marketing related; business/managerial economics; international business; international/global studies; marketing.

TOMPKINS CORTLAND COMMUNITY COLLEGE
Dryden, New York
Instructional and Learning Resources
http://www.sunytccc.edu/e-tc3/e-tc3.asp

Tompkins Cortland Community College was founded in 1968. It is accredited by Middle States Association of Colleges and Schools. It first offered distance learning courses in 1997. In fall 2006, there were 1,772 students enrolled in distance learning courses. Institutionally administered financial aid is available to distance learners.

Services Distance learners have accessibility to bookstore, career placement assistance, e-mail services, library services, tutoring.

Contact Eric Machan Howd, Coordinator of Online Learning Services, Tompkins Cortland Community College, 170 North Street, PO Box 139, Dryden, NY 13053. Telephone: 607-844-8211 Ext. 4297. Fax: 607-844-6540. E-mail: howde@tc3.edu.

DEGREES AND AWARDS

AAS Business Administration–Applied Management; Chemical Dependency Studies Counseling; Hotel and Restaurant Management; Paralegal Studies

COURSE SUBJECT AREAS OFFERED OUTSIDE OF DEGREE PROGRAMS

Undergraduate—accounting and related services; business/commerce; business/corporate communications; communication and media; computer and information sciences; computer programming; computer software and media applications; developmental and child psychology; English; English as a second language; English composition; fine and studio art; hospitality administration; international business; legal studies (non-professional general, undergraduate); management sciences and quantitative methods; marketing; mathematics; mental and social health services and allied professions; nursing; psychology; psychology related; social psychology; sociology; visual and performing arts.

Non-credit—business, management, and marketing related; business operations support and assistant services; computer software and media applications; computer systems networking and telecommunications; data processing.

TOURO UNIVERSITY INTERNATIONAL
Cypress, California
http://www.tourou.edu/

Touro University International is accredited by Western Association of Schools and Colleges. It first offered distance learning courses in 1999. In fall 2006, there were 7,200 students enrolled in distance learning courses. Institutionally administered financial aid is available to distance learners.
Services Distance learners have accessibility to academic advising, bookstore, campus computer network, e-mail services, library services.
Contact Wei Ren, Registrar, Touro University International, 5665 Plaza Drive, 3rd Floor, Cypress, CA 90630. Telephone: 714-816-0366. Fax: 714-827-7407. E-mail: registration@tourou.edu.

DEGREES AND AWARDS

BS Business Administration; Computer Science; Health Sciences; Information Technology Management
MAE Education
MBA Business Administration
MHS Health Sciences
MS Information Technology Management
PhD Business Administration; Educational Leadership; Health Sciences
See full description on page 464.

TREASURE VALLEY COMMUNITY COLLEGE
Ontario, Oregon
Division of Extended Learning
http://www.tvcc.cc

Treasure Valley Community College was founded in 1962. It is accredited by Northwest Commission on Colleges and Universities. It first offered distance learning courses in 1985. In fall 2006, there were 800 students enrolled in distance learning courses. Institutionally administered financial aid is available to distance learners.
Services Distance learners have accessibility to academic advising, bookstore, campus computer network, e-mail services, library services.
Contact Linda C. Simmons, Director, Continuing/Community Education, Treasure Valley Community College, 650 College Boulevard, Ontario, OR 97914. Telephone: 541-881-8822 Ext. 358. Fax: 541-881-2721. E-mail: lsimmons@tvcc.cc.

DEGREES AND AWARDS
Programs offered do not lead to a degree or other formal award.

COURSE SUBJECT AREAS OFFERED OUTSIDE OF DEGREE PROGRAMS

Undergraduate—agricultural and domestic animal services; agricultural production; agriculture and agriculture operations related; alternative and complementary medical support services; biology; business administration, management and operations; business/commerce; chemistry; cognitive psychology and psycholinguistics; community psychology; computer and information sciences and support services related; computer programming; creative writing; education; ethnic, cultural minority, and gender studies; family and consumer sciences/human sciences; foods, nutrition, and related services; geological and earth sciences/geosciences; health and physical education/fitness; mathematics and statistics related; music; nutrition sciences; physical sciences; psychology; psychology related; real estate; social sciences; sociology.
Non-credit—real estate.

TRINITY EPISCOPAL SCHOOL FOR MINISTRY
Ambridge, Pennsylvania

Trinity Episcopal School for Ministry was founded in 1975. It is accredited by Association of Theological Schools in the United States and Canada. It first offered distance learning courses in 1997. Institutionally administered financial aid is available to distance learners.
Services Distance learners have accessibility to academic advising, bookstore, campus computer network, career placement assistance, e-mail services, library services, tutoring.

Contact Mr. Travis S. Hines, Director, Center for Distance Learning, Trinity Episcopal School for Ministry, 311 11th Street, Ambridge, PA 15003. Telephone: 724-266-3838 Ext. 228. Fax: 724-266-4617. E-mail: thines@tesm.edu.

DEGREES AND AWARDS
Diploma Anglican Studies; Christian Ministry

COURSE SUBJECT AREAS OFFERED OUTSIDE OF DEGREE PROGRAMS

Graduate—biblical and other theological languages and literatures; biblical studies; missionary studies and missiology; religious studies; theological and ministerial studies; theology and religious vocations related.
Non-credit—biblical studies; missionary studies and missiology; religious studies; theological and ministerial studies; theology and religious vocations related.

TRI-STATE UNIVERSITY
Angola, Indiana
http://www.tristate.edu/

Tri-State University was founded in 1884. It is accredited by North Central Association of Colleges and Schools. It first offered distance learning courses in 1995. In fall 2006, there were 95 students enrolled in distance learning courses. Institutionally administered financial aid is available to distance learners.
Services Distance learners have accessibility to bookstore, e-mail services, library services.
Contact Mr. Scott Goplin, Dean of Admission, Tri-State University, 1 University Avenue, Angola, IN 46703. Telephone: 260-665-4132. Fax: 260-665-4578. E-mail: admit@tristate.edu.

DEGREES AND AWARDS
Programs offered do not lead to a degree or other formal award.

COURSE SUBJECT AREAS OFFERED OUTSIDE OF DEGREE PROGRAMS

Undergraduate—accounting and related services; business administration, management and operations; business/commerce; economics; fine and studio art; geological and earth sciences/geosciences; history; legal studies (non-professional general, undergraduate); liberal arts and sciences, general studies and humanities; marketing; social sciences.

TRITON COLLEGE
River Grove, Illinois
Alternative Learning at Triton
http://www.triton.edu

Triton College was founded in 1964. It is accredited by North Central Association of Colleges and Schools. It first offered distance learning courses in 1997. In fall 2006, there were 1,221 students enrolled in distance learning courses. Institutionally administered financial aid is available to distance learners.
Services Distance learners have accessibility to academic advising, bookstore, campus computer network, e-mail services, library services, tutoring.
Contact Mr. Douglas Olson, Dean, Student Services, Triton College, 2000 Fifth Avenue, River Grove, IL 60171. Telephone: 708-456-0300 Ext. 3230. Fax: 708-582-3162. E-mail: dolson@triton.edu.

DEGREES AND AWARDS
AA the Arts
AAS General Program

COURSE SUBJECT AREAS OFFERED OUTSIDE OF DEGREE PROGRAMS

Undergraduate—accounting and related services; anthropology; architecture; area studies; astronomy and astrophysics; biology; chemistry; clinical/medical laboratory science and allied professions; developmental and child psychology; drafting/design engineering technologies; dramatic/

theater arts and stagecraft; economics; educational psychology; English composition; fine and studio art; health and physical education/fitness; history; languages (Romance languages); legal studies (non-professional general, undergraduate); liberal arts and sciences, general studies and humanities; linguistic, comparative, and related language studies; marketing; music; nursing; philosophy; philosophy and religious studies related; psychology; real estate; social psychology; social sciences; sociology; speech and rhetoric; statistics.

Non-credit—communication and journalism related; computer and information sciences; languages (foreign languages related); medical basic sciences; real estate.

TROY UNIVERSITY
Troy, Alabama
eCampus/Graduate
http://www.tsulearn.net

Troy University was founded in 1887. It is accredited by Southern Association of Colleges and Schools. It first offered distance learning courses in 1998. In fall 2006, there were 1,200 students enrolled in distance learning courses. Institutionally administered financial aid is available to distance learners.

Services Distance learners have accessibility to academic advising, bookstore, career placement assistance, e-mail services, library services.

Contact Dr. Barbara Echord, Director of Student Services, Troy University, eCampus Online Programs, 304 Wallace Hall, Troy, AL 36082. Telephone: 334-670-5875. Fax: 334-670-5679. E-mail: bechord@troy.edu.

DEGREES AND AWARDS

MBA Business Administration
MPA Public Administration
MS Criminal Justice; Human Resource Management; International Relations; Management; Postsecondary Education

See full description on page 466.

TROY UNIVERSITY
Troy, Alabama
eCampus/Undergraduate
http://www.troy.edu/

Troy University was founded in 1887. It is accredited by Southern Association of Colleges and Schools. It first offered distance learning courses in 1988. In fall 2006, there were 7,700 students enrolled in distance learning courses. Institutionally administered financial aid is available to distance learners.

Services Distance learners have accessibility to academic advising, bookstore, campus computer network, career placement assistance, e-mail services, library services, tutoring.

Contact Miss Michelle K. Sewell, Enrollment Coordinator, Troy University, Undergraduate eCampus, 326 Green Acres Road, FT Walton Beach, FL 32547. Telephone: 888-3ecampus. Fax: 850-863-2702. E-mail: ecampusundergraduate@troy.edu.

DEGREES AND AWARDS

ABA Business Administration
AGS General Education
BBA Business Administration
BS Bachelor of Applied Science in Computer Science; Criminal Justice; History; Political Science; Psychology; Social Science; Sport and Fitness Manager
BSAST Applied Science and Resource Technology Management

COURSE SUBJECT AREAS OFFERED OUTSIDE OF DEGREE PROGRAMS

Undergraduate—accounting and related services; biological and physical sciences; business administration, management and operations; computer science; English composition; history; mathematics; political science and government; social sciences.

TUNXIS COMMUNITY COLLEGE
Farmington, Connecticut
http://www.tunxis.commnet.edu/tole

Tunxis Community College was founded in 1969. It is accredited by New England Association of Schools and Colleges. It first offered distance learning courses in 1996. In fall 2006, there were 1,800 students enrolled in distance learning courses. Institutionally administered financial aid is available to distance learners.

Services Distance learners have accessibility to academic advising, bookstore, e-mail services, library services, tutoring.

Contact Peter McCluskey, Director of Admissions, Tunxis Community College, 271 Scott Swamp Road, Farmington, CT 06032. Telephone: 860-255-3563. E-mail: tx-admissions@txcc.commnet.edu.

DEGREES AND AWARDS

AA Criminal Justice; General Studies/Liberal Arts
Certificate Corrections Pre-Certification

COURSE SUBJECT AREAS OFFERED OUTSIDE OF DEGREE PROGRAMS

Undergraduate—anthropology; area, ethnic, cultural, and gender studies related; business administration, management and operations; communication and media; computer and information sciences; computer systems networking and telecommunications; criminal justice and corrections; criminology; dental support services and allied professions; developmental and child psychology; English; English composition; history; industrial and organizational psychology; linguistic, comparative, and related language studies; management information systems; music; philosophy; psychology; sociology.
Non-credit—business/commerce; computer and information sciences; criminal justice and corrections; education related; information science/studies.

TYLER JUNIOR COLLEGE
Tyler, Texas
Learning Resources
http://www.tjc.edu/academics/distance-learning.htm

Tyler Junior College was founded in 1926. It is accredited by Southern Association of Colleges and Schools. It first offered distance learning courses in 1969. In fall 2006, there were 2,300 students enrolled in distance learning courses. Institutionally administered financial aid is available to distance learners.

Services Distance learners have accessibility to academic advising, bookstore, career placement assistance, e-mail services, library services, tutoring.

Contact Gay Howard, Secretary of Learning Resources, Tyler Junior College, PO Box 9020, Tyler, TX 75711. Telephone: 903-510-2529. Fax: 903-510-2643. E-mail: ghow@tjc.edu.

DEGREES AND AWARDS

AA General Studies
AAS Business Management; Computer Information Systems Network Administration; Emergency Medical Service Professions (Paramedic option)

COURSE SUBJECT AREAS OFFERED OUTSIDE OF DEGREE PROGRAMS

Undergraduate—accounting and related services; American literature (United States and Canadian); astronomy and astrophysics; biology; business administration, management and operations; business/commerce; business/corporate communications; business operations support and assistant services; cell biology and anatomical sciences; computer and information sciences; computer and information sciences and support services related; computer/information technology administration and management; computer programming; computer science; computer software and media applications; computer systems analysis; computer systems networking and telecommunications; creative writing; criminal justice and corrections; economics; education; educational/instructional media design; English composition; fine and studio art; fire protection; health services/allied health/health sciences; history; languages (Romance languages); legal studies (non-professional general, undergraduate); legal support services; liberal arts and sciences, general studies and humanities; mathematics and statistics related; music; political science and government; psychology; sociology.

Non-credit—accounting and related services; business administration, management and operations; business/commerce; computer and information sciences; computer programming; computer software and media applications; educational/instructional media design; information science/studies; management information systems.

UNION INSTITUTE & UNIVERSITY
Cincinnati, Ohio
http://www.tui.edu

Union Institute & University was founded in 1969. It is accredited by North Central Association of Colleges and Schools. It first offered distance learning courses in 1993. In fall 2006, there were 1,300 students enrolled in distance learning courses. Institutionally administered financial aid is available to distance learners.

Services Distance learners have accessibility to academic advising, bookstore, e-mail services, library services, tutoring.

Contact Admissions, Union Institute & University, 440 East McMillan Street, Cincinnati, OH 45206. Telephone: 800-486-3116. Fax: 513-861-0779. E-mail: admissions@tui.edu.

DEGREES AND AWARDS

BA Liberal Arts and Sciences

BS Bachelor of Science

MA Interdisciplinary

EdD Education

PhD Interdisciplinary Studies

Psy D Psychology

UNION UNIVERSITY
Jackson, Tennessee
http://www.uu.edu

Union University was founded in 1823. It is accredited by Southern Association of Colleges and Schools. It first offered distance learning courses in 1999. In fall 2006, there were 500 students enrolled in distance learning courses. Institutionally administered financial aid is available to distance learners.

Services Distance learners have accessibility to academic advising, bookstore, campus computer network, career placement assistance, e-mail services, library services.

Contact Ms. Robin Navel, Director of Online Instruction and Training, Union University, 1050 Union University Drive, Jackson, TN 38305. Telephone: 731-661-5402. E-mail: rnavel@uu.edu.

DEGREES AND AWARDS

Programs offered do not lead to a degree or other formal award.

COURSE SUBJECT AREAS OFFERED OUTSIDE OF DEGREE PROGRAMS

Undergraduate—accounting and computer science; behavioral sciences; biological and physical sciences; business, management, and marketing related; computer science; education; library science; management information systems; marketing; mathematics and computer science; medical clinical sciences/graduate medical studies; nursing; physical science technologies; physics; psychology; religious studies; social psychology.

Graduate—education; educational administration and supervision; educational assessment, evaluation, and research; health professions related; religious studies.

Non-credit—religious studies.

UNITED STATES SPORTS ACADEMY
Daphne, Alabama
Continuing Education and Distance Learning
http://www.ussa.edu

United States Sports Academy was founded in 1972. It is accredited by Southern Association of Colleges and Schools. It first offered distance learning courses in 1995. In fall 2006, there were 900 students enrolled in distance learning courses. Institutionally administered financial aid is available to distance learners.

Services Distance learners have accessibility to academic advising, bookstore, campus computer network, e-mail services, library services.

Contact Ms. Bobbie Spurgeon-Harris, Director of Student Services, United States Sports Academy, One Academy Drive, Daphne, AL 36526-7055. Telephone: 800-223-2668 Ext. 147. Fax: 251-625-1035. E-mail: spurgeon@ussa.edu.

DEGREES AND AWARDS

BS Sports Coaching; Sports Management; Sports Studies

Certification Coaching–National Coaching certification; International Sport Diploma; Sports Coaching (International certification); Sports Coaching; Sports Management (International certification); Sports Management; Sports Medicine

MSS Sports Coaching; Sports Fitness; Sports Management; Sports Medicine; Sports Studies

DSM Sports Management–Sports Medicine emphasis; Sports Management

COURSE SUBJECT AREAS OFFERED OUTSIDE OF DEGREE PROGRAMS

Undergraduate—business, management, and marketing related; health and physical education/fitness.

Graduate—business administration, management and operations; entrepreneurial and small business operations; health and physical education/fitness; marketing.

Non-credit—business, management, and marketing related; health and physical education/fitness; parks, recreation and leisure; parks, recreation and leisure facilities management; parks, recreation, and leisure related.

THE UNIVERSITY OF ALABAMA
Tuscaloosa, Alabama
College of Continuing Studies
http://academicoutreach.ua.edu

The University of Alabama was founded in 1831. It is accredited by Southern Association of Colleges and Schools. It first offered distance learning courses in 1991. In fall 2006, there were 5,000 students enrolled in distance learning courses. Institutionally administered financial aid is available to distance learners.

Services Distance learners have accessibility to academic advising, bookstore, campus computer network, e-mail services, library services.

Contact Ms. Nina Smith, Program Manager, Adult Student Services, The University of Alabama, Division of Academic Outreach, Box 870388, Tuscaloosa, AL 35487-0388. Telephone: 205-348-0089. Fax: 205-348-0249. E-mail: nsmith@ccs.ua.edu.

DEGREES AND AWARDS

BA Interdisciplinary Studies

BS Commerce and Business Administration (General Business); Human Environmental Sciences–General Studies option; Human Environmental Sciences–Restaurant and Hospitality Management; Interdisciplinary Studies; Mechanical Engineering; Nursing; Nursing

MA Health Studies–Health Promotion; Rehabilitation Counseling

MLIS Library and Information Studies–Master of Library and Information Studies

MS Human Environmental Sciences–Food and Nutrition; Human Environmental Sciences–Interactive Technology; Nursing; Operations Management

MSAE Aerospace Engineering

MSW Social Work

COURSE SUBJECT AREAS OFFERED OUTSIDE OF DEGREE PROGRAMS

Undergraduate—accounting and related services; American literature (United States and Canadian); astronomy and astrophysics; biological and physical sciences; biology; business/commerce; business, management, and marketing related; communication and media; computer and information sciences; computer science; computer systems networking and telecommunications; creative writing; criminal justice and corrections; economics; education (specific levels and methods); engineering; English; English composition; English language and literature related; English literature (British and Commonwealth); family and consumer economics; family and consumer sciences/human sciences; family and consumer sciences/human sciences business services; family and consumer sciences/human sciences related; finance and financial management services; foods, nutrition, and related services; geography and cartography; health professions related; history; hospitality administration; human development, family studies, and related services; journalism; languages (Romance languages); liberal arts and sciences, general studies and humanities; linguistic, comparative, and related language studies; mathematics; philosophy; philosophy and religious studies related; political science and government; psychology; public relations, advertising, and applied communication related; religious studies; sales, merchandising, and related marketing operations (specialized); social sciences; social sciences related.

Graduate—aerospace, aeronautical and astronautical engineering; computer and information sciences and support services related; engineering mechanics; family and consumer economics; finance and financial management services; health professions related; library science; nursing.

See full description on page 468.

UNIVERSITY OF ALASKA ANCHORAGE, KODIAK COLLEGE
Kodiak, Alaska

University of Alaska Anchorage, Kodiak College was founded in 1968. It is accredited by Northwest Commission on Colleges and Universities. In fall 2006, there were 700 students enrolled in distance learning courses. Institutionally administered financial aid is available to distance learners.
Services Distance learners have accessibility to academic advising, bookstore, e-mail services, library services, tutoring.
Contact Jennifer Myrick, Registrar, University of Alaska Anchorage, Kodiak College, 117 Benny Benson Drive, Kodiak, AK 99615. Telephone: 907-486-1235. Fax: 907-486-1264. E-mail: jmyrick@kodiak.alaska.edu.

DEGREES AND AWARDS
Programs offered do not lead to a degree or other formal award.

COURSE SUBJECT AREAS OFFERED OUTSIDE OF DEGREE PROGRAMS

Undergraduate—accounting and computer science; allied health and medical assisting services.

UNIVERSITY OF ALASKA FAIRBANKS
Fairbanks, Alaska
Center for Distance Education and Independent Learning
http://distance.uaf.edu

University of Alaska Fairbanks was founded in 1917. It is accredited by Northwest Commission on Colleges and Universities. It first offered distance learning courses in 1970. In fall 2006, there were 3,500 students enrolled in distance learning courses. Institutionally administered financial aid is available to distance learners.
Services Distance learners have accessibility to bookstore, campus computer network, e-mail services, library services, tutoring.
Contact Tina Johnson, Communications Coordinator, University of Alaska Fairbanks, PO Box 756700, Fairbanks, AK 99775. Telephone: 800-277-8060. Fax: 907-479-3443. E-mail: distance@uaf.edu.

DEGREES AND AWARDS
Programs offered do not lead to a degree or other formal award.

COURSE SUBJECT AREAS OFFERED OUTSIDE OF DEGREE PROGRAMS

Undergraduate—accounting and related services; American literature (United States and Canadian); anthropology; applied mathematics; bilingual, multilingual, and multicultural education; biology; business administration, management and operations; business/commerce; business, management, and marketing related; communication and journalism related; computer and information sciences; computer science; computer software and media applications; criminal justice and corrections; design and applied arts; drafting/design engineering technologies; dramatic/theater arts and stagecraft; economics; education; educational administration and supervision; English; English composition; English language and literature related; ethnic, cultural minority, and gender studies; film/video and photographic arts; fine and studio art; geography and cartography; gerontology; health professions related; health psychology; history; human development, family studies, and related services; human resources management; journalism; languages (classics and classical); languages (Romance languages); legal studies (non-professional general, undergraduate); liberal arts and sciences, general studies and humanities; library science; linguistic, comparative, and related language studies; marketing; mathematics; mathematics and computer science; mathematics and statistics related; music; nutrition sciences; personality psychology; political science and government; psychology; psychometrics and quantitative psychology; public relations, advertising, and applied communication related; radio, television, and digital communication; real estate; social psychology; social sciences; social sciences related; social work; sociology; statistics; technical and business writing; technology education/industrial arts.

Graduate—computer and information sciences; counseling psychology; curriculum and instruction; educational administration and supervision; education related; education (specific levels and methods); family psychology; health psychology; human development, family studies, and related services; intercultural/multicultural and diversity studies; legal professions and studies related; psychology; psychology related.

See full description on page 470.

UNIVERSITY OF ALASKA SOUTHEAST
Juneau, Alaska
Distance Learning at UAS
http://www.uas.alaska.edu/distance

University of Alaska Southeast was founded in 1972. It is accredited by Northwest Commission on Colleges and Universities. It first offered distance learning courses in 1986. In fall 2006, there were 1,021 students enrolled in distance learning courses. Institutionally administered financial aid is available to distance learners.
Services Distance learners have accessibility to academic advising, bookstore, campus computer network, e-mail services, library services, tutoring.
Contact Deema Ferguson, Admissions Clerk, University of Alaska Southeast, 11120 Glacier Highway, Juneau, AK 99801-8625. Telephone: 907-796-6100. Fax: 907-796-6365. E-mail: infoo.uas@uas.alaska.edu.

DEGREES AND AWARDS
AA Education, general
AAS Business Administration; Computer Information and Office Systems; Early Childhood Education; Environmental Technology; Health Information Management
BBA Accounting; Business, general; Management; Marketing
BLS General Studies
Certificate of Completion Administrative Office Support; Child Development Associate; Computer Applications; Environmental Technology; Medical Office Specialist; Web Authoring; Web Foundations
Certificate Accounting Technician; Community Wellness Advocate; Computer Information and Office Systems; Early Childhood Education; Environmental Technology; Health Information Management Coding Specialist; Healthcare Privacy; Small Business Management
Endorsement Early Childhood Education; Educational Technology; Mathematics Education; Reading; Special Education
License Elementary Education
MAT Elementary Education

MBA Business Administration
MEd Early Childhood Education; Educational Technology; Reading
MPA Public Administration

THE UNIVERSITY OF ARIZONA
Tucson, Arizona
Extended University, Distance Learning Program
http://www.ceao.arizona.edu/dist/
The University of Arizona was founded in 1885. It is accredited by North Central Association of Colleges and Schools. It first offered distance learning courses in 1972. In fall 2006, there were 900 students enrolled in distance learning courses. Institutionally administered financial aid is available to distance learners.
Services Distance learners have accessibility to bookstore, campus computer network, e-mail services, library services.
Contact Colleen Reed, Program Coordinator, The University of Arizona, PO Box 210158, University Services Building, Room 301, Tucson, AZ 85721-0158. Telephone: 520-626-2079. Fax: 520-626-1102. E-mail: distance@email.arizona.edu.

DEGREES AND AWARDS
Graduate Certificate Digital Information Management; Gerontology; Optical Sciences
MEngr Engineering
MS Optical Sciences

COURSE SUBJECT AREAS OFFERED OUTSIDE OF DEGREE PROGRAMS
Undergraduate—agriculture; psychology; psychology related.
Graduate—educational psychology; education (specific levels and methods); engineering; engineering mechanics; gerontology; industrial engineering; library science; mechanical engineering; special education.

UNIVERSITY OF ARKANSAS
Fayetteville, Arkansas
Division for Continuing Education
http://www.uacted.uark.edu
University of Arkansas was founded in 1871. It is accredited by North Central Association of Colleges and Schools. It first offered distance learning courses in 1998. In fall 2006, there were 1,000 students enrolled in distance learning courses. Institutionally administered financial aid is available to distance learners.
Services Distance learners have accessibility to bookstore, e-mail services, library services.
Contact Gary McHenry, Director, University of Arkansas, Office of Credit Studies, 2 East Center Street, Fayetteville, AR 72701. Telephone: 479-575-3648. Fax: 479-575-7232. E-mail: gmchenry@uark.edu.

DEGREES AND AWARDS
BS Human Resource Development
MBA/M Ed Elementary Education/Reading; Physical Education; Special Education; Workforce Development Education
MBA/MS Agricultural, Food, and Life Sciences Non-Thesis (Food Safety emphasis)
MSN Nursing

COURSE SUBJECT AREAS OFFERED OUTSIDE OF DEGREE PROGRAMS
Undergraduate—curriculum and instruction; developmental and child psychology; dramatic/theater arts and stagecraft; English composition; geography and cartography; history; industrial and organizational psychology; journalism; languages (Germanic); languages (Romance languages); legal studies (non-professional general, undergraduate); mathematics and statistics related; microbiological sciences and immunology; philosophy and religious studies related; social work; sociology.
Graduate—agricultural and food products processing; education (specific subject areas).

UNIVERSITY OF BRIDGEPORT
Bridgeport, Connecticut
Office of Distance Learning
http://www.bridgeport.edu/pages/50.asp
University of Bridgeport was founded in 1927. It is accredited by New England Association of Schools and Colleges. It first offered distance learning courses in 1997. In fall 2006, there were 300 students enrolled in distance learning courses. Institutionally administered financial aid is available to distance learners.
Services Distance learners have accessibility to academic advising, bookstore, campus computer network, e-mail services, library services, tutoring.
Contact Claude A. Perrottet, Coordinator of Student Services, University of Bridgeport, 126 Park Avenue, Bridgeport, CT 06604. Telephone: 203-576-4853. Fax: 203-576-4537. E-mail: ubonline@bridgeport.edu.

DEGREES AND AWARDS
BS Dental Hygiene Online (degree completion program); General Studies
Certification Marriage Education (for credit); Marriage Education (non-credit)
MS Computer Science; Human Nutrition; Technology Management

COURSE SUBJECT AREAS OFFERED OUTSIDE OF DEGREE PROGRAMS
Undergraduate—area, ethnic, cultural, and gender studies related; business/commerce; business, management, and marketing related; counseling psychology; dental support services and allied professions; developmental and child psychology; economics; entrepreneurial and small business operations; foods, nutrition, and related services; history; human development, family studies, and related services; human services; liberal arts and sciences, general studies and humanities; mathematics and statistics related; music; philosophy; philosophy and religious studies related; political science and government; psychology; religious studies; sales, merchandising, and related marketing operations (general); social psychology; social sciences; sociology.
Graduate—foods, nutrition, and related services.
Non-credit—human development, family studies, and related services.

THE UNIVERSITY OF BRITISH COLUMBIA
Vancouver, British Columbia, Canada
Distance Education and Technology
http://det.ubc.ca
The University of British Columbia was founded in 1915. It is provincially chartered. It first offered distance learning courses in 1949. In fall 2006, there were 4,172 students enrolled in distance learning courses. Institutionally administered financial aid is available to distance learners.
Services Distance learners have accessibility to academic advising, bookstore, campus computer network, career placement assistance, e-mail services, library services, tutoring.
Contact Linda Haftner, Student Advisor, The University of British Columbia, Enrolment Services, 1874 East Mall, Room 2016, Brock Hall, Vancouver, BC V6T 1Z1, Canada. Telephone: 604-822-3768. Fax: 604-822-5945. E-mail: linda.haftner@ubc.ca.

DEGREES AND AWARDS
Graduate Certificate Rehabilitation Sciences; Technology-Based Distributed Learning; Technology-Based Learning for Schools
MA Educational Technology–Master of Educational Technology

COURSE SUBJECT AREAS OFFERED OUTSIDE OF DEGREE PROGRAMS
Undergraduate—agricultural business and management; agriculture; animal sciences; area studies; civil engineering; computer and information sciences; dental support services and allied professions; education; educational/instructional media design; English; environmental control technologies; ethnic, cultural minority, and gender studies; film/video and photographic arts; foods, nutrition, and related services; forestry; geography and cartography; history; landscape architecture; languages (Romance languages); library science related; medieval and Renaissance studies; metallurgical engineering; music; nursing; phi-

losophy; political science and government; psychology; rehabilitation and therapeutic professions; social work; soil sciences.

Graduate—education; educational/instructional media design; rehabilitation and therapeutic professions.

Non-credit—English composition.

UNIVERSITY OF CALIFORNIA, DAVIS
Davis, California
UC Davis Extension
http://www.extension.ucdavis.edu/distancelearning
University of California, Davis was founded in 1905. It is accredited by Western Association of Schools and Colleges. It first offered distance learning courses in 1987. In fall 2006, there were 573 students enrolled in distance learning courses. Institutionally administered financial aid is available to distance learners.
Services Distance learners have accessibility to academic advising, bookstore, library services.
Contact Bill Heekin, Director of Student Services, University of California, Davis, 1333 Research Park Drive, Davis, CA 95616. Telephone: 530-757-8777. Fax: 530-757-8696. E-mail: bheekin@unexmail.ucdavis.edu.

DEGREES AND AWARDS
Programs offered do not lead to a degree or other formal award.

COURSE SUBJECT AREAS OFFERED OUTSIDE OF DEGREE PROGRAMS
Undergraduate—allied health and medical assisting services; computer and information sciences; computer programming; computer systems analysis; education; food science and technology; health professions related; languages (Romance languages); public health.

Non-credit—allied health and medical assisting services; computer engineering technologies; computer/information technology administration and management; computer programming; computer science.

UNIVERSITY OF CALIFORNIA, LOS ANGELES
Los Angeles, California
University Extension
http://www.uclaextension.edu
University of California, Los Angeles was founded in 1919. It is accredited by Western Association of Schools and Colleges. It first offered distance learning courses in 1996. In fall 2006, there were 2,500 students enrolled in distance learning courses. Institutionally administered financial aid is available to distance learners.
Services Distance learners have accessibility to academic advising, bookstore, campus computer network, e-mail services, library services, tutoring.
Contact Program Representative, University of California, Los Angeles, 10995 LeConte, Los Angeles, CA 90024. Telephone: 310-825-2648. Fax: 310-267-4793. E-mail: dstlrng@unex.ucla.edu.

DEGREES AND AWARDS
Programs offered do not lead to a degree or other formal award.

COURSE SUBJECT AREAS OFFERED OUTSIDE OF DEGREE PROGRAMS
Graduate—archeology; business administration, management and operations; business/commerce; design and applied arts; economics; film/video and photographic arts; health and physical education/fitness; languages (foreign languages related); liberal arts and sciences, general studies and humanities; mathematics; philosophy and religious studies related; psychology; social sciences; technical and business writing; visual and performing arts.

UNIVERSITY OF CALIFORNIA, RIVERSIDE
Riverside, California
University Extension
http://www.unex.ucr.edu
University of California, Riverside was founded in 1954. It is accredited by Western Association of Schools and Colleges. It first offered distance learning courses in 1994. In fall 2006, there were 150 students enrolled in distance learning courses. Institutionally administered financial aid is available to distance learners.
Services Distance learners have accessibility to academic advising, bookstore, library services.
Contact Jon Kindschy, Director of Sciences, University of California, Riverside, Riverside, CA 92507. Telephone: 951-827-5804 Ext. 1622. E-mail: sciences@ucx.ucr.edu.

DEGREES AND AWARDS
Programs offered do not lead to a degree or other formal award.

COURSE SUBJECT AREAS OFFERED OUTSIDE OF DEGREE PROGRAMS
Non-credit—agriculture and agriculture operations related; applied horticulture/horticultural business services; atmospheric sciences and meteorology; computer software and media applications; education related; geography and cartography; nursing; plant sciences.

UNIVERSITY OF CENTRAL ARKANSAS
Conway, Arkansas
Division of Continuing Education
http://www.uca.edu/aoep
University of Central Arkansas was founded in 1907. It is accredited by North Central Association of Colleges and Schools. It first offered distance learning courses in 1992. In fall 2006, there were 1,087 students enrolled in distance learning courses. Institutionally administered financial aid is available to distance learners.
Services Distance learners have accessibility to bookstore, career placement assistance, e-mail services, library services.
Contact Sondra Pugh, Extended Study Secretary, University of Central Arkansas, 201 Donaghey Avenue, Brewer-Hegeman Conference Center, Suite 102, Conway, AR 72035. Telephone: 501-450-3118. Fax: 501-450-5277. E-mail: sondrap@uca.edu.

DEGREES AND AWARDS
Programs offered do not lead to a degree or other formal award.

COURSE SUBJECT AREAS OFFERED OUTSIDE OF DEGREE PROGRAMS
Undergraduate—accounting and related services; American literature (United States and Canadian); creative writing; educational psychology; English composition; history; languages (Germanic); mathematics; political science and government; psychology; social psychology; sociology.

Graduate—business, management, and marketing related; computer and information sciences and support services related; curriculum and instruction; educational administration and supervision; education related; geography and cartography; health professions related; library science related; nursing; rehabilitation and therapeutic professions.
Non-credit—business administration, management and operations; computer and information sciences; English; insurance; journalism.

UNIVERSITY OF CENTRAL FLORIDA
Orlando, Florida
Center for Distributed Learning
http://online.ucf.edu
University of Central Florida was founded in 1963. It is accredited by Southern Association of Colleges and Schools. It first offered distance learning courses in 1996. In fall 2006, there were 9,431 students enrolled in distance learning courses. Institutionally administered financial aid is available to distance learners.
Services Distance learners have accessibility to academic advising, bookstore, campus computer network, e-mail services, library services.

Contact Ms. Lori Allison, Coordinator, University of Central Florida, 3100 Technology Parkway, Suite 234, Orlando, FL 32826-3271. Telephone: 407-823-4910. Fax: 407-207-4911. E-mail: lallison@mail.ucf.edu.

DEGREES AND AWARDS

BA Interdisciplinary Studies
BS Health Services Administration; Information Systems Technology; Interdisciplinary Studies; Radiologic Sciences; Technical Education and Industry Training
BSET Engineering Technology
BSN Nursing
Graduate Certificate Community College Education; Educational Media; Gifted Education; Initial Teacher Professional Preparation; Instructional Design for Simulations; Instructional/Educational Technology; Nonprofit Management; Nursing Education; Pre-Kindergarten Handicapped Endorsement; Professional Writing; Special Education; e-Learning Professional Development
MA Career and Technical Education; Exceptional Education; Instructional Technology/Media E-Learning or Instructional Systems; Instructional Technology/Media–Educational Technology track
MEd Instructional Technology/Media–Educational Media track
MM Nonprofit Management
MS Criminal Justice; Forensic Science–Forensic Analysis track; Forensic Science–Forensic Biochemistry track
MSN Nursing–Leadership and Management track; Nursing–Nurse Educator track

COURSE SUBJECT AREAS OFFERED OUTSIDE OF DEGREE PROGRAMS

Undergraduate—computer and information sciences and support services related; education related; health and medical administrative services; legal professions and studies related; nursing; philosophy and religious studies related; sociology; statistics.
Graduate—chemistry; educational/instructional media design; education related; health and medical administrative services; nursing; public administration; public administration and social service professions related; technical and business writing.

UNIVERSITY OF CENTRAL MISSOURI
Warrensburg, Missouri
Department of Nursing
http://www.ucmo.edu/extcamp

University of Central Missouri was founded in 1871. It is accredited by North Central Association of Colleges and Schools. It first offered distance learning courses in 1993. In fall 2006, there were 2,180 students enrolled in distance learning courses. Institutionally administered financial aid is available to distance learners.

Services Distance learners have accessibility to academic advising, bookstore, campus computer network, career placement assistance, e-mail services, library services, tutoring.

Contact Ms. Barbara Carder, Assistant Director for Distance Learning, University of Central Missouri, Office of Extended Campus, 410 Humphreys, Warrensburg, MO 64093. Telephone: 877-729-8266 Ext. 21. Fax: 660-543-8333. E-mail: bcarder@ucmo.edu.

DEGREES AND AWARDS

BSN Nursing
MSN Nursing–Rural Family Nursing

COURSE SUBJECT AREAS OFFERED OUTSIDE OF DEGREE PROGRAMS

Undergraduate—computer science; criminal justice and corrections; curriculum and instruction; educational assessment, evaluation, and research; educational psychology; education (specific subject areas); foods, nutrition, and related services; library science; technology education/industrial arts.
Graduate—criminal justice and corrections; curriculum and instruction; educational assessment, evaluation, and research; educational psychology; library science; nursing; special education; technology education/industrial arts.

Non-credit—accounting and related services; computer programming; computer software and media applications; computer systems networking and telecommunications; entrepreneurial and small business operations.

See full description on page 472.

UNIVERSITY OF CENTRAL MISSOURI
Warrensburg, Missouri
Department of Criminal Justice
http://www.ucmo.edu/extcamp

University of Central Missouri was founded in 1871. It is accredited by North Central Association of Colleges and Schools. It first offered distance learning courses in 1993. In fall 2006, there were 2,180 students enrolled in distance learning courses. Institutionally administered financial aid is available to distance learners.

Services Distance learners have accessibility to academic advising, bookstore, campus computer network, career placement assistance, e-mail services, library services, tutoring.

Contact Ms. Barbara Carder, Assistant Director for Distance Learning, University of Central Missouri, Office of Extended Campus, 410 Humphreys, Warrensburg, MO 64093. Telephone: 877-729-8266 Ext. 21. Fax: 660-543-8480. E-mail: bcarder@ucmo.edu.

DEGREES AND AWARDS

MS Criminal Justice

COURSE SUBJECT AREAS OFFERED OUTSIDE OF DEGREE PROGRAMS

Undergraduate—computer science; criminal justice and corrections; curriculum and instruction; educational assessment, evaluation, and research; educational psychology; education (specific subject areas); foods, nutrition, and related services; library science; technology education/industrial arts.
Graduate—criminal justice and corrections; curriculum and instruction; educational assessment, evaluation, and research; educational psychology; library science; nursing; special education; technology education/industrial arts.
Non-credit—accounting and related services; computer programming; computer software and media applications; computer systems networking and telecommunications; entrepreneurial and small business operations.

See full description on page 474.

UNIVERSITY OF CENTRAL MISSOURI
Warrensburg, Missouri
School of Technology
http://www.ucmo.edu/extcamp

University of Central Missouri was founded in 1871. It is accredited by North Central Association of Colleges and Schools. It first offered distance learning courses in 1993. In fall 2006, there were 2,180 students enrolled in distance learning courses. Institutionally administered financial aid is available to distance learners.

Services Distance learners have accessibility to academic advising, bookstore, campus computer network, career placement assistance, e-mail services, library services, tutoring.

Contact Ms. Barbara Carder, Assistant Director for Distance Learning, University of Central Missouri, Office of Extended Campus, 410 Humphreys, Warrensburg, MO 64093. Telephone: 877-729-8266 Ext. 21. Fax: 660-543-8333. E-mail: bcarder@ucmo.edu.

DEGREES AND AWARDS

MS Industrial Management

COURSE SUBJECT AREAS OFFERED OUTSIDE OF DEGREE PROGRAMS

Undergraduate—computer science; criminal justice and corrections; curriculum and instruction; educational assessment, evaluation, and research; educational psychology; education (specific subject areas); foods, nutrition, and related services; library science; technology education/industrial arts.

Graduate—criminal justice and corrections; curriculum and instruction; educational assessment, evaluation, and research; educational psychology; library science; nursing; special education; technology education/industrial arts.

Non-credit—accounting and related services; computer programming; computer software and media applications; computer systems networking and telecommunications; entrepreneurial and small business operations.

See full description on page 476.

UNIVERSITY OF CENTRAL OKLAHOMA
Edmond, Oklahoma
Distance Learning Technologies
http://www.bronze.ucok.edu/corrstudies

University of Central Oklahoma was founded in 1890. It is accredited by North Central Association of Colleges and Schools. It first offered distance learning courses in 1996. In fall 2006, there were 2,000 students enrolled in distance learning courses. Institutionally administered financial aid is available to distance learners.

Services Distance learners have accessibility to academic advising, bookstore, career placement assistance, e-mail services, library services.

Contact Sandra L. Burkey, Director, University of Central Oklahoma, 100 North University, Box 170, Edmond, OK 73034. Telephone: 405-974-2529. E-mail: sburkey@ucok.edu.

DEGREES AND AWARDS
Programs offered do not lead to a degree or other formal award.

COURSE SUBJECT AREAS OFFERED OUTSIDE OF DEGREE PROGRAMS
Undergraduate—biological and physical sciences; business/commerce; communication and journalism related; comparative psychology; computer and information sciences; computer programming; criminology; educational administration and supervision; education related; English; English as a second language; English composition; family and consumer economics; family and consumer sciences/human sciences; fine and studio art; funeral service and mortuary science; geography and cartography; history; languages (Romance languages); legal studies (non-professional general, undergraduate); library science; library science related; mathematics; music; nursing; psychology; psychology related; sociology; special education; speech and rhetoric; technical and business writing.
Graduate—educational administration and supervision; education related; English; English as a second language; fine and studio art; funeral service and mortuary science; library science; sociology.
Non-credit—computer and information sciences.

UNIVERSITY OF CINCINNATI
Cincinnati, Ohio
Distance Learning Programs
http://www.uc.edu/distance

University of Cincinnati was founded in 1819. It is accredited by North Central Association of Colleges and Schools. It first offered distance learning courses in 1984. In fall 2006, there were 2,950 students enrolled in distance learning courses. Institutionally administered financial aid is available to distance learners.

Services Distance learners have accessibility to academic advising, bookstore, campus computer network, e-mail services, library services, tutoring.

Contact Dr. Melody Clark, Academic Director, Distance Learning, University of Cincinnati, PO Box 210635, Cincinnati, OH 45221-0635. Telephone: 513-556-9154. Fax: 513-556-6050. E-mail: melody.clark@uc.edu.

DEGREES AND AWARDS
AAS Early Childhood Education; Fire Science Technology
BEd Early Childhood Education

BS Addiction Studies; Clinical Laboratory Science; Fire Science Technology; Health Information Management
Certificate Medical/Biller Coder; Software Productivity
MEd Curriculum and Instruction (for Health Care Professionals); Educational Leadership
MS Criminal Justice; Phramaceutical Sciences, Cosmetic Science emphasis
MSN Nurse Midwifery; Women's Health Nurse Practitioner
PharmD Pharmacy

COURSE SUBJECT AREAS OFFERED OUTSIDE OF DEGREE PROGRAMS
Undergraduate—accounting and related services; anthropology; business/commerce; communication disorders sciences and services; computer software and media applications; criminal justice and corrections; education; engineering related; English; geography and cartography; geological and earth sciences/geosciences; history; mathematics; philosophy; philosophy and religious studies related; psychology.
Graduate—communication disorders sciences and services; engineering related.
Non-credit—accounting and computer science; accounting and related services; business/commerce; business operations support and assistant services; computer and information sciences; computer programming; publishing; technical and business writing.

UNIVERSITY OF CINCINNATI RAYMOND WALTERS COLLEGE
Cincinnati, Ohio
Outreach and Continuing Education
http://www.rwc.uc.edu/maps/news/courses.htm

University of Cincinnati Raymond Walters College was founded in 1967. It is accredited by North Central Association of Colleges and Schools. It first offered distance learning courses in 1995. In fall 2006, there were 350 students enrolled in distance learning courses. Institutionally administered financial aid is available to distance learners.

Services Distance learners have accessibility to academic advising, bookstore, campus computer network, career placement assistance, e-mail services, library services, tutoring.

Contact Janice Ooten, Program Manager, University of Cincinnati Raymond Walters College, 9555 Plainfield Road, Cincinnati, OH 45236-1096. Telephone: 513-936-1533. Fax: 513-745-8315. E-mail: janice.ooten@uc.edu.

DEGREES AND AWARDS
Programs offered do not lead to a degree or other formal award.

COURSE SUBJECT AREAS OFFERED OUTSIDE OF DEGREE PROGRAMS
Undergraduate—biology; business administration, management and operations; business/commerce; computer/information technology administration and management; computer software and media applications; English composition; film/video and photographic arts; foods, nutrition, and related services; health professions related; library science; physics; psychology; sociology.

UNIVERSITY OF COLORADO AT BOULDER
Boulder, Colorado
Center for Advanced Engineering and Technology Education (CAETE)
http://caete.colorado.edu

University of Colorado at Boulder was founded in 1876. It is accredited by North Central Association of Colleges and Schools. It first offered distance learning courses in 1983. In fall 2006, there were 400 students enrolled in distance learning courses. Institutionally administered financial aid is available to distance learners.

Services Distance learners have accessibility to academic advising, bookstore, campus computer network, career placement assistance, e-mail services, library services.

Contact Robin M.W. McClanahan, Marketing Manager, University of Colorado at Boulder, CAETE, 435 UCB, Boulder, CO 80309. Telephone: 303-492-0212. Fax: 303-492-5987. E-mail: caete@colorado.edu.

DEGREES AND AWARDS

Graduate Certificate Engineering Management; Managing Applied Research in Technology; Performance Excellence in Technology Management; Power Electronics; Project Management; Quality Systems for Product and Process Engineering; Research and Development; Software Engineering

ME Aerospace Engineering; Computer Science; Electrical and Computer Engineering; Engineering Management; Telecommunications

MS Aerospace Engineering; Electrical and Computer Engineering; Telecommunications

COURSE SUBJECT AREAS OFFERED OUTSIDE OF DEGREE PROGRAMS

Graduate—aerospace, aeronautical and astronautical engineering; biomedical/medical engineering; civil engineering; computer engineering; computer science; computer systems networking and telecommunications; electrical and electronic engineering technologies; engineering/industrial management; environmental/environmental health engineering; mechanical engineering.

Non-credit—aerospace, aeronautical and astronautical engineering; biomedical/medical engineering; civil engineering; computer engineering; computer science; computer systems networking and telecommunications; electrical and electronic engineering technologies; engineering/industrial management; environmental/environmental health engineering; mechanical engineering.

UNIVERSITY OF COLORADO AT COLORADO SPRINGS

Colorado Springs, Colorado
http://www.uccs.edu/~online/
University of Colorado at Colorado Springs was founded in 1965. It is accredited by North Central Association of Colleges and Schools. It first offered distance learning courses in 1996. In fall 2006, there were 610 students enrolled in distance learning courses. Institutionally administered financial aid is available to distance learners.
Services Distance learners have accessibility to academic advising, campus computer network, e-mail services, library services.
Contact Dana Rocha, Director of Extended Studies, University of Colorado at Colorado Springs, 1420 Austin Bluffs Parkway, MH 316, ADM 10, Colorado Springs, CO 80933-7150. Telephone: 719-262-4662. E-mail: drocha@uccs.edu.

DEGREES AND AWARDS

MA Curriculum and Instruction–Educational Leadership; English as a Second Language Education program; Online Principal Licensure program and Masters Degree in Curriculum and Instruction

MBA Business Administration

ME Engineering Management; Space Studies; Systems Engineering

MSN Nurse Practitioner and Clinical Specialist

COURSE SUBJECT AREAS OFFERED OUTSIDE OF DEGREE PROGRAMS

Undergraduate—American literature (United States and Canadian); area, ethnic, cultural, and gender studies related; biological and biomedical sciences related; chemistry; communication and media; economics; English composition; geography and cartography; gerontology; health professions related; history; languages (Middle/Near Eastern and Semitic); mathematics; mechanical engineering; military studies; nursing; psychology; sociology.

Graduate—aerospace, aeronautical and astronautical engineering; business/commerce; criminal justice and corrections; educational administration and supervision; health professions related; mechanical engineering; nursing; public administration.

UNIVERSITY OF COLORADO AT DENVER AND HEALTH SCIENCES CENTER

Denver, Colorado
CU Online
http://cuonline.edu/petersons
University of Colorado at Denver and Health Sciences Center was founded in 1912. It is accredited by North Central Association of Colleges and Schools. It first offered distance learning courses in 1996. In fall 2006, there were 2,510 students enrolled in distance learning courses. Institutionally administered financial aid is available to distance learners.
Services Distance learners have accessibility to academic advising, bookstore, career placement assistance, e-mail services, library services, tutoring.
Contact Kate Miller, Operations Manager, Student Services Support Coordinator, University of Colorado at Denver and Health Sciences Center, Campus Box 198, PO Box 173364, Denver, CO 80217-3364. Telephone: 303-556-6505. Fax: 303-556-6530. E-mail: inquiry@cuonline.edu.

DEGREES AND AWARDS

BA English–Writing; Sociology

Certificate Designing and Implementing Web-based Learning Environments

Certification Early Literacy Certificate program

License Early Childhood Special Education, Generalist; Special Education Generalist licensure program

MA Early Childhood Education; Information and Learning Technologies, School Library; eLearning Design and Implementation

MBA Business Administration

MEngr Geographic Information Systems (GIS)

MPA Public Administration

MS Finance; Information Systems

COURSE SUBJECT AREAS OFFERED OUTSIDE OF DEGREE PROGRAMS

Undergraduate—accounting and related services; American literature (United States and Canadian); anthropology; biochemistry, biophysics and molecular biology; biology; cell biology and anatomical sciences; civil engineering; communication and media; computer programming; creative writing; dramatic/theater arts and stagecraft; economics; electrical, electronics and communications engineering; engineering; engineering science; English; English composition; ethnic, cultural minority, and gender studies; fine and studio art; geography and cartography; geological and earth sciences/geosciences; history; industrial and organizational psychology; languages (classics and classical); liberal arts and sciences, general studies and humanities; linguistic, comparative, and related language studies; mathematics and statistics related; mechanical engineering; music; philosophy and religious studies related; physics; political science and government; psychology; social psychology; sociology; statistics; technical and business writing.

Graduate—accounting and related services; architecture; business administration, management and operations; business/commerce; business/corporate communications; business, management, and marketing related; business/managerial economics; education; education related; electrical, electronics and communications engineering; engineering; engineering design; engineering/industrial management; engineering related; engineering technologies related; history; management information systems; management sciences and quantitative methods; marketing; political science and government; public administration; public administration and social service professions related; public policy analysis; sales, merchandising, and related marketing operations (general); sales, merchandising, and related marketing operations (specialized).

See full description on page 478.

UNIVERSITY OF CONNECTICUT
Storrs, Connecticut
Center for Continuing Studies
http://continuingstudies.uconn.edu/onlinecourses
University of Connecticut was founded in 1881. It is accredited by New England Association of Schools and Colleges. It first offered distance learning courses in 2001. In fall 2006, there were 500 students enrolled in distance learning courses. Institutionally administered financial aid is available to distance learners.

Services Distance learners have accessibility to academic advising, bookstore, campus computer network, career placement assistance, e-mail services, library services, tutoring.

Contact Dr. Judy Buffolino, Director of Distance Education, University of Connecticut, Center for Continuing Studies, Distance Education Office, One Bishop Circle, Unit 4056, Storrs, CT 06269-4056. Telephone: 860-486-1080. Fax: 860-486-0756. E-mail: judy.buffolino@uconn.edu.

DEGREES AND AWARDS
BGS Law and Society; Occupational Safety and Health focus; Web Technology focus
MPS Homeland Security Leadership; Human Resource Management; Humanitarian Services Administration

COURSE SUBJECT AREAS OFFERED OUTSIDE OF DEGREE PROGRAMS
Undergraduate—area, ethnic, cultural, and gender studies related; behavioral sciences; computer and information sciences and support services related; computer/information technology administration and management; computer programming; computer software and media applications; criminal justice and corrections; ethnic, cultural minority, and gender studies; health professions related; health services/allied health/health sciences; liberal arts and sciences, general studies and humanities; multi-/interdisciplinary studies related; sociology.
Graduate—criminology; health professions related; human resources management; human services; security and protective services related.
Non-credit—health professions related.

See full description on page 480.

UNIVERSITY OF DALLAS
Irving, Texas
Center for Distance Education
http://www.thedallasmba.com
University of Dallas was founded in 1955. It is accredited by American Academy for Liberal Education. It first offered distance learning courses in 1970. In fall 2006, there were 800 students enrolled in distance learning courses. Institutionally administered financial aid is available to distance learners.

Services Distance learners have accessibility to academic advising, bookstore, career placement assistance, library services, tutoring.

Contact Ms. Vanessa Cox, Associate Director of Online Learning, University of Dallas, 1845 East Northgate Drive, Irving, TX 75062-4736. Telephone: 877-408-2335. Fax: 972-721-5265. E-mail: vcox@gsm.udallas.edu.

DEGREES AND AWARDS
Graduate Certificate Accounting; CFP Certified Financial Planning; Corporate Finance; Global Business; Health Services Management; Information Assurance; Information Technology; Interdisciplinary (Custom curriculum); Marketing Management; Not-for-Profit; Project Management; Sports and Entertainment Management; Supply Chain Management/Market Logistics; Telecommunications Management
MBA Accounting; CFP Certified Financial Planning; Corporate Finance; Global Business; Health Services Management; Information Assurance; Information Technology; Interdisciplinary (Custom curriculum); Marketing Management; Not-for-Profit; Project Management; Sports and Entertainment Management; Supply Chain Management/Market Logistics; Telecommunications Management
MM Accounting; CFP Certified Financial Planning; Corporate Finance; Global Business; Health Services Management; Information Assurance;

Information Technology; Interdisciplinary (Custom curriculum); Marketing Management; Not-for-Profit; Project Management; Sports and Entertainment Management; Supply Chain Management/Market Logistics; Telecommunications Management

COURSE SUBJECT AREAS OFFERED OUTSIDE OF DEGREE PROGRAMS
Graduate—accounting and related services; business administration, management and operations; computer and information sciences; computer and information sciences and support services related; computer systems analysis; computer systems networking and telecommunications; finance and financial management services; health and medical administrative services; international business; management information systems; marketing; sales, merchandising, and related marketing operations (general); sales, merchandising, and related marketing operations (specialized).

See full description on page 482.

UNIVERSITY OF DELAWARE
Newark, Delaware
Division of Professional and Continuing Studies
http://www.continuingstudies.udel.edu/udonline/
University of Delaware was founded in 1743. It is accredited by Middle States Association of Colleges and Schools. It first offered distance learning courses in 1988. In fall 2006, there were 3,000 students enrolled in distance learning courses. Institutionally administered financial aid is available to distance learners.

Services Distance learners have accessibility to academic advising, bookstore, campus computer network, career placement assistance, e-mail services, library services, tutoring.

Contact Mrs. Melanie Rehberg, Program Manager, University of Delaware, 210 Clayton Hall, Newark, DE 19716. Telephone: 302-831-1079. Fax: 302-831-3292. E-mail: melanier@udel.edu.

DEGREES AND AWARDS
AA Associate in Arts Online
BS Hotel, Restaurant, and Institutional Management; Nursing
MME Mechanical Engineering
MS Health Services Administration
MSEE Electrical Engineering
MSN Nursing–Health Services Administration; Nursing–RN to MSN

COURSE SUBJECT AREAS OFFERED OUTSIDE OF DEGREE PROGRAMS
Undergraduate—accounting and related services; animal sciences; apparel and textiles; biology; chemical engineering; chemistry; civil engineering; communication and media; criminal justice and corrections; economics; education; engineering science; English; English composition; English language and literature related; foods, nutrition, and related services; history; hospitality administration; human development, family studies, and related services; marketing; mathematics and statistics related; mechanical engineering; music; nursing; philosophy and religious studies related; political science and government; sociology; technical and business writing; urban studies/affairs.

Graduate—chemical engineering; civil engineering; education; engineering mechanics; foods, nutrition, and related services; health professions related; mechanical engineering; nursing; political science and government; public administration.

Non-credit—business, management, and marketing related; foods, nutrition, and related services; hospitality administration; mechanical engineering; nursing.

UNIVERSITY OF DENVER
Denver, Colorado
University College
http://www.universitycollege.du.edu

University of Denver was founded in 1864. It is accredited by North Central Association of Colleges and Schools. It first offered distance learning courses in 1996. In fall 2006, there were 375 students enrolled in distance learning courses. Institutionally administered financial aid is available to distance learners.

Services Distance learners have accessibility to academic advising, bookstore, campus computer network, career placement assistance, e-mail services, library services.

Contact Mr. Mark Guthrie, Director of Enrollment and Advising, University of Denver, 2211 South Josephine, Denver, CO 80208. Telephone: 303-871-7582. Fax: 303-871-3070. E-mail: maguthri@du.edu.

DEGREES AND AWARDS

BA Bachelor of Arts Completion Program

Certificate Alternative Dispute Resolution–Certificate of Advanced Study; Arts and Literature–Certificate of Advanced Study; Broadband–Certificate of Advanced Study; Computer Information Systems–Certificate of Advanced Study; Database Administration–Certificate of Advanced Study; Distributed Object-Oriented Analysis and Design–Certificate of Advanced Study; Environmental Information Management–Certificate of Advanced Study; Environmental Management–Certificate of Advanced Study; Environmental Policy–Certificate of Advanced Study; Environmental Project Management–Certificate of Advanced Study; Environmental, Health, and Safety Management–Certificate of Advanced Study; Geographic Information Systems–Certificate of Advanced Study; Human Resource Administration–Certificate of Advanced Study; Information Security–Certificate of Advanced Study; Information Systems Security–Certificate of Advanced Study; Leadership–Certificate of Advanced Study; Modern Languages–Certificate of Advanced Study; Natural Resource Management–Certificate of Advanced Study; Organizational Security–Certificate of Advanced Study; Project Management–Certificate of Advanced Study; Public Relations and Marketing Communications–Certificate of Advanced Study; Technology Management–Certificate of Advanced Study; Telecommunications Management and Policy–Certificate of Advanced Study; Telecommunications Networks–Certificate of Advanced Study; Telecommunications Technology–Certificate of Advanced Study; Training and Development–Certificate of Advanced Study; Web Design and Development Technologies–Certificate of Advanced Study

MLS Liberal Studies–Master of Liberal Studies

MPS Applied Communication–Master of Professional Studies in Applied Communication; Human Resource Administration–Master of Professional Studies in Human Resource Administration; Organizational Leadership–Master of Professional Studies in Organizational Leadership

MS Computer Information Systems–Master of Applied Science in Computer Information Systems; Environmental Policy and Management–Master of Applied Science in Environmental Policy and Management; Knowledge and Information Technologies–Master of Applied Science in Knowledge and Information Technologies; Security Management–Master of Applied Science in Security Management; Technology Management–Master of Applied Science in Technology Management; Telecommunications–Master of Applied Science in Telecommunications

COURSE SUBJECT AREAS OFFERED OUTSIDE OF DEGREE PROGRAMS

Undergraduate—business/corporate communications; public policy analysis; science, technology and society; social sciences related.

Graduate—business administration, management and operations; communication and media; computer and information sciences; computer and information sciences and support services related; computer/information technology administration and management; computer systems networking and telecommunications; creative writing; liberal arts and sciences, general studies and humanities; linguistic, comparative, and related language studies; natural resources management and policy.

See full description on page 484.

THE UNIVERSITY OF FINDLAY
Findlay, Ohio
Global Campus
http://ufonline.findlay.edu

The University of Findlay was founded in 1882. It is accredited by North Central Association of Colleges and Schools. It first offered distance learning courses in 1998. In fall 2006, there were 1,045 students enrolled in distance learning courses. Institutionally administered financial aid is available to distance learners.

Services Distance learners have accessibility to academic advising, bookstore, campus computer network, career placement assistance, e-mail services, library services, tutoring.

Contact Mrs. Heather L. Riffle, Director, Graduate and Special Programs, The University of Findlay, 1000 North Main Street, Findlay, OH 45840. Telephone: 419-434-4600. Fax: 419-434-5517. E-mail: riffle@findlay.edu.

DEGREES AND AWARDS

BS Business Management; Criminal Justice Administration; Environmental, Safety, and Health Management

MAE Education–Human Resource Development Strand

MBA Business Administration

MS Environmental, Safety, and Health Management

COURSE SUBJECT AREAS OFFERED OUTSIDE OF DEGREE PROGRAMS

Undergraduate—accounting and related services; biblical studies; business administration, management and operations; business/commerce; business/managerial economics; chemistry; communication and journalism related; computer science; criminal justice and corrections; criminology; economics; ethnic, cultural minority, and gender studies; fine and studio art; history; human resources management; international business; marketing; mathematics; philosophy and religious studies related; religious studies; social sciences; sociology; statistics; visual and performing arts.

Graduate—accounting and related services; business administration, management and operations; business/corporate communications; business/managerial economics; educational assessment, evaluation, and research; educational/instructional media design; environmental control technologies; human resources management; marketing; public administration; sales, merchandising, and related marketing operations (general).

Non-credit—business, management, and marketing related; business/managerial economics; management information systems; management sciences and quantitative methods.

UNIVERSITY OF FLORIDA
Gainesville, Florida
UF EDGE
http://www.ufl.edu/

University of Florida was founded in 1853. It is accredited by Southern Association of Colleges and Schools. It first offered distance learning courses in 1964. In fall 2006, there were 275 students enrolled in distance learning courses. Institutionally administered financial aid is available to distance learners.

Services Distance learners have accessibility to academic advising, bookstore, campus computer network, career placement assistance, e-mail services, library services, tutoring.

Contact Lisa Boles, Program Assistant, University of Florida, College of Engineering, E-117 CSE, PO Box 116100, Gainesville, FL 32611-6100. Telephone: 352-392-1678. Fax: 352-392-1724. E-mail: lbole@eng.ufl.edu.

DEGREES AND AWARDS

MS Civil Engineering; Computer Engineering (Bioinformatics track); Computer Engineering (General track); Computer Engineering–Bioinformatics; Electrical and Computer Engineering; Environmental Engineering–Water Resources Planning and Management track; Environmental Engineering–Water, Wastewater, and Stormwater Engineering; Materials Science and Engineering; Mechanical and Aerospace Engineering-Dynamics and Control; Mechanical and Aerospace Engineering-

Fundamentals of Thermal Fluids Transport track; Mechanical and Aerospace Engineering-Solid Mechanics and Design track

COURSE SUBJECT AREAS OFFERED OUTSIDE OF DEGREE PROGRAMS

Graduate—environmental/environmental health engineering; materials science.

See full description on page 486.

UNIVERSITY OF GREAT FALLS
Great Falls, Montana
Center for Distance Learning
http://www.ugf.edu/distancelearning/

University of Great Falls was founded in 1932. It is accredited by Northwest Commission on Colleges and Universities. It first offered distance learning courses in 1979. In fall 2006, there were 81 students enrolled in distance learning courses. Institutionally administered financial aid is available to distance learners.

Services Distance learners have accessibility to academic advising, bookstore, campus computer network, career placement assistance, e-mail services, library services, tutoring.

Contact Jim Gretch, Director of Distance Learning, University of Great Falls, 1301 20th Street South, Great Falls, MT 59405. Telephone: 406-791-5320. Fax: 406-791-5394. E-mail: jgretch@ugf.edu.

DEGREES AND AWARDS

BA Criminal Justice; Paralegal Studies; Psychology
MA Criminal Justice Administration; Secondary Teaching
MAM Organizational Management

COURSE SUBJECT AREAS OFFERED OUTSIDE OF DEGREE PROGRAMS

Undergraduate—American literature (United States and Canadian); biological and physical sciences; computer and information sciences; computer science; computer software and media applications; counseling psychology; criminal justice and corrections; developmental and child psychology; English; fine and studio art; health and physical education/fitness; history; human services; legal studies (non-professional general, undergraduate); liberal arts and sciences, general studies and humanities; mathematics; mathematics and statistics related; natural sciences; philosophy and religious studies related; psychology; social sciences; sociology; technical and business writing; theological and ministerial studies.
Graduate—counseling psychology; criminal justice and corrections; education (specific levels and methods); human services; psychology.

UNIVERSITY OF HAWAII–WEST OAHU
Pearl City, Hawaii
http://www.uhwo.hawaii.edu/distanceed

University of Hawaii–West Oahu was founded in 1976. It is accredited by Western Association of Schools and Colleges. It first offered distance learning courses in 1981. In fall 2006, there were 200 students enrolled in distance learning courses. Institutionally administered financial aid is available to distance learners.

Services Distance learners have accessibility to academic advising, bookstore, campus computer network, career placement assistance, e-mail services, library services, tutoring.

Contact Robyn Oshiro, Student Services Specialist, University of Hawaii–West Oahu, 96-129 Ala Ike, Student Services Office, Pearl City, HI 96782. Telephone: 808-454-4700. Fax: 808-453-6075. E-mail: robyno@hawaii.edu.

DEGREES AND AWARDS

BA Business Administration; Social Sciences–Applied track; Social Sciences
Certificate Disaster Preparedness and Emergency Management; Health Care Administration; Substance Abuse and Addictions Studies

COURSE SUBJECT AREAS OFFERED OUTSIDE OF DEGREE PROGRAMS

Undergraduate—accounting and related services; anthropology; business administration, management and operations; business, management, and marketing related; clinical psychology; counseling psychology; criminal justice and corrections; criminology; developmental and child psychology; economics; history; human resources management; philosophy; political science and government; psychology; psychology related; public administration; public administration and social service professions related; social sciences; social sciences related; sociology; statistics.

UNIVERSITY OF HOUSTON–VICTORIA
Victoria, Texas
School of Business Administration

University of Houston–Victoria was founded in 1973. It is accredited by Southern Association of Colleges and Schools. It first offered distance learning courses in 1996. In fall 2006, there were 2,000 students enrolled in distance learning courses. Institutionally administered financial aid is available to distance learners.

Services Distance learners have accessibility to academic advising, bookstore, campus computer network, career placement assistance, e-mail services, library services, tutoring.

Contact Ms. Chari Norgard, Director of Instructional Support Services, University of Houston–Victoria, 3007 North Ben Wilson, Victoria, TX 77901-4450. Telephone: 361-570-4290. Fax: 361-570-4314. E-mail: norgardc@uhv.edu.

DEGREES AND AWARDS

BA History
BBA Business, general; Management; Marketing
BS Criminal Justice
MBA Business Administration; Global MBA
MEd Special Education
MS Computer Information System; Economic Development and Entrepreneurship

COURSE SUBJECT AREAS OFFERED OUTSIDE OF DEGREE PROGRAMS

Undergraduate—accounting and related services; biology; communication and journalism related; computer and information sciences; education; English composition; history; nursing; psychology.
Graduate—accounting and related services; computer and information sciences; education; entrepreneurial and small business operations; psychology.

UNIVERSITY OF HOUSTON–VICTORIA
Victoria, Texas
School of Education and Human Development

University of Houston–Victoria was founded in 1973. It is accredited by Southern Association of Colleges and Schools. It first offered distance learning courses in 1998. In fall 2006, there were 480 students enrolled in distance learning courses. Institutionally administered financial aid is available to distance learners.

Services Distance learners have accessibility to academic advising, bookstore, career placement assistance, e-mail services, library services, tutoring.

Contact Dr. Carol Klages, Chair, Initial Certification Programs, University of Houston–Victoria, 3007 North Ben Wilson, Victoria, TX 77901. Telephone: 877-970-4848 Ext. 284. Fax: 361-570-4257. E-mail: klagesc@uhv.edu.

DEGREES AND AWARDS
Programs offered do not lead to a degree or other formal award.

COURSE SUBJECT AREAS OFFERED OUTSIDE OF DEGREE PROGRAMS

Undergraduate—anthropology; education; educational/instructional media design; education related; education (specific levels and methods); education (specific subject areas); English language and literature related;

human development, family studies, and related services; mathematics; natural sciences; physical sciences; physical sciences related; physics; special education.

Graduate—anthropology; counseling psychology; curriculum and instruction; developmental and child psychology; education; educational administration and supervision; educational assessment, evaluation, and research; educational/instructional media design; educational psychology; education related; education (specific levels and methods); education (specific subject areas); English language and literature related; family psychology; geological and earth sciences/geosciences; intercultural/multicultural and diversity studies; mathematics; mathematics and statistics related; multi-/interdisciplinary studies related; natural sciences; physical sciences; physical sciences related; physics; school psychology; special education; student counseling and personnel services; teaching assistants/aides.

UNIVERSITY OF IDAHO
Moscow, Idaho
Engineering Outreach
http://www.uidaho.edu/eo/

University of Idaho was founded in 1889. It is accredited by Northwest Commission on Colleges and Universities. It first offered distance learning courses in 1976. In fall 2006, there were 391 students enrolled in distance learning courses. Institutionally administered financial aid is available to distance learners.

Services Distance learners have accessibility to academic advising, bookstore, campus computer network, e-mail services, library services.

Contact Ms. Diane Bancke, Administrative Manager, University of Idaho, Engineering Outreach, PO Box 441014, Moscow, ID 83844-1014. Telephone: 800-824-2889. Fax: 208-885-9249. E-mail: outreach@uidaho.edu.

DEGREES AND AWARDS

Certificate Applied Geotechnics; Communication Systems; Electric Machines and Drives; Heating, Ventilation, and Air Conditioning (HVAC) Systems; Material Design, advanced; Power System Protection and Relaying; Secure and Dependable Computing Systems; Structural Engineering; Water Resources Engineering

MAT Teaching Mathematics

MEngr Biological and Agricultural Engineering (Water Management emphasis); Civil Engineering; Computer Engineering; Electrical Engineering; Mechanical Engineering

MS Biological and Agricultural Engineering (Water Management emphasis); Computer Engineering; Computer Science; Electrical Engineering; Geological Engineering

COURSE SUBJECT AREAS OFFERED OUTSIDE OF DEGREE PROGRAMS

Undergraduate—agricultural/biological engineering and bioengineering; biology; chemical engineering; civil engineering; computer engineering; computer programming; computer science; geography and cartography; mathematics and statistics related; mechanical engineering; psychology; statistics.

Graduate—accounting and computer science; agricultural/biological engineering and bioengineering; applied mathematics; business administration, management and operations; business, management, and marketing related; chemical engineering; civil engineering; computer engineering; computer science; electrical and electronic engineering technologies; engineering; engineering technology; environmental/environmental health engineering; geological/geophysical engineering; materials engineering; mathematics; mathematics and computer science; mathematics and statistics related; mechanical engineering; mechanical engineering related technologies; psychology; psychology related; statistics.

UNIVERSITY OF IDAHO
Moscow, Idaho
Independent Study in Idaho
http://www.uidaho.edu/isi

University of Idaho was founded in 1889. It is accredited by Northwest Commission on Colleges and Universities. It first offered distance learning courses in 1973. In fall 2006, there were 538 students enrolled in distance learning courses. Institutionally administered financial aid is available to distance learners.

Services Distance learners have accessibility to bookstore, library services.

Contact Jeanne Workman, Registration Coordinator, University of Idaho, Independent Study in Idaho, PO Box 443225, Moscow, ID 83844-3225. Telephone: 877-464-3246. Fax: 208-885-5738. E-mail: indepst@uidaho.edu.

DEGREES AND AWARDS
Programs offered do not lead to a degree or other formal award.

COURSE SUBJECT AREAS OFFERED OUTSIDE OF DEGREE PROGRAMS

Undergraduate—accounting and related services; agricultural business and management; anthropology; biology; business/commerce; criminal justice and corrections; dental support services and allied professions; economics; education related; English; English composition; environmental/environmental health engineering; family and consumer economics; finance and financial management services; health and medical administrative services; health and physical education/fitness; history; human development, family studies, and related services; journalism; library science; library science related; linguistic, comparative, and related language studies; mathematics; microbiological sciences and immunology; museum studies; music; philosophy; physics; political science and government; psychology; real estate; social sciences; social sciences related; sociology; special education.

Graduate—library science; library science related.

UNIVERSITY OF ILLINOIS
Urbana, Illinois
University of Illinois Online
http://www.online.uillinois.edu

University of Illinois is accredited by North Central Association of Colleges and Schools. It first offered distance learning courses in 1997. In fall 2006, there were 6,000 students enrolled in distance learning courses. Institutionally administered financial aid is available to distance learners.

Services Distance learners have accessibility to academic advising, bookstore, campus computer network, career placement assistance, e-mail services, library services, tutoring.

Contact Jeff Harmon, Director of Marketing, University of Illinois, 807 South Wright Street, Suite 370, MC 307, Champaign, IL 61820. Telephone: 800-633-8465. Fax: 217-333-5040. E-mail: uiol-info@uillinois.edu.

DEGREES AND AWARDS

BA English; History; Liberal Studies; Philosophy
BS Computer Science; Mathematics
Certificate of Completion Medical–Graduate Medical Education Core Curriculum
CAGS Library and Information Science; Library and Information Science
CCCPE Blood Bank Technology Specialist; Business English; Career Specialist Studies; Certified Fire Fighter II; Computer Security; Dairy Science professional development sequence; E-Business Strategy; Electromagnetics Technology; Engineering Law and Management; Fund Development; GME Core Curriculum; Hazardous Waste Risk and Remediation; Health Informatics; Information Systems; Information Systems; Integrated Circuits; Marketing Strategy in the Digital Age; Materials Failure; Materials; Math Teacher Link; NetMath; Networks and Distributed Systems; Nonprofit Management; Nursing–School Nurse; Nursing–Teaching certificate in Nursing Education; Power and Energy Systems; Project Management Online; Secondary Math–Online Secondary Math; Software Engineering; Specialty Needs for Primary Care

Physicians (CME Online); Strategic Technology Management; Systems Software; Telecommunications and Signal Processing; Translation, French professional development sequence; Veterinary Education Online; Wireless Communication Technology; Writers Series

MAE Education Leadership–Master of Arts in Education Leadership

MBA Business Administration

MCC Computer Science

ME Engineering

MEd Community College Teaching and Learning (Ed.M); Curriculum, Technology, and Education Reform; Global Human Resource Development; Global Studies in Education

MHA Health Professions Education–Master of Health Professions Education

MLIS LEEP–Library and Information Science

MPH Public Health Informatics

MS Agricultural Education; Management Information Systems

MSME Mechanical Engineering

COURSE SUBJECT AREAS OFFERED OUTSIDE OF DEGREE PROGRAMS

Undergraduate—anthropology; area, ethnic, cultural, and gender studies related; business administration, management and operations; classical and ancient studies; computer and information sciences; educational psychology; English; English composition; ethnic, cultural minority, and gender studies; history; human development, family studies, and related services; languages (foreign languages related); languages (Germanic); languages (Romance languages); liberal arts and sciences, general studies and humanities; mathematics; mathematics and statistics related; philosophy; philosophy and religious studies related; political science and government; psychology; sociology.

Graduate—agriculture; business administration, management and operations; clinical/medical laboratory science and allied professions; computer and information sciences; computer/information technology administration and management; computer science; computer systems networking and telecommunications; curriculum and instruction; education; education (specific subject areas); engineering; health professions related; human resources management; international business; library science; materials engineering; mathematics; mechanical engineering; nursing; pharmacy, pharmaceutical sciences, and administration; public administration.

Non-credit—business/commerce; computer programming; computer software and media applications; creative writing; English; English composition; fine and studio art; fire protection; marketing; public administration; public health; technical and business writing.

UNIVERSITY OF ILLINOIS AT CHICAGO
Chicago, Illinois
Office of External Education
http://www.uic.edu/depts/uionline/
University of Illinois at Chicago was founded in 1946. It is accredited by North Central Association of Colleges and Schools. It first offered distance learning courses in 1998. In fall 2006, there were 4,700 students enrolled in distance learning courses. Institutionally administered financial aid is available to distance learners.

Services Distance learners have accessibility to academic advising, bookstore, campus computer network, e-mail services, library services.

Contact Katie Kaminski, Senior Communications Coordinator, University of Illinois at Chicago, External Education, 1333 South Halsted Street, MC 140, Suite 205, Chicago, IL 60607. Telephone: 312-355-1771. Fax: 312-413-9730. E-mail: khartz@uic.edu.

DEGREES AND AWARDS
BSN Nursiing–RN to BSN

Certificate Advanced Nursing Leadership; Advanced Practice Palliative Care; Bioinformatics; Electromagnetics Technology Campus certificate; Emergency Preparedness and Continuity Planning; Engineering Law and Management Campus certificate; Environmental Health Informatics Campus certificate; Health Informatics; Public Health Informatics Campus certificate; School Nurse Campus certificate; Teaching in Nursing; Wireless Communication Technology campus certificate

MEngr Engineering

MHPE Health Professions Education

MPH Public Health Informatics

MS Health Informatics

COURSE SUBJECT AREAS OFFERED OUTSIDE OF DEGREE PROGRAMS

Graduate—accounting and related services; business administration, management and operations; business/commerce; business, management, and marketing related; business/managerial economics; chemical engineering; economics; education (specific subject areas); electrical and electronic engineering technologies; electrical, electronics and communications engineering; engineering; engineering related; engineering technology; finance and financial management services; health professions related; health services/allied health/health sciences; information science/studies; marketing; medical illustration and informatics; nursing; pharmacy, pharmaceutical sciences, and administration; public health; social work; statistics.

Non-credit—business administration, management and operations; business/commerce; business/corporate communications; business, management, and marketing related; education (specific subject areas); English as a second language; marketing; medical clinical sciences/graduate medical studies; nursing; pharmacy, pharmaceutical sciences, and administration; public administration and social service professions related; public health; social work; technical and business writing.

UNIVERSITY OF ILLINOIS AT SPRINGFIELD
Springfield, Illinois
Office of Technology-Enhanced Learning
http://online.uis.edu
University of Illinois at Springfield was founded in 1969. It is accredited by North Central Association of Colleges and Schools. It first offered distance learning courses in 1984. In fall 2006, there were 1,971 students enrolled in distance learning courses. Institutionally administered financial aid is available to distance learners.

Services Distance learners have accessibility to academic advising, bookstore, campus computer network, career placement assistance, e-mail services, library services, tutoring.

Contact Dr. Ray Schroeder, Director of Office of Technology and Enhanced Learning, University of Illinois at Springfield, OTEL, Brookens, Room 426, One University Plaza, MS BRK 425, Springfield, IL 62703-5407. Telephone: 217-206-7531. Fax: 217-206-7539. E-mail: schroeder.ray@uis.edu.

DEGREES AND AWARDS

BA Economics; English; History; Liberal Studies; Mathematical Sciences; Philosophy

BBA Business Administration

BS Computer Science

MA Environmental Studies–Natural Resources and Sustainable Development concentration; Legal Studies; Teacher Leadership

MPA Public Administration

MS Computer Science; Human Services–Social Services Administration concentration; Management Information Systems

COURSE SUBJECT AREAS OFFERED OUTSIDE OF DEGREE PROGRAMS

Undergraduate—accounting and computer science; accounting and related services; business administration, management and operations; business, management, and marketing related; chemistry; communication and journalism related; communication and media; computer science; economics; education related; fine and studio art; languages (foreign languages related); liberal arts and sciences, general studies and humanities; mathematics; philosophy; psychology; sociology.

Graduate—communication and media; computer science; education related; environmental/environmental health engineering; human services; legal professions and studies related; management information systems; political science and government; public administration.

UNIVERSITY OF ILLINOIS AT URBANA–CHAMPAIGN
Champaign, Illinois
Graduate School of Library and Information Science
http://www.lis.uiuc.edu/

University of Illinois at Urbana–Champaign was founded in 1867. It is accredited by North Central Association of Colleges and Schools. It first offered distance learning courses in 1996. In fall 2006, there were 250 students enrolled in distance learning courses. Institutionally administered financial aid is available to distance learners.

Services Distance learners have accessibility to academic advising, bookstore, campus computer network, career placement assistance, e-mail services, library services, tutoring.

Contact Valerie Youngen, GSLIS Admissions, University of Illinois at Urbana–Champaign, 501 East Daniel Street, Champaign, IL 61820. Telephone: 800-982-0914. Fax: 217-244-3302. E-mail: lis-apply@uiuc.edu.

DEGREES AND AWARDS

CAGS Library and Information Science

MS Library and Information Science

COURSE SUBJECT AREAS OFFERED OUTSIDE OF DEGREE PROGRAMS

Graduate—communications technology; computer and information sciences; computer/information technology administration and management; computer software and media applications; educational/instructional media design; library science; science, technology and society.

UNIVERSITY OF ILLINOIS AT URBANA–CHAMPAIGN
Champaign, Illinois
College of Engineering

University of Illinois at Urbana–Champaign was founded in 1867. It is accredited by North Central Association of Colleges and Schools. It first offered distance learning courses in 1998. In fall 2006, there were 200 students enrolled in distance learning courses. Institutionally administered financial aid is available to distance learners.

Services Distance learners have accessibility to academic advising, bookstore, campus computer network, career placement assistance, e-mail services, library services.

Contact Mrs. Laura A. Miller, Director of Engineering Online Programs, University of Illinois at Urbana–Champaign, Office of Continuing Engineering Education, 400 Engineering Hall, MC-268, 1308 West Green Street, Urbana, IL 61801. Telephone: 217-333-6634. Fax: 217-333-0015. E-mail: ocee@uiuc.edu.

DEGREES AND AWARDS

Graduate Certificate Computer Security; Environmental and Water Resources Engineering; Information Systems; Materials Engineering; Materials Failure Analysis; Networks and Distributed Systems; Software Engineering; Strategic Technology Management; System Software; Systems Engineering

MCS Computer Science–Master of Computer Science

MSME Mechanical Engineering

COURSE SUBJECT AREAS OFFERED OUTSIDE OF DEGREE PROGRAMS

Graduate—civil engineering; computer science; computer systems analysis; computer systems networking and telecommunications; data processing; engineering; entrepreneurial and small business operations; genetics; management sciences and quantitative methods; materials engineering; materials science; mathematics; mechanical engineering; systems engineering.

Non-credit—genetics; management sciences and quantitative methods; mechanical engineering.

UNIVERSITY OF LA VERNE
La Verne, California
Distance Learning Center
http://www.ulv.edu/dlc/dlc.html

University of La Verne was founded in 1891. It is accredited by Western Association of Schools and Colleges. It first offered distance learning courses in 1996. In fall 2006, there were 1,119 students enrolled in distance learning courses. Institutionally administered financial aid is available to distance learners.

Services Distance learners have accessibility to academic advising, bookstore, campus computer network, career placement assistance, e-mail services, library services, tutoring.

Contact Mrs. Cheryl DeVroom, Marketing Assistant, University of La Verne, 1950 3rd Street, La Verne, CA 91750. Telephone: 800-468-4858. Fax: 909-971-2294. E-mail: degreeinfo@ulv.edu.

DEGREES AND AWARDS

BS Criminology; Organizational Management; Public Administration

MBA Business Administration

COURSE SUBJECT AREAS OFFERED OUTSIDE OF DEGREE PROGRAMS

Graduate—anthropology; biological and physical sciences; biology; chemistry; communication and media; creative writing; curriculum and instruction; developmental and child psychology; education (specific subject areas); English composition; history; liberal arts and sciences, general studies and humanities; museum studies; music; natural resources and conservation related; philosophy; physical sciences; psychology; public administration; speech and rhetoric.

UNIVERSITY OF LETHBRIDGE
Lethbridge, Alberta, Canada
http://www.uleth.ca/

University of Lethbridge was founded in 1967. It is provincially chartered. It first offered distance learning courses in 2001. In fall 2006, there were 217 students enrolled in distance learning courses. Institutionally administered financial aid is available to distance learners.

Services Distance learners have accessibility to academic advising, bookstore, campus computer network, career placement assistance, e-mail services, library services, tutoring.

Contact Inquiries, University of Lethbridge, 4401 University Drive, Lethbridge, AB T1K 3M4, Canada. Telephone: 403-329-2233. E-mail: inquiries@uleth.ca.

DEGREES AND AWARDS
Programs offered do not lead to a degree or other formal award.

COURSE SUBJECT AREAS OFFERED OUTSIDE OF DEGREE PROGRAMS

Undergraduate—computer software and media applications; education related.

Graduate—education; educational assessment, evaluation, and research; education related.

UNIVERSITY OF MAINE
Orono, Maine
Continuing Education Division
http://Learnonline.umaine.edu

University of Maine was founded in 1865. It is accredited by New England Association of Schools and Colleges. It first offered distance learning courses in 1989. In fall 2006, there were 2,786 students enrolled in distance learning courses. Institutionally administered financial aid is available to distance learners.

Services Distance learners have accessibility to academic advising, bookstore, campus computer network, e-mail services, library services.

Contact James F. Toner, Associate Director, University of Maine, 5713 Chadbourne Hall, Orono, ME 04469-5713. Telephone: 207-581-3142. Fax: 207-581-3141. E-mail: jim.toner@umit.maine.edu.

DEGREES AND AWARDS

BUS University Studies
Certificate Maine Studies

COURSE SUBJECT AREAS OFFERED OUTSIDE OF DEGREE PROGRAMS

Undergraduate—accounting and related services; area studies; biology; civil engineering technology; communication disorders sciences and services; computer and information sciences and support services related; creative writing; developmental and child psychology; education (specific subject areas); English as a second/foreign language (teaching); English as a second language; English composition; ethnic, cultural minority, and gender studies; languages (foreign languages related); mechanical engineering; music; nursing; plant sciences; psychology; public administration; social psychology; sociology; special education; technical and business writing; visual and performing arts.

Graduate—animal sciences; anthropology; business/commerce; civil engineering; education; liberal arts and sciences, general studies and humanities; mechanical engineering; social work.

THE UNIVERSITY OF MAINE AT AUGUSTA
Augusta, Maine
University of Maine System Network for Education and Technology (UNET)
http://www.uma.maine.edu

The University of Maine at Augusta was founded in 1965. It is accredited by New England Association of Schools and Colleges. It first offered distance learning courses in 1986. In fall 2006, there were 2,400 students enrolled in distance learning courses. Institutionally administered financial aid is available to distance learners.

Services Distance learners have accessibility to academic advising, bookstore, campus computer network, e-mail services, library services, tutoring.

Contact Sheri Fraser, Director of Admissions and Advising, The University of Maine at Augusta, 46 University Drive, Augusta, ME 04330. Telephone: 207-621-3390. Fax: 207-621-3333. E-mail: fraser@maine.edu.

DEGREES AND AWARDS

AA Social Services

AS Business Administration; Liberal Studies; Library and Information Services

BA Liberal Studies

BS Accounting; Applied Science–Bachelor of Applied Science; Library and Information Services; Management; Mental Health and Human Services

COURSE SUBJECT AREAS OFFERED OUTSIDE OF DEGREE PROGRAMS

Undergraduate—accounting and related services; American literature (United States and Canadian); anthropology; applied mathematics; business administration, management and operations; business/commerce; business/corporate communications; business, management, and marketing related; communication and media; community health services; comparative literature; computer and information sciences; computer software and media applications; counseling psychology; creative writing; criminal justice and corrections; developmental and child psychology; economics; English; English composition; finance and financial management services; history; human development, family studies, and related services; human resources management; human services; liberal arts and sciences, general studies and humanities; library science related; mathematics; mental and social health services and allied professions; music; nursing; philosophy; physical sciences; political science and government; psychology; social sciences; sociology; statistics; taxation; technical and business writing.

UNIVERSITY OF MAINE AT FORT KENT
Fort Kent, Maine

University of Maine at Fort Kent was founded in 1878. It is accredited by New England Association of Schools and Colleges. It first offered distance learning courses in 1989. In fall 2006, there were 531 students enrolled in distance learning courses. Institutionally administered financial aid is available to distance learners.

Services Distance learners have accessibility to academic advising, bookstore, campus computer network, career placement assistance, e-mail services, library services, tutoring.

Contact Donald K. Eno, Academic Outreach Coordinator, University of Maine at Fort Kent, 23 University Drive, Fort Kent, ME 04743. Telephone: 207-834-7835. Fax: 207-834-8604. E-mail: deno@maine.edu.

DEGREES AND AWARDS

AA General Studies, Criminal Justice Sequence
BS Rural Public Safety Administration
BSN Nursing–RN to BSN
BUS University Studies

COURSE SUBJECT AREAS OFFERED OUTSIDE OF DEGREE PROGRAMS

Undergraduate—anthropology; astronomy and astrophysics; behavioral sciences; business/commerce; business, management, and marketing related; communication and media; creative writing; criminal justice and corrections; developmental and child psychology; economics; education related; education (specific levels and methods); English; geography and cartography; geological and earth sciences/geosciences; health professions related; history; liberal arts and sciences, general studies and humanities; music; nursing; philosophy; political science and government; psychology; public administration; public policy analysis; real estate; sociology; special education.

Non-credit—criminal justice and corrections.

UNIVERSITY OF MANAGEMENT AND TECHNOLOGY
Arlington, Virginia
http://www.umtweb.edu

University of Management and Technology was founded in 1998. It is accredited by Distance Education and Training Council. It first offered distance learning courses in 1998. In fall 2006, there were 5,000 students enrolled in distance learning courses. Institutionally administered financial aid is available to distance learners.

Services Distance learners have accessibility to academic advising, bookstore, library services, tutoring.

Contact Dr. J. Davidson Frame, Academic Dean, University of Management and Technology, 1901 North Fort Myer Drive, Suite 700, Arlington, VA 22209. Telephone: 703-516-0035. Fax: 703-516-0985. E-mail: davidson.frame@umtweb.edu.

DEGREES AND AWARDS

ABA Business Administration

AS Computer Science; General Studies

BBA Information Technology Management; International Management; Management; Marketing Management

BS Computer Science–Information Systems; Computer Science–Information Technology; Computer Science–Software Engineering; Computer Science; General Studies

Certificate Acquisition Management; Project Management

Graduate Certificate Project Management

MBA Management; Project Management

MS Information Technology–IT Management; Information Technology–IT Project Management; Information Technology–Management Information Systems

MSCS Computer Science; Multimedia Technology; Software Engineering

MSM Acquisition Management; Management; Project Management; Public Administration; Telecommunications Management

COURSE SUBJECT AREAS OFFERED OUTSIDE OF DEGREE PROGRAMS

Undergraduate—accounting and computer science; applied mathematics; behavioral sciences; business administration, management and operations; business, management, and marketing related; computer and information sciences; computer/information technology administration and management; computer programming; computer science; computer software and media applications; computer systems analysis; computer systems networking and telecommunications; economics; English; finance and financial management services; history; human resources management; international business; international/global studies; management information systems; management sciences and quantitative methods; mathematics; psychology; public administration; science technologies related; science, technology and society; statistics; technical and business writing.

Graduate—accounting and computer science; business administration, management and operations; business/commerce; economics; linguistic, comparative, and related language studies; management information systems; psychology.

UNIVERSITY OF MARYLAND, COLLEGE PARK
College Park, Maryland
E-Learning
http://www.onlinestudies.umd.edu

University of Maryland, College Park was founded in 1856. It is accredited by Middle States Association of Colleges and Schools. It first offered distance learning courses in 2000. In fall 2006, there were 250 students enrolled in distance learning courses. Institutionally administered financial aid is available to distance learners.

Services Distance learners have accessibility to academic advising, bookstore, library services.

Contact Paul E. Roche, EdD, Senior Project Manager, University of Maryland, College Park, 2103 Reckord Armory, Office of Professional Studies, College Park, MD 20742. Telephone: 301-405-8989. Fax: 301-314-9572. E-mail: proche@umd.edu.

DEGREES AND AWARDS

Graduate Certificate Graduate Certificate in Public Health Informatics
MEngr Professional Master of Engineering in Fire Protection
MLS Life Sciences

See full description on page 488.

UNIVERSITY OF MARYLAND EASTERN SHORE
Princess Anne, Maryland
http://www.umes.edu

University of Maryland Eastern Shore was founded in 1886. It is accredited by Middle States Association of Colleges and Schools. It first offered distance learning courses in 2000. In fall 2006, there were 376 students enrolled in distance learning courses. Institutionally administered financial aid is available to distance learners.

Services Distance learners have accessibility to academic advising, bookstore, campus computer network, career placement assistance, e-mail services, library services, tutoring.

Contact Dr. Andrew T. Carrington, Associate Vice President, Academic Affairs, University of Maryland Eastern Shore, JT Williams Hall, Room #2104, Princess Anne, MD 21853. Telephone: 410-651-8446. Fax: 410-651-6085. E-mail: atcarrington@umes.edu.

DEGREES AND AWARDS
Programs offered do not lead to a degree or other formal award.

COURSE SUBJECT AREAS OFFERED OUTSIDE OF DEGREE PROGRAMS

Undergraduate—agricultural and domestic animal services; agriculture and agriculture operations related; computer and information sciences and support services related; developmental and child psychology; family and consumer sciences/human sciences; hospitality administration; physical sciences related; rehabilitation and therapeutic professions; social sciences; sociology; statistics.

Graduate—counseling psychology; educational assessment, evaluation, and research; fishing and fisheries sciences and management; health and medical administrative services; health professions related; health psychology; pharmacology and toxicology; psychology related; rehabilitation and therapeutic professions.

UNIVERSITY OF MARYLAND UNIVERSITY COLLEGE
Adelphi, Maryland

University of Maryland University College was founded in 1947. It is accredited by Middle States Association of Colleges and Schools. It first offered distance learning courses in 1972. In fall 2006, there were 32,000 students enrolled in distance learning courses. Institutionally administered financial aid is available to distance learners.

Services Distance learners have accessibility to academic advising, bookstore, campus computer network, career placement assistance, e-mail services, library services, tutoring.

Contact Advisor, University of Maryland University College, 3501 University Boulevard East, Adelphi, MD 20783. Telephone: 800-888-UMUC. E-mail: umucinfo@umuc.edu.

DEGREES AND AWARDS
BA Communication Studies; English; History; Humanities
BS Accounting; Business Administration; Computer Studies; Computer and Information Science; Criminal Justice; Environmental Management; Finance; Fire Science; Global Business and Public Policy; Human Resource Management; Information Systems Management; Legal Studies; Management Studies; Marketing; Psychology; Social Science
GMBA Business Administration
Graduate Certificate Accounting and Information Technology; Accounting; Advertising; Applied Computer Systems; Bioinformatics; Biotechnology Management; Database Systems Technologies; Distance Education and Technology; Distance Education in Developing Countries; Electronic Commerce; Energy Resources Management and Policy; Environmental Management; Financial Management in Organizations; Foundations for Human Resource Management; Global Management; Health Care Administration; Homeland Security Management; Information Assurance; Information Resources Management; Information Technology; Integrated Direct Marketing; Integrative Supply Chain Management; International Marketing; International Trade; Leadership and Management; Library Services in Distance Education; Nonprofit and Association Financial Management; Procurement and Contract Management; Project Management; Public Relations; Software Development Management; Software Engineering; Systems Analysis; Teaching at a Distance; Technology Systems Management; Telecommunications Management; Training at a Distance
MBA Business Administration
MDE Distance Education
MEd Education
MIM International Management
MS Accounting and Financial Management; Accounting and Information Technology; Biotechnology Studies; Computer Systems Management; E-Commerce; Environmental Management; Financial Management and Information Systems; Health Administration Informatics; Health Care Administration; Information Technology; Management; Software Engineering; Technology Management; Telecommunications Management
DM Management

COURSE SUBJECT AREAS OFFERED OUTSIDE OF DEGREE PROGRAMS

Undergraduate—accounting and related services; anthropology; area studies; biology; business administration, management and operations; chemistry; communication and media; computer and information sciences; criminal justice and corrections; economics; fire protection; gerontology; human resources management; information science/studies; international business; journalism; mathematics; psychology; sales, merchandising, and related marketing operations (general); social sciences; sociology.

Graduate—accounting and related services; business administration, management and operations; business, management, and marketing related; computer/information technology administration and management; computer systems networking and telecommunications; educational/instructional media design; education (specific levels and methods); education (specific subject areas); entrepreneurial and small business operations; health and medical administrative services; human resources management; international business; marketing; public administration; sales, merchandising, and related marketing operations (general).

UNIVERSITY OF MASSACHUSETTS BOSTON
Boston, Massachusetts
Corporate, Continuing and Distance Education
http://www.ccde.umb.edu

University of Massachusetts Boston was founded in 1964. It is accredited by New England Association of Schools and Colleges. It first offered distance learning courses in 2001. In fall 2006, there were 1,000 students enrolled in distance learning courses. Institutionally administered financial aid is available to distance learners.

Services Distance learners have accessibility to academic advising, bookstore, campus computer network, career placement assistance, e-mail services, library services, tutoring.

Contact Ms. Katharine Grant Galaitsis, Director of Online Education, University of Massachusetts Boston, Corporate, Continuing, and Distance Education, 100 Morrissey Boulevard, Boston, MA 02125-3393. Telephone: 617-287-7918. Fax: 617-287-7297. E-mail: kitty.galaitsis@umb.edu.

DEGREES AND AWARDS
BA Community Studies completer program
BS Nursing–RN to BS
Certificate Community, Media, and Technology; Fundamentals of Information Technology
Graduate Certificate Critical and Creative Thinking (Focus on Creativity at Work); Education–Adapting Curriculum Frameworks for All Learners; Gerontology–Management of Aging Services track; Instructional Technology Design; Instructional Technology for Educators
MA Linguistics–Applied Linguistics, ESL concentration
MEd Counseling–Family Therapy track; Counseling–Mental Health Counseling track; Counseling–Rehabilitation Counseling track; Counseling–School Guidance track; Instructional Design
MS Gerontology–Management of Aging Services track
PMC Nursing–Gerontological/Adult and Family Nurse Practitioner

COURSE SUBJECT AREAS OFFERED OUTSIDE OF DEGREE PROGRAMS
Undergraduate—anthropology; archeology; biology; business administration, management and operations; classical and ancient studies; communication and media; community organization and advocacy; community psychology; computer and information sciences; computer/information technology administration and management; computer science; criminal justice and corrections; economics; English; environmental/environmental health engineering; history; international relations and affairs; languages (classics and classical); languages (Romance languages); liberal arts and sciences, general studies and humanities; linguistic, comparative, and related language studies; management information systems; marketing; mathematics; music; natural resources and conservation related; nursing; nutrition sciences; physics; political science and government; psychology; social sciences; sociology; statistics; technology education/industrial arts.
Graduate—biological and physical sciences; counseling psychology; criminal justice and corrections; education; educational/instructional media design; educational psychology; education (specific subject areas); English as a second/foreign language (teaching); gerontology; history; international relations and affairs; linguistic, comparative, and related language studies; nursing; peace studies and conflict resolution; school psychology; sociology; special education; statistics; student counseling and personnel services; technology education/industrial arts.
Non-credit—agriculture and agriculture operations related; city/urban, community and regional planning; human services; landscape architecture; natural resources and conservation related; parks, recreation, and leisure related; urban studies/affairs.

UNIVERSITY OF MASSACHUSETTS DARTMOUTH
North Dartmouth, Massachusetts
Professional and Continuing Education

University of Massachusetts Dartmouth was founded in 1895. It is accredited by New England Association of Schools and Colleges. It first offered distance learning courses in 1995. In fall 2006, there were 334 students enrolled in distance learning courses. Institutionally administered financial aid is available to distance learners.

Services Distance learners have accessibility to academic advising, bookstore, campus computer network, e-mail services.

Contact Mr. David Pedro, PCE Advisor/Online Program Coordinator, University of Massachusetts Dartmouth, 800 Purchase Street, New Bedford, MA 02740. Telephone: 508-990-1160. Fax: 508-990-1254. E-mail: dpedro@umassd.edu.

DEGREES AND AWARDS
Programs offered do not lead to a degree or other formal award.

COURSE SUBJECT AREAS OFFERED OUTSIDE OF DEGREE PROGRAMS
Undergraduate—anthropology; astronomy and astrophysics; criminal justice and corrections; criminology; English; ethnic, cultural minority, and gender studies; geography and cartography; history; music; nursing; philosophy; physics; social sciences; sociology; technical and business writing.
Graduate—computer and information sciences; education; nursing; technical and business writing.

UNIVERSITY OF MASSACHUSETTS LOWELL
Lowell, Massachusetts
Continuing Studies and Corporate Education
http://continuinged.uml.edu/online

University of Massachusetts Lowell was founded in 1894. It is accredited by New England Association of Schools and Colleges. It first offered distance learning courses in 1995. In fall 2006, there were 3,500 students enrolled in distance learning courses. Institutionally administered financial aid is available to distance learners.

Services Distance learners have accessibility to academic advising, bookstore, campus computer network, e-mail services, library services.

Contact UMass Lowell Continuing Studies, University of Massachusetts Lowell, One University Avenue, Lowell, MA 01854-2881. Telephone: 800-480-3190. Fax: 978-934-4006. E-mail: continuing_education@uml.edu.

DEGREES AND AWARDS
AS Information Technology
BA Liberal Arts (BLA); Psychology
BS Information Technology; Information Technology, Business minor
Certificate Contemporary Communications; Data/Telecommunications; Information Technology; Multimedia Applications; Paralegal Studies; Security Management and Homeland Security; UNIX; Website Design and Development
Graduate Certificate Behavioral Intervention in Autism; Business–Foundations of Business; Clinical Pathology; Domestic Violence Prevention; Forensic Criminology; Plastics Engineering Fundamentals; Security Studies
MA Criminal Justice
MBA Business Administration
MEd Curriculum and Instruction–Science Education concentration; Curriculum and Instruction; Educational Administration; Reading and Language

COURSE SUBJECT AREAS OFFERED OUTSIDE OF DEGREE PROGRAMS
Undergraduate—accounting and computer science; business/commerce; business/corporate communications; communication and media; computer and information sciences; computer programming; computer systems networking and telecommunications; education (specific levels and methods); English composition; ethnic, cultural minority, and gender studies; information science/studies; liberal arts and sciences, general

studies and humanities; mathematics and computer science; philosophy; security and protective services related; social sciences related; sociology.

Graduate—accounting and computer science; behavioral sciences; clinical/medical laboratory science and allied professions; criminal justice and corrections; criminology; curriculum and instruction; education; educational administration and supervision; electrical and electronic engineering technologies; finance and financial management services; forensic psychology; health professions related; health services/allied health/health sciences; management information systems; marketing; polymer/plastics engineering; security and protective services related; special education.

Non-credit—educational/instructional media design; education related.

UNIVERSITY OF MEDICINE AND DENTISTRY OF NEW JERSEY
Newark, New Jersey
http://www.umdnj.edu/

University of Medicine and Dentistry of New Jersey was founded in 1970. It is accredited by Middle States Association of Colleges and Schools. It first offered distance learning courses in 1998. In fall 2006, there were 300 students enrolled in distance learning courses. Institutionally administered financial aid is available to distance learners.

Services Distance learners have accessibility to academic advising, bookstore, campus computer network, e-mail services, library services.

Contact Mr. Brian Lewis, Assistant Dean of Enrollment Services, University of Medicine and Dentistry of New Jersey, 65 Bergen Street, Room 149, Newark, NJ 07107. Telephone: 973-972-8575. Fax: 973-972-7463. E-mail: lewisbj@umdnj.edu.

DEGREES AND AWARDS

BS Health Sciences
MS Clinical Nutrition; Health Sciences; Health Systems; Psychiatric Rehabilitation
DH Sc Clinical Nutrition (DCN)
PhD Health Sciences

COURSE SUBJECT AREAS OFFERED OUTSIDE OF DEGREE PROGRAMS

Undergraduate—health professions related; nutrition sciences.
Graduate—health professions related; nutrition sciences.

UNIVERSITY OF MICHIGAN–DEARBORN
Dearborn, Michigan
http://dln.engin.umd.umich.edu

University of Michigan–Dearborn was founded in 1959. It is accredited by North Central Association of Colleges and Schools. It first offered distance learning courses in 2003. In fall 2006, there were 200 students enrolled in distance learning courses. Institutionally administered financial aid is available to distance learners.

Services Distance learners have accessibility to academic advising, bookstore, campus computer network, e-mail services, library services.

Contact Susan Guinn, Distance Learning Program Manager, University of Michigan–Dearborn, College of Engineering and Computer Science, 4901 Evergreen Road, 2040 PEC, Dearborn, MI 48128-1491. Telephone: 313-593-4000. Fax: 313-593-4070. E-mail: sguinn@umich.edu.

DEGREES AND AWARDS

MS Engineering Management; Software Engineering
MSE Automotive Systems Engineering; Computer Engineering; Industrial and Systems Engineering

COURSE SUBJECT AREAS OFFERED OUTSIDE OF DEGREE PROGRAMS

Undergraduate—computer and information sciences; computer science.
Graduate—computer and information sciences; computer engineering; computer science; engineering; engineering/industrial management; engineering science; mechanical engineering.
Non-credit—engineering science.

UNIVERSITY OF MICHIGAN–FLINT
Flint, Michigan
Distance Learning Program
http://online.umflint.edu/

University of Michigan Flint was founded in 1956. It is accredited by North Central Association of Colleges and Schools. It first offered distance learning courses in 2000. In fall 2006, there were 2,350 students enrolled in distance learning courses. Institutionally administered financial aid is available to distance learners.

Services Distance learners have accessibility to academic advising, bookstore, campus computer network, career placement assistance, e-mail services, library services.

Contact Office of Extended Learning, University of Michigan–Flint, 3102 William S. White Bldg., 303 E. Kearsley, Flint, MI 48502-1950. Telephone: 810-762-3200 Ext. 3200. Fax: 810-766-6803. E-mail: elearning@umflint.edu.

DEGREES AND AWARDS

BBA Administration
BSN Nursing
Certificate Africana Studies
MA Technology in Education (Global)
MBA Business Administration

COURSE SUBJECT AREAS OFFERED OUTSIDE OF DEGREE PROGRAMS

Undergraduate—accounting and related services; allied health diagnostic, intervention, and treatment professions; business/commerce; computer science; management sciences and quantitative methods; marketing; mathematics; nursing; social work.

Graduate—accounting and related services; business administration, management and operations; human resources management; management sciences and quantitative methods; marketing.

Non-credit—accounting and related services; business administration, management and operations; business/commerce; business/corporate communications; business, management, and marketing related; computer software and media applications; educational administration and supervision; educational assessment, evaluation, and research; educational/instructional media design; education (specific subject areas); management information systems; sales, merchandising, and related marketing operations (specialized); teaching assistants/aides.

UNIVERSITY OF MINNESOTA, CROOKSTON
Crookston, Minnesota
Office of Continuing Education
http://www.crk.umn.edu/cal

University of Minnesota, Crookston was founded in 1966. It is accredited by North Central Association of Colleges and Schools. It first offered distance learning courses in 1990. In fall 2006, there were 415 students enrolled in distance learning courses. Institutionally administered financial aid is available to distance learners.

Services Distance learners have accessibility to academic advising, campus computer network, career placement assistance, e-mail services, library services, tutoring.

Contact Michelle A. Christopherson, Director, Center for Adult Learning, University of Minnesota, Crookston, 2900 University Avenue, Crookston, MN 56716-5001. Telephone: 218-281-8679. Fax: 218-281-8676. E-mail: mchristo@umn.edu.

DEGREES AND AWARDS

BS Applied Health–Bachelor of Applied Health Online; Business Online; Manufacturing Management–Bachelor of Manufacturing Management Online
Certificate Hotel, Restaurant, and Institutional Management

COURSE SUBJECT AREAS OFFERED OUTSIDE OF DEGREE PROGRAMS

Undergraduate—accounting and related services; agricultural and food products processing; biology; business administration, management and operations; data entry/microcomputer applications; data processing; economics; English composition; entrepreneurial and small business operations; foods, nutrition, and related services; health and medical administrative services; industrial production technologies; information science/studies; management information systems; marketing; mathematics; microbiological sciences and immunology; philosophy; physics; psychology; sociology; speech and rhetoric; statistics.

UNIVERSITY OF MINNESOTA, DULUTH
Duluth, Minnesota
http://www.d.umn.edu/

University of Minnesota, Duluth was founded in 1947. It is accredited by North Central Association of Colleges and Schools. It first offered distance learning courses in 1980. In fall 2006, there were 600 students enrolled in distance learning courses. Institutionally administered financial aid is available to distance learners.

Services Distance learners have accessibility to academic advising, bookstore, campus computer network, e-mail services, library services.

Contact Torina Stark, Program Coordinator, University of Minnesota, Duluth, 251 Darland Administration, 1049 University Drive, Duluth, MN 55812. Telephone: 218-726-8146. E-mail: tstark@d.umn.edu.

DEGREES AND AWARDS
Programs offered do not lead to a degree or other formal award.

COURSE SUBJECT AREAS OFFERED OUTSIDE OF DEGREE PROGRAMS

Undergraduate—area, ethnic, cultural, and gender studies related; astronomy and astrophysics; education (specific subject areas); English composition; health and physical education/fitness; history; psychology; sociology; special education.

Graduate—education (specific subject areas); special education.

UNIVERSITY OF MINNESOTA, MORRIS
Morris, Minnesota
College of Continuing Education-GenEdWeb Program
http://genedweb.mrs.umn.edu

University of Minnesota, Morris was founded in 1959. It is accredited by North Central Association of Colleges and Schools. It first offered distance learning courses in 1997. In fall 2006, there were 100 students enrolled in distance learning courses. Institutionally administered financial aid is available to distance learners.

Services Distance learners have accessibility to academic advising, bookstore, campus computer network, e-mail services, library services, tutoring.

Contact Ms. Karen M. Cusey, Program Associate/GenEdWeb Program Coordinator, University of Minnesota, Morris, 225 Community Services Building, 600 East 4th Street, Morris, MN 56267. Telephone: 800-842-0030. Fax: 320-589-1661. E-mail: genedweb@morris.umn.edu.

DEGREES AND AWARDS
Programs offered do not lead to a degree or other formal award.

COURSE SUBJECT AREAS OFFERED OUTSIDE OF DEGREE PROGRAMS

Undergraduate—business, management, and marketing related; creative writing; developmental and child psychology; economics; education; education (specific subject areas); English composition; history; legal studies (non-professional general, undergraduate); mathematics; multi-/interdisciplinary studies related; political science and government; psychology; sociology; statistics.

UNIVERSITY OF MINNESOTA, TWIN CITIES CAMPUS
Minneapolis, Minnesota
Independent and Distance Learning
http://www.cce.umn.edu/petersons

University of Minnesota, Twin Cities Campus was founded in 1851. It is accredited by North Central Association of Colleges and Schools. It first offered distance learning courses in 1941. In fall 2006, there were 4,000 students enrolled in distance learning courses. Institutionally administered financial aid is available to distance learners.

Services Distance learners have accessibility to academic advising, bookstore, campus computer network, career placement assistance, e-mail services, library services, tutoring.

Contact Information Center Receptionist, University of Minnesota, Twin Cities Campus, College of Continuing Education, 20 Classroom Office Building, 1994 Buford Avenue, Saint Paul, MN 55108. Telephone: 800-234-6564. Fax: 612-625-1511. E-mail: info@cce.umn.edu.

DEGREES AND AWARDS
Certificate Applied Business; Paper Science and Engineering
MS Paper Science and Engineering

COURSE SUBJECT AREAS OFFERED OUTSIDE OF DEGREE PROGRAMS

Undergraduate—accounting and related services; agriculture; allied health diagnostic, intervention, and treatment professions; applied horticulture/horticultural business services; biochemistry, biophysics and molecular biology; biology; biology/biotechnology laboratory technician; biopsychology; business administration, management and operations; business/corporate communications; business, management, and marketing related; business/managerial economics; business operations support and assistant services; cell biology and anatomical sciences; communication and journalism related; communication and media; comparative literature; computer software and media applications; computer systems networking and telecommunications; developmental and child psychology; ecology, evolution, and population biology; economics; educational psychology; English; English language and literature related; English literature (British and Commonwealth); entrepreneurial and small business operations; ethnic, cultural minority, and gender studies; family and consumer economics; family and consumer sciences/human sciences; finance and financial management services; fine and studio art; food science and technology; foods, nutrition, and related services; forest engineering; genetics; geological and earth sciences/geosciences; health and medical administrative services; health/medical preparatory programs; health professions related; health services/allied health/health sciences; human resources management; journalism; languages (classics and classical); languages (Germanic); languages (Romance languages); languages (Slavic, Baltic and Albanian); liberal arts and sciences, general studies and humanities; linguistic, comparative, and related language studies; marketing; materials science; mathematics; music; nursing; operations research; personality psychology; philosophy; physics; physiology, pathology and related sciences; psychology; public health; public relations, advertising, and applied communication related; publishing; rehabilitation and therapeutic professions; social work; speech and rhetoric; technical and business writing; work and family studies.

Graduate—communication and media; forest engineering; liberal arts and sciences, general studies and humanities; public health; speech and rhetoric.

See full description on page 490.

UNIVERSITY OF MISSOURI–COLUMBIA
Columbia, Missouri
Center for Distance and Independent Study
http://cdis.missouri.edu

University of Missouri–Columbia was founded in 1839. It is accredited by North Central Association of Colleges and Schools. It first offered distance learning courses in 1941. In fall 2006, there were 6,475 students enrolled in distance learning courses. Institutionally administered financial aid is available to distance learners.

Services Distance learners have accessibility to academic advising, bookstore, e-mail services, library services.

Contact Ms. Terrie Nagel, Student Services Adviser, University of Missouri–Columbia, 136 Clark Hall, Columbia, MO 65211-4200. Telephone: 800-609-3727 Ext. 4. Fax: 573-882-6808. E-mail: nagelt@missouri.edu.

DEGREES AND AWARDS
BGS General Studies–Online Bachelor of General Studies completion program

COURSE SUBJECT AREAS OFFERED OUTSIDE OF DEGREE PROGRAMS
Undergraduate—accounting and related services; agricultural/biological engineering and bioengineering; American literature (United States and Canadian); animal sciences; anthropology; area, ethnic, cultural, and gender studies related; astronomy and astrophysics; atmospheric sciences and meteorology; behavioral sciences; biblical and other theological languages and literatures; biology; business administration, management and operations; business/commerce; business, management, and marketing related; business/managerial economics; classical and ancient studies; creative writing; curriculum and instruction; developmental and child psychology; economics; education; educational psychology; education related; engineering; engineering mechanics; English; English composition; English language and literature related; English literature (British and Commonwealth); ethnic, cultural minority, and gender studies; film/video and photographic arts; geography and cartography; geological and earth sciences/geosciences; gerontology; health and medical administrative services; health and physical education/fitness; health professions related; history; human development, family studies, and related services; human resources management; intercultural/multicultural and diversity studies; international relations and affairs; languages (classics and classical); languages (foreign languages related); languages (Germanic); languages (Romance languages); liberal arts and sciences, general studies and humanities; linguistic, comparative, and related language studies; marketing; mathematics; mathematics and statistics related; mental and social health services and allied professions; parks, recreation and leisure; philosophy; physics; political science and government; psychology; psychology related; religious studies; social work; sociology; statistics; technical and business writing.
Graduate—animal sciences; counseling psychology; curriculum and instruction; education; educational administration and supervision; educational assessment, evaluation, and research; educational psychology; education related; gerontology; human development, family studies, and related services; mental and social health services and allied professions; philosophy; sociology.
Non-credit—city/urban, community and regional planning; fire protection; forestry; human resources management; languages (Romance languages); work and family studies.

UNIVERSITY OF MISSOURI–COLUMBIA
Columbia, Missouri
MU Direct: Continuing and Distance Education
http://MUdirect.missouri.edu/mu/pg3.htm
University of Missouri–Columbia was founded in 1839. It is accredited by North Central Association of Colleges and Schools. It first offered distance learning courses in 1990. In fall 2006, there were 2,134 students enrolled in distance learning courses. Institutionally administered financial aid is available to distance learners.
Services Distance learners have accessibility to academic advising, bookstore, campus computer network, e-mail services, library services, tutoring.
Contact Juanita Smarr, Administrative Assistant, University of Missouri–Columbia, 105 Whitten Hall, Columbia, MO 65211-6300. Telephone: 800-545-2604. Fax: 573-882-5071. E-mail: mudirect@missouri.edu.

DEGREES AND AWARDS
BHS Radiologic Sciences Bachelors completion program (Radiography); Respiratory Therapy Bachelors completion program
BSN Nursing–RN to BSN Online option (Bachelors completion program)
MA Architectural Studies; Journalism (Media Management); Journalism (Strategic Communications); Library Science

MEd Business and Marketing Education; Early Childhood Education; Early Childhood Special Education; Educational Leadership; Gifted Education; Journalism Education; Learning Systems Design and Development; Literacy; Mental Health Practices in Schools; Social Studies; Teaching English to Speakers of Other Languages (TESOL); Technology in Schools
MHA Health Services Management (Executive Program)
MS Architectural Studies; Family Nurse Practitioner; Gerontological Nurse Practitioner; Health Informatics (Executive Program); Leadership in Nursing and Healthcare Systems; Mental Health Nurse Practitioner; Nursing Education; Nursing–Public Health or School Health Nursing; Pediatric Nurse Practitioner; Personal Financial Planning
PhD Architectural Studies

COURSE SUBJECT AREAS OFFERED OUTSIDE OF DEGREE PROGRAMS
Undergraduate—agricultural and food products processing; agricultural business and management; food science and technology; foods, nutrition, and related services; health professions related; nuclear engineering; nursing; plant sciences.
Graduate—agricultural and food products processing; agricultural business and management; economics; education; educational administration and supervision; educational/instructional media design; educational psychology; education related; education (specific subject areas); food science and technology; foods, nutrition, and related services; health and medical administrative services; information science/studies; journalism; library science; library science related; mental and social health services and allied professions; nuclear engineering; nursing; public relations, advertising, and applied communication related; radio, television, and digital communication; school psychology; technology education/industrial arts.
Non-credit—agricultural business and management; business, management, and marketing related; city/urban, community and regional planning; criminal justice and corrections; criminology; education; educational assessment, evaluation, and research; education related; education (specific levels and methods); fire protection; forestry; health/medical preparatory programs; health professions related; health services/allied health/health sciences; human resources management; languages (foreign languages related); medical illustration and informatics; personal and culinary services related; soil sciences; wildlife and wildlands science and management.

THE UNIVERSITY OF MONTANA
Missoula, Montana
Continuing Education
http://www.umt.edu/ce/deo/external
The University of Montana was founded in 1893. It is accredited by Northwest Commission on Colleges and Universities. It first offered distance learning courses in 1989. In fall 2006, there were 1,000 students enrolled in distance learning courses. Institutionally administered financial aid is available to distance learners.
Services Distance learners have accessibility to academic advising, bookstore, campus computer network, career placement assistance, e-mail services, library services.
Contact Ms. Candice Merrill, Program Coordinator, The University of Montana, Extended Degrees, Continuing Education, Missoula, MT 59812. Telephone: 406-243-6431. Fax: 406-243-2047. E-mail: candice.merrill@umontana.edu.

DEGREES AND AWARDS
AAS Surgical Technology
Certificate Customer Relations; Forensic Studies
Endorsement Library Media
MBA Business Administration (Off Campus MBA)
MEd Curriculum Studies; Educational Leadership
MM Master of Music in Music Education
MPA Public Administration
EdD Educational Leadership (weekend cohort program)

COURSE SUBJECT AREAS OFFERED OUTSIDE OF DEGREE PROGRAMS

Undergraduate—accounting and related services; anthropology; biology; business/commerce; communication and media; computer science; curriculum and instruction; educational administration and supervision; English composition; environmental psychology; health and physical education/fitness; health professions related; human resources management; journalism; library science related; mathematics; nursing; philosophy; philosophy and religious studies related; physical sciences; political science and government; psychology; public administration; public health; science, technology and society; social work; sociology; speech and rhetoric.

Graduate—anthropology; business administration, management and operations; curriculum and instruction; education; educational administration and supervision; education related; information science/studies; library science related; mathematics; music; philosophy; political science and government; public administration; public administration and social service professions related; public policy analysis.

See full description on page 492.

THE UNIVERSITY OF MONTANA–WESTERN
Dillon, Montana
Division of Outreach
http://www.wmc.edu/Academics/Outreach/

The University of Montana–Western was founded in 1893. It is accredited by Northwest Commission on Colleges and Universities. It first offered distance learning courses in 1989. In fall 2006, there were 250 students enrolled in distance learning courses. Institutionally administered financial aid is available to distance learners.

Services Distance learners have accessibility to academic advising, bookstore, career placement assistance, e-mail services, library services.
Contact Vickie Lansing, Director of Continuing Education and Extension Programs, The University of Montana–Western, 710 South Atlantic Street, Dillon, MT 59725. Telephone: 406-683-7537. Fax: 406-683-7809. E-mail: v_lansing@umwestern.edu.

DEGREES AND AWARDS
Programs offered do not lead to a degree or other formal award.

COURSE SUBJECT AREAS OFFERED OUTSIDE OF DEGREE PROGRAMS

Undergraduate—business, management, and marketing related; computer software and media applications; education; education (specific levels and methods); English composition; geological and earth sciences/geosciences; history; liberal arts and sciences, general studies and humanities; library science related; mathematics; philosophy; psychology.
Non-credit—computer software and media applications; legal professions and studies related; medical basic sciences.

UNIVERSITY OF NEBRASKA AT KEARNEY
Kearney, Nebraska
Division of Continuing Education
http://learn.unk.edu

University of Nebraska at Kearney was founded in 1903. It is accredited by North Central Association of Colleges and Schools. It first offered distance learning courses in 1986. In fall 2006, there were 900 students enrolled in distance learning courses. Institutionally administered financial aid is available to distance learners.

Services Distance learners have accessibility to academic advising, bookstore, campus computer network, career placement assistance, e-mail services, library services, tutoring.
Contact Gloria Vavricka, Director of eCampus, University of Nebraska at Kearney, Communications Center, Kearney, NE 68849-4220. Telephone: 308-865-8390. Fax: 308-865-8090. E-mail: vavrickag@unk.edu.

DEGREES AND AWARDS
Endorsement English as a Second Language–ESL; Gifted Graduate Endorsement; Library Media Graduate Endorsement; Vocational Diversified Occupations endorsement
MAE Curriculum and Instruction; Reading K-12; Special Education–Gifted Education
MS Biology
MSE Instructional Technology

UNIVERSITY OF NEBRASKA AT OMAHA
Omaha, Nebraska
http://www.unomaha.edu/

University of Nebraska at Omaha was founded in 1908. It is accredited by North Central Association of Colleges and Schools. It first offered distance learning courses in 1996. In fall 2006, there were 861 students enrolled in distance learning courses. Institutionally administered financial aid is available to distance learners.

Services Distance learners have accessibility to academic advising, bookstore, campus computer network, e-mail services, library services.
Contact Shelley Schafer, Manager of Distance Education, University of Nebraska at Omaha, Eppley Administration Building, #110-H, 6001 Dodge Street, Omaha, NE 68123. Telephone: 402-554-4831. Fax: 402-554-3475. E-mail: sschafer@mail.unomaha.edu.

DEGREES AND AWARDS
BGS General Studies; General Studies
MFA Creative Writing
MPA Public Administration

COURSE SUBJECT AREAS OFFERED OUTSIDE OF DEGREE PROGRAMS

Undergraduate—astronomy and astrophysics; creative writing; English composition; English language and literature related; history; management information systems; political science and government; psychology; social psychology; social sciences; sociology.
Graduate—air transportation; creative writing; education (specific subject areas); public administration; special education.

UNIVERSITY OF NEBRASKA–LINCOLN
Lincoln, Nebraska
Extended Education and Outreach
http://extended.unl.edu

University of Nebraska–Lincoln was founded in 1869. It is accredited by North Central Association of Colleges and Schools. It first offered distance learning courses in 1941. In fall 2006, there were 4,000 students enrolled in distance learning courses. Institutionally administered financial aid is available to distance learners.

Services Distance learners have accessibility to academic advising, bookstore, campus computer network, career placement assistance, e-mail services, library services, tutoring.
Contact Customer Service Representative, University of Nebraska–Lincoln, Extended Education and Outreach, 900 North 22nd Street, Lincoln, NE 68588. Telephone: 402-472-2175. Fax: 402-472-4345. E-mail: extservice@unl.edu.

DEGREES AND AWARDS
Endorsement Educational Administration; Special Education; Teaching, Learning, and Teacher Education
Graduate Certificate Community College Leadership; Community College Leadership; Educational Technology; Financial Planning–Family Financial Planning; Meat Culinology; NCA CASI School Improvement Specialist; Youth Development
MA Educational Administration; Journalism and Mass Communications; Textiles, Clothing, and Design
MAg Agriculture
MBA Business Administration
MBA/M Ag Agribusiness specialization
MEd Educational Administration; Special Education; Teaching, Learning, and Teacher Education

MEngr Engineering Management

MS Architecture; Entomology; Family and Consumer Sciences

EdD Educational Administration; Educational Studies

PhD Educational Studies

COURSE SUBJECT AREAS OFFERED OUTSIDE OF DEGREE PROGRAMS

Undergraduate—accounting and related services; agricultural business and management; area studies; biology; business administration, management and operations; chemistry; communication and journalism related; communication and media; curriculum and instruction; developmental and child psychology; ecology, evolution, and population biology; economics; engineering; engineering/industrial management; English; English composition; finance and financial management services; fine and studio art; fire protection; foods, nutrition, and related services; geography and cartography; health and physical education/fitness; history; human development, family studies, and related services; insurance; international business; journalism; management information systems; marketing; mathematics; mathematics and statistics related; medieval and Renaissance studies; nursing; philosophy; physics; plant sciences; political science and government; psychology; radio, television, and digital communication; real estate; sociology; statistics.

Graduate—accounting and related services; agricultural business and management; apparel and textiles; business administration, management and operations; business, management, and marketing related; business/managerial economics; communication and journalism related; communication and media; communication disorders sciences and services; culinary arts and related services; curriculum and instruction; economics; education; educational administration and supervision; educational/instructional media design; educational psychology; education related; engineering; family and consumer sciences/human sciences; interior architecture; international business; journalism; marketing; political science and government; psychology related; special education; statistics.

Non-credit—business/commerce; English composition; mathematics and statistics related.

UNIVERSITY OF NEBRASKA MEDICAL CENTER
Omaha, Nebraska
CON Rural Nursing Education/CON Graduate Program
http://www.unmc.edu/nursing

University of Nebraska Medical Center was founded in 1869. It is accredited by North Central Association of Colleges and Schools. It first offered distance learning courses in 1970. In fall 2006, there were 425 students enrolled in distance learning courses. Institutionally administered financial aid is available to distance learners.

Services Distance learners have accessibility to academic advising, bookstore, campus computer network, career placement assistance, e-mail services, library services, tutoring.

Contact Ms. Dani S. Eveloff, RN, Recruitment Coordinator, University of Nebraska Medical Center, 985330 Nebraska Medical Center, College of Nursing, Omaha, NE 68198-5330. Telephone: 402-559-5184.

DEGREES AND AWARDS

BSN Nursing

MSN Nursing

COURSE SUBJECT AREAS OFFERED OUTSIDE OF DEGREE PROGRAMS

Undergraduate—nursing.

Graduate—nursing.

Non-credit—nursing.

UNIVERSITY OF NEVADA, LAS VEGAS
Las Vegas, Nevada
Distance Education
http://Distance_Ed.unlv.edu

University of Nevada, Las Vegas was founded in 1957. It is accredited by Northwest Commission on Colleges and Universities. It first offered distance learning courses in 1996. In fall 2006, there were 9,000 students enrolled in distance learning courses. Institutionally administered financial aid is available to distance learners.

Services Distance learners have accessibility to academic advising, bookstore, campus computer network, e-mail services, library services.

Contact Barbara Trumble, Program Manager of Distance Education, University of Nevada, Las Vegas, 4505 Maryland Parkway, Box 451038, Las Vegas, NV 89154. Telephone: 702-895-0334. Fax: 702-895-2918. E-mail: distanceeducation@unlv.edu.

DEGREES AND AWARDS

BA Social Science Studies

Graduate Certificate Instructional Technology

See full description on page 494.

UNIVERSITY OF NEW HAMPSHIRE
Durham, New Hampshire
Interactive Instructional Television Center
http://e-learn.unh.edu

University of New Hampshire was founded in 1866. It is accredited by New England Association of Schools and Colleges. It first offered distance learning courses in 1980. In fall 2006, there were 70 students enrolled in distance learning courses. Institutionally administered financial aid is available to distance learners.

Services Distance learners have accessibility to academic advising, bookstore, campus computer network, career placement assistance, e-mail services, library services.

Contact Debra JohnyBear, Public Relations Assistant, University of New Hampshire, College of Engineering and Physical Sciences, 33 College Road, Kingsbury W283C, Durham, NH 03824. Telephone: 603-862-3102. Fax: 603-862-2486. E-mail: debra.johnybear@unh.edu.

DEGREES AND AWARDS

Programs offered do not lead to a degree or other formal award.

COURSE SUBJECT AREAS OFFERED OUTSIDE OF DEGREE PROGRAMS

Graduate—computer science; electrical, electronics and communications engineering; health professions related; mechanical engineering; statistics.

UNIVERSITY OF NEW ORLEANS
New Orleans, Louisiana
UNO Metropolitan College
http://alt.uno.edu

University of New Orleans was founded in 1958. It is accredited by Southern Association of Colleges and Schools. It first offered distance learning courses in 1980. In fall 2006, there were 7,000 students enrolled in distance learning courses. Institutionally administered financial aid is available to distance learners.

Services Distance learners have accessibility to academic advising, bookstore, campus computer network, e-mail services, library services, tutoring.

Contact Dr. Carl Drichta, Interim Dean, University of New Orleans, Lakefront Campus, Education 122, New Orleans, LA 70148. Telephone: 504-280-7100. Fax: 504-280-7317. E-mail: alt@uno.edu.

DEGREES AND AWARDS

Programs offered do not lead to a degree or other formal award.

COURSE SUBJECT AREAS OFFERED OUTSIDE OF DEGREE PROGRAMS

Undergraduate—accounting and computer science; American literature (United States and Canadian); American Sign Language (ASL); anthropology; applied mathematics; architectural engineering; architectural engineering technology; area, ethnic, cultural, and gender studies related; behavioral sciences; bioethics/medical ethics; biological and biomedical sciences related; biological and physical sciences; biology; business administration, management and operations; business/corporate communications; business, management, and marketing related; business/managerial economics; chemistry; city/urban, community and regional planning; civil engineering; classical and ancient studies; community organization and advocacy; comparative literature; computer and information sciences; computer programming; computer science; computer systems analysis; creative writing; curriculum and instruction; developmental and child psychology; economics; education; educational administration and supervision; educational assessment, evaluation, and research; education (specific levels and methods); education (specific subject areas); electrical and electronic engineering technologies; engineering; engineering-related fields; English; English as a second language; English composition; English language and literature related; English literature (British and Commonwealth); entrepreneurial and small business operations; finance and financial management services; geography and cartography; geological and earth sciences/geosciences; geological/geophysical engineering; gerontology; health professions related; history; hospitality administration; human resources management; journalism; languages (foreign languages related); languages (Germanic); languages (Romance languages); liberal arts and sciences, general studies and humanities; linguistic, comparative, and related language studies; management information systems; management sciences and quantitative methods; marketing; mathematics; mathematics and computer science; mathematics and statistics related; mechanical engineering; medieval and Renaissance studies; music; natural resources and conservation related; naval architecture and marine engineering; personality psychology; philosophy; philosophy and religious studies related; physical sciences; physics; political science and government; psychology; psychometrics and quantitative psychology; public administration; public administration and social service professions related; real estate; social sciences; sociology; special education; speech and rhetoric; statistics; systems engineering; technical and business writing; urban studies/affairs.

Graduate—accounting and computer science; American literature (United States and Canadian); American Sign Language (ASL); anthropology; applied mathematics; architectural engineering; architectural engineering technology; area, ethnic, cultural, and gender studies related; behavioral sciences; biological and biomedical sciences related; biological and physical sciences; biology; business administration, management and operations; business/corporate communications; business, management, and marketing related; business/managerial economics; chemistry; city/urban, community and regional planning; civil engineering; classical and ancient studies; comparative literature; computer and information sciences; computer programming; computer science; computer systems analysis; creative writing; curriculum and instruction; developmental and child psychology; dramatic/theater arts and stagecraft; economics; education; educational administration and supervision; educational assessment, evaluation, and research; educational/instructional media design; education (specific levels and methods); education (specific subject areas); electrical and electronic engineering technologies; engineering; engineering-related fields; English; English as a second language; English composition; English language and literature related; English literature (British and Commonwealth); entrepreneurial and small business operations; finance and financial management services; geography and cartography; geological and earth sciences/geosciences; geological/geophysical engineering; gerontology; health professions related; history; hospitality administration; human resources management; journalism; languages (foreign languages related); languages (Germanic); languages (Romance languages); liberal arts and sciences, general studies and humanities; linguistic, comparative, and related language studies; management information systems; management sciences and quantitative methods; marketing; mathematics; mathematics and computer science; mathematics and statistics related; mechanical engineering; medieval and Renaissance studies; music; natural resources and conservation related; naval architecture and marine engineering; personality psychology; philosophy;

philosophy and religious studies related; physical sciences; physics; political science and government; psychology; psychometrics and quantitative psychology; public administration; public administration and social service professions related; real estate; social sciences; sociology; special education; speech and rhetoric; statistics; systems engineering; technical and business writing; urban studies/affairs.

Non-credit—business, management, and marketing related; communication and journalism related; creative writing; English composition; finance and financial management services; liberal arts and sciences, general studies and humanities; mathematics.

UNIVERSITY OF NORTH ALABAMA
Florence, Alabama
Educational Technology Services/Distance Learning
http://distance.una.edu

University of North Alabama was founded in 1830. It is accredited by Southern Association of Colleges and Schools. It first offered distance learning courses in 1997. In fall 2006, there were 1,000 students enrolled in distance learning courses. Institutionally administered financial aid is available to distance learners.

Services Distance learners have accessibility to academic advising, bookstore, campus computer network, career placement assistance, e-mail services, library services, tutoring.

Contact Ms. B.J. Wilson, Coordinator of Distance Learning, University of North Alabama, UNA Box 5005, Florence, AL 35632-0001. Telephone: 877-765-6110. Fax: 256-718-3923. E-mail: bhwilson@una.edu.

DEGREES AND AWARDS
BSN Nursing–RN to BSN
MBA Business Administration–Online MBA program

COURSE SUBJECT AREAS OFFERED OUTSIDE OF DEGREE PROGRAMS

Undergraduate—accounting and related services; area studies; business, management, and marketing related; communication and media; computer and information sciences; criminal justice and corrections; economics; education; English; English composition; finance and financial management services; foods, nutrition, and related services; geography and cartography; gerontology; history; marketing; nursing; philosophy; political science and government; social work; sociology.

Graduate—accounting and related services; area studies; business administration, management and operations; business/commerce; education; English; geography and cartography.

THE UNIVERSITY OF NORTH CAROLINA AT CHAPEL HILL
Chapel Hill, North Carolina
The William and Ida Friday Center for Continuing Education
http://fridaycenter.unc.edu

The University of North Carolina at Chapel Hill was founded in 1789. It is accredited by Southern Association of Colleges and Schools. It first offered distance learning courses in 1941. In fall 2006, there were 3,800 students enrolled in distance learning courses. Institutionally administered financial aid is available to distance learners.

Services Distance learners have accessibility to academic advising, bookstore, career placement assistance, library services.

Contact Carol McDonnell, Student Services Manager, The University of North Carolina at Chapel Hill, CB #1020, Chapel Hill, NC 27599-1020. Telephone: 800-862-5669. Fax: 919-962-5549.
E-mail: carol_mcdonnell@unc.edu.

DEGREES AND AWARDS
Programs offered do not lead to a degree or other formal award.

COURSE SUBJECT AREAS OFFERED OUTSIDE OF DEGREE PROGRAMS

Undergraduate—accounting and related services; anthropology; area studies; astronomy and astrophysics; biology; business administration, management and operations; business/corporate communications; chemistry; communication and media; computer and information sciences; creative writing; criminal justice and corrections; dramatic/theater arts and stagecraft; economics; English as a second language; English composition; ethnic, cultural minority, and gender studies; fine and studio art; foods, nutrition, and related services; geography and cartography; geological and earth sciences/geosciences; history; hospitality administration; journalism; languages (classics and classical); languages (foreign languages related); languages (Romance languages); languages (Slavic, Baltic and Albanian); mathematics and statistics related; music; parks, recreation and leisure; philosophy; physics; political science and government; psychology; religious studies; sociology; statistics.

Non-credit—area, ethnic, cultural, and gender studies related; business/corporate communications; business, management, and marketing related; creative writing; ethnic, cultural minority, and gender studies; fine and studio art; history; music; nursing; philosophy; political science and government.

See full description on page 496.

THE UNIVERSITY OF NORTH CAROLINA AT CHARLOTTE
Charlotte, North Carolina
Continuing Education, Extension and Summer Programs
http://www.DistanceEd.uncc.edu

The University of North Carolina at Charlotte was founded in 1946. It is accredited by Southern Association of Colleges and Schools. It first offered distance learning courses in 1985. In fall 2006, there were 595 students enrolled in distance learning courses. Institutionally administered financial aid is available to distance learners.

Services Distance learners have accessibility to academic advising, bookstore, campus computer network, career placement assistance, e-mail services, library services, tutoring.

Contact Mary Faye Englebert, Associate Director, The University of North Carolina at Charlotte, 9201 University City Boulevard, Charlotte, NC 28223. Telephone: 704-687-4594. Fax: 704-687-4305. E-mail: mfengleb@uncc.edu.

DEGREES AND AWARDS
BA Elementary Education
BSET Electrical Engineering Technology; Fire Science
BSN Nursing–RN to BSN completion
License Education, Middle and Secondary Education Teacher Licensure; Special Education, Adapted Curriculum; Special Education, General Curriculum Teacher licensure
Graduate Certificate Education, Academically or Intellectually Gifted Add-On Teacher Licensure; Information Security and Privacy
MEd Education, Middle Grades; Elementary Education; Reading, Language, and Literacy
MSA Education and School Administration
MSN Community and Public Health, School Nurse option; Nurse Educator

COURSE SUBJECT AREAS OFFERED OUTSIDE OF DEGREE PROGRAMS
Undergraduate—business, management, and marketing related; classical and ancient studies; computer and information sciences; education; engineering; English as a second language; history; mathematics; nursing; political science and government; psychology related; sociology.
Graduate—biology; education; information science/studies; nursing; statistics.
Non-credit—accounting and computer science; accounting and related services; architecture; building/construction finishing, management, and inspection; business administration, management and operations; business/commerce; business/corporate communications; business, management, and marketing related; business operations support and assistant services; civil engineering; computer software and media applications; counseling psychology; electrical and electronic engineering technologies; engineering; film/video and photographic arts; finance and financial management services; fire protection; geography and cartography; health and medical administrative services; hospitality administration; human

resources management; legal support services; marketing; mechanical engineering; nursing; public administration and social service professions related; sales, merchandising, and related marketing operations (specialized); taxation.

THE UNIVERSITY OF NORTH CAROLINA AT GREENSBORO
Greensboro, North Carolina
Division of Continual Learning and Summer Session
http://www.calldcl.com

The University of North Carolina at Greensboro was founded in 1891. It is accredited by Southern Association of Colleges and Schools. It first offered distance learning courses in 1972. In fall 2006, there were 1,323 students enrolled in distance learning courses. Institutionally administered financial aid is available to distance learners.

Services Distance learners have accessibility to academic advising, bookstore, campus computer network, career placement assistance, e-mail services, library services.

Contact William H. Taylor, Director of Distance Learning and Summer Session, The University of North Carolina at Greensboro, Division of Continual Learning, 1100 West Market Street, Suite 300, PO Box 26170, Greensboro, NC 27402-6170. Telephone: 336-334-5414. Fax: 336-334-5628. E-mail: whtaylor@uncg.edu.

DEGREES AND AWARDS
BA Liberal Studies (Humanities concentration)
BS Education–Birth-Kindergarten Teacher Licensure
BSN Nursing
Certificate Conflict Resolution; Nonprofit Management (post-Baccalaureate)
MA Conflict Resolution; Dance Education; Liberal Studies
MEd Curriculum and Instruction; Educational Administration–School Administration; Special Education (Cross-Categorical emphasis)
MLIS Library and Information Studies
MSN Nursing
PMC Counseling–School Counseling, advanced

COURSE SUBJECT AREAS OFFERED OUTSIDE OF DEGREE PROGRAMS
Undergraduate—anthropology; business/managerial economics; classical and ancient studies; communication disorders sciences and services; dance; economics; film/video and photographic arts; geological and earth sciences/geosciences; health professions related; history; human development, family studies, and related services; liberal arts and sciences, general studies and humanities; mathematics; mathematics and statistics related; philosophy; philosophy and religious studies related; psychology; public health; social sciences; sociology; statistics.
Graduate—curriculum and instruction; dance; education related; liberal arts and sciences, general studies and humanities; library science; library science related; nursing; peace studies and conflict resolution; special education; student counseling and personnel services.
Non-credit—business administration, management and operations; computer and information sciences and support services related; health and medical administrative services; pharmacy, pharmaceutical sciences, and administration.

UNIVERSITY OF NORTH DAKOTA
Grand Forks, North Dakota
Division of Continuing Education
http://www.conted.und.edu

University of North Dakota was founded in 1883. It is accredited by North Central Association of Colleges and Schools. It first offered distance learning courses in 1970. In fall 2006, there were 679 students enrolled in distance learning courses. Institutionally administered financial aid is available to distance learners.

Services Distance learners have accessibility to academic advising, bookstore, campus computer network, career placement assistance, e-mail services, library services, tutoring.

Contact Ms. Heidi Flaten, Coordinator, University of North Dakota, Gustafson Hall, Room 205, 3264 Campus Road, Stop 9021, Grand Forks, ND 58202-9021. Telephone: 877-450-1842. Fax: 701-777-6401. E-mail: distancedegreeprograms@mail.und.edu.

DEGREES AND AWARDS
BA Social Science
BBA Information Systems
BGS General Studies
BS Chemical Engineering; Civil Engineering; Electrical Engineering; Mechanical Engineering; Nursing
Endorsement English Language Learner/English as a Second Language
Graduate Certificate Autistic Spectrum Disorders; Geographic Information Sciences; Health Administration
MA Counseling; Forensic Psychology
MBA Business Administration
MEd Education Leadership; Special Education
MPA Public Administration
MS Early Childhood Education; Elementary Education; General Studies (Secondary Education); Instructional Design and Technology; Space Studies
MSN Nursing–Education specialization
MSW Social Work
EdD Educational Leadership
PhD Higher Education

COURSE SUBJECT AREAS OFFERED OUTSIDE OF DEGREE PROGRAMS
Undergraduate—accounting and related services; anthropology; business administration, management and operations; chemical engineering; chemistry; civil engineering; communication and media; economics; education (specific levels and methods); education (specific subject areas); English composition; geography and cartography; history; industrial and organizational psychology; linguistic, comparative, and related language studies; mathematics; mechanical engineering; nursing; physical sciences; physics; psychology; religious studies; social work; sociology.
Graduate—business administration, management and operations; education (specific subject areas); English as a second/foreign language (teaching); public administration; social work.
Non-credit—computer programming; computer software and media applications; graphic communications; health and medical administrative services; health professions related; heating, air conditioning, ventilation and refrigeration maintenance technology; human resources management; legal support services; mathematics; real estate.

UNIVERSITY OF NORTHERN IOWA
Cedar Falls, Iowa
Division of Continuing Education
http://www.uni.edu/contined/cp/distance.shtml
University of Northern Iowa was founded in 1876. It is accredited by North Central Association of Colleges and Schools. It first offered distance learning courses in 1941. In fall 2006, there were 1,200 students enrolled in distance learning courses. Institutionally administered financial aid is available to distance learners.
Services Distance learners have accessibility to academic advising, bookstore, campus computer network, career placement assistance, e-mail services, library services.
Contact Dr. Kent Johnson, Associate Director of Continuing Education Credit Programs, University of Northern Iowa, Cedar Falls, IA 50614-0223. Telephone: 319-273-5970. Fax: 319-273-2872. E-mail: kent.johnson@uni.edu.

DEGREES AND AWARDS
BLS Liberal Studies

COURSE SUBJECT AREAS OFFERED OUTSIDE OF DEGREE PROGRAMS
Undergraduate—accounting and related services; area studies; communication and media; criminology; education; English; family and con-

sumer economics; geography and cartography; health and physical education/fitness; marketing; mathematics; music; psychology; religious studies; social work; sociology.
Graduate—criminology; education; geography and cartography; religious studies; social work; sociology.

UNIVERSITY OF NORTH FLORIDA
Jacksonville, Florida
http://www.unf.edu/
University of North Florida was founded in 1965. It is accredited by Southern Association of Colleges and Schools. It first offered distance learning courses in 1997. In fall 2006, there were 1,268 students enrolled in distance learning courses. Institutionally administered financial aid is available to distance learners.
Services Distance learners have accessibility to academic advising, bookstore, campus computer network, career placement assistance, e-mail services, library services, tutoring.
Contact Dr. Julia A. Watkins, Assistant Professor, University of North Florida, 4567 St. Johns Bluff Road South, Jacksonville, FL 32224-2465. Telephone: 904-620-1468. E-mail: jwatkins@unf.edu.

DEGREES AND AWARDS
Programs offered do not lead to a degree or other formal award.

COURSE SUBJECT AREAS OFFERED OUTSIDE OF DEGREE PROGRAMS
Undergraduate—building/construction finishing, management, and inspection; computer and information sciences; computer programming; creative writing; curriculum and instruction; education; English composition; health and medical administrative services; health services/allied health/health sciences; music; nursing; nutrition sciences; philosophy; public health; special education.
Graduate—dietetics and clinical nutrition services; health services/allied health/health sciences.

UNIVERSITY OF NORTH TEXAS
Denton, Texas
Center for Distributed Learning
http://courses.unt.edu
University of North Texas was founded in 1890. It is accredited by Southern Association of Colleges and Schools. It first offered distance learning courses in 1995. In fall 2006, there were 12,233 students enrolled in distance learning courses. Institutionally administered financial aid is available to distance learners.
Services Distance learners have accessibility to academic advising, bookstore, campus computer network, career placement assistance, e-mail services, library services, tutoring.
Contact Dr. Arlita W. Harris, Senior Marketing Specialist, University of North Texas, PO Box 310889, Denton, TX 76203-0889. Telephone: 940-565-2942. Fax: 940-565-4990. E-mail: arlita@unt.edu.

DEGREES AND AWARDS
BA General Studies
BAA Applied Technology and Performance Improvement; Organizational Development
Certificate E-Commerce; Retailing–Five Course Sequence in Retailing; TESOL
Certification Texas Teacher Certification–Secondary Education
Endorsement Gifted and Talented Education
Graduate Certificate Behavior Analysis; Gifted Education; Hospitality Management; Library and Information Sciences; Merchandising; Specialist Certificate in Aging; Volunteer and Community Resource Management
MA Anthropology; Applied Gerontology
MBA Management
MEd Education–Secondary Education; Educational Administration
MLS Library Science

MS Applied Gerontology; Computer Education and Cognitive Systems; Educational Administration and Supervision; Educational Psychology; Hospitality Management; Information Sciences; Merchandising; Teaching and Learning with Technology
MSE Applied Technology, Training, and Development

COURSE SUBJECT AREAS OFFERED OUTSIDE OF DEGREE PROGRAMS

Undergraduate—anthropology; apparel and textiles; behavioral sciences; biology; business administration, management and operations; business/commerce; business, management, and marketing related; chemistry; computer and information sciences; computer/information technology administration and management; computer software and media applications; curriculum and instruction; data entry/microcomputer applications; developmental and child psychology; economics; education; educational administration and supervision; educational assessment, evaluation, and research; educational/instructional media design; educational psychology; electrical and electronic engineering technologies; engineering-related technologies; engineering technologies related; family and consumer economics; fine and studio art; food science and technology; geological and earth sciences/geosciences; health and physical education/fitness; history; hospitality administration; human development, family studies, and related services; journalism; library science; library science related; linguistic, comparative, and related language studies; marketing; mathematics; music; nutrition sciences; psychology related; public administration; rehabilitation and therapeutic professions; sales, merchandising, and related marketing operations (specialized); social sciences; social work; sociology; special education; technical and business writing.
Graduate—anthropology; apparel and textiles; behavioral sciences; business administration, management and operations; business, management, and marketing related; chemistry; communications technology; community organization and advocacy; computer and information sciences; computer software and media applications; curriculum and instruction; developmental and child psychology; education; educational administration and supervision; educational assessment, evaluation, and research; educational/instructional media design; educational psychology; education related; electrical and electronic engineering technologies; family and consumer economics; food science and technology; gerontology; health and medical administrative services; hospitality administration; human development, family studies, and related services; human resources management; industrial and organizational psychology; information science/studies; library science; library science related; linguistic, comparative, and related language studies; marketing; rehabilitation and therapeutic professions; sales, merchandising, and related marketing operations (specialized); social and philosophical foundations of education; social sciences; special education.
Non-credit—behavioral sciences; business administration, management and operations; education; educational administration and supervision; educational psychology; gerontology; library science; library science related; marketing; rehabilitation and therapeutic professions; school psychology; special education.

UNIVERSITY OF NORTHWESTERN OHIO
Lima, Ohio
Division of Distance Learning
http://www.unoh.edu
University of Northwestern Ohio was founded in 1920. It is accredited by North Central Association of Colleges and Schools. It first offered distance learning courses in 1993. In fall 2006, there were 600 students enrolled in distance learning courses. Institutionally administered financial aid is available to distance learners.
Services Distance learners have accessibility to academic advising, bookstore, campus computer network, career placement assistance, e-mail services, library services, tutoring.
Contact Mr. Rick Morrison, Director of Admissions, University of Northwestern Ohio, 1441 North Cable Road, Lima, OH 45805. Telephone: 419-998-3120. Fax: 419-229-6926. E-mail: rmorris@unoh.edu.

DEGREES AND AWARDS
AAS Agribusiness; Automotive Management; Information Systems Technology; Legal Assisting; Marketing; Marketing, Management, and Tech-

nology; Medical Assistant Technology; Secretarial (Administrative, Legal, Medical); Travel Management; Word Processing–Administrative Support
BS Accounting; Business Administration; Health Care Administration

COURSE SUBJECT AREAS OFFERED OUTSIDE OF DEGREE PROGRAMS
Undergraduate—accounting and related services; agricultural business and management; allied health and medical assisting services; business administration, management and operations; business operations support and assistant services; computer and information sciences; electrical and power transmission installation.

UNIVERSITY OF OKLAHOMA
Norman, Oklahoma
College of Continuing Education
http://www.occe.ou.edu
University of Oklahoma was founded in 1890. It is accredited by North Central Association of Colleges and Schools. It first offered distance learning courses in 1941. In fall 2006, there were 50,000 students enrolled in distance learning courses. Institutionally administered financial aid is available to distance learners.
Services Distance learners have accessibility to academic advising, bookstore, campus computer network, career placement assistance, e-mail services, library services.
Contact Larry D. Hayes, Information Assistant, Office of the Vice President for University Outreach, University of Oklahoma, University OUTREACH, 1700 Asp Avenue, Norman, OK 73072. Telephone: 800-522-0772 Ext. 4414. Fax: 405-325-7196. E-mail: lhayes@ou.edu.

DEGREES AND AWARDS
BLS Liberal Studies
MA Advanced Programs
MLS Liberal Studies
PhD Advanced Programs

COURSE SUBJECT AREAS OFFERED OUTSIDE OF DEGREE PROGRAMS
Undergraduate—anthropology; astronomy and astrophysics; business administration, management and operations; business/corporate communications; chemistry; communication and media; dramatic/theater arts and stagecraft; economics; education; engineering; English composition; finance and financial management services; geography and cartography; geological and earth sciences/geosciences; health and physical education/fitness; history; journalism; library science related; marketing; mathematics; philosophy; political science and government; sociology.

See full description on page 498.

See full description on page 498.

UNIVERSITY OF OREGON
Eugene, Oregon
Distance Education
http://de.uoregon.edu
University of Oregon was founded in 1872. It is accredited by Northwest Commission on Colleges and Universities. It first offered distance learning courses in 1996. In fall 2006, there were 750 students enrolled in distance learning courses. Institutionally administered financial aid is available to distance learners.
Services Distance learners have accessibility to academic advising, bookstore, campus computer network, e-mail services, library services.
Contact Sonya Faust, Program Coordinator, University of Oregon, 1277 University of Oregon, Eugene, OR 97403-1277. Telephone: 541-346-4231. Fax: 541-346-3545. E-mail: disted@uoregon.edu.

DEGREES AND AWARDS
MS Information Management–Applied Information Management

COURSE SUBJECT AREAS OFFERED OUTSIDE OF DEGREE PROGRAMS
Undergraduate—astronomy and astrophysics; economics; geography and cartography; geological and earth sciences/geosciences; linguistic,

comparative, and related language studies; multi-/interdisciplinary studies related; physics; political science and government; visual and performing arts related.
Graduate—information science/studies; management information systems.

UNIVERSITY OF PHOENIX ONLINE CAMPUS
Phoenix, Arizona
http://www.uoponline.com
University of Phoenix Online Campus was founded in 1989. It is accredited by North Central Association of Colleges and Schools. It first offered distance learning courses in 1989. In fall 2006, there were 165,373 students enrolled in distance learning courses. Institutionally administered financial aid is available to distance learners.
Services Distance learners have accessibility to academic advising, bookstore, campus computer network, library services, tutoring.
Contact Mr. Brian Mayer, Director of Marketing, University of Phoenix Online Campus, Mail Stop AA-B418, 4615 East Elwood Street, Phoenix, AZ 85040-1958. Telephone: 480-557-1510. Fax: 602-383-6364. E-mail: brian.mayer@phoenix.edu.

DEGREES AND AWARDS
AA Accounting; Business; Criminal Justice; General Studies; Health Administration; Information Technology; Information Technology/Networking; Information Technology/Visual Communications; Paraprofessional Education
BEd Education
BS Business Hospitality Management; Business/Accounting; Business/Business Administration; Business/Communication; Business/E-Business; Business/Finance; Business/Global Business Management; Business/Information Systems; Business/Integrated Supply Chain and Operations Management; Business/Management; Business/Marketing; Business/Organizational Innovation; Business/Public Administration; Business/Retail Management; Criminal Justice Administration; Health Administration; Health Administration/Health Information Systems; Health Administration/Long-Term Care; Human Services/Management; Information Technology; Information Technology/Information Systems Security; Information Technology/Multimedia and Visual Communication; Information Technology/Software Engineering; Organizational Security and Management; Psychology
BSN Nursing–RN to Bachelor of Science in Nursing
MA Curriculum and Instruction–Adult Education; Education–Administration and Supervision specialization; Education–Computer Education; Education–Curriculum and Instruction; Education–Early Childhood Education specialization; Education/Adult Education and Training; Education/Curriculum and Instruction–English and Language Education; Education/Curriculum and Instruction–Mathematics Education; Education/ESL; Education/Elementary Teacher Education; Education/Secondary Teacher Education
MBA Accounting; Business Administration; Business Administration/Marketing; Global Management; Human Resource Management; Public Administration; Technology Management
MBA/MHMS Business Administration/Health Care Management
MHA Health Administration–Master of Health Administration
MISM Master of Information Systems
MM Human Resource Management; International; Management; Public Administration
MS Administration of Justice and Security; Psychology
MSN Nursing–Master of Business Administration, Health Care Management; Nursing–Nursing/Health Care Education; Nursing
DBA Business Administration
DH Sc Health Administration–Doctor of Health Administration (DHA)
DM Organizational Leadership, Information Systems and Technology specialization; Organizational Management
EdD Educational Leadership; Educational Leadership, Curriculum and Instruction specialization

COURSE SUBJECT AREAS OFFERED OUTSIDE OF DEGREE PROGRAMS
Undergraduate—business operations support and assistant services; human resources management.

Graduate—education; nursing.
See full description on page 500.

UNIVERSITY OF PITTSBURGH AT BRADFORD
Bradford, Pennsylvania
http://www.upb.pitt.edu/
University of Pittsburgh at Bradford was founded in 1963. It is accredited by Middle States Association of Colleges and Schools. It first offered distance learning courses in 1995. In fall 2006, there were 39 students enrolled in distance learning courses. Institutionally administered financial aid is available to distance learners.
Services Distance learners have accessibility to academic advising, bookstore, campus computer network, career placement assistance, e-mail services, library services.
Contact Mr. Don Lewicki, Director, Computing, Telecommunications, and Media Services, University of Pittsburgh at Bradford, 300 Campus Drive, Bradford, PA 16701-2898. Telephone: 814-362-7660. Fax: 814-362-5279. E-mail: lewicki@upb.pitt.edu.

DEGREES AND AWARDS
AA Liberal Studies

COURSE SUBJECT AREAS OFFERED OUTSIDE OF DEGREE PROGRAMS
Undergraduate—biology; business, management, and marketing related; chemistry; computer and information sciences; computer science; criminal justice and corrections; economics; management information systems; marketing; nursing.

UNIVERSITY OF ST. AUGUSTINE FOR HEALTH SCIENCES
St. Augustine, Florida
Division of Distance Education
http://www.usa.edu
University of St. Augustine for Health Sciences was founded in 1978. It is accredited by Distance Education and Training Council. It first offered distance learning courses in 1979. In fall 2006, there were 400 students enrolled in distance learning courses. Institutionally administered financial aid is available to distance learners.
Services Distance learners have accessibility to academic advising, bookstore, e-mail services, library services, tutoring.
Contact Dr. Debra Gray, Transitional DPT Program Director, University of St. Augustine for Health Sciences, 1 University Boulevard, St. Augustine, FL 32086. Telephone: 904-826-0084 Ext. 262. Fax: 904-826-0085. E-mail: info@usa.edu.

DEGREES AND AWARDS
DPT Physical Therapy–Transitional Doctor of Physical Therapy
OTD Occupational Therapy

COURSE SUBJECT AREAS OFFERED OUTSIDE OF DEGREE PROGRAMS
Graduate—rehabilitation and therapeutic professions.
Non-credit—health professions related.

UNIVERSITY OF ST. FRANCIS
Joliet, Illinois
http://www.stfrancis.edu/
University of St. Francis was founded in 1920. It is accredited by North Central Association of Colleges and Schools. It first offered distance learning courses in 1997. In fall 2006, there were 1,538 students enrolled in distance learning courses. Institutionally administered financial aid is available to distance learners.
Services Distance learners have accessibility to academic advising, bookstore, campus computer network, career placement assistance, e-mail services, library services, tutoring.

Contact Ms. Sandra Sloka, Director, Graduate and Degree Completion Admissions, University of St. Francis, 500 Wilcox Street, Joliet, IL 60435. Telephone: 800-735-7500. Fax: 815-740-5032. E-mail: ssloka@ stfrancis.edu.

DEGREES AND AWARDS

BS Applied Organizational Management; Health Arts; Health Care Leadership; Organizational Leadership
BSN Nursing Fast Track
MBA Business Administration
MS Health Services Administration; Training and Development
MSM Management
MSN Nurse Practitioner

COURSE SUBJECT AREAS OFFERED OUTSIDE OF DEGREE PROGRAMS

Undergraduate—business administration, management and operations; communication and media; computer and information sciences; English; fine and studio art; health professions related; history; nursing; philosophy and religious studies related; social sciences.

Graduate—business administration, management and operations; educational assessment, evaluation, and research; health and medical administrative services; nursing.

UNIVERSITY OF ST. MICHAEL'S COLLEGE
Toronto, Ontario, Canada

University of St. Michael's College was founded in 1852. It is provincially chartered. It first offered distance learning courses in 2005. In fall 2006, there were 20 students enrolled in distance learning courses. Institutionally administered financial aid is available to distance learners.
Services Distance learners have accessibility to campus computer network, e-mail services, library services.
Contact Dr. Anne Anderson, CSJ, Dean, Faculty of Theology, University of St. Michael's College, 81 St. Mary Street, Toronto, ON M5S 1J4, Canada. Telephone: 416-926-7265. Fax: 416-926-7294. E-mail: anne. anderson@utoronto.ca.

DEGREES AND AWARDS

Programs offered do not lead to a degree or other formal award.

COURSE SUBJECT AREAS OFFERED OUTSIDE OF DEGREE PROGRAMS

Undergraduate—theology and religious vocations related.
Graduate—theology and religious vocations related.

UNIVERSITY OF ST. THOMAS
Houston, Texas

University of St. Thomas was founded in 1947. It is accredited by Southern Association of Colleges and Schools. It first offered distance learning courses in 2003. In fall 2006, there were 124 students enrolled in distance learning courses. Institutionally administered financial aid is available to distance learners.
Services Distance learners have accessibility to bookstore, career placement assistance, e-mail services, library services.
Contact Arthur Ortiz, Assistant Director of Admissions, University of St. Thomas, 3800 Montrose, houston, TX 77006. Telephone: 713-9423-483. Fax: 713-942-3464. E-mail: ortiza@stthom.edu.

DEGREES AND AWARDS

Programs offered do not lead to a degree or other formal award.

COURSE SUBJECT AREAS OFFERED OUTSIDE OF DEGREE PROGRAMS

Undergraduate—education; management information systems.
Graduate—education.

UNIVERSITY OF SASKATCHEWAN
Saskatoon, Saskatchewan, Canada
Extension Credit Studies
http://www.extension.usask.ca

University of Saskatchewan was founded in 1907. It is provincially chartered. It first offered distance learning courses in 1941. In fall 2006, there were 1,500 students enrolled in distance learning courses. Institutionally administered financial aid is available to distance learners.
Services Distance learners have accessibility to academic advising, bookstore, campus computer network, e-mail services, library services, tutoring.
Contact Ms. Grace Milashenko, Independent Studies Coordinator, University of Saskatchewan, Room 444, Williams Building, 221 Cumberland Avenue North, Saskatoon, SK S7N 1M3, Canada. Telephone: 306-966-5562. Fax: 306-966-5590. E-mail: grace.milashenko@usask.ca.

DEGREES AND AWARDS

Programs offered do not lead to a degree or other formal award.

COURSE SUBJECT AREAS OFFERED OUTSIDE OF DEGREE PROGRAMS

Undergraduate—agricultural business and management; agriculture; anthropology; archeology; computer science; curriculum and instruction; economics; education (specific levels and methods); education (specific subject areas); English; English as a second/foreign language (teaching); English as a second language; English literature (British and Commonwealth); geography and cartography; geological and earth sciences/geosciences; history; mathematics; music; nursing; philosophy; political science and government; psychology; religious studies; sociology.

Graduate—educational psychology; education related.

Non-credit—agricultural business and management; agriculture and agriculture operations related; applied horticulture/horticultural business services; botany/plant biology; educational/instructional media design; education related; education (specific subject areas); English as a second/foreign language (teaching); English as a second language; landscape architecture; soil sciences.

UNIVERSITY OF SIOUX FALLS
Sioux Falls, South Dakota
http://www.usiouxfalls.edu/

University of Sioux Falls was founded in 1883. It is accredited by North Central Association of Colleges and Schools. It first offered distance learning courses in 2000. In fall 2006, there were 160 students enrolled in distance learning courses. Institutionally administered financial aid is available to distance learners.
Services Distance learners have accessibility to academic advising, bookstore, campus computer network, career placement assistance, e-mail services, library services.
Contact Phyllis Thompson, Associate Dean of Academic Affairs and Registrar, University of Sioux Falls, 1101 West 22nd Street, Jorden Hall, Sioux Falls, SD 57105. Telephone: 605-331-6651. Fax: 605-331-6615. E-mail: phyllis.thompson@usiouxfalls.edu.

DEGREES AND AWARDS

Programs offered do not lead to a degree or other formal award.

COURSE SUBJECT AREAS OFFERED OUTSIDE OF DEGREE PROGRAMS

Undergraduate—education (specific subject areas); English; fine and studio art; geography and cartography; health and physical education/fitness; health professions related; history; sociology.

Graduate—education; educational administration and supervision; educational assessment, evaluation, and research.

UNIVERSITY OF SOUTH ALABAMA
Mobile, Alabama
USA Online
http://usaonline.southalabama.edu

University of South Alabama was founded in 1963. It is accredited by Southern Association of Colleges and Schools. It first offered distance learning courses in 1999. In fall 2006, there were 1,300 students enrolled in distance learning courses. Institutionally administered financial aid is available to distance learners.

Services Distance learners have accessibility to academic advising, bookstore, e-mail services, library services.

Contact Melissa Jones, Director of Admissions, University of South Alabama, AD 182, Mobile, AL 36688-0002. Telephone: 251-460-6141. Fax: 251-460-7876. E-mail: admiss@usamail.usouthal.edu.

DEGREES AND AWARDS
BSN Nursing
Certification Educational Administration; Educational Media (Library Media)
MEd Educational Leadership; Educational Media (Library Media); Special Education (Gifted)
MS Instructional Design and Development
MSN Nursing

COURSE SUBJECT AREAS OFFERED OUTSIDE OF DEGREE PROGRAMS
Graduate—accounting and related services; business administration, management and operations; educational administration and supervision; educational/instructional media design; education (specific levels and methods); finance and financial management services; nursing; special education.

UNIVERSITY OF SOUTH CAROLINA SUMTER
Sumter, South Carolina
http://www.uscsumter.edu/

University of South Carolina Sumter was founded in 1966. It is accredited by Southern Association of Colleges and Schools. It first offered distance learning courses in 1993. In fall 2006, there were 37 students enrolled in distance learning courses. Institutionally administered financial aid is available to distance learners.

Services Distance learners have accessibility to academic advising, bookstore, campus computer network, e-mail services, library services.

Contact Mr. Keith Britton, Director of Distance Learning, University of South Carolina Sumter, 200 Miller Road, Sumter, SC 29150. Telephone: 803-938-3882. E-mail: kbritton@uscsumter.edu.

DEGREES AND AWARDS
Programs offered do not lead to a degree or other formal award.

COURSE SUBJECT AREAS OFFERED OUTSIDE OF DEGREE PROGRAMS
Undergraduate—American literature (United States and Canadian); community health services; education; educational administration and supervision; educational assessment, evaluation, and research; engineering; history; public administration; public health; social and philosophical foundations of education; social psychology; social sciences.
Graduate—business administration, management and operations; educational administration and supervision; education related; nursing; social work; sociology.

THE UNIVERSITY OF SOUTH DAKOTA
Vermillion, South Dakota
Division of Continuing and Distance Education
http://www.usd.edu/swes

The University of South Dakota was founded in 1862. It is accredited by North Central Association of Colleges and Schools. It first offered distance learning courses in 1957. In fall 2006, there were 1,602 students enrolled in distance learning courses. Institutionally administered financial aid is available to distance learners.

Services Distance learners have accessibility to academic advising, bookstore, campus computer network, career placement assistance, e-mail services, library services, tutoring.

Contact Secretary, The University of South Dakota, Division of Continuing & Distance Education, 414 East Clark Street, Vermillion, SD 57069. Telephone: 800-233-7937. Fax: 605-677-6118. E-mail: ceinfo@usd.edu.

DEGREES AND AWARDS
AA General Studies
Certificate Alcohol and Drug Abuse Studies
Graduate Certificate Alcohol and Drug Abuse Studies; Long-Term Care Management
MA Educational Administration/Adult and Higher Education; Educational Administration/Elementary School Principal; Educational Administration/School District Superintendent; Educational Administration/Secondary School Principal
MBA Business Administration; Health Services Administration specialization
MS Administrative Studies/Health Services Administration; Administrative Studies/Interdisciplinary Studies; Administrative Studies/Long-Term Care Administration; Administrative Studies/Organizational Leadership; Technology for Education and Training

COURSE SUBJECT AREAS OFFERED OUTSIDE OF DEGREE PROGRAMS
Undergraduate—behavioral sciences; biology; chemistry; creative writing; criminal justice and corrections; criminology; dramatic/theater arts and stagecraft; education; English; English composition; history; liberal arts and sciences, general studies and humanities; mathematics; microbiological sciences and immunology; music; nursing; physical sciences; physiology, pathology and related sciences; psychology; public relations, advertising, and applied communication related; social sciences related; sociology; speech and rhetoric; statistics.
Graduate—counseling psychology; criminal justice and corrections; education; speech and rhetoric.

THE UNIVERSITY OF SOUTH DAKOTA
Vermillion, South Dakota
School of Education

The University of South Dakota was founded in 1862. It is accredited by North Central Association of Colleges and Schools. It first offered distance learning courses in 1957. In fall 2006, there were 1,602 students enrolled in distance learning courses. Institutionally administered financial aid is available to distance learners.

Services Distance learners have accessibility to academic advising, bookstore, campus computer network, career placement assistance, e-mail services, library services, tutoring.

Contact Secretary, The University of South Dakota, Division of Continuing and Distance Education, 414 East Clark Street, Vermillion, SD 57069. Telephone: 800-233-7937. Fax: 605-677-6118. E-mail: ceinfo@usd.edu.

DEGREES AND AWARDS
AA General Studies
Certificate Alcohol and Drug Abuse Studies
Graduate Certificate Long-Term Care Management
MA Educational Administration/Adult and Higher Education; Educational Administration/Elementary School Principal; Educational Administration/School District Superintendent; Educational Administration/Secondary School Principal
MBA General Studies; Health Services Administration specialization
MS Administrative Studies/Health Services Administration; Administrative Studies/Interdisciplinary Studies; Administrative Studies/Long-Term Care Administration; Technology for Education and Training

COURSE SUBJECT AREAS OFFERED OUTSIDE OF DEGREE PROGRAMS
Undergraduate—behavioral sciences; biology; chemistry; creative writing; criminal justice and corrections; criminology; dramatic/theater arts and stagecraft; education; English; English composition; history; liberal arts and sciences, general studies and humanities; mathematics; microbiological sciences and immunology; music; nursing; physical sciences; physiology, pathology and related sciences; psychology; public

relations, advertising, and applied communication related; social sciences related; sociology; speech and rhetoric; statistics.
Graduate—counseling psychology; criminal justice and corrections; education; speech and rhetoric.

UNIVERSITY OF SOUTHERN CALIFORNIA
Los Angeles, California
Technology Enhanced Learning and Distance Learning Initiative
http://www.usc.edu/

University of Southern California was founded in 1880. It is accredited by Western Association of Schools and Colleges. It first offered distance learning courses in 1972. In fall 2006, there were 1,510 students enrolled in distance learning courses. Institutionally administered financial aid is available to distance learners.
Services Distance learners have accessibility to academic advising, bookstore, campus computer network, career placement assistance, e-mail services, library services, tutoring.
Contact Dr. Suh-Pyng Ku, Chief Technology Officer for Enhanced Learning, University of Southern California, Los Angeles, CA 90089-1427. Telephone: 213-740-6540. E-mail: tel.dl@marshall.usc.edu.

DEGREES AND AWARDS
Graduate Certificate Astronautical Engineering; Engineering Technology Commercialization; Gerontology; Petroleum Engineering (Smart Oilfield Technologies); System Safety and Security; Systems Architecture Engineering Certificate
MA Gerontology; Long-Term Care Administration
MCM Construction Management
ME Computer-Aided Engineering
MS Aerospace Engineering; Aerospace and Mechanical Engineering (Computational Fluid and Solid Mechanics); Aerospace and Mechanical Engineering (Dynamics and Control); Astronautical Engineering; Biomedical Engineering (Medical Imaging and Imaging Informatics); Biomedical Engineering; Chemical Engineering; Civil Engineering (Construction Engineering); Civil Engineering (Structural Engineering); Computer Engineering; Computer Science (Computer Networking); Computer Science (Computer Security); Computer Science (Multimedia and Creative Technologies); Computer Science (Software Engineering); Computer Science; Engineering Management; Industrial and Systems Engineering; Materials Engineering; Mechanical Engineering; Medical Device and Diagnostic Engineering; Petroleum Engineering (Smart Oilfield Technologies); Petroleum Engineering; Product Development Engineering; Regulatory Science; System Safety and Security; Systems Architecture Engineering
MSEE Electrical Engineering (Computer Networks); Electrical Engineering (Multimedia and Creative Technologies); Electrical Engineering (VLSI Design); Electrical Engineering

COURSE SUBJECT AREAS OFFERED OUTSIDE OF DEGREE PROGRAMS
Graduate—gerontology.

UNIVERSITY OF SOUTHERN INDIANA
Evansville, Indiana
Distance Education Programming
http://www.usi.edu/distance

University of Southern Indiana was founded in 1965. It is accredited by North Central Association of Colleges and Schools. It first offered distance learning courses in 1994. In fall 2006, there were 1,564 students enrolled in distance learning courses. Institutionally administered financial aid is available to distance learners.
Services Distance learners have accessibility to academic advising, bookstore, campus computer network, e-mail services, library services.
Contact Dr. Saxon Reasons, Programming Manager, Instructional Technology Services, University of Southern Indiana, 8600 University Boulevard, Evansville, IN 47712. Telephone: 800-813-4238. Fax: 812-465-7131. E-mail: saxrea@usi.edu.

DEGREES AND AWARDS
BS Health Professions and Related Sciences; Radiologic and Imaging Sciences
BSN Nursing
MHA Health Administration
MSN Nursing
MSOT Occupational Therapy

COURSE SUBJECT AREAS OFFERED OUTSIDE OF DEGREE PROGRAMS
Undergraduate—biology; communication and media; computer/information technology administration and management; dental support services and allied professions; economics; education; educational psychology; education (specific levels and methods); English; English composition; English literature (British and Commonwealth); fine and studio art; gerontology; health and medical administrative services; history; journalism; languages (foreign languages related); linguistic, comparative, and related language studies; nursing; political science and government; psychology; public relations, advertising, and applied communication related; radio, television, and digital communication; speech and rhetoric; visual and performing arts.
Graduate—economics; education; education (specific subject areas); health professions related; marketing; nursing; social work.
Non-credit—accounting and computer science; audiovisual communications technologies; communication and journalism related; computer and information sciences; computer software and media applications; film/video and photographic arts; health professions related; human resources management; legal professions and studies related; nursing; sales, merchandising, and related marketing operations (general).

UNIVERSITY OF SOUTHERN MISSISSIPPI
Hattiesburg, Mississippi
Department of Continuing Education
http://www.usm.edu/cice/ce/index.html

University of Southern Mississippi was founded in 1910. It is accredited by Southern Association of Colleges and Schools. It first offered distance learning courses in 1941. In fall 2006, there were 2,551 students enrolled in distance learning courses. Institutionally administered financial aid is available to distance learners.
Services Distance learners have accessibility to academic advising, bookstore, campus computer network, e-mail services, library services.
Contact Ms. Sheri L. Rawls, Director, Learning Enhancement Center, University of Southern Mississippi, Learning Enhancement Center, 118 College Drive, #9649, Hattiesburg, MS 39406-0001. Telephone: 601-266-5518. Fax: 601-266-4560. E-mail: sheri.rawls@usm.edu.

DEGREES AND AWARDS
BS Construction Technology
MAT Teaching of Languages (MATL)
MEd Music Education–Master of Music Education
MLIS Library Information Science
MS Child and Family Studies; Sport Coaching Education; Sport Management

COURSE SUBJECT AREAS OFFERED OUTSIDE OF DEGREE PROGRAMS
Undergraduate—accounting and related services; anthropology; biblical studies; biology; chemistry; community health services; community organization and advocacy; comparative literature; creative writing; criminal justice and corrections; criminology; educational administration and supervision; educational assessment, evaluation, and research; education related; engineering technologies related; English; English composition; English literature (British and Commonwealth); foods, nutrition, and related services; geography and cartography; health and physical education/fitness; health professions related; human development, family studies, and related services; liberal arts and sciences, general studies and humanities; library science related; linguistic, comparative, and related language studies; management information systems; marketing; mathematics and statistics related; microbiological sciences and immunology;

music; nursing; philosophy and religious studies related; social work; sociology; special education; technical and business writing.

Graduate—biochemistry, biophysics and molecular biology; biology; city/urban, community and regional planning; cognitive psychology and psycholinguistics; communication and media; community health services; construction engineering technology; criminal justice and corrections; curriculum and instruction; demography and population; economics; education; educational administration and supervision; educational assessment, evaluation, and research; geography and cartography; health and physical education/fitness; human development, family studies, and related services; linguistic, comparative, and related language studies; marketing; music; nursing; parks, recreation, and leisure related; public health; social and philosophical foundations of education; social work; special education; statistics.

UNIVERSITY OF SOUTH FLORIDA
Tampa, Florida
Educational Outreach
http://www.outreach.usf.edu/dlstudents

University of South Florida was founded in 1956. It is accredited by Southern Association of Colleges and Schools. It first offered distance learning courses in 1983. In fall 2006, there were 10,950 students enrolled in distance learning courses. Institutionally administered financial aid is available to distance learners.

Services Distance learners have accessibility to academic advising, bookstore, campus computer network, career placement assistance, e-mail services, library services.

Contact Office of the Registrar, University of South Florida, 4202 East Fowler Avenue, SVC 1034, Tampa, FL 33620. Telephone: 813-974-2000. Fax: 813-974-5271. E-mail: asktheregistrar@admin.usf.edu.

DEGREES AND AWARDS

BSN Nursing–RN completion program for Associate Degree Holding Nurses

Graduate Certificate Children's Mental Health; Clinical Investigation; Digital Music Education; Disaster Management; Engineering Technology Management; Entrepreneurship; Gifted Education; Homeland Security; Humanitarian Assistance; Instructional Technology–Distance Education; Instructional Technology–Florida Digital Educator; Instructional Technology–Web Design; Process Engineering; Public Health Generalist; Public Health Policy and Programs; Regulatory Affairs–Medical Devices; Total Quality Management Engineering; Transportation Systems Analysis; Wireless Engineering

MA Career and Technical Education; Gifted Education; Library and Information Science; Music Education; Physical Education

MPH Public Health Administration; Public Health Practice

MSEE Electrical Engineering (MSEE)

MSEM Engineering Management (MSEM)

MSN Nursing

COURSE SUBJECT AREAS OFFERED OUTSIDE OF DEGREE PROGRAMS

Undergraduate—anthropology; archeology; area, ethnic, cultural, and gender studies related; area studies; biology; chemistry; criminal justice and corrections; curriculum and instruction; education; engineering; English; English composition; ethnic, cultural minority, and gender studies; fine and studio art; geography and cartography; geological and earth sciences/geosciences; history; languages (Romance languages); liberal arts and sciences, general studies and humanities; library science; mathematics; mathematics and computer science; music; natural sciences; nursing; nutrition sciences; philosophy; philosophy and religious studies related; social sciences; sociology.

Graduate—accounting and computer science; biomedical/medical engineering; business administration, management and operations; business, management, and marketing related; business/managerial economics; chemical engineering; chemistry; civil engineering technology; computer and information sciences; computer engineering; computer programming; computer software and media applications; construction engineering; criminal justice and corrections; criminology; curriculum and instruction; education; educational administration and supervision; educational assessment, evaluation, and research; educational/instructional media

design; educational psychology; education (specific levels and methods); education (specific subject areas); electrical and electronic engineering technologies; electrical, electronics and communications engineering; engineering; engineering design; engineering/industrial management; English; English as a second/foreign language (teaching); environmental/environmental health engineering; health services/allied health/health sciences; industrial engineering; information science/studies; languages (Germanic); library science; marketing; materials engineering; mechanical engineering; music; nursing; psychology; public administration; public health; public policy analysis; quality control and safety technologies; social and philosophical foundations of education; special education; systems engineering; visual and performing arts.

Non-credit—business administration, management and operations; communication and journalism related; computer programming; computer software and media applications; creative writing; English as a second language; entrepreneurial and small business operations; finance and financial management services; journalism; publishing.

THE UNIVERSITY OF TENNESSEE
Knoxville, Tennessee
Department of Distance Education and Independent Study
http://www.anywhere.tennessee.edu

The University of Tennessee was founded in 1794. It is accredited by Southern Association of Colleges and Schools. It first offered distance learning courses in 1941. In fall 2006, there were 2,300 students enrolled in distance learning courses. Institutionally administered financial aid is available to distance learners.

Services Distance learners have accessibility to academic advising, bookstore, campus computer network, e-mail services, library services.

Contact Ms. Caroline C. Bowers, Assistant Director, Distance Education, The University of Tennessee, 208 Conference Center Building, 600 Henley Street, Knoxville, TN 37996-4126. Telephone: 800-670-8657. Fax: 865-974-4684. E-mail: cbowers1@utk.edu.

DEGREES AND AWARDS

Graduate Certificate Applied Statistical Strategies; Computational Fluid Dynamics; Engineering Management; Nuclear Criticality Safety; Reliability and Maintainability Engineering

MBA Aerospace; Physician Executive; Professional (weekend) program; Senior Executive

MCE Public Works option

MS Agricultural and Extension Education; Engineering Management; Environmental Engineering; Information Sciences

COURSE SUBJECT AREAS OFFERED OUTSIDE OF DEGREE PROGRAMS

Undergraduate—agricultural business and management; American literature (United States and Canadian); anthropology; applied mathematics; astronomy and astrophysics; business administration, management and operations; chemistry; creative writing; curriculum and instruction; economics; education; English; English composition; English language and literature related; English literature (British and Commonwealth); environmental control technologies; geography and cartography; history; languages (Germanic); languages (Romance languages); liberal arts and sciences, general studies and humanities; mathematics; physics; political science and government; psychology; religious studies; sociology; technical and business writing.

Non-credit—computer/information technology administration and management; creative writing; mathematics.

THE UNIVERSITY OF TENNESSEE AT MARTIN
Martin, Tennessee
Office of Extended Campus and Continuing Education
http://www.utm.edu/~ecce

The University of Tennessee at Martin was founded in 1900. It is accredited by Southern Association of Colleges and Schools. It first offered distance learning courses in 1992. In fall 2006, there were 835 students enrolled in distance learning courses. Institutionally administered financial aid is available to distance learners.

Services Distance learners have accessibility to academic advising, bookstore, campus computer network, career placement assistance, e-mail services, library services.

Contact Dr. Tommy Cates, Director, The University of Tennessee at Martin, Office of Online and University Studies, 227 Administration Building, Martin, TN 38238-5050. Telephone: 731-881-7589. E-mail: tcates@utm.edu.

DEGREES AND AWARDS
BUS University Studies
MS Agriculture and Natural Resources Systems Management, Agriculture and Natural Resources Management major
MSE Education

COURSE SUBJECT AREAS OFFERED OUTSIDE OF DEGREE PROGRAMS
Non-credit—accounting and related services; business administration, management and operations; computer and information sciences; crafts, folk art and artisanry; criminal justice and corrections; education; education (specific levels and methods); human development, family studies, and related services.

THE UNIVERSITY OF TEXAS AT ARLINGTON
Arlington, Texas
Center for Distance Education
http://distance.uta.edu
The University of Texas at Arlington was founded in 1895. It is accredited by Southern Association of Colleges and Schools. It first offered distance learning courses in 1973. In fall 2006, there were 2,500 students enrolled in distance learning courses. Institutionally administered financial aid is available to distance learners.
Services Distance learners have accessibility to academic advising, bookstore, campus computer network, e-mail services, library services, tutoring.
Contact Dr. Pete Smith, Assistant Vice President of Academic Affairs, The University of Texas at Arlington, Box 19027, Arlington, TX 76019. Telephone: 817-272-5727. Fax: 817-272-5728. E-mail: info@distance.uta.edu.

DEGREES AND AWARDS
BA Criminology and Criminal Justice (completion degree)
MBA Management, general
ME Aerospace Engineering; Computer Science and Engineering; Mechanical Engineering
MEd Curriculum and Instruction/Reading
MPA Public Administration
MS Industrial Engineering
MSCE Civil Engineering
MSEE Electrical Engineering

COURSE SUBJECT AREAS OFFERED OUTSIDE OF DEGREE PROGRAMS
Undergraduate—biology; business, management, and marketing related; communication and journalism related; criminology; dramatic/theater arts and stagecraft; economics; fine and studio art; languages (Romance languages); nursing; political science and government; social work; sociology.
Graduate—aerospace, aeronautical and astronautical engineering; curriculum and instruction; engineering mechanics; environmental/environmental health engineering; finance and financial management services; mechanical engineering; political science and government; social work.

THE UNIVERSITY OF TEXAS AT EL PASO
El Paso, Texas
The University of Texas at El Paso was founded in 1913. It is accredited by Southern Association of Colleges and Schools. It first offered distance learning courses in 1997. In fall 2006, there were 634 students enrolled in distance learning courses. Institutionally administered financial aid is available to distance learners.
Services Distance learners have accessibility to campus computer network, e-mail services, library services.

Contact Instructional Support Services, The University of Texas at El Paso. Telephone: 915-747-5059. E-mail: iss@utep.edu.

DEGREES AND AWARDS
BSN Nursing–RN-BSN program
Certificate Nurse Clinician Educator
MFA Creative Writing

COURSE SUBJECT AREAS OFFERED OUTSIDE OF DEGREE PROGRAMS
Undergraduate—accounting and related services; anthropology; criminal justice and corrections; developmental and child psychology; education; educational administration and supervision; educational assessment, evaluation, and research; educational psychology; education related; English; liberal arts and sciences, general studies and humanities; linguistic, comparative, and related language studies; nursing; political science and government.
Graduate—creative writing; education; nursing.

THE UNIVERSITY OF TEXAS AT SAN ANTONIO
San Antonio, Texas
Distance Learning Center
http://www.dlc.utsa.edu
The University of Texas at San Antonio was founded in 1969. It is accredited by Southern Association of Colleges and Schools. It first offered distance learning courses in 1993. In fall 2006, there were 4,494 students enrolled in distance learning courses. Institutionally administered financial aid is available to distance learners.
Services Distance learners have accessibility to academic advising, bookstore, campus computer network, career placement assistance, e-mail services, library services, tutoring.
Contact Mr. Bill Angrove, Assistant Vice Provost, The University of Texas at San Antonio, 6900 North Loop 1604 West, San Antonio, TX 78249-0617. Telephone: 210-458-5855. Fax: 210-458-7378. E-mail: bill.angrove@utsa.edu.

DEGREES AND AWARDS
Certificate Paralegal Online Certificate program
MS Management of Technology

COURSE SUBJECT AREAS OFFERED OUTSIDE OF DEGREE PROGRAMS
Undergraduate—accounting and related services; anthropology; biological and physical sciences; biology; business administration, management and operations; business/commerce; business, management, and marketing related; cell biology and anatomical sciences; civil engineering; civil engineering technology; communication and media; computer programming; computer science; economics; education related; engineering; English composition; geography and cartography; geological and earth sciences/geosciences; health and physical education/fitness; health services/allied health/health sciences; information science/studies; languages (Romance languages); linguistic, comparative, and related language studies; marketing; mathematics; mechanical engineering; physical sciences; political science and government; psychology; sales, merchandising, and related marketing operations (specialized); technical and business writing.
Graduate—biology; business administration, management and operations; business, management, and marketing related; computer science; curriculum and instruction; economics; engineering; engineering/industrial management; engineering technologies related; languages (Romance languages); management information systems; management sciences and quantitative methods; mathematics; neuroscience; political science and government; psychology; technology education/industrial arts.
Non-credit—engineering related.

THE UNIVERSITY OF TEXAS AT TYLER
Tyler, Texas
Interactive Television
http://www.uttyler.edu

The University of Texas at Tyler was founded in 1971. It is accredited by Southern Association of Colleges and Schools. It first offered distance learning courses in 1991. In fall 2006, there were 1,090 students enrolled in distance learning courses. Institutionally administered financial aid is available to distance learners.

Services Distance learners have accessibility to academic advising, bookstore, e-mail services, library services.

Contact Bonnie Purser, Admissions Assistant, The University of Texas at Tyler, Enrollment Management, 3900 University Boulevard, Tyler, TX 75799. Telephone: 903-566-7202. Fax: 903-566-7068. E-mail: bpurser @uttyler.edu.

DEGREES AND AWARDS

BBA Business Administration
BS Health Professions; Interdisciplinary Studies–Early Childhood through Grade Four (Education); Technology–Human Resource Development
BSN LVN to Bachelor of Science in Nursing; Nursing–RN Option; Nursing
MBA Business Administration
MEd Educational Leadership
MS Kinesiology; Technology–Human Resource Development
MSN Nursing–Administration and Education options; Nursing–RN-MSN Option

COURSE SUBJECT AREAS OFFERED OUTSIDE OF DEGREE PROGRAMS

Undergraduate—accounting and related services; anthropology; archeology; biology; business/commerce; business/corporate communications; community health services; computer science; criminal justice and corrections; criminology; curriculum and instruction; education (specific levels and methods); finance and financial management services; fire protection; geography and cartography; health and physical education/ fitness; health professions related; history; human resources management; industrial production technologies; marketing; mathematics; nursing; political science and government; psychology; sales, merchandising, and related marketing operations (specialized); sociology; special education; statistics; technology education/industrial arts.

Graduate—business administration, management and operations; computer science; health professions related; human resources management; management sciences and quantitative methods; nursing; public administration; quality control and safety technologies; special education.

THE UNIVERSITY OF TEXAS SYSTEM
Austin, Texas
UT TeleCampus
http://www.telecampus.utsystem.edu

The University of Texas System is accredited by Southern Association of Colleges and Schools. It first offered distance learning courses in 1999. In fall 2006, there were 3,321 students enrolled in distance learning courses. Institutionally administered financial aid is available to distance learners.

Services Distance learners have accessibility to academic advising, bookstore, campus computer network, library services, tutoring.

Contact Dr. Darcy Hardy, Director, The University of Texas System, 702 Colorado, Suite 4.100, Austin, TX 78701. Telephone: 888-TEXAS-16. Fax: 512-499-4715. E-mail: telecampus@utsystem.edu.

DEGREES AND AWARDS

BS Criminal Justice (completion degree)
BSAST Health Services Technology (BAT)
BSN Nursing–RN to BSN
Certificate Blood Bank Technology; Border Administration; Border Studies; Chess in Education Online; Paralegal; Physical Therapy (IMPRINTS); Reading Specialist
Certification Education–Alternative Teacher; Education–Master Reading Teacher; Health Science Technology Teacher; Trade & Industrial (T&I)
Endorsement English as a Second Language (ESL)

Graduate Certificate Nursing Education
MAT Science Education
MBA Business Administration and Management
MEd Curriculum and Instruction, Literacy emphasis; Educational Technology; Kinesiology
MFA Creative Writing-Bilingual
MPA Public Administration
MS Human Resource Development; Kinesiology

COURSE SUBJECT AREAS OFFERED OUTSIDE OF DEGREE PROGRAMS

Undergraduate—accounting and related services; biology; clinical/ medical laboratory science and allied professions; computer and information sciences; computer and information sciences and support services related; computer systems networking and telecommunications; creative writing; curriculum and instruction; developmental and child psychology; economics; education; educational/instructional media design; education related; education (specific subject areas); English; English as a second language; English composition; English language and literature related; fine and studio art; geological and earth sciences/geosciences; health professions related; history; information science/studies; liberal arts and sciences, general studies and humanities; linguistic, comparative, and related language studies; mathematics; mathematics and statistics related; music; physical sciences; physical sciences related; political science and government; psychology; social and philosophical foundations of education; social sciences; social sciences related; sociology; statistics.

Graduate—allied health and medical assisting services; computer and information sciences; curriculum and instruction; education; educational/ instructional media design; educational psychology; education related; education (specific subject areas); English as a second/foreign language (teaching); health professions related; nursing; political science and government; social and philosophical foundations of education; teaching assistants/ aides.

Non-credit—allied health and medical assisting services; clinical/ medical laboratory science and allied professions; legal support services; political science and government.

See full description on page 502.

UNIVERSITY OF THE CUMBERLANDS
Williamsburg, Kentucky
http://www.cumberlandcollege.edu

University of the Cumberlands was founded in 1889. It is accredited by Southern Association of Colleges and Schools. It first offered distance learning courses in 2004. In fall 2006, there were 250 students enrolled in distance learning courses. Institutionally administered financial aid is available to distance learners.

Services Distance learners have accessibility to academic advising, bookstore, campus computer network, e-mail services, library services.

Contact Dr. Janette Ralston, Chair, Department of Education, University of the Cumberlands, Education Department, Cumberland College Station, Williamsburg, KY 40769. Telephone: 606-539-4391. Fax: 606-539-4014. E-mail: jralston@cumberlandcollege.edu.

DEGREES AND AWARDS

Certification Add-On Special Education–L/BD; Alternative Certification– Special Education–L/BD; Director of Pupil Personnel; Director of Special Education; School Superintendent; School Supervisor
MAE Elementary P-5; Instructional Leadership–Principal (all grades); Middle Grades 5-9; Reading and Writing Specialist P-12; Secondary; Special Education Learning and Behavior Disorders P-12
MAT Elementary P-5; Middle Grades 5-9; Secondary; Special Education– Learning and Behavior Disorders

COURSE SUBJECT AREAS OFFERED OUTSIDE OF DEGREE PROGRAMS

Graduate—business, management, and marketing related; English; history; mathematics; music; science, technology and society; special education.

UNIVERSITY OF THE INCARNATE WORD
San Antonio, Texas
Universe Online
http://www.uiw.edu/online
University of the Incarnate Word was founded in 1881. It is accredited by Southern Association of Colleges and Schools. It first offered distance learning courses in 2000. In fall 2006, there were 1,250 students enrolled in distance learning courses. Institutionally administered financial aid is available to distance learners.
Services Distance learners have accessibility to academic advising, bookstore, career placement assistance, library services, tutoring.
Contact Dr. Cyndi Wilson Porter, Dean, Virtual University/Director, Universe Online, University of the Incarnate Word, CPO #324, 4301 Broadway, San Antonio, TX 78209. Telephone: 877-827-2709. Fax: 210-829-2756. E-mail: virtual@uiwtx.edu.

DEGREES AND AWARDS

AA Business; Information Systems; Liberal Studies
BA Administration; Human Resources; Organizational Development
BAA Applied Arts and Sciences (BAAS)
BBA Business Administration
MA Administration–Communication Arts; Instructional Technology; Organizational Development
MBA General Program; International
See full description on page 504.

UNIVERSITY OF THE PACIFIC
Stockton, California
Center for Professional and Continuing Education
http://www.pacific.edu/
University of the Pacific was founded in 1851. It is accredited by Western Association of Schools and Colleges. It first offered distance learning courses in 1995. In fall 2006, there were 5,500 students enrolled in distance learning courses. Institutionally administered financial aid is available to distance learners.
Contact Crislyn Parker, Program Coordinator, University of the Pacific, 3601 Pacific Avenue, Stockton, CA 95211. Telephone: 209-946-2424 Ext. 5040. Fax: 209-946-3916. E-mail: cpce@pacific.edu.

DEGREES AND AWARDS
Programs offered do not lead to a degree or other formal award.

COURSE SUBJECT AREAS OFFERED OUTSIDE OF DEGREE PROGRAMS
Undergraduate—creative writing.
Graduate—education related.
Non-credit—personal and culinary services related.

UNIVERSITY OF THE SCIENCES IN PHILADELPHIA
Philadelphia, Pennsylvania
http://www.usip.edu
University of the Sciences in Philadelphia was founded in 1821. It is accredited by Middle States Association of Colleges and Schools. It first offered distance learning courses in 2000. In fall 2006, there were 115 students enrolled in distance learning courses. Institutionally administered financial aid is available to distance learners.
Services Distance learners have accessibility to academic advising, bookstore, campus computer network, e-mail services, library services.
Contact Ms. Joyce D'Angelo, Admission Counselor, College of Graduate Studies, University of the Sciences in Philadelphia, 600 South 43rd Street, Philadelphia, PA 19104-4418. Telephone: 215-596-8937. Fax: 215-895-1185. E-mail: j.dangel@usip.edu.

DEGREES AND AWARDS
MBA Pharmaceutical Business
MS Biomedical Writing

COURSE SUBJECT AREAS OFFERED OUTSIDE OF DEGREE PROGRAMS
Undergraduate—information science/studies.
Graduate—allied health diagnostic, intervention, and treatment professions; health professions related; health services/allied health/health sciences.

THE UNIVERSITY OF TOLEDO
Toledo, Ohio
Division of Distance and eLearning
http://www.dl.utoledo.edu
The University of Toledo was founded in 1872. It is accredited by North Central Association of Colleges and Schools. It first offered distance learning courses in 1995. In fall 2006, there were 3,464 students enrolled in distance learning courses. Institutionally administered financial aid is available to distance learners.
Services Distance learners have accessibility to academic advising, bookstore, campus computer network, career placement assistance, e-mail services, library services, tutoring.
Contact Janet Green, Director eLearning Student Services Management, The University of Toledo, eLearning and Academic Support, MS 516, Toledo, OH 43606-3390. Telephone: 419-530-8835. Fax: 419-530-8836. E-mail: utdl@utoledo.edu.

DEGREES AND AWARDS
AAB Accounting Technology; Business Management Technology–FastTrack option; Business Management Technology; Computer Software Specialist; Information Services and Support; Marketing and Sales Technology; Programming and Software Development
AIS Interdisciplinary program in Technical Studies
BA Adult Liberal Studies
BS Computer Science and Engineering Technology; Health Care Administration; Health Information Management
Certificate Accounting Software Applications; Accounting Technology; Accounting for Health Care and Non-Profit; Applied Organizational Technology; Business Management Technology; Computer Software Specialist; Diversity Management; Information Services and Support; Legal Secretarial Certificate; Management Accounting Certificate; Marketing and Sales Technology; Nursing Education; Post Baccalaureate Certificate in Health Information Administration; Preparation for Certified Bookkeeper Exam; Preparation for Certified Bookkeeper Exam; Programming and Sofware Development; Web Design Certificate
Graduate Certificate Psychiatric-Mental Health Clinical Nurse Specialist
MEd Early Childhood Education Pre-K-3 (Non-licensure); Special Education—Early Childhood Intervention Specialist
MLS Liberal Studies
MSE Engineering
MSN Nurse Educator; Nurse Educator; Psychiatric-Mental Health Clinical Nurse Specialist

COURSE SUBJECT AREAS OFFERED OUTSIDE OF DEGREE PROGRAMS
Undergraduate—allied health and medical assisting services; area, ethnic, cultural, and gender studies related; communication and media; computer and information sciences; computer/information technology administration and management; criminology; curriculum and instruction; developmental and child psychology; economics; education; education related; engineering technologies related; English; English composition; ethnic, cultural minority, and gender studies; film/video and photographic arts; geography and cartography; health professions related; history; human resources management; journalism; legal studies (non-professional general, undergraduate); liberal arts and sciences, general studies and humanities; mathematics; music; nutrition sciences; philosophy; philosophy and religious studies related; political science and government; psychology; public administration and social service professions related; religious studies; social sciences; social work; sociology; statistics; technical and business writing; visual and performing arts related.
Graduate—counseling psychology; curriculum and instruction; education; educational assessment, evaluation, and research; education related;

engineering; engineering related; liberal arts and sciences, general studies and humanities; philosophy; political science and government; special education.

See full description on page 506.

UNIVERSITY OF TORONTO
Toronto, Ontario, Canada
School of Continuing Studies
http://learn.utoronto.ca
University of Toronto was founded in 1827. It is provincially chartered. It first offered distance learning courses in 1944. In fall 2006, there were 5,000 students enrolled in distance learning courses. Institutionally administered financial aid is available to distance learners.
Services Distance learners have accessibility to academic advising, bookstore, e-mail services.
Contact Alison Baird, Operations Manager, University of Toronto, School of Continuing Studies, Toronto, ON M5S 2V8, Canada. Telephone: 416-978-7698. Fax: 416-978-5673. E-mail: alison.baird@ utoronto.ca.

DEGREES AND AWARDS
Programs offered do not lead to a degree or other formal award.

COURSE SUBJECT AREAS OFFERED OUTSIDE OF DEGREE PROGRAMS
Undergraduate—accounting and related services; business administration, management and operations; business/commerce; business/corporate communications; business, management, and marketing related; business/managerial economics; communication and media; computer/information technology administration and management; economics; finance and financial management services; human resources management; information science/studies; languages (foreign languages related); management sciences and quantitative methods; marketing; taxation.

Non-credit—accounting and related services; business administration, management and operations; business/corporate communications; business/managerial economics; communication and media; computer/information technology administration and management; economics; finance and financial management services; human resources management; insurance; languages (East Asian); languages (foreign languages related); languages (Germanic); languages (Romance languages); languages (South Asian); management sciences and quantitative methods; marketing.

UNIVERSITY OF TULSA
Tulsa, Oklahoma
College of Business Administration
http://www.imba.utulsa.edu
University of Tulsa was founded in 1894. It is accredited by North Central Association of Colleges and Schools. It first offered distance learning courses in 2000. In fall 2006, there were 15 students enrolled in distance learning courses. Institutionally administered financial aid is available to distance learners.
Services Distance learners have accessibility to academic advising, bookstore, campus computer network, career placement assistance, e-mail services, library services.
Contact Heidi Herrin, Enrollment Management Coordinator, University of Tulsa, 600 South College, BAH 217, Tulsa, OK 74104-3189. Telephone: 918-631-3211. Fax: 918-631-2142. E-mail: graduate-business@ utulsa.edu.

DEGREES AND AWARDS
M Tax Taxation
MBA MBA Online
See full description on page 508.

UNIVERSITY OF VERMONT
Burlington, Vermont
Distance Learning Network
http://learn.uvm.edu
University of Vermont was founded in 1791. It is accredited by New England Association of Schools and Colleges. It first offered distance learning courses in 1995. In fall 2006, there were 950 students enrolled in distance learning courses. Institutionally administered financial aid is available to distance learners.
Services Distance learners have accessibility to academic advising, bookstore, campus computer network, career placement assistance, e-mail services, library services, tutoring.
Contact Carol Vallett, Dean, Continuing Education, University of Vermont, Continuing Education, 322 South Prospect Street, Burlington, VT 05401. Telephone: 800-639-3210. Fax: 802-656-0266. E-mail: carol.vallett@ uvm.edu.

DEGREES AND AWARDS
Programs offered do not lead to a degree or other formal award.

COURSE SUBJECT AREAS OFFERED OUTSIDE OF DEGREE PROGRAMS
Undergraduate—accounting and computer science; anthropology; business/managerial economics; community organization and advocacy; computer science; education; English; gerontology; international relations and affairs; languages (Romance languages); library science; nursing; nutrition sciences; psychology; psychology related; public administration; religious studies; social work; sociology; statistics; teaching assistants/aides.

Graduate—communication disorders sciences and services; education (specific levels and methods); electrical and electronic engineering technologies; library science; nursing; public administration; religious studies; social work; speech and rhetoric.

Non-credit—accounting and related services; business administration, management and operations; business/managerial economics; communication disorders sciences and services; computer/information technology administration and management; computer programming; computer science; computer software and media applications; engineering; English; food science and technology; languages (Romance languages); mathematics; mathematics and statistics related; music; nursing; nutrition sciences; psychology; social work; statistics.

THE UNIVERSITY OF VIRGINIA'S COLLEGE AT WISE
Wise, Virginia
http://www.uvawise.edu
The University of Virginia's College at Wise was founded in 1954. It is accredited by Southern Association of Colleges and Schools. It first offered distance learning courses in 1995. In fall 2006, there were 100 students enrolled in distance learning courses. Institutionally administered financial aid is available to distance learners.
Services Distance learners have accessibility to academic advising, bookstore, campus computer network, career placement assistance, e-mail services, library services, tutoring.
Contact Mr. P. Scott Bevins, Director of Institutional Research/External Programs, The University of Virginia's College at Wise, 1 College Avenue, Wise, VA 24219. Telephone: 276-376-1066. Fax: 276-376-4518. E-mail: pb8q@uvawise.edu.

DEGREES AND AWARDS
Programs offered do not lead to a degree or other formal award.

COURSE SUBJECT AREAS OFFERED OUTSIDE OF DEGREE PROGRAMS
Undergraduate—business administration, management and operations; computer science; economics; library science.

UNIVERSITY OF WASHINGTON
Seattle, Washington
Extension
http://onlinelearning.washington.edu/ol/

University of Washington was founded in 1861. It is accredited by Northwest Commission on Colleges and Universities. In fall 2006, there were 9,700 students enrolled in distance learning courses. Institutionally administered financial aid is available to distance learners.

Services Distance learners have accessibility to academic advising, bookstore, campus computer network, e-mail services, library services.

Contact General Information, University of Washington, 4311 11th Avenue, NE, Seattle, WA 98105-4608. Telephone: 800-543-2320. Fax: 206-685-9359. E-mail: onlinelearning@extn.washington.edu.

DEGREES AND AWARDS

Certificate Brain Research in Education; Business Foundations; Computer Programming–C Programming; Computer Programming–C++ Programming; Computer Programming–Java 2 Programming; Construction Management; Curriculum Integration in Action; Data Resource Management; Database Management; Distance Learning Design and Development; Embedded and Real-Time Systems Programming; Facility Management; Fiction Writing; Gerontology; Heavy Construction Project Management; Infrastructure Construction; Internet Programming; Object-Oriented Analysis and Design Using UML; Project Management; Quantitative Construction Management; School Library Media Specialist; Site Planning; Web Administration; Web Consultant for Small Business; Web Technology Essentials

CCCPE Paralegal

MAE Aerospace Engineering

MEE Electrical Engineering

MLIS Library and Information Science

MS Aeronautics and Astronautics; Construction Engineering; Strategic Planning for Critical Infrastructure

MSE Manufacturing Engineering; Materials Science and Engineering

MSME Mechanical Engineering

COURSE SUBJECT AREAS OFFERED OUTSIDE OF DEGREE PROGRAMS

Undergraduate—accounting and related services; American literature (United States and Canadian); anthropology; applied mathematics; archeology; astronomy and astrophysics; atmospheric sciences and meteorology; building/construction finishing, management, and inspection; business/corporate communications; chemistry; cognitive psychology and psycholinguistics; communication and media; computer engineering; computer programming; computer science; construction engineering technology; creative writing; criminology; curriculum and instruction; developmental and child psychology; economics; education; educational psychology; English; English as a second language; English composition; ethnic, cultural minority, and gender studies; geography and cartography; geological and earth sciences/geosciences; gerontology; history; international business; journalism; languages (Modern Greek); languages (Slavic, Baltic and Albanian); library science; marketing; materials engineering; mathematics; mathematics and statistics related; mechanical engineering; pharmacy, pharmaceutical sciences, and administration; philosophy; political science and government; psychology; religious studies; social psychology; sociology; speech and rhetoric; statistics; technical and business writing; urban studies/affairs.

Graduate—building/construction finishing, management, and inspection; city/urban, community and regional planning; civil engineering; computer science; construction engineering technology; electrical and electronic engineering technologies; engineering/industrial management; engineering related; gerontology; library science; library science related; materials engineering; mechanical engineering; political science and government.

Non-credit—business administration, management and operations; city/urban, community and regional planning; computer and information sciences; computer and information sciences and support services related; computer/information technology administration and management; computer programming; computer software and media applications; computer systems analysis; creative writing; English; English as a second language; information science/studies.

See full description on page 510.

UNIVERSITY OF WATERLOO
Waterloo, Ontario, Canada
Distance and Continuing Education
http://dce.uwaterloo.ca

University of Waterloo was founded in 1957. It is provincially chartered. It first offered distance learning courses in 1968. In fall 2006, there were 4,500 students enrolled in distance learning courses. Institutionally administered financial aid is available to distance learners.

Services Distance learners have accessibility to academic advising, bookstore, campus computer network, e-mail services, library services, tutoring.

Contact Information and Student Services, University of Waterloo, Distance and Continuing Education Office, University of Waterloo, Waterloo, ON N2L 3G1, Canada. Telephone: 519-888-4050. Fax: 519-746-4607. E-mail: distance@uwaterloo.ca.

DEGREES AND AWARDS

BA English; General Studies, Non-Major; Humanities; Philosophy; Religious Studies; Social Development Studies; Social Sciences

BS Science, general non-major

MM Management Sciences–Master of Management Sciences Online (MMSC)

COURSE SUBJECT AREAS OFFERED OUTSIDE OF DEGREE PROGRAMS

Undergraduate—accounting and related services; American literature (United States and Canadian); anthropology; applied mathematics; area, ethnic, cultural, and gender studies related; area studies; astronomy and astrophysics; biblical and other theological languages and literatures; biblical studies; biochemistry, biophysics and molecular biology; biological and biomedical sciences related; biological and physical sciences; biology; business/managerial economics; cell biology and anatomical sciences; chemistry; community organization and advocacy; computer and information sciences; computer science; criminology; dance; developmental and child psychology; ecology, evolution, and population biology; economics; educational psychology; English composition; English literature (British and Commonwealth); ethnic, cultural minority, and gender studies; finance and financial management services; geological and earth sciences/geosciences; gerontology; history; human development, family studies, and related services; insurance; languages (classics and classical); languages (foreign languages related); languages (Germanic); languages (Modern Greek); languages (Romance languages); languages (Slavic, Baltic and Albanian); liberal arts and sciences, general studies and humanities; linguistic, comparative, and related language studies; mathematics; mathematics and statistics related; medieval and Renaissance studies; microbiological sciences and immunology; multi-/interdisciplinary studies related; peace studies and conflict resolution; philosophy; philosophy and religious studies related; physical sciences; physics; physiology, pathology and related sciences; psychology; psychology related; religious studies; social psychology; social sciences; social sciences related; social work; sociology; statistics.

Graduate—management information systems.

Non-credit—chemistry; mathematics and statistics related; physics.

UNIVERSITY OF WEST FLORIDA
Pensacola, Florida
Online Campus/Academic Technology Center
http://onlinecampus.uwf.edu

University of West Florida was founded in 1963. It is accredited by Southern Association of Colleges and Schools. It first offered distance learning courses in 1995. In fall 2006, there were 3,500 students enrolled in distance learning courses. Institutionally administered financial aid is available to distance learners.

Services Distance learners have accessibility to academic advising, bookstore, campus computer network, e-mail services, library services, tutoring.

Contact Mrs. Sharon Cobb, Program Coordinator, Academic Technology Center, University of West Florida, 11000 University Parkway, Building 77, Room 138A, Pensacola, FL 32514. Telephone: 850-473-7468. Fax: 850-474-2807. E-mail: scobb@uwf.edu.

DEGREES AND AWARDS

BA Career and Technical Studies Education specialization; Exceptional Student Education

BS Health Sciences, Allied Health; IIT Networking and Telecommunications with e-Learning Systems; Information Engineering Technology; Maritime Studies; Oceanography

MA Special Education

MEd Career and Technical Education (CTE); Education and Training Management Subspecialty/Human Performance Technology; Education and Training Management Subspecialty/Instructional Technology; Education–Comprehensive Masters in Education; Instructional Technology

MS Acquisition and Contract Administration (MSA); Biomedical/Pharmaceutical (MSA); Criminal Justice Administration (MSA); Education Leadership (MSA); Health Care Administration (MSA); Human Performance Technology (MSA); Nursing Administration; Public Administration (MSA); Public Health

COURSE SUBJECT AREAS OFFERED OUTSIDE OF DEGREE PROGRAMS

Undergraduate—anthropology; archeology; biological and biomedical sciences related; biology; business/corporate communications; communication and media; communications technology; computer programming; computer science; computer software and media applications; computer systems networking and telecommunications; data entry/microcomputer applications; economics; engineering technologies related; English; English composition; fine and studio art; history; liberal arts and sciences, general studies and humanities; mathematics; mathematics and statistics related; philosophy; physical sciences; physical sciences related; political science and government; religious studies; statistics; technical and business writing.

Graduate—accounting and computer science; allied health diagnostic, intervention, and treatment professions; behavioral sciences; business administration, management and operations; computer science; educational/instructional media design; education related; health services/allied health/health sciences; information science/studies; political science and government; public administration and social service professions related; special education.

Non-credit—business, management, and marketing related; communications technology; computer engineering; education related; education (specific subject areas); human resources management; technology education/industrial arts.

UNIVERSITY OF WINDSOR
Windsor, Ontario, Canada
Continuing Education
http://www.uwindsor.ca/
University of Windsor was founded in 1857. It is provincially chartered. It first offered distance learning courses in 1985. In fall 2006, there were 1,000 students enrolled in distance learning courses. Institutionally administered financial aid is available to distance learners.
Services Distance learners have accessibility to academic advising, bookstore, campus computer network, career placement assistance, e-mail services, library services, tutoring.
Contact Mr. Marty Lowman, Supervisor, Student Information Resource Centre (SIRC), University of Windsor, Student Information Resource Centre (SIRC), Windsor, ON N9B 3P4, Canada. Telephone: 519-253-3000 Ext. 1414. Fax: 519-971-3623. E-mail: askme@uwindsor.ca.

DEGREES AND AWARDS

BA Liberal and Professional Studies; Political Science

BBA Accounting–General Accounting Track (BBS)

BComm Business Administration–Honours Business Administration; Commerce–Bachelor of Commerce Program for University Graduates

BS General Science

Certificate Arts Management; Business Administration; Labour Studies

UNIVERSITY OF WISCONSIN COLLEGES
Madison, Wisconsin
UWC On-line
http://www.online.uwc.edu
University of Wisconsin Colleges is accredited by North Central Association of Colleges and Schools. It first offered distance learning courses in 1998. In fall 2006, there were 1,400 students enrolled in distance learning courses. Institutionally administered financial aid is available to distance learners.
Services Distance learners have accessibility to academic advising, bookstore, campus computer network, e-mail services, library services, tutoring.
Contact Ms. Leanne Johnson, DE Coordinator, University of Wisconsin Colleges, 780 Regent Street, Suite 130, Madison, WI 53715-2635. Telephone: 608-263-9553. Fax: 608-262-7872. E-mail: decoordiator@uwc.edu.

DEGREES AND AWARDS
AAS Liberal Arts

COURSE SUBJECT AREAS OFFERED OUTSIDE OF DEGREE PROGRAMS

Undergraduate—anthropology; biology; business/commerce; chemistry; communication and journalism related; creative writing; economics; English; English composition; ethnic, cultural minority, and gender studies; geography and cartography; geological and earth sciences/geosciences; history; journalism; mathematics; mathematics and computer science; mathematics and statistics related; music; natural sciences; philosophy; political science and government; psychology; social sciences; sociology; statistics; visual and performing arts related.
Non-credit—English; mathematics.

UNIVERSITY OF WISCONSIN–LA CROSSE
La Crosse, Wisconsin
http://www.uwlax.edu/
University of Wisconsin–La Crosse was founded in 1909. It is accredited by North Central Association of Colleges and Schools. It first offered distance learning courses in 1995. In fall 2006, there were 65 students enrolled in distance learning courses. Institutionally administered financial aid is available to distance learners.
Services Distance learners have accessibility to academic advising, bookstore, campus computer network, career placement assistance, e-mail services, library services, tutoring.
Contact Terry Wirkus, DE Site Support Coordinator, University of Wisconsin–La Crosse, 1725 State Street, La Crosse, WI 54601. Telephone: 608-785-8049. Fax: 608-785-8825. E-mail: wirkus.terr@uwlax.edu.

DEGREES AND AWARDS
Programs offered do not lead to a degree or other formal award.

COURSE SUBJECT AREAS OFFERED OUTSIDE OF DEGREE PROGRAMS

Undergraduate—health professions related; linguistic, comparative, and related language studies.
Graduate—accounting and related services; business administration, management and operations; economics; educational psychology; finance and financial management services; microbiological sciences and immunology; parks, recreation and leisure facilities management; sales, merchandising, and related marketing operations (general).

UNIVERSITY OF WISCONSIN–PARKSIDE
Kenosha, Wisconsin
http://www.uwp.edu/
University of Wisconsin–Parkside was founded in 1968. It is accredited by North Central Association of Colleges and Schools. It first offered distance learning courses in 1996. In fall 2006, there were 28 students enrolled in distance learning courses. Institutionally administered financial aid is available to distance learners.
Services Distance learners have accessibility to academic advising, bookstore, campus computer network, career placement assistance, e-mail services, library services, tutoring.

Contact Bradley R. Piazza, Assistant Dean of the School of Business, University of Wisconsin–Parkside, 900 Wood Road, PO Box 2000, Kenosha, WI 53141-2000. Telephone: 262-595-2046. Fax: 262-595-2680. E-mail: bradley.piazza@uwp.edu.

DEGREES AND AWARDS
Programs offered do not lead to a degree or other formal award.

COURSE SUBJECT AREAS OFFERED OUTSIDE OF DEGREE PROGRAMS
Graduate—accounting and computer science; accounting and related services; business administration, management and operations; business, management, and marketing related; business/managerial economics; economics; finance and financial management services; management information systems; management sciences and quantitative methods; sales, merchandising, and related marketing operations (general); statistics.

UNIVERSITY OF WISCONSIN–PLATTEVILLE
Platteville, Wisconsin
Distance Learning Center
http://www.uwplatt.edu/~disted
University of Wisconsin–Platteville was founded in 1866. It is accredited by North Central Association of Colleges and Schools. It first offered distance learning courses in 1978. In fall 2006, there were 1,100 students enrolled in distance learning courses. Institutionally administered financial aid is available to distance learners.
Services Distance learners have accessibility to academic advising, bookstore, campus computer network, career placement assistance, e-mail services, library services.
Contact Darla Banfi, Marketing Coordinator, University of Wisconsin–Platteville, B12 Karrmann Library, One University Plaza, Platteville, WI 53818. Telephone: 800-362-5460. Fax: 608-342-1071. E-mail: disted@uwplatt.edu.

DEGREES AND AWARDS
BS Business Administration; Criminal Justice
Certificate Engineering Management; Human Resource Management; International Business; Leadership and Human Performance; Project Management
Advanced Graduate Diploma Criminal Justice
CAGS Structural/Geotechnical Engineering
MS Criminal Justice; Engineering; Project Management

COURSE SUBJECT AREAS OFFERED OUTSIDE OF DEGREE PROGRAMS
Undergraduate—accounting and related services; business administration, management and operations; communication and media; economics; finance and financial management services; human resources management; marketing; mathematics; music; sales, merchandising, and related marketing operations (specialized); speech and rhetoric.
Graduate—business/commerce; civil engineering; communication and media; criminal justice and corrections; education (specific levels and methods); management sciences and quantitative methods; mathematics; mechanical engineering; psychology.
Non-credit—criminal justice and corrections.

UNIVERSITY OF WISCONSIN–PLATTEVILLE
Platteville, Wisconsin
Online Program in Criminal Justice
http://www.uwplatt.edu/~disted/
University of Wisconsin–Platteville was founded in 1866. It is accredited by North Central Association of Colleges and Schools. It first offered distance learning courses in 1978. In fall 2006, there were 138 students enrolled in distance learning courses. Institutionally administered financial aid is available to distance learners.
Services Distance learners have accessibility to academic advising, bookstore, campus computer network, career placement assistance, e-mail services, library services.

Contact Dr. Cheryl Banachowski-Fuller, Director of Criminal Justice Distance Education Program, University of Wisconsin–Platteville, 1 University Plaza, Platteville, WI 53818. Telephone: 608-342-1652. Fax: 608-342-1986. E-mail: criminaljstc@uwplatt.edu.

DEGREES AND AWARDS
BS Criminal Justice
Advanced Graduate Diploma Criminal Justice
MS Criminal Justice

COURSE SUBJECT AREAS OFFERED OUTSIDE OF DEGREE PROGRAMS
Undergraduate—business/corporate communications; business, management, and marketing related; international business.
Graduate—business administration, management and operations; business/commerce; criminal justice and corrections; criminology; political science and government; psychology; sociology.
Non-credit—criminal justice and corrections.

UNIVERSITY OF WISCONSIN–PLATTEVILLE
Platteville, Wisconsin
Online Program in Project Management
http://www.uwplatt.edu/~disted/
University of Wisconsin–Platteville was founded in 1866. It is accredited by North Central Association of Colleges and Schools. It first offered distance learning courses in 1978. In fall 2006, there were 314 students enrolled in distance learning courses. Institutionally administered financial aid is available to distance learners.
Services Distance learners have accessibility to academic advising, bookstore, campus computer network, career placement assistance, e-mail services, library services.
Contact Bill Haskins, Program Coordinator of Project Management Program, University of Wisconsin–Platteville, 1 University Plaza, Platteville, WI 53818. Telephone: 608-342-1961. Fax: 608-342-1466. E-mail: projectmgmt@uwplatt.edu.

DEGREES AND AWARDS
Certificate Project Management
CAGS Project Management
MS Project Management

COURSE SUBJECT AREAS OFFERED OUTSIDE OF DEGREE PROGRAMS
Graduate—accounting and related services; business administration, management and operations; business/commerce; business/corporate communications; mathematics.
Non-credit—quality control and safety technologies.

UNIVERSITY OF WISCONSIN–PLATTEVILLE
Platteville, Wisconsin
Online Program in Engineering
http://www.uwplatt.edu/~disted/
University of Wisconsin–Platteville was founded in 1866. It is accredited by North Central Association of Colleges and Schools. It first offered distance learning courses in 1978. In fall 2006, there were 130 students enrolled in distance learning courses. Institutionally administered financial aid is available to distance learners.
Services Distance learners have accessibility to academic advising, bookstore, campus computer network, career placement assistance, e-mail services, library services.
Contact Dr. Lisa Riedle, Program Coordinator of Engineering Distance Education Program, University of Wisconsin–Platteville, 1 University Plaza, Platteville, WI 53818. Telephone: 608-342-1686. Fax: 608-342-1566. E-mail: engineering@uwplatt.edu.

DEGREES AND AWARDS
CAGS Engineering Management; Structural/Geotechnical Engineering
MS Engineering

COURSE SUBJECT AREAS OFFERED OUTSIDE OF DEGREE PROGRAMS

Graduate—business administration, management and operations; business/commerce; business/corporate communications; computer engineering; electrical, electronics and communications engineering; engineering; engineering design; engineering/industrial management; engineering related; mathematics; statistics.

UNIVERSITY OF WISCONSIN–PLATTEVILLE
Platteville, Wisconsin
Bachelor of Science in Business Administration
http://www.uwplatt.edu/~disted/

University of Wisconsin–Platteville was founded in 1866. It is accredited by North Central Association of Colleges and Schools. It first offered distance learning courses in 1978. In fall 2006, there were 500 students enrolled in distance learning courses. Institutionally administered financial aid is available to distance learners.

Services Distance learners have accessibility to academic advising, bookstore, campus computer network, career placement assistance, e-mail services, library services.

Contact Marge Karsten, Chair of Business and Accounting Department, University of Wisconsin–Platteville, 1 University Plaza, Platteville, WI 53818. Telephone: 608-342-1749. Fax: 608-342-1466. E-mail: businessadmn@uwplatt.edu.

DEGREES AND AWARDS

BSBA Business Administration
Certificate Human Resource Management; International Business; Leadership and Human Performance

COURSE SUBJECT AREAS OFFERED OUTSIDE OF DEGREE PROGRAMS

Undergraduate—accounting and related services; business administration, management and operations; business/commerce; business/corporate communications; communication and media; economics; finance and financial management services; human resources management; international business; marketing; mathematics; public relations, advertising, and applied communication related.

Graduate—business administration, management and operations; business/corporate communications.

UNIVERSITY OF WISCONSIN–STOUT
Menomonie, Wisconsin
Office of Continuing Education
http://www.uwstout.edu/solutions/ces

University of Wisconsin–Stout was founded in 1891. It is accredited by North Central Association of Colleges and Schools. It first offered distance learning courses in 1980. In fall 2006, there were 3,500 students enrolled in distance learning courses. Institutionally administered financial aid is available to distance learners.

Services Distance learners have accessibility to academic advising, bookstore, campus computer network, career placement assistance, e-mail services, library services, tutoring.

Contact Sandra White, Credit Outreach Program Manager III, University of Wisconsin–Stout, Outreach Services, 140 Vocational Rehabilitation Building, Menomonie, WI 54751-0790. Telephone: 715-232-2693. Fax: 715-232-3385. E-mail: whites@uwstout.edu.

DEGREES AND AWARDS

BS Career and Technical Education; Golf Enterprise Management; Information and Communication Technologies; Management
Certificate Gaming Management Certificate program; Human Resource Management; Quality Management Certificate
Certification Early Childhood/Middle Childhood; Health Science Occupations; Reading Teacher certification
Graduate Certificate E-Learning and Online Teaching Graduate Certificate

MS Career and Technical Education; Education; Information Communication Technologies; Manufacturing Engineering; Technology Management; Training and Development; Vocational Rehabilitation Counseling

COURSE SUBJECT AREAS OFFERED OUTSIDE OF DEGREE PROGRAMS

Undergraduate—business, management, and marketing related; chemistry; developmental and child psychology; economics; education; human resources management.

Graduate—business administration, management and operations; developmental and child psychology; education; human resources management; library science; management sciences and quantitative methods; science technologies related; social sciences; technology education/industrial arts.

Non-credit—computer systems networking and telecommunications; education (specific levels and methods); gerontology; human development, family studies, and related services; human resources management.

UNIVERSITY OF WISCONSIN–SUPERIOR
Superior, Wisconsin
http://dlc.uwsuper.edu/

University of Wisconsin–Superior was founded in 1893. It is accredited by North Central Association of Colleges and Schools. It first offered distance learning courses in 1978. In fall 2006, there were 277 students enrolled in distance learning courses. Institutionally administered financial aid is available to distance learners.

Services Distance learners have accessibility to academic advising, bookstore, campus computer network, career placement assistance, e-mail services, library services, tutoring.

Contact Barbara Doherty, Student Services Program Manager, University of Wisconsin–Superior, Distance Learning Center, PO Box 2000, Belknap and Catlin, Superior, WI 54880. Telephone: 715-394-8487. Fax: 715-394-8139. E-mail: dlc@uwsuper.edu.

DEGREES AND AWARDS
Programs offered do not lead to a degree or other formal award.

COURSE SUBJECT AREAS OFFERED OUTSIDE OF DEGREE PROGRAMS

Undergraduate—accounting and computer science; American literature (United States and Canadian); astronomy and astrophysics; biology; business administration, management and operations; communication and journalism related; communication and media; counseling psychology; curriculum and instruction; education; English; fine and studio art; history; human services; mathematics and computer science; physical sciences; social sciences.

Graduate—education; educational administration and supervision; health psychology.

Non-credit—gerontology.

See full description on page 512.

UNIVERSITY OF WISCONSIN–WHITEWATER
Whitewater, Wisconsin

University of Wisconsin–Whitewater was founded in 1868. It is accredited by North Central Association of Colleges and Schools. It first offered distance learning courses in 1980. In fall 2006, there were 1,455 students enrolled in distance learning courses. Institutionally administered financial aid is available to distance learners.

Services Distance learners have accessibility to bookstore, campus computer network, e-mail services, library services.

Contact Lorna Y. Wong, Director, Instructional Technology Services, University of Wisconsin–Whitewater, 800 West Main Street, Whitewater, WI 53190. Telephone: 262-472-7795. Fax: 262-472-1285. E-mail: disted@uww.edu.

DEGREES AND AWARDS
MBA Business Administration–Online Masters of Business Administration

COURSE SUBJECT AREAS OFFERED OUTSIDE OF DEGREE PROGRAMS

Undergraduate—accounting and computer science; anthropology; area, ethnic, cultural, and gender studies related; business administration, management and operations; business, management, and marketing related; communication and journalism related; communication and media; creative writing; curriculum and instruction; economics; education; education related; English; English as a second language; ethnic, cultural minority, and gender studies; history; journalism; languages (foreign languages related); library science; management information systems; marketing; political science and government.

Graduate—accounting and related services; area, ethnic, cultural, and gender studies related; business administration, management and operations; business, management, and marketing related; communication and journalism related; creative writing; economics; English; English as a second language; finance and financial management services; history; journalism; management information systems; marketing; political science and government; psychology related.

UNIVERSITY OF WYOMING
Laramie, Wyoming
Outreach School
http://outreach.uwyo.edu/occ

University of Wyoming was founded in 1886. It is accredited by North Central Association of Colleges and Schools. In fall 2006, there were 3,930 students enrolled in distance learning courses. Institutionally administered financial aid is available to distance learners.

Services Distance learners have accessibility to academic advising, bookstore, campus computer network, career placement assistance, e-mail services, library services, tutoring.

Contact Ms. Judith E. Atencio, Program Manager, Outreach Credit Programs, University of Wyoming, Department 3274, 1000 East University Avenue, Laramie, WY 82071. Telephone: 800-448-7801. Fax: 307-766-4048. E-mail: occ@uwyo.edu.

DEGREES AND AWARDS

BA Criminal Justice; Social Sciences

BGS Bachelor of Applied Science, Organizational Leadership concentration

BS Business Administration; Family and Consumer Sciences (Family and Community Services option); Family and Consumer Sciences (Professional Child Development option); Psychology; Social Sciences

BSN Nursing–RN to BSN

Certificate Family and Consumer Sciences (Early Childhood Program Director's certificate); Land Surveying; Real Estate

Endorsement Early Childhood Birth to Five Endorsement; Early Childhood Special Education; Literacy Program (Wyoming Reading Endorsement); Principal Endorsement Program

MA Education–Adult and Post-Secondary Education; Education–Educational Leadership; Education–Special Education; Education–Teaching and Learning

MBA Executive Master of Business Administration

MPA Public Administration

MS Education–Instructional Technology; Kinesiology and Health; Nursing–Nurse Educator option; Speech-Language Pathology

MSW Social Work

COURSE SUBJECT AREAS OFFERED OUTSIDE OF DEGREE PROGRAMS

Undergraduate—agriculture; American literature (United States and Canadian); astronomy and astrophysics; biological and biomedical sciences related; botany/plant biology; business/commerce; chemistry; communication and media; criminal justice and corrections; education; English composition; English literature (British and Commonwealth); ethnic, cultural minority, and gender studies; family and consumer economics; foods, nutrition, and related services; geography and cartography; history; liberal arts and sciences, general studies and humanities; mathematics; music; nursing; physics; real estate; social psychology; statistics.

Graduate—business administration, management and operations; education; educational/instructional media design; health professions related; nursing; public administration; social work.

See full description on page 514.

UPPER IOWA UNIVERSITY
Fayette, Iowa
External Degree
http://www.uiu.edu

Upper Iowa University was founded in 1857. It is accredited by North Central Association of Colleges and Schools. It first offered distance learning courses in 1973. In fall 2006, there were 1,900 students enrolled in distance learning courses. Institutionally administered financial aid is available to distance learners.

Services Distance learners have accessibility to academic advising, bookstore, campus computer network, career placement assistance, e-mail services, library services.

Contact Barbara J. Schultz, Director, External Degree Program, Upper Iowa University, PO Box 1861, Fayette, IA 52142. Telephone: 888-877-3742. Fax: 563-425-5353. E-mail: moreinfo@uiu.edu.

DEGREES AND AWARDS

AA Business, general; Liberal Arts

BS Accounting; Business Administration; Criminal Justice; Emergency and Disaster Management; Finance; Health Services Administration; Human Resources Management; Human Services; Interdisciplinary Studies; Management; Marketing; Psychology; Public Administration; Public Administration–Fire Science emphasis; Public Administration–Law Enforcement emphasis; Social Sciences; Technology and Information Management

Certificate Emergency and Disaster Management; Human Resources Management; Marketing; Organizational Communications; Organizational Leadership

COURSE SUBJECT AREAS OFFERED OUTSIDE OF DEGREE PROGRAMS

Undergraduate—accounting and related services; astronomy and astrophysics; biology; business administration, management and operations; business/corporate communications; business, management, and marketing related; communication and media; counseling psychology; criminal justice and corrections; criminology; English; English composition; entrepreneurial and small business operations; finance and financial management services; health professions related; health services/allied health/health sciences; history; human resources management; human services; industrial and organizational psychology; international business; legal studies (non-professional general, undergraduate); liberal arts and sciences, general studies and humanities; management information systems; management sciences and quantitative methods; marketing; mathematics; mathematics and statistics related; natural sciences; philosophy and religious studies related; physical sciences; political science and government; psychology; psychology related; public administration; public administration and social service professions related; public relations, advertising, and applied communication related; social psychology; social sciences; social sciences related; sociology; statistics.

Non-credit—accounting and computer science; accounting and related services; biological and physical sciences; biology; communication and media; English composition; history; industrial and organizational psychology; international business; management information systems; marketing; political science and government; psychology; public administration; sociology; statistics.

See full description on page 516.

UTAH STATE UNIVERSITY
Logan, Utah
Independent and Distance Education
http://extension.usu.edu

Utah State University was founded in 1888. It is accredited by Northwest Commission on Colleges and Universities. It first offered distance learning courses in 1983. In fall 2006, there were 7,500 students enrolled in distance learning courses. Institutionally administered financial aid is available to distance learners.

Services Distance learners have accessibility to academic advising, bookstore, campus computer network, e-mail services, library services.

Contact Staff Assistant, Independent and Distance Education, Utah State University, 5055 Old Main Hill, Logan, UT 84322-5055. Telephone: 800-233-2137. Fax: 435-797-1399. E-mail: de-info@ext.usu.edu.

DEGREES AND AWARDS

AAS Office Support Systems; Ornamental Horticulture

AS General Studies

BS Accounting; Business; Communicative Disorders and Deaf Education (Post-Bachelors); Computer Science; Entrepreneurship; Psychology; Special Education

Endorsement Distance Learning; Reading, Elementary Education; Reading, Secondary Education; School Library Media; Utah Mathematics Endorsement Project

ME Electrical/Computer Engineering

MEd Elementary Education; Health, Physical Education, and Recreation; Instructional Technology–Educational Technology emphasis; Secondary Education; Special Education

MFHD Family and Human Development

MS Agricultural Systems Technology, Family and Consumer Sciences Education and Extension emphasis; Agricultural Systems Technology, Secondary/Post-Secondary Agricultural Education emphasis; Business Information Systems; Computer Science; English/Technical Writing Specialization Online; Psychology–School Counseling specialization; Special Education

MSW Social Work

EdD Distance Doctorate

COURSE SUBJECT AREAS OFFERED OUTSIDE OF DEGREE PROGRAMS

Undergraduate—accounting and related services; anthropology; applied mathematics; biology; business administration, management and operations; business operations support and assistant services; chemistry; communication disorders sciences and services; data entry/microcomputer applications; data processing; economics; English; English literature (British and Commonwealth); family and consumer economics; family and consumer sciences/human sciences; history; human resources management; liberal arts and sciences, general studies and humanities; mathematics; mathematics and statistics related; philosophy; physical sciences; physics; psychology; social psychology; social sciences; social work; sociology; special education; statistics.

Graduate—agriculture and agriculture operations related; business administration, management and operations; computer programming; computer science; computer software and media applications; computer systems analysis; computer systems networking and telecommunications; curriculum and instruction; education; educational administration and supervision; educational assessment, evaluation, and research; educational/instructional media design; educational psychology; education (specific levels and methods); education (specific subject areas); English; family and consumer sciences/human sciences; human development, family studies, and related services; human resources management; library science related; psychology; school psychology; social sciences related; special education.

See full description on page 518.

UTAH VALLEY STATE COLLEGE
Orem, Utah
Department of Distance Education
http://www.uvsc.edu/disted

Utah Valley State College was founded in 1941. It is accredited by Northwest Commission on Colleges and Universities. It first offered distance learning courses in 1988. In fall 2006, there were 10,000 students enrolled in distance learning courses. Institutionally administered financial aid is available to distance learners.

Services Distance learners have accessibility to academic advising, bookstore, campus computer network, career placement assistance, e-mail services, library services, tutoring.

Contact Karen Merrick, Assistant Director of Support Services, Utah Valley State College, 800 West University Parkway, MS 149, Orem, UT 84058. Telephone: 801-863-HELP. Fax: 801-863-7298. E-mail: dehelp @uvsc.edu.

DEGREES AND AWARDS

AS Communication; Criminal Justice; General Studies
BS Aviation Science

COURSE SUBJECT AREAS OFFERED OUTSIDE OF DEGREE PROGRAMS

Undergraduate—accounting and related services; air transportation; American literature (United States and Canadian); anthropology; astronomy and astrophysics; atmospheric sciences and meteorology; behavioral sciences; biological and physical sciences; biology; business administration, management and operations; business/corporate communications; business, management, and marketing related; communication and journalism related; communication and media; computer and information sciences; creative writing; dramatic/theater arts and stagecraft; electrical/electronics maintenance and repair technology; English; English composition; fire protection; history; hospitality administration; languages (foreign languages related); legal studies (non-professional general, undergraduate); management information systems; ocean engineering; philosophy; political science and government; psychology; public relations, advertising, and applied communication related; social sciences; sociology; zoology/animal biology.

Non-credit—computer and information sciences; computer software and media applications.

UTAH VALLEY STATE COLLEGE
Orem, Utah
Global Aviation Degree Center
http://www.aviationuniversity.com

Utah Valley State College was founded in 1941. It is accredited by Northwest Commission on Colleges and Universities. It first offered distance learning courses in 1997. In fall 2006, there were 1,500 students enrolled in distance learning courses. Institutionally administered financial aid is available to distance learners.

Services Distance learners have accessibility to academic advising, bookstore, campus computer network, career placement assistance, e-mail services, library services, tutoring.

Contact Theo Okawa, Aviation Advisor, Utah Valley State College, 800 West University Parkway, MS 114, Orem, UT 84058-5999. Telephone: 888-901-7192 Ext. 7837. Fax: 801-764-7815. E-mail: okawath@uvsc. edu.

DEGREES AND AWARDS

AAS Aviation Job Ready degree
AS Aviation (Baccalaureate Degree transfer)
BS Aviation Administration/Management; Aviation Professional Pilot

COURSE SUBJECT AREAS OFFERED OUTSIDE OF DEGREE PROGRAMS

Undergraduate—aerospace, aeronautical and astronautical engineering; biology; English composition; English language and literature related; fine and studio art; health and physical education/fitness; history; mathematics; philosophy; physical sciences; social sciences; social sciences related.

Graduate—aerospace, aeronautical and astronautical engineering.

UTICA COLLEGE
Utica, New York
Utica College was founded in 1946. It is accredited by Middle States Association of Colleges and Schools. It first offered distance learning courses in 2000. In fall 2006, there were 425 students enrolled in distance learning courses. Institutionally administered financial aid is available to distance learners.

Services Distance learners have accessibility to academic advising, bookstore, campus computer network, e-mail services, library services, tutoring.

Contact Dr. Stephen P. Neun, Assistant Vice President for Academic Affairs, Utica College, 1600 Burrstone Road, Office of Graduate and Extended Studies, Utica, NY 13502. Telephone: 315-792-3002. E-mail: sneun@utica.edu.

DEGREES AND AWARDS
BS Criminal Justice, Economic Crime Investigation; Cybersecurity and Information Assurance
Certificate Financial Crime Investigation certificate program
MBA Business Administration–Economic Crime and Fraud Management; Business Administration–Professional Accountancy
MS Economic Crime Management
DPT Physical Therapy–Transitional Doctorate of Physical Therapy

COURSE SUBJECT AREAS OFFERED OUTSIDE OF DEGREE PROGRAMS
Undergraduate—biology; economics; English; gerontology; liberal arts and sciences, general studies and humanities; mathematics; psychology.

VALLEY CITY STATE UNIVERSITY
Valley City, North Dakota
North Dakota Interactive Video Network
http://distancelearning.vcsu.edu
Valley City State University was founded in 1890. It is accredited by North Central Association of Colleges and Schools. It first offered distance learning courses in 2000. In fall 2006, there were 95 students enrolled in distance learning courses. Institutionally administered financial aid is available to distance learners.

Services Distance learners have accessibility to academic advising, bookstore, campus computer network, career placement assistance, e-mail services.

Contact Monte Johnson, Registrar, Valley City State University, 101 College Street SW, Valley City, ND 58072. Telephone: 701-845-7295 Ext. 7297. Fax: 701-845-7299. E-mail: monte.johnson@vcsu.edu.

DEGREES AND AWARDS
Programs offered do not lead to a degree or other formal award.

COURSE SUBJECT AREAS OFFERED OUTSIDE OF DEGREE PROGRAMS
Undergraduate—communication and journalism related; English as a second language; English composition; health and physical education/fitness; library science; psychology; speech and rhetoric; technology education/industrial arts.
Graduate—education; technology education/industrial arts.

VANCE-GRANVILLE COMMUNITY COLLEGE
Henderson, North Carolina
http://www.vgcc.edu
Vance-Granville Community College was founded in 1969. It is accredited by Southern Association of Colleges and Schools. It first offered distance learning courses in 1998. In fall 2006, there were 1,101 students enrolled in distance learning courses. Institutionally administered financial aid is available to distance learners.

Services Distance learners have accessibility to academic advising, bookstore, e-mail services, library services.

Contact Evelyn Harris, Director of Distance Education, Vance-Granville Community College, PO Box 917, Henderson, NC 27536. Telephone: 252-492-2061. Fax: 252-738-3372. E-mail: harris@vgcc.edu.

DEGREES AND AWARDS
AA General Studies
AAS Business Administration; Business Administration; Information Systems; Information Systems/Network Administration and Support
Certificate Early Childhood Associate–Administration; Early Childhood Associate–General Education; Early Childhood Associate–Special Needs

COURSE SUBJECT AREAS OFFERED OUTSIDE OF DEGREE PROGRAMS
Undergraduate—accounting and related services; American literature (United States and Canadian); biology; business administration, management and operations; business operations support and assistant services; computer/information technology administration and management; computer programming; computer systems networking and telecommunications; criminal justice and corrections; criminology; economics; English composition; history; human development, family studies, and related services; human services; information science/studies; liberal arts and sciences, general studies and humanities; marketing; political science and government; psychology; sociology; statistics; teaching assistants/aides.
Non-credit—accounting and related services; building/construction finishing, management, and inspection; business/commerce; business/corporate communications; computer and information sciences; computer programming; computer software and media applications; computer systems networking and telecommunications; data entry/microcomputer applications; entrepreneurial and small business operations; personal and culinary services related; sales, merchandising, and related marketing operations (specialized); technical and business writing.

VERMONT TECHNICAL COLLEGE
Randolph Center, Vermont
http://www.vtc.vsc.edu/
Vermont Technical College was founded in 1866. It is accredited by New England Association of Schools and Colleges. It first offered distance learning courses in 1996. In fall 2006, there were 100 students enrolled in distance learning courses. Institutionally administered financial aid is available to distance learners.

Services Distance learners have accessibility to academic advising, bookstore, campus computer network, e-mail services, library services.

Contact Mr. Michael Dempsey, Registrar, Vermont Technical College, PO Box 500, Randolph Center, VT 05061. Telephone: 802-728-1302. Fax: 802-728-1597. E-mail: mdempsey@vtc.edu.

DEGREES AND AWARDS
Programs offered do not lead to a degree or other formal award.

COURSE SUBJECT AREAS OFFERED OUTSIDE OF DEGREE PROGRAMS
Undergraduate—computer and information sciences; dental support services and allied professions; history; social sciences related.

VILLANOVA UNIVERSITY
Villanova, Pennsylvania
Division of Part-time Studies/Summer Sessions
http://engineering.villanova.edu/distanceed/
Villanova University was founded in 1842. It is accredited by Middle States Association of Colleges and Schools. It first offered distance learning courses in 1997. In fall 2006, there were 273 students enrolled in distance learning courses. Institutionally administered financial aid is available to distance learners.

Services Distance learners have accessibility to academic advising, bookstore, campus computer network, career placement assistance, e-mail services, library services, tutoring.

Contact Mr. Sean O'Donnell, Director of Distance Education, Villanova University, Villanova, PA 19085. E-mail: sean@villanova.edu.

DEGREES AND AWARDS
Certificate Biochemical Engineering certificate
Graduate Certificate Urban Water Resources Design
MCE Civil Engineering
MSEE MSEE
MSME MSME
MSWREE Water Resources and Environmental Engineering

COURSE SUBJECT AREAS OFFERED OUTSIDE OF DEGREE PROGRAMS
Undergraduate—engineering related.
Graduate—electrical, electronics and communications engineering; mechanical engineering related technologies.
Non-credit—engineering.

VINCENNES UNIVERSITY
Vincennes, Indiana
Distance Education/Degree Completion
http://www.vinu.edu/distance
Vincennes University was founded in 1801. It is accredited by North Central Association of Colleges and Schools. It first offered distance learning courses in 1989. In fall 2006, there were 1,300 students enrolled in distance learning courses. Institutionally administered financial aid is available to distance learners.
Services Distance learners have accessibility to academic advising, bookstore, campus computer network, career placement assistance, e-mail services, library services, tutoring.
Contact Mr. Donald E. Kaufman, Dean of Continuing Studies, Vincennes University, 1002 North First Street, Classroom Building A, Vincennes, IN 47591. Telephone: 812-888-5343. Fax: 812-888-2054. E-mail: dkaufman@vinu.edu.

DEGREES AND AWARDS
AAS Funeral Service Education; General Studies–Business Studies; General Studies; Law Enforcement Studies; Technology Apprenticeship–General Studies option
AS Behavioral Sciences; Business Administration; General Studies–Surgical Technology Degree completion; General Studies; Health Information Management; Law Enforcement Studies; Recreation Management–Therapeutic option; Technology Apprenticeship
Certificate of Completion Administrative Office Technology–Office Software Specialist; Behavioral Science–Substance Abuse Certificate; Community Rehabilitation; Pharmacy Technician
Certificate General Studies–Customized Certificate
Graduate Certificate Surgical Technology accelerated option, Certificate of Graduation

COURSE SUBJECT AREAS OFFERED OUTSIDE OF DEGREE PROGRAMS
Undergraduate—accounting and related services; allied health and medical assisting services; applied mathematics; business/commerce; business operations support and assistant services; chemistry; community health services; computer and information sciences; creative writing; criminal justice and corrections; developmental and child psychology; economics; education; English composition; entrepreneurial and small business operations; fire protection; funeral service and mortuary science; history; information science/studies; mathematics; parks, recreation and leisure facilities management; pharmacy, pharmaceutical sciences, and administration; psychology; rehabilitation and therapeutic professions; sales, merchandising, and related marketing operations (specialized); social sciences; social work; sociology; speech and rhetoric.

VIRGINIA HIGHLANDS COMMUNITY COLLEGE
Abingdon, Virginia
Virginia Highlands Community College was founded in 1967. It is accredited by Southern Association of Colleges and Schools. It first offered distance learning courses in 1995. In fall 2006, there were 580 students enrolled in distance learning courses. Institutionally administered financial aid is available to distance learners.
Services Distance learners have accessibility to academic advising, bookstore, campus computer network, career placement assistance, e-mail services, library services, tutoring.

Contact Mr. Charles Boling, Coordinator of Distance Learning, Virginia Highlands Community College, 100 VHCC Drive, PO Box 828, Abingdon, VA 24210. Telephone: 276-739-2514. Fax: 276-739-2590. E-mail: cboling@vhcc.edu.

DEGREES AND AWARDS
Programs offered do not lead to a degree or other formal award.

COURSE SUBJECT AREAS OFFERED OUTSIDE OF DEGREE PROGRAMS
Undergraduate—accounting and related services; allied health and medical assisting services; allied health diagnostic, intervention, and treatment professions; American literature (United States and Canadian); applied mathematics; business, management, and marketing related; community health services; computer and information sciences; computer/information technology administration and management; computer programming; computer software and media applications; computer systems networking and telecommunications; criminal justice and corrections; English composition; English literature (British and Commonwealth); health/medical preparatory programs; history; pharmacology and toxicology; philosophy; physics; political science and government; psychology; sociology.

VIRGINIA POLYTECHNIC INSTITUTE AND STATE UNIVERSITY
Blacksburg, Virginia
Institute for Distance and Distributed Learning
http://iddl.vt.edu
Virginia Polytechnic Institute and State University was founded in 1872. It is accredited by Southern Association of Colleges and Schools. It first offered distance learning courses in 1983. In fall 2006, there were 5,396 students enrolled in distance learning courses. Institutionally administered financial aid is available to distance learners.
Services Distance learners have accessibility to academic advising, bookstore, campus computer network, career placement assistance, e-mail services, library services, tutoring.
Contact Mrs. Angie Starr, eLearning Enrollment Coordinator, Virginia Polytechnic Institute and State University, Institute for Distance and Distributed Learning, Blacksburg, VA 24061. Telephone: 540-231-1264. Fax: 540-231-2079. E-mail: vto@vt.edu.

DEGREES AND AWARDS
Certificate Humanistic Traditions (undergraduate); Political Science–Enviromental Politics and Policies
Certification Political Science–Foundations of Political Analysis; Political Science–Information Policy and Society; Political Science–Security Studies
License Alternative Teaching; Career and Technical Education
Graduate Certificate Computer Engineering; IT Business Information Systems; IT Communication; IT Decision Support Systems; IT Networking; Liberal Arts; Natural Resources; Software Development
MA Instructional Technology
MIT Information Technology
MS Agricultural and Life Sciences; Career and Technical Education; Civil Infrastructure Engineering; Civil and Environmental Engineering; Computer Engineering; Curriculum and Instruction–Health Promotion emphasis; Electrical and Computer Engineering; Engineering Administration; Ocean Engineering; Political Science; Systems Engineering

COURSE SUBJECT AREAS OFFERED OUTSIDE OF DEGREE PROGRAMS
Undergraduate—agriculture; agriculture and agriculture operations related; apparel and textiles; applied horticulture/horticultural business services; civil engineering; communication and media; computer engineering; computer science; education (specific levels and methods); education (specific subject areas); electrical and electronic engineering technologies; engineering; English composition; ethnic, cultural minority, and gender studies; fishing and fisheries sciences and management; geography and cartography; history; hospitality administration; human resources management; languages (Romance languages); linguistic, com-

parative, and related language studies; marketing; mathematics; music; philosophy; physics; political science and government; religious studies; science technologies related; sociology.

Graduate—accounting and related services; aerospace, aeronautical and astronautical engineering; agriculture and agriculture operations related; applied horticulture/horticultural business services; computer engineering; computer science; curriculum and instruction; educational administration and supervision; education related; education (specific subject areas); English; ethnic, cultural minority, and gender studies; forestry; geography and cartography; liberal arts and sciences, general studies and humanities; management information systems; marketing; mathematics; mechanical engineering; natural resources management and policy; political science and government; public administration; science technologies related; urban studies/affairs; veterinary biomedical and clinical sciences.

Non-credit—animal sciences; applied horticulture/horticultural business services; architecture; business administration, management and operations; business/commerce; computer and information sciences; computer software and media applications; education; engineering; engineering technologies related; forestry; history; marketing; music; natural resources conservation and research; plant sciences; public health; real estate; work and family studies.

See full description on page 520.

VITERBO UNIVERSITY
La Crosse, Wisconsin

Viterbo University was founded in 1890. It is accredited by North Central Association of Colleges and Schools. It first offered distance learning courses in 2000. In fall 2006, there were 150 students enrolled in distance learning courses. Institutionally administered financial aid is available to distance learners.

Services Distance learners have accessibility to academic advising, bookstore, campus computer network, career placement assistance, e-mail services, library services, tutoring.

Contact Dr. Jan P. Eriksen, Director of School of Adult Learning, Viterbo University, School of Adult Learning, 900 Viterbo Drive, La Crosse, WI 54601. Telephone: 608-796-3087. Fax: 608-796-3372. E-mail: jperiksen@viterbo.edu.

DEGREES AND AWARDS

BBA Organizational Management, Management and Information Technology

COURSE SUBJECT AREAS OFFERED OUTSIDE OF DEGREE PROGRAMS

Undergraduate—accounting and computer science; biblical studies; business, management, and marketing related; dramatic/theater arts and stagecraft; fine and studio art; liberal arts and sciences, general studies and humanities; nursing; social sciences.

Graduate—business administration, management and operations; education; nursing; theological and ministerial studies.

WAKE TECHNICAL COMMUNITY COLLEGE
Raleigh, North Carolina
http://www.waketech.edu

Wake Technical Community College was founded in 1958. It is accredited by Southern Association of Colleges and Schools. It first offered distance learning courses in 1986. In fall 2006, there were 2,897 students enrolled in distance learning courses. Institutionally administered financial aid is available to distance learners.

Services Distance learners have accessibility to academic advising, bookstore, career placement assistance, e-mail services, library services, tutoring.

Contact Diana Osborne, Head, Distance Education Support Department, Wake Technical Community College, 9101 Fayetteville Road, Raleigh, NC 27603-5696. Telephone: 919-866-5616. Fax: 919-773-6190. E-mail: dgosborn@waketech.edu.

DEGREES AND AWARDS

AA College/University Transfer
AAS Web Technologies

COURSE SUBJECT AREAS OFFERED OUTSIDE OF DEGREE PROGRAMS

Undergraduate—accounting and related services; allied health and medical assisting services; American literature (United States and Canadian); anthropology; astronomy and astrophysics; biology; biomathematics and bioinformatics; business/commerce; business operations support and assistant services; chemistry; computer and information sciences and support services related; computer software and media applications; computer systems networking and telecommunications; criminal justice and corrections; culinary arts and related services; drafting/design engineering technologies; economics; engineering technology; English composition; English literature (British and Commonwealth); geological and earth sciences/geosciences; heating, air conditioning, ventilation and refrigeration maintenance technology; history; marketing; mathematics; philosophy; political science and government; polymer/plastics engineering; psychology; religious studies; social work; sociology.

Non-credit—accounting and related services; business administration, management and operations; computer and information sciences and support services related; computer programming; computer software and media applications; data entry/microcomputer applications; data processing; English as a second language; entrepreneurial and small business operations; family and consumer economics; film/video and photographic arts; languages (foreign languages related); legal support services; sales, merchandising, and related marketing operations (general); technical and business writing.

WALDEN UNIVERSITY
Minneapolis, Minnesota
http://www.waldenu.edu/

Walden University was founded in 1970. It is accredited by North Central Association of Colleges and Schools. It first offered distance learning courses in 1970. In fall 2006, there were 25,400 students enrolled in distance learning courses. Institutionally administered financial aid is available to distance learners.

Services Distance learners have accessibility to academic advising, bookstore, campus computer network, career placement assistance, e-mail services, library services, tutoring.

Contact Enrollment Advisor, Walden University, 1001 Fleet Street, Baltimore, MD 21202. Telephone: 866-492-5336. E-mail: info@waldenu.edu.

DEGREES AND AWARDS

BS Business Administration Completion–Finance; Business Administration Completion–Human Resource Management; Business Administration Completion–Information Systems; Business Administration Completion–Management; Business Administration Completion–Marketing; Business Administration Completion, general

MBA Business Administration, general; Entrepreneurship; Finance; Human Resource Management; Leadership; Management of Technology; Marketing; Project Management

MPA General Program; Health Services; Homeland Security, Policy, and Coordination; International Nongovernmental Organizations (NGOs); Knowledge Management; Nonprofit Management and Leadership; Public Management and Leadership; Public Policy; Public Safety Management

MPH Community Health

MS Computer Engineering; Computer Science; Education–Curriculum, Instruction, and Assessment (Grades K–12); Education–Educational Leadership; Education–Elementary Reading and Literacy (Grades K-6); Education–Elementary Reading and Mathematics (Grades K 6); Education–Integrating Technology in the Classroom (Grades 3-12); Education–Literacy and Learning in the Content Areas (Grades 6-12); Education–Mathematics (Grades 6-8); Education–Mathematics (Grades K-5); Education–Middle Level Education (Grades 5-8); Education–Science (Grades K-8); Electrical Engineering–Communications track; Electrical Engineering–Integrated Circuits track; Electrical Engineering–Microelectronic and Semiconductor Engineering; Nursing–BSN Nursing

Informatics; Nursing–BSN track, Education; Nursing–BSN track, Leadership and Management; Nursing–RN Nursing Informatics; Nursing–RN track, Education; Nursing–RN track, Leadership and Management; Psychology Mental Health Counseling; Psychology–General; Psychology–Organizational Psychology and Development; Software Engineering; Systems Engineering

EdD Administrator Leadership for Teaching and Learning; Teacher Leadership

PhD Applied Management and Decision Sciences–Accounting; Applied Management and Decision Sciences–Engineering Management; Applied Management and Decision Sciences–Finance; Applied Management and Decision Sciences–Information Systems Management; Applied Management and Decision Sciences–Knowledge Management; Applied Management and Decision Sciences–Leadership and Organizational Change; Applied Management and Decision Sciences–Learning Management; Applied Management and Decision Sciences–Operations Research; Applied Management and Decision Sciences–self-designed; Applied Management and Decision Sciences, general; Education–Adult Education Leadership; Education–Community College Leadership; Education–Early Childhood Education; Education–Educational Technology; Education–Higher Education; Education–K-12 Educational Leadership; Education–Self-Designed; Education–Special Education; Education, general; Health Services–Community Health Promotion and Education; Health Services–Health Management and Policy; Health Services, general; Human Services–Clinical Social Work; Human Services–Counseling; Human Services–Criminal Justice; Human Services–Family Studies and Intervention Strategies; Human Services–Human Services Administration; Human Services–Social Policy Analysis and Planning; Human Services–self-designed; Human Services, general; Psychology–Clinical Psychology (Licensure); Psychology–Counseling Psychology (Licensure); Psychology–General Program, Educational Psychology track; Psychology–General Program, Research and Evaluation track; Psychology–Health Psychology; Psychology–Organizational; Psychology–School Psychology (Licensure); Public Health–Community Health Promotion and Education; Public Health–Epidemiology; Public Policy and Administration–Health Services; Public Policy and Administration–Homeland Security, Policy, and Coordination; Public Policy and Administration–International Nongovernmental Organizations (NGOs); Public Policy and Administration–Knowledge Management; Public Policy and Administration–Nonprofit Management and Leadership; Public Policy and Administration–Public Management and Leadership; Public Policy and Administration–Public Policy; Public Policy and Administration–Public Safety Management; Public Policy and Administration, general

COURSE SUBJECT AREAS OFFERED OUTSIDE OF DEGREE PROGRAMS

Undergraduate—business administration, management and operations.
Graduate—business administration, management and operations; education; engineering; nursing; psychology; public administration; public health.

See full description on page 522.

WASHBURN UNIVERSITY
Topeka, Kansas
Division of Continuing Education
http://www.washburn.edu/ce

Washburn University was founded in 1865. It is accredited by North Central Association of Colleges and Schools. It first offered distance learning courses in 1999. In fall 2006, there were 2,600 students enrolled in distance learning courses. Institutionally administered financial aid is available to distance learners.
Services Distance learners have accessibility to academic advising, bookstore, campus computer network, career placement assistance, e-mail services, library services.
Contact Dr. Timothy W. Peterson, Dean of Continuing Education, Washburn University, 1700 SW College Avenue, Topeka, KS 66621. Telephone: 785-670-1399. Fax: 785-670-1028. E-mail: tim.peterson@washburn.edu.

DEGREES AND AWARDS
BAA Human Services; Technology Administration

BHS Health Services Administration/Health Services Administration and Medical Imaging
BLS Administrative Communications–Liberal Studies
BS Criminal Justice

COURSE SUBJECT AREAS OFFERED OUTSIDE OF DEGREE PROGRAMS

Undergraduate—allied health diagnostic, intervention, and treatment professions; American literature (United States and Canadian); biology; business, management, and marketing related; chemistry; education; English composition; health and physical education/fitness; history; human services; military studies; music; nursing; political science and government; psychology; public administration; social work; sociology; technology education/industrial arts.
Graduate—criminal justice and corrections; education; liberal arts and sciences, general studies and humanities.
Non-credit—human resources management; social sciences related.

WASHINGTON STATE UNIVERSITY
Pullman, Washington
Distance Degree Programs
http://www.distance.wsu.edu

Washington State University was founded in 1890. It is accredited by Northwest Commission on Colleges and Universities. It first offered distance learning courses in 1991. In fall 2006, there were 2,700 students enrolled in distance learning courses. Institutionally administered financial aid is available to distance learners.
Services Distance learners have accessibility to academic advising, bookstore, campus computer network, career placement assistance, e-mail services, library services, tutoring.
Contact Student Services, Washington State University, 104 Van Doren Hall, PO Box 645220, Pullman, WA 99164-5220. Telephone: 800-222-4978. Fax: 509-335-4850. E-mail: distance@wsu.edu.

DEGREES AND AWARDS
BA Business Administration; Criminal Justice; Human Development; Humanities; Social Sciences
BSN Nursing–RN to BS
Certificate Professional Writing
MS Agriculture

COURSE SUBJECT AREAS OFFERED OUTSIDE OF DEGREE PROGRAMS

Undergraduate—English composition.

See full description on page 524.

WASHTENAW COMMUNITY COLLEGE
Ann Arbor, Michigan
Office of Distance Learning
http://www.wccnet.edu

Washtenaw Community College was founded in 1965. It is accredited by North Central Association of Colleges and Schools. It first offered distance learning courses in 1982. In fall 2006, there were 1,100 students enrolled in distance learning courses. Institutionally administered financial aid is available to distance learners.
Services Distance learners have accessibility to academic advising, bookstore, campus computer network, e-mail services, library services, tutoring.
Contact John Miller, PhD, Manager of Instructional Design and Technology, Washtenaw Community College, Ann Arbor, MI 48106. Telephone: 734-477-8724. E-mail: jamiller@wccnet.edu.

DEGREES AND AWARDS
Programs offered do not lead to a degree or other formal award.

COURSE SUBJECT AREAS OFFERED OUTSIDE OF DEGREE PROGRAMS

Undergraduate—building/construction finishing, management, and inspection; business administration, management and operations; business operations support and assistant services; clinical psychology; communication and journalism related; communication and media; computer and information sciences; computer programming; computer software and media applications; construction management; dental support services and allied professions; English; English composition; health professions related; legal studies (non-professional general, undergraduate); mathematics; nursing; philosophy; political science and government; psychology; sociology.

WAUBONSEE COMMUNITY COLLEGE
Sugar Grove, Illinois
Center for Distance Learning
http://www.waubonsee.edu/

Waubonsee Community College was founded in 1966. It is accredited by North Central Association of Colleges and Schools. It first offered distance learning courses in 1996. In fall 2006, there were 2,200 students enrolled in distance learning courses. Institutionally administered financial aid is available to distance learners.

Services Distance learners have accessibility to academic advising, bookstore, e-mail services, library services, tutoring.

Contact Ms. Susan V. Harmon, Manager of Distance Learning, Waubonsee Community College, Route 47 at Waubonsee Drive, COL226, Sugar Grove, IL 60554-9799. Telephone: 630-466-7900 Ext. 5758. E-mail: sharmon@waubonsee.edu.

DEGREES AND AWARDS

AA General Program
AGS General Studies
AS General Program
Certificate of Achievement Beginning Web Page; General Studies
Certificate Midmanagement

COURSE SUBJECT AREAS OFFERED OUTSIDE OF DEGREE PROGRAMS

Undergraduate—accounting and related services; American literature (United States and Canadian); biology; business administration, management and operations; communication and media; computer and information sciences; computer programming; creative writing; criminal justice and corrections; criminology; developmental and child psychology; economics; English as a second language; English composition; health and physical education/fitness; history; human resources management; human services; legal studies (non-professional general, undergraduate); liberal arts and sciences, general studies and humanities; management information systems; mathematics; nursing; physical sciences; psychology; social psychology; social work; sociology; speech and rhetoric; statistics.

WAYLAND BAPTIST UNIVERSITY
Plainview, Texas
http://www.wbu.edu/

Wayland Baptist University was founded in 1908. It is accredited by Southern Association of Colleges and Schools. It first offered distance learning courses in 1998. In fall 2006, there were 1,325 students enrolled in distance learning courses. Institutionally administered financial aid is available to distance learners.

Services Distance learners have accessibility to academic advising, library services.

Contact Dr. David Howle, Virtual Campus Director, Wayland Baptist University, 1900 West 7th Street, CMB 420, Plainview, TX 79072. Telephone: 806-291-1031. Fax: 806-291-1957. E-mail: dhowle@wbu.edu.

DEGREES AND AWARDS

MA Management
MCM Christian Ministry
MPA Public Administration

COURSE SUBJECT AREAS OFFERED OUTSIDE OF DEGREE PROGRAMS

Undergraduate—accounting and related services; business administration, management and operations; criminal justice and corrections; economics; education related; finance and financial management services; health and medical administrative services; history; management information systems; marketing; music; political science and government; psychology; religious education; religious studies; sociology.
Graduate—accounting and related services; business administration, management and operations; counseling psychology; economics; education related; health and medical administrative services; human resources management; management information systems; public administration; religious education; religious studies.

WAYNE STATE COLLEGE
Wayne, Nebraska
Regional Education and Distance Learning
http://www.wsc.edu

Wayne State College was founded in 1910. It is accredited by North Central Association of Colleges and Schools. It first offered distance learning courses in 1997. In fall 2006, there were 795 students enrolled in distance learning courses. Institutionally administered financial aid is available to distance learners.

Services Distance learners have accessibility to academic advising, bookstore, campus computer network, career placement assistance, e-mail services, library services.

Contact Dr. Craig Kinsella, Director of Continuing Education, Wayne State College, 1111 Main Street, Wayne, NE 68787. Telephone: 402-375-7217. Fax: 402-375-7204. E-mail: crkinse1@wsc.edu.

DEGREES AND AWARDS

MBA Business Administration

COURSE SUBJECT AREAS OFFERED OUTSIDE OF DEGREE PROGRAMS

Undergraduate—accounting and related services; business administration, management and operations; chemistry; computer and information sciences; economics; education; education (specific subject areas); English; family and consumer sciences/human sciences; human resources management; industrial production technologies; languages (foreign languages related); mathematics; multi-/interdisciplinary studies related; natural sciences; philosophy; physical sciences; physics.
Graduate—accounting and related services; business administration, management and operations; counseling psychology; economics; education; educational administration and supervision; education (specific subject areas); English; family and consumer sciences/human sciences; human resources management; industrial production technologies; mathematics; multi-/interdisciplinary studies related; special education.

WEBER STATE UNIVERSITY
Ogden, Utah
Distance Learning and Independent Study
http://departments.weber.edu/ce/dl

Weber State University was founded in 1889. It is accredited by Northwest Commission on Colleges and Universities. It first offered distance learning courses in 1990. In fall 2006, there were 8,000 students enrolled in distance learning courses. Institutionally administered financial aid is available to distance learners.

Services Distance learners have accessibility to academic advising, bookstore, campus computer network, career placement assistance, e-mail services, library services, tutoring.

Contact Susan Smith, Office of Distance Learning, Weber State University, 4005 University Circle, Ogden, UT 84408-4005. Telephone: 801-626-6600. Fax: 801-626-8035. E-mail: dist-learn@weber.edu.

DEGREES AND AWARDS

AAS Clinical Laboratory Technician; Health Information Technology
AS Criminal Justice; General Studies

BS Clinical Laboratory Sciences; Health Administrative Services; Health Information Management; Health Promotion; Radiological Sciences

Certificate Health Care Coding and Classification; Radiological Sciences

COURSE SUBJECT AREAS OFFERED OUTSIDE OF DEGREE PROGRAMS

Undergraduate—accounting and related services; anthropology; building/construction finishing, management, and inspection; business administration, management and operations; chemistry; communication and media; computer and information sciences; computer and information sciences and support services related; computer science; English; English composition; geography and cartography; geological and earth sciences/geosciences; gerontology; health and medical administrative services; history; human development, family studies, and related services; linguistic, comparative, and related language studies; mathematics; microbiological sciences and immunology; music; philosophy; physics; political science and government; psychology; technical and business writing; zoology/animal biology.

Graduate—clinical/medical laboratory science and allied professions; health and medical administrative services.

See full description on page 526.

WEBSTER UNIVERSITY
St. Louis, Missouri
Academic Distance Learning Center
http://www.webster.edu/worldclassroom

Webster University was founded in 1915. It is accredited by North Central Association of Colleges and Schools. It first offered distance learning courses in 1998. In fall 2006, there were 1,800 students enrolled in distance learning courses. Institutionally administered financial aid is available to distance learners.

Services Distance learners have accessibility to academic advising, bookstore, career placement assistance, e-mail services, library services, tutoring.

Contact Matt Nolan, Director, Graduate and Evening Student Admissions, Webster University, 470 East Lockwood Avenue, St. Louis, MO 63119. Telephone: 314-968-7089. Fax: 314-968-7462. E-mail: nolan@webster.edu.

DEGREES AND AWARDS

Certificate Web Site Design; Web Site Development

Graduate Certificate Decision Support Systems; Global Commerce–MBA Certificate in Global Commerce; Government Contracting; Web Services

MA Business and Organizational Security Management; Communications Management; Human Resources Development; Human Resources Management; International Relations; Management and Leadership; Procurement and Acquisitions Management; Public Relations

MAT Educational Technology and Multidisciplinary Studies

MBA Business Administration

MS Finance

COURSE SUBJECT AREAS OFFERED OUTSIDE OF DEGREE PROGRAMS

Undergraduate—computer and information sciences; languages (foreign languages related); philosophy; public relations, advertising, and applied communication related; religious education.

Graduate—business, management, and marketing related; communication and journalism related; computer and information sciences and support services related; education; educational administration and supervision; finance and financial management services; management information systems; marketing; security and protective services related.

WENATCHEE VALLEY COLLEGE
Wenatchee, Washington
http://www.wvc.edu/

Wenatchee Valley College was founded in 1939. It is accredited by Northwest Commission on Colleges and Universities. It first offered distance learning courses in 1982. In fall 2006, there were 568 students enrolled in distance learning courses. Institutionally administered financial aid is available to distance learners.

Services Distance learners have accessibility to academic advising, bookstore, campus computer network, career placement assistance, e-mail services, library services.

Contact Jimmy Hill, Education Online Specialist, Wenatchee Valley College, 1300 5th Street, Wenatchee, WA 98801. Telephone: 509-682-6706. Fax: 509-682-6801. E-mail: distanceed@wvc.edu.

DEGREES AND AWARDS

AAS Liberal Arts and Sciences

COURSE SUBJECT AREAS OFFERED OUTSIDE OF DEGREE PROGRAMS

Non-credit—business administration, management and operations; business/commerce; computer programming; computer software and media applications; computer systems networking and telecommunications; creative writing; entrepreneurial and small business operations; linguistic, comparative, and related language studies; real estate.

WESTCHESTER COMMUNITY COLLEGE
Valhalla, New York
http://www.sunywcc.edu/

Westchester Community College was founded in 1946. It is accredited by Middle States Association of Colleges and Schools. It first offered distance learning courses in 1997. In fall 2006, there were 650 students enrolled in distance learning courses. Institutionally administered financial aid is available to distance learners.

Services Distance learners have accessibility to academic advising, bookstore, library services.

Contact Carol Klein, Acting Distance Learning Coordinator, Westchester Community College, 75 Grasslands Road, Valhalla, NY 10595. Telephone: 914-785-6827. Fax: 914-785-8550. E-mail: carol.klein@sunywcc.edu.

DEGREES AND AWARDS

AA Liberal Arts/Social Science; Liberal Arts/Social Science

COURSE SUBJECT AREAS OFFERED OUTSIDE OF DEGREE PROGRAMS

Undergraduate—accounting and related services; American literature (United States and Canadian); anthropology; behavioral sciences; biological and physical sciences; biology; business/commerce; chemistry; communication and media; computer and information sciences; computer and information sciences and support services related; computer programming; computer science; computer systems networking and telecommunications; criminal justice and corrections; data processing; economics; English; English as a second language; English composition; English language and literature related; geography and cartography; health and physical education/fitness; history; management information systems; mathematics; mathematics and computer science; philosophy; psychology; sales, merchandising, and related marketing operations (specialized); social sciences; sociology; technical and business writing.

WESTERN CAROLINA UNIVERSITY
Cullowhee, North Carolina
Continuing Education and Summer School
http://edoutreach.wcu.edu

Western Carolina University was founded in 1889. It is accredited by Southern Association of Colleges and Schools. It first offered distance learning courses in 1997. In fall 2006, there were 750 students enrolled in distance learning courses. Institutionally administered financial aid is available to distance learners.

Services Distance learners have accessibility to academic advising, bookstore, career placement assistance, e-mail services, library services.

Contact Bronwen Sheffield, Director of Off-Campus Services, Western Carolina University, 138 Camp Building, Cullowhee, NC 28723. Telephone: 828-227-3074. Fax: 828-227-7115. E-mail: bsheffie@email.wcu.edu.

DEGREES AND AWARDS

BBA Entrepreneurship
BEd Birth–Kindergarten; Elementary Education
BS Criminal Justice; Emergency Medical Care; Engineering Technology Program; Public Safety and Security Management; Public Safety and Security Management
BSN Nursing–RN to BSN
MAT Special Education program
MCM Master of Construction Management Program
MHS Gerontology concentration
MPM Project Management
MS Two-Year Community College Administration Program
MSA Master of School Administration Program
MSN Nurse Educator track

COURSE SUBJECT AREAS OFFERED OUTSIDE OF DEGREE PROGRAMS

Undergraduate—communication disorders sciences and services; gerontology; human resources management; special education.
Graduate—communication disorders sciences and services; gerontology; human resources management.
Non-credit—finance and financial management services; management sciences and quantitative methods.

WESTERN KENTUCKY UNIVERSITY
Bowling Green, Kentucky
Distance Learning
http://www.wku.edu/reachu

Western Kentucky University was founded in 1906. It is accredited by Southern Association of Colleges and Schools. It first offered distance learning courses in 1999. In fall 2006, there were 3,453 students enrolled in distance learning courses. Institutionally administered financial aid is available to distance learners.
Services Distance learners have accessibility to academic advising, bookstore, career placement assistance, e-mail services, library services, tutoring.
Contact Ms. Pam Wilson, Coordinator, Distance Learning, Western Kentucky University, Distance Learning, 1906 College Heights Boulevard, 61084, Bowling Green, KY 42101-1084. Telephone: 270-745-2106. Fax: 270-745-2107. E-mail: pam.wilson@wku.edu.

DEGREES AND AWARDS

AAS Paramedicine completion
AS Interdisciplinary Early Childhood Education
BS Computer Information Technology; Consumer and Family Sciences with Child Studies emphasis; Technology Management
Certificate Canadian Studies
Endorsement Gifted and Talented Graduate Teaching Endorsement
Graduate Certificate Women's Studies
MA Exceptional Education; Mathematics Education
MBA eMBA
MS Biology Education; Communication Disorders; Library Media Education; Physical Education Pedagogy; Technology Management

WESTERN MICHIGAN UNIVERSITY
Kalamazoo, Michigan
Department of Distance Education
http://dde.wmich.edu

Western Michigan University was founded in 1903. It is accredited by North Central Association of Colleges and Schools. It first offered distance learning courses in 1996. In fall 2006, there were 1,766 students enrolled in distance learning courses. Institutionally administered financial aid is available to distance learners.
Services Distance learners have accessibility to academic advising, bookstore, campus computer network, career placement assistance, e-mail services, library services.

Contact Teri Cleveland, Office Assistant, Western Michigan University, Academic Technology and Instructional Services, 1343 Ellsworth Hall, Kalamazoo, MI 49008-5232. Telephone: 269-387-4199. Fax: 269-387-4226. E-mail: teresa.cleveland@wmich.edu.

DEGREES AND AWARDS

MAE Educational Technology

COURSE SUBJECT AREAS OFFERED OUTSIDE OF DEGREE PROGRAMS

Undergraduate—air transportation; anthropology; apparel and textiles; area studies; computer software and media applications; economics; education; educational administration and supervision; educational assessment, evaluation, and research; educational/instructional media design; engineering; English composition; ethnic, cultural minority, and gender studies; family and consumer economics; family and consumer sciences/human sciences; family and consumer sciences/human sciences related; film/video and photographic arts; geography and cartography; history; industrial engineering; languages (Romance languages); medieval and Renaissance studies; music; natural sciences; public administration and social service professions related; rehabilitation and therapeutic professions; religious studies; sales, merchandising, and related marketing operations (specialized); science, technology and society; social work; sociology.

Graduate—computer engineering; computer science; counseling psychology; developmental and child psychology; economics; educational/instructional media design; engineering/industrial management; family and consumer economics; film/video and photographic arts; history; human resources management.

WESTERN PIEDMONT COMMUNITY COLLEGE
Morganton, North Carolina
http://www.wp.cc.nc.us/

Western Piedmont Community College was founded in 1964. It is accredited by Southern Association of Colleges and Schools. It first offered distance learning courses in 1995. In fall 2006, there were 1,000 students enrolled in distance learning courses. Institutionally administered financial aid is available to distance learners.
Services Distance learners have accessibility to academic advising, bookstore, campus computer network, career placement assistance, e-mail services, library services.
Contact Susan Williams, Director of Admissions, Western Piedmont Community College, 1001 Burkemont Avenue, Morganton, NC 28655. Telephone: 828-438-6051. Fax: 828-438-6015. E-mail: swilliams@wpcc.edu.

DEGREES AND AWARDS

AAS Business Administration; Paralegal Technology

COURSE SUBJECT AREAS OFFERED OUTSIDE OF DEGREE PROGRAMS

Undergraduate—accounting and computer science; accounting and related services; allied health and medical assisting services; business administration, management and operations; business/commerce; business/managerial economics; business operations support and assistant services; computer and information sciences; computer programming; computer software and media applications; computer systems networking and telecommunications; criminal justice and corrections; economics; education (specific levels and methods); English composition; fine and studio art; geography and cartography; history; human resources management; management information systems; marketing; mathematics; mathematics and statistics related; nursing; psychology; quality control and safety technologies; sociology; taxation.

WESTERN SEMINARY
Portland, Oregon
Center for Lifelong Learning
http://www.westernseminary.edu

Western Seminary was founded in 1927. It is accredited by Northwest Commission on Colleges and Universities. It first offered distance learning courses in 1981. In fall 2006, there were 191 students enrolled in distance learning courses. Institutionally administered financial aid is available to distance learners.

Services Distance learners have accessibility to academic advising, bookstore, career placement assistance, e-mail services, library services.

Contact James Stewart, Director of Distance Education, Western Seminary, 5511 SE Hawthorne Boulevard, Portland, OR 97215. Telephone: 877-517-1800. Fax: 503-517-1801. E-mail: jstewart@westernseminary.edu.

DEGREES AND AWARDS

Programs offered do not lead to a degree or other formal award.

COURSE SUBJECT AREAS OFFERED OUTSIDE OF DEGREE PROGRAMS

Graduate—biblical and other theological languages and literatures; biblical studies; religious education; religious studies; theological and ministerial studies; theology and religious vocations related.

Non-credit—biblical and other theological languages and literatures; biblical studies; religious education; religious studies; theological and ministerial studies; theology and religious vocations related.

WESTERN WYOMING COMMUNITY COLLEGE
Rock Springs, Wyoming
Extended Education
http://www.wwcc.cc.wy.us/dist.htm

Western Wyoming Community College was founded in 1959. It is accredited by North Central Association of Colleges and Schools. It first offered distance learning courses in 1988. In fall 2006, there were 1,200 students enrolled in distance learning courses. Institutionally administered financial aid is available to distance learners.

Services Distance learners have accessibility to academic advising, bookstore, campus computer network, career placement assistance, e-mail services, library services, tutoring.

Contact Ms. Christine Lustik, Director of Distance Education, Western Wyoming Community College, 2500 College Drive, PO Box 428, Rock Springs, WY 82902. Telephone: 307-382-1757. Fax: 307-382-1812. E-mail: clustik@wwcc.wy.edu.

DEGREES AND AWARDS

AA General Studies

AAS Office Information Systems

AS Accounting; Business Administration; Computer Information Systems; Economics; General Studies; Marketing

Certificate Accounting; Western American Studies

Certification Web Site Development certificate

COURSE SUBJECT AREAS OFFERED OUTSIDE OF DEGREE PROGRAMS

Undergraduate—accounting and related services; anthropology; applied mathematics; biological and physical sciences; business administration, management and operations; business/commerce; business operations support and assistant services; computer science; computer software and media applications; economics; education (specific levels and methods); English composition; ethnic, cultural minority, and gender studies; philosophy; psychology.

WEST HILLS COMMUNITY COLLEGE
Coalinga, California
Learning Resources Division
http://www.westhillscollege.com/

West Hills Community College was founded in 1932. It is accredited by Western Association of Schools and Colleges. It first offered distance learning courses in 1989. In fall 2006, there were 2,500 students enrolled in distance learning courses. Institutionally administered financial aid is available to distance learners.

Services Distance learners have accessibility to academic advising, bookstore, campus computer network, e-mail services, library services, tutoring.

Contact M. Susan Kincade, Dean of Learning Resources, West Hills Community College, 9900 Cody Avenue, Coalinga, CA 93210. Telephone: 559-925-3404. Fax: 559-925-3830. E-mail: susankincade@westhillscollege.com.

DEGREES AND AWARDS

AA Administration of Justice–Law Enforcement; Liberal Arts; Psychology; Social Science

AS Administration of Justice–Law Enforcement

COURSE SUBJECT AREAS OFFERED OUTSIDE OF DEGREE PROGRAMS

Non-credit—accounting and computer science; accounting and related services; applied horticulture/horticultural business services; computer software and media applications; gerontology; health services/allied health/health sciences; languages (Romance languages); mathematics and computer science; real estate; veterinary biomedical and clinical sciences.

WEST LIBERTY STATE COLLEGE
West Liberty, West Virginia

West Liberty State College was founded in 1837. It is accredited by North Central Association of Colleges and Schools. It first offered distance learning courses in 2004. In fall 2006, there were 300 students enrolled in distance learning courses. Institutionally administered financial aid is available to distance learners.

Services Distance learners have accessibility to academic advising, bookstore, e-mail services, library services.

Contact Ms. Ann Calder Rose, Coordinator of Distance Learning, West Liberty State College, PO Box 295, West Liberty, WV 26074. Telephone: 304-336-8432. E-mail: arose@westliberty.edu.

DEGREES AND AWARDS

Programs offered do not lead to a degree or other formal award.

COURSE SUBJECT AREAS OFFERED OUTSIDE OF DEGREE PROGRAMS

Undergraduate—accounting and computer science; business administration, management and operations; business/managerial economics; dental support services and allied professions; design and applied arts; education; educational assessment, evaluation, and research; geography and cartography; nursing; social work; sociology.

WEST LOS ANGELES COLLEGE
Culver City, California
Distance Learning Center
http://www.wlac.edu/online

West Los Angeles College was founded in 1969. It is accredited by Western Association of Schools and Colleges. It first offered distance learning courses in 1999. In fall 2006, there were 1,157 students enrolled in distance learning courses. Institutionally administered financial aid is available to distance learners.

Services Distance learners have accessibility to academic advising, bookstore, campus computer network, library services, tutoring.

Contact Mr. Eric Jean Ichon, Distance Learning Coordinator, West Los Angeles College, 9000 Overland Avenue, Culver City, CA 90230. Telephone: 310-287-4305. Fax: 310-841-0396. E-mail: ichone@wlac.edu.

DEGREES AND AWARDS
Programs offered do not lead to a degree or other formal award.

COURSE SUBJECT AREAS OFFERED OUTSIDE OF DEGREE PROGRAMS
Undergraduate—accounting and computer science; air transportation; allied health and medical assisting services; American literature (United States and Canadian); applied mathematics; area, ethnic, cultural, and gender studies related; behavioral sciences; business administration, management and operations; business/commerce; business, management, and marketing related; business operations support and assistant services; computer and information sciences; computer/information technology administration and management; computer science; creative writing; criminal justice and corrections; data entry/microcomputer applications; dental support services and allied professions; dentistry and oral sciences (advanced/graduate); design and applied arts; dramatic/theater arts and stagecraft; economics; English; English as a second language; English composition; English language and literature related; health and physical education/fitness; health/medical preparatory programs; health services/allied health/health sciences; history; international relations and affairs; languages (foreign languages related); legal professions and studies related; library science; marketing; mathematics; music; philosophy; political science and government; psychology; real estate; sales, merchandising, and related marketing operations (specialized); speech and rhetoric; technical and business writing; visual and performing arts.

WEST SHORE COMMUNITY COLLEGE
Scottville, Michigan
http://www.westshore.edu
West Shore Community College was founded in 1967. It is accredited by North Central Association of Colleges and Schools. It first offered distance learning courses in 1998. In fall 2006, there were 320 students enrolled in distance learning courses. Institutionally administered financial aid is available to distance learners.
Services Distance learners have accessibility to academic advising, bookstore, career placement assistance, e-mail services, library services, tutoring.
Contact Patti Davidson, Director of Distance Learning and Information Technology, West Shore Community College, 3000 North Stiles Road, Scottville, MI 49454-0277. Telephone: 231-845-0806. Fax: 231-845-0207. E-mail: pldavidson@westshore.edu.

DEGREES AND AWARDS
AGS General Studies

COURSE SUBJECT AREAS OFFERED OUTSIDE OF DEGREE PROGRAMS
Undergraduate—American literature (United States and Canadian); biology; botany/plant biology; business administration, management and operations; business, management, and marketing related; computer and information sciences; criminal justice and corrections; English composition; geological and earth sciences/geosciences; history; liberal arts and sciences, general studies and humanities; marketing; mathematics; mathematics and statistics related; music; public relations, advertising, and applied communication related; sociology.

WEST TEXAS A&M UNIVERSITY
Canyon, Texas
West Texas A&M University was founded in 1909. It is accredited by Southern Association of Colleges and Schools. It first offered distance learning courses in 1997. In fall 2006, there were 3,096 students enrolled in distance learning courses. Institutionally administered financial aid is available to distance learners.
Services Distance learners have accessibility to academic advising, bookstore, career placement assistance, e-mail services, library services.
Contact Mr. Shawn Thomas, Director, Admissions, West Texas A&M University, Office of Admissions, WTAMU Box 60907, Canyon, TX 79016-0001. Telephone: 806-651-2020. Fax: 806-651-5285. E-mail: admissions@mail.wtamu.edu.

DEGREES AND AWARDS
BGS General Studies
BSN Nursing–RN to BSN degree completion program
MBA Business Administration
MEd Instructional Technology
MS Agricultural Business Economics

COURSE SUBJECT AREAS OFFERED OUTSIDE OF DEGREE PROGRAMS
Undergraduate—education.
Graduate—accounting and computer science; educational assessment, evaluation, and research; education (specific subject areas).

WEST VALLEY COLLEGE
Saratoga, California
Distance Learning
http://www.westvalley.edu/wvc/dl/dl.html
West Valley College was founded in 1963. It is accredited by Western Association of Schools and Colleges. It first offered distance learning courses in 1985. In fall 2006, there were 3,069 students enrolled in distance learning courses. Institutionally administered financial aid is available to distance learners.
Services Distance learners have accessibility to academic advising, bookstore, campus computer network, e-mail services, library services.
Contact Steve Peltz, Program Director, Distance Learning and Instructional Technology, West Valley College, 14000 Fruitvale Avenue, Saratoga, CA 95070. Telephone: 408-741-2065. Fax: 408-741-2134. E-mail: steve_peltz@westvalley.edu.

DEGREES AND AWARDS
AA Business Management; General Programs; Web Design

COURSE SUBJECT AREAS OFFERED OUTSIDE OF DEGREE PROGRAMS
Undergraduate—anthropology; business administration, management and operations; business/commerce; computer and information sciences; computer science; computer software and media applications; creative writing; developmental and child psychology; economics; English composition; film/video and photographic arts; fine and studio art; history; information science/studies; languages (Romance languages); legal studies (non-professional general, undergraduate); library science related; marketing; mathematics; philosophy; political science and government; psychology; sociology.

WEST VIRGINIA STATE UNIVERSITY
Institute, West Virginia
http://www.wvsc.edu/
West Virginia State University was founded in 1891. It is accredited by North Central Association of Colleges and Schools. It first offered distance learning courses in 1998. In fall 2006, there were 160 students enrolled in distance learning courses. Institutionally administered financial aid is available to distance learners.
Services Distance learners have accessibility to bookstore, campus computer network, e-mail services, library services, tutoring.
Contact Dr. John Teeuwissen, Assistant Vice President for Academic Affairs, West Virginia State University, 131 Ferrell Hall, PO Box 1000, Institute, WV 25112. Telephone: 304-766-3147. Fax: 304-766-4251. E-mail: johntee@wvstateu.edu.

DEGREES AND AWARDS
Programs offered do not lead to a degree or other formal award.

COURSE SUBJECT AREAS OFFERED OUTSIDE OF DEGREE PROGRAMS
Undergraduate—business administration, management and operations; communication and journalism related; communication and media; computer and information sciences; education; English; English composition; film/video and photographic arts; health professions related; social work; technical and business writing.
Graduate—communication and media; film/video and photographic arts.

WEST VIRGINIA UNIVERSITY
Morgantown, West Virginia
Extended Learning
http://www.e-learn.wvu.edu

West Virginia University was founded in 1867. It is accredited by North Central Association of Colleges and Schools. It first offered distance learning courses in 1987. In fall 2006, there were 5,118 students enrolled in distance learning courses. Institutionally administered financial aid is available to distance learners.

Services Distance learners have accessibility to academic advising, bookstore, campus computer network, career placement assistance, e-mail services, library services, tutoring.

Contact Ms. Cindy K. Hart, Coordinator of Distance Learning, West Virginia University, 707 Allen Hall, PO Box 6808, Morgantown, WV 26506-6808. Telephone: 304-293-3852. Fax: 304-293-3853. E-mail: lkhart@mail.wvu.edu.

DEGREES AND AWARDS
BA Multidisciplinary Studies; Regents Bachelor of Arts
BSN Nursing–RN to BSN
Certificate Integrated Marketing Communications
EMBA Business Administration
MA Elementary Education; Secondary Education–Science Emphasis; Secondary Education–Social Studies emphasis; Special Education
MLS Legal Studies
MPH Public Health
MS Athletic Coaching; Integrated Marketing Communications; Rehabilitation Counseling; Software Engineering; Sports Management
MSE Physical Education Teacher Education
MSN Nursing
MSOT Occupational Therapy

COURSE SUBJECT AREAS OFFERED OUTSIDE OF DEGREE PROGRAMS
Non-credit—computer software and media applications; education; engineering related; finance and financial management services; forensic psychology; health professions related; health services/allied health/health sciences; legal support services; management information systems; nursing; technology education/industrial arts.

WEST VIRGINIA UNIVERSITY AT PARKERSBURG
Parkersburg, West Virginia
http://www.wvup.edu

West Virginia University at Parkersburg was founded in 1961. It is accredited by North Central Association of Colleges and Schools. It first offered distance learning courses in 1999. In fall 2006, there were 1,500 students enrolled in distance learning courses. Institutionally administered financial aid is available to distance learners.

Services Distance learners have accessibility to academic advising, bookstore, campus computer network, e-mail services, library services, tutoring.

Contact Theresa Cross, WebCT System Administrator, West Virginia University at Parkersburg, 300 Campus Drive, Parkersburg, WV 26104. Telephone: 304-424-8358. Fax: 304-424-8354. E-mail: theresa.cross@mail.wvu.edu.

DEGREES AND AWARDS
AAS Business Technology; Criminal Justice

COURSE SUBJECT AREAS OFFERED OUTSIDE OF DEGREE PROGRAMS
Undergraduate—accounting and related services; biological and physical sciences; biology; business administration, management and operations; business/commerce; business/corporate communications; business, management, and marketing related; business/managerial economics; business operations support and assistant services; communication and journalism related; community health services; computer and information sciences; computer/information technology administration and management; criminal justice and corrections; dramatic/theater arts and stagecraft; English composition; English language and literature related; health and physical

education/fitness; health professions related; history; human resources management; intercultural/multicultural and diversity studies; management information systems; marketing; mathematics; nursing; philosophy; psychology; social sciences; sociology; technology education/industrial arts.

Non-credit—accounting and computer science; business/corporate communications; business operations support and assistant services; communication and media; communications technologies and support services related; computer and information sciences; computer/information technology administration and management; construction trades related; crafts, folk art and artisanry; dance; fishing and fisheries sciences and management; foods, nutrition, and related services; quality control and safety technologies; technical and business writing.

WESTWOOD ONLINE
Denver, Colorado
http://www.westwood.edu

Westwood Online is accredited by Accrediting Commission of Career Schools and Colleges of Technology. It first offered distance learning courses in 2002. In fall 2006, there were 350 students enrolled in distance learning courses. Institutionally administered financial aid is available to distance learners.

Services Distance learners have accessibility to academic advising, bookstore, campus computer network, career placement assistance, e-mail services, library services, tutoring.

Contact Kim Beckman, Area Vice President, Westwood Online, Denver, CO 80221. Telephone: 303-635-7750 Ext. 11510. E-mail: kbeckman@westwood.edu.

DEGREES AND AWARDS
AAS Computer Network Engineering; Graphic Design and Multimedia; Software Engineering
BS Animation; Business Administration–Accounting concentration; Business Administration–Marketing and Sales concentration; Business–Fashion Merchandising; Computer Network Management; Criminal Justice; E-Business Management; Game Art and Design; Game Software Development; Information Systems Security; Visual Communications; Web Design and Multimedia
MBA Business Administration

COURSE SUBJECT AREAS OFFERED OUTSIDE OF DEGREE PROGRAMS
Undergraduate—accounting and related services; business administration, management and operations; computer programming; computer software and media applications; computer systems networking and telecommunications; criminal justice and corrections; design and applied arts.

See full description on page 528.

WHARTON COUNTY JUNIOR COLLEGE
Wharton, Texas
http://www.wcjc.cc.tx.us/

Wharton County Junior College was founded in 1946. It is accredited by Southern Association of Colleges and Schools. It first offered distance learning courses in 1993. In fall 2006, there were 930 students enrolled in distance learning courses. Institutionally administered financial aid is available to distance learners.

Services Distance learners have accessibility to bookstore, e-mail services, library services, tutoring.

Contact Ken Rosier, Distance Learning Program Director, Wharton County Junior College, 911 Boling Highway, Wharton, TX 77488. Telephone: 979-532-6944. Fax: 979-532-6567. E-mail: rosierk@wcjc.edu.

DEGREES AND AWARDS
Programs offered do not lead to a degree or other formal award.

COURSE SUBJECT AREAS OFFERED OUTSIDE OF DEGREE PROGRAMS
Undergraduate—accounting and computer science; allied health and medical assisting services; American literature (United States and

Canadian); behavioral sciences; biology; business administration, management and operations; business/commerce; business, management, and marketing related; computer and information sciences; computer science; computer software and media applications; computer systems networking and telecommunications; creative writing; criminal justice and corrections; English; English composition; English language and literature related; English literature (British and Commonwealth); geological and earth sciences/geosciences; history; liberal arts and sciences, general studies and humanities; marketing; psychology; sociology; speech and rhetoric.

Non-credit—English as a second language; fire protection.

WICHITA STATE UNIVERSITY
Wichita, Kansas
Media Resources Center
http://www.mrc.twsu.edu/mrc/telecourse
Wichita State University was founded in 1895. It is accredited by North Central Association of Colleges and Schools. It first offered distance learning courses in 1982. In fall 2006, there were 668 students enrolled in distance learning courses. Institutionally administered financial aid is available to distance learners.
Services Distance learners have accessibility to bookstore, library services.
Contact Mary Morriss, Telecourse Coordinator, Wichita State University, 1845 Fairmount, Wichita, KS 67260-0057. Telephone: 316-978-7766. Fax: 316-978-3560. E-mail: morriss@mrc.twsu.edu.

DEGREES AND AWARDS
Programs offered do not lead to a degree or other formal award.

COURSE SUBJECT AREAS OFFERED OUTSIDE OF DEGREE PROGRAMS
Undergraduate—accounting and related services; anthropology; astronomy and astrophysics; communication and media; family and consumer economics; geography and cartography; gerontology; history; music; psychology; sociology; speech and rhetoric.

WILFRID LAURIER UNIVERSITY
Waterloo, Ontario, Canada
Office of Teaching Support Services
http://www.wlu.ca/pts
Wilfrid Laurier University was founded in 1911. It is provincially chartered. It first offered distance learning courses in 1978. In fall 2006, there were 3,000 students enrolled in distance learning courses. Institutionally administered financial aid is available to distance learners.
Services Distance learners have accessibility to academic advising, bookstore, campus computer network, career placement assistance, e-mail services, library services.
Contact Lisa Fanjoy, Manager, Distance and Continuing Education, Wilfrid Laurier University, Office of Teaching Support Services, 75 University Avenue West, Waterloo, ON N2L 3C5, Canada. Telephone: 519-884-0710 Ext. 4106. Fax: 519-884-6063. E-mail: lfanjoy@wlu.ca.

DEGREES AND AWARDS
BA General Studies

COURSE SUBJECT AREAS OFFERED OUTSIDE OF DEGREE PROGRAMS
Undergraduate—accounting and related services; American literature (United States and Canadian); anthropology; astronomy and astrophysics; biology; biopsychology; botany/plant biology; business/commerce; cognitive psychology and psycholinguistics; communication and media; developmental and child psychology; economics; English; English literature (British and Commonwealth); finance and financial management services; fine and studio art; geography and cartography; geological and earth sciences/geosciences; history; languages (Germanic); languages (Romance languages); philosophy; psychology; psychology related; religious studies; social work; sociology; visual and performing arts.

Non-credit—English composition.

WILKES COMMUNITY COLLEGE
Wilkesboro, North Carolina
Individualized Studies Department
http://www.wilkes.cc.nc.us
Wilkes Community College was founded in 1965. It is accredited by Southern Association of Colleges and Schools. It first offered distance learning courses in 1984. In fall 2006, there were 1,624 students enrolled in distance learning courses. Institutionally administered financial aid is available to distance learners.
Services Distance learners have accessibility to academic advising, bookstore, campus computer network, career placement assistance, e-mail services, library services.
Contact Debi McGuire, Director of Distance Learning, Wilkes Community College, PO Box 120, Wilkesboro, NC 28697. Telephone: 336-838-6524. E-mail: debi.mcguire@wilkescc.edu.

DEGREES AND AWARDS
AA Arts
AAS Business Administration

COURSE SUBJECT AREAS OFFERED OUTSIDE OF DEGREE PROGRAMS
Undergraduate—accounting and related services; American literature (United States and Canadian); biology; business administration, management and operations; business/commerce; business, management, and marketing related; business/managerial economics; communication and media; communications technology; computer and information sciences; computer and information sciences and support services related; computer programming; computer science; creative writing; data processing; dramatic/theater arts and stagecraft; education related; English; English composition; English language and literature related; English literature (British and Commonwealth); ethnic, cultural minority, and gender studies; fine and studio art; history; human development, family studies, and related services; management information systems; marketing; mathematics; philosophy and religious studies related; physical sciences; psychology; psychology related; public relations, advertising, and applied communication related; religious studies; sales, merchandising, and related marketing operations (specialized); sociology; technical and business writing.

WILLISTON STATE COLLEGE
Williston, North Dakota
Williston State College was founded in 1957. It is accredited by North Central Association of Colleges and Schools. It first offered distance learning courses in 2000. In fall 2006, there were 409 students enrolled in distance learning courses. Institutionally administered financial aid is available to distance learners.
Services Distance learners have accessibility to academic advising, bookstore, campus computer network, e-mail services, library services, tutoring.
Contact Mrs. Wanda Mae Meyer, Director for Distance Learning, Williston State College, 1410 University Avenue, Williston, ND 58801. Telephone: 701-774-4231. Fax: 701-772-4211. E-mail: wanda.meyer@wsc.nodak.edu.

DEGREES AND AWARDS
AAS Administrative Assistant–Accounting option; Administrative Assistant–Health Information Management option; Administrative Assistant–Information Processing option; Entrepreneurship; Marketing/Management; Medical Transcription; Paraeducator; Speech Language Pathology Assistant
Certificate of Completion Entrepreneurship
Certificate Administrative Assistant–Front Office option; Administrative Assistant–Information Processing option; Administrative Assistant–Medical Billing and Coding option; Entrepreneurship; Marketing/Management; Medical Transcription

COURSE SUBJECT AREAS OFFERED OUTSIDE OF DEGREE PROGRAMS

Undergraduate—accounting and computer science; biology; business, management, and marketing related; business/managerial economics; chemistry; computer science; English composition; history; mathematics; music; psychology; sociology.

WISCONSIN INDIANHEAD TECHNICAL COLLEGE
Shell Lake, Wisconsin
http://www.witc.edu

Wisconsin Indianhead Technical College was founded in 1912. It is accredited by North Central Association of Colleges and Schools. It first offered distance learning courses in 1991. In fall 2006, there were 651 students enrolled in distance learning courses. Institutionally administered financial aid is available to distance learners.

Services Distance learners have accessibility to academic advising, bookstore, career placement assistance, e-mail services, library services, tutoring.

Contact Dr. Diane Vertin, Vice President, Academic Affairs, Wisconsin Indianhead Technical College, 505 Pine Ridge Drive, Shell Lake, WI 54871. Telephone: 715-468-2815 Ext. 2331. Fax: 715-468-2819. E-mail: diane.vertin@witc.edu.

DEGREES AND AWARDS

AD Information Technology–Web Analyst/Programmer

COURSE SUBJECT AREAS OFFERED OUTSIDE OF DEGREE PROGRAMS

Undergraduate—accounting and related services; agricultural and food products processing; agricultural business and management; agriculture; applied mathematics; business administration, management and operations; business/commerce; business operations support and assistant services; communication and media; computer and information sciences; computer programming; foods, nutrition, and related services; human development, family studies, and related services; nursing; psychology; public relations, advertising, and applied communication related; sales, merchandising, and related marketing operations (specialized); sociology; statistics.

Non-credit—accounting and related services; agricultural and food products processing; agricultural business and management; agriculture; applied mathematics; business administration, management and operations; business/commerce; business operations support and assistant services; communication and media; computer and information sciences; computer programming; foods, nutrition, and related services; human development, family studies, and related services; nursing; psychology; public relations, advertising, and applied communication related; sales, merchandising, and related marketing operations (specialized); sociology; statistics.

WORCESTER POLYTECHNIC INSTITUTE
Worcester, Massachusetts
Advanced Distance Learning Network
http://www.wpi.edu/+ADLN

Worcester Polytechnic Institute was founded in 1865. It is accredited by New England Association of Schools and Colleges. It first offered distance learning courses in 1979. In fall 2006, there were 400 students enrolled in distance learning courses. Institutionally administered financial aid is available to distance learners.

Services Distance learners have accessibility to academic advising, bookstore, campus computer network, career placement assistance, e-mail services, library services.

Contact Pamela S. Shelley, Assistant Director of Distance Learning, Worcester Polytechnic Institute, 100 Institute Road, Worcester, MA 01609-2280. Telephone: 508-831-6789. Fax: 508-831-5694. E-mail: online@wpi.edu.

DEGREES AND AWARDS

CGMS Management

Graduate Certificate Environmental Engineering; Fire Protection Engineering
MBA Technology Management
MS Environmental Engineering; Fire Protection Engineering

COURSE SUBJECT AREAS OFFERED OUTSIDE OF DEGREE PROGRAMS

Graduate—business administration, management and operations; environmental/environmental health engineering; fire protection; marketing.

WRIGHT STATE UNIVERSITY
Dayton, Ohio
Center for Teaching and Learning
http://www.wright.edu/dl

Wright State University was founded in 1964. It is accredited by North Central Association of Colleges and Schools. It first offered distance learning courses in 1995. In fall 2006, there were 1,700 students enrolled in distance learning courses. Institutionally administered financial aid is available to distance learners.

Services Distance learners have accessibility to academic advising, bookstore, campus computer network, e-mail services, library services.

Contact Terri Klaus, Associate Director of Center for Teaching and Learning and Distance Learning, Wright State University, 023 Library, 3640 Colonel Glenn Highway, Dayton, OH 45435. Telephone: 937-775-4965. Fax: 937-775-3152. E-mail: terri.klaus@wright.edu.

DEGREES AND AWARDS

BS Nursing–RN to BSN completion program
MEd Teacher Leader
MS Family Nurse Practitioner–First Masters; Family Nurse Practitioner–Second Masters; Human Factors Engineering; Logistics and Supply Chain Management; Rehabilitation Counseling
MSIS Information Systems

COURSE SUBJECT AREAS OFFERED OUTSIDE OF DEGREE PROGRAMS

Undergraduate—biological and physical sciences; biology; communication and media; computer and information sciences; economics; education; education (specific levels and methods); English; English composition; history; liberal arts and sciences, general studies and humanities; linguistic, comparative, and related language studies; mathematics; music; nursing; philosophy; political science and government; religious studies; statistics; technical and business writing.

Graduate—communication and media; economics; educational/instructional media design; education related; geological and earth sciences/geosciences; nursing; technical and business writing.

Non-credit—economics; education related.

XAVIER UNIVERSITY OF LOUISIANA
New Orleans, Louisiana
Drexel Center for Extended Learning
http://www.xula.edu/

Xavier University of Louisiana was founded in 1925. It is accredited by Southern Association of Colleges and Schools. It first offered distance learning courses in 1989. In fall 2006, there were 100 students enrolled in distance learning courses. Institutionally administered financial aid is available to distance learners.

Services Distance learners have accessibility to academic advising, bookstore, campus computer network, e-mail services, library services.

Contact Dr. Elizabeth Moore Rhodes, Program Director, Xavier University of Louisiana, 1 Drexel Drive, Box 99C, New Orleans, LA 70125. Telephone: 504 520 7534. E-mail: erhodes@xula.edu.

DEGREES AND AWARDS

Programs offered do not lead to a degree or other formal award.

COURSE SUBJECT AREAS OFFERED OUTSIDE OF DEGREE PROGRAMS

Undergraduate—education; educational administration and supervision; education (specific levels and methods).
Graduate—education; educational administration and supervision; educational/instructional media design; education (specific levels and methods).

YORK COUNTY COMMUNITY COLLEGE
Wells, Maine
http://www.yccc.edu

York County Community College was founded in 1994. It is accredited by New England Association of Schools and Colleges. It first offered distance learning courses in 1999. In fall 2006, there were 300 students enrolled in distance learning courses. Institutionally administered financial aid is available to distance learners.
Services Distance learners have accessibility to academic advising, bookstore, campus computer network, e-mail services, library services.
Contact Fred Quistgard, Director of Admissions, York County Community College, 112 College Drive, Wells, ME 04090. Telephone: 207-646-9282 Ext. 311. Fax: 207-641-0837. E-mail: fquistgard@yccc.edu.

DEGREES AND AWARDS

Programs offered do not lead to a degree or other formal award.

COURSE SUBJECT AREAS OFFERED OUTSIDE OF DEGREE PROGRAMS

Undergraduate—accounting and related services; American literature (United States and Canadian); applied mathematics; business administration, management and operations; business/commerce; business/corporate communications; business, management, and marketing related; business operations support and assistant services; computer and information sciences; computer/information technology administration and management; computer programming; computer software and media applications; culinary arts and related services; English composition; hospitality administration; human development, family studies, and related services; management information systems; mathematics; psychology; sociology; technical and business writing.

YORK TECHNICAL COLLEGE
Rock Hill, South Carolina
Distance Learning Department
http://www.yorktech.com

York Technical College was founded in 1961. It is accredited by Southern Association of Colleges and Schools. It first offered distance learning courses in 1995. In fall 2006, there were 3,400 students enrolled in distance learning courses. Institutionally administered financial aid is available to distance learners.
Services Distance learners have accessibility to academic advising, bookstore, campus computer network, career placement assistance, e-mail services, library services, tutoring.
Contact Anita McBride, Department Manager, York Technical College, 452 South Anderson Road, Rock Hill, SC 29730. Telephone: 803-981-7044. Fax: 803-981-7193. E-mail: mcbride@yorktech.com.

DEGREES AND AWARDS

AAB Accounting–Associate of Business

COURSE SUBJECT AREAS OFFERED OUTSIDE OF DEGREE PROGRAMS

Undergraduate—accounting and related services; biological and physical sciences; business administration, management and operations; business/commerce; computer science; developmental and child psychology; economics; English; English composition; environmental/environmental health engineering; history; mathematics; nursing; philosophy; psychology; sociology.
Non-credit—computer and information sciences and support services related.

YORK UNIVERSITY
Toronto, Ontario, Canada
http://www.yorku.ca/

York University was founded in 1959. It is provincially chartered. It first offered distance learning courses in 1994. In fall 2006, there were 10,000 students enrolled in distance learning courses. Institutionally administered financial aid is available to distance learners.
Services Distance learners have accessibility to academic advising, bookstore, campus computer network, e-mail services, library services, tutoring.
Contact Ms. Amalia Syligardakis, Manager, e-Learning Services, York University, Office of Computing Technology and e-Learning Services, 4700 Keele Street, Room 2120, TEL Building, Toronto, ON M3J 1P3, Canada. Telephone: 416-736-2100 Ext. 30705. Fax: 416-736-5637. E-mail: amalias@yorku.ca.

DEGREES AND AWARDS

BA Business Economics
BBA Administrative Studies

COURSE SUBJECT AREAS OFFERED OUTSIDE OF DEGREE PROGRAMS

Undergraduate—accounting and related services; business administration, management and operations; business/corporate communications; business/managerial economics; communication and media; economics; English language and literature related; film/video and photographic arts; geography and cartography; health professions related; history; human development, family studies, and related services; human resources management; liberal arts and sciences, general studies and humanities; management sciences and quantitative methods; marketing; mathematics; nursing; philosophy; political science and government; psychology related; public administration; public administration and social service professions related; religious studies; social sciences; social work; sociology; statistics; visual and performing arts related.

YOUNGSTOWN STATE UNIVERSITY
Youngstown, Ohio
http://www.ysu.edu/metro

Youngstown State University was founded in 1908. It is accredited by North Central Association of Colleges and Schools. It first offered distance learning courses in 1999. In fall 2006, there were 500 students enrolled in distance learning courses. Institutionally administered financial aid is available to distance learners.
Services Distance learners have accessibility to academic advising, bookstore, campus computer network, career placement assistance, e-mail services, library services, tutoring.
Contact Dr. Salvatore A. Sanders, Assistant Professor and Director of Distance Learning for The Bitonte College of Health and Human Services, Youngstown State University, Department of Health Professions, 1 University Plaza, Youngstown, OH 44555. Telephone: 330-941-7157. Fax: 330-941-2921. E-mail: sasanders@ysu.edu.

DEGREES AND AWARDS

BS BSAS in Allied Health; BSAS in Criminal Justice; BSAS in Public Health
MHSA Master of Health and Human Services
MPH Public Health

COURSE SUBJECT AREAS OFFERED OUTSIDE OF DEGREE PROGRAMS

Undergraduate—criminal justice and corrections; economics; foods, nutrition, and related services; geological and earth sciences/geosciences; health and physical education/fitness; health professions related; history; mathematics; nursing; philosophy.
Graduate—educational administration and supervision; educational/instructional media design; health professions related; public administration; public health.
Non-credit—accounting and related services; allied health and medical assisting services; American literature (United States and Canadian); business administration, management and operations; business, man-

agement, and marketing related; business/managerial economics; business operations support and assistant services; computer and information sciences; computer software and media applications; computer systems networking and telecommunications; creative writing; English language and literature related; entrepreneurial and small business operations; health and medical administrative services; public relations, advertising, and applied communication related; sales, merchandising, and related marketing operations (specialized); technical and business writing.

YUBA COLLEGE
Marysville, California
Learning Resource Center
http://www.yubaonline.edu

Yuba College was founded in 1927. It is accredited by Western Association of Schools and Colleges. It first offered distance learning courses in 1975. In fall 2006, there were 2,181 students enrolled in distance learning courses. Institutionally administered financial aid is available to distance learners.

Services Distance learners have accessibility to academic advising, bookstore, campus computer network, career placement assistance, e-mail services, library services, tutoring.

Contact Miss Jeanette O'Bryan, Distributive Education Support Specialist, Yuba College, 2088 North Beale Road, Marysville, CA 95901. Telephone: 530-741-6754. Fax: 530-741-6824. E-mail: jobryan@yccd.edu.

DEGREES AND AWARDS
AAS General Studies

COURSE SUBJECT AREAS OFFERED OUTSIDE OF DEGREE PROGRAMS
Undergraduate—accounting and computer science; agricultural business and management; agriculture and agriculture operations related; animal sciences; anthropology; applied mathematics; astronomy and astrophysics; behavioral sciences; biology; chemistry; communication and media; computer and information sciences and support services related; computer programming; computer systems networking and telecommunications; ecology, evolution, and population biology; economics; education related; education (specific subject areas); English composition; foods, nutrition, and related services; liberal arts and sciences, general studies and humanities; mathematics and computer science; music; personality psychology; plant sciences; psychology; psychology related; sociology; veterinary biomedical and clinical sciences.

In-Depth Descriptions

The following two-page descriptions were prepared for this book by the institutions. An institution's absence from this section does not constitute an editorial decision. Rather, in-depth descriptions were offered as an open forum for institutions to expand upon the information provided in the previous section of this book. The descriptions are arranged alphabetically by institution name.

ADAMS STATE COLLEGE COLORADO
Great Stories Begin Here
EXTENDED STUDIES

ADAMS STATE COLLEGE

Extended Studies

Alamosa, Colorado

Adams State College (ASC), which was founded in 1921, is located in the San Luis Valley in south-central Colorado in the city of Alamosa. Alamosa, at an elevation of 7,500 feet above sea level, is surrounded by mountain ranges with peaks rising up to 14,000 feet above sea level. The student body is composed of approximately 2,500 individuals from various ethnic and racial backgrounds. Adams State College is accredited by the Higher Learning Commission of the North Central Association of Colleges and Schools. The School of Education is currently accepted as a candidate in the Teacher Education Accreditation Council (TEAC).

Distance Learning Program

Adams State College has been providing programs to off-campus students for more than twenty-five years. In the past year, more than 18,000 students took advantage of one of the options offered through Extended Studies.

The Distance Degree Program offers a Bachelor of Arts (B.A.) degree in business administration, interdisciplinary studies, and sociology; a Bachelor of Science (B.S.) degree in business administration; and the Associate of Arts (A.A.) and Associate of Science (A.S.) degrees.

Certificate programs are available in alternative dispute resolution (mediation), legal investigation, legal nurse consultant training, legal secretary studies, management information systems, paralegal studies, and victim advocacy. Students who are not interested in degree completion can enroll in a choice of more than 200 independent-study/correspondence courses in accounting, business, business finance, business management, business strategy, criminology, economics, education, English, geology, history, management, marketing, math, psychology, social theory, social welfare, and sociology.

Delivery Media

A variety of delivery options are available to students for all the accounting, business administration, criminology, economics, education, English, geology, history, management, sociology, and general education courses, including online delivery, print materials, and face-to-face instruction at various sites. Students enrolling in an online or independent-study (correspondence) course are provided with a printed study guide outlining course requirements. Students send completed course work directly to the instructor. Some courses require proctored examinations, while others have online examinations. Online and traditional tools are available for courses, such as e-mail, textbooks, and videotapes. All ASC instructors are available by telephone, fax, e-mail, and surface mail.

Programs of Study

The B.A. and B.S. degrees in business administration require 120 semester credits for graduation; 45 must be junior- or senior-level credits, and a minimum of 30 credits must be completed with ASC. B.A./B.S. degree requirements include 40 semester credits in general education and approximately 40 in electives and 40 in the major field (specific requirements subject to the academic major). A maximum of 90 semester credits can be transferred to ASC, of which a maximum of 60 may be from junior/community colleges. Admitted students must maintain active status by enrolling in at least one ASC course per semester.

A.A. and A.S. degree program requirements include 43 semester credits in general education and 17 in elective Students must complete general educ tion course work to satisfy requir ments from the following eight area oral and written communication, h man behavior and institutions, histor and culture, and arts and literature (credits each); quantitative thinking (credits) and speech fundamentals (credits; speech is required for A.A. ar A.S. degrees only); science foundatior and issues (8 credits); and health ar fitness (2 credits). For specific cours titles that meet these requirement students should visit the ASC Web si at http://exstudies.adams.edu/degre html.

Transfer credit is accepted fro accredited institutions recommende by the American Association of Coll giate Registrars and Admissions Offi ers. Credits from a nonaccredite institution may be petitioned for trar fer after the student has completed least 24 semester credits at ASC with C (2.0 GPA) average or better. Studen may petition the appropriate academ dean for approval of courses that a not accepted during the normal adm sion and transfer process.

Special Programs

Courses that have attracted the inte ests of many students include t popular certificate programs in para gal studies, alternative dispute reso tion (mediation), legal investigatio legal nurse consultant training, leg secretary studies, and victim advocac

More than 200 six-week, noncred online interactive courses are availab to students who are not interested ir standard academic program but a seeking a short-term solution to current need. These courses are d signed to provide the student with ne skills and knowledge or to impro current skills. The categories of cours clude business management, computer and software applications, entrepreneur studies, health, Internet, personal enrichment, small business, and web page design. For a complete listing, students should visit http://www. d2go.com/adams/.

ASC offers a wide range of online and independent-study graduate courses that have been developed for teachers. Many schools and school districts allow these courses to be used for in-service training or recertification purposes. Customized graduate certificate programs are designed to meet the professional development needs of educators.

Student Services

Free unofficial transfer evaluations are offered to students who are interested the degree program. The ASC adviser provides students with a free, preliminary, unofficial credit evaluation upon request. Students must provide copies transcripts or grade reports showing previous college work. These "unofficial" documents are reviewed by the program adviser, entered on a degree advisement form, and returned to the student. Students have the opportunity see how their previous college work might meet the ASC requirements. The unofficial evaluation is subject to change based on the outcome of the official admission evaluation and acceptance of transfer credits by the Admissions office.

Degree-seeking students have access ASC faculty members via mail, e-mail, fax or by calling the Extended studies Office toll-free at 800-548-6679. Books may be purchased from the ASC bookstore via telephone, mail, or fax. pertinent forms are located on the tended Studies Web site.

Credit Options

For the bachelor's degrees, students may transfer in a maximum of 90 semester credits to ASC. The remaining semester credits must be completed th ASC. Only 60 credits from community colleges may be applied to the degree. For the associate degree, students may transfer in a maximum of 45

semester credits, with the remaining 15 credits completed at ASC.

ASC participates in the College-Level Examination Program (CLEP) (general or subject exams). Students who have performed satisfactorily in college-level courses before college entrance and have demonstrated a requisite achievement (minimum scores of 50th percentile) on tests of the College Board College-Level Examination Program may submit the results to ASC for consideration for college credit. The Records Office records the college credit based on determinations made by the appropriate school's department chair. The maximum credit on the general exams is 18 semester hours (in the areas of humanities, natural science, and social science). The semester hours of credit for each subject exam, as well as credit by examination in total, are determined by the appropriate school's dean.

Military and civilian training is also considered for credit. The chair of the academic department in which the degree is earned evaluates any military and civilian training and makes the decision as to how credit will be awarded. ASC uses the American Council on Education Guides for credit recommendations. Military service credit is processed when official documents or transcripts are received at ASC. Courses found in the American Council on Education Guide or on transcripts (CCAF, AARTS, SMART) can be evaluated. Locally conducted (base- or post-level) courses are generally not acceptable due to their unstructured and changing content.

Faculty

Approximately 65 percent of the faculty members in the Distance Degree Program have a Ph.D. and are full-time professors on campus at ASC. All professors have experience working with distance learners.

Admission

Transfer students with at least 12 transferable college credits are not required to submit ACT or SAT scores or their high school transcript but must submit the admission application, appli-

cation fee, and official transcripts from all colleges previously attended. First-time freshman students must submit the program application fee, the application for admission, and high school transcripts with ACT or SAT scores. The Distance Degree Program application fee is $25. For admission and application information and details, students should visit http://exstudies.adams.edu/degree.html.

Tuition and Fees

Independent-study course tuition for undergraduate credit is $105 per semester hour; for graduate credit, it is $125 per semester hour. Tuition must be submitted with the registration for the course. Some courses may have additional fees for materials. For course details, applicants should see the specific course description at http://extudies.adams.edu/ind_study/independ.html.

Financial Aid

Currently, students admitted to the Distance Degree Program are eligible to apply for financial aid. Also, company-sponsored tuition and military tuition assistance programs may be used for ASC courses. Eligible military personnel should process DANTES applications through their education office.

Applying

Students can find course and degree application information, application and registration forms, and more answers to their questions by visiting the Extended Studies Web site.

CONTACT

Distance Degree Programs
Extended Studies
Adams State College
208 Edgemont Boulevard
Alamosa, Colorado 81102

Phone: 800-548-6679 (toll-free)
Fax: 719-587-7974
E-mail: ascadvisor@adams.edu
Web site: http://exstudies.adams.
edu

AIU ONLINE—AMERICAN INTERCONTINENTAL UNIVERSITY

Accelerated Degrees

Hoffman Estates, Illinois

American InterContinental University (AIU) Online is one of the premier online universities in the United States. With a tradition of educating students for more than thirty-five years, AIU has created an online education environment that combines the most sophisticated in Internet technology with the tradition of excellent higher education. American InterContinental University is accredited by the Commission on Colleges of the Southern Association of Colleges and Schools to award associate, bachelor's, and master's degrees.

Distance Learning Program

AIU Online's virtual campus provides a rich, interactive education. AIU Online offers degrees with classrooms as close as any Internet-connected computer, so students have access to a complete campus experience 24 hours a day, seven days a week. An education from AIU Online provides students with an opportunity to continue their education and advance their careers without disrupting their current lifestyles and schedules.

Delivery Media

The Web-based degree programs delivered by AIU Online are specifically designed for the student who accesses the course from a home or work personal computer. Recommended PC specifications are provided to students at the time of enrollment.

Programs of Study

All AIU Online programs can be taken at an accelerated pace, so students can make their move upward sooner. A master's degree or M.B.A. can be completed in ten months.

Business: Today's increasingly complicated business environments demand that existing and future business professionals have a comprehensive knowledge of the economic climate in the modern workforce.

The business administration program includes many sought-after concentrations that students can choose from to tailor their business degree to a specific career interest. Business concentrations include accounting and finance, health-care management, human resource management, international business, management, marketing, operations management, organizational psychology and development, and project management.

The Bachelor of Business Administration (B.B.A.) programs provide an in-depth study of business, management, and marketing and give students a strong foundation for continued studies should they wish to advance their business education in the future.

AIU Online's accelerated M.B.A. program helps ensure that a student is professionally up-to-date and prepared to meet the challenges of today's increasingly complicated business environments. An online education from AIU Online gives students the knowledge and understanding of the economic climate in the modern workplace.

Information Technology (IT): As the modern business world becomes increasingly dependent on computers, the demand for IT professionals may continue to grow. AIU Online's degree programs in information technology offer a real-world education and can help qualify a student to meet the demands.

The Bachelor of Information Technology (B.I.T.) provides students with the relevant, up-to-date knowledge to pursue exciting, in-demand IT careers. This curriculum focuses on the development of appropriate business and programming skills, the use of networks, education in data administration, and the completion of IT projects. Concentrations in computer forensics, computer systems, Internet security, network administration, and programming empower students to self-direct their degree program in a specific area of interest

The Master of Information Technology (M.I.T.), with a concentration in Internet security, combines the technology and Internet security portions of the course work

with key information management courses to help ensure success in the job market.

Visual Communications: AIU Online is one of the first universities to offer a Bachelor of Fine Arts in visual communication, with available concentrations in digital design and Web design, completely online. These program are designed to educate and develop artistic and imaginative students who are interested in such careers as flash animator, Web designer, and computer-based training developer. All required graphics software is included in the cost of course materials, providing students with training in the latest design software necessary to pursue a chosen career upon completion of the degree program

Criminal Justice: The growing emphasis on homeland security has created an unprecedented demand for criminal justice and security professionals. This accelerated program helps students prepare for such vital, in-demand careers as FBI officers, correction officers, security analysts, U.S. customs agents, and directors of security.

The Bachelor of Science in criminal justice provides students with a superb foundation in some of the most interesting aspects of the industry, including criminology, the causes of crime, and typologies and victims. Courses are taught by experts in the criminal justice field who bring their significant knowledge and expertise to each course.

Education: For students who have a passion for learning and inspiring others, AIU Online offers a Master of Education degree program. This program can provide the spark for an individual to advance a career as a teacher, corporate instructor, or military trainer. Available concentrations include curriculum and instruction, educational assessment and evaluation, instructional technology, and leadership in educational organizations.

Health-Care Management: Health care is one of the fastest-growing fields. Whether a student is looking to start a new career in health-care management or upgrade an existing one, AIU Online's accelerated health-care management degree programs can help ensure he or she is prepared to meet the challenge in months, not years.

The B.B.A. in health-care management helps provide a solid foundation for those interested in a management position in health care, whether in a hospital, long-term-care facility, insurance company, managed-care organization, pharmaceutical company, or one of the many other health-care–related industries.

The ten-month M.B.A. in health-care management was designed to provide a unique, market-relevant combination of a comprehensive business education with real-world, health-care–focused deliverables. The M.B.A. in health-care management is designed to help turn managers into executives; to arm them with the knowledge, skills, and experience necessary to reach high-level success.

Marketing: Today's complicated business models demand qualified marketing professionals in the management, planning, implementation, and evaluation of marketing and advertising functions. AIU Online offers accelerated, career-focused bachelor's (B.B.A.) and master's (M.B.A.) degree programs for students interested in pursuing rewarding careers in the ever-changing, fast-paced marketing industry.

The B.B.A. in marketing is designed to deliver a solid foundation for business marketing professionals by combining a core education in business with a focus on topics relevant to various marketing careers. This degree provides the experience-based education that helps students qualify for a wide variety of challenging, interesting careers.

AIU Online's M.B.A. in marketing is a ten-month program that combines the specialized curriculum of an executive M.B.A. with a focused training in marketing management disciplines. The result is a program that provides the advanced knowledge, skills, and practical experience-based education necessary to qualify for top marketing positions.

Organizational Psychology and Development: As the career-focused society spends more and more time at the office, there is a growing need for knowledgeable professionals with a modern, up-to-date understanding of the principles of psychology as they apply to the workplace. AIU Online's accelerated degree programs in

organizational psychology and development prepare graduates for career advancement in business or management, with specific emphasis on jobs requiring relevant knowledge of such issues as group dynamics, performance appraisal, training and development, and conflict management.

The B.B.A. in organizational psychology and development is designed to prepare business and management professionals to drive their careers forward with up-to-date knowledge and applicable, real-world, experience-based learning.

The M.B.A. in organizational psychology and development can be completed in just ten months. This real-world degree program is designed to be immediately applicable to issues facing today's modern workplaces. The experience-based curriculum focuses on preparing business and management professionals to achieve leadership roles within their organizations.

Student Services

To help ensure an overall high-quality educational experience and academic success, AIU Online provides a range of student support services, including admissions, academics, financial aid, career services, and technical support. All services are accessible through the University's virtual campus. Students also have access to their account information, degree plan, and personal information 24 hours a day through this secure Web site.

Credit Options

In addition to college credit earned at accredited postsecondary institutions, the following can be evaluated for academic advanced standing: CLEP Examination, Advanced Placement (AP) tests, Computer Competency Examination, extra-institutional credit/experiential learning, and DANTES/military credit.

Faculty

AIU Online provides experienced faculty members with advanced degrees, who bring their real-world experience and expertise to their students. All faculty members teaching online receive training and guidance in online delivery methods and pedagogy.

Admission

To be considered for admission to AIU Online, applicants must submit an application

and a $50 application fee and fulfill all admission requirements for the program. Selection of students for admission into degree programs of study is based on an individual assessment of each applicant. Each applicant must submit proof of high school graduation or the equivalent and participate in an admissions interview arranged by admissions personnel. If the applicant's first language is not English or if the applicant graduated from a non-English-speaking university, a minimum TOEFL score of 500 (undergraduate) or 550 (graduate) or other acceptable proof of English proficiency must be submitted

Tuition and Fees

Tuition and fee schedules for programs of study are reviewed with students at the time of acceptance.

Financial Aid

AIU Online's Financial Aid Department is committed to providing financial aid to those who qualify. AIU Online participates in various federal, state, and private student financial assistance programs. These financial aid programs are designed to provide assistance to students who are currently enrolled or accepted for enrollment but whose financial resources are unable to meet the full cost of their education. In addition, alternative financing options are available to those who qualify.

Applying

To apply for admission, a prospective student should submit an online application at http://www.aiuonline.edu along with a $50 application fee and complete a personal telephone interview.

CONTACT

Debbie Love
Vice President of Admissions
American InterContinental University Online
5550 Prairie Stone Parkway, Suite 400
Hoffman Estates, Illinois 60192

Phone: 877-701-3800 (toll-free)
E-mail: info@aiuonline.edu
Web site: http://www.aiuonline.edu

AMERICAN MILITARY UNIVERSITY
Distance Learning Programs
Charles Town, West Virginia

American Military University (AMU) is part of the American Public University System, and is a private institution of higher learning licensed by the West Virginia Higher Education Policy Commission. AMU is accredited by the Distance Education and Training Council (DETC) and The Higher Learning Commission of the North Central Association of Colleges and Schools (NCA). In addition, AMU is a member of the Servicemembers Opportunity Colleges (SOC). The University focuses on the educational needs of the military, national security, and public safety communities and has developed a flexible distance learning model uniquely suited to the working adult. Founded in 1991, the University System serves more than 20,000 students studying in 130 countries around the world. The University has continuously broadened its curricula, expanding to include management, business administration, information technology management, homeland security, national security, criminal justice, intelligence, security management, psychology, sports management, and many others in addition to its core military studies and history programs. The University's headquarters is located in Charles Town, West Virginia, with administrative offices in Manassas, Virginia.

Distance Learning Program
AMU is exclusively a distance learning institution. All courses are Web-based and accessible around the clock through the Electronic Campus from wherever students have Internet access. Students are led through the eight-week or sixteen-week courses via an online classroom with a qualified instructor.

Delivery Media
AMU delivers and supports its courses through its Electronic Campus, with classrooms served by Educator® courseware by Ucompass. Through these electronic classrooms, students communicate with professors and each other using LISTSERV, discussion boards, streaming video, student lounge chat rooms, and e-mail. Through this system, students are able to interact with each other and with professors, submit assignments, receive feedback, and take examinations. Electronic communications are supplemented by phone consultations during professors' office hours, with classes restricted to 25 students to ensure adequate student-professor interaction.

Programs of Study
AMU offers more than 100 associate, bachelor's, and master's degree programs and certificates.

Graduate programs, consisting of 36 semester hours/twelve courses and a comprehensive final examination, thesis, or practicum project are offered in criminal justice, homeland security, intelligence, management (including public, logistics, and crisis), military studies (including air warfare and special operations), national security studies, political science, public administration, space studies, and transportation management.

Certificate programs, consisting of 15–18 semester hours, five or six courses, are offered in many specialties within the curriculum and in area studies, period studies, and both historical and contemporary study areas.

Undergraduate programs include the Associate of Arts in general studies, a 60-semester-hour program with 30 semester hours of specified general education courses and electives, and the Bachelor of Arts, a 120–122 semester-hour program that mirrors the associate degree's lower-division requirements and includes upper-division major requirements and electives. The bachelor's degree is offered in American studies, criminal justice, English, family development, history, intelligence studies, interdisciplinary studies, management, marketing, military history (with American and world concentrations), military management, philosophy, political science, psychology, religious studies, and sociology.

Student Services
The Student Services department is staffed to assist students as needed by e-mail, phone, and even via online chat rooms. All students experience AMU's online orientation program that prepares them for distance learning, including navigating the electronic campus, using the classroom functions, and understanding transfer credit and tuition and financial aid options. Many Student Services' functions are available online, and it is easy for students to submit changes and check their status.

Credit Options
Credits may be earned through AMU by traditional courses, challenge examinations, and independent study. Courses may be audited without credit. AMU accepts transfer credit from accredited institutions, training and experience credit recommended by the American Council on Education, and credit by examinations (CLEP, DANTES, etc.).

Credit acceptance by program is as follows: associate degree, up to 45 semester hours; bachelor's degree, up to 90 semester hours; and graduate degree, up to 15 semester hours.

Faculty
AMU's faculty brings real-world experience and world-class credentials to the

online learning experience. More than 300 adjunct faculty members, along with 67 full-time faculty members, work together to ensure AMU students achieve appropriate learning outcomes. All faculty members meet traditional accreditation standards with regard to degrees and professional preparedness.

Admission

Graduate students must possess an accredited baccalaureate degree. Undergraduate students must have a high school diploma or GED certificate. No examinations are required for admission.

Tuition and Fees

Tuition is $250 per semester hour for undergraduate programs. Graduate pro-gram tuition is $275 per semester hour. There is no admission fee. All undergraduate students earning academic credit receive AMU's book grant, covering 100 percent of the costs of all textbooks. Transfer credit evaluations are subject to a one-time fee of $75, and all students who have attended other institutions of higher learning are required to submit a transfer evaluation by the end of their first semester at AMU. A graduation fee of $100 is assessed, which includes a framed and matted diploma.

Financial Aid

AMU accepts military tuition assistance, GI Bill and VA educational benefits, and corporate tuition assistance. Students may be eligible for Sallie Mae education loans and federal student aid loans and grants, and AMU has an installment payment plan as well. AMU is committed to providing the military and public safety communities with a quality, low-cost education, assisting in achieving their educational goals.

Applying

The application process is easy and is completed online. There is no cost to apply for admission and applicants are conditionally admitted upon submission of the online application form. A student ID is issued, and applicants receive a password via e-mail, allowing them to log in to the electronic campus, complete their online orientation, and register for courses.

CONTACT

Admissions
American Military University
American Public University System
111 West Congress Street
Charles Town, West Virginia 25414

Phone: 877-468-6268, menu option 2 (toll-free)
E-mail: info@apus.edu
Web site: http://www.amu.apus.edu/

Athabasca University
Canada's Open University

ATHABASCA UNIVERSITY

Quality Learning. Anywhere. Anytime.

Athabasca, Alberta, Canada

Athabasca University (AU), Canada's Open University, is a publicly funded university in the province of Alberta, Canada. AU is one of the world's foremost and fastest growing online and distance education specialists, serving 34,000 students worldwide.

As an open university, AU strives to eliminate barriers that prevent people from pursuing university studies. By providing access to flexible online and distance learning, AU helps people continue their studies regardless of where they live, their educational backgrounds, and their career or family obligations. AU is committed to innovation, flexibility in learning, and excellence in teaching, research, and scholarship.

AU is a full member of the Association of Universities and Colleges of Canada, the Association of Commonwealth Universities, the International Council for Open and Distance Education, the Canadian Association for Distance Education, the Canadian Association for Graduate Studies, the Canadian Virtual University, the Circumpolar Universities Association, the Global University Alliance, and the Inter-American Distance Education Consortium.

Distance Learning Program

AU, Canada's largest online and distance education university, offers more than 700 courses in over sixty undergraduate and graduate degree, diploma, and certificate programs. The flexibility of online and distance learning allows students to complete courses or programs on a full-time or part-time basis and to study when and where it is convenient for them. Many students also complete selected AU courses to satisfy specific program requirements at other universities and colleges.

Enrollment in AU courses has increased by 41 percent in the last five years, totaling 34,000 students in the 2005–06 academic year. Ninety-eight percent of AU graduates say they would recommend AU to others.

Delivery Media

AU uses a variety of distance learning methods, including multimedia online activities, print materials, Web, e-mail, the Internet, CD-ROMs, CDs, DVDs, computer software, audio/videoconferencing, TV, and radio. A particular course might use any combination of these methods. Students have support from professors, tutors, advisers, and a variety of specialized student services support staff members by e-mail and phone (toll-free in Canada and the United States).

Programs of Study

Graduate degree programs offered are Master of Arts–Integrated Studies, Executive Master of Business Administration, Executive Master of Business Administration in Project Management, Master of Counselling, Master of Distance Education, Master of Health Studies, Master of Nursing, and Master of Science–Information Systems.

Graduate diplomas offered are Advanced Graduate Diploma in Advanced Nursing Practice, Advanced Graduate Diploma in Distance Education (Technology), Advanced Graduate Diploma in Management, and Advanced Graduate Diploma in Project Management.

Undergraduate degrees offered are Bachelor of Arts (three- or four-year) in anthropology, English, French, history, humanities, information systems, labour studies, political economy, political science, psychology, sociology, and women's studies; Bachelor of Arts (four-year) in Canadian studies; Bachelor of Commerce in accounting or e-commerce; Bachelor of General Studies (three-year) in applied studies or arts and science; Bachelor of Health Administration; Bachelor of Human Resources and Labour Relations; Bachelor of Management (three- or four-year) with majors in human resources management or marketing; Bachelor of Nursing (four-year; post-RN or post-LPN); Bachelor of Professional Arts (four-year) in communication studies, criminal justice, human services, or governance, law, and management; Bachelor of Science (four-year) in human science or computing and information systems.

Undergraduate University certificates are offered in accounting, advanced accounting, administration, career development, computers and management information systems, computing and information systems, counseling women, English language studies, French language proficiency, health development administration, human resources and labour relations, labour studies, and public administration.

Undergraduate University diplomas are offered in arts and inclusive education.

Special Programs

AU is a founding partner in Canadian Virtual University (CVU), an innovative partnership of Canada's leading universities in online and distance learning. Students can select from among 2,000 courses in the CVU catalogue and apply them to programs at any partner university. Students who take courses from more than one partner university can save money on fees. Some courses are available in both French and English. Students should visit CVU's

Web site at http://www.cvu-uvc.ca for course and program information.

AU's many partnerships with other postsecondary institutions and organizations provide a variety of learning options for students. For more information, students should visit http://www.athabascau.ca/collab/collab.php.

Student Services

AU takes pride in providing exceptional service to students. Services such as advising, counselling, registration support, help for students with disabilities, a long-distance library, and more are available. The first point of contact is the Information Centre at 800-788-9041 (toll-free in Canada and the U.S.) or 780-675-6100 (international). Students can also visit http://www.askau.ca for a quick answer to most general questions.

Credit Options

AU grants academic credit for courses completed at other recognized postsecondary institutions. AU course credits are also eligible for transfer to programs at other higher education institutions worldwide.

Some of AU's undergraduate degree programs include a post-diploma option, which allows a student who has previously completed an appropriate two-year diploma from an accredited college to receive advanced standing (typically receiving credit for the first two years of university study).

Students can also apply for a prior learning assessment, a process through which relevant, informal university-level learning, such as learning derived from work or life experience, is evaluated for credit toward an AU credential.

Faculty

As of March 31, 2006, AU's faculty comprised 123 full-time professors, 120 part-time professors, and 332 part-time tutors.

Admission

Undergraduate students may apply for admission to programs or register in courses year-round. Anyone 16 years or older is eligible for admission. (Some programs and courses may have academic or geographic restrictions).

Graduate programs typically require students to have a bachelor's degree from a recognized postsecondary institution. Additional admission requirements vary from program to program. Students should consult AU's academic calendar or Web site for more information.

Tuition and Fees

Course fees include the cost of textbooks, course materials, and tuition. Until August 31, 2007, the cost for an undergraduate 3-credit course is Can$578 (Alberta), Can$661 (rest of Canada), and Can$884 (international). Graduate program fees vary by program. Students should consult the academic calendar or the program office of a particular graduation program for precise fee information.

Financial Aid

Financial assistance is available to full- and part-time students from Alberta Students Finance or the financial aid agency where a student resides. The amount of assistance available varies according to need and provincial regulations in force. Alberta students can obtain a financial aid package from Athabasca University. Out-of-province students should contact their local financial aid agency.

AU offers nearly 200 scholarships, leadership awards, and bursaries to graduate and undergraduate students on the basis of academic achievement or financial need. All students are automatically considered for many of the academic scholarships; several others are available by application or nomination. Students should visit http://www.athabascau.ca/registrar/studawrds.php for more information on student awards.

Applying

Students may apply for admission to undergraduate programs year-round and start most courses on the first day of any month. To apply, students must complete a General Application Form and submit it along with the application fee. Students may apply online at the AU Web site or by fax or mail. Application forms are available in the academic calendar and on the Web site.

Application deadlines for graduate programs can be found in the academic calendar or on the AU Web site.

CONTACT

Athabasca University Information Centre
1 University Drive
Athabasca, Alberta
   Canada T9S 3A3

Phone: 780-675-6100 (international)
       800-788-9041 (toll-free in Canada and the U.S.)
Fax: 780-675-6437
E-mail: inquire@athabascau.ca
Web site: http://www.athabascau.ca

AUBURN UNIVERSITY
Graduate Outreach Program
Auburn, Alabama

Auburn University was chartered in 1856 as the East Alabama Male College. In 1872, Auburn became a state institution—the first land-grant university in the South to be separate from a state university. Auburn University is Alabama's premier engineering and business institution. U.S. News & World Report's "America's Best Colleges" ranks both Auburn's College of Business and its College of Engineering among the nation's top fifty programs at public institutions. Auburn's Graduate Outreach Program has been ranked by GetEducated.com's "Top 25 Best Buys" for Web-based distance learning graduate-degree programs. Auburn is dedicated to serving the state and the nation through instruction, research, and extension. Auburn University is accredited by the Commission on Colleges of the Southern Association of Colleges and Schools.

The campus consists of more than 1,800 acres, with a student body of approximately 24,000. Auburn University, the largest school in the state of Alabama, is located in east-central Alabama. The city of Auburn has a population of about 40,000. Auburn is known for its small-town, friendly atmosphere and is often referred to as "the loveliest village on the Plain."

Distance Learning Program

In response to industry's request, Auburn's College of Engineering began offering courses to off-campus students through the Graduate Outreach Program in 1984. The Graduate Outreach Program allows professionals the opportunity to continue their education while maintaining full-time employment. The program serves more than 400 students in forty-eight states. The M.B.A. program is accredited by AACSB International–The Association to Advance Collegiate Schools of Business. The programs in the College of Engineering are accredited by the Accreditation Board of Engineering and Technology (ABET).

Note for international inquirers: Due to material distribution methods, the current distance learning program service area is limited to the U.S. and Canada and to U.S. military personnel with APO or FPO mailing addresses.

Delivery Media

The Graduate Outreach Program makes every effort to ensure that the off-campus students receive the same high-quality education as on campus students. Live classes are recorded daily and distributed by streaming video and in DVD format. Professors establish telephone office hours and/or e-mail communication so that off-campus students may receive answers to any questions they may have. E-mail accounts are established for the Graduate Outreach Program students. Most faculty members also utilize the Internet to post handouts and class materials.

Programs of Study

The Graduate Outreach Program offers master's degrees in seven disciplines in engineering—aerospace engineering, chemical engineering, civil engineering, computer science and software engineering, industrial and systems engineering, materials engineering, and mechanical engineering—as well as the Master of Management Information Systems, Master of Accounting, and Master of Business Administration. These programs are all nonthesis and without residency requirements. Each candidate must pass an on-campus, comprehensive, final oral examination covering the program of study to graduate. The examination covers the major and minor subjects, including any research or special projects involved.

In the Master of Business Administration program, students may earn a concentration in finance, health-care administration, human resource management, management information systems, management of technology, marketing, or operations management. The program consists of 36 to 42 semester hours of course work, including eight core courses and four electives. Applicants are required to complete a course in calculus and statistics prior to entering the program. Students with nonbusiness undergraduate degrees may be required to pass foundations exams in economics, finance, marketing, management, and accounting. Incoming students are also advised to have a working knowledge of word processing and spreadsheet software and an elementary understanding of database applications. M.B.A. students must visit the campus for five days during their final semester prior to graduating for on-campus presentations.

Nondegree professional development courses are available for those who need to meet job requirements or professional certification.

Special Programs

Career and job placement assistance is available through Auburn University's Career and Student Development Services. Accessibility to the R. B. Draughon Library is also available. A valid Auburn University student identification card is required to check out resources. The Division of University Computing provides University-wide computing and networking services to students. Computer accounts are free of charge to currently enrolled students.

Credit Options

Graduate credit taken in residence at another approved graduate school may be transferred to Auburn University but is not accepted until the student has completed at least 9 hours of work in the Graduate School at Auburn University. No prior commitment is made concerning whether transfer credit can be accepted. A student must earn at least 21 semester hours or half of the total hours required for a master's degree (whichever is greater) at Auburn University. No transfer credit is approved without two official transcripts. No course in which a grade lower than B was earned may be transferred.

Faculty

The Auburn University faculty consists of more than 1,200 members. Eighty percent of the faculty members hold a doctoral degree, and 88 percent hold a terminal degree in their field.

Admission

An applicant to the Graduate School must hold a bachelor's degree or its equivalent from an accredited college or university. The Graduate Record Examinations (GRE) is required for admission to the College of Engineering, and the Graduate Management Admission Test (GMAT) is required for admission to the M.B.A. program. Students whose native language is not English must submit scores of the Test of English as a Foreign Language (TOEFL) for admission to the M.B.A. program. Admission is based on the grade point average of university-level courses, GRE or GMAT scores, and recommendation letters from instructors and supervisors. Students can be informed by the Graduate Outreach Program on how they can enroll as off-campus students once they are accepted by the Graduate School.

Tuition and Fees

The Graduate Outreach Program fees are $546 per credit hour for engineering and $568 for business. Registration schedules and fee bills are mailed to the student prior to the beginning of each quarter.

Financial Aid

Military personnel who have been accepted into the Graduate School may apply for tuition aid through DANTES at their local education office. Many of the Graduate Outreach Program students receive tuition assistance through their employer's tuition reimbursement plan. The Auburn University Office of Student Financial Aid assists in the awarding of grants, loans, and scholarships for qualified full-time students.

Applying

To apply for admission, a prospective student must return a Graduate School application, an M.B.A. application (if applicable), a nonrefundable application fee of $25 for U.S. citizens or $50 for non-U.S. citizens, three letters of recommendation, GRE or GMAT scores, and two official transcripts of all undergraduate and subsequent course work from the respective institutions. Graduate School applicants may apply online at http://www.grad.auburn.edu. This ensures a quicker response in most cases.

CONTACT

Wanda Lambert
Graduate Outreach Program
202 Ramsay Hall
Auburn University
Auburn, Alabama 36849-5331

Phone: 888-844-5300 (toll-free)
Fax: 334-844-2502
E-mail: lambewf@eng.auburn.edu
Web site: http:// www.gop.auburn.edu

BAKER COLLEGE

Baker Online
Flint, Michigan

Baker College, which was founded in the true American tradition as a small business college in 1911, is a private, nonprofit, accredited, coeducational institution. The College has more than a dozen campuses and branch locations in the Midwest and has a total enrollment of more than 31,500 students. The College is uniquely designed for one purpose: to provide high-quality higher education that enables graduates to be successful throughout their challenging and rewarding careers. The College offers diploma, certificate, and associate, bachelor's, and master's degree programs in business, technical, and health service fields. Total commitment to students' employment success is uniquely evident in all aspects of the College's operations.

Baker College is accredited by the Higher Learning Commission of the North Central Association of Colleges and Schools. Baker College is an equal opportunity/affirmative action institution.

Distance Learning Program

Baker Online offers the convenience of classroom accessibility 24 hours a day, seven days a week, from virtually anywhere in the world. It is not a self-paced program. Courses begin and end on specific dates and classwork is assigned deadlines, but as long as students have Internet access, they have access to their courses.

Delivery Media

Students are required to have a computer with the following minimum requirements: a Pentium III or higher system, Windows XP Professional or higher, a 56K (minimum) modem, Internet Explorer 5.5 or Netscape 4.7 or higher (AOL is not compatible), and Microsoft Office XP Professional. A CD-ROM drive and an Internet service provider are required. The virtual classroom is the common meeting area for all students taking classes online. Communication is accomplished by sending messages back and forth from the student's computer to the classroom computer. Each classroom has a unique name, and only students taking that class have access to the virtual classroom. This ensures privacy for all students.

Programs of Study

Baker Online offers the delivery of high-quality, respected courses and programs that enable a student to earn an associate, bachelor's, or master's degree at home, on the road, or anywhere in the world.

The Associate of Business Administration degree has been designed specifically for the online college environment, where students have a variety of choices in filling out the degree plan. The curriculum gives students a good background of business facts and knowledge upon which to build or enhance a career in business.

The Bachelor of Business Administration degree is a program designed for the working professional that combines core course work with independent research and experiential credit to provide a contemporary business degree for today's business environment. Each core course contains focused study in the content area, accompanied by independent research.

The Master of Business Administration degree program seeks to combine the best of conventional academic training with the best of field-based learning. Most typical business disciplines are represented in the curriculum because the College believes that a successful manager must be conversant with different aspects of running any of today's organizations or companies. Students may also elect to focus their studies in one of the following areas: computer information systems, healthcare management, human resource management, industrial management, integrated health care, international business, leadership studies, or marketing.

The Master of Science in Information Systems degree is designed for information systems professionals who are responsible for managing the development, acquisition, implementation, and operation of information systems in a variety of organizational settings. The program emphasizes information systems theory and its application to business opportunities and challenges. In addition, the program addresses mission-critical issues such as strategic planning, risk management, financial considerations, project management, and quality assurance.

Special Programs

Baker Online offers undergraduate courses at all levels to support all of the campuses and their program offerings as a convenience for students who may have trouble commuting to a campus. Baker Online publishes a listing each quarter showing which classes will be offered.

Student Services

Every Baker College student is assigned an e-mail account on the BakerNet system. Through this system, students can communicate with each other and their instructors and with members of the graduate school staff. Students may also use their accounts to access the World Wide Web. They also have access to the Baker College Library System and FALCON, a consortium of libraries that supports an online catalog database of more than 500,000 holdings. Students also have access to InfoTrac periodical indexing databases, the UMI/ProQuest General Periodicals On-Disc full-article imaging station, Books-in-Print with Reviews, and all available Internet and World Wide Web resources.

Baker College offers a renowned Lifetime Employment Service, with access to thousands of career opportunities and employment databases, to all students. This service can be used for the rest of one's life.

Credit Options

Baker College recognizes the expediency of understandable and universally accepted standards related to transfer of academic credit. The College follows the Michigan Association of Collegiate Registrars and Admissions Officers Official Policies and recognizes the College-Level Examination Program (CLEP) or other standardized tests.

Faculty

The focus of Baker's faculty is somewhat different from that of traditional universities. Instead of placing an emphasis on empirical research, Baker values practitioner-oriented education. Faculty members remain continually active in their professions by consulting, conducting seminars, running their own businesses, writing, volunteering in their communities, and working with other organizations. The faculty-student ratio in distance education is 1:12.

Admission

Graduate program candidates must have a bachelor's degree from an accredited institution and a 2.5 or better GPA in their undergraduate work, be able to display appropriate communication skills, submit three letters of reference, submit a current resume, and have completed no less than three years of full-time work. Undergraduates must have graduated from high school, completed a GED program, or passed an Ability to Benefit assessment before entering.

Tuition and Fees

Undergraduate tuition for the 2007–08 school year is $185 per credit hour. Graduate tuition is $315 per credit hour. The cost of books ranges from $200 to $250 per quarter.

Financial Aid

Students who are accepted into Baker College may be considered for several forms of state, federal, and institutional financial aid. Students are requested to complete the Free Application for Federal Student Aid (FAFSA) and return it directly to the College.

Applying

Baker College uses a rolling admission process, so there are no deadlines for applications. Students are allowed to begin in any quarter. Once the Admissions Committee receives an application, applicants usually receive a decision in approximately four weeks. Once accepted, students participate in a three-week online orientation. They are not required to visit a campus at any time.

CONTACT

Chuck J. Gurden
Vice President for Admissions
Center for Graduate Studies
Baker Online
1116 West Bristol Road
Flint, Michigan 48507-9843

Phone: 810-766-4390
      800-469-3165 (toll-free)
Fax: 810-766-4399
E-mail: adm-ol@baker.edu
Web site: http://www.bakercollegeonline.com

BELLEVUE UNIVERSITY
Online Programs
Bellevue, Nebraska

Bellevue University is one of Nebraska's largest fully accredited independent colleges. It is accredited by the Higher Learning Commission of the North Central Association of Colleges and Schools (30 North LaSalle Street, Suite 2400, Chicago, Illinois 60602-2504; telephone: 800-621-7440). Programs serve the needs of nearly 7,000 students annually and cater to working adult students as well as traditional undergraduate students. Benefits include accelerated degree completion programs, online programs, an online library, and cooperative credit transfer agreements. Associate degrees are accepted in full, and credit is given for corporate and military training as well as life experience.

Distance Learning Program

Bellevue University is an information-age institution of higher learning with progressive options for online graduate and undergraduate degrees. Graduate and undergraduate programs, online, on campus, and in centers throughout the region, prepare students for an ever-changing environment.

Delivery Media

Online education is about taking classes and earning a degree entirely through the Internet. With Internet access, students go online to take classes, participate in discussions with professors and fellow students, conduct research at the online library, and interact with their online adviser. Online classes are small to give the Cyber-Active® Learning advantage that characterizes Bellevue University.

Programs of Study

Undergraduate programs are offered in an accelerated, cohort-based format. The program in advertising management provides students the skills and knowledge necessary to understand advertising campaigns. The program in business administration of technical studies emphasizes techniques, procedures, and methods for managing the technical functions of business. The business information systems program prepares students who do not have computer technology degrees or course work for management within information technology (IT) and positions with technical applications. The correc-

tions administration and management program provides students the skills and knowledge necessary for the professional oversight of modern correctional programs. The program in criminal justice administration focuses on management and opportunities in the criminal justice system. The program is designed for individuals working in, or closely associated with, the criminal justice system. The health-care management program provides a systems perspective for those interested in pursuing management opportunities in health care. The program in management of health-care informatics is designed for students interested in the management of electronic records and information in the health-care arena. The program in Internet systems and software technology provides a comprehensive study of the information technology industry. Topics are included in an integrated format built around a common project management theme. The degree program in investigations gives students an advanced knowledge of investigations, both in the private and public sectors. The leadership program provides students the theoretical and practical preparation they need to assume positions of leadership in the professional ranks of organizations. The management program gives students a comprehensive background in the skills, methods, and theories that undergird all effective management. The management of human resources program covers methods and practices of the human

resource management professional. The management information systems program emphasizes business knowledge and management skills for individuals working in the management information systems field. The security management program provides students with the theoretical and practical knowledge necessary for a career in the security field. The strengths-based management program focuses on management issues as they relate to the Gallup Organization's talent-based management principles. The marketing management program emphasizes the techniques and methods of managing and planning in marketing. The focus is on proven practices and application of theory. The logistics management program is designed for individuals interested in, or already working in, the field of logistics management and supply chain management.

The Master of Business Administration (M.B.A.) program covers the tools and methods required to run a business. The program requires 36 credit hours of course work. The schedule of course offerings permits an individual working full-time to complete all the requirements for the M.B.A. degree in eighteen months (two classes per term). Students who do not have an undergraduate degree in business generally take the Foundation (9 credits), the core (18 credits), and a concentration (9 credits) to complete the degree. M.B.A. concentrations are offered in accounting, advanced programming, finance, health care, human resource management, interdisciplinary business, international management, management information systems, marketing, and supply chain management. The Master of Science in computer information systems program has strong elements of both business and computer/telecommunication subjects. Students with business or computer undergraduate preparation typically finish the program with 36 credits of graduate work. For students without a computer background, there are 9 additional prerequisite credits. The Master of Science in management of information systems was created for midlevel IT managers and future chief information officers who need to keep pace with the rapidly changing world of enterprise technology. The program requires 36 hours of course work. The Master in Health-Care Administration (M.H.A.) program provides clinical health-care providers with an opportunity to pursue in depth the various areas of planning, organizing, leading, and controlling as they provide administrative guidance to others within their health-related organization. Students in the Master of Arts in management program develop a working knowledge of the application of quantitative techniques, marketing analysis, human resource management, financial analysis, influencing behavior in organizations, and sensitivity to the legal environment in which operations occur. The Master of Arts in leadership program encourages individual thought, synthesis of group contribution, and assimilation of practical and theoretical teachings. Its mission is to combine leadership philosophy, derived from great leaders and their writings, with concepts and theoretical models of organizational leadership. The Master of Arts and the Master of Science in communication studies programs address competencies in the areas of critical thinking, research, professional and social skills, diversity and intercultural communication, applied theory, leadership, and emotional intelligence. The programs are designed to produce graduates who can bridge the modern workplace communication gap, meet internal training and development needs, and identify and utilize effective skills to address important communication issues inherent in all work environments. The Master of Science in security management prepares students to function effectively at the director level in a broad spectrum of homeland security and related occupations. The Master of Science in instructional design prepares students to be a master educator in the application of instructional technology for both online and traditional class-

rooms, emphasizing the integration of theory and practice. The Master of Public Administration prepares students to become outstanding managers and leaders prepared to handle the complexities and challenges present in the public sector.

Credit Options

Bellevue University grants credit for college-level learning that a student has obtained through sources other than college classes. Students may be granted credit for college-level learning acquired outside of a regionally accredited college setting. Procedures are in place to assess student learning from non–regionally accredited institutions, American Council on Education recommendations, corporate training or programs, CLEP/DANTES tests, and the Experiential Learning Assessment.

Faculty

The Bellevue University full-time and adjunct faculty consists of 398 full- and part-time members who teach students from freshman to graduate level. The student-faculty ratio is 22:1. For most classes and programs, Bellevue University employs adjunct faculty members who are professionals in their respective fields. Faculty members are screened to ensure each is current on issues and technology.

Admission

Online degree completion programs are offered in an accelerated format. To qualify for undergraduate programs, students must have at least 60 credit hours from an accredited institution or an associate degree. To qualify for graduate programs, students must have a baccalaureate degree from an accredited institution, a minimum 2.5 GPA over the course of the last two years of undergraduate work, two letters of recommendation, and a completed essay.

Tuition and Fees

Online undergraduate tuition for a 36-hour major program is $10,620; for the 9-hour Signature Series, it is $2655. Undergraduate fees include the nonrefundable application/assessment fee, $50; stu-

dent fees, $150; and graduation fees, $75. The estimated total cost for an online undergraduate program is $13,550. This figure excludes the cost of books.

Tuition for the graduate online programs is as follows: the Master of Business Administration and the Master of Science in computer information systems, $340 per credit hour; the Master of Arts in leadership, the Master of Public Administration, and the Master of Arts in management, $12,240 or $340 per credit hour (excluding books); and the Master in Health-Care Administration, $12,240. The application fee is $50 and the graduation fee is $75 for all online graduate programs. The general college fee is $45 per semester for the M.B.A. and the M.S. in computer information systems programs and $150 for the M.A. in management, the M.A. in leadership, and the Master in Health-Care Administration.

Financial Aid

Financial aid assists students with the costs of attending college. This assistance comes from the federal and state government, the institution, and private sources. Financial aid includes grants, scholarships, work-study programs, and student loans. Grants and scholarships do not have to be repaid.

Applying

Individuals interested in applying should transmit the application online or by mail, pay fees, and submit transcripts for evaluation. Admissions counselors work with students to complete the official admissions process. An educational degree plan is completed for each student, defining the requirements needed to achieve each student's degree goal.

CONTACT

Bellevue University
1000 Galvin Road South
Bellevue, Nebraska 68005
Phone: 402-293-2000
        800-756-7920 (toll-free)
E-mail: info@bellevue.edu
Web site: http://www.bellevue.edu

BRENAU UNIVERSITY

Online Studies

Gainesville, Georgia

Brenau University, founded in 1878, is a historic, private, comprehensive university in Gainesville, Georgia, with a mission of preparing students to live extraordinary lives.

The University serves two populations: a coeducational population of adult and nontraditional students and a single-gender population of women. Brenau students are able to take classes in an array of formats: day, evening, weekend, and online.

Brenau's Online Studies division offers degree and certificate programs entirely online, with a focus on collaborative learning. Evening and weekend classes serve a growing population of working adult men and women by offering degree and certificate programs and other classes in four locations across the state (Atlanta, Augusta, Gainesville, and Kings Bay). Daytime classes have provided a single-gender liberal arts education since the University's founding.

Brenau University is regionally accredited by the Southern Association of Colleges and Schools.

Distance Learning Program

Brenau University provides high-quality educational experiences through the delivery of graduate and undergraduate programs utilizing the latest distance learning technology. Programs delivered in the online format are designed to provide maximum flexibility without compromising learning outcomes or academic rigor.

Delivery Media

Online classes are delivered via the Internet. Common software programs are used to enhance the delivery of course materials. Dialogue among students, using an asynchronous discussion board system, is central to the collaborative learning goal. Online students, like their professors, bring with them varied life and work experiences that, when shared with classmates, provide relevant applications of theory to real-world situations.

Programs of Study

Brenau University currently offers undergraduate degree programs entirely online in the areas of business, criminal justice, liberal studies, and nursing. Graduate degree programs are offered in business and education.

The Associate of Arts (A.A.) in liberal studies degree program is designed for the nontraditional, first-time college student or the student with very little college experience. This 60-hour degree program allows for flexibility in scheduling and course selection and can be completed in as little as five semesters.

Brenau's RN-to-B.S.N. bridge program provides registered nurses the opportunity for career advancement by earning a bachelor's degree. An experienced and academically qualified faculty of registered nurses offers this 31-hour program. The clinical portion of this program may be completed in the student's local community, supervised by a Brenau nursing faculty member.

The Bachelor of Business Administration (B.B.A.) in accounting, management, or marketing is a 120-hour degree program. These undergraduate business degree programs, which include courses in organizational behavior, ethics, and international business, can be completed in approximately four years.

The Bachelor of Science degree in criminal justice is a 120-hour degree program. This undergraduate degree program features courses in judicial process, law, management, and public administration/policy and can be completed in four years entirely online.

M.B.A. degrees in accounting, advanced management studies, business administration, and health-care management are available from the Department of Business Administration, which has a long history of offering high-quality M.B.A. programs. Students can reach their professional goals easily with Brenau's accelerated ten-course, 30-hour general M.B.A.; the thirteen-course, 39-hour M.B.A. in advanced management studies; the eleven-course, 33-hour M.B.A. in health-care management; or the twelve-course, 36-hour M.B.A. in accounting. Many states have adopted the 150-hour educational requirement to sit for the CPA exam; Brenau students meet this requirement by earning their M.B.A. degrees.

The M.Ed. degree in early childhood or middle grades education is available from the School of Education. The early childhood M.Ed., a long-standing degree offering at Brenau, is a twelve-course, 34- or 36-hour program, depending on the student's choice of a capstone activity (comprehensive exam or research project). The M.Ed. in middle grades education prepares professionals to teach children in grades four through eight. Students develop a variety of appropriate teaching methods and strategies that are specifically geared to the middle-grade learner. This program is an eleven-course, 34- or 36-hour degree program, depending on the student's choice of a capstone activity.

Special Programs

Brenau University's accelerated M.B.A. program in business administration is designed so that students may complete it in five semesters. Classes are small and offer students asynchronous discussion and work-related collaborative projects. These activities are designed to guarantee participation in online classes.

BA 500, the business administration department's intensive business foundations course, covers all undergraduate basics in the fields of statistics, management, accounting, and marketing. This course was designed for nonbusiness majors seeking to earn an M.B.A. Experienced faculty members from each of these fields collaborate to teach this unique 6-hour course.

Student Services

In addition to online application, advising, registration, and tuition payment, other student services include writing and math tutors, career services (job search and career selection), mental health counseling, and disability support services through the campus Learning Center. The Brenau Trustee Library catalog is available online using the popular Voyager software, and supplemental materials are offered via the GALILEO database, document delivery, and interlibrary loan.

Credit Options

For undergraduate programs, 45 credit hours must be completed at Brenau University. The residency requirement (Brenau credit hours) for the nursing degree is 31 hours. Alternative credit options toward a Brenau University undergraduate degree (credit earned from advanced-placement exams, international baccalaureate programs, CLEP, military credit, experiential credit, or challenge exams) are limited to a total of 27 hours.

Brenau University may accept up to 6 hours of transfer credit from other regionally accredited institutions as part of a planned graduate program of study upon approval of the respective department chair.

Faculty

Classes are taught by professors who are trained and certified in online course facilitation. Professors teaching in graduate programs have doctorates in their fields and corporate and/or practical experience.

Admission

Prospective students should submit a completed application, a $35 application fee, and transcripts from all institutions previously attended. Standardized test scores (GMAT, GRE, MAT, TOEFL) must be sent from testing services for graduate program applicants.

Tuition and Fees

Online tuition is $440 per semester credit hour ($100 technology fee per semester). Tuition rates are addressed prior to each academic year. Tuition is payable by check, money order, or credit card (Visa, MasterCard, and Discover). Brenau offers a military tuition discount for online classes.

Financial Aid

Online students who qualify are eligible for all need-based financial aid programs, including Pell Grants, other federal grants and loan programs, state-direct loans for students in nursing, and institutional grants. Program-specific funds are also available. The FAFSA financial aid application is available online.

A total of 2,169 (71.5 percent) Brenau University students received some type of financial aid this past academic year. The Office of Financial Aid receives student loan applications (phone: 800-252-5119 Ext. 6152, toll-free).

Applying

The completed application, a $35 application fee, and official transcripts and test scores should be sent directly to the Office of Admissions, 500 Washington Street, SE, Gainesville, Georgia 30501. Military applicants should include a copy of a valid military I.D. or DD214. Online College representatives are available by phone at 800-252-5119 (toll-free) and e-mail.

CONTACT

Heather S. Gibbons, Ph.D.
Associate Vice President for IT and Online Studies
Brenau University
500 Washington Street, SE
Gainesville, Georgia 30501

Phone: 770-718-5327
Fax: 770-718-5329
E-mail: online@brenau.edu
Web site: http://online.brenau.edu

 **CALIFORNIA INSTITUTE OF INTEGRAL STUDIES**
Online Degree Programs
San Francisco, California

California Institute of Integral Studies (CIIS) in San Francisco is an accredited university offering an online M.A. in transformative leadership and an online Ph.D. in transformative studies in a unique learning community. Residential Ph.D., Psy.D., M.A., and B.A. completion degrees in psychology and the humanities are also offered. The Institute's commitment to the study and practice of multiple cultural and spiritual traditions and to their expression throughout the activities of the community promotes a stimulating learning environment with rigorous scholarship and a supportive community—including the online programs.

Distance Learning Program

The master's degree program in transformative leadership has been created for individuals who want to take the initiative and find ways to express their passion for making a contribution to the world. The program provides a context where they can prepare themselves in a community of like-minded individuals, exploring their own mission in life and developing the skills needed to make it a reality. The culminating capstone project grounds students' work in an action site, where they can apply their learning on a continuous basis.

The primary focus of the doctoral program in transformative studies is to develop thought-leaders who are committed to exploring leading-edge issues in innovative ways, combining scholarship, creativity, and self-inquiry. The program places great value in developing the ability to participate in scholarly discourse through publication and on the importance of viewing academic inquiry as an opportunity for personal and social transformation, while grounding transformative processes in academic depth, rigor, and imagination.

Current information about the programs and courses is available on the CIIS Web site, by telephone, or in person at CIIS in San Francisco.

Delivery Media

The M.A. and Ph.D. are offered as 36-semester-unit programs. The doctoral program also requires a dissertation. Both programs are offered in online format using community-based learning through CIIS's Web-based virtual campus, in which students, faculty members, and staff members interact.

Students from both online programs participate in weeklong intensives in a San Francisco Bay Area retreat setting. Intensives are held at the beginning of each semester. Distance students generally take all their courses on the virtual campus.

Student Services

The CIIS Library, Registrar's, Business Office, and Financial Aid Department are well prepared to support online students with their specific needs.

Faculty

CIIS programs attract a faculty of scholars who wish to act from a spiritual foundation while helping to improve the effectiveness and well-being of individuals, communities, and organizations. The online-degree faculty members bring practical experience and intellectual expertise relevant to transformation and change and the

pedagogies appropriate for an online learning environment.

Admission

Individuals who wish to deepen their understanding and effectiveness as transformative change agents are welcome to apply. Typically, candidates have professional experience and are seeking to enhance their abilities through study, action, reflection, and scholarship.

Both master's and doctoral programs are also attractive to those wishing to make a career transition or looking to approach change differently in their current site of practice. The ideal candidate also is seeking a program that uses an integral pedagogy, one that honors body, mind, and spirit. And finally, those who require a program that caters to the working professionals find the virtual campus a convenient venue.

Tuition and Fees

For 2007–08, full-time tuition for the M.A. program, at 9 units per semester, is $7020 ($14,040 per year). For the Ph.D. program, at 9 units per semester, tuition is $8325 ($16,650 per year).

Financial Aid

Financial assistance through scholarships, loans, and grants is awarded on the basis of merit and/or need. A serious attempt is made to extend a personalized, concerned approach to student financial needs while complying with governmental and donor regulations. General financial aid programs include Federal Pell Grants, Federal Supplemental Educational Opportunity Grants (FSEOG), Institute scholarships, diversity scholarships, international scholarships, Veterans Administration Educational Benefits, Federal Family Education Loan Programs (FFELP), Federal Stafford Student Loans, and other loan and scholarship opportunities based on merit or need.

Applying

Applicants must meet the general admissions requirements of the Institute. In addition to official transcripts and an autobiographical statement, applicants must submit the following: two letters of recommendation, a critical writing essay, a resume, and a goal statement. Ph.D. applicants should include a statement telling how they will use the resources of the curriculum to advance a chosen inquiry.

Complete admission information and applications are available through the CIIS Web site or through the Admissions Office.

CONTACT

Admissions Counselor
California Institute of Integral Studies
1453 Mission Street
San Francisco, California 94103

Phone: 415-575-6150
Fax: 415-575-1264
E-mail: admissions@ciis.edu
Web site: http://www.ciis.edu

CALIFORNIA STATE UNIVERSITY, DOMINGUEZ HILLS
College of Extended and International Education
Carson, California

California State University, Dominguez Hills (CSUDH), is a national leader in distance learning, named by Forbes *magazine as one of the top cyber universities. Founded in 1960, the University is one of twenty-three California State University (CSU) campuses and has the largest distance learning program in the CSU system. The University offered its first distance learning degree in 1974, and in 1995 offered one of the first online master's degree programs ever approved by the Western Association of Schools and Colleges.*

CSU Dominguez Hills continues to be in the forefront of distance learning technology and academic excellence, garnering numerous awards, including the Best Distance Learning Teacher from the U.S. Distance Learning Association, an Omni Intermedia Award, an Aegis Award, two Telly Awards, and a Top 100 Video Producer Award.

The CSU Dominguez Hills campus is located in the South Bay area of Los Angeles and is accredited by the Western Association of Schools and Colleges.

Distance Learning Program

The distance learning unit is part of the College of Extended and International Education, whose mission is to extend the resources of the University to better serve the educational needs of its communities. The University has more than 4,000 students enrolled in distance learning programs in all fifty states and more than sixty countries.

Delivery Media

All distance learning courses have a Web site, and participants can interact with faculty and staff members via e-mail, telephone, and correspondence. Courses are conducted via live Webcast, where students participate in a live, interactive educational environment, including video transmission of the lecture; via asynchronous Internet, where participants log in at their convenience to complete class assignments and engage in discussion groups with their peers; via television, where CSUDH broadcasts 24 hours a day on cable systems throughout southern California; and via correspondence.

Programs of Study

CSU Dominguez Hills currently offers ten degree and ten certificate programs via distance learning. There are no on-campus requirements for any CSUDH distance learning program. Programs include the following:

Master of Arts in Behavioral Science: Negotiation, Conflict Resolution, and Peacebuilding. Taught via asynchronous Internet, the program teaches participants valuable skills and knowledge that may be applied directly to police work, counseling, human resources management, labor relations, supervision, administration, alternative dispute resolution, arbitration, public policy, social work, teaching, intercultural and community conflicts, corporate contracts, and purchasing (telephone: 310-243-2162; e-mail: negotiation@csudh.edu; Web site: http://www.csudh.edu/negcon).

Master of Arts in the Humanities. Taught via correspondence, the degree offers an interdisciplinary approach to the disciplines of the humanities—history, literature, philosophy, music, and art—with emphasis on their interrelating effects and influences (telephone: 310-243-3190; e-mail: huxonline@csudh.edu; Web site: http://www.csudh.edu/hux).

Master of Business Administration. Taught via asynchronous Internet, the M.B.A. at CSUDH provides a solid qualification in business management with courses that are wide-ranging in content, covering the essential areas of knowledge and skills required in today's competitive business environment (telephone: 310-243-2714; e-mail: cyan@csudh.edu; Web site: http://mbaonline.csudh.edu).

Master of Public Administration. Taught via asynchronous Internet, the program is designed to provide a high-quality graduate professional education for individuals entering or currently employed in public service and nonprofit professions (telephone: 310-243-2395; e-mail: mpaonline@csudh.edu; Web site: http://mpaonline.csudh.edu).

Master of Science in Engineering Management (M.S.E.M.). Taught via asynchronous Internet, the M.S.E.M. is an interdisciplinary degree program designed to integrate the development of management and engineering skills focusing on problem solving in the synthesis of technical, financial, and organizational requirements for engineering projects in a rapidly changing environment. The program is currently offered jointly by California State University, Long Beach (for the engineering component), and CSU, Dominguez Hills (for business), and the degree is granted at CSU, Long Beach in the name of both institutions (telephone: 310-243-3165; e-mail: kpoertner@csudh.edu; Web site: http://csulb.edu/colleges/coe/).

Master of Science in Nursing and Bachelor of Science in Nursing. Taught via asynchronous Internet, the bachelor's completion program prepares graduates to function as leaders, managers, and resource people in a variety of health-care settings. The graduate program prepares professional nurses for advanced and specialized practice. Role emphasis options include clinical nurse specialist in gerontological nursing and nursing education (telephone: 310-243-3741; e-mail: eeinfo@csudh.edu; Web site: http://www.csudh.edu/msn or http://www.csudh.edu/bsn).

Master of Science in Quality Assurance and Bachelor of Science in Quality Assurance. Taught via asynchronous Internet, the bachelor's program provides the academic environment and the requisite course of study to blend the basic sciences, technologies, management principles, quality concepts, and statistical tools needed to prepare professionals for careers in quality assurance and to serve working professionals seeking career enhancement. Master's degree students receive education in both the technical and administrative foundations of quality assurance, an interdisciplinary profession used in management in manufacturing, service, government, and health-care organizations (telephone: 310-243-3880; e-mail: msqa@csudh.edu; Web site: http://www.csudh.edu/msqa or http://www.csudh.edu/bsqa).

Bachelor of Science in Applied Studies. Taught via live broadcasts on the Web and cable television, as well as archived broadcasts and Web sites, the program enables students with associate degrees to complete their bachelor's degree entirely via distance learning. Eighteen courses representing a wide spectrum of management and liberal arts courses help students to become leaders in their profession and advance in their careers. (telephone: 866-278-6789; e-mail: appliedstudiestv@csudh.edu; Web site: http://www.appliedstudies.tv).

Quality Management, Quality Engineering, Quality Auditing, Reliability Engineering, and Software Quality Engineering Certificates of Completion. Taught via asynchronous Internet, the certificate completion programs in quality assurance allow professionals to gain certification in specialized areas of quality and prepare for American Society for Quality exams. Students who successfully complete three master's degree–level courses and the associated capstone course can earn a certificate of completion (telephone: 310-243-3880; e-mail: msqa@csudh.edu; Web site: http://www.csudh.edu/msqa).

Assistive Technology Certificate. Taught via asynchronous Internet, the program prepares individuals to comply with state and federal laws that require that school personnel be prepared to offer a full range of assistive technology services to disabled people. The program is useful to educational administrators, teachers, special education teachers, occupational and physical therapists, speech and language specialists, rehabilitation specialists, program specialists, resource specialists, and psychologists (telephone: 310-243-3741; e-mail: paul_richard@ocde.k12.ca.us; Web site: http://www.csudh.edu/at).

Community College Teaching Certificate. Taught via asynchronous Internet, the program is designed to enhance the skills and the employability of potential community college instructors (telephone: 310-243-2781; e-mail: dulloa@csudh.edu; Web site: http://www.csudh.edu/ccteaching).

Production and Inventory Control Certificate. Taught via asynchronous Internet, the program provides a broad education in the principles of production and inventory control. The program is taught by professionals currently employed in the field who are certified in production and inventory management (telephone: 310-243-3741; e-mail: smackay@csudh.edu; Web site: http://www.csudh.edu/lapicsonline).

Purchasing Certificate. Taught via asynchronous Internet, the program provides a broad education in the principles of procurement management and also helps students prepare for the Certified Purchasing Manager exam (telephone: 310-243-3741; e-mail: smackay@csudh.edu; Web site: http://www.csudh.edu/purchasingonline).

Technical Writing Certificate of Completion. The Technical Writing Certificate of Completion introduces students to the many aspects of contemporary technical writing practices and helps them develop the skills and confidence to communicate complex technical concepts simply and effectively (telephone: 310-243-3730; e-mail: bwald@lists.csudh.edu; Web site: http://www.csudh.edu/extension/technicalwriting.htm).

Special Programs

The Center for Training and Development at CSUDH works closely with the business community to develop custom-designed training programs to help meet the demands of the fast-paced workplace of the new millennium. Programs are delivered via distance learning, on-site, and on the CSUDH campus.

Student Services

Faculty members are available to students via e-mail, telephone, and mail. Student services available at a distance include academic advising, technical support, online tutoring, and access to the library and bookstore.

Credit Options

Depending on the specific program, students may transfer credit earned at other accredited colleges and universities. For more information, students should visit the CSUDH distance learning Web site.

Faculty

CSU Dominguez Hills has more than 100 faculty members teaching distance learning courses. Most of these faculty members have doctoral degrees in their chosen fields.

Admission

Admission requirements vary for each program. Students should consult the CSUDH distance learning Web site for specific program requirements.

Tuition and Fees

Tuition and fees vary for each program. For specific cost information, students should consult the CSUDH distance learning Web site.

Financial Aid

More than $30 million in financial aid is disbursed to CSUDH students each year. Approximately 68 percent of CSUDH students receive some form of financial assistance, and most financial aid programs are available to qualified distance learning students. For further information, students should visit the financial aid Web site (http://www.csudh.edu/fin_aid/default.htm).

Applying

Application processes vary for each program, and campus visits are not required for any program. Students should consult the CSUDH distance learning Web site for specific application information.

CONTACT

Registration Office
College of Extended and International Education
California State University,
  Dominguez Hills
1000 East Victoria Street
Carson, California 90747

Phone: 310-243-3741
       877-GO-HILLS (toll-free)
Fax: 310-516-3971
E-mail: eeinfo@csudh.edu
Web site: http://dominguezonline.
       csudh.edu

CALIFORNIA STATE UNIVERSITY, SACRAMENTO

College of Business Administration

Sacramento, California

California State University, Sacramento (Sacramento State), is the seventh-largest university in the CSU system. It was founded as Sacramento State College in 1947 during a time of intense demand for higher education after World War II. Sacramento State is committed to providing an excellent education to all eligible applicants who aspire to expand their knowledge and prepare themselves for meaningful lives, careers, and service to their communities.

For more than five decades, the College of Business Administration at Sacramento State has consistently achieved its fundamental goal—to cultivate excellence in its graduates and to develop business leaders possessing not only top management skills but also a broad understanding of their responsibilities to business and their communities. It has maintained its accreditation under the stringent standards of AACSB International—The Association to Advance Collegiate Schools of Business since 1963. In the course of its history, the College has graduated nearly 40,000 undergraduate and graduate students.

Distance Learning Program

The College of Business Administration offers Master of Science in Accountancy and Master of Science in Business Administration (M.S.B.A.) Taxation programs online.

The Master of Science in Accountancy program was developed in response to new developments in the accounting and business worlds. Increasingly, accountants who hold undergraduate degrees in accounting seek advanced degrees as the complexity of the accounting field increases. Accounting professionals are involved with an ever-widening range of careers, including public accounting, corporate accounting, income tax accounting, not-for-profit accounting, and government accounting.

Significant changes in the regulatory climate, including the Sarbanes-Oxley Act, have increased the need for graduate-level education. One result is a heightened interest in forensic accounting, fraud detection, and information system security. The 150-credit-hour education requirement established by the American Institute of Certified Public Accountants (AICPA) also has significantly increased the demand for graduate education in accounting. The

M.S. in Accountancy program helps to qualify students to sit for professional accounting examinations that lead to credentials such as the Certified Public Accountant (CPA) and the Certified Management Accountant (CMA) designations.

The degree is granted by the Sacramento State College of Business Administration. The Sacramento State College of Continuing Education (CCE) coordinates the administrative aspects of the M.S. in Accountancy program, such as registration and tuition payment.

The Master of Science in Business Administration (M.S.B.A.) Taxation program is a highly specialized and intensive master's program designed for individuals seeking a career in taxation as a tax practitioner with a corporation or with one of the many federal or state tax agencies.

The benefits of an M.S.B.A. Taxation degree are practical and economical. Many companies pay out more than 50 percent of their profits in taxes, making proper tax planning critical to maximizing the bottom line. Law firms and accounting consultants need this type of training to increase their clients' bottom lines, and in government offices, this type of training ensures that

tax laws are being complied with and properly enforced. This program gives practical exposure to the critical aspects of taxation with an orientation toward planning and strategy and is supplemented by compliance knowledge where relevant. The material is consistently updated to reflect current taxation issues. The role of taxation in national development, the e-commerce economy, multilateral treaties, and intellectual property are some of the current topics under examination by Sacramento State students and the global tax community.

The M.S. in Accountancy and M.S.B.A. Taxation degrees are granted by the College of Business Administration. The College of Continuing Education coordinates the administrative aspects of the programs.

Delivery Media

The program's primary e-classroom platforms are WebCT 6 and Macromedia Breeze 5. Both are easily navigated and accessible with standard software, hardware, and bandwidth. Course functionality includes quizzes, a built-in e-mail system, discussion groups, live chatting, announcements, lecture notes, and an online grade book.

Breeze Meeting provides for a real-time interactive e-classroom or e-meeting experience. Instructor and students can carry on live conversations, share documents, and collaborate on projects. This learning platform provides participants with all of the benefits of an on-site course or meeting without having to leave their homes or offices.

Programs of Study

The M.S. in Accountancy program requires 28 to 36 credits for completion: 18 units of program requirements,

6 in the concentration, 3 to 6 of electives, and 1 to 3 for the culminating thesis or project. For students without an undergraduate business degree, several foundation course requirements need to be satisfied before the program requirements are begun.

The M.S.B.A. Taxation program requires 30 to 33 units: 15 of required courses, 12 to 15 of electives, and 1 to 3 for the culminating thesis or comprehensive exam. Each course is offered in a six-week format, and the entire program can be completed in as little as eighteen months. For students without an undergraduate business degree, three foundation courses are required for the program.

Faculty

Instructors in the M.S. in Accountancy and M.S.B.A. Taxation programs are among the finest faculty members and professionals in these fields. They have all completed advanced degrees and/or are practicing professionals, bringing current and cutting-edge education to the classroom. The instructors are experienced in the emerging issues in the accounting, taxation, and information systems fields and the daily demands of a practitioner's work environ-

ment, and they bring the relevance of contemporary issues into the program content.

Admission

There are six criteria for admission based on an evaluation of GMAT scores (or LSAT or CPA scores) and undergraduate GPA. Students should visit the programs' Web site for the specific requirements and the formulas used to determine an applicant's acceptance.

Tuition and Fees

Tuition is approximately $150 per credit.

Financial Aid

The College of Continuing Education is self-supported and unable to offer direct financial aid. However, there are loan programs and scholarships for which students may qualify. The programs are described on the Sacramento State Financial Aid Office's Web site (https://webapps1.csus.edu/faid_general/default.asp).

Applying

Applicants should complete an online College of Business Administration application (http://www.cba.csus.edu/mba/applications.asp) and submit one

set of official transcripts and GMAT or LSAT or CPA scores, two letters of recommendation, and a resume to the College of Business Administration. Applicants must also complete the California State University Graduate Application (http://www.csus.edu/gradstudies) and submit one set of official transcripts and a $55 application fee to the Sacramento State Office of Graduate Studies.

CONTACT

Graduate Programs Office
Tahoe Hall, Room 1035
College of Business Administration
California State University, Sacramento
6000 J Street
Sacramento, California 95819-6088
Phone: 916-278-6772
Fax: 916-278-4233
E-mail: cbagrad@csus.edu
Web site: http://www.cba.csus.edu

Office of Graduate Studies
River Front Center, Room 206
California State University, Sacramento
6000 J Street
Sacramento, California 95819-6112
Phone: 916-278-6470
E-mail: gradctr@csus.edu

CAPELLA UNIVERSITY

Online Learning

Minneapolis, Minnesota

Capella University is an accredited university that offers online graduate and undergraduate programs for professionals pursuing advancement in the fields of business management, health care administration, higher education, information technology, K-12 education, mental health, and public safety. Capella was founded in 1993 and today is a national leader in online education, with more than 19,000 students from all 50 states and 56 other countries. For more information, students should visit http://www.capella.edu or call 888-CAPELLA (227-3552).

Capella University is accredited by the The Higher Learning Commission and is a member of the North Central Association of Colleges and Schools (NCA), http://www.ncahlc.org.

Distance Learning Program

The mission of Capella University is to extend access to high-quality doctoral, master's, bachelor's, and certificate programs for adults seeking to maximize their personal and professional potential. This mission is fulfilled through innovative programs that are responsive to the needs of adult learners. Faculty members are selected for a strong combination of academic and professional experience. A key part of their instructional method is to encourage students to share current workplace challenges as problem-solving opportunities for the entire class.

Capella offers seventeen degree programs, eighty-nine graduate and undergraduate specializations, and sixteen certificate programs. The online university currently serves more than 19,000 adults from all fifty states and fifty-six other countries.

Delivery Media

The Capella online courseroom places the student at the center of the learning experience. The content of each course is developed to align with industry and professional standards, so students learn what is relevant in the field. Many course assignments may be tailored to apply to the student's work situation.

The instructor serves as an expert guide and discussion leader. Active online discussions involve the instructor and other students each week in sharing diverse perspectives and feedback on course assign-

ments. Many Capella courses incorporate interactive media that bring the topic to life and graphically illustrate key concepts.

Programs of Study

Capella University's programs are offered through five schools.

The School of Education offers the Ph.D. in education (nine specializations), the M.S. in education (ten specializations), and three graduate certificates. More than 2,500 educators have chosen Capella University to advance their education and achieve personal and professional goals. Capella's online education degree and certificate programs in K-12, higher education, and continuing and adult education are designed to improve teaching and leadership effectiveness in diverse educational settings. Capella graduates are found throughout the U.S. in leadership roles such as superintendent, principal, and dean.

The School of Human Services offers the Ph.D. in human services (five specializations), the Ph.D. in public safety (three specializations), the M.S. in human services (seven specializations, including two counseling specializations accredited by the American Counseling Association's Council for Accreditation of Counseling and Related Educational Programs [CACREP]), the M.S. in public safety (three specializations), and eight graduate certificates. These programs prepare students to pursue their passion for social change

in a variety of institutional, agency, community, and educational settings. Capella University is one of few online universities to offer M.S. and Ph.D. programs with a specialization in criminal justice. In addition, CACREP has accredited two of Capella's clinical counseling specializations: marital, couple, and family counseling/therapy and mental health counseling.

The Harold Abel School of Psychology offers the clinically oriented Psy.D. program (two specializations), the Ph.D. in psychology (three specializations), the M.S. in psychology (ten specializations), and one specialist certificate. The school offers a range of academic and professionally oriented online psychology degree specializations. Students develop critical thinking skills to understand and apply key psychological principles in diverse work settings.

The School of Business and Technology offers the Ph.D. in organization and management (five specializations), the Ph.D. in information technology (two specializations), the M.B.A. (seven specializations), the M.S. in organization and management (three specializations), the M.S. in information technology (five specializations), and four graduate certificates. In these programs, faculty members combine professional business and technology experience with a solid academic foundation in fundamental principles that drive business success. The programs are competency-based so that students can take practical solutions from the courseroom into the workplace. The information technology curriculum reflects the skills associated with leading IT certifications, such as CCNA®, CCNP®, MCSE, CISSP®, and PMP.

The School of Undergraduate Studies offers the B.S. in business (seven specializations), the B.S. in information technology (seven specializations), and the B.S. in public safety. Through relevant and practical course work, students gain knowledge and skills that can make an immediate impact in their career—even before they graduate. Students in the information technology bachelor's program benefit from a relevant curriculum that addresses essential IT competencies in project management, information security, enterprise systems integration, application development, network architecture and design, systems design and programming, and graphics multimedia. The B.S. in business program develops foundational knowledge and scholarship related to current issues in the areas of accounting, business administration, finance, human resource management, management and leadership, and marketing.

Special Programs

Capella's enrollment counselors take a respectful, consultative approach in helping prospective students investigate their educational options. They offer details on Capella programs and specializations, provide a customized estimate of the time and cost to complete a Capella program, and supply other information that prospective students seek in order to make a well-informed decision.

Academic advisers work with each Capella University student to guide them in planning and completing their educational program. Academic advisers help students plan course sequences, develop a long-term educational plan, and understand the requirements for degree completion.

The Capella University Library offers a team of librarians dedicated exclusively to working with Capella students and faculty and staff members. The library provides the full range of academic resources and services, including databases and online services, reference services, interlibrary loans, and training in research methodology.

Capella University's Writing Program fosters the connection between clear thinking and clear writing. Program faculty members have extensive writing and teaching experience and are eager to help students achieve a level of writing excellence that will advance their academic pursuits and life goals.

Effective, skilled career counselors can be essential allies during educational pursuits. Capella's career services staff members help students recognize their strengths and focus energy in the right direction. Although job placement is not provided, career services professionals provide award-winning online resources, assist with career planning and development, and deliver one-to-one career guidance and job search assistance. Capella graduates have lifetime access to Capella Career Center services.

The Capella Alumni Association creates lifelong opportunities for continued professional and academic networking and growth. Capella University graduates become part of a nationwide and international network of educated practitioners.

All doctoral programs and some master's and certificate programs involve academic residencies, on-site learning experiences that vary in length and number. A residency advances academic learning, research or clinical skills, and community building—all integral to the Capella model of the personal, professional, and intellectual transformation into a "scholar-practitioner." For example, Ph.D. students participate in three 1-week residential colloquia at specific points in their program. Each one is timed to support success in the next stage of the doctoral program.

Credit Options

Adults typically bring a wealth of experience and knowledge to their education. Not only is this prior learning welcomed and valued in the Capella educational environment, but it may also apply toward a Capella degree program. Course work from regionally accredited or internationally recognized institutions may transfer directly into a Capella program. In some business and IT programs, Capella students may also earn credit by demonstrating relevant, college-level knowledge gained outside the classroom, such as through professional certifications. At the bachelor's degree level, students may be able to gain credit for military training and national testing exams such as ACE, DSST, and CLEP. In these ways, prior learning may shorten the time and reduce the cost of earning a Capella degree.

Faculty

Capella has 942 faculty members—132 core, full-time faculty members and faculty administrators as well as 810 adjunct faculty members. Capella faculty members live in all fifty U.S. states and seven foreign countries. Eighty percent of the faculty hold doctoral degrees.

Admission

Capella University was founded with a commitment to extend access to high-quality higher education. To achieve this goal, Capella admits applicants who have received the appropriate qualifying degree or course work from accredited institutions or programs and who have a qualifying grade point average. Some programs or specializations have additional requirements; an enrollment counselor can provide details.

Tuition and Fees

The application fee is $75 ($175 for international applicants). Tuition costs vary for each school within the University. Current tuition rates are found at http://www.capella.edu/inc/pdf/tuition_chart.pdf.

Financial Aid

More than three quarters (78 percent) of Capella University students receive some form of financial aid to support their education investment. Sources include federal loans and grants, employer tuition reimbursement, military education benefits, scholarships, and grants. Capella offers an online financial aid application and assistance to those who would like to secure educational funding to help finance their academic program. Enrollment counselors can provide more information about financial aid and other ways to reduce tuition costs.

Applying

Capella's eAdmissions tool makes it easy to apply online at http://www.capella.edu. Admission requirements vary depending on the program and the school. The details of admission can be found in the catalog, available on request. For more information, prospective students should contact the University.

CONTACT

Capella University
225 South 6th Street, 9th Floor
Minneapolis, Minnesota 55402
Phone: 888-227-2736 (toll-free)
    612-339-8650 (international)
Fax: 612-977-5060
E-mail: info@capella.edu
Web site: http://www.capella.edu

CENTRAL MICHIGAN UNIVERSITY

CMU *CMU Off-Campus Programs*

CENTRAL MICHIGAN UNIVERSITY Mount Pleasant, Michigan

Since its founding in 1892, Central Michigan University (CMU) has grown from a small teachers' college into a world-class Midwestern university offering more than 150 programs at the bachelor's level and nearly sixty programs at the master's, specialist's, and doctoral level. CMU is accredited by the North Central Association of Colleges and Schools. This accreditation includes all on- and off-campus programs. Central Michigan University is an institutional member of the Council for Adult and Experiential Learning; the Adult Education Association; the Alliance: An Association of Alternative Degree Programs for Adults; and the National Association of Institutions in Military Education.

Distance Learning Program

Programs are offered in a compressed format to help balance the demands of work, school, family, and other obligations. The compressed format does not mean easier courses. Distance learning courses are held to the same academic standards that on-campus courses must meet. To help insure success in the compressed format, procedures and support services are fast and accessible.

Delivery Media

Students have a choice of delivery formats: online, print-based learning packages, or classroom-based courses at more than sixty locations in North America.

Online courses use Web technology to involve the student in interactive learning. Students can interact with instructors and others through e-mail, chat sessions, and message forums. Student lecture materials and assignments are all online. Textbooks are still required.

Learning packages are print-based courses that use textbooks and study guides but may also include audio and videocassettes as well as the use of e-mail and Internet chat rooms to enrich the content.

Classes are also available in evening or weekend formats at locations throughout the United States, Canada, and Mexico. An up-to-date listing of locations is available at http://www.cel.cmich.edu/locations/default.html.

Programs of Study

CMU Off-Campus Programs offers undergraduate-, graduate-, and doctoral-level degree programs. Undergraduate program offerings are available at centers in Michigan and online through CMU's distance learn-ing program. All bachelor's degrees are based on 124 semester hours of credit and are available online and face-to-face in classrooms in the State of Michigan.

The Bachelor of Science degree with a major in administration is for students wishing to pursue an administrative career. The core courses provide a foundation in the concepts and applications critical to becoming a successful, effective administrator. Graduates of this program are prepared for careers as production supervisors, human resource administrators, and small business administrators. General education and elective courses allow students to acquire basic skills and learn to communicate with people in other disciplines and jobs and they provide an emphasis in liberal arts and natural or social sciences. A sampling of courses within the organizational administration concentration includes managerial economics, human resource management, and organizational behavior among other business topics.

The Bachelor of Science degree with an option in community development prepares students for work in the public sector or human services area. Graduates go on to careers in political office, the public health professions, directing community education, and more. Courses focus on the general theory and practice of community along with interaction of community institutions in a community setting. The community services concentration prepares students for employment at community agencies, for providing community services, and for work in non-profit organizations; many of the courses are focused in sociology. The public administration concentration is for those wishing to work in local, state, or federal government positions; many of the courses are centered on political science.

The Master of Science in Administration (M.S.A.) degree is a 36-semester-hour program that approaches administration and management from a broader perspective than other graduate degrees. This interdisciplinary program was developed to meet the needs of administrators in both the public and nonprofit sectors. M.S.A. concentrations are available at locations throughout North America, with two concentrations (general administration and information resource management) available completely online. Within the M.S.A. curriculum are core courses (about half of the degree) and concentration courses (the remaining half). The core courses provide students with quantitative analysis while the concentration courses allow them to tailor the program to their individual areas of interest. Among the concentrations offered, the general administration concentration gives an excellent foundation in management principals and is applicable to a wide variety of administrative settings. The health services concentration equips students to proactively meet the challenges faced in a health-care facility or in hospital administration. The concentration in human resource administration helps students develop their human resource management skills, focusing on the areas of labor relations, staffing, training, and organizational development. An information resource management concentration enables students to develop a comprehensive approach to the management of information systems in an organization to ensure that the chosen technology solution is the most appropriate one. The leadership concentration enhances abilities to think creatively, manage knowledge effectively, develop a vision, establish direction, and motivate staff. The public administration concentration prepares students for careers in public administration. Students get in-depth information on public policy-making and regulatory, budgetary, and personnel issues. Many of the courses are centered in political science.

CMU plans to offer an Online M.B.A. program starting in January 2008. The program, which is suited for working professionals seeking a program in advanced managerial study, will have a concentration in management information systems (MIS) and an emphasis in enterprise software (SAP). This eighteen-month, 31-credit program is planned to be offered 100 percent online with a two-week face-to-face SAP. To participate in this program, students must show evidence of computer literacy with a working knowledge of advanced business computer applications in spreadsheet, database, and presentation graphics. Applicants must also submit their GMAT score and have a minimum of four years of work experience.

The M.S. in Nutrition and Dietetics (M.S.N.D.) degree is designed to provide advanced training in human nutritional sciences for new and experienced professionals. Its objective is to enhance the graduate's knowledge base and expertise in the continually advancing field of nutrition and clinical dietetics. In addition, the program is designed to provide graduates with the quantitative and methodological knowledge necessary to better interpret the scientific literature to conduct their own nutritional research. This program is available completely online.

CMU's long-standing tradition of teacher excellence continues with its Master of Arts in Education degree (M.A.Ed.). This program is designed to provide knowledge and skills for individuals required to function effectively in various positions of educational leadership. The M.A.Ed. is a continuing education program for teachers; it presumes the individual is already trained and qualified in the technical aspects of her or his field. Concentrations available within the program are adult education (teaching in an adult education environment), community college (currently only available in Canada, this concentration is for effective teaching in a community college environment), and instructional (for K–12 curriculum and instruction), The M.A.Ed. degree is offered at select locations throughout the United States and Canada.

The M.A. in educational leadership with an emphasis in charter school administration is one of CMU's newest online offerings starting in January 2008. The program is geared toward the growing needs of charter school administration. Course topics include leadership in a charter school, administration within diverse populations, school and community relations, and principles of educational administration. This is a 33-credit hour program offered 100 percent online.

Special Programs
The Doctor of Health Administration (D.H.A.) is a 63-credit program that is cutting edge, academically sound, practice based, and flexible. Designed for leaders in the health-care field, the online format, combined with six weekend seminars, provides the ultimate combination of academic rigor and practical convenience.

Student Services
All services are available online and/or by a toll-free phone call. The service ranked highest by CMU's current students and graduates is the nationally recognized Off-Campus Library Services. Document delivery provides students with books, copies of journal articles, and other materials free of charge.

Credit Options
Credits earned through distance learning are recorded on Central Michigan University's transcripts in the same manner as credits earned in on-campus courses. These courses are part of the regular offerings of Central Michigan University. Relevant transfer credit and prior learning credits are also options.

Faculty
Faculty members are selected from the main campus in Mount Pleasant, Michigan; from other universities; and from the executive ranks of government, business, and industry. They enjoy the challenge of working with adult students and respect the knowledge and skills the students bring to the classroom. Approval of all faculty members is done by department chairpersons on the basis of their academic and professional qualifications.

Admission
Students must be admitted to CMU in order to take distance learning courses. The minimum requirement for admission to CMU undergraduate programs is a high school diploma or GED certificate. Undergraduate applicants must posses a GPA of 2.0 or higher. For those with GPAs lower than the required 2.0, conditional admission may be granted. One official transcript from all previously attended institutions should be provided to CMU.

Graduate applicants must have a baccalaureate or equivalent degree from an insti-tution that has received regional accreditation or recognized standing at the time the student attended. Graduate applicants must have an overall grade point average of at least 2.7 in their bachelor's studies. Applicants whose GPA is between 2.3 and 2.7 may be considered for conditional admission. GMAT or GRE scores are not required (except for the Online M.B.A. program.

D.H.A. applicants must have a master's degree of at least 27 semester hours or have earned a professional doctorate (such as M.D., D.O., J.D., or Pharm.D.) from a U.S. regionally accredited university.

Tuition and Fees
Tuition for the 2007–08 academic year is as follows: undergraduate, $309 per credit hour; graduate, $403 per credit hour; and D.H.A., $850 per credit hour. Military personnel (active duty and retired) and their dependents are eligible for a discounted tuition rate at both the undergraduate and graduate levels of select programs of $250 per credit hour. This rate does not apply at the doctoral level. Proper identification is required to receive this lower discounted rate.

Additional fees include a $50 admission fee, $50 graduation fee, $100 prior learning application fee, and a $75 prior learning assessment fee (per credit hour).

Financial Aid
Financial aid is available to those students who qualify. Students interested in financial aid are encouraged to contact CMU for more information.

Applying
Students interested in taking classes through CMU Off-Campus Programs are encouraged to apply for admission to Central Michigan University. Admission applications can be downloaded from the Web site listed in the Contact section.

CONTACT

CMU Off-Campus Programs
Central Michigan University
Mount Pleasant, Michigan 48859

Phone: 877-268-4636 (toll-free)
Fax: 989-774-1822
E-mail: cmuoffcampus@cmich.edu
Web site: http://www.cmuoffcampus.
com

CHARTER OAK STATE COLLEGE
New Britain, Connecticut

Charter Oak State College, one of America's leading distance learning colleges for adults, was established in 1973 by the Connecticut Legislature to provide an alternate way for adults to earn a college degree. Recognized as the College that offers "degrees without boundaries," Charter Oak responds to the degree-completion needs of adult learners. The College, which is regionally accredited by the New England Association of Schools and Colleges and is a Servicemembers Opportunity College, awards bachelor's and associate degrees.

Charter Oak's flexible degree-completion programs are designed to assist adult learners in achieving their educational objectives as they continue to meet career, family, and financial obligations.

Students can complete their degree credit requirements by combining credits earned—no matter how long ago—from regionally accredited colleges and universities, noncollegiate-sponsored instruction, standardized testing such as CLEP and Dantes, work or military experience, contract learning, portfolio assessment, and Charter Oak online courses.

Individualized professional advisement is a hallmark of Charter Oak State College. Each student benefits from one-on-one support from an academic counselor who specializes in the student's chosen field of study. Counselors, who are accessible via telephone, e-mail, fax, and U.S. mail, work closely with students to customize a degree-completion program geared to personal goals.

Distance Learning Program

Charter Oak State College provides all of its services using distance technology. The College offers an expansive selection of five-, eight-, and fifteen-week quality online courses. Textbooks may be purchased electronically from an authorized bookstore.

Programs of Study

Charter Oak State College offers four degrees in general studies: Associate in Arts, Associate in Science, Bachelor of Arts, and Bachelor of Science. To earn an associate degree, a student must complete at least 60 credits; a bachelor's degree requires at least 120 credits. The College accepts up to 90 community college credits toward a bachelor's degree.

A Charter Oak degree is more than an accumulation of the required number of credits. At least one half of the credits toward a degree must be earned in subjects traditionally included in the liberal arts and sciences—humanities, mathematics, natural sciences, and social sciences. Achievement in these areas demonstrates breadth of learning. To demonstrate depth of learning, students who pursue a baccalaureate degree must complete a concentration consisting of at least 36 credits.

A concentration plan, accompanied by an essay, must be submitted to the faculty for approval. Concentrations may be constructed in many areas, including applied arts, art history, the behavioral sciences, business, child study, communication, computer science, engineering studies, fire service administration, health-care administration, human services, individualized studies, languages, liberal studies, literature, music history, the natural sciences, organizational management and leadership, public safety administration, religious studies, the social sciences, and technology studies. As a graduation requirement, students must also submit an academic autobiography that provides them the opportunity to reflect on their educational experiences and demonstrate their writing ability and understanding of their degree program.

Special Programs

The College has evaluated a number of noncollegiate courses and programs for which it awards credit toward Charter Oak degree programs. Many health-care specialties from hospital-based programs are included, such as medical laboratory technician, nurse practitioner, physician assistant, radiologic technologist, registered nurse, and respiratory therapist or technician. The College also evaluates state and municipal police officer training. Other evaluations include the Child Development Associate (CDA) credential; the FAA Airman Certificate; Famous Artists School in Westport, Connecticut; Institute of Children's Literature in West Redding, Connecticut; the National Opticianry Competency Examination; the Contact Lens Registry Examination; and several fire certifications, including Fire Marshal, Deputy Fire Marshal, Fire Inspector, Fire Fighter III, Fire Officer I or II, and Fire Service Instructor I or II.

Credit Options

Students can transfer credits from other regionally accredited colleges and universities. Age of credits is not a factor in most concentrations. There is no limit to the number of credits that can be earned using standardized examinations, prior learning—including ACE-evaluated military credits and ACE- and PONSI-evaluated noncollegiate learning—and portfolio assessment

Faculty

Full-time faculty members, from public and independent institutions of higher education in Connecticut, serve as consulting examiners at Charter Oak. Distance learning faculty members come from all over the United States and possess appropriate degrees and/or experience.

Admission

Admission is open to any person 16 years or older, regardless of level of formal education, who is able to demonstrate college-level achievement. To be admitted, a student must have earned 9 college-level credits from acceptable sources of credit.

Tuition and Fees

All students pay a $75 application fee. Connecticut residents pay a first-year matriculation fee of $675 for an associate degree or $985 for a bachelor's degree. Nonresidents pay a first-year matriculation fee of $955 for an associate degree or $1300 for a bachelor's degree. Active-duty service members and their spouses pay in-state resident's rates for all Charter Oak fees and services. All students pay a graduation fee of $185. Tuition for online and video-based courses is $165 per credit for Connecticut residents and $235 per credit for nonresidents. There is a $40 registration fee for all students. A Comprehensive Enrollment Fee, combining matriculation and 12 credits per year is available at a rate reflecting a 10 percent discount.

Financial Aid

Financial aid is available to eligible Charter Oak students from federal, state, and institutional sources. All students who wish to apply for aid must complete the Free Application for Federal Student Aid (FAFSA). The FAFSA may be completed online and can be accessed at http://www.fafsa.ed.gov. Charter Oak's forms can be accessed online at http://www.charteroak.edu/sfa. The Charter Oak State College school code is 032343.

Applying

Charter Oak reviews applications on a rolling basis; students may matriculate at anytime during the year.

CITY UNIVERSITY
Distance Learning Option
Bellevue, Washington

City University is a private not-for-profit institution of higher education. Its mission is to change lives for good by offering high quality and relevant lifelong education to anyone with the desire to learn.

City University's programs cover a variety of academic fields, ranging from business management and technology to psychology and communications. The majority of faculty members actively work in the fields they teach. The combination of innovative program design and outstanding instruction makes City University an exceptional institution of higher learning.

Distance Learning Program

In keeping with its mission of providing convenient, accessible education, City University offers most of its degree programs through distance learning (DL), utilizing the World Wide Web. City University serves approximately 5,000 students annually through DL.

Delivery Media

City University delivers distance learning course work utilizing the Blackboard Course Management System. Delivered through asynchronous interaction on the World Wide Web, City University distance learning courses are designed for optimum learning anywhere, anytime. Highly qualified faculty members, who are working in the fields they teach, provide distance learning students with real-world application of course material. In addition, structured discussions provide students the opportunity to exchange in dialogue with peers without the need of traveling to a classroom.

Programs of Study

City University's undergraduate programs prepare students to compete in today's marketplace. Students may complete a Bachelor of Science (B.S.) or a Bachelor of Arts (B.A.) degree. Within these degrees, students may pursue one of several areas of study, including accounting, business administration, communications, computer systems, and psychology. Undergraduate courses are 5 credits each; 180 credits are required for completion of a B.S. degree, and students typically transfer the first two years of study.

City University's graduate business program prepares management professionals for leadership roles at local, national, and international levels. Students may pursue a Master of Business Administration (M.B.A.) or a Master of Science in either project management or computer systems. Most graduate courses are worth 3 credits; total required credits range from 45 to 60. Students may also pursue a Master of Education (M.Ed.) in literacy. Total required credits for this program is 48.

Special Programs

City University has an "open-door" admissions policy for most programs. Students may begin course work at the start of any quarter once accepted to their program of study.

All of City University's programs are geared for adult students. From its student body to its faculty and staff, City University is a community of professionals. All who are associated with the University understand the needs of adult learners who are seeking high-quality education that applies to their individual lifestyle.

Student Services

Students may register online or by phone. Academic advising and assistance is available from a distance learning adviser by phone, fax, or e-mail. Students have full access to the library via the Internet and a toll-free phone number, and a mailing service for circulation of books and articles is available as well.

Credit Options

Students may transfer up to 90 approved lower-division and 45 approved upper-division credits from approved institutions for baccalaureate programs. The Prior Learning Experience Program lets students earn credits through documented experimental learning. Students may receive credit for the CLEP or other standardized tests. Graduate students may transfer up to 12 credits from approved programs.

Faculty

There are more than 350 faculty members included in the distance learning program. Faculty members have, at minimum, a master's degree and professional experience in the fields they teach.

Admission

Undergraduate programs are generally open to applicants over 18 years of age who hold a high school diploma or GED. Admission to graduate programs requires that students hold a baccalaureate degree from an accredited or otherwise recognized institution. Additional requirements apply to education programs. International students whose first language is not English are required to submit a TOEFL score of at least 540 for admission to undergraduate programs and 565 for graduate programs.

Tuition and Fees

For 2007–08, tuition is $290 per undergraduate credit hour and $494 per graduate credit hour. The tuition rate is the same for both in-class and distance learning study. Other fees may apply, depending on the specific course of study. Additional fees apply for certificate completion, graduation application, course registration, and various tests or examinations that the student may request. All initial applicants for certificate or degree programs pay a nonrefundable application fee of $50. Tuition and fees are subject to annual review on July 1.

Textbooks and other instructional materials are additional. While the number of required texts and other course materials vary with each course, textbooks typically cost between $100 and $150 each.

Financial Aid

For information, students should contact the Financial Aid Office at 800-426-5596 (toll-free).

Applying

DL students may enroll on a rolling admissions basis. Students must speak with an academic adviser to complete the initial enrollment. Students should then submit the application form, nonrefundable application fee, transcripts, and admission documents to the Office of Admissions.

CONTACT

Office of Admissions
City University
11900 NE First Street
Bellevue, Washington 98005

Phone: 425-737-1010
           800-422-4898 (toll-free)
Fax: 425-709-5361
E-mail: info@cityu.edu
Web site: http://www.cityu.edu

COLORADO STATE UNIVERSITY
College of Business, Distance M.B.A. Program
Fort Collins, Colorado

Colorado State University's College of Business offers a comprehensive M.B.A. program to professionals around the world who desire not only to learn the concepts and theories behind sound business practices but also to understand how to apply these ideas to their day-to-day operations. The Distance M.B.A. Program is offered through mixed-media DVD technology; students gain the benefit of the full lectures, student discussions, questions, and special topics presented by the guest speakers. Students are at a distance—not in isolation.

CSU strives to make all of its students feel part of the activities experienced on the main campus. The degree earned is not a diluted form of the on-campus degree but rather encompasses the same academic content and rigor as the on-campus M.B.A. program. Our distance M.B.A. students earn an M.B.A. from Colorado State University, not an online or distance degree.

Accredited by AACSB International–The Association of Advance Collegiate Schools of Business more than thirty years ago, the Distance M.B.A. Program at Colorado State University was the first to earn this coveted accreditation and remains one of the only distance M.B.A. programs to be so accredited. The program strives to provide students with the knowledge, skills, and functional competencies they need to become effective decision makers and leaders in a business environment that is becoming more global, more competitive, and increasingly dynamic.

Distance Learning Program

Founded more than thirty-five years ago and one of the nation's oldest distance degree programs, the Distance M.B.A. Program delivers a high-quality education while providing students with the flexibility needed to earn their degrees. This program was the first distance M.B.A. program to earn the coveted AACSB International accreditation more than thirty years ago and remains one of the only distance/online M.B.A. programs with the prestigious accreditation. Program content is cross-functional and has a strong emphasis on leadership, entrepreneurship, and global issues. Nearly 2,000 professionals have earned their M.B.A. degrees through the CSU Distance M.B.A. Program.

Most individuals in the CSU Distance M.B.A. Program are working professionals, with an average of thirteen years of work experience. They are drawn from all fifty states, many provinces in Canada, and, increasingly, from around the world. Over the years, U.S. military personnel have been frequent participants in the program and continue to be heavy supporters of this flexible and convenient M.B.A. program. The average age of the distance students is 33; their average GMAT score is 610.

The Distance M.B.A. Program at CSU offers active duty military personnel, National Guard personnel, reservists, and veterans a Military Tuition Reduction Program to help bridge the funding gap found in graduate education. Likewise, a Federal and State Employee Tuition Reduction Program is available.

Delivery Media

Distance M.B.A. students are linked to each other and to the epicenter of the M.B.A. programs at CSU through a technologically advanced classroom and an online communications network. By virtue of the unique connectedness, all students come together as one class, even though they may be located across the country or in another part of the world.

The classroom lectures and discussions are recorded using a mixed-media DVD format for the distance M.B.A. students and are shipped the following day. The DVD format gives CSU's distance M.B.A. students a direct link to the classroom, the on-campus students, and the professors. In addition to lectures and discussions being delivered using the DVD technology, students also are part of the unique M.B.A. intranet for communication with professors, other students in the sections, and team members. The chat rooms and threaded discussions keep students engaged with others in the program, assignments, and group collaboration.

Program of Study

The Distance M.B.A. Program is designed to serve the needs of working professionals who need flexibility in schedule and location. There is no requirement to come to the campus during the course of the program; however, over 50 percent of the Distance M.B.A. Program graduates come to take part in commencement each year. The 36-credit program may be completed in as little as twenty-one months, or a student may take up to five years to complete the program; summer classes are required regardless of the time sequence selected. The College's M.B.A. adviser works with students throughout the program to match course offerings with professional and personal schedules. There is no thesis required in this program.

In this comprehensive and progressive M.B.A. degree program, students study the five major functional areas of a business and the interrelationship among those areas. Students are not only exposed to the concepts and theories of modern business practices but they also have the opportunity to apply those concepts and theories to their own companies/businesses or to others around them. This application-based course of study is lauded by CSU's students as immediately valuable in their day-to-day professional lives.

Student Services

A student in the Colorado State University Distance M.B.A. Program is afforded all the student-support services offered to those on campus. Each student is assigned to an M.B.A. adviser to help with course sequencing or special situations impacting program participation. In addition, each student has electronic access to the main CSU library's business databases and the library's reference materials, journals, and periodicals. Students can even sign up to receive books and articles directly from the library. In addition, each student has access to technical support and an operations assistant for the M.B.A. intranet.

Credit Options

The Distance M.B.A. Program offers courses in a lock-step sequencing mode, so each class builds on the previous classes. Because of the lock-step sequencing of the program and because of the group collaboration, CSU does not accept transfer credits; however, there are no prerequisites for the program. For students who feel they could benefit from a refresher with accounting, finance, and statistics, an MBA Survival Kit is available through the bookstore. These self-paced CDs take students through the basics of each of these subject areas providing foundation knowledge and confidence.

Faculty

What differentiates CSU's Distance M.B.A. Program from other programs is the high quality of its faculty members, who not only teach the material but also demonstrate how to apply it to the business world. With the exception of a few extraordinary individuals with private-industry experience, the professors who teach in the M.B.A. program are full-time faculty members with Ph.D.'s in their disciplines. Their research efforts and work in their respective industries keep the faculty members in the forefront of what is happening in business today.

Admission

Admission to the Distance M.B.A. Program is predicated on an individual's performance at the undergraduate level; their professional experience, including management of projects or people; their GMAT scores; and their application materials. A balance of these four criteria is sought in the determination for admission. In special cases, petitions for GMAT waivers are considered.

Colorado State University seeks to balance each class with a representation of industries, years of experience, and a mix of undergraduate degree concentrations. In addition, attention is paid to provide a balance along gender lines and a rich mix of backgrounds. Applicants with all types of undergraduate backgrounds are encouraged to apply. The program does not have prerequisites.

Tuition and Fees

For the 2006–07 academic year, the tuition for the distance M.B.A. courses was $547 per credit hour. There is a small increase expected in the 2007–08 academic year. The $547 per-credit-hour cost includes the production of the course-delivery DVDs, shipping, the M.B.A. intranet, technical support, production assistance, and all other student services. Students are responsible for their own textbooks and course materials.

Financial Aid

Federal financial aid is available to qualified students admitted to the Distance M.B.A. Program who take at least 5 credits per semester. More information can be obtained from the Financial Aid Office (http://sfs.colostate.edu/B2000.cfm; 970-491-6321). Students may also complete the Free Application for Federal Student Aid on the Web at http://www.fafsa.ed.gov.

Applying

The application deadlines for the Distance M.B.A. Program are July 15 for the fall semester and December 8 for the spring semester. Applicants must submit a resume; a cover letter that reflects carefully considered reasons for pursuing a business degree at the master's level; GMAT scores (unless a petition for a waiver to the GMAT is submitted and approved); TOEFL scores (for international students); a completed data sheet for the College of Business; three references from individuals who know the applicant's work, each in a sealed envelope; two copies of official transcripts in sealed envelopes; a completed Graduate School Web Application; and a $50 application fee. To request an admissions packet, students should contact the College.

CONTACT

Rachel Stoll
Graduate Admission Coordinator
Colorado State University College of Business
1270 Campus Delivery
Fort Collins, Colorado 80523-1270

Phone: 800-491-4622 (toll-free)
Fax: 970-491-3481
E-mail: rachel.stoll@colostate.edu
Web site: http://www.CSUdistanceMBA.com

COLORADO STATE UNIVERSITY
Continuing Education
Fort Collins, Colorado

Colorado State University has served the people of Colorado as the state's land-grant university since 1870. Today, the campus in Fort Collins is home to 25,000 students pursuing degrees at all levels in a wide range of subjects in liberal arts, engineering, business, natural resources, agriculture, and the sciences. The University's instructional outreach activities go far beyond the campus and the state of Colorado.

Distance Learning Program

Colorado State University's online and distance learning courses are designed to begin or to finish a degree, to explore new topics, to enrich life, and to give students an opportunity to develop a level of proficiency in professional development. Approximately 7,450 individuals from all over the country and overseas are enrolled in distance education courses from Colorado State University.

Delivery Media

Colorado State offers courses in online, print, and mixed media formats. All courses are supported by Colorado State University faculty members. Students may contact course faculty members via telephone, fax, e-mail, or regular mail. Students should call Continuing Education or visit the Web site for contact information for an instructor.

Programs of Study

As an institution, Colorado State has been involved in online and distance learning since 1967 and was one of the first schools to utilize technology in distance education.

Independent Study: Correspondence Study, Telecourses, and Online Courses remove the traditional boundaries of time and location for the distance learner. Through the use of a study guide, textbooks, the Internet, and applicable reference materials, students have the opportunity to participate in an individualized mode of instruction offering a high degree of flexibility. Students interested in correspondence courses and telecourses may enroll at any time, set their own pace, and choose the most convenient time and place to study. Online courses are taught according to the regular University semester schedule.

Distance Degrees offer working professionals the opportunity to earn credit from Colorado State without coming to campus. These are semester-based courses that use DVD/VCD, online, and mixed-media formats. Whether students are working on their degree or taking courses to stay current in their field, distance degrees offer the flexibility to pursue educational objectives as work schedules permit.

Courses are available in several disciplines, including agriculture, business, communication/public affairs, computer science, engineering, fire and emergency services administration, human resource development, statistics, and telecommunications. Distance Degree students are located throughout the United States and Canada and at U.S. military APO and FPO addresses. At this time, only correspondence courses and online courses and degrees are available to overseas students. Thousands of motivated people have earned their degrees, and countless others have taken individual courses to enhance their skill base or keep current with the latest technology.

Special Programs

Colorado State also provides other distance education opportunities. These courses are open-entry/open-exit, meaning students may register at any time and take six months to complete the course. Many of the courses can be used for specific programs, such as Child Care Administration Certification or Seed Analyst Training.

The state of Colorado requires certification of all child-care center directors and substitute directors by the State Department of Human Services. Certification requires both experience working with young children and specific education. Colorado State University is proud to offer courses through distance education that may satisfy some of the educational requirements. Other states may have individual specific educational requirements. Students should contact the appropriate agency in their area for further information.

For instructors wanting to enhance their teaching, Colorado State offers a Postsecondary Teaching Certificate Program, consisting of three 3-credit courses: Models of Teaching, Communication and Classrooms, and Educators, Systems, and Change. In this program, new instructors acquire a practical overview of a range of effective teaching models, ideas for engaging students while addressing measurable learning objectives, and approaches to promote critical and creative thinking. Experienced instructors update and energize their teaching repertoires, connecting personal knowledge with established research on effective classroom practices. Students in the program can earn graduate credit for advanced course work in postsecondary education and apply the 9 credits toward a master's or doctoral degree.

An innovative Seed Analyst Training Program consisting of four distance learning (correspondence) courses has been developed by the National Seed Storage Laboratory and Colorado State University. The courses were prepared over a two-year period by University professors and other experts with the support of the Colorado seed industry. The four courses cover the basics of seed analyst training: 1) Seed Anatomy and Identification, 2) Seed Development and Metabolism, 3) Seed Purity Analysis, and 4) Seed Germination and Viability.

Counseling through the University Center for Advising and Student Achievement is offered to all those interested in continuing their education. There is no fee for academic advising services. Students may schedule an appointment with an academic adviser by calling 970-491-7095. The Extended University Programs librarian is available to assist students with identifying and accessing library materials. Students should call 970-491-6952 to speak with the librarian.

Credit Options

All credits earned through distance education are recorded on a Colorado State University transcript. Distance education courses are the same as on-campus courses and are accredited by the same organizations as the University. A student currently enrolled in a degree program elsewhere is responsible for checking with the appropriate official at the degree-granting institution to make certain the course applies.

Faculty

Distance education faculty members must meet the same high standards any Colorado State University faculty member must meet. Most of the distance faculty members are faculty members within the department granting the course credit. Faculty members are available to answer questions and give feedback via telephone, fax, e-mail, or regular mail.

Admission

Anyone who has the interest, desire, background, and ability may register for distance learning courses. However, if prerequisites are listed for a course, they must be met. Registration in distance learning courses does not constitute admission to Colorado State University.

Tuition and Fees

Tuition for distance degrees for the 2006–07 academic year was $547 per credit (business courses), $520 per credit (weekly videotaped courses), or $411 per credit (online courses). Tuition for other distance education courses for the 2006–07 academic year was $223 per credit for undergraduate courses and $280 per credit for graduate courses. For current tuition information, students should visit the Web site.

Financial Aid

Colorado State University courses are approved for the DANTES program. Eligible military personnel should process DANTES applications through their education office. For information regarding veterans' benefits, students should contact the VA office at Colorado State University. With the exception of distance degrees, distance learning is not a degree-granting program and is therefore not eligible for federal grants. Students are encouraged to seek scholarship aid from organizations and local civic groups that may sponsor such study.

Applying

To complete a distance degree, admittance to the University is required. There is no application for distance education. Students should simply register for the course(s) of interest by mail or fax or online and pay the tuition. For more information about these and other distance courses from Colorado State University, or for registration information, students should contact the University.

CONTACT

Phone: 970-491-5288
        877-491-4336 (toll-free)
Fax: 970-491-7885
E-mail: info@learn.colostate.edu
Web site: http://www.learn.colostate.edu

COLORADO TECHNICAL UNIVERSITY

Colorado Technical University Online
Accelerated Degrees
Colorado Springs, Colorado

Since 1965, Colorado Technical University has helped thousands of students achieve success in business, management, and technology careers. Academic programs are continually evaluated and updated for relevance and currency. Colorado Technical University is accredited by the Higher Learning Commission of the North Central Association of Colleges and Schools. For more information, students should visit the NCA Higher Learning Commission Web site.

Distance Learning Program

Colorado Technical University Online provides students with a high-quality education relevant to the needs and demands of the ever-evolving business and technical job markets. Colorado Tech Online offers innovative, career-relevant degree programs completely online, so students can learn anywhere, anytime, on any PC with Internet access. Each program's content is continually updated and instantly applicable.

Delivery Media

Colorado Tech Online offers one of the best online platforms available. All courses are taught in a multimedia format that provides a rich, dynamic, interactive classroom experience. The programs offer many opportunities for students to adapt their learning experiences to their own personal styles. Students who prefer to have a hard copy of notes can print the presentations. Students also control the pace of an instructor's presentation. Students participate in discussions with the instructors and other students. Since the participants are employed in a variety of interesting professions, students gain insightful knowledge and learn from each other's experiences.

Programs of Study

Colorado Tech Online offers accelerated bachelor's and master's degrees in a variety of career-relevant fields, including business, criminal justice, informa-

tion technology, and marketing. The bachelor's degrees and master's degrees can be completed in fifteen months. (The fifteen-month bachelor's degree is a 2+2 program and assumes that all associate-level requirements have been met through an associate degree or the equivalent. Colorado Tech Online students with no previous college experience can complete this degree in about 2½ years.) All of Colorado Tech Online's degree programs incorporate professional certificates that students earn as they progress through the programs, without additional courses or added costs.

Colorado Tech Online is a registered educational provider of the Project Management Institute™ (PMI), the world's leading not-for-profit project management professional association. Select course content has been reviewed by PMI and found to be relevant to project management and consistent with the knowledge and process areas described in the *Guide to the Project Management Book of Knowledge*.

Business: Colorado Tech Online's School of Business can prepare versatile managers with the business and management skills they need to provide creative leadership vision, while solving modern business problems effectively and efficiently.

The Bachelor of Science in Business Administration (B.S.B.A.) degree programs emphasize practical competencies, creative leadership approaches, and the development of critical-

thinking skills. Students can select from several career-relevant concentrations, including finance, health-care management, human resource management, international business, management, and project management.

The Master of Science in Management (M.S.M.) degree programs are designed to help provide immediate management applications, along with the knowledge and understanding of the critical skills necessary to analyze and solve various business problems. Available concentrations include business management and project management.

The Master of Business Administration (M.B.A.) degree program features an array of career-relevant concentrations, including accounting, finance, health-care management, and human resource management.

Students can also select the Executive M.B.A. degree program, which delivers immediate management applications, along with the knowledge and understanding of the critical skills necessary to analyze and solve various business problems. The emphasis is on real-world skills and knowledge that managers need to succeed in today's business world. This Executive M.B.A. program also incorporates information technology management and project management competencies.

Criminal Justice: The Colorado Tech Online School of Criminal Justice prepares students for a wide variety of careers in law enforcement, corrections, the court systems, and security by providing in-depth criminal justice knowledge in addition to strong business and management skills appropriate to the industry.

The Bachelor of Science in Criminal Justice (B.S.C.J.) offers students a component of forensic study not usually available at the undergraduate level.

This degree program can help prepare students for positions such as police officer, deputy sheriff, fraud investigator, highway patrol officer, and more.

Information Technology: Information technology is a rapidly growing industry. Colorado Tech Online develops curricula to reflect current market conditions by incorporating relevant, up-to-date material into course content.

The Bachelor of Science in Business Administration (B.S.B.A.), with a concentration in information technology, gives students the technical skills and strong management skills they need to help position themselves for career advancement in this growing industry.

With the Bachelor of Science in Information Technology (B.S.I.T.), students acquire a practical, real-world education from professors who are also IT professionals. In addition to important undergraduate foundation studies, students learn computer programming languages, computer network systems operations, and software engineering skills. Available concentrations include network management, security, and software systems engineering.

The Master of Science in Management (M.S.M.) degree program includes two technology-related concentrations: information systems security and IT management. The M.S.M. in information systems security provides a strong foundation for students to help advance their technical skills to plan, manage, certify, and accredit an organization's security plan. The M.S.M. in IT management is designed as a broad-based IT management curriculum that provides an understanding of computer architecture, networking and telecommunication, database management, and business and financial management strategies.

Marketing: As the consumer marketplace continues to evolve into an increasingly complex environment, demand grows for professionals with the up-to-date knowledge and skills to drive it forward. The Colorado Tech Online School of Marketing was developed to help prepare marketing professionals who want to establish and advance successful careers.

The Bachelor of Science in Business Administration (B.S.B.A.), with a concentration in marketing, provides students with an understanding of the intricate relationships between organizations and their customers. Course content has been developed to emphasize current marketing trends and opportunities for success. The M.B.A. degree program also offers a concentration in marketing for students who wish to pursue top-tier positions in this field.

Student Services

Colorado Tech Online provides technical support 24/7 via an online help desk as well as a toll-free telephone number.

For research and curriculum support, Colorado Tech Online students have access to a full academic library completely online. The texts, journals, articles, and thousands of other resources are accessible whenever a student needs them.

The Career Services Department is staffed by skilled professionals who assist students with their career planning process. The department's full range of services includes career development strategies, job search strategies, interviewing tips, and resume and cover letter assistance.

Credit Options

Students with college credit or military experience may be eligible for the Colorado Tech Online Baccalaureate Degree Completion Program. If eligible, this program may reduce the time required to complete a degree program.

Faculty

Colorado Tech Online's faculty members have advanced degrees and are established professionals in their fields, giving students valuable opportunities to derive insights and real-world perspectives from their experiences. They bring situation-specific relevance to every course, so students receive an education they can apply in the real world. Colorado Tech Online also limits the number of students enrolled in each class to encourage interaction with, and personal attention from, instructors.

Admission

To be considered for admission to Colorado Tech Online, applicants must submit an application and $50 application fee and fulfill all admission requirements for the program. Applicants are contacted to arrange for a personal telephone interview and for the necessary school transcripts to be submitted. TOEFL scores are required from nonnative speakers of English.

Tuition and Fees

Tuition amounts vary depending on the program. Students should call an Admissions Representative for more information.

Financial Aid

Financial aid is available for those who qualify.

CONTACT

Colorado Technical University Online
4435 North Chestnut Street, Suite E
Colorado Springs, Colorado 80907

Phone: 800-416-8904 (toll-free)
Web site: http://www.ctuonline.edu

CORBAN COLLEGE

Adult Studies Online Programs

Salem, Oregon

Corban College is an independent, Christian liberal arts college and is accredited by the Northwest Commission on Colleges and Universities. Its core purpose is to educate Christians who will make a difference in the world for Jesus Christ.

The College offered its first distance learning program in 1994, which developed into a uniquely online format in 1997. It now offers two online degree-completion programs for Christian students in the areas of management and communication and family studies.

Distance Learning Program

Corban's online degree-completion programs are specifically and conveniently formatted for the Christian student who has two years of college credit and desires a Christian college education but is unable to attend on-campus classes. With only a three-day residency orientation, the entirety of the sixteen-month program is completed from home via computer.

Delivery Media

Online course work requires an IBM-compatible computer system, Internet access, and completion of an initial orientation, which is held on campus. Complete precourse training is provided for all students via self-paced tutorials, hands-on workshops, and follow-up technical support. Course instruction is accomplished by utilizing facilitated discussion forums, live chat conferences, and collaborative project reports, which are supported by Internet course-management software, audio-video and keyboard conferencing programs, e-mail, and telephone.

Programs of Study

Corban offers two degree-completion programs entirely online. Individual online courses are also offered to assist students in completing general education requirements. The online degree-completion programs lead to a B.S. or B.A. degree. Students enrolling in the degree-completion program must have completed 60 semester hours of transferable credit. A total of 128 semester hours is required for the bachelor's degree.

Both online degree-completion programs in management and communication and family studies are excellent preparation for graduate study. The management and communication online degree-completion program is 41 semester hours in length. The curriculum is structured to develop leadership, analytical, and problem-solving skills with a Christian perspective. Course work provides expertise in management, organization development, and communication—three of the most important aspects of business and public administration. The family studies online degree-completion program is 44 semester hours in length. It uses an applied interdisciplinary approach, focusing on the study of family dynamics and the relationships between families and the society at large. The curriculum is integrated with biblical principles and is taught by Christian professionals. New optional tracks for these programs include mental health and strategic management.

Special Programs

Students are given the opportunity to earn college credit for prior learning through the Prior Learning Assessment program. Students learn how to identify, document, and describe appropriate prior learning experiences. Weekend classes are offered both online and on campus and are designed to meet general education requirements. The course offerings vary in length. Internships and research projects are required in the online degree-completion programs. They are generally completed within the workplace or in a related local business or agency.

Student Services

Online students enjoy complete access to the same College services as campus students via Web-based communication, fax, or telephone. In addition to academic advising and project mentoring, financial aid, the registrar's office, technical support, the campus bookstore, and library services are available. Online library resources include EBSCOhost, ERIC, Academic Universe, ProQuest Direct, and other comprehensive databases.

Credit Options

Qualifying college credit may be transferred, subject to the approval of the College registrar. Students may earn a maximum of 32 semester hours of credit through college-level exams (CLEP, DANTES) and 30 semester hours of credit through the Prior Learning Assessment program.

Admission

Enrollment in the online degree-completion program requires applicants to have a minimum of 60 semester hours of transferable college credit as well as profession of a personal faith in Jesus Christ.

Tuition and Fees

The 2007 tuition for the online degree-completion program is $15,658. Tuition includes all textbooks and graduation fees.

Financial Aid

Financial aid is available through federal and state financial aid programs. For further information, students should contact the financial aid office at 800-845-3005 (toll-free) or via e-mail at aid@corban.edu.

Applying

Applicants for online degree-completion programs must complete an application and submit transcripts, two references, an acceptable writing sample, and a profession of faith in Jesus Christ.

CONTACT

Adult Studies Online Program
Corban College
5000 Deer Park Drive, SE
Salem, Oregon 97301

Phone: 800-764-1383 (toll-free)
Fax: 503-375-7583
E-mail: asd@corban.edu
Web site: http://www.corban.edu

DEPAUL UNIVERSITY

School for New Learning
Center for Distance Education
Chicago, Illinois

DePaul University is nationally recognized for its innovative academic programs that combine hands-on learning and personal attention to help students achieve their personal and career goals. With more than 23,000 students hailing from all fifty states in the U.S. and sixty-five other countries, DePaul combines multiple perspectives, experience-based learning, and small class sizes to give them a practical education for a global marketplace.

Nowhere is the value of life experience more respected than in School for New Learning (SNL), one of DePaul's eight colleges and schools. Established more than thirty years ago, SNL is a national leader in the design and delivery of competence-based learning for adults. At SNL, students are able to earn college credit for their past life and work experiences, reap the value of prior college courses, and tailor a personalized course of study to achieve their own goals. The program is designed for adults, age 24 and older, to accommodate the complexities of their lives.

Because DePaul and SNL are fully accredited and nationally known for their high academic standards, the Bachelor of Arts degree students earn will be honored by employers and other universities worldwide. SNL's unique program is recognized as an NGO (Non-Governmental Organization) by the United Nations.

Distance Learning Program

SNL's distance education program allows students to earn a Bachelor of Arts degree entirely online. They work intensively with their faculty mentors, plan their degree program, collaborate with others, and take classes online. If they live in the Chicago area, they can choose to take a combination of on-campus and online courses to fulfill their degree requirements. SNL's online courses are interdisciplinary and aimed at developing competence that can be applied immediately in their lives. Students also may register for online courses through other DePaul colleges and schools, such as the School of Computer Science, Telecommunications, and Information Systems.

Flexible and rigorous, the School for New Learning provides excellent learning opportunities and individualized attention. Networking and real-world relevance are built into the program through the professional adviser, an expert in the student's chosen focus area.

Delivery Media

Students complete the distance education program using a range of electronic media, including course management systems, such as Blackboard; e-mail; podcasts; Web conferencing; VoIP; WIKIs; and blogs. SNL's delivery media change with the development of new technology. The highly interactive system keeps students well-connected with faculty members, advisers, professional experts, and classmates.

Programs of Study

Graduates receive a Bachelor of Arts degree from DePaul University. The degree is competence-based, consisting of fifty requirements allocated across three areas: lifelong learning, liberal arts, and focus area. Students determine their focus areas based on their personal and career goals; about 60 percent of current SNL students graduate with a focus related to business.

There are various ways to earn credit toward a degree, including interdisciplinary, competence-based DePaul courses; transfer courses; proficiency examinations; demonstration of prior learning; and independent study. Students generally master two competencies per course; most part-time students complete the degree in three to four years.

In order to ensure both academic quality and focus-area expertise, students work with a personal academic committee consisting of a faculty mentor and professional adviser throughout their time at SNL. As an adult learner, they chair their own committee, decide on your own externship and major project, and identify the skills they need to develop in order to further their personal goals through their focus area. The faculty mentor helps plan the student's degree program. The professional adviser is an expert in the student's focus-area field who helps determine the competencies needed to meet career goals.

Student Services

Distance learning students are able to access admission and registration services, identification cards, extensive online and campus-based library resources, career counseling, writing and math assistance, financial aid, academic advising, the bookstore, and more areas—entirely online. Unlike with many online programs, the admissions staff members are skilled and experienced student advisers. Advisers have no quotas to meet; their goal is only to help students achieve their own goals. The DePaul Writing Centers provide writing support via e-mail and Web cams; services include tutoring and editing of papers.

Credit Options

Any course, with a grade of C- or better, from an accredited institution is eligible for transfer credit, regardless of how long ago the course was completed.

Faculty

SNL faculty members are dedicated to teaching adults in a student-centered, individualized, and collaborative environment. All are experienced in the fields in which they teach, and nearly all have terminal or graduate degrees.

Admission

Applicants must be 24 years old or older, proficient in the use of the English language and have completed a high school diploma or its equivalent.

Students must have access to a computer with an Internet connection and an e-mail account. Hardware and software requirements are a Pentium III computer with Win ME, Windows 2000 Professional, or XP Home or Professional; at least 256 MB of RAM; a 20 gigabyte hard drive; a 56K baud dial-up modem or high-speed connection (DSL or cable); a sound card; speakers; a CD-ROM drive; a monitor with 1024 x 728 pixel resolution or better; and a printer. Macintosh users must have OS 9.2.2 (or higher) with comparable features.

Tuition and Fees

Tuition and fees for the 2006–07 academic year were $405 per credit hour. Most SNL courses are four credit hours, or $1,620. The cost of textbooks varies from class to class.

Financial Aid

Students are eligible to apply for financial aid. For more information, students should visit DePaul's financial aid Web site at http://www.depaul.edu/financial_aid.

Applying

Applications are accepted year-round. Interested students should visit SNL's Web site to request additional information about the program as well as an application for admission.

CONTACT

School for New Learning
Center for Distance Education
DePaul University
25 East Jackson Boulevard
Chicago, Illinois 60604
Phone: 312-362-8001
        866-SNL-FORU (toll-free)
Fax: 312-362-5053
E-mail: snlonline@depaul.edu
Web site: http://www.snlonline.net

DEPAUL UNIVERSITY

School of Computer Science, Telecommunications, and Information Systems

Chicago, Illinois

DePaul University is nationally recognized for its innovative academic programs that combine hands-on learning and personal attention to help students achieve their personal and career goals. With more than 23,000 students hailing from all fifty U.S. states and sixty-five other countries, DePaul combines multiple perspectives, experience-based learning, and small class sizes to give students a practical education for a global marketplace.

Students create the career they want through practical, cutting-edge courses that reflect changing market demand at the School of Computer Science, Telecommunications, and Information Systems (CTI). With 2,000 students, CTI has grown to become one of the nation's largest graduate computer science programs, offering a curriculum that is both broad and deep. Its faculty members are recognized leaders in the field, combining a solid foundation in theory with extensive opportunities for research and application. CTI has forged high-level partnerships in industries ranging from digital cinema and computer animation to network security and information assurance, providing students with the experiences and contacts to succeed.

Distance Learning Program

Students choose from among nine complete master's degree programs as well as a wide range of individual graduate classes online. Nearly ninety Web-based courses are offered each quarter, all in conjunction with courses on campus, giving students a sense of the classroom experience. Requirements are the same for distance learning and on-campus courses and degrees, enabling students to pursue their degree completely online or with a mix of online and classroom-based courses.

Delivery Media

CTI's innovative Course OnLine (COL) system enables students to view the vital components of any live class online. COL captures all of the important events in a class session: what the instructor says, points to, writes on the board, or displays on the projector. The parts are synchronized after class and posted to the Web for the remainder of the quarter. Distance-learning students follow the assignment and exam schedule for the on-campus section of the course but have the flexibility of viewing the weekly lectures at a time that works best for them.

Distance learning courses are integrated into CTI's course-management system, which also contains assignments, grades, course documents, announcements, instructor information, and links to external Web sites. In addition, courses take advantage of asynchronous communication tools, including threaded discussion groups, e-mail, and the live interaction of online chat sessions. Learners interact with other distance learning students as well as on-campus students.

Programs of Study

Nine master's degrees can be completed entirely online: the Master of Arts in information technology and the Master of Science degree in computer, information, and network security; computer science; distributed systems; e-commerce technology; information systems; instructional technology systems; software engineering; and telecommunication systems.

More information about each degree program is available on CTI's Web site at http://www.cti.depaul.edu/admissions/dl/dl_home.asp.

Student Services

Distance learning students can remotely access many vital University services, including online course registration, account management, course grades and history, the help desk, degree planning, academic advising, course evaluations, faculty evaluation history, online exam scheduling, library resources, career services, and the Graduate Student Association.

Credit Options

Students with qualifying experience may be exempted from prerequisite courses. Students should review their education and experience with their faculty adviser to see if they should take an equivalency exam or if they qualify for a course waiver.

Faculty

Distance learning students learn from the same distinguished CTI professors who teach on-campus courses. The school has approximately 80 full-time faculty members and 115 adjunct lecturers who come from distinguished research, academic, and industry backgrounds. They conduct pioneering research and solve real-time problems in a broad array of industries and technical areas.

Admission

The primary criterion in determining eligibility is previous academic achievement. Applicants must possess a bachelor's degree from a regionally accredited institution or be in the final stage of completing the undergraduate degree. They should present a superior academic record for at least the final two years of undergraduate work and preferably for their overall undergraduate experience.

Other factors, such as work experience and career progression, are also considered. There are no additional requirements for admission of distance learning students. An applicant's intent to complete the program via distance learning is not considered in the admission decision.

Tuition and Fees

Graduate tuition for 2006–07 was $575 per quarter hour or $2300 for the average four-credit course. Additional fees may apply. There are no special costs for distance learning. However, distance learning students are responsible for any fees associated with taking exams at another college or university.

Financial Aid

For more information regarding financial aid options, interested students should contact the DePaul Financial Aid Office at 312-362-8091, or visit online at http://www.depaul.edu/financial_aid.

Applying

More information and online applications are available at http://www.cti.depaul.edu/admissions. Students may pay the $25 nonrefundable application fee online at the end of the application process.

CONTACT

School of Computer Science, Telecommunications, and
   Information Systems
DePaul University
243 South Wabash Avenue
Chicago, Illinois 60604

Phone: 312-362-8714
Fax: 312-362-5327
E-mail: ctiadmissions@cti.depaul.edu
Web site: http://www.cti.depaul.edu/admissions/dl/dl_
   home.asp

DEVRY UNIVERSITY

Online Center

Oakbrook Terrace, Illinois

DeVry University provides high-quality, career-oriented associate, bachelor's, and master's degree programs in technology, health-care technology, business, and management. More than 48,000 students are enrolled across eighty-five locations in twenty-four states and Canada. DeVry University is accredited by the Higher Learning Commission and is a member of the North Central Association of Colleges and Schools (NCA). DeVry University, a division of DeVry Inc. (NYSE: DV), is based in Oakbrook Terrace, Illinois. For more information about DeVry University, students should visit http://www.devry.edu.

Distance Learning Program

Distance learning, delivered through DeVry University's Online Center, integrates today's high-tech, Internet-based capabilities with DeVry's proven educational methodologies. The innovative "anytime, anywhere" educational delivery system extends the offering of DeVry programs to students who reside beyond the geographic reach of DeVry locations or whose schedules preclude their attending on site. The result is solid education enhanced by the latest in interactive information technology, which enables students to send messages and receive feedback from instructors as well as participate in various group and team activities with fellow online students. DeVry University Online has more than 8,800 enrolled undergraduate and graduate students.

Delivery Media

Typical distance learning technologies include the undergraduate site (http://www.devry.edu/online) and graduate site (http://online.keller.edu), which are accessible 24 hours a day, seven days a week. DeVry Online offers course syllabi and assignments; a virtual library and other Web-based resources; e-mail, threaded conversations, and chat rooms; text and course materials available through an online bookstore; CD-ROM companion disks; and study notes or instructor lectures for student review.

Programs of Study

DeVry University Online currently offers associate degree programs in accounting technology, health-information technology, and network systems administration. Bachelor degrees are available in business administration, computer information systems, game and simulation programming, information technology, network and communications management, and technical management. DeVry University's graduate-level programs include master's degrees in accounting and financial management, business administration, human resource management, information systems management, network and communications management, project management, and public administration. Graduate certificates are also available for students who wish to develop their expertise in these graduate-level programs without completing a degree or who wish to specialize in one of these areas within their degree program.

Undergraduate students must achieve a cumulative grade point average of at least 2.0 (on a 4.0 scale) and satisfactorily complete all curriculum requirements to graduate. Graduate students must achieve a cumulative grade point average of at least 3.0 as well as fulfill the graduation requirements for their specific programs.

Student Services

In addition to offering high-quality education online, DeVry is committed to providing online students with access to a full range of support services, including admission and registration information, academic advising, and financial aid information. DeVry University maintains an online library with full-text periodical databases and online short courses for self-instruction. DeVry Online staff members are available to assist students with administrative matters as well as with education-related issues. Students can complete all administrative details online, including purchasing books.

Faculty

Instructors for online courses are drawn from DeVry's faculty throughout North America as well as from leading organizations in business and technology, creating a systemwide student-faculty community. To ensure their effective delivery of course material as well as their ability to facilitate relevant and meaningful participation from all class members, faculty members teaching online courses complete specialized instruction to prepare them to teach via this medium. As a result, online students are provided with a comprehensive learning experience that enables them to master course content.

Admission

DeVry University's admission process is streamlined, so students learn quickly whether they have been accepted. Applicants must complete a personal interview with an admissions representative and complete a written application. Applicants should visit DeVry University's Web site for further details (http://www.devry.edu).

For admission to undergraduate programs, specific requirements must be met regarding age, prior education, demonstrated proficiency in the basic and prerequisite skills needed for college-level work in the chosen field of study, and computer literacy. Each undergraduate applicant pays a $50 application fee.

For regular graduate admission, applicants must hold a baccalaureate degree from a U.S. regionally accredited institution (international applicants must hold a degree equivalent to a U.S. baccalaureate degree). Applicants who meet baccalaureate degree requirements and whose undergraduate cumulative grade point average is 2.7 or higher are eligible for admission. Appli-

cants with a cumulative GPA below 2.7 must demonstrate quantitative and verbal skills proficiency in one of several possible standardized tests.

Tuition and Fees

For undergraduate online students attending 14 to 19 credit hours, standard tuition is $7160 per semester. For online students attending 1 to 13 credit hours, tuition is $525 per credit hour. Online students attending more than 19 credit hours are charged the standard tuition rate plus the per-credit-hour rate for each additional credit hour. All new students pay a $50 deposit, which is credited toward the first semester's tuition.

For graduate online students, tuition is $2050 per course. After acceptance into the graduate school, new students pay a $100 deposit, which is credited toward the first term's tuition.

Financial Aid

Federal Stafford Student Loan money is available to graduate students through the Federal Family Education Loan Program (FFELP). Undergraduate students who qualify can take advantage of the five major federal financial aid programs in which DeVry is eligible to participate. Undergraduate students may also qualify for state-funded programs and DeVry scholarships.

CONTACT

DeVry University
One Tower Lane
Oakbrook Terrace, Illinois 60181

Phone: 800-839-9009 (toll-free)
Web site: http://www.devry.edu/online
        http://online.keller.edu

DREXEL UNIVERSITY

Drexel University Online
Philadelphia, Pennsylvania

Founded in 1891, Drexel University is a leader in the integration of technology into academics. Fully accredited by the Middle States Association of Colleges and Secondary Schools, Drexel consists of eleven colleges and schools offering 161 degree programs to approximately 16,000 students. Drexel University has more than 90,000 alumni and 1,000 full-time faculty members. Known as Philadelphia's technological university, Drexel is among the top fifty private, nonprofit, national doctoral/research universities in the United States and is ranked by U.S. News & World Report *as one of "America's Best Colleges for 2007."*

Distance Learning Program

Drexel University Online, a subsidiary of Drexel University, specializes in innovative, Internet-based distance education programs for working professionals in the United States and abroad. A pioneer in online education, Drexel has offered programs online since 1996. Using the same rigorous academic standards (admission criteria, curricula, accreditation, and exams), Drexel's online programs are taught by the same distinguished faculty members and lead to the same high-quality degree as those received on the campus.

Delivery Media

Drexel University's online courses require a student to have a personal computer with an Internet connection and use a Web browser to access the e-learning environment. Course instruction is delivered primarily asynchronously (i.e., where the teacher and learner are not physically at the same place at the same time). Instructional materials come in text, graphics, audio, and video formats and are available online 24/7. Students interact directly with each other and faculty members through e-mail, threaded discussions (online discussion boards), chat, and Web-based whiteboard facilities. All readings, assignments, quizzes, and exams are prespecified, monitored on a continuous basis, and submitted online.

Programs of Study

Drexel's online Bachelor of Science degree programs offered through the College of Nursing include RN-B.S.N. and RN-B.S.N.-M.S.N. programs, which focus on industry-current issues in nursing. In these programs, which are accredited by the National League for Nursing Accrediting Commission (NLNAC) and Commission on Collegiate Nursing Education (CCNE), students arrange to complete clinicals in their area. An RN license is required for admission to the programs. A B.S. in health services administration program is also available.

Bachelor of Science programs are also offered in communication, communications and applied technology, computing technology and security, education, general studies–individualized studies, general studies with a minor in business, and psychology. The programs are designed for adult learners, who can transfer up to 135 out of 180 quarter credits.

Drexel's master's degree online programs offered through the College of Nursing include M.S.N. in contemporary nursing faculty, nursing leadership in health systems management, clinical trials research, acute-care nurse practitioner (NP)*, adult psychiatric–mental health (NP)*, completion program for NPs, and innovation and intraepreneurship/entrepreneurship in advanced nurs-

ing practice. Programs are accredited by the National League for Nursing Accrediting Commission (NLNAC) and the CCNE and prepare nurses to move into managerial or leadership roles in their desired fields. Post-master's certificates are also available.

The MBA Anywhere™* program provides a broadly based management curriculum with available concentrations in marketing, finance, information systems strategy, engineering management, and entrepreneurship. This program optimizes the students' leadership potential in a twenty-four-month, part-time cohort format and is accredited by AACSB International, the highest accreditation for U.S. business schools.

Online master's degrees through Drexel's College of Engineering are available in engineering management, electrical engineering, software engineering, and computer science. Drexel University's College of Engineering is the third-largest private engineering college in the United States, with numerous faculty recognitions, highly ranked programs, and research accomplishments. Its curricula are accredited by the Accreditation Board for Engineering and Technology, Inc. (ABET), the leading authority on educational standards for the engineering and science professions.

Drexel, an internationally recognized center for education and research in all facets of information science and systems, also offers online M.S. degree programs in library and information science and in information systems. The M.S. program in library and information science is a top-ranked, ALA-accredited program that allows students to specialize in management of digital information or information/library services. The M.S. program in information systems features a wide range of courses that cover all stages of systems engineering as a life-cycle process.

Ranked as one of America's Best Graduate Schools for 2007 by *U.S. News & World Report,* Drexel's College of Education offers M.S. degrees in educational administration: collaborative leadership, global and international education, higher education, the science of instruction, and teaching, learning, and curriculum.

The teacher certification program certifies students in elementary education or secondary education in the areas of biology, chemistry, physics, earth and space science, general science, environmental education, and/or mathematics. The certification program can be incorporated into the master's program or can be completed as a stand-alone program.

Add-on certificates available include instructional technology specialist, principal's certification, and teaching English as a second language. These programs incorporate current research on teaching and expose teachers to the latest developments in instructional technology.

Drexel's online M.S. in clinical research organization and management program allows students to earn the experience and knowledge necessary to conduct investigations in the increasingly complex and highly regulated clinical field. A five-course certificate of study is also available.

Programs accompanied by an * require on-campus attendance.

Special Programs

Drexel offers an undergraduate certificate program in retail leadership and medical billing and coding. Graduate nursing certificates are available in clinical trials research, complementary and integrative therapies, contemporary nursing faculty, innovation and intrapreneurship/entrepreneurship in advanced nursing practice, and nursing leadership in health systems management. Additional graduate certificates are available in epidemiology and biostatistics, health-care informatics, engineering management, and toxicology and industrial hygiene.

Student Services

Online students have access to library facilities, career services, individual tutoring, learning resources, the writing center, 24/7 technical support, and more.

Credit Options

Students pursuing bachelor's degree programs may receive transfer credit for previous studies at an accredited college, CLEP exams, portfolio assessment, military training, Skillsoft, and more. The maximum number of transfer credits varies according to the student's program.

Faculty

Drexel has more than 1,000 full-time faculty members—90 percent of whom hold Ph.D.'s. Many of them are distinguished authorities in their fields, including several members of the National Academies of Science and Engineering. Drexel's online programs are taught by the same distinguished faculty members who teach on campus.

Admission

All Drexel online programs run on ten-week quarters beginning in January, March, June, and September, with the exception of the M.S. and certificate in clinical research, which begin three times a year, in January, May, and August. Admissions requirements vary across programs. Students should visit the Web site for specific program information.

Tuition and Fees

Tuition rates vary across programs. Interested students should visit the Web site listed in the Contact section (http://www.drexel.com/petersons) for specific program rates. Students are required to purchase textbooks. There are no application fees.

Financial Aid

Students may apply for scholarships, loans, grants, federal and state aid, and more. Drexel is part of the Servicemembers Opportunity Colleges (SOC) Consortium, welcoming adult students from the military who are using military aid or the Montgomery G.I. Bill benefits to cover their education costs. Deferred tuition payment plans are also available for students receiving reimbursement.

Applying

Application deadlines are typically six weeks before the start of classes. There is no application fee, and applications are accepted on a rolling basis. Students should visit the Web site for more information.

CONTACT

Drexel University Online
Drexel University
3001 Market Street
One Drexel Plaza, Suite 300
Philadelphia, Pennsylvania 19104
Phone: 866-440-1949 (toll-free)
Fax: 215-895-0525
E-mail: info@drexel.com
Web site: http://www.drexel.com/
petersons

EAST CAROLINA UNIVERSITY
Division of Continuing Studies
Greenville, North Carolina

Founded in 1907, East Carolina University (ECU) is the third-largest of the sixteen institutions in the University of North Carolina system and offers baccalaureate, master's, specialist, and doctoral degrees in the liberal arts and sciences and professional fields, including medicine. Fully accredited by the Southern Association of Colleges and Schools, the University's goal is to provide students with a rich and distinctive educational experience. ECU's commitment to providing outstanding off-campus educational opportunities is long-standing; the University offered its first distance education course in 1947. The Division of Continuing Studies provides a portal at http://www.options.ecu.edu to the resources of the University as well as assistance that allows adult learners to choose programs that fit their schedules and academic goals. East Carolina University is constantly evaluating and updating its distance learning programs to take advantage of the latest technology and is committed to meeting the evolving needs of the lifelong learner.

Distance Learning Program

East Carolina University's academic community has developed a diverse offering of distance learning programs in direct response to the needs of students. A number of fully online programs are currently available, with additional programs under development. ECU is committed to providing programs designed to meet the professional needs and demanding schedules of busy, working adults. For more information on the latest offerings, students should visit the Web site for the Division of Continuing Studies, which is listed in the Contact section of this description.

Delivery Media

East Carolina University's Web-based courses are faculty-member created Web sites that contain course materials and interactive tools. Most utilize the Blackboard Course Management System. Faculty members may employ a variety of communication tools within their courses, including threaded discussion groups, small-group work, asynchronous Web based chats, and instant messaging. In addition, faculty members may elect to deliver essential components of their courses via audio and video streaming, by distribution of CDs, or by using desktop videoconferencing technologies.

Programs of Study

Graduate programs are offered in art education (M.A.Ed.), business administration/finance (M.B.A.), business administration/health-care management (M.B.A.), business administration/management information systems (M.B.A.), business administration/security studies (M.B.A.), business education (M.A.Ed.), construction mangement (M.C.M.), criminal justice (M.S.), educational specialist/educational leadership (Ed.S.), English/technical and professional communications (M.A.), health education (M.A. or M.A.Ed.), instructional technology (M.A.Ed. or M.S.), library science (M.L.S.), music education* (M.M.), nursing/clinical nurse specialist (M.S.N.), nursing/family nurse practitioner* (M.S.N.), nursing/nursing leadership* (M.S.N.), nursing/neonatal nurse practitioner* (M.S.N.), nursing/nurse midwifery* (M.S.N.), nursing/nursing education (M.S.N.), nutrition and dietetics (M.S.), occupational safety (M.S.O.S.), psychology* (M.A.), science education (M.A.Ed.), software engineering (M.S.), special education (M.A.Ed.), speech-language pathology* (M.S.), technology systems/computer networking management (M.S.), technology systems/digital communications (M.S.), technology systems/distribution and logistics (M.S.), technology systems/information security (M.S.), technology systems/manufacturing (M.S.), technology systems/performance improvement (M.S.), and vocational education/information technologies (M.S.).

Undergraduate degree completion programs are available in birth–kindergarten education (B.S.), business administration (B.S.B.A.), communication (B.S.), health information management (B.S.), health services management (B.S.), hospitality management (B.S.), industrial technology/bioprocess manufacturing (B.S.), industrial technology/industrial distribution and logistics (B.S.), industrial technology/industrial supervision (B.S.), industrial technology/information and computer technology (B.S.), information technologies (B.S.B.E.), and registered nurse/Bachelor of Science in Nursing (RN/B.S.N.).

Graduate certificates are offered in assistive technology, community college teaching, computer network professional, distance learning, information assurance, multicultural literature, performance improvement, professional communication, security studies, virtual reality in education and training, and Web site developer.

Post-master's nursing certificates can be earned in family nurse practitioner*, neonatal nurse practitioner*, nurse midwifery*, and nursing education.

Add-on teacher licensure programs are offered in driver's education, preschool*, and technology facilitator.

For the programs listed above, the * denotes programs for which some on-campus attendance is required.

Student Services

Distance learners at East Carolina University have access to library services, the campus network, e-mail accounts, the bookstore, registration, and academic advising at a distance. Academic advisers are available by phone, e-mail, fax, and in person to assist students with course selection.

Credit Options

Transfer credit is granted on academic course work within degree-specific limits, and no credit is granted on the basis of professional experience. CLEP course credit may also be available.

Faculty

ECU's approximately 1,300 full-time faculty members, the majority of whom hold terminal degrees, teach both the on-campus and distance-learning courses.

Admission

Before registering for a course, students must first apply and be admitted to ECU. Students may be admitted as degree-seeking or as nondegree/visiting students. Admission for students seeking a degree is based on their previous academic record and standardized test scores. In addition, graduate students are required to submit letters of recommendation.

Tuition and Fees

Undergraduate tuition and technology fees are $94 per semester hour for in-state residents and $450 per semester hour for out-of-state students. Graduate tuition and technology fees are $154 per semester hour for in-state residents and $659 per semester hour for out-of-state students. Graduate business-student tuition and technology fees are $214 per semester hour for in-state residents and $719 per semester hour for out-of-state students. Graduate students taking undergraduate courses are charged graduate tuition. Rates are projected and subject to change without prior written notice.

Financial Aid

Distance learning students are eligible to apply for financial aid and are encouraged to contact the Office of Financial Aid at 252-328-9379, faques@ ecu.edu, or via the Web at http://www. ecu.edu/financial/ for more information.

Applying

Prospective students must submit an application, accompanied by a fee of $50, for admission. Applications can also be obtained online from the Division of Continuing Studies at the Web site listed in the Contact section. While most programs accept students year-round, students are urged to apply early.

CONTACT

Carolyn Dunn
Division of Continuing Studies
404-E Self-Help Center
East Carolina University
Greenville, North Carolina 27858-4353
Phone: 252-328-9218
        800-398-9275 (toll-free)
E-mail: options@ecu.edu
Web site: http://www.options.ecu.edu

EASTERN MICHIGAN UNIVERSITY

EMU-Online and Independent Learning

Ypsilanti, Michigan

Eastern Michigan University (EMU) is a public, comprehensive, metropolitan university that offers programs in the arts, sciences, and professions. Founded in 1849, the University comprises more than 24,000 students, who are served by 680 full-time faculty members as well as 1,200 staff members—on campus, off campus, and electronically. EMU offers undergraduate, graduate, specialist, doctoral, and certificate programs in its Colleges of Arts and Sciences, Business, Education, Health and Human Services, and Technology.

Eastern Michigan University continues to be the largest producer of educational personnel in the United States, including the largest producer of special education personnel, mathematics teachers, and science teachers, and is among the top ten producers of educational administrators. The University is fully accredited by the North Central Association of Colleges and Schools.

Eastern Michigan University's Continuing Education Office offers programs and courses online, at off-campus locations throughout the state, on weekends, in the evenings during the week, and in accelerated formats.

Distance Learning Program

EMU's Distance Education program offers students two convenient distance learning options. First, EMU's online courses allow students to attend class when it's convenient for their busy schedule—early in the morning, during the weekend, or even at 2 a.m. Whether students live just 5 or 500 miles from EMU's campus, they are able to learn conveniently, using a computer from their home, office, hotel room, military base, or "virtually" any other location in the world. Second, Independent Learning courses allow students to enroll anytime, learn at their own pace, avoid commuting and parking inconveniences, satisfy general education requirements, and submit course work via Internet, fax, or U.S. mail.

Delivery Media

Courses are delivered via World Wide Web, videotapes and DVDs, and print. Students may interact via e-mail, World Wide Web, mail, telephone, or fax.

Programs of Study

EMU-Online offers the Master of Arts in educational media and technology; Master of Science in earth science education; Master of Science in engineering management; Master of Science in human nutrition; Master of Science in human nutrition through the Coordinated Program in Dietetics (CPD); Master of Science in integrated marketing communications; Master of Science in quality management; Bachelor of Science in applied technology (degree-completion program); Bachelor of Science in dietetics (CPD); Bachelor of Science in technology management (degree-completion program); graduate certificate in educational media and technology; graduate certificate in geographic information systems (GIS) for educators; and graduate certificate in human resource management.

Special Programs

Prior Learning and Portfolio Development is offered to students seeking credit for prior learning through portfolio assessment. A free workshop helps students identify competencies and document experience to create a portfolio to present for assessment by faculty members in appropriate departments.

Student Services

Distance learners can complete their online education entirely via the Internet. Registration, book buying, discussions, homework assignments, library services, and exams are all available at the click of a computer mouse.

Credit Options

Students may transfer credits from another institution or may earn credits through examinations, portfolio assessment, military training, or business training.

Faculty

More than 200 faculty members from EMU's academic departments currently teach online, and Independent Learning courses at EMU.

Admission

Students may register by World Wide Web, mail, fax, and e-mail and in person.

Tuition and Fees

Out-of-state students can take EMU-Online courses at in-state tuition rates. In 2006–07, per-credit-hour rates for Michigan and Ohio residents were $194.50 for all levels (100–400) of undergraduate courses, $340.50 for lower-level (500–600) graduate courses, and $391.75 for upper-level (700–999) graduate courses.

A registration fee of $40 per semester and a general fee of $21 per credit hour are also assessed. Other fees include $110 for late registration, $10 per credit hour for technology, $27 for payment plan (for fall/winter only), $33 per month for late payments, and $20 for returned checks and declined charge cards. Program support fees also apply and vary by program. In addition to tuition and other applicable fees, online students are assessed an additional $40-per-credit-hour program fee. For specific continuing education program fees, candidates should visit http://www.emich.edu/controller/sbs/tutfee.htm.

All tuition and fees are subject to change by action of the EMU Board of Regents without prior notice and at any time.

Financial Aid

For financial aid information, students should visit http://www.emich.edu/finaid/ or call 734-487-0455.

Applying

For information on undergraduate admissions, prospective students should visit http://www.emich.edu/admissions or call 800-GO-TO-EMU (toll-free).

Each graduate program has its own requirements for admissions. Students should contact the graduate coordinator in their department of interest to determine which of these are required. For more information, students should call 800-GO-TO-EMU (toll-free).

CONTACT

EMU-Online and Independent Learning
Continuing Education
Eastern Michigan University
101 Boone Hall
Ypsilanti, Michigan 48197

Phone: 800-777-3521 (toll-free)
E-mail: distance.education@emich.edu
Web site: http://www.emuonline.edu
http://www.ce.emich.edu

EXCELSIOR COLLEGE
Learning Services
Albany, New York

As a private institution with no residency requirement, Excelsior College—an accredited leader in distance education—has devoted itself to making college degrees more accessible to busy, working adults. Top-ranked by U.S. News & World Report for transfer students, the College accepts credits from a broad array of sources, including Excelsior College distance courses and Excelsior College Exams. As a result, many students find that most or all of their prior college-level credits transfer into their Excelsior College degree program.

Excelsior College offers associate, bachelor's, master's, and certificate programs in liberal arts (including criminal justice), business, health science and technology, and nursing. The College's self-paced degree programs are accessible worldwide, allowing students to complete their degrees from any location.

Excelsior College is accredited by the Commission on Higher Education of the Middle States Association of Colleges and Schools, 3624 Market Street, Philadelphia, Pennsylvania 19104; telephone: 215-662-5606. All of the College's academic programs are registered (i.e., approved) by the New York State Education Department, and its examinations are recognized by the American Council on Education, Center for Adult Learning and Educational Credentials, for the award of college-level credit.

The associate, baccalaureate, and master's degree programs in nursing are accredited by the National League for Nursing Accrediting Commission (NLNAC), 61 Broadway, New York, New York 10006; telephone 800-669-1656 (toll-free). The NLNAC is a specialized accrediting agency recognized by the U.S. Secretary of Education. The baccalaureate degree programs in electronics engineering technology and nuclear engineering technology are accredited by the Technology Accreditation Commission (TAC) of the Accreditation Board for Engineering and Technology (ABET) 111 Market Place, Baltimore, Maryland 21202; telephone: 410-347-7700. The TAC of ABET is a specialized accrediting agency recognized by the U.S. Secretary of Education.

Distance Learning Program

Excelsior College programs are designed to help busy adults pursue their degree at a distance through whatever combination of courses, exams, and training fits their situation. The College accepts credits from Excelsior College Courses and Excelsior College Examinations; classroom and distance courses from other accredited colleges and universities; other college-level proficiency examinations, such as CLEP and DANTES; and military, academy, and corporate training recognized for college credit by the American Council on Education (ACE), Center for Adult Learning and Educational Credentials, National Program on Noncollegiate

Sponsored Instruction (PONSI), or training evaluated for college credit by Excelsior College.

Currently, the College has more than 27,000 students enrolled in its associate, baccalaureate, and master's degree programs and has more than 115,000 graduates worldwide.

Programs of Study

Excelsior College offers thirty-four degree programs through distinct schools in three major areas.

In the School of Business and Technology, twelve undergraduate business programs lead to degrees in such fields as accounting, finance, global business,

management information systems, management of human resources, marketing, operations management, and risk management and insurance. The College also offers both a Master of Business Administration (M.B.A.) program and a certificate in entrepreneurship that can be completed entirely at a distance. The GMAT is not required for the M.B.A. A dozen undergraduate technology degree programs educate students in fields such as computer technology, electronics engineering technology, electronics technology, information technology, nuclear engineering technology, and nuclear technology. The College awards college credit for approved industry training in several fields, including fossil fuel plant technology, information technology, and nuclear power.

Students in the School of Liberal Arts can earn associate or baccalaureate degrees in majors that include biology, chemistry, communication, criminal justice, economics, geography, geology, history, literature, mathematics, music, philosophy, physics, political science, psychology, sociology, or world language and literature. In addition, a liberal studies option provides flexibility for students to pursue a range of interests while focusing on a particular discipline. The School offers two associate and two baccalaureate degrees, a certificate in homeland security, and a Master of Arts in liberal studies that can be earned entirely online. Master's students can now focus studies to match their interests and career goals by choosing one of five new tracks: Issues in Today's Society, Global Strategies, Educational Leadership, Natural Science and Society, and Self-Design. The Graduate Record Examinations (GRE) are not required.

The School of Nursing is an NLN Center of Excellence and one of the largest distance education nursing programs in the world. The nursing components of the associate degree programs are made up of guided independent study and nationally recognized Excelsior College Examinations. The nursing component of the bachelor's degree comprises 30 transfer credits (validated by successful completion of the NCLEX-RN), Excelsior College courses, and Excelsior College Examinations. Students can earn credit for General Education requirements through of wide variety of sources.

Excelsior College offers an online Master of Science degree in nursing, with specializations in clinical systems management and nursing education, plus an RN-M.S. in nursing program.

The new School of Health Sciences expands the College's offerings in health care with online certificate programs in end-of-life care, health-care informatics, and nursing management. The Bachelor of Science in health sciences, available to students with at least 20 undergraduate credits in the health sciences, offers concentrations in end-of-life care, gerontology, health education, and management.

Special Programs
Through its Office of Military Education, Excelsior College has addressed educational needs of the members of the U.S. armed forces. The College awards credit for military training recognized for college credit by the American Council on Education. Four programs, including associate degrees in aviation, technical studies, and administrative/management studies, are specially designed to meet the needs of military personnel. DANTES-funded Excelsior College Examinations are free to all in active duty military, National Guard, and Reserve Component personnel. Special discounted fees and tuition are available to military personnel, military family members, veterans, and DoD civilians. Special partnerships allow active duty personnel to take Excelsior College distance courses that may be 100 percent covered by military tuition assistance. A college military deployment policy holds the status of deployed students without extension or penalty fees until their return.

Student Services
Excelsior College students draw on a team of experienced academic advisers who assist in the development of individualized degree completion plans.

Enrolled students can use Excelsior College Course Search, a searchable database of distance courses and examinations, to find credit sources to meet their degree requirements. It is the most comprehensive database of such offerings available today.

Students take advantage of a variety of online services through a customized Web user account, including paying bills online and viewing billing transactions, viewing transcript and graduation status, viewing course and exam registration status, and utilizing resources for career development, job hunting, resume writing, and other opportunities.

The Excelsior College Virtual Library gives students online access to millions of the world's most current and authoritative resources. The Electronic Peer Network (EPN) provides a Web-based community where students can join online study groups and buy and sell textbooks, among other things. For those who seek help as they study for Excelsior College Exams, the Online Writing and Online Tutoring Services connect students to experienced tutors and to select online practice exams.

Tuition and Fees
Undergraduate tuition for Excelsior College distance courses is $275 per credit hour. Excelsior College charges an $895 (associate programs) or $995 (baccalaureate programs) fee at enrollment, which covers a student's initial evaluation, academic advisement, and program planning services for one year; a $450 (associate) or $515 (baccalaureate) annual fee for each year after, which covers the ongoing evaluation of academic records submitted by a student; and a $465 to $490 (associate) or $495 (baccalaureate) fee for a final evaluation and verification of all academic records prior to program completion and graduation. Different fees and fee structures apply to military students and graduate programs. Students can choose to pay their Excelsior College enrollment and annual service expenses, tuition, and exams fees through special payment plans. Complete details can be found on the Excelsior College Web site.

Financial Aid
Excelsior College offers more than fifteen options for financing a degree, including ten scholarship and five private loan programs. Veterans Affairs educational benefits and New York State financial aid programs are also available. Excelsior College offers several flexible payment plan options that allow students to spread the cost of fees and tuition over several installments.

Applying
Students apply to the degree program of their choice, then receive an unofficial evaluation of how prior credit may apply to their degree program. They then enroll as a matriculated student. Application and enrollment are available online, by mail, or by fax.

CONTACT
Admissions Office
Excelsior College
7 Columbia Circle
Albany, New York 12203
Phone: 518-464-8500 (press 2-7 at the prompt)
888-647-2388 (toll-free)
E-mail: leads@excelsior.edu
Web site: http://www.excelsior.edu

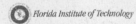

FLORIDA INSTITUTE OF TECHNOLOGY

University College–Distance Learning Division– Virtual Campus

Melbourne, Florida

Florida Institute of Technology is an accredited, coeducational, independently controlled and supported university. It is committed to the pursuit of excellence in teaching and research in the sciences, engineering, technology, business, and related disciplines as well as to providing the challenges that motivate students to reach their full academic and professional potential. Today, more than 4,700 students are enrolled, with more than 3,300 students on the Melbourne campus and the others at Florida Tech's off-campus sites. All of the off-campus students and more than 1,000 on-campus students are enrolled in graduate programs. Florida Tech offers 140 degree programs in science and engineering, aviation, business, education, humanities, psychology, and communication. Doctoral degrees are offered in twenty disciplines, while more than sixty master's degrees are offered. The university is organized into six academic units: the College of Aeronautics, College of Business, College of Engineering, College of Psychology and Liberal Arts, College of Science, and University College, which encompasses the Distance Learning and Extended Studies Divisions.

Distance Learning Program

University College is an extraordinary collaboration between business, government, and academia—all with the intent to further advance Florida Tech's national and international reputation as an educational leader across all disciplines. An integral part of Florida Tech, University College consists of five divisions: Extended Studies, Distance Learning, Florida Tech Consulting, Professional Development, and Applied Research.

The mission of University College is to prepare working professionals for rewarding and productive careers in a work environment that is driven by rapidly changing technology. Steeped in value and excellence, University College seeks to provide the best in academics, training, and research addressing today's dynamic global economy. Guided by steadfast values and beliefs, the faculty and staff of University College believe that learning is a lifelong process that need not be constrained by time or place. Learning is a cooperative process involving the joint responsibility of both students and teachers. These goals are achievable because of University College's highly defined capabilities. Academic offerings include graduate degree and certificate programs at ten U.S. sites

in five East Coast states, as well as a well-established distance learning program with online classes taught via the Virtual Campus. Over 16,000 master's degrees have been awarded to candidates representing the military services, federal and local government, and a wide variety of business and industry sectors.

Delivery Media

With Blackboard as the learning management system, courses are offered via the Internet. Text information is supported by audio and video clips. Interaction between instructors and students is provided through e-mail, synchronous chats, and asynchronous threaded discussions.

Programs of Study

Degrees offered online include the Professional Master of Business Administration (PMBA), with concentrations in acquisition and contract management, e-business, human resource management, and information systems; the Master of Public Administration (M.P.A.); and the Master of Science (M.S.) in acquisition and contract management, computer information systems, human resources management, logistics management, management (with concen-

trations in acquisition and contract management, e-business, human resources management, information systems, logistics management, and transportation management), materiel acquisition management, systems management (with concentration in operations research), project management (with concentrations in information systems and operations research), and operations research.

Programs require a set of core requirements and a set of electives, with some programs and courses requiring the completion of specific prerequisites prior to enrollment. All courses are 3 semester hours.

Additional information about Florida Tech's academic and admission policies may be found at http://uc.fit.edu/dl/ academics/academic_policies.html and http://uc.fit.edu/dl/admissions/index. html. Course prerequisites are available in the University College catalog at http:// uc.fit.edu/pdf/catalog/0607Catalog.pdf.

Graduate certificate programs are offered online in the following areas of study: business management, contract management, e-business, human resources management, information systems management, logistics, materiel acquisition management, program management, quality management, systems management, and transportation management. Each certificate program requires the completion of five 3-hour courses.

Student Services

Florida Tech's Library Information Network (LINK) and its many valuable resources and features are provided via remote access through http://www.lib.fit. edu. Access is granted to registered students via a personal identification number and password for certain restricted databases.

Academic advising for distance learning students is provided through e-mail, fax, or telephone contact on a request basis.

All students are eligible to use the university's career placement services.

Credit Options

If the courses constitute a logical part of the student's program, up to a maximum of 12 semester hours of transfer credit from regionally accredited institutions may be transferred to Florida Tech (for one master's degree only), under certain conditions. For details, students should see http://uc.fit.edu/dl/academics/academic_policies.html. Transfer credit from foreign universities is considered on a case-by-case basis, subject to certain limitations. The same rules apply as given above.

Some courses presented by certain military schools, plus the resident courses of the U.S. Army Command and General Staff College, Fort Leavenworth, Kansas, have been evaluated by Florida Tech, and specific courses have been found acceptable for transfer to designated degree programs without charge to the student. Information about the specific courses found acceptable and the Florida Tech equivalents is available from University College in Melbourne.

Faculty

The faculty members of University College have a passion for educating. Each day, they make an impact. Their choice for a career in higher education is one of dedication and determination, allowing them to share their passion and excitement for teaching. Faculty members are aware that their adult learners, no matter where they are employed, come to Florida Tech expecting a cutting-edge education because they must have up-to-date information in order to compete in a knowledge-based environment. Teaching at Florida Tech is an exciting adventure because they are working with willing minds in a quest to do more and to be better than ever before. The synergistic partnership between students and teachers leaves both parties with a well-deserved sense of achievement.

Admission

Admission to graduate study is granted to qualified applicants. Successful applicants for the master's degree will have received a bachelor's degree from a regionally accredited institution or its equivalent internationally. As a general rule, an undergraduate cumulative grade point average (GPA) of at least 3.0 is required for regular admission. Individual academic units may have higher minimum standards. For further details, students should visit http://uc.fit.edu/dl/admissions/index.html.

Tuition and Fees

For the latest information about tuition and fees policies, students should refer to the university's Web site at http://uc.fit.edu/dl/academics/tuition.html.

Financial Aid

As a general rule, a graduate student must be enrolled half-time (at least 5 credit hours per term) as a regular student in a degree program and must be a U.S. citizen or an eligible noncitizen to qualify for federal and/or state financial aid. Financial aid forms are available through the University's Office of Financial Aid.

Applying

Application information is available online at http://uc.fit.edu/dl/admissions/index.html. Applicants must sign and mail an affidavit attesting to the accuracy of the application to the university's Graduate Admission Office. Official transcripts are required from all colleges and universities attended. Students may begin the online application process anytime at https://ssb-p.adm.fit.edu/.

CONTACT

University College
Distance Learning Division–Virtual Campus
Florida Institute of Technology
150 West University Boulevard
Melbourne, Florida 32901

Phone: 888-225-2239 (toll-free in the U.S.)
Fax: 864-226-2258
E-mail: pvassar@fit.edu
       uc@fit.edu
Web site: http://uc.fit.edu/dl

FRANKLIN UNIVERSITY
The Virtu@l Campus®
Columbus, Ohio

Franklin University's primary objective is to provide services and programs for students who work full- or part-time. Franklin is focused on providing students with a supportive environment that allows achievement of goals and provides a practical education with immediate application in the workplace. Students learn from professionals who practice what they teach, are accessible, have a wealth of experience, and exhibit a true commitment to teaching and learning. Franklin University is an independent, nonprofit institution that celebrated its 100th anniversary in 2002. It has offered online courses since 1996 and currently offers sixteen undergraduate majors as well as an online Vantage M.B.A.® Program through its Virtu@l Campus®. In 1998, the University unveiled the Community College Alliance (CCA) Program, which encourages community college graduates to obtain a bachelor's degree by combining on-campus classes at their community colleges with online classes through Franklin. In addition, Franklin was chosen as one of the initial institutions partnering with the U.S. Army to offer online learning opportunities for soldiers through the eArmyU Program and has served more than 1,500 students to date through the Virtu@l Campus®.

Distance Learning Program
Franklin University has a total distance education enrollment of nearly 4,000 students, an online Vantage M.B.A.® Program enrollment of over 200 students, and an eArmyU enrollment of nearly 600.

Delivery Media
Students in Franklin's Virtu@l Campus® access courses, programs, and student services via the Internet. All of Franklin's Virtu@l Campus® classes are designed to incorporate electronic communication tools that include chat rooms, bulletin boards, whiteboards, e-mail, and a grade book that can be accessed by students and faculty members online.

The Balanced Learning Format (BLF) course design and delivery format provides students with a wide range of offerings to meet their learning needs and busy schedules. With three-, six-, twelve-, and fifteen-week course lengths, new classes start every few weeks. The BLF allows students to anticipate consistent time commitments from week to week and from class to class. Franklin University uses a team of instructional

designers, faculty members, and developers to create courses. This guarantees students consistent course outcomes, experiential learning, and consistent grading criteria.

Programs of Study
Franklin serves degree-seeking candidates, students who want to continue their education, and those who are interested in experiencing online learning. Franklin's Virtu@l Campus® offers fifteen undergraduate programs and one graduate degree program, the Vantage Master of Business Administration® (M.B.A.). The online Vantage M.B.A.® Program is a seventeen-month program consisting of six-week courses and two 3-day, high-intensity learning residencies. Admitted students can enter the M.B.A. program at multiple points along the academic calendar. The online graduate program enables students to continue their careers, balance family and social commitments, and still reach their educational goals.

Sixteen bachelor's degree completion majors are offered online: accounting, applied management, business administration, business forensics, computer science, eMarketing, financial management, forensic accounting, health-care management, human resources management, information technology, management, management information sciences (MIS), marketing, public safety management, and Web development.

Franklin University continually updates its programs and schedules to stay current with industry trends and the ever-changing job market.

Student Services
Through Franklin University's student-centered approach, each student is matched with a Student Services Associate (SSA) who, along with the course faculty members, becomes an important contact at the University. SSAs serve as both an initial and long-term resource, working from initial application through graduation.

The Community College Alliance (CCA) program is an educational alliance with more than 240 two-year colleges in thirty-two states. The CCA enables community college graduates, or those with equivalent credit, to earn a bachelor's degree from Franklin without leaving their community. Students complete their degrees through a combination of on-site courses at the community college and online courses through Franklin. For more information, students may visit the program's Web site at http://alliance.franklin.edu.

Credit Options
Franklin University has a credit transfer policy that is more student-friendly than those at most other institutions. More than 75 percent of Franklin students have transferred credit from other colleges and universities. Students also can earn credit outside the classroom through the College-Level

Examination Program (CLEP), Franklin University Proficiency Exams (FUPE), and Prior Learning Portfolios.

Faculty

Franklin faculty members enrich the virtual classroom with special talents and abilities drawn from successful careers in business, industry, government, and social service. Franklin University faculty members are working professionals who provide both excellence in teaching and real-world experience.

Admission

Admission to the Franklin M.B.A. program is based on the following selection criteria: a baccalaureate degree from a regionally accredited college or university, a minimum of three years of full-time work experience, a minimum cumulative undergraduate GPA of 2.75

on a 4.0 scale (GMAT scores are considered if the GPA is below 2.75), and a score of 550 (paper-based) or 213 (computer-based) or better on the Test of English as a Foreign Language (TOEFL).

To apply transfer credits from another institution, all official transcripts should be directly forwarded to Franklin University from the previous institution(s); however, a student can begin a distance learning course before the transcripts have been received.

Tuition and Fees

For the 2007–08 academic year, tuition for undergraduate online courses from Franklin University is $266 per credit hour for standard courses and $318 per credit hour for computer science, MIS, and information technology courses. For online Vantage M.B.A.® Program courses, tuition is $413 per credit hour.

Financial Aid

Franklin offers a variety of financial aid options, including a deferred-payment plan for students whose employers offer a tuition reimbursement program. More than 75 percent of Franklin students receive some type of financial assistance through grants, scholarships, loans, employer tuition reimbursement, and student employment. Franklin University awards approximately 250 scholarships every year to new and current students.

Applying

Anyone who is a graduate of an accredited high school or has passed the GED test is eligible for admission as a degree-seeking undergraduate student. Those seeking a bachelor's degree must complete an admission application and forward an official high school transcript or an official GED test score report to Franklin.

CONTACT

Franklin University Virtu@l Campus®
201 South Grant Avenue
Columbus, Ohio 43215

Phone: 877-341-6300 (toll-free)
E-mail: info@franklin.edu
Web site: http://www.franklin.edu

GEORGIA INSTITUTE OF TECHNOLOGY

Center for Distance Learning
Atlanta, Georgia

Founded in 1885, the Georgia Institute of Technology is the Southeast's largest technological institution. Georgia Tech is located on a 330-acre campus near downtown Atlanta—the financial, communications, and cultural hub of the Southeast. The Institute's mission is to be a leader among those few technological universities whose alumni, faculty, students, and staff define, expand, and communicate the frontiers of knowledge and innovation.

U.S. News & World Report consistently lists Georgia Tech among the fifty best universities in the nation. Georgia Tech also makes their list of the top graduate engineering programs in the country. Eight of the engineering options were ranked in the top ten, with four in the top five.

In addition to its high-quality undergraduate and graduate instructional programs, Tech has a world-class research program, with $435 million in new grants and contracts awarded during the 2006 fiscal year. This ranks Tech as the South's number one public institution in engineering research.

Distance Learning Program

Georgia Tech's Center for Distance Learning serves more than 600 distance learning students and is housed within a unit that reports directly to the provost. Georgia Tech is accredited by the Southern Association of Colleges and Schools. Engineering disciplines are accredited by the Accrediting Board for Engineering and Technology, Inc.

Delivery Media

Video cameras record instructor presentations and student-instructor interaction during regular Georgia Tech graduate classes. The captured lectures are encoded and placed on a video-on-demand server and made available to off-campus students, who take courses without having to come to the campus. Selected courses are available at some locations via videoconferencing, satellite, Web-casting, and the Internet. Students enrolled in the program communicate with their Georgia Tech professor by telephone, fax, and/or e-mail. Students have access to the Georgia Tech Electronic Library and the computer system via a business or home computer and an Internet connection. Access is also provided over the Internet. Every student is expected to have access to a high-

quality computer with a printer and Internet access. (High-speed connection is highly recommended.)

Programs of Study

The Georgia Tech video-based distance delivery program provides high-quality graduate-level courses that can be applied to several master's degree programs. The School of Aerospace Engineering offers two master's degrees, the Master of Science in Aerospace Engineering (M.S.A.E.) and the Master of Science (M.S.). The M.S.A.E is generally referred to as a designated degree, while the M.S. is referred to as an undesignated degree. The difference between the two degree programs is that the designated degree program includes the completion of all academic course work required for a Bachelor of Science in Aerospace Engineering degree. The Master of Science in Electrical and Computer Engineering is offered with options in computer engineering, digital signal processing, power, and telecommunications; all options require 30 hours of course work. The M.S. and the Master of Science in Environmental Engineering (M.S.Env.E.) degrees are offered with concentrations in water quality, surface and subsurface systems, hazardous and solid waste, and air qual-

ity; all programs require 30 hours of course work or the equivalent. The Master of Science in Industrial Engineering is offered with specializations in automation, production and logistics systems, and statistical process control and quality assurance; it requires 30 hours of course work and students must hold an undergraduate degree from an ABET-accredited engineering curriculum. The Master of Science in Operations Research (M.S.O.R.) is a program for students who likely have a background in engineering, mathematics, the physical sciences, or computer science. The Master of Science in Mechanical Engineering is offered with specializations in thermal science and mechanical systems; it requires 30 hours of course work. The Master of Science in Medical Physics (M.S.M.P.) degree program is intended to prepare students with a bachelor's degree in science or engineering for productive careers as medical physicists. Students have the choice of a thesis or a nonthesis option in the medical physics curriculum. Both options include seven required courses (21 credit hours) and a clinical rotation (3 credit hours). The thesis option includes an additional 6 credit hours for the preparation of a thesis and the elective for a total of 33 credit hours.

The Master of Science degree in building construction and integrated facility management requires 36 semester hours. Students can choose either the thesis option or the nonthesis option. The thesis option is 18 hours of required courses in addition to two elective courses and a master's thesis. The nonthesis option is 18 hours of required courses and 18 hours of professional electives. The course emphasis is on professional trends, environmental and safety concerns, planning and project management, real estate and facility maintenance and management, and financial topics.

Specific information on admission and degree requirements can be obtained by calling the academic coordinators for each area. Students should call the contact name for additional information.

Special Programs

Georgia Tech offers every graduate-level credit course in all of the above listed disciplines via video-on-demand download via the Internet. This new system enables qualified students around the world to earn a Georgia Tech master's degree completely online.

All Georgia Tech online graduate courses use state-of-the-art streaming audio and video technologies synchronized with slides, simulations, and other multimedia and make maximum use of the pedagogical advantages offered by Web-based courseware and instruction. Further information about these new online degree programs is available at the Georgia Tech Center for Distance Learning Web site at the address listed in the Contact section.

A Certificate in Manufacturing provides students with the fundamentals in support of education and research in manufacturing. Each student pursuing the certificate develops knowledge and skills in a particular discipline coupled with a general knowledge of the entire manufacturing enterprise and an ability to work well as a member of a team. The certificate emphasizes the philosophy that it is not possible to educate engineers, managers, or scientists in all aspects of manufacturing. Accordingly, the program is structured to broaden and enhance the education of students who are enrolled in traditional academic disciplines. The program encourages students to develop knowledge in multiple disciplines from class work and experiences in multidisciplinary team activities. Thus, the program balances technical depth with a broad exposure and comprehension of the realistic problems and solution methodologies that are faced by manufacturing industries every day. The Certificate in Manufacturing is obtained as part of a graduate degree program (M.S. or Ph.D.) from the Georgia Institute of Technology. Students must complete a graduate degree to obtain the certificate. The certificate program consists of a set of key courses that are fundamental to manufacturing, from which the students select 12 semester hours. Students are also required to attend seminars.

Credit Options

Students earn credit toward their degree by registering for and completing courses online. Requirements for each course are the same as for on-campus students enrolled in the course. A student may receive transfer credit of up to 6 hours for graduate-level courses (approved by the academic adviser) taken at an accredited institution in the United States or Canada and not used for credit toward another degree.

Faculty

There are 940 full-time faculty members at Georgia Tech. Of these, 96 percent hold doctoral degrees. Sixteen percent, or 150 faculty members, teach in the Distance Learning Program.

Admission

Admission requirements vary among the academic disciplines. To apply, individuals should contact the academic adviser or admissions office in the School to which he or she is applying.

Tuition and Fees

Tuition for in-state and out-of-state students for the 2006–07 academic year was $801 per credit hour. Fees are subject to change each year. Students were assessed a technology fee of $100 per semester; students must also purchase their own textbooks and software.

Financial Aid

There are financial aid programs available through Georgia Tech for distance learning students. Most employers have programs that will help students pay the course fees. The Department of Veterans Affairs has approved the Georgia Tech Video Program as independent study. Georgia Tech has a memorandum of understanding with DANTES and with the Air Force.

Applying

Application materials can be obtained from the School to which the student is applying. Applicants must submit an Application for Admission, three letters of recommendation, a biographical sketch, two official transcripts of all previous college work, and scores from the Graduate Record Examinations (GRE). Decisions are made by the individual Schools.

CONTACT

Student Support Services Manager
Center for Distance Learning
Georgia Institute of Technology
Atlanta, Georgia 30308-1031

Phone: 404-894-3378
Fax: 404-894-8924
Web site: http://www.cdl.gatech.edu/

GRANTHAM UNIVERSITY

The College of Computer Science and Engineering Technology
The Mark Skousen School of Business
The College of Arts and Sciences

Kansas City, Missouri

Established in 1951, Grantham University, with 10,000 active students, is a private institution that specializes in educating the working adult student. Grantham's mission is to level the playing field by making a high-quality college education available to adult learners, based on the combined academic and economic principles of accessibility, affordability, and academic accountability. Since 1951, Grantham has contributed to the formal education of thousands of working adults. Students from each of the fifty states and many countries around the world have discovered the benefits and convenience of the Grantham distance education model.

Grantham University has designed its degree programs to meet the needs of busy working adults. Students can complete their course work at the times and places that fit their busy schedules.

Grantham University is accredited by the Accrediting Commission of the Distance Education and Training Council, 1601 18th Street NW, Washington, D.C. 20009 (http://www.detc.org).

Distance Learning Program

Grantham University's degree programs are offered through distance education, or e-learning, formats. Its programs are 100 percent online and do not require on-campus or in-classroom attendance. Grantham's students are not required to log on to the Internet on specific days or at specific times. Students enjoy self-paced, self-directed methods of study and course completion. This unique method of learning is advantageous for those students with full-time jobs or who have family or other commitments that do not allow them to participate in a regular classroom environment.

Other students who are attracted to Grantham University are those who travel extensively or find that the nearest college or university may be hundreds of miles away. Grantham University also attracts thousands of military students who appreciate the benefit of being able to complete classes from almost anywhere in the world. Grantham's military students never have to worry about frequent deployments or transfers, because they can take their course work with them and complete it when and where it is convenient.

Grantham offers both undergraduate and graduate degree programs. All of Grantham University's degree programs include an emphasis on both theory and applications, and each program also incorporates general studies courses designed to help students learn to communicate clearly, formulate and analyze problems, and develop well-thought-out solutions.

Delivery Media

Grantham utilizes the latest technologies to deliver courses electronically to students worldwide. Students have access to course materials, announcements, e-mails, and grades through Grantham's online student information system. Online testing and grading provides students with immediate results to ensure that they can work at their own pace. New students are required to take DE-100, a course designed to help them understand Grantham's distance learning model and to inform them of the wide array of services offered by Grantham.

Programs of Study

Associate and bachelor's degree programs are offered in business administration, computer engineering technology, computer science, criminal justice, electronics engineering technology, general studies (business, economics, English, the humanities, physical sciences, and social sciences), and interdisciplinary studies.

Master of Business Administration and Master of Science degree programs are offered in information management-project management and information technology.

A student is given eight weeks to complete each course, but can accelerate course completion based on study habits and time devoted to the material.

Students must complete 60 credit hours for an associate degree, of which, 15 credit hours must be completed with Grantham. The bachelor's programs require 120–125 credit hours, of which 30 credit hours must be completed with Grantham. The master's degree programs require 36 credit hours of which 27 credit hours must be completed with Grantham.

Credit Options

Grantham University makes every effort to apply college credit for military training and previous course work whenever possible. CLEP testing, DSST exams, and Grantham Challenge tests along with military and work-related training courses may be eligible for transfer credit. More information about transfer of credit is available on Grantham's Web site.

Faculty

Grantham's faculty, administration, and advisers comprise educators, business executives, industry professionals, and entrepreneurs. Among them are Mr. D. Bruce Merrifield, former Assistant Secretary of Commerce under President Reagan and an endowed chair at the Wharton School of the University of Pennsylvania; Dr. Herbert I. London, founder, endowed chair, and former Dean of Students at New York University's Gallatin School of Individualized Study, and Dr. Mark Skousen, economist, financial adviser, author, and economics professor at Columbia University's Barnard College.

Admission

Students wishing to apply to Grantham must have earned a high school diploma or GED equivalent. Applicants with high school or previous education in another country and who do not reside in the United States, the United Kingdom, or Canada must demonstrate English-language proficiency. A minimum score of 500 on the Test of English as a Foreign Language (TOEFL) is required for admission.

Tuition and Fees

Grantham University's tuition rates include all courses, required textbooks, course guides, software, and postage for each semester (North America and APO/FPO only). Interested students should contact the Admissions Department or visit http://www.grantham.edu for current tuition rates and fees.

Financial Aid

Grantham University offers its students financing options through SLM Financial Corporation, a Sallie Mae company, and Education One, a Chase company. Prospective students who require financing for tuition and fees may e-mail contact Grantham's Admissions Department for more information about applying for these student loans.

Grantham University provides scholarships for active duty military service members, National Guard members, Reservists, veterans, military family members, and law enforcement professionals.

Applying

Students may apply to Grantham at any time. Grantham University offers continuous enrollment. Students may apply 24 hours a day, 365 days a year using the school's online enrollment services.

CONTACT

Admissions Department
Grantham University
7200 Northwest 86th Street
Kansas City, Missouri 64153

Phone: 800-955-2527 (toll-free)
Fax: 816-595-5757
E-mail: admissions@grantham.edu
Web site: http://www.grantham.edu

INDIANA STATE UNIVERSITY
Distance Learning Program
Terre Haute, Indiana

Indiana State University is a medium-sized, comprehensive university accredited by the North Central Association of Colleges and Schools. Founded in 1865, the University has grown to serve a student population of approximately 11,000, including students from throughout the United States and sixty-one other countries.

Attention to and concern for the individual is reflected in the institution's offerings. Flexible and responsive programs are designed to facilitate student attainment of academic, vocational, and personal goals. Classes are designed to meet the needs of full-time and part-time students.

In addition to offering distance programs and courses, the University offers undergraduate and graduate programs in more than 100 areas of study on the Indiana State University campus in Terre Haute, Indiana.

Distance Learning Program

Indiana State University (ISU) has offered distance learning since 1969. Many courses and programs can be completed entirely via distance learning; others require minimal campus visits. All distance programs are available in Indiana. Numerous programs and courses can be completed by out-of-state and international students. More than 1,000 students enroll in ISU distance learning courses each semester.

Delivery Media

Courses are offered primarily via the Internet. Selected courses are offered via print-based correspondence, DVD, and live television (available at selected receive sites). Television courses offer live, two-way interaction among students and the instructor. Students enrolled in correspondence courses work independently, interacting with their instructors via written communications. Students in online courses and some DVD courses interact via e-mail and Internet chat rooms. Equipment requirements vary, depending on course format.

Programs of Study

Students may complete individual undergraduate or graduate courses. Each semester, approximately 200 ISU courses are offered via distance learning, including professional development courses for teachers, principals, administrators, counselors, and other educational specialists.

In addition, eligible students may complete numerous undergraduate and graduate degrees and professional development programs.

Undergraduate degree programs include an Associate of Science in general aviation flight technology and bachelor's degree completion programs in business administration, career and technical education, community health promotion, criminology, electronics technology, industrial technology, human resource development, industrial supervision,

insurance and risk management, mechanical engineering technology, and nursing.

Undergraduate certificate programs are offered in corrections, law enforcement, and private security and loss prevention. Also offered is a driver education instructor license program.

Graduate degree programs include a doctoral program in technology management and master's programs in criminology, electronics and computer technology, health and safety, human resource development, nursing, and student affairs and higher education.

Graduate certificate/licensure programs are offered in the following areas: driver education instructor license, family nurse practitioner studies, library media services, middle/secondary teaching, public administration, public personnel administration, school administration, teaching English as a second or foreign language, visual impairment, and vocational business education.

Special Programs

DegreeLink is a bachelor's degree completion program that enables individuals to transfer previously earned credit to Indiana State University, and complete selected bachelor degrees via distance learning. Students may transfer credit earned from Ivy Tech Community College, Vincennes University, and other accredited institutions.

The Library Media Services Certification Program consists of 27 hours of library and media courses leading to graduate licensure/certification in library media services.

The Master of Science in nursing includes specializations in adult health, community health, family nurse practitioner studies, and nursing administration.

The Master of Science in electronics and computer technology program is a 32-semester-hour (minimum) program that includes a focus, or concentration, in instrumentation, systems, and automation.

The Ph.D. in technology management is offered through the College of Technology in cooperation with a consortium of four other universities. Course work includes a general technology core, a technical specialization, cognate studies, an internship, and a research core and dissertation.

Student Services

Indiana State University offers distance learners a comprehensive package of services, including online registration, credit transfer assistance, academic advisement, a virtual bookstore, library services, technical support, and career counseling. The Office of Distance Support Services offers one-stop assistance to individuals interested in pursuing undergraduate and graduate courses and programs via distance learning.

Credit Options

Students earn credit by registering for and completing semester-based courses offered on campus or via distance learning. In addition, undergraduate students may opt to earn credit via year-based study. Selected programs enable undergraduates to earn credit for prior work experience, by examination, and through portfolios. Graduate students are eligible to transfer selected credit; each department determines the number of hours transferable.

Faculty

Distance courses are developed and taught by Indiana State University faculty members. Working with instructional designers and media specialists, faculty members transform on-campus courses to distance formats.

Admission

Admission requirements vary by program of study. For information, prospective students should visit http://www.indstate.edu/distance.

Tuition and Fees

Distance learners are eligible for fee waivers that equate to in-state fees. For details, students should visit http://www.indstate.edu/distance.

Applying

Individuals may obtain undergraduate and graduate applications, information, and assistance by contacting the Office of Distance Support Services or visiting http://www.indstate.edu/distance.

CONTACT

Office of Distance Support Services
Erickson Hall, Room 122
Indiana State University
Terre Haute, Indiana 47809

Phone: 812-237-8080
      888-237-8080 (toll-free)
Fax: 812-237-8540
E-mail: studentservices@indstate.edu
Web site: http://www.indstate.edu/distance

INDIANA UNIVERSITY

School of Continuing Studies

Bloomington, Indiana

Indiana University (IU) was established in 1820 in Bloomington, Indiana. There are now eight IU campuses located throughout the state of Indiana. Indiana University has more than 920 authorized degree programs. For fall semester 2005, the all-campus enrollment was 98,543 students (graduate and undergraduate).

Indiana University has offered University distance education courses since 1912 and high school distance education courses since 1925. It is accredited by the North Central Association of Colleges and Schools.

Distance Learning Program

The IU Independent Study Program (ISP) is one of the world's largest. It offers more than 195 undergraduate courses by correspondence, more than 100 high school courses by correspondence, and a growing inventory of undergraduate and high school online courses. Each year, enrollments in the program top 14,000. The Independent Study Program has won fifty-four course awards from the University Continuing Education Association.

Delivery Media

The IU Independent Study Program courses use such technologies as the World Wide Web, e-mail, CD-ROMs, computer software, and audio cassettes and videotapes. Students may interact with their instructors by toll-free phone, e-mail, and the World Wide Web.

Programs of Study

Through the IU Independent Study Program, students can take individual courses, earn an Indiana University high school diploma, or complete all degree requirements leading to an IU Associate of Arts in General Studies (60 semester credit hours) or an IU Bachelor of General

Studies (120 semester credit hours). Students may now earn both degrees online.

ISP courses are open to all students. In fact, many students at other educational institutions use ISP courses to fulfill degree or diploma requirements at their home institution.

Student Services

Students should visit the IU School of Continuing Studies Web site to find course information and enrollment forms. Students can contact the School 24 hours a day, seven days a week. They enjoy a one-on-one relationship with their instructors either by phone or e-mail. Students enrolling in Independent Study Program courses receive a free IU e-mail account. Through the IU Bloomington Libraries Distance Education Services, students can obtain a library code for borrowing books; order books, articles, and other library materials to be delivered free of charge; get reference help; and learn how to search the library's catalog and databases.

Credit Options

Students can use a variety of options for earning credit toward their Asso-

ciate of Arts in General Studies and their Bachelor of General Studies. Students who started their college education at another accredited college or university should be able to transfer a considerable number of credits to Indiana University. Other options include credit by examination, credit for self-acquired competency, and military service credit.

Students pursuing the Associate of Arts in General Studies must successfully complete at least 15 of the 60 required credit hours at Indiana University or through the IU Independent Study Program. Students pursuing the Bachelor of General Studies degree must successfully complete at least 30 of the 120 required credit hours at Indiana University or through the IU Independent Study Program.

Faculty

The 2005–06 ISP teaching faculty included 43 high school instructors and 135 University instructors.

Admission

Admission to Indiana University is not required for taking ISP courses. Students need only fill out a registration form for the desired courses.

Students wanting to earn an Associate of Arts in General Studies or a Bachelor of General Studies must submit an admission application to the General Studies Degree Program office. For more information, students should contact the General Studies Degree Program as listed below.

Tuition and Fees

Fees are the same for all students, regardless of where they live. The 2006–07 fee for University ISP courses was $138.65 per credit hour. The 2006–07 fee for high school ISP courses was $125 per 1-credit course and $62.50 per half-credit course. Students seeking admission to the General Studies Degree Program pay a $50 application fee ($65 for international students). Fees are subject to change.

Financial Aid

At this time, Indiana University is unable to administer federal or state financial aid for students pursuing degrees entirely through distance education, including those students enrolled in ISP courses.

Applying

There are no residency requirements for enrolling in Independent Study Program courses or applying to the General Studies Degree Program, and no on-campus meetings are required; these programs are open to students worldwide.

CONTACT

School of Continuing Studies
Owen Hall
Indiana University
790 East Kirkwood Avenue
Bloomington, Indiana 47405-7101

Phone: 812-855-2292
        800-334-1011 (toll-free)
E-mail: scs@indiana.edu
Web site: http://scs.indiana.edu/guest/petersons_indepth.
          html

KANSAS STATE UNIVERSITY

Division of Continuing Education Distance Education

Manhattan, Kansas

Kansas State University (K-State) was founded on February 16, 1863, as a land-grant institution under the Morrill Act. Originally located on the grounds of the old Bluemont Central College, which was chartered in 1858, the University was moved to its present site in 1875.

The 664-acre campus is in Manhattan, 125 miles west of Kansas City, via Interstate 70, in the rolling Flint Hills of northeast Kansas. The Salina campus, 70 miles west of Manhattan, was established through a merger of the former Kansas College of Technology with the University. This was made possible by an enactment of the 1991 Kansas Legislature.

K-State is accredited by the North Central Association of Colleges and Schools (NCA). One of the six universities governed by the Kansas Board of Regents, Kansas State University continues to fulfill its historic educational mission in teaching, research, and public service.

Distance Learning Program

Kansas State University innovatively offers high-quality courses and degree programs to students who are not geographically located near the Manhattan campus. K-State utilizes cutting-edge technologies that enhance the learning environment and extend it far beyond the University's physical boundaries.

Adults across the country want to complete their education, advance their careers, or change their professions. Success requires dedication, self-direction, and perseverance on the part of the student. Distance education offered by K-State provides people with an opportunity to pursue these goals without leaving a current job or family. K-State offers bachelor's degrees, master's degrees, and certificate programs at a distance.

Delivery Media

K-State offers courses through a variety of delivery methods. Most courses follow regular K-State semester dates. Some courses require minimum computer system requirements. Kansas State University offers more than 250 courses per year through distance education. Courses are offered in a variety of subject areas, and students can take many of these without enrolling in a degree program.

Delivery methods include use of videotapes and audiotapes, the Web, listservs, e-mail, discussion rooms, guided study, desktop video, community-based outreach courses, independent study, and correspondence course work.

Programs of Study

K-State has been offering degree completion programs through distance education for more than thirty years. The goal of the Distance Education Degree Completion Programs is to help students complete the last two years of a Bachelor of Science degree. K-State staff is available to help students get started, stay directed, and earn a Bachelor of Science degree.

A student's requirements include a minimum of 30 K-State hours, with 20 of the last 30 hours earned from K-State. Students may transfer a maximum of 60 credit hours to K-State from other institutions. The average student completes a bachelor's degree in two to six years; the pace is up to the student.

Bachelor's degree completion programs are offered in animal sciences and industry, early childhood education, dietetics, food science and industry, general business, interdisciplinary social science, and technology management.

Master's degree programs offered include agribusiness, chemical engineering, civil engineering, counseling and student development, educational leadership, electrical engineering, engineering management, food science, gerontology, industrial/organizational psychology, mechanical engineering, merchandising, personal financial planning, software engineering, and youth development.

Special Programs

Certificate/endorsement programs are also offered. These programs include an academic advising certificate, applied statistics graduate certificate, business administration graduate certificate, conflict resolution graduate and undergraduate certificates, early childhood education credential and endorsement, engineering professional-development hours, food science certificate, gerontology graduate certificate, merchandising graduate certificate, occupational health certificate, organizational leadership graduate certificate, personal financial planning certificate, public administration graduate certificate, and youth development graduate certificate.

K-State is a member of Service Members Opportunity College for the SOCAD-2 flexible-degree network. This network guarantees worldwide transfer of credit for military personnel who take courses from participating colleges and universities.

Student Services

Students in degree programs receive advising from the college offering the degree. The Division of Continuing

Education also has Program Coordinators for each college, who can provide assistance.

Library services are available to students enrolled in degree completion programs.

The technical support help desk can provide a variety of technical support services once a student is enrolled in a distance education course.

For information about all the student services, students should visit the Student Services Web site at http://www.dce.ksu.edu/studentservices.

Faculty

Kansas State University is an accredited institution offering credit courses through distance education. Distance education courses are taught by faculty members who teach K-State on-campus courses.

Admission

Each distance education degree program has specific admission requirements and procedures. Admission information is available for each program at the Web address listed in the Contact section.

Tuition and Fees

Distance education tuition at K-State is the same for both in-state and out-of-state students. Tuition is the cost for an academic course and includes a per-credit-hour charge. It also includes additional tuition components such as student services, TELENET 2 media fee, engineering equipment and maintenance, licensing, tape/Web media, and distance education support.

Financial Aid

Students may be eligible for financial aid for distance education courses if federal requirements are met, they are admitted and enrolled in a degree program in Kansas State University, and they are enrolled in a minimum of 6 credit hours of Kansas State University course work.

Scholarships are also available to students enrolled in degree programs.

Applying

The application process for each program varies. For complete information on a specific program, students can access the Web site listed below or contact the Division of Continuing Education at 785-532-5575 or at the toll-free number listed in the Contact section, or by e-mail at the address listed in the Contact section.

CONTACT

Division of Continuing Education
Kansas State University
13 College Court Building
Manhattan, Kansas 66506-6002

Phone: 785-532-5575
        800-622-2KSU   (toll-free)
Fax: 785-532-5637
E-mail: informationdce@ksu.edu
Web site: http://www.dce.ksu.edu/distance

KAPLAN UNIVERSITY

Fort Lauderdale, Florida

In a recent national survey (http://www.kaplan.edu/ku/surveyresults), Kaplan University surpassed all for-profit secondary institutions for the quality and value of the education provided. Founded in 2000, the University provides innovative undergraduate, graduate, and continuing professional educational programs designed to offer working students the opportunity to launch, enhance, or change careers. Kaplan University is committed to general education, a student-centered service and support approach, and applied scholarship in a practical environment. The University is accredited by the Higher Learning Commission (HLC) (312-263-0456, http://www.ncahlc.org) and is a member of the North Central Association of Colleges and Schools (NCA).

Distance Learning Program

As a distance learning institution, Kaplan University provides challenging academic programs developed and assessed by faculty and staff members and by members of educational, professional, and business communities. These programs provide intensive and comprehensive instruction to more than 21,000 students, instilling the value of lifelong learning by stimulating intellectual curiosity, creative and critical thinking, and awareness of culture and diversity. The University plans and provides facilities and resources that respond to the needs of students and assist them in developing professional attitudes, values, skills, and strategies that will foster success in their careers and in life.

Delivery Media

Kaplan University focuses on adding a human touch to the high technology of learning online. Faculty members are committed to providing students with personal attention and academic support when they need it. The flexibility and dynamic interaction of online education at Kaplan University also allows for innovative learning opportunities, including online quizzes with instant feedback, message boards for discussions and advice from professors, and interactive seminar sessions.

Programs of Study

Master's degrees are offered in business, criminal justice, and education, each averaging eighteen months to two years to complete (less with transfer credits).

Bachelor's degrees are awarded in arts and sciences, business, criminal justice, education, information systems and technology, nursing, and legal studies, typically requiring 180 credits and four years to complete (less with transfer credits). Advanced Start bachelor's degrees can be earned in twelve months to two years.

Associate degree programs are offered in arts and sciences, business, criminal justice, health sciences, information systems and technology, and legal studies. Each usually requires 90 credits and two years to finish.

Certificate programs in criminal justice and education may be completed in nine to fifteen months.

Continuing and professional studies programs in business, finance, and health care are self-paced.

Special Programs

Kaplan University offers a 15 percent tuition discount to active-duty service members, as well as discounts on other Kaplan, Inc., products, including educational test-preparation services. The University is a Servicemembers Oppor-tunity College (SOC), part of an association of schools working together to help service members and their families enroll in college programs by simplifying credit transfers and reducing residency requirements.

Student Services

The University offers rich academic support through no-fee tutoring and online writing and mathematics labs, as well as a distinct virtual community composed of honor societies and professional associations. Kaplan University provides students a full complement of library services via the University of Alabama, whose entire library catalog is available online. Students can easily access a description of any item in the collection.

Credit Options

Kaplan University's policy is to transfer experiential and prior learning credit according to American Council on Education (ACE) guidelines. Students may also earn credit toward degrees through CLEP and DANTES examinations. These methods can greatly reduce the time it takes to earn a degree.

Faculty

Kaplan University programs are taught by practicing professionals. As of May 2006, the faculty is composed of approximately 1,700 part-time and 170 full-time instructors. Nearly 45 percent have doctoral-level degrees.

Admission

Admissions advisers are trained to counsel and help students with all aspects of their educational and career goals, from selecting the program that is right for them to assisting them in securing financial aid.

Tuition and Fees

All undergraduate programs, the Pathway to Paralegal Postbaccalaureate Certificate Program, the Master of Arts in Teaching and Learning program, the Master of Education program, the Professional Development for Teachers Program, the Iowa Teacher Intern Certificate Program, and the Professional Development for Teachers Program are $305 per credit, while the Master of Science in Criminal Justice program is $350 per credit, the Master of Business Administration program is $395 per credit, and the *Newsweek* M.B.A. program is $475 per credit. Books are included in the price of tuition for all undergraduate degree programs. (Not all courses require textbooks; some use electronic instructional materials.) All online students pay an $85 technology fee per term. (For the M.B.A. programs, this fee is prorated to $42.50 per six-week term. For the Professional Development for Teachers Program, this fee is waived.) A minimum deposit of $95 is required at the time of enrollment and is credited toward tuition when classes begin.

A fee of $300 is required for each clinical course taken in the Nurse Assistant Preparation Certificate Program. Students enrolled in the School of Health Sciences programs pay a one-time program fee. This fee may be paid using financial aid funds and can be incorporated into the student's monthly payment plan. The fee for the A.A.S. in medical assisting program is $300, the fee for the A.A.S. in medical office management program is $50, and the fee for the A.A.S. in medical transcription program is $100.

Financial Aid

Kaplan University actively assists students in securing financial support for their education. Sources include federal grants; federal, state, and private lending programs; and military financial aid. The University also awards scholarships to eligible undergraduate students.

CONTACT

Online Program Admissions
Kaplan University
6301 Kaplan University Avenue
Fort Lauderdale, Florida 33309

Phone: 866-527-5268 (toll-free)
      954-515-4015 (international)
      866-572-6026 (TYY-TDD; toll-free)
Fax: 888-887-6494 (toll-free)
E-mail: kuadmissions@degrees.kaplan.edu
Web site: http://www.getinfo.kaplan.edu

KEISER UNIVERSITY

Keiser University eCampus

Fort Lauderdale, Florida

For over thirty years, Keiser University has provided high-quality career education and now offers degree programs online to prepare students for high-demand professions. Associate and bachelor's degrees are offered with a student-centered approach and curriculum that is in pace with technology and workforce demand trends.

Keiser University is accredited by the Commission on Colleges of the Southern Association of Colleges and Schools (1866 Southern Lane, Decatur, Georgia 30033-4097; 404-679-4501) to award associate, bachelor's, and master's degrees.

Keiser University eCampus offers degrees in fields that are in high demand and provides job placement assistance to all its students and alumni. The University researches trends for growing fields and tailors its curriculum to prepare students for entry into rewarding careers.

Distance Learning Program

Online learning is not impersonal at Keiser University Online. From admissions to faculty, Keiser University Online staff members are dedicated to superior student care accomplished through accessible staff and faculty members who foster a student-centered learning community, state-of-the-practice online classroom technology and user-friendly format to enhance learning, a one-class-at-a-time approach that allows busy students to focus on their education and develop the skills to excel, and extensive online resources that include information and access to all student services.

Delivery Media

Students should contact eCampus for technical requirements at admissions@keiseruniversity.edu.

Programs of Study

Keiser University eCampus offers fully online programs and is a division of the Fort Lauderdale campus. Students interact with their instructors and each other using advanced technology, from anywhere at anytime.

Bachelor's degrees online are offered in accounting, business administration (this program is also offered in Spanish), criminal justice, health science, health-services administration, homeland security, information technology, management information systems (MIS), and in nursing (B.S.N.). Associate degrees online are offered in accounting, aquatics engineering, criminal justice, health services administration, homeland security, information technology, medical assistant studies, and paralegal studies.

All online students must log in at least three times a week and actively participate in class. Each student must maintain satisfactory progress. Students must maintain at least a C average or better during each grading period.

Student Services

Keiser University Online programs are Web-based courses, designed by qualified faculty and staff members to create an interesting and interactive learning environment. Keiser's virtual classroom is comfortable, and courses can be taken easily by anyone with access to the World Wide Web. Lesson plans, assignments, and class schedules are posted online, while student-teacher interaction and student-student interaction also occur over the Internet. Scheduled discussions, e-mail messages, live chats, and real-time group discussions are a few of the opportunities for interacting during an online course.

Online students have access to all Keiser University resources, from the bookstore to on-campus libraries. In addition, online access to information and services includes application, enrollment and registration procedures, financial aid information, tuition and fee information, course schedules and outlines, course demonstrations, faculty information, and an e-mail directory. Online students also have access to online academic advising and technical support through e-mail or telephone.

Credit Options

Credit for courses or degrees completed at another institution by students enrolling at Keiser University are subject to approval by the Dean of Academic Affairs. These courses or degrees must be similar in content and duration to those offered in the program for which the student has applied. The Dean of Academic Affairs considers only official transcripts mailed directly to Keiser University. Students are responsible for having official transcripts sent to Keiser University from their transfer institutions. Keiser University requires that, as a minimum, the student must complete the last 25 percent of credits in a program of study at the University. All transfer students are informed in writing of any credits accepted as transferable. Preliminary notification is presented, in most cases, prior to enrollment, but in no case, later than the end of the transfer student's first semester.

Admission

In order to be considered for enrollment at Keiser University, all applicants must supply verification of high school graduation (such as a transcript or diploma), verification of GED completion (GED scores or GED diploma), or proof of graduation from an international institution comparable to a U.S. secondary school.

Home schooled applicants who have a high school diploma are also considered for admission. Home schooled applicants should present their SAT or ACT scores with their application.

Students should make arrangements to take Keiser University's entrance examination (administered at the University) or provide results of their SAT or ACT exam. The University requirements for admission are a combined score of 800 on the SAT and a composite score of 17 on the ACT. In addition, students in Keiser University's medical programs must sign a Statement of Good Health prior to entrance into the program.

Keiser University is proud of the international character of its student body and welcomes students from other nations. All international students must be fluent in English before they enroll. Applicants must furnish proof that they can read, write, and speak English fluently. Keiser University has been approved by the United States Department of Immigration for students to pursue their studies at any of the University's campuses. The University can accept only F-1 visas based upon the student's program of study. International student applicants must meet the following requirements for admission to Keiser University: successful completion of a secondary school program that is equivalent to high school in the U.S., certification of financial ability to meet tuition and other necessary expenses or ability to qualify for financial aid as an eligible noncitizen, and the required minimum TOEFL score of 500 on the paper-based test or 225 on the computer-based test if the primary language is not English.

Applications for international students can be obtained through the Admissions Office. Students should apply at least two months prior to the start of the program.

Tuition and Fees

Students should contact the Admissions Department for current information on tuition and fees.

Financial Aid

Keiser University offers a number of financial aid programs to its students, including Federal Pell Grants, Federal Supplemental Educational Opportunity Grants (FSEOG), Keiser University Academic Scholarships, Federal Stafford Student Loans, Federal PLUS Loans, and Federal Perkins Loans.

Applying

Applications are accepted on an ongoing basis and can be accessed online at the University Web site at http://online.keiseruniversity.edu.

CONTACT

Admissions Director
Keiser University eCampus
1900 West Commercial Boulevard
Fort Lauderdale, Florida 33309
Phone: 954-351-4040
       866-KEISER-1 (866-534-7371, toll-free)
E-mail: admissions@keiseruniversity.edu
Web site: http://online.keiseruniversity.edu

KETTERING UNIVERSITY
Graduate Studies Department
Flint, Michigan

Kettering University, formerly known as GMI Engineering & Management Institute, is a highly respected private college located in Flint, Michigan. For nearly ninety years, Kettering University has proudly been recognized for providing students worldwide with specialized, practical, high-quality, and real-world education in engineering, automotive systems, manufacturing, business, management, and the sciences.

Kettering University is accredited by the North Central Association of Colleges and Schools of North America (NCA), the Accreditation Board for Engineering and Technology (ABET), and the Association of Collegiate Business Schools and Programs (ACBSP).

As featured in the 2007 edition of "America's Best Colleges Guide," published by U.S. News & World Report, Kettering University maintains its top Number One ranking for its Industrial and Manufacturing Engineering program—marking its seventh consecutive year at first place. In addition, two other Kettering undergraduate programs rank tops in the country for undergraduate engineering schools at which the highest degree awarded is a bachelor's or master's degree. These rankings include third for the Mechanical Engineering program and seventh for the Electrical and Computer Engineering program.

Known in the industry as "America's Co-Op College," Kettering University works with more than 700 undergraduate co-op employers—including various manufacturing and automotive companies, banks, hospitals, government agencies, and corporations.

Kettering University also offers first-class graduate and continuing education programs that develop leaders for the real world. Designed for the working professional, Kettering's master's degree programs are offered on campus as well as off campus through distance learning methods. The convenience, flexibility, and portability of distance learning makes Kettering's graduate programs available virtually anywhere in the world through CD-ROM, DVD, or online video-streaming. Participating employers make Kettering's graduate programs available to their employees at more than 130 off-site learning centers around the world.

Distance Learning Program

Kettering University's convenient and flexible graduate programs are available virtually anywhere through distance learning methods that include DVD, online video-streaming, Internet/Web, and CD-ROM (students must have access to RealPlayer for viewing class lectures on CD and online video-streaming formats). Kettering's distance learning is also supported by Blackboard.

Delivery Media

On-campus graduate courses are presented to students in a high-tech classroom/television studio on the Kettering campus to digitally capture the entire class presentation, lecture materials, case studies, question-answer sessions, and other contents presented. These class sessions are recorded onto CD-ROMs, DVDs, and Internet video-streaming formats.

Distance learning students get the same class experience and materials that on-campus students receive, without ever setting foot on campus. Since courses are recorded, distance learning students receive the course content/materials one week after on-campus students.

Students can select the delivery format that best suits their needs. Kettering ships course materials (such as CDs and DVDs) to the student on a weekly basis, or students can simply view their courses online through video-streaming on Blackboard. Exams are sent to and proctored by a site coordinator/proctor assigned to a specific learning center or by a designated proctor for independent students.

Programs of Study

Most of Kettering University's graduate degrees are Master of Science degree programs that consist of ten core classes, totaling 40 credit hours. (This does not include any prerequisite courses that may apply for some programs.) Kettering also offers a new M.B.A. program with several concentrations, totaling 48 credit hours. Kettering designed the master's programs to be terminal professional degrees for engineers, managers, and business professionals. The programs are particularly attractive to working professionals who want to extend and broaden their related skills. Although designed as terminal degrees, they also provide preparation for study at the doctoral level.

Graduate students have up to six years to complete the degree requirements. The textbooks are free, and the GMAT or GRE is not required for admission.

Kettering University's master's degree programs include an M.B.A. (with general or technical concentrations), engineering (with concentrations available in automotive systems (on-campus only)), electrical and computer engineering, industrial engineering (on-campus only), manufacturing engineering, manufacturing engineering–lean manufacturing (on-campus only), mechanical cognate, and mechanical design; engineering management, with a concentration available in lean manufacturing (on-campus only); information technology; manufacturing management; manufacturing operations; and operations management.

To learn more about Kettering University's graduate programs, including courses, prerequisites, and admission requirements, prospective students should visit the University's Web site.

Credit Options

Credits are earned by completing courses; however, students may transfer up to 8 credit hours. Credit may be transferred for grades of B or better and is granted only for completed graduate study. Credit is not given for experience. Anyone interested in transfer credit should obtain an application for transfer credit from the Graduate Office.

Faculty

Kettering University's excellent faculty and staff members are truly committed to educating and preparing future leaders for a global workplace. The majority of the University's graduate programs are taught by nationally ranked faculty members who hold doctorate degrees in addition to having practical experience in their respective fields of study.

Professors announce office hours for students to clarify materials, ask questions, or obtain assistance. Students may contact professors during office hours via e-mail, phone or voice-mail, fax, or online bulletin boards.

Admission

Only students with at least a bachelor's degree are accepted into Kettering's graduate programs. A bachelor's degree in engineering from an ABET-accredited institution is required for admission to any of the Master of Science in engineering degree programs. Two letters of recommendation are also required for engineering students as well as for the manufacturing operations program. Other requirements include a minimum 3.0 grade point average in undergraduate work and two supervisor recommendations. Certain other requirements must be met for some programs. The same requirements apply to on-campus and distance learning students.

Tuition and Fees

Tuition for graduate studies during the 2007–08 academic year is $648 per credit hour. There are no application or registration fees for U.S. applicants. There is a $50 application fee for international applicants.

Applying

Application deadlines are as follows: for the summer 2007 term, the deadline was June 8, for fall 2007, the deadline is September 14; for the winter 2008 term, the deadline is December 14; and for spring 2008, the deadline is March 21.

CONTACT

Kettering University
1700 West Third Avenue
Flint, Michigan 48504-4898

Phone: 866-584-7237 Ext. 4 (toll-free)
Fax: 810-762-9935
E-mail: gradoff@kettering.edu
Web site: http://www.kettering.edu

LESLEY UNIVERSITY
Cambridge, Massachusetts

Lesley prepares women and men for professional careers in education, the arts, human services, management, environmental activism, and liberal arts. Since 1909, when the school was founded to train early-childhood educators, Lesley has been a leader and innovator in preparing people to have a positive impact on the world. A commitment to scholarship, citizenship, and lifelong learning forms the foundation of Lesley's educational philosophy. Lesley offers a variety of graduate and undergraduate programs on its Cambridge and Boston campuses and in regional, national, and international locations. Central to the mission of all its programs is a commitment to excellence, creative instruction, the integration of academic and field-based learning, and responsiveness to the needs of society and the student.

Distance Learning Program

Throughout the 1980s and early 1990s, Lesley instructors increasingly enhanced their courses with electronic educational resources and communicated with students by e-mail. In 1996, the first totally online course was offered at Lesley. In 1997, students began to take entire master's degrees online.

Students from all fifty states and more than twenty countries have taken Lesley's online classes and become part of a community of skilled, knowledgeable, and inspired educators. Online courses and master's and doctoral degree programs combine creative and thought-provoking online teaching strategies with timely, practical content. With a reliable Internet connection, students can enjoy the flexibility and convenience of taking courses from anywhere in the world.

Delivery Media

Courses are asynchronous, so time zones and personal schedules do not interfere with class participation. Math, technology in education, and science in education master's degree programs are fully online, without residency requirements. The ecological teaching and learning program combines online learning with two 3-week summer field experiences. The Ph.D. program blends its online course work with seven periods of residency over a three-year period.

Online education tools provide opportunities for communication, including discussion boards and e-mails, between students and faculty members. Students discover new methods of collaboration as learning expands beyond traditional classrooms, creating communities of worldwide learners.

The most important technical requirements are access to a reliable high-speed Internet connection and an e-mail address that can be checked daily. Students can work with either a PC or Macintosh operating system and should have access to an integrated word processor/spreadsheet package, preferably Microsoft Office.

Programs of Study

Four master's degree programs and a doctoral degree program are offered, as are individual online courses such as Autism Spectrum Disorders and Children with Behavior Problems: Responding to the Challenges.

Master's Programs: The Mathematics Education Online Master's Degree Program (M.Ed.) for elementary and middle school teachers emphasizes deep mathematics content knowledge, helping teachers connect this knowledge to classroom practice and their own students' understanding of mathematics. The program includes math content courses covering the five national content standards that support teachers in becoming highly qualified educators in mathematics.

Students in the Technology in Education Program, designed for K–12 educators, earn the M.Ed. degree. The program provides students with the knowledge and skills to create a technology-rich environment for K–12 students that sparks imagination and inspires creativity.

The innovative Science in Education Program, culminating in an M.Ed. degree specifically for K–8 educators, builds an understanding of core science concepts. Students experience the nature of scientific process in their own learning and learn how to carry out hands-on science investigations at home. Each course has a built-in practicum.

Students can earn a Master of Science degree through the Audubon Expedition Institute's (AEI) Ecological Teaching and Learning (ETL) Program, an eighteen-month program for working educators in schools, museums, and nature centers. Students explore the integration of ecological concepts into the curriculum.

Doctoral Program: The Ph.D. program in educational studies, adult learning specialization, reflects Lesley's focus on learning as a vehicle for changing oneself and the world. The adult-learning-focused program, an intensive residency-based specialization, integrates the areas of cognition, learning, and human development with the study of institutions, organizations, and cultures. Participants critically examine educational research and literature and address a commitment to reflective practice, critical thinking, and lifelong education, while answering four central questions: How do adults learn?

What is the relationship between learning and development? How does culture affect learning? and How do the environments in which adults learn impact their learning? The program, which prepares future leaders in the field of adult and continuing education, was designed to meet the needs of administrators, instructors of adults, staff developers, and program planners in learning environments such as business and industry, community development, staff development, professional continuing education, corrections education, literacy and adult basic education, religious education, human services, correspondence and distance learning, higher education, and university extension. The program is designed to be completed in 3 years, including seven residency periods.

Special Programs

Lesley University offers students the opportunity to participate in a number of non-Lesley-affiliated programs of off-campus study.

Student Services

Distance learning students have access to the University's resources, including the Eleanor DeWolfe Ludcke Library, which houses more than 100,000 titles and 700 print-journal subscriptions and offers a growing list of electronic resources.

Every distance learning student is assigned an individual academic adviser who works with them throughout their program of study. All student also have access to 24/7 tech support.

Credit Options

For master's programs, Lesley University may allow a transfer of up to 6 graduate-level credits from an appropriately accredited institution; credits must be relevant to the program of study. All 45 credits of post-master's course work in the doctoral program must be completed at Lesley. The University's policy on transfer credits can be found at http://www.lesley.edu/policies/catalog/transfer_credits.html.

Faculty

Lesley's online faculty members are experienced with both face-to-face instruction and online teaching. Their responsibilities go far beyond facilitating learning—they serve multiple roles as teacher-mentors, researchers, consultants, writers, speakers, and community leaders. They are the primary force in promoting the vision and setting the high academic goals that enable Lesley University to deliver online programs with the same quality and standards as its face-to-face education programs.

Admission

To enroll in a master's degree program, students must have a bachelor's degree from a regionally accredited institution. Students may enroll in a course on a space-available basis, but Lesley strongly urges that everyone apply for the degree program before beginning any courses.

Tuition and Fees

Tuition is currently $465 per credit, with a $30 technology fee per course.

Financial Aid

Fully accepted students who are enrolled at least part-time each semester are eligible for financial aid. Graduate-degree candidates may qualify for up to $20,500 per academic year in 2007–08. More information is available at http://www.lesley.edu/financial.html.

Applying

Lesley University admits students to online programs on a rolling admissions basis, so there is no application deadline. In general, students must submit the completed application, the $50 application fee, official transcripts, two letters of recommendation, and a two-page personal statement. Other requirements, including interviews, vary by program. International students may have to submit TOEFL scores.

CONTACT

Sara Violante
Assistant Director, Online Learning
Lesley University
29 Everett Street
Cambridge, Massachusetts 02138

Phone: 801-626-6600
        800-999-1959 Ext. 8301 (toll-free)
Fax: 617-349-8391
E-mail: violante@lesley.edu
Web site: http://web.lesley.edu/admissions/online.asp

LOCK HAVEN UNIVERSITY OF PENNSYLVANIA

eCampus Programs
Lock Haven, Pennsylvania

Lock Haven University of Pennsylvania (LHUP) encourages academic excellence. The University's educational programs are designed to develop the intellectual skills and talents of all students. Through formal and informal instruction, students are guided to achieve their full potential. Students gain a better self-understanding, a sense of individual and community responsibility, and knowledge of cultural diversity and the global community. The institution is accredited by the Middle States Association of Colleges and Schools, and distance education is included in the scope of the accreditation.

"This educational experience at LHUP has helped me to focus my goals and redefine them more clearly and has also given me the opportunity to achieve greater insight into this world. This has been the best experience of my life."
Carolyne M. Timko, M.L.A.; Blossburg, Pennsylvania.

Distance Learning Program
Lock Haven University (LHUP) provides students with the opportunity to complete a full degree program (associate, bachelor's, or master's) or to complete individual courses either at a local education center or in the convenience of their homes.

Delivery Media
Lock Haven University offers distance learning programs via videoconferencing-based technologies or Web-based technologies to create a fully online experience. The videoconferencing sites are limited to sites contracting with the University. Web-based technologies include a full-featured course-management system, Web-casting of lectures, resource materials, threaded discussions, journaling, real-time chat discussions, document sharing, and other instructional methods that create active and engaged learning communities.

Programs of Study
LHUP offers associate degrees in criminal justice (online) and surgical technology (online) and a bachelor's degree in general studies (online). Students can complete some of their LHUP General Education requirements through the distance learning program as a nonmatriculating student. Four master's degree programs are also available. These include the Master of Education in Alternative Education program (online), Master of Education in Teaching and Learning program (online), Master of Liberal Arts (online), and Master of Health Science in Physician Assistant Studies program (distributed learning).

Noncredit certificates are available in business, construction technology (including International Code Council preparation courses for residential and commercial inspection), health care, Internet design and technical programs, networking and CompTIA certification prep, Microsoft certification prep, paralegal studies and legal secretary studies, and video game design and development. K–12 teachers can also take continuing education classes and receive Act 48 credit.

Special Programs
Lock Haven University encourages students to consider studying abroad. LHUP has a large and diverse international program, providing many opportunities for its students to study abroad for periods ranging from several weeks in a semester to a year or more. The University has direct exchange programs with institutions in Australia, China, Costa Rica, Croatia, England, Finland, France, Germany, Italy, Japan, Mexico, Poland, Russia, Scotland, Spain, and Ukraine. The University offers interested and qualified students an opportunity to participate in various internship programs that provide field experiences to supplement classroom learning.

Student Services
The course management system organizes information, services, and resources relevant to distance learners. Forms are available online to apply for admissions and/or register for courses. The Stevenson Library caters to online students, providing a catalog of resources and access to databases and full-text journals online.

Credit Options
The various subject examinations offered through the College Board's Advanced Placement (AP) program are approved and credit is awarded based on a test score of 3 or higher. With the exception of only one General Examination (English Composition) and four subject tests (Business Law, Educational Psychology, College Composition, and Freshman English) offered through the College Board's College-Level Examination Program (CLEP), degree credit may be earned by candidates who achieve a scaled score equivalent to the 50th percentile or higher using current national norms for each test. There is no limit to the number of courses for which CLEP or AP may award credit. A maximum of 6 graduate semester hours may be transferred and applied toward most graduate degrees.

Faculty
Of the 259 faculty members, 91 percent are full-time. Faculty members are

noted for their diverse expertise, their interest in interdisciplinary study and their dedication to working with adult students. In addition to teaching, faculty members advise students, formulate program policy, and supervise independent study and capstone projects.

Admission

Admission requirements vary by program. Generally, undergraduates should have completed college-preparatory course work in high school, have a satisfactory command of the English language, and should have taken either the SAT or the ACT. In general, graduate students must have a baccalaureate degree from an accredited institution and a minimum GPA of 3.0.

Tuition and Fees

Tuition and fees are set by the Board of Governors of the Pennsylvania State System of Higher Education once a year.

For the 2006–07 academic year, undergraduate tuition was $210 per credit for Pennsylvania residents and $214.20 per credit for nonresidents; the distance education fee was 10 percent of the tuition. Graduate in-state tuition was $386 per credit, and out-of-state students paid $394 per credit. For graduate and undergraduate students, the tuition technology fee was $31 for residents and $47 for nonresidents.

For current information, students should check the Web site at http://www.lhup.edu/financial-services/bursar/. The cost of noncredit courses and certificate programs may vary.

Financial Aid

Financial aid to meet the costs of attending LHUP is available from a variety of programs, including grants, loans, and scholarships. The majority of these programs provide funds based on computed financial need, but some non-need-based programs are also available. To apply for financial aid, students must complete the Free Application for Federal Student Aid (FAFSA). Pennsylva-

nia residents should complete this form as provided by the Pennsylvania Higher Education Assistance Agency and any supplemental forms required for the Pennsylvania State Grant. Of all full-time matriculated undergraduates who enrolled in 2003, 77 percent of undergraduates had their financial need fully met.

Applying

Application procedures vary by program, and students should contact the distance education office for specific information. Applicants are required to submit the completed application, a $25 application fee, all high school transcripts, and official SAT or ACT scores. In addition, graduate programs require official transcripts of all undergraduate and graduate work; students applying to the Master of Education programs must also submit three letters of recommendation and a writing sample. International students must also submit TOEFL scores. All applications are processed on a rolling basis.

CONTACT

Dr. Ellen P. O'Hara-Mays, Executive Director
eCampus
Lock Haven University of Pennsylvania
Lock Haven, Pennsylvania 17745

Phone: 570-484-2072
   877-268-4688 (toll-free)
Fax: 570-484-2638
E-mail: poharama@lhup.edu
Web site: http://ecampus.lhup.edu/

LYNN UNIVERSITY
Institute for Distance Learning
Boca Raton, Florida

Founded in 1962 and located in Boca Raton, Florida, Lynn University is a private coeducational institution whose primary purposes are education; the preservation, discovery, dissemination, and creative application of knowledge; and the preparation of its graduates with the academic foundation for lifelong learning. Service, scholarly activity that includes research, and ongoing professional development allow the faculty, in conjunction with the entire University community, to fulfill its purposes: facilitating student-centered learning and fostering the intellectual life of the University.

Distance Learning Program

The Institute for Distance Learning provides students with easy access to online courses from anywhere in the world where Internet access is available. Online courses follow a term calendar of six 8-week terms per year. Start dates for graduate courses and adult undergraduate courses are in September, November, January, March, May, and July. Online courses associated with the Day Division follow the Day Division schedule.

Online courses reside on the Blackboard Platform and can only be accessed by students and faculty members engaged in online course work.

The Online Degree Program Division of Lynn University's Institute for Distance Learning offers undergraduate and graduate degrees that combine a comprehensive general education with a study in a major and validation of prior learning experience.

A student's credit hours are earned through instruction (distance learning or traditional classroom), transfer credits from an accredited college or university, military service course credits (DANTES), Florida Department of Law Enforcement (FDLE) or a similar state training facility, professional training or certification as recognized by the American Council on Education (ACE) or the College Level Examination Program (CLEP), and/or a student's professional experience or experiential learning.

Lynn University is approved by the Commission on Colleges of the Southern Association of Colleges and Schools (SACS) (1866 Southern Lane, Decatur, Georgia 30033-4097; telephone: 404-679-4501) to offer complete distance learning degree programs via the Web.

Delivery Media

Internet technology encourages interactions between faculty members and students, students and other students, and students and resources (books, journals, electronic library services, and the Internet). Courses are delivered using Blackboard, a student-friendly platform that affords students the opportunity to complete assignments and engage in various discussions at convenient times and locations. Distance learning courses are delivered in an accelerated format, with six 8-week class terms per academic year. Students may begin their studies during any of the terms.

Programs of Study

Lynn University offers online courses leading to seven graduate and undergraduate degrees. Students can find the course schedule at http://www.lynn.edu/pm.

The Ph.D. program in global leadership offers a specialization in corporate and organizational management. Master's-level online graduate degree programs are also offered in administra-

tion, with a specialization in criminal justice or in emergency planning and administration, and in educational leadership, with specializations in higher education administration, school administration, or school administration with ESOL endorsement.

Undergraduate degree programs include business administration, criminal justice administration, and psychology. An online post-baccalaureate certificate in emergency planning and administration rounds out the course of study.

Credit Options

Most online courses are 3 credits each. Courses with labs are 4 credits. Courses offered with less than 3 credits are identified in the Academic Catalog, which can be found online at http://www.lynn.edu/pm.

Lynn University accepts transfer credits from most other regionally accredited schools. Specific information about transfer credits may be found in the catalog. Credits earned in the online program are combined with credits earned on campus to complete a degree.

Faculty

The faculty members at Lynn University are highly qualified and committed to providing high-quality instruction and learning opportunities for self-directed learners. Along with excellent academic credentials, the faculty members are primarily practitioners in their fields of expertise, thus providing the theoretical context for the practical applications of the subject matter.

Admission

To enroll in an undergraduate degree program, students must have earned a high school diploma or GED certificate.

Attendees of foreign schools are required to submit an international transcript evaluation and course equivalency report. International students whose first language is not English must submit official test results of the Test of English as a Foreign Language (TOEFL) or IELTS. Applicants with TOEFL scores of 470–499 (paper based) or 150–170 (computer- based) are placed in the English for Academic Purposes Program. Applicants with TOEFL scores of 500 or higher (paper-based) or 173 (computer-based) are considered for regular admission.

Graduate students must have earned a college diploma from a regionally accredited or internationally listed college or university. Applicants whose undergraduate grade point average (GPA) was less than 3.0 must also submit the appropriate entrance examination score from the GRE, GMAT, or MAT. All graduate degree program applicants must submit two recommendation letters, a resume, and a statement of professional goals. Other admission requirements vary by degree program and are outlined in the Academic Catalog.

In addition, online students enrolled in the Ph.D. program have a required campus residency of four on-campus immersions, consisting of three to five days each, and a fifth for the defense of the dissertation. These immersions are associated with a program orientation and the research core: RES 700Q, RES 702Q, RES 704Q, RES 900Q, and RES 902 (dissertation defense). Students who are unable to meet this enrollment requirement may develop an alternative plan with their program coordinator.

Tuition and Fees

All new students pay a one-time nonrefundable $50 application fee. The tuition fees and registration fees follow the pricing established for the respective colleges and noncredit programs. For the 2006–07 academic year, the fees were as follows: undergraduate, $270 per credit hour; graduate, $525 per credit hour; and doctoral, $735 per credit hour. Noncredit tuition varies with the individual courses. There is a registration fee of $50 at the beginning of each term enrolled and an experiential portfolio administration fee is $75 per credit hour. More information and specific details regarding fees are available in the Academic Catalog on the University's Web site, http://www.lynn.edu.

Financial Aid

The Financial Aid Office is committed to tailoring a financial package to meet students' individual needs. For those who take advantage of available financial aid (federal, state, and institutional), private higher education is affordable. Students should visit the "Resources for Future Students" section of the Web site for tools that will help them calculate costs and for detailed information on financial aid.

Applying

Students may apply online or download a printable application at http://www. lynn.edu/pm. To obtain an application by mail, students should call the Admissions Office at 800-888-LYNN (5966) (toll-free in the United States) or 561-237-7900 (outside the U.S.).

CONTACT

Mary L. Tebes, Ph.D.
Director, Institute for Distance Learning
Lynn University
3601 North Military Trail
Boca Raton, Florida 33431
Phone: 561-237-7902
E-mail: mtebes@lynn.edu
Web site: http://www.lynn.edu

Millersville University
SEIZE THE OPPORTUNITY

MILLERSVILLE UNIVERSITY OF PENNSYLVANIA
Master of Science in Emergency Management
Millersville, Pennsylvania

Innovation in education is the philosophy of Millersville University (MU) of Pennsylvania. Established in 1855, the University has grown to a 250-acre campus with more than sixty buildings. The University's modern research facilities, blended with Romanesque Revival structures and late-Victorian wooden frame houses, reflect its integration of contemporary and classical elements of education. Simultaneously innovative and traditional, this setting encourages close faculty-student relationships as an important component of academic and personal development. Millersville University is accredited by the Middle States Association of Colleges and Schools.

Distance Learning Program

MUOnline is a growing part of the University's commitment to educational access. The mission of MUOnline is to maximize access to high-quality traditional and nontraditional education for students and professionals. The distance learning program at MU offers opportunities to further the mission of Millersville University in significant ways, such as expanding access to new and existing clientele, giving growing attention to the increasingly diverse and nontraditional students, and enhancing and expanding learning opportunities for Pennsylvanians and others through information and communication technologies.

Delivery Media

Students and professors meet in a virtual classroom for live interaction. Students should have access to a computer and the Internet. Required software may include Mozilla Firefox, Macromedia Shockwave Director and Shockwave Flash, QuickTime, RealPlayer, Adobe Acrobat Reader, and Microsoft PowerPoint Viewer.

Programs of Study

MU's first degree offered wholly online, the Master of Science in Emergency Management program (MSEM) is a nonthesis practitioner's degree program that offers students live virtual classroom interaction involving both the professor and students, creating a unique learning environment. The 30-credit-hour curriculum consists of 24 credit hours of required courses and 6 credit hours of electives. Each course incorporates knowledge and skills from or relevant to academic research, best practices, human behavior, and key organizations as well as legal issues, policies, rules, and regulations. The program is developed primarily for graduate students who are already in an emergency management-related career. Students must maintain at least a 3.0 grade point average for all applicable course work and have five years to complete the degree.

Student Services

The Millersville University library catalog, databases, and periodical indexes are all available on campus, off campus, or anywhere in the world with an Internet connection. Students need a library identification number, found on their Millersville University ID cards, for access. Technical support is available to all students through the help desk, which is accessible via phone and e-mail and has hours on weekdays and evenings as well as Saturday and Sunday.

Credit Options

A student may transfer up to 9 credit hours of graduate course work from a regionally accredited college or university, with approval from the MSEM program coordinator and the graduate dean. Credits may not be older than five years.

Faculty

Faculty and staff members recognize that every student arrives with energy, intelligence, and promise. With a close, collaborative learning environment, students are taught, mentored, and inspired by professors who pay attention to the context of their students' lives beyond the classroom. Innovative programs are taught by leading professors in their fields, who produce learning opportunities that are both comprehensive and deep, often beyond the depth available in larger universities or private colleges. Ninety-four percent of Millersville's professors have earned terminal degrees in their fields.

Admission

Students must have a baccalaureate degree from a regionally accredited college or university. Scores from either the Miller Analogies Test (MAT) or the Graduate Record Exam (GRE) are required. Applicants should also have experience in an emergency management or related job or have served as a volunteer in an emergency management-related organization.

Tuition and Fees

Tuition and fee information can be found online at http://www.millersville.edu/~bursar. Students should check with the Graduate Studies Office (717-872-3099, gradst@millersville.edu) for information about reduced tuition rates for nonresidents.

Financial Aid

Financial assistance is available to graduate students via student loans. More information is available at http://muweb.millersville.edu/~finaid/.

Applying

Students must submit a completed graduate application; the application fee; an official transcript from all institutions of higher education attended, with verification of completion of a baccalaureate degree from an accredited institution; an official score from either the GRE or MAT taken within five years of the date of application; and three professional letters of recommendation from nonrelatives. Applicants whose first language is not English must submit their score from the Test of English as a Foreign Language (TOEFL), which must have been completed within the previous five years. Prior to acceptance to the program, a telephone interview is arranged with the MSEM program director. All application materials are available electronically at http://www.millersville.edu/~graduate and must be in the Office of Graduate Studies and Research by February 1 for full consideration for fall admission.

CONTACT

Graduate Studies Office
Millersville University of Pennsylvania
Millersville, Pennsylvania 17551

Phone: 717-872-3099
Fax: 717-872-3453
E-mail: gradstu@millersville.edu
Web site: http://www.millersville.edu/~msem

Millersville University
SEIZE THE OPPORTUNITY

MILLERSVILLE UNIVERSITY OF PENNSYLVANIA
Master of Science in Nursing Education
Millersville, Pennsylvania

Innovation in education is the philosophy of Millersville University (MU) of Pennsylvania. Established in 1855, the University has grown to a 250-acre campus with more than sixty buildings. The University's modern research facilities, blended with Romanesque Revival structures and late-Victorian wooden frame houses, reflect its integration of contemporary and classical elements of education. Simultaneously innovative and traditional, this setting encourages close faculty-student relationships as an important component of academic and personal development. Millersville University is accredited by the Middle States Association of Colleges and Schools. The Department of Nursing's degree programs are accredited by the National League for Nursing Accrediting Commission.

Distance Learning Program

MUOnline is a growing part of the University's commitment to educational access. The mission of MUOnline is to maximize access to high-quality traditional and nontraditional education for students and professionals. The distance learning program at MU offers opportunities to further the mission of Millersville University in significant ways, such as expanding access to new and existing clientele, giving growing attention to the increasingly diverse and nontraditional students, and enhancing and expanding learning opportunities for Pennsylvanians and others through information and communication technologies.

Delivery Media

Students and professors meet in a virtual classroom for live interaction. Students should have access to a computer and the Internet. Required software may include Mozilla Firefox, Macromedia Shockwave Director and Shockwave Flash, QuickTime, RealPlayer, Adobe Acrobat Reader, and Microsoft PowerPoint Viewer.

Programs of Study

The education track of the Master of Science in Nursing—developed for part-time study for nurses balancing work and family life—is designed for those interested in teaching in diploma and associate-and baccalaureate-degree programs or working in staff development positions in hospitals, long-term-care facilities, community centers, and other settings. The degree program consists of 35 or 38 credits. Students can begin by taking the core courses, followed by the graduate nursing and the advanced nursing practice core courses, if they so choose. Core courses are available completely online; other classes are taught in a blended format, with some conducted on campus and others online. Some students, based on their State Board of Nursing regulations for nurse educators or their personal preference, can complete a nursing course with a clinical focus area (NURS 515: Advanced Practice Nursing Clinical Internship).

Special Programs

Internships and co-ops, as well as service-learning opportunities, are available. More information can be obtained from the Office of Community and Academic Partnerships (http://www.millersville.edu/~cap).

Student Services

The Millersville University library catalog, databases, and periodical indexes are all available on campus, off campus, or anywhere in the world with an Internet connection. Students need a library identification number, found on their Millersville University ID cards, for access. Technical support is available to all students through the help desk, which is accessible via phone and e-mail and has hours on weekdays and evenings as well as Saturday and Sunday.

Credit Options

To continue to take courses after 9 credits have been earned, students must apply to one of the programs in nursing.

Faculty

The faculty believes that professional nursing is a practice discipline with a unique body of knowledge derived from the humanities; the physical, biological, psychological, and social sciences; and nursing science. Faculty members recognize that learning is a lifelong process, and they ensure that the nursing education program is interactive among students, teachers, and the environment, and is individualized, creative, goal oriented, and outcome based. The faculty believes that students bring with them experiences that serve as a foundation for the examination, development, and understanding of professional development, personal growth, and affective awareness.

Admission

Applicants should have a baccalaureate degree in nursing from an accredited school of nursing, with an undergraduate GPA of at least 3.0. The undergraduate curriculum should have included courses in health assessment, statistics, and nursing research. In addition, applicants must have at least one year of clinical experience in nursing and licensure as a registered nurse in Pennsylvania or in the state where clinical practice or internship is to be arranged.

Tuition and Fees

In 2007–08, tuition and fees for 9 credits hours are $3813 and $5683 for residents and nonresidents, respectively. For 12 to 15 credit hours, Pennsylvania pay $4022, and nonresidents pay $5892.

Financial Aid

Financial assistance is available to graduate students via scholarships and graduate student loans. The former include the Lancaster Regional Medical Center/Community Hospital of Lancaster Scholarship, which covers tuition and offers a stipend; the Forty et Eight Tuition Scholarships; and the Luelle Hamilton Scholarship in Nursing. Students can also apply to the Pennsylvania Higher Education Foundation Nursing Education Grant Program. Scholarship applications are available at http://muweb.millersville.edu/~nursing/scholarships.php.

Applying

Applicants must submit the completed application, the application fee, official transcripts, official GRE or MAT scores, three academic and/or professional references, and a current resume or CV that reflects at least one year of clinical experience. All application materials must be in the Office of Graduate Studies and Research by February 1 in order to be considered for admission for the fall semester.

CONTACT

Dr. Deborah T. Castellucci, CRNP
Department Chairperson
Millersville University of Pennsylvania
127 Caputo Hall
Millersville, Pennsylvania 17551
Phone: 717-872-3410
Fax: 717-871-4877
E-mail: deborah.castellucci@millersville.edu
Web site: http://muweb.millersville.edu/~nursing/
nursing_education.php

MONTANA STATE UNIVERSITY-BILLINGS

MSU–B Online Program

Billings, Montana

Established in 1927, Montana State University-Billings provides excellent instructional and learning opportunities in the arts and sciences as well as in its professional programs in business, technology, human services, rehabilitation, and education. MSU-Billings is accredited by the Northwest Association of Schools and Colleges, and its various degree programs, including teacher education, are accredited by other individual organizations. The University offers a wide variety of preprofessional and certification programs and awards degrees at the associate, bachelor's, and master's levels to more than 4,000 students annually. For more information on Montana State University-Billings, prospective students should visit the University Web site.

Distance Learning Program

Through the Montana State University–Billings (MSU-B) Online University, established in 1998, MSU-Billings is pleased to offer students an opportunity to take college courses via the Internet as a way of overcoming barriers of time and place. The program ensures that students can achieve their personal, professional, and academic goals while not having to sacrifice the other things that are important in their lives. The program currently offers more than 240 individual online courses, including nineteen fully online degree programs, with more than 9,000 annual student enrollments.

Delivery Media

All MSU-B online classes are delivered entirely via the Internet, using the sophisticated eCollege online course delivery system. This system provides for complete course content hosting whereby all readings, assignments, multimedia tutorials, audio and video streaming media, and instructional documents are provided online. In addition to hosting course content, the delivery system provides access to a variety of cutting-edge online interaction tools, including centralized e-mail, Internet and course search tools, chat rooms, and threaded discussions, in addition to an online journal, calendar, Webliography, document sharing, exam manager, and gradebook features. Minimal hardware, software, and Internet connectivity requirements exist for all online classes.

Programs of Study

The MSU-Billings Online University currently offers fifteen fully online degree programs.

Online bachelor's degree programs are the Bachelor of Applied Science (B.A.S.), Bachelor of Arts (B.A.) in communication-mass communications, B.A. in communication-organizational communications, Bachelor of Science in Business Administration (B.S.B.A.), Bachelor of Science (B.S.) in education (*on-site requirements), Bachelor of Science (B.S.) in public relations, Bachelor of Science in Health Administration (B.S.H.A.) (*on-site enrichment available), and the Bachelor of Science in Liberal Studies (B.S.L.S.).

B.S.L.S. concentrations are available in health administration and organizational communication, health administration and public relations, management and mass communications, management and organizational communication, management and public relations, mass communications and public relations, organizational communications and accounting technology, organizational communications and human resource management, and organizational communication and public relations.

Online Associate of Applied Science (A.A.S.), Associate of Arts (A.A.), and Associate of Science (A.S.) degree programs include Accounting Technology (A.A.S.), General Studies (A.A. or A.S.), Human Resource Management–General Applied Emphasis (A.S.), and Human Resource Management–College of Business Articulated Emphasis (A.S.).

Online graduate programs offered are Education–Interdisciplinary Studies (*onsite requirements), Post-Baccalaureate: Teacher Certification (*on-site requirements), Master of Health Administration (M.H.A.) (*on-site enrichment available), and Master of Science in Public Relations.

The B.S.L.S. degree completion program uses the same curriculum as the full four-year B.S.L.S. degree, but it allows students to transfer or substitute prior academic course work into the program while completing the thematic concentration. To complete the B.S.L.S. degree or the B.S.L.S. degree completion program, individuals must earn a minimum of 120 credits with a cumulative grade point average of 2.0 or better. In addition, all students must satisfy the general education requirements at MSU-Billings. MSU-Billings accepts transfer students with completed A.A. or A.S. degrees from other institutions as having fulfilled their MSU-Billings general education requirements, provided the A.A. or A.S. is comparable in total credit hours and content to the MSU-Billings general education requirements. Students should consult with an academic adviser for an evaluation of transfer credits. Students must complete a minimum of 30 credits through MSU-Billings.

The B.A. in communication degree program shares many of the same requirements as the B.S.L.S. degree program, but it allows students to complete a major core of courses in organizational communication, mass communication, or public relations. The degree is designed to educate students entering the fields of business and social service as managers, public relations personnel, trainers, human resource officers, and corporate communication staff members. The degree also provides students with an excellent preparation for graduate study in communication or law.

For more information on any of the online courses and degree programs, prospective students should visit the MSU-B Online University Web site at http://www.msubonline.org.

Special Programs

MSU-Billings offers individuals who have already earned an associate degree an opportunity to complete an interdisciplinary bachelor's degree through the new Health Career Pathways 2+2 Online Degree Completion Programs.

The Bachelor of Science in Liberal Studies degree in health-care management and in public relations and the Bachelor of Applied Science degree in health-care administration are fully online degree-completion programs that have been strategically designed to prepare graduates for success in leadership roles in health-care management, administration, and public relations. Some of the unique features of these programs include:

2+2 Transferability: Students seamlessly transfer after graduating from their two-year college to complete their bachelor's degree from MSU-Billings.

Affordability: Students can receive up to $2000 in scholarship support for the 2+2 online degree completion, and they may also qualify for federal financial aid through this unique program.

e-Learning: Students enjoy the freedom, flexibility, comfort, and convenience of e-Learning—with more time for work and family while completing the bachelor's degree entirely online through MSU-Billings' Online University.

Adult Learning Format: By enrolling in 6 credits per term in consecutive eight-week terms, students can complete their bachelor's degree within two years with only a part-time course workload.

Student Services

The MSU-B Online University provides online students with access to all student services offered to MSU-Billings on-site students, including admissions, degree planning and advising, financial aid, ordering books and supplies, fee payment, library, 24-hour HelpDesk technical support, and a number of other student support services. In addition, all students enrolling in an online class receive access to an online orientation course that is designed to help students learn how to use the course delivery system and to maximize their success and satisfaction in online learning.

Faculty

Most of the 120 faculty members who teach classes online for the MSU-B Online University are also full-time faculty members of Montana State University-Billings. In addition to teaching their online classes, these faculty members teach equivalent courses in traditional on-site classes. Eighty-six percent of the University's faculty members hold the highest degrees in their fields.

Admission

The requirements for admission to MSU-B are the same as those for individuals taking classes on-site. Online students should apply for admission and register for online courses through the MSU-B Online University Web site at http://www.msubonline.org.

Tuition and Fees

Tuition and fees for online classes are the same as for taking classes on-site, with an additional $40-per-credit nonrefundable fee that is assessed for all Internet courses. The exact rate of tuition and fees depends upon the number of credits taken and whether the student is a resident or nonresident of Montana. For a current schedule of tuition and fees, prospective students should visit the MSU-B Online University Web site at http://www.msubonline.org.

Financial Aid

Financial aid is awarded to more than 60 percent of the University population—including students taking courses online—in the form of grants, scholarships, tuition waivers, employment, and loans. For more information or to apply for financial aid, prospective students should visit the MSU-B Online University Web site at http://www.msubonline.org.

Applying

All students wishing to enroll in MSU-B Online courses or degree programs should do so by submitting an online application and registration form accessible from the MSU-Billings Online University Web site at http://www.msubonline.org.

CONTACT

Admissions Counselor
New Student Services
McMullen 101
Montana State University-Billings
1500 University Drive
Billings, Montana 59101

Phone: 406-896-5911
      800-708-0068 Ext. 5911 (toll-free)
Fax: 406-657-2302
E-mail: inquiry@msubonline.org
Web site: http://www.msubonline.org
      http://www.msubillings.edu

NAROPA UNIVERSITY

Boulder, Colorado

Naropa University is a private, nonprofit, nonsectarian, liberal arts institution dedicated to advancing contemplative education. This approach to learning integrates the best of Eastern and Western educational traditions, helping students know themselves more deeply and engage constructively with others. Accredited by the Higher Learning Commission of the North Central Association of Colleges and Schools, the University comprises a four-year undergraduate college and graduate degree programs in the arts, education, environmental leadership, psychology, and religious studies, as well a study-abroad program in Prague, Czech Republic.

Distance Learning Program

In addition to its many in-residence programs, Naropa University offers four low-residency graduate degree programs: M.A. in contemplative education, M.A. in transpersonal psychology, M.A. in transpersonal psychology with a concentration in ecopsychology, and an M.F.A. in creative writing.

Delivery Media

Courses are offered from the heart of Naropa University's liberal arts curriculum. They are taught by experienced Naropa faculty members and translated and refined for delivery through state-of-the-art Internet technology. Naropa utilizes the latest interactive Internet technologies, with private, password-secure Web pages for the exclusive use of the students and instructors of each class. Communication tools include audio lectures, multimedia, chat rooms, threaded discussion groups, private online journals, written lectures, local assignments, and group projects in a dynamic online learning community. Enrolled students have access to 24/7 technical support.

Programs of Study

The Master of Arts in contemplative education is a two-year, 36-credit degree program for practicing teachers from all levels of instruction and for others interested in a nonsectarian, contemplative approach to teaching and learning. This professional development program joins together the wisdom and skillful means of Eastern meditative traditions with Western holistic educational methods and insights. Based on the principles and practices of mindfulness and awareness primarily from Tibetan contemplative traditions, the curriculum offers a path of personal nourishment and effective pedagogy. The program begins in the summer with a three-week residential program, which is followed by two online courses in each of the fall and spring semesters. Online semesters apply contemplative approaches to each student's classroom, as well as extend academic studies of spiritual approaches to teaching, learning, and human emotional development. The second year repeats this sequence, except the Thesis Seminar is the only spring online course. The program is completed during the third summer conference with the thesis presentation. Summer retreats are typically held from late-June to mid-July in Colorado and focus on the contemplative transformation of the teacher. For further information, students should contact Richard Brown, Chair, MA Contemplative Education Program (phone: 303-545-4765; e-mail: rbrown@naropa.edu.)

The low-residency Master of Arts in transpersonal psychology is a two-year, 36-credit program that integrates intellectual rigor, contemplative practice, personal development, and applications of transpersonal psychology. The curriculum includes required courses on foundations, theories and applications of transpersonal psychology, and meditation practice. Two 1-week summer intensives on the campus provide community building and exploration of transpersonal practices and issues. The transpersonal psychology program does not result in a clinical degree. Those who already have professional clinical or counseling training and credentials may use this degree to expand their understanding and practice. Prospective students should contact John Davis, the Director of the Master of Arts program in transpersonal psychology (phone: 303-245-4654; e-mail: jdavis@naropa.edu).

The Master of Arts in transpersonal psychology with a concentration in ecopsychology integrates psychology and ecology in the study of human/nature relationships. At Naropa University, contemplative practice and transpersonal psychology provide a foundation for this integration, and the result is a unique contemplative and transpersonal orientation. Following the general format of the MATP program, the ecopsychology program is a two-year, 38-credit program that begins in the summer. Students also attend a three-day intensive course in Boulder each winter. Course work integrates theory, experience, and contemplative practice in the study of ecopsychology, ecology, transpersonal psychology, and meditative practices. The ecopsychology concentration does not result in a clinical degree. Additional information is available from Jed Swift, the Director of the ecopsychology program (phone:

303-245-4837 or 614-921-1997; e-mail: jedscottswift@earthlink.net).

The Master of Fine Arts in creative writing is a 49-credit degree program. Courses are taken online during the regular academic year, and 16 credit hours of the Summer Writing Program (spread out over two or three summers) are completed at Naropa University's Boulder campus. The curriculum balances online writing workshops and literature seminars. This reflects the department's conviction that creative writing, reading, and critical analysis must be involved in a writer's growth. The contact person for the program is Junior Burke, Chair of the Department of Writing and Poetics and the Director of the M.F.A. in creative writing program (phone: 303-245-4820; e-mail: jrburke@naropa.edu).

Faculty

The Naropa University faculty is distinguished by a wealth of experience in the professional, artistic, and scholastic applications of their disciplines. In addition to the outstanding core faculty, an international community of scholars and artists is consistently drawn to Naropa because of its strong vision and leadership in contemplative education. The average class size is 13, and Naropa's student-teacher ratio is 12:1.

Admission

When making admissions decisions, Naropa considers inquisitiveness and engagement with the world as well as previous academic achievement. A student's statement of interest, interview, letters of recommendation, and supplemental application materials play important roles in the admissions process. GRE scores are not required.

Tuition and Fees

Beginning summer 2007, graduate tuition is $685 per credit hour, plus a registration fee ($120 for summer, $250 for fall, $250 for spring). In addition, technology fees are: 1 credit, $60; 1.5 credits, $75; 2 credits, $90; 2.5 credits, $105; 3 credits, $120; 4 credits, $150; and 5 credits, $180.

Financial Aid

Naropa University makes every attempt to assist students who do not have the financial resources to accomplish their educational objectives. Naropa offers institutional grants and scholarships, as well as all types of federal student aid, including subsidized and unsubsidized Federal Stafford Student Loans. Some financial aid for international students is available. Approximately 70 percent of Naropa's degree-seeking students receive financial assistance in the form of loans, student employment, scholarships, and grants. Naropa also offers Tuition Management Systems, which allows students to make monthly payments for tuition with no interest charges.

Applying

The suggested deadline for receiving completed applications for the summer and fall semesters is January 15, and for the spring semester, October 15. Any application received after the suggested deadline will be reviewed on a space-available basis.

CONTACT

Office of Admissions
Naropa University
2130 Arapahoe Avenue
Boulder, Colorado 80302
Phone: 303-546-3572
        800-772-6951 (toll-free)
E-mail: admissions@naropa.edu
Web site: http://www.naropa.edu

THE NEW SCHOOL
A UNIVERSITY

THE NEW SCHOOL: A UNIVERSITY
Bachelor's Degree Program for Adults
New York, New York

The New School is a legendary, progressive university comprising eight schools that are bound by a common, unusual intent—to prepare and inspire the University's 9,300 undergraduate and graduate students to bring actual, positive change to the world. From its Greenwich Village campus, The New School launches economists and actors, fashion designers and urban planners, dancers and anthropologists, orchestra conductors, filmmakers, political scientists, organizational experts, jazz musicians, scholars, psychologists, historians, journalists, and above all, world citizens—individuals whose ideas and innovations forge new paths of progress in the arts, design, humanities, public policy, and the social sciences.

In addition to offering seventy graduate and undergraduate degrees, the University offers certificate programs and more than 1,000 continuing education courses to 25,000 adult learners every year. The University began offering online courses and programs in 1994 with the support of grants from FIPSE, ATT, Citibank, and the Alfred P. Sloan Foundation. The New School and its degree programs are fully accredited by the Commission on Higher Education of the Middle States Association of Colleges and Schools. Its credits and degrees are recognized and accepted by other accredited colleges, universities, and professional schools throughout the United States.

Distance Learning Program

The New School offers online degrees, certificates, and individual courses to more than 1,110 students. More than 200 Web-based classes taught by New School professors are available annually and can be taken for degree credit, general credit (courses for transfer to other institutions), or no credit. The seminar style of teaching translates especially well to the Web.

All online courses are drawn from the University's curriculum and are designed to integrate with the rest of the student's program of study. A recent issue of *ComputerLife* magazine cited The New School as having "one of the best and most extensive course offerings in the field of liberal arts online."

Delivery Media

Students must have a computer and an Internet connection in order to access MyNewSchool.edu, where the University's online classes "meet." Similar to any class taken on campus, the professor presents the material and then leads a discussion. However, instead of speaking, students post comments using the My Courses feature of MyNewSchool. The experience is much like that of a traditional class—in fact, the conversation is sometimes more in depth, because the posting mechanism makes it easier for all students to participate. Online classes meet asynchronously, meaning that students can read materials, join discussions, and post responses at any time. Although each class is different, it is strongly recommended that students log in to the class a minimum of three times each week.

Programs of Study

Intended for students returning to college to complete their undergraduate degrees, the Bachelor's Program online at The New School for General Studies is an individualized program of study in the liberal arts. The understanding of the individual, society, and the world that comes from the study of the liberal arts should be at the heart of undergraduate education. With the assistance of a faculty adviser, each student selects a program of study based on intellectual interests and professional goals. The New School requires a total of 120 credits for the bachelor's degree, with at least 30 credits of course work as a matriculated student. However, the credit requirement may be waived for students age 24 or older.

The following areas of study are currently available to bachelor's degree students: cinema and media studies, the city, creative writing, democracy and cultural pluralism, literature, media production, psychology, visual arts, and visual studies. Others area are being developed for the future. For detailed information on the courses within these areas, students should visit http://adultba.newschool.edu.

Special Programs

The New School Bachelor's Program online offers non-liberal arts credit for internships arranged through the degree program office. To apply for an internship, students should have earned at least 12 credits in residence at The New School and have an internship in mind that contributes to their overall plan of study. Students are allowed to take up to two internships while matriculated in the Bachelor's Program. Credit for independent study courses can be arranged through the degree program office in conjunction with the academic departments.

Student Services

The same student services that are available to those who take classes on campus—advising, admissions, registration, tuition payment, and enrollment—are also available to the University's online students. Online students have the advantage of being able to arrange everything online or by phone, fax, mail, or e-mail—all without having to visit the campus.

Through an online student orientation, students learn how to navigate the online classroom, gain familiarity with online communication, and get a sense of the dynamics of online interaction before a course begins. The orientation remains available for reference throughout the semester. Technical support and student service professionals are available by phone or e-mail 24 hours a day, seven days a week.

Credit Options

The New School awards up to 6 credits for college-level learning comparable to the courses offered at the University. Students considering applying for credit for prior learning should discuss their options with their adviser.

Faculty

Instructors at the New School come from diverse fields within and outside the field of education. They all share one common motivation—teaching what they are most interested in and what they consider most valuable to know. In addition to academic scholars, many are working professionals who bring to the classroom the benefit of their experience.

Admission

The New School Bachelor's Program online welcomes applications from individuals with at least 33 credits toward a bachelor's degree (the credit requirement may be waived for students age 24 or older) who have the maturity to be in charge of their own learning process and can demonstrate their ability to work successfully in an intellectually challenging academic environment. The New School seeks students who are inquisitive, independent, and self-directed. Applicants should have strong verbal skills (spoken and written) and a capacity for clear, critical thinking.

Tuition and Fees

In 2006–07, students paid $800 per credit plus $115 in University fees, which covered the registration and technology fee, as well as a Student Activity Fee of $15. New tuition and fee schedules are published several months in advance of each academic year.

Financial Aid

Financial aid is granted on the basis of need and merit, with financial need determined in accordance with federal regulations. Packages awarded are based on estimated total educational costs for the academic year. Most forms of financial aid require recipients to take a minimum of 6 credits each semester, and some require full-time study (12 credits or more). To maintain eligibility for federal and state financial aid, students must be in good academic standing and must be making satisfactory progress toward their baccalaureate degree.

Applying

Students must submit the completed application form, the nonrefundable $50 application fee, official transcripts from each college or university attended, a resume, and three essays (Educational Objective, New Way of Thinking, and Course Plan). An interview may be required. Additional information can be found on the link for Admissions at http://adultba.newschool.edu/.

For the fall semester, the priority deadline is June 1 and the final deadline is July 1. The deadline for spring admission is November 1.

CONTACT

Gerianne Brusati, Associate
    Director of Admissions
The New School
66 West 12th Street, Room 401
New York, New York 10011
Phone: 212-229-5630
Fax: 212-989-3887
E-mail: brusatig@newschool.edu
Web site: http://adultba.newschool.
    edu

THE NEW SCHOOL: A UNIVERSITY

Master of Arts in Media Studies Program

New York, New York

The New School is a legendary, progressive university comprising eight schools that are bound by a common, unusual intent—to prepare and inspire the University's 9,300 undergraduate and graduate students to bring actual, positive change to the world. From its Greenwich Village campus, The New School launches economists and actors, fashion designers and urban planners, dancers and anthropologists, orchestra conductors, filmmakers, political scientists, organizational experts, jazz musicians, scholars, psychologists, historians, journalists, and above all, world citizens—individuals whose ideas and innovations forge new paths of progress in the arts, design, humanities, public policy, and the social sciences.

In addition to offering seventy graduate and undergraduate degrees, the University offers certificate programs and nearly 1,000 continuing education courses to 15,000 adult learners every year. The University began offering online courses and programs in 1994 with the support of grants from FIPSE, ATT, Citibank, and the Alfred P. Sloan Foundation. The New School and its degree programs are fully accredited by the Commission on Higher Education of the Middle States Association of Colleges and Schools. Its credits and degrees are recognized and accepted by other accredited colleges, universities, and professional schools throughout the United States.

Distance Learning Program

The New School offers degrees, certificates, and individual courses online to more than 1,110 students. Over 200 Web-based classes taught by New School professors are available annually and can be taken for degree credit, general credit (courses for transfer to other institutions), or no credit. The seminar style of teaching translates especially well to the Web.

All online courses are drawn from the University's curriculum and are designed to integrate with the rest of the student's program of study. A recent issue of *ComputerLife* magazine cited The New School as having "one of the best and most extensive course offerings in the field of liberal arts online."

Delivery Media

Students must have a computer and an Internet connection in order to access MyNewSchool.edu, where the University's online classes "meet." As in any class taken on campus, the professor presents the material and then leads a discussion. However, instead of speaking, students post comments using the My Courses feature of MyNewSchool. The experience is much like that of a traditional class—in fact, the conversation is sometimes more in depth, because the posting mechanism makes it easier for all students to participate. Online classes meet asynchronously, meaning that students can read materials, join discussions, and post responses at any time. Although each class is different, it is strongly recommended that students log in to the class a minimum of three times each week.

Program of Study

The New School's Master of Arts (M.A.) in Media Studies program is one of the few in the country that allows students to integrate course work in media theory, media production, and media management. The program helps students put theory into practice, guided by a faculty of media professionals from all walks of academic, artistic, and commercial life, who strive to be humane and thoughtful citizens in an increasingly mediated world. In an era defined by rapidly changing information and communication technologies, a master's degree in media studies can give students the competitive edge they need.

Students must successfully complete a minimum of 36 credits (thesis option) or 39 credits (nonthesis option) to fulfill degree requirements. All degree candidates are required to take Foundations of Media Theory, Foundations of Media Design, Media Research Methods, and two courses in a production sequence (video, audio, film, digital design, or multimedia). The online program of study provides an opportunity for students to satisfy all the requirements for the M.A. degree. Required theory and research courses and a full complement of electives are offered online over two academic years.

The New School M.A. in Media Studies program reflects a commitment to a number of core values: an emphasis on the essential relationship between media theory and practice in the belief that a conceptual understanding of media is necessary for creating discerning productions and, in turn, that producing media messages grounds an understanding of theory; a respect for both aesthetic and pragmatic dimensions of communication; a recognition of the integrity and potential contribution of all media formats; an awareness of the ethical imperatives of communication throughout the "global village;" an appreciation of the ways in which media theory and practice can contribute to intercultural understanding; an acknowledgment of the challenging marketplace conditions facing today's graduates; and a belief in the importance of openness to change and innovation.

Special Programs

Each semester the students in Media Studies create videos, films, and multimedia as part of their requirements for the degree. These showcases, which highlight selected group projects and special events, include the Critical Themes in

Media Studies Student Conference, Mixed Messages, the Hirshon Film Festival, and Immediacy, an online journal.

Media studies students have held internships over the past years at such organizations as Showtime, MTV, Oxygen Television, NBC, Children's Television Workshop, Bloomberg Television, *POV, 60 Minutes,* Polygram Records, and the United Nations.

Student Services

The same student services that are available to those who take classes on campus—advising, admissions, registration, tuition payment, and enrollment—are also available to online students. Online students have the advantage of being able to arrange everything online or by phone, fax, mail, or e-mail, without the need to schedule a campus visit.

Through an online student orientation, students have the opportunity to learn how to navigate the online classroom, gain familiarity with online communication, and get a sense of the dynamics of online interaction before a course begins. The orientation remains available for reference throughout the semester. Technical support and student service professionals are available by phone or e-mail 24 hours a day, seven days a week.

Credit Options

Admitted degree candidates may apply for transfer of up to 9 credits to be used toward the elective requirement.

Faculty

Instructors at the New School come from diverse fields within and outside education. They all share one common motivation—teaching what they are most interested in and what they consider most valuable to know. In addition to academic scholars, many are working professionals who bring to the classroom the benefit of their experience.

Admission

The Media Studies Program takes an inclusive view of media and communication studies, and welcomes strong applicants from all undergraduate majors, especially in the liberal arts. The program seeks mature and motivated individuals who demonstrate a clear vision and potential for original thinking and work. For more information and/or to arrange a class visit, prospective students should contact an admissions counselor at 212-229-5630.

Tuition and Fees

In 2006–07, students pay $968 per credit plus $115 per semester in University fees, which cover the registration and technology fee, as well as a Student Activity Fee of $15. New tuition and fee schedules are published several months in advance of each academic year.

Financial Aid

Media Studies scholarships are awarded to those who demonstrate academic merit. To apply for assistantships, students must complete an application form that is available from the Media Studies Student Services Office. Students must be registered for a minimum of 6 credits during the fall and spring semesters. Candidates eligible for college work-study may work hours in addition to, but not combined with, award hours. Awards are available to degree candidates only. All awards are for the academic year, not the semester. Students are invited to apply for more than one award.

All applications should be submitted to the Media Studies Scholarship Committee, Department of Media Studies and Film, The New School, 70 Fifth Avenue, New York, New York 10011.

Applying

An applicant must hold a bachelor's degree from an accredited college or university. A completed application (available online), the $50 application fee, a statement of purpose, official transcripts of all undergraduate and graduate studies, and one academic and one professional letter of recommendation should be submitted. International students must submit a minimum TOEFL score of 230 (570 on the paper-based test) and official transcripts of all undergraduate and graduate studies translated into English as well as a WES credential evaluation.

The application deadline for the fall semester is February 15; the spring semester deadline is October 15.

CONTACT

Gerianne Brusati, Associate Dean for Admissions
The New School
66 West 12th Street, Room 401
New York, New York 10011

Phone: 212-229-5630
Fax: 212-989-3887
E-mail: nsadmissions@newschool.edu
Web site: http://www.mediastudies.newschool.edu

THE NEW SCHOOL: A UNIVERSITY

THE NEW SCHOOL A UNIVERSITY

M.A. in Teaching English to Speakers of Other Languages
New York, New York

The New School is a legendary, progressive university comprising eight schools that are bound by a common, unusual intent—to prepare and inspire the University's 9,300 undergraduate and graduate students to bring actual, positive change to the world. From its Greenwich Village campus, The New School launches economists and actors, fashion designers and urban planners, dancers and anthropologists, orchestra conductors, filmmakers, political scientists, organizational experts, jazz musicians, scholars, psychologists, historians, journalists, and above all, world citizens—individuals whose ideas and innovations forge new paths of progress in the arts, design, humanities, public policy, and the social sciences.

In addition to offering seventy graduate and undergraduate degrees, the University offers certificate programs and nearly 1,000 continuing education courses to 15,000 adult learners every year. The University began offering online courses and programs in 1994 with the support of grants from FIPSE, ATT, Citibank, and the Alfred P. Sloan Foundation. The New School and its degree programs are fully accredited by the Commission on Higher Education of the Middle States Association of Colleges and Schools. Its credits and degrees are recognized and accepted by other accredited colleges, universities, and professional schools throughout the United States.

Distance Learning Program

The New School offers degrees, certificates, and individual courses online to more than 1,110 students. Over 200 Web-based classes taught by New School professors are available annually and can be taken for degree credit, general credit (courses for transfer to other institutions), or no credit. The seminar style of teaching translates especially well to the Web.

All online courses are drawn from the University's curriculum and are designed to integrate with the rest of the student's program of study. A recent issue of *ComputerLife* magazine cited The New School as having "one of the best and most extensive course offerings in the field of liberal arts online."

Delivery Media

Students must have a computer and an Internet connection in order to access MyNewSchool.edu, where the University's online classes "meet." As in any classes taken on campus, the professor presents the material and then leads a discussion. However, instead of speaking, students post comments using the My Courses feature of MyNewSchool. The experience is much like that of a traditional class—in fact, the conversation is sometimes more in depth, because the posting mechanism makes it easier for all students to participate. Online classes meet asynchronously, meaning that students can read materials, join discussions, and post responses at any time. Although each class is different, it is strongly recommended that students log in to the class a minimum of three times each week.

Programs of Study

The New School's 30-credit Master of Arts in Teaching English to Speakers of Other Languages (MATESOL) program is designed to raise the standards of trained professionals in the TESOL field and consequently to raise the standards of the profession itself. Some elements that make the New School MATESOL distinctive include training in specialized concentrations (publishing and writing, program development and management, curriculum development, or teaching), political and cultural orientation, flexible scheduling, and theory leading to practical, hands-on training. A thesis is not required.

The program provides students with the practical, relevant training they will need to advance in careers in publishing, writing, managing, and developing ESOL programs, or designing curriculum in the public or private sector. The goal of the program is to produce well-trained, culturally and politically aware professionals who are proficient in their specialties and knowledgeable about crucial issues in language teaching and learning in the evolving global environment.

Students who take six courses online and four courses during the summer in New York City can complete the MATESOL in one calendar year or three semesters. Students generally need four semesters to complete the entire program online.

Special Programs

A six-week intensive summer program at The New School in Greenwich Village in New York City gives MATESOL students the option of completing 12 credits of course work while experiencing one of the most exciting cities in the world. Students also have the chance to do internships at well-known ESOL publishers or in ESL programs at some of the best teaching sites in the city. Housing is available in university dormitories.

Student Services

The same student services that are available to those who take classes on campus—advising, admissions, registration, tuition payment, and enrollment—are also available to the University's online students. Online students have the advantage of being able to arrange everything online or by phone, fax, mail, or e-mail, without the need to schedule a campus visit.

Through an online student orientation, students have the opportunity to learn how to navigate the online classroom, gain familiarity with online communication, and get a sense of the dynamics of online interaction before a course begins. The orientation remains available for reference throughout the semester. Technical support and student service professionals are available by phone or e-mail 24 hours a day, seven days a week.

Faculty

Instructors at The New School come from diverse fields within and outside education. They all share one common motivation—teaching what they are most interested in and what they consider most valuable to know. In addition to academic scholars, many are working professionals who bring to the classroom the benefit of their experience. The MATESOL faculty members and course developers have been chosen from among the best, most experienced, and most respected TESOL professionals around the world, including teacher educators, publishers, writers, curriculum designers, and program administrators.

Admission

The MATESOL program welcomes applications from individuals interested in preparing for careers in teaching English to adults and from ESL or EFL professionals with two or more years of teaching experience. Proficiency in a language other than English is assumed for all applicants. Applications are reviewed and admission decisions are made by a faculty committee.

Tuition and Fees

Tuition for the 2007–08 academic year (pending approval of the Board of Trustees) is $1000 per credit plus $115 per semester in University fees, which cover the registration and technology fee, as well as a Student Activity Fee of $15. New tuition and fee schedules are published several months in advance of each academic year.

Financial Aid

Financial aid is granted on the basis of need and merit, with financial need determined in accordance with federal regulations. Packages awarded are based on estimated total educational costs for the academic year. Most forms of financial aid require recipients to take a minimum of 6 credits each semester, and some require full-time study (12 credits or more). To maintain eligibility for federal and state financial aid, students must be in good academic standing.

The MATESOL program gives scholarship consideration to all applicants as part of the admissions review process. Strong academic and professional achievements identify those candidates for admission who, in the estimation of the admissions committee, merit special recognition. Scholarship amounts vary and cover partial costs of tuition. A student must register for a minimum of 6 credits to maintain the scholarship.

Applying

Applicants must hold a bachelor's degree from an accredited university. Students must submit the completed application, the $50 application fee, official transcripts from every institution attended for undergraduate and graduate studies, a resume, a statement of purpose, and two letters of recommendation. In addition, applicants for the concentrations in publishing and writing, program development and management, or curriculum development must have completed a minimum of 100 hours of English language teacher training as well as two years of English language teaching and must submit a lesson plan, an essay on the philosophy of teaching, and one recommendation from a teaching supervisor.

The deadline for fall admission is March 15. All applicants are encouraged to submit applications well in advance of the stated deadline. Only completed applications received by the deadline are considered for the upcoming academic term.

CONTACT

Gerianne Brusati, Associate Dean of Admissions

The New School

66 West 12th Street, Room 401

New York, New York 10011

Phone: 212-229-5630

Fax: 212-989-3887

E-mail: nsadmissions@newschool. edu

Web site: http://www.newschool. edu/matesol

NORTHERN ARIZONA UNIVERSITY
Distance Learning
Flagstaff, Arizona

Established in 1899, Northern Arizona University (NAU) has maintained a tradition of excellence over the past century, through its commitment to providing quality academic programs, a wide range of majors, personalized services, and close faculty-student interaction. With thirty campus locations throughout Arizona and a growing number of online programs, NAU serves approximately 19,000 students from all fifty states and sixty-three countries. An integral part of NAU's mission, distance learning is recognized nationally and internationally for its outstanding programs in education, the health professions, the hospitality professions, forestry management, and more. Long-standing community partnerships, dedicated faculty and staff members, continued new-program development to meet market demand, powerful technology, and a philosophy of "expand on demand" create a unique, progressive learning environment.

Distance Learning Program

With more than twenty-five years of experience, NAU offers a growing number of programs in a range of venues, including Web-based learning opportunities. Convenient and comprehensive, this format provides students greater flexibility and options for earning a degree from an accredited university.

Delivery Media

NAU offers a variety of formats for distance learning students that includes the latest technological advances. Through NAU, videoconferencing connects rural and urban areas alike. DISH network, satellite broadcasting, and high-speed Internet access allow NAU to deploy the latest technology to deliver higher-education opportunities across traditional social and geographic boundaries. All delivery methods allow the instructors and students to interact via e-mail or online chat rooms. Textbooks and materials are available through the NAU bookstore.

Programs of Study

Dedicated to providing students with a high-quality education, NAU offers the same accredited degree via distance learning technology as the degree awarded on the NAU campus, holding all students and faculty members to the same standards of excellence. NAU currently offers the following programs: the Bachelor of Arts in Liberal Studies (B.A.I.L.S.) degree, with emphases in arts and letters, enterprise in society, parks and recreation management, and public agency service; the Bachelor of Applied Science (B.A.S.) degree in computer technology, early childhood education, health promotion, and public agency service; the Bachelor of Science (B.S.) degree in health promotion, hotel and restaurant management, and parks and recreation management; the Bachelor of Science in Education (B.S.Ed.) degree in career and technical education; the Bachelor of Science in Dental Hygiene (B.S.D.H.) degree-completion program; the Bachelor of Science in Nursing (B.S.N.) degree, an RN to B.S.N. program; the Master of Administration (M.Admin.) degree; the Master of Arts (M.A.) degree in applied communication; the Master of Arts in Teaching (M.A.T.) degree in mathematics; the Master of Education (M.Ed.) degree in career and technical education, educational technology, and elementary education; the Master of Engineering (M.Eng.) degree; endorsements in English as a second language, middle school, and reading; and certificates in educational technology, inter-national tourism management, parks and recreation management, professional writing, public management, and restaurant management. Each of these programs of study was developed based on student needs.

Special Programs

A member of the Arizona Regents University, NAU works in conjunction with Arizona State University and the University of Arizona to offer students access to courses and degrees not offered by NAU. Students select a home campus through which they receive all services, including registration. Students may earn credit from all three institutions, which transfers to degree programs at any one of the three universities.

Western Governors University (WGU) is an online university offering Web-based classes from a variety of educational institutions in sixteen states, Guam, and Canada. NAU is a provider of classes for WGU. Students enrolled in these classes are considered non-degree-seeking for NAU purposes, though they may be earning a degree from WGU. Students pay 1½ times in-state tuition.

Student Services

NAU distance learning students are provided electronic access to academic records, enrollment, online research through Cline Library, and other online student services. Academic advising is available to distance students either online or through NAU's toll-free number. Students who do not have a computer and live in Arizona can complete their classes at one of the twenty-five NAU statewide computer labs.

Credit Options

To be eligible for financial aid, students must be admitted to a degree or certification program. Classes may be taken for audit or professional development credit; however, space may be limited due to for-credit student demand. Most classes are evaluated with a letter grade, but some classes are offered on a pass-fail basis. These classes are outlined in the current NAU undergraduate and graduate catalogs.

Faculty

All distance learning instructors are faculty members, 80 percent of whom hold a doctorate or other terminal degree in their field. All faculty members have continued involvement within their fields of expertise.

Admission

NAU has a rolling admissions policy.

Tuition and Fees

Nonresident students taking only Web or satellite courses are eligible for a special reduced tuition rate of 1½ times in-state tuition. The graduate degree- or certificate-seeking applicants pay a $50 admission fee. The non-degree-seeking or readmitting applicants pay a $25 admission fee. The undergraduate application fee is $25 for U.S. citizens and legal residents and $50 for international students. Some classes may have additional fees attached (students should see the online course catalog for those fees).

Financial Aid

NAU maintains an extensive financial assistance program. The amount of financial aid awarded to students is based upon their need as computed from the Free Application for Federal Student Aid (FAFSA). Students requiring financial aid or other benefits must comply with policies and deadlines.

Applying

Undergraduate applicants must provide transcripts from high school and all higher education institutions attended. Graduate applicants must hold a baccalaureate degree from an accredited institution and provide transcripts of college course work. Students should refer to the NAU catalog for specific program requirements.

CONTACT

Distance Learning
Northern Arizona University
P.O. Box 4117
Flagstaff, Arizona 86001-4117

Phone: 800-426-8315 (toll-free)
Fax: 928-523-1169
E-mail: distance.program@nau.edu
Web site: http://www.distance.nau.edu

NORTHWESTERN COLLEGE
Center for Distance Education
St. Paul, Minnesota

Northwestern College, which was founded in 1902, is an independent, Christian four-year college. It is accredited by the North Central Association of Colleges and Schools. It first offered distance learning courses in 1994. In 2005–06, the College offered forty-seven courses at a distance and had over 3,000 new distance enrollments.

Distance Learning Program

The Center for Distance Education (CDE) at Northwestern College is at the forefront of delivering high-quality, Christ-centered education in a flexible and convenient format. More than a correspondence school, the center utilizes the latest strategies in adult education and user-friendly technology to bring college courses to students. Since 1994, the CDE has enrolled more than 6,000 students and delivered more than 17,000 courses to students all over the world. With more than forty-five courses to choose from, students can take courses in Bible, English, history, math, science, speech, music, and physical fitness.

Delivery Media

The Center for Distance Education makes use of the most convenient delivery methods possible. Course media is determined by the content of the course but usually consists of printed study guides, video lectures, CD-ROMs, and textbooks. Course work is usually submitted through the Internet, though some is submitted through postal mail. All courses host a course site that is used for interaction between students and instructors, although each course varies in the level of participation.

Programs of Study

The Center for Distance Education seeks to meet the educational needs of adult learners by offering Christ-centered curriculum. The center currently offers a Certificate of Bible, the INSIGHT program, an Associate of Arts in bible, a Bachelor of Arts in biblical studies, a Bachelor of Arts in global studies, and dual-enrollment options for high school students.

The Certificate of Bible prepares students for Christian ministry through the completion of 32 credits. The program provides in-depth training in Bible study and develops credentials for ministry-related endeavors. All credits earned in the certificate program may be applied to a degree program at Northwestern.

The Associate in Arts and Bible Program is designed to prepare the graduate for transfer to an upper-level degree program at Northwestern or another institution. The degree is granted upon completion of 60 credits. Students should contact the Center for Distance Education for details. Students should also check the course requirements of the program and school where further study is planned.

The INSIGHT program is an on-site study in Pasadena, California, and Minneapolis, Minnesota, that is designed to provide first-year students with a comprehensive Christian worldview as a foundation for the major they eventually choose. The curriculum consists of four modules to be taken consecutively over the course of one year. Each INSIGHT module follows the unfolding of God's work through human developments, revealing His redemptive plan and consequently His glory. Each module is worth 8 semester credits, for a total of 32 lower-division college credits.

The Bachelor of Arts in biblical studies is designed to provide in-depth study and preparation in bible and related areas and subjects. It is intended for students who wish to pursue graduate studies in preparation for teaching, for those who desire a solid pre-seminary program, or for persons who wish to gain a high proficiency in biblical studies.

The Bachelor of Arts in global studies is designed for students who have previously completed two years of postsecondary course work and are serious about full-time ministry. The major is targeted at those preparing for or currently involved in missions endeavors. However, any Christian, whether at home or abroad, who desires to more fully understand God's evangelistic purposes benefits from this program.

Special Programs

The Post Secondary Enrollment Option (PSEO) is a program that is open to high school juniors and seniors who are public-, private-, or home-schooled and who are residents of the state of Minnesota. This program allows high school students to take courses through the Center for Distance Education and earn credit that applies to both high school and college. Credits earned under this program are applicable to degree programs at Northwestern or other institutions. The state of Minnesota finances the program.

The NextStep program offers college courses to qualified high school juniors and seniors anywhere. It is meant to be a stepping stone to their college career. These courses are offered at a discounted rate, and course materials are provided on a loan basis.

Student Services

The Center for Distance Education helps students achieve their educational goals without feeling like a number in someone's system. From enrollment through course completion, Student Services staff members provide caring, proactive service. The CDE processes course assignments, helps find mentors and exam proctors, and helps maintain contact with faculty members.

Northwestern College's Bernsten Library aids distance learners with research and resource acquisition for projects and papers. The CDE Web site and Course Management System contain independent-study tools and helpful resources to facilitate learning.

Free unofficial transfer evaluations are offered to students who are interested in a degree program. Students must provide copies of transcripts or grade reports showing previous college work. These documents are reviewed by the CDE Registrar, entered on a curriculum chart, and returned to the student. Students have the chance to see how previous college work meets the CDE's requirements.

Credit Options

Some students may transfer credits from another institution or may earn credits through examinations, portfolio assessment, life experience, or military training.

Faculty

Distance education faculty members are credentialed professionals who are highly qualified in their academic disciplines. More than 35 faculty members teach distance education courses. Of this group, 19 have earned doctoral degrees. The faculty members at Northwestern College care about each student's spiritual, intellectual, and emotional development as well as their academic development.

Admission

To qualify for a certificate or degree program, students must meet the admission requirements of Northwestern College. Students should contact the Center for Distance Education for specific requirements. Students not seeking to earn credits toward a degree or a certificate at Northwestern are allowed to take up to 16 credits without formal admission to the College. PSEO and NextStep applicants must be at least 16 years old, have suitable scores on a state-recognized benchmark exam or a letter of recommendation from a high school official, and demonstrate competence in college-level work.

Tuition and Fees

There is a one-time, nonrefundable $30 fee at the time of registration. Tuition is $235 per semester credit. There is a required fee of $85 for each course's materials. Discounts apply to full- or part-time Christian workers.

Financial Aid

Admitted students who register for at least 6 credit hours for a degree program in one semester may be eligible for financial aid. Northwestern College cooperates with the U.S. Department of Veterans Affairs when eligible admitted students request VA benefits for distance education courses. The College also works with the Defense Activity for Non-Traditional Education Support (DANTES). Students should contact the CDE for more information.

Applying

Information can be obtained either at the CDE Web site or by contacting the Center for Distance Education. Students may register for distance education by mail or fax, online, or in person. To register, students should complete a registration form either online or by mail, pay the nonrefundable processing fee, and contact the CDE to begin the registration process.

CONTACT

Center for Distance Education
Northwestern College
3003 Snelling Avenue North
Saint Paul, Minnesota 55113

Phone: 800-308-5495 (toll-free)
Fax: 651-631-5133
E-mail: distance@nwc.edu
Web site: http://www.distance.nwc.edu

NORTHWESTERN UNIVERSITY

Master of Science in Medical Informatics

Evanston, Illinois

Northwestern University is a world-class institution committed to providing access to high-quality educational opportunities. Innovative teaching and pioneering research come together in a highly collaborative environment that transcends traditional academic boundaries.

Founded in 1851, Northwestern University is a private institution located just 12 miles north of Chicago. The University has 2,250 full-time faculty members, including Nobel and Pulitzer Prize winners, MacArthur Fellowship recipients, and members of numerous honorary and professional societies. Northwestern has more than 160,000 alumni who have become leaders in business, government, law, science, education, medicine, media, and the performing arts. Northwestern is recognized both nationally and internationally for the high quality of its educational programs at all levels.

Distance Learning Program

Medical Informatics blends health-care management and information systems, providing medical and technology professionals with the knowledge and skills necessary for leadership roles. The field of medical informatics is experiencing significant growth as health care and related industries have become increasingly dependent on information management. To prepare leaders in this exciting new field, Northwestern University School of Continuing Studies, in partnership with the Feinberg School of Medicine, offers the Master of Science in Medical Informatics (MMI) program in an online format.

Designed with the working professional in mind, the online option for this graduate degree program parallels its campus-based counterpart in every way, providing the same curriculum designed and taught by Northwestern faculty members. The MMI program is designed to be completed in two to three years of uninterrupted part-time study, although students are allowed five years from the first quarter of registration to finish the program.

Delivery Media

The MMI program at Northwestern University offers a dynamic interactive learning experience with small class sizes, individual and team projects, and faculty interaction combined with rich online materials.

Program of Study

Medical informatics requires a new generation of leaders dedicated to improving health-care outcomes through the application of information technologies. The MMI program provides a balance of both conceptual and applied knowledge, preparing graduates for exceptional career paths in the field of medical information management.

This eleven course graduate program includes classes in clinical thinking, decision support systems in health care, health-care enterprise operations, management of medical technologies, and legal, ethical, and social issues related to health care. It also features a capstone course with opportunities for an applied research project and a leadership development experience.

The program has two paths. Students with a technical background take two courses to introduce them to the American health-care system and the clinical landscape, while students with clinical backgrounds enroll in two courses that describe basic concepts in computer databases and networking. Students with little background in either area may be asked to take all four courses.

The technical and clinical paths then merge into the program's common core of seven courses in medical informatics. In addition, students complete a capstone project and a leadership series. Students may pursue their final project either independently or in a team-based class environment.

Student Services

Northwestern University School of Continuing Studies provides library services online 24 hours a day, seven days a week. All graduate students are also encouraged to take advantage of the Northwestern University Career Placement Office and its services.

Credit Options

No course work may be transferred from outside Northwestern University to fulfill MMI program requirements.

Faculty

The MMI program has been created in partnership with the Feinberg School of Medicine, and a program advisory board that includes Feinberg and other Northwestern faculty members oversees the curriculum. MMI courses are taught by faculty members from the Feinberg School of Medicine as well as medical informatics practitioners. These instructors regularly bring guest speakers to class who serve as administrators in profes-

sional organizations, executive managers in medical technology companies, and representatives from health-care information management.

Admission

Admission to the program is on a rolling basis, so students may start in any of the four terms. Applicants to the MMI program must hold a bachelor's degree from an accredited U.S. college or university or its foreign equivalent. A competitive undergraduate record that indicates strong academic ability is required, but applicants need not have extensive academic or professional experience in health care or information technology. Work or research experience in these areas or the medical informatics field is highly desirable but not a requirement for admission. The Graduate Record Examinations (GRE) is not required but strong scores will bolster chances for admission.

Tuition and Fees

In the 2006–07 academic year, the MMI program tuition is $2810 per course.

Financial Aid

There are a number of financial support options available to prospective students. Students should contact a Northwestern University enrollment adviser at 877-664-3347 to get the latest information on loans or grants.

Applying

Students must submit the completed application, a nonrefundable $60 application fee ($75 for international students), one sealed copy of official transcripts from all previous colleges or universities attended, a resume or curriculum vitae, two letters of recommendation, and a 300-word statement of intent.

CONTACT

School of Continuing Studies
Northwestern University
405 Church Street
Evanston, Illinois 60208

Phone: 877-664-3347 (toll-free)
Fax: 321-239-1870
E-mail: scs@northwestern.edu
Web site: https://www.medinformatics.northwestern.
edu/default.php?src=D_Petersons

OREGON STATE UNIVERSITY
Extended Campus
Corvallis, Oregon

Founded in 1868 and accredited by the Northwest Commission on Colleges and Universities, Oregon State University (OSU) is one of a select number of schools nationwide to receive the Carnegie Foundation's highest rating for education and research. A land-grant, sea-grant, space-grant, and sun-grant university, Oregon State serves the state of Oregon, the nation, and the world through its teaching, research, and outreach efforts. Today, OSU is the home of 19,236 students who are pursuing their degrees in one of more than 200 undergraduate and graduate academic degree programs. The American Productivity and Quality Center recently named Oregon State a top university for providing electronic services to students.

Distance Learning Program

During spring term 2007, more than 2,500 individuals throughout Oregon and the world were enrolled in Oregon State University courses off campus. Each year, through OSU Extended Campus (Ecampus), students have access to more than 400 distance and online courses in more than sixty subjects. Subject areas are as diverse as education, fisheries and wildlife, history, math, chemistry, and psychology. Courses are designed as part of bachelor's completion programs, undergraduate minors, certificate programs, and some graduate-level degrees and course work.

Delivery Media

Oregon State offers the majority of its distance courses via the Web, DVDs, videotapes, and streaming media. Courses often entail a combination of delivery methods, such as a video course with class interaction through an electronic listserv or Web site. Students communicate with instructors and administrative staff members via e-mail, phone, fax, or regular mail. Certain courses and programs are also delivered through face-to-face instruction or interactive television broadcasting (ITV) at statewide locations.

Programs of Study

Oregon State University is one of a handful of universities nationwide pioneering the field of online education. The majority of the more than 400 distance courses offered through Ecampus each year are delivered partially or entirely on the Web. The remainder of distance courses involve some online requirement, such as e-mail communication with faculty members or discussion board communication with peers.

Degree partnership programs are available through many Oregon community colleges; however, many students work with Ecampus Student Services staff to utilize past college experiences and to plan individual programs. Students can complete their degree from anywhere in the world by taking upper-division course work through OSU Extended Campus. Students may select from a Bachelor of Arts/Bachelor of Science (B.A./B.S.) in liberal studies (a preprofessional elementary education option is available statewide), a B.S. in environmental sciences, a B.S. in general agriculture, and a B.S. in natural resources. Students in bachelor's programs must accumulate a minimum of 180 quarter credit hours to graduate.

Undergraduate minors in anthropology, environmental sciences, fisheries and wildlife, natural resources, political science, sociology, U.S. history, and writing are available worldwide. Minors usually include at least 27 quarter credit hours of study and can be pursued as part of a bachelor's program or added to a transcript after graduation.

OSU Ecampus also offers online graduate degrees in education and in radiation health physics. An online graduate certificate in sustainable natural resources, an online/on-site health management and policy graduate certificate, and an online professional certificate in geographic information science are also available.

Special Programs

Web-based graduate-level course work in education is available through Ecampus for teachers, trainers, and other professional educators who wish to pursue an advanced degree or simply gain skills in advanced teaching strategies or teaching course work online. The School of Education offers an on-site/online program for those seeking to earn their Oregon Continuing Teaching License. The Master of Arts in Teaching (M.A.T.) in early childhood/ elementary education and the ESOL bilingual endorsement programs are also delivered online and on-site. In these programs, students may enroll in Web courses and related practicums at a rate based on their individual needs, tailoring their education to meet both time and financial constraints. Students should visit the program's Web site for specific contact information on these and other graduate-level programs, including an online Ed.M. and graduate degrees in adult and higher education leadership.

OSU's Professional Programs in Ecampus operates as an outreach to corporations, public agencies, organizations, and professionals seeking to upgrade their skill level and increase their employability and productivity. Professional Programs offers a variety of online noncredit programs, such as management and human resource skills for pharmacists. Professional Programs also offers online short skill-building courses that fit the busy adult's lifestyle and pocketbook.

OSU Extended Campus offers OSU K–12 Online, a top-quality high school curriculum that is available to home-schooled students or high school students seeking courses that may not be available through their district. These online courses can be taken for elective credit and/or high school graduation completion.

Student Services

Oregon State makes it a priority to provide excellent student services to distance learners via e-mail, a toll-free phone number, and a comprehensive Web site that includes live chat, online forums, and a searchable knowledge base. Students have access to online library services, online tutoring, a toll-free hotline for computer consulting, online writing support, step-by-step assistance with procedures, and an online schedule of classes. Students can subscribe to *OSU E-News,* a free electronic newsletter that provides timely course and program information, student and faculty member profiles, and technical tips.

Credit Options

All credits earned through OSU distance or online education are recorded identically on the Oregon State University transcript as courses that were taken on campus. Each course falls under the same accreditation ratings of the individual department from which it originates. Transfer students enrolled in academic programs must have previous credits evaluated by an OSU adviser to ensure that program requirements are met. Forty-five of the last 75 credit hours for bachelor's completion programs must be from Oregon State University.

Faculty

Oregon State has more than 2,700 faculty members, with nearly 1,100 in the tenure system. Eighty-five percent of faculty members in professorial ranks have doctoral degrees. OSU distance education faculty members must adhere to the same quality standards as any faculty member teaching on campus.

Admission

Students taking distance or online courses to meet OSU degree requirements must be admitted to the University through the regular admission process and must meet the requirements for admission. Nondegree enrollment requires no formal admission and can be attained by contacting the Office of Admissions. For more information on regular or nondegree admission, students can visit the Office of Admissions Web site at http://oregonstate.edu/admissions.

Tuition and Fees

Tuition for undergraduate distance degree courses is $200 per quarter credit hour for most courses. Graduate-level courses are generally $408 per quarter credit, depending upon the program. Additional fees may be assessed for tape rental or other course materials. Students may check the Ecampus Web site for additional information.

Financial Aid

Distance learners are eligible for financial aid programs according to the same rules as on-campus students. Generally, to be considered, a student must be taking at least 6 quarter hours. Some scholarships are open to part-time distance learning students. Students can consult specific information on the Web site at http://oregonstate.edu/admin/finaid.

Applying

Online or distance learners seeking an OSU degree should apply through the regular application process. Some of the distance programs at the graduate level are cohort based and require admission prior to fall quarter. The undergraduate distance degree programs accept students year-round. It is recommended that students seek initial advising prior to the application process. Registration for individual courses generally requires no application other than to contact the registrar for admission as a nondegree or part-time student.

CONTACT

OSU Extended Campus
Attention: Student Services Center
4943 The Valley Library
Oregon State University
Corvallis, Oregon 97331-4504
Phone: 541-737-9204
          800-667-1465 (toll-free)
Fax: 541-737-2734
E-mail: ecampus@oregonstate.edu
Web site: http://ecampus.oregonstate.edu

PACIFIC GRADUATE SCHOOL OF PSYCHOLOGY

Master of Science in Psychology

Palo Alto, California

Founded in 1975, the Pacific Graduate School of Psychology (PGSP) is committed to unifying the research-oriented scientific model with direct service-oriented training. PGSP is a diverse learning community, dedicated to the search for knowledge and its dissemination, forming a community of highly talented faculty members and graduate students working side by side to bring scientific rigor and theoretical knowledge to the analysis and practice of clinical psychology. A private institution, PGSP also offers the Ph.D. and Psy.D. in clinical psychology. The Ph.D. program has been APA-accredited since 1988. The Western Association of Schools and Colleges accredits PGSP's Master of Science (M.S.) in psychology distance-learning program.

Distance Learning Program

The M.S. in psychology distance-learning program has had participants from all over the United States as well as from Canada, Europe, Asia, Africa, and South America. About 30 students participated in the program in 2006–07. Evidence indicates that those enrolled in the distance-learning degree program perform as well as those taking on-campus courses.

Delivery Media

The program uses a number of techniques to accomplish its educational goals and partners with the educational technology company Docutek, which hosts the course materials. Many classes offer Microsoft PowerPoint presentations complete with lecture notes. Assigned readings are available on the Web in .PDF format, which students can easily read using the free Adobe Acrobat software. Some classes use threaded discussion groups, among other methods, to help students to discuss course material and ask questions. Students must have access to a computer as well as an Internet connection. High-speed Internet access, such as DSL or a cable modem, is strongly recommended.

Programs of Study

Classes begin in September and end in mid-June; students cannot enter the program once classes have started. The program consists of 39 units of course work, with no thesis requirement. Courses are taken over a two-year period during the regular academic year, and there are no summer classes. During most quarters, students take no more than two classes at a time. With one exception, most courses offered are the same as those taken by first-year graduate students enrolled in PGSP's residential Ph.D. program. Courses do not contain a clinical component. Student performance can be assessed through papers, exams, or both, depending on the instructor and the course. Tests are proctored by independent third parties. At the end of each course, students evaluate both the class and the instructor.

Special Programs

The distance-learning program was developed to provide students with the opportunity to demonstrate their ability to handle Ph.D.-level work at PGSP. Those who do well can transfer into the on-campus Ph.D. program. The doctoral program trains psychologists whose work is firmly grounded in theory and is informed by current research, who can function effectively as independent practitioners, and who can critically evaluate and perform research that contributes to the academic discipline of scientific psychology.

Students are strongly encouraged to attend an on-campus two-day orientation in September. This orientation gives students a chance to meet members of the faculty and administration, to be trained in the use of the Web-based library resources, and to spend some time getting to know each other. PGSP reimburses student attendees for one-half the cost of hotel accommodations and travel expenses so that everyone in the class can attend.

Student Services

Some classes use chat rooms to facilitate student-student and student-instructor communication. Chat times vary and instructors try to accommodate students from around the world.

Credit Options

Up to 6 units of prior graduate work that is not more than five years old can be transferred into the program. Students must submit a course description and supporting documentation. Credit is granted on a case-by-case basis.

Faculty

The PGSP faculty includes 15 full-time and approximately 12 part-time research and clinical teaching professors, drawn from the Bay Area's rich resource pool of active researchers and practitioners from a range of specializations. The faculty members are actively engaged in clinical practice and research; they provide the enthusiasm, knowledge, and insights of those actively working to find answers to central questions in the field of psychology. For the most part, full-time PGSP faculty members teach the distance-learning curriculum.

Admission

Applicants must have graduated from an accredited undergraduate institution. An applicant must submit the completed application, the $50 application fee, all official transcripts, three letters of reference, and an essay that outlines the goals and reasons for pursuing the Master of Science in psychology. For students coming from a nonpsychology background, there are four prerequisite courses that must be completed: developmental psychology, physiological psychology, personality or abnormal psychology, and statistics.

Tuition and Fees

In the 2006–07, academic year, tuition was $796 per unit, with 21 units in the first year. The technology fee is $267 per quarter. Tuition and fees totaled $17,517 for first-year students.

Financial Aid

Financial assistance is available to eligible PGSP students in the form of grants, fellowships, scholarships, loans (repayable with interest), and on-campus employment. U.S. citizens enrolled in the distance-learning program may be eligible for federal financial aid. For more information, students should contact the Financial Aid Office at 800-340-6986. Prospective students can also e-mail the Financial Aid Office to request further financial aid information (financialaid@pgsp.edu).

Applying

Although the application deadline is August 15, it is recommended that students apply in the spring or early summer. An online application form is available at http://www.pgsp.edu/admissions_online_application.php, or students may request an application form from the Office of Admissions at 650-843-3419.

CONTACT

William Froming, Ph.D., Academic Vice President and
    Director
Distance Learning Program
Pacific Graduate School of Psychology
935 East Meadow Drive
Palo Alto, California 94303

Phone: 650-843-3530
        800-818-6136 (toll-free)
Fax: 650-493-6147
E-mail: wfroming@pgsp.edu
Web site: http://www.pgsp.edu/program_distance_learning_
        home.php

PARK UNIVERSITY
College for Distance Learning
Parkville, Missouri

Park University was founded in 1875 and is accredited by the Higher Learning Commission of the North Central Association of Colleges and Schools. Park's College for Distance Learning offers Bachelor of Science (B.S.) and Master of Science (M.S.) degrees. Numerous undergraduate courses and degrees are offered through the Internet. Graduate programs in public affairs, education, and business administration are also offered.

Park University is a nonprofit entrepreneurial institution of learning that is devoted to providing access to academic excellence to prepare learners to think critically, communicate effectively, and engage in lifelong learning while serving a global community.

Distance Learning Program

Hectic schedules are the biggest reason most adults fail to complete their college education. With busy schedules, family responsibilities, and travel obligations, it is often impossible for many adults to attend regularly scheduled classes.

The Online learning environment at Park University allows course participants to go to class when and where their schedule permits. Commuting time disappears, travel conflicts no longer matter, and childcare issues disappear.

The Online learning programs offered by Park University represent more than thirty years of experience in extended learning—experience honed through operating forty-one satellite "campus centers" on military bases where course work needs to be compact and mobile. As a result of this experience, Park developed, and now offers, accelerated eight-week courses as well as standard sixteen-week offerings. Online courses, first developed in 1996, now number more than 225 different courses. Virtually all in-person courses that are taught at Park University are also taught Online, along with other unique course offerings that were developed specifically for Online delivery or a combination of on-ground activities with online interaction.

Surveys of Online students indicate a higher degree of satisfaction for the general learning experience. In traditional classroom settings, people are often treated according to others' preconceived perceptions of age, gender, ethnicity, and even income level. In Park University's Online learning program, students are judged only by the caliber of their thoughts and the quality of their contributions. This learning environment is active and student-centered. Some students find the online format particularly effective for certain types of courses. In fact, the level of interactivity is actually higher in Park University's Online courses. Online learning requires extensive work— including much reading and writing— but many Online students actually learn better through the Online format than they do in traditional, face-to-face classes.

Delivery Media

Park University offers more than 225 Online courses at five entry points— terms—during each year. Most courses are in accelerated eight-week format. Some courses follow nine- and sixteen-week formats. All courses require minimum computer-system capabilities.

To ensure the highest degree of success, prospective Online students need a basic level of computer literacy. Learners will be asked to open and transfer files and have a working knowledge of the use of e-mail within a course environment. Online students will do well if they have access to a Windows-capable computer with at least a 56.6 kbps modem; Netscape Navigator, Internet Explorer, or an equivalent, reliable Internet browser. Students should not borrow someone else's account, use a public-access account (such as a public library terminal), or use a temporary free account when taking the Online courses.

Courses are offered in a variety of subject areas, and learners can take many courses without enrolling in a degree program.

Each undergraduate course is concluded with a proctored exam.

Programs of Study

Park University has provided degree completion programs via distance learning for more than thirty years. The goal of Park's degree completion program is to provide students with the opportunity and assistance to enable them to complete the last two years of their undergraduate degrees. In addition, students can enter Park their freshman year and complete a degree entirely online. Current fields of study include the Bachelor of Science degree in computer information systems, criminal justice, health care, human resources, management, marketing, and social psychology.

Graduate Online degree programs include the Master of Arts in communication and leadership; Master of Business Administration with an emphasis in entrepreneurship, health care/health services management, international business, and management of information services; Master of Healthcare Leadership; Master of Public Affairs with an emphasis in government/business relations, health care, management of information services, nonprofit and community services management, and public management; and Master of Education with an emphasis in arts in teaching, educational administration, and special education.

Online learning is a dynamic, growing program at Park University. New courses continue to be developed on an on-going basis.

Special Programs

Online students have access to an Online bookstore and library and all traditional student services, such as academic advising, online application, registration, and financial aid.

Credit Options

Park University Online courses are transferable to programs at other regionally accredited institutions. In turn, Park accepts credit from other regionally accredited institutions. Specifically, the University accepts up to 84 hours of course completion with a grade of C or better from two-year schools. Official transcripts from previous colleges or universities; official test reports or transcripts from CLEP, USAFI, or DANTES; and ACT/PEP documentation can accompany an application. Up to 24 hours of credit may be awarded for military service and for Validated Learning Equivalency.

Faculty

Park University has hundreds of Internet faculty instructors, all of whom have advanced degrees and have taught previously. In addition, each Online instructor has completed an intensive eight-week training program to develop the skills necessary for meeting the challenges of teaching Online. This course, which is taught Online, of course, enables instructors to learn firsthand the challenges of being an Online student.

Admission

Park's Online undergraduate programs are open to students who have earned a high school diploma, a GED certificate, or the equivalent; have a minimum 2.0 cumulative GPA in all previous college study; have completed the online Application for Admission; and have paid the application fee. To receive a degree from Park University, students must complete at least 30 semester hours through the University, with 12 hours in their major.

For admission to graduate programs, students must have a bachelor's degree from a regionally accredited U.S. institution of higher learning or four years of equivalent full-time college work from an accredited foreign institution. They must also have a 2.75 minimum GPA on a 4.0 scale. Individual programs may require appropriate entrance test scores, such as the GRE or GMAT.

Although entrance test scores, by themselves, do not constitute the sole or final criterion for granting or denying admission to any student, each program that uses test scores will consider them, in combination with other criteria, as an essential part of the requirements for granting full admission.

Students are required to meet course and program standards to remain in the Online program.

Tuition and Fees

For the 2006–07 academic year, undergraduate Online tuition is $242 per credit hour, with an Internet fee of $14 per credit hour. Graduate Online tuition is $336 per credit hour, with a $16 per credit hour Internet fee.

Financial Aid

Financial assistance may be awarded to full-time and part-time students who qualify.

Applying

Degree-seeking students must meet all admission standards for Park University and pay a one-time $25 application fee.

For more information, students should contact Park University at the telephone number listed below or visit the Web site at the address listed below.

CONTACT

For undergraduate online programs:
College for Distance Learning
Park University
8700 Northwest River Park Drive
Parkville, Missouri 64152-3795
Phone: 866-505-1059 (toll-free)
E-mail: online@park.edu
Web site: http://www.park.edu/online

For graduate online programs:
Graduate School
Park University
8700 Northwest River Park Drive
Parkville, Missouri 64152-3795
Phone: 816-842-6182 Ext. 5525
E-mail: gradschool@park.edu
Web site: http://www.park.edu/grad

PEIRCE COLLEGE

Peirce Online
Philadelphia, Pennsylvania

Founded in 1865, Peirce is a private, four-year, specialized institution providing practical, leading-edge curricula to primarily working adult learners. The College has been offering online programs since 2000 through Peirce Online.

Peirce is accredited by the Commission on Higher Education of the Middle States Association of Colleges and Schools and the Pennsylvania Department of Education to award bachelor's and associate degrees. The business administration program is accredited by the Association of Collegiate Business Schools and Programs (ACBSP). The American Bar Association (ABA) approves the paralegal studies program.

Distance Learning Program

Peirce Online offers students high-quality programs from an accredited college, the flexibility to fit higher education into their busy lifestyles, and the personalized attention from faculty and staff members needed to successfully complete their degrees.

Peirce Online courses are seven weeks in length, with new courses starting every month. Students can earn an associate degree in eighteen months and a bachelor's degree in thirty-six months.

Delivery Media

Peirce Online students must have access to the Internet and an e-mail account.

Courses and degree programs can be completed entirely online, with no residency requirement. While there are weekly deadlines, students complete course work at their own pace. As part of each course, students submit homework assignments, papers, and exams online and participate in asynchronous online discussions. Through the online courseware, students can join with classmates in threaded conversations, privately correspond with instructors, and review their progress with the online grade book.

Program of Study

Peirce College offers bachelor's and associate degrees in business administration, information technology, and paralegal studies. Degrees in business administration and information technology can be completed entirely online. A minimum of 61 credits is required for an associate degree and 121 credits for a bachelor's degree.

In business administration, students can choose from concentrations in accounting, business law, entrepreneurship/small business management, human resource management, management, marketing, or real estate management.

In information technology, students can select from concentrations in application programming with .NET technology, desktop applications for business, information security, networking, network security, or technology management.

In paralegal studies, students can complete most courses online. After taking four initial courses in a traditional classroom setting at Peirce's Philadelphia campus, or from other accredited paralegal programs, students can conveniently complete the remainder of their degree online.

Peirce maintains strong business community relationships and continually upgrades courses to reflect hiring trends. In all degree programs, students take general education core courses in English, communication, social sciences, mathematics, and science. Supervised cooperative education is available in all programs. Most of the bachelor's degree programs include a capstone course in the last term of the program.

Student Services

Peirce offers student services in an online format, including academic advising, workshops, and tutoring; career development counseling and workshops; and services for students with disabilities. Library services include an extensive collection of online databases incorporating full-text periodicals, e-books, industry and financial reports, legal research, and reference materials. All Peirce College students are welcome to request a free copy of Microsoft Office Professional.

Credit Options

Peirce College reserves the right, in its sole discretion, to allow students to earn 90 credits toward a bachelor's degree and 30 credits toward an associate degree through any combination of transfer credits, credit by examination, work experience, and portfolio assessment. Students wishing to receive a degree or certificate from Peirce must complete 15 credits in their concentration through courses offered by Peirce College.

Faculty

Peirce Online emphasizes personal attention from faculty and staff members. Small classes and convenient online courseware ensure that faculty members are readily available to offer professional guidance to individual students. Faculty members also serve as career and academic advisers.

Peirce College employs full-time and adjunct faculty members with diverse professional backgrounds. Most faculty members have advanced degrees and are practitioners in their field. Attorneys, certified public accountants, psychologists, market analysts, computer experts, health-care professionals, business managers, and other professionals are among the teaching staff members at Peirce.

Admission
In compliance with relevant federal, state, and local laws, the College does not unlawfully discriminate in its admissions decisions on the basis of age, sex, race, color, religion, creed, national origin, citizenship, disability, sexual orientation, marital status, veteran's status, military status, or membership in any other protected group.

Applicants for a degree program must submit the following official documents for consideration: a completed application for admission with application fee; an official transcript documenting high school graduation or a copy of the GED or state equivalency diploma and scores; official college transcripts for college transfer credit; and evaluation of transfer credits for final admission and acceptance into the College.

Complete admissions requirements are available in the Peirce *Student Handbook,* which is posted at the College Web site http://www.peirce. edu.

Tuition and Fees
For the 2006–07 academic year, tuition and fees were $408 per credit hour for day, evening, and online courses plus a $100 technology fee. Books and supplies average about $100 per course. Costs are subject to change.

Financial Aid
Financial assistance includes scholarships, grants, loans, and on-campus employment. Peirce College participates in most federal and state aid programs. Approximately 70 percent of students receive financial aid. Applicants for aid must submit the Free Application for Federal Student Aid (FAFSA).

Applying
The Peirce Online application process is convenient and flexible. When students apply to Peirce Online, they can register and begin their studies while transcripts and other documents are being processed. There is no long wait—the initial application should take only 15 minutes. The application/ registration process can be completed online at http://www.peirceonline.net. There is a $50 fee due at time of application.

CONTACT

Online Programs
Peirce College
1420 Pine Street
Philadelphia, Pennsylvania 19102-4699

Phone: 888-GO-PEIRCE Ext. 9800 (toll-free)
Fax: 215-670-9101
E-mail: online@peirce.edu
Web site: http://www.peirce.edu
       http://www.peirceonline.net (Online Learning)

PE N STATE WORLD CA PUS

Department of Distance and Online Education
University Park, Pennsylvania

The Pennsylvania State University, founded in 1855, is a land-grant institution that offers undergraduate and graduate programs. The University has more than 4,500 faculty members and offers degrees in about 160 baccalaureate and 150 graduate programs. Penn State regularly ranks among the nation's top fifteen public research universities, with yearly research expenditures of more than $500 million. Penn State is a member of the Association of American Universities, and it is accredited by the Middle States Association of Colleges and Schools.

Distance Learning Program

In 1998, Penn State launched its twenty-fifth campus of the University, Penn State World Campus. The World Campus is "Penn State Online," delivering more than fifty distance education programs to learners around the world. The World Campus carries on Penn State's proud tradition of more than a century of delivering distance education programs designed to meet the educational goals of a diverse set of learners.

As one of the nation's leading public research universities, Penn State has a longstanding commitment to reach beyond its traditional campuses and to engage in helping to solve the needs of the individuals and communities it serves. From its pioneering innovation with correspondence study—the first generation of distance education—in 1892 to its leadership in online learning in the twenty-first century, Penn State has made creative use of technology to address the changing nature of work, home life, and learning.

The World Campus provides adult learners worldwide (all fifty states, more than forty countries, and all seven continents) with some of Penn State's most highly regarded graduate, undergraduate, and continuing professional education degrees, certificates, and courses available anytime, anywhere. As part of Penn State's global learning community, World Campus students interact with faculty members and exchange ideas and expertise with one

another in the same high-quality, academically challenging courses as those taught in the classroom, as they strive to meet their educational and career goals. Credits earned through the World Campus are identical to those earned at Penn State's traditional campuses.

Delivery Media

Students enrolled in online group and online individual classes must have access to the Web; Internet access for independent learners is optional. In online groups, students interact with their instructors and other students, and group work and/or student-student interaction may be required. In online individual courses, students interact one-on-one with their instructors, with no student interaction required. For independent learners, an optional Web site and e-mail lesson submission may be included.

Programs of Study

Penn State's World Campus offers fifty-four programs, 691 courses, sixteen graduate/postbaccalaureate certificates, and sixteen undergraduate certificates.

Thirteen undergraduate degree programs are offered through the World Campus, including the Associate in Arts in letters, arts, and sciences; the Associate in Science (A.S.) in business administration; the A.S. in dietetic food systems management–dietetic technician emphasis, the A.S. in dietetic food

systems management–school food service emphasis, the A.S. in hotel, restaurant, and institutional management; the A.S. in human development and family studies; the Associate in Information Sciences and Technology; the Bachelor of Arts (B.A.) in letters, arts, and sciences; the B.A. in law and society; the Bachelor of Science (B.S.) in criminal justice; the B.S. in nursing (RN to B.S.); the B.S. in organizational leadership; and the B.S. in turfgrass science.

Nine graduate degrees are offered; they are the Master of Business Administration (iMBA), which is accredited by AACSB International; the Master of Education, with concentrations in adult education, curriculum and instruction–children's literature, curriculum and instruction–teacher leadership, and instructional systems–educational technology; the Master of Engineering in oil and gas engineering management; the Master of Geographic Information Systems; the Master of Homeland Security in Public Health Preparedness; and the Master of Project Management.

Student Services

Penn State World Campus programs are supported by a full range of student services. Support services, such as library access, advising, and assessment, are structured to meet students' needs while providing support that is often lacking in more traditional distance education programs. The World Campus HelpDesk offers technical support resources to ensure that students have a successful online learning experience. Staff members can answer questions regarding the online learning environment; software, Web browsers, and operating systems; and computer hardware and Internet issues. Online resources include tutorials, news/alerts, and additional training resources. More information is available at http://www.worldcampus.psu.edu/StudentServices.shtml.

Credit Options

Penn State accepts only certain types of professional experience for credit toward fulfilling degree requirements, determined by a process called Credit by Portfolio Evaluation, which is typically restricted to students with particular types of formal professional training such as nurses or police officers. Some aspects of military training may also result in transfer credits if officially documented. Other types of professional training are considered on a case-by-case basis, but the review is costly and rarely results in credit conferral.

Students who wish to earn their degrees from Penn State must complete a minimum number of credits through World Campus—for an associate degree, at least 18 of the student's last 30 credits earned must be from Penn State, and for a bachelor's degree, at least 36 of the last 60 credits.

In order to transfer college credits to Penn State, the college must be accredited by one of the following accrediting agencies: Middle States Association of Colleges and Schools, Northwest Association of Schools and Colleges, New England Association of Schools and Colleges, Southern Association of Schools and Colleges, North Central Association of Colleges and Schools, and the Western Association of Schools and Colleges.

Each Penn State academic unit has its own requirements for accepting transfer credits. General information about applying as a graduate transfer student can be found on the Web site for The Graduate School at Penn State at http://www.gradsch.psu.edu/.

Faculty

The Penn State World Campus faculty consists of the same faculty members teaching courses at the Penn State campuses. Recognizing that a primary key to the success of an online teaching and learning program is a skilled and competent faculty, Penn State's World Campus has sponsored a faculty development initiative since 1995. The main goal of the Faculty Development Program is to build a teaching and learning community of faculty and staff members who can effectively author, design, develop, and deliver distance education courses via Penn State's World Campus. In addition, members of the Instructional Design and Development (ID&D) unit of the World Campus work closely with faculty members to produce high-quality distance education courses.

Admission

Application requirements vary by program. In general, students must submit an application, the application fee, and official transcripts. Additional materials, such as test scores or letters of recommendation, may be required. Students should visit the Web page for the World Campus program of interest

and click on the "Apply Now" button for specific instructions.

Tuition and Fees

Graduate tuition ranges between $550 and $1000 per credit hour, depending on the program. Upper-division undergraduate tuition is $430 per credit hour; lower-division undergraduate tuition is $404 per credit hour for online groups and $250 per credit hour for individuals and for independent learners. The information technology fee is $104 per year. At this time, the World Campus online iMBA program is the only program that offers a payment plan.

Financial Aid

Penn State World Campus degree students who take at least 6 credits per semester and who meet all other federal eligibility requirements may be eligible to receive federal student aid. The University offers some scholarships for which distance-learning students are eligible, including the Fischer Family Scholarship Program, the World Campus Student Fund, and the Trustee Scholarship Program. More information is available online at http://www.worldcampus.psu.edu/StudentServices_Paying.shtml.

Applying

Program deadlines vary. Students should check online for more detailed information.

CONTACT

Penn State World Campus
128 Outreach Building
The Pennsylvania State University
University Park, Pennsylvania 16802

Phone: 814-865-5403
          800-252-3592 (toll-free within the United States)
Fax: 814-865-3290
E-mail: psuwd@psu.edu
Web site: http://www.worldcampus.psu.edu/

PENNSYLVANIA COLLEGE OF TECHNOLOGY
An Affiliate of The Pennsylvania State University
Distance Learning
Williamsport, Pennsylvania

Pennsylvania College of Technology
PENN STATE

The mission of distance learning at the Pennsylvania College of Technology (Penn College)—a special mission affiliate of Penn State that is committed to applied technology education—is to provide educational opportunities, using a variety of media, as an alternative to traditional classroom-based learning. Distance learning courses are accessible to students both off and on campus and are intended to meet the needs of students who desire an alternative to traditional face-to-face courses due to work schedules, geographical distance from the campus, or other special needs.

Distance Learning Program

The Penn College distance learning program was founded on the central principle of providing excellence in instruction and appropriate educational opportunities to students. Serving approximately 450 students per semester, the College offers an average of forty-five distance courses per semester across a range of academic disciplines as well as five bachelor's degree–completion programs that are available entirely via distance learning.

Delivery Media

Penn College operates on the WebCT Campus Edition instructional platform. In addition, supported applications include Adobe Photoshop, Adobe Acrobat, Macromedia Director, Flash, Apple QuickTime, Windows Media Player, and Respondus. Certain discipline-specific software programs also are employed.

Programs of Study

The Bachelor of Science degree in residential construction technology and management allows students who have earned appropriate applied technology skills in their first two years to move into advanced course work related to residential construction and management. Course work includes basic management and accounting as well as advanced estimating and scheduling, residential building systems, cost control, codes compliance, construction law, purchasing, and energy management.

The Bachelor of Science degree in technology management allows students who enter with an associate degree in a technical/professional area to obtain a baccalaureate degree, with the last two years emphasizing the development of business management skills. Technical/ professional associate degrees include those with a concentrated area of study in a technical/ professional area.

The Bachelor of Science degree in applied health studies is a 127-credit major for individuals who are certified, licensed, or registered in a health-care profession or for students enrolled in the College's occupational therapy assistant studies, paramedic studies, or radiography majors who wish to earn a bachelor's degree. Students acquire the advanced-level core knowledge that guides all health-care practitioners. This degree allows the student to increase knowledge in management and administrative issues; assist in planning, problem solving, and evaluating health-care delivery methods and systems; and establish a more marketable, multiskilled background.

The baccalaureate-level dental hygiene program is designed to prepare licensed dental hygienists to contribute to the improvement of oral health in a rapidly changing health-care environment. This program enables hygienists to build upon their current knowledge base and assume positions of responsibility in a variety of alternate care settings as well as in positions created to meet future health-care needs.

The Bachelor of Science degree in automotive technology management is structured to meet the needs of the automotive service and manufacturing industries. The curriculum provides an in-depth study of technical skills, technical knowledge, and management skills as applied in the automotive industry. It emphasizes supervision and personnel management, financial analysis and accounting principles, sales promotion and marketing plan, problem-solving methods, and organization and planning techniques as well as communications and mathematics, which are essential for a management career.

Special Programs

The Office of Distance Learning assists in scheduling and determining each semester's class offerings in concert with the academic deans. Courses are offered on a regular and predictable basis to ensure academic progress and adequate course selection for those learning at a distance.

To accommodate the needs of distance learners, selected enrollments are restricted at the start of each semester scheduling period. Resident students also may enroll in distance courses on a space-available basis.

Student Services

Penn College distance learners have full student standing and are entitled to all the privileges and services of a Penn College student. The Financial Aid Office, Career Services, the Advisement Center, and the College Store all have a Web presence and respond to student inquiries via telephone or e-mail. Distance students may order textbooks via the Web site. The library catalog and other references, periodical abstracts, and full-text databases are available through the Penn College Library Web site. An electronic reserve system is provided for assigned readings and supplemental assignments. A College librarian is assigned to each distance learning course to address distance learning and library instruction needs.

Credit Options

Transfer credits, advanced placement, credit for military experience, professional certifications, and credit by exam may be considered during transcript review. Acceptance of credits varies by major.

Faculty

Approximately 55 faculty members teach distance learning courses; 92 percent are full-time faculty members.

Admission

Distance learners are accepted to Penn College and the academic department that houses their major. There is no separate admission process for distance learning students.

Tuition and Fees

Tuition and fee rates for 2005–06, including computer, lab, and activity fees, were $336 per credit hour for in-state students and $422 per credit hour for out-of-state students.

Financial Aid

As students in full standing, distance learners may be eligible for financial aid, including federal aid programs.

Applying

Students should submit an application for admission online at http://www.pct.edu/forms or contact the Office of Admissions at the College's toll-free number.

CONTACT

Paula Neal
Distance Learning Services Assistant
Pennsylvania College of Technology
One College Avenue
Williamsport, Pennsylvania 17701

Phone: 570-320-8019
       800-367-9222 (toll-free)
Fax: 570-321-5559
E-mail: distancelearning@pct.edu
Web site: http://www.pct.edu/away

PRESCOTT COLLEGE
Adult Degree, Master of Arts, and Ph.D. Programs
Prescott, Arizona

Prescott College's mission is to educate students of diverse ages and backgrounds to understand, thrive in, and enhance the world community and environment. Prescott regards learning as a continuing process and strives to provide an education that enables students to live productive lives while achieving a balance between self-fulfillment and service to others. Students are encouraged to think critically and act ethically, with sensitivity to both the human community and the biosphere. The College's philosophy stresses experiential learning and self-direction within an interdisciplinary curriculum.

Prescott College is an independent liberal arts college that grants Bachelor of Arts (B.A.), Master of Arts (M.A.), and Ph.D. degrees. The College is accredited by the Higher Learning Commission of the North Central Association of Colleges and Schools. The teacher education program is approved by the Arizona State Board of Education and the Arizona State Directors of Teacher Education and Certification. The Association of Experiential Education also accredits the College.

Distance Learning Program
The Prescott College distance learning programs consist of the Adult Degree Program (ADP), a B.A. completion program; a Master of Arts program (MAP); and a Ph.D. in education program. In all programs, students maintain their personal and professional lives while earning a degree. The programs are self-designed (with the assistance of faculty members), student-centered, and flexible. The programs require very limited residencies in Prescott, Arizona. The College offers ongoing support from faculty members and other students.

Delivery Media
The Adult Degree Program Students in the B.A. Adult Degree Program work with mentors (local professionals) in their home communities along with core faculty members at Prescott College on an individualized course of study. Students study with these mentors one-on-one in their home communities and at times and places that are convenient to them. It is not an online program. Students are required to be in Arizona for just two 3-day weekends during their program.

The Master of Arts Program Faculty-chosen graduate advisers assist students in the Master of Arts program in planning, executing, and evaluating their graduate study programs. These faculty members are recruited from everywhere in the U.S. and are selected based upon the student's spe-

cific area of interest. Students and graduate advisers send material via postal or electronic mail to one another. Master's students must attend two 3-day colloquia per semester. Program length varies depending upon the degree sought and ranges from 1½ to 2½ years.

The Ph.D. in Education Program Ph.D. students are guided by committees that consist of a core faculty member and 3 affiliate faculty members. Doctoral students attend thirty-seven days of residency (eight trips to Arizona) over the course of the four-year program.

Programs of Study
The Adult Degree Program B.A. students can complete degrees in adventure education, education, environmental studies, human development, human services, humanities, and management. Working with faculty members, students design concentrations in individualized areas within each of these degrees. Within each degree area, students have developed a wide range of concentrations.

Adventure education: adventure-based tourism, ecotourism, outdoor education, outdoor program administration, recreation management, and wilderness leadership.

Education: Teacher education students may complete all courses leading to Arizona teaching credentials in elementary, secondary, or special education while earn-

ing their bachelor's degree. Students may also complete post-bachelor's teacher certification. Other areas of concentration within education include adult education, alternative education, and early childhood education.

Environmental studies: agroecology, appropriate technologies and assessment, biology, bioregional studies, botany, conservation biology, Earth sciences, ecological design, ecological economics, ecology, environmental education, environmental policy, global studies, international sustainable development, natural resource assessment and management, permaculture, restoration ecology, rural planning, sustainable communities and agriculture, sustainable community development, urban planning, and wildlife studies.

Human development/human services: advocacy, border studies, child development, community health education, counseling, criminal justice, ecopsychology, expressive arts therapy, family and community services, family studies, gender studies, gerontology, healing arts, holistic health, human development, human relations, leadership, political science, psychology, social justice, social science, sociology, somatic psychology, spiritual studies, transpersonal psychology, and wilderness therapy.

Humanities: anthropology, art (performance, studio, visual), art history, comparative religion, creative writing, cultural studies, dance, drama, expressive arts, English, film studies, geography, history, independent media studies, journalism, language studies (e.g., Spanish, Ute), literature, mathematics, museum studies, music, peace studies, philosophy, photo journalism, photography, and theater arts.

Management: accounting, business management, communications, computer information systems, ecological economics, environmental planning, environmental resource conservation, finance, human resource management, leadership for change, legal studies, marketing, nonprofit management, organizational development, public administration, safety and risk management, small business management, and technologies studies.

The Master of Arts Program Students may design programs in five broadly defined programs of study—adventure education, counseling and psychology, education, environmental studies, and the humanities. Within these degree areas, the possibilities for areas of concentration are extensive. Students propose their area of study during the application process and further refine and develop it with the assistance of their graduate advisers.

Adventure education: adventure-based tourism, community recreation programs, corrections and outfitting, Earth-based studies, ecotourism, guiding and outfitting, integral adventure education, outdoor education, outdoor program administration, recreation management, school and college curricula, therapeutic applications of adventure education, and wilderness leadership.

Counseling and psychology: Students may prepare for certification or licensure in professional counseling or marriage and family therapy or in a nonclinical, more theoretical, aspect of the field. Counseling and psychology students focus on specialties such as adventure-based psychotherapy, child development, equine-assisted mental health, expressive arts therapies, grief counseling, and somatic psychology.

Education: curriculum design, English as a second language, pedagogy, literacy, school guidance counseling, school renewal, and bilingual, early childhood, elementary, environmental, experiential, global, international, multicultural, secondary, and special education.

Environmental studies: agroecology, conservation biology, Earth sciences, ecological design, ecological restoration, ecology, environmental education, environmental ethics and philosophy, environmental history, ethnobotany, marine studies, natural history, natural resource management, social ecology, sustainability education, sustainability science and practice, sustainable community development, and wildlife conservation.

Humanities: Concentrations within the humanities fall within four academic areas.

The traditional humanities (arts and letters): art education, art history, art theory, communication, creative non-fiction, creative writing, dance, environmental writing, journalism, literature, painting, photo journalism, photography, poetry sculpture, technical writing, theater, and video or film theory or production.

Cultural studies: African-American studies, class studies, conflict resolution, gender studies, geography, historic preservation, history of the Southwest, international studies, justice and activism studies, languages (e.g., Spanish, Navajo), literature, men's studies, peace studies, political science, queer studies, social ecology, social sustainability, solidarity studies, and women's studies.

Business and management: business administration, economics, globalism and economics, health-care administration, health-care management, human resources, international development, management, marketing, organizational development, public administration, and sustainable business practices.

Other social sciences: anthropology, archaeology, cosmology, depth psychology, dialogical ecology, eco-feminism, ecopsychology, forensic psychology, mythology, philosophy, psychology of women, religious studies, spirituality, theology, and wellness.

The Ph.D. Program Students design their own studies within the area of sustainability education. Areas of concentration have been in the areas of community activism, economics, education, environmental studies, and social justice.

Admission

For admission requirements and to contact the admission counselors, students should visit the Prescott College Web site at http://www.prescott.edu/admissions.

Tuition and Fees

For 2007–08, tuition for the B.A. program is $9396 per year, tuition for the M.A. program is $12,960, and tuition for the Ph.D. program is $16,980. Tuition increases may occur in July of each year.

Financial Aid

The types of financial aid available are Federal Pell Grants, Prescott College grants and scholarships, Arizona State Student Incentive Grants, Federal Supplemental Educational Opportunity Grants, the Arizona Voucher Program, the Postsecondary Education Grant, Federal Stafford Student Loans, and student employment. Students seeking any form of financial assistance are encouraged to speak with the Financial Aid Office. The financial aid process begins with filling out the Free Application for Federal Student Aid (FAFSA), which is available online at http://www.fafsa.ed.gov. The Prescott College school code is 013659.

Applying

Application requirements vary by program (B.A., M.A., and Ph.D.) and are available in the program catalogs or online at Prescott's Web site. Applicants may apply online or use the application from the College's catalog. Students in Tucson and southern Arizona who are interested in the B.A. or M.A. programs should contact the Tucson office. All other geographic areas may work with the Prescott admissions office.

The Admissions Office strongly encourages applicants to submit all required application materials by the priority filing date. Files that are received after the priority filing date are still considered on a rolling basis.

CONTACT

Admissions Office
Prescott College
220 Grove Avenue
Prescott, Arizona 86301
Phone: 928-350-2112
　　　877-350-2100　Ext. 2112 (toll-free)
Fax: 928-776-5242
E-mail: admissions@prescott.edu
Web site: http://www.prescott.edu

Admissions
Prescott College Tucson Center
2233 East Speedway Boulevard
Tucson, Arizona 85719
Phone: 888-797-4680　(toll-free)
Fax: 520-319-1032

REGIONS UNIVERSITY
Distance Learning Programs
Montgomery, Alabama

SCU

Founded in 1967, Regions University is an independent, nonsectarian, coeducational institution dedicated to the spirit of its ideals and Christian heritage. All of Regions University's programs are taught from a Christian perspective. Regions University is the home of one of the nation's leading universities offering distance learning programs and services to adults nationally. In 1999, Regions University was selected by the U.S. Department of Education as a Distance Education Demonstration Program Institution. One of fifteen initial participants in the nation, Regions University partnered with the U.S. Department of Education, serving as a national model for distance education. As a result, the U.S. Congress recently changed the law regarding distance education, making it more accessible to more students. Accredited by the Southern Association of Colleges and Schools, Regions University grants bachelor's, master's, and doctoral degrees—all available via a distance learning format.

Distance Learning Program

Regions University programs are designed with the adult learner in mind. Eighty percent of Region's students are employed while they are attending. Courses can be taken anywhere there is Internet access and at any time. Regions University has enrolled thousands of students in distance learning courses throughout the United States and internationally.

Delivery Media

Utilizing state-of-the-art technologies, Region University's distance learning programs are delivered to students over the Internet. Students participate via online discussion groups, testing, e-mail, and telephone. Some courses are streamed live over the Internet and can be viewed as the class is being taught or at the student's convenience. The flexibility of the programs ensures continuity for students in transit, such as military personnel, clergy, or salespeople who must move while still in school.

Programs of Study

Regions University programs are structured with the traditional program in mind. Distance education is approved by the Southern Association of Colleges

and Schools and the U.S. Department of Education, ensuring that distance education students receive the same high-quality education as on-campus students. Faculty and student services for online students are available to distance learning students. Regions University ensures that students have regular contact with faculty and staff members via e-mail and telephone. Residency is only required in certain programs. No residency is required for undergraduates. Undergraduate degrees are awarded in biblical studies, business administration, homeland security, human development, human resource management, liberal studies, management communication, and public safety and criminal justice. These degrees promote biblical and Christian ministry skills, human development skills, knowledge in the arts, and management communication skills. Graduate degrees are awarded in counseling/family therapy, organizational leadership, and religious studies. These degrees prepare students for careers and professions that provide support and services for the well-being of individuals, families, or society; foster leadership, counseling, and family therapy skills; and develop knowledge and biblical and Christian ministry skills. Some of the counseling degrees

are designed to help prepare students for licensure. Doctoral degrees include family therapy and ministry. These degrees are advanced professional degrees for community organizations and church-related vocations, with a concentration designed to prepare participants to counsel families and individuals. Regions University students are fully matriculated students of Regions University with full student privileges, rights, and responsibilities.

Special Programs

Regions University has developed fully accredited programs of study to help working adults obtain their bachelor's degree in a timely manner through its programs. All undergraduate courses are 4 semester hours, rather than 3. A student only has to take three courses (12 semester hours) to be a full-time student and eligible for maximum financial aid benefits. Also, fewer courses are required for degree completion.

Regions University is one of only a few institutions participating in the expansion of eArmyU colleges and universities. eArmyU is the Army's popular e-learning virtual university, offering thousands of soldiers the opportunity to earn a college degree during their enlistment. With the flexibility of eArmyU, soldier-students are able to continue their education uninterrupted and complete their degrees in a timely manner while they serve.

Student Services

Regions University provides support for all aspects of the distance learning experience. ProQuest Religion Database and First Search library programs give students access to 65 online databases, including the Library of Congress. Students have access to the collections of 150 theological schools online. Personal academic advising is performed via phone or e-mail. Students also receive personal evaluations of their degree program.

Credit Options

Fulfillment of some degree requirements is possible by passing the CLEP/DANTES tests or Excelsior examinations and through credit for lifetime learning and credit for military experience.

Faculty

The instructional faculty members total 85. Seventy-six percent of the full-time faculty members hold doctoral degrees, 100 percent hold master's degrees, and 100 percent hold terminal degrees. Faculty members are specialized in their areas and have training in distance learning delivery.

Admission

There is a rolling admission plan. Admission requirements are verification of high school graduation or passage of the GED test for undergraduates and demonstrated proficiency in computer literacy. Ninety percent of applicants are accepted.

Tuition and Fees

The graduate tuition cost per semester hour is $495. Undergraduate tuition per semester hour is $250. A comprehensive fee of $400 per semester is required of all graduate students.

Financial Aid

Aid from institutionally generated funds is provided on the basis of academic merit, financial need, or other criteria. A limited number of scholarships are available. Priority is given to early applicants. Federal funding available for undergraduates and graduates includes Pell and FSEOG grants, Academic Competitiveness Grants, and National SMART grants for undergraduates, the Federal Work-Study Program, and FFEL subsidized and unsubsidized loans for undergraduates and graduates. Eighty percent of students receive financial aid.

Applying

Prospective students must submit a $50 nonrefundable fee along with the completed application for admission. During the first semester, graduate students must submit letters of recommendation, transcripts, and test scores.

CONTACT

Rick Johnson
Regions University
1200 Taylor Road
Montgomery, Alabama 36117

Phone: 800-351-4040 Ext. 7513 (toll-free)
E-mail: admissions@regionsuniveristy.edu
Web site: http://www.regionsuniversity.edu

R·I·T ROCHESTER INSTITUTE OF TECHNOLOGY
Online Learning
Rochester, New York

Online Learning at the Rochester Institute of Technology (RIT) offers a broad selection of courses and full-degree programs, all regionally accredited by the Middle States Association of Colleges and Schools. With more than twenty years of experience in distance education, RIT offers one of the largest and most established online learning programs in the U.S.

Distance Learning Program

Rochester Institute of Technology is one of the nation's leaders in online learning education programs. RIT online learning students have access to more than forty-five full degree and certificate programs, including thirteen graduate degrees, four undergraduate degrees, twenty-four certificate programs, and more than 300 courses. The commitment to quality education is an integral part of RIT online learning programs.

Delivery Media

Professors deliver course materials through the Internet and a combination of textbooks, videotapes, audiotapes, audio conferences, chats, electronic library resources, and other components that enhance that particular course experience. Students submit most assignments online, but professors may request students to fax or mail assignments. Students may order course materials online and have complete access to a full range of library services and academic advising online.

In order to participate, students must have full access to the Internet and a personal computer. Students must also have basic computer skills and some Internet experience to be successful. For specific computer requirements, students should visit the Web site.

Programs of Study

All programs offered through RIT are available to students worldwide. Applications for all programs are available online. Most students have some college experience before coming to RIT, but admission into the undergraduate certificate and bachelor's-level programs can be accommodated without previous college experi-ence. Master's degree candidates must meet the admissions standards required by that program and must have completed a baccalaureate degree or equivalent from an accredited institution. International applicants must demonstrate English proficiency, usually through the Test of English as a Foreign Language (TOEFL). TOEFL scores vary by program, but most programs require a score of 550 (paper-based) or better, or the computer-based equivalent.

The B.S. in applied arts and science program presents a flexible opportunity for a student to create a program tailored to meet his or her educational needs. It requires the completion of 180 credit hours. Twelve concentrations are available.

The B.S. in electrical/mechanical engineering technology program requires experiences that must be completed over several weekends at RIT or by taking an alternative course from an approved institution. The undergraduate degree requires 194 credit hours. This program is accredited by ABET-TAC.

The B.S. in telecommunications engineering technology program (the technical option) is currently available to both working professionals and full-time students. Upper-division course work is available online. The academic emphasis is placed on backbone technologies that transmit, switch, and manage networks and the information they carry. Individuals who have no background or have not completed basic lab work in this field may need to come to RIT for intensive weekend labs. This program is accredited by ABET-TAC.

The B.S. in safety technology program is structured to be at the leading edge of this field, providing high-quality aca-demic preparation and relevant work experience. All students completing RIT's safety technology bachelor's degree program are eligible to take the associate safety professional examination upon graduation. Individuals may enter the upper-division program from an associate degree program or with two years of college, including appropriate courses in math, science, and liberal arts.

The M.S. in print media program is oriented toward educating individuals for production and management positions in the ever-evolving printing and publishing industry. This master's program addresses publishing from the technological/production viewpoint, including its management, and considers interrelationships among e-commerce, cross-media publishing, and the many digital and variable data aspects of printing as well as traditional printing models. The program is open to students with a variety of undergraduate degree backgrounds. While all courses are provided online, students attend a one-week summer technology practicum course on campus after completing the first five required courses. This M.S. degree requires completion of 48 credit hours.

The M.S. in applied statistics program is designed for full-time professionals who want to learn state-of-the art statistical techniques to enhance their careers and their value to their companies. Students must complete 45 credits. Admission to the degree program is granted to qualified holders of a baccalaureate degree from an accredited college or university and who have acceptable mathematics credits, including one academic year of calculus.

The M.S. in software development and management program consists of 48 credit hours, comprising the software engineering core foundation, the software engineering project, and electives. A minimal background is required in mathematics (discrete structures, statistics) and computing (programming in a high-level language, data structures, elementary computer architecture, and digital logic).

The M.S. in information technology program consists of 48 credit hours of graduate study in core courses, with a choice of electives and concentrations in application development, electronic commerce, and telecommunications. Entering students are expected to have programming skills at an intermediate level in an appropriate language and understand the fundamentals of computer hardware.

The M.S. in health systems administration program is designed to meet the needs of health professionals who desire a nonclinical degree in management and administration. Students typically enter in cohort groups, which improve the learning environment, and take two courses per quarter until completion of the 48 credit hours.

The M.S. in professional studies program consists of 48 credit hours, which comprise two or three concentrations from various areas. These areas are designed to give the student a comprehensive and customized plan of graduate study tailored to meet either career or educational objectives. Students must take a course in interdisciplinary research techniques and finish a capstone project to complete this degree.

The M.S. in environmental health and safety management program requires 48 credit hours drawn from core courses like environmental health and safety management system design and performance measurement, 20 credits from professional electives, and 6 credits from the graduate thesis and graduate project.

The M.S. in imaging science program emphasizes a systems approach to the study of imaging science, and, with a background in science or engineering, this degree prepares the student for positions in research, product development, and management in the imaging industry. The program requires completion of 45 credits.

The M.E. in microelectronics manufacturing engineering program is designed for students with a B.S. degree in electrical or chemical engineering or other related engineering areas. The degree requires the completion of nine 4-credit courses and a 9-credit thesis for a total of 45 credits.

The M.S. in learning and knowledge management systems is a 45-credit-hour program that develops knowledge and skills in the area of planning, creating, and implementing innovative instructional, performance support, and knowledge-sharing environments.

The M.S. in telecommunications engineering technology is a 48-quarter-credit-hour program. Six core courses that introduce essential fundamental concepts and skills are required. In addition, students choose technical electives in network design, fiber-optic telecommunications, wireless telecommunications, and management.

The M.S. in facility management consists of 52 quarter credit hours of graduate study. The program is available predominately in the distance learning format, although some courses and electives are available in the classroom. The curriculum consists of a sequence of core courses (40 credits), professional electives chosen from the program or other departments (8 credits), and a graduate project (4 credits). Project topics should complement the student's interests and professional position and are generally considered applied in nature.

The M.S. in networking and systems administration enables the matriculated student to study, develop, and become proficient in the practices, methodologies, and techniques in the management of modern IT infrastructure. The focus is on enterprise-level problems and solutions. The graduate program of study consists of twelve courses (48 quarter credit hours), which include eight courses (32 quarter credit hours) of required core courses, plus another four courses (16 quarter credit hours) as electives from an approved set. Two quarters of optional cooperative work experience are possible.

RIT also offers twenty-four certificates for those wanting to improve or obtain skills in specialized areas. Courses in the certificate programs may be applied toward a degree.

Credit Options

Students have a number of options available for credit, including transfer credit, credit by exam, College-Level Examination Program (CLEP), Excelsior College Examinations, credit for educational experiences in the armed forces and noncollegiate organizations, and credit for nontraditional learning. Advisers work with students to evaluate the number of credits that can be transferred, since the number of non-RIT credits accepted varies by program.

Faculty

RIT's faculty members are world-renowned and teach both on-campus and online courses. More than 200 full- and part-time faculty members teach online learning courses.

Admission

Requirements for admission and completion of degree or certificate programs vary by academic department. Students should refer to Programs of Study descriptions.

Tuition and Fees

Graduate tuition is $800 per credit hour. Undergraduate tuition is $391 per credit hour.

Financial Aid

RIT offers a full range of traditional financial aid programs as well as a number of innovative financing plans. Scholarships and assistantships are available to matriculated students in most graduate departments.

Applying

Online learning students follow the same procedures as all other students attending RIT. Decisions for selection rest within each college. Correspondence between the student and the Institute is conducted through the Office of Part-Time and Graduate Enrollment Services, which reviews applications as they are received.

CONTACT

Office of Part-Time and Graduate
  Enrollment Services
Rochester Institute of Technology
58 Lomb Memorial Drive
Rochester, New York 14623-5604
Phone: 585-475-2229
       866-260-3950 (toll-free)
Fax: 585-475-7164
E-mail: distance@rit.edu
Web site: http://www.rit.edu/online

SAINT JOSEPH'S COLLEGE
Division of Graduate and Professional Studies
Standish, Maine

Saint Joseph's College is a Roman Catholic liberal arts college that nurtures intellectual, spiritual, and social growth in students of all faiths and all ages. Saint Joseph's was founded in 1912 by the Sisters of Mercy and chartered by the Maine Legislature in 1915. It is the Catholic college of Maine. Saint Joseph's grants degrees in fulfillment of the educational ideals of the Sisters of Mercy, founded by Mary Catherine McAuley in Dublin, Ireland, in 1831. The College's 350-acre campus is situated on the shore of Sebago Lake in Standish, Maine, a half hour from Portland, Maine's largest city, and 2 hours north of Boston. Approximately 1,000 young adults reside at the College's campus, where they pursue their undergraduate studies.

In 1976, distance education was introduced at Saint Joseph's to serve the needs of nontraditional adult learners in the U.S. and abroad. The distance education program at Saint Joseph's College, the Division of Graduate and Professional Studies, is known for its high-quality education geared to working professionals and is one of the most established in the country. With three decades of experience providing distance education to adult students, the College has the procedures and polices that work for busy professionals who are interested in furthering their education for career advancement and for personal growth.

Saint Joseph's College is accredited by the New England Association of Schools and Colleges to award baccalaureate and master's degrees. The nursing program is approved by the Maine State Board of Nursing, Augusta, Maine, and accredited by the Commission on Collegiate Nursing Education. The long-term-care administration program is accredited by the National Association of Boards of Examiners of Long-Term Care Administrators.

Distance Learning Program

Saint Joseph's College offers the adult learner an opportunity to integrate formal education in the liberal arts tradition with professional experience. The Graduate and Professional Studies Program provides academic options in a variety of disciplines leading to undergraduate and graduate certificates and to associate, baccalaureate, and graduate degrees. Students may also choose individual courses for personal goals and/or industry continuing education requirements. Each option is designed to reflect the special nature of Saint Joseph's commitment to its students. Approximately 8,500 Saint Joseph's alumni have earned their degrees through the distance program.

Delivery Media

Distance education courses through the Division of Graduate and Professional Studies and the Department of Nursing are available online via the World Wide Web, using WebCT. This integrated online platform is a flexible learning system through which students have access to course content, study tips, resources tailored to the individual course, and various communication tools. Instructors use asynchronous instruction, so students enjoy a highly flexible, accessible mode of education that allows them to complete their programs of study where they reside, completely on their individual schedules. Upon enrollment, students receive the necessary texts and materials for their courses, including course access instructions. (Some courses are available in a text format for students with limited Internet access. Interested students should contact the Admissions Office for more information.) All online courses require a computer with Internet access. Faculty members assist each student with their studies through a com-

bination of written feedback on assignments, telephone consultations, and e-mail. An academic adviser is assigned to work with each student from enrollment through graduation. Some undergraduate and graduate degree programs require attending the two-week summer program at the campus in Maine.

Programs of Study

Saint Joseph's College offers the following degree programs at the graduate level: a Master of Arts in Pastoral Studies, which is designed for those involved with parishes, diocesan agencies, hospitals, retreat/spiritual centers, or social service agencies; a Master of Science in Education (33 credits), with specializations in teaching and learning and administrative management, which is intended for teachers and/or administrators who are interested in initiating or enhancing a career in K–12 education, community college, or adult education; a Master of Health Administration (42 credits) for senior management roles in complex health-care organizations; a Master of Science in Nursing (39 credits), with specializations in nursing administration and nursing education; and a Master of Business Administration (42 credits), with a specialization in quality leadership. Graduate certificates (18 credits) include programs in nursing and health-care education and nursing administration and leadership.

At the undergraduate level, Saint Joseph's College offers the following degrees through distance learning: the Bachelor of Science (128 credits), offering majors in business administration, with specializations in banking through a joint venture with the Center for Financial Training, and management; general studies (a degree-completion program for adult students transferring a minimum of 30 credits), with specializations in adult education and training, business administration, criminal justice, human services, and psychology; health administration; long-term-care administration; and radiologic science (a postcertification baccalaureate degree for radiology technicians). A Bachelor of Arts in theological studies (128 credits) is also available at the undergraduate level. In addition, a Bachelor of Science in Nursing (129 credits) is available for RNs; it can also be earned in the RN to M.S.N. program, a curriculum that allows students to more rapidly progress through the B.S.N. and M.S.N. requirements and earn both degrees. Students can also choose from seven majors within the Associate of Science degree (66 credits), including adult education and training, business administration, criminal justice, general studies, human services, management, and psychology.

Undergraduate certificate programs (18 credits) are available in adult education and training, business administration, Christian tradition, health-care management, and long-term-care administration. Students who would like to take individual courses at either the graduate or undergraduate level may enroll as continuing education students.

Special Programs

The Division of Graduate and Professional Studies has developed partnerships with numerous organizations and corporations to provide educational opportunities to their employees throughout the country at multiple locations. (For more information, students should contact the Admissions Office.) Saint Joseph's College is also a member of Servicemembers Opportunity Colleges (SOC), which guarantees transfer of credit for military personnel completing courses from other SOC schools. The Division is also a member of eArmyU, the Navy College Program Distance Learning Partnership, and Troops to Teachers and assists active and nonactive military personnel in their educational pursuits.

Credit Options

The Graduate and Professional Studies Program acknowledges the value of certain formal learning and career-based experience. For most programs, the College follows the American Council on Education (ACE) guidelines in granting transfer credit for courses of study from accredited colleges or universities with a grade of C or better; ACE/PONSI-approved credit; ACE-approved military training and experience credit; CEUs earned through professional seminars, workshops, internships, and in-service education classes as elective credit; and CLEP, ACT/PEP, and DANTES exams. The total number of credits that can be awarded varies depending on the program.

Faculty

Nearly 200 full-time and part-time faculty members serve students in the Graduate and Professional Studies Program. Many teach in the residential program at Saint Joseph's College as well as in distance education. Each online instructor is required to complete a comprehensive five-week online training program to develop and refine the necessary skills to teach in an online environment. All instructors excel in their fields and have substantial experience with nontraditional students. Students communicate with faculty members via e-mail, phone, fax, and/or regular postal mail.

Admission

Admission requirements vary by program of study. Prospective students should contact the Admissions Office for the Graduate and Professional Studies Program at 800-752-4723 (toll-free) with specific questions about admission requirements. Information can also be obtained online at http://www.sjcme.edu/gps.

Tuition and Fees

For the 2006–07 academic year, tuition was $260 per credit ($780 per 3-credit

course) at the undergraduate level. Graduate course tuition varies depending on the program and ranged from $300 to $350 per credit ($900 to $1050 per 3-credit course). Application fees are $50 for degree programs and $25 for certificate programs and continuing education. A complete fee schedule is available at the College's Web site.

Financial Aid

Students may be eligible for the Federal Pell Grant and/or Federal Stafford Student Loan. Applying for financial aid is an individualized process requiring consultation and evaluation. For more information and assistance, students should call the Financial Aid Office at 800-752-1266 (toll-free).

Applying

Applicants for all programs and all courses are required to submit an application and a nonrefundable application fee. Application fees are $50 for degree programs and $25 for certificate programs and continuing education. For many programs, students are accepted on a rolling admissions basis and, therefore, can apply and begin their studies at any time during the year. Students may download the application forms online or apply online at the College's Web site. For further information, students may contact the Admissions Office.

CONTACT

Admissions Office
Division of Graduate and Professional Studies
Saint Joseph's College
278 Whites Bridge Road
Standish, Maine 04084-5263

Phone: 800-752-4723 (toll-free)
Fax: 207-892-7480
E-mail: info@sjcme.edu
Web site:
http://www.sjcme.edu/gps

ST. LOUIS COMMUNITY COLLEGE SYSTEM

Telelearning Services
St. Louis, Missouri

St. Louis Community College (SLCC) is a public coeducational college supported by local taxes, state funds, and student fees. Created by area voters in 1962, the College offers freshman- and sophomore-level career and college transfer, developmental, and continuing education programs at its four campuses, three education centers, and numerous other locations throughout St. Louis city and county. Nearly 130,000 students enroll each year in credit and noncredit courses. The College also serves the business community by offering St. Louis area business stakeholders performance improvement, consulting, and training services. St. Louis Community College and its campuses are accredited by the Higher Learning Commission of North Central Association of Colleges and Schools. The College is also a founding member of the League for Innovation in the Community College, serving on the League's Board of Directors and as a Board member of Project SAIL

Distance Learning Program

St. Louis Community College offers instruction via the World Wide Web, videotapes, CD-ROMs, DVDs, e-mail, live interactive video, and streaming video in addition to face-to-face classroom instruction. Since 1973, St. Louis Community College has offered distance education to students locally, nationally, and internationally. Approximately 5,000 students currently enroll in distance learning courseware through SLCC.

Delivery Media

Web-based courses and TeleWEB-courses: Course orientation and exams may be administered via the Web or held on campus or at instructor-approved sites, depending on the specific course. Assignments, announcements, projects, tutorials, e-mail, student discussion forums, essay submission and retrieval, operating instructions, bulletins, and library research are accomplished via asynchronous communication in distance learning courses.

Telecourses: Video lessons—televised, videocassette, or CD/DVD—accompany related readings and assignments, discussions, and examinations. When students need help, instructors are just a phone call or e-mail away.

Special print materials (textbooks, study guides, and student manuals) have been prepared to accompany each course.

Interactive Television (ITV) classes enable students to participate in SLCC courses from multiple locations at the same time. High-end videoconferencing technology bridges distances and allows students and teachers to see and hear each other from remote locations. Students may participate in an SLCC course from different SLCC locations, area high schools, or other institutions.

Programs of Study

SLCC offers an Associate in Applied Science (A.A.S.) in hospitality studies and in information reporting technology as well as certificates of proficiency in funeral directing, information reporting technology, and business administration.

Hospitality Studies: Graduates of the Associate of Applied Science degree program are prepared to enter the hospitality industry at a supervisory level and perform management functions and duties. Students with a Certificate of Proficiency in hotel and restaurant management are prepared for entry-level positions such as front office management, guest services, bar and beverage management, and restaurant or facility management.

Funeral Directing: This certificate of proficiency program prepares the student for licensure as a funeral director and entry-level employment in a funeral establishment. This is a nontechnical certificate geared toward the business and public relations aspects of operating a funeral home. There are no courses in embalming. Graduates are eligible to take the licensing examinations for Missouri or for any other states with similar licensing requirements.

Information Reporting Technology: CART and Captioning Reporting: An Associate in Applied Science degree and a certificate of proficiency are offered through the Information Reporting Technology program. Communication Access Realtime Translation (CART), also referred to as realtime captioning, is a word-for-word speech-to-text interpreting service for people who need communication access. For students who are fascinated with words and have good English skills, manual dexterity, keyboarding experience, and the ability to hear the spoken word, CART and captioning reporting may be the perfect career. This program prepares the student for entry-level positions in realtime captioning.

Business Administration: This program, which offers a certificate of proficiency and a certificate of specialization, addresses the educational and occupational needs of several groups of people in the business field. Students can enroll in short-term, intensive training for job opportunities, or they can complete specific undergraduate requirements toward an advanced degree in business.

Special Programs

St. Louis Community College offers an honors program; students are admitted based on their high school GPA and SAT or ACT scores. Students who earn 15 hours of honors credit receive the designation of Honors Program Scholar on their diplomas and transcripts.

In recognition of the importance of the United States' position within the international community, SLCC offers transcultural and international study. This includes semesters abroad and study tours. The International Education Office (314-539-5176) has additional information.

Student Services

Students can access many SLCC student services via the Web, including admissions, registration, financial aid, library services, and the 24/7 HelpDesk.

Credit Options

Students may be eligible for credit for academic knowledge gained outside the classroom. The number of credits earned through examination is limited; College policy states that 15 of the final 25 semester hours earned toward an associate degree must be earned at St. Louis Community College. Students should get official transcripts mailed to the College and request an evaluation of previously earned credits by the campus admission/registration office.

Faculty

Faculty members specialize in teaching at the undergraduate level and hold advanced degrees—master's or doctoral—or advanced licensing degrees in technical fields. Career instructors have worked in business and industry and keep current with changes in their fields. Of the College's 570 faculty members, 32 percent are full-time.

Admission

St. Louis Community College has an open-admissions policy in keeping with its original purpose to provide a high-quality, low-cost education to area residents. Although admission to the College is not based on minimum academic qualifications, certain programs have required standards for admission and retention.

Tuition and Fees

Maintenance fees are $81 per credit hour for students in the SLCC service area, $118 per credit hour for out-of-district students, $148 per credit hour for out-of-state students, and $158 per credit hour for international students.

Financial Aid

St. Louis Community College provides a comprehensive financial aid program funded by federal, state, and private agencies. Aid awards fall into four categories—grants, scholarships, loans, and work. Although superior ability and talent are recognized through College and other scholarship programs, most aid is awarded on the basis of financial need. Students are encouraged to apply for aid as early as possible (by April 1 for the fall semester). Students who wish to know more about their financial aid eligibility should contact the College's financial aid office.

Applying

Students can apply online, by mail or fax, or in person. Applicants must submit an official high school transcript or GED score. International students must also submit TOEFL scores and certification of finances.

CONTACT

Daniel A. Bain, Ph.D., Director
Telelearning Services
St. Louis Community College System
300 South Broadway
St. Louis, Missouri 63102

Phone: 314-539-5056
Fax: 314-539-5125
E-mail: dbain@stlcc.edu
Web site: http://www.stlcc.edu/distance

SAVANNAH COLLEGE OF ART AND DESIGN

SCAD-eLearning Program

Savannah, Georgia

Savannah College of Art and Design (SCAD) exists to prepare talented students for professional careers, emphasizing learning through individual attention in a positively oriented university environment. SCAD is a private, coeducational institution with locations in Atlanta and Savannah, Georgia. Online programs are offered through SCAD-eLearning. A balanced fine arts and liberal arts curriculum has attracted students from every state and from more than ninety countries, making SCAD one of the largest art and design colleges in the United States.

Distance Learning Program

The Savannah College of Art and Design offers individual courses and degree and certificate programs at the undergraduate and graduate levels through SCAD-eLearning. SCAD, a member of the Sloan Consortium of institutions, is an award-winning, recognized leader in online course design, instructional technology, and online education. SCAD-eLearning is committed to academic excellence, technology integration, and twenty-first century design practices. Its distance education programs give students the flexibility to further their creative talents online in order to suit their locations, schedules, and preferences.

SCAD, including SCAD-eLearning, is regionally accredited by the Commission on Colleges of the Southern Association of Colleges and Schools (1866 Southern Lane, Decatur, Georgia 30033-4097; 404-679-4500) to award bachelor's and master's degrees. SCAD-eLearning students earn a SCAD degree, with no distinction made between degree requirements met on campus and online.

Delivery Media

Courses are delivered via the Internet and are offered year-round; each is organized into ten units, usually one per week. Courses adhere to a ten-week quarter with start and end dates, but are not held at scheduled times. Instead, students attend class when it is convenient for them. Students are expected to complete course work according to a schedule that stipulates due dates, assessments, and discussions. Student participation is expected in all assignments, examinations, and field trips or other activities. Attendance is determined by active login time and participation.

SCAD-eLearning provides a secure and user-friendly way for faculty members and students to communicate with one another. Regular online discussions, live chat sessions with professors and peers, assessments, and feedback help students maximize their experience. Students have access to an extensive range of online services and resources.

Instructional designers and technologists, media designers, and e-services staff members collaborate with faculty members to ensure that all courses are fully ADA compliant and adhere to the same high standards as SCAD's on-site course offerings.

SCAD-eLearning students must possess basic computer skills and have regular access to appropriate hardware, software, and Internet connectivity. SCAD-eLearning courses are designed to run on a variety of computers and operating systems and may be accessed with a 56K modem connection or better. Prospective students may find specific technical requirements online at http://www.scadelearning.org.

Programs of Study

SCAD-eLearning programs include Bachelor of Arts degrees in digital media and visual communications; Master of Arts degrees in broadcast design and motion graphics, digital photography, graphic design, historic preservation, illustration design, interactive design and game development, interior design, and painting; a Master of Fine Arts degree in graphic design; an undergraduate certificate in digital publishing; and graduate certificates in historic preservation, interactive design, digital publishing management, and typeface design.

The four-year Bachelor of Arts (B.A.) degree program incorporates fine arts foundation studies, general education courses,

an area of concentration, and electives. The majority of the B.A. curriculum consists of fine arts, humanities, general education, and liberal arts courses. An area of study concentration complements the course work. Students pursuing a B.A. degree in digital media may choose a concentration in game development or interactive design; those interested in a visual communication degree may concentrate in graphic design or sequential art.

The Master of Arts degree in broadcast design and motion graphics is a mixture of graphic design in motion and experimental animation. The program combines taught and self-directed studies, critical approaches to spatial and material culture, project management, design methodology, research, communication, and design theory.

The Master of Arts degree in digital photography allows students to gain a thorough knowledge of the medium and the photographic applications of digital technology. Students achieve a mastery of craft, technology, and aesthetics by exploring creative possibilities, developing a personal vision, and studying the history and criticism of the medium.

The eLearning certificates and degree programs in graphic design prepare students for careers in a variety of fields including publishing, education, advertising, and new media. In the certificate programs, students learn to produce a broad range of materials, including newsletters, brochures, and Web sites with industry-standard computer applications. The undergraduate certificate in digital publishing features an emphasis on production, while the graduate certificate in digital publishing management emphasizes management of content, design and development processes, and creative teams. With the graduate certificate in typeface design, students pursue historical and practical research opportunities and a comprehensive understanding of the nature of typeface design processes. Students invent, develop, and promote their own typeface solutions. The Master of Arts program in graphic design is professionally oriented and allows a broad course of study; the Master of Fine

Arts program includes a field or teaching internship and a thesis component.

The graduate certificate in historic preservation is designed for individuals working in historic preservation or related fields and those with an interest in historic preservation who would like to expand their knowledge or prepare to enter the field or enhance their careers. The Master of Arts program includes courses in building assessment and preservation planning, and requires a final project.

The Master of Arts degree in illustration design allows students to create a substantial body of work, producing comprehensive portfolios in preparation for a career in freelance illustration. Students are introduced to the practical side of the illustration business, from portfolio presentation to marketing and invoicing. Course work parallels professional practice and sometimes involves actual clients.

The graduate certificate and Master of Arts degree in interactive design and game development prepares students for careers in interactive art and design, particularly with large design firms, advertising agencies, product manufacturers, and education. The online method of course delivery is compelling, as students are educated in the electronically mediated environment in which they typically work or plan to work. Students are prepared for or may enhance their careers in interactive design, art direction, creative technology, exhibit design, and projection media.

The Master of Arts degree in interior design prepares students for advanced professional practice, teaching, or research. The curriculum includes commercial, residential, and institutional projects, both large and small, that address a wide range of behavioral, environmental, decorative, and technical issues.

Painting students in the Master of Arts degree program develop their work through informed, individual instruction and a curriculum that promotes exploration based on practical knowledge and awareness of historical and contemporary factors. The program begins with a five-week residency in Savannah, continues online, and finishes with a five-week residency in Atlanta.

All courses may be credited toward other applicable degree programs upon successful application and acceptance to the program.

Student Services

SCAD-eLearning provides a forum for students to participate in College events and discussions through Web casts, online forums, and other digital-programming outlets. Through the College's MySCAD Intranet, students may access comprehensive e-campus services, including course registration, peer tutoring, career services, Writing Center instruction, and SCAD's Jen Library online services. Students are encouraged to communicate with their peers through course discussions, e-mail, quarterly online chats, and the eLearning Club, which holds regular meetings online in real time.

Credit Options

Through SCAD-eLearning, the Savannah College of Art and Design offers students the option of taking courses without enrolling in a degree or certificate program. Depending on their admission status, students may take courses for credit. Course offerings change quarterly; students should consult the SCAD-eLearning Web site for an updated course listing.

Faculty

SCAD-eLearning courses are taught by highly qualified professors who guide students toward academic and professional success. Seventy-four percent of SCAD faculty members hold terminal degrees and 81 percent are full time. Every SCAD professor offers the professional experience, academic credentials, expertise, and passion for teaching that are characteristic of SCAD faculty members. Professors actively teach, publish academic papers, work as professional artists and designers, and exhibit their work in museums and galleries.

Admission

Application and admission policies and procedures for SCAD-eLearning are the same as for all undergraduate and graduate programs offered by the College. New students may enter for the fall, winter, spring, or summer quarter. Applicants are encouraged to submit their applications online and to apply as early as possible. Students applying for federal or state financial aid should plan to complete their application file and submit all financial aid information at least six months prior to their intended entry quarter. Students who wish to be considered for institutional scholarships must indicate this on the application for admission and must submit all required materials as requested. Scholarship funds are limited and are awarded to the earliest qualifiers.

As a general rule, applications for fall quarter should be completed no later than March 1 in order for admission decisions to be rendered by April 1. This same time frame applies with corresponding dates for students entering for the winter, spring, or summer quarters. Applications received less than one month prior to the intended entry date are considered only on a space-available basis.

Tuition and Fees

Undergraduate tuition for 2008–09 is $2885 per 5-credit-hour course; graduate tuition is $2935 per 5-credit-hour course. All degree-seeking students pay a one-time, non-refundable matriculation fee of $500. Non-degree-seeking students pay a tuition deposit of $200.

Financial Aid

Qualified SCAD-eLearning students are eligible to receive scholarships, fellowships, and federal and state financial aid. Only degree-seeking and certificate students who are enrolled at least half-time (two classes) may be eligible for federal financial aid. For application requirements and detailed information about scholarships, fellowships, and financial aid, prospective students should visit http://www.scadelearning. org. Students enrolling less than half-time and non-degree-seeking students should contact an alternative lender for financial assistance. Alternative lender information may be found on the College Web site at http://www.scad.edu. Aid programs offered by the state of Georgia may be available to Georgia students who are enrolled full-time (three classes). Non-Georgia students are encouraged to research their states' incentive program scholarships.

Applying

To apply for admission, learn more about online programs, or take the SCAD-eLearning self-assessment test, students should visit SCAD's Web site at http://www. scadelearning.org.

CONTACT

SCAD-eLearning
Savannah College of Art and Design
P.O. Box 2072
Savannah, Georgia 31402-2072
Phone: 912-525-5100
　　　　800-869-7223 (toll-free)
E-mail: elearn@scad.edu
Web site: http://www.scadelearning.
　　　　org

SAYBROOK GRADUATE SCHOOL AND RESEARCH CENTER
Graduate Programs in Psychology, Human Science, and Organizational Systems
San Francisco, California

Accredited by the Western Association of Schools and Colleges, Saybrook Graduate School and Research Center is a private, nonprofit institution offering M.A. and Ph.D. degrees in human science, organizational systems, and psychology. Saybrook provides an educational framework in which students have the flexibility to engage in research to explore new ideas and/or in innovative practice in their chosen profession. Saybrook's philosophy of learning emphasizes and integrates three areas of excellence—education, scholarship, and practice—to foster proactive engagement in and with the world. The goal of a Saybrook education is a learning process that is continuous and ongoing from the classroom out into the world and back into the classroom. At Saybrook, students are educated to become leaders for life-enhancing change, self-reflective scholars and practitioners, extraordinary thinkers who move beyond traditional disciplinary and paradigmatic boundaries, and professionals who place their work within an expanded geopolitical, temporal, and socioenvironmental context.

Distance Learning Program

For more than thirty-five years, students have earned M.A. and Ph.D. degrees through Saybrook's distance learning model. This blended interactive learning environment combines unique and individualized one-on-one faculty mentoring, online academic courses, and residential conferences with intensive seminars and workshops. With the School's one-on-one faculty mentoring format, students develop their own curricula aligned with their personal and professional interests.

Delivery Media

In Saybrook's virtual classroom, students begin and end the course together as a group. Saybrook requires students to use technology to perform research, send assignments, communicate regularly with faculty members, and connect with fellow students and administrators. Consistent with the unique distance learning process, students are able to use many different learning modes: Web-based classrooms, e-mail, bulletin boards, residential conferences, faculty mentoring, and other methods.

Programs of Study

Students can earn M.A. and Ph.D. degrees in human science, organizational systems, and psychology programs. Each program emphasizes the study of and inquiry into understanding people in their entirety. Courses center on humanistic philosophical, scientific, social, and political contexts as well as practical, real-world implica-

tions. Students are eligible to take classes in any program that Saybrook offers; however, students usually focus their study by selecting a concentration from one of the following areas: consciousness and spirituality, humanistic and transpersonal psychology, integrative health studies, organizational systems, or social transformation.

The Saybrook human science program is designed for students interested in interdisciplinary studies that foster understanding of the human condition in deeply subjective, personal, historical, contextual, cross-cultural, political, and spiritual terms. The program explores the human condition through various lenses that include self-reflection, art, music, literature, poetry, drama, language, philosophy, spirituality, and imagery. The program encompasses theoretical and practical critiques of self, culture, and society; focuses critical attention on the nature of theory, methodology, social practices, and the meaning of being human; and proposes that other, more expansive approaches are necessary for psychologists and other social-behavioral scientists to study the world in which people actually live. Students in the human science program usually seek and have professions in a wide range of disciplines that include sociology, anthropology, and other social science fields. Its primarily qualitative methodology approach is gaining credence in many disciplines across the country, such as in nursing and occupational therapy. Students may choose to deepen

their learning by selecting any of Saybrook's five concentration areas.

The unique focus of the organizational systems program at Saybrook is the combination of academic and professional achievement within a humanistic and transpersonal orientation and the integration of organizational behavior and systems science knowledge. The program is designed for current and future leaders in all types of organizations: business, educational, health care, community service, and government. Students learn skills that are important for the creation, design, and management of organizations that are able to adapt to change while respecting core human values. Its multidisciplinary approach blends elements of graduate study in business, public administration, organizational psychology, systems science, anthropology, and sociology. The program is particularly for people in the fields of human resources, social policy, strategic planning, administration, and education; line managers, psychologists, lawyers, and accountants who consult to public and/or private organizations; and change agents, including educators, consultants, administrators, and system designers who see their professional future linked to the development of broad skills in creating organizational designs and social change. Students in the organizational systems program may only select the organizational systems concentration.

Saybrook's psychology program is committed to the study of and inquiry into human experience from multiple frameworks that are informed by a historical and evolving humanistic perspective. It is designed for individuals interested in cutting-edge research, clinical professions, and practices based on expanded definitions of health and well-being that embrace both individuals and culture. The program's flexibility is well-suited to people planning or engaged in careers in research, teaching, health, clinical work, community development, consultation, mediation and conflict resolution, human resources, and counseling and guidance. The emphasis is on disciplined inquiry, scholarly research and writing, and the conceptualization of issues in psychology within the framework of their philosophical, scientific, social, and political contexts as well as practical real-world implications. Students may select any of Saybrook's five concentration areas.

The marriage and family therapy (MFT) specialization is designed to prepare graduates to be academically eligible to sit for the MFT license examination in California. It may prepare students to sit for licensure for other types of master's-level counseling licenses, including licensed professional counselor or mental health counselor. However, Saybrook cannot guarantee the acceptance of its program for license tracks outside of California because states' requirements vary widely. It is the responsibility of the student to check their state's licensing requirements. The program focuses on the promotion of personal growth and family well-being in a culturally grounded, whole-person-centered approach that integrates body, mind, and spirit within the social context. It offers a comprehensive body of knowledge, theory, and research tailored to meet the unique needs of each student through techniques that combine individual mentoring and tutorials, interactive distance learning, and on-site classroom and practicum classes. Saybrook champions a growth-oriented multicultural view of psychology that believes everyone has the capacity, given the chance, to realize their unique and diverse potential and to collaborate with others to create a better world. Toward that end, the Saybrook MFT curriculum emphasizes the need to be culturally competent in a diverse global society and addresses the changing nature of the concept of marriage and family

The M.A. in psychology with emphasis in creativity studies focuses on human potential in terms of its broadest and most expansive capacities. Students receive a theoretical and practical understanding of the creative process, including significant theoretical models, psychological components, sociological implications, factors that encourage and discourage creativity, creativity in organizations, and creativity in specific domains. The program is targeted to students seeking to work with individuals and organizations to enhance their creative process, work with corporations to facilitate institutional creativity, lead groups in effective collaboration, and teach at the college level.

The clinical psychology Ph.D. specialization is part of the humanistic and transpersonal psychology concentration, which meets modal requirements for licensure in

some states. While Saybrook does not have a formal clinical psychology program, it does have the courses needed to satisfy licensure requirements and has laid out a recommended clinical psychology Ph.D. track for students seeking licensure. Students whose career goals require obtaining a clinical license must become thoroughly familiar with requirements for licensing in the state in which they wish to first become licensed. Although most states have adopted a uniform national written examination, individual state requirements for academic preparedness, specific courses and course titles, and practicum and internship hours vary considerably.

Student Services
Saybrook's intent is to foster community among students, faculty and staff members, and alumni and to be responsive to student and institutional needs. Most administrative business can be conducted online. Students can find information at http://www.saybrook.edu/student_resources/ and students can e-mail or phone the appropriate department at any time.

Faculty
Students have the opportunity to work with an internationally recognized faculty of scholars and practitioners, all of which hold a doctoral degree in their field. In addition to teaching, faculty members have extensive experience as researchers, practitioners, consultants, authors, business people, and organizational leaders. They are committed to Saybrook's ideals and values and strongly support students' personal and scholarly growth.

Admission
All applicants seeking admission into a master's program must hold a bachelor's degree from a regionally accredited institution. The minimum expected grade point average (GPA) requirement is 3.0 from the last degree-granting institution; however, exceptions may be made with the approval of the Vice President of Academic Affairs.

Doctoral degree applicants must have an appropriate master's degree from a regionally accredited institution. Candidates wishing to pursue the doctoral degree but who lack a master's degree should apply to one of Saybrook's M.A. programs and, upon graduation from the master's program, apply for the Ph.D. program and transfer a maximum of 31 Saybrook credits toward Saybrook's Ph.D. degree.

Tuition and Fees
Annual tuition for 2007–08 is $17,600. Also required are fees of approximately $825 each for twice-a-year Residential Conferences (RCs). The fee covers the cost of registration, meals, conference materials, and meeting space, but does not include travel and lodging costs.

Financial Aid
Saybrook offers a variety of tuition assistance options that include scholarships, an expanded tuition assistance program, tuition grants, federal financial aid in the form of loans and work-study, and state and private loans. Saybrook's new multi-year scholarship program is available for new students who have outstanding merit and financial need, complete a FAFSA, and continue to show ability to complete a Saybrook degree program in a timely manner, with a minimum of 12 units completed for the first academic year. Scholarships are renewable as long as students remain in good academic standing and have continual financial need. Students are also considered for other forms of financial assistance, such as Federal Stafford and PLUS Loans.

Applying
It is strongly recommended that applications are completed at least three months before the proposed enrollment date. Priority is given to applications received by June 1 for fall semester enrollment. Applications received by December 15 have priority for spring semester enrollment. Applications are reviewed on a case-by-case basis until the Residential Orientation begins for each term. The financial aid process should be initiated at least three months prior to the proposed enrollment date to guarantee timely disbursement of tuition funds.

An online admission fee of $50 is required for first- and second-degree candidates. An application fee is required every time an application is submitted for review.

CONTACT
Saybrook Graduate School and Research Center
747 Front Street, 3rd Floor
San Francisco, California 94111-1920
Phone: 415-433-9200
          800-825-4480 (toll-free)
Fax: 415-433-9271
E-mail: admissions@saybrook.edu
Web site: http://www.saybrook.edu

SCHILLER INTERNATIONAL UNIVERSITY

M.B.A. Online Programs in Financial Planning, International Business, International Hotel and Tourism Management, and Management of Information Technology

Dunedin, Florida

Schiller International University (SIU), a leader in global education, with eight campuses in six countries, was founded in 1964. SIU is an independent, licensed, and accredited institution offering a curriculum of more than 300 courses in sixteen areas of study that leads to associate, bachelor's, and master's degrees. The mission of SIU is to prepare students, personally and professionally, for future leadership roles in an international setting. Schiller students have the unique opportunity of transferring among SIU's campuses without losing any credits while continuing their chosen program of study. SIU's campuses are in Dunedin, Florida; London, England; Paris, France; Strasbourg, France; Heidelberg, Germany; Engelberg, Switzerland; Leysin, Switzerland; and Madrid, Spain.

Schiller is a university where personal initiative is encouraged and where faculty members know students by name. The close attention paid to each individual student is one of the hallmarks of an SIU education. SIU is accredited by the Accrediting Council for Independent Colleges and Schools (ACICS) and is licensed by the Florida Commission for Independent Education. The accreditation and licensing applies to both traditional and online programs.

Distance Learning Program

Distance learning is a natural extension of the University's high-quality education, both on the undergraduate and graduate levels, for students from all over the world. This program has been developed in response to the needs of the adult learner in the Information Age. The creative use of modern education technology makes selected SIU programs available, anytime, anywhere, through the World Wide Web. Students may complete the entire M.B.A. program online, or online courses may be combined with one or more terms in residence at an SIU campus in the United States or in Europe. Online courses are usually limited to no more than 20 students per class.

Delivery Media

Online M.B.A.'s in international business, international hotel and tourism management, and management of information technology are available to all students who have access to a Pentium-based computer, a 28.8-Kbps (or faster) modem, the usual office software, and an Internet connection. All courses are Web-based and are delivered via the Internet, using the eCollege.com platform. Technical support is provided 24 hours a day, seven days a week, by eCollege.com's help desk. The course Web site contains a home page with the most essential information about the course, e-mail links to the instructor and other students taking the course, a discussion forum that allows instructor and students to communicate with the group as a whole, Web links, and glossaries. Each course utilizes a textbook, a study guide on CD-ROM, and the Web-based course materials, which also provide the medium of interaction. Although most interaction is asynchronous, chat rooms are available for student and faculty member use.

Programs of Study

Completion of an Online M.B.A. requires 45 credit hours. The curriculum for the international business degree concentrates on the more detailed aspects of international marketing, management, finance, and economics. For the concentrations in financial planning, international hotel and tourism management (IHTM), or management of information technology (MIT), stu-

dents complete seven core M.B.A. courses, two elective courses, and six concentrated courses in either financial planning, IHTM, or MIT. Students whose undergraduate background does not include preparation in accounting/finance, economics, or statistics are required to take additional preparatory courses, which are available online. The degree requirements are designed to provide practical knowledge and training for future business executives. SIU M.B.A. programs promote a professional academic environment without borders in which world-class education is offered in worldwide classrooms online.

In addition to the Online M.B.A., selected courses on the undergraduate level are offered in a distance learning format. More information about all programs can be accessed from SIU's Web site.

Special Programs

SIU offers an Executive M.B.A. program, which combines online courses as well as evening, weekend, and accelerated summer courses at selected campuses. During specific semesters, several undergraduate- and graduate-level courses are available online in a variety of subjects, including accounting, business administration and management, business communications, computer/information technology administration and management, economics, English composition, history, hospitality services management, human resources management, international business, international relations and diplomacy, marketing management and research, mathematics, physical sciences, psychology, statistics, and tourism and travel services marketing operations.

Student Services

The University has developed a number of methods to assist students in distance learning programs. Each student receives a copy of SIU's publication, *A Guide to Distance Learning.* Specially trained faculty mentors are always available by e-mail for consultation, and the Web-based host for the courses offers technical assistance 24 hours a day. Students in the distance learning programs have access to the full range of support services, including the Library and Information Resource Network (LIRN) and NET Library, that are used by all Schiller students. Each online course has its own library of study aids and resources. Lecture notes, sample quizzes, assignment checks, and hyperlinks to other interesting sites are available for viewing and downloading.

Credit Options

For the master's program, students must earn at least 36 credit hours, and undergraduates must earn at least 33 credits at SIU. Credit may be awarded to students who receive appropriate scores in CLEP subject examinations. Students admitted to the Executive M.B.A. program at the Florida campus may earn up to 6 credits by portfolio.

Faculty

All virtual courses are taught by instructors with advanced degrees and extensive practical experience in their fields. The faculty members' ability to teach in both online and ground-based formats ensures consistency across the programs. All courses in the distance learning program are Web-based. An online course has learning objectives identical to those of a ground-delivered course, incorporating both asynchronous and the possibility of synchronous technology to facilitate learning. Each course has a syllabus describing the course content, assignments, and grading policy. The faculty members choose from many course-delivery technolo-

gies, including journals and e-mail for assignment submission and correspondence; and discussion forums and chat rooms for ongoing questions and answers. The instructor uses these technologies to enhance the learning experience.

Admission

Admission to the Online M.B.A. program requires completion of a B.B.A. degree or equivalent; a bachelor's degree or equivalent, with a major in business studies or economics, providing that core courses have been completed in economics, statistics, business law, marketing, management, and accounting; or a bachelor's degree or equivalent in a nonbusiness field, provided that course work in the areas listed above has been completed. Non-native English speakers must provide scores of at least 550 (213 for the computerized test) on a TOEFL taken within the past two years. Test scores should be sent directly to the University.

A completed application form must be sent to the SIU Office of Admissions together with a $60 application fee, payable by check, credit card, or international money order. Applicants must also request that official transcripts of academic work be sent via airmail to the Office of Admissions. Applicants must submit transcripts of all college courses attended as well as proof of an earned degree. Undergraduate applicants must submit proof of high school graduation as well as TOEFL scores, if applicable. Original documents or certified copies must be submitted as well as a certified English translation of those documents not in English.

Tuition and Fees

Distance learning students pay the same tuition as on-campus students. Tuition for the 2006–07 academic year was $474 per graduate credit and $470 per undergraduate credit. It is payable

by check, credit card, or international money order. Tuition includes all instruction and faculty-produced materials. Students are responsible for the additional cost of textbooks, and information about online booksellers is provided. Room and board fees vary by campus. Students wishing to complete a portion of their degree in residence should contact the individual campus. Additional fees include a $60 application fee, a $90 graduation fee, and a late registration fee of $125, which is applicable only after classes commence.

Financial Aid

SIU participates in Title IV programs and is eligible to participate in the Veteran's Training Program. Both programs are for U.S. citizens and residents who qualify. Students should e-mail the Office of Financial Aid for further information.

Applying

Applications for admission are accepted year-round. Classes begin in September, January, and June. Students interested in online courses must complete two surveys, which are found on the distance learning page of the SIU Web site. Students can visit this site or contact the Office of Admissions for further information.

CONTACT

Office of Admissions
Schiller International University
453 Edgewater Drive
Dunedin, Florida 34698
Phone: 727-736-5082
      800-336-4133 (toll-free in the U.S.)
Fax: 727-734-0359
E-mail: admissions@schiller.edu
     financial_aid@schiller.edu
Web site: http://www.schiller.edu

SETON HALL UNIVERSITY

M.A. in Counseling

South Orange, New Jersey

Founded in 1856, Seton Hall is a private coeducational Catholic institution—the nation's oldest diocesan institution of higher education in the United States. One of the region's most prestigious academic institutions and a recognized leader in online education, Seton Hall University enrolls approximately 10,000 undergraduate and graduate students. Seton Hall University is accredited by the Middle States Commission on Higher Education.

Distance Learning Program

SetonWorldWide, Seton Hall's online campus, provides learners with the opportunity to earn a Seton Hall University degree in an e-learning environment that allows the working professional to fit their education into their busy lifestyle.

Delivery Media

Learners access their online course rooms using an Internet connection—anytime, anywhere. This 24/7 access allows course study and interaction in a flexible user-friendly environment.

Programs of Study

Seton Hall University's online counseling degrees follow a predetermined set of courses and are designed to expertly train students of diverse backgrounds, providing them with a solid, general knowledge base and clinical preparation for advanced work in the mental-health field or in the field of school counseling. The program's primary goal is to provide students with a thorough grounding in the theories, skills, and models of interventions essential to function effectively as counselors in a variety of settings.

The 48-credit curriculum provides students with a thorough background in individual counseling and group counseling skills and theory; clinical practice and ethical, professional, and legal issues in counseling; social and cultural factors in counseling; human development across the life span; work,

leisure, and career development theories and interventions; appraisal and assessment issues in counseling; the application of research methodology and statistics to understand mental-health issues; and the role and function of community mental-health agencies.

Seton Hall University's 48-credit online Master of Arts in School Counseling program prepares students for work in educational settings as school guidance counselors and may lead to certification as a school counselor in certain states. The program in school counseling emphasizes the development of competence, social consciousness, and reflection. Students are trained to work in ethnically, geographically, and socially diverse K–12 settings. This program promotes three major counseling functions within the context of school settings: prevention and intervention of personal and interpersonal concerns, fostering of optimal human development, and coordination of care services for students within school systems. Students begin the program learning the basics of counseling skills and foundational theories, and they end the program transitioning from a three-semester applied clinical experience.

Special Programs

A clinical experience is a part of the master's degree. Students receive individual counseling, guidance, and support from dedicated faculty members throughout this aspect of the program

to ensure the most professional experience possible during the practicum and internship.

The program curriculum meets many state requirements for licensure. For students requiring an additional number of courses, Seton Hall University offers a 12-credit sequence of courses or a post-masters licensure program online.

Students who are completing the M.A. in Counseling program can also enroll in the 12-credit post-master's School Counselor Certificate program that meets many state requirements for certification as a school counselor in grades K–12, and they can enroll in a post-masters licensing sequence if additional courses are needed.

Student Services

Seton Hall provides online support and assistance throughout the program and learners have online access to Seton Hall University's extensive library resources.

Credit Options

This program is open only to those who are matriculating as new students. Transfer credits are accepted on a selective individual basis.

Faculty

The program uses Seton Hall University faculty members as well as qualified adjunct professors who are leading experts and practitioners in the field of counseling. Faculty members also engage in traditional classroom teaching and learning. Students have a variety of instructors, all highly qualified. All course facilitators meet requirements as instructors.

Admission

All applicants must have a bachelor's degree from an accredited college or university and submit three letters of recommendation, a personal statement, and a resume. GRE or MAT scores may be waived in individual cases.

Tuition and Fees

The total cost of the 48-credit program is $32,500. This includes all fees, except for the application fee, and all expenses, including books and other materials and room and meals for the short on-campus residencies. Computer equipment, software, Internet access, and travel expenses to the residencies are not covered.

Financial Aid

There are various options for financing a degree from Seton Hall University. In order to be eligible for financial aid, a student must be accepted into a degree program. Financial aid for graduate students is available in the form of a FFELP/Stafford Loan, an alternative loan, or a personal loan. Another option available to students is a budget plan that divides tuition costs into monthly payments. Students are encouraged to check with their human resources departments to determine what educational assistance or tuition reimbursement programs may be available.

To be considered for any federal, state or University financial aid programs administered by Seton Hall, students must fill out the Free Application for Federal Student Aid (FAFSA). This free form is used to determine a student's eligibility for all financial aid programs. The FAFSA application can be completed online at http://www.fafsa.ed.gov. The Seton Hall University school code for FAFSA is 002632.

Applying

Applicants must submit the completed online application, the $50 nonrefundable application fee, transcripts from all undergraduate or graduate institutions attended, GRE or MAT scores (may be waived in individual cases), TOEFL scores (if applicable), three letters of recommendation, a resume, and a personal statement.

CONTACT

Rosalie Maiorella, Program Administrator
Presidents Hall, Room 324
Seton Hall University
400 South Orange Avenue
South Orange, New Jersey 07079

Phone: 973-313-6239
Fax: 973-761-9325
E-mail: maiorero@shu.edu
Web site: http://www.setonworldwide.net

SETON HALL UNIVERSITY

M.A. in Educational Leadership, Management, and Policy

South Orange, New Jersey

Founded in 1856, Seton Hall is a private coeducational Catholic institution—the nation's oldest diocesan institution of higher education. One of the region's most prestigious academic institutions and a recognized leader in online education, the University enrolls about 10,000 students.

Seton Hall University and its associated online programs are accredited by the National Council for Accreditation of Teacher Education (NCATE) and the Middle States Association of Colleges and Schools.

Distance Learning Program

SetonWorldWide, Seton Hall's online campus, provides learners with the opportunity to earn a Seton Hall University degree in an e-learning environment that allows the working professional to fit their education into their busy lifestyle.

Delivery Media

Learners access their online course rooms using an Internet connection—anytime, anywhere. This 24/7 access allows course study and interaction in a flexible user-friendly environment. The student-professor ratio is kept at 10:1 to ensure a timely response from the professor to each student.

Programs of Study

The M.A. in Education, Leadership, Management, and Policy (ELMP) program provides students with extensive knowledge of educational administration, including academic theories, skills, and techniques. This graduate degree concentration can lead to a supervisor certification with the New Jersey State Department of Education, and course work can be applied toward similar certification in other states. Students also train for the principal certification, which is built into this degree program.

The two-year program consists of eleven 3-credit courses and 6-credit principal internship for a total of 39 credits. All candidates take a comprehensive written examination at the end of the sixth semester.

The Department of Education Leadership, Management, and Policy holds two mandatory on-campus residency weekends. These weekend residencies usually begin in mid-July. Each weekend begins on Friday afternoon and runs through noon on Sunday. Residencies provide learning team members the opportunity to meet face-to-face, share experiences, continue discussions, provide feedback on program progress, and meet with instructors.

Special Programs

SetonWorldWide and Seton Hall University's College of Education and Human Services have teamed up to create an online supervisor's certificate program for teachers who have a master's degree but require additional credits to obtain the certificate. Successful completion of the 12-credit program enables students to be eligible for a supervisor of instruction position.

Student Services

Seton Hall provides online support and assistance throughout the program, and learners have access to Seton Hall University's extensive library resources.

Credit Options

Transfer credits are accepted on a selective, individual basis.

Faculty

All courses are taught by Seton Hall University faculty members with expertise in education, leadership, and management and policy as well as in online teaching and learning. There are 13 faculty members in the department.

Admission

Applicants must have a bachelor's degree from an accredited institution and at least a 3.0 GPA.

Tuition and Fees

The cost for the entire program is $21,000 and includes all fees and expenses, tuition, books and other materials, room and meals for the on-campus residencies, and graduation costs. Travel expenses to the residencies, the nonrefundable application fee, computer equipment, software, and Internet access are not included. Tuition for teachers in Catholic schools is $14,000, according to Seton Hall University policy.

Financial Aid

Most applicants who are American citizens are eligible for low-interest federal loans.

Applying

Interested students should apply online at http://www.setonworldwide.net, following the online instructions. A toll-free number and e-mail are available if questions arise. Applicants must submit the completed application, the nonrefundable $50 application fee, transcripts from all undergraduate institutions attended, a letter of intent that explains the reasons for applying to the program, a current resume, scores from the GRE or MAT, and three letters of recommendation from academic and/or professional references.

CONTACT

Mel Klein, Assistant Academic Director
Jubilee Hall, Room 357
Seton Hall University
400 South Orange Avenue
South Orange, New Jersey 07079
Phone: 888-738-6699 Ext. 2469
    (toll-free)
Fax: 973-761-9325
E-mail: kleinmel@shu.edu

Al Galloway, Program Director
Jubilee Hall, Room 357
Seton Hall University
400 South Orange Avenue
South Orange, New Jersey 07079
Phone: 888-738-6699 Ext. 2469
    (toll-free)
Fax: 973-761-9325
E-mail: gallowal@shu.edu
Web site:
    http://www.setonworldwide.net

SETON HALL UNIVERSITY
Master of Healthcare Administration
South Orange, New Jersey

Founded in 1856, Seton Hall is a private coeducational Catholic institution—the oldest diocesan institution of higher education in the United States. One of the nation's most prestigious academic institutions and a recognized leader in online education, the University enrolls about 10,000 students.

Seton Hall University is accredited by the Middle States Commission on Higher Education. A member of the Association of University Programs in Health Administration (AUPHA), a national association of university-based educational programs dedicated to continuously improving the field of health management and practice, the Seton Hall University Master of Healthcare Administration Program is ranked seventh among AUPHA's survey of the nation's twenty-five largest M.H.A. programs in the nation.

Distance Learning Program

SetonWorldWide, Seton Hall's online campus, provides learners with the opportunity to earn a Seton Hall University degree in an e-learning environment that allows the working professional to fit their education into their busy lifestyle.

Delivery Media

Learners access their online course rooms using any Internet connection—anytime, anywhere. This 24/7 access allows course study and interaction in a flexible user-friendly environment.

Programs of Study

The Seton Hall University Online Master of Healthcare Administration (M.H.A.) and Online Certificate in Healthcare Administration programs prepare managers for leadership roles within the health-care industry. Providing a rigorous and thorough understanding of the health-care environment, the programs address "real-world" strategies and skills that help health-care managers make significant contributions to their organizations.

Using state-of-the-art learning technologies in a highly interactive learning environment, the program is designed around an applied-focused, rigorous curriculum. The 39-credit, twenty-three-month program consists of six competency areas: Understanding the Environment, Managing Change, Financial Competencies, Decision Making, Strategic Leadership, and Analysis as well as a capstone project. All course work is completed online. There are three required on-campus weekend residencies. Learners begin the program with an orientation residency, followed by a midprogram residency, and a final residency at the end of the program.

Special Programs

The 15-credit online Graduate Certificate Program in Healthcare Administration is designed for individuals who might wish to pursue a career in health-care administration, those who already have a graduate degree but need to develop specific management skills, or individuals who would like to enroll in a selected set of graduate health-care administration courses but choose not to commit to an entire graduate degree program.

Student Services

Seton Hall provides online support and assistance throughout the program, and learners have access to Seton Hall University's extensive library resources.

Credit Options

Learners enroll in a cohort class and follow a prescribed sequential course of study. In most cases previously earned academic course credits are not accepted toward fulfilling the degree requirements.

Faculty

The faculty is composed of full-time Seton Hall faculty members as well as experienced practitioners with extensive knowledge in their respective fields. The SetonWorldwide Online M.H.A. program faculty members provide an in-depth theoretical and real-world practice knowledge base.

Admission

Candidates should have a baccalaureate degree from an accredited college or university with an undergraduate GPA of at least 3.0 or equivalent and health-care managerial experience.

Tuition and Fees

The cost for the six-semester program is $29,500 and includes all fees and expenses, tuition, books and other materials, room and meals for the on-campus residencies, and graduation costs. Travel expenses to the residencies, the application fee, computer equipment, software, and Internet access are not included in this figure.

Financial Aid

Many learners fund their tuition through employer tuition-reimbursement benefits or through federal and private institutional loan programs. The University does not offer financial aid in the form of scholarships or grants for online M.H.A. students.

Applying

Application to the program can be submitted online. The application process includes submission of a completed online application, a $50 nonrefundable application fee, transcripts from all universities attended, a letter of intent, a current resume, and three letters of recommendation from academic or professional references. In addition, individuals who have graduated from a baccalaureate program within the last five years must submit test scores from the GRE (aptitude), GMAT, or LSAT.

CONTACT

James J. Howard, Ph.D., Program Director
SetonWorldWide Online Master of Healthcare Administration Program
Presidents Hall, Room 328
Seton Hall University
400 South Orange Avenue
South Orange, New Jersey 07079
Phone: 973-275-2559
Fax: 973-761-9325
E-mail: howardjj@shu.edu
Web site: http://www.setonworldwide.net

SETON HALL UNIVERSITY

M.A. in Strategic Communication and Leadership

South Orange, New Jersey

Founded in 1856, Seton Hall is a private coeducational Catholic institution—the nation's oldest diocesan institution of higher education in the United States. One of the region's most prestigious academic institutions and a recognized leader in online education, Seton Hall University enrolls approximately 10,000 undergraduate and graduate students. Seton Hall University is accredited by the Middle States Commission on Higher Education.

Distance Learning Program

SetonWorldWide, Seton Hall's online campus, provides learners with the opportunity to earn a Seton Hall University degree in an e-learning environment that allows the working professional to fit their education into their busy lifestyle.

Delivery Media

Learners access their online course rooms using an Internet connection—anytime, anywhere. This 24/7 access allows course study and interaction in a flexible user-friendly environment.

Programs of Study

A basic building block for success in today's highly competitive world is the manager who can lead and communicate effectively. Executives, managers, and military command personnel are increasingly expected to bring to their organizations these unique competencies. The Master of Arts in Strategic Communication and Leadership (MASCL) program has been designed to meet the needs of today's busy professional. Through a highly interactive curriculum that allows for significant discussion of strategies and solutions to current issues in effective leadership and communication, the program provides an opportunity to network and

study with colleagues and experts in specialized disciplines. Using state-of-the-art online learning technologies, this rigorous program is aimed at helping the high-potential individual earn a Seton Hall University degree in a convenient format.

A serious program for the serious learner, MASCL requires 36 credits and takes eighteen months to complete. Students interact with a learning team of their peers (successful executives, managers, and professionals), experienced instructors, and other experts in an anytime, anyplace e-learning environment. Three on-campus weekend-long residencies, five 12-week modules, and an ongoing leadership and communication skills enhancement program combine to develop the superior abilities required for dynamic leadership. Faculty members mentor participants throughout the program to polish interpersonal, presentation, and writing skills.

The three on-site weekends—Orientation, Mid-Program Residency, and Final Residency—include sessions for students to practice their communication and leadership skills. Individual coaching is provided during all of the residencies. The Orientation Weekend prepares the learning team for the program. Students meet one another, faculty members, and administrators. They

learn how to access and use the online learning technologies, and they make a presentation and receive feedback and coaching. At the Mid-Program residency, students give group and individual presentations, and they also take part in a mock press conference. During the Final Residency, students present their strategic-communication plan, with an emphasis on how they intend to communicate it to their organization's stakeholders. The weekend concludes with commencement exercises.

Student Services

Seton Hall provides online support and assistance throughout the program, and learners have access to Seton Hall University's extensive library resources.

Credit Options

All course waivers, including work experience, and transfer credits are subject to the review and approval of the program director.

Faculty

The Department of Communication faculty members combine practical experience with academic preparation. Each curricular area utilizes faculty members who have impressive professional records and those with doctoral degrees for a blend of the academic and practical.

Admission

Applicants should have a baccalaureate degree from an accredited college or university. The ideal candidate has significant experience in a corporate, military, governmental, association, or nonprofit organization. Candidates are ready for increased workplace responsibilities or a new executive position and seek to develop and enhance their leadership communication skills in preparation for these challenges and opportunities. They typically do not have the time to attend an on-campus program and seek a rigorous online program in communication, leadership, business strategy, and organizational development.

Tuition and Fees

The cost for the entire program is $27,500 and includes all fees and expenses, tuition, books and other materials, room and meals for the on-campus residencies, and graduation costs. Travel expenses to the on-campus residencies, the application fee, computer equipment, software, and Internet access are not included in this figure.

Financial Aid

Financial aid for graduate students is available in the form of a FFELP/Stafford Loan, an alternative loan, or a personal loan. Another option available to students is a budget plan that divides tuition costs into monthly payments. Students are encouraged to check with their human resources departments to determine what educational assistance or tuition reimbursement programs may be available.

Applying

Students must submit the completed online application, the $50 nonrefundable application fee, official transcripts from all colleges and universities attended, two letters of recommendation (preferably one each from a present and a former supervisor), a current resume, a work sample in any medium that demonstrates the candidate's excellence in his or her field, and a short (about 500 words) essay that states the candidate's goals for engaging in the MASCL learning experience.

CONTACT

Regina Walker, Account Executive
Presidents Hall, Room 327
Seton Hall University
400 South Orange Avenue
South Orange, New Jersey 07079

Phone: 973-275-2419
Fax: 973-761-9325
E-mail: walkerre@shu.edu
Web site: http://www.setonworldwide.net

SETON HALL UNIVERSITY
Programs in Nursing
South Orange, New Jersey

Founded in 1856, Seton Hall is a private coeducational Catholic institution—the nation's oldest diocesan institution of higher education in the United States. One of the region's most prestigious academic institutions and a recognized leader in online education, the University enrolls about 10,000 students. Seton Hall University and its associated online programs are accredited by the Middle States Association of Colleges and Schools.

Distance Learning Program

SetonWorldWide, Seton Hall's online campus, offers degree programs and certificates designed for professionals who have demonstrated achievement in their respective fields and have the ability, desire, and dedication to accept the rigors of a fast-paced, challenging curriculum. Working professionals can benefit from "anytime, anywhere" education. As learning team members, students and faculty members have extensive interaction, and these relationships provide a rich and dynamic online learning experience. All SetonWorldWide degree program graduates receive an accredited Seton Hall University degree.

Delivery Media

Online learning takes advantage of different methods of presentation, but the educational objectives are the same as traditional, in-classroom learning at Seton Hall University. SetonWorldWide provides for student-teacher interaction through a discussion section for each unit, which poses questions and comments initiated by the instructor. Students then respond both to the instructor and to each other with answers that show critical thinking and synthesis of course content. E-mail is used for individual and small-group interactions. Instructors review student material submitted electronically, and students receive feedback via e-mail or telephone.

Programs of Study

The Bachelor of Science in Nursing (B.S.N.) program is designed for the busy RN who wants to balance career and personal commitments with a flexible educational program of study. The five-semester program offers the required 34 credits of nursing (nine courses) online, and students may complete their clinical requirements within their respective geographical locations.

The nationally ranked Master of Science in Nursing (M.S.N.)–Nurse Practitioner program provides highly interactive online multimedia programs in five clinical specialty areas: adult, gerontological, pediatric, women's health, and acute-care nurse practitioner. Students complete the didactic portion of the program online in their home or office at their convenience. The required clinical practice component is fulfilled within the students' geographical location. All nurse practitioner graduates are eligible to apply for advanced-practice certification.

The 33-credit M.S.N. in health systems administration is designed to prepare nurse managers, directors, and executives with the needed leadership skills demanded by today's complex health-care industry. Students become knowledgeable about the business and financial operations necessary to effectively manage large patient-care departments. Nurses looking to bring their career to a new level in management are ideal candidates.

Three on-campus weekend residencies enable students to meet their classmates and the faculty in person. On Orientation Weekend, students participate in hands-on training in accessing their online courses and resources, tour the Seton Hall campus, and meet other online learning teams. For the Mid-Program Weekend Residency, clinical assessment skills are refined and role development sessions are scheduled. The Final Residency Weekend is the culminating event of the program, with scheduled final student project presentations and graduation activities. The health systems administration students attend only the first and last weekend residencies.

Student Services

Students find everything they need online, including admission information, academic assistance, financial aid assistance, career guidance, and other services. The Help Desk's technical support staff has the knowledge and experience to help make every student's transition into the virtual classroom a smooth one. All SetonWorldWide participants have access to Seton Hall University library resources. During the orientation, students meet the librarians and technical staff members who provide assistance throughout the program. Students can use the library's ASK ME service to request and receive assistance from a fully qualified librarian.

Credit Options

Graduate credits earned recently at another accredited college or university may be accepted in partial satisfaction of graduate credit requirements. A total of 6 credits may be approved for transfer.

Faculty

The College of Nursing faculty includes distinguished educators and prolific researchers who bring real-world management perspectives to the learning environment. Students receive truly individualized personal attention as well as supportive career direction and guidance. The College has about 60 full- and part-time faculty members.

Admission

In addition to having a diploma or an associate degree from a nursing program, applicants to the B.S.N. program must have a minimum overall GPA of 3.0 and RN licensure. M.S.N. applicants must have graduated from an NLN- or CCNE-accredited baccalaureate pro-

gram in nursing and have earned at least a B average in nursing courses and overall. GRE or MAT testing is required.

Tuition and Fees

The all-inclusive tuition includes all fees, except for the application fee and room and meals for the short on-campus residencies. Computer equipment, software, Internet access, and travel expenses to the residencies are not covered. The cost for tuition for the 2005–06 academic year was $717 per credit for undergraduate courses and $743 per credit for graduate courses.

Financial Aid

Almost 90 percent of the students who entered Seton Hall in 2005 received some form of financial aid, and 75 percent of these students received money directly from the University. The four types of financial aid include scholar-

ships, grants and discounts, loans, and part-time jobs on campus. In addition, many working RNs use tuition remission through their places of employment. Specific nursing scholarships are available for nursing students during the clinical portion of the curriculum.

Applying

B.S.N. applicants must submit the completed application, the $45 nonrefundable application fee, all official high school and college transcripts, two letters of recommendation from academic and professional references, and a resume or curriculum vitae. M.S.N. applicants must submit the completed application, the $50 nonrefundable application fee, a typewritten statement of goals, a curriculum vitae or resume, all official college transcripts, two letters of recommendation, and scores from the Miller Analogies Test.

CONTACT

Mary Jo Bugel, Director of Recruitment
Schwartz Hall
Seton Hall University
400 South Orange Avenue
South Orange, New Jersey 07079

Phone: 973-275-9306
Fax: 973-761-9607
E-mail: nursing@shu.edu
Web site: http://www.setonworldwide.net

SKIDMORE COLLEGE

University Without Walls

Saratoga Springs, New York

University Without Walls (UWW) is the degree completion program for adults at Skidmore College. UWW was in the vanguard in establishing a program for distance learners. The program began in 1971 as an experiment in nontraditional education jointly funded by the Ford Foundation and the U.S. Department of Education. When the funding for this experiment ended in 1975, Skidmore College took over the program as its own. Over the years, UWW has evolved to serve adult students pursuing baccalaureate degrees in a variety of liberal arts, performing arts, and preprofessional fields.

The UWW program is characterized by its flexibility and the high quality of education students receive. The unique advising system at UWW guarantees that each program meets the student's individual needs and the high standards of Skidmore College.

Distance Learning Program

UWW serves 220 full- and part-time undergraduate students from as near as the city of Saratoga Springs and as far away as Europe, Africa, and Asia. The UWW program does not require its students to be in residence on campus. Student programs may include UWW online courses, independent study with Skidmore faculty members, courses at other accredited institutions, internships, and distance learning courses from major universities. Every program includes a final project in the area of the student's focus.

Delivery Media

With support from an Alfred P. Sloan Foundation grant in 2001–04, UWW has created a rich offering of online courses designed to meet the educational needs of its students. Students can also take on-site or online courses through other accredited institutions. Independent study with Skidmore faculty members or faculty members at other institutions takes place through telephone, mail, and e-mail communications.

Programs of Study

UWW offers Bachelor of Arts degrees in most traditional liberal arts fields, including American studies, anthropology, art history, classics, computer science, economics, English, French, geology, government, history, mathematics, philosophy, psychology, religion, sociology, and Spanish. Bachelor of Science degrees are available in art, business, dance, human services, and theater. Students can also combine fields to create an interdisciplinary program, such as arts management, Asian studies, communications, environmental studies, health studies, human behavior, international affairs, Latin American studies, management information systems, nonprofit management, organizational behavior, public administration, and religion and culture. Individually designed majors are welcomed.

All degrees are 120-credit programs. Programs are expected to include at least 12 credits in the humanities, 6 credits in history, 12 credits in the social sciences, and 9 credits in math or science, including laboratory experience. Professional programs must include at least 60 credits in the liberal arts. Courses taken prior to enrollment in UWW may be considered in satisfaction of these requirements.

Special Programs

UWW's flexibility allows many students to take advantage of unusual learning opportunities. Recent UWW students have studied abroad in Austria, Canada, Costa Rica, the Czech Republic, Germany, India, Ireland, Poland, Spain, and Switzerland, among other locations. Business students often have the opportunity to include professional management and banking seminars in satisfaction of their degree requirements.

UWW students are often able to participate in programs sponsored by Skidmore College and the Office of Special Programs, including a summer study program in Florence, the New York State Writers Institute, the Skidmore Jazz Institute, the Summer Dance Workshop, and the SITI Summer Theater Workshop. UWW students are eligible for substantial discounts on courses offered by Skidmore Summer Academic Sessions and the Summer Six Art Program.

UWW business students are eligible to apply for 3/2 M.B.A. programs in cooperation with Rensselaer Polytechnic Institute in Troy and Rensselaer–Hartford.

Student Services

UWW is a small, personal program, and the staff members are happy to assist students in any way possible. Typical services include academic advising, registration assistance, financial aid counseling, and book-order assistance. Local students also enjoy library privileges, career counseling, access to recreational facilities, access to computer labs, and an e-mail account. Some summer housing is available for special program participants.

Credit Options

UWW accepts transfer credit for courses completed with a grade of C or better. There is no limit to the number of credits transferred or the age of the work, provided that the course is appropriate to a liberal arts curriculum. Credit is also available for experiential learning and internships. In addition, students may document knowledge through CLEP, ACT-PEP, DANTES, and Regents examinations. Many college-level courses offered through the military are accepted. Credit from international universities is usually accepted.

Faculty

Skidmore has approximately 200 full- and part-time faculty members. Most participate as advisers and instructors in the UWW program. Ninety-three percent of the Skidmore faculty members have a terminal degree.

Admission

UWW considers any applicant able to succeed at demanding college-level work. However, the program works best for students who have had some college experience. Applicants must have a high school diploma or the equivalent.

Tuition and Fees

Tuition is determined by the number of credits the student is taking. In general, annual costs range from $12,000 for a full-time program (12–16 credits per semester for fall and spring semesters) to $6700 for less than half-time (fewer than 6 credits). These fees include full access to UWW online courses and independent study with Skidmore faculty members. UWW reimburses students for courses taken at other institutions ($250 per credit hour, with a semester cap that varies depending on the student's total number of credits). A different fee schedule applies to summer courses, and a fee of $100 is charged for experiential credit review.

Financial Aid

Students are eligible for Federal Pell Grants, New York State TAP awards, and all federal loan programs. A small amount of scholarship assistance is available.

Applying

Application forms are available from UWW or can be downloaded from the UWW Web site. All applicants are required to attend a personal admissions interview on the Skidmore campus.

CONTACT

University Without Walls
Skidmore College
815 North Broadway
Saratoga Springs, New York 12866

Phone: 518-580-5450
          866-310-6444 (toll-free)
Fax: 518-580-5449
E-mail: uww@skidmore.edu
Web site: http://www.skidmore.edu/uww

SOUTHERN METHODIST UNIVERSITY
School of Engineering
Dallas, Texas

Founded in 1911, SMU is a private, comprehensive university. SMU comprises six degree-granting schools: the School of Engineering, Dedman College of Humanities and Sciences, Meadows School of the Arts, the Edwin L. Cox School of Business, the Dedman School of Law, and Perkins School of Theology. Southern Methodist University is accredited by the Commission on Colleges of the Southern Association of Colleges and Schools.

For more than thirty years, the School of Engineering has been a national pioneer in offering distance education courses for graduate study. In 1964, the School of Engineering established one of the first two regional closed-circuit TV distance learning networks in the nation. In 1978, it instituted its own for-credit videotape program for students living outside the Dallas/Ft. Worth area. Today, the program is delivered via distance learning and students are enrolled nationally from coast to coast.

Distance Learning Program

The School of Engineering's distance learning program serves more than 600 graduate students. Master of Science degree programs are offered nationally via distance learning. No campus attendance is required to complete the degree programs. Twenty M.S. degrees can be earned via distance learning.

Delivery Media

Distance learning students are enrolled in classes that are given on the SMU campus. The lectures are recorded and loaded to a server within 24 hours. Distance learning students log in to the secured server to download the recorded on-campus lectures. Distance learning students interact with their professors via phone, fax, e-mail, or the Internet. Many professors make course materials available to the student via the School of Engineering's Web site.

Programs of Study

Engineering schools have an obligation to be responsive to challenges and opportunities in a technological society. As a private university, SMU can respond quickly to engineering needs with high-quality academic programs.

The School of Engineering offers the following Master of Science degree programs via distance learning: civil engineering, computer engineering, computer science, electrical engineering, engineering management, environmental engineering, environmental science, environmental science (major in environmental systems management), environmental science (major in hazardous and waste materials management), facilities management, information engineering and management, manufacturing systems management, mechanical engineering, operations research, packaging of electronic and optical devices, security engineering, software engineering, systems engineering, and telecommunications.

The Master of Science degree requires 30–36 (depending on the program) semester credit hours for completion, with a minimum 3.0 grade point average on a 4.0 scale. Distance learning students may meet the credit requirement entirely by course work or have the option of preparing a thesis for 6 semester hours of credit.

Credit Options

Generally, up to 6 semester hours of graduate courses may be transferred from an institution approved by the School of Engineering's Graduate Division, provided that such course work was completed in the five years prior to matriculation, that the transferred courses carried graduate credit, that those courses were not used to meet the requirements of an undergraduate degree, and that grades of B– or higher were received in the courses to be transferred.

Faculty

Of the 45 full-time faculty members, 100 percent hold the doctorate or terminal professional degree in their fields. In addition, in the professional degree programs, the School of Engineering utilizes outstanding adjunct faculty members to bring into the classroom valuable experience from industry and government.

Admission

Admission to a Master of Science degree program requires the bachelor's degree appropriate to the program to which the student is applying, as well as a minimum grade point average of 3.0 (on a 4.0 scale) in previous undergraduate and graduate study. Scores on the Graduate Record Examinations (GRE) are required for the M.S. programs in civil engineering, computer engineering, computer science, electrical engineering, environmental engineering, environmental science, and mechanical engineering.

Tuition and Fees

Tuition for distance learning students is $985 per credit hour or $2955 for a 3-credit-hour course.

Financial Aid

Financial aid opportunities are available to distance learning students, including Federal Stafford Student Loans. SMU's distance learning programs are approved for Veterans Administration educational benefits.

Applying

Distance learning students must complete an application for admission to the Graduate Division of the School of Engineering and submit transcripts of all previous undergraduate and graduate work. Application deadline dates are as follows: for the fall semester, July 1; for the spring semester, November 15; and for the summer semester, April 15.

CONTACT

Teresa Harvey, Assistant Director
Graduate Student Experience and Enrollment Management
School of Engineering
Southern Methodist University
P.O. Box 750335
Dallas, Texas 75275-0335
Phone: 214-768-4661
        800-601-4040 (toll-free)
Fax: 214-768-3778
E-mail: tharvey@engr.smu.edu
Web site: https://engr.smu.edu

SOUTHERN NEW HAMPSHIRE UNIVERSITY
SNHU Online
Manchester, New Hampshire

Southern New Hampshire University, founded in 1932, is a private, regional institution that is recognized for its solid academic programs and dedication to teaching. Southern New Hampshire University offers certificate and degree programs in business, community economic development, culinary arts, education, hospitality, and liberal arts, with degrees at the associate level through the doctoral level. Southern New Hampshire University is regionally and nationally accredited by the Accreditation Commission for Programs in Hospitality Administration, American Culinary Federation Education Institute, Association of Collegiate Business Schools and Programs, European Council for Business Education, New England Association of Schools and Colleges, New Hampshire Postsecondary Education Commission, New Hampshire State Department of Education for Teacher Certification, and the North American Society for Sport Management.

Southern New Hampshire University's online program was established in 1996 and is one of New England's largest and fastest-growing programs. Southern New Hampshire University is a recognized leader in online learning and offers more than fifty undergraduate and graduate degree and certificate programs. SNHU Online reports more than 14,000 enrollments annually from all over the world.

Southern New Hampshire University is also approved for the education of veterans and the children of veterans and for the rehabilitation training of handicapped students. The program is listed in the Department of Education's Education Directory, Part 3, Higher Education®. *Staff and faculty members are dedicated to delivering high-quality academic and administrative support. Students have access to online applications, registration, academic advising, technical support, course work, tutoring, orientation, the bookstore, and the library.*

Distance Learning Program

Southern New Hampshire University's online program is recognized as a leader in online learning. Courses with SNHU Online are offered in six undergraduate terms (eight weeks in length) and four graduate terms (eleven weeks in length) each year. The residency requirement for undergraduate students, which may be satisfied by taking online courses, is 30 semester hours (ten classes) through Southern New Hampshire University, including 12 semester hours from the major for a bachelor's degree or 9 semester hours from the major for an associate degree. Each student's final 24 semester hours must be taken through Southern New Hampshire University except for active duty military students. The graduate program limits transfer credits to 6 semester hours, which must have been completed at an accredited institution within the last five years. In addition, the grade(s) earned must be a B or better.

Delivery Media

SNHU Online offers many advantages to students and faculty members. Classes are limited to 18 students, providing significant faculty-student interaction not found at many onsite-based class environments.

Blackboard Learning System™ is the learning management system for all online courses. In order to participate in Southern New Hampshire University's online courses, students must have a computer with Internet access. Courses with SNHU Online are not correspondence or CD-ROM–based. Instead, they are asynchronous, with no mandatory or set times that students are required to be online, and courses are self-paced, allowing students to complete their work at their own time and pace, within specific deadlines determined by the instructor.

For the recommended technical specifications, a listing of personal characteristics that contribute to becoming a successful online student, or for additional information about SNHU Online, students should visit the SNHU Online Web site (http://www.snhu.edu/online).

Programs of Study

Southern New Hampshire University's online programs provide students with a solid educational foundation in different aspects of business and liberal arts. Undergraduate degree and certificate programs available online within the School of Business include accounting, accounting/finance, accounting information systems, business administration, business information systems, business studies, finance/economics, human resource management, information technology, international business, marketing, and technical management. Online degree and certificate programs offered through the School of Liberal Arts include communication, English language and literature, psychology, psychology with a concentration in child and adolescent development, and social science. Graduate degree programs available online include the Global M.B.A. and the Master of Science in business education, justice studies, marketing, organizational leadership, and sport management. Graduate certificates in accounting, human resource management, integrated marketing communications, international business, marketing, operations management, sport management, and training and development are also offered.

Southern New Hampshire University's online courses carry the same accreditation and provide the same semester hours toward a degree as classes taken through the day school or through any one of the University's Continuing Education centers. For an overview of degree requirements, prospective students should visit the SNHU Online Web site (http://www.snhu.edu/online).

Credit Options

Students can transfer undergraduate credits earned at other accredited postsecondary institutions to Southern New Hampshire University and can also receive undergraduate credit by taking CLEP, DANTES, Regents College Examinations, institutional exams, military service training programs, ACE-certified career-related workshops and seminars, or other standardized tests. Southern New Hampshire University is designated as a Servicemembers Opportunity College (SOC, SOCCAD, SOCNAV, and SOCCOAST)–approved and cooperating institution. As an SOC institution, Southern New Hampshire University awards credit for service-related education and for completion of an associate degree through the Community College of the Air Force.

A maximum of 90 semester hours may be transferred toward a bachelor's degree, and 30 semester hours may be applied to an associate degree. Academic advisers are available to conduct free transfer-credit evaluations. Prospective students should e-mail Southern New Hampshire University's advisers at advising@snhu.edu and fax transcripts to 603-645-9706.

Faculty

SNHU Online provides students with the opportunity to interact with more than 300 highly qualified and specially trained instructors throughout the world who bring extensive work and life experiences into the classroom.

Admission

Applicants for undergraduate degree programs must have graduated from high school or passed the GED. Applicants for graduate programs require a bachelor's degree from an accredited institution. Official transcripts are required for admission.

International undergraduate applicants must have completed the equivalent of a U.S. secondary school. Students who have attended a recognized postsecondary institution may be eligible to receive transfer credits or exemptions. All applicants must submit a completed application and official or attested copies of academic records translated into English, including proof of graduation or completion of a program and proof of English proficiency. A minimum TOEFL score of 550 is required for undergraduate students. International graduate applicants must have completed the equivalent of a U.S. bachelor's degree and have a minimum TOEFL score of 550.

Tuition and Fees

The tuition for each SNHU Online undergraduate course is $774 for non-military students and $750 for military students. SNHU Online graduate courses cost $1458 per course. Tuition rates are subject to change. Some courses may require the purchase of specific software.

Financial Aid

Southern New Hampshire University accepts employer tuition reimbursement, federal and private loans, grants, VA Programs/Montgomery GI Bill, Navy College Fund (as part of the GI Bill), and scholarships. A federal financial aid application form is available online at http://www.fafsa.gov. Applicants may contact the University's financial aid office (telephone: 603-645-9645; e-mail: finaid@snhu.edu) to explore financial aid options.

Applying

Students may enroll in undergraduate classes on a rolling basis. Official acceptance is not necessary to begin undergraduate course work. All applicants (new and transfer students) must submit an application along with an official high school transcript or original copy of GED scores and, if applicable, official college transcripts. Graduate students who wish to enroll in course work only are limited to taking a maximum of two graduate courses (6 semester hours). Official or unofficial transcripts must be mailed or faxed to the SNHU Online office before a student may register for a graduate course, including course-work-only students. Prospective students may apply online. Once students are admitted and after an initial consultation, they can register for courses online.

Southern New Hampshire University does not discriminate on the basis of race, color, national origin, citizenship, religion, marital status, age, sex, sexual orientation, or disability in admission to, access to, treatment in, or employment in its programs and activities.

CONTACT

SNHU Online
Southern New Hampshire
   University
2500 North River Road
Manchester, New
   Hampshire 03106-1045
Phone: 603-645-9766
       866-860-0449 (toll-free)
Fax: 603-645-9706
E-mail: online@snhu.edu
Web site: http://www.snhu.edu/
       online

Bring Your University Home

SOUTHERN POLYTECHNIC STATE UNIVERSITY
Extended University's Office of Distance Learning
Marietta, Georgia

At Southern Polytechnic State University, distance students are able to study the sciences, technologies, construction, quality and systems management, information technology, and technical communications in a unique and practical manner. They acquire an education that is career-based and balanced.

Since its founding in 1948, the University has earned an exceptional academic reputation. SPSU, Georgia's technology university, has approximately 4,000 students (traditional, nontraditional, and distance) from approximately thirty-five states and eighty-two countries.

Distance Learning Program

The Office of Distance Learning (ODL) provides administrative, marketing, and technical support for distance learning activities at Southern Polytechnic State University (SPSU). SPSU has offered distance learning options in a variety of formats since 1995. Current methods of distance delivery at SPSU include several Web applications and videoconferencing.

Delivery Media

Online students are required to have regular access to the Internet and a computer capable of running current versions of Web browsers as well as standard office and design applications. Students communicate with their professors and class members through discussions, chat, live classroom (voice chat), and e-mail. Assignments are completed using word processing, spreadsheet, and graphic software, such as Microsoft Word, Excel, and Photoshop. Other software may be required depending on the course.

Distance learning courses at SPSU use Vista, a Web-based course-management system from WebCT that is accessible through an Internet browser, such as Internet Explorer, Netscape, or Mozilla.

Programs of Study

SPSU offers the following degrees and certificates via distance learning: Master of Science (M.S.) in Quality Assurance (MSQA), Master of Science In Systems Engineering (MSSYE), Graduate Certificate in Technical Communication, Graduate Certificate in Informational Design and Communication (GCIDC), Graduate Certificate in Technical Communications (GCTC), Graduate Certificate in Content Development (GCCD), Graduate Certificate in Communications Management (GCCM), Graduate Certificate in Visual Communication and Graphics (GCVCG), and an undergraduate Certificate in Specialty Construction (SCC). Through two state consortia, SPSU also offers eCore, (University System of Georgia (USG) core-curriculum classes) and a Bachelor of Science degree in Information Technology (WebBSIT).

The M.S. in quality assurance has been offered at a distance since 1997 and was the first degree in quality assurance to be offered in the country as a distance program. The MSQA program is designed for anyone working in quality, training, and related disciplines and meets the needs of professionals who support total quality, continuous improvement, and process management within an organization.

The M.S. in systems engineering (MSSYE) is the first program of its kind in Georgia and joins an elite list of distance MSSYE programs in the country. The MSSYE helps professionals enhance the development of systems thinking and the ability to apply system-analysis techniques in a real-world environment. Participants learn to design, analyze, and manage the implementation of complex systems for business and technology.

Consisting of 20 credit hours or six graduate courses, the Graduate Certificate in Technical Communications (GCTC) is offered entirely in a Web-based learning environment that allows professionals already working in the field to update and expand their skills. For those new to the field, the program is an opportunity to learn desirable information design and communication skills that are sought by today's employers. This is the prerequisite for the other four certificate programs (18 hours each) also offered completely online.

The Specialty Construction Certificate (SCC) requires 19 semester hours and includes courses in building; mechanical, electrical, and plumbing loads; the estimating process; project management; and energy conservation.

The WebBSIT degree is offered in a consortium with four other schools in the University of Georgia System. This program of study provides a solid background in the technical, user-centric, and managerial skills required by today's information technology managers. Graduates can pursue careers in programming, systems design, database design, and e-commerce, among others.

eCore (Electronic Core Curriculum) is another USG-consortium effort that offers the first two years of core curriculum entirely online. eCore consists of online freshman- and sophomore-level courses designed, developed, taught, and supported by USG faculty and staff members. eCore courses comply with ADA standards to meet the needs of students with disabilities or special needs.

Student Services

The Office of Distant Learning's Web site at http://dl.spsu.edu provides links to all distance-learning student services available at SPSU, including admissions, registration, financial aid, career services, counseling services, the bookstore, and the Johnson Library's Resources for Distance Learners Web page (http://www.spsu.edu/library/Dl/dlguide.html).

The ODL web site also offers an online orientation to SPSU, a self-assessment test to determine how well a student's learning style is suited to distance learning, links and descriptions of the various degree and certificate programs, technical support, a self-directed Vista tutorial, and a Web form to request additional or more specific information about distance learning at Southern Polytechnic State University. Students can access this information on the Distance Learning Web site at http://dl.spsu.edu/.

Credit Options

In general, students can be awarded some transfer credit for course work already completed elsewhere. Distance learning M.S. students can choose the online graduate seminar class as the final course, which delves into special technical topics not normally covered in other courses. A technical semester project is required. Alternatively, distance learning students can choose to complete QA7503, a two-semester research methods project class, as their final course. This course requires two intensive full-day Saturday on-campus meetings, one in October and the other in March. At the second meeting, students present their completed research projects to faculty members and students.

Faculty

The faculty strives for excellence in teaching and service, providing a laboratory-centered and/or professionally oriented education that fosters problem solving, ethical awareness, and a desire for lifelong learning. All classes are taught by experienced, dedicated faculty members, not teaching assistants. At SPSU, teaching is the top criterion for promotion and tenure. All faculty members are required to have relevant work or research experience.

Admission

Incoming freshmen must have completed a minimum of 16 units in English, math, science, history, and foreign language and must have a minimum GPA of 2.5 and a minimum SAT score of 1000 (42 on the ACT).

Tuition and Fees

In 2006–07, undergraduate tuition was $189 per credit hour; graduate tuition was $227 per credit hour. Those enrolled in the WebBSIT program paid $290 per credit hour. The eCore program cost $144 per credit hour. All programs required the payment of a technology fee of $75 per semester.

Financial Aid

Each year, approximately 90 percent of undergraduate students receive aid, consisting of loans, scholarships, grants, and work-study assignments. Graduate students can receive aid through loans or a work-study program. Information about aid available to distance learners is available through the Office of Scholarships and Financial Aid.

Applying

Undergraduate applicants must submit the completed application form, a $20 nonrefundable application fee, all official high school and college transcripts, and official SAT or ACT scores. Graduate applicants must send in the completed application form, a $20 nonrefundable application fee, two copies of all official college transcripts, and three letters of reference. Applications may also be made online. The application deadlines for the summer, fall, and spring semesters are May 1, August 1, and December 1, respectively.

CONTACT

Office of Distance Learning
Southern Polytechnic State University
1100 South Marietta Parkway
Marietta, Georgia 30060-2896

Phone: 678-915-3713
Fax: 678-915-3576
Web site: http://dl.spsu.edu

Dawn Ramsey, Dean
Phone: 678-915-4287
E-mail: dramsey@spsu.edu

Stephen Rehberg, Instructional Designer
Phone: 678-915-3169
E-mail: srehberg@spsu.edu

Jennie Vitty-Rogers, eCore Coordinator
Phone: 678-915-4984
E-mail: jrogers4@spsu.edu

STATE UNIVERSITY OF NEW YORK AT OSWEGO

B.A. in Broadcasting and Mass Communication
B.A. in Public Justice
B.S. in Vocational Teacher Preparation
Oswego, New York

The State University of New York at Oswego was founded in 1861 as the Oswego Normal School. The institution became Oswego State Teachers College and one of SUNY's charter members in 1948. While maintaining its high standards as a center for teacher education, the college began to broaden its academic perspective in 1962 when it became one of the colleges of arts and science of the State University of New York.

Today, Oswego is one of thirteen university colleges in the SUNY system. About 8,000 students enroll annually. Oswego offers more than 100 academic programs leading to bachelor's degrees, master's degrees, and certificates of advanced study. The college is accredited by the Middle States Association of Colleges and Schools and by the Commission on Higher Education. The School of Education is accredited by the National Council for Accreditation of Teacher Education.

Distance Learning Program

The Bachelor of Arts (B.A.) in broadcasting and mass communication, the Bachelor of Arts (B.A.) in public justice, and the Bachelor of Science (B.S.) in six majors in vocational teacher preparation (agricultural, business and marketing, family and consumer sciences, health careers, technical, and trade education) are available to students with two-year degrees in appropriate disciplines. Degrees in vocational teacher preparation are offered in the following areas: agriculture education, business education, family and consumer sciences, health occupations subjects education, technical subjects education, and trade subjects education. All required courses, cognates, and electives as well as courses in other disciplines to fulfill general education requirements are offered online. Students also have the opportunity to complete an economics minor online.

Delivery Media

All courses are taught via the World Wide Web in asynchronous mode through the SUNY Learning Network (SLN) (http://sln.suny.edu). Students are required to have reliable access to computers connected to the Internet. Courses use texts/reading materials and involve substantial writing assignments. Students may be required to arrange laboratory experiences with colleges or universities close to home with credits transferred to Oswego.

Students taking VTP 312 online must attend a one-week summer residency in Oswego.

Students taking PBJ 401 online must attend a weekend residency in Oswego during the semester in which the course is offered.

Program of Study

Some required courses may be transferred into the program through substitution or through articulation agreements with two-year and four-year colleges. A transfer evaluation of credit assigns previously earned credits to the appropriate program and to general education and college requirements. Students must complete a total of 122 credit hours for broadcasting and 127 credit hours for vocational teacher preparation to graduate, with a minimum of 30 credit hours taken from SUNY Oswego. At least 60 hours must be from a four-year college. General education requirements also apply.

Specific requirements in the broadcasting major, the public justice major, and the vocational teacher preparation major, including cognates and electives, are available at the Oswego State Web site. Students can find requirements for broadcasting at http://www.oswego.edu/ODP/. Requirements for public justice can be found at http://www.oswego.edu/academics/colleges_and_departments/departments/public_justice/. Vocational teacher preparation requirements can be found at http://www.oswego.edu/vtp/.

Special Programs

Some degree program students may benefit from internship opportunities arranged through the Office of Experience-Based Education. Up to 15 hours of internship credit may be applied as electives both in the major and under the general studies curriculum. Past students have performed internships in network television, local and regional media, advertising, media research, and government. Such experiences often lead to job offers and referrals.

Student Services

Some of the campus services and resources that are available online include certain resources in Penfield Library, the Registrar's Office, Student Accounts, the Financial Aid Office, and the Career Services Center. The State University of New York at Oswego Web site is http://www.oswego.edu. Advisement options include e-mail and telephone consultation for all students.

Credit Options

Up to 62 transfer credits from a two-year school may be applied toward the broadcasting and public justice degrees, and up to 67 transfer credits from a two-year school and 97 transfer credits from a four-year school may be applied toward the vocational teacher preparation degree. The public justice programs may accept up to 92 transfer credits from a four-year school. The College-Level Examination Program (CLEP) is offered and accepted. Up to 32 credits may be earned through CLEP, which is considered transfer credit.

Faculty

Approximately 40 full-time and 30 part-time faculty and professional staff members currently teach distance courses at SUNY Oswego. Of these, 70 percent have doctoral degrees. The student/teacher ratio is 20:1.

Admission

Applicants must submit official transcripts indicating that they have gradu-ated with a two-year degree appropri-ate for their program. Students may enroll full-time or part-time and must become matriculated after completing 22 hours of study at Oswego.

Tuition and Fees

Part-time undergraduate tuition (in-state) is $181 per credit hour. Part-time undergraduate tuition (out-of-state) is $429 per credit hour. Full-time under-graduate tuition (in-state) is $2175 per semester. Full-time undergraduate tu-ition (out-of-state) is $5150 per semes-ter.

Part-time fees (in-state and out-of-state) are $25.39 per credit hour.

Tuition and fee amounts are subject to change.

Financial Aid

Students should contact the Office of Financial Aid for information regarding income, credit hours, and other guide-lines. In most instances, students must be enrolled in at least 6 credit hours to be eligible for financial aid.

Applying

A SUNY application needs to be submitted for both programs. Both programs have an additional applica-tion that must be obtained by contact-ing the applicable department. Stu-dents are notified in writing if and when they are accepted into the program. An orientation session is optional.

CONTACT

For information on broadcasting and mass communication:

Dr. Michael S. Ameigh, Assistant Provost and Coordinator, Online Degree Program
State University of New York at Oswego
35A Lanigan Hall
Oswego, New York 13126
Phone: 315-312-3500
Fax: 315-312-3195
E-mail: ameigh@oswego.edu
Web site: http://www.oswego.
        edu/ODP/

For information on vocational teacher preparation:

Dr. Margaret Martin, Chair, Vocational Teacher Preparation Department
State University of New York at Oswego
307 Park Hall
Oswego, New York 13126
Phone: 315-312-2480
Fax: 315-312-3062
E-mail: mmartin4@oswego.edu
Web site: http://www.oswego.
        edu/vtp/

For information on vocational public justice:

Dr. Margaret Ryniker, Chair, Public Justice Department
State University of New York at Oswego
307 Park Hall
Oswego, New York 13126
Phone: 315-312-2480
Fax: 315-312-3062
E-mail: pubjust@oswego.edu
Web site: http://www.oswego.
        edu/publicjustice

STATE UNIVERSITY OF NEW YORK
EMPIRE STATE COLLEGE
Center for Distance Learning
Saratoga Springs, New York

Empire State College, of the State University of New York, is an internationally recognized innovator in adult education and a pioneer in distance learning. Since 1971, the College has served students who need alternatives to campus-based education because of work, family, or other responsibilities. Providing flexible degree programs at the associate, bachelor's, and master's levels, Empire State College features a number of student-focused study methods, such as one-to-one instruction, online courses, intensive mentoring by a faculty adviser, and undergraduate credit for college-level learning gained from life experience.

The College currently enrolls more than 16,000 students per year at thirty-five locations in New York State. Through its Center for Distance Learning (CDL), the College also serves students across the nation and around the world. Empire State College was the first public, nontraditional institution to receive regional accreditation by the Middle States Association of Colleges and Schools.

Distance Learning Program

More than 6,000 students are served annually by the College's Center for Distance Learning (CDL). Established in 1978, CDL now offers full degrees as well as individual courses entirely online. As a founding member of the SUNY Learning Network, the College was among the first in the State University of New York to offer online courses. It was also the first within the University to offer an entire degree (in business, management, and economics) online. Today, students may earn degrees online in all areas of study offered by the College. Through the Center for Graduate Programs, the College offers four Master of Arts degrees, including a Master of Arts in Teaching with online and on-site components. An M.B.A. is offered primarily via the World Wide Web.

Delivery Media

The Center for Distance Learning makes use of the latest distance learning technology on the World Wide Web. Empire State College's online courses can be accessed at any time of the day, allowing students and faculty members to share ideas and concepts at times that are convenient to them. In addi-

tion, all student services, such as registration, academic advising, career and library services, and peer support, are available on the Internet.

Programs of Study

The Center for Distance Learning offers both two- and four-year degrees: Associate in Arts, Associate in Science, Bachelor of Arts, Bachelor of Science, and Bachelor of Professional Studies. The College also offers four Master of Arts programs, with concentrations in labor and policy studies, liberal studies, and social policy, in addition to an M.B.A. with online courses and a Master of Arts in Teaching.

One of the strengths of the Empire State College distance learning program is that students are assigned a faculty adviser, who guides them through all phases of their degree program, from academic planning to graduation. With their adviser, undergraduate students design individualized degree programs in any of eleven areas of study: the arts; business, management, and economics; community and human services; cultural studies; educational studies; historical studies; human development; interdisciplinary studies; labor studies; science, mathematics, and technology;

and social theory, social structure, and change. Within these degree programs, a number of concentrations can be developed. Some examples of these are fire service administration, criminal justice, emergency management, health services administration, and information systems.

To earn an associate degree, a student must successfully complete 64 credits, with at least 24 earned through study with Empire State College. A bachelor's degree requires successful completion of 128 credits, with at least 32 being earned through the College.

Special Programs

The Center for Distance Learning is one of a select number of institutions of higher education to offer online degree programs to the United States Army, the United States Navy, the United States Coast Guard, and the Army National Guard. Through eArmyU, soldiers may take part in portable learning that suits the requirements of military life. The College also participates in the Navy College Program Distance Learning Partnership (NCPDLP) for sailors who need maximum flexibility in the ways they study. Many other organizations and corporations work with CDL to sponsor educational options for their employees, including a number of telecommunications companies and unions. A complete list is available at http://www.esc.edu/CDL.

Credit Options

Students can transfer credits earned at other regionally accredited institutions to Empire State College and can receive credit for college-level learning gained through work and life experience and through the College-Level Examination Program (CLEP), standardized tests, or individualized evaluation. A total of 40 prior learning credits may be granted in the associate degree program; 96 credits may be applied to a bachelor's degree program.

Faculty

There are 875 full- and part-time faculty members at Empire State College, including adjunct faculty. Ninety-six percent of full-time faculty members and nearly half of part-time faculty members have doctoral or other terminal academic degrees.

Admission

There are two principal requirements for admission to Empire State College: possession of a high school diploma or its equivalent and the ability of the College to meet the applicant's educational needs and objectives.

Tuition and Fees

In 2006–07, undergraduate tuition was $181 per credit. A per-term telecommunications development and support fee of $75 was also charged, which provided access to electronic mail, computer conferencing, the Internet, and other information sources. Other fees also apply. Students should visit the College's Web site at http://www.esc.edu for further details

Financial Aid

More than $30 million in financial aid was awarded to Empire State College students in 2005–06, with more than 50 percent of the enrolled students receiving some form of financial assistance. General financial aid programs available through Empire State College include the Federal Pell Grant, Federal Supplemental Educational Opportunity Grant, Federal Perkins Loan, and the Federal Work-Study Program. New York State financial aid programs include the Tuition Assistance Program (TAP), Aid for Part-Time Study (APTS), and the SUNY Supplemental Tuition Award. The Empire State College Foundation awards more than $241,982 in scholarships and grants annually.

Applying

Empire State College reviews applications in order of date received, and students may apply online. The number of new students accepted depends on available space. There are five deadlines per year posted on the Web site (address listed below). Nonmatriculated students can take up to 16 credits without applying to the College.

CONTACT

Shelley Dixon
Center for Distance Learning
Empire State College
111 West Avenue
Saratoga Springs, New York 12866-6048

Phone: 800-847-3000 Ext. 2300 (toll-free)
Fax: 518-587-2660
E-mail: cdl@esc.edu
Web site: http://www.esc.edu/CDL

STEVENS INSTITUTE OF TECHNOLOGY
Graduate School Distance Learning Programs
Hoboken, New Jersey

Stevens Institute of Technology, one of the world's premier technical universities, offers an array of Web-based distance learning graduate programs from WebCampus. Stevens is ranked among the top twenty-five schools with entrepreneurial programs. Optimize magazine selected Stevens as one of the five schools that prepare technology managers. Stevens is one of only three schools accredited by the Project Management Institute. Stevens has won the Sloan Consortium's top award for best "institution-wide online teaching and learning programming," the US Distance Learning Association's "21st Century Award for Best Practices in Distance Learning," and the "2006 Best Practices in Programming" award. Stevens offers fifteen master's degree programs and thirty-four graduate certificate programs in engineering, management, and science online..

Students are instructed by noted faculty members who deliver the same superior courses taught on the main campus. Blended-learning programs (with online and conventional classroom components) are also available, as well as conveniently located off-campus courses at corporate sites. Many classes include a real-time Web conferencing component. Stevens is accredited by the Middle States Commission on Higher Education of the Middle States Association of Colleges and Schools. WebCampus is cosponsored by the Association of Computing Machinery (ACM), the Institute of Electrical and Electronics Engineers (IEEE), the American Society for Mechanical Engineers (ASME), the Society of Naval Architects and Marine Engineers (SNAME), the American Society of Civil Engineers (ASCE), and the National Exchange Carrier Association (NECA).

Distance Learning Program
Graduate certificates and master's degrees for professionals seeking advanced knowledge in science, engineering, and management are available online through WebCampus. In addition, a wide range of off-campus graduate degree programs in engineering, management, and information technology, among other disciplines, are taught at corporate sites.

Delivery Media
Stevens has been at the forefront of distance learning for a number of years, offering instructor-led courses that take advantage of the benefits of Web conferencing and other net applications. WebCampus online graduate students use rich Web features such as real-time and recorded lectures, threaded discussions, chat rooms, bulletin boards, e-mail, file sharing, whiteboards, and work groups for in-depth online participation. Students also have online library privileges, with instant search and retrieval of important databases such as the IEEE Electronic Library and Hoovers Company Records.

Programs of Study
Master's degree and certificate programs include biomedical engineering, construction management, cybersecurity, database systems, digital signal processing, engineering management, environmental engineering, financial engineering, information management, microelectronics, multimedia technology, networked information systems, pharmaceutical management, pharmaceutical manufacturing, photonics, professional communications, project management, software engineering, systems engineering, technology management, and telecommunications management.

Graduate certificate programs offer students the opportunity to focus on a specific area of study without having to complete a master's degree program. Credits earned toward a graduate certificate at Stevens may also be applied to a master's degree should students wish to continue their studies.

Off campus, at corporate and other sites, graduate students may enroll as part of company-sponsored programs, some of which are delivered using Web conferencing. Employees at some of the nation's most progressive and prominent companies, including Boeing, Johnson & Johnson, Con Ed, Verizon, and dozens of others, may take graduate certificate courses and master's degree courses in a number of disciplines at corporate sites. These include computer engineering, computer science, electrical engineering, management, mechanical engineering, project management, technology management, and telecommunications management.

For high school seniors who wish to get a head start on their college studies, Stevens created the Euclid Program of Online Courses. The Euclid Program covers the following areas: calculus and advanced math, computer science, and physics.

Student Services
Online learning graduate students access the entire range of Stevens' student services online, including faculty advising, books and materials ordering, admissions, registration, and financial aid. Graduate students also have instant online access to the school's digital library. A cyberlibrarian is available via e-mail and telephone to guide students in the use of electronic databases and other research tools and media. Technical and other help desk support services are also available

online. Stevens' Student Information System allows distance learners to access course schedules, grades, account statements, and other documents entirely online.

Credit Options

All graduate courses are worth 3 credits. Most graduate certificates are awarded after students have completed four courses online, on campus, or both. To earn a master's degree in engineering and science, students are required to complete ten courses. Students must complete twelve courses for a master's degree in management.

Faculty

An impressive graduate faculty teaches courses at Stevens, providing the same superior instruction online and on and off campus. WebCampus faculty members are required to participate in teaching and learning colloquia, which are held periodically during each semester, in order to share their experiences and to demonstrate their online teaching capabilities. Faculty members who teach online are also trained in how to exploit the technological and pedagogical benefits of Web-based courseware applications.

Admission

To be admitted to an online learning program at Stevens, students are required to satisfy the same qualifications as those who wish to enroll in Stevens' conventional courses. Prospective graduate students need to have completed an undergraduate degree at an accredited institution. Applicants may either apply by mail or complete an application form online at https://apply.embark. com/grad/stevens/14/. Two letters of recommendation are required. Applicants must also provide official transcripts in English for each college or university attended. Transcripts translated into English must be prepared by the school attended or by an official translator with a recognized seal. Applicants must provide official confirmation of the degree earned if it was awarded by a non-U.S. institution. The applicant's name, Social Security number, or date of birth must be on all submitted documents. All documents must be in English or have attested English translations.

Tuition and Fees

Each semester, students are required to pay nominal enrollment and technology fees. Tuition for management

courses is $825 per credit hour. Tuition for engineering and science courses is $965 per credit hour. Other fees may apply for late enrollment and late payment, among other services.

Financial Aid

Stevens has a strong commitment to assisting and investing in talented students. The school offers a number of scholarships, many of which are made available through generous friends and successful alumni. Many graduate students receive tuition reimbursement from their companies. Members of the WebCampus cosponsoring professional societies receive a 10 percent discount upon successful completion of the course.

Applying

Before applying to the online or off-campus distance learning programs, it is recommended that students review the Graduate School Web site or Stevens' WebCampus site in order to obtain information, instructions, and online application forms.

CONTACT

Online programs:
Wendy Pate
Stevens Institute of Technology
Castle Point on Hudson
Hoboken, New Jersey 07030

Phone: 201-216-5015
      800-494-4935 (toll-free)
Fax: 201-216-5011
E-mail: webcampus@stevens.edu
Web site: http://www.webcampus.
    stevens.edu

Off-campus programs:
Stephanie Robinson
Stevens Institute of Technology
Castle Point on Hudson
Hoboken, New Jersey 07030

Phone: 201-216-5510
Fax: 201-216-5011
E-mail: srobins2@stevens.edu
Web site: http://gradschool.stevens-
    tech.edu/home/

 **STRAYER UNIVERSITY**
Over 45 Campuses and Online

Established in 1892, Strayer University was designed to answer the educational needs of working students. To do this, Strayer University offers a real-world education in the areas of accounting, business, information systems, management, public administration, health services administration, and education in a format that allows students to balance college classes with their jobs and personal lives. In addition, Strayer University supports their students' success with individualized instruction and personalized support services, from enrollment through graduation and beyond. By continuously updating and expanding the curricula, Strayer University ensures that its students are well equipped to excel in today's dynamic workplace.

Today, Strayer University is one of the largest and most respected accredited universities in the United States. With more than forty-five campuses in eleven states and Washington, D.C., as well as online instruction offered around the world, Strayer University currently helps 31,000 working students achieve their goals.

Strayer University is regionally accredited by the Middle States Commission on Higher Education, an institutional accrediting agency recognized by the U.S. Department of Education.

pared to excel in today's dynamic workplace. Strayer University's instructors combine impressive academic credentials with years of practical work experience, and they are committed to the success of their students. In addition, Strayer University supports its students with the highest level of academic and administrative services.

Strayer University offers a wide variety of graduate and undergraduate degree programs in today's high-demand career fields. Some of the most popular disciplines include accounting, business, information systems, health services administration, public administration, and education. Students should visit Strayer University's Web site, http://www.strayer.edu, to learn more about the academic programs. Program availability varies by state and by campus.

Distance Learning Program

To accommodate the student's lifestyle, location, and learning preferences, Strayer University offers two different online class formats: **asynchronous** and **synchronous.** Both formats are designed to provide a high-quality education in the most convenient and efficient way possible, allowing students to balance their educational goals with their personal and professional obligations. In each format, classes are kept small to provide the highest level of personalized instruction and promote a dynamic learning experience.

With the **online asynchronous format,** students and instructors participate at different times that fit their schedules. Students can attend class any time they want, 24/7, by accessing recorded audio lectures, video presentations, and supporting materials via the Internet. In addition, students have the option of participating in real-time chats with their classmates and professors, similar to a classroom discussion on campus.

With the **online synchronous format,** students and instructors participate at the same day and time and interact in real time, just as in a regular classroom.

With this virtual classroom, students hear live audio from the professor, supported by an on-screen multimedia presentation. In addition, students can communicate in real time via text with the professor and classmates.

Delivery Media

The only equipment that students need to take online classes at Strayer University is a computer with access to the Internet. The necessary software is available free from the Web site or through Web site links. Strayer University's virtual classrooms use RealAudio. More detailed system requirements can be found at http://www.strayer.edu.

Programs of Study

When time and money are invested into an education, quality and value are very important. Students want the best instructors, the most relevant curriculum, and the most effective learning methods. Strayer University offers the highest caliber of education, in a proven educational format. By continuously updating and expanding its curricula, Strayer University ensures that its students are well pre-

Student Services

As experienced professionals, Strayer University's faculty advisers help students design the appropriate plan to achieve their objectives and career goals. In addition, tutoring is available on campus and online for many introductory-level courses.

Credit Options

Students who have attended other educational institutions may receive transfer credit or advanced standing in Strayer University's degree and diploma programs. College credit may be awarded for CLEP and DANTES tests, certain training received in the military, or prior work/life learning. The required number of credits taken in residence, online, or on campus is 36 for a master's degree, 54 for a bachelor's degree, 27 for an associate degree, and 31.5 for a diploma.

Faculty

Strayer University has more than 130 full-time and more than 925 part-time faculty members. Of these, more 330 than teach classes online.

Admission

Students who apply to undergraduate degree programs must provide certification of high school graduation or the equivalent. For admission to graduate degree programs, students must have graduated from an accredited college or university with a U.S. baccalaureate degree.

Tuition and Fees

For the 2007 academic year, tuition for graduate courses is $384 per credit hour. Full-time undergraduate students (13.5 credits or more) pay $284 per credit hour, and part-time undergraduate students pay $301 per credit hour.

Financial Aid

In today's business world, a college education is one of the best investments that can be made in one's career. To make education more affordable, Strayer University's Student Services Office can help identify and understand a wide variety of financing and financial aid options. Among these options are the following:

Federal Grants and Loans. Federal grants do not have to be repaid; federal loans are available that offer funds at a reduced interest rate or with deferred payment. Applications can be submitted online through the Virtual Financial Aid Office via links to the U.S. Department of Education.

Signature Student Loan. As an alternative to federal loan programs, undergraduate and graduate students are eligible, subject to credit approval, for low-cost, flexible loans through the Signature Student Loan program designed for Strayer University. This program does not offer the benefits of federal loan programs but provides an alternative and convenient way to finance tuition.

The Bailey Family Foundation Scholarship. The Bailey Family Foundation, founded in 1996 by Strayer University past President Ron K. Bailey, offers scholarship programs to high school seniors as well as current college students of any age with demonstrated scholastic achievement and financial need. A limited number of these scholarships are reserved for Strayer University students. To qualify, a current student must be in good standing with the University, and a new student must be accepted into one of Strayer University's programs. Scholarship applications and additional information are available online at http://www.bailey-family.org/.

Active-Duty Military Scholarship. Strayer University's military scholarship supplements the military tuition assistance program and other educational resources to offer 100 percent tuition coverage for undergraduate tuition and a majority of graduate tuition, for up to two courses per quarter. Strayer University is a GoArmyEd school.

Veterans Educational Benefits. Veterans' educational benefits are available for eligible programs at the University. Strayer University remains in contact with the Department of Veterans Affairs and can advise students about current requirements and regulations.

Employer Tuition Assistance. Many companies provide tuition benefits to their employees in the form of either direct payment to the school or reimbursing tuition expenses directly to the employee/student. Strayer University encourages all students to check with their employer's human resources or training and education department for more information about educational benefits.

Applying

Applications are accepted on an ongoing basis and can be accessed online at http://www.strayer.edu. There is a $50 application fee.

CONTACT

Strayer University Information
   Processing
P.O. Box 1310
Newington, Virginia 22122
Phone: 866-344-3286 (toll-free)
Fax: 703-339-4948
E-mail: info@strayer.edu
Web site: http://www.strayer.edu

SYRACUSE UNIVERSITY
Undergraduate and Master of Social Science Degree Programs
Syracuse, New York

Founded in 1870, Syracuse University (SU) is a major private research university of 14,400 residential students and an additional 3,700 part-time adult students located in central New York State. Organized into twelve separate schools and colleges, each offering a variety of baccalaureate, master's, and doctoral degrees, Syracuse has excellent research facilities, including sophisticated computer networks and a library containing more than 2.8 million volumes. Syracuse is one of the select group of American and Canadian universities chosen for membership in the prestigious Association of American Universities. Syracuse has a long-standing commitment to adult education. The University's innovative distance education degree programs are a form of nontraditional education in which Syracuse was a pioneer. Offered through five of the University's academic units, SU's distance programs make up one of the three oldest external degree programs in the United States. The programs have been active since 1966 and reflect the University's response to the demands for creative educational techniques and programs in a constantly changing society.

Distance Learning Program
Syracuse's distance education degree programs have a limited-residency structure: they combine short periods of intensive on-site instruction with longer periods of home study, during which students and faculty members communicate online. There are currently about 1,000 adults actively enrolled in twelve different degree programs through distance education, approximately one sixth of whom are international students or Americans living abroad. Syracuse degrees earned through distance study are the same as those earned by traditional Syracuse students in comparable campus programs and have the same accreditation.

Programs of Study
University College offers three undergraduate programs, a certificate, and a master's program by means of the limited-residency distance education format. Undergraduate degrees include an Associate of Arts in liberal arts, a Bachelor of Arts in liberal studies, and a certificate and a Bachelor of Professional Studies in organizational leadership. The associate degree is 60 credits.

The bachelor's degrees are 120-credit programs. The certificate is 15 credits.

The graduate degree is a 30-credit Master of Social Science (M.S.Sc.) with an international relations emphasis. It offers an interdisciplinary, international, and multicultural approach to complex global issues. An internationally renowned faculty teaches courses for the degree from Syracuse University's Maxwell School of Citizenship and Public Affairs.

The degrees and the certificate are state and regionally accredited. Students may initially enroll on a nonmatriculated basis.

Special Programs
A number of online credit and noncredit courses are offered each semester. Detailed information on these is available at http://www.yesu.syr.edu/online.

Student Services
All distance education students are provided with free computer accounts and have access to the Syracuse University library and computer facilities.

Online students have access to a help desk for technical problems. All distance students at Syracuse have access to a full range of online student services, including academic advising, financial aid, assistance, and registration.

Credit Options
The associate degree program accepts a maximum of 30 credits to be transferred from another postsecondary institution. The baccalaureate programs accept a maximum of 90 transfer credits, which may include 66 credits from a junior college. Transfer credit is granted for most courses in which a grade of C or better has been earned, provided courses are from an accredited college and fit the degree requirements. For credit to be accepted from an international institution of higher learning, the institution must be a recognized third-level institution.

A maximum of 30 credits gained through testing may be applied toward an undergraduate degree program. DANTES, CLEP, and Syracuse advanced credit exams may be used for this purpose. However, credit awarded through testing does not count toward the minimum number of credits that must be taken at Syracuse in order to earn a degree. On the graduate level, there is no provision for experiential credit. However, 6 credits may be taken in transfer from other accredited graduate programs, with a grade of C or better.

Faculty
Distance courses are taught by full-time Syracuse University faculty members, who participate in the distance education programs in addition to their full-time campus responsibilities.

Admission

Candidates for admission to the certificate, associate, and baccalaureate programs should have a high school diploma or its equivalent. Transfer students must have at least a 2.0 (C) average for the liberal studies program. Graduate applicants whose primary language is a language other than English must also take the TOEFL.

Applicants for all programs must submit official transcripts of prior academic work, three letters of recommendation, and a personal statement that accompanies the application form.

Tuition and Fees

For 2007–08, the undergraduate tuition rate is $550 per credit, and the graduate rate is $1012 per credit. Additional expenses for room and board during the on-site residences vary depending upon the choice of facility, and book charges average $150 per course.

Financial Aid

Distance education students who are U.S. citizens are eligible for all the standard federal grants and loans available to part-time students. Selective institutional aid is available; detailed information is available upon request. Syracuse University awards more than $100,000 to distance education students each year. International students (non-U.S. citizens) are not eligible for financial aid.

Applying

Applicants should request application materials from the address below. The programs admit students on a continuous basis, and students can begin in the fall, spring, or summer terms. In-person interviews are not required, although they can be arranged on request.

CONTACT

Marketing Department
Syracuse University/University College
700 University Avenue
Syracuse, New York 13244-2530
Phone: 315-443-3480
          800-442-0501 (toll-free, U.S. only)
Fax: 315-443-4174
E-mail: parttime@uc.syr.edu
Web site: http://www.yesu.syr.edu/distance

TAYLOR UNIVERSITY
Center for Lifelong Learning
Fort Wayne, Indiana

Taylor University is one of America's oldest evangelical Christian institutions. In 1846, it began as a women's college with the conviction that women as well as men should have an opportunity for higher education. In 1855, it became coeducational and, in 1938, it offered its first distance learning course.

Today, U.S. News & World Report *repeatedly ranks Taylor as one of America's best regional liberal arts colleges. The Templeton Foundation has named it one of the nation's top colleges for building character in students, and* Barron's *has listed it as a "best buy in college education."*

Taylor University's mission is to educate men and women for lifelong learning and for ministering the redemptive love of Jesus Christ. It is accredited by the Higher Learning Commission of the North Central Association of Colleges and Schools.

Distance Learning Program

The Center for Lifelong Learning is the virtual campus of Taylor University; it emphasizes the integration of faith and learning through distance education. The Center offers a Bachelor of Business Administration (B.B.A.) degree, three Associate of Arts (A.A.) degrees, seven certificate programs, the Head Start on College program for high school juniors and seniors, and more than 150 online courses from most academic disciplines. Annually, it enrolls more than 1,300 students.

Delivery Media

At the Taylor University Center for Lifelong Learning, the antiquated method of correspondence education has been replaced by the advantages of Internet technology and online learning. Rather than repackaging traditional classroom learning methods or simply creating digital versions of correspondence courses, Taylor has designed each course to ensure that it is learner-oriented and specifically designed for online, distance learning students. The eLearning platform brings together the elements that create the most valuable educational experience for the online distance learner—dynamic interaction and discussion with other students; close, continuous access to the instructor; and the convenience of having it all right at the student's fingertips.

Programs of Study

The 120-credit-hour B.B.A. degree is designed primarily for adults who meet the following criteria: have earned an associate degree from the Center for Lifelong Learning or another accredited institution, can transfer in at least 60 credit hours from an accredited institution, or have a combination of these options. Students may also be eligible for up to 30 hours of prior learning credit or other entry options. The curriculum is designed to empower the student with the ability to express an idea, negotiate a settlement, motivate others, manage time, and build collaborative networks. Taylor's B.B.A. program provides opportunities to recognize and define problems, examine data, and persuasively communicate in order to achieve results in organizations and people's lives. It includes 40 credit hours in the discipline, consisting of four 9-hour modules in cohort format and a 4-hour practicum/internship. A student admitted with an associate degree, therefore, can expect to complete the B.B.A. degree in twenty-three months through the blended format, meeting for a five-day seminar once each term and completing the majority of the program online.

The 64-credit-hour A.A. degree in biblical studies is designed for individuals preparing for vocational or lay Christian ministry. The curriculum is designed to give the student a foundational understanding of the Bible, Christian theology, and the knowledge and skills required for serving in a church or parachurch setting. It consists of 43 credit hours of general education course work, 15 hours in the discipline, and 6 elective hours.

The 64-credit-hour A.A. degree in justice administration is designed for individuals currently serving in or seeking to enter criminal justice, courts, corrections, law enforcement, or juvenile justice. It consists of 43 credit hours of general education course work and 21 hours in the discipline. Students select a ministry or public policy concentration. The A.A. with a concentration in ministry is the only degree program in the nation from an accredited institution specifically designed to prepare the student for correctional ministry. The degree is designed for individuals currently serving in or seeking to enter corrections, outreach, or ministry to offenders and at-risk populations.

The 64-credit-hour A.A. degree in the liberal arts is for students who desire a breadth of knowledge. It consists of 43 credit hours of general education course work, 15 hours in the chosen discipline, and 6 elective hours. Students select an interdisciplinary, history, or social science concentration.

The 65-credit-hour 2+2 program offers an online A.A. degree in the liberal arts in one of several concentrations, which is totally online during the first two years but leads directly to one of several baccalaureate degrees taken during the second two years on the campus of Taylor University Fort Wayne. A significant cost savings can be realized through the 2+2 program over attending the residential campus all four years.

The seven certificate programs include the 24-credit-hour Certificate in Biblical and Cultural Leadership, which is designed to equip women and men with a thorough grounding of Biblical content, a systematic theological review, an opportunity for personal spiritual development, and a philosophical defense of the faith;

the 24-credit-hour Biblical Studies Certificate, designed for busy pastors, church workers, and lay people who desire in-depth studies in the Bible; the 18-credit-hour Christian Worker Certification, designed for potential missionaries, pastors, and laypeople who desire a greater knowledge of the Bible and a better understanding of the professional challenges of ministry; the 18-credit-hour Justice and Ministry Certificate, specifically aimed at equipping individuals for correctional ministry; the 18-credit-hour Leadership Development Certificate, designed to equip current or potential leaders with the interpersonal skills and organizational abilities necessary for coping with business or ministry issues; the 18-credit-hour Certificate in Missions Studies, designed to assist those who desire to work in the mission field either as a full-time missionary or through frequent trips overseas for ministry purposes; and the 24-credit-hour Professional Writing Certificate, designed to strengthen students' abilities to write and communicate clearly in a style that is marketable to a contemporary audience.

Special Programs

All courses through the Taylor University Center for Lifelong Learning are competency-based, which means that students can complete the course as soon as the competencies are attained. The motivated student can progress at his or her own pace to ensure that the subject matter is understood well. Credit for each course is given when the expected learning results are documented and demonstrated. (Prospective students should note that the B.B.A. program follows the cohort schedule for module course work

only.) Many CLL courses can be used to achieve dual credit for both high school and college.

Student Services

The Taylor University Center for Lifelong Learning staff is committed to providing qualified, efficient, and responsive service in a timely manner. Online registration facilitates course enrollments at any time of the day or night. Once enrolled, students become part of the Center's virtual campus, meeting the needs of today's Internet-savvy students. Within the virtual campus, students enjoy a relational, faith-based learning environment.

Credit Options

Students earn credits with the successful completion of courses. Up to 34 hours of transfer credit may be approved toward the 64-credit-hour A.A. degree programs. Only course work with a grade of C- or better is accepted.

To receive credit for work done at other accredited institutions, students should send their transcripts to the Taylor University Center for Lifelong Learning for review. CLEP, AP, and DANTES credit must meet Taylor's standards to be accepted as transfer credit.

Faculty

The faculty of the Taylor University Center for Lifelong Learning consists of more than 65 highly credentialed, dedicated Christians. These instructors, most of whom hold doctoral degrees, are among the most qualified academic professionals in the field of Christian higher education.

Admission

Admission is open to all students registering for individual courses or beginning a certificate program. Degree-seeking

students must meet certain minimum admission standards and complete an application, which includes a personal reference recommendation.

Tuition and Fees

All courses are $210 per credit hour, with the exceptions of B.B.A. module courses, which are $325 per credit hour, and the Head Start on College courses, which are discounted to $180 per credit hour for high school juniors and seniors. Other expenses may include textbooks, supplemental materials, and shipping and handling fees. Taylor's most current fee structure is maintained at its Web site.

Financial Aid

Students who have been accepted into online degree programs and who will be registered for at least 6 credit hours in one term may apply for financial aid available through the University's Title IV agreement with the U.S. Department of Education.

The Department of Veterans Affairs has approved courses offered by the Taylor University Center for Lifelong Learning for those students entitled to receive veteran's educational benefits.

Applying

The Taylor University Center for Lifelong Learning offers open enrollment year-round through a secure, online registration process. Students may enroll online at any time in individual courses, certificate programs, or degree programs. Students seeking a degree must apply and be accepted. Secure, online registration is available at http://cll.taylor.edu/catalog. Students may also call toll-free at 800-845-3149. Students may also register and/or apply by fax, e-mail, mail, or in person.

CONTACT

Kevin Mahaffy, M.Min., M.B.A.
Director
Taylor University Center for Lifelong Learning
1025 West Rudisill Boulevard
Fort Wayne, Indiana 46807-2197

Phone: 260-744-8750
       800-845-3149 (toll-free enrollment hotline)
Fax: 260-744-8796
E-mail: info@cll.taylor.edu
Web site: http://cll.taylor.edu

THOMAS EDISON STATE COLLEGE

Trenton, New Jersey

Thomas Edison State College specializes in providing flexible, high-quality, collegiate learning opportunities for self-directed adults. One of New Jersey's twelve senior public institutions of higher education, the College offers sixteen associate, baccalaureate, and master's degrees in more than 100 areas of study. Students earn degrees through a wide variety of rigorous and high-quality academic methods that can by customized to meet their individual needs. Identified by Forbes magazine as one of the top twenty colleges and universities in the nation in the use of technology to create learning opportunities for adults, Thomas Edison State College is a national leader in the assessment of adult learning and a pioneer in the use of educational technologies. Founded in 1972, Thomas Edison State College is regionally accredited by the Commission on Higher Education of the Middle States Association of Colleges and Schools.

Distance Learning Program

Thomas Edison State College offers one of the most highly regarded, comprehensive distance learning programs in the United States. Adults may choose from more than 356 distance learning courses, including online classes. Students also take tests and submit portfolios to demonstrate and earn credit for college-level knowledge they already have and may transfer credits earned at other accredited institutions.

Delivery Media

Distance education courses are provided through several options, including Thomas Edison State College courses offered through the mail and online. Also available are online credit-by-examination e-Pack® courses, which allow students to prepare for a comprehensive final examination by taking a series of chapter quizzes delivered via the Internet.

Programs of Study

Thomas Edison State College offers sixteen associate, baccalaureate, and master's degrees in more than 100 areas of study. Undergraduate degrees offered include the Associate in Applied Science; Associate in Arts; Associate in Science in Applied Science and Technology; Associate in Science in Business Administration; Associate in Science in Natural Science and Mathematics; Associate in Science in Public and Social Services; Bachelor of Arts; Bachelor of Science in Applied Sci-

ence and Technology; Bachelor of Science in Business Administration; Bachelor of Science in Health Sciences, a joint-degree program with the University of Medicine and Dentistry of New Jersey (UMDNJ) School of Health Related Professions (SHRP); Bachelor of Science in Human Services; and Bachelor of Science in Nursing.

Each undergraduate degree requires work in general education, the area of study, and elective subjects. Students are encouraged to work in conjunction with one of the College's program advisers to develop an individual program plan.

In addition, the College offers four online master's programs. The Master of Science in Human Resources Management degree serves human resources professionals who wish to become strategic partners in their organizations. This program uses a cohort model and is designed to position human resources professionals as leaders within their organizations. The 36-semester-hour program provides practitioners with technical human resources skills in staffing, providing professional development, managing organizational culture, and measuring and rewarding performance. The Master of Science in Management degree program serves employed adults with professional experience in management. It integrates the theory and practice of management as it applies to diverse organizations. The College's Master of Arts in Liberal Studies de-

gree program provides working professionals an opportunity to study the liberal arts from an applied perspective. The Master of Science in Nursing RN–B.S.N./M.S. N.) degree program is designed for experienced RNs who want a quality education with the convenience and flexibility that an online program can provide.

Special Programs

Thomas Edison State College's Military Degree Completion Program (MDCP) serves military personnel worldwide and was developed to accommodate the special needs of military personnel whose location, relocation, and time constraints make traditional college attendance difficult, if not impossible. The program allows students to engage in a degree program wherever they may be stationed and receive maximum credit for military training and education. Thomas Edison State College is a partner college for the Navy College Program Distance Learning Partnership (NCPDLP) and the Navy College Program Afloat College Education (NCPACE) and is a participant in the Army University Access Online (eArmyU) program.

The College's unique Degree Pathways Program allows community college students and graduates to complete a baccalaureate degree at home, in the workplace, or at their local two-year college. The Degree Pathways Program lets community college students and graduates make a smooth transition directly into a Thomas Edison State College baccalaureate program by transferring up to 80 credits toward the 120 credits needed for a baccalaureate degree. The program provides coordinated support in admissions, academic programming, advisement, registration, and the sharing of technologies. Students who have earned an associate degree within the past five years or are six months from completing an associate degree are eligible for the Degree Pathways Program. Students may continue to take classes and use technologies that are available at their community or county college as they move closer to the 80-credit limit of the 120 credits required for a baccalaureate degree.

Student Services

Academic advisement is provided to enrolled students by the College's Advisement Center, which assists students in integrating their learning style, background, and educational goals with the credit-earning methods and programs available. Students may access advisement through in-person appointments or through the Advisement Phone Center. They also have 24-hour access through fax and e-mail.

Credit Options

Students have the opportunity to earn degrees through traditional and nontraditional methods and use several convenient methods of meeting degree requirements, depending upon their individual learning styles and preferences. Once a student is enrolled in a specific degree program, an evaluator determines the number of credits the student has already earned and fits those into the degree program requirement.

Credit-earning options for nondegree students benefit individuals who would like to earn credit through examinations, prior learning assessment, and Thomas Edison State College courses. Students may do so by paying the appropriate fee for these programs. An application to the College is not required to take advantage of these nondegree, credit-earning options.

Credit Banking is for students who wish to document college-level learning and consolidate college-level work into a Thomas Edison State College transcript. Credits transcribed under the Credit Banking program may or may not apply to a degree program at Thomas Edison State College.

Thomas Edison State College grants credit for current professional licenses or certificates that have been approved for credit by ACE and the College's Academic Council. Students must submit notarized copies of their license or certificate and current renewal card, if appropriate, to receive credit. A list of licenses and certificates approved for credit may be found in the College's *Undergraduate Prospectus*.

Faculty

There are approximately 200 mentors at Thomas Edison State College. Drawn from other highly regarded colleges and universities, mentors provide many services, including assessment of prior knowledge and advisement.

Admission

Adults 21 years of age or older who are seeking an associate, baccalaureate, or master's degree and are high school graduates are eligible to become Thomas Edison State College students. Because Thomas Edison State College delivers high-quality education directly to students wherever they live or work, students may complete degree requirements at their convenience. There are two brief residency requirements for the organizational leadership professional focus area of the Master of Science in Management degree. A computer is required to complete graduate degrees and to take undergraduate online courses.

Tuition and Fees

Tuition is payment for all costs directly associated with the academic delivery of a Thomas Edison State College education. Fees are designated as payment for administrative services and for materials used by students for courses and other activities. Thomas Edison State College offers one annual tuition plan, the Comprehensive Tuition Plan, for students who want access to all components of the tuition package. For those students who have determined that their particular situation is one where only components of the Comprehensive Tuition Plan are required, the College offers the Enrolled Options Plan. A complete listing of tuition and fees is included in the College's information packet and is available by calling the Office of Admissions or by visiting the College Web site.

Financial Aid

Thomas Edison State College participates in a number of federal and state aid programs. Eligible students may receive Federal Pell Grants or federal education loans such as the Federal Stafford Student Loan (subsidized and unsubsidized). Eligible New Jersey residents may also tap a variety of state grant and loan programs. Students may use state aid to meet all or part of their college costs, provided they are taking at least 12 credits per semester. Detailed information about the financial aid process may be found in the financial aid packet, which is available from the Office of Financial Aid & Veterans' Affairs or on the College Web site. To receive this information, students should contact the office at 609-633-9658 or finaid@tesc.edu.

Applying

Students may apply to Thomas Edison State College by mail or fax or online at http://www.tesc.edu. The Office of Admissions assists potential applicants in determining whether Thomas Edison State College suits their particular academic goals.

CONTACT

Renee San Giacomo
Director of Admissions
Thomas Edison State College
101 West State Street
Trenton, New Jersey 08608-1176

Phone: 888-442-8372 (toll-free)
Fax: 609-984-8447
E-mail: info@tesc.edu
Web site: http://www.tesc.edu

TOURO UNIVERSITY INTERNATIONAL

Distance Learning Program

Cypress, California

Touro University International (TUI), located in southern California, is regionally accredited by the Commission for Senior Colleges and Universities of the Western Association of Schools and Colleges.

TUI offers affordable degree programs on the Internet, using the latest technology and innovative live interactive delivery methodology.

TUI is committed to sustaining the high quality of its pedagogical model, its faculty, and its support services. A worldwide university operating 24 hours a day, 365 days a year, TUI offers students an excellent learning experience accessed from their own homes, while allowing them to maintain their work and family responsibilities.

Distance Learning Program

TUI offers high-quality education utilizing online Internet instruction as its primary means of delivery. There is no residency requirement and no need for campus visits. The student-centered teaching model has two major elements: modular case-based learning and the cyber classroom. These essential elements are part of every module of every course.

Delivery Media

The cyber classroom approach includes the use of multimedia for academic transactions and interactive collaboration (live exchange with professors and peers). The multimedia approach includes audio and video on demand, Internet links, PowerPoint presentations, and live conferences among students and between professors and students. This allows students to work as a team with fellow students from around the world. Case-based learning provides real-world application to each topic.

Programs of Study

TUI consists of the College of Business Administration, the College of Education, the College of Health Sciences, and the College of Information Systems. The College of Business Administration offers three degree programs: the Bachelor of Science in Business Administration (120 semester credits), with concentrations in criminal justice, finance, general management, human resources information technology management, logistics, and degree completion specially designed for students with an A.A. or A.S. degree; the Master of Science in Business Administration (44 semester credits), with concentrations in conflict and negotiations management, criminal justice administration, entrepreneurship, finance, general management, human resource management, information technology management, international business, logistics management, public management, and strategic leadership; and the Doctor of Philosophy in Business Administration (44 semester credits of course work plus a research dissertation). The concentration depends on the candidate's specific research interests.

The College of Education offers two degree programs: the Master of Arts in Education (36 semester credits), with concentrations in teaching and instruction, educational leadership, higher education, and e-learning, and the Doctor of Philosophy in Educational Leadership (48 semester credits of course work plus a research dissertation), with specializations in K–12 leadership, higher education leadership, and e-learning leadership.

The College of Health Sciences offers three degree programs: the Bachelor of Science in Health Sciences (124 semester credits), with concentrations in health education, health-care management, and professional degree completion; the Master of Science in Health Sciences (40 semester credits), with specializations in clinical research administration, emergency and disaster management, health-care management, health-care informatics, health education, international health, law and expert witness studies, and public health, and graduate certificates in clinical research administration, emergency and disaster management, health-care administration, health informatics, law and expert witness studies, and quality assurance; and the Doctor of Philosophy in Health Sciences (44 semester credits in course work plus a research dissertation), with specializations in international health and educator/researcher/practitioner studies.

The College of Information Systems offers three degree programs: the Bachelor of Science in Computer Science (120 semester credits), the Bachelor of Science in Information Technology Management (120 semester credits), and the Master of Science in Information Technology Management (36 semester credits).

Student Services

Touro University International maintains five specific student services. Preadmission advisement assists students with enrollment procedures and any other student concerns. Preadmission English competency evaluation is provided for students whose first language is not English, who do not meet TUI's English competency requirements, or who feel that they do not possess adequate English skills. Post-admission advisement assists students with course selection and sequencing, developing good study habits, and other student concerns. Information technology assistance is provided to ensure that students have access to all information technology features of TUI courses. The Information Technology department also assists students with installation and configuration. Library resource assistance is provided via e-mail in the use of all cyber library holdings.

TUI provides financial assistance under three federal programs that are available to citizens and eligible noncitizens of the United States.

Faculty

All TUI faculty members hold doctoral degrees and have experience in their respective fields in addition to having sound academic teaching, research, and dissertation advisement records. Exceptional full-time faculty members

teach nearly all TUI classes. The highest level of faculty expertise in each field is also available through guest lecturers and visiting faculty members via the cyber classroom delivery mode.

Admission

TUI offers four sessions per year, beginning in April, July, October, and January, with each session lasting twelve weeks. All TUI courses are valued at 4 semester credits. A full-time load is two courses per session, whereby students can earn 32 semester credits per year while continuing with family and work responsibilities.

The Office of Admissions assists potential students in determining their compatibility with the program based on past academic performance and educational goals. For specific details about each degree program, students may visit the Web site.

Tuition and Fees

TUI's tuition is one of the most affordable in the nation. Tuition is $250 per semester credit for B.S.-level courses, $300 per semester credit for M.S.-level courses, and $500 per semester credit for Ph.D.-level courses. Students may contact TUI registration for information about scholarships and financial aid.

Active-duty military, retired military, military dependents, and civilian military employees receive special tuition rates through TUI's DANTES agreement. Students should contact their base or post education officer or TUI for details.

Applying

Applications may be completed online at http://www.tourou.edu and are accepted year-round. A complete application package must be received by TUI two weeks prior to the start of the first session. TUI will respond within 24 business hours of receiving the complete package of application materials.

CONTACT

College of Business Administration
5665 Plaza Drive, 3rd Floor
Cypress, California 90630
Phone: 714-816-0366
      800-375-9878 (toll-free)
Fax: 714-816-0367
E-mail: infocba@tourou.edu
Web site: http://www.tourou.edu

College of Education
5665 Plaza Drive, 3rd Floor
Cypress, California 90630
Phone: 714-226-9840
      800-375-9878 (toll-free)
Fax: 714-226-9844
E-mail: infocoe@tourou.edu
Web site: http://www.tourou.edu

College of Health Sciences
5665 Plaza Drive, 3rd Floor
Cypress, California 90630
Phone: 714-226-9840
      800-375-9878 (toll-free)
Fax: 714-226-9844
E-mail: infochs@tourou.edu
Web site: http://www.tourou.edu

College of Information Systems
Cypress, California 90630
Phone: 714-816-0366
      800-375-9878 (toll-free)
Fax: 714-816-0367
E-mail: infocis@tourou.edu
Web site: http://www.tourou.edu

For program information:
Phone: 800-375-9878 (toll-free)
E-mail: infoDEV@tourou.edu

TROY UNIVERSITY
eCampus
Troy, Alabama

Since its founding in 1887, Troy University has been recognized for the quality of its academic programs and its focus on the individual student. The University is dedicated to the preparation of students in a variety of fields in the arts and sciences, fine arts, business, communication, applied science, nursing, and allied health sciences, as well as to its historic role in the preparation of teachers. The administrators, faculty and staff members, and students of the University, through a system of shared governance, are committed to excellence in education. A major commitment exists to provide undergraduate and graduate education for the national and international community, especially for mature students, not only by traditional means of delivery but also by technological means. Additional information about the University may be found at its Web site: http://www.troyst. edu.

Distance Learning Program

The distance learning program at Troy University is an important and growing part of the mission of the University. A variety of courses are offered, including seven complete graduate degrees that may be completed online. Along with personalized attention from faculty members, the distance learning program (http://www.tsulearn.net) is supported by the eCampus at Troy University in Alabama.

Delivery Media

eCampus course offerings are Web interactive and are delivered through the Blackboard Internet-learning platform. Students may complete course work on an anytime/anyplace basis worldwide. Additional distance learning courses at Troy University are also provided using videoconferencing, cable TV, and Web-enhanced and videotape/DVD media.

Programs of Study

There are currently seven master's degree programs and a variety of individual courses offered by eCampus. Complete details can be found by visiting the eCampus Web site.

The Master of Science in Business Administration (M.B.A.) program is designed to provide advanced study to students who have already acquired a common body of knowledge in business administration. It also offers students an opportunity to obtain advanced proficiency in decision-making skills as well as business management skills. The program also prepares students to carry out managerial responsibilities in government, business, and industry and develop the problem solving skills required in a dynamic and uncertain business environment.

The Master of Science in Criminal Justice (M.S.C.J.) program is designed to provide qualified students with an interdisciplinary graduate-level education in criminal justice. It provides students with knowledge or enhancement in the criminal justice field or leads to a terminal degree.

The Master of Science in International Relations (M.S.I.R.) program is designed to offer the graduates of diversified undergraduate programs an opportunity to obtain proficiency in international relations. Topics include foreign policy analysis, defense and security policy, comparative politics, regional and state-specific studies, international economics, and specific instruments of international affairs, such as international organizations and interna-

tional law. The degree program offers a ten-course option and a twelve-course option.

The Master of Public Administration (M.P.A.) degree program offers a twelve course program with nine concentrations. There is no comprehensive examination, but there is a final capstone course. The M.P.A. is designed to offer graduates of various undergraduate programs an opportunity to obtain high levels of proficiency in public management as the basis for an application of technical and managerial skills to enhance public service work.

The Master of Science in Human Resources Management (M.S.H.R.M.) is a professional degree program designed to offer graduates of diversified undergraduate programs an opportunity to obtain a proficiency in human resources management skills. The program emphasizes fundamental problem-solving, technical, and decision-making skills; communication and interpersonal competencies; and knowledge critical for success in today's and tomorrow's entrepreneurial and business organizations.

The Master of Science in Management (M.S.M.) is a professional program designed to offer the graduate of diversified undergraduate programs an opportunity to obtain proficiency in management skills and decision making that enables them to carry out managerial responsibilities in both the private and public sectors. Students complete a five-course core, a three-course concentration, and two elective courses suitable to their individual academic and employment backgrounds and specific career objectives.

The Master of Science in Postsecondary Education Program (MSPSE) is designed to strengthen and enrich current and future educators in the instructional technology, adult education, and foundation of education areas of study. The degree provides graduate study for students, teachers, and administrators whose career goals call for further education, improved abilities to use new instructional technology effectively, and performance of research and policymaking in this field. This is a noncertification program.

Special Programs

eCampus is a part of University College. The University College component of Troy University is unique to Alabama universities as it provides a global focus to Troy University's routine operations. University College sites span from Korea to Guantanamo Bay, Cuba, giving meaning to the phrase "the sun never sets on Troy University." Additional information about the University's programs may be found at its Web site, listed in the contact section.

Student Services

Troy University is committed to providing a wide range of learning opportunities for a diverse student population. Students come to Troy University with hopes and high expectations. Professors teach courses using the latest course materials and techniques for rich interaction between students and professors. Professors can advise students on course options and degree requirements. The staff members at eCampus also provide advice and assistance with admissions, registra-

tion, evaluation of transfer credit, changes of program, and processing of Intents to Graduate.

Credit Options

eCampus offers credits through distance learning that are recorded on a Troy University transcript in the same manner as credits earned in on-campus courses. Most students enroll as degree-seeking students, but there is opportunity for students to take individual courses that may apply to degrees at other institutions of higher learning. Students should contact the Student Services staff at eCampus to learn more about transient authorizations or other credit opportunities.

Faculty

All eCampus faculty members meet the standards set forth by the Southern Association of Colleges and Schools, the state of Alabama, and the review agencies of the various Troy University colleges. Faculty members are full-time or adjunct members of the department granting the course credit.

Admission

Admission to the distance learning degree programs at Troy University has the same criteria as admission for any on-campus student. Interested students should access the eCampus Web site for more information. There is a $50 admission fee.

Tuition and Fees

Tuition and fees are subject to change and are published on the eCampus Web site. With the exception of the M.B.A. program, graduate credit for the 2007–08 academic year was $315 per credit hour ($945 per 3-credit hour course), offered only through the main campus in Troy, Alabama. The fees for the M.B.A. program were $440 per credit, or $1320 for each 3-credit hour course. Additional fees include $50 for admissions, $50 for graduation, and $7.50 for transcripts.

Financial Aid

Troy University offers a comprehensive program of financial assistance for students pursuing a graduate degree. Application for Financial Aid forms may be obtained by e-mailing a request to the e-mail address listed in the contact section. The G.I. Bill, Veterans Administration, and tuition assistance (TA) are also means by which students who are qualified for these forms of financial aid may pay for tuition.

Applying

Students can submit an Application for Admission as well as register for courses using the Distance Learning Web site. The Web site provides complete details regarding degree programs and application and registration requirements.

CONTACT

Student Services
eCampus
Troy University
Troy, Alabama 36082

Phone: 334-670-5876
      800-265-9811 (toll-free)
Fax: 334-670-5679
E-mail: tsulearn@troyst.edu
Web site: http://www.troy.edu/ecampus/onlinegraduatepro-
      grams/

THE UNIVERSITY OF ALABAMA
College of Continuing Studies
Division of Academic Outreach
Tuscaloosa, Alabama

Founded in 1831, the University of Alabama has been selected repeatedly as one of the top fifty public universities in the country. By using technology and flexible formats, the Division of Academic Outreach provides diverse and convenient academic programs to students pursuing educational and personal development.

Distance Learning Program

The Division of Academic Outreach accommodates distance and adult learners who are limited by time, geography, work schedules, or personal obligations. Degrees and courses are available via the Internet, DVD, and videoconferencing.

Delivery Media

Academic Outreach delivers high school and college courses over the Internet directly to the student's computer. Students are instructed through a secure Internet site, and they interact with their professors and complete lessons through the online course-management system.

Academic Outreach delivers undergraduate and graduate courses via DVD to students who cannot attend classes on campus. Courses are filmed as they occur, and DVDs are mailed to students the same week. Students take proctored exams at convenient locations. Video courses are semester based. Interested students should visit http://www.BamaByDistance.ua.edu for registration information or call 800-452-5971 (toll-free).

The Intercampus Interactive Telecommunication System (IITS) is a network of conference rooms connected to Vianet, a statewide videoconferencing network. Approximately 120 sites throughout Alabama are equipped with cameras, monitors, and other devices that allow teachers and students to interact as if they were in the same room. Interested students should visit http://www.BamaByDistance.ua.edu for registration information or call 800-452-5971 (toll-free).

Through Independent Study, students may select their hours of study and work at their own pace to complete courses through written correspondence. With certain stipulations, the undergraduate courses may be used to complete a maximum of 25 percent of the work leading to the bachelor's degree. Nine of the last 18 hours required for a degree may be taken by written correspondence, provided that all residence requirements have been met.

Programs of Study

The University of Alabama offers the following programs through distance learning: B.A. or B.S. in interdisciplinary studies (requires a three-day, on-campus orientation), B.S. in commerce and business administration (general business), B.S. in consumer sciences with a concentration in family financial planning and counseling, B.S. in human environmental sciences (general studies), B.S. in mechanical engineering (available in Dothan, Alabama), Bachelor of Science in Nursing (RN to B.S.N.), Bachelor and Master of Science in Nursing (RN to B.S.N./M.S.N.), B.S. in restaurant and hospitality management (executive restaurant and hospitality management), B.S. in restaurant and hospitality management (restaurant, hotel, and meetings management), M.A. in counselor education (rehabilitation) (Alabama only), M.A. in health studies (health promotion), Master of Law and Taxation, Master of Library and Information Studies, M.S. in aerospace engineering, M.S. in human environmental sciences (general studies with a certificate in family financial planning and counseling), M.S. in human environmental sciences (general studies with a concentration in consumer quality management, M.S. in human environmental sciences (general studies with a specialization in interactive technology), M.S. in human environmental sciences (human nutrition), M.S. in nursing (case management for rural populations/clinical nurse leader), M.S. in operations management, Ed.S. in counselor education, and Ed.S. in secondary education science concentration.

Special Programs

The External Degree Program is an interdisciplinary undergraduate distance learning program. Students may apply previously earned academic credits transferred from regionally accredited colleges or earned through national tests such as the College-Level Examination Program (CLEP), independent study, out-of-class learning contracts, correspondence studies, classroom work, and demonstrated prior learning toward a B.A. or a B.S. in interdisciplinary studies.

Applicants must have high school diplomas or General Educational Development (GED) equivalency scores of at least 50 if the test was taken prior to January 2002 or at least 500 if the test was taken after January 2002, be 25 years of age or older, have cumulative GPAs of 2.0 or higher on all previous college work, and have educational goals that are attainable through the program. As with most of the University's distance programs, applicants need not be Alabama residents.

Credit Options

Applicability of credit toward an undergraduate degree refers to the prerogative of the respective academic divisions to count specific credit toward a student's degree requirements. A maximum of 64 semester hours of two-year college credit may be applied toward graduation requirements. At the graduate level, a maximum of 12 semester hours of work taken as a nondegree student may be applied to the credit-hour requirements for a degree. Responsibility rests with the student to observe the limitations imposed on credit hours, course work, and transfer of credit. Procedures and forms are furnished upon request.

Faculty

At The University of Alabama, distinguished faculty members require the same level of academic excellence from their distance students as they do from on-campus students. Faculty members receive special training in facilitating distance learning, and students receive high-quality degree programs from an accredited, world-class institution.

Admission

Admission policies and procedures for degree programs and courses offered through Academic Outreach vary. Students are responsible for reading and understanding admissions polices and procedures for the degree program and courses in which they plan to enroll. For more information, students should visit the Web site at http://BamaByDistance.ua.edu and click on the Prospective Student tab.

The Division of Academic Outreach provides services to assist students with the admission process, registration, advising and schedule building, and financial aid. Students should contact Nina Smith for assistance (telephone: 205-348-0089 or 800-467-0227 (toll-free); e-mail: nsmith@ccs.ua.edu or AOinfo@ccs.ua.edu).

Tuition and Fees

Tuition varies by program and format. Students should visit the Division of Academic Outreach Web site at http://BamaByDistance.ua.edu for current tuition rates.

Financial Aid

Loans are administered through the Office of Student Financial Services. Academic Outreach offers several scholarships for adult students each academic year. Applications are generally available in the fall semester, and the deadline is usually in early December.

Applying

Students may obtain information on admission and registration by contacting the Division of Academic Outreach online at http://www.BamaByDistance.ua.edu, by e-mail at aoinfo@ccs.ua.edu, or by telephone at 800-467-0227 (toll-free).

CONTACT

Division of Academic Outreach
College of Continuing Studies
The University of Alabama
Box 870388
Tuscaloosa, Alabama 35487-0388

Phone: 205-348-0089
      800-467-0227 (toll-free)
Fax: 205-348-0249
E-mail: AOinfo@ccs.ua.edu
Web site: http://www.BamaByDistance.ua.edu

UNIVERSITY OF ALASKA FAIRBANKS

Center for Distance Education and Independent Learning
Fairbanks, Alaska

In 1917, just fifteen years after the discovery of gold in the heart of the Alaskan wilderness, the Alaska Agricultural College and School of Mines was created by a special act of the Alaska Territorial Legislature. In 1922, the college opened with 6 faculty members and 6 students. Today, the University of Alaska Fairbanks (UAF), whose name was changed in 1931, continues to grow, both in size and stature. In addition to the main campus in Fairbanks, UAF has branch campuses in Bethel, Dillingham, Kotzebue, Nome, and the Interior/Aleutians. UAF is the state's land-, sea-, and space-grant institution. Its College of Rural and Community Development has the primary responsibility for Alaska Native education and study, and UAF remains the only university in Alaska that offers doctoral degrees. UAF's colleges and schools offer more than seventy fields of study and a wide variety of technical and vocational programs. All courses are approved and meet the accreditation standards of the Northwest Commission on Colleges and Universities. UAF is an Affirmative Action/Equal Opportunity employer and educational institution.

Distance Learning Program

UAF developed a Correspondence Study Program in the late 1950s, but the current Center for Distance Education and Independent Learning (CDE) was created in 1987. The Independent Learning Program offers more than 135 courses in nearly forty disciplines, with approximately 6,000 student enrollments throughout the world each year.

Independent Learning courses are open for enrollment any time of the year. Students have up to one year from the date of enrollment to finish course work. Extensions may be available, depending on the circumstances. Students are encouraged to use e-mail to submit lessons to circumvent delays in the standard mailing process.

CDE also supports close to 150 distance-delivered courses offered on a semester basis. CDE is part of the College of Rural and Community Development, with branch campuses in Bethel, Dillingham, Interior-Aleutians (Fairbanks), Kotzebue, and Nome, as well as participating with extended campuses of the University of Alaska Anchorage and University of Alaska Southeast.

Delivery Media

A wide range of media, including basic written materials, audiotapes, videotapes, CD-ROMS, e-mail, and the World Wide Web, is utilized to deliver instruction. Many courses are available online, most utilizing the Blackboard Learning System, and more are being developed regularly. Not all modes of delivery are available for every course, and students must have access to the appropriate equipment as specified in individual course descriptions. Most interaction between students and instructors is asynchronous in nature and may be via written communication, e-mail, or by phone interview.

Programs of Study

Approximately 135 independent learning courses can be used to fulfill degree program requirements within the University of Alaska's statewide system or at any other university that accepts the credits. The Center for Distance Education and Independent Learning is not a degree-granting organization. Future plans include delivery of certificates and degrees online.

Individual course requirements vary for Independent Learning courses and are detailed in the course description. Many courses list prerequisites, and it is up to the student to determine if he or she has fulfilled the requirements.

Special Programs

The Center for Distance Education and Independent Learning participates in the Defense Activity for Non-Traditional Education Support (DANTES) programs; information is available from base personnel or education officers. Veterans' educational benefits are also applicable. DANTES students must complete a UAF enrollment form as well as the DANTES forms.

People interested in being certified to teach in Alaska find courses available that fulfill teacher certificate and recertification requirements for the State of Alaska Department of Education. Students may choose among several courses that satisfy the Alaska studies and multicultural requirements.

Student Services

Students have access to the state library system and the UAF Rasmuson Library directly or through the Statewide Library Electronic Doorway (SLED). All students can obtain accounts on the University of Alaska computer network, which also gives access to the wider Internet and the World Wide Web. The UAF Writing Center offers free tutoring for student use. Papers are faxed to the center, and a telephone appointment is made between the tutor and the student. Students may not schedule more than one appointment per day. A toll-free UAF math hotline for problem solving and math help is also available for student use. Available hours may change each semester.

Credit Options

Since the Center for Distance Education and Independent Learning is not a degree-granting organization, there is no transfer of credit or credit for prior learning available.

Faculty

The Independent Learning Program includes approximately 90 faculty members, about half of whom are also full-time members of the UAF faculty and have terminal academic degrees. Adjunct faculty members and discipline professionals are hired to supplement the University's full-time faculty.

Admission

Students may enroll in individual courses any time during the year and have one year to complete the course. There are no admissions requirements or procedures, since the Center for Distance Education and Independent Learning is not a degree-granting organization.

Tuition and Fees

All students enrolled in UAF Independent Learning courses are charged the same tuition whether they are Alaska residents or not. Tuition for 100- to 200-level courses is $120 per credit, 300- to 400-level courses are $135 per credit, and 600-level courses are $268 per credit. There is an additional UA Network fee, which is assessed at 2 percent of tuition. The only other costs for courses are materials fees that vary by course and a $25 service fee per course. Students outside the U.S. must submit payment in U.S. dollars and are charged an extra $30 per course plus any additional shipping charges for the delivery of materials. (Actual costs of delivery are determined upon registration.)

Financial Aid

Alaska students who are full-time (enrolled in at least 12 credits per semester) and are taking independent learning courses on a semester basis are eligible for all the types of financial aid available to other students, including Federal Pell Grants, Federal Supplemental Educational Opportunity Grants, State Educational Incentive grants, Bureau of Indian Affairs grants, Federal Stafford Student Loans, and State of Alaska student loans. Students enrolled in regular yearlong courses are not eligible to receive financial aid.

Applying

No application is required of students taking Independent Learning courses. Completion of a UAF enrollment form and payment of fees are all that are required of students to take courses. Verification of enrollment and course materials are mailed to the students outside of the local Fairbanks area.

CONTACT

Curt Madison, Director
Center for Distance Education and Independent Learning
College of Rural and Community Development
P.O. Box 756700
University of Alaska Fairbanks
Fairbanks, Alaska 99775-6700
Phone: 907-474-5353
        800-277-8060 (toll-free)
Fax: 907-474-5402
E-mail: distance@uaf.edu
Web site: http://distance.uaf.edu

UNIVERSITY OF CENTRAL MISSOURI

Office of Extended Campus–Distance Learning
Department of Nursing

Warrensburg, Missouri

> *Founded in 1871, the University of Central Missouri (formerly Central Missouri State University) is a state university offering approximately 150 areas of study to 11,100 undergraduate and graduate students. In 1996, the University was designated Missouri's lead institution for professional technology, an area long recognized as one of the University's greatest strengths. The new mission has expanded this commitment and means that Central will continue to integrate the latest technologies into every level of its comprehensive liberal arts curriculum. Central is committed to acquiring, disseminating, and utilizing technology to enhance the University's comprehensive educational mission. Central is accredited by the North Central Association of Colleges and Schools.*

Distance Learning Program

Central's main distance learning program provides undergraduate- and graduate-level courses through two-way interactive television and Internet-based courses. The online program currently includes one doctoral degree, three master's degrees, and numerous graduate and undergraduate courses. From fall 1994 through fall 2006, Central provided instruction to more than 40,000 graduate, undergraduate, and high school students in a distance learning environment.

Institutional and financial information about the University of Central Missouri can be accessed via the Web at http://www.ucmo.edu/rsearch/ir/toc.htm.

Delivery Media

Central uses a variety of technologies to deliver its distance learning courses. These include two-way, interactive television; broadcast television; and Internet technologies, including video and audio streaming. Central links to the Missouri Research and Educational Network (MOREnet) statewide backbone, which connects all of Missouri's public higher education institutions and many K–12 schools, to provide Internet-based and interactive television programming. Central's complement of six 2-way videoconferencing facilities, which are capable of ISDN,

H.323, T.120, and audioconferencing, allow Central to provide distance learning content anywhere in the world.

Programs of Study

There are two degrees offered by the Department of Nursing primarily through distance learning technologies. The RN completion program resulting in a bachelor's degree is delivered through online courses. The Master of Science in Nursing degree is also delivered online.

The Bachelor of Science in Nursing degree is designed for the registered nurse who wants to upgrade to a bachelor's degree. The bachelor's degree provides more flexibility and leads to more career opportunities in nursing. Employment opportunities increase as the level of education increases. A baccalaureate degree provides many more options in the areas of public health, home health, nursing management, program planning, and health teaching. Registered nurses face increasingly complex demands that require a broad-based bachelor's degree preparation. Central's Bachelor of Science in Nursing includes general education courses and an introduction to other disciplines in addition to the focus on nursing. The program enhances a nurse's ability to think critically, teaches more effective communication skills, broadens the scope of

nursing into areas of wellness, and provides a deeper understanding of professional nursing leadership.

The program features flexible scheduling that allows students to start any semester and set their own pace for completion. Full-time students can complete the course work in one year; part-time students can take up to four years to complete the program. The program allows the transfer of up to 64 credit hours of university studies and nursing prerequisites from other institutions. Students receive credit for courses completed within another nursing program and for professional experience. Nursing faculty members understand the needs of working professionals who are students. The program is accredited by the Commission on Collegiate Nursing Education (CCNE). More information is available online in the undergraduate catalog at http://www.ucmo.edu/catalogs/.

The Master of Science in Nursing online degree program is designed for nurses with a baccalaureate degree who seek advanced practice as a specialist. Central, with more than forty-five years of experience providing high-quality nursing education, uses state-of-the-art technology to deliver the program. Students specialize in one of two professional tracks: family nurse practitioner or nurse educator.

There are many benefits for students earning a Master of Science in Nursing degree at Central. All professional tracks offer flexibility at an affordable cost. The online classes provide "anytime, anywhere" access, and the online format eliminates travel time and expense. Online classes expand the student's technical skills, increasing valuable workplace skills. Classes are student centered and user friendly, providing individual attention from the instructors. Earning this degree provides students with the foundation for advanced practice, specialty practice, and advanced study at the doctoral level. More information can be found in the graduate catalog online at http://www.ucmo.edu/catalogs/.

Special Programs

Central's distance learning program builds upon the existing curriculum offerings at Central as well as offerings that address special distance learning needs. Central's distance learning students are eligible to participate in the same opportunities as on-campus students. These include study tours and internships in many disciplines. The Office of Career Services reports a 93 percent placement rate for Central graduates within six months of graduation.

Student Services

The toll-free University number, 800-729-8266, allows access to offices involved with student services: Extended Campus, Distance Learning, admissions, financial aid, revenue, University housing, and the Graduate School. All students enrolled at Central are issued a network account to access University resources. The Help Desk is available to Central students needing technical computer assistance. Distance learning students receive individualized course information prior to the start of each semester as well as information about University resources available to them. Online library resources are available for distance learning and off-campus students. An online writing lab (OWL) provides writing assistance to distance learning students. A toll-free number provides ordering

and delivery service for textbooks from the University Bookstore.

Credit Options

For entering graduate students, Central accepts up to 9 hours of transfer credits in graduate work.

Faculty

Faculty members at Central exemplify the goals of the institution as they balance personal attention with expertise in their respective fields. Approximately 68 percent of the 439 full-time faculty members hold doctoral degrees. The student-faculty ratio is 18:1.

Admission

Students interested in pursuing an online degree through Central's Department of Nursing should contact the Office of Extended Campus and Distance Learning for information. Applicants must be admitted to the University before enrolling in a nursing program. If this is a student's first enrollment at Central, a $30 nonrefundable application fee (international students, $50) must accompany the application and official transcripts of all undergraduate and graduate course work. Admission to the University or Graduate School is not equivalent to admission to a particular program or degree.

Tuition and Fees

For 2006–07, graduate tuition was $257 per credit hour for Internet-based courses. Undergraduate tuition was $215 per credit hour for Internet-based programs. Prospective students should note that tuition rates may be changed at any time by action of the Board of Governors.

Financial Aid

Central recognizes a student's continuing need for financial assistance. Federal grant and loan funds are available for eligible students who have been accepted for regular degree programs at Central. Application eligibility information may be obtained by contacting the Office of Financial Aid, 660-543-4040 or 800-729-8266 (toll-free). Students who are veterans may also be considered for VA educational benefits to help with tuition costs. The University participates in all federal student financial aid grant, loan, and employment programs. Visiting and non-degree-seeking students are not eligible to receive federal student aid.

Applying

Undergraduate students should call 660-543-4290/4677 or 800-729-8266 Ext. 1 (toll-free). Graduate students should call 660-543-4621 or 800-729-8266 Ext. 3 (toll-free).

CONTACT

Barbara Carder
Assistant Director for Distance
   Learning
Office of Extended Campus and
   Distance Learning
Humphreys 410
University of Central Missouri
Warrensburg, Missouri 64093
Phone: 660-543-8480
      800-729-8266 Ext. 21
      (toll-free)
Fax: 660-543-8333
E-mail: bcarder@ucmo.edu
Web site: http://www.ucmo.edu/
   ucmonline

UNIVERSITY OF CENTRAL MISSOURI

Office of Extended Campus–Distance Learning
Master of Science in Criminal Justice

Warrensburg, Missouri

Founded in 1871, the University of Central Missouri (formerly Central Missouri State University) is a state university offering approximately 150 areas of study to 11,100 undergraduate and graduate students. In 1996, the University was designated Missouri's lead institution for professional technology, an area long recognized as one of the University's greatest strengths. The new mission has expanded this commitment and means that Central will continue to integrate the latest technologies into every level of its comprehensive liberal arts curriculum. Central is committed to acquiring, disseminating, and utilizing technology to enhance the University's comprehensive educational mission. Central is accredited by the North Central Association of Colleges and Schools.

Distance Learning Program

Central's main Distance Learning Program provides undergraduate- and graduate-level courses through two-way interactive television and Internet-based courses. The online program currently includes one doctoral degree, three master's degrees, and numerous graduate and undergraduate courses. From fall 1994 through fall 2006, Central provided instruction to more than 40,000 graduate, undergraduate, and high school students in a distance learning environment.

Institutional and financial information about the University of Central Missouri can be accessed via the Web at http://www.ucmo.edu/rsearch/ir/toc.htm.

Delivery Media

Central uses a variety of technologies to deliver its distance learning courses. These include two-way, interactive television; broadcast television; and Internet technologies, including video and audio streaming. Central links to the Missouri Research and Educational Network (MOREnet) statewide backbone, which connects all of Missouri's public higher education institutions and many K–12 schools, to provide Internet-based and interactive television programming. Central's complement of six 2-way videoconferencing facilities, which are capable of ISDN, H.323, T.120, and audioconferencing, allow Central to provide distance learning content to anywhere in the world.

Programs of Study

The Master of Science in Criminal Justice program is designed to provide the requisite knowledge, skills, and abilities for those students who intend to enter and/or advance in the criminal justice fields of law enforcement, corrections, and juvenile justice or who seek leadership, professional specialization, research, or teaching positions in criminal justice. Course work emphasizes leading justice system issues, including legal aspects; organization, administration, management, and leadership; and information acquisition, analysis, and interpretation. Distance delivery of the Master of Science in Criminal Justice includes complete online delivery of the degree program. Site-based programs are also held at Central Summit Center in Lee's Summit, Missouri.

The graduate with a Master of Science in Criminal Justice can use the knowledge and skills obtained in the program to articulate knowledge of the major issues facing the criminal justice system in the nation and world; conduct and present an independent research project; communicate and interact professionally in scholarly, academic settings; and delineate the ethical principles of human subject protection in social science research.

First offered in 1962, the program is one of the most respected criminal justice programs in the world. Among Central's criminal justice alumni are members of numerous police and corrections agencies, national and state government officials, judges, attorneys, professors, and approximately 400 chief administrators in all parts of the world.

To be accepted into the program of study for the Master of Criminal Justice, a student must have an undergraduate degree in criminal justice or a related field and have earned a minimum grade point average of 2.75 on all undergraduate course work and 3.0 on all graduate course work. A student without a criminal justice degree may be required to complete up to 15 hours of background courses in criminal justice prior to taking graduate-level courses. The requirement to take background courses may be waived by the department's graduate coordinator based on previous courses taken and/or relevant professional experience. Students not meeting program admission requirements may request that the department's graduate committee admit them provisionally to the program. GRE scores are generally not required.

The 36-hour Master of Science in Criminal Justice program allows for 6 semester hours of departmentally approved electives under the thesis option and 9 hours under the nonthesis or comprehensive examination option.

Special Programs

Central's distance learning program builds upon the existing curriculum offerings at Central as well as offerings that address special distance learning needs.

Central's distance learning students are eligible to participate in the same opportunities as on-campus students. These include study tours and internships in many disciplines.

The Office of Career Services reports a 94 percent placement rate for Central graduates within six months of graduation.

Student Services

A toll-free University number, 800-729-8266, allows access to offices involved with student services: Extended Campus and Distance Learning, admissions, financial aid, revenue, University housing, and the Graduate School. All students enrolled at Central are issued a network account to access University resources. The Help Desk is available to Central students needing technical computer assistance. Distance learning students receive individualized course information prior to the start of each semester as well as information regarding University resources available to them. Online library resources are available for distance learning and off-campus students. An online writing lab (OWL) provides writing assistance to distance learning students. A toll-free number provides ordering and delivery service for textbooks from the University Bookstore.

Credit Options

For entering graduate students of the Master of Science in criminal justice program, Central will accept up to 6 hours of transfer credits in graduate work.

Faculty

Faculty members at Central exemplify the goals of the institution as they balance personal attention with expertise in their respective fields. Approximately 68 per-cent of the 439 full-time faculty members hold doctoral degrees. The student-faculty ratio is 18:1.

The criminal justice faculty has a unique blend of academic credentials and field experience, with all members holding terminal degrees. In addition, 90 percent of the faculty members had significant experience with a criminal justice agency prior to joining the faculty of the University of Central Missouri.

Admission

Individuals interested in pursuing a graduate degree at the University of Central Missouri should contact the Graduate School for application information at 800-729-8266 (toll-free) or visit the Web site at http://www.ucmo.edu/graduate. The Graduate School should receive all application materials at least three weeks prior to the beginning of the semester in which the student wishes to register.

All degree-seeking student applicants must submit a formal application for admission to the Graduate School and official transcripts of all undergraduate/graduate course work. If this is a student's first enrollment at Central, a $30 nonrefundable application fee is required (international students must remit $50). Admission to the Graduate School, which permits enrollment in classes, is not equivalent to admission to a particular program or degree.

Tuition and Fees

For 2006–07, graduate tuition was $257 per credit hour for Internet-based courses. Prospective students should note that tuition rates may be changed at any time by action of the Board of Governors.

Financial Aid

Central recognizes a student's continuing need for financial assistance. Federal grant and loan funds are available for eligible students who have been accepted for regular degree programs at Central. Application eligibility information may be obtained by contacting the Office of Financial Aid, 660-543-4040 or 800-729-8266 (toll-free). Students who are veterans may also be considered for VA educational benefits to help with tuition costs.

The University participates in all federal student financial aid grant, loan, and employment programs. Visiting and non-degree-seeking students are not eligible to receive federal financial aid.

Applying

Graduate students should contact the Graduate School, 660-543-4621 or toll-free at 800-729-8266 Ext. 3.

CONTACT

Dr. Betsy W. Kreisel
Faculty Graduate Coordinator
University of Central Missouri
Warrensburg, Missouri 64093
Phone: 660-543-8836
E-mail: kreisel@ucmo.edu
Web site: http://www.ucmo.edu/cj/index.html

Barbara Carder
Assistant Director for Distance Learning
Office of Extended Campus and
    Distance Learning
Humphreys 410
University of Central Missouri
Warrensburg, Missouri 64093
Phone: 660-543-8480
    800-729-8266 Ext. 21 (toll-free)
Fax: 660-543-8333
E-mail: bcarder@ucmo.edu
Web site: http://www.ucmo.edu/ucmonline

UNIVERSITY OF CENTRAL MISSOURI

Office of Extended Campus–Distance Learning
Master of Science in Industrial Management

Warrensburg, Missouri

Founded in 1871, the University of Central Missouri (formerly Central Missouri State University) is a state university offering approximately 150 areas of study to 11,100 undergraduate and graduate students. In 1996, the University was designated Missouri's lead institution for professional applied science and technology programs, an area long recognized as one of the University's greatest strengths. The new mission has expanded this commitment and means that Central will continue to integrate the latest technologies into every level of its comprehensive liberal arts curriculum. Central is committed to acquiring, disseminating, and utilizing technology to enhance the University's comprehensive educational mission. Central is accredited by the North Central Association of Colleges and Schools.

Distance Learning Program

Central's main Distance Learning Program provides undergraduate- and graduate-level courses through two-way interactive television and Internet-based courses. The online program currently includes one doctoral degree, three master's degrees, and numerous graduate and undergraduate courses. From fall 1994 through fall 2006, Central provided instruction to more than 40,000 graduate, undergraduate, and high school students in a distance learning environment.

Institutional and financial information about the University of Central Missouri can be accessed via the Web at http://www.ucmo.edu/rsearch/ir/toc.htm.

Delivery Media

Central uses a variety of technologies to deliver its distance learning courses. These include two-way, interactive television; broadcast television; and Internet technologies, including video and audio streaming. Central links to the Missouri Research and Educational Network (MOREnet) statewide backbone, which connects all of Missouri's public higher education institutions and many K–12 schools, to provide Internet-based and interactive television programming. Finally, Central's complement of six 2-way videoconferencing facilities, which are capable of ISDN, H.323, T.120, and audioconferencing, allow Central to provide distance learning content to anywhere in the world.

Programs of Study

The Master of Science in industrial management is designed for students who are preparing for upward mobility in supervisory or management positions in business and industry, manufacturing, quality control or quality systems management, or related positions.

In a recent survey of graduates from this degree, the average response age was 40 years old, with a mean salary of $65,000 per year. Some occupational titles include vice president of operations, production manager, shift supervisor, quality systems manager, and plant manager.

Participants in the Master of Science degree in industrial management develop skills useful to business and industry. The program provides a balanced curriculum focusing on the human element of the workplace as well as a variety of industrial systems. Specific skills are developed in the fields of leadership, problem solving, and decision making.

The graduate with a Master of Science degree in industrial management can use the knowledge and skills obtained in the program to apply management skills and concepts to specific situations, plan and implement a project, analyze and develop a human relations strategy, demonstrate the ability to communicate effectively, explain and apply the basic concepts of an industrial economy, introduce and adapt technical expertise to a given process or product, and perform, interpret, and explain research.

The Master of Science in industrial management is a 33-credit-hour degree program. Complete online delivery of the program began in fall 2002. Students may enter the course cycle at the beginning of any semester. Courses are scheduled with the capability of completing the degree program in two calendar years, including one summer session. Degree information is available on the Web at http://www.ucmo.edu/msim.

A strength of this program is the flexibility built into the cognate course work and culminating experience. The program allows several curricular paths leading to graduation and facilitates articulation to a cooperative doctoral program in technology management.

To be accepted into this program, a student shall have a minimum GPA of 2.6 in the undergraduate major. A student not meeting this requirement may petition the department for admittance on a conditional basis. GRE or GMAT scores are not required.

Special Programs

Central's distance learning program builds upon the existing curriculum offerings at Central as well as offerings that address special distance learning needs.

Central's distance learning students are eligible to participate in the same opportunities as on-campus students.

These include study tours and internships in many disciplines.

The Office of Career Services reports a 93 percent placement rate for Central graduates within six months of graduation.

Student Services

A toll-free University number, 800-729-8266, allows access to offices involved with student services: Extended Campus and Distance Learning, admissions, financial aid, revenue, University housing, and the Graduate School. All students enrolled at Central are issued a network account to access University resources. The Help Desk is available to Central students needing technical computer assistance. Distance learning students receive individualized course information prior to the start of each semester as well as information regarding University resources available to them. Online library resources are available for distance learning and off-campus students. An online writing lab (OWL) provides writing assistance to distance learning students. A toll-free number provides ordering and delivery service for textbooks from the University Bookstore.

Credit Options

For entering graduate students, Central will accept up to 9 hours of transfer credits in graduate work.

Faculty

Faculty members at Central exemplify the goals of the institution as they balance personal attention with expertise in their respective fields. Approximately 68 percent of the 439 full-time faculty members hold doctoral degrees. The student-faculty ratio is 18:1.

Admission

Individuals interested in pursuing a graduate degree at the University of Central Missouri should contact the Graduate School for application information at 800-729-8266 (toll-free) or visit the Web site, http://www.ucmo.edu/graduate. The Graduate School should receive all application materials at least three weeks prior to the beginning of the semester in which the student wishes to register.

All degree-seeking student applicants must submit a formal application for admission to the Graduate School and official transcripts of all undergraduate/graduate course work. If this is a student's first enrollment at Central, a $30 nonrefundable application fee is required (international students must remit $50). Admission to the Graduate School, which permits enrollment in classes, is not equivalent to admission to a particular program or degree.

Tuition and Fees

For 2006–07, graduate tuition was $237 per credit hour for Internet-based courses. Prospective students should note that tuition rates may be changed at any time by action of the Board of Governors.

Financial Aid

Central recognizes a student's continuing need for financial assistance. Federal grant and loan funds are available for eligible students who have been accepted for regular degree programs at Central. Application eligibility information may be obtained by contacting the Office of Financial Aid, 660-543-4040 or 800-729-8266 (toll-free). Students who are veterans may also be considered for VA educational benefits to help with tuition costs.

The University participates in all federal student financial aid grant, loan, and employment programs. Visiting and non-degree-seeking students are not eligible to receive federal financial aid.

Applying

Graduate students should contact the Graduate School, 660-543-4621 or toll-free at 800-729-8266 Ext 3.

CONTACT

Dr. Ronald Woolsey
Faculty Coordinator
University of Central Missouri
Warrensburg, Missouri 64093
Phone: 660-543-4340
E-mail: woolsey@ucmo.edu
Web site: http://www.ucmo.edu/msim

Barbara Carder
Assistant Director for Distance Learning
Office of Extended Campus and
   Distance Learning
Humphreys 410
University of Central Missouri
Warrensburg, Missouri 64093
Phone: 660-543-8480
     800-729-8266 Ext. 21 (toll-free)
Fax: 660-540-8333
E-mail: bcarder@ucmo.edu
Web site: http://www.ucmo.edu/
     cmsuonline

UNIVERSITY OF COLORADO AT DENVER AND HEALTH SCIENCES CENTER

CU Online

Denver, Colorado

The University of Colorado at Denver and Health Sciences Center (UCDHSC) is one of three institutions in the University of Colorado system and the only public university in the Denver metropolitan area. Ranked among America's best graduate schools, UCDHSC features a 15:1 student-faculty ratio, respected academic programs, and a collaborative community relationship. With the Denver skyline as its backdrop, three major sports arenas within walking distance, and numerous outdoor activities at its doorstep, UCDHSC is quickly growing into the model for metro campuses. But with CU Online, UCDHSC's virtual campus, that doorstep has been extended globally. CU Online was among the first fully accredited online programs in the country. It has grown and evolved to be a respected and renowned institution and continues in that tradition. The University of Colorado at Denver was founded in 1965 and is accredited by the North Central Association of Colleges and Schools.

Distance Learning Program

CU Online allows students the opportunity to attend the University of Colorado at Denver and Health Sciences Center on their time schedule and at their convenience, while also providing the recognition and respect that only a brick and mortar university can offer.

CU Online offers not just one or two courses; there are over 350 courses. Students can actually complete an entire degree—or ten degrees—online, without setting a foot on campus. CU Online allows students to enjoy the same stimulating courses, top-notch faculty members, and dedicated resources as the on-campus students— but with the freedom and convenience that online courses naturally provide.

That is only the beginning. CU Online is well on its way to achieving its initial goal of providing students with the most compressive set of online courses, services, and resources of any institution of higher education in the world. Whether students are looking to start a degree, finish one, or just take the occasional course or two, CU Online provides them the opportunity to tailor courses around their lives— rather than tailor life around their courses.

Delivery Media

CU Online courses run on a traditional semester schedule. Although courses are not self-paced, they are flexible. Students are able to log into their courses on a regular basis, at their convenience. They are assigned a homepage to access courses, find lectures and assignments, and contribute to threaded discussions and real-time course chat rooms.

Each course is developed to offer everything students would expect from UCDHSC, but it is online instead of on-campus, so instructors deliver course content through cutting-edge technologies such as streaming audio, video, Web conferencing, virtual animations, and multimedia slide shows. And for lectures, a variety of delivery methods (such as Real Audio, Real Video, and PowerPoint presentations) are available to each UCDHSC instructor.

Programs of Study

CU Online offers courses in liberal arts and science, arts and media, business, education, engineering, public affairs, and architecture and planning. A variety of degrees and certificates can be obtained exclusively through online courses.

Fully online degree programs include the Bachelor of Arts (B.A.) in English writing; Bachelor of Arts (B.A.) in sociology; the Master of Arts (M.A.) in early childhood education; the Master of Arts (M.A.) in information and learning technologies (ILT), with an emphasis in e-learning design and implementation or in school library; Master of Business Administration (M.B.A.); Master of Engineering (M. Eng.), with an emphasis in geographic information systems; Master of Public Administration (M.P.A.); Master of Science (M.S.) in finance; and Master of Science(M.S.) in information systems.

Other online programs include certificates in designing and implementing Web-based learning environments, early literacy, and nonprofit management.

Online licensing modules are offered in early childhood special education specialist and special education generalist.

All online courses may be applied to a degree program at UCDHSC or may be transferred to a student's home institution, pending approval.

Credits and degrees earned through CU Online courses are identical to credits and degrees earned through traditional on-campus courses. UCDHSC is a fully accredited institution making credits easily transferable to other universities.

Special Programs

A hybrid course is just like it sounds: half on-campus and half online. Hybrid courses might be what students are looking for if they are taking online courses and enjoying the scheduling flexibility, but feel they are missing out on some of the intangibles of being in a classroom. Hybrid courses meet approximately 50 percent of the normal classroom hours on campus, and the remainder of the time is completed online.

Student Services

An online education wouldn't be complete without support and services dedicated exclusively to online students. To make the online experience more integrated and beneficial, CU Online students can do the following online: search the University catalog, register for courses, buy textbooks, receive guided advising, apply for financial aid, receive tutoring, view academic records, visit the virtual library (which has online journals, books and subject guides), and more. If students ever have problems or issues with their online courses, they can contact the 24/7 support staff.

Credit Options

Credit, noncredit, and continuing and professional education courses are all available. Most online courses are measured by traditional letter grades. Some courses also offer the pass/fail option.

Faculty

The professors and faculty members of traditional classes are the same ones teaching the online courses. Four out of five full-time faculty members hold

doctoral degrees and have many years of teaching experience, and many are actively engaged in their fields outside the classroom. Not only do they have real-world experience, but many are consultants, advisers, and partners to the leading organizations that frequently hire CU Online graduates.

Admission

A smooth transition to UCDHSC is a primary goal. Students currently living in the state of Colorado must apply and be admitted as either a degree-seeking or a non-degree-seeking student. Students living outside of Colorado do not need to be admitted to the University to take CU Online courses; however, if they wish to complete their degree through CU Online, they need to apply and be formally admitted to the University.

Tuition and Fees

Tuition rates vary depending on the specific college students are interested in and the students' residency status. For residents, most undergraduate courses cost from $201 to $290 per credit hour. There is also a standard $100 course fee for the online technology and 24-7 customer service. (Regardless of how many online courses are taken—one course or four—the fee is still just $100). Any student that registers strictly for online courses is

only responsible for the IT Fee and the Student Information System Fee. All other traditional fees are waved, including the incidental fees associated with driving, mass transit, and parking. Students should visit the CU Online Web site at http://www.cuonline.edu/stu_htm/online_tuition_fees.shtml for current cost information.

Financial Aid

UCDHSC firmly believes that finances should never stand in the way of motivated, talented individuals. As a result, the financial aid programs are strong and well established. To be eligible for financial aid, students must be enrolled as a degree-seeking student at UCDHSC. Students who have any questions or who would like to request further information about financial aid should contact the financial aid office (303-556-2886; finaid@carbon.cudenver.edu).

Applying

Students can apply to the University online at http://www.cuonline.edu/petersons or by paper application. Admission requirements vary by college and school. To find specific information about applying to the University of Colorado at Denver and Health Sciences Center, students can visit the CU Online Web site at http://cuonline.edu.

CONTACT

For more information about CU Online, students should contact:

CU Online, Campus Box 198
University of Colorado at Denver
    and Health Sciences Center
P.O. Box 173364
Denver, Colorado 82017-3364

Phone: 303-556-6505
Fax: 303-556-6530
E-mail: inquiry@cuonline.edu
Web site: http://www.cuonline.edu/petersons

UNIVERSITY OF CONNECTICUT
Center for Continuing Studies
Storrs, Connecticut

Founded in 1881, the University of Connecticut (UConn) is categorized by the Carnegie Foundation among the Doctoral/Research Universities–Extensive, a distinction shared by fewer than 4 percent of America's higher education institutions that confer the widest number and range of degrees. UConn is the only public institution in New England with its own Schools of Law, Social Work, Medicine, and Dental Medicine. The University is accredited by the New England Association of Schools and Colleges.

The Center for Continuing Studies (CCS) offers a bachelor's degree program and three master's degree programs that are available online. The Center identifies, develops, and provides high-quality, research-based interdisciplinary, academic, professional, and enrichment programs as well as appropriate support services to diverse communities of learners in a fiscally responsible manner. Working with academic and student support units across the University, the Center for Continuing Studies provides a gateway linking the University with individuals as well as with corporate and public service sectors statewide, nationally, and internationally. CCS is dedicated to engaging learners in a lifelong academic partnership with the University of Connecticut.

Distance Learning Program

Based on educational demand and market research, the Center for Continuing Studies provides a variety of learning opportunities that utilize the most effective and efficient mode of delivery, given the course/program content and the intended learners. Individuals in CCS programs achieve relevant academic, professional, and technical competence and/or the personal enrichment they seek through a student-centered approach that reflects a high-quality education. Students may take individual courses or enroll in one of the online graduate or undergraduate degree or certificate programs. The asynchronous course format allows students to take courses from anywhere in the world. Faculty members are a key component of the online courses and programs and ensure that online students receive a high-quality education and personalized attention.

Delivery Media

All online courses are offered completely through the Internet using WebCT Vista in a paced, asynchronous environment. The asynchronous format allows access to courses seven days a week, 24 hours a day, including holidays. Discussion and interactivity among the students and the instructor are a key component of all of the online courses. Much of this interactivity is accomplished using an asynchronous threaded discussion tool within the course. An e-mail system that is internal to the course is used for private communication. Some assignments have been designed for students working in groups. Online programs offered through the Center for Continuing Studies are geared toward working adults who need the flexibility to juggle work, family, and academic responsibilities. Courses are accessible using either a PC or a Macintosh. Prospective students are encouraged to review the list of frequently asked questions located at http://continuingstudies.uconn.edu/onlinecourses/faqs./index.html.

Programs of Study

The Center for Continuing Studies offers a Master of Professional Studies (M.P.S.) and a Bachelor of General Studies (B.G.S.). The online M.P.S. degree offers three fields of study: homeland security leadership, human resource management and humanitarian services administration. The M.P.S. degree is specifically designed for individuals and practitioners who are developing marketable skills to meet evolving workforce demands, seeking professional development or expanded promotional opportunities, or interested in changing careers. The M.P.S. requires 36 graduate-level credits, including 30 credits of course work and 6 credits of a capstone project toward the end of the program. The M.P.S. also includes an issues-based two-week on-site residency requirement.

The M.P.S. in homeland security leadership is designed to meet the professional development need of individuals who are U.S. citizens and have experience in law enforcement, emergency management, corporate security, transportation security, fire service, public safety, public health preparedness, and the military.

The M.P.S. in human resource management is designed to meet the professional development needs of individuals who are currently working in the field of human resource management or who are interested in pursuing a career in human resource management. Interested individuals who do not have human resource management or supervisory experience are strongly encouraged to participate in an internship, which may be taken for course credit. Students may select a career track in either labor relations or personnel or may select a program combining electives from both tracks, depending upon their career interests.

The M.P.S. in humanitarian services administration is designed to meet the educational needs of individuals involved or interested in humanitarian assistance programs, whether in disaster relief or sustainability programs. Students develop theoretical and professional knowledge to operate and conduct humanitarian response missions with nongovernmental, governmental, and international organizations. Students can choose courses related to disaster relief or sustainability, or they may select courses from both areas, depending on their interests.

The B.G.S. degree can be completed online. Two foci are offered: occupational and environmental safety and health and Web technology. The B.G.S. program, established in 1977, is an interdisciplinary major designed for returning adults. A student needs at least 60 college credits or an associate degree from a regionally accredited college to be admitted to the program. B.G.S. students work one on one with the same academic adviser through graduation. The adviser and student work together to develop an academic program that suits the student's educational and career goals through an individualized major or by following a B.G.S. focus. B.G.S. alumnae have been accepted into graduate programs at Yale, Princeton, Columbia, MIT, Berkeley, and William and Mary in such fields as medicine, dentistry, law, ministry, and business.

The B.G.S. degree with a focus in occupational and environmental safety and health has served more than 450 students since its inception in 1995. The courses are designed for practitioners and nonpractitioners and provide students with marketable skills and knowledge that are relevant to a broad spectrum of industries and work environments. Students can also use the courses to prepare for the national Certified Safety Professional (CSP) examination, a prestigious designation in the occupational safety and health field.

The B.G.S. degree with a focus in Web technology is geared toward preparing students for the variety of information technologies they will encounter in their career paths. This program provides immediate practical benefits and a solid foundation for corporate IT training programs and advanced study by taking a hands-on approach toward the understanding of IT. Courses generally fall under the areas of Web content development and Web system administration.

General education courses are also available online and may be taken individually or as part of an undergraduate degree program.

Students may enroll in a degree program, or they may take individual courses. Online noncredit programs are offered in health-care information technology.

Special Programs

Students can take individual courses as nondegree students, allowing working adults to enroll in University of Connecticut undergraduate and graduate courses and earn academic credit without being formally admitted to a degree program. Nondegree study allows high school graduates of all ages to return to college at their own pace and gain the confidence they need to complete their education. If students later choose to apply for a degree program, it is likely that these credits can be applied toward their degree. Taking a course as a nondegree student at UConn is also a convenient way for students from other colleges and universities to take credit courses at UConn and then transfer the credits to their own university. Students in the online programs can take on-campus courses. If students are degree students, they need permission from their advisers. Nondegree students do not need to see an adviser before registering.

Student Services

All major student services are available to online students, including registration services, advising, bookstore ordering, library, e-mail, and tutoring. Technical support is available to all students in online courses.

Credit Options

Students in the B.G.S. program may transfer up to 90 credits that they have earned through other regionally accredited institutions.

Faculty

The Center for Continuing Studies employs full-time and adjunct faculty members. Faculty members who teach online are approved by the department and also teach on-campus courses. All full-time faculty members and all faculty members teaching in the graduate program have earned doctorates. Adjunct faculty members are accomplished practitioners and have the requisite educational experience to make them effective online instructors.

Admission

Applicants to the M.P.S. program must have completed a baccalaureate degree from a regionally accredited college or university. For further admission information for the M.P.S. program, students should visit http://continuingstudies.uconn.edu/mps/academicinfo.html. Applicants to the B.G.S. degree must have an associate degree from a regionally accredited college or university or must have completed at least 60 college credits from a regionally accredited college or university. For further admission information for the B.G.S. program, students should visit http://continuingstudies.uconn.edu/bgs/admissions.html. Students may register for individual courses without matriculating into a program, provided they meet specific course requirements. For course registration information, students should visit http://continuingstudies.uconn.edu/overview/register.html.

Tuition and Fees

Undergraduate course fees are $1029 per 3-credit course. Graduate course fees are $1581 per 3-credit course. There is a $45 infrastructure maintenance fee for undergraduate and graduate courses. Course fees are calculated on a per-credit basis; current fees are subject to change. Students who enroll in the center's online courses pay the same fees as in-state students. Students should visit the Web site for current fees.

Financial Aid

Financial aid is available to online students who have matriculated into a degree program. For further information, students should contact the Office of Student Financial Aid Services at 860-486-2819 or visit the Web site at http://www.financial-aid.uconn.edu.

Applying

Application to the M.P.S. degree program is available online at http://continuingstudies.uconn.edu/mps/academicinfo.html. Application to the B.G.S. degree program is available online at https://continuingstudies.uconn.edu/bgs/admissions.html.

CONTACT

Dr. Judy Buffolino, Director
Distance Education Office
Center for Continuing Studies
University of Connecticut
One Bishop Circle, Unit 4056
Storrs, Connecticut 06269-4056

Phone: 860-486-1080
Fax: 860-486-0756
E-mail: ccsonline@uconn.edu
Web site: http://continuingstudies.
uconn.edu/onli-
necourses

UNIVERSITY OF DALLAS

Graduate School of Management
Center for Distance Learning
Irving, Texas

The University of Dallas (UD) was founded in 1956 as in independent Catholic university dedicated to excellence in its educational programs.

The Graduate School of Management (GSM) is the largest Master of Business Administration–granting institution in the Southwest. GSM was founded in 1966 with a distinctive mission: to create a professionally sound M.B.A. program accessible to individuals who are already employed in business. More than 80 percent of GSM students work full-time. The student body is made up of Americans and international students representing more than sixty-five countries. The UD main campus is in Irving, adjacent to the thriving Las Colinas business community and near downtown Dallas and Dallas/Fort Worth International Airport.

The Commission on Colleges of the Southern Association of Colleges and Schools (SACS) accredits UD. In addition, UD is accredited by the International Assembly for Collegiate Business Education (IACBE) and the Association of Collegiate Business Schools and Programs (ACBSP).

Distance Learning Program

UD is committed to providing the kind of education, programming, and service that motivates and enables success. The online environment offers professionals the flexibility to maintain current schedules and perform to their fullest in a fast-paced educational program. The aspects of flexible course delivery help to create an environment conducive to an inflexible world.

The UD courses are available from any Internet connection worldwide at anytime. The learning model is designed to serve students with a program offering the greatest level of flexibility to participate in the online classroom. It allows participation whenever it is most convenient for the individual student while maintaining the highest educational standards. All courses are developed and taught by professors who have real-world business experience in addition to their academic qualifications. This allows students to learn tools and techniques proven in the changing business world.

In addition, the online program is an integral part of the academic environment at UD. Students can choose to complete all classes online or integrate online learning with the traditional classroom environment. Each method, online or traditional classroom, provides consistent, high-quality learning outcomes. This flexibility meets the needs of students living in the Dallas/Fort Worth area and students who are part of the global learning community.

GSM began its Internet-based M.B.A. program (IMBA) in 1997 with three courses and 30 students. Now GSM offers the entire M.B.A. core curriculum and thirteen concentrations online.

While taking an IMBA class, there is no requirement to come to the campus. However, many students take a blend of on-campus and Internet-based courses. Other students take their entire M.B.A. online. There is no distinction made on the transcript between classroom and IMBA courses.

Students are attracted to the GSM because it offers a comprehensive background in the general business disciplines, as well as industry-specific fields of knowledge, such as corporate finance, global business, health services, information assurance, interdisciplinary (custom curriculum), marketing, not-for-profit management, project management, sports and entertainment management, supply chain management, and telecommunications—all online.

Delivery Media

The virtual campus was created with the understanding that students need the ability to organize their class schedules without being confined to a certain time, campus, or even country. Students access the IMBA using a standard Internet connection and Web browser. The courses use an instructor-led, asynchronous method of teaching, which means that students and their professors do not have to be online at the same time. This allows flexibility for those students who travel or have other obligations. Classes fit into everyday life. However, both professors and students are expected to be online multiple times during the weekly sessions.

For additional information on the online delivery method or the IMBA, students should visit http://www.thedallasmba.com/imba.cfm.

Programs of Study

The University of Dallas offers Master of Business Administration (M.B.A.), Master of Management (M.M.), and Master of Science (M.S.) degree programs.

The University of Dallas Graduate School of Management (GSM) is a professional school whose primary purpose is to prepare its students to become competent, responsible practitioners in the profession of management. GSM's academic programs do not emphasize theoretical courses; instead, they offer highly pragmatic programs, both on-campus and online, that focus on the practical realities of managerial life and success. While scholarly writings on business topics are carefully examined in classes, the principal emphasis is on how to manage wisely and effectively.

Academic programs at GSM differ from those at more traditional management schools in three other ways: the faculty members have extensive business experience, and many professors are actively engaged in business pursuits; specialized M.B.A. concentrations provide detailed insights into the practical aspects of these fields; and project-driven courses give students hands-on experience with real problems in strategy and management. Since the 1960s, GSM has developed a distinct educational method in which student teams are assigned to actual consulting projects requested by a wide variety of local, national, and global firms. Students define client problems, analyze various solutions, and propose specific solutions to the client.

The Dallas M.B.A. program's practical approach makes it unique among graduate business schools and distinguishes its graduates from traditional M.B.A. students. The M.B.A. degree is offered online, with concentrations in accounting, corporate finance, financial services, global business, health services management, information assurance, information technology, information technology service management, market logistics, marketing management, not-for-profit management, project management, sports and entertainment management, supply chain management, and telecommunications management. An interdisciplinary option is also available. The M.B.A. program can be completed in three to four trimesters of full-time study. Part-time students normally take 2½ to 3½ years to complete the M.B.A. degree. However, students can complete the program at their desired pace. For more details, students should visit http://www.thedallasmba.com/programs.cfm.

The Master of Management (M.M.) degree (post-M.B.A.) and graduate certificates are also available online in any of the above concentrations. The M.M. degree provides profession-specific graduate education for those who already hold an M.B.A. from a regionally accredited U.S. college or university or the international equivalent. Adding an M.M. degree to an M.B.A. can strengthen an individual's academic credentials and help him or her stay ahead in today's and tomorrow's workplace. For more information, students should visit: http://www.thedallasmba.com/programs.cfm.

The Master of Science (M.S.) degree is a specialized graduate degree program for students who seek in-depth knowledge in a specific field. For more details, students should visit: http://www.thedallasmba.com.

Special Programs

GSM has partnerships with Fortune 500 corporations to provide classes to their employees through the Internet. Inquiries are welcomed from other organizations that may be interested in offering graduate business studies to their employees.

Student Services

The primary support structure is the IMBA professor. Class size is kept moderate, thus permitting professors and students to interact with one another.

At the Graduate School of Management there are talented individuals—all of whom have had personal experience with GSM programs—who provide customer support and service for prospective, current, and past students. Each enrollment manager specializes in one of the concentrations offered.

These professionals work for the students and are their advocates within the GSM community. Each enrollment manager stands ready to answer students' questions, address their unique concerns, and guide them through the application, admissions, and registration process—and beyond. Staff members in the Online Learning Department are available to address questions unique to distance learning. A help desk that operates 24 hours a day handles Web- and PC-based questions.

Credit Options

For the M.B.A. program, a maximum of four courses or 12 hours of transfer credits may be applied. A transfer course must be a 3-semester-hour (5-quarter-hour) graduate-level course from an accredited school. The transfer course must not be more than six years old. A grade of at least a B (3.0) is required. For further information, students can contact the GSM Admissions Office at the address below.

Faculty

GSM professors have business experience in addition to their academic qualifications. They have held positions ranging from entrepreneurs to senior-level executives in large companies. Full-time faculty members engage in consulting within their field, while adjunct professors hold jobs in their area of teaching, thus keeping the classes current and relevant.

Admission

Admission to the Dallas M.B.A. program is competitive. The program seeks highly motivated individuals demonstrating potential for management and leadership responsibility and possessing the intellectual ability, initiative, and creativity to excel in its programs as well as in the globally competitive marketplace.

Success in the Master of Business Administration program depends on a number of factors ranging from motivation to practical knowledge to academic ability. The primary purpose of the School's admission criteria and application process is to determine a prospective student's potential to successfully complete the requirements for the M.B.A. degree.

While an undergraduate degree is a prerequisite, no specific undergraduate major or concentration is required to pursue the Dallas M.B.A. program in any M.B.A. concentration.

Because the Graduate School of Management enrolls full-time, part-time, and international students, a variety of paths are available to individuals seeking admission.

Prospective students may apply for admission to the Graduate School of Management for any fall, fall II, spring, spring II, or summer II trimester, or intermester. For more information, students should go online to http://www.thedallasmba.com/admissions.cfm.

Tuition and Fees

Graduate tuition was $505 per credit hour in 2006–07 for residents and nonresidents.

Financial Aid

U.S. graduate students may obtain financial assistance through various loan programs. The University's Financial Aid Office (telephone: 972-721-5266; Web site: http://www.udallas.edu/admiss/gradaid.html) has information and application forms for loans.

Applying

Those interested are encouraged to contact GSM at the address in the Contact section or to visit the Web site for additional information. Students can apply online from anywhere in the world.

CONTACT

Office of Admissions
Graduate School of Management
University of Dallas
1845 East Northgate Drive
Irving, Texas 75062-4799
Phone: 972-721-5174
        877-408-2335 (toll-free)
E-mail: admiss@gsm.udallas.edu
Web site:
    http://www.thedallasmba.com

UNIVERSITY OF DENVER

University College

Denver, Colorado

The University of Denver (DU), the oldest independent university in the Rocky Mountain region, is a premier liberal arts university that was founded in 1864. In addition to its rich history, DU is known for its research and high-quality teaching. To augment the traditional undergraduate and graduate programs, this outstanding institution offers innovative graduate programs through its division for professional and continuing studies—University College. University College was founded in 1983. With more than forty national awards and many other distinctions from its peers, University College of the University of Denver is recognized as one of the very best providers of adult education in the nation. University College offered its first online master's degree program in 1996. Today, it offers master's degrees in ten different areas, more than thirty Certificates of Advanced Study, and numerous individual courses in a variety of subject areas. In fall 2006, University College added a Bachelor of Arts Completion Program for students who have started their bachelor's degree, but for some reason have not finished. University College is accredited by the North Central Association of Colleges and Schools.

Distance Learning Program

The University College distance learning program provides the same premier, internationally recognized University of Denver program quality to students who, because of geographic location, work schedule, or personal commitments, would otherwise not have the opportunity to attend DU. The learning experience for the distance student goes beyond the traditional classroom by capitalizing on the advantages of distance learning technology. University College provides an anytime, anywhere support service as well as consistent high-quality instruction. University College has more than 600 students actively taking courses online from a wide list of states and countries.

Delivery Media

All of the University College distance learning bachelor's degrees, master's degrees, and Certificates of Advanced Study can be taken entirely online. A wide array of learning techniques is used to help students develop their knowledge, understanding, and problem-solving skills. University College has an entire team dedicated to utilizing emerging technologies and understanding individualized learning styles to enhance the educational experience. University College uses eCollege® as its courseware management tool. The system is interactive, allows students to work collaboratively in lively discussion boards and chat rooms, and promotes the exchange of ideas and the development of a learning community. This interaction includes extensive communication with faculty members over the Internet, virtual teams, individual and group assignments, online projects, and online papers and connects students to experts from around the world.

Programs of Study

The University College online programs offer master's degrees in ten different program areas and more than thirty graduate Certificates of Advanced Study. There are no on-campus requirements for any of the distance learning programs. The on-campus and online master's degree programs require 48 credit hours of study to be completed in five years or less. Typically, a program can be completed in less than two years. Certificates are 24 quarter credit hours and typically take twelve to eighteen months to complete. A bachelor's degree is required for a certificate, and certificate course credits may be applied toward a master's degree.

Professionals with at least one year of transferable undergraduate credits can now complete their degrees online and earn a Bachelor of Arts in communication arts, global studies, leadership and organization studies, public policy and social services, or science and technology in a program that provides a dynamic new experience. Designed with the input of business and civic leaders, the program focuses on developing the talents needed for success in the information age: effective communication, problem solving, creative thinking, multi-tasking, decision making, technology utilization, and teamwork. These talents are approached from an interdisciplinary perspective, providing the most balanced and well-rounded experience possible.

The Applied Communication master's degree program is designed to teach the real-time and practical knowledge and skills that provide the specific industry expertise required for career success in a wide range of communication professions. The program's curriculum emphasizes a balance of theory, principles, and practice combined with professional experience to generate focused outcomes that are not offered in generic communication degree programs. Concentrations are available online in alternative dispute resolution, public relations and marketing, and training and development.

The Computer Information Systems program is designed for computer professionals as well as for those planning a new career in the computer industry. This flexible program keeps current with today's changing technology and how it relates to new technologies, existing systems, and customers' needs. In addition to the master's degree program, five online certificate programs of advanced study are offered: computer information systems, database administration, distributed object-oriented analysis and design, information systems security, and Web design and development technologies.

The Environmental Policy and Management program provides a seamlessly blended graduate education that emphasizes ethical management, science-based environmental policies, and professional applications of technical knowledge. Six certificate programs of advanced study are offered in environmental, health, and safety management; environmental information management; environmental management;

environmental policy; environmental project management; and natural resource management.

The Geographic Information Systems (GIS) program provides great job opportunities for those interested in managing physical facilities, providing services, analyzing markets, and managing information in public agencies or private organizations. The master's degree, designed in conjunction with DU's Department of Geography, allows students in the University College GIS certificate program to transfer up to 24 quarter hours from their certificate. The certificate program, also designed in conjunction with the DU's Department of Geography, offers working professionals the opportunity to acquire the background information and hands-on-expertise necessary to capitalize on the emerging technology.

The Human Resource Administration program offers a Master of Professional Studies (M.P.S.) in human resource administration. It provides a comprehensive examination of the HR profession and positions graduates for career advancement in a variety of organizational settings that include business, government, and not-for-profit organizations.

University of Denver University College, in collaboration with the Library and Information Science Program in the College of Education, now offers the Master's of Applied Science in knowledge and information technologies. This program is the first of its kind in the Rocky Mountain region. An engaging learning environment filled with professionals who value their educational experience ensures the development of effective critical and creative thinking, strategic and tactical decision making, and global awareness. Degree tracks are available in computer information systems, geographic information systems, and technology management.

The Organizational Leadership program is a flexible management and leadership degree presenting both the analytic and interpersonal skills necessary to be an effective manager in a variety of enterprises. The degree is structured around a core of management and leadership courses. Students select from a wide range of specializations, such as project management, leadership, alternative dispute resolution, environmental policy and management, telecommunications, computer information systems, and others. Most of the concentrations offered in other University College degrees are potential concentrations in the M.P.S.

The Security Management degree is designed for business and organizational security management professionals. The program provides students with the latest skills for effectively leading and managing security operations and addressing personnel, property, facility, information, and business-continuity security. The program provides the management skills and technical knowledge required to function as a chief security officer, director of loss prevention, director of security, security consultant, investigator, firefighter, or police officer.

The Technology Management program is designed for those who understand the power of leveraging technology in business to create their own competitive advantage. Career opportunities are limitless for those who can create, manage, and use emerging technology. In addition, five certificate programs of advanced study are offered in international markets, leadership, project management, research and development management, and twenty-first century strategic management.

The Telecommunications program fosters an integration of telecommunications technologies and effective management. In an industry driven by new technology, new applications, and an increasing demand for services, professionals need to maintain a current understanding of fundamental issues surrounding those technologies and the regulations which govern them. The telecommunications offerings at University College are designed to help students keep abreast of changes and take advantage of the opportunities change offers. Certificate programs of advanced study are offered in four areas: broadband, telecommunications management, telecommunications technology, and wireless networks.

Student Services

University College is dedicated to providing complete student services online. This includes admissions, registration, student advising, online resources through the library, access to the bookstore, and an individualized career counselor. There is a complete support team for technical issues as well as student support and training for eCollege.

Credit Options

Students may be able to transfer credit earned at other accredited graduate colleges and universities. The credit hours for the certificates may apply toward the related master's degree.

Faculty

University College has 300 faculty members, all with advanced degrees, who are practicing professionals in the areas in which they teach. At any given time there are 20 to 30 faculty members teaching online. University College engages in advanced and continual training for its faculty members in the methods and application of distance learning.

Admission

Entrance examinations are not required. Students who are applying for admission to the master's degree programs must have a bachelor's degree from a regionally accredited institution and a minimum 3.0 undergraduate GPA. Applicants must also submit an essay, a career goal statement, and letters of recommendation.

Tuition and Fees

Tuition is $359 per credit hour for on-campus classes and $393 per credit hour for online classes. There is also a technology fee of $4 per credit hour.

Financial Aid

Some financial aid programs are available to assist University College students. The University of Denver's Office of Student Financial Services handles all financial aid applications (http://www.du.edu/sfs/).

Applying

To apply for admission to University College, students must complete a full application, including a degree plan. Registration is available on the University College Web site at http://www.universitycollege.du.edu/registernow/registerinstructions.asp# online. For more information or an application, students should visit the University College Web site.

CONTACT

Enrollment Manager
University College
University of Denver
2211 South Josephine
Denver, Colorado 80208
Phone: 303-871-3315
     800-347-2042 (toll-free)
Fax: 303-871-3070
E-mail: ucolinfo@du.edu
Web site: http://www.university
    college.du.cdu

UNIVERSITY OF FLORIDA

College of Engineering UF EDGE
(Electronic Delivery of Graduate Engineering)
Gainesville, Florida

The University of Florida (UF) is a major, public, comprehensive, land-grant, research university. Founded in 1853, it is the state's oldest, largest, and most comprehensive university, and it is among the nation's most academically diverse public universities. With more than 48,000 students, Florida is now the fourth-largest university in the nation. Florida has a 2,000-acre campus and more than 900 buildings (including 170 with classrooms and laboratories). The northeast corner of the campus is listed as a Historic District on the National Register of Historic Places.

UF is accredited by the Southern Association of Colleges and Schools (SACS; 1866 Southern Lane, Decatur, Georgia 30033-4097; telephone: 404-679-4501), and the College of Engineering is accredited by ABET.

Distance Learning Program

The College of Engineering distance learning program, the UF EDGE, serves more than 250 graduate students. UF EDGE programs have been delivered to practicing engineers in Florida and throughout the world since 1982. Master of Science degrees are offered via streaming video. No campus attendance is required to complete the degree programs.

Delivery Media

Distance learning students are enrolled in classes that are given on the UF campus. The lectures are recorded and are available via streaming video at the close of business on that same day at the course's WebCT Vista course site. Distance learning students interact with their professors via phone, fax, e-mail, or the Internet. Many professors make course materials available to their students via course Web sites.

Programs of Study

The College of Engineering offers the following Master of Science (M.S.) degree programs via distance learning: civil engineering; computer engineering/computer science; computer engineering/computer science, with a bioinfor-

matics track; electrical and computer engineering, with a communications track; environmental engineering, with a specialization in water resources planning and management; environmental engineering, with a specialization in water, wastewater, and stormwater engineering; mechanical and aerospace engineering, with a specialization in fundamentals of thermal fluids transport; mechanical and aerospace engineering, with a specialization in solid mechanics; mechanical and aerospace engineering, with a specialization in dynamics and control; and material science engineering. The Master of Science degree requires 30 semester credit hours for completion, with a minimum 3.0 grade point average on a 4.0 scale. Distance learning students may meet the credit requirement entirely by course work.

Special Programs

The College of Engineering offers graduate certificate programs in the areas of environmental policy and management. Each certificate program requires the completion of three to five 3-semester-hour courses. The curricu-

lum consists of required courses and two or more electives chosen from a specified list.

Student Services

Library service is provided via remote access to all internal holdings and to several electronic databases through http://www.uflib.ufl.edu. Access is provided to currently registered students via a personal identification number and password for certain restricted databases.

Academic advising is provided through e-mail, fax, and telephone contact on a request basis. Distance learning students are also eligible to use the University's career placement services.

Credit Options

Students earn credit toward their degree by registering for and completing courses delivered via distance learning. Requirements for each course are the same as for on-campus students enrolled in the course.

Only graduate-level work to the extent of 9 semester credits, earned with a grade of A, B+, or B, may be transferred from an institution approved by the Graduate School or 15 semester credits from postbaccalaureate work at the University of Florida. Credits transferred from other universities are applied toward meeting the degree requirement, but the grades earned are not computed in the student's grade point average. Acceptance of transfer of credit requires approval from the student's department and the Dean of the Graduate School.

Faculty

There are 2,685 full-time faculty members at the University, with 319 in the College of Engineering. In the College of Engineering, 126 faculty members (39 percent) have taught in the distance learning program.

Admission

Admission decisions are made by the individual departments based on GRE or Fundamentals of Engineering (FE) score, GPA, and letters of reference.

Tuition and Fees

Tuition and fees for the 2005–06 academic year were $300 per credit hour for in-state students and $961 per credit hour for out-of-state students. Achievement awards, which provided a discounted tuition of $500 per credit hour up to 30 credit hours, were available for qualified out-of-state students. Costs are subject to change each year. Students must purchase their own textbooks.

Financial Aid

As a general rule, a graduate student must be enrolled half-time (at least 5 semester hours per term) as a regular student in a degree program and must be a United States citizen or an eligible non-U.S. citizen to qualify for federal and/or state financial aid. Specific information is available through the Office of Student Financial Affairs. Although students may apply for Federal Direct Stafford/Ford Loans throughout the year, they must observe the deadlines set each semester for applying for loans for the following semester and should always apply as early as possible. Many employers have programs that can help students pay for courses.

Applying

Application materials can be obtained from the school to which the student is applying. For specific program information, prospective students should visit http://www.admissions.ufl.edu/grad/gradegreeprograms.html#engineering. Application information is available online through http://www.admissions.ufl.edu/start.html. Official transcripts are required from all colleges or universities attended. Admission decisions are made by the individual departments.

CONTACT

UF EDGE Registrar
College of Engineering
E-117, CSE
University of Florida
P.O. Box 116100
Gainesville, Florida 32611-6100

Phone: 352-392-9670
E-mail: ufedge@ufl.edu
Web site: http://ufedge.eng.ufl.edu

UNIVERSITY OF MARYLAND, COLLEGE PARK

Online Studies

College Park, Maryland

The University of Maryland is the flagship institution among the University System of Maryland's eleven state public colleges and universities. Founded in 1856 as the original land-grant institution in Maryland, the University is the top public research institution in the mid-Atlantic region and one of the nation's best. Sixty-nine of its programs are ranked in the top twenty-five in the country, with fifty Maryland programs ranked in the top fifteen. The University of Maryland is accredited by the Middle States Association of Colleges and Schools and is a member of the Association of American Universities.

In 2000, the University of Maryland Office of Professional Studies introduced a University-wide online-learning strategy and launched its first program: Master of Life Sciences. The Web-based Master of Life Sciences is a content-rich, interdisciplinary program, with options in biology and chemistry, that focuses on the most current issues in modern science. Designed to enable practicing teachers to conveniently pursue an advanced degree, the program has attracted students worldwide. In 2007, the University launched an online graduate certificate in food safety risk analysis, one of a few food science programs in the country to include risk analysis in the curriculum.

Distance Learning Program

The University of Maryland is dedicated to increasing the visibility and reputation of its high-quality professional and graduate programs, measured not only by advances in research but also by innovations in the delivery of programs to a worldwide audience. The University's online studies program provides the platform for conveniently delivering educational solutions to students anywhere, at any time.

Delivery Media

Courses are delivered asynchronously through the Internet using a range of technologies, including chat rooms, threaded discussions, and links to campus libraries and academic resources. Faculty members are available in person, through e-mail, and by prescribed phone appointments.

Programs of Study

Online Studics at the University of Maryland offers three completely Web-based graduate programs: a 30-credit Master of Life Sciences, a 12-credit graduate certificate in food safety risk analysis, and a 12-credit graduate certificate in public health informatics.

Master of Life Sciences. The Master of Life Sciences provides in-depth knowledge of current research areas in the chemical, biological, biochemical, and biomedical sciences. Courses cover modern biology, modern molecular genetics, transmission genetics, human physiology, biodiversity and conservation biology, chemical ecology, principles of chemical biology, biochemistry, natural products chemistry, electrochemical cells, evolutionary biology and behavior, and experimental biology. Students may follow concentrations in chemistry or biology.

Graduate Certificate in Food Safety Risk Analysis. While risk analysis has been used for hundreds of years in the insurance industry and engineering fields, its application to food production and distribution is a recent phenomenon. In the past decade, federal agencies responsible for food safety have adopted risk analysis as the official

science-based paradigm for decision making. However, few food science academic programs include risk analysis in their curricula. The new graduate certificate of professional studies in food safety risk analysis from the University of Maryland is one of the few such programs in the United States.

Offered by the University of Maryland's Office of Professional Studies, in conjunction with the Department of Nutrition and Food Science and the Joint Institute for Food Safety and Applied Nutrition (JIFSAN), the graduate certificate can be completed entirely online in only one year. Through a series of four 10-week online courses, students will be instructed in the three basic components of risk analysis: risk management and risk communication.

Graduate Certificate in Public Health Informatics. The graduate certificate in public health informatics offers online, graduate-level courses in applied health informatics. The curriculum supports the emerging international movement toward evidence-based approaches to health information management, including evaluation and integration of health information systems for health data collection, analysis, and presentation. It familiarizes students with the most recent technologies and computer applications in public health education and practice. The course work provides students with a thorough understanding of the theory and practice of health informatics in the real world. Additionally, students are required to demonstrate the ability to use scientific and population health principles to evaluate and implement health information systems for their organizations. They learn how to use qualitative and quantitative methods for conducting health surveillance activities and enhancing public health preparedness, as well as use computer models to measure and present health outcomes. There is no research component required and the courses can be completed entirely online in 10 weeks. This intensive program has been approved to award continuing education contact hours (CECHs) to meet requirements for health educators who are certified health education specialists through the Society for Public Health Education (SOPHE). The credits earned may also meet the degree requirements for the M.P.H. and Ph.D. degrees.

Student Services

Through Single Point of Contact (SPOC), listed in the Contact section, students may inquire about the programs, apply for admission, register, pay their bills, and purchase textbooks. Students also have access to equipment and software specifications needed for successful completion of course work, online library resources, and technical support.

Faculty

The Master of Life Sciences program has 11 full-time University of Maryland faculty members with doctoral degrees. The graduate certificate in food safety risk analysis and the graduate certificate in public health informatics program are taught by faculty members with outstanding teaching and research credentials.

Admission

The Master of Life Sciences program requires an undergraduate degree in biological science, chemistry, biochemistry, or science education; one year of teaching experience or the equivalent; letters of recommendation from a school principal and a science supervisor; and successful completion of a gateway review class, LFSC510 Concepts of Modern Biology or LFSC520 Concepts of Modern Chemistry, or acceptable performance on an admission exam based on LFSC510 or LFSC520.

The graduate certificate in food safety risk analysis requires an earned bachelor's degree with a GPA of 3.0 or better from an accredited institution. Applicants with an undergraduate GPA of less than 3.0 may be admitted on a provisional basis if they have demonstrated satisfactory performance in another graduate program and/or salutary work experience.

The graduate certificate in public health informatics is open to qualified applicants with an earned bachelor's degree, GPA of 3.0 or better, from an accredited institution. Applicants with foreign credentials must submit academic records in the original language with literal English translations. Allow at least three months for evaluation.

Tuition and Fees

The Master of Life Sciences program costs $361 per credit hour, and there are a $60-per-term technology/distance learning fee and an admission exam fee of $20.

The graduate certificate in food safety risk analysis costs $600 per credit hour, and there is a $60-per-term technology/distance learning fee.

The graduate certificate in public health informatics costs $425 per credit hour. There is a $60-per-term technology/distance learning fee.

All tuition and fees are subject to change. All graduate students pay a one-time $60 application fee.

Financial Aid

Information regarding financial assistance may be obtained online at http://www.onlinestudies.umd.edu/financialaid.html.

CONTACT

Single Point of Contact (SPOC)
Mitchell Building, First Floor
University of Maryland
College Park, Maryland 20742-5231

Phone: 301-314-3572
          877-989-SPOC (toll-free)
Fax: 301-314-1282
E-mail: onlinestudies@umd.edu
Web site: http://www.onlinestudies.umd.edu

UNIVERSITY
OF MINNESOTA

UNIVERSITY OF MINNESOTA, TWIN CITIES CAMPUS

Independent and Distance Learning,
College of Continuing Education

Saint Paul, Minnesota

The University of Minnesota, with its four campuses, is one of the most comprehensive universities in the United States and ranks among the most prestigious. It is both a land-grant university with a strong tradition of education and public service and a major research institution. It was founded as a preparatory school in 1851 and was reorganized as a university in 1869, benefiting from the Morrill (or Land-Grant) Act of 1862.

The University of Minnesota has campuses in the Twin Cities (Minneapolis and St. Paul), Duluth, Morris, and Crookston, Minnesota. The Twin Cities campus, home of the College of Continuing Education, is a classic Big Ten campus with comprehensive academic programs offering unlimited opportunities for students and faculty.

Distance Learning Program

Independent and Distance Learning (IDL) offers outstanding University credit courses using mail and electronic technologies. In a recent year, the department received approximately 5,500 registrations from students throughout the United States and abroad. The 180 courses are fully accredited each year by approximately sixty different academic departments in fifteen colleges at the University. IDL is part of the College of Continuing Education (CCE), the division of the University of Minnesota that serves adult and part-time learners.

Delivery Media

Most courses are self-paced and available as printed packets by mail and assignment exchange via e-mail and postal mail with faculty members. Many faculty members provide the option of e-mail for lesson exchange. The program is adding more and more online courses that are fully interactive. Many of the online courses are one semester (fifteen weeks) in length, with some, nine months in length. All students who register for college credit with Independent and Distance Learning receive an e-mail and Internet account.

Programs of Study

Approximately 180 credit courses are offered in such varied subjects as applied business, child psychology, ecology, English literature and writing courses, foreign languages, management, math, and physics. Most courses are at the undergraduate level. Independent and Distance Learning courses are known for their high academic quality and variety of topics. No bachelor's degrees can be completed entirely through IDL. There is one professional master's degree available in paper science and engineering. There are two upper-level undergraduate certificates available online: applied business and paper science and engineering.

Student Services

The Continuing Education Information Center helps with finding information about specific courses, how to register, academic advising, and financial aid.

University of Minnesota libraries fully support distance learners with reference services, research assistance, and home delivery of documents.

If students have a disability, Independent and Distance Learning coordinates efforts to provide accommodations that remove academic and physical barriers

to earning credits. Such accommodations may include more time to complete exams or an alternate format for an exam, a separate testing room, audiotaping required materials, and taped rather than written comments from an instructor. Requests for such accommodations should be made well in advance of when they are needed so that necessary documentation may be obtained and accommodations facilitated.

Faculty

IDL has more than 100 faculty members. Approximately 40 percent are University of Minnesota professors, 30 percent are graduate student teaching assistants, and 30 percent are adjunct faculty members, lecturers, or others. All instructors hold advanced degrees.

Admission

For individual courses, no application is needed, and there are no admission requirements to register. Students who want to earn a certificate in applied business or paper science and engineering should go online to http://www.cce.umn.edu/certificates.

Tuition and Fees

Students who are not admitted to University of Minnesota certificate or degree programs qualify for in-state tuition rates, regardless of location of their residence. Tuition for 2007–08 is $305.77 per undergraduate semester credit. A University-wide fee of $50 per credit is assessed. An administrative fee of up to $247.50 per semester is assessed. Texts and other materials are purchased separately from the University of Minnesota bookstore.

Financial Aid

Financial aid is limited. Eligibility requirements may vary, but most aid programs place restrictions on some types of IDL enrollment and require admission to a University of Minnesota, Twin Cities, degree program or eligible certificate program. Non-admitted students who reside in Minnesota may be eligible for College of Continuing Education grants or scholarships, which have more flexible eligibility criteria. Employer assistance may also be an option for some students.

Applying

No application is needed to register in individual courses. For most courses, students can register any day of the year and have nine months to complete. For information about applying for the online certificate programs in applied business or paper science and engineering, students can visit the Web site at http://www.cce.umn.edu/certificates.

CONTACT

College of Continuing Education Information Center
20 Classroom Office Building
University of Minnesota
1994 Buford Avenue
Saint Paul, Minnesota 55108

Phone: 612-624-4000
        800-234-6564 (toll-free)
Fax: 612-625-1511
E-mail: cceinfo@cce.umn.edu
Web site: http://www.cce.umn.edu/petersons

THE UNIVERSITY OF MONTANA-MISSOULA

Continuing Education, Educational Outreach

Missoula, Montana

The University of Montana–Missoula (UM-M), the main campus of The University of Montana System, founded in 1893, is a midsize, state-supported university located in Missoula, Montana, a small city of about 65,000 people located in the Rocky Mountain West. Approximately 10,500 undergraduate and 1,250 graduate students are enrolled, some of whom are taking courses through distance programs. UM-M is a Carnegie doctoral level–intensive university offering a variety of undergraduate and graduate degree programs through centers of excellence in its colleges and professional schools: Arts and Sciences, Business Administration, Education, Fine Arts, Forestry, Health Professions and Biomedical Sciences, Journalism, Law, and Technology. The University of Montana–Missoula is governed by the Montana University System Board of Regents and accredited by the Northwest Association of Schools and Colleges (professional schools and departments are approved by specialized accrediting organizations). The University of Montana–Missoula ranks seventeenth in the nation and fifth among public universities in producing Rhodes scholars.

Distance Learning Program

For students who live throughout Montana, across the United States, or around the world or for students who are unable to attend class during the traditional school day, academic departments at The University of Montana team with Continuing Education to offer individual online courses, online certificate programs, and degree programs both fully online or through a combination of traditional classrooms and videoconferencing.

UMOnline is The University of Montana–Missoula's online teaching and learning environment. More than 200 unique online courses have been offered. The mix of courses changes regularly, so students should check the UMOnline Web site at http://muonline.umt.edu for the current offerings. Courses are open to qualified, regularly admitted UM students. Non-degree students are welcome. Students are advised to consult The University of Montana undergraduate and graduate catalogs for complete program details and admission requirements.

Programs of Study

Seven fully online programs of study are offered: M.B.A. Foundation (graduate-level preparation courses for the M.B.A.), Master of Education in curriculum studies, Master of Education in educational leadership, Master of Public Administration, library media endorsement, certificate in customer relations, and certificate in forensic sciences.

Three additional programs of study are offered by The University of Montana. The Master of Music in music education is offered online during autumn and spring semesters and on the UM campus during summer semester, with some courses to be arranged. The Off-Campus M.B.A. Program is a dynamic evening program delivered via interactive-video-systems sites in Montana, including Billings, Bozeman, Butte, Dillon, Helena, Kalispell, and Missoula. The Doctor of Education in educational leadership is available as a cohort model and is delivered through a blend of traditional classroom, video conferencing, and online instruction.

Student Services

Students enjoy access to a wide variety of services, including financial aid, admission, registration, career planning, and placement. The Mansfield Library provides special services to distance students, such as round-the-clock chat reference help; access to digital journals, books, and other resources; and delivery of books, photocopies, and other materials right to the student's doorstep or via e-mail.

Credit Options

Courses are offered for undergraduate and graduate academic credit.

Faculty

Courses are developed and taught by University of Montana faculty members.

Admission

Courses and programs are available to qualified, regularly admitted UM students. For online admission, students should visit http://umonline.umt.edu/StudentInfo/. Students applying to an advanced degree program should contact the academic coordinator for individual degree programs listed at http://www.umt.edu/ce/deo/external/Default.asp.

Tuition and Fees

Students taking only online courses may choose to enroll as "distance students" and pay reduced fees. Distance students are not eligible for UM health insurance, Curry Health Center services, athletic event ticket discounts, or campus recreation. Students must waive the health service/insurance option prior to registering for classes. In addition, students enrolled in this status are eligible to enroll only in online/ Internet courses. Information about tuition is available at http://cyberbear. umt.edu (select: tuition/fee costs).

Financial Aid

Students receiving any form of financial assistance are advised to check with the UM Financial Aid Office to determine coverage. Students can find more information at http://www. umt.edu/finaid/.

CONTACT

Educational Outreach, Continuing Education
The University of Montana–Missoula
Missoula, Montana 59812

Phone: 406-243-2900
E-mail: outreach@umontana.edu
Web site: http://www.montanaeducation.com

UNIVERSITY OF NEVADA, LAS VEGAS

Distance Education

Las Vegas, Nevada

The University of Nevada, Las Vegas (UNLV), has grown dramatically since its founding in 1957 and now enrolls more than 26,000 students. The campus is on 333 acres in urban Las Vegas, in a metropolitan area of more than 1.5 million. The University concentrates its resources on instructional and research programs that are student centered but responsive to the needs of the local, regional, national, and international communities. In addition to its educational offerings, the University plays a vital role in the economic development of the community and assumes a major role in identifying and solving many of the region's social and environmental problems. UNLV offers stimulating intellectual activities, diverse cultural and arts experiences, and exciting athletic competition, all of which invite community participation.

All programs are fully accredited by the Northwest Commission on Colleges and Universities. The University is a member of the American Association of State Colleges and Universities, the Council of Graduate Schools, the Western Association of Graduate Schools, the American Council on Education, and the Western College Association.

Distance Learning Program

Distance education (DE) at UNLV was started in 1996 to develop and deliver educational programs to southern Nevada's rapidly growing communities and as a result of Nevada's prior commitment to extended education and UNLV's desire to respond to community needs. Over time, an electronic network emerged, and online learning became a part of many of the regular course offerings.

The mission of the Office of Distance Education is to provide learning opportunities that are less restricted by time and place than are on-campus UNLV courses and programs. Through its network of distance education professionals, who use the latest in educational technology, students may work toward a college degree, enhance their professional standing, or enrich their understanding of the world. The office increases educational access for students unable to attend classes on campus, fully uses the resources of the University, and improves instruction by integrating technology into the curriculum. Distance education offers off-campus students the chance to complete their degrees in their own homes or at other computer-accessible locations.

There are currently more than 21,000 distance education students. UNLV's 86 percent retention rate is far above the national average of about 50 percent.

Delivery Media

Students need access to a computer capable of using Internet Explorer 6.0 or above to access the Internet. Las Vegas students without Internet access at home may use any one of UNLV's computer labs. All DE courses use online delivery, and 99 percent use streaming video, both of which are captioned. Lectures can be watched online with the free RealPlayer plug-in.

Programs of Study

The University of Nevada, Las Vegas, offers a Bachelor of Arts (B.A.) in social science studies degree tailored to students seeking a wide range of knowledge applicable to a variety of careers. An interdisciplinary degree, it is designed to develop lifelong skills in critical and creative thinking, problem solving, effective communication, and intercultural understanding through an individualized course of study. Students acquire a broad, interdisciplinary understanding of many of the central issues addressed by research in the social sciences. They develop a critical awareness of the different methodologies used to answer questions about society, social interaction, and human subjectivity. Major areas of concentration in the social science program include anthropology, history, political science, and psychology. This program is intended primarily for students who have completed, or nearly completed, the equivalent of the first two years of college and are unable to complete a degree because they cannot attend classes on campus.

In 2005, UNLV began offering a Ph.D. in nursing education completely online through distance education. A highly competitive Master of Hospitality Administration is also offered through DE. Additional degrees are planned; students should check the UNLV DE Web site for the latest information.

UNLV offers more than 100 undergraduate and more than forty graduate classes online. Students should check the Web site to see which courses are available in a given semester.

Student Services

Support is available in a number of ways to students who are enrolled in distance classes. From student labs to online and telephone support, help is always available. The Student Computing Support Center is the central source of information for distance education course registration (except course listings) and all student WebCampus information.

Leid Library makes every effort to ensure that off-campus students have access to all online electronic services provided to on-campus students, including the availability of databases, tutorials, and Internet links offered through the library Web site, as well as an expanding array of full-text information, reference by e-mail, and instructional assistance. Students can, if necessary, arrange to come to the campus to use the library at any time during its open hours (105 hours per week). Interlibrary loan and document-delivery services can be easily arranged. In addition, the library has classroom space designed to accommodate the instructional needs of the distance learner.

Credit Options
Most distance education courses, both undergraduate and graduate, are 3 credits. Those enrolling in the bachelor's degree in social science studies program should have the equivalent of about two years of college work completed.

Faculty
Many of the University's faculty members teach distance education courses. UNLV is committed to staffing the program with full-time tenure-track faculty members, and there are also some tenure-track faculty members from collaborating universities. Part-time faculty members can participate only if they have previously taught on campus. Of the University's 850 faculty members, 54 percent are full-time. Professors bring degrees and teaching experience from leading universities around the world. Faculty members are involved in important research for government and public service agencies and for scholarly books and journals, and many have won major awards.

Admission
Information on admission to the bachelor's degree program is available from the Office of Distance Education.

Tuition and Fees
Tuition for Nevada residents is $113 per credit for undergraduate courses and $151 per credit for graduate courses, which includes the $15 per credit DE fee. In addition to these costs, nonresidents must pay $136.50 per credit for 6 or fewer credits ($4734 per semester for 7 or more credits) for undergraduate classes and $150 per credit for 6 or fewer credits ($4734 per semester for 7 or more credits) for graduate work. Out-of-state students should contact the Office of Distance Education to find out about special tuition rates. Fees vary.

Financial Aid
UNLV offers more than $70 million each year to students who apply for scholarships, grants, student loans, part-time work, or veterans' benefits. Funds come from federal, state, and private sources. Financial assistance can be used to help cover the costs of registration, fees, tuition, and books. To apply for federal, state, and institutional financial aid, students must complete the Free Application for Federal Student Aid (FAFSA).

Applying
Students already enrolled at UNLV can register for classes online. Other students must first fill out a non-admitted student information form, which lets them use UNLV's registration system. Nevada residents must also fill out a residency form. More information is available from the Distance Education Office.

CONTACT

Barbara Trumble
Program Manager of Distance Education
University of Nevada, Las Vegas
4505 Maryland Parkway, Box 451038
Las Vegas, Nevada 89154

Phone: 702-895-2918 or 0334
Fax: 702-895-3647
E-mail: barbara.trumble@unlv.edu
Web site: http://distance-ed.unlv.edu

THE UNIVERSITY OF NORTH CAROLINA AT CHAPEL HILL
The William and Ida Friday Center for Continuing Education
Chapel Hill, North Carolina

As the nation's first state university, the University of North Carolina (UNC) at Chapel Hill was chartered in 1789 and opened to students in 1795. UNC–Chapel Hill was the only public university to award degrees to students in the eighteenth century. Today, there are more than 3,100 faculty members and 27,000 students at UNC. Carolina's academic offerings span a broad range of fields, including seventy-one bachelor's, 110 master's, and seventy-seven doctoral degree programs as well as professional degrees in dentistry, medicine, pharmacy, and law. Distance learning has been available since 1913. The University is accredited by the Southern Association of Colleges and Schools.

Distance Learning Program

The Friday Center for Continuing Education offers a variety of credit programs for part-time students. Carolina Courses Online and Self-paced Courses are college-level distance courses that enable students to earn college credit without having to be admitted to UNC or travel to the campus. The Friday Center administers courses from eight institutions of the University of North Carolina: Appalachian State University, East Carolina University, Elizabeth City State University, North Carolina State University, UNC–Chapel Hill, UNC–Greensboro, Western Carolina University, and Winston-Salem State University. Approximately 5,000 students enroll in distance education courses through the Friday Center each year.

Delivery Media

The Self-paced Courses program offers correspondence and online courses. Students enrolled in print-based Self-paced Courses receive a printed course manual that contains all lessons, assignments, and instructions. Students enrolled in online Self-paced Courses receive information on how to access the Web pages containing this information.

Students work through the course at their own pace. Each course has an instructor who grades assignments and answers questions. The minimum completion time for a Self-paced Course is twelve weeks, and students have nine months to complete the course. Students may take two courses at a time. More than 140 Self-paced Courses are available, and most courses are offered for credit at the undergraduate college level.

The Carolina Courses Online program follows the UNC calendar. Students enrolled in a Carolina Courses Online course receive information on how to access the Web pages that contain all lessons, assignments, and instructions. They communicate with classmates and their instructor via e-mail and discussion forums and are encouraged to use the vast resources available through the Internet as they complete their course work. More than seventy Carolina Courses Online courses are available, and most courses are offered for credit at the undergraduate college level.

Programs of Study

The Friday Center offers a variety of courses in more than thirty subjects, including accounting, African and Afro-American studies, art, biology, business, chemistry, classics, criminal justice, communication studies, drama, economics, education, English, environmental sciences, French, geography, geology, history, hospitality management, Italian, journalism, Latin, law, mathematics, music, nursing, nutrition, philosophy, physics, political science, psychology, recreation administration, religious studies, Russian, sociology, Spanish, and statistics. Credit earned in courses offered through the Friday Center can be applied toward degree requirements at UNC–Chapel Hill and other institutions.

Special Programs

Credit courses offered by the Friday Center may be used for teacher license renewal at the discretion of the local district. Students should visit the Friday Center Web site listed in the Contact section for more information.

Student Services

Friday Center staff members are available to answer questions, provide academic advising, and process enrollments. Online library services are available through the UNC–Chapel Hill library system.

Credit Options

Most courses are offered for credit at the undergraduate college level. Credit earned in these courses may be applied toward a degree, if the course is applicable to the requirements of the particular degree program.

Faculty

Faculty members are appointed by the department or school offering the course. Approximately 120 faculty members teach in the program at any given time.

Admission

Carolina Courses Online and Self-paced Courses are open to anyone who wishes to enroll; there are no admission requirements.

Tuition and Fees

Tuition must be paid in full at the time of enrollment. The 2007 tuition and fees are $126 per credit hour for North Carolina residents and $259 per credit hour for nonresidents. Most courses are 3 credit hours. Tuition and other charges are subject to change without notice. Textbooks must be purchased separately.

Financial Aid

Financial aid may be available through VA benefits, vocational rehabilitation grants, local education agencies, and Defense Activity for Non-Traditional Education Support (DANTES).

Applying

Enrollments in Self-paced Courses are accepted at any time by mail, fax, in person, or online. Carolina Courses Online enrollments must be received by specified deadlines. Students should visit the Friday Center Web site for more information.

CONTACT

Student Services Manager
CB #1020
University of North Carolina at Chapel Hill
Chapel Hill, North Carolina 27599-1020

Phone: 919-962-1134
       800-862-5669 (toll-free)
Fax: 919-962-5549
E-mail: ceinfo@unc.edu
Web site: http://fridaycenter.unc.edu

OU The University of Oklahoma
OUTREACH

THE UNIVERSITY OF OKLAHOMA

University Outreach
College of Continuing Education
College of Liberal Studies
Norman, Oklahoma

The University of Oklahoma's (OU) College of Continuing Education (CCE) is a lifelong learning organization dedicated to helping individuals, businesses, groups, and communities transform themselves through knowledge. Formally organized in 1913, CCE is the outreach arm of the University of Oklahoma. Nationally recognized for its pioneering efforts in continuing education, CCE extends the educational resources of the University through more than thirty different program formats, including undergraduate and graduate degree programs, correspondence and other distance programs, and on- and off-campus courses as well as through a wide variety of programs conducted under the auspices of federal and state grants and contracts. On the Norman campus, adult and other learners attend programs at the Oklahoma Center for Continuing Education, one of eleven W. K. Kellogg Foundation–funded, University-based residential conference centers in the world. Annually, CCE offers some 2,000 courses and activities to more than 250,000 nontraditional learners in Oklahoma and in locations all over the world.

The mission of the College of Liberal Studies is to provide the highest-quality interdisciplinary education to nontraditional undergraduate and graduate students through innovative delivery formats. By combining independent study with weekend classes or brief seminars on campus or Internet-guided study, adult students can earn a Bachelor of Liberal Studies or Master of Liberal Studies degree. The College of Liberal Studies is a fully accredited, academic division of the University of Oklahoma.

Distance Learning Program

In carrying out its mission to help nontraditional learners transform themselves through knowledge, CCE offers a variety of credit and noncredit distance learning courses and programs within the state of Oklahoma and beyond. Each year, CCE extends the educational resources of the University of Oklahoma through more than thirty different program formats. Annually, CCE offers some 2,000 courses and activities to more than 250,000 nontraditional learners in Oklahoma and worldwide.

Delivery Media

Courses are delivered via television, videotapes, videoconferencing, interactive television, audiotapes, audioconferencing, computer software, CD-ROM, computer conferencing, World Wide Web, e-mail, and print. Students and faculty members may meet in person or interact via videoconferencing, audio-conferencing, mail, telephone, fax, e-mail, interactive television, or World Wide Web. The following equipment may be required: audiocassette player, fax machine, television, cable television, videocassette player, computer, modem, Internet access, e-mail, and CD-ROM.

Programs of Study

A variety of programs are available in various distance formats. Independent study courses (credit and noncredit)—some of which are offered online—are available in the following subjects: anthropology, astronomy, business administration, business communication, chemistry, Chinese, classical culture, communication, drama, economics, education, engineering, English, finance, French, geography, geology, German, Greek, health and sport sciences, history, human relations, journalism and mass communication, Latin, library and information studies, management, marketing, mathematics, modern languages, music, philosophy, political science, psychology, Russian, sociology, and Spanish. Master's degree programs in the following areas are presented on-site at military and civilian locations around the world: communication, economics, human relations (including a human resource development emphasis and a community services emphasis), public administration, and social work. In addition, a doctorate in organizational leadership is available at some overseas sites. (These programs combine on-site course delivery with online and correspondence study.) In addition, students in Oklahoma have access to telecourses and OneNet courses.

Special Programs

CCE offers a number of distance learning special programs. Among these are the DHS/SATTRN (Satellite Training Network) programs held for Oklahoma Department of Human Services and other state employees. CCE's Independent Study Department works closely with the DANTES program and the Navy College PACE program. In addition, this department offers a number of noncredit writing courses and more than seventy-five high school courses, many of them available online.

Student Services

Students enrolled in CCE's Advanced Programs have access to the facilities and resources of OU's Norman-based library. Advanced Programs students order all their textbooks online through Follett, and Independent Study offers students a complete array of bookstore services.

Credit Options

CCE's Independent Study Department provides students various options to earn credit through testing. Among these are the College-Level Examination Program (CLEP), DANTES, and institutionally developed advanced-standing examinations.

Faculty

The faculty for distance programs includes regular University of Oklahoma faculty members, adjunct faculty members, and instructors with special appointments. All are experienced and highly qualified instructional professionals who are knowledgeable about the needs, concerns, and capabilities of distance education students.

Admission

Admission to the University of Oklahoma is necessary for credit courses other than those offered through Independent Study. Independent Study students need not be first admitted to OU. To participate in graduate programs, admission to OU's Graduate College is required. For more information, prospective students should use the information listed in the Contact section.

Tuition and Fees

Tuition and fees vary based on the chosen program. Prospective students are encouraged to inquire about the costs associated with the program in which they are interested. Expenses relating to continuing education courses taken to maintain and improve professional skills may be tax deductible (Treas. Reg. 1.162-5, Coughlin v. Commissioner, 203f.2d 307). A tax adviser can make this determination based on the particular facts relating to one's professional situation. All tuition and fees at the University of Oklahoma are subject to changes made by the State Regents for Higher Education.

Financial Aid

Financial aid is available for many of the semester-based programs offered through CCE. Financial aid is not available to Independent Study students. Each program has different eligibility requirements. Interested students are encouraged to use the contact information below. They will then be put in touch with the appropriate CCE department that can fully answer their financial aid questions.

Applying

Distance learners interested in credit and noncredit programs may enroll by telephone (800-522-0772 Ext. 2248) or by fax (405-325-7164). Prospective students should use the contact information below to determine the appropriate telephone number.

CONTACT

Larry Hayes
College of Continuing Education
The University of Oklahoma
1700 Asp Avenue
Norman, Oklahoma 73072-6400

Phone: 405-325-4414
Fax: 405-325-7196
E-mail: lhayes@ou.edu
Web site: http://www.outreach.ou.edu

UNIVERSITY OF PHOENIX
Online Campus
Phoenix, Arizona

Founded in 1976, University of Phoenix is the largest private university in North America dedicated to meeting the needs of working students. The University is accredited by the Higher Learning Commission and is a member of the North Central Association (312-263-0456; http://www.ncahigherlearningcommission. org). University of Phoenix serves thousands of students every year with more than 20,000 highly qualified instructors at more than 190 campuses and learning centers and through Internet delivery worldwide.

High academic standards, commitment to quality, and programs designed specifically to address the needs of today's marketplace have earned University of Phoenix a reputation for leadership in both the academic and business communities. A distinguishing blend of proven academic models and innovative instructional delivery systems, combined with a focus on excellent service to students, has pioneered the University's phenomenal growth. The mission of University of Phoenix is to provide access to higher education opportunities that enable students to develop the knowledge and skills necessary to achieve their professional goals, improve the productivity of their organizations, and provide leadership and service to their communities. In fact, University of Phoenix has helped thousands of students achieve the higher education they need to achieve higher success.

Distance Learning Program

The online learning format utilizes computer communications to link faculty members and students from around the world into interactive forums. Class size is limited to 20 for maximum interaction. Course work is completed entirely online for the convenience of working students who find it difficult or impossible to attend classes at fixed times and places.

Delivery Media

Once enrolled in an online degree program, students are required to log on at least four days each week to participate in class discussions focused on the topics they are studying. All interaction among students and instructors is completed through e-mails and online forums, while assignments are completed offline. This balance of both online and offline interaction is referred to as asynchronous communication.

Programs of Study

The Bachelor of Science (B.S.) and Bachelor of Science in Business (B.S.B.) degree programs require 120 credits (124 in Kansas) for degree completion. The Associate of Arts (A.A.) degree consists of 60 credits and has a specialization in general studies.

The Bachelor of Science (B.S.) degree programs feature specializations in criminal justice administration, elementary education (Arizona residents only), health administration, health administration/health information systems, health administration/long-term care, human services management, information technology, information technology/visual communication, management, nursing, and organizational security and management.

The Bachelor of Science in Business (B.S.B.) degree programs feature specializations in accounting, administration, communications, e-Business, finance, global business management, hospitality management, information systems, integrated supply chain and operations management, management, marketing, public administration, and retail management.

The Master of Arts in Education (M.A.Ed.) degree programs consist of a number of specializations and vary in the number of credit hours required. The specializations are administration and supervision, curriculum and instruction, curriculum and Instruction/adult education, curriculum and instruction/ESL, early childhood education, elementary education, secondary education, and special education.

The Master of Business Administration (M.B.A.) degree program features specializations consisting of varying credit hours. In addition to the M.B.A., the following specializations are available: accounting, global management, health care management, human resources management, marketing, and technology management.

The Master of Health Administration (M.H.A.) degree program prepares leaders who can effectively respond to the dynamic and ever-changing health-care industry.

The Master of Information Systems (M.I.S.) degree focuses on technology theory and its application in real-world business opportunities and challenges.

The Master of Management (M.M.) degree features specializations in human resource management and public administration management. Credit hours can vary between the M.M. degree and the M.M. degree with the specialization.

Master of Science in Nursing (M.S.N.) degree programs feature a number of specializations. In addition, bridge programs are available for students who hold a degree in another subject other than nursing. The specializations include nursing/health-care education, integrative health care, M.B.A./health-care management, and Master of Health Administration.

Doctoral degree programs are available with a number of specializations. They include the following: Doctor of Business Administration, Doctor of Education in Educational Leadership, Doctor of Education in Educational Leadership with a Specialization in Curriculum and Instruction, Doctor of Health Administration, Doctor of Management in Organizational Leadership, and Doctor of Management in Organizational Leadership with a Specialization in Information Systems.

For more information on the programs, including program descriptions, prospective students should visit the Web site at http://www.uopxonline.com/programs.asp.

Credit Options

Through the University of Phoenix's Prior Learning Assessment Center (PLAC) or through a number of national testing programs (such as CLEP, DANTES, and Excelsior) that test students for college-level knowledge, students may be able to earn a number of credits depending on University policy and individual program requirements.

Faculty

All faculty members have both academic credentials and demonstrated success in the fields they teach. The University recruits only those who are working in their area of expertise—bringing practical, real-world experience to the students they teach. In addition, all faculty members undergo extensive training in online instruction, and all participate in periodic evaluations that include a peer-review component.

Admission

For graduate applicants, an undergraduate degree from a regionally accredited college or university, with a minimum cumulative GPA of 2.5 (3.0 for prior graduate work) is required. Students must also be currently employed or have access to an organization where they can apply concepts they have learned. Undergraduate applicants must have a high school diploma or its equivalent, be at least 18 years old, and be currently employed or have access to an organizational environment. Students must complete the University-proctored Comprehensive Cognitive Assessment.

For international applicants and those whose primary language is not English, a minimum score of 213 on the computer-based TOEFL; 750 on the TOEIC; 6.5 on the IELTS; or 550 on the Berlitz Online English Proficiency Exam within the last two years is required.

Admission requirements may vary depending on state and program requirements. Prospective students should contact the University for a complete list of admission requirements.

Tuition and Fees

Graduate business tuition is $612 per credit; graduate nursing and graduate education tuition is $485 per credit. Undergraduate business tuition is $494 per credit; undergraduate nursing tuition is $430 per credit. Doctoral programs are $692 per credit. Additional costs include an application fee of $45 and a graduation fee of $65. A resource fee ($75 for undergraduate courses and $95 for graduate courses) is required to access online readings and texts. Textbook costs vary by course.

Applying

Unless students are relying on foreign transcripts for admission, all that is needed to begin the first course is to complete an application, enrollment agreement, and disclosure form. While students are in their first three classes, academic counselors work with them to complete transcript requests, the Comprehensive Cognitive Assessment, and any other items necessary for formal registration.

CONTACT

Enrollment Department
University of Phoenix Online
3157 East Elwood Street
Phoenix, Arizona 85034

Phone: 800-833-0287 (toll-free in the U.S.)
Fax: 602-387-6440
Web site: http://www.uopx.com/petersons

THE UNIVERSITY OF TEXAS SYSTEM
UT TeleCampus (UTTC)–Online Courses and Degrees
Austin, Texas

The University of Texas (UT) System offers online courses and degree programs via the award-winning UT TeleCampus (UTTC). The UT TeleCampus is the central support center for online learning within UT System institutions. Students can access virtual classrooms, links to University services and offices, a UT TeleCampus digital library, and many other service features. Launched in May 1998, the UT TeleCampus gives students the assurance of accredited universities, expert faculty members, and high-quality online education, along with the support services students need to succeed. The UT TeleCampus has received numerous national and regional awards since its development. All UT academic institutions participating in UT TeleCampus–based programs are Southern Association of Colleges and Schools (SACS) accredited. To learn more about online degrees or courses, prospective students should visit the UTTC Web site.

Distance Learning Program

UT TeleCampus–based programs and courses are composed of the same rigorous content found on-site at the UT System's fifteen institutions. From application to graduation, students face the same general expectations and receive the same high-quality courses on-site or online. Online courses follow a semester schedule, allowing flexibility during the week for study and participation in Web-based group discussions. An online syllabus maps out test and project deadlines.

The majority of the courses offered through the UT TeleCampus can be taken entirely online. Students can learn from anywhere in the world with access to the Internet.

Delivery Media

The UT TeleCampus uses Internet technologies for course delivery and student support via the World Wide Web. Courses may also utilize additional distance education tools, including CDs, audiotapes and videotapes, streaming video and audio, e-mail, discussion groups, and chat rooms.

Programs of Study

The UT TeleCampus offers online master's degrees, bachelor's degree-completion programs, and various graduate, undergraduate, and professional development courses and certificate programs.

The M.B.A. in general management is a 48-hour program that received the 2001 U.S. Distance Learning Association's Excellence in Distance Learning Programming award.

The Master of Public Administration is a 36-hour nonthesis program designed to provide students with the skills needed for effective public leadership.

The Master of Science in human resource development is a 36-hour nonthesis program that is ideal for corporate trainers, HR directors, and administrators in education as well as others with an interest in technology for human resource development. Certification programs in office education, trade and industrial, and health science technology are available with this degree plan.

Designed for individuals with significant ability in a science discipline as well as a serious commitment to teaching, the online Master of Arts in teaching science education prepares educators in research and pedagogy focused on science content.

Physical educators, athletics directors, wellness trainers, and coaches can earn their master's degree in kinesiology online from their choice of four UT institutions. This 36-hour program received the 2002 U.S. Distance Learning Association's Excellence in Distance Learning Programming award.

The 36-hour M.Ed. in educational technology is designed for teachers, technology coordinators, administrators, and corporate trainers who want to excel at integrating technology into their curriculum.

The 36-hour M.Ed. in curriculum and instruction with a literacy emphasis includes a Master Reading Teacher (MRT) certification program, a reading specialist certification program, and a four-course English as a second language (ESL) endorsement program. Certificate and endorsement course work can also be taken separately.

A bilingual Master of Fine Arts in creative writing program is offered to prepare writers for the publishing marketplace and teaching and editing careers in both the United States and Latin America.

A four-course superintendent certification program, UTOPS, prepares candidates for superintendent certification in Texas.

An alternative teacher certification program (ATCP) is available to individuals with bachelor's degrees in areas other than education who want to become fully certified teachers.

A postprofessional certificate program, Improved Training of Physical Therapists in Early Intervention Settings (IMPRINTS), prepares physical therapists to provide services to infants and toddlers with disabilities.

Online nursing programs include an RN-to-B.S.N. program, which offers the five required nursing courses for registered nurse students to complete their

B.S. in nursing degree, and a graduate certificate in nursing education, a three-course program designed for registered nurses who are interested in pursuing the role of a nurse educator.

A bachelor's degree–completion program in criminology and criminal justice is available entirely online. The program consists of 66 hours of upper-level course work.

A bachelor's-completion program in applied technology health services technology is offered for graduates of Associate of Applied Science degrees in the allied health and nursing fields.

Other areas of academic study include most general undergraduate curriculum required in Texas, an undergraduate track in management information systems, a chess in education program, a blood bank technology program, and border studies and border administration certificates.

Special Programs

The UT TeleCampus also facilitates the delivery of professional development training in a wide range of topics, including paralegal studies, blood bank technology, and border studies certificates. Interested students should visit the UTTC Web site and follow the links to Professional Development Online (PDO) to view the catalog.

Student Services

The UT TeleCampus was designed with the online student in mind. It provides all of the services students need to succeed, including technical support available 24/7, an extensive digital library, and free online academic support that provides students with tutorials and writing labs. In addition, department liaisons are available at each campus to aid online students with questions about the library, registration, financial aid, and veteran's affairs.

Credit Options

Transfer credit toward online courses and programs is generally the same as comparable on-site programs. Students should contact the program advisers listed on the UT TeleCampus Web site for specifics.

Faculty

The same expert faculty members who teach on-campus courses at the University of Texas campuses teach online academic courses offered through the UT TeleCampus. Courses are designed and developed by these faculty members, with production support and faculty development provided by the institutions and the UT TeleCampus.

Admission

Admission criteria and processes for online offerings are generally the same as on-site courses. It is advisable to start the initial application process at least ninety days prior to the beginning of a semester.

Tuition and Fees

The amount of tuition and fees charged by each UT System institution varies and is based on residency status. Students should access the UT TeleCampus Web site for links to campus tuition and fee information.

Financial Aid

Financial aid opportunities are available for students enrolled in UT TeleCampus courses.

Applying

Prospective students need to apply and be admitted to the UT System institution offering their course or degree program. Depending on the program of interest, different institutions participate.

CONTACT

Student Services
UT TeleCampus
The University of Texas System
702 Colorado Street, Suite 4.100
Austin, Texas 78701

Phone: 888-TEXAS-16 (toll-free)
Fax: 512-499-4715
E-mail: telecampus@utsystem.edu
Web site: http://www.telecampus.utsystem.edu

THE UNIVERSITY OF THE INCARNATE WORD

Universe Online

San Antonio, Texas

The University of the Incarnate Word (UIW) was founded in 1881 as an outgrowth of the original mission of the Sisters of Charity of the Incarnate Word, who settled in San Antonio, Texas, in 1869. The school maintains the mission of the founders by providing high-quality educational opportunities to all students, developing graduates who are concerned and enlightened citizens. UIW is accredited by a variety of regional and national associations but most notably by the regional accrediting body of the Commission on Colleges of the Southern Association of Colleges and Schools. Through its College of Professional Studies, UIW is nationally accredited by the Association of Collegiate Business Schools and Programs. Universe Online is accredited by the Association of Accredited Online Programs International.

Distance Learning Program

Universe Online is a natural extension of the mission and the entrepreneurial nature of UIW. By utilizing personal computers and asynchronous instruction, the program addresses the changing needs of adult learners. Maintaining the quality for which it is known, UIW allows students to complete a degree program totally online.

Delivery Media

Students accepted into the program use computer-conferencing software that allows for asynchronous interaction, in an eight-week-term format. Students interact throughout the week in both private and group discussions. Students are required to have an Internet service provider (ISP) to connect and upload/download assignments.

Programs of Study

Universe Online offers a variety of undergraduate degree programs and graduate programs.

Understanding the needs of the transfer student, UIW has developed a variety of degree programs that accept transfer credit and use it to complete the degree program. This allows students to finish faster and not lose credit for their past work.

The Bachelor of Arts in organizational development and the Bachelor of Arts in human resources combine courses that are relevant to today's business world and the specialty with the opportunity for students to include transfer work or a minor.

The Bachelor of Arts degree in applied science is designed for the person who has an associate degree in a specialized field or up to 60 credits in a concentration area. This degree then allows students to complete a professional sequence, giving them a tailored degree that will meet the needs of the business community using the student's specific skill set.

The Bachelor of Business Administration (B.B.A.) prepares the student for today's changing business climate. The required core and choice of specialization prepare students for positions of leadership in the business world. Areas of specialization include accounting, information systems, international business, management, and marketing.

The Master of Business Administration (M.B.A.) degree program seeks to develop in each student a broad understanding of how the elements and processes of business organizations relate to one another and to the external environment. Degree requirements are designed to develop stu-

dents' proficiency and confidence in all of the functional areas of business. Students can elect the general or international focus.

The Master of Arts in Administration (M.A.A.) degree program provides participants with the knowledge and skills required for managers, administrators, and supervisors to function more effectively in all types of organizations, plus the specialized managerial expertise needed for management positions within or related to the organizational development profession. Concentrations are communication arts, organizational development, and urban administration.

Students must complete both the course work in their major field of study and the University's general studies core as required in all courses. A minimum of 128 credits of course work is required to graduate in all undergraduate programs. All classes, including graduate classes, are 3 credits (semester hours). Students must complete 36 semester hours to graduate from the graduate programs.

Student Services

All students at UIW, including Universe Online students, have a wide variety of student service options. Online students have access to academic and financial aid advising, library and bookstore services, and online admission application and registration. In addition, students have access to career planning services.

Credit Options

Universe Online welcomes transfer students. UIW accepts all transfer work, requiring students to complete a minimum of 45 semester hours to receive the UIW degree.

Upon acceptance as a degree-seeking student at the University, a student must obtain prior written approval to transfer any additional credits from other institutions.

Faculty

Given the stringent requirements of national/regional accreditation, faculty members must meet a very exacting set of requirements; this has led to a high-quality educational program delivered by highly credentialed and dedicated faculty members.

Admission

Undergraduate students must possess a high school diploma or its equivalent.

Students having previous college work must have a GPA of 2.5 or better. Students must have worked for three years prior to application, in or outside of the home. Students who have not completed English composition I and II and college algebra must take these courses early in their program of study and may be tested for level.

International student transcripts and course descriptions must be translated.

Tuition and Fees

Undergraduate tuition is $360 per credit and graduate tuition is $545 per credit. There is a one-time transcript fee of $30. There are no other fees assessed.

Financial Aid

Financial aid and payment plans are available for all qualified students. Military benefits, as well as employer reimbursement benefits, may be used for online courses.

Applying

To apply for admission, students can fill out an application for admission through the University's Web site. In order to be considered for admission, students must fill out an application online at the school Web site and submit official high school or postsecondary school transcripts from all institutions attended. Students are notified of application decisions via e-mail and U.S. mail.

CONTACT

Universe Online
University of the Incarnate Word
CPO #324
4301 Broadway
San Antonio, Texas 78209

Phone: 877-827-2702 (toll-free)
Fax: 210-829-2756
E-mail: virtual@uiwtx.edu
Web site: http://www.uiw.edu/online

THE UNIVERSITY OF TOLEDO
Distance and eLearning
Toledo, Ohio

Established in 1872, the University of Toledo (UT) has a diverse enrollment of more than 19,000 students representing nearly ninety countries. Located in the heart of Toledo in northwest Ohio, the University plays an important role in the region. Faculty members participate in research, are involved in the community, and are committed to teaching. The Colleges of Arts and Sciences, Business, Education, Engineering, Health Science and Human Service, Nursing, Medicine, Pharmacy, Law, and University College offer a variety of certificate, associate, bachelor's, master's, and doctoral degree programs. UT is regionally accredited by the Higher Learning Commission and a member of the North Central Association of Colleges and Schools and is authorized to offer degrees online.

Distance Learning Program

Distance and eLearning was established in June 1995 to meet the distance learning mission of The University of Toledo (UT). Distance and eLearning provides greater access to educational opportunities for learners in Ohio and worldwide. The University is the leader in distance learning among Ohio's four-year public universities and colleges, offering more than 850 courses online.

Delivery Media

Student-faculty interaction is accomplished through e-mail, chat room discussions, bulletin board postings, CD-ROM, and phone. Most courses are offered via the Internet in an asynchronous environment. Students are responsible for having access to a computer and Internet service provider.

Programs of Study

Distance learning at The University of Toledo provides a flexible environment to fit its students' busy lifestyles for a variety of undergraduate and graduate degree and certificate programs as well as an array of individual courses. Distance and eLearning works with colleges throughout the University to offer courses taught by leading UT faculty members. Programs offered online are also offered in the traditional on-campus setting. Students can apply credits from some of the following programs to a related associate (*) or bachelor's (**) degree program.

Accounting Technology Certificate Program This program provides participants with the skills necessary to prepare financial statements and record business transactions and offers a foundation in the current technology pertaining to the profession.*

Business Management Technology Certificate Program This 24-credit program, which can be completed in one year, consists of eight courses.*

Computer Software Specialist Certificate Program This program gives students the necessary skills to organize and perform activities related to the office environment. Graduates are prepared to sit for the Microsoft certification examination.*

Diversity Management Certificate Program Participants in this program learn how to create a bias-free workplace, develop diversity training for all types of organizations, and set up mentorship programs and diversity councils.*

Health Information Administration Certificate Program The program in Health Information Administration (HIA) prepares student with bachelor's degrees for administrative positions in the health-care industry. The program is accredited by CAHIM. Upon completion, students are eligible to sit for the national certification examination of the AHIMA to become registered health information administrators (RHIA).

Information Services and Support Certificate Program This certificate prepares students for careers as software and hardware support professionals, operating-systems experts, information technologists, and computer technicians.*

Marketing and Sales Technology Certificate Program This program prepares students for careers in new product development, merchandising, advertising, and wholesale/retail trade management.

Nursing Education Graduate Certificate Program This program is designed for registered nurses with a baccalaureate degree or higher degree and provides an opportunity for current and potential nurse educators in academic and health-care settings to develop and refine the practice of teaching.

Programming and Software Development Certificate Program This certificate prepares students to work in the computer industry as programmers, software developers, data managers, and information system designers.*

Psychiatric–Mental Health Clinical Nurse Specialist Graduate Certificate Program The program is for individuals with a master's degree in nursing and a desire to obtain specialized knowledge to seek certification as an adult psychiatric and mental health NCS. Graduates are qualified to take national certification examinations.

Associate Degree in Accounting Technology Program Students receive a well-rounded education in all areas of accounting, including payroll, accounts receivable/payable, purchasing, and taxation, and are prepared for careers in the public and private sectors.**

Associate Degree in Business Management Technology Program This two-year, 65-credit program explores aspects of human resources, computer technology, marketing, accounting, and workplace diversity.**

Associate Degree in Business Management Technology Program—Fast-Track Option This degree can be completed in fifteen months or less. Cohort groups provide supportive, interactive distance-learning experiences. Courses are presented in either eight- or sixteen-week sessions.

Associate Degree in Computer Software Specialist Program Students in this program obtain skills necessary to organize and perform activities related to the office environment. Its highly marketable graduates are prepared to sit for the Microsoft certification examination.**

Associate Degree in Information Services and Support Program This degree program prepares students for careers as software and hardware support professionals, operating-systems experts, information technologists, and computer technicians.**

Associate Degree in Interdisciplinary Technical Studies Program In this program, students individualize a program to meet their unique interests and career goals. Depending on the courses selected, the entire program can be completed online.**

Associate Degree in Marketing and Sales Technology Program This two-year program enables students to develop the business skills necessary to recognize changes in the marketplace and technology; students can specialize in the process of bringing raw materials from the producer to the final customer.**

Associate Degree in Programming and Software Development Program This program prepares students to work in the computer industry as programmers, software developers, data managers, and information system designers.**

Bachelor of Arts in Liberal Studies Program Students complete topical seminars in humanities, natural sciences, and social sciences along with an individualized component of traditional courses. Students may qualify for experiential credit via portfolio or credit through CLEP testing.

Bachelor of Science in Engineering Technology Program This program provides the last two years of the computer science and engineering technology program curriculum, focusing on aspects of computer networking and Web-based programming. Applicants must have an associate degree in electrical engineering technology or a closely related field. UT partners with several Ohio community colleges that provide the first two years of the curriculum.

Bachelor of Science in Health Information Management Program Graduates play a critical role in maintaining, collecting, and analyzing data that health-care providers need to deliver high-quality health care. An associate degree in health information technology or a closely related field may be applied to this degree. Graduates are eligible to sit for the national certification examination to become registered health administrators (RHIA).

Bachelor of Science in Nursing Program (for current RNs): Graduates provide theory-based nursing care in diverse health-care settings, including hospitals, clinics, nursing homes, schools, and outpatient facilities. UT students can take many of the general education, liberal arts, and science courses online. Students enrolled through Bowling Green take the courses on campus. College of Nursing courses are taken online. The B.S.N. is awarded by the respective university

Master of Liberal Studies Program In this flexible, customized College of Arts and Sciences program, students complete seminars in humanities, natural and social sciences, and visual and performing arts and a master's thesis. A minimum 2.7 undergraduate GPA is required. Applicants with a lower GPA can enroll provisionally and must take the GRE.

Master of Science in Engineering Program This part-time, cross-disciplinary program, with a concentration in engineering practice, integrates engineering, business, and elective courses. The program, designed for students with a bachelor's degree in engineering, engineering technology, or a closely related area, combines study in business management and engineering and presents an alternative to a traditional business management or technical M.S. degree. Students typically seek to build management skills while sharpening their technical capabilities.

M.S.N., Nurse Educator Program For nurses with a bachelor's degree and clinical nursing experience who want to teach undergraduate nursing students in classroom and clinical settings, this program focuses on curriculum development, teaching-learning processes, classroom and clinical teaching strategies, and evaluation principles. Full-time and part-time enrollment options are offered.

M.S.N., Psychiatric–Mental Health Clinical Nurse Specialist Program A two-year, full-time program with part-time options, the curriculum expands knowledge and prepares advanced-practice nurses to work in a wide variety of community and hospital-based psychiatric settings, and includes theoretically based and clinically focused courses.

Student Services

Distance and eLearning provides comprehensive student services to enable students to become involved participants in the online learning process. Students have access to a number of services, including online applications, applications for financial aid, registration, academic advising, and software information and to the UT Bookstore, Career Services, UT's online library, and the eWriting Center. The University is a member of the OhioLINK consortium, which provides students online access to library resources from Ohio's university and college libraries. The University has been awarded the designation of meeting Best Practices in Student Services by the Ohio Learning Network.

Credit Options

College credits earned through distance learning courses are recorded on a University of Toledo transcript in the same manner as credits earned in on-campus courses. There is no special designation on the transcript. Students who have attended a regionally accredited college or university may be able to transfer credits. Online courses are equivalent in content to the on-campus courses.

Admission

All distance learners must be admitted to the University and meet the same requirements as traditional students. Special-status admission is available for non-degree-seeking students.

Tuition and Fees

Tuition and fees for online courses are the same as for on-campus courses. Students who are not Ohio residents are eligible for the Distance Learning scholarship, which covers the out-of-state tuition surcharge and the admission application fee. Tuition rates may vary depending on the program. A one-time $25 matriculation fee is charged at the time of registration. University scholarships are available for both in-state and out-of-state students. Prospective students should visit the Distance and eLearning Web site for additional information.

Applying

Prospective students should submit an official application along with the $40 admission fee, an official high school transcript, GED scores, or official transcripts from all previous colleges or universities. Applications are available online or by mail.

CONTACT

Janet Green, Director, eLearning
    Student Services Management
eLearning and Academic Support
The University of Toledo
M.S. 516
2801 Bancroft Street
Toledo, Ohio 43606-3390

Phone: 866-886-5336 (toll-free)
Fax: 419-530-8835
E-mail: utdl@utoledo.edu
Web site: http://www.dl.utoledo.edu

UNIVERSITY OF TULSA

MBA Online
Master of Taxation (MTAX) Online

Tulsa, Oklahoma

The University of Tulsa is a private institution that was founded in 1894 in Indian Territory. The College of Business Administration was established in 1935 and is fully accredited by AACSB International–The Association to Advance Collegiate Schools of Business at both the graduate and undergraduate levels. As faculty members in the College of Business have sought to provide programs that are on the leading edge of technology, they have acted on the need to address new ways of delivering advanced education. The MBA Online and Master of Taxation (MTAX) Online are their response to professionals whose schedules do not permit regular classroom attendance. Interaction between student and professor is emphasized and encouraged in both programs. The MTAX program prepares students to become successful, integral members of the business team, and the MBA Online program prepares graduates to be the effective leaders businesses have come to expect from the University of Tulsa. Graduates of the MBA Online program receive a fully accredited University of Tulsa M.B.A. degree. Graduates of the MTAX program receive a fully accredited Master of Taxation degree.

Distance Learning Program

The MBA Online and MTAX Online programs make graduate business education accessible to the motivated professional who wishes to earn an M.B.A. or graduate tax degree but whose schedule does not permit regular classroom attendance. Students in classes of no more than 25 people enjoy more options for interaction with their professors and classmates than ever before.

Delivery Media

The technology-based online programs require students to have a computer with Internet access; Win98 SE, Win2K, or WinXP; Office 2K or Office XP; Netscape or Internet Explorer; speakers; and a sound card. All courses have been developed utilizing WebCT. Students are able to access chat rooms, e-mail, online forums, and bulletin boards. To access a sample course, interested individuals may visit the MBA Online Web site at http://www.imba.utulsa.edu or the MTAX Web site at http://bus.cba.utulsa.edu/mtax.

Programs of Study

The University of Tulsa MBA Online is a part-time program consisting of two courses per term, three terms per year, in which students can complete their degree in only two years, depending on their undergraduate degree and grades. Those applying for this program must have at least two years of working experience following completion of their baccalaureate degree. Students earn a high-quality M.B.A. from the University of Tulsa, which is internationally recognized and accredited by AACSB International.

Interactivity is a key component of the MBA Online program. Chat rooms, e-mail, electronic bulletin boards, and online forums provide a powerful arena for discussion, analysis, and collaboration. Students also have online access to the campus library. Students come to the campus for two 2-day sessions during the course of the program to meet with their professors and classmates, receive orientation materials, and participate in various workshops and seminars.

Building on the successes of the MBA Online program, the University of Tulsa now offers a two-year online Master of Taxation program. This 30-hour specialized program can be completed in as little as twenty-four months. (Students can choose to complete the degree in more than two years.) The program offers high-potential professionals currently holding a bachelor's degree the opportunity to earn a Master of Taxation, from an institution that is accredited by AACSB International, while continuing to meet the demands of the workplace. Because the specifics of tax code vary from year to year, and state to state, the curriculum focus is on big-picture issues with enduring applicability.

Interactivity is also a key component of the MTAX program. The virtual classroom includes application-sharing software, CD-ROM multimedia courseware, audio/video, electronic bulletin boards, e-mail, an online library, and lecture resources with direct links to other course materials. The entire program is taught online; no campus time is required.

Students are able to complete a high-quality degree in an extremely flexible format without the need to miss work in order to attend regular classes. Course materials are available anytime and anywhere. Course work can be completed at home, at work, or while away on business or personal travel.

Student Services

Students have an e-mail address within WebCT for communicating directly with classmates and faculty members. In addition, all students enrolled at the University of Tulsa are assigned a University e-mail account. With the establishment of a University e-mail account, students may access McFarlin

Library electronically. Both part-time and full-time students and alumni of the University of Tulsa may utilize Career Services.

Credit Options

University policy allows for transfer of up to 6 credit hours at the master's level. Any such graduate credit must have been earned at an AACSB-accredited graduate school and have been completed within the last six years. The Graduate Program Director is responsible for determining the applicability of transfer work to the student's program, subject to final approval by the faculty and the Dean of Research and Graduate Studies.

Faculty

All faculty members who teach in the MBA Online program have obtained a Ph.D. and/or a J.D. and are the same professors who teach in the on-campus M.B.A. program. All faculty members who teach in the MTAX program have advanced degrees and extensive professional experience.

Admission

Enrollment in the MBA Online is limited to the fall term, with the exception of foundation courses, which are offered year-round. Students must have a baccalaureate degree in any field (a business degree is not required), two years of work experience, preferably a 3.0 or better GPA, an acceptable GMAT score, three letters of reference, and a resume.

Admission to the MTAX program is offered for the fall and summer terms. Students must have a baccalaureate degree in any field (a business degree is not required), preferably a 3.0 or better GPA, an acceptable GMAT or LSAT score, three letters of reference, and a resume. Two foundation courses are also required: any accounting course and a federal tax course.

Tuition and Fees

Tuition for the MBA Online and MTAX degrees is $741 per credit hour. There is a one-time enrollment fee of $375 and a $40 application fee. There are no additional fees except for books, articles, or other materials required by professors.

Financial Aid

Students are eligible to apply for Federal Stafford Student Loans (subsidized and unsubsidized) as well as other funded loans. Graduate students can normally apply year-round for these loans. Students who are residents of the state of Oklahoma may apply for an Oklahoma Tuition Aid Grant. The annual deadline for these grants is March 1. Students receiving reimbursement from their employers may arrange to defer tuition to match their employer's reimbursement policy. For more information on available financial aid, students should visit http://www.utulsa.edu/financialaid.

Applying

For more detailed information on the MBA Online program or to apply online, students should visit http://www.imba.utulsa.edu.

For more information on the MTAX program or to apply online, students should visit http://bus.cba.utulsa.edu/mtax.

CONTACT

Graduate Business Programs, Bah 217
University of Tulsa
600 South College Avenue
Tulsa, Oklahoma 74104-3189

Phone: 918-631-2242
Fax: 918-631-2142
E-mail: graduate-business@utulsa.edu
Web site: http://www.imba.utulsa.edu

UNIVERSITY OF WASHINGTON

UW Extension
Seattle, Washington

Founded in 1861, the University of Washington (UW) is one of the oldest state-supported institutions of higher education on the Pacific coast. The University comprises three campuses: the Seattle campus, which is made up of seventeen schools and colleges offering educational opportunities to students ranging from first-year undergraduates through doctoral-level candidates; the Bothell campus; and the Tacoma campus.

The primary mission of the University of Washington is the preservation, advancement, and dissemination of knowledge. UW advances new knowledge through many forms of research, inquiry, and discussion. Accreditation is by the Northwest Association of Schools and Colleges.

Distance Learning Program

The University of Washington offers twelve degree programs, twenty-five certificate programs, and hundreds of courses online, making it one of the leading public institutions in the online field. The UW online program has been rated among the top ten online learning education offerings available through U.S. universities. Distance learning courses at UW are developed by a team of online learning designers working with UW faculty members and academic departments. They create courses that are academically rigorous, suitable for a distance format, and convenient. Several courses have won the prestigious Helen Williams Award for Excellence in Collegiate Independent Study from the well-respected American Association for Collegiate Independent Study (AACIS) as well as awards from the University Continuing Education Association (UCEA). The distance learning program at UW has 4,074 students enrolled.

Delivery Media

Most programs rely on the Internet and e-mail to access instruction and to communicate with teachers and fellow students. Some classes start and finish at set times; others enable students to start according to their own schedule. Students can contact their instructors at any time with questions about the courses. Many courses use online discussion, and some courses incorporate chats into their curriculum.

Programs of Study

UW offers a Master in Strategic Planning for Critical Infrastructures degree program that was developed in partnership with the Washington National Guard for leaders who are responsible for ensuring the reliability and security of critical infrastructures and emergency services. This program was developed for officials in public and private infrastructure, emergency management, and homeland security.

Master's degrees in engineering are available through UW's Education at a Distance for Growth and Excellence (UW/EDGE), with four areas of specialization: aeronautics and astronautics, aerospace engineering, manufacturing engineering, and mechanical engineering.

The master's in construction engineering is designed for professionals in the heavy construction industry, combining courses in construction management and civil engineering.

The Master of Science in applied mathematics is designed for professionals in scientific fields who cannot attend classes on campus.

The Master of Library and Information Science degree was established to meet the high demand for library and information professionals. Delivery of instruction is primarily Internet-based, with on-campus three-day residencies at the beginning of each quarter.

Twenty-five certificate programs are offered, with each requiring three to nine intensive courses. Certificate programs include Brain Research in Education, Business Foundations, C++ Programming, Construction Management, Curriculum Integration in Action, Data Resource Management, E-learning Design and Development, Facility Management, Gerontology, Heavy Construction Project Management, Infrastructure Construction, Internet Programming, Java 2 Programming, Object-Oriented Analysis and Design Using UML, Paralegal Studies, Project Management, Quantitative Construction Management, School Library Media Professional, Site Planning, Web Administration, Web Consultant for Small Business, Web Technology Essentials, and Writers' Program: Literary Fiction Writing and Nonfiction Writing.

More than 200 courses are available in architecture and urban planning, arts and sciences, business and management, computing, engineering and technology, education, health sciences, languages, and library and information science. The OpenUW program at the UW offers twelve free noncredit classes.

Student Services

Academic advising is available via e-mail and telephone and, for those who are able to come to the campus, in person. Advisers can answer questions about prerequisites and course content. Students enrolled in online learning courses receive student numbers and have library checkout privileges at UW libraries. Distance learning students living outside the Seattle area may request specific library materials by mail. Technical support for courses is provided. Textbooks may be ordered online.

Credit Options

Credit earned by taking a distance learning course can be applied to an undergraduate degree or can help students prepare for UW admission. Online learning credits are not considered residence credits. It is not possible to earn an undergraduate degree from the University of Washington through online learning alone. However, nine master's degrees may be completed solely through online learning.

Faculty

Most UW online learning courses are designed and taught by faculty members who teach the same courses on the UW campus. The instructors are familiar with student questions and needs. With the help of instructional designers, they have developed the appropriate methods and materials, interactive strategies, and online activities to help students achieve the course objectives in a distance learning format.

Admission

It is not necessary to be admitted to the University of Washington before taking distance learning courses. (There are prerequisites for some courses, and TOEFL scores are required for international students.) Certificate and graduate degree programs have an application process.

Tuition and Fees

All registrants pay a nonrefundable $30 registration fee. Fees for credit courses through distance learning are $176 per credit for undergraduate students and $387 per credit for Tier 1 graduate and graduate courses. Prices for graduate instruction vary by degree program.

Financial Aid

UW distance learning students are ineligible for the University's financial aid programs in most cases. For information about alternative funding, students should visit http://www.outreach. washington.edu/extinfo/loan_sources. asp.

Applying

Prospective students can register online for courses. Application forms for certificates and degree programs can be downloaded.

CONTACT

University of Washington Online Learning
4311 11th Avenue, NE
Seattle, Washington 98105-4608
Phone: 206-897-8936
      800-506-1338 (toll-free)
E-mail: uwonline@extn.washington.edu
Web site: http://www.onlinelearning.washington.edu

Wisconsin's Public Liberal Arts College

UNIVERSITY OF WISCONSIN-SUPERIOR
Distance Learning Center
Superior, Wisconsin

The Distance Learning Center (formerly known as the Extended Degree Program) at the University of Wisconsin-Superior (UW-Superior) was established in 1978. UW-Superior is part of the highly acclaimed University of Wisconsin System.

The Distance Learning Program is a nationwide program with one tuition for all students. It is accredited by the North Central Association of Colleges and Schools and serves adults who do not have access to a four-year institution because of where they live or because of career and/or family responsibilities.

UW-Superior recognizes that adults are dedicated to achieving educational goals but must also address other priorities. By enrolling in UW-Superior's Distance Learning Program, students can obtain a degree without having to come to the campus. The individually designed major is designed by the student to fit his or her career goals and educational needs. Elementary education is an option for the student who wants to teach in Wisconsin. Communications is the third major offered by the Distance Learning Center.

Distance Learning Program

The Distance Learning Program is a semester-based program. The three enrollment periods include fall, spring, and summer. Each class is taught by a UW-Superior faculty member to ensure that students are receiving the best instruction possible, with an up-to-date curriculum. At any given time, more than 200 students are enrolled in the program. Advisers work closely with students as they complete their degrees.

Delivery Media

Courses are delivered mainly via online format, although a few courses are print-based. Access to the Desire 2 Learn software is provided through the UW-Superior network system. Students are encouraged to utilize e-mail and message boards while enrolled in the online courses. Print-based course materials can be mailed or faxed to the Distance Learning Office.

Programs of Study

The Distance Learning Program offers three bachelor's degree options: communications, elementary education, and the individually designed major.

The communications degree is the newest major offered. Students work with faculty members who specialize in improving communications. It not only allows students to dig deeper into the communications discipline but also gives students a wide range of communication venues to explore—interpersonal, conflict, persuasion, organizational, and intercultural communication.

The individualized major allows students to plan a major using both past and new learning experiences. It is designed by students to meet their educational and career goals. Examples of individualized majors include human services, child development, and health management.

The elementary education degree at a distance has been in existence for more than twenty-five years. It provides preparation for Wisconsin licensure for birth through ages 11–12 or ages 6 through 12–13. UW-Superior's Teacher Education Department has an excellent reputation for quality and innovation.

Credit Options

Credit for prior learning is made possible through credit by exam, credit for military service, and credit for non-university programs. Students also have the option to petition for technical college credit and to seek credit through portfolio development.

Admission

Students seeking admission to the Distance Learning Program can apply online at the University's Web site (http://www.uwsuper.edu). They can also request admission information via e-mail.

Tuition and Fees

All distance learning students pay the same tuition regardless of residency. An additional course fee is charged for each course.

Financial Aid

Financial aid is available to distance learning students.

CONTACT

Distance Learning Program
University of Wisconsin–Superior
Belknap and Catlin Avenues
Superior, Wisconsin 54880

Phone: 877-528-6597 (toll-free)
E-mail: dlc@uwsuper.edu
Web site: http://www.uwsuper.edu/distancelearning

UNIVERSITY OF WYOMING
New Thinking

THE UNIVERSITY OF WYOMING
Outreach School
Division of Outreach Credit Programs
Laramie, Wyoming

The University of Wyoming (UW), a land-grant university founded in 1886, is accredited by the Higher Learning Commission and is a member of the North Central Association of Colleges and Schools. The University of Wyoming was the first university west of the Missouri River to offer correspondence courses. In its outreach mission, the University of Wyoming is guided by the following vision: the state of Wyoming is the campus of the University of Wyoming. The University has one faculty and staff, one student body, and one set of academic programs. Teaching, research, and service are the missions of the University, regardless of location. The University recognizes that its "one student body" is composed of a wide variety of students whose needs differ.

Distance Learning Program

The UW Outreach School's Outreach Credit Programs division delivers the University's distance learning programs. The mission of the Outreach School is to extend the University of Wyoming's educational programs and services to people in the state of Wyoming and beyond. The School delivers more than 300 University courses and complete degree and certificate programs to approximately 4,000 students per semester through Outreach Credit Programs and the other academic division of the Outreach School, UW/CC Center, the University's largest location of onsite courses outside the main campus..

Delivery Media

Outreach Credit Programs launched Online UW in the spring of 1999 in cooperation with eCollege to serve students interested in learning online. In addition, Outreach Credit Programs delivers programs via correspondence study, audio-teleconference, videoconference, and onsite instruction. Additional courses also are offered through Web-based instruction.

For a list of audio, video, Web-based, onsite, and correspondence study courses, students should visit http://outreach.uwyo.edu/ocp. All correspondence study courses, a limited number of audio-teleconference courses, and all Web-based courses are available to students outside the state of Wyoming.

Programs of Study

Degrees, certificates, and endorsements are available to students through distance education. For a complete list of programs, requirements, tuition charges, and academic advising contacts, students should visit the Web at http://outreach.uwyo.edu/ocp/degrees&programs.asp.

Certificate programs include land surveying (offered nationwide through audio-teleconference with videotaped lectures), family and consumer sciences/early childhood program director's certificate (available online), and real estate (available online).

Endorsement programs include early childhood birth to 5 endorsement, early childhood special education endorsement, principal endorsement, and Wyoming reading endorsement literacy program, all available statewide through a combination of delivery media.

Graduate programs include an Executive M.B.A. (available online); an M.S. in education, with a specialization in instructional technology (available online); an M.S. in kinesiology and health (statewide, some courses nationwide); an M.S. in nursing, with an advanced practice in rural health/nurse educator option (online); an M.S. in speech-language pathology (available nation-wide through audio-teleconference with videotaped lectures); and an M.S.W. in social work (statewide).

Other available distance degrees are baccalaureate completion degrees in business administration and family and consumer science (online), criminal justice, psychology, and social science (statewide, some courses nationwide) and an RN/B.S.N. completion program (online).

Special Programs

Outreach Credit Programs currently delivers more than 100 University courses and ten degrees and certificates completely online. Courses are available worldwide in the areas of adult learning, astronomy, biochemistry, business administration, child development, directing preschool and day-care programs, economics, education, engineering, family and consumer sciences, human resources management, instructional technology, nutrition, physics, psychology, real estate, religion, and statistics. Students should visit http://outreach.uwyo.edu/ocp/degrees&programs.asp for a list of programs offered.

Student Services

All student services (such as admission, enrollment, tuition payment, grade reporting, financial aid, bookstore, and library outreach) are available to distance learning students. The library outreach service is available at http://www.lib.uwyo.edu. Students can purchase textbooks and course packets online at the University Bookstore at http://www.uwyobookstore.com. In addition, services from the Center for Advising and Career Services, Disability Support Services, Educational Opportunity Center, Testing Center, Writing Center, and Student Affairs are also available to distance students. A complete list of all services is available at http://outreach.uwyo.edu/ocp/resources.asp.

Credit Options

Students may transfer courses from accredited institutions of higher education to the University of Wyoming. Credit is also available through AP, CLEP, portfolio assessment, and departmental examinations. Degrees require a minimum of 48 hours of upper-division credit, with a minimum of 30 credits from the University of Wyoming. Most degree programs require 120–124 credits for graduation.

Faculty

The majority of those who teach through Outreach Credit Programs are full-time faculty members at the University of Wyoming. A limited number of adjunct faculty members, who are approved by the University's academic departments, teach distance courses. In any given semester, approximately 75 regular full-time faculty members and 15 part-time adjunct faculty members teach distance courses through the Outreach School. The programs offered at a distance are academically challenging, and the requirements for enrollment, admission, and completion are the same as for the programs offered on the main University campus in Laramie, Wyoming.

Admission

All students interested in enrolling in UW courses through Outreach Credit Programs must first be admitted to the University. Students should check with the appropriate academic departments for their study plan requirements.

Students who decide to pursue UW undergraduate degrees must apply and be admitted to a specific degree program at the University. A maximum of 12 UW credit hours can be applied to a UW degree program prior to admission. Undergraduate admission generally requires completion of at least 13 high school units in a precollege curriculum, a cumulative high school grade point average of at least 2.75, and an ACT score of at least 20 or an SAT score of at least 960. Conditional admission is available for adult learners who do not meet these criteria.

Students who decide to pursue UW graduate degrees must apply and be admitted to a specific degree program at the University. Credits taken prior to admission may or may not apply to a graduate program of study. Graduate programs require a Graduate Record Examinations (GRE) combined verbal and quantitative score of at least 900. The University offers GRE testing through the University of Wyoming Testing Center. For more information, students can visit the Web site at http://www.uwyo.edu/ucc/utc/.

Tuition and Fees

All outreach students are charged tuition at an in-state rate. Undergraduate tuition for outreach courses is $94 per credit hour, with an $11-per-credit-hour delivery fee or a $40-per-credit-hour delivery fee for Online UW courses. Graduate tuition for outreach courses is $159 per credit hour, with an $11-per-credit-hour delivery fee or a $40-per-credit-hour delivery fee for Online UW courses. Tuition for the Executive M.B.A. program is $500 per credit hour plus a $40-per-credit-hour delivery fee, and tuition for the land surveying program is $192 per credit hour.

Financial Aid

All forms of federal financial aid and other scholarship aid are available to Outreach students. Outreach Credit Programs also has a number of scholarships available to Outreach students. Information describing available aid and award criteria is available on the Web at http://www.uwyo.edu/sfa or from the Office of Student Financial Aid, Department 3335, University of Wyoming, 1000 East University Avenue, Laramie, Wyoming 82071.

Applying

Non-degree-seeking and degree-seeking students should apply through the Admissions Office (telephone: 800-DIAL-WYO (toll-free) or 307-766-2287; Web site: http://www.uwyo.edu) or Graduate Admissions (telephone: 307-766-2287; Web site: http://www.uwyo.edu/uwgrad).

CONTACT

Outreach School
Division of Outreach Credit
   Programs
Department 3274
University of Wyoming
1000 East University Avenue
Laramie, Wyoming 82071
Phone: 307-766-4300
       800-448-7801 (toll-free)
Fax: 307-766-4048
E-mail: occ@uwyo.edu
Web site: http://outreach.uwyo.
      edu/ocp

UPPER IOWA UNIVERSITY
Extended University

Fayette, Iowa

UPPER IOWA UNIVERSITY
Established in 1857™

Upper Iowa University (UIU) was established in 1857 and has since become the largest private university in the state of Iowa. Unlike some of the newer schools offering distance learning programs, UIU has a beautiful residential campus on 90 acres with eight academic buildings and three residence halls. Upper Iowa also has seventeen sports teams, known as the Peacocks, who compete in the NCAA Division II. As a nonprofit, rapidly growing, four-year liberal arts institution of higher learning, UIU offers a wide range of high-quality degree programs to nearly 6,000 students worldwide. UIU provides educational opportunities to the global community, focusing on the future while preserving the traditions of the past. Upper Iowa University is accredited by the Higher Learning Commission and is a member of the North Central Association of Colleges and Schools (Web site: http://www.ncahigherlearningcommission.org; telephone: 312-263-0456).

Distance Learning Program

The Extended University's distance learning programs are offered through two primary modes of delivery. Its External Degree program offers Associate of Arts and Bachelor of Science degree programs with seventeen majors through independent study/correspondence, and its Online program currently offers a Bachelor of Science (B.S.) with seven business majors, criminal justice, emergency and disaster management, health-services administration, interdisciplinary studies, public administration, a Master of Business Administration (M.B.A.) and a Master of Public Administration (M.P.A.). Courses offered through both External Degree and Online formats meet the same standards as courses offered through the residential University in Fayette, Iowa. The External Degree program, which began in 1972, has been successfully delivered to more than 10,000 learners. Upper Iowa's External Degree program was one of the first and most successful in the United States. Both the External Degree and Online programs continue to be vital components in serving both civilian and military learners worldwide.

Delivery Media

In the External Degree program, students communicate with instructors via e-mail, fax, and regular mail. Classes are self-paced with no minimum completion time. Upper Iowa's Online program is noted for its e-mail–like feel. Online students log on (via the Internet) just long enough to send and receive materials, anytime, anywhere, day or night. Most work is accomplished off-line, or through asynchronous communication. Online students may also communicate with their instructors through course software, e-mail, fax, or phone.

Programs of Study

Upper Iowa University has a long history of offering high-quality degree programs through distance learning.

In the External Degree program, associate and bachelor's degree programs are available in a wide range of academic areas, including accounting, business administration, criminal justice, emergency and disaster management, finance, health-services administration, human resources management, human services, interdisciplinary stud-

ies, management, marketing, psychology, public administration (general, law enforcement, or fire science), social science, and technology and information management.

Upper Iowa's Online program offers a Bachelor of Science degree with fifteen majors to choose from: accounting, business administration, criminal justice, emergency and disaster management, finance, health-services administration, human resources management, human services, interdisciplinary studies, management, marketing, psychology, public administration (general, law enforcement, or fire science), and technology and information management.

The M.B.A. offers six areas of emphasis: accounting, corporate finance management, global business, human resources management, organizational development, and quality management.

The M.P.A. offers four areas of emphasis: health and human services, homeland security, justice administration, and public personnel management. The course work focuses on the theories and skills that are the foundation for tomorrow's organizations, including organizational design, total quality management, self-managed teams, employee empowerment, change management, facilitation skills, high-performance work systems, and more.

Special Programs

Each summer, the External Degree program sponsors the Institute for Experiential Learning (IEXL) for undergraduate students. During an intensive weeklong session held on the Fayette campus, students have the opportunity to earn 3 semester hours of undergraduate credit while visiting the residential campus and networking with other learners from around the world.

Student Services

External Degree and Online students are provided with one-on-one academic advising via U.S. mail, e-mail, telephone, fax communication, and through use of a special software/courseware package (for Online program students). In addition to local university libraries, undergraduate and graduate students and faculty members have access to the Henderson Wilder Library holdings through Upper Iowa University's Web site.

Credit Options

Full credit is given to students for college-level courses completed at regionally accredited colleges and universities. Students can transfer a maximum of 45 semester hours for an associate degree, 90 semester hours for a bachelor's degree, and 12 semester hours for a master's degree. Other sources of credit include the American Council on Education (ACE), the College-Level Examination Program (CLEP), Dantes Subject Standardized Test (DSST) subject exams, and experiential learning.

Faculty

Upper Iowa University's distance learning program has more than 100 adjunct faculty members, many of whom have doctoral or terminal degrees. Faculty members are experienced in the areas in which they teach.

Admission

Admission criteria for undergraduate degrees include graduation from an accredited public or private high school or completion of the GED test or its equivalent. For the graduate program, prospective students must hold an undergraduate degree from a regionally accredited college or university. More information regarding grade point requirements, TOEFL scores for international students, and transfer credit is available upon request or on the UIU Web site.

Tuition and Fees

Associate- and baccalaureate-level tuition for courses taken through External Degree (independent study/correspondence) or at off-campus learning centers (classroom) for 2006–07 was $681 per 3-semester-credit course. Undergraduate and graduate online (Internet-based) courses were $849 and $1050 respectively, per 3-semester-credit course.

Financial Aid

Financial aid in the form of Federal Stafford Student Loans, Federal Pell Grants, Iowa Tuition Grants (Iowa residents only), Veterans Assistance, and Military Tuition Assistance is available.

Applying

Students may enroll in UIU distance learning programs at any time. In the External Degree program, students may start courses at any time. In the Online program, eight-week terms begin six times a year. Students should send official transcripts (including CLEP, DSST, or DD-214), GRE/GMAT score reports (if required), and a completed Application for Admission form (available online or by contacting the school via telephone or e-mail) directly to Upper Iowa University.

CONTACT

Extended University
Upper Iowa University
605 Washington Street
P.O. Box 1857
Fayette, Iowa 52142-1857

Phone: 877-366-0581 (toll-free)
Fax: 563-425-5771
E-mail: moreinfo@uiu.edu
Web site: http://www.uiu.edu

UTAH STATE UNIVERSITY
Regional Campuses and Distance Education
Logan, Utah

Utah State University (USU) was founded in 1888 as part of the public educational system of Utah and operates under the constitution and laws of the state. It belongs to the family of institutions known as land-grant universities, which had their origin in 1862. USU is governed by the State Board of Regents and accredited by Northwest Association of Accredited Schools.

USU integrates teaching, research, extension, and service to meet its unique role as Utah's land-grant university.

Distance Learning Program

USU Distance Education is an integral part of USU's outreach mission. ESU Distance Education provides educational opportunities for time- and place-bound students who are not able to come to the campus to attend classes.

Distance Education offers several bachelor's and master's degree programs via interactive broadcast and a master's degree over the Internet. Many other interactive broadcast, Internet-based, and independent-study CD-ROM courses are offered.

USU is one of the leading institutions in the United States for its off-campus programs.

Delivery Media

Distance Education is made up of three program delivery units: interactive broadcast (satellite, video teleconferencing), online, and independent study.

Interactive broadcast degree programs are offered at USU education centers and are only available to Utah students. Online courses are designed for access any time of the day or night. Online students submit assignments electronically and interact with their instructors and classmates via e-mail and online discussions.

Students who register for independent study courses receive a CD-ROM or printed course outline at registration. Independent study students mail in assignments, take proctored examinations, and may contact their instructors by phone or e-mail.

Programs of Study

Complete degree and certificate programs can be earned entirely through Regional Campuses and Distance Education (RCDE). For a detailed list, interested students should visit http://distance.usu.edu.

Student Services

Student services available to distance learners include access to the University bookstore, Library Support System for Distance Learners, and the Academic Resource Center. For more information on student services available to distance learners, prospective students should visit the Web site at http://distance.usu.edu.

Credit Options

Credit earned through USU Distance Education is measured in semester units and is transferable to most colleges and universities in the U.S.

Students who plan to transfer credit should make arrangements with the transfer institution prior to registration.

Faculty

The majority of Distance Education instructors are USU faculty members; many are leading researchers in their field. Distance Education faculty members recognize that the needs of individuals are of major importance; programs have been established to give students optimal individual attention.

Admission

Non-degree-seeking students do not need to be admitted to enroll in Distance Education courses. Degree-seeking students must apply for admission. Admission requirements are program specific and may be obtained by contacting the Admissions Office at 435-797-1079. Prospective students may complete an application for admission online at http://www.usu.edu/admissions.

Tuition and Fees

For tuition and fee information, prospective students should visit the Web site at http://distance.usu.edu.

Financial Aid

Financial aid is available for distance education students. Utah State University participates in the following financial aid programs: Federal Pell Grants, Federal Supplemental Educational Opportunity Grants (FSEOG), LEAAP Grants, Federal Perkins Loans,

Federal Work-Study, Federal Stafford Loans, Plus Loans, scholarships, and emergency loans. For more information, prospective students should contact the financial aid office at 435-797-0173 or visit the Web site at http://www.usu.edu/finaid/.

Applying

Students working toward any of the degree programs offered through Independent and Distance Education must be admitted to the University. Prospective students may complete an application for admission online at http://www.usu.edu/admissions or request a printed application by contacting the Admissions Office at 435-797-1129 or toll-free at 800-488-8108.

CONTACT

Regional Campuses and Distance Education
5055 Old Main Hill
Utah State University
Logan, Utah 84322-3080

Phone: 800-233-2137 (toll-free)
Fax: 435-797-1399
E-mail: distance.info@usu.edu
Web site: http://distance.usu.edu

VIRGINIA POLYTECHNIC INSTITUTE AND STATE UNIVERSITY
Institute for Distance and Distributed Learning
Blacksburg, Virginia

Founded in 1872 as a land-grant college, Virginia Tech is the most comprehensive university in the Commonwealth of Virginia and is among the top research universities in the nation. Today, Virginia Tech's eight colleges are dedicated to quality, innovation, and results through teaching, research, and outreach activities. At its 2,600-acre main campus located in Blacksburg and other campus centers in Northern Virginia, Southwest Virginia, Hampton Roads, Richmond, and Roanoke, Virginia Tech enrolls more than 28,000 undergraduate and graduate students from all fifty states and more than 100 countries in 180 academic degree programs.

The University's growing reputation for excellence includes national recognition as a leader in distance and distributed learning. Virginia Tech is helping to meet the changing needs of undergraduate and graduate students with online and distance-delivered master's degree programs, certificates, and licensures as well as noncredit offerings for personal and professional growth. Innovative use of technology is transforming the educational process, while making it more accessible and learner-centered. Virginia Tech is fully accredited by the Commission on Colleges of the Southern Association of Colleges and Schools.

Distance Learning Program

As part of the Office of the University Provost and Vice President for Academic Affairs, Virginia Tech's Institute for Distance and Distributed Learning (IDDL) provides leadership, coordination, management, and support to the distance and distributed learning (eLearning) activities of Virginia Tech. Through these activities, Virginia Tech extends its campus to communities throughout the world and provides an open campus environment that allows individuals to engage in learning at anytime and from anywhere. In addition, Virginia Tech shares the practical application of the University's knowledge and expertise in support of economic development, increases the University's access to the world and the world's access to the University, and researches new teaching and learning environments through the application of technology.

More than 15,000 annual enrollments are accounted for in close to 550 courses and twenty-nine master's degree programs, certificates, licensures, and specialized programs. Virginia Tech actively participates in the Electronic Campus of Virginia and collaboratively delivers courses and degree programs at a distance with other Virginia colleges and universities through the Commonwealth Graduate Engineering Program and Virginia Consortium of Engineering and Science Universities. Virginia Tech also participates in the Southern Region Electronic Campus and the Natural Resources Distance Learning Consortium.

Programs of Study

Virginia Tech offers certificate programs in business information systems, communications, computer engineering, decision support systems, natural resources, networking, and software development.

An online graduate certificate in liberal arts was a new addition to the 2005–06 eLearning academic offerings.

Licensures are available in career and alternative licensure professional studies and in career and technical education.

Programs leading to a Master of Arts degree are available in instructional technology and political science.

The Master of Science can be earned in agriculture and life sciences, career and technical education, civil and environmental engineering, civil infrastructure engineering, computer engineering, electrical and computer engineering, engineering administration, health promotion, ocean engineering, and systems engineering.

The Master of Business Administration and the Master of Information Technology are also awarded.

A wide variety of credit and noncredit courses is also offered through distance learning in the areas of accounting, architecture, art, biology, black studies, building construction, business, communications, computer science, economics, education, engineering, English, entomology, finance, geography, history, hotel management, horticulture, information science, landscape architecture, management, marketing, math, music, philosophy, physics, psychology, science and technology, sociology, Spanish, statistics, women's studies, and more.

Student Services

Recognizing the diverse needs of distance learners, Virginia Tech employs a holistic approach to distance learning in which the student's total educational experience is considered. This approach provides learners with accessible learning resources, support services, and interactive technologies in addition to renowned faculty members who create and teach the wide array of distance and distributed learning courses. Through cross-University collaboration, Virginia Tech works to create accessible online support services that include academic program information, the admissions process, preadmissions advising, enrollment services, an orientation to distance learning, a distance learning compatibility self-test, course delivery format descriptions, technical requirements, degree requirements, program of study descriptions, library resources and services, bookstore services, academic advising, tutoring, writing center, study skills, an online wellness resource center, services for students with disabilities, career services, technical help, and FAQ.

Credit Options

Distance learners can transfer credits earned at other accredited postsecondary institutions to Virginia Tech following the established University policies. Students admitted to the University who have been certified by the Virginia Community College System or Richard Bland College as completing the transfer module are deemed to have completed the University core curriculum components and receive 35 total credits for the module.

Faculty

The faculty is the foundation of Virginia Tech's distance learning programs and assures its academic excellence. The same faculty members, including some of the most highly honored faculty at the University, who teach traditional classroom-based campus courses also teach distance learning courses. Currently, 88 percent of Virginia Tech's academic teaching departments are involved in teaching distance learning courses.

Admission

To become undergraduate or graduate degree candidates at Virginia Tech, students must apply formally for admission. Students' records at Virginia Tech and all other colleges and universities attended are reviewed within the context of current admission policies. Virginia Tech allows qualified students at other Virginia universities and colleges to enroll in its courses as non-degree-seeking or Commonwealth Campus students. For more information on undergraduate admission, students should visit the IDDL Web site http://www.iddl.vt.edu; those interested in graduate programs should visit http://www.grads.vt.edu.

Tuition and Fees

For the latest information, students should visit http://www.bursar.vt.edu.

Financial Aid

Virginia Tech is a direct lending institution and awards financial aid from federally funded and state-funded programs as well as privately funded sources. Financial aid sources include the Federal Direct Stafford Loan, Federal Perkins Loan, Federal Direct PLUS Loan, Federal Pell Grant, Federal Work-Study, Virginia Guaranteed Assistance Program, Commonwealth Award, and the College Scholarship Assistance Program.

Applying

Students applying for undergraduate admission can access current information at http://www.admiss.vt.edu. Students applying for graduate admission can access current information at http://www.grads.vt.edu. Students can register for Internet-based courses at http://www.vto.vt.edu.

There is a nonrefundable fee ($50 undergraduate, $25 graduate) for non-degree-seeking students.

CONTACT

Angie Starr
eLearner Support Specialist
Institute for Distance and Distributed Learning
Virginia Tech (0445)
Blacksburg, Virginia 24061

Phone: 540-231-1264
Fax: 540-231-2079
E-mail: vto@vt.edu
Web site: http://www.iddl.vt.edu
　　　　　　http://www.vto.vt.edu (online catalog)

WALDEN UNIVERSITY

Graduate Distance Education

Minneapolis, Minnesota

WALDEN UNIVERSITY
A higher degree. A higher purpose.

Walden University's online doctoral, master's, and bachelor's programs are designed to help students achieve their goals of personal enrichment and professional advancement and make a difference in the lives of others.

Walden's degree programs combine high-quality curricula, expert faculty members, and innovative distance-delivery models to offer highly applied, rigorous programs that allow adult learners to pursue advanced degrees while maintaining their personal and professional commitments.

Founded in 1970, Walden University offers master's and doctoral degrees in education, health and human services, management, psychology, and public policy and administration as well as master's programs in engineering and IT and bachelor's completion programs in business.

Walden University is accredited by the Higher Learning Commission and is a member of the North Central Association, http://www.ncahlc.org; 312-263-0456.

Distance Learning Program

With a global network of peers and faculty mentors, Walden's students collaborate with a diverse range of professionals to gain the critical insights and skills that are highly relevant to the work they do every day.

Delivery Media

Students and faculty members exchange ideas and collaborate with their colleagues through e-mail, online courses, study teams, and, in some programs, face-to-face residency sessions. Individual mentoring, online courses, and progress based on demonstrations of knowledge are among the components of Walden's delivery system. Students who enroll in a Walden program should be comfortable using a personal computer, a word processor, and e-mail.

Programs of Study

The Ph.D. in Applied Management and Decision Sciences Program offers an interdisciplinary approach that prepares students to advance the knowledge and practice of management and leadership. Students can complete a general or self-designed program or specialize in accounting, engineering management, finance, information systems management, knowledge management, leadership and organizational change, learning management, or operations research.

The Ph.D. in Education Program produces leaders who can address the nation's most pressing educational challenges. Options include general and self-designed programs and specializations in adult education leadership, community college leadership, early childhood education, educational technology, higher education, K-12 educational leadership, and special education.

The Ph.D. in Health Services Program prepares students to serve at the forefront of the design and delivery of cutting-edge private and public health services. General study is available as well as specializations in community health promotion and education and health management and policy. Graduates gain insight into issues of health and human behavior and develop the expertise to move to the forefront of health-services delivery.

The Ph.D. in Human Services Program prepares students to serve at the forefront of the design and delivery of cutting-edge public services and to excel within a diverse service-delivery system. Students can complete a general or self-designed program or specialize in clinical social work, counseling, criminal justice, family studies and intervention strategies, human services administration, or social policy analysis and planning.

The Ph.D. in Public Health Program focuses on seeking solutions to significant public health problems and applying and integrating new knowledge into public health research and practice settings. Specializations are available in community health promotion and education and in epidemiology. Graduates are able to leverage their experience to assume leadership roles in academia or positions in the public or private sector.

The Ph.D. in Psychology Program prepares psychology professionals to fully excel in today's health-care settings, private practices, and global industries. Specializations include clinical psychology, counseling psychology, general psychology (with tracks in educational psychology and in research and evaluation), health psychology, organizational psychology, and school psychology. The clinical, counseling, and school psychology specializations are designed to meet the academic licensure requirements of most state psychology boards.

The Ph.D. in Public Policy and Administration Program prepares students to meet the challenges of governance and effective service delivery. General study is available as well as specializations in criminal justice, health services, homeland security policy and coordination, international nongovernmental organizations, knowledge management, nonprofit management and leadership, public management and leadership, public policy, and public safety management.

The Doctor of Education (Ed.D.) Program has specializations in teacher leadership and in administrator leadership for teaching and learning. Both are designed for K-12 educators who want to continue their practice while assuming leadership roles in their schools and communities.

The Master of Business Administration (M.B.A.) Program offers students new insights and comprehensive cross-discipline skills to meet the complex issues and challenges of the global economy. Students may choose a general program or select from several specializations: entrepreneurship, finance, human resource management, leadership, marketing, product management, and technology.

The Master of Public Administration (M.P.A.) Program prepares professionals to across the boundaries of public, private, and governmental sectors. Students may choose a general program or specialize in a variety of areas, including criminal justice, health services, homeland security policy and coordination, international nongovernmental organizations, knowledge management, nonprofit management and leadership, public management and leadership, public policy, and public safety management.

The course-based M.S. in Psychology Degree Program includes a general program as well as a specialization in organizational psychology and development.

Through a mix of research, fieldwork, and courses taught by national experts, the M.S. in Mental Health Counseling Program prepares students to address and treat behavioral disorders knowledgeably, ethically, and with respect for diversity.

The M.S. in Education Program develops scholar-practitioners among educators serving students in K–12 classrooms. The program offers specializations in curriculum, instruction, and assessment (grades K–12); educational leadership; elementary reading and literacy (grades K–6); elementary reading and mathematics (grades K–6); integrating technology in the classroom (grades 3–12); literacy and learning in the content areas (grades 6–12); mathematics (grades K–5); mathematics (grades 6–8); middle level education (grades 5–8); science (grades K–8), and starting in September 2007, a teacher leadership specialization for grades K–12.

The M.S. in Public Health Program prepares students to lead communities in the development of population-based assessment techniques and intervention strategies to improve health-care access and service delivery.

The Master of Public Health (M.P.H.) Program with a specialization in community health education features a practice-oriented approach using real-world examples and case studies and is designed to address the growing need for well-prepared public health professionals. Graduates are provided with the credentials to serve as an advocate for the development for healthy individuals, organizations, and communities and are able to develop and evaluate culturally relevant interventions to promote public health.

The M.S. in Nursing Program is based on the American Association of Colleges of Nursing (AACN) Essentials of Master's Education and American Nurses Association's (ANA) Scope and Standards for Nurse Administrators. It offers specializations in education, leadership and management, and nursing informatics. Graduates gain new knowledge, skills, and influence to affect more lives and make a greater contribution as nurse educators, administrators, or specialists in nursing informatics. The nursing program is also accredited by the Commission on Collegiate Nursing Education (CCNE).

Walden University offers five M.S. in engineering programs: Computer Engineering, which prepares students to work in the dynamic and rapidly expanding field of digital technology; Computer Science, where students develop an advanced body of knowledge in the design, analysis, and implementation of algorithmic processes that transform raw data into valuable information; Electrical Engineering, which provides students with a technical background for analysis, design, development, operation, or research on electrical or electronic systems; Software Engineering, where students become experts in the latest software development theories and the fundamental engineering principles that support progressive software design; and Systems Engineering, which provides the necessary processes and tools to define and validate system requirements, develop effective designs, and ensure those designs are safe and meet customer requirements.

Student Services

Student services include academic advising, course management, financial aid, technical assistance, orientation programming, disability services, tutoring, the Writing Center, and a career center. Walden University's partnership with the Indiana University Bloomington libraries provides reference, search, catalog, and distribution services.

Credit Options

Transfer of credit from other institutions is permitted in most programs. Applicants can request an informal transfer of credit evaluation prior to admission. Official notification of credits accepted for transfer may be issued at admission or once required documents are received.

Faculty

Walden attracts esteemed scholars, researchers, and distinguished professionals as faculty members. The distance-delivery model allows students to fully benefit from the diverse talents and experiences of the finest faculty members, regardless of where they reside. Some are deans or faculty members at major universities, while others are corporate executives, educators, clinicians, and military leaders. All faculty members are credible subject experts who demonstrate vast experience and a profound commitment to adult learners.

Admission

Walden University has a long-standing commitment to providing educational opportunities to a diverse population of learners. Walden's admission process focuses on selecting learners who can benefit from a distributed educational or online learning approach and who, with the benefit of a Walden education, are most likely to contribute to their current or future academic or professional fields and communities. Admission requirements vary by program and major. To learn more, students should contact a Walden enrollment adviser.

Tuition and Fees

Tuition and fees vary by program.

Financial Aid

Walden offers students a variety of options to assist in funding their educational expenses. Most Walden students receive some form of financial assistance. Available options include federal programs, veterans' education benefits, and institutional fellowships. Tuition reductions are also available for group/spousal enrollment. Walden can also assist students in securing private scholarships, employer tuition benefits, and loans from private lenders.

Applying

Submission of a completed and signed application, a $50 application fee, and a personal/professional statement of purpose is required. Applicants must also send a resume, official transcripts from the institution that conferred their bachelor's or master's degree, and, in health and human services, two required recommendation forms. Students can also apply online.

CONTACT

Walden University
155 Fifth Avenue South, Suite 100
Minneapolis, Minnesota 55401

Phone: 866-492-5336 (toll-free)
E-mail: info@waldenu.edu
Web site: http://www.WaldenU.edu

WASHINGTON STATE UNIVERSITY

WSU Center for Distance and Professional Education

Pullman, Washington

Washington State University (WSU), the state's land-grant institution, is dedicated to the preparation of students for productive lives and professional careers, to basic and applied research, and to the dissemination of knowledge. Founded in 1890, the University is a statewide institution with a main campus in Pullman, three branch campuses, ten community learning centers, and numerous Cooperative Extension and research facilities throughout the state. WSU is accredited by the Northwest Association of Schools and Colleges. In addition, the University is an acknowledged leader in developing and delivering distance education programs. Since 1992, WSU's Office of Distance Degree Programs (DDP) has served students in Washington and across the nation and continues to expand online credit and noncredit options as the Center for Distance and Professional Education (CDPE). The University's undergraduate core curriculum, including world civilization courses and expanded writing requirements, is nationally recognized. Money magazine has called WSU a "public ivy" and rated the honors program as one of the nation's best.

Distance Learning Program

WSU's Center for Distance and Professional Education offers degree-completion programs leading to a Bachelor of Arts (B.A.) in business administration (with majors in management information systems (MIS) or management and operations), criminal justice, human development, humanities, social sciences, or women's studies; a Bachelor of Science in Nursing (B.S.N.); and a Master of Science (M.S.) in agriculture and in engineering and technology management. Formal minors are available. The undergraduate degree programs are designed primarily for students who have completed the equivalent of the first two years of college. They are the same degrees offered on three WSU campuses; requirements are the same, but students can complete their degrees without attending WSU in person.

CDPE also offers three online credit certificate programs, Early Childhood Development and Care Certificate, Instructional Design Certificate (graduate level), and Professional Writing Certificate, as well as two online noncredit certificate programs, Volunteer Management Certificate Program (VMCP) and Telework Certificate Program.

Delivery Media

Courses are delivered directly to students' homes through a variety of distance learning technologies, primarily the Internet, with Web access and e-mail requirements. Courses also incorporate multimedia resources (DVDs, CDs, videotapes), lab kits, library resources, and print materials.

Programs of Study

WSU's online B.A. in business administration with a major in management information systems is designed to enable graduates to enter the working world as systems analysts, systems project managers, or Web masters. The program is fully accredited by AACSB International–The Association to Advance Collegiate Schools of Business

The online B.A. in business administration with a major in management and operations provides a broad foundation for employment in the world of business, either at a large corporation or in the student's own business. The program is also fully accredited by AACSB International.

WSU's online B.A. in criminal justice offers a broad exposure in the social sciences through a policy-focused curriculum that prepares students for positions in the criminal justice system, other government agencies, and the private sector.

The online B.A. in human development is especially effective for individuals who work in child- or elder-care programs or in direct-service roles with a variety of special-needs clients. The degree program includes an internship component supervised by a WSU faculty member.

The B.A. in humanities is a broad-based, interdisciplinary liberal arts degree program with no set list of required courses. The program focuses on the humanities as it develops skills in communication, writing, problem solving, and critical thinking.

WSU's online B.A. in social sciences is a liberal arts degree that offers students multiple options and emphases in the social sciences and provides a broad background applicable to a variety of careers through an interdisciplinary approach.

The online B.A. in women's studies is the interdisciplinary study of gender and how class, race, ethnicity, nationality, sexual orientation, age, and ability shape the female and male experience. Students learn how female and male social roles affect personal lives and world-wide issues. They also develop an understanding of how a wide variety of inequalities were created and are reproduced and learn the manner in which societal change has addressed problems of discrimination and marginalization.

A B.S.N. degree program is available for registered nurses. The Intercollegiate College of Nursing/WSU College of Nursing offers nine theory courses using Web-based software and two clinical courses, which, in some circumstances, may be taken close to home. Out-of-state students may be required to complete the two clinical courses in Washington, which are scheduled based on negotiations between the student and faculty. RNs work with B.S.N.-prepared preceptors; nursing faculty members supervise the course. RN students must meet specific criteria prior to application to this program.

The online M.S. in agriculture program is designed for students who wish to prepare for or further their careers in agriculture without having to relocate or interfere with their current employment. A student can concentrate in one or two fields or otherwise tailor the curriculum to fit their particular needs. They may choose a thesis or nonthesis program.

The online M.S. in engineering and technology management program provides engineers and professionals in technology management with formal academic experience in managing projects, people, organizations, operations, and quality. The program often results in immediate on-the-job improvements and provides graduates the ability to gain management responsibility.

The online early childhood development and care certificate addresses the complex ways in which child development is influenced and how this knowledge can be applied to designing innovative and effective programs for young children and their families. The program is ideal for students pursuing a degree in human development who would like to specialize in early childhood, individuals who already hold a bachelor's degree in another discipline, and persons currently working in the field of early childhood education who have at least 27 semester credits of college course work.

The online graduate certificate in instructional design is designed for working professionals, educators, Web designers, and corporate trainers to strengthen their traditional face-to-face education and training skills and improve their ability to work in alternative learning environments. The 12-credit graduate program incorporates courses in constructivist learning design, educational technology and media, and leadership.

WSU's Professional Writing Certificate allows students to develop a base of skills and knowledge of effective communication (including editorial and technical skills and the broader skills of analysis and synthesis) useful in the professional world. The certificate requires completion of 15 credits (made up of five courses taken in a specific order), with a grade of B (3.0) or better in each course.

The online Volunteer Management Certificate Program (http://capps.wsu.edu/vmcp/) and the online noncredit Telework Certificate Program (http://capps.wsu.edu/telework/) provide noncredit professional education options. These programs have requirements different from the credit and degree programs; students should visit their Web pages for details.

Nearly 200 courses are available to the students. Courses are also available from the National Universities Degree Consortium (NUDC), a group of eight land-grant and state universities formed to address the needs of adult and part-time learners.

To earn a bachelor's degree, WSU requires the completion of at least 120 semester credits, 40 at the upper-division level. At least 30 of the 120 credits must be taken

through WSU. The 120 credits must include courses that meet WSU general education requirements. Graduate credit programs require admission to the WSU Graduate School.

Student Services

Academic advising is available to all prospective and currently enrolled degree-seeking students. The WSU Office of Admissions prepares an official evaluation of a student's transcript when he or she is admitted to the University. A Distance Degree Programs (DDP) adviser assists DDP students in developing a study plan based on the program options and University requirements. A student services coordinator is available to help students with logistical details.

Students register online or with support from DDP student services. DVDs, CDs, videotapes, lab kits, and other supplementary materials are available through the DDP office. Students may order textbooks and course guides from the WSU Students Book Corporation online or via the toll-free telephone number.

All DDP students have access to the WSU libraries. The DDP librarian is available via toll-free telephone to assist students with database searches, checking out materials, and copying.

The ASWSU-DDP Career Counselor is available to WSU DDP students to discuss career-related concerns ranging from developing a school-to-career identity to finding a graduate school program.

Credit Options

Undergraduate students may transfer to WSU a maximum of 60 semester credits of lower-division credit and up to 30 credits from other four-year institutions. The exact number of transfer credits accepted by WSU may vary depending upon an individual's choice of degree.

The University has developed a method of accepting credit by examination, including Advanced Placement (AP), College-Level Examination Program (CLEP), DANTES, and American Council on Education (ACE). Interested students should check with their advisers for details.

Faculty

There are 1,131 full-time and 231 part-time instructional faculty members in the Washington State University system. Eighty-four percent have terminal academic degrees.

Admission

Admission to the Center for Distance and Professional Education Distance degree programs requires at least 27 semester or 40 quarter credits of transferable college course work from an accredited community or four-year college, with at least a 2.0 cumulative GPA.

Tuition and Fees

In 2007–08, undergraduate tuition (semester-based) was $315 per semester credit for Washington residents and $460 per semester credit for nonresidents. Graduate tuition (semester-based) was $378 per semester credit for Washington residents and $554 per semester credit for nonresidents. DVD, CD, and videotape rental charges vary by course. Correspondence (flexible enrollment) course tuition is $232 per credit. Payment options for full-time students are available as well.

Financial Aid

A financial aid adviser is available to all DDP students. WSU students receive aid from all federal programs. Washington residents are eligible for institutional and state need grants. In 2004–05, WSU awarded approximately $190 million in financial aid. Approximately 61 percent of all WSU students receive financial aid.

Applying

WSU degree-seeking students must submit an admissions form, have official copies of transcript(s) sent directly from the postsecondary institution(s) attended, and pay the $50 undergraduate application fee. Graduate requirements differ, so students should visit http://www.gradsch.wsu.edu/howtoapply.htm for information on WSU Graduate School admission requirements.

CONTACT

Student Support Services
Center for Distance and Professional
  Education
Van Doren 104
Washington State University
P.O. Box 645220
Pullman, Washington 99164-5220
Phone: 509-335-3557
  800-222-4978 (toll-free)
Fax: 509-335-4850
E-mail: distance@wsu.edu
Web site: http://www.distance.wsu.
  edu

WEBER STATE UNIVERSITY
Distance Learning
Ogden, Utah

Weber State University (WSU) provides lifelong opportunities for diverse learners on and off campus. It offers degrees through seven colleges and forty departments via distance learning options, including online and independent study courses. Students may earn their Associate of Science in general studies or receive specialized training in health professions, criminal justice, and manufacturing. WSU's academic programs prepare students for immediate employment or further study and equip them with liberal education concepts and skills to support their lifelong learning.

WSU serves as Utah's premier public undergraduate university. The institution was founded in 1889, became a state junior college in 1933, and added upper-division courses and began bachelor's degree programs in 1959. On January 1, 1991, Weber State further expanded its offerings and was granted university status.

Weber State University is accredited by the Northwest Association of Schools and Colleges. In addition, professional agencies such as the Commission on Accreditation for Allied Health Education Programs and the Association of University Programs in Health Administration accredit specific disciplines.

Distance Learning Program

The WSU Distance Learning Program serves students who cannot attend college classes in person. During the 2005–06 academic year, more than 25,000 students enrolled in print- and Internet-based courses. Students use distance learning to earn general education credits, as well as degrees and professional credentials in manufacturing, criminal justice, and health science areas.

Delivery Media

Students follow study guides, read textbooks, view videotapes, hear cassettes, and/or participate in online courses. They interact with other students, instructors, and advisers by using mail, telephone, e-mail, and online discussion groups. Exams are delivered online or through the mail and are administered by approved proctors. Access to a videocassette/DVD player, audiocassette player, word processor, or a computer with browser software and an Internet service provider may be required.

Programs of Study

The WSU Distance Learning degree program evolved from a commitment to providing education for health-care professionals and other working adults regardless of location. Combining independent study with Internet courses, a bachelor's degree requires 120 semester hours (40 upper-division, 30 through WSU) with a minimum GPA of at least a 2.0 (or C).

Bachelor's degrees are available in clinical laboratory science, diagnostic medical sonography (medical-vascular), health information management, health promotion, health services administration, nuclear medicine, radiation therapy, and radiologic science (emphases in advanced radiography, cardiovascular-interventional technology, computed tomography, magnetic resonance imaging, mammography, and quality management).

Associate of Science degrees are available in health information technology and respiratory therapy. An Associate of Applied Science degree is also available in clinical laboratory science.

The associate degree in general studies serves the needs of students who want to individualize the first two years of their academic programs, students who want to obtain a broad liberal education, and students who want to lay broad foundations for continued higher education.

The Weber State University Distance Learning Associate of Science degree program in criminal justice and the professional certificate programs in production and inventory management are designed for professionals whose work and travel schedules and remote locations make it difficult for them to participate in classroom course work.

Law enforcement and security professionals can register online with the Utah Electronic College (UEC) and take courses through Weber State University or one of its six collaborating institutions, completing their training on their home or work computers.

Weber State University works in partnership with the 70,000-member APICS (The Association for Operations Management) to offer its certification program through WSU Online for people who work in production and resource management.

WSU certificate programs include health information technology, health-care coding and classification, and radiologic sciences. Radiologic sciences classes can be used toward continuing education units (CEU).

Special Programs

WSU Online, the award-winning extension of the University on the Internet, allows students to take online courses, use online support services, and participate in online discussions and activities with faculty and staff members and other students. WSU Online makes it possible for students with busy schedules and/or long commutes to take advantage of the convenience of online courses with support services and interpersonal experiences that are essential to their success. For current course listings and additional information, students can visit the WSU Web site at http://wsuonline.weber.edu.

Courses from a wide range of academic disciplines are available through Weber State University's independent study program, allowing students to complete their course work at their convenience. Each year, more than 2,000 students enroll in these Internet or print-based courses and take advantage of this self-paced, individualized mode of study.

Student Services

WSU recognizes that most of its students have work, family, and other responsibilities that limit their participation in traditional classroom college courses; therefore, convenience is a major factor in the design of the Distance Learning Program.

Students receive guidance from distance learning staff and faculty members. Degree-seeking students are assigned academic advisers who review transcripts and past learning experiences. This information is used to design individualized programs of study.

Students may access Stewart Library's catalog, interlibrary loan, reference help, document delivery, and other services electronically at http://library.weber.edu. Textbooks can be purchased directly from the WSU bookstore, by telephone (800-848-7770 Ext. 6352), or online (http://bookstore.weber.edu) for a small handling charge.

Credit Options

WSU may grant credit for active military, National Guard, or reserve experience; 38 or more credits to registered radiographers; a maximum of 45 credits to diploma nursing school graduates; and varying credits to registered respiratory therapy technicians and graduates of accredited therapy/specialty programs. Official transcripts should be sent directly from universities and colleges attended. WSU also recognizes College-Level Examination Program (CLEP) credits.

Faculty

WSU Distance Learning currently employs 200 full-time university faculty members and 50 adjunct faculty members. Nearly all faculty members hold terminal degrees in their respective fields.

Admission

Degree-seeking Distance Learning applicants must meet WSU admission requirements. The programs in health professions require separate applications and information specific to their academic areas. Students not seeking to complete a degree at WSU may be eligible for simplified, nonmatriculated admission.

Tuition and Fees

Distance Learning tuition averages $177 per semester hour. Additional materials may include course study guides ($3–$40) and audiotape, videotape, or DVD deposits of $60 to $100, with a $40 refund upon their return.

Tuition fees for online courses are $177 per semester hour for non-Utah residents. Utah residents pay regular on-campus tuition and fees. All fees are subject to change. Students can consult the current catalog or visit the Web site at http://www.weber.edu/distancelearning/ for more information.

Financial Aid

Eligible students may apply for federal financial aid such as Pell Grants, Supplemental Educational Opportunity Grants (SEOG), Perkins Loans, and Stafford Student Loans. Students can contact the office of financial aid toll-free at 800-848-7770 Ext. 7569.

Veterans may also be considered for VA educational benefits (office of Veteran Affairs telephone: 800-848-7770 Ext. 6039, toll-free). Health professions degree programs are approved by DANTES.

Applying

Students should apply online at http://weber.edu/admissions/ and send an individual program application (if required); official transcripts from previous colleges; and an application fee of $30 (may be paid online by credit card) to the contact address. Distance Learning students need not attend an orientation.

CONTACT

Office of Distance Learning
Weber State University
4005 University Circle
Ogden, Utah 84408-4005
Phone: 801-626-6600
          800-848-7770 Ext. 6600 (toll-free)
Fax: 801-626-8035
E-mail: dist-learn@weber.edu
Web site: http://wsuonline.weber.edu
              http://weber.edu/distancelearning

WESTWOOD COLLEGE–DENVER NORTH ONLINE PROGRAMS

Westwood College Online

Denver, Colorado

Westwood College has been providing accelerated career-focused education since 1953. In addition to online degree programs, Westwood College operates seventeen campuses, with locations in Anaheim, Inland Empire (Upland), South Bay, and Los Angeles, California; Atlanta, Georgia; DuPage, O'Hare Airport, River Oaks, and Chicago–Loop, Illinois; Denver–North and Denver–South, Colorado; Dallas, Fort Worth, and Houston, Texas; and the Washington, D.C., area.

Westwood's accelerated programs enable a student to complete an associate degree in as little as twenty months and a bachelor's degree in as little as three years. By offering year-round classes focused on the most critical skills needed to advance your career, you can complete your course work in less time than students at traditional schools.

Online degree programs are offered through Westwood College–Denver North. Online Programs and are accredited by the Accrediting Commission of Career Schools and Colleges of Technology (ACCSCT).

Distance Learning Program

Westwood College started offering online degree programs in May 2002. Westwood College Online is an excellent option for students who are outside of the metro areas served by Westwood campuses or students whose work or family obligations do not allow time to attend scheduled classes on campus.

Delivery Media

The online courses are instructor led, not self-paced. Assignments are due weekly. The online courses may include the use of threaded discussions simulating in-class discussion and interaction; group projects; student-to-student, student-to-instructor, and instructor-to-student e-mails, chat rooms, short online audio and video lectures, and graphical demonstrations of concepts.

Programs of Study

Westwood College Online offers twenty degree programs ranging from business administration to criminal justice to game art and design. The curriculum provides hands-on projects incorporating some of the latest skills and technologies students learn during course work. Education at Westwood College Online challenges students, enriches them, and helps launch them into a successful career.

Westwood College Online's programs include the following:

Institute of Business: Business administration, with concentrations in accounting and marketing and sales; fashion merchandising; health-care management; e-business management; technical management; Master of Business Administration.

Institute of Design: Animation, graphic design and multimedia, interior design, Web design and multimedia, visual communications, game art and design.

Institute of Justice: Criminal justice, paralegal.

Institute of Technology: Computer network engineering, computer network management, information systems security, software engineering, game software development.

For a complete overview of each program as well as program topics, details, and career opportunities, students should visit http://www. westwoodonline.edu for an up-to-date listing and information.

Special Programs

Alumni retraining is a special program at Westwood. All Westwood alumni are entitled to tuition-free graduate retraining in the program they completed at Westwood. Graduates are able to audit classes to update their skills as curriculum changes in their field of study. Charges for books and student fees may apply.

Student Services

Westwood distance learning students receive online access to the same student services that are provided to on-campus students. With its academic advising, Westwood is dedicated to helping students remove obstacles to success. There are several programs that provide students with the opportunity to solve problems, share ideas, and set goals with members of the college staff. Westwood has a free tutoring program that provides online help. There is a full research library that is available online to students 24 hours a day, seven days a week. Distance learning students also have access to technical assistance 24 hours a day, seven days a week.

The primary objective of the Career Development Services Office is to help students achieve their career goals. At Westwood, successful job-search assistance begins long before graduation. In fact, Westwood's unique approach to career planning and job-placement assistance begins at registration and continues beyond graduation.

Credit Options

There are four ways to achieve advanced academic standing at Westwood College: with transfer credits from accredited colleges or universities, through articulation agreements with selected high schools and colleges, through Westwood College Proficiency Exams, and through Advanced Placement (AP) exams, College Level Examination Program (CLEP) exams, or nationally recognized certification exams.

Faculty

Westwood instructors bring a wealth of real-world experience in their fields and eagerly share that knowledge in the classroom. They are also experts in online teaching and consistently receive high marks from their students: according to Westwood College Online's May 2006 Mid-Term Faculty Course Evaluation Survey, 97 percent of Westwood College Online graduates said they would recommend their teacher to other students.

Admission

Admission into any program requires that the applicant meet certain admissions requirements. Applicants must provide documentation of prior educa-tion and must demonstrate proficiency in basic college-level skills. Applicants from countries where English is not the primary language spoken and applicants whose native languages is not English must demonstrate English language proficiency. For a complete list of admissions requirements found in the Colorado catalog, students should visit http://www.westwood.edu/pdf/catalogs/default.asp.

Tuition and Fees

A complete listing of tuition and charges is contained in a catalog addendum. The College reserves the right to adjust tuition rates at the beginning of any academic term, but such increases are announced at least sixty days in advance. Students should visit http://www.westwood.edu/pdf/catalogs/default.asp for a list of the catalogs.

Financial Aid

Tuition assistance is available for those who qualify. In order to help guide applicants through the tuition assistance application process, Westwood provides a step-by-step guide as well as links to all of the forms that can be filled out online.

Applying

To qualify for admission, students must submit an application fee of $25 and a registration fee of $75, provide proof of a high school diploma or GED completion, and provide passing test scores from college-level exams outlined in the Admission section.

CONTACT

Westwood College Online
Westwood College–Denver
  North–Online Programs
7350 North Broadway
Denver, Colorado 80221

Phone: 888-996-6546 (toll-free)
Fax: 303-426-1832
E-mail: wolinternet@westwood.edu
Web site:
  http://www.westwoodonline.
  edu

Consortium In-Depth Description

The organization listed in this section represents a consortium of institutions offering Distance Learning programs. Consortia are formed so that an expanded set of distance learning options can be offered beyond the resources available through any single member institution. They do not have a central application process and/or do not directly award credits and degrees. The application process, credits, or conferred degrees are awarded through one of the member institutions. Further, consortia generally are not directly granted accreditation; rather, credits and degrees reflect the accreditation of the awarding institution. The reader should obtain specific information directly from the consortium itself.

SREB'S ELECTRONIC CAMPUS
Atlanta, Georgia

In February 2004, the Southern Regional Education Board (SREB) launched a more robust Electronic Campus, recreating it as a regional "learning network for the South" with improved levels of function. The Electronic Campus Web site (http://www.ElectronicCampus.org) is the gateway to e-learning opportunities and online services designed to meet the unique needs of the adult learners who want to start, continue, or complete their education. It provides a one-stop place for adults to learn about and understand educational opportunities, to select campuses and/or e-learning opportunities that best match their needs, and to apply online and enroll in courses or programs. While the Electronic Campus is an online resource for all students, it is targeted at the unique needs of adult and e-learners to help them get the education they need to meet the demands of the twenty-first-century workforce.

Established in 1998, SREB's Electronic Campus has grown from 104 courses to more than 15,000 courses and over 550 degree programs from colleges and universities from the sixteen member states. New courses and programs are added continually.

The Southern Regional Education Board, the nation's first interstate compact for education, was created in 1948 at the request of Southern business, education, and governmental leaders. It is designed to help leaders in government and education work together to advance education and thus improve the social and economic life of the region. SREB's member states are Alabama, Arkansas, Delaware, Florida, Georgia, Kentucky, Louisiana, Maryland, Mississippi, North Carolina, Oklahoma, South Carolina, Tennessee, Texas, Virginia, and West Virginia.

Distance Learning Program

The *Electronic Campus* provides detailed common and comparable information about distance learning courses and programs offered by participating colleges and universities. The goal is to provide enhanced educational opportunities for adult e-learners as well as traditional and nontraditional students by removing many of the barriers that have long hindered access to higher education.

Delivery Media

Courses and programs are available in a variety of delivery formats. The predominant delivery method is the World Wide Web. Courses and programs are available via the Web in both synchronous and asynchronous modes. Other delivery formats are videotapes, satellite, CD-ROMs, compressed video, and open broadcast. Information on the delivery formats for each course and program is available on the *Electronic Campus* Web site (http://www.ElectronicCampus.org).

Programs of Study

The *Electronic Campus* provides access to more than 550 academic programs from regionally accredited public and private colleges and universities. Programs are available in a variety of disciplines and majors at the associate, bachelor's, master's, and doctoral levels. Certificate programs at various levels are also available. More than 15,000 credit courses at the undergraduate and graduate levels, all offered electronically, are available and fully searchable on the site.

All courses and programs available at the *Electronic Campus* meet SREB's Principles of Good Practice and have undergone a review at the institutional, state, and regional levels. The Principles are the quality cornerstone of the *Electronic Campus*. Institutions offering courses and programs must meet a variety of requirements: the course or program must provide appropriate interaction between faculty members and students and among students, high-quality faculty members must provide appropriate supervision of the program or course that is offered electronically, and academic standards for all programs or courses offered electronically must be the same as those for other courses or programs delivered at the institution from which they originate.

Special Programs

The *Electronic Campus* also offers specialized portals to help individuals meet their professional development needs in specific career areas. The first is The Teacher Center (http://www. TheTeacherCenter.org), a site that links teachers, administrators, counselors, librarians, teacher aides, and aspiring teachers to a comprehensive set of services. Educators can search for and enroll in online courses and programs that are offered at the undergraduate and graduate level and that provide either college credit or continuing education units. The portal also provides information about scholarships and financial aid; information about the federal No Child Left Behind Act and each state's requirements for highly qualified teachers; information about each SREB state's licensure, certification, and alternative routes to teaching; career opportunities; and numerous other online services.

The Academic Common Market/ *Electronic Campus* program enables a student in the SREB states to get a waiver of out-of-state tuition if certain conditions are met. Those conditions include the following: no public college or university in a student's home state (state of residence) offers a degree program in the chosen field of study; the program is available in another SREB state participating in the Academic Common Market; the program is available through the *Electronic Campus;* the home state adopts/accepts the program for its residents; the student meets admissions requirements; and the student can be certified as a resident in their home state to participate. More than sixty degree programs are now available through the Academic Common Market/*Electronic Campus.*

Faculty

Many of the SREB region's most respected professors teach courses and programs on the *Electronic Campus.* The faculty members respond to students' questions online and often list times that they can be reached by telephone and e-mail in their campus offices. Students say communication with online professors is as effective as or even more effective than in a classroom setting.

Admission

Each college or university handles admission to its degree programs offered on the *Electronic Campus.* Students can access this information directly from the *Electronic Campus* Web site. Many institutions allow potential students to complete the application for admission online with just a few mouse clicks. Students who wish to enroll in a specific course may be able to do so without formal application and admission. The enrollment procedure and requirements for all colleges and universities participating in the *Electronic Campus* are outlined on the Web site.

Tuition and Fees

Each college or university offering courses and programs sets its tuition and fees. Tuition and fee charges are available at the *Electronic Campus* site.

A growing number of colleges and universities participating in the *Electronic Campus* are offering courses at a single or "electronic rate." These rates apply to students enrolling in courses irrespective of their residence. These courses are clearly marked to help

more students gain access and afford these learning opportunities.

Financial Aid

Participating colleges and universities coordinate financial aid. Specific information on financial aid is available from the institutions. General information is available on the *Electronic Campus* site.

Applying

Anyone with Internet access may search courses and programs available through the *Electronic Campus.* There is no charge for accessing or using the services available at the site. A simple registration can be completed when visiting. Creating a free *Electronic Campus* or Teacher Center account allows users to use (and reuse) data to complete online applications for colleges and universities and financial aid, save course and program information, establish e-mail and personal calendars, and take advantage of other services at the *Electronic Campus.*

CONTACT

Mary Agnes Larson
Associate Director, *Electronic Campus*
Southern Regional Education Board
592 10th Street, NW
Atlanta, Georgia 30318-5776

Phone: 404-875-9211
Fax: 404-872-1477
E-mail: electroniccampus@sreb.org
Web site: http://www.ElectronicCampus.org

Indexes

INSTITUTIONS OFFERING DEGREE AND CERTIFICATE PROGRAMS INDEX

Index of degree and certificate programs offered by institutions. A=Associate degree; B=Bachelor's degree; GC=Graduate certificate; M=Master's degree; UC=Undergraduate certificate

A+ CERTIFICATION

Jefferson Community and Technical College (UC)

A+ CERTIFICATION AND COMPUTER TECHNOLOGY

Cleveland Institute of Electronics (UC)

AAS NURSING, HEALTH CARE PROVIDER TO RN ARTICULATION

St. Clair County Community College (A)

ACADEMIC ADVISING

Kansas State University (GC)

ACCELERATED PROGRAM

California State University, San Marcos (B)

ACCOUNTANCY

Auburn University (M)
California State University, Sacramento (M)
National University (B)

ACCOUNTANT

Lake Superior College (A)

ACCOUNTING

Athabasca University (B,UC)
Blackhawk Technical College (A)
Brenau University (M)
Central Georgia Technical College (A)
City University (B,UC)
Colorado Technical University (A,B)
Darton College (A)
DeVry University Online (A)
Dickinson State University (B)
EduKan (A)
Excelsior College (B)
Franklin Pierce University (UC)
Franklin University (A,B)
Indiana Wesleyan University (A)
Keiser University (A)
Lakeland College (B)
Liberty University (M,A,B)
Madison Area Technical College (A)
Mercy College (A)
Middlesex Community College (A)
Minnesota School of Business–Richfield (B)
Montgomery County Community College (A)
Mountain Empire Community College (A)
Mount Saint Vincent University (UC)
Myers University (B)
Northeastern University (A)
Northwest Missouri State University (B)
Northwest Technical College (A)
Randolph Community College (A)
Seminole Community College (A)
Southern New Hampshire University (GC,A,B)
Southwestern College (B)
Strayer University (A,B,UC)
Thomas Edison State College (B)
University of Alaska Southeast (B)
University of Dallas (GC,M)
The University of Maine at Augusta (B)
University of Maryland University College (GC,B)
University of Northwestern Ohio (B)
University of Phoenix Online Campus (M,A)
Upper Iowa University (B)
Utah State University (B)
Western Wyoming Community College (A,UC)
Southern New Hampshire University (UC)

ACCOUNTING (BACHELOR COMPLETION)

Indiana Wesleyan University (B)

ACCOUNTING AND FINANCE

New England College of Finance (GC)

ACCOUNTING AND FINANCE CONCENTRATION (10-MONTH PROGRAM)

American InterContinental University Online (M)

ACCOUNTING AND FINANCE CONCENTRATION (COMPLETION PROGRAM)

American InterContinental University Online (B)

ACCOUNTING AND FINANCIAL MANAGEMENT

DeVry University Online (M)
University of Maryland University College (M)

ACCOUNTING AND INFORMATION TECHNOLOGY

University of Maryland University College (GC,M)

ACCOUNTING AND TAX SPECIALIST

Minnesota School of Business–Richfield (A)

ACCOUNTING APPLICATIONS

Seminole Community College (UC)

ACCOUNTING CONCENTRATION

Colorado Technical University (M)

ACCOUNTING FOR HEALTH CARE AND NON-PROFIT

The University of Toledo (UC)

ACCOUNTING NYS CPA TRACK

Excelsior College (B)

ACCOUNTING ONLINE

Bryant and Stratton Online (A)

ACCOUNTING SOFTWARE APPLICATIONS

The University of Toledo (UC)

ACCOUNTING TECHNICIAN

Minot State University–Bottineau Campus (A)
University of Alaska Southeast (UC)

ACCOUNTING TECHNOLOGY

Montana State University–Billings (A)
The University of Toledo (A,UC)

ACCOUNTING TRAINEE I

Jefferson Community and Technical College (UC)

ACCOUNTING TRAINEE II

Jefferson Community and Technical College (UC)

ACCOUNTING–ASSOCIATE OF BUSINESS

York Technical College (A)

ACCOUNTING–GENERAL ACCOUNTING TRACK (BBS)

University of Windsor (B)

ACCOUNTING–HEALTHCARE ACCOUNTING AND FINANCIAL MANAGEMENT

Indiana University System (UC)

ACCOUNTING, ADVANCED

Athabasca University (UC)
College of Southern Maryland (UC)

ACCOUNTING, BASIC

College of Southern Maryland (UC)

ACCOUNTING, FINANCE, INFORMATION SYSTEMS, MARKETING

Old Dominion University (B)

ACCOUNTING/FINANCE

Southern New Hampshire University (M,B)

ACCOUNTING/INFORMATION SYSTEMS

Southern New Hampshire University (B)

ACQUISITION AND CONTRACT ADMINISTRATION (MSA)

University of West Florida (M)

ACQUISITION AND CONTRACT MANAGEMENT

Florida Institute of Technology (M)
Strayer University (A,B,UC)

ACQUISITION AND CONTRACTING CONCENTRATION OR PROJECT MANAGEMENT CONCENTRATION

American Graduate University (M)

ACQUISITION MANAGEMENT

University of Management and Technology (M,UC)

ACQUISITION MANAGEMENT– MASTER OF ACQUISITION MANAGEMENT

American Graduate University (M)

ACUTE CARE NURSE PRACTITIONER

Drexel University (M,)

ADD-ON SPECIAL EDUCATION– L/BD

University of the Cumberlands (UC)

ADDICTION STUDIES

University of Cincinnati (B)

ADMINISTRATION

Athabasca University (UC)
Northern Arizona University

University of Michigan–Flint (B)
University of the Incarnate Word (B)

ADMINISTRATION OF CRIMINAL JUSTICE

Northwest Mississippi Community College (A)

ADMINISTRATION OF JUSTICE

Arizona Western College (A)
Cerro Coso Community College (A)
Thomas Edison State College (A,B)

ADMINISTRATION OF JUSTICE AND SECURITY

University of Phoenix Online Campus (M)

ADMINISTRATION OF JUSTICE– LAW ENFORCEMENT

West Hills Community College (A)

ADMINISTRATION–BUILDING CODE ADMINISTRATION

Central Michigan University (B)

ADMINISTRATION– COMMUNICATION ARTS

University of the Incarnate Word (M)

ADMINISTRATION–GENERAL ADMINISTRATION CONCENTRATION

Central Michigan University (M)

ADMINISTRATION–HEALTH SERVICES ADMINISTRATION CONCENTRATION

Central Michigan University (M)

ADMINISTRATION–HUMAN RESOURCE ADMINISTRATION

Central Michigan University (M)

ADMINISTRATION–INFORMATION RESOURCE MANAGEMENT CONCENTRATION

Central Michigan University (M)

ADMINISTRATION–LEADERSHIP CONCENTRATION

Central Michigan University (M)

ADMINISTRATION– ORGANIZATIONAL ADMINISTRATION

Central Michigan University (B)

ADMINISTRATION–PUBLIC ADMINISTRATION CONCENTRATION

Central Michigan University (M)

ADMINISTRATIVE ASSISTANT

Jefferson Community and Technical College (A)
Madison Area Technical College (A)
Minot State University–Bottineau Campus (A)
North Dakota State College of Science (A)
Northwest Technical College (A)

ADMINISTRATIVE ASSISTANT– ACCOUNTING OPTION

Williston State College (A)

ADMINISTRATIVE ASSISTANT– FRONT OFFICE OPTION

Williston State College (UC)

ADMINISTRATIVE ASSISTANT– HEALTH INFORMATION MANAGEMENT OPTION

Williston State College (A)

ADMINISTRATIVE ASSISTANT– INFORMATION PROCESSING OPTION

Williston State College (A,UC)

ADMINISTRATIVE ASSISTANT– MEDICAL BILLING AND CODING OPTION

Williston State College (UC)

ADMINISTRATIVE COMMUNICATIONS–LIBERAL STUDIES

Washburn University (B)

ADMINISTRATIVE MEDICAL SPECIALIST WITH MEDICAL BILLING AND CODING CERTIFICATE

California State University, Dominguez Hills (GC)

ADMINISTRATIVE OFFICE SUPPORT

University of Alaska Southeast (UC)

ADMINISTRATIVE OFFICE TECHNOLOGY

Central Georgia Technical College (A)

ADMINISTRATIVE OFFICE TECHNOLOGY–OFFICE SOFTWARE SPECIALIST

Vincennes University (UC)

ADMINISTRATIVE PRINCIPAL PROGRAM

California University of Pennsylvania (M)

ADMINISTRATIVE PRINCIPALS PROGRAM

California University of Pennsylvania (UC)

ADMINISTRATIVE SERVICES CERTIFICATE

National University (UC)

ADMINISTRATIVE STUDIES

Missouri State University (M)
St. John's University (B)
Thomas Edison State College (A)
York University (B)

ADMINISTRATIVE STUDIES/ HEALTH SERVICES ADMINISTRATION

The University of South Dakota (M)
The University of South Dakota (M)

ADMINISTRATIVE STUDIES/ INTERDISCIPLINARY STUDIES

The University of South Dakota (M)
The University of South Dakota (M)

ADMINISTRATIVE STUDIES/LONG-TERM CARE ADMINISTRATION

The University of South Dakota (M)
The University of South Dakota (M)

ADMINISTRATIVE STUDIES/ ORGANIZATIONAL LEADERSHIP

The University of South Dakota (M)

ADMINISTRATIVE SUPPORT

Rappahannock Community College (UC)

ADMINISTRATIVE SUPPORT TECHNOLOGY

Mountain Empire Community College (A)

ADMINISTRATIVE SUPPORT TECHNOLOGY MEDICAL OFFICE SPECIALIST

Mountain Empire Community College (A)

ADMINISTRATIVE/MANAGEMENT STUDIES

Excelsior College (A)

ADMINISTRATOR LEADERSHIP FOR TEACHING AND LEARNING

Walden University (D)

ADULT AND CONTINUING EDUCATION

Kansas State University (M)

ADULT DEVELOPMENT AND AGING SERVICES

Penn State University Park (UC)

ADULT EDUCATION

Brock University (UC)
Buffalo State College, State University of New York (GC,M)
Indiana University System (M)
Oregon State University (M)
Penn State University Park (M)

ADULT EDUCATION (BED IN ADULT EDUCATION)

Brock University (B)

ADULT EDUCATION AND TRAINING

Saint Joseph's College of Maine (A,UC)

ADULT LEARNING AND DEVELOPMENT

Cleveland State University (GC,M)

ADULT LIBERAL STUDIES

The University of Toledo (B)

ADULT NURSE PRACTITIONER

Clarkson College (M,)
East Carolina University (M)

ADULT PSYCHIATRIC MENTAL HEALTH NURSE PRACTITIONER

Drexel University (M,)

ADULT RELIGIOUS EDUCATION

Saint Joseph's College of Maine (B)

ADVANCED CATECHIST CERTIFICATE

The Catholic Distance University (UC)

ADVANCED CODING FOR THE PHYSICIAN'S OFFICE CERTIFICATE

California State University, Dominguez Hills (GC)

ADVANCED HOSPITAL CODING AND CCS PREP

California State University, Dominguez Hills (GC)

ADVANCED NURSING LEADERSHIP

University of Illinois at Chicago (UC)

ADVANCED PRACTICE PALLIATIVE CARE

University of Illinois at Chicago (UC)

ADVANCED PROGRAMS

University of Oklahoma (D,M)

ADVENTURE EDUCATION

Prescott College (M,B)

ADVERTISING

Academy of Art University (M,A,B)
University of Maryland University College (GC)

ADVERTISING AND PUBLIC RELATIONS

Seminole Community College (A)

ADVERTISING DESIGN

Syracuse University (M)

AERONAUTICAL SCIENCE

Embry-Riddle Aeronautical University (M)

AERONAUTICS AND ASTRONAUTICS

Stanford University (M)
University of Washington (M)

AEROSPACE

The University of Tennessee (M)

AEROSPACE AND MECHANICAL ENGINEERING (COMPUTATIONAL FLUID AND SOLID MECHANICS)

University of Southern California (M)

AEROSPACE AND MECHANICAL ENGINEERING (DYNAMICS AND CONTROL)

University of Southern California (M)

AEROSPACE ENGINEERING

Auburn University (M)
Georgia Institute of Technology (M)
North Carolina State University (M)
The University of Alabama (M)
University of Colorado at Boulder (M)
University of Southern California (M)
The University of Texas at Arlington (M)
University of Washington (M)

AFRICAN AMERICAN MINISTRY LEADERSHIP MODULE

Defiance College (UC)

AFRICANA STUDIES

University of Michigan–Flint (UC)

AGRIBUSINESS

Kansas State University (M)
University of Northwestern Ohio (A)

AGRIBUSINESS SPECIALIZATION

University of Nebraska–Lincoln (M)

AGRICULTURAL AND EXTENSION EDUCATION

The University of Tennessee (M)

AGRICULTURAL AND EXTENSION EDUCATOR

New Mexico State University (M)

AGRICULTURAL AND LIFE SCIENCES

Virginia Polytechnic Institute and State University (M)

AGRICULTURAL BUSINESS ECONOMICS

West Texas A&M University (M)

AGRICULTURAL EDUCATION

Texas Tech University (D,M)
University of Illinois (M)

AGRICULTURAL EXTENSION EDUCATION

Colorado State University (M)

AGRICULTURAL SALES AND SERVICES–EQUINE OPTION

Dickinson State University (A)

AGRICULTURAL SYSTEMS TECHNOLOGY, FAMILY AND CONSUMER SCIENCES EDUCATION AND EXTENSION EMPHASIS

Utah State University (M)

AGRICULTURAL SYSTEMS TECHNOLOGY, SECONDARY/ POST-SECONDARY AGRICULTURAL EDUCATION EMPHASIS

Utah State University (M)

AGRICULTURAL TEACHER EDUCATION

North Carolina State University (M)

AGRICULTURAL, FOOD, AND LIFE SCIENCES NON-THESIS (FOOD SAFETY EMPHASIS)

University of Arkansas (M)

AGRICULTURE

Iowa State University of Science and Technology (M)
Texas Tech University (M)
University of Nebraska–Lincoln (M)
Washington State University (M)

AGRICULTURE AND NATURAL RESOURCES SYSTEMS MANAGEMENT, AGRICULTURE AND NATURAL RESOURCES MANAGEMENT MAJOR

The University of Tennessee at Martin (M)

AGRICULTURE, GENERAL

Oregon State University (B)

AGRONOMY

Iowa State University of Science and Technology (M)

AIR TRAFFIC CONTROL

Thomas Edison State College (A,B)

AIRCRAFT MAINTENANCE

Embry-Riddle Aeronautical University (A)

ALCOHOL AND DRUG ABUSE STUDIES

The University of South Dakota (GC)
The University of South Dakota (UC)
The University of South Dakota (UC)

ALLIED HEALTH

National University (B)

ALLIED HEALTH LEADERSHIP–BS COMPLETION PROGRAM

East Tennessee State University (B)

ALTERNATIVE CERTIFICATION– SPECIAL EDUCATION–L/BD

University of the Cumberlands (UC)

ALTERNATIVE DISPUTE RESOLUTION–CERTIFICATE OF ADVANCED STUDY

University of Denver (UC)

ALTERNATIVE EDUCATION

Lock Haven University of Pennsylvania (M)

ALTERNATIVE ENERGY SYSTEMS

Prescott College (M)

ALTERNATIVE TEACHERS CERTIFICATION PROGRAM

The University of Texas at El Paso

ALTERNATIVE TEACHING

Virginia Polytechnic Institute and State University (UC)

AMERICAN STUDIES

Columbia College (B)
Skidmore College (B)

ANGLICAN STUDIES

Trinity Episcopal School for Ministry (UC)

ANIMAL SCIENCE AND INDUSTRY

Kansas State University (B)

ANIMATION

Westwood Online (B)

ANIMATION AND VISUAL EFFECTS

Academy of Art University (M,A,B)

ANTHROPOLOGY

Darton College (A)
Prescott College (M)
Thomas Edison State College (B)
University of North Texas (M)
Skidmore College (B)

ANTHROPOLOGY (3 YEAR)

Athabasca University (B)

ANTHROPOLOGY (4 YEAR)

Athabasca University (B)

ANTHROPOLOGY PRE-MAJOR

Seminole Community College (A)

APPAREL AND MERCHANDISING

Colorado State University (M,UC)

APPAREL AND MERCHANDISING (GRADUATE)

Colorado State University (UC)

APPLICATION SOFTWARE SPECIALIST

Minot State University (GC)

APPLIED ARTS AND SCIENCES (BAAS)

University of the Incarnate Word (B)

APPLIED BEHAVIOR ANALYSIS FOR SPECIAL EDUCATION

Penn State University Park (GC)

APPLIED BUSINESS

University of Minnesota, Twin Cities Campus
   (UC)

APPLIED COMMUNICATION

Northern Arizona University (M)

APPLIED COMMUNICATION–MASTER OF PROFESSIONAL STUDIES IN APPLIED COMMUNICATION

University of Denver (M)

APPLIED COMPUTER SCIENCE

Northwest Missouri State University (M)

APPLIED COMPUTER STUDIES

Thomas Edison State College (A)

APPLIED COMPUTER SYSTEMS

University of Maryland University College
   (GC)

APPLIED ELECTRONIC STUDIES

Thomas Edison State College (A)

APPLIED GEOTECHNICS

University of Idaho (UC)

APPLIED GERONTOLOGY

University of North Texas (M)

APPLIED HEALTH STUDIES

Pennsylvania College of Technology (B)
Thomas Edison State College (A)

APPLIED HEALTH–BACHELOR OF APPLIED HEALTH ONLINE

University of Minnesota, Crookston (B)

APPLIED INFORMATION TECHNOLOGY, TELECOMMUNICATIONS DEGREE

Pace University (A)

APPLIED MANAGEMENT

Central Texas College (A)
Franklin University (B)

APPLIED MANAGEMENT AND DECISION SCIENCES–ACCOUNTING

Walden University (D)

APPLIED MANAGEMENT AND DECISION SCIENCES–ENGINEERING MANAGEMENT

Walden University (D)

APPLIED MANAGEMENT AND DECISION SCIENCES–FINANCE

Walden University (D)

APPLIED MANAGEMENT AND DECISION SCIENCES–INFORMATION SYSTEMS MANAGEMENT

Walden University (D)

APPLIED MANAGEMENT AND DECISION SCIENCES–KNOWLEDGE MANAGEMENT

Walden University (D)

APPLIED MANAGEMENT AND DECISION SCIENCES–LEADERSHIP AND ORGANIZATIONAL CHANGE

Walden University (D)

APPLIED MANAGEMENT AND DECISION SCIENCES–LEARNING MANAGEMENT

Walden University (D)

APPLIED MANAGEMENT AND DECISION SCIENCES–OPERATIONS RESEARCH

Walden University (D)

APPLIED MANAGEMENT AND DECISION SCIENCES–SELF-DESIGNED

Walden University (D)

APPLIED MANAGEMENT AND DECISION SCIENCES, GENERAL

Walden University (D)

APPLIED MANAGEMENT WITH COMPUTER APPLICATIONS (NON-TEXAS STUDENTS ONLY)

Central Texas College (A)

APPLIED ORGANIZATIONAL MANAGEMENT

University of St. Francis (B)

APPLIED ORGANIZATIONAL TECHNOLOGY

The University of Toledo (UC)

APPLIED SCIENCE

Nashville State Technical Community College
   (A)

APPLIED SCIENCE AND RESOURCE TECHNOLOGY MANAGEMENT

Troy University (B)

APPLIED SCIENCE IN TECHNOLOGY (BAST)

Dickinson State University (B)

APPLIED SCIENCE–BACHELOR OF APPLIED SCIENCE

East Tennessee State University (B)
The University of Maine at Augusta (B)

APPLIED SCIENCE–DIPLOMA IN APPLIED SCIENCE AND ASSOCIATE IN APPLIED SCIENCE

Central Carolina Community College (A)

APPLIED STATISTICAL STRATEGIES

The University of Tennessee (GC)

APPLIED STATISTICS

Kansas State University (GC)
Penn State University Park (GC)
Rochester Institute of Technology (M)

APPLIED STATISTICS AND DATA ANALYSIS

Colorado State University (UC)

APPLIED STUDIES

Abilene Christian University (UC)
Athabasca University (B)
California State University, Dominguez Hills (B)

APPLIED TECHNOLOGY

Central Texas College (A)
Rogers State University (A,B)

APPLIED TECHNOLOGY AND PERFORMANCE IMPROVEMENT

University of North Texas (B)

APPLIED TECHNOLOGY, OPTION IN ALLIED HEALTH SERVICES

Granite State College (B)

APPLIED TECHNOLOGY, OPTION IN EDUCATION AND TRAINING

Granite State College (B)

APPLIED TECHNOLOGY, OPTION IN MANAGEMENT

Granite State College (B)

APPLIED TECHNOLOGY, TRAINING, AND DEVELOPMENT

University of North Texas (M)

ARCHITECTURAL DESIGN

Thomas Edison State College (A,B)

ARCHITECTURAL DRAFTING AND ESTIMATING TECHNOLOGY

North Dakota State College of Science (A)

ARCHITECTURAL STUDIES

University of Missouri–Columbia (D,M)

ARCHITECTURE

Texas Tech University (B)
University of Nebraska–Lincoln (M)

ART

Darton College (A)
Prescott College (B)
Thomas Edison State College (B)

ART (STUDIO)

Skidmore College (B)

ART EDUCATION

East Carolina University (M)
Mansfield University of Pennsylvania (M)
Texas Tech University (M)

ART HISTORY

Mansfield University of Pennsylvania (B)
Prescott College (M)
Skidmore College (B)

ART THERAPY

Prescott College (M)

ARTIFICIAL INTELLIGENCE

Stanford University (GC)

ARTS

Athabasca University (UC)
Spartanburg Community College (A)
Wilkes Community College (A)

ARTS AND LITERATURE–CERTIFICATE OF ADVANCED STUDY

University of Denver (UC)

ARTS AND SCIENCE

Athabasca University (B)

ARTS AND SCIENCE DEGREE PROGRAM

Southwest Virginia Community College (A)

ARTS AND SCIENCE–APPLIED ARTS AND SCIENCE

Rochester Institute of Technology (B)

ARTS AND SCIENCE–APPLIED ARTS AND SCIENCES

Midwestern State University (B)

ARTS AND SCIENCES

Clarion University of Pennsylvania (A)
College of Southern Maryland (A)
Mountain View College (A)
Northeastern University (A)

ARTS AND SCIENCES DEGREE FOR TRANSFER

John Tyler Community College (A)

ARTS AND SCIENCES–APPLIED SCIENCE AND TECHNOLOGY

College of Southern Maryland (A)

ARTS AND SCIENCES–ARTS AND HUMANITIES

College of Southern Maryland (A)

ARTS AND SCIENCES–SOCIAL SCIENCES

College of Southern Maryland (A)

ARTS MANAGEMENT

Prescott College (M)
University of Windsor (UC)

ASIAN STUDIES

Skidmore College (B)

ASSET MANAGEMENT

The American College (GC)

ASSISTIVE TECHNOLOGY

California State University, Dominguez Hills (UC)
East Carolina University (GC)

ASSISTIVE TECHNOLOGY SPECIALIZATION

Bowling Green State University (M)

ASSOCIATE IN ARTS

St. Clair County Community College (A)

ASSOCIATE IN ARTS ONLINE

University of Delaware (A)

ASSOCIATE IN BUSINESS (TRANSFER PROGRAM)

St. Clair County Community College (A)

ASSOCIATE IN SCIENCE–GENERAL STUDIES

Central Carolina Community College (A)

ASSOCIATE OF ARTS

Fairfield University (A)
Nashville State Technical Community College (A)

ASSOCIATE OF ARTS AND BACHELOR OF GENERAL STUDIES

Indiana University–Purdue University Fort Wayne (B)

ASSOCIATE OF ARTS–GENERAL STUDIES

Central Carolina Community College (A)

ASTRONAUTICAL ENGINEERING
University of Southern California (GC,M)

AT-RISK YOUTH SPECIALIZATION
Central Texas College (A,UC)

ATHLETIC COACHING
West Virginia University (M)

ATMOSPHERIC AND ENVIRONMENTAL SCIENCE AND ENGINEERING
Stevens Institute of Technology (GC)

AUTISM
Texas Tech University (GC)
Penn State University Park (GC)

AUTISTIC SPECTRUM DISORDERS
University of North Dakota (GC)

AUTOMOTIVE MANAGEMENT
University of Northwestern Ohio (A)

AUTOMOTIVE SYSTEMS ENGINEERING
University of Michigan–Dearborn (M)

AUTOMOTIVE TECHNOLOGY MANAGEMENT
Pennsylvania College of Technology (B)

AVIATION (BACCALAUREATE DEGREE TRANSFER)
Utah Valley State College (A)

AVIATION ADMINISTRATION/ MANAGEMENT
Utah Valley State College (B)

AVIATION FLIGHT TECHNOLOGY
Thomas Edison State College (A,B)

AVIATION JOB READY DEGREE
Utah Valley State College (A)

AVIATION MAINTENANCE MANAGEMENT
Embry-Riddle Aeronautical University (B)
St. Cloud State University (B)

AVIATION MAINTENANCE TECHNOLOGY
Thomas Edison State College (A,B)

AVIATION MANAGEMENT
Lynn University (M)
Schoolcraft College (A,UC)

AVIATION PROFESSIONAL PILOT
Utah Valley State College (B)

AVIATION SCIENCE
Utah Valley State College (B)

AVIATION STUDIES
Excelsior College (A)

BACHELOR OF APPLIED SCIENCE IN COMPUTER SCIENCE
Troy University (B)

BACHELOR OF APPLIED SCIENCE IN TECHNOLOGY MANAGEMENT (TWO-YEAR COMPLETION)
Missouri State University (B)

BACHELOR OF APPLIED SCIENCE, ORGANIZATIONAL LEADERSHIP CONCENTRATION
University of Wyoming (B)

BACHELOR OF ARTS COMPLETION PROGRAM
University of Denver (B)

BACHELOR OF HOSPITALITY & TOURISM MANAGEMENT
Cape Breton University (B)

BACHELOR OF SCIENCE
Union Institute & University (B)

BACHELOR OF TECHNOLOGY– EMERGENCY MANAGEMENT
Cape Breton University (B)

BACHELOR OF TECHNOLOGY– ENVIRONMENTAL STUDIES
Cape Breton University (B)

BACHELOR OF TECHNOLOGY– MANUFACTURING
Cape Breton University (B)

BACHELOR OF TECHNOLOGY– PUBLIC HEALTH
Cape Breton University (B)

BACHELORS DEGREE IN MULTILINGUAL EDUCATION
Northern Arizona University

BAILS ARTS AND LETTERS
Northern Arizona University (B)

BAILS CRIMINAL JUSTICE
Northern Arizona University (B)

BAILS ENTERPRISE IN SOCIETY
Northern Arizona University (B)

BAILS ENVIRONMENTAL SCIENCES
Northern Arizona University (B)

BAILS LEARNING AND PEDAGOGY
Northern Arizona University (B)

BAILS MATHEMATICS/ STATISTICS
Northern Arizona University (B)

BAILS ORGANIZATIONAL COMMUNICATION
Northern Arizona University (B)

BAILS PARKS AND RECREATION MANAGEMENT
Northern Arizona University (B)

BAILS PSYCHOLOGY
Northern Arizona University (B)

BAILS SOCIOLOGY
Northern Arizona University (B)

BANKING
Strayer University (B)

BANKING AND FINANCE
Central Georgia Technical College (A)

BANKING STUDIES
New England College of Finance (GC)

BEGINNING WEB PAGE
Waubonsee Community College (UC)

BEHAVIOR ANALYSIS

St. Cloud State University (M)
University of North Texas (GC)

BEHAVIORAL INTERVENTION IN AUTISM

University of Massachusetts Lowell (GC)

BEHAVIORAL LEADERSHIP AND MANAGEMENT

Regions University (M)

BEHAVIORAL SCIENCE

Granite State College (A)
Mercy College (B)

BEHAVIORAL SCIENCE–SUBSTANCE ABUSE CERTIFICATE

Vincennes University (UC)

BEHAVIORAL SCIENCES

Vincennes University (A)

BIBLE

Briercrest Distance Learning (UC)
Northwestern College (UC)

BIBLE AND THEOLOGY

Global University of the Assemblies of God (A,B)

BIBLE/PASTORAL MINISTRIES

Global University of the Assemblies of God (B)

BIBLICAL AND CULTURAL LEADERSHIP

Taylor University (UC)

BIBLICAL AND THEOLOGICAL STUDIES

Covenant Theological Seminary (GC)

BIBLICAL STUDIES

The Baptist College of Florida (B)
Dallas Baptist University (B)
Global University of the Assemblies of God (M)
Hope International University (A,UC)
Life Pacific College (A)
Northwestern College (A,B)
Regent University (M)
Regions University (D,M,B)
Taylor University (A,UC)
Temple Baptist Seminary (UC)

BIBLICAL STUDIES–OVER 20 CONCENTRATIONS AVAILABLE

Temple Baptist Seminary (M)

BILINGUAL EDUCATION

Prescott College (M)

BILINGUAL EDUCATION ENDORSEMENT

Northern Arizona University (UC)

BILINGUAL/MULTICULTURAL EDUCATION

Northern Arizona University (M)

BIOCHEMICAL ENGINEERING CERTIFICATE

Villanova University (UC)

BIODESIGN

Stanford University (GC)

BIOETHICS

Cleveland State University (GC,UC)

BIOINFORMATICS

Stanford University (GC)
University of Illinois at Chicago (UC)
University of Maryland University College (GC)

BIOLOGICAL AND AGRICULTURAL ENGINEERING

North Carolina State University (GC,M)

BIOLOGICAL AND AGRICULTURAL ENGINEERING (WATER MANAGEMENT EMPHASIS)

University of Idaho (M)

BIOLOGICAL SCIENCE

Darton College (A)

BIOLOGY

Skidmore College (B)
Thomas Edison State College (A,B)
University of Nebraska at Kearney (M)

BIOLOGY EDUCATION

Western Kentucky University (M)

BIOMEDICAL ELECTRONICS

Thomas Edison State College (A,B)

BIOMEDICAL ENGINEERING

Columbia University (M)
University of Southern California (M)

BIOMEDICAL ENGINEERING (MEDICAL IMAGING AND IMAGING INFORMATICS)

University of Southern California (M)

BIOMEDICAL INFORMATICS

Stanford University (M)

BIOMEDICAL WRITING

University of the Sciences in Philadelphia (M)

BIOMEDICAL/PHARMACEUTICAL (MSA)

University of West Florida (M)

BIOTECHNOLOGY LABORATORY TECHNICIAN

California State University, San Marcos (UC)

BIOTECHNOLOGY MANAGEMENT

University of Maryland University College (GC)

BIOTECHNOLOGY STUDIES

University of Maryland University College (M)

BIOTERRORISM PREPAREDNESS

Penn State University Park (GC)

BIRTH–KINDERGARTEN

Western Carolina University (B)

BLOOD BANK TECHNOLOGY

The University of Texas System (UC)

BLOOD BANK TECHNOLOGY SPECIALIST

University of Illinois (GC)

BOOKKEEPING

Minot State University–Bottineau Campus (UC)

BOOKKEEPING–PARAPROFESSIONAL ACCOUNTING PROGRAM

Bellevue Community College (UC)

BOOKKEEPING–PROFESSIONAL BOOKKEEPER

Lake Superior College (UC)

BOOKKEEPING/ACCOUNTING

Rappahannock Community College (UC)

BORDER ADMINISTRATION

The University of Texas System (UC)

BORDER STUDIES

The University of Texas System (UC)

BRAIN RESEARCH IN EDUCATION

University of Washington (UC)

BRANCH MANAGEMENT

New England College of Finance (GC)

BRIDGE DOCTOR OF PHYSICAL THERAPY

Simmons College (D)

BROADBAND–CERTIFICATE OF ADVANCED STUDY

University of Denver (UC)

BROADCAST DESIGN AND MOTION GRAPHICS

Savannah College of Art and Design (M)

BROADCAST ENGINEERING

Cleveland Institute of Electronics (UC)

BSAS IN ALLIED HEALTH

Youngstown State University (B)

BSAS IN CRIMINAL JUSTICE

Youngstown State University (B)

BSAS IN PUBLIC HEALTH

Youngstown State University (B)

BUILDING A SUSTAINABLE WORLD

Saybrook Graduate School and Research Center (GC)

BUILDING CODE ENFORCEMENT

Red Rocks Community College (A)

BUILDING CONSTRUCTION

Georgia Institute of Technology (M)

BUSINESS

Andrew Jackson University (A)
Ashford University (A)
Buena Vista University (B)
Capella University (M,B)
Cerro Coso Community College (A)
Chemeketa Community College (A)
Clinton Community College (A)
Colorado State University (UC)
Drexel University (M)
Emporia State University (B)
Excelsior College (M,A)
Granite State College (A)
Indiana Wesleyan University (A)
Judson College (B)
Kaplan University (B)
Keiser University (A)
Lansing Community College (A)
Liberty University (A,B)
Mercy College (A)
Missouri Southern State University (B)
New York Institute of Technology (M)
Prescott College (B)
Red Rocks Community College (A)
Rose State College (A)
St. John's University (A)
University of Phoenix Online Campus (A)
University of the Incarnate Word (A)
Utah State University (B)

BUSINESS ADMINISTRATION

Adams State College (B)
American Public University System (M,B)
Arizona Western College (A)
Athabasca University (M)
Auburn University (M)
Baker College of Flint (M,A,B)
Ball State University (M)
Bellevue University (M,B)
Bemidji State University (B)
Berkeley College (A,B)
Brookdale Community College (A)
California State University, Dominguez Hills (M)
Capitol College (M)
Carl Albert State College (A)
Cayuga County Community College (A)
Central New Mexico Community College (A)
Cerro Coso Community College (A)
Chadron State College (M)
Clarion University of Pennsylvania (M)
College of Southern Maryland (A)
College of The Albemarle (A)
Colorado State University (M)
Colorado Technical University (A)
Columbia College (M,A,B)
The Community College of Baltimore County (A)
Community College of Denver (A,UC)
Concordia University, St. Paul (M)
Concordia University Wisconsin (M)
County College of Morris (A)
Culver-Stockton College (B)
Dallas Baptist University (B)
Darton College (A)
De Anza College (UC)
Delaware County Community College (A)
Des Moines Area Community College (A)
DeVry University Online (M,B)
Dickinson State University (B)

Drexel University (M)
East Carolina University (M,B)
Eastern Oregon University (B)
Eastern Wyoming College (A)
Edmonds Community College (A)
Florida State University (M)
Franklin University (A,B)
Grantham University (M,A,B)
Harford Community College (A)
Harrisburg Area Community College (A)
Herkimer County Community College (A)
Indiana State University (B)
Indiana Tech (A,B)
Indiana Wesleyan University (M)
Jacksonville State University (M)
Jefferson Community College (A)
Jones College (A,B)
Jones International University (M,B)
Kansas State University (GC)
Kaplan University (M)
Keiser University (B)
Lakeland College (M,B)
Lake Superior College (A)
Lehigh Carbon Community College (A)
Lehigh University (M)
LeTourneau University (M)
Liberty University (M)
Limestone College (A)
Lynn University (B)
Marist College (M)
Mayville State University (B)
Memorial University of Newfoundland (B,UC)
Mercy College (M,B)
Metropolitan State University (B)
Miami Dade College (A)
Midstate College (B)
Minnesota School of Business–Richfield (M,A,B)
Mississippi State University (M)
Missouri State University (M)
Monroe Community College (A)
Montana State University–Billings (B)
Montgomery Community College (A)
Montgomery County Community College (A)
Mountain Empire Community College (A)
Mount Saint Vincent University (B)
Mount Wachusett Community College (A)
National University (M,B)
New England College of Finance (A)
New Mexico State University (B)
New York Institute of Technology (B)
Northeastern University (A)
Northern Virginia Community College (A)
The Ohio State University (M)
Oral Roberts University (M,B)
Park University (M)
Patrick Henry Community College (A)
Penn State University Park (A)
Randolph Community College (A)
Regent University (M)
Regis University (M,B)
Rogers State University (A)
St. Cloud State University (M)
Saint Joseph's College of Maine (A,B,UC)
Schiller International University (M)
Shippensburg University of Pennsylvania (M)
Sinclair Community College (A)
Southeastern Community College (A)
Southern New Hampshire University (A,B)
Southwestern College (M,B)

State University of New York Empire State College (M)
Strayer University (M,,A,UC)
Suffolk University (M)
Taylor University (B)
Tennessee Technological University (M)
Texas Woman's University (M)
Touro University International (D,M,B)
Troy University (M)
Troy University (A,B)
University of Alaska Southeast (M,A)
University of Colorado at Colorado Springs (M)
University of Colorado at Denver and Health Sciences Center (M)
The University of Findlay (M)
University of Hawaii–West Oahu (B)
University of Houston–Victoria (M)
University of Illinois (M)
University of Illinois at Springfield (B)
University of La Verne (M)
The University of Maine at Augusta (A)
University of Management and Technology (A)
University of Maryland University College (M,B)
University of Massachusetts Lowell (M)
University of Michigan–Flint (M)
University of Nebraska–Lincoln (M)
University of North Dakota (M)
University of Northwestern Ohio (B)
University of Phoenix Online Campus (D,M)
University of St. Francis (M)
The University of South Dakota (M)
The University of Texas at Tyler (M,B)
University of the Incarnate Word (B)
University of Windsor (UC)
University of Wisconsin–Platteville (B)
University of Wisconsin–Platteville (B)
University of Wyoming (B)
Upper Iowa University (B)
Vance-Granville Community College (A)
Vincennes University (A)
Washington State University (B)
Wayne State College (M)
Webster University (M)
Western Piedmont Community College (A)
Western Wyoming Community College (A)
West Texas A&M University (M)
West Virginia University (M)
Westwood Online (M)
Wilkes Community College (A)

BUSINESS ADMINISTRATION (ASBA)

Thomas Edison State College (A)

BUSINESS ADMINISTRATION (BACHELOR COMPLETION)

Indiana Wesleyan University (B)

BUSINESS ADMINISTRATION (BACHELOR OF APPLIED SCIENCE)

Mayville State University (B)

BUSINESS ADMINISTRATION (HUMAN RESOURCE MANAGEMENT CONCENTRATION)

Southern New Hampshire University (B)

BUSINESS ADMINISTRATION (INFORMATION SYSTEMS/ TECHNOLOGY EMPHASIS)

City University (B)

BUSINESS ADMINISTRATION (MARKETING EMPHASIS)

City University (B)

BUSINESS ADMINISTRATION (OFF CAMPUS MBA)

The University of Montana (M)

BUSINESS ADMINISTRATION (ORGANIZATIONAL LEADERSHIP CONCENTRATION)

Southern New Hampshire University (B)

BUSINESS ADMINISTRATION (PROJECT MANAGEMENT EMPHASIS)

City University (B)

BUSINESS ADMINISTRATION (SMALL BUSINESS MANAGEMENT CONCENTRATION)

Southern New Hampshire University (B)

BUSINESS ADMINISTRATION AND BUSINESS EDUCATION CONCENTRATIONS

Parkland College (A)

BUSINESS ADMINISTRATION AND LIBERAL ARTS; HUMANITIES AND SOCIAL SCIENCE

Clinton Community College (A)

BUSINESS ADMINISTRATION AND MANAGEMENT

Alaska Pacific University (B)
Hope International University (B)
The University of Texas System (M)

BUSINESS ADMINISTRATION AND MANAGEMENT–NONPROFIT EMPHASIS

Alaska Pacific University (B)

BUSINESS ADMINISTRATION CAREER

Middlesex Community College (A)

BUSINESS ADMINISTRATION COMPLETION–FINANCE

Walden University (B)

BUSINESS ADMINISTRATION COMPLETION–HUMAN RESOURCE MANAGEMENT

Walden University (B)

BUSINESS ADMINISTRATION COMPLETION–INFORMATION SYSTEMS

Walden University (B)

BUSINESS ADMINISTRATION COMPLETION–MANAGEMENT

Walden University (B)

BUSINESS ADMINISTRATION COMPLETION–MARKETING

Walden University (B)

BUSINESS ADMINISTRATION COMPLETION, GENERAL

Walden University (B)

BUSINESS ADMINISTRATION FOUNDATION COURSES

Missouri State University (M)

BUSINESS ADMINISTRATION IN AVIATION

Embry-Riddle Aeronautical University (M)

BUSINESS ADMINISTRATION MANAGEMENT

Ball State University (A)

BUSINESS ADMINISTRATION OF TECHNICAL STUDIES

Bellevue University (B)

BUSINESS ADMINISTRATION TRANSFER

Anne Arundel Community College (A)
Middlesex Community College (A)

BUSINESS ADMINISTRATION– ACCELERATED MBA FOR ATTORNEYS

Suffolk University (M)

BUSINESS ADMINISTRATION–ACCELERATED MBA FOR CPAS

Suffolk University (M)

BUSINESS ADMINISTRATION–ACCELERATED ONLINE BACHELORS OF BUSINESS ADMINISTRATION

LeTourneau University (B)

BUSINESS ADMINISTRATION–ACCOUNTING

Limestone College (B)

BUSINESS ADMINISTRATION–ACCOUNTING CONCENTRATION

Peirce College (A,B)
Westwood Online (B)

BUSINESS ADMINISTRATION–APPLIED MANAGEMENT

Tompkins Cortland Community College (A)

BUSINESS ADMINISTRATION–BUSINESS LAW CONCENTRATION

Peirce College (A,B,UC)

BUSINESS ADMINISTRATION–COMPUTER PROGRAMMING

Limestone College (B)

BUSINESS ADMINISTRATION–COMPUTER SOFTWARE APPLICATIONS

Limestone College (B)

BUSINESS ADMINISTRATION–DISTANCE MBA PROGRAM

Colorado State University (M)

BUSINESS ADMINISTRATION–E-COMMERCE EMPHASIS (BULGARIA)

City University (B)

BUSINESS ADMINISTRATION–E. MBA

Pace University (M)

BUSINESS ADMINISTRATION–ECONOMIC CRIME AND FRAUD MANAGEMENT

Utica College (M)

BUSINESS ADMINISTRATION–ENTREPRENEURSHIP/SMALL BUSINESS MANAGEMENT CONCENTRATION

Peirce College (A,B)

BUSINESS ADMINISTRATION–GENERAL BUSINESS

Limestone College (B)

BUSINESS ADMINISTRATION–GENERAL MANAGEMENT EMPHASIS

City University (B)

BUSINESS ADMINISTRATION–HONOURS BUSINESS ADMINISTRATION

University of Windsor (B)

BUSINESS ADMINISTRATION–HUMAN RESOURCE EMPHASIS

City University (B)

BUSINESS ADMINISTRATION–HUMAN RESOURCE MANAGEMENT CONCENTRATION

Peirce College (A,B)

BUSINESS ADMINISTRATION–INDIVIDUALIZED STUDY EMPHASIS

City University (B)

BUSINESS ADMINISTRATION–INFORMATION SYSTEMS MANAGEMENT

Berkeley College-New York City Campus (A,B)
Berkeley College-Westchester Campus (A,B)

BUSINESS ADMINISTRATION–INTERNATIONAL OPTION

Montgomery County Community College (A)

BUSINESS ADMINISTRATION–MANAGEMENT

Berkeley College-New York City Campus (A,B)
Berkeley College-Westchester Campus (A,B)
Limestone College (B)

BUSINESS ADMINISTRATION–MANAGEMENT CONCENTRATION

Peirce College (A,B)

BUSINESS ADMINISTRATION–MANAGEMENT EMPHASIS

Community College of Denver (A)

BUSINESS ADMINISTRATION–MARKETING

Berkeley College-New York City Campus (A,B)
Berkeley College-Westchester Campus (A,B)

BUSINESS ADMINISTRATION–MARKETING AND SALES CONCENTRATION

Westwood Online (B)

BUSINESS ADMINISTRATION–MARKETING CONCENTRATION

Peirce College (A,B)

BUSINESS ADMINISTRATION–OFFERED IN THE SPANISH LANGUAGE

Keiser University (B)

BUSINESS ADMINISTRATION–ONLINE MASTERS OF BUSINESS ADMINISTRATION

University of Wisconsin–Whitewater (M)

BUSINESS ADMINISTRATION–ONLINE MBA

Franklin University (M)

BUSINESS ADMINISTRATION–ONLINE MBA PROGRAM

University of North Alabama (M)

BUSINESS ADMINISTRATION–PROFESSIONAL ACCOUNTANCY

Utica College (M)

BUSINESS ADMINISTRATION–PROFESSIONAL MASTER OF BUSINESS ADMINISTRATION

Florida Institute of Technology (M)

BUSINESS ADMINISTRATION–REAL ESTATE MANAGEMENT CONCENTRATION

Peirce College (B)

BUSINESS ADMINISTRATION–TECHNICAL MANAGEMENT

College of Southern Maryland (A)

BUSINESS ADMINISTRATION, ADVANCED

Jefferson Community and Technical College (UC)

BUSINESS ADMINISTRATION, BASIC

Jefferson Community and Technical College (UC)

BUSINESS ADMINISTRATION, ENTREPRENEURSHIP

Community College of Denver (UC)

BUSINESS ADMINISTRATION, GENERAL

Walden University (M)

BUSINESS ADMINISTRATION, INTERNATIONAL BUSINESS

Community College of Denver (UC)

BUSINESS ADMINISTRATION/ ACCOUNTING

Kaplan University (A)

BUSINESS ADMINISTRATION/ GENERAL BUSINESS

Regions University (B)

BUSINESS ADMINISTRATION/ HEALTH CARE MANAGEMENT

University of Phoenix Online Campus (M)

BUSINESS ADMINISTRATION/ INFORMATION COMMUNICATION

Regions University (B)

BUSINESS ADMINISTRATION/ INFORMATION SYSTEMS MANAGEMENT

Regions University (B)

BUSINESS ADMINISTRATION/ MANAGEMENT

Chadron State College (B)
Kaplan University (A)

BUSINESS ADMINISTRATION/ MANAGEMENT INFORMATION SYSTEMS

Chadron State College (B)

BUSINESS ADMINISTRATION/ MARKETING

Chadron State College (B)
University of Phoenix Online Campus (M)

BUSINESS ADMINISTRATIONS

Ashford University (M)

BUSINESS AND ECONOMICS

Eastern Oregon University (B)

BUSINESS AND INDUSTRIAL TECHNOLOGY (ADVANCED)

Pima Community College (UC)

BUSINESS AND INDUSTRY TECHNOLOGY

Pima Community College (A)

BUSINESS AND INDUSTRY TECHNOLOGY (BASIC)

Pima Community College (UC)

BUSINESS AND MANAGEMENT

Skidmore College (B)

BUSINESS AND MARKETING EDUCATION

University of Missouri–Columbia (M)

BUSINESS AND ORGANIZATIONAL SECURITY MANAGEMENT

Webster University (M)

BUSINESS AND TECHNOLOGY

Columbia University (UC)

BUSINESS ASPECTS OF PUBLISHING

Pace University (GC)

BUSINESS COMMUNICATION

Jones International University (M,B)

BUSINESS COMPLETION

Presentation College (B)

BUSINESS COMPUTER SPECIALIST OPTION

Darton College (A)

BUSINESS CONCENTRATION

American InterContinental University Online (A)

BUSINESS ECONOMICS

York University (B)

BUSINESS EDUCATION

Darton College (A)
East Carolina University (M)
Edmonds Community College (A)
Emporia State University (M)
Southern New Hampshire University (M)

BUSINESS ENGLISH

University of Illinois (GC)
Northeastern University (UC)

BUSINESS FOUNDATIONS

University of Washington (UC)

BUSINESS GENERALIST EMPHASIS

Community College of Denver (A)

BUSINESS HOSPITALITY MANAGEMENT

University of Phoenix Online Campus (B)

BUSINESS INFORMATION SYSTEMS

Bellevue University (B)
Southern New Hampshire University (UC)
Utah State University (M)

BUSINESS INFORMATION SYSTEMS (BACHELOR COMPLETION)

Indiana Wesleyan University (B)

BUSINESS INFORMATION TECHNOLOGY

Edmonds Community College (A)
Minot State University (B)

BUSINESS INTELLIGENCE ANALYST

Bellevue Community College (UC)

BUSINESS INTELLIGENCE DEVELOPER

Bellevue Community College (UC)

BUSINESS MANAGEMENT

Anne Arundel Community College (A)
Burlington County College (A)
Central Texas College (A,UC)
Cerro Coso Community College (A)
Columbus State Community College (A)
Concordia University Wisconsin (B)
Dawson Community College (A)
Edmonds Community College (A)
Granite State College (B)
Lehigh Carbon Community College (A,UC)

Malone College (B)
Northern Virginia Community College (A)
Northwest Missouri State University (B)
Parkland College (A)
Penn State University Park (UC)
Tyler Junior College (A)
The University of Findlay (B)
West Valley College (A)

BUSINESS MANAGEMENT CONCENTRATION

Colorado Technical University (M)

BUSINESS MANAGEMENT MARKETING AND SALES

Central Texas College (UC)

BUSINESS MANAGEMENT MARKETING AND SALES MANAGEMENT

Central Texas College (A)

BUSINESS MANAGEMENT TECHNOLOGY

The University of Toledo (A,UC)

BUSINESS MANAGEMENT TECHNOLOGY–FASTTRACK OPTION

The University of Toledo (A)

BUSINESS MANAGEMENT– EBUSINESS EMPHASIS

North Dakota State College of Science (A)

BUSINESS MANAGEMENT–PUBLIC MANAGEMENT SPECIALIZATION

Northern Virginia Community College (A)

BUSINESS ONLINE

Bryant and Stratton Online (A)
University of Minnesota, Crookston (B)

BUSINESS QUALITY MANAGEMENT

Southwestern College (B)

BUSINESS SECURITY AND ASSURANCE

Kaplan University (B)

BUSINESS SOFTWARE

Chemeketa Community College (UC)

BUSINESS SOFTWARE APPLICATIONS SPECIALIST

Madison Area Technical College (UC)

BUSINESS SOFTWARE SPECIALIST–BUSINESS TECHNOLOGY SYSTEMS

Bellevue Community College (UC)

BUSINESS STUDIES (ACCOUNTING CONCENTRATION)

Southern New Hampshire University (B)

BUSINESS STUDIES (BUSINESS ADMINISTRATION CONCENTRATION)

Southern New Hampshire University (B)

BUSINESS STUDIES (BUSINESS FINANCE CONCENTRATION)

Southern New Hampshire University (B)

BUSINESS STUDIES (HUMAN RESOURCE MANAGEMENT CONCENTRATION)

Southern New Hampshire University (B)

BUSINESS STUDIES (INFORMATION TECHNOLOGY CONCENTRATION)

Southern New Hampshire University (B)

BUSINESS STUDIES (INTERNATIONAL MANAGEMENT CONCENTRATION)

Southern New Hampshire University (B)

BUSINESS STUDIES (MARKETING CONCENTRATION)

Southern New Hampshire University (B)

BUSINESS STUDIES (ORGANIZATIONAL LEADERSHIP CONCENTRATION)

Southern New Hampshire University (B)

BUSINESS STUDIES (SMALL BUSINESS MANAGEMENT CONCENTRATION)

Southern New Hampshire University (B)

BUSINESS SUCCESSION PLANNING

The American College (GC)

BUSINESS TECHNOLOGY

Motlow State Community College (A)
West Virginia University at Parkersburg (A)

BUSINESS TRANSFER

Jefferson Community and Technical College (UC)

BUSINESS–ACCOUNTING

Herkimer County Community College (A)

BUSINESS–ASSOCIATE IN ARTS

EduKan (A)

BUSINESS–ASSOCIATE IN BUSINESS, GENERAL BUSINESS MAJOR

Piedmont Technical College (A)

BUSINESS–ASSOCIATE IN BUSINESS, OFFICE SYSTEMS TECHNOLOGY MAJOR

Piedmont Technical College (A)

BUSINESS–BACHELOR OF SCIENCE IN BUSINESS

Murray State University (B)

BUSINESS–BUSINESS ADMINISTRATION

Erie Community College (A)
Herkimer County Community College (A)

BUSINESS–BUSINESS ADMINISTRATION (TRANSFER OPTION)

Erie Community College (A)

BUSINESS–ENTREPRENEURSHIP

Andrew Jackson University (B)

BUSINESS–FASHION MERCHANDISING

Westwood Online (B)

BUSINESS–FOUNDATIONS OF BUSINESS

University of Massachusetts Lowell (GC)

BUSINESS–GENERAL BUSINESS CONCENTRATION

Andrew Jackson University (B)

BUSINESS–HEALTH SERVICES MANAGEMENT TECHNOLOGY

Herkimer County Community College (A)

BUSINESS–HUMAN RESOURCE MANAGEMENT

Herkimer County Community College (A)

BUSINESS–MANAGEMENT/ LEADERSHIP CONCENTRATION

Andrew Jackson University (B)

BUSINESS–MARKETING

Herkimer County Community College (A)

BUSINESS–OFFICE MANAGEMENT

Erie Community College (A)

BUSINESS–SALES CONCENTRATION

Andrew Jackson University (B)

BUSINESS–SALES MANAGEMENT

Andrew Jackson University (B)

BUSINESS–SMALL BUSINESS MANAGEMENT

Herkimer County Community College (A)

BUSINESS, GENERAL

Berkeley College-New York City Campus (B)
Berkeley College-Westchester Campus (B)
Chadron State College (B)
Excelsior College (B)
Jefferson Community and Technical College (UC)
Kansas State University (B)
Missouri Southern State University (A)
Schoolcraft College (A)
Seminole Community College (A)
University of Alaska Southeast (B)
University of Houston–Victoria (B)
Upper Iowa University (A)

BUSINESS, MANAGEMENT, AND COMMUNICATION

Corban College (B)

BUSINESS, MANAGEMENT, AND ECONOMICS

State University of New York Empire State College (A,B)

BUSINESS/ACCOUNTING

Kaplan University (B)
University of Phoenix Online Campus (B)

BUSINESS/BUSINESS ADMINISTRATION

University of Phoenix Online Campus (B)

BUSINESS/COMMUNICATION

University of Phoenix Online Campus (B)

BUSINESS/E-BUSINESS

University of Phoenix Online Campus (B)

BUSINESS/FINANCE

Kaplan University (B)
University of Phoenix Online Campus (B)

BUSINESS/GLOBAL BUSINESS MANAGEMENT

University of Phoenix Online Campus (B)

BUSINESS/INFORMATION SYSTEMS

University of Phoenix Online Campus (B)

BUSINESS/INTEGRATED SUPPLY CHAIN AND OPERATIONS MANAGEMENT

University of Phoenix Online Campus (B)

BUSINESS/MANAGEMENT

University of Phoenix Online Campus (B)

BUSINESS/MANAGEMENT OF INFORMATION SYSTEMS

Kaplan University (B)

BUSINESS/MARKETING

University of Phoenix Online Campus (B)

BUSINESS/ORGANIZATIONAL INNOVATION

University of Phoenix Online Campus (B)

BUSINESS/PUBLIC ADMINISTRATION

University of Phoenix Online Campus (B)

BUSINESS/RETAIL MANAGEMENT

University of Phoenix Online Campus (B)

CANADIAN STUDIES

Western Kentucky University (UC)

CANADIAN STUDIES (3 YEAR)

Athabasca University (B)

CANADIAN STUDIES (4 YEAR)

Athabasca University (B)

CARDIOVASCULAR BIOENGINEERING

Stanford University (GC)

CAREER AND TECHNICAL EDUCATION

Ball State University (M)
Indiana State University (B)
Northern Arizona University (M)
University of Central Florida (M)
University of South Florida (M)
University of Wisconsin–Stout (M,B)
Virginia Polytechnic Institute and State University (M,UC)

CAREER AND TECHNICAL EDUCATION (BS ED.)

Northern Arizona University (B)

CAREER AND TECHNICAL EDUCATION (CTE)

University of West Florida (M)

CAREER AND TECHNICAL STUDIES EDUCATION SPECIALIZATION

University of West Florida (B)

CAREER DEVELOPMENT

Athabasca University (UC)
Memorial University of Newfoundland (UC)

CAREER SPECIALIST STUDIES

University of Illinois (GC)

CAREER STUDIES CERTIFICATE– ACCOUNTING

Mountain Empire Community College (UC)

CAREER STUDIES CERTIFICATE– CHILD DEVELOPMENT

Mountain Empire Community College (UC)

CAREER STUDIES CERTIFICATE– COMPUTER SOFTWARE SPECIALIST

Mountain Empire Community College (UC)

CAREER STUDIES CERTIFICATE– GEOGRAPHICAL INFORMATION SYSTEMS

Mountain Empire Community College (UC)

CAREER STUDIES CERTIFICATE– HEALTH INFORMATION TECHNOLOGY

Mountain Empire Community College (UC)

CAREER STUDIES CERTIFICATE–LEGAL OFFICE ASSISTING

Mountain Empire Community College (UC)

CAREER STUDIES CERTIFICATE–MEDICAL RECORDS CLERK

Mountain Empire Community College (UC)

CAREER STUDIES CERTIFICATE–MEDICAL TRANSCRIPTIONIST

Mountain Empire Community College (UC)

CAREER STUDIES CERTIFICATE–OFFICE AUTOMATION SPECIALIST

Mountain Empire Community College (UC)

CAREER STUDIES CERTIFICATE–PERSONAL COMPUTING FOR HOME AND OFFICE

Mountain Empire Community College (UC)

CAREER STUDIES CERTIFICATE–POLYSOMNOGRAPHY

Mountain Empire Community College (UC)

CAREER STUDIES CERTIFICATE–WASTEWATER PLANT OPERATOR

Mountain Empire Community College (UC)

CAREER STUDIES CERTIFICATE–WATER PLANT OPERATOR

Mountain Empire Community College (UC)

CAREER STUDIES CERTIFICATE–WORD PROCESSING

Mountain Empire Community College (UC)

CAREER STUDIES–ALLIED HEALTH

Patrick Henry Community College (UC)

CAREER STUDIES–MANAGEMENT ASSISTANT

Patrick Henry Community College (UC)

CAREER STUDIES–MEDICAL TRANSCRIPTIONIST

Patrick Henry Community College (UC)

CAREER STUDIES–OFFICE ASSISTING

Patrick Henry Community College (UC)

CAREER STUDIES–WELLNESS

Patrick Henry Community College (UC)

CASE MANAGEMENT

Kaplan University (UC)

CASE MANAGEMENT FOR AGING CLIENTS

Lewis and Clark Community College (UC)

CATECHETICAL DIPLOMA

The Catholic Distance University (UC)

CATHOLIC SCHOOL LEADERSHIP

Marymount University (M)

CERTIFIED FIRE FIGHTER II

University of Illinois (GC)

CERTIFIED INFORMATION SYSTEMS SECURITY PROFESSIONAL (CISSP)

Peirce College (UC)

CFP CERTIFIED FINANCIAL PLANNING

University of Dallas (GC,M)

CFP(R) CERTIFICATION CURRICULUM

The American College (UC)

CHARITABLE PLANNING

The American College (GC)

CHARTERED ADVISOR FOR SENIOR LIVING (CASL) DESIGNATION

The American College (UC)

CHARTERED ADVISOR IN PHILANTHROPY(R)(CAP) DESIGNATION

The American College (GC)

CHARTERED FINANCIAL CONSULTANT (CHFC(R)) DESIGNATION

The American College (UC)

CHARTERED LEADERSHIP FELLOW(R) (CLF(R)) DESIGNATION

The American College (UC)

CHARTERED LIFE UNDERWRITER (CLU(R)) DESIGNATION

The American College (UC)

CHEMICAL DEPENDENCY SPECIALIZATION

Central Texas College (A,UC)

CHEMICAL DEPENDENCY STUDIES COUNSELING

Tompkins Cortland Community College (A)

CHEMICAL ENGINEERING

Auburn University (M)
Columbia University (M)
Kansas State University (M)
Lehigh University (M)
North Carolina State University (M)
University of North Dakota (B)
University of Southern California (M)

CHEMISTRY

Lehigh University (M)
Skidmore College (B)

CHESS IN EDUCATION ONLINE

The University of Texas System (UC)

CHILD AND FAMILY STUDIES

University of Southern Mississippi (M)

CHILD CARE ADMINISTRATION TRAINING

Colorado State University (UC)

CHILD CARE ASSISTANT

Jefferson Community and Technical College (UC)

CHILD DEVELOPMENT

Concordia University, St. Paul (B)

CHILD DEVELOPMENT ASSOCIATE

University of Alaska Southeast (UC)

CHILD DEVELOPMENT SERVICES

Thomas Edison State College (A,B)

CHILDREN'S LITERATURE

Penn State University Park (GC)

CHILDREN'S MENTAL HEALTH

University of South Florida (GC)

CHILDREN, YOUTH, AND FAMILY SERVICES

Penn State University Park (UC)

CHRISTIAN CARE AND COUNSELING

Oral Roberts University (B)

CHRISTIAN EDUCATION

Dallas Baptist University (M)

CHRISTIAN EDUCATION–4 DISTINCT CONCENTRATIONS

Temple Baptist Seminary (M)

CHRISTIAN LEADERSHIP

Liberty University (M)

CHRISTIAN MINISTRIES

Anderson University (M)
Dallas Baptist University (B)
Temple Baptist Seminary (UC)

CHRISTIAN MINISTRY

Hope International University (A,B,UC)
Regions University (D)
Trinity Episcopal School for Ministry (UC)
Wayland Baptist University (M)

CHRISTIAN OUTREACH

Concordia University, St. Paul (M)

CHRISTIAN PROFESSIONAL STUDIES

Shasta Bible College (B)

CHRISTIAN SCHOOL ADMINISTRATION

Oral Roberts University (M)

CHRISTIAN SCHOOL ADMINISTRATION (PK–12)

Oral Roberts University (D)

CHRISTIAN SCHOOL CURRICULUM

Oral Roberts University (M)

CHRISTIAN SCHOOL POSTSECONDARY ADMINISTRATION

Oral Roberts University (M)

CHRISTIAN SCHOOL PROGRAM

Regent University (M)

CHRISTIAN STUDIES

Briercrest Distance Learning (A,B)

CHRISTIAN TRADITION

Saint Joseph's College of Maine (B,UC)

CHRISTIAN WORKER

Taylor University (UC)

CHURCH EDUCATION

Defiance College (UC)

CHURCH MINISTRIES

Oral Roberts University (B)

CINEMA ARTS

Regent University (M)

CIVIL AND CONSTRUCTION ENGINEERING TECHNOLOGY

Thomas Edison State College (A)

CIVIL AND ENVIRONMENTAL ENGINEERING

Virginia Polytechnic Institute and State University (M)

CIVIL ENGINEERING

Auburn University (M)
Colorado State University (M)
Columbia University (M,UC)
Georgia Institute of Technology (M)
Kansas State University (M)
North Carolina State University (M)
Southern Methodist University (M)
University of Florida (M)
University of Idaho (M)
University of North Dakota (B)
The University of Texas at Arlington (M)
Villanova University (M)

CIVIL ENGINEERING (CONSTRUCTION ENGINEERING)

University of Southern California (M)

CIVIL ENGINEERING (STRUCTURAL ENGINEERING)

University of Southern California (M)

CIVIL ENGINEERING TECHNOLOGY

Old Dominion University (B)
Thomas Edison State College (B)

CIVIL ENGINEERING– CONSTRUCTION ENGINEERING AND MANAGEMENT

Columbia University (M)

CIVIL INFRASTRUCTURE ENGINEERING

Virginia Polytechnic Institute and State University (M)

CLASSICS

Skidmore College (B)

CLASSROOM TECHNOLOGY SPECIALTY

Kansas State University (UC)

CLERICAL ASSISTANT

Mountain Empire Community College (UC)

CLERICAL STUDIES

Patrick Henry Community College (UC)

CLINICAL GENETICS

Simmons College (GC)

CLINICAL INFORMATICS

Stanford University (GC)

CLINICAL INVESTIGATION

MGH Institute of Health Professions (GC)
University of South Florida (GC)

CLINICAL INVESTIGATIONS

MGH Institute of Health Professions (M)

CLINICAL LAB SCIENCE

Thomas Edison State College (A,B)

CLINICAL LABORATORY SCIENCE

University of Cincinnati (B)

CLINICAL LABORATORY SCIENCES

Weber State University (B)

CLINICAL LABORATORY SCIENCES (ADVANCED AND CATEGORICAL)

Rosalind Franklin University of Medicine and Science (M)

CLINICAL LABORATORY SCIENCES (ENTRY-LEVEL)

Rosalind Franklin University of Medicine and Science (M)

CLINICAL LABORATORY TECHNICIAN

Weber State University (A)

CLINICAL NURSE SPECIALIST

East Carolina University (M,)

CLINICAL NUTRITION

University of Medicine and Dentistry of New Jersey (M)

CLINICAL NUTRITION (DCN)

University of Medicine and Dentistry of New Jersey (D)

CLINICAL NUTRITION/NUTRITION EDUCATION

Rosalind Franklin University of Medicine and Science (M)

CLINICAL PATHOLOGY

University of Massachusetts Lowell (GC)

CLINICAL PSYCHOLOGY

Fielding Graduate University (D)

CLINICAL RESEARCH ORGANIZATION AND MANAGEMENT

Drexel University (M)

CLINICAL TRIALS RESEARCH

Drexel University (M,UC)

CLINICAL VISION RESEARCH

Nova Southeastern University (M)

COACHING AND MENTORING

Regent University (UC)

COACHING–NATIONAL COACHING CERTIFICATION

United States Sports Academy (UC)

COACHING–NEW YORK STATE COACHING CERTIFICATION

Monroe Community College (UC)

COLLABORATIVE EDUCATIONAL LEADERSHIP

Fielding Graduate University (M)

COLLABORATIVE LEARNING AND TEACHING

Graceland University (M)

COLLABORATIVE TEACHER AND EARLY CHILDHOOD EDUCATION

Auburn University (M)

COLLEGE STUDENT PERSONNEL

Arkansas Tech University (M)

COLLEGE TRANSFER

Randolph Community College (A)
Southeastern Community College (A)

COLLEGE/UNIVERSITY TRANSFER

Wake Technical Community College (A)

COMMERCE AND BUSINESS ADMINISTRATION (GENERAL BUSINESS)

The University of Alabama (B)

COMMERCE–BACHELOR OF COMMERCE PROGRAM FOR UNIVERSITY GRADUATES

University of Windsor (B)

COMMERCIAL LENDING

New England College of Finance (GC)

COMMUNICATION

Andrew Jackson University (A)
Dallas Baptist University (B)
Drexel University (B)
North Dakota State University (M)
Regent University (D)
Spring Arbor University (M)
Utah Valley State College (A)

COMMUNICATION ARTS (BA OR BS)

Austin Peay State University (B)

COMMUNICATION DISORDERS

Western Kentucky University (M)

COMMUNICATION SCIENCES AND DISORDERS

Longwood University (M)

COMMUNICATION STUDIES

Athabasca University (B)
Regent University (M)
University of Maryland University College (B)

COMMUNICATION STUDIES–PROFESSIONAL COMMUNICATION STUDIES

Pace University (B)

COMMUNICATION SYSTEMS

University of Idaho (UC)

COMMUNICATION–PROFESSIONAL COMMUNICATION

East Carolina University (GC)

COMMUNICATION/ ORGANIZATIONAL COMMUNICATIONS/MASS COMMUNICATION/PUBLIC RELATIONS

Montana State University–Billings (B)

COMMUNICATION/PUBLIC RELATIONS/JOURNALISM CONCENTRATION

East Carolina University (B)

COMMUNICATIONS

Andrew Jackson University (B)
Indiana Wesleyan University (UC)
Prescott College (B)
Regent University (B)
Southern New Hampshire University (B)
State University of New York at Oswego (B)
Thomas Edison State College (B)

COMMUNICATIONS AND APPLIED TECHNOLOGY

Drexel University (B)

COMMUNICATIONS MANAGEMENT

Southern Polytechnic State University (GC)
Syracuse University (M)
Webster University (M)

COMMUNICATIONS–PROFESSIONAL COMMUNICATIONS

Stevens Institute of Technology (GC)

COMMUNICATIVE DISORDERS AND DEAF EDUCATION (POST-BACHELORS)

Utah State University (B)

COMMUNITY AND ECONOMIC DEVELOPMENT

Penn State University Park (GC)

COMMUNITY AND HUMAN SERVICES

State University of New York Empire State College (A,B)

COMMUNITY AND PUBLIC HEALTH, SCHOOL NURSE OPTION

The University of North Carolina at Charlotte (M)

COMMUNITY AND REGIONAL PLANNING

Iowa State University of Science and Technology (M)

COMMUNITY CHANGE AND CIVIC LEADERSHIP

Antioch University McGregor (M)

COMMUNITY COLLEGE EDUCATION

University of Central Florida (GC)

COMMUNITY COLLEGE LEADERSHIP

Mississippi State University (M)
Old Dominion University (D)
University of Nebraska–Lincoln (GC)

COMMUNITY COLLEGE LEADERSHIP CONCENTRATION

Oregon State University (D)

COMMUNITY COLLEGE MANAGEMENT

Antioch University McGregor (M)

COMMUNITY COLLEGE TEACHING

California State University, Dominguez Hills (UC)
East Carolina University (GC)
North Carolina State University (GC)

COMMUNITY COLLEGE TEACHING AND LEARNING (ED.M)

University of Illinois (M)

COMMUNITY COUNSELING

St. Mary's University of San Antonio (M)

COMMUNITY DEVELOPMENT

Fort Hays State University (UC)
Kansas State University (M)

COMMUNITY DEVELOPMENT, COMMUNITY SERVICES MAJOR

Central Michigan University (B)

COMMUNITY DEVELOPMENT, HEALTH SCIENCES MAJOR

Central Michigan University (B)

COMMUNITY DEVELOPMENT, PUBLIC ADMINISTRATION MAJOR

Central Michigan University (B)

COMMUNITY HEALTH

Old Dominion University (M)
Walden University (M)

COMMUNITY HEALTH AND DEVELOPMENT

Saybrook Graduate School and Research Center (GC)

COMMUNITY HEALTH PROMOTION

Indiana State University (B)

COMMUNITY LEADERSHIP

Duquesne University (M)

COMMUNITY MENTAL HEALTH

New York Institute of Technology (B)

COMMUNITY PSYCHOLOGY

St. Cloud State University (B)

COMMUNITY REHABILITATION

Vincennes University (UC)

COMMUNITY SERVICES

Thomas Edison State College (A,B)

COMMUNITY STUDIES

Cape Breton University (B)

COMMUNITY STUDIES COMPLETER PROGRAM

University of Massachusetts Boston (B)

COMMUNITY WELLNESS ADVOCATE

University of Alaska Southeast (UC)

COMMUNITY, MEDIA, AND TECHNOLOGY

University of Massachusetts Boston (UC)

COMMUNITY-BASED DEVELOPMENT

Colorado State University (UC)

COMPLEMENTARY AND INTEGRATIVE THERAPIES

Drexel University (UC)

COMPLETION PROGRAM

American InterContinental University Online (A)

COMPUTATIONAL FLUID DYNAMICS

The University of Tennessee (GC)

COMPUTER AND INFORMATION SCIENCE

University of Maryland University College (B)

COMPUTER AND INFORMATION SCIENCES

Knowledge Systems Institute (M)

COMPUTER AND NETWORK TECHNOLOGY

Minnesota State Community and Technical College–Fergus Falls (A)

COMPUTER APPLICATIONS

University of Alaska Southeast (UC)

COMPUTER APPLICATIONS FOR THE OFFICE

Erie Community College (UC)

COMPUTER ARCHITECTURE

Stanford University (GC)

COMPUTER ARTS/NEW MEDIA

Academy of Art University (M,A,B)

COMPUTER ASSISTED DRAFTING (CAD)

Chemeketa Community College (UC)

COMPUTER DATABASE SPECIALIST

Lansing Community College (A)

COMPUTER DATABASE SPECIALIST–CERTIFICATE OF ACHIEVEMENT

Lansing Community College (UC)

COMPUTER EDUCATION AND COGNITIVE SYSTEMS

University of North Texas (M)

COMPUTER ENGINEERING

Iowa State University of Science and Technology (M)
Southern Methodist University (M)

University of Idaho (M)
University of Michigan–Dearborn (M)
University of Southern California (M)
Virginia Polytechnic Institute and State
  University (GC,M)
Walden University (M)

COMPUTER ENGINEERING (BIOINFORMATICS TRACK)

University of Florida (M)

COMPUTER ENGINEERING (GENERAL TRACK)

University of Florida (M)

COMPUTER ENGINEERING TECHNOLOGY

Grantham University (A,B)

COMPUTER ENGINEERING–BIOINFORMATICS

University of Florida (M)

COMPUTER GAME DEVELOPMENT

Edmonds Community College (UC)

COMPUTER GRAPHICS

Stevens Institute of Technology (GC)

COMPUTER HARDWARE AND VLSI DESIGN

Stanford University (GC)

COMPUTER INFORMATION AND OFFICE SYSTEMS

University of Alaska Southeast (A,UC)

COMPUTER INFORMATION SYSTEM

University of Houston–Victoria (M)

COMPUTER INFORMATION SYSTEMS

Bellevue University (M)
Cerro Coso Community College (A)
The College of St. Scholastica (M,UC)
Darton College (A)
DeVry University Online (B)
Harford Community College (A)
Ivy Tech Community College–Bloomington
  (A)
Ivy Tech Community College–Central Indiana
  (A)
Ivy Tech Community College–Columbus (A)
Ivy Tech Community College–East Central
  (A)
Ivy Tech Community College–Kokomo (A)
Ivy Tech Community College–Lafayette (A)

Ivy Tech Community College–North Central
  (A)
Ivy Tech Community College–Northeast (A)
Ivy Tech Community College–Northwest (A)
Ivy Tech Community College–Southeast (A)
Ivy Tech Community College–Southern
  Indiana (A)
Ivy Tech Community College–Southwest (A)
Ivy Tech Community College–Wabash Valley
  (A)
Ivy Tech Community College–Whitewater (A)
Jamestown Community College (A)
Jones College (A,B)
Kaplan University (A)
Mercy College (B)
Missouri State University (M)
Moberly Area Community College (A)
Mount Wachusett Community College (A)
Nova Southeastern University (D,M)
Prescott College (B)
Regis University (B)
Thomas Edison State College (B)
Western Wyoming Community College (A)

COMPUTER INFORMATION SYSTEMS (BACHELOR OF APPLIED SCIENCE)

Mayville State University (B)

COMPUTER INFORMATION SYSTEMS NETWORK ADMINISTRATION

Tyler Junior College (A)

COMPUTER INFORMATION SYSTEMS–CERTIFICATE OF ADVANCED STUDY

University of Denver (UC)

COMPUTER INFORMATION SYSTEMS–MASTER OF APPLIED SCIENCE IN COMPUTER INFORMATION SYSTEMS

University of Denver (M)

COMPUTER INFORMATION SYSTEMS–WEB DESIGN

North Dakota State College of Science (UC)

COMPUTER INFORMATION SYSTEMS/COMPUTER PROGRAMMING

Bristol Community College (A)

COMPUTER INFORMATION SYSTEMS/JAVA

Kaplan University (A)

COMPUTER INFORMATION SYSTEMS/MULTIMEDIA AND INTERNET

Bristol Community College (A)

COMPUTER INFORMATION SYSTEMS/NETWORKING

Kaplan University (A)

COMPUTER INFORMATION SYSTEMS/PROGRAMMING

Kaplan University (A)

COMPUTER INFORMATION SYSTEMS/WEB DEVELOPMENT

Kaplan University (A)

COMPUTER INFORMATION SYSTEMS/WIRELESS NETWORKING

Kaplan University (A)

COMPUTER INFORMATION TECHNOLOGY

Franklin Pierce University (B)
Regis University (M)
Western Kentucky University (B)

COMPUTER INFORMATION TECHNOLOGY AND SYSTEMS MANAGEMENT

Cleveland Institute of Electronics (A)

COMPUTER LANGUAGES AND OPERATING SYSTEMS

Stanford University (GC)

COMPUTER NETWORK ENGINEERING

Westwood Online (A)

COMPUTER NETWORK MANAGEMENT

Westwood Online (B)

COMPUTER NETWORK PROFESSIONAL

East Carolina University (GC)

COMPUTER NETWORKING

George Mason University (GC)
Regis University (B,UC)

COMPUTER NETWORKING AND SECURITY MANAGEMENT

Keiser University (A)

COMPUTER OPERATIONS TECHNOLOGY

Southwestern College (B)

COMPUTER PROGRAMMER/ ANALYST

Lansing Community College (UC,A)

COMPUTER PROGRAMMING

Bristol Community College (UC)
College of Southern Maryland (A)
Minnesota State Community and Technical College–Fergus Falls (A)
Seminole Community College (UC)
North Carolina State University (UC)

COMPUTER PROGRAMMING AND ANALYSIS

Seminole Community College (A)

COMPUTER PROGRAMMING AND ANALYSIS (C++ PROGRAMMING SPECIALIZATION)

Seminole Community College (A)

COMPUTER PROGRAMMING AND ANALYSIS VISUAL BASIC PROGRAMMING SPECIALIZATION

Seminole Community College (A)

COMPUTER PROGRAMMING TECHNOLOGY

Southwestern College (B)

COMPUTER PROGRAMMING WITH JAVA AND C#

Cleveland Institute of Electronics (UC)

COMPUTER PROGRAMMING–C PROGRAMMING

University of Washington (UC)

COMPUTER PROGRAMMING–C++ PROGRAMMING

City University (GC)
University of Washington (UC)

COMPUTER PROGRAMMING– JAVA 2 PROGRAMMING

University of Washington (UC)

COMPUTER PROGRAMMING– JAVA PROGRAMMING

Regis University (UC)

COMPUTER PROGRAMMING– UNIX (SOLARIS)

Regis University (UC)

COMPUTER RELATED CRIME INVESTIGATIONS

St. Petersburg College (UC)

COMPUTER SCIENCE

California State University, Chico (M,B)
Capitol College (M)
Colorado State University (M)
Columbia University (GC,M)
DePaul University (M)
DePaul University (M)
Dickinson State University (B)
Drexel University (M)
Franklin University (A,B)
George Mason University (M)
Grantham University (A,B)
Jamestown Community College (A)
Lakeland College (B)
Mercy College (B)
National University (M,B)
North Carolina State University (M)
Northwest Missouri State University (B)
Nova Southeastern University (D,M)
Old Dominion University (B)
Regis University (B)
Rogers State University (A)
Skidmore College (B)
Southern Methodist University (M)
Stanford University (M)
Stevens Institute of Technology (M)
Texas Tech University (D,M)
Thomas Edison State College (A,B)
Touro University International (B)
University of Bridgeport (M)
University of Colorado at Boulder (M)
University of Idaho (M)
University of Illinois (M,B)
University of Illinois at Springfield (M,B)
University of Management and Technology (M,A,B)
University of Southern California (M)
Utah State University (M,B)
Walden University (M)

COMPUTER SCIENCE (COMPUTER NETWORKING)

University of Southern California (M)

COMPUTER SCIENCE (COMPUTER SECURITY)

University of Southern California (M)

COMPUTER SCIENCE (MULTIMEDIA AND CREATIVE TECHNOLOGIES)

University of Southern California (M)

COMPUTER SCIENCE (SOFTWARE ENGINEERING)

University of Southern California (M)

COMPUTER SCIENCE AND ENGINEERING

Auburn University (M)
The University of Texas at Arlington (M)

COMPUTER SCIENCE AND ENGINEERING TECHNOLOGY

The University of Toledo (B)

COMPUTER SCIENCE INFORMATION TECHNOLOGY

Limestone College (B)

COMPUTER SCIENCE INTERNET MANAGEMENT

Limestone College (A)

COMPUTER SCIENCE INTERNET MANAGEMENT–DATABASE

Limestone College (B)

COMPUTER SCIENCE INTERNET MANAGEMENT–E-COMMERCE

Limestone College (B)

COMPUTER SCIENCE INTERNET MANAGEMENT–OPERATIONS MANAGEMENT

Limestone College (B)

COMPUTER SCIENCE INTERNET MANAGEMENT–WEB DEVELOPMENT

Limestone College (B)

COMPUTER SCIENCE INTERNET MANAGEMENT, GENERAL

Limestone College (B)

COMPUTER SCIENCE MANAGEMENT INFORMATION SYSTEMS

Limestone College (A)

COMPUTER SCIENCE PROGRAMMING

Limestone College (A,B)

COMPUTER SCIENCE TECHNOLOGY

Thomas Edison State College (A,B)

COMPUTER SCIENCE–AUTOCAD OPERATOR

Central Georgia Technical College (UC)

COMPUTER SCIENCE–CISCO CERTIFIED NETWORK ASSOCIATE PREPARATION, ACCELERATED

Fort Hays State University (UC)

COMPUTER SCIENCE–CISCO CERTIFIED NETWORK ASSOCIATE PREPARATION, MILITARY

Fort Hays State University (UC)

COMPUTER SCIENCE–CISCO SPECIALIST

Central Georgia Technical College (UC)

COMPUTER SCIENCE–CYBERSECURITY CONCENTRATION

Stevens Institute of Technology (M)

COMPUTER SCIENCE–ELEMENTS OF COMPUTER SCIENCE

Stevens Institute of Technology (GC)

COMPUTER SCIENCE–FOUNDATIONS IN COMPUTER SCIENCE

Stanford University (GC)

COMPUTER SCIENCE–INFORMATION SYSTEMS

Austin Peay State University (B)
University of Management and Technology (B)

COMPUTER SCIENCE–INFORMATION TECHNOLOGY

Central Texas College (A)
University of Management and Technology (B)

COMPUTER SCIENCE–MASTER OF COMPUTER SCIENCE

University of Illinois at Urbana–Champaign (M)

COMPUTER SCIENCE–MICROSOFT CERTIFIED SYSTEMS ADMINISTRATOR

Seminole Community College (UC)

COMPUTER SCIENCE–MICROSOFT CERTIFIED SYSTEMS ENGINEER

Seminole Community College (UC)

COMPUTER SCIENCE–MICROSOFT USER SPECIALIST

Central Georgia Technical College (UC)

COMPUTER SCIENCE–SOFTWARE ENGINEERING

University of Management and Technology (B)

COMPUTER SCIENCE, COMPUTER AND INFORMATION SYSTEMS SECURITY

Limestone College (B)

COMPUTER SECURITY

University of Illinois (GC)
University of Illinois at Urbana–Champaign (GC)

COMPUTER SKILLS FOR MANAGERS

College of Southern Maryland (UC)

COMPUTER SOFTWARE

Excelsior College (A)

COMPUTER SOFTWARE APPLICATION SPECIALIST

Central Georgia Technical College (UC)

COMPUTER SOFTWARE SPECIALIST

The University of Toledo (A,UC)

COMPUTER STUDIES

University of Maryland University College (B)

COMPUTER SUPPORT SPECIALIST

Three Rivers Community College (A)

COMPUTER SYSTEMS (NETWORKING/ TELECOMMUNICATIONS EMPHASIS)

City University (B)

COMPUTER SYSTEMS (PROGRAMMING IN C++ EMPHASIS)

City University (B)

COMPUTER SYSTEMS (WEB DESIGN EMPHASIS)

City University (B)

COMPUTER SYSTEMS MANAGEMENT

University of Maryland University College (M)

COMPUTER SYSTEMS–C++ PROGRAMMING EMPHASIS

City University (M)

COMPUTER SYSTEMS–DATABASE TECHNOLOGY EMPHASIS

City University (B)

COMPUTER SYSTEMS– INDIVIDUALIZED STUDY EMPHASIS

City University (M,B)

COMPUTER SYSTEMS– INFORMATION TECHNOLOGY SECURITY EMPHASIS

City University (B)

COMPUTER SYSTEMS– TECHNOLOGY MANAGEMENT EMPHASIS

City University (M)

COMPUTER SYSTEMS–WEB DEVELOPMENT EMPHASIS

City University (M)

COMPUTER SYSTEMS–WEB LANGUAGES EMPHASIS

City University (B)

COMPUTER SYSTEMS–WEB PROGRAMMING IN E-COMMERCE EMPHASIS

City University (M)

COMPUTER TECHNOLOGY

Broome Community College (A)
Excelsior College (B)

COMPUTER TECHNOLOGY (BAS)

Northern Arizona University (B)

COMPUTER TECHNOLOGY MANAGEMENT

Dickinson State University (B)

COMPUTER, INFORMATION, AND NETWORK SECURITY

DePaul University (M)
DePaul University (M)

COMPUTER-AIDED ENGINEERING

University of Southern California (M)

COMPUTER/TECHNOLOGY

Cleveland State University (UC)

COMPUTERS AND MANAGEMENT INFORMATION SYSTEMS

Athabasca University (UC)

COMPUTING AND INFORMATION SYSTEMS

Athabasca University (B,UC)

COMPUTING AND INFORMATION SYSTEMS–POST-DIPLOMA

Athabasca University (B)

COMPUTING AND SECURITY TECHNOLOGY

Drexel University (B)

COMPUTING TECHNOLOGY IN EDUCATION

Nova Southeastern University (D,M)

COMPUTING–DOCTOR OF PROFESSIONAL STUDIES IN COMPUTING

Pace University (UC)

CONFLICT RESOLUTION

Antioch University McGregor (M)
Kansas State University (GC)
The University of North Carolina at Greensboro (M,UC)

CONFLICT RESOLUTION AND RECONCILIATION

Abilene Christian University (M,UC)

CONSTRUCTION

Thomas Edison State College (B)

CONSTRUCTION ENGINEERING

National University (B)
University of Washington (M)

CONSTRUCTION MANAGEMENT

East Carolina University (M)
University of Southern California (M)
University of Washington (UC)

CONSTRUCTION MANAGEMENT–SURVEYING

Northern Kentucky University (B)

CONSTRUCTION SCIENCE AND MANAGEMENT

Clemson University (M)

CONSTRUCTION SUPERVISION

California State University, San Marcos (UC)

CONSTRUCTION TECHNOLOGY

University of Southern Mississippi (B)

CONSTRUCTION TECHNOLOGY–CONSTRUCTION ELECTRICIAN EMPHASIS

Red Rocks Community College (A)

CONSTRUCTION TECHNOLOGY–POWER TECHNOLOGY EMPHASIS

Red Rocks Community College (A)

CONSTRUCTION WORKER–CERTIFIED CONSTRUCTION WORKER

Central Georgia Technical College (UC)

CONSUMER AND FAMILY SCIENCES WITH CHILD STUDIES EMPHASIS

Western Kentucky University (B)

CONTEMPLATIVE EDUCATION

Naropa University (M)

CONTEMPORARY COMMUNICATIONS

University of Massachusetts Lowell (UC)

CONTEMPORARY NURSING FACULTY

Drexel University (M,,UC)

CONTENT DEVELOPMENT

Southern Polytechnic State University (GC)

CONTINUING TEACHING LICENSURE

Oregon State University (UC)

CONTRACT MANAGEMENT–MASTER OF CONTRACT MANAGEMENT

American Graduate University (M)

CONTROL AND SYSTEM ENGINEERING

Stanford University (GC)

CORPORATE COMMUNICATION

Austin Peay State University (M)

CORPORATE COMMUNICATIONS

Mercy College (B)

CORPORATE FINANCE

University of Dallas (GC,M)

CORPORATE MANAGEMENT

Myers University (B)

CORRECTIONAL ADMINISTRATION AND MANAGEMENT

Bellevue University (B)

CORRECTIONAL OFFICER

Lansing Community College (UC)

CORRECTIONAL SERVICES

Mountain Empire Community College (A)

CORRECTIONS

Herkimer County Community College (UC)
Indiana State University (UC)

CORRECTIONS OFFICER ACADEMIC PROGRAM

Alpena Community College (UC)

CORRECTIONS PRE-CERTIFICATION

Tunxis Community College (UC)

COSMETOLOGY BUSINESS

Minnesota School of Business–Richfield (A)

COTA TO MOT

Texas Woman's University (M)

COUNSELING

Athabasca University (M,)
Liberty University (D)
Mercy College (M)
Northern Arizona University (M)
Seton Hall University (M)
University of North Dakota (M)

COUNSELING AND PSYCHOLOGY

Prescott College (M)

COUNSELING EDUCATION AND SUPERVISION

Regent University (D)

COUNSELING PSYCHOLOGY

Memorial University of Newfoundland (M)

COUNSELING PSYCHOLOGY/ HUMAN SERVICES

Prescott College (B)

COUNSELING WOMEN

Athabasca University (UC)

COUNSELING–FAMILY THERAPY TRACK

University of Massachusetts Boston (M)

COUNSELING–MENTAL HEALTH COUNSELING TRACK

University of Massachusetts Boston (M)

COUNSELING–REHABILITATION COUNSELING TRACK

University of Massachusetts Boston (M)

COUNSELING–SCHOOL COUNSELING (K-12)

Emporia State University (M)

COUNSELING–SCHOOL COUNSELING, ADVANCED

The University of North Carolina at Greensboro (GC)

COUNSELING–SCHOOL GUIDANCE COUNSELING

Prescott College (M)

COUNSELING–SCHOOL GUIDANCE TRACK

University of Massachusetts Boston (M)

COUNSELING/HUMAN RELATIONS

Northern Arizona University (M)

COUNSELING/SCHOOL COUNSELING

Northern Arizona University (M)

COUNSELOR EDUCATION

The University of Alabama

CREATIVE STUDIES

Buffalo State College, State University of New York (GC,M)

CREATIVE WRITING

Naropa University (M)
National University (M)
Prescott College (B)
University of Nebraska at Omaha (M)
The University of Texas at El Paso (M)

CREATIVE WRITING-BILINGUAL

The University of Texas System (M)

CREATIVITY STUDIES

Saybrook Graduate School and Research Center (GC)

CRIME PREVENTION THROUGH SOCIAL DEVELOPMENT

Cape Breton University (UC)

CRIME SCENE TECHNOLOGY

St. Petersburg College (A,UC)

CRIMINAL JUSTICE

American Public University System (M,B)
Andrew Jackson University (M,A,B)
Athabasca University (B)
Bemidji State University (A,B)
Bismarck State College (A)
Brenau University (B)
Central Texas College (A)
Clovis Community College (A)
College of The Albemarle (A)
College of the Southwest (B)
Colorado Technical University (A,B)
Columbia College (A,B)
The Community College of Baltimore County (A)
Concordia University, St. Paul (B)
Darton College (A)
East Carolina University (M)
Eastern Wyoming College (A)
Excelsior College (B)
Franklin Pierce University (A,B)
Granite State College (B)
Grantham University (A,B)
Herkimer County Community College (A)
Hodges University (M)
Indiana Wesleyan University (A,UC)
Ivy Tech Community College–Bloomington (A)
Ivy Tech Community College–Central Indiana (A)
Ivy Tech Community College–Columbus (A)
Ivy Tech Community College–East Central (A)
Ivy Tech Community College–Kokomo (A)
Ivy Tech Community College–Lafayette (A)
Ivy Tech Community College–North Central (A)
Ivy Tech Community College–Northeast (A)
Ivy Tech Community College–Northwest (A)
Ivy Tech Community College–Southeast (A)
Ivy Tech Community College–Southern Indiana (A)
Ivy Tech Community College–Southwest (A)
Ivy Tech Community College–Wabash Valley (A)
Ivy Tech Community College–Whitewater (A)
Jefferson Community College (A)
Judson College (B)
Kaplan University (M,A,B)
Keiser University (A,B)
Lakeland College (B)
Liberty University (A,B)
Limestone College (B)

Lock Haven University of Pennsylvania (A)
Lynn University (B)
Mercy College (B)
Missouri Southern State University (B)
Monroe Community College (A)
Montgomery Community College (A)
New Mexico Junior College (A)
New Mexico State University (M)
New York Institute of Technology (B)
Northern Arizona University (B)
Old Dominion University (B)
Ouachita Technical College (A)
Peninsula College (A)
Penn State University Park (B)
Prescott College (B)
Randolph Community College (A)
St. John's University (A,B)
Saint Joseph's College of Maine (A)
Southwestern College (B)
Thomas Edison State College (B)
Troy University (M)
Troy University (B)
Tunxis Community College (A)
University of Central Florida (M)
University of Central Missouri (M)
University of Cincinnati (M)
University of Great Falls (B)
University of Houston–Victoria (B)
University of Maryland University College (B)
University of Massachusetts Lowell (M)
University of Phoenix Online Campus (A)
University of Wisconsin–Platteville (GC)
University of Wisconsin–Platteville (GC)
University of Wisconsin–Platteville (M)
University of Wisconsin–Platteville (M)
University of Wisconsin–Platteville (B)
University of Wisconsin–Platteville (B)
University of Wyoming (B)
Upper Iowa University (B)
Utah Valley State College (A)
Washburn University (B)
Washington State University (B)
Weber State University (A)
Western Carolina University (B)
West Virginia University at Parkersburg (A)
Westwood Online (B)

CRIMINAL JUSTICE (BACHELOR COMPLETION)

Indiana Wesleyan University (B)

CRIMINAL JUSTICE (COMPLETION DEGREE)

The University of Texas System (B)

CRIMINAL JUSTICE ADMINISTRATION

Bellevue University (B)
Lynn University (M)
Myers University (B)
National University (B)
Park University (B)
The University of Findlay (B)
University of Great Falls (M)
University of Phoenix Online Campus (B)

CRIMINAL JUSTICE ADMINISTRATION (MSA)

University of West Florida (M)

CRIMINAL JUSTICE ADMINISTRATION CONCENTRATION

American InterContinental University Online (A)

CRIMINAL JUSTICE CORRECTIONS SPECIALIZATION

Central Texas College (A,UC)

CRIMINAL JUSTICE LEADERSHIP

Roosevelt University (B,UC)

CRIMINAL JUSTICE STUDIES

St. Cloud State University (M,B)

CRIMINAL JUSTICE STUDIES SPECIALIZATION

Central Texas College (UC)

CRIMINAL JUSTICE TECHNOLOGY

Gaston College (A)

CRIMINAL JUSTICE–ADMINISTRATION OPTION

Middlesex Community College (A)

CRIMINAL JUSTICE–COMPUTER SCIENCE

Grantham University (A,B)

CRIMINAL JUSTICE–ECONOMIC CRIME

Herkimer County Community College (A)

CRIMINAL JUSTICE–HOMELAND SECURITY

Austin Peay State University (B)
Grantham University (A,B)

CRIMINAL JUSTICE–LAW ENFORCEMENT OPTION

Middlesex Community College (A)

CRIMINAL JUSTICE–POLICE

Cayuga County Community College (A)

CRIMINAL JUSTICE, ADMINISTRATION OPTION

Granite State College (B)

CRIMINAL JUSTICE, ECONOMIC CRIME INVESTIGATION

Utica College (B)

CRIMINAL JUSTICE, LAW ENFORCEMENT

Lansing Community College (A)

CRIMINAL JUSTICE, SPECIAL POPULATIONS CONCENTRATION

American InterContinental University Online (B)

CRIMINAL JUSTICE/CORRECTIONS

Kaplan University (A,B)

CRIMINAL JUSTICE/CRIME ANALYSIS

Kaplan University (B)

CRIMINAL JUSTICE/CRIME SCENE INVESTIGATION

Kaplan University (B)

CRIMINAL JUSTICE/FORENSIC PSYCHOLOGY

Kaplan University (B)

CRIMINAL JUSTICE/FRAUD EXAMINATION AND INVESTIGATION

Kaplan University (B)

CRIMINAL JUSTICE/GLOBAL ISSUES IN CRIMINAL JUSTICE

Kaplan University (M)

CRIMINAL JUSTICE/LAW

Kaplan University (M)

CRIMINAL JUSTICE/LAW ENFORCEMENT

Kaplan University (A,B)

CRIMINAL JUSTICE/LEADERSHIP AND EXECUTIVE MANAGEMENT

Kaplan University (M)

CRIMINAL JUSTICE/POLICING

Kaplan University (M)

CRIMINAL JUSTICE/PRIVATE SECURITY

Kaplan University (A,B)

CRIMINOLOGY

Indiana State University (M)
Memorial University of Newfoundland (UC)
University of La Verne (B)

CRIMINOLOGY AND CRIMINAL JUSTICE

Indiana State University (M,B)

CRIMINOLOGY AND CRIMINAL JUSTICE (COMPLETION DEGREE)

The University of Texas at Arlington (B)

CRIMINOLOGY, CRIMINAL JUSTICE STUDIES MAJOR

Florida State University (M)

CRITICAL AND CREATIVE THINKING (FOCUS ON CREATIVITY AT WORK)

University of Massachusetts Boston (GC)

CRITICAL CARE (ADVANCED TECHNICAL CERTIFICATION)

St. Petersburg College (UC)

CROP SCIENCE

Texas Tech University (M)

CROSS CULTURAL TEACHING

National University (M)

CROSS DISCIPLINARY PROFESSIONAL STUDIES

Rochester Institute of Technology (M)

CROSS-CATEGORICAL SPECIAL EDUCATION

Regent University (M)

CULTURAL AND REGIONAL STUDIES

Prescott College (B)

CULTURAL STUDIES

Prescott College (M)
State University of New York Empire State College (A,B)

CURRICULUM AND INSTRUCTION

Black Hills State University (GC)
The College of St. Scholastica (M)
Concordia University Wisconsin (M)
Emporia State University (M)
North Carolina State University (M)
University of Arkansas
University of Massachusetts Lowell (M)
University of Nebraska at Kearney (M)
The University of North Carolina at Greensboro (M)

CURRICULUM AND INSTRUCTION (FOR HEALTH CARE PROFESSIONALS)

University of Cincinnati (M)

CURRICULUM AND INSTRUCTION CONCENTRATION (10-MONTH PROGRAM)

American InterContinental University Online (M)

CURRICULUM AND INSTRUCTION–ADULT EDUCATION

University of Phoenix Online Campus (M)

CURRICULUM AND INSTRUCTION–CHILDREN'S LITERATURE

Penn State University Park (M)

CURRICULUM AND INSTRUCTION–EDUCATIONAL LEADERSHIP

University of Colorado at Colorado Springs (M)

CURRICULUM AND INSTRUCTION–EFFECTIVE TEACHING AND INSTRUCTIONAL LEADERSHIP EMPHASIS

Buena Vista University (M)

CURRICULUM AND INSTRUCTION–HEALTH PROMOTION EMPHASIS

Virginia Polytechnic Institute and State University (M)

CURRICULUM AND INSTRUCTION–LEARNING TECHNOLOGIES EMPHASIS

New Mexico State University (D)

CURRICULUM AND INSTRUCTION–SCIENCE EDUCATION CONCENTRATION

University of Massachusetts Lowell (M)

CURRICULUM AND INSTRUCTION–TEACHER LEADERSHIP

Penn State University Park (M)

CURRICULUM AND INSTRUCTION–TEACHING ENGLISH AS A SECOND LANGUAGE EMPHASIS

Buena Vista University (M)

CURRICULUM AND INSTRUCTION, LITERACY EMPHASIS

The University of Texas System (M)

CURRICULUM AND INSTRUCTION/READING

The University of Texas at Arlington (M)

CURRICULUM INTEGRATION IN ACTION

University of Washington (UC)

CURRICULUM STUDIES

The University of Montana (M)

CURRICULUM TEACHING AND LEARNING STUDIES

Memorial University of Newfoundland (M)

CURRICULUM, TECHNOLOGY, AND EDUCATION REFORM

University of Illinois (M)

CUSTOMER RELATIONS

The University of Montana (UC)

CYBER SECURITY

Stevens Institute of Technology (GC)

CYBERSECURITY AND INFORMATION ASSURANCE

Utica College (B)

CYTOTECHNOLOGY

Thomas Edison State College (B)

DAIRY SCIENCE PROFESSIONAL DEVELOPMENT SEQUENCE

University of Illinois (GC)

DANCE

Skidmore College (B)

DANCE EDUCATION

The University of North Carolina at Greensboro (M)

DATA ENTRY OPERATOR

Jefferson Community and Technical College (UC)

DATA MINING

Connecticut State University System (M)
New Jersey Institute of Technology (GC)

DATA MINING AND APPLICATIONS (STATISTICS)

Stanford University (GC)

DATA RESOURCE MANAGEMENT

University of Washington (UC)

DATA/TELECOMMUNICATIONS

University of Massachusetts Lowell (UC)

DATABASE ADMINISTRATION–CERTIFICATE OF ADVANCED STUDY

University of Denver (UC)

DATABASE MANAGEMENT

University of Washington (UC)

DATABASE SYSTEMS

Stevens Institute of Technology (GC)

DATABASE SYSTEMS TECHNOLOGIES

University of Maryland University College (GC)

DATABASE TECHNOLOGIES (MSCIT)

Regis University (GC)

DATABASES

Stanford University (GC)

DEAF AND HARD OF HEARING

Texas Tech University (GC)

DEAF EDUCATION

Texas Woman's University (M)

DECISION ANALYSIS

Stanford University (GC)

DECISION SUPPORT SYSTEMS

Webster University (GC)

DEGREE COMPLETION

Duquesne University (B)

DENTAL ASSISTING

Monroe Community College (UC)

DENTAL HYGIENE

Pennsylvania College of Technology (B)
St. Petersburg College (B)
Thomas Edison State College (B)

DENTAL HYGIENE COMPLETION PROGRAM

Northern Arizona University (B)

DENTAL HYGIENE ONLINE (DEGREE COMPLETION PROGRAM)

University of Bridgeport (B)

DENTAL HYGIENE–BS COMPLETION PROGRAM

East Tennessee State University (B)

DENTAL HYGIENE–DEGREE COMPLETION IN DENTAL HYGIENE

Oregon Institute of Technology (B)

DENTISTRY–PRE-DENTISTRY

Darton College (A)

DESIGN FOR CUSTOMER VALUE AND MARKET SUCCESS

Stanford University (GC)

DESIGNING AND IMPLEMENTING WEB-BASED LEARNING ENVIRONMENTS

University of Colorado at Denver and Health Sciences Center (UC)

DESKTOP PUBLISHING TECHNOLOGY

Bristol Community College (UC)

DEVELOPMENTAL DISABILITIES

Minot State University (A,UC)

DIAGNOSTIC MEDICAL SONOGRAPHY

Darton College (A)

DIETARY MANAGEMENT

Auburn University (UC)

DIETETIC FOOD SYSTEMS MANAGEMENT, DIETETIC TECHNICIAN EMPHASIS

Penn State University Park (A)

DIETETIC FOOD SYSTEMS MANAGEMENT, SCHOOL FOOD SERVICE EMPHASIS

Penn State University Park (A)

DIETETIC TECHNICIAN–ASSOCIATE IN APPLIED SCIENCE DEGREE

Gaston College (A)

DIETETICS

Eastern Michigan University (B)
Kansas State University (B)

DIFFERENTIATED INSTRUCTION

Concordia University, St. Paul (M)

DIGITAL CINEMA

National University (M)

DIGITAL COMMUNICATION

Franklin University (B)
Stanford University (GC)

DIGITAL INFORMATION MANAGEMENT

The University of Arizona (GC)

DIGITAL LIBRARIES

Syracuse University (GC)
Syracuse University (GC)

DIGITAL MEDIA

Savannah College of Art and Design (B)

DIGITAL MUSIC EDUCATION

University of South Florida (GC)

DIGITAL PHOTOGRAPHY

Savannah College of Art and Design (M)

DIGITAL PRINT AND PUBLISHING

Rochester Institute of Technology (GC)

DIGITAL PUBLISHING

Savannah College of Art and Design (UC)

DIGITAL PUBLISHING MANAGEMENT

Savannah College of Art and Design (GC)

DIGITAL SIGNAL PROCESSING

Stevens Institute of Technology (GC)

DIRECT MARKETING

Mercy College (M)

DIRECT TRANSFER

Everett Community College (A)

DIRECTOR OF PUPIL PERSONNEL

University of the Cumberlands (UC)

DIRECTOR OF SPECIAL EDUCATION

University of the Cumberlands (UC)

DISASTER AND EMERGENCY MANAGEMENT

Park University (M)
Rochester Institute of Technology (UC)

DISASTER MANAGEMENT

University of South Florida (GC)

DISASTER MEDICINE AND MANAGEMENT

Philadelphia University (M)

DISASTER PREPAREDNESS AND EMERGENCY MANAGEMENT

University of Hawaii–West Oahu (UC)

DISASTER READINESS

Penn State University Park (GC)

DISTANCE DOCTORATE

Utah State University (D)

DISTANCE EDUCATION

Athabasca University (M)
Indiana University System (UC)
Penn State University Park (GC)
University of Maryland University College (M)

DISTANCE EDUCATION (TECHNOLOGY)

Athabasca University (GC)

DISTANCE EDUCATION AND TECHNOLOGY

University of Maryland University College (GC)

DISTANCE EDUCATION IN DEVELOPING COUNTRIES

University of Maryland University College (GC)

DISTANCE LEARNING

East Carolina University (GC)
Utah State University (UC)

DISTANCE LEARNING DESIGN AND DEVELOPMENT

University of Washington (UC)

DISTANCE MBA PROGRAM

Colorado State University (M)

DISTRIBUTED OBJECT-ORIENTED ANALYSIS AND DESIGN–CERTIFICATE OF ADVANCED STUDY

University of Denver (UC)

DISTRIBUTED SYSTEMS

DePaul University (M)

DIVERSITY MANAGEMENT

The University of Toledo (UC)

DIVINITY

The Baptist College of Florida (A)
Global University of the Assemblies of God (M)
Liberty University (M)
Oral Roberts University (M)

DIVINITY–MASTER OF DIVINITY–ENGLISH BIBLE TRACK WITH OVER 20 CONCENTRATIONS AVAILABLE

Temple Baptist Seminary (M)

DOCTORAL COMPLETION PROGRAM

Saybrook Graduate School and Research Center (D)

DOMESTIC VIOLENCE PREVENTION

University of Massachusetts Lowell (GC)

DREAM STUDIES

Saybrook Graduate School and Research Center (GC)

DRIVER EDUCATION INSTRUCTOR

Indiana State University (UC)

DUAL IMPAIRMENTS

Texas Tech University (GC)

DUKE ENVIRONMENTAL LEADERSHIP MASTER OF ENVIRONMENTAL MANAGEMENT

Duke University (M)

E-BUSINESS

Bellevue University (B)
Dallas Baptist University (M,UC)
Lansing Community College (A,UC)

E-BUSINESS

Rochester Institute of Technology (UC)
Strayer University (B)

E-BUSINESS MANAGEMENT

The Community College of Baltimore County (A)
Westwood Online (B)

E-BUSINESS SOFTWARE (DATABASE TRACK)

Seminole Community College (UC)

E-BUSINESS SOFTWARE (WEB DESIGN TRACK)

Seminole Community College (UC)

E-BUSINESS STRATEGY

University of Illinois (GC)

E-BUSINESS TECHNOLOGY

The Community College of Baltimore County (A)

E-BUSINESS TECHNOLOGY (MICROSOFT TRACK)

Seminole Community College (UC)

E-BUSINESS TECHNOLOGY (SECURITY SPECIALIZATION)

Seminole Community College (A)

E-BUSINESS TECHNOLOGY (SOFTWARE SPECIALIZATION)

Seminole Community College (A)

E-BUSINESS TECHNOLOGY (TECHNOLOGY SPECIALIZATION)

Seminole Community College (A)

E-COMMERCE

Athabasca University (B)
Columbus State Community College (GC)

University of Maryland University College (M)
University of North Texas (UC)

E-COMMERCE AND WEBMASTER TECHNOLOGY

Rose State College (A)

E-COMMERCE ENGINEERING (MSCIT)

Regis University (GC)

E-COMMERCE TECHNOLOGY

DePaul University (M)

E-COMMERCE WEB DEVELOPMENT

Fort Hays State University (UC)

E-LEARNING

Jones International University (M)
Roosevelt University (GC)

E-LEARNING AND ONLINE TEACHING GRADUATE CERTIFICATE

University of Wisconsin–Stout (GC)

E-LEARNING PROFESSIONAL DEVELOPMENT

University of Central Florida (GC)

EARLY CHILDHOOD

Broome Community College (A)
Concordia University, St. Paul (M)

EARLY CHILDHOOD (BAS)

Northern Arizona University (B)

EARLY CHILDHOOD ADMINISTRATOR

Jefferson Community and Technical College (UC)

EARLY CHILDHOOD ASSOCIATE–ADMINISTRATION

Vance-Granville Community College (UC)

EARLY CHILDHOOD ASSOCIATE–GENERAL EDUCATION

Vance-Granville Community College (UC)

EARLY CHILDHOOD ASSOCIATE–SPECIAL NEEDS

Vance-Granville Community College (UC)

EARLY CHILDHOOD BIRTH TO FIVE ENDORSEMENT

University of Wyoming (UC)

EARLY CHILDHOOD DEVELOPMENT

J. Sargeant Reynolds Community College (A)
National University (B)

EARLY CHILDHOOD EDUCATION

Arkansas Tech University (A,B)
Brenau University (M)
Casper College (A)
Clarion University of Pennsylvania (A)
Emporia State University (M)
Haywood Community College (A)
Ivy Tech Community College–Bloomington (A)
Ivy Tech Community College–Central Indiana (A)
Ivy Tech Community College–Columbus (A)
Ivy Tech Community College–East Central (A)
Ivy Tech Community College–Kokomo (A)
Ivy Tech Community College–Lafayette (A)
Ivy Tech Community College–North Central (A)
Ivy Tech Community College–Northeast (A)
Ivy Tech Community College–Northwest (A)
Ivy Tech Community College–Southeast (A)
Ivy Tech Community College–Southern Indiana (A)
Ivy Tech Community College–Southwest (A)
Ivy Tech Community College–Wabash Valley (A)
Ivy Tech Community College–Whitewater (A)
Kansas State University (B,UC)
Lehigh Carbon Community College (A,UC)
Mayville State University (B)
Northern Arizona University (M)
Oral Roberts University (M)
University of Alaska Southeast (M,A,UC)
University of Cincinnati (A,B)
University of Colorado at Denver and Health Sciences Center (M)
University of Missouri–Columbia (M)
University of North Dakota (M)

EARLY CHILDHOOD EDUCATION ADMINISTRATION CREDENTIAL

Kansas State University (UC)

EARLY CHILDHOOD EDUCATION ASSOCIATE

Mayville State University (A)

EARLY CHILDHOOD EDUCATION PRE-K-3 (NON-LICENSURE)

The University of Toledo (M)

EARLY CHILDHOOD EDUCATION, ELEMENTARY EDUCATION, SECONDARY EDUCATION, SPECIAL EDUCATION, AND MASS COMMUNICATION (INTEGRATED) CONCENTRATIONS

Parkland College (A)

EARLY CHILDHOOD EDUCATION, GROUP/LEADER/CHILD DEVELOPMENT ASSOCIATE–INFANT/TODDLER

Community College of Denver (UC)

EARLY CHILDHOOD EDUCATION, GROUP/LEADER/CHILD DEVELOPMENT ASSOCIATE–PRESCHOOL

Community College of Denver (UC)

EARLY CHILDHOOD INTERVENTION

Auburn University (M)

EARLY CHILDHOOD SPECIAL EDUCATION

National University (UC)
University of Wyoming (UC)
University of Missouri–Columbia (M)

EARLY CHILDHOOD SPECIAL EDUCATION, GENERALIST

University of Colorado at Denver and Health Sciences Center (UC)

EARLY CHILDHOOD/ ELEMENTARY EDUCATION

Oregon State University (M)

EARLY CHILDHOOD/MIDDLE CHILDHOOD

University of Wisconsin–Stout (UC)

EARLY LITERACY CERTIFICATE PROGRAM

University of Colorado at Denver and Health Sciences Center (UC)

EARTH AND ENVIRONMENTAL ENGINEERING

Columbia University (M)

EARTH SCIENCE EDUCATION

Eastern Michigan University (M)

ECOLOGICAL TEACHING AND LEARNING

Lesley University (M)

ECOLOGY

Prescott College (M)

ECOMMERCE

Franklin Pierce University (GC)

ECONOMIC CRIME MANAGEMENT

Utica College (M)

ECONOMIC DEVELOPMENT AND ENTREPRENEURSHIP

University of Houston–Victoria (M)

ECONOMICS

Community College of Denver (A)
Darton College (A)
Skidmore College (B)
Strayer University (A,B)
Thomas Edison State College (B)
University of Illinois at Springfield (B)
Western Wyoming Community College (A)

ECONOMICS (BUSINESS TRACK)

Seminole Community College (A)

ECONOMICS (LIBERAL ARTS TRACK)

Seminole Community College (A)

EDUCATION

Arizona Western College (A)
Bemidji State University (M)
Capella University (D,M)
Cardinal Stritch University (M)
Casper College (A)
Central Michigan University (M)
Chatham University (M)
Drexel University (B)
Fort Hays State University (M)
Indiana Wesleyan University (M)
Judson College (B)
Lehigh Carbon Community College (A)
Liberty University (D,M)
Millersville University of Pennsylvania (M)
Mount Saint Vincent University (M)
New Mexico State University (M)
Oregon State University (M)
Prescott College (M,B)
Regent University (GC)
Regis University (M)
Saint Joseph's College of Maine (M)
Strayer University (M)
Touro University International (M)
Union Institute & University (D)
University of Maryland University College (M)
University of Phoenix Online Campus (B)
The University of Tennessee at Martin (M)
University of Wisconsin–Stout (M)

EDUCATION (K-8)

Alaska Pacific University (A,B)

EDUCATION ADMINISTRATION

Concordia University Wisconsin (M)

EDUCATION AND HUMAN RESOURCE STUDIES (ADULT EDUCATION AND TRAINING–AET)

Colorado State University (M)

EDUCATION AND HUMAN RESOURCE STUDIES (ORGANIZATIONAL PERFORMANCE AND CHANGE–OPC)

Colorado State University (M)

EDUCATION AND SCHOOL ADMINISTRATION

The University of North Carolina at Charlotte (M)

EDUCATION AND TRAINING MANAGEMENT SUBSPECIALTY/ HUMAN PERFORMANCE TECHNOLOGY

University of West Florida (M)

EDUCATION AND TRAINING MANAGEMENT SUBSPECIALTY/ INSTRUCTIONAL TECHNOLOGY

University of West Florida (M)

EDUCATION COUNSELING

Concordia University Wisconsin (M)

EDUCATION DOCTORATE

Regent University (D)

EDUCATION LEADERSHIP

Concordia University (M)
University of North Dakota (M)

EDUCATION LEADERSHIP (MSA)

University of West Florida (M)

EDUCATION LEADERSHIP– MASTER OF ARTS IN EDUCATION LEADERSHIP

University of Illinois (M)

EDUCATION LEADERSHIP, MANAGEMENT, AND POLICY (ELMP)

Seton Hall University (M)

EDUCATION SPECIALIST

Liberty University
Utah State University

EDUCATION SPECIALIST –SCHOOL SUPERINTENDENT

University of Nebraska at Kearney

EDUCATION–ADAPTING CURRICULUM FRAMEWORKS FOR ALL LEARNERS

University of Massachusetts Boston (GC)

EDUCATION–ADMINISTRATION AND SUPERVISION SPECIALIZATION

University of Phoenix Online Campus (M)

EDUCATION–ADULT AND POST-SECONDARY EDUCATION

University of Wyoming (M)

EDUCATION–ADULT EDUCATION LEADERSHIP

Walden University (D)

EDUCATION–ALTERNATIVE TEACHER

The University of Texas System (UC)

EDUCATION–BIRTH-KINDERGARTEN EDUCATION

East Carolina University (B)

EDUCATION–BIRTH-KINDERGARTEN TEACHER LICENSURE

The University of North Carolina at Greensboro (B)

EDUCATION–COMMUNITY COLLEGE LEADERSHIP

Walden University (D)

EDUCATION–COMPREHENSIVE MASTERS IN EDUCATION

University of West Florida (M)

EDUCATION–COMPUTER EDUCATION

University of Phoenix Online Campus (M)

EDUCATION–CURRICULUM AND INSTRUCTION

University of Phoenix Online Campus (M)

EDUCATION–CURRICULUM, INSTRUCTION, AND ASSESSMENT (GRADES K–12)

Walden University (M)

EDUCATION–EARLY CHILDHOOD EDUCATION

Walden University (D)

EDUCATION–EARLY CHILDHOOD EDUCATION SPECIALIZATION

University of Phoenix Online Campus (M)

EDUCATION–EDUCATIONAL LEADERSHIP

University of Wyoming (M)
Walden University (M)

EDUCATION–EDUCATIONAL TECHNOLOGY

Walden University (D)

EDUCATION–ELEMENTARY READING AND LITERACY (GRADES K-6)

Walden University (M)

EDUCATION–ELEMENTARY READING AND MATHEMATICS (GRADES K-6)

Walden University (M)

EDUCATION–GRADUATE INTERN TEACHING CERTIFICATE

Drexel University (UC)

EDUCATION–GRADUATE PA SECONDARY TEACHER CERTIFICATION PROGRAM

Clarion University of Pennsylvania (UC)

EDUCATION–HIGHER EDUCATION

Walden University (D)

EDUCATION–HUMAN RESOURCE DEVELOPMENT STRAND

The University of Findlay (M)

EDUCATION–INSTRUCTIONAL TECHNOLOGY

University of Wyoming (M)

EDUCATION–INTEGRATING TECHNOLOGY IN THE CLASSROOM (GRADES 3-12)

Walden University (M)

EDUCATION–K-12 EDUCATIONAL LEADERSHIP

Walden University (D)

EDUCATION–LEVEL I EDUCATION SPECIALIST CREDENTIAL: MILD/MOD

National University (UC)

EDUCATION–LITERACY AND LEARNING IN THE CONTENT AREAS (GRADES 6-12)

Walden University (M)

EDUCATION–MASTER READING TEACHER

The University of Texas System (UC)

EDUCATION–MATHEMATICS (GRADES 6-8)

Walden University (M)

EDUCATION–MATHEMATICS (GRADES K-5)

Walden University (M)

EDUCATION–MIDDLE LEVEL EDUCATION (GRADES 5-8)

Walden University (M)

EDUCATION–MIDDLE SCHOOL EDUCATION

Buena Vista University (UC)

EDUCATION–MISSOURI VISUAL IMPAIRMENT CERTIFICATION TRAINING PROGRAM

Missouri State University (UC)

EDUCATION–POST-BACHELOR'S TEACHING CERTIFICATE

Drexel University (UC)

EDUCATION–POSTSECONDARY SCHOOL ADMINISTRATION

Oral Roberts University (D)

EDUCATION–PRE-K THROUGH 6

Old Dominion University (M)

EDUCATION–SCIENCE (GRADES K-8)

Walden University (M)

EDUCATION–SECONDARY EDUCATION

Buena Vista University (UC)
Judson College (B)
University of North Texas (M)

EDUCATION–SELF-DESIGNED

Walden University (D)

EDUCATION–SPECIAL EDUCATION

University of Wyoming (M)
Walden University (D)

EDUCATION–SUSTAINABILITY EDUCATION

Prescott College (D)

EDUCATION–TEACHER PREPARATION

Old Dominion University (B)

EDUCATION–TEACHING AND LEARNING

University of Wyoming (M)

EDUCATION–TED MULTIPLE OR SINGLE SUBJECT TEACHING CREDENTIAL

National University (UC)

EDUCATION, ACADEMICALLY OR INTELLECTUALLY GIFTED ADD-ON TEACHER LICENSURE

The University of North Carolina at Charlotte (GC)

EDUCATION, GENERAL

Gadsden State Community College (A)
Gaston College (A)
Ouachita Technical College (A)
Park University (M)
University of Alaska Southeast (A)
Walden University (D)

EDUCATION, MIDDLE AND SECONDARY EDUCATION TEACHER LICENSURE

The University of North Carolina at Charlotte (UC)

EDUCATION, MIDDLE GRADES

The University of North Carolina at Charlotte (M)

EDUCATION-ELEMENTARY EDUCATION

Dickinson State University (B)

EDUCATION/ADULT EDUCATION AND TRAINING

University of Phoenix Online Campus (M)

EDUCATION/CURRICULUM AND INSTRUCTION–ENGLISH AND LANGUAGE EDUCATION

University of Phoenix Online Campus (M)

EDUCATION/CURRICULUM AND INSTRUCTION–MATHEMATICS EDUCATION

University of Phoenix Online Campus (M)

EDUCATION/ELEMENTARY TEACHER EDUCATION

University of Phoenix Online Campus (M)

EDUCATION/ESL

University of Phoenix Online Campus (M)

EDUCATION/SECONDARY TEACHER EDUCATION

University of Phoenix Online Campus (M)

EDUCATIONAL ADMINISTRATION

Andrews University (M)
Emporia State University (M)
Fort Hays State University (M)
Kansas State University (M)
New Mexico State University (M)
Prescott College (M)
St. Cloud State University (M)
Skidmore College (B)
University of Massachusetts Lowell (M)
University of Nebraska–Lincoln (D,M,UC)
University of North Texas (M)
University of South Alabama (UC)

EDUCATIONAL ADMINISTRATION (EDUCATIONAL LEADERSHIP)

New Mexico State University (D)

EDUCATIONAL ADMINISTRATION AND ADMINISTRATIVE SERVICES

National University (M)

EDUCATIONAL ADMINISTRATION AND COUNSELING

College of the Southwest (M)

EDUCATIONAL ADMINISTRATION AND SUPERVISION

Ball State University (M)
University of North Texas (M)

EDUCATIONAL ADMINISTRATION–COLLABORATIVE LEADERSHIP

Drexel University (M)

EDUCATIONAL ADMINISTRATION–EDUCATIONAL TECHNOLOGY EMPHASIS

Minnesota State University Moorhead (M)

EDUCATIONAL ADMINISTRATION–SCHOOL ADMINISTRATION

The University of North Carolina at Greensboro (M)

EDUCATIONAL ADMINISTRATION/ ADULT AND HIGHER EDUCATION

The University of South Dakota (M)
The University of South Dakota (M)

EDUCATIONAL ADMINISTRATION/ ELEMENTARY SCHOOL PRINCIPAL

The University of South Dakota (M)
The University of South Dakota (M)
The University of South Dakota
The University of South Dakota

EDUCATIONAL ADMINISTRATION/ SCHOOL DISTRICT SUPERINTENDENT

The University of South Dakota (M)
The University of South Dakota (M)
The University of South Dakota
The University of South Dakota

EDUCATIONAL ADMINISTRATION/ SECONDARY SCHOOL PRINCIPAL

The University of South Dakota (M)
The University of South Dakota (M)
The University of South Dakota
The University of South Dakota

EDUCATIONAL ADMINISTRATIVE LICENSURE

New Mexico State University (UC)

EDUCATIONAL AND INSTRUCTIONAL TECHNOLOGY

National University (M)

EDUCATIONAL ASSESSMENT AND EVALUATION CONCENTRATION (10-MONTH PROGRAM)

American InterContinental University Online (M)

EDUCATIONAL COUNSELING, CURRICULUM, OR TECHNOLOGY

Cape Breton University (M)

EDUCATIONAL DIAGNOSTICIAN

College of the Southwest (M)
Texas Tech University (UC)

EDUCATIONAL LEADERSHIP

Clemson University (D)
Dallas Baptist University (M)
LeTourneau University (M)
Midwestern State University (M)
Northern Arizona University (D,M)
Regent University (M)
Texas Tech University (D)
Touro University International (D)
University of Cincinnati (M)
University of Missouri–Columbia (M)
The University of Montana (M)
University of North Dakota (D)
University of Phoenix Online Campus (D)
University of South Alabama (M)
The University of Texas at Tyler (M)

EDUCATIONAL LEADERSHIP (WEEKEND COHORT PROGRAM)

The University of Montana (D)

EDUCATIONAL LEADERSHIP AND CHANGE

Fielding Graduate University (D)

EDUCATIONAL LEADERSHIP AND PRINCIPAL PROFESSIONAL CERTIFICATION PREPARATION

Texas Tech University (M)

EDUCATIONAL LEADERSHIP STUDIES

Memorial University of Newfoundland (M)

EDUCATIONAL LEADERSHIP, CHARTER SCHOOL ADMINISTRATION EMPHASIS

Central Michigan University (M)

EDUCATIONAL LEADERSHIP, CURRICULUM AND INSTRUCTION SPECIALIZATION

University of Phoenix Online Campus (D)

EDUCATIONAL LEADERSHIP, HIGHER EDUCATION ADMINISTRATION SPECIALIZATION

Lynn University (M)

EDUCATIONAL LEADERSHIP, SCHOOL ADMINISTRATION SPECIALIZATION

Lynn University (M)

EDUCATIONAL LEADERSHIP, SCHOOL ADMINISTRATION WITH ESOL ENDORSEMENT SPECIALIZATION

Lynn University (M)

EDUCATIONAL LEADERSHIP/ ADMINISTRATION

Florida State University (M)

EDUCATIONAL MEDIA

University of Central Florida (GC)

EDUCATIONAL MEDIA (LIBRARY MEDIA)

University of South Alabama (M,UC)

EDUCATIONAL MEDIA AND TECHNOLOGY

The College of St. Scholastica (M)
Eastern Michigan University (GC,M)

EDUCATIONAL MEDIA, NEW MEDIA AND GLOBAL EDUCATION

Appalachian State University (M)

EDUCATIONAL PSYCHOLOGY

University of North Texas (M)

EDUCATIONAL SPECIALIST/ EDUCATION LEADERSHIP

East Carolina University

EDUCATIONAL STUDIES

State University of New York Empire State College (A,B)
University of Nebraska–Lincoln (D)

EDUCATIONAL STUDIES, ADULT LEARNING SPECIALIZATION

Lesley University (D)

EDUCATIONAL TECHNOLOGY

Azusa Pacific University (M)
Boise State University (M)
Cape Breton University (M)
Chadron State College (M)
Cleveland State University (M)
Connecticut State University System (M)
Dakota State University (M)
National University (M)
New Jersey City University (M)
Northern Arizona University (M,UC)
Northwestern Connecticut Community College (A)
Pittsburg State University (M)
University of Alaska Southeast (M,UC)
University of Nebraska–Lincoln (GC)

The University of Texas System (M)
Western Michigan University (M)

EDUCATIONAL TECHNOLOGY AND MULTIDISCIPLINARY STUDIES

Webster University (M)

EDUCATIONAL TECHNOLOGY INTEGRATION

Penn State University Park (GC)

EDUCATIONAL TECHNOLOGY– MASTER OF EDUCATIONAL TECHNOLOGY

Boise State University (M)
The University of British Columbia (M)

ELEARNING DESIGN AND IMPLEMENTATION

University of Colorado at Denver and Health Sciences Center (M)

ELECTRIC MACHINES AND DRIVES

University of Idaho (UC)

ELECTRIC POWER TECHNOLOGY

Bismarck State College (A,UC)

ELECTRIC TRANSMISSION SYSTEM TECHNOLOGY

Bismarck State College (A,UC)

ELECTRICAL AND COMPUTER ENGINEERING

Northeastern University (M)
University of Colorado at Boulder (M)
University of Florida (M)
Virginia Polytechnic Institute and State University (M)

ELECTRICAL AND COMPUTER ENGINEERING (TELECOMMUNICATIONS)

Colorado State University (M)

ELECTRICAL ENGINEERING

Capitol College (M)
Clemson University (M)
Columbia University (GC,M)
Drexel University (M)
Georgia Institute of Technology (M)
Iowa State University of Science and Technology (M)
Kansas State University (M)
Michigan Technological University (D,M)
Southern Methodist University (M)
Stanford University (M)
University of Delaware (M)

University of Idaho (M)
University of North Dakota (B)
University of Southern California (M)
The University of Texas at Arlington (M)
University of Washington (M)

ELECTRICAL ENGINEERING (COMPUTER NETWORKS)

University of Southern California (M)

ELECTRICAL ENGINEERING (MSEE)

University of South Florida (M)

ELECTRICAL ENGINEERING (MULTIMEDIA AND CREATIVE TECHNOLOGIES)

University of Southern California (M)

ELECTRICAL ENGINEERING (VLSI DESIGN)

University of Southern California (M)

ELECTRICAL ENGINEERING TECHNOLOGY

Old Dominion University (B)
The University of North Carolina at Charlotte (B)

ELECTRICAL ENGINEERING– COMMUNICATIONS TRACK

Walden University (M)

ELECTRICAL ENGINEERING– INTEGRATED CIRCUITS TRACK

Walden University (M)

ELECTRICAL ENGINEERING– MICROELECTRONIC AND SEMICONDUCTOR ENGINEERING

Walden University (M)

ELECTRICAL TECHNOLOGY

Thomas Edison State College (A,B)

ELECTRICAL/COMPUTER ENGINEERING

Utah State University (M)

ELECTRICAL/MECHANICAL ENGINEERING TECHNOLOGY

Rochester Institute of Technology (B)

ELECTROMAGNETICS TECHNOLOGY

University of Illinois (GC)

ELECTROMAGNETICS TECHNOLOGY CAMPUS CERTIFICATE

University of Illinois at Chicago (UC)

ELECTRONIC BUSINESS

National University (M)

ELECTRONIC CIRCUITS

Stanford University (GC)

ELECTRONIC COMMERCE

Southeastern Community College (A)
University of Maryland University College (GC)

ELECTRONIC DEVICES AND TECHNOLOGY

Stanford University (GC)

ELECTRONIC ENGINEERING TECHNOLOGY

Cleveland Institute of Electronics (A)
Thomas Edison State College (A,B)

ELECTRONICS AND COMPUTER TECHNOLOGY

Indiana State University (M)

ELECTRONICS ENGINEERING

Cleveland Institute of Electronics (UC)

ELECTRONICS ENGINEERING TECHNOLOGY

Excelsior College (B)
Grantham University (A,B)

ELECTRONICS TECHNOLOGY

Excelsior College (A)
Indiana State University (B)

ELECTRONICS TECHNOLOGY AND ADVANCED TROUBLESHOOTING

Cleveland Institute of Electronics (UC)

ELECTRONICS TECHNOLOGY WITH DIGITAL MICROPROCESSOR LAB

Cleveland Institute of Electronics (UC)

ELECTRONICS TECHNOLOGY WITH FCC LICENSE PREPARATION

Cleveland Institute of Electronics (UC)

ELECTRONICS TECHNOLOGY WITH LABORATORY

Cleveland Institute of Electronics (UC)

ELEMENTARY EDUCATION

Ball State University (M)
Bemidji State University (B)
Buena Vista University (B)
Community College of Denver (A)
Emporia State University (B)
Fort Hays State University (B)
Kansas State University (B)
Mayville State University (B)
Mississippi State University (B)
Missouri State University (M,B)
Montgomery County Community College (A)
New Mexico State University (B)
Northern Arizona University (M)
Prescott College (B)
University of Alaska Southeast (M,UC)
The University of North Carolina at Charlotte (M,B)
University of North Dakota (M)
Utah State University (M)
Western Carolina University (B)
West Virginia University (M)

ELEMENTARY EDUCATION (BS ED.)

Northern Arizona University (B)

ELEMENTARY EDUCATION (POST-BACCALAUREATE)

Pima Community College (UC)

ELEMENTARY EDUCATION POSTDEGREE

Northern Arizona University (UC)

ELEMENTARY EDUCATION WITH CERTIFICATION

Oral Roberts University (B)

ELEMENTARY EDUCATION/ READING

University of Arkansas (M)

ELEMENTARY LICENSURE (POST BA)

New Mexico State University (UC)

ELEMENTARY OR SECONDARY EDUCATION

Marshall University (M)

ELEMENTARY P-5

University of the Cumberlands (M)

ELEMENTARY, MIDDLE GRADES, AND SPECIAL EDUCATION

Southeastern Community College (A)

ELEMENTS OF HEALTH CARE LEADERSHIP

Rochester Institute of Technology (GC)

EMBA

Western Kentucky University (M)

EMBEDDED AND REAL-TIME SYSTEMS PROGRAMMING

University of Washington (UC)

EMERGENCY ADMINISTRATION AND MANAGEMENT

Arkansas Tech University (B)
St. Petersburg College (A,UC)

EMERGENCY AND DISASTER MANAGEMENT

American Public University System (M,B)
Lynn University (GC)
Upper Iowa University (B,UC)

EMERGENCY DISASTER SERVICES

Thomas Edison State College (A,B)

EMERGENCY MANAGEMENT

Jacksonville State University (GC,M)
Millersville University of Pennsylvania (M)
New Jersey Institute of Technology (GC)

EMERGENCY MANAGEMENT (HOMELAND SECURITY MINOR)

Jacksonville State University (B)

EMERGENCY MANAGEMENT (PUBLIC SAFETY COMMUNICATIONS MINOR)

Jacksonville State University (B)

EMERGENCY MANAGEMENT AND PLANNING

Red Rocks Community College (A)

EMERGENCY MEDICAL CARE

Western Carolina University (B)

EMERGENCY MEDICAL SERVICE PROFESSIONS (PARAMEDIC OPTION)

Tyler Junior College (A)

EMERGENCY PLANNING AND ADMINISTRATION

Lynn University (GC,M)

EMERGENCY PREPAREDNESS AND CONTINUITY PLANNING

University of Illinois at Chicago (UC)

EMERGING NETWORK TECHNOLOGIES

Franklin Pierce University (GC)

ENERGY ELECTIVE

Athabasca University (M)

ENERGY MANAGEMENT

New York Institute of Technology (M)

ENERGY RESOURCES MANAGEMENT AND POLICY

University of Maryland University College (GC)

ENERGY UTILITY TECHNOLOGY

Thomas Edison State College (B)

ENGINEERING

Eastern Michigan University (M)
Michigan Technological University (B)
Northern Arizona University (M)
Texas Tech University (M)
The University of Arizona (M)
University of Illinois (M)
University of Illinois at Chicago (M)
The University of Toledo (M)
University of Wisconsin–Platteville (M)
University of Wisconsin–Platteville (M)

ENGINEERING ADMINISTRATION

Virginia Polytechnic Institute and State University (M)

ENGINEERING AND MANAGEMENT SYSTEMS

Columbia University (M)

ENGINEERING DESIGN

Michigan Technological University (UC)

ENGINEERING GRAPHICS

Thomas Edison State College (A,B)

ENGINEERING LAW AND MANAGEMENT

University of Illinois (GC)

ENGINEERING LAW AND MANAGEMENT CAMPUS CERTIFICATE

University of Illinois at Chicago (UC)

ENGINEERING MANAGEMENT

Drexel University (GC,M)
Kansas State University (M)
Kettering University (M)
National University (M)
New Jersey Institute of Technology (M)
Old Dominion University (M)
Southern Methodist University (M)
Stevens Institute of Technology (M)
University of Colorado at Boulder (GC,M)
University of Colorado at Colorado Springs (M)
University of Michigan–Dearborn (M)
University of Nebraska–Lincoln (M)
University of Southern California (M)
The University of Tennessee (GC,M)
University of Wisconsin–Platteville (UC)
University of Wisconsin–Platteville (GC)

ENGINEERING MANAGEMENT (MSEM)

University of South Florida (M)

ENGINEERING MECHANICS– MATHEMATICAL FOUNDATIONS AND APPLICATIONS

Stanford University (GC)

ENGINEERING ONLINE

North Carolina State University (M)

ENGINEERING TECHNOLOGY

Michigan Technological University (A)
Pittsburg State University (M)
University of Central Florida (B)

ENGINEERING TECHNOLOGY COMMERCIALIZATION

University of Southern California (GC)

ENGINEERING TECHNOLOGY MANAGEMENT

University of South Florida (GC)

ENGINEERING TECHNOLOGY PROGRAM

Western Carolina University (B)

ENGINEERING TECHNOLOGY, GENERAL

Old Dominion University (B)

ENGINEERING–COMPUTATIONAL AND MATHEMATICAL ENGINEERING

Stanford University (M)

ENGINEERING–ELECTRICAL AND COMPUTER ENGINEERING CONCENTRATION

Kettering University (M)

ENGINEERING–MANUFACTURING ENGINEERING CONCENTRATION

Kettering University (M)

ENGINEERING–MECHANICAL DESIGN CONCENTRATION

Kettering University (M)

ENGLISH

American Public University System (B)
Buena Vista University (B)
Darton College (A)
Judson College (B)
Mercy College (B)
National University (M,B)
Northeastern University (B)
Northern Arizona University (M)
Regent University (B)
Rose State College (A)
Skidmore College (B)
Thomas Edison State College (B)
University of Illinois (B)
University of Illinois at Springfield (B)
University of Maryland University College (B)
University of Waterloo (B)

ENGLISH (3 YEAR)

Athabasca University (B)

ENGLISH (4 YEAR)

Athabasca University (B)

ENGLISH AS A SECOND LANGUAGE

Murray State University (UC)
Northern Arizona University (UC)

ENGLISH AS A SECOND LANGUAGE (ESL)

The University of Texas System (UC)

ENGLISH AS A SECOND LANGUAGE EDUCATION PROGRAM

University of Colorado at Colorado Springs (M)

ENGLISH AS A SECOND LANGUAGE–ESL

University of Nebraska at Kearney (UC)

ENGLISH LANGUAGE AND LITERATURE

Southern New Hampshire University (B)

ENGLISH LANGUAGE LEARNER/ ENGLISH AS A SECOND LANGUAGE

University of North Dakota (UC)

ENGLISH LANGUAGE STUDIES

Athabasca University (UC)

ENGLISH LITERATURE

Eastern Oregon University (B)
Mercy College (M)

ENGLISH–PROFESSIONAL AND TECHNICAL COMMUNICATION CONCENTRATION

East Carolina University (M)

ENGLISH–SINGLE SUBJECT PREPARATION IN ENGLISH

National University (B)

ENGLISH–WRITING

University of Colorado at Denver and Health Sciences Center (B)

ENGLISH/LITERATURE EMPHASIS

Community College of Denver (A)

ENGLISH/TECHNICAL WRITING SPECIALIZATION ONLINE

Utah State University (M)

ENTERPRISE SYSTEMS ARCHITECTURE

New Jersey Institute of Technology (GC)

ENTOMOLOGY

University of Nebraska–Lincoln (M)

ENTREPRENEURSHIP

Kaplan University (M)
Northern Kentucky University (UC)
Thomas Edison State College (B)
University of South Florida (GC)
Utah State University (M)
Walden University (M)
Western Carolina University (B)
Williston State College (A,UC)

ENTREPRENEURSHIP CONCENTRATION

Andrew Jackson University (M)

ENVIRONMENTAL AND TECHNOLOGICAL STUDIES

St. Cloud State University (M)

ENVIRONMENTAL AND WATER RESOURCES ENGINEERING

University of Illinois at Urbana–Champaign (GC)

ENVIRONMENTAL EDUCATION

Prescott College (M)

ENVIRONMENTAL ENGINEERING

Georgia Institute of Technology (M)
Iowa State University of Science and Technology (GC)
Southern Methodist University (M)
The University of Tennessee (M)
Worcester Polytechnic Institute (GC,M)

ENVIRONMENTAL ENGINEERING– WATER RESOURCES PLANNING AND MANAGEMENT TRACK

University of Florida (M)

ENVIRONMENTAL ENGINEERING– WATER, WASTEWATER, AND STORMWATER ENGINEERING

University of Florida (M)

ENVIRONMENTAL HEALTH AND SAFETY MANAGEMENT

Rochester Institute of Technology (M)

ENVIRONMENTAL HEALTH INFORMATICS CAMPUS CERTIFICATE

University of Illinois at Chicago (UC)

ENVIRONMENTAL INFORMATION MANAGEMENT–CERTIFICATE OF ADVANCED STUDY

University of Denver (UC)

ENVIRONMENTAL MANAGEMENT

University of Maryland University College (GC,M,B)

ENVIRONMENTAL MANAGEMENT–CERTIFICATE OF ADVANCED STUDY

University of Denver (UC)

ENVIRONMENTAL POLICY AND MANAGEMENT

American Public University System (M)

ENVIRONMENTAL POLICY AND MANAGEMENT–MASTER OF APPLIED SCIENCE IN ENVIRONMENTAL POLICY AND MANAGEMENT

University of Denver (M)

ENVIRONMENTAL POLICY– CERTIFICATE OF ADVANCED STUDY

University of Denver (UC)

ENVIRONMENTAL PROJECT MANAGEMENT–CERTIFICATE OF ADVANCED STUDY

University of Denver (UC)

ENVIRONMENTAL SCIENCE

Southern Methodist University (M)

ENVIRONMENTAL SCIENCE (ENVIRONMENTAL SYSTEMS MANAGEMENT MAJOR)

Southern Methodist University (M)

ENVIRONMENTAL SCIENCE (HAZARDOUS AND WASTE MATERIALS MANAGEMENT MAJOR)

Southern Methodist University (M)

ENVIRONMENTAL SCIENCE AND MANAGEMENT

Duquesne University (M)

ENVIRONMENTAL SCIENCES

Northern Arizona University (B)
Oregon State University (B)
Thomas Edison State College (A,B)

ENVIRONMENTAL STUDIES

American Public University System (B)
Columbia College (A)
Prescott College (M,B)
Skidmore College (B)
Thomas Edison State College (B)

ENVIRONMENTAL STUDIES IN CONSERVATION BIOLOGY

Green Mountain College (M)

ENVIRONMENTAL STUDIES– NATURAL RESOURCES AND SUSTAINABLE DEVELOPMENT CONCENTRATION

University of Illinois at Springfield (M)

ENVIRONMENTAL TECHNOLOGY

University of Alaska Southeast (A,UC)

ENVIRONMENTAL, HEALTH, AND SAFETY MANAGEMENT– CERTIFICATE OF ADVANCED STUDY

University of Denver (UC)

ENVIRONMENTAL, SAFETY, AND HEALTH MANAGEMENT

The University of Findlay (M,B)

EPIDEMIOLOGY AND BIOSTATISTICS

Drexel University (UC)

EQUINE ASSISTED MENTAL HEALTH

Prescott College (M)

ERGONOMICS (BASIC)

Colorado State University (UC)

ESL ENDORSEMENT IN ELEMENTARY AND SECONDARY EDUCATION

Kansas State University (UC)

ESOL/BILINGUAL EDUCATION

Oregon State University (UC)

ESR ACCESS

Earlham School of Religion (M)

ESTATE PLANNING AND TAXATION

The American College (GC)

ÉTUDES FRANÇAISES (EN DÉVELOPPEMENT)

Laurentian University

EVANGELISM AND CHURCH PLANTING

Liberty University (M)

EXCEPTIONAL EDUCATION

University of Central Florida (M)
Western Kentucky University (M)

EXCEPTIONAL NEEDS WITH MILD INTERVENTIONS (SPECIAL ED)

Indiana Wesleyan University (UC)

EXCEPTIONAL STUDENT EDUCATION

University of West Florida (B)

EXECUTIVE COACHING

Kaplan University (UC)

EXECUTIVE INTERNATIONAL MANAGEMENT (MSM)

Regis University (GC)

EXECUTIVE LEADERSHIP (MSM)

Regis University (GC)

EXECUTIVE MASTER OF BUSINESS ADMINISTRATION

Colorado Technical University (M)
University of Wyoming (M)

EXECUTIVE MASTER OF BUSINESS ADMINISTRATION (SPANISH VERSION)

National University (M)

EXECUTIVE MASTER OF ORGANIZATION DEVELOPMENT

Bowling Green State University (M)

EXERCISE SCIENCE

Skidmore College (B)

EXERCISE SCIENCE AND HEALTH PROMOTION–PERFORMANCE ENHANCEMENT AND INJURY PREVENTION

California University of Pennsylvania (M)

EXERCISE SCIENCE AND HEALTH PROMOTION–REHABILITATION SCIENCES

California University of Pennsylvania (M)

EXERCISE SCIENCE AND HEALTH PROMOTION–SPORTS PSYCHOLOGY

California University of Pennsylvania (M)

EXERCISE SCIENCE AND HEALTH PROMOTION–WELLNESS AND FITNESS

California University of Pennsylvania (M)

EXPRESSIVE ARTS FOR HEALING AND SOCIAL CHANGE

Saybrook Graduate School and Research Center (GC)

FACILITIES MANAGEMENT

Southern Methodist University (M)

FACILITY MANAGEMENT

Rochester Institute of Technology (M)
University of Washington (UC)

FAMILY AND CONSUMER SCIENCE EDUCATION

North Dakota State University (M)

FAMILY AND CONSUMER SCIENCES

Iowa State University of Science and Technology (M)
University of Nebraska–Lincoln (M)

FAMILY AND CONSUMER SCIENCES (EARLY CHILDHOOD PROGRAM DIRECTOR'S CERTIFICATE)

University of Wyoming (UC)

FAMILY AND CONSUMER SCIENCES (FAMILY AND COMMUNITY SERVICES OPTION)

University of Wyoming (B)

FAMILY AND CONSUMER SCIENCES (PROFESSIONAL CHILD DEVELOPMENT OPTION)

University of Wyoming (B)

FAMILY AND FINANCIAL PLANNING

Montana State University (M)

FAMILY AND HUMAN DEVELOPMENT

Utah State University (M)

FAMILY DEVELOPMENT

American Public University System (B)

FAMILY DEVELOPMENT CREDENTIAL

Kansas State University (UC)

FAMILY FINANCIAL PLANNING

Iowa State University of Science and Technology (GC)
North Dakota State University (GC,M)

FAMILY LIFE EDUCATION

Concordia University, St. Paul (B)

FAMILY LIFE STUDIES AND HUMAN SEXUALITY

Laurentian University (UC)

FAMILY LITERACY

Penn State University Park (GC,UC)

FAMILY NURSE PRACTITIONER

Clarkson College (M,)
Graceland University (GC,M)
University of Missouri–Columbia (M)
Indiana State University

FAMILY NURSE PRACTITIONER–FIRST MASTERS

Wright State University (M)

FAMILY NURSE PRACTITIONER–SECOND MASTERS

Wright State University (M)

FAMILY STUDIES

Texas Woman's University (M)

FAMILY STUDIES AND CONSUMER SCIENCE EDUCATION

Texas Tech University (M)

FAMILY SUPPORT STUDIES/ HUMAN DEVELOPMENT

Edmonds Community College (A)

FAMILY THERAPY

Regions University (D)

FASHION

Academy of Art University (M,A,B)

FICTION WRITING

University of Washington (UC)

FILM AND CINEMA STUDIES

Prescott College (M)

FINANCE

Dallas Baptist University (M)
Excelsior College (B)
Kaplan University (M)
Myers University (B)
New Jersey City University (M)
Northeastern University (A)
Regis University (B)
Strayer University (B)
Thomas Edison State College (B)
University of Colorado at Denver and Health Sciences Center (M)
University of Maryland University College (B)
Upper Iowa University (B)
Walden University (M)
Webster University (M)

FINANCE AND ACCOUNTING MANAGEMENT

Northeastern University (B)

FINANCE CONCENTRATION

Andrew Jackson University (M)
Colorado Technical University (M,B)

FINANCE–METHODS IN FINANCE

Columbia University (M)

FINANCE/ECONOMICS

Southern New Hampshire University (B)

FINANCIAL ASSISTANT

Jefferson Community and Technical College (A)

FINANCIAL ASSISTANT CLERK

Jefferson Community and Technical College (UC)

FINANCIAL ASSISTANT TRAINEE

Jefferson Community and Technical College (UC)

FINANCIAL CRIME INVESTIGATION CERTIFICATE PROGRAM

Utica College (UC)

FINANCIAL ENGINEERING

Columbia University (UC)
Stevens Institute of Technology (GC)

FINANCIAL INSTITUTION MANAGEMENT

Thomas Edison State College (B)

FINANCIAL MANAGEMENT

City University (GC)
National University (B)

FINANCIAL MANAGEMENT AND INFORMATION SYSTEMS

University of Maryland University College (M)

FINANCIAL MANAGEMENT IN ORGANIZATIONS

University of Maryland University College (GC)

FINANCIAL PLANNING

Kaplan University (UC)
Schiller International University (M)

FINANCIAL PLANNING–FAMILY FINANCIAL PLANNING

University of Nebraska–Lincoln (GC)

FINANCIAL PLANNING– GRADUATE FINANCIAL PLANNING TRACK

The American College (GC)

FINANCIAL RECORD KEEPER

Jefferson Community and Technical College (UC)

FINANCIAL SERVICES

The American College (M)
Berkeley College (A)
Labette Community College (A)

FINANCIAL SERVICES STUDIES

New England College of Finance (GC)

FINANCIAL VALUATION AND INVESTMENT MANAGEMENT

Lynn University (M)

FINE ART

Academy of Art University (M,A,B)

FIRE AND EMERGENCY SERVICES ADMINISTRATION

Colorado State University (B)

FIRE AND EMERGENCY SERVICES ADMINISTRATION (FESA)

Colorado State University (UC)

FIRE AND SAFETY ENGINEERING TECHNOLOGY

Eastern Kentucky University (B)

FIRE INSPECTOR I

St. Petersburg College (UC)

FIRE INSPECTOR II

St. Petersburg College (UC)

FIRE INVESTIGATOR I

St. Petersburg College (UC)

FIRE INVESTIGATOR II

St. Petersburg College (UC)

FIRE OFFICER I

St. Petersburg College (UC)

FIRE OFFICER II

St. Petersburg College (UC)

FIRE PROTECTION

Middlesex Community College (A)

FIRE PROTECTION ENGINEERING

Worcester Polytechnic Institute (GC,M)

FIRE PROTECTION SCIENCE

Thomas Edison State College (A,B)

FIRE PROTECTION TECHNOLOGY–FIRE PREVENTION

Chemeketa Community College (A)

FIRE PROTECTION TECHNOLOGY–FIRE SUPPRESSION

Chemeketa Community College (A)

FIRE SCIENCE

Casper College (A)
Cogswell Polytechnical College (B)
Prescott College (M)
University of Maryland University College (B)
The University of North Carolina at Charlotte (B)

FIRE SCIENCE ADMINISTRATION

Columbia College (A)
Salem State College (B)

FIRE SCIENCE MANAGEMENT

American Public University System (B)
Red Rocks Community College (A)

FIRE SCIENCE TECHNOLOGY

University of Cincinnati (A,B)

FIRE SERVICES ADMINISTRATION

Eastern Oregon University (B)

FITNESS AND WELLNESS SERVICES

Thomas Edison State College (A)

FOLKLORE ET ETHNOLOGIE DE L'AMERIQUE FRANCAISE

Laurentian University (B,UC)

FOOD AND NUTRITION

Bowling Green State University (GC)

FOOD PROTECTION

North Dakota State University (GC)

FOOD SCIENCE

Kansas State University (GC,UC)

FOOD SCIENCE AND INDUSTRY

Kansas State University (M,B)

FOOD SCIENCE, NUTRITION, AND HEALTH PROMOTION

Mississippi State University (M)

FOOD SERVICE AND LODGING MANAGEMENT

Iowa State University of Science and Technology (D)

FOREIGN LANGUAGE

Auburn University (M)
Darton College (A)
Thomas Edison State College (B)

FOREIGN LANGUAGES

Prescott College (M)

FOREIGN LANGUAGES AND LITERATURE

Skidmore College (B)

FORENSIC ACCOUNTING

Myers University (B)
New England College of Finance (GC)
Northeastern University (GC)

FORENSIC CRIMINOLOGY

University of Massachusetts Lowell (GC)

FORENSIC NURSING

Cleveland State University (M)

FORENSIC PSYCHOLOGY

University of North Dakota (M)

FORENSIC SCIENCE

Darton College (A)

FORENSIC SCIENCE–FORENSIC ANALYSIS TRACK

University of Central Florida (M)

FORENSIC SCIENCE–FORENSIC BIOCHEMISTRY TRACK

University of Central Florida (M)

FORENSIC SCIENCES–MASTER OF FORENSIC SCIENCES

National University (M)

FORENSIC STUDIES

The University of Montana (UC)

FORESTRY

Thomas Edison State College (A,B)

FOUNDATIONS FOR HUMAN RESOURCE MANAGEMENT

University of Maryland University College (GC)

FRENCH

Skidmore College (B)

FRENCH (3 YEAR)

Athabasca University (B)

FRENCH (4 YEAR)

Athabasca University (B)

FRENCH LANGUAGE PROFICIENCY

Athabasca University (UC)

FUND DEVELOPMENT

University of Illinois (GC)

FUNDAMENTALS OF INFORMATION TECHNOLOGY

University of Massachusetts Boston (UC)

FUNERAL SERVICE EDUCATION

Vincennes University (A)

FUNERAL SERVICES

St. Petersburg College (A)

FUTURE STUDIES

Regent University (UC)

GAME AND SIMULATION PROGRAMMING

DeVry University Online (B)

GAME ART AND DESIGN

Westwood Online (B)

GAME SOFTWARE DEVELOPMENT

Westwood Online (B)

GAMING MANAGEMENT CERTIFICATE PROGRAM

University of Wisconsin–Stout (UC)

GAY AND LESBIAN STUDIES

Prescott College (M)

GENDER STUDIES

Prescott College (M)

GENERAL AVIATION FLIGHT TECHNOLOGY

Indiana State University (A)

GENERAL BUSINESS (COMPLETION DEGREE)

Missouri State University (B)

GENERAL CONCENTRATION

Kettering University (M)

GENERAL EDUCATION

Pulaski Technical College (A)
St. Clair County Community College (A)
Troy University (A)

GENERAL EDUCATION REQUIREMENTS

Adams State College (A)

GENERAL MANAGEMENT

City University (GC)
Thomas Edison State College (B)

GENERAL PROGRAM

Ball State University (A)
Dickinson State University (A)
North Idaho College (A)
St. Petersburg College (A)
Seattle Central Community College (A)

Snead State Community College (A)
Triton College (A)
University of the Incarnate Word (M)
Walden University (M)
Waubonsee Community College (A)

GENERAL PROGRAMS

West Valley College (A)

GENERAL SCIENCE

University of Windsor (B)

GENERAL STUDIES

American Public University System (A)
Anne Arundel Community College (A)
Ball State University (B)
Bellevue Community College (A)
Black Hills State University (A)
Butler County Community College (A)
Casper College (A)
Central Texas College (A)
Charter Oak State College (A,B)
Chemeketa Community College (A)
City University (A,B)
College of Southern Maryland (A,UC)
Columbia College (A,B)
Columbus State Community College (A)
The Community College of Baltimore County (A)
Dakota State University (A)
Darton College (A)
Dawson Community College (A)
Delaware County Community College (A)
Delta College (A)
EduKan (A)
Everett Community College (A)
Fairmont State University (A)
Fort Hays State University (A,B)
Franklin Pierce University (A,B)
Gadsden State Community College (A)
Granite State College (A)
Grantham University (A,B)
Gulf Coast Community College (A)
Harford Community College (A)
Indiana Tech (A)
Indiana University System (A)
Indiana Wesleyan University (A,B)
Ivy Tech Community College–Bloomington (A)
Ivy Tech Community College–Central Indiana (A)
Ivy Tech Community College–Columbus (A)
Ivy Tech Community College–East Central (A)
Ivy Tech Community College–Kokomo (A)
Ivy Tech Community College–Lafayette (A)
Ivy Tech Community College–North Central (A)
Ivy Tech Community College–Northeast (A)
Ivy Tech Community College–Northwest (A)
Ivy Tech Community College–Southeast (A)
Ivy Tech Community College–Southern Indiana (A)
Ivy Tech Community College–Southwest (A)
Ivy Tech Community College–Wabash Valley (A)
Ivy Tech Community College–Whitewater (A)
Lansing Community College (A)
Liberty University (A)

Luzerne County Community College (A)
Marshall University (A)
Minot State University (B)
Missouri Southern State University (A,B)
Montgomery County Community College (A)
Mountain Empire Community College (A)
Mount Wachusett Community College (A)
Northern Virginia Community College (A)
North Harris Montgomery Community College District (A)
North Seattle Community College (A)
NorthWest Arkansas Community College (A)
Parkland College (A)
Patrick Henry Community College (A)
Pima Community College (A)
Rappahannock Community College (A)
Rio Salado College (A)
Saint Joseph's College of Maine (A,B)
Seminole Community College (A)
Southwest Virginia Community College (A)
Strayer University (A)
Texas Tech University (B)
Texas Woman's University (B)
Three Rivers Community College (A)
Tyler Junior College (A)
University of Alaska Southeast (B)
University of Bridgeport (B)
University of Management and Technology (A,B)
University of Nebraska at Omaha (B)
University of North Dakota (B)
University of North Texas (B)
University of Phoenix Online Campus (A)
The University of South Dakota (M,A)
The University of South Dakota (A)
Utah State University (A)
Utah Valley State College (A)
Vance-Granville Community College (A)
Vincennes University (A)
Waubonsee Community College (A,UC)
Weber State University (A)
Western Wyoming Community College (A)
West Shore Community College (A)
West Texas A&M University (B)
Wilfrid Laurier University (B)
Yuba College (A)

GENERAL STUDIES (SECONDARY EDUCATION)

University of North Dakota (M)

GENERAL STUDIES DEGREE PROGRAM

Indiana University System (B)

GENERAL STUDIES–ASSOCIATE OF ARTS

National University (A)

GENERAL STUDIES–BACHELOR OF GENERAL STUDIES

East Tennessee State University (B)

GENERAL STUDIES–BUSINESS STUDIES

Vincennes University (A)

GENERAL STUDIES–CUSTOMIZED CERTIFICATE

Vincennes University (UC)

GENERAL STUDIES–INDIVIDUALIZED STUDIES

Drexel University (B)

GENERAL STUDIES–ONLINE BACHELOR OF GENERAL STUDIES COMPLETION PROGRAM

University of Missouri–Columbia (B)

GENERAL STUDIES–SURGICAL TECHNOLOGY DEGREE COMPLETION

Vincennes University (A)

GENERAL STUDIES, BUSINESS MINOR

Drexel University (B)

GENERAL STUDIES, CRIMINAL JUSTICE SEQUENCE

University of Maine at Fort Kent (A)

GENERAL STUDIES, NON-MAJOR

University of Waterloo (B)

GENERAL STUDIES/LIBERAL ARTS

Tunxis Community College (A)

GENERALIST

Community College of Denver (A)

GEOGRAPHIC INFORMATION SCIENCE

Northwest Missouri State University (M)

GEOGRAPHIC INFORMATION SCIENCES

Oregon State University (UC)
University of North Dakota (GC)

GEOGRAPHIC INFORMATION SYSTEMS

Columbus State Community College (GC)
Eastern Michigan University (GC)
North Carolina State University (GC)
Penn State University Park (GC,M)

GEOGRAPHIC INFORMATION SYSTEMS (GIS)

Fort Hays State University (UC)
University of Colorado at Denver and Health Sciences Center (M)

GEOGRAPHIC INFORMATION SYSTEMS–CERTIFICATE OF ADVANCED STUDY

University of Denver (UC)

GEOLOGICAL ENGINEERING

University of Idaho (M)

GEOSCIENCES

Mississippi State University (B)

GEOSCIENCES, BROADCAST METEOROLOGY

Mississippi State University (UC)

GEOSCIENCES, OPERATIONAL METEOROLOGY

Mississippi State University (UC)

GEOSCIENCES, TEACHERS IN GEOSCIENCE

Mississippi State University (M)

GERIATRIC CARE MANAGEMENT

Kaplan University (UC)

GERIATRIC REHABILITATION AND WELLNESS

Sacred Heart University (M)

GERMAN

Skidmore College (B)

GERONTOLOGICAL NURSE PRACTITIONER

University of Missouri–Columbia (M)

GERONTOLOGY

Iowa State University of Science and
  Technology (GC)
Kansas State University (GC,M)
Laurentian University (B,UC)
Mount Saint Vincent University (UC)
North Dakota State University (GC,M)
Texas Tech University (GC)
Thomas Edison State College (A,B)
The University of Arizona (GC)
University of Southern California (GC,M)
University of Washington (UC)

GERONTOLOGY CONCENTRATION

Western Carolina University (M)

GERONTOLOGY–MANAGEMENT OF AGING SERVICES TRACK

University of Massachusetts Boston (GC,M)

GERONTOLOGY–MASTER OF ARTS IN GERONTOLOGY (MAG)

Chatham University

GIFTED AND TALENTED

Murray State University (UC)

GIFTED AND TALENTED EDUCATION

Northern Kentucky University (UC)
University of North Texas (UC)

GIFTED AND TALENTED GRADUATE TEACHING ENDORSEMENT

Western Kentucky University (UC)

GIFTED EDUCATION

Northern Arizona University (UC)
University of Central Florida (GC)
University of Missouri–Columbia (M)
University of North Texas (GC)
University of South Florida (GC,M)

GIFTED EDUCATION ENDORSEMENT

Bowling Green State University (GC)

GIFTED GRADUATE ENDORSEMENT

University of Nebraska at Kearney (UC)

GLOBAL AND INTERNATIONAL EDUCATION

Drexel University (M)

GLOBAL BUSINESS

Excelsior College (B)
Regent University (B)
University of Dallas (GC,M)

GLOBAL BUSINESS AND PUBLIC POLICY

University of Maryland University College
  (B)

GLOBAL BUSINESS MANAGEMENT

Bellevue University (B)

GLOBAL COMMERCE–MBA CERTIFICATE IN GLOBAL COMMERCE

Webster University (GC)

GLOBAL HUMAN RESOURCE DEVELOPMENT

University of Illinois (M)

GLOBAL LEADERSHIP, CORPORATE AND ORGANIZATIONAL MANAGEMENT SPECIALIZATION

Lynn University (D)

GLOBAL MANAGEMENT

University of Maryland University College
  (GC)
University of Phoenix Online Campus (M)

GLOBAL MASTER OF BUSINESS ADMINISTRATION FOR LATIN AMERICAN MANAGERS

Thunderbird School of Global Management
  (M)

GLOBAL MASTER OF BUSINESS ADMINISTRATION ON-DEMAND

Thunderbird School of Global Management
  (M)

GLOBAL MBA

Southern New Hampshire University (M)
University of Houston–Victoria (M)

GLOBAL STUDIES

National University (B)

GLOBAL STUDIES IN EDUCATION

University of Illinois (M)

GME CORE CURRICULUM

University of Illinois (GC)

GOLF ENTERPRISE MANAGEMENT

University of Wisconsin–Stout (B)

GOVERNANCE, LAW, AND MANAGEMENT

Athabasca University (B)

GOVERNMENT

Regent University (M)
Skidmore College (B)

GOVERNMENT CONTRACTING

Webster University (GC)

GOVERNMENT–BUSINESS RELATIONS

Park University (M)

GOVERNMENTAL SERVICES

Darton College (A)

GRADUATE CERTIFICATE IN PUBLIC HEALTH INFORMATICS

University of Maryland, College Park (GC)

GRADUATE TEACHING LICENSURE

The College of St. Scholastica (M,UC)

GRANT PROPOSAL WRITING AND PROGRAM EVALUATION

Fort Hays State University (UC)

GRAPHIC DESIGN

Academy of Art University (M,A,B)
Savannah College of Art and Design (M)

GRAPHIC DESIGN AND MULTIMEDIA

Westwood Online (A)

GREENHOUSE TECHNOLOGY

Minot State University–Bottineau Campus (UC)

GROUNDS WORKER SKILLS, BASIC

Minot State University–Bottineau Campus (UC)

GUIDANCE AND CONTROL (AERONAUTICS AND ASTRONAUTICS)

Stanford University (GC)

GUIDANCE AND COUNSELING–SCHOOL GUIDANCE AND COUNSELING

Buena Vista University (M)

HACCP/FOOD SAFETY MANAGERS

North Carolina State University (UC)

HAZARDOUS WASTE RISK AND REMEDIATION

University of Illinois (GC)

HEALTH

Chatham University (M)

HEALTH ADMINISTRATION

Athabasca University (B)
Montana State University–Billings (M)
University of North Dakota (GC)
University of Phoenix Online Campus (A,B)
University of Southern Indiana (M)

HEALTH ADMINISTRATION INFORMATICS

University of Maryland University College (M)

HEALTH ADMINISTRATION POST-DIPLOMA

Athabasca University (B)

HEALTH ADMINISTRATION–DOCTOR OF HEALTH ADMINISTRATION (DHA)

University of Phoenix Online Campus (D)

HEALTH ADMINISTRATION–MASTER OF HEALTH ADMINISTRATION

University of Phoenix Online Campus (M)

HEALTH ADMINISTRATION/HEALTH INFORMATION SYSTEMS

University of Phoenix Online Campus (B)

HEALTH ADMINISTRATION/LONG-TERM CARE

University of Phoenix Online Campus (B)

HEALTH ADMINISTRATIVE SERVICES

Weber State University (B)

HEALTH AND HUMAN PERFORMANCE

Fort Hays State University (M)

HEALTH AND NUTRITION COUNSELING

Thomas Edison State College (B)

HEALTH AND PHYSICAL EDUCATION (EXERCISE SCIENCE)

Darton College (A)

HEALTH AND PHYSICAL EDUCATION (RECREATION)

Darton College (A)

HEALTH AND PHYSICAL EDUCATION (SPORTS MANAGEMENT)

Darton College (A)

HEALTH AND PHYSICAL EDUCATION (TEACHER ED OPTION)

Darton College (A)

HEALTH AND SAFETY (OCCUPATIONAL SAFETY MANAGEMENT SPECIALIZATION)

Indiana State University (M)

HEALTH ARTS

University of St. Francis (B)

HEALTH CARE ADMINISTRATION

Bellevue University (M,B)
Graceland University (GC,M)
Saint Joseph's College of Maine (B)
University of Hawaii–West Oahu (UC)
University of Maryland University College (M,GC)
University of Northwestern Ohio (B)
The University of Toledo (B)

HEALTH CARE ADMINISTRATION (MSA)

University of West Florida (M)

HEALTH CARE BUSINESS LEADERSHIP

Clarkson College (M)

HEALTH CARE BUSINESS–HEALTH INFORMATION MANAGEMENT MAJOR

Clarkson College (B)

HEALTH CARE BUSINESS–INFORMATICS MAJOR

Clarkson College (B)

HEALTH CARE BUSINESS–MANAGEMENT MAJOR

Clarkson College (B)

HEALTH CARE CODING

Lehigh Carbon Community College (UC)

HEALTH CARE CODING AND CLASSIFICATION

Weber State University (UC)

HEALTH CARE LEADERSHIP

University of St. Francis (B)

HEALTH CARE MANAGEMENT

Dallas Baptist University (B)
East Carolina University (GC)
Franklin University (B)
Graceland University (B)
Minnesota School of Business–Richfield (B)
Saint Joseph's College of Maine (UC)

HEALTH CARE MANAGEMENT CONCENTRATION

Colorado Technical University (M,B)

HEALTH CARE MANAGEMENT, ADVANCED

Saint Joseph's College of Maine (UC)

HEALTH CARE/HEALTH SERVICES MANAGEMENT

Park University (M)

HEALTH DEVELOPMENT ADMINISTRATION

Athabasca University (UC)

HEALTH EDUCATION

East Carolina University (M)

HEALTH INFORMATICS

University of Illinois (GC)
University of Illinois at Chicago (M,,UC)

HEALTH INFORMATICS (EXECUTIVE PROGRAM)

University of Missouri–Columbia (M)

HEALTH INFORMATION ADMINISTRATION

Dakota State University (B)

HEALTH INFORMATION MANAGEMENT

Clarkson College (A)
The College of St. Scholastica (M)
Darton College (A)
East Carolina University (B)
University of Alaska Southeast (A)
University of Cincinnati (B)
The University of Toledo (B)
Vincennes University (A)
Weber State University (B)

HEALTH INFORMATION MANAGEMENT CODING SPECIALIST

University of Alaska Southeast (UC)

HEALTH INFORMATION MANAGEMENT DEGREE COMPLETION

The College of St. Scholastica (B)

HEALTH INFORMATION MANAGEMENT TECHNOLOGY

Quinebaug Valley Community College (UC)

HEALTH INFORMATION MANAGEMENT–FOUNDATIONS

Clarkson College (UC)

HEALTH INFORMATION MANAGEMENT–HIM

Clarkson College (UC)

HEALTH INFORMATION RESOURCES

Rochester Institute of Technology (GC)

HEALTH INFORMATION TECHNICIAN

North Dakota State College of Science (A)

HEALTH INFORMATION TECHNOLOGY

Dakota State University (A)
Darton College (A)
DeVry University Online (A)
Edgecombe Community College (A)
Hodges University (A)
Minnesota State Community and Technical College–Fergus Falls (A)
Passaic County Community College (A)
Weber State University (A)

HEALTH INFORMATION–MASTER OF HEALTH INFORMATION (MHIM)

Louisiana Tech University (M)

HEALTH MANAGEMENT AND POLICY

Oregon State University (GC)

HEALTH PRACTICE MANAGEMENT

Franklin Pierce University (GC)

HEALTH PROFESSIONS

The University of Texas at Tyler (B)

HEALTH PROFESSIONS AND RELATED SCIENCES

University of Southern Indiana (B)

HEALTH PROFESSIONS EDUCATION

Simmons College (GC)
University of Illinois at Chicago (M)

HEALTH PROFESSIONS EDUCATION–MASTER OF HEALTH PROFESSIONS EDUCATION

University of Illinois (M)

HEALTH PROMOTION

Northern Arizona University (B)
Weber State University (B)

HEALTH PROMOTION (BAS)

Northern Arizona University (B)

HEALTH SCIENCE

Cleveland State University (M)
Mercy College (B)

HEALTH SCIENCE OCCUPATIONS

University of Wisconsin–Stout (UC)

HEALTH SCIENCE TECHNOLOGY TEACHER

The University of Texas System (UC)

HEALTH SCIENCES

Excelsior College (B)
Keiser University (B)
Old Dominion University (B)
Touro University International (D,M,B)
University of Medicine and Dentistry of New Jersey (D,M,B)

HEALTH SCIENCES–MASTER OF HEALTH SCIENCES

Chatham University (M)

HEALTH SCIENCES, ALLIED HEALTH

University of West Florida (B)

HEALTH SERVICE ADMINISTRATION

Austin Peay State University (M)
Keiser University (A)

HEALTH SERVICES

Thomas Edison State College (B)
Walden University (M)

HEALTH SERVICES ADMINISTRATION

Alaska Pacific University (B)
Berkeley College (A)

Berkeley College-New York City Campus
 (A,B)
Berkeley College-Westchester Campus (A)
Drexel University (B)
Keiser University (B)
Saint Joseph's College of Maine (M)
Strayer University (M)
Thomas Edison State College (B)
University of Central Florida (B)
University of Delaware (M)
University of St. Francis (M)
Upper Iowa University (B)

HEALTH SERVICES ADMINISTRATION AND NURSING DUAL DEGREE

Saint Joseph's College of Maine (M)

HEALTH SERVICES ADMINISTRATION SPECIALIZATION

The University of South Dakota (M)
The University of South Dakota (M)

HEALTH SERVICES ADMINISTRATION–MEDICAL INSURANCE, BILLING, AND CODING

Berkeley College (A)
Berkeley College-New York City Campus (A)
Berkeley College-Westchester Campus (A)

HEALTH SERVICES ADMINISTRATION/HEALTH SERVICES ADMINISTRATION AND MEDICAL IMAGING

Washburn University (B)

HEALTH SERVICES EDUCATION

Thomas Edison State College (B)

HEALTH SERVICES MANAGEMENT

Berkeley College-Westchester Campus (B)
East Carolina University (B)
Herkimer County Community College (A)
Mercy College (M)
Myers University (B)
University of Dallas (GC,M)

HEALTH SERVICES MANAGEMENT (EXECUTIVE PROGRAM)

University of Missouri–Columbia (M)

HEALTH SERVICES MANAGEMENT CONCENTRATION

Andrew Jackson University (M)

HEALTH SERVICES TECHNOLOGY (BAT)

The University of Texas System (B)

HEALTH SERVICES–COMMUNITY HEALTH PROMOTION AND EDUCATION

Walden University (D)

HEALTH SERVICES–HEALTH MANAGEMENT AND POLICY

Walden University (D)

HEALTH SERVICES, GENERAL

Walden University (D)

HEALTH STUDIES

Texas Woman's University (M,B)

HEALTH STUDIES–HEALTH PROMOTION

The University of Alabama (M)

HEALTH STUDIES–MASTER OF HEALTH STUDIES

Athabasca University (M)

HEALTH SYSTEMS

University of Medicine and Dentistry of New
 Jersey (M)

HEALTH SYSTEMS ADMINISTRATION

Rochester Institute of Technology (M,UC)

HEALTH SYSTEMS FINANCE

Rochester Institute of Technology (GC)

HEALTH, PHYSICAL EDUCATION, AND RECREATION

Utah State University (M)

HEALTH, SAFETY, AND ENVIRONMENTAL TECHNOLOGY

Eastern Iowa Community College District (A)

HEALTH/TEACHER EDUCATION

East Carolina University (M)

HEALTHCARE ADMINISTRATION

Central Michigan University (D)
New England College (B)
Seton Hall University (M)

HEALTHCARE ADMINISTRATION CONCENTRATION

American InterContinental University Online
 (A)

HEALTHCARE INFORMATICS

The College of St. Scholastica (UC)
Drexel University (UC)

HEALTHCARE MANAGEMENT

Brenau University (M)
Rosalind Franklin University of Medicine and
 Science (GC,M)

HEALTHCARE MANAGEMENT CONCENTRATION (10-MONTH PROGRAM)

American InterContinental University Online
 (M)

HEALTHCARE MANAGEMENT CONCENTRATION (COMPLETION PROGRAM)

American InterContinental University Online
 (B)

HEALTHCARE PRIVACY

University of Alaska Southeast (UC)

HEATING, VENTILATION, AND AIR CONDITIONING (HVAC) SYSTEMS

University of Idaho (UC)

HEAVY CONSTRUCTION PROJECT MANAGEMENT

University of Washington (UC)

HEMODIALYSIS PATIENT CARE TECHNICIAN

Lake Superior College (UC)

HIGHER EDUCATION

Dallas Baptist University (M)
Drexel University (M)
University of North Dakota (D)

HIGHER EDUCATION ADMINISTRATION

Northeastern University (GC)
Prescott College (M)

HISTOLOGIC TECHNOLOGY

Darton College (A)

HISTOLOGY

Darton College (UC)

HISTORIC PRESERVATION

Savannah College of Art and Design (GC,M)

HISTORICAL STUDIES

State University of New York Empire State
  College (A,B)

HISTORY

American Public University System (M,B)
Buena Vista University (B)
Butler Community College (A)
Columbia College (B)
Darton College (A)
Judson College (B)
Mercy College (B)
National University (B)
Northeastern University (B)
Prescott College (B)
Rose State College (A)
Skidmore College (B)
Thomas Edison State College (B)
Troy University (B)
University of Houston–Victoria (B)
University of Illinois (B)
University of Illinois at Springfield (B)
University of Maryland University College
  (B)

HISTORY (3 YEAR)

Athabasca University (B)

HISTORY (4 YEAR)

Athabasca University (B)

HISTORY (IN DEVELOPMENT)

Laurentian University (B)

HISTORY EMPHASIS

Community College of Denver (A)

HISTORY, LIBERAL ARTS AND SCIENCES, MASS COMMUNICATIONS (ADVERTISING/PUBLIC RELATIONS; JOURNALISM), POLITICAL SCIENCE, AND PSYCHOLOGY CONCENTRATIONS

Parkland College (A)

HIT–MEDICAL CODING

North Dakota State College of Science (UC)

HOLOCAUST STUDIES

Gratz College (GC)

HOMELAND SECURITY

American Public University System (M,B)
Keiser University (A)
Schoolcraft College (A)
University of South Florida (GC)

HOMELAND SECURITY AND SAFETY ENGINEERING

National University (M)

HOMELAND SECURITY IN PUBLIC HEALTH PREPAREDNESS

Penn State University Park (M)

HOMELAND SECURITY LEADERSHIP

University of Connecticut (M)

HOMELAND SECURITY MANAGEMENT

University of Maryland University College
  (GC)

HOMELAND SECURITY, POLICY, AND COORDINATION

Walden University (M)

HORTICULTURE

Texas Tech University (M,B)
Thomas Edison State College (A,B)

HORTICULTURE SCIENCE

North Carolina State University (GC)

HOSPITAL HEALTH CARE ADMINISTRATION

Thomas Edison State College (B)

HOSPITALITY AND TOURISM MANAGEMENT

Strayer University (B)

HOSPITALITY MANAGEMENT

American Public University System (B)
Central Texas College (A)
Chemeketa Community College (A,UC)
East Carolina University (B)
Excelsior College (B)
Lynn University (M)
Middlesex Community College (A)
New York Institute of Technology (B)
Penn State University Park (UC)
Thomas Edison State College (B)
University of North Texas (GC,M)

HOSPITALITY MANAGEMENT– FOOD AND BEVERAGE MANAGEMENT

Central Texas College (A,UC)

HOSPITALITY MANAGEMENT– PROPERTY MANAGEMENT ADVANCED

Central Texas College (UC)

HOSPITALITY MANAGEMENT– ROOMS DIVISION

Central Texas College (UC)

HOTEL AND RESTAURANT MANAGEMENT

Northern Arizona University (B)
Tompkins Cortland Community College (A)
Auburn University (M)

HOTEL, RESTAURANT AND TOURISM MANAGEMENT

New Mexico State University (B)

HOTEL, RESTAURANT, AND INSTITUTIONAL MANAGEMENT

Penn State University Park (A,UC)
University of Delaware (B)
University of Minnesota, Crookston (UC)

HUMAN AND COMMUNITY SERVICES–BACHELOR OF HUMAN AND COMMUNITY SERVICES

New Mexico State University (B)

HUMAN AND ORGANIZATIONAL DEVELOPMENT

Fielding Graduate University (D)

HUMAN BEHAVIOR

National University (M)

HUMAN DEVELOPMENT

Hope International University (B)
Pacific Oaks College (M,B)
Regions University (B)
State University of New York Empire State
  College (A,B)
Washington State University (B)

HUMAN DEVELOPMENT AND FAMILY STUDIES

Colorado State University (B)
Penn State University Park (A)

HUMAN DEVELOPMENT AND FAMILY STUDIES (GERONTOLOGY EMPHASIS)

Texas Tech University (M)

HUMAN ENVIRONMENTAL SCIENCES–FOOD AND NUTRITION

The University of Alabama (M)

HUMAN ENVIRONMENTAL SCIENCES–GENERAL STUDIES OPTION

The University of Alabama (B)

HUMAN ENVIRONMENTAL SCIENCES–INTERACTIVE TECHNOLOGY

The University of Alabama (M)

HUMAN ENVIRONMENTAL SCIENCES–RESTAURANT AND HOSPITALITY MANAGEMENT

The University of Alabama (B)

HUMAN FACTORS ENGINEERING

Wright State University (M)

HUMAN NUTRITION

Eastern Michigan University (M)
University of Bridgeport (M)

HUMAN PERFORMANCE TECHNOLOGY (MSA)

University of West Florida (M)

HUMAN RELATIONS AND BUSINESS

Amberton University (M)

HUMAN RESOURCE ADMINISTRATION–CERTIFICATE OF ADVANCED STUDY

University of Denver (UC)

HUMAN RESOURCE ADMINISTRATION–MASTER OF PROFESSIONAL STUDIES IN HUMAN RESOURCE ADMINISTRATION

University of Denver (M)

HUMAN RESOURCE DEVELOPMENT

Buffalo State College, State University of New York (GC)
Clemson University (M)
Indiana State University (M,B)
Limestone College (B)
Rochester Institute of Technology (GC)
Southwestern College (B)
University of Arkansas (B)
The University of Texas System (M)

HUMAN RESOURCE LEADERSHIP

Regions University (B)

HUMAN RESOURCE MANAGEMENT

Concordia University, St. Paul (B)
Dallas Baptist University (M)
DeVry University Online (M)
Dickinson State University (B)
Eastern Michigan University (GC)
Fort Hays State University (UC)
Franklin Pierce University (GC)
Mercy College (M)
Myers University (B)
Southern New Hampshire University (GC,UC)
Stony Brook University, State University of New York (GC)
Strayer University (B)
Troy University (M)
University of Connecticut (M)
University of Maryland University College (B)
University of Phoenix Online Campus (M)
University of Wisconsin–Platteville (UC)
University of Wisconsin–Platteville (UC)
University of Wisconsin–Stout (UC)
Walden University (M)

HUMAN RESOURCE MANAGEMENT AND ORGANIZATIONAL DEVELOPMENT

National University (M)

HUMAN RESOURCE MANAGEMENT CONCENTRATION

Andrew Jackson University (M)
Colorado Technical University (M,B)

HUMAN RESOURCE MANAGEMENT CONCENTRATION (10-MONTH PROGRAM)

American InterContinental University Online (M)

HUMAN RESOURCE MANAGEMENT CONCENTRATION (COMPLETION PROGRAM)

American InterContinental University Online (B)

HUMAN RESOURCE STUDIES

Regent University (UC)

HUMAN RESOURCES

Indiana Tech (B)
Minnesota State Community and Technical College–Fergus Falls (A)
Penn State University Park (UC)
University of the Incarnate Word (B)

HUMAN RESOURCES AND LABOUR RELATIONS

Athabasca University (B,UC)

HUMAN RESOURCES CONCENTRATION

American InterContinental University Online (A)

HUMAN RESOURCES DEVELOPMENT

Webster University (M)

HUMAN RESOURCES MANAGEMENT

Florida Institute of Technology (M)
Northeastern University (A)
Pima Community College (UC)
Stevens Institute of Technology (GC)
Thomas Edison State College (M)
Upper Iowa University (B,UC)
Webster University (M)
Kaplan University (M)

HUMAN RESOURCES MANAGEMENT/MARKETING (3 YEAR)

Athabasca University (B)

HUMAN RESOURCES MANAGEMENT/MARKETING (4 YEAR)

Athabasca University (B)

HUMAN RESOURCES MANAGEMENT/ORGANIZATIONAL MANAGEMENT

Thomas Edison State College (B)

HUMAN SCIENCE

Athabasca University (B)
Saybrook Graduate School and Research Center (D,M)

HUMAN SCIENCE–POST-DIPLOMA

Athabasca University (B)

HUMAN SERVICES

Alaska Pacific University (B)
Athabasca University (B)
Bismarck State College (A)
Broome Community College (A)
Capella University (D,M)
Columbia College (A)
Dawson Community College (A)
Franklin Pierce University (A,B,UC)
Herkimer County Community College (A)
Indiana Wesleyan University (UC)
Ivy Tech Community College–Bloomington (A)
Ivy Tech Community College–Central Indiana (A)
Ivy Tech Community College–Columbus (A)

Ivy Tech Community College–East Central (A)
Ivy Tech Community College–Kokomo (A)
Ivy Tech Community College–Lafayette (A)
Ivy Tech Community College–North Central (A)
Ivy Tech Community College–Northeast (A)
Ivy Tech Community College–Northwest (A)
Ivy Tech Community College–Southeast (A)
Ivy Tech Community College–Southern Indiana (A)
Ivy Tech Community College–Southwest (A)
Ivy Tech Community College–Wabash Valley (A)
Ivy Tech Community College–Whitewater (A)
Liberty University (M)
Mount Wachusett Community College (A)
Northeastern University (B)
Saint Joseph's College of Maine (A)
Upper Iowa University (B)
Washburn University (B)

HUMAN SERVICES COUNSELING

Old Dominion University (B)
Regent University (M)

HUMAN SERVICES SHORT-TERM CERTIFICATE

Sinclair Community College (UC)

HUMAN SERVICES–CLINICAL SOCIAL WORK

Walden University (D)

HUMAN SERVICES–COUNSELING

Walden University (D)

HUMAN SERVICES–CRIMINAL JUSTICE

Walden University (D)

HUMAN SERVICES–CRIMINAL JUSTICE LEADERSHIP EMPHASIS

Concordia University, St. Paul (M)

HUMAN SERVICES–FAMILY LIFE EDUCATION EMPHASIS

Concordia University, St. Paul (M)

HUMAN SERVICES–FAMILY STUDIES AND INTERVENTION STRATEGIES

Walden University (D)

HUMAN SERVICES–HUMAN SERVICES ADMINISTRATION

Walden University (D)

HUMAN SERVICES–SELF-DESIGNED

Walden University (D)

HUMAN SERVICES–SOCIAL POLICY ANALYSIS AND PLANNING

Walden University (D)

HUMAN SERVICES–SOCIAL SERVICES ADMINISTRATION CONCENTRATION

University of Illinois at Springfield (M)

HUMAN SERVICES, GENERAL

Walden University (D)

HUMAN SERVICES/MANAGEMENT

University of Phoenix Online Campus (B)

HUMANE AND ENVIRONMENTAL STUDIES (MNM)

Regis University (GC)

HUMANE LEADERSHIP

Duquesne University (B)

HUMANISTIC TRADITIONS (UNDERGRADUATE)

Virginia Polytechnic Institute and State University (UC)

HUMANITARIAN ASSISTANCE

University of South Florida (GC)

HUMANITARIAN SERVICES ADMINISTRATION

University of Connecticut (M)

HUMANITIES

American Public University System (M)
California State University, Dominguez Hills (M)
Cerro Coso Community College (A)
County College of Morris (A)
Prescott College (M,B)
Thomas Edison State College (B)
University of Maryland University College (B)
University of Waterloo (B)
Washington State University (B)

HUMANITIES (3 YEAR)

Athabasca University (B)

HUMANITIES (4 YEAR)

Athabasca University (B)

HUMANITIES OPTION

Passaic County Community College (A)

HUMANITIES/PHILOSOPHY EMPHASIS

Community College of Denver (A)

I-MBA

Penn State University Park (M)

I.T. CONCENTRATION

Kettering University (M)

IIT NETWORKING AND TELECOMMUNICATIONS WITH E-LEARNING SYSTEMS

University of West Florida (B)

ILLUSTRATION

Academy of Art University (M,A,B)
Syracuse University (M)

ILLUSTRATION DESIGN

Savannah College of Art and Design (M)

IMAGING SCIENCE

Rochester Institute of Technology (M)

IMBA

Syracuse University (M)
Syracuse University (M)

IMS ACCOUNTING

Syracuse University (M)

INCLUSIVE EDUCATION

Athabasca University (UC)

INDEPENDENT BUSINESS MANAGEMENT

Parkland College (UC)

INDEPENDENT STUDIES–BACHELOR OF INDEPENDENT STUDIES/GENERAL STUDIES

Murray State University (B)

INDIVIDUAL STUDIES

Jamestown Community College (GC,A)
Jefferson Community College (A)

INDIVIDUALIZED DEGREE PROGRAM

Regent University (M)

INDIVIDUALIZED LIBERAL AND PROFESSIONAL STUDIES (VARIOUS SELF-DESIGNED TOPICS)

Antioch University McGregor (M)

INDIVIDUALIZED OCCUPATIONAL PREPARATION

Northwest Technical College (A)

INDIVIDUALIZED STUDIES

Governors State University (B)
Metropolitan State University (B)
Skidmore College (B)

INDIVIDUALLY DESIGNED FOCUS AREA

DePaul University (B)

INDUSTRIAL AND SYSTEMS ENGINEERING

Auburn University (M)
Georgia Institute of Technology (M)
University of Michigan–Dearborn (M)
University of Southern California (M)

INDUSTRIAL DESIGN

Academy of Art University (M,A,B)

INDUSTRIAL ELECTRONICS WITH PLC TECHNOLOGY

Cleveland Institute of Electronics (UC)

INDUSTRIAL ENGINEERING

Columbia University (UC)
Iowa State University of Science and
  Technology (M)
Mississippi State University (M)
New Mexico State University (M)
The University of Texas at Arlington (M)

INDUSTRIAL ENGINEERING AND OPERATIONS RESEARCH

Columbia University (GC)

INDUSTRIAL ENGINEERING– MASTER OF SCIENCE IN INDUSTRIAL ENGINEERING

New Mexico State University (M)

INDUSTRIAL ENVIRONMENTAL MANAGEMENT

Rochester Institute of Technology (UC)

INDUSTRIAL HYGIENE

Montana Tech of The University of Montana
  (M)

INDUSTRIAL MANAGEMENT

Myers University (B)
University of Central Missouri (M)

INDUSTRIAL TECHNOLOGY

Bemidji State University (M)

INDUSTRIAL TECHNOLOGY MANAGEMENT

Indiana State University (B)

INDUSTRIAL TECHNOLOGY– BIOPROCESS MANUFACTURING

East Carolina University (B)

INDUSTRIAL TECHNOLOGY– INDUSTRIAL DISTRIBUTION AND LOGISTICS

East Carolina University (B)

INDUSTRIAL TECHNOLOGY– INDUSTRIAL SUPERVISION

East Carolina University (B)

INDUSTRIAL TECHNOLOGY– INFORMATION AND COMPUTER TECHNOLOGY

East Carolina University (B)

INDUSTRIAL TECHNOLOGY– MANUFACTURING SYSTEMS

East Carolina University (B)

INDUSTRIAL/ORGANIZATIONAL PSYCHOLOGY

Kansas State University (M)

INFORMATICS

Northeastern University (M)

INFORMATION AND COMMUNICATION TECHNOLOGIES

University of Wisconsin–Stout (B)

INFORMATION AND COMMUNICATION TECHNOLOGY– BACHELOR OF INFORMATION AND COMMUNICATION TECHNOLOGY

New Mexico State University (B)

INFORMATION AND LEARNING TECHNOLOGIES, SCHOOL LIBRARY

University of Colorado at Denver and Health
  Sciences Center (M)

INFORMATION AND SYSTEMS ENGINEERING (MS OR MENG)

Lehigh University (M)

INFORMATION AND TELECOMMUNICATION SYSTEMS MANAGEMENT

Capitol College (M)

INFORMATION ASSURANCE

Capitol College (M)
East Carolina University (GC)
Iowa State University of Science and
  Technology (GC)
University of Dallas (GC,M)
University of Maryland University College
  (GC)

INFORMATION ASSURANCE AND COMPUTER SECURITY

Dakota State University (M)

INFORMATION CENTER SPECIALIST

Central Texas College (UC)

INFORMATION COMMUNICATION TECHNOLOGIES

University of Wisconsin–Stout (M)

INFORMATION ENGINEERING AND MANAGEMENT

Southern Methodist University (M)

INFORMATION ENGINEERING TECHNOLOGY

University of West Florida (B)

INFORMATION MANAGEMENT

Buena Vista University (B)
Grantham University (M)
Syracuse University (M)
Syracuse University (M)

INFORMATION MANAGEMENT FOR MANAGERS

New Jersey Institute of Technology (GC)

INFORMATION MANAGEMENT TECHNOLOGY

Grantham University (M)

INFORMATION MANAGEMENT–APPLIED INFORMATION MANAGEMENT

University of Oregon (M)

INFORMATION MANAGEMENT–PROJECT MANAGEMENT

Grantham University (M)

INFORMATION MEDIA

St. Cloud State University (M)

INFORMATION NETWORKING AND TELECOMMUNICATIONS (COMPUTER NETWORKING AND TELECOMMUNICATIONS CONCENTRATION)

Fort Hays State University (B)

INFORMATION NETWORKING AND TELECOMMUNICATIONS (WEB DEVELOPMENT CONCENTRATION)

Fort Hays State University (B)

INFORMATION PROCESSING SPECIALIST

Bismarck State College (UC)

INFORMATION RESOURCES MANAGEMENT

University of Maryland University College (GC)

INFORMATION SCIENCE AND TECHNOLOGY

Colorado State University (UC)
Drexel University (GC)
Penn State University Park (UC)

INFORMATION SCIENCES

University of North Texas (M)
The University of Tennessee (M)

INFORMATION SCIENCES AND TECHNOLOGY

Penn State University Park (A)

INFORMATION SECURITY

James Madison University (M)
Nova Southeastern University (M)

INFORMATION SECURITY AND PRIVACY

The University of North Carolina at Charlotte (GC)

INFORMATION SECURITY MANAGEMENT

Northeastern University (GC)
Syracuse University (GC)
Syracuse University (GC)

INFORMATION SECURITY–CERTIFICATE OF ADVANCED STUDY

University of Denver (UC)

INFORMATION SERVICES AND SUPPORT

The University of Toledo (A,UC)

INFORMATION SERVICES TECHNOLOGY

College of Southern Maryland (A,UC)

INFORMATION SERVICES TECHNOLOGY–WEB DEVELOPER

College of Southern Maryland (A)

INFORMATION STUDIES

Florida State University (M)

INFORMATION SYSTEMS

Athabasca University (M)
City University (GC)
Columbia University (UC)
Dakota State University (M)
DePaul University (M)
Drexel University (M)
Minot State University (M)
National University (M,B)
Northeastern University (M)
Nova Southeastern University (D)
Randolph Community College (A)
Shippensburg University of Pennsylvania (M)
Stevens Institute of Technology (M)
Strayer University (M,,A,B,UC)
University of Colorado at Denver and Health Sciences Center (M)
University of Illinois (GC)
University of Illinois at Urbana–Champaign (GC)
University of North Dakota (B)
University of the Incarnate Word (A)
Vance-Granville Community College (A)
Wright State University (M)

INFORMATION SYSTEMS (3 YEAR)

Athabasca University (B)

INFORMATION SYSTEMS (4 YEAR)

Athabasca University (B)

INFORMATION SYSTEMS AND TELECOMMUNICATIONS MANAGEMENT

Syracuse University (GC)
Syracuse University (GC)

INFORMATION SYSTEMS CONCENTRATION

American InterContinental University Online (A)

INFORMATION SYSTEMS IMPLEMENTATION

New Jersey Institute of Technology (GC)

INFORMATION SYSTEMS MANAGEMENT

DeVry University Online (M)
Hodges University (M,B)
University of Maryland University College (B)

INFORMATION SYSTEMS SECURITY

Westwood Online (B)

INFORMATION SYSTEMS SECURITY CONCENTRATION

Colorado Technical University (M)

INFORMATION SYSTEMS SECURITY–CERTIFICATE OF ADVANCED STUDY

University of Denver (UC)

INFORMATION SYSTEMS TECHNOLOGY

Northern Virginia Community College (UC)
Patrick Henry Community College (A)
Regent University (UC)
Southern Illinois University Carbondale (B)
University of Central Florida (B)
University of Northwestern Ohio (A)

INFORMATION SYSTEMS/NETWORK ADMINISTRATION AND SUPPORT

Vance-Granville Community College (A)

INFORMATION TECHNOLOGIES

East Carolina University (B)

INFORMATION TECHNOLOGY

Capella University (D,M,B)
Colorado Technical University (A)
DePaul University (M)
Excelsior College (B)
Florida Institute of Technology (M)
Franklin University (A,B)
Grantham University (M)
Jamestown Community College (GC,A)
Jones International University (B)
Kaplan University (B,M)
Kettering University (M)
Memorial University of Newfoundland (M)

Minnesota School of Business–Richfield (A,B)
Myers University (B)
Northeastern University (B)
Rochester Institute of Technology (M)
Rogers State University (B)
Southern New Hampshire University (A,B)
Southern Polytechnic State University (B)
University of Dallas (GC,M)
University of Maryland University College (GC,M)
University of Massachusetts Lowell (A,B,UC)
University of Phoenix Online Campus (A,B)
Virginia Polytechnic Institute and State University (M)

INFORMATION TECHNOLOGY AND BACHELOR OF INFORMATION TECHNOLOGY (BIT), COMPUTER FORENSICS CONCENTRATION (COMPLETION PROGRAM)

American InterContinental University Online (B)

INFORMATION TECHNOLOGY AND BACHELOR OF INFORMATION TECHNOLOGY (BIT), INTERNET SECURITY CONCENTRATION (COMPLETION PROGRAM)

American InterContinental University Online (B)

INFORMATION TECHNOLOGY AND INFORMATION SERVICES LIBRARY PARAPROFESSIONAL

Belmont Technical College (A)

INFORMATION TECHNOLOGY BASICS

Lansing Community College (UC)

INFORMATION TECHNOLOGY CONCENTRATION

Colorado Technical University (B)

INFORMATION TECHNOLOGY COORDINATOR

New Mexico State University (UC)

INFORMATION TECHNOLOGY FLUENCY

Bristol Community College (UC)

INFORMATION TECHNOLOGY MANAGEMENT

American Public University System (B)
Concordia University, St. Paul (B)
Franklin Pierce University (M)

Keiser University (B)
Mount Saint Vincent University (UC)
National University (B)
Saint Joseph's College of Maine (A,UC)
Touro University International (M,B)
University of Management and Technology (B)

INFORMATION TECHNOLOGY MANAGEMENT CONCENTRATION

Colorado Technical University (M)

INFORMATION TECHNOLOGY ONLINE

Bryant and Stratton Online (A)
Oregon Institute of Technology (B)

INFORMATION TECHNOLOGY PATHWAY CERTIFICATE

Kaplan University (UC)

INFORMATION TECHNOLOGY PROJECT MANAGEMENT

DePaul University (M)

INFORMATION TECHNOLOGY–.NET TECHNOLOGY CONCENTRATION

Peirce College (UC)

INFORMATION TECHNOLOGY–BACHELOR OF INFORMATION TECHNOLOGY (BIT)–COMPUTER SYSTEMS CONCENTRATION (COMPLETION PROGRAM)

American InterContinental University Online (B)

INFORMATION TECHNOLOGY–BACHELOR OF INFORMATION TECHNOLOGY (BIT)–NETWORK ADMINISTRATION CONCENTRATION (COMPLETION PROGRAM)

American InterContinental University Online (B)

INFORMATION TECHNOLOGY–BACHELOR OF INFORMATION TECHNOLOGY (BIT)–PROGRAMMING CONCENTRATION (COMPLETION PROGRAM)

American InterContinental University Online (B)

INFORMATION TECHNOLOGY–DESKTOP APPLICATIONS FOR BUSINESS CONCENTRATION

Peirce College (A,B)

INFORMATION TECHNOLOGY–HELP DESK TECHNICIAN CONCENTRATION

Peirce College (UC)

INFORMATION TECHNOLOGY–INFORMATION SECURITY CONCENTRATION

Peirce College (B)

INFORMATION TECHNOLOGY–IT MANAGEMENT

University of Management and Technology (M)

INFORMATION TECHNOLOGY–IT PROJECT MANAGEMENT

University of Management and Technology (M)

INFORMATION TECHNOLOGY–MANAGEMENT INFORMATION SYSTEMS

University of Management and Technology (M)

INFORMATION TECHNOLOGY–NETWORK SECURITY CONCENTRATION

Peirce College (A,B)

INFORMATION TECHNOLOGY–NETWORKING CONCENTRATION

Peirce College (A,B)

INFORMATION TECHNOLOGY–PROGRAMMING AND APPLICATION DEVELOPMENT CONCENTRATION

Peirce College (B)

INFORMATION TECHNOLOGY–PROGRAMMING APPLICATION AND DEVELOPMENT CONCENTRATION

Peirce College (A)

INFORMATION TECHNOLOGY–TECHNOLOGY MANAGEMENT CONCENTRATION

Peirce College (A,B)

INFORMATION TECHNOLOGY–WEB ANALYST/PROGRAMMER

Wisconsin Indianhead Technical College (A)

INFORMATION TECHNOLOGY–WINDOWS NETWORK OPERATING SYSTEM CONCENTRATION

Peirce College (UC)

INFORMATION TECHNOLOGY, BUSINESS MINOR

University of Massachusetts Lowell (B)

INFORMATION TECHNOLOGY, GENERAL

The Community College of Baltimore County (A)

INFORMATION TECHNOLOGY, NETWORK MANAGEMENT CONCENTRATION

Colorado Technical University (B)

INFORMATION TECHNOLOGY, SECURITY CONCENTRATION

Colorado Technical University (B)

INFORMATION TECHNOLOGY, SOFTWARE SYSTEMS ENGINEERING CONCENTRATION

Colorado Technical University (B)

INFORMATION TECHNOLOGY/INFORMATION SYSTEMS SECURITY

University of Phoenix Online Campus (B)

INFORMATION TECHNOLOGY/MULTIMEDIA AND VISUAL COMMUNICATION

University of Phoenix Online Campus (B)

INFORMATION TECHNOLOGY/NETWORKING

University of Phoenix Online Campus (A)

INFORMATION TECHNOLOGY/SOFTWARE ENGINEERING

University of Phoenix Online Campus (B)

INFORMATION TECHNOLOGY/VISUAL COMMUNICATIONS

University of Phoenix Online Campus (A)

INFRASTRUCTURE CONSTRUCTION

University of Washington (UC)

INITIAL TEACHER PROFESSIONAL PREPARATION

University of Central Florida (GC)

INNOVATION AND INTRA/ENTREPRENEURSHIP IN ADVANCED NURSING PRACTICE

Drexel University (M,,UC)

INSTITUTIONAL ADMINISTRATION (NUTRITION)

Texas Woman's University (M)

INSTITUTIONAL RESEARCH

Penn State University Park (GC)

INSTRUCTIONAL AND PERFORMANCE TECHNOLOGY

Boise State University (M)

INSTRUCTIONAL DESIGN

Roosevelt University (GC)
Southern Polytechnic State University (GC)
University of Massachusetts Boston (M)

INSTRUCTIONAL DESIGN AND DEVELOPMENT

University of South Alabama (M)

INSTRUCTIONAL DESIGN AND TECHNOLOGY

Emporia State University (M)
University of North Dakota (M)

INSTRUCTIONAL DESIGN FOR SIMULATIONS

University of Central Florida (GC)

INSTRUCTIONAL LEADERSHIP

Northern Kentucky University (M)

INSTRUCTIONAL LEADERSHIP–PRINCIPAL (ALL GRADES)

University of the Cumberlands (M)

INSTRUCTIONAL SYSTEMS

Florida State University (M)

INSTRUCTIONAL SYSTEMS–EDUCATIONAL TECHNOLOGY

Penn State University Park (M)

INSTRUCTIONAL TECHNOLOGY

Duquesne University (D)
East Carolina University (M)
Fort Hays State University (M)

University of Nebraska at Kearney (M)
University of Nevada, Las Vegas (GC)
University of the Incarnate Word (M)
University of West Florida (M)
Virginia Polytechnic Institute and State University (M)
West Texas A&M University (M)

INSTRUCTIONAL TECHNOLOGY (DISTANCE EDUCATION EMPHASIS)

Texas Tech University (M)

INSTRUCTIONAL TECHNOLOGY CONCENTRATION (10-MONTH PROGRAM)

American InterContinental University Online (M)

INSTRUCTIONAL TECHNOLOGY DESIGN

University of Massachusetts Boston (GC)

INSTRUCTIONAL TECHNOLOGY EDUCATION SPECIALIST

Bloomsburg University of Pennsylvania (M)

INSTRUCTIONAL TECHNOLOGY FOR EDUCATORS

University of Massachusetts Boston (GC)

INSTRUCTIONAL TECHNOLOGY SPECIALIST

Clarion University of Pennsylvania (UC)
Drexel University (UC)
Missouri State University (GC)

INSTRUCTIONAL TECHNOLOGY SYSTEMS

DePaul University (M)

INSTRUCTIONAL TECHNOLOGY–DISTANCE EDUCATION

University of South Florida (GC)

INSTRUCTIONAL TECHNOLOGY–EDUCATIONAL TECHNOLOGY EMPHASIS

Utah State University (M)

INSTRUCTIONAL TECHNOLOGY–FLORIDA DIGITAL EDUCATOR

University of South Florida (GC)

INSTRUCTIONAL TECHNOLOGY–WEB DESIGN

University of South Florida (GC)

INSTRUCTIONAL TECHNOLOGY/MEDIA E-LEARNING OR INSTRUCTIONAL SYSTEMS

University of Central Florida (M)

INSTRUCTIONAL TECHNOLOGY/MEDIA–EDUCATIONAL MEDIA TRACK

University of Central Florida (M)

INSTRUCTIONAL TECHNOLOGY/MEDIA–EDUCATIONAL TECHNOLOGY TRACK

University of Central Florida (M)

INSTRUCTIONAL/EDUCATIONAL TECHNOLOGY

University of Central Florida (GC)

INSURANCE AND RISK MANAGEMENT

Indiana State University (B)

INSURANCE SPECIALIST

Central Georgia Technical College (UC)

INTEGRAL STUDIES

Fielding Graduate University (UC)

INTEGRATED CIRCUITS

University of Illinois (GC)

INTEGRATED DIRECT MARKETING

University of Maryland University College (GC)

INTEGRATED MARKETING COMMUNICATIONS

Eastern Michigan University (M)
Southern New Hampshire University (GC)
West Virginia University (M,UC)

INTEGRATED OFFICE SKILLS

Jefferson Community and Technical College (UC)

INTEGRATED STUDIES

Athabasca University (M)
Emporia State University (B)

INTEGRATED STUDIES–ASSOCIATE IN INTEGRATED STUDIES (DTA)

Cascadia Community College (A)

INTEGRATIVE SUPPLY CHAIN MANAGEMENT

University of Maryland University College (GC)

INTELLIGENT SYSTEMS

Columbia University (UC)

INTERACTIVE DESIGN

Savannah College of Art and Design (GC)

INTERACTIVE DESIGN AND GAME DEVELOPMENT

Savannah College of Art and Design (M)

INTERCULTURAL CONFLICT MANAGEMENT

Antioch University McGregor (M)

INTERCULTURAL MINISTRIES DEGREE COMPLETION

Northwestern College (B)

INTERDEPARTMENTAL STUDIES

Schiller International University (B)

INTERDISCIPLINARY

Union Institute & University (M)

INTERDISCIPLINARY (CUSTOM CURRICULUM)

University of Dallas (GC,M)

INTERDISCIPLINARY EARLY CHILDHOOD EDUCATION

Western Kentucky University (A)

INTERDISCIPLINARY PROGRAM IN TECHNICAL STUDIES

The University of Toledo (A)

INTERDISCIPLINARY SOCIAL SCIENCE

Florida State University (B)

INTERDISCIPLINARY SOCIAL SCIENCES

Kansas State University (B)

INTERDISCIPLINARY STUDIES

Adams State College (B)
Central Texas College (A)
Columbia College (B)
Eastern Wyoming College (A)
Grantham University (A,B)
Hodges University (A,B)
Jones College (B)
Kaplan University (A)
Mississippi State University (B)
New York Institute of Technology (B)
Regent University (B)
State University of New York Empire State College (A,B)
Tennessee Technological University (B)
Union Institute & University (D)
The University of Alabama (B)
University of Central Florida (B)
Upper Iowa University (B)

INTERDISCIPLINARY STUDIES–ACTION FOR A VIABLE FUTURE

Sonoma State University (M)

INTERDISCIPLINARY STUDIES–EARLY CHILDHOOD THROUGH GRADE FOUR (EDUCATION)

The University of Texas at Tyler (B)

INTERDISCIPLINARY STUDIES, COMMUNITY DEVELOPMENT SPECIALIZATION

Iowa State University of Science and Technology (M)

INTERDISCIPLINARY STUDIES/EDUCATIONAL PARAPROFESSIONAL (TEACHER'S AIDE)

Kaplan University (A)

INTERIOR ARCHITECTURE AND DESIGN

Academy of Art University (M,A,B)

INTERIOR DESIGN

Northern Arizona University (B)
Savannah College of Art and Design (M)

INTERNATIONAL

University of Phoenix Online Campus (M)
University of the Incarnate Word (M)

INTERNATIONAL AFFAIRS

Skidmore College (B)

INTERNATIONAL BUSINESS

Berkeley College (A)
Berkeley College-New York City Campus (A,B)
Berkeley College-Westchester Campus (A,B)
Dallas Baptist University (M)
Lansing Community College (A)
Lynn University (M)
Park University (M)
Schiller International University (A,B,M)
Southern New Hampshire University (GC,B)
Strayer University (B)

Thomas Edison State College (B)
University of Wisconsin–Platteville (UC)
University of Wisconsin–Platteville (UC)

INTERNATIONAL BUSINESS CONCENTRATION

Colorado Technical University (B)

INTERNATIONAL BUSINESS CONCENTRATION (10-MONTH PROGRAM)

American InterContinental University Online (M)

INTERNATIONAL BUSINESS CONCENTRATION (COMPLETION PROGRAM)

American InterContinental University Online (B)

INTERNATIONAL DEVELOPMENT

Hope International University (M)

INTERNATIONAL HOTEL AND TOURISM MANAGEMENT

Schiller International University (M,B)

INTERNATIONAL LOGISTICS AND TRANSPORTATION MANAGEMENT

Rochester Institute of Technology (UC)

INTERNATIONAL MANAGEMENT

University of Management and Technology (B)
University of Maryland University College (M)

INTERNATIONAL MARKETING

University of Maryland University College (GC)

INTERNATIONAL NONGOVERNMENTAL ORGANIZATIONS (NGOS)

Walden University (M)

INTERNATIONAL ORGANIZATIONS

Regent University (UC)

INTERNATIONAL REGULATORY AFFAIRS

Northeastern University (GC)

INTERNATIONAL RELATIONS

American Public University System (B)
St. Mary's University of San Antonio (M)
Troy University (M)
Webster University (M)

INTERNATIONAL RELATIONS AND CONFLICT RESOLUTION

American Public University System (M)

INTERNATIONAL RELATIONS AND DIPLOMACY

Schiller International University (B)

INTERNATIONAL SCIENTIFIC AND TECHNICAL COMMUNICATION

Bowling Green State University (GC)

INTERNATIONAL SECURITY

Stanford University (GC)

INTERNATIONAL SPORT DIPLOMA

United States Sports Academy (UC)

INTERNATIONAL STUDIES

Montgomery County Community College (UC)

INTERNATIONAL TOURISM MANAGEMENT

Northern Arizona University (UC)

INTERNATIONAL TRADE

University of Maryland University College (GC)

INTERNET AND WEBSITE DEVELOPMENT

Kaplan University (UC)

INTERNET BUSINESS SYSTEMS

Mercy College (M)

INTERNET ENGINEERING

Capitol College (M)

INTERNET FOR BUSINESS– CERTIFICATE OF ACHIEVEMENT

Lansing Community College (UC)

INTERNET FOR BUSINESS– CERTIFICATE OF COMPLETION

Lansing Community College (UC)

INTERNET PROGRAMMING

University of Washington (UC)

INTERNET SECURITY CONCENTRATION (10-MONTH PROGRAM)

American InterContinental University Online (M)

INTERNET SYSTEMS AND SOFTWARE TECHNOLOGY

Bellevue University (B)

INTERNET SYSTEMS ENGINEERING

New Jersey Institute of Technology (GC)

INTERNET TECHNOLOGIES

Pace University (GC)

INTERNET TECHNOLOGY

Pace University (GC)

INTERNET TECHNOLOGY FOR E-COMMERCE

Pace University (M)

INTERPERSONAL COMMUNICATIONS

Seminole Community College (A)

INTERPRETER EDUCATION MASTER MENTOR

Northeastern University (GC)

INTERPRETER TRAINING (GENERAL TECHNOLOGY–AD IN OCCUPATIONAL TECHNOLOGY)

Spartanburg Community College (A)

INTRODUCTION TO COMPUTER PROGRAMMING LANGUAGE

Kaplan University (UC)

INTRODUCTION TO HOME AUTOMATION INSTALLATION

Cleveland Institute of Electronics (UC)

INTRODUCTION TO PROGRAMMING–NTID

Rochester Institute of Technology (UC)

INTRODUCTORY C++ PROGRAMMING

Bellevue Community College (UC)

IOWA TEACHER INTERN CERTIFICATE

Kaplan University (UC)

IRISH STUDIES

Regis University (UC)

IT BUSINESS INFORMATION SYSTEMS

Virginia Polytechnic Institute and State University (GC)

IT COMMUNICATION

Virginia Polytechnic Institute and State University (GC)

IT DECISION SUPPORT SYSTEMS

Virginia Polytechnic Institute and State University (GC)

IT NETWORKING

Virginia Polytechnic Institute and State University (GC)

IT PROJECT MANAGEMENT CONCENTRATION (10 MONTH PROGRAM)

American InterContinental University Online (M)

IT/DATABASE

Kaplan University (B)

IT/MULTIMEDIA AND ANIMATION

Kaplan University (B)

IT/NETWORKING

Kaplan University (B)

IT/PROGRAMMING

Kaplan University (B)

IT/WEB DEVELOPMENT

Kaplan University (B)

JEWISH EARLY CHILDHOOD EDUCATION

Gratz College (GC)

JEWISH EDUCATION

Gratz College (GC)

JEWISH EDUCATION–MASTER OF SCIENCE IN JEWISH EDUCATION (MSJE)

Spertus Institute of Jewish Studies (M)

JEWISH MUSIC

Gratz College (GC)

JEWISH NON-PROFIT MANAGEMENT

Gratz College (GC)

JEWISH STUDIES

Gratz College (GC,M,B)
Hebrew College (M)
Spertus Institute of Jewish Studies (D,M)

JOURNALISM

Prescott College (B)
Regent University (M)
Seminole Community College (A)
Thomas Edison State College (B)

JOURNALISM (MEDIA MANAGEMENT)

University of Missouri–Columbia (M)

JOURNALISM (STRATEGIC COMMUNICATIONS)

University of Missouri–Columbia (M)

JOURNALISM AND MASS COMMUNICATION

Darton College (A)

JOURNALISM AND MASS COMMUNICATIONS

University of Nebraska–Lincoln (M)

JOURNALISM EDUCATION

University of Missouri–Columbia (M)

JUSTICE ADMINISTRATION— MINISTRY CONCENTRATION

Taylor University (A)

JUSTICE ADMINISTRATION— PUBLIC POLICY CONCENTRATION

Taylor University (A)

JUSTICE AND MINISTRY

Taylor University (UC)

JUSTICE STUDIES

Fort Hays State University (B)
Southern New Hampshire University (M)

JUSTICE STUDIES–CRIMINAL JUSTICE

Berkeley College (A,B)

JUSTICE SYSTEMS AND POLICY PLANNING (BAS)

Northern Arizona University (B)

K-12 EDUCATORS AND ADMINISTRATION

Jones International University (M)

K-12 SPECIALIZATION

Northeastern University (M)

KELLEY DIRECT MBA/M-GM DUAL DEGREE–THUNDERBIRD AND INDIANA UNIVERSITY

Thunderbird School of Global Management (M)

KENTUCKY CHILD CARE PROVIDER

Jefferson Community and Technical College (UC)

KINESIOLOGY

Texas Woman's University (M)
The University of Texas at Tyler (M)
The University of Texas System (M)

KINESIOLOGY AND HEALTH

University of Wyoming (M)

KNOWLEDGE AND INFORMATION TECHNOLOGIES–MASTER OF APPLIED SCIENCE IN KNOWLEDGE AND INFORMATION TECHNOLOGIES

University of Denver (M)

KNOWLEDGE MANAGEMENT

Minot State University (GC)
Walden University (M)

LABOR STUDIES

State University of New York Empire State College (A,B)
Thomas Edison State College (B)

LABOR STUDIES AND INDUSTRIAL RELATIONS

Penn State University Park (UC)

LABORATORY ANIMAL SCIENCE

Thomas Edison State College (A,B)

LABOUR STUDIES

Athabasca University (UC)
University of Windsor (UC)

LABOUR STUDIES (3 YEAR)

Athabasca University (B)

LABOUR STUDIES (4 YEAR)

Athabasca University (B)

LAND SURVEYING

University of Wyoming (UC)

LAND USE PLANNING

Prescott College (M)

LANDSCAPE TECHNICIAN

Minot State University–Bottineau Campus (UC)

LANGUAGE LITERACY EDUCATION

Texas Tech University (M)

LASER AND FIBER OPTIC TECHNOLOGY

Three Rivers Community College (GC)

LAW AND JUSTICE

Laurentian University (B,UC)

LAW AND SOCIETY

Penn State University Park (B)
University of Connecticut (B)

LAW ENFORCEMENT

Dawson Community College (A)
Indiana State University (UC)
Missouri Southern State University (A)

LAW ENFORCEMENT ADMINISTRATION

Austin Peay State University (A)

LAW ENFORCEMENT STUDIES

Vincennes University (A)

LAW–PRE-LAW

Darton College (A)

LAW–SCHOOL LAW

Park University (M)

LEADERSHIP

The American College (M)
Bellevue University (M,B)
Fort Hays State University (M,UC)
Franklin Pierce University (M)
Jefferson Community and Technical College (UC)
Northeastern University (GC,M,B)

Regent University (GC)
Southwestern College (M)
Walden University (M)

LEADERSHIP (MNM)

Regis University (GC)

LEADERSHIP AND BUSINESS ETHICS

Duquesne University (M)

LEADERSHIP AND HUMAN PERFORMANCE

University of Wisconsin–Platteville (UC)
University of Wisconsin–Platteville (UC)

LEADERSHIP AND INFORMATION TECHNOLOGY–MASTERS OF LEADERSHIP AND INFORMATION TECHNOLOGY

Duquesne University (M)

LEADERSHIP AND LIBERAL STUDIES

Duquesne University (M)

LEADERSHIP AND MANAGEMENT

Regions University (M)
University of Maryland University College (GC)

LEADERSHIP DEVELOPMENT

Brenau University (M)
Taylor University (UC)

LEADERSHIP IN NURSING AND HEALTHCARE SYSTEMS

University of Missouri–Columbia (M)

LEADERSHIP IN THE PUBLIC SECTOR

North Carolina State University (B)

LEADERSHIP OF EDUCATIONAL ORGANIZATIONS CONCENTRATION (10-MONTH PROGRAM)

American InterContinental University Online (M)

LEADERSHIP OF LEARNING

Abilene Christian University (M)

LEADERSHIP–CERTIFICATE OF ADVANCED STUDY

University of Denver (UC)

LEADING ORGANIZATIONAL TRANSFORMATION

Saybrook Graduate School and Research Center (GC)

LEAN SIX SIGMA

East Carolina University (GC)

LEARNING AND KNOWLEDGE MANAGEMENT SYSTEMS

Rochester Institute of Technology (GC,M)

LEARNING SYSTEMS DESIGN AND DEVELOPMENT

University of Missouri–Columbia (M)

LEARNING SYSTEMS DESIGN AND DEVELOPMENT (EDUCATIONAL SPECIALIST)

University of Missouri–Columbia

LEEP–LIBRARY AND INFORMATION SCIENCE

University of Illinois (M)

LEGAL ADMINISTRATIVE ASSISTANT

Minnesota State Community and Technical College–Fergus Falls (A)

LEGAL ASSISTANT

Jones College (A)

LEGAL ASSISTING

University of Northwestern Ohio (A)

LEGAL NURSE CONSULTING

Kaplan University (UC)

LEGAL OFFICE

North Harris Montgomery Community College District (A)

LEGAL SECRETARIAL CERTIFICATE

The University of Toledo (UC)

LEGAL SERVICES

Thomas Edison State College (A,B)

LEGAL STUDIES

American Public University System (B)
Strayer University (B)
University of Illinois at Springfield (M)

University of Maryland University College
(B)
West Virginia University (M)

LEGAL STUDIES (MLS)

West Virginia University

LEGAL STUDIES–HOMELAND SECURITY

California University of Pennsylvania (M)

LEGAL STUDIES–LAW AND PUBLIC POLICY

California University of Pennsylvania (M)

LETTERS, ARTS, AND SCIENCES

Penn State University Park (A,B)

LIBERAL AND PROFESSIONAL STUDIES

University of Windsor (B)

LIBERAL ARTS

Austin Peay State University (A)
Brookdale Community College (A)
Burlington County College (A)
Butler Community College (A)
Cerro Coso Community College (A)
Colorado State University (B)
De Anza College (A)
Eastern Iowa Community College District (A)
Excelsior College (A,B)
Kirkwood Community College (A)
Lehigh Carbon Community College (A)
Lock Haven University of Pennsylvania (M)
Minot State University–Bottineau Campus (A)
Monroe Community College (A)
Mountain Empire Community College (A)
The New School: A University (B)
Northern Virginia Community College (A)
Peninsula College (A)
Piedmont Technical College (A)
Pima Community College (A,UC)
Rogers State University (A,B)
Rose State College (A)
St. Cloud State University (A)
Schoolcraft College (A)
Seattle Central Community College (A)
Southern New Hampshire University (A)
Syracuse University (A)
University of Wisconsin Colleges (A)
Upper Iowa University (A)
Virginia Polytechnic Institute and State
University (GC)
West Hills Community College (A)

LIBERAL ARTS (BLA)

University of Massachusetts Lowell (B)

LIBERAL ARTS—HISTORY CONCENTRATION

Taylor University (A)

LIBERAL ARTS— INTERDISCIPLINARY CONCENTRATION

Taylor University (A)

LIBERAL ARTS—SOCIAL SCIENCE CONCENTRATION

Taylor University (A)

LIBERAL ARTS AND GENERAL STUDIES

Mount Saint Vincent University (B)

LIBERAL ARTS AND HUMANITIES

Cayuga County Community College (A)

LIBERAL ARTS AND SCIENCE/ HUMANITIES AND SOCIAL SCIENCE

Erie Community College (A)

LIBERAL ARTS AND SCIENCES

Burlington County College (A)
Mercy College (A)
Middlesex Community College (A)
Rockland Community College (A)
Sinclair Community College (A)
Union Institute & University (B)
Wenatchee Valley College (A)

LIBERAL ARTS AND SCIENCES– GENERAL STUDIES

Herkimer County Community College (A)

LIBERAL ARTS AND SCIENCES– HUMANITIES

Herkimer County Community College (A)

LIBERAL ARTS AND SCIENCES– SOCIAL SCIENCE

Herkimer County Community College (A)

LIBERAL ARTS AND SCIENCES/ MATHEMATICS AND SCIENCES

Cayuga County Community College (A)

LIBERAL ARTS WITH BUSINESS MINOR

Northeastern University (B)

LIBERAL ARTS–ASSOCIATE OF ARTS IN LIBERAL ARTS

Arkansas State University–Beebe (A)

LIBERAL ARTS–GENERAL STUDIES

Broome Community College (A)

LIBERAL ARTS–HUMANITIES AND SOCIAL SCIENCE

Jefferson Community College (A)

LIBERAL ARTS–MASTER OF LIBERAL ARTS

Texas Christian University (GC)

LIBERAL ARTS, GENERAL

DePaul University (B)

LIBERAL ARTS, GENERAL STUDIES, HUMANITIES

Andrews University (A,B)

LIBERAL ARTS/GENERAL STUDIES

Thomas Edison State College (A)

LIBERAL ARTS/HUMANITIES AND SOCIAL SCIENCE

Clinton Community College (A)

LIBERAL ARTS/SOCIAL SCIENCE

Westchester Community College (A)

LIBERAL EDUCATION

Lake Superior College (A)

LIBERAL SCIENCE

Laurentian University (B)

LIBERAL STUDIES

California State University, Chico (B)
Eastern Oregon University (B)
East Tennessee State University (M)
Excelsior College (M,B)
Fort Hays State University (M)
Limestone College (A,B)
Middlesex Community College (A,UC)
Middle Tennessee State University (B)
Montgomery County Community College (A)
Neumann College (A)
Northeastern University (B)
Oral Roberts University (B)
Oregon State University (B)
Regions University (A,B)
St. John's University (A,B)
Sonoma State University (B)
State University of New York Empire State
College (M)
Stony Brook University, State University of
New York (M)
Syracuse University (B)
Thomas Edison State College (M,B)
University of Illinois (B)
University of Illinois at Springfield (B)

The University of Maine at Augusta (A,B)
The University of North Carolina at
  Greensboro (M)
University of Northern Iowa (B)
University of Oklahoma (M,B)
University of Pittsburgh at Bradford (A)
University of the Incarnate Word (A)
The University of Toledo (M)

LIBERAL STUDIES (HUMANITIES CONCENTRATION)

The University of North Carolina at
  Greensboro (B)

LIBERAL STUDIES DEGREE COMPLETION

California State University, Monterey Bay (B)

LIBERAL STUDIES–BACHELOR OF LIBERAL STUDIES ONLINE DEGREE PROGRAM

Bowling Green State University (B)

LIBERAL STUDIES–MANAGEMENT AND COMMUNICATION CONCENTRATION

Montana State University–Billings (B)

LIBERAL STUDIES–MASTER OF LIBERAL STUDIES

University of Denver (M)

LIBERAL STUDIES, LIBRARY SCIENCE CONCENTRATION

Clarion University of Pennsylvania (B)

LIBRARY AND INFORMATION SCIENCE

Drexel University (M)
Emporia State University (M)
Syracuse University (M)
Syracuse University (M)
University of Illinois (GC)
University of Illinois at Urbana–Champaign
  (GC,M)
University of South Florida (M)
University of Washington (M)

LIBRARY AND INFORMATION SCIENCE IN SCHOOL MEDIA

Syracuse University (M)

LIBRARY AND INFORMATION SCIENCES

University of North Texas (GC)

LIBRARY AND INFORMATION SERVICES

The University of Maine at Augusta (A,B)

LIBRARY AND INFORMATION STUDIES

The University of North Carolina at
  Greensboro (M)

LIBRARY AND INFORMATION STUDIES–MASTER OF LIBRARY AND INFORMATION STUDIES

The University of Alabama (M)

LIBRARY AND INFORMATION TECHNOLOGIES–SCHOOL LIBRARY AND INFORMATION TECHNOLOGIES

Mansfield University of Pennsylvania (M)

LIBRARY ASSISTANT

Ivy Tech Community College–Bloomington
  (A)
Ivy Tech Community College–Central Indiana
  (A)
Ivy Tech Community College–Columbus (A)
Ivy Tech Community College–Southeast (A)
Ivy Tech Community College–Southern
  Indiana (A)
Ivy Tech Community College–Southwest (A)
Ivy Tech Community College–Wabash Valley
  (A)
Ivy Tech Community College–Whitewater (A)

LIBRARY INFORMATION MANAGEMENT

Chadron State College (B)

LIBRARY INFORMATION SCIENCE

University of Southern Mississippi (M)

LIBRARY MEDIA

The University of Montana (UC)

LIBRARY MEDIA CERTIFICATION

Montana State University (UC)

LIBRARY MEDIA EDUCATION

Western Kentucky University (M)

LIBRARY MEDIA GRADUATE ENDORSEMENT

University of Nebraska at Kearney (UC)

LIBRARY MEDIA TEACHING

Azusa Pacific University (UC)

LIBRARY SCIENCE

Clarion University of Pennsylvania (M)
Connecticut State University System (M)
East Carolina University (M)
Texas Woman's University (M)

University of Missouri–Columbia (M)
University of North Texas (M)

LIBRARY SCIENCE–SCHOOL LIBRARIANSHIP

Azusa Pacific University (M)

LIBRARY SERVICES IN DISTANCE EDUCATION

University of Maryland University College
  (GC)

LIBRARY STUDIES

Memorial University of Newfoundland (UC)

LIBRARY TECHNICAL ASSISTANT

Ivy Tech Community College–East Central
  (A)
Ivy Tech Community College–Kokomo (A)
Ivy Tech Community College–Lafayette (A)
Ivy Tech Community College–North Central
  (A)
Ivy Tech Community College–Northeast (A)
Ivy Tech Community College–Northwest (A)
Rose State College (A)

LIFE CARE PLANNING

Kaplan University (UC)

LIFE ISSUES

Fort Hays State University (UC)

LIFE SCIENCES

University of Maryland, College Park (M)

LINGUISTICS–APPLIED LINGUISTICS, ESL CONCENTRATION

University of Massachusetts Boston (M)

LITERACY

University of Missouri–Columbia (M)

LITERACY AND CULTURE

Longwood University (M)

LITERACY PROGRAM (WYOMING READING ENDORSEMENT)

University of Wyoming (UC)

LOCAL CHURCH MINISTRY

Grace College (M)

LOGISTICS AND SUPPLY CHAIN MANAGEMENT

Wright State University (M)

LOGISTICS MANAGEMENT

Florida Institute of Technology (M)

LONG-TERM CARE ADMINISTRATION

Saint Joseph's College of Maine (B,UC)
University of Southern California (M)

LONG-TERM CARE ADMINISTRATION, ADVANCED

Saint Joseph's College of Maine (UC)

LONG-TERM CARE MANAGEMENT

The University of South Dakota (GC)
The University of South Dakota (GC)

LOSS PREVENTION AND SAFETY

Eastern Kentucky University (M)

LUTC FELLOW DESIGNATION

The American College (UC)

LVN TO BACHELOR OF SCIENCE IN NURSING

The University of Texas at Tyler (B)

MAED

Northern Kentucky University (M)

MAINE STUDIES

University of Maine (UC)

MANAGEMENT

Amberton University (M,B)
American Public University System (M,B)
Athabasca University (GC)
Austin Peay State University (M)
Bellevue University (M,B)
Berkeley College (B)
Brenau University (B)
Dallas Baptist University (M,B)
Darton College (A)
Des Moines Area Community College (UC)
Embry-Riddle Aeronautical University (M)
Florida Institute of Technology (M)
Fort Hays State University (B,UC)
Franklin Pierce University (A,B,UC)
Franklin University (B)
Hodges University (M,B)
Hope International University (M)
Indiana Tech (B)
Indiana Wesleyan University (M)
Kaplan University (B)
Liberty University (M)
Metropolitan State University (B)
Minot State University (M,B)
National University (M,B)
Northeastern University (B)
North Harris Montgomery Community
  College District (A)
Old Dominion University (B)
Park University (B)

Prescott College (B)
Regis University (M)
Saint Joseph's College of Maine (A)
Southwestern College (M)
Spartanburg Community College (A)
Stevens Institute of Technology (M)
Strayer University (B)
Thomas Edison State College (M)
Troy University (M)
University of Alaska Southeast (B)
University of Houston–Victoria (B)
The University of Maine at Augusta (B)
University of Management and Technology
  (M,B)
University of Maryland University College
  (D,M)
University of North Texas (M)
University of Phoenix Online Campus (M)
University of St. Francis (M)
University of Wisconsin–Stout (B)
Upper Iowa University (B)
Wayland Baptist University (M)
Worcester Polytechnic Institute (GC)

MANAGEMENT (BACHELOR COMPLETION)

Indiana Wesleyan University (B)

MANAGEMENT (BSBA)

Northern Arizona University (B)

MANAGEMENT ACCOUNTING

Minnesota School of Business–Richfield (A)

MANAGEMENT ACCOUNTING CERTIFICATE

The University of Toledo (UC)

MANAGEMENT AND HUMAN RESOURCE SKILLS FOR PHARMACISTS

Oregon State University (UC)

MANAGEMENT AND LEADERSHIP

Judson College (B)
Webster University (M)

MANAGEMENT AND ORGANIZATIONAL DEVELOPMENT

Spring Arbor University (B)

MANAGEMENT COMMUNICATION

Regions University (B)

MANAGEMENT CONCENTRATION

Andrew Jackson University (M)

MANAGEMENT CONCENTRATION

Colorado Technical University (B)

MANAGEMENT CONCENTRATION (10-MONTH PROGRAM)

American InterContinental University Online
  (M)

MANAGEMENT CONCENTRATION (COMPLETION PROGRAM)

American InterContinental University Online
  (B)

MANAGEMENT DEVELOPMENT

College of Southern Maryland (A,UC)

MANAGEMENT DEVELOPMENT– MARKETING

College of Southern Maryland (UC)

MANAGEMENT EMPHASIS, GENERAL MANAGEMENT

Community College of Denver (A)

MANAGEMENT ESSENTIALS

New Jersey Institute of Technology (GC)

MANAGEMENT IN COMPUTER SCIENCE/TELECOM WITH SECURITY MANAGEMENT AND FORENSICS

Stevens Institute of Technology (M)

MANAGEMENT INFORMATION SCIENCES

Franklin University (B)

MANAGEMENT INFORMATION SYSTEMS

Auburn University (M)
Bellevue University (B)
Culver-Stockton College (B)
Dakota State University (B)
Dallas Baptist University (M,B)
Excelsior College (B)
Florida State University (M)
Liberty University (A,B)
Minot State University (B)
Myers University (B)
Northeastern University (A)
Northwest Missouri State University (B)
Nova Southeastern University (M)
Regis University (UC)
Seminole Community College (A)
Stevens Institute of Technology (GC)
University of Illinois (M)
University of Illinois at Springfield (M)

MANAGEMENT OF HUMAN RESOURCES

Bellevue University (B)
Excelsior College (B)

MANAGEMENT OF INFORMATION SYSTEMS

Keiser University (B)

MANAGEMENT OF INFORMATION TECHNOLOGY

Schiller International University (M)

MANAGEMENT OF TECHNOLOGY

New Jersey Institute of Technology (GC)
The University of Texas at San Antonio (M)
Walden University (M)

MANAGEMENT OF TECHNOLOGY (MSCIT)

Regis University (GC)

MANAGEMENT POST-DIPLOMA (3 YEAR)

Athabasca University (B)

MANAGEMENT POST-DIPLOMA (4 YEAR)

Athabasca University (B)

MANAGEMENT SCIENCE

Neumann College (M)

MANAGEMENT SCIENCE AND ENGINEERING

Stanford University (GC,M)

MANAGEMENT SCIENCES–MASTER OF MANAGEMENT SCIENCES ONLINE (MMSC)

University of Waterloo (M)

MANAGEMENT STUDIES

University of Maryland University College (B)

MANAGEMENT STUDIES, ADVANCED

Brenau University (M)

MANAGEMENT–GENERAL MANAGEMENT EMPHASIS

City University (M)

MANAGEMENT–MASTER OF MANAGEMENT

Oral Roberts University (M)

MANAGEMENT, COMMUNICATION AND QUALITY

Kaplan University (M)

MANAGEMENT, GENERAL

Dallas Baptist University (M)
The University of Texas at Arlington (M)

MANAGEMENT/COMPUTER INFORMATION SYSTEMS

Park University (B)

MANAGEMENT/E-BUSINESS

Kaplan University (B)

MANAGEMENT/HEALTH CARE MANAGEMENT

Kaplan University (B)

MANAGEMENT/HUMAN RESOURCES

Park University (B)

MANAGEMENT/HUMAN RESOURCES MANAGEMENT

Kaplan University (B)

MANAGEMENT/MARKETING

Park University (B)

MANAGEMENT/SALES AND MARKETING

Kaplan University (B)

MANAGING APPLIED RESEARCH IN TECHNOLOGY

University of Colorado at Boulder (GC)

MANUFACTURING

Regent University (UC)

MANUFACTURING ENGINEERING

Boston University (M)
Columbia University (UC)
University of Washington (M)
University of Wisconsin–Stout (M)

MANUFACTURING ENGINEERING (INDUSTRIAL AND MANUFACTURING ENGINEERING CONCENTRATION)

Kettering University (M)

MANUFACTURING ENGINEERING TECHNOLOGY

Thomas Edison State College (A,B)

MANUFACTURING MANAGEMENT

Kettering University (M)
Missouri State University (UC)

MANUFACTURING MANAGEMENT–BACHELOR OF MANUFACTURING MANAGEMENT ONLINE

University of Minnesota, Crookston (B)

MANUFACTURING OPERATIONS

Kettering University (M)

MANUFACTURING SYSTEMS ENGINEERING

Lehigh University (M)

MANUFACTURING SYSTEMS MANAGEMENT

Southern Methodist University (M)

MANUFACTURING SYSTEMS TECHNOLOGY

Jacksonville State University (M)

MARINE ENGINEERING TECHNOLOGY

Thomas Edison State College (A,B)

MARITIME STUDIES

University of West Florida (B)

MARITIME STUDIES–BACHELOR OF MARITIME STUDIES (BMS)

Memorial University of Newfoundland (B)

MARKETING

American Public University System (B)
Brenau University (B)
City University (GC,UC)
Columbus State Community College (A)
Dallas Baptist University (M)
Excelsior College (B)
Franklin Pierce University (A,B,UC)
Indiana Tech (B)
J. Sargeant Reynolds Community College (A)
Kaplan University (M)
Lakeland College (B)
Lynn University (M)
Metropolitan State University (B)
Mount Saint Vincent University (B)
Myers University (B)
National University (B)
Northeastern University (A)
Regis University (B)
Southern New Hampshire University (GC,M,A,B)
Strayer University (A,B)
Thomas Edison State College (B)
University of Alaska Southeast (B)
University of Houston–Victoria (B)
University of Maryland University College (B)
University of Northwestern Ohio (A)
Upper Iowa University (B,UC)

Walden University (M)
Western Wyoming Community College (A)

MARKETING AND MANAGEMENT

Butler Community College (A)

MARKETING AND SALES TECHNOLOGY

The University of Toledo (A,UC)

MARKETING CONCENTRATION

Andrew Jackson University (M)
Colorado Technical University (M,B)

MARKETING CONCENTRATION (10-MONTH PROGRAM)

American InterContinental University Online (M)

MARKETING CONCENTRATION (COMPLETION PROGRAM)

American InterContinental University Online (B)

MARKETING EMPHASIS

Community College of Denver (A)

MARKETING MANAGEMENT

Bellevue University (B)
Concordia University, St. Paul (B)
University of Dallas (GC,M)
University of Management and Technology (B)

MARKETING STRATEGY IN THE DIGITAL AGE

University of Illinois (GC)

MARKETING, MANAGEMENT, AND TECHNOLOGY

University of Northwestern Ohio (A)

MARKETING/MANAGEMENT

Williston State College (A,UC)

MARRIAGE AND FAMILY THERAPY

Liberty University (M)
Regions University (M)
Saybrook Graduate School and Research Center (M)

MARRIAGE EDUCATION (FOR CREDIT)

University of Bridgeport (UC)

MARRIAGE EDUCATION (NON-CREDIT)

University of Bridgeport (UC)

MASS COMMUNICATION AND MEDIA MANAGEMENT

Lynn University (M)

MASTER OCCUPATIONAL THERAPY

Texas Woman's University

MASTER OF CONSTRUCTION MANAGEMENT PROGRAM

Western Carolina University (M)

MASTER OF ENGINEERING

Mississippi State University (M)

MASTER OF HEALTH AND HUMAN SERVICES

Youngstown State University (M)

MASTER OF HEALTH CARE ADMINISTRATION

National University (M)

MASTER OF INFORMATION SYSTEMS

University of Phoenix Online Campus (M)

MASTER OF INTERNATIONAL MANAGEMENT IN INTERNATIONAL BUSINESS

Schiller International University (M)

MASTER OF MUSIC IN MUSIC EDUCATION

The University of Montana (M)

MASTER OF PUBLIC ADMINISTRATION

California State University, Dominguez Hills (M)

MASTER OF SCHOOL ADMINISTRATION PROGRAM

Western Carolina University (M)

MASTER OF SCIENCE ENGINEERING MANAGEMENT

California State University, Dominguez Hills (M)

MASTER OF WORLDVIEW STUDIES IN EDUCATION

Institute for Christian Studies (M)

MASTER READING TEACHER

Texas Tech University (UC)

MASTER TEACHER ELEMENTARY

Emporia State University (M)

MATERIAL ACQUISITION MANAGEMENT

Florida Institute of Technology (M)

MATERIAL DESIGN, ADVANCED

University of Idaho (UC)

MATERIALS

University of Illinois (GC)

MATERIALS ENGINEERING

Auburn University (M)
University of Illinois at Urbana–Champaign (GC)
University of Southern California (M)

MATERIALS FAILURE

University of Illinois (GC)

MATERIALS FAILURE ANALYSIS

University of Illinois at Urbana–Champaign (GC)

MATERIALS SCIENCE AND ENGINEERING

Columbia University (M,UC)
University of Florida (M)
University of Washington (M)

MATH

Chadron State College (M,B)

MATH TEACHER LINK

University of Illinois (GC)

MATHEMATICAL SCIENCES

University of Illinois at Springfield (B)

MATHEMATICS

Mercy College (B)
Montana State University (M)
Northern Arizona University (M)
Skidmore College (B)
Thomas Edison State College (A,B)
University of Illinois (B)

MATHEMATICS EDUCATION

Florida State University (M)
University of Alaska Southeast (UC)
Western Kentucky University (M)

MATHEMATICS EDUCATION (K-8)

Lesley University (M)

MATHEMATICS–APPLIED MATHEMATICS

Columbia University (M,UC)

MBA ONLINE

University of Tulsa (M)

MBA–POLICING ELECTIVE

Athabasca University (M)

MEAT CULINOLOGY

University of Nebraska–Lincoln (GC)

MECHANICAL AND AEROSPACE ENGINEERING-DYNAMICS AND CONTROL

University of Florida (M)

MECHANICAL AND AEROSPACE ENGINEERING-FUNDAMENTALS OF THERMAL FLUIDS TRANSPORT TRACK

University of Florida (M)

MECHANICAL AND AEROSPACE ENGINEERING-SOLID MECHANICS AND DESIGN TRACK

University of Florida (M)

MECHANICAL DESIGN (ME CONCENTRATION)

Kettering University (M)

MECHANICAL ENGINEERING

Auburn University (M)
Columbia University (GC,M)
Georgia Institute of Technology (M)
Iowa State University of Science and
  Technology (M)
Kansas State University (M)
Michigan Technological University (D,M)
North Carolina State University (M)
Southern Methodist University (M)
Stanford University (M)
The University of Alabama (B)
University of Delaware (M)
University of Idaho (M)
University of Illinois (M)
University of Illinois at Urbana–Champaign
  (M)
University of North Dakota (B)

University of Southern California (M)
The University of Texas at Arlington (M)
University of Washington (M)

MECHANICAL ENGINEERING (ENGINEERING MANAGEMENT PROGRAM)

Colorado State University (M)

MECHANICAL ENGINEERING (IND ENGG AND OPERATIONS RES PROGRAM)

Colorado State University (D,M)

MECHANICAL ENGINEERING (MATERIALS ENGINEERING)

Colorado State University (M)

MECHANICAL ENGINEERING (MS OR MENG)

Lehigh University (M)

MECHANICAL ENGINEERING TECHNOLOGY

Indiana State University (B)
Old Dominion University (B)
Thomas Edison State College (A,B)

MECHANICAL ENGINEERING, PHARMACEUTICAL CONCENTRATION

Stevens Institute of Technology

MECHANICS AND MAINTENANCE

Thomas Edison State College (A)

MEDIA ARTS

Cerro Coso Community College (A)

MEDIA MANAGEMENT

The New School: A University (GC)

MEDIA PSYCHOLOGY

Fielding Graduate University (D)

MEDIA STUDIES

The New School: A University (M)

MEDIATION

Colorado State University (UC)

MEDICAID NURSE AIDE

Jefferson Community and Technical College
  (UC)

MEDICAL ADMINISTRATIVE ASSISTANT

Minnesota State Community and Technical
  College–Fergus Falls (A)

MEDICAL ADMINISTRATIVE SECRETARY TECHNOLOGY

Northwest Technical College (A)

MEDICAL ASSISTANT

Minot State University–Bottineau Campus
  (A,UC)

MEDICAL ASSISTANT TECHNOLOGY

University of Northwestern Ohio (A)

MEDICAL ASSISTING

Keiser University (A)

MEDICAL BILLING AND CODING

Colorado Technical University (A)
Drexel University (UC)

MEDICAL BILLING AND CODING CERTIFICATE

California State University, Dominguez Hills
  (GC)

MEDICAL CODING

Darton College (UC)
Minot State University–Bottineau Campus
  (UC)

MEDICAL CODING AND BILLING CONCENTRATION

American InterContinental University Online
  (A)

MEDICAL CODING SPECIALIST

Southwest Wisconsin Technical College (UC)

MEDICAL DEVICE AND DIAGNOSTIC ENGINEERING

University of Southern California (M)

MEDICAL IMAGING

Clarkson College (B)
Thomas Edison State College (A,B)

MEDICAL IMAGING POST-BACCALAUREATE CERTIFICATE

MGH Institute of Health Professions (UC)

MEDICAL INFORMATICS

Northwestern University (M)

MEDICAL LAB TECHNOLOGY

Broome Community College (A)

MEDICAL LABORATORY TECHNOLOGY

Central Virginia Community College (A)
Clark State Community College (A)
Darton College (A)
St. Petersburg College (A)

MEDICAL OFFICE

North Harris Montgomery Community
College District (A)

MEDICAL OFFICE ADMINISTRATION

Presentation College (A)

MEDICAL OFFICE ASSISTANT

Edison State Community College (A)

MEDICAL OFFICE CODING SPECIALIST

Sinclair Community College (UC)

MEDICAL OFFICE SPECIALIST

University of Alaska Southeast (UC)

MEDICAL PHYSICS

Georgia Institute of Technology (M)

MEDICAL SECRETARY

Minot State University–Bottineau Campus (A)

MEDICAL TECHNOLOGY

Darton College (A)

MEDICAL TRANSCRIPTION

Central Texas College (UC)
Minot State University–Bottineau Campus
(UC)
North Dakota State College of Science (UC)
Presentation College (UC)
Southwest Wisconsin Technical College (UC)
Williston State College (A,UC)

MEDICAL TRANSCRIPTION CERTIFICATE

California State University, Dominguez Hills
(GC)

MEDICAL TRANSCRIPTIONIST

Jefferson Community and Technical College
(A)

MEDICAL–GRADUATE MEDICAL EDUCATION CORE CURRICULUM

University of Illinois (UC)

MEDICAL/BILLER CODER

University of Cincinnati (UC)

MENTAL HEALTH AND HUMAN SERVICES

The University of Maine at Augusta (B)

MENTAL HEALTH AND REHABILITATION SERVICES

Thomas Edison State College (B)

MENTAL HEALTH COUNSELING

Prescott College (M)

MENTAL HEALTH NURSE PRACTITIONER

University of Missouri–Columbia (M)

MENTAL HEALTH PRACTICES IN SCHOOLS

University of Missouri–Columbia (M)

MENTAL HEALTH PRACTICES IN SCHOOLS (EDUCATIONAL SPECIALIST)

University of Missouri–Columbia

MERCHANDISING

Kansas State University (M)
North Dakota State University (GC,M)
University of North Texas (GC,M)

METEOROLOGY–BROADCAST METEOROLOGY PROGRAM

Mississippi State University

METEOROLOGY–OPERATIONAL METEOROLOGY PROGRAM

Mississippi State University

MICROCOMPUTER OFFICE SPECIALIST

Lake Superior College (UC)

MICROELECTRONICS AND PHOTONICS

Stevens Institute of Technology (M)

MICROELECTRONICS MANUFACTURING ENGINEERING

Rochester Institute of Technology (M)

MICROFINANCE MANAGEMENT

Southern New Hampshire University (GC)

MICROSOFT NETWORKING MCSA

Jefferson Community and Technical College
(UC)

MICROSOFT OFFICE SPECIALIST CERTIFICATION PREPARATION

Lansing Community College (UC)

MIDDLE EASTERN STUDIES

American Public University System (B)

MIDDLE GRADES 5-9

University of the Cumberlands (M)

MIDDLE GRADES EDUCATION

Brenau University (M)

MIDDLE SCHOOL EDUCATION

Northern Arizona University (UC)

MIDDLE/SECONDARY TEACHING

Indiana State University (UC)

MIDMANAGEMENT

Waubonsee Community College (UC)

MIDWIFERY

Philadelphia University (M)

MILITARY HISTORY

Austin Peay State University (M)

MILITARY HISTORY, MILITARY MANAGEMENT, INTELLIGENCE STUDIES

American Public University System (B)

MILITARY SPECIALTIES

Fort Hays State University (B)

MILITARY STUDIES

American Public University System (M)

MINISTERIAL EDUCATION

God's Bible School and College (B)

MINISTERIAL LEADERSHIP

Regions University (M)

MINISTERIAL STUDIES

Global University of the Assemblies of God
(M,A)

MINISTRY

Global University of the Assemblies of God
 (UC)
Liberty University (D)
Oral Roberts University (D)
Regions University (M)

MINISTRY (MINISTERIAL LEADERSHIP AND YOUTH MINISTRY CONCENTRATIONS)

Indiana Wesleyan University (M)

MINISTRY AND LEADERSHIP DEGREE COMPLETION PROGRAM

Life Pacific College (B)

MINISTRY STUDIES

Judson College (B)

MINISTRY STUDIES–6 DISTINCT CONCENTRATIONS AVAILABLE

Temple Baptist Seminary (D)

MINISTRY–LEADERSHIP AND RENEWAL

Regent University (D)

MINISTRY–MASTER OF MINISTRY–VARIOUS CONCENTRATIONS AVAILABLE

Temple Baptist Seminary (M)

MINISTRY/BIBLE

Regions University (B)

MIS CONCENTRATION AND SAP EMPHASIS

Central Michigan University (M)

MISSIONS

Global University of the Assemblies of God
 (B)

MISSIONS STUDIES

Taylor University (UC)

MODERN LANGUAGES– CERTIFICATE OF ADVANCED STUDY

University of Denver (UC)

MOLECULAR BIOLOGY

Lehigh University (M)

MOTION PICTURES AND TELEVISION

Academy of Art University (M,A,B)

MPA ONLINE

California State University, San Bernardino
 (M)

MSBA/TAXATION

California State University, Sacramento (M)

MSEE

Villanova University (M)

MSME

Villanova University (M)

MULTI-CULTURAL EDUCATION

Park University (M)

MULTICULTURAL AND TRANSNATIONAL LITERATURES EMPHASIS

East Carolina University (M)

MULTICULTURAL LITERATURE

East Carolina University (GC)

MULTIDISCIPLINARY STUDIES

Liberty University (B)
West Virginia University (B)

MULTIDISCIPLINARY STUDIES– EDUCATION CONCENTRATION

Liberty University (B)

MULTIMEDIA APPLICATIONS

University of Massachusetts Lowell (UC)

MULTIMEDIA COMMUNICATIONS

Bristol Community College (UC)

MULTIMEDIA NETWORKING

Columbia University (UC)

MULTIMEDIA TECHNOLOGY

Stevens Institute of Technology (GC)
University of Management and Technology
 (M)

MUSEUM STUDIES

Prescott College (M)

MUSIC

Auburn University (M)
Darton College (A)
Judson College (B)
Prescott College (B)
Skidmore College (B)
Thomas Edison State College (B)

MUSIC EDUCATION

East Carolina University (M)
University of South Florida (M)

MUSIC EDUCATION–MASTER OF MUSIC EDUCATION

University of Southern Mississippi (M)

MUSIC EDUCATION–MASTERS IN MUSIC EDUCATION

Duquesne University (M)

MUSIC THERAPY

Georgia College & State University (M)

MUTUAL FUNDS AND INVESTMENTS

New England College of Finance (GC)

NANOSCALE MATERIALS SCIENCE

Stanford University (GC)

NANOTECHNOLOGY

Columbia University (UC)

NATIONAL SECURITY STUDIES

American Public University System (M)

NATIVE STUDIES

Laurentian University (B)

NATIVE STUDIES (HONOURS)

Laurentian University (B)

NATURAL RESOURCE MANAGEMENT–CERTIFICATE OF ADVANCED STUDY

University of Denver (UC)

NATURAL RESOURCES

Oregon State University (B)
Virginia Polytechnic Institute and State
 University (GC)

NATURAL RESOURCES AND CONSERVATION

Prescott College (M,B)

NATURAL RESOURCES AND THE ENVIRONMENT

Colorado State University (UC)

NATURAL SCIENCES/ MATHEMATICS

Thomas Edison State College (B)

NCA CASI SCHOOL IMPROVEMENT SPECIALIST

University of Nebraska–Lincoln (GC)

NEGOTIATION, CONFLICT RESOLUTION AND PEACEBUILDING

California State University, Dominguez Hills (M)

NEONATAL NURSE PRACTITIONER

East Carolina University (M)

NETMATH

University of Illinois (GC)

NETWORK AND COMMUNICATIONS MANAGEMENT

DeVry University Online (M,B)

NETWORK AND INTERNET ADMINISTRATION

Southwest Virginia Community College (UC)

NETWORK SECURITY

Capitol College (M)

NETWORK SECURITY AND INFORMATION ASSURANCE

New Jersey Institute of Technology (GC)

NETWORK SECURITY MANAGEMENT

Northeastern University (GC)

NETWORK SYSTEMS ADMINISTRATION

DeVry University Online (A)

NETWORK+ CERTIFICATION AND COMPUTER TECHNOLOGY

Cleveland Institute of Electronics (UC)

NETWORKED INFORMATION SYSTEMS

Stevens Institute of Technology (GC,M)

NETWORKING & SYSTEMS ADMINISTRATION

Rochester Institute of Technology (M)

NETWORKING (ELECTRICAL ENGINEERING)

Stanford University (GC)

NETWORKING AND SYSTEMS

Columbia University (UC)

NETWORKING TECHNOLOGIES (MSCIT)

Regis University (GC)

NETWORKING/ TELECOMMUNICATIONS

City University (UC)

NETWORKS AND DISTRIBUTED SYSTEMS

University of Illinois (GC)
University of Illinois at Urbana–Champaign (GC)

NEUROPSYCHOLOGY

Fielding Graduate University (UC)

NEW BUSINESS DEVELOPMENT

Regent University (UC)

NEW MEDIA ENGINEERING

Columbia University (UC)

NEW TESTAMENT

Johnson Bible College (M)

NEWFOUNDLAND STUDIES

Memorial University of Newfoundland (UC)

NON-PROFIT ORGANIZATION MANAGEMENT

Green Mountain College (M)

NONDESTRUCTIVE TESTING TECHNOLOGY

Thomas Edison State College (A,B)

NONPROFIT AND ASSOCIATION FINANCIAL MANAGEMENT

University of Maryland University College (GC)

NONPROFIT AND COMMUNITY SERVICES MANAGEMENT

Park University (M)

NONPROFIT MANAGEMENT

George Mason University (GC)
Hope International University (M)
Northeastern University (GC)
Oral Roberts University (M)
Regis University (M)
University of Central Florida (GC,M)
University of Illinois (GC)

NONPROFIT MANAGEMENT (POST-BACCALAUREATE)

The University of North Carolina at Greensboro (UC)

NONPROFIT MANAGEMENT AND LEADERSHIP

Walden University (M)

NONTRADITIONAL PHARMD

The Ohio State University (D)

NOT-FOR-PROFIT

University of Dallas (GC,M)

NUCLEAR CRITICALITY SAFETY

The University of Tennessee (GC)

NUCLEAR ENGINEERING TECHNOLOGY

Excelsior College (B)
Thomas Edison State College (A,B)

NUCLEAR MEDICINE TECHNOLOGY

Darton College (A)
Thomas Edison State College (A,B)

NUCLEAR POWER TECHNOLOGY

Bismarck State College (A)

NUCLEAR TECHNOLOGY

Excelsior College (A)

NURSE CLINICIAN EDUCATOR

The University of Texas at El Paso (UC)

NURSE EDUCATOR

Florida State University (M)
Graceland University (GC,M)
The University of North Carolina at Charlotte (M)
The University of Toledo (M)
Missouri State University (GC)

NURSE EDUCATOR TRACK

Western Carolina University (M)

NURSE MIDWIFERY

East Carolina University (M,)
University of Cincinnati (M)

NURSE PRACTITIONER

University of St. Francis (M)

NURSE PRACTITIONER ADVANCEMENT

Northern Kentucky University (UC)

NURSE PRACTITIONER AND CLINICAL SPECIALIST

University of Colorado at Colorado Springs (M)

NURSE-MIDWIFERY

Philadelphia University (UC)

NURSIING–RN TO BSN

University of Illinois at Chicago (B)

NURSING

Allen College (M)
Athabasca University (M)
Ball State University (M,B)
California State University, Chico (M,B)
California State University, Dominguez Hills (M)
Clarion University of Pennsylvania (B)
Clemson University (M,B)
Concordia University Wisconsin (M)
Darton College (A)
Duquesne University (D,M)
Excelsior College (M,A,B)
Graceland University (B)
Jacksonville State University (M)
Liberty University (M)
Lock Haven University of Pennsylvania (A)
Memorial University of Newfoundland (M)
Mercy College (B)
Metropolitan State University (M)
Middle Tennessee State University (M,B)
Minnesota State University Moorhead (M)
Mississippi University for Women (B)
Missouri State University (B)
Montana State University (M)
National University (B)
New Mexico State University (B)
Northern Arizona University (M,B)
Northern Kentucky University (M,)
Northwest Technical College (A)

Old Dominion University (B)
Oregon Health & Science University (B)
Pennsylvania College of Technology (B)
Sacred Heart University (B)
Saint Francis Medical Center College of Nursing (M)
Saint Joseph's College of Maine (M,B)
Samuel Merritt College (M)
Seton Hall University (M)
State University of New York at Plattsburgh (B)
Tennessee Technological University (M)
Texas Christian University (M)
Texas Woman's University (D)
Thomas Edison State College (M,B)
The University of Alabama (M,B)
University of Arkansas (M)
University of Central Florida (B)
University of Central Missouri (B)
University of Delaware (B)
University of Michigan–Flint (B)
University of Nebraska Medical Center (M,B)
The University of North Carolina at Greensboro (M,B)
University of North Dakota (B)
University of Phoenix Online Campus (M)
University of South Alabama (M,B)
University of Southern Indiana (M,B)
University of South Florida (M)
The University of Texas at Tyler (B)
West Virginia University (M)

NURSING (FAMILY NURSE PRACTITIONER SPECIALIZATION)

Indiana State University (M)

NURSING (LPN-BS)

Indiana State University (B)

NURSING (NURSING ADMINISTRATION SPECIALIZATION)

Indiana State University (M)

NURSING (NURSING EDUCATION SPECIALIZATION)

Indiana State University (M)

NURSING (RN TO BS COMPLETION)

Indiana Wesleyan University (B)

NURSING (RN TO BSN)

Penn State University Park (B)

NURSING (RN-BS)

Indiana State University (B)

NURSING (STEP NURSING PROGRAM)

Jacksonville State University (B)

NURSING ADMINISTRATION

Fort Hays State University (M)
Mercy College (M)
University of West Florida (M)

NURSING ADMINISTRATION AND LEADERSHIP

Saint Joseph's College of Maine (GC)

NURSING AND HEALTHCARE EDUCATION

Saint Joseph's College of Maine (GC)

NURSING CARE HEALTH CARE LEADERSHIP

Clarkson College

NURSING COMPLETION PROGRAM

California State University, Dominguez Hills (B)

NURSING EDUCATION

Andrews University (M)
Clarkson College (M,)
East Carolina University (M,)
Fort Hays State University (M)
Mansfield University of Pennsylvania (M)
Mercy College (M)
University of Central Florida (GC)
University of Missouri–Columbia (M)
The University of Texas System (GC)
The University of Toledo (UC)

NURSING EDUCATION AND HOSPITALITY ADMINISTRATION– PH.D. NURSING EDUCATION, MASTER'S IN HOSPITALITY ADMINISTRATION

University of Nevada, Las Vegas

NURSING EDUCATION AND NURSING ADMINISTRATION MAJORS

Indiana Wesleyan University (M)

NURSING FAST TRACK

University of St. Francis (B)

NURSING FOR REGISTERED NURSES

Minot State University (B)

NURSING HEALTH CARE LEADERSHIP

Clarkson College (M)

NURSING LEADERSHIP

East Carolina University (M)

NURSING LEADERSHIP IN HEALTH SYSTEMS MANAGEMENT

Drexel University (M,UC)

NURSING–ACCELERATED OPTION

Northern Arizona University (B)

NURSING–ADMINISTRATION AND EDUCATION OPTIONS

The University of Texas at Tyler (M)

NURSING–BACHELOR OF SCIENCE

Minnesota State University Moorhead (B)

NURSING–BSN COMPLETION FOR RN'S

Concordia University Wisconsin (B)

NURSING–BSN FOR REGISTERED NURSES

Laurentian University (B)

NURSING–BSN NURSING INFORMATICS

Walden University (M)

NURSING–BSN TRACK, EDUCATION

Walden University (M)

NURSING–BSN TRACK, LEADERSHIP AND MANAGEMENT

Walden University (M)

NURSING–CONTINENCE CARE NURSE

Metropolitan State University (UC)

NURSING–EDUCATION SPECIALIZATION

University of North Dakota (M)

NURSING–FAMILY NURSE PRACTITIONER

Clarion University of Pennsylvania (M)
East Carolina University (M,)

NURSING–FOR PRELICENSURE AND LICENSED

Missouri Southern State University (B)

NURSING–FOR REGISTERED NURSES

Missouri Southern State University (B)

NURSING–FORENSIC NURSING

Duquesne University
Kaplan University (UC)

NURSING–GERONTOLOGICAL/ ADULT AND FAMILY NURSE PRACTITIONER

University of Massachusetts Boston (GC)

NURSING–HEALTH SERVICES ADMINISTRATION

University of Delaware (M)

NURSING–LEADERSHIP AND MANAGEMENT TRACK

University of Central Florida (M)

NURSING–LPN CERTIFICATE TO BSN NURSING COMPLETION

Presentation College (B)

NURSING–MASTER OF BUSINESS ADMINISTRATION, HEALTH CARE MANAGEMENT

University of Phoenix Online Campus (M)

NURSING–NEONATAL NURSE PRACTIONER

East Carolina University

NURSING–NURSE EDUCATOR OPTION

University of Wyoming (M)

NURSING–NURSE EDUCATOR TRACK

University of Central Florida (M)

NURSING–NURSE LEADER AND NURSE EDUCATOR OPTIONS

Old Dominion University (M)

NURSING–NURSING PRACTICE, ADVANCED

Athabasca University (GC)

NURSING–NURSING/HEALTH CARE EDUCATION

University of Phoenix Online Campus (M)

NURSING–ONLINE ADN NURSING PROGRAM

John Tyler Community College (A)

NURSING–ONLINE RN TO BSN PROGRAM

California State University, San Bernardino (B)

NURSING–OSTOMY CARE NURSE

Metropolitan State University (UC)

NURSING–PATIENT CARE SERVICES ADMINISTRATION– FAMILY NURSE PRACTITIONER

Sacred Heart University (M)

NURSING–PERIOPERATIVE NURSING

St. Petersburg College (UC)

NURSING–POST-BSN

Duquesne University (UC)

NURSING–POST-LPN

Athabasca University (B)

NURSING–POST-MASTERS

Duquesne University (GC)

NURSING–POST-RN

Athabasca University (B)
Memorial University of Newfoundland (B)

NURSING–PRACTICAL NURSING

North Dakota State College of Science (A)

NURSING–PUBLIC HEALTH OR SCHOOL HEALTH NURSING

University of Missouri–Columbia (M)

NURSING–REGISTERED NURSE TO BACHELOR OF SCIENCE IN NURSING

Austin Peay State University (B)

NURSING–REGISTERED NURSING

Clark State Community College (A)

NURSING–RN COMPLETION PROGRAM FOR ASSOCIATE DEGREE HOLDING NURSES

University of South Florida (B)

NURSING–RN NURSING INFORMATICS

Walden University (M)

NURSING–RN OPTION

The University of Texas at Tyler (B)

NURSING–RN TO BA COMPLETION

The College of St. Scholastica (B)

NURSING–RN TO BACHELOR OF SCIENCE IN NURSING

Keiser University (B)
University of Phoenix Online Campus (B)

NURSING–RN TO BS

University of Massachusetts Boston (B)
Washington State University (B)

NURSING–RN TO BSN

Brenau University (B)
Clarkson College (B)
Drexel University (B)
East Carolina University (B)
Florida State University (B)
Fort Hays State University (B)
Liberty University (B)
Mansfield University of Pennsylvania (B)
Northern Arizona University (B)
Regis University (B)
Seton Hall University (B)
Southwestern College (B)
University of Maine at Fort Kent (B)
University of North Alabama (B)
The University of Texas System (B)
University of Wyoming (B)
Western Carolina University (B)
West Virginia University (B)

NURSING–RN TO BSN BACHELORS COMPLETION PROGRAM

Connecticut State University System (B)

NURSING–RN TO BSN COMPLETION

Kaplan University (B)

NURSING–RN TO BSN COMPLETION

The University of North Carolina at Charlotte (B)

NURSING–RN TO BSN COMPLETION PROGRAM

Wright State University (B)

NURSING–RN TO BSN DEGREE COMPLETION PROGRAM

West Texas A&M University (B)

NURSING–RN TO BSN NURSING COMPLETION

Presentation College (B)

NURSING–RN TO BSN ONLINE OPTION (BACHELORS COMPLETION PROGRAM)

University of Missouri–Columbia (B)

NURSING–RN TO BSN/MSN

Duquesne University (B)

NURSING–RN TO MSN

University of Delaware (M)

NURSING–RN TRACK, EDUCATION

Walden University (M)

NURSING–RN TRACK, LEADERSHIP AND MANAGEMENT

Walden University (M)

NURSING–RN–BS IN NURSING

Texas Woman's University (B)

NURSING–RN-BSN

Marymount University (B)
Northern Kentucky University (B)

NURSING–RN-BSN PROGRAM

The University of Texas at El Paso (B)

NURSING–RN-BSN–RN TO BACHELOR OF SCIENCE IN NURSING

Chatham University (B)

NURSING–RN-MSN OPTION

The University of Texas at Tyler (M)

NURSING–RN-TO-BSN COMPLETION

Bowling Green State University (B)

NURSING–RURAL FAMILY NURSING

University of Central Missouri (M)

NURSING–SCHOOL NURSE

University of Illinois (GC)

NURSING–TEACHING CERTIFICATE IN NURSING EDUCATION

University of Illinois (GC)

NURSING–WOUND CARE NURSE

Metropolitan State University (UC)

NURSING–WOUND OSTOMY CONTINENCE NURSE

Metropolitan State University (UC)

NURSING&AD-LPN TO BSN NURSING COMPLETION

Presentation College (B)

NUTRITION AND DIETETICS

Central Michigan University (M)
East Carolina University (M)

OBJECT-ORIENTED ANALYSIS AND DESIGN USING UML

University of Washington (UC)

OBJECT-ORIENTED DESIGN

New Jersey Institute of Technology (GC)

OBJECT-ORIENTED TECHNOLOGIES (MSCIT)

Regis University (GC)

OCCUPATION AND TECHNICAL STUDIES

Old Dominion University (D)

OCCUPATIONAL AND TECHNICAL STUDIES

Old Dominion University (M,B)

OCCUPATIONAL HEALTH PSYCHOLOGY

Kansas State University (UC)

OCCUPATIONAL MEDICINE

Medical College of Wisconsin (M)

OCCUPATIONAL SAFETY

East Carolina University (M)

OCCUPATIONAL SAFETY AND HEALTH FOCUS

University of Connecticut (B)

OCCUPATIONAL STUDIES

Thomas Edison State College (A)

OCCUPATIONAL STUDIES IN AVIATION STUDIES

Excelsior College (A)

OCCUPATIONAL THERAPY

Darton College (A)
Texas Woman's University (M)
University of St. Augustine for Health
  Sciences (D)
University of Southern Indiana (M)
West Virginia University (M)

OCEAN ENGINEERING

Virginia Polytechnic Institute and State
  University (M)

OCEANOGRAPHY

University of West Florida (B)

OFFICE ADMINISTRATION

Central New Mexico Community College (A)
Ivy Tech Community College–Bloomington
  (A)
Ivy Tech Community College–Central Indiana
  (A)
Ivy Tech Community College–Columbus (A)
Ivy Tech Community College–East Central
  (A)
Ivy Tech Community College–Kokomo (A)
Ivy Tech Community College–Lafayette (A)
Ivy Tech Community College–North Central
  (A)
Ivy Tech Community College–Northeast (A)
Ivy Tech Community College–Northwest (A)
Ivy Tech Community College–Southeast (A)
Ivy Tech Community College–Southern
  Indiana (A)
Ivy Tech Community College–Southwest (A)
Ivy Tech Community College–Wabash Valley
  (A)
Ivy Tech Community College–Whitewater (A)

OFFICE ADMINISTRATION (ADMINISTRATIVE SUPPORT)

Darton College (A)

OFFICE ADMINISTRATION (SECRETARIAL SCIENCE)

Darton College (A)

OFFICE ASSISTANT

Central Texas College (UC)
Jefferson Community and Technical College
  (A)

OFFICE INFORMATION SYSTEMS

Northwest Missouri State University (B)
Western Wyoming Community College (A)

OFFICE MANAGEMENT

Central Texas College (A)

OFFICE MANAGEMENT LEVELS 1&2

Central Texas College (UC)

OFFICE SOFTWARE APPLICATIONS

Seminole Community College (UC)

OFFICE SUPPORT

Seminole Community College (UC)

OFFICE SUPPORT SYSTEMS

Utah State University (A)

OFFICE SYSTEMS TECHNOLOGY

Randolph Community College (A)

OFFICE TECHNOLOGY

State University of New York College of
  Agriculture and Technology at Morrisville

OHIO READING ENDORSEMENT PROGRAM

Bowling Green State University (GC)

ONLINE PRINCIPAL LICENSURE PROGRAM AND MASTERS DEGREE IN CURRICULUM AND INSTRUCTION

University of Colorado at Colorado Springs
  (M)

ONLINE TEACHING

Roosevelt University (GC)

ONLINE TEACHING AND LEARNING

California State University, East Bay (M)

OPERATIONS MANAGEMENT

Excelsior College (B)
Kettering University (M)
Southern New Hampshire University (GC)
Southwestern College (B)
Thomas Edison State College (B)
The University of Alabama (M)

OPERATIONS MANAGEMENT CONCENTRATION (10-MONTH PROGRAM)

American InterContinental University Online
  (M)

OPERATIONS MANAGEMENT CONCENTRATION (COMPLETION PROGRAM)

American InterContinental University Online
  (B)

OPERATIONS RESEARCH

Columbia University (UC)
Florida Institute of Technology (M)
Georgia Institute of Technology (M)
Southern Methodist University (M)

OPERATIONS TECHNOLOGY

Northeastern University (B)

OPTICAL SCIENCES

The University of Arizona (GC,M)

OPTICIANRY

Arkansas State University–Mountain Home
  (A)
Hillsborough Community College (A)

OPTICS, IMAGING, AND COMMUNICATIONS

Stanford University (GC)

OPTOMETRIC TECHNICIAN

Madison Area Technical College (UC)

OPTOMETRY–PRE-OPTOMETRY

Darton College (A)

OREGON TRANSFER

Chemeketa Community College (A)

OREGON TRANSFER MODULE

Chemeketa Community College (UC)

ORGANIZATION AND MANAGEMENT

Capella University (D,M)

ORGANIZATION DEVELOPMENT AND ORGANIZATIONAL MANAGEMENT

Fielding Graduate University (UC)

ORGANIZATION DYNAMICS

Immaculata University (B)

ORGANIZATIONAL ADMINISTRATION

Metropolitan State University (B)

ORGANIZATIONAL BEHAVIOR

National University (B)

ORGANIZATIONAL COMMUNICATION

Penn State University Park (UC)
Regent University (UC)
Seminole Community College (A)

ORGANIZATIONAL COMMUNICATIONS

Northeastern University (B)
Upper Iowa University (UC)

ORGANIZATIONAL CONSULTING

Saybrook Graduate School and Research
Center (GC)

ORGANIZATIONAL DEVELOPMENT

University of North Texas (B)
University of the Incarnate Word (M,B)

ORGANIZATIONAL DEVELOPMENT CONSULTING

Regent University (UC)

ORGANIZATIONAL LEADERSHIP

Fort Hays State University (B)
Kansas State University (GC)
Mercy College (M)
National University (M)
Northern Kentucky University (B)
Penn State University Park (B)
Regent University (D,M)
Roosevelt University (B,UC)
Southern New Hampshire University (M)
Syracuse University (B,UC)
University of St. Francis (B)
Upper Iowa University (UC)

ORGANIZATIONAL LEADERSHIP AND MANAGEMENT

Regent University (B)

ORGANIZATIONAL LEADERSHIP IN ANIMAL ADVOCACY

Duquesne University (GC)

ORGANIZATIONAL LEADERSHIP–MASTER OF PROFESSIONAL STUDIES IN ORGANIZATIONAL LEADERSHIP

University of Denver (M)

ORGANIZATIONAL LEADERSHIP, INFORMATION SYSTEMS AND TECHNOLOGY SPECIALIZATION

University of Phoenix Online Campus (D)

ORGANIZATIONAL MANAGEMENT

Ashford University (B)
Concordia University, St. Paul (M)
Mercy College (B)
Spring Arbor University (M)
University of Great Falls (M)
University of La Verne (B)
University of Phoenix Online Campus (D)

ORGANIZATIONAL MANAGEMENT–HUMAN RESOURCES EMPHASIS

Concordia University, St. Paul (M)

ORGANIZATIONAL MANAGEMENT, HUMAN SERVICES OPTION

Chadron State College (M)

ORGANIZATIONAL MANAGEMENT, MANAGEMENT AND INFORMATION TECHNOLOGY

Viterbo University (B)

ORGANIZATIONAL MANAGEMENT/ ORGANIZATIONAL DEVELOPMENT

Fielding Graduate University (M)

ORGANIZATIONAL MANAGMENT AND LEADERSHIP

Concordia University, St. Paul (B)

ORGANIZATIONAL PSYCHOLOGY AND DEVELOPMENT CONCENTRATION (10-MONTH PROGRAM)

American InterContinental University Online (M)

ORGANIZATIONAL PSYCHOLOGY AND DEVELOPMENT CONCENTRATION (COMPLETION PROGRAM)

American InterContinental University Online (B)

ORGANIZATIONAL SECURITY AND MANAGEMENT

University of Phoenix Online Campus (B)

ORGANIZATIONAL SECURITY–CERTIFICATE OF ADVANCED STUDY

University of Denver (UC)

ORGANIZATIONAL STUDIES

Saybrook Graduate School and Research
Center (D)

ORGANIZATIONAL SYSTEMS

Saybrook Graduate School and Research
Center (M)

ORIENTATION AND MOBILITY

Texas Tech University (UC)

ORNAMENTAL HORTICULTURE

Utah State University (A)

PACKAGING OF ELECTRONIC AND OPTICAL DEVICES

Southern Methodist University (M)

PACS ADMINISTRATOR

Clarkson College (UC)

PACS MANAGER

Clarkson College (UC)

PAINTING

Savannah College of Art and Design (M)

PAPER SCIENCE AND ENGINEERING

University of Minnesota, Twin Cities Campus (M,UC)

PARAEDUCATION

Minot State University–Bottineau Campus (A)

PARAEDUCATOR

Williston State College (A)

PARALEGAL

Franklin Pierce University (UC)
Herkimer County Community College (A)
Ivy Tech Community College–Bloomington (A)
Ivy Tech Community College–Central Indiana (A)
Ivy Tech Community College–Columbus (A)
Ivy Tech Community College–Kokomo (A)
Ivy Tech Community College–Southeast (A)
Ivy Tech Community College–Southern Indiana (A)
Ivy Tech Community College–Southwest (A)
Ivy Tech Community College–Wabash Valley (A)
Ivy Tech Community College–Whitewater (A)
Jones College (B)
Minnesota School of Business–Richfield (A,B)
Minnesota State Community and Technical College–Fergus Falls (A)

The University of Texas System (UC)
University of Washington (GC)

PARALEGAL CERTIFICATE

California State University, Dominguez Hills (GC)

PARALEGAL ONLINE

Bryant and Stratton Online (A)

PARALEGAL ONLINE CERTIFICATE PROGRAM

The University of Texas at San Antonio (UC)

PARALEGAL STUDIES

California State University, San Marcos (UC)
Colorado State University-Pueblo (UC)
Hodges University (A)
Ivy Tech Community College–East Central (A)
Ivy Tech Community College–Kokomo (A)
Ivy Tech Community College–Lafayette (A)
Ivy Tech Community College–North Central (A)
Ivy Tech Community College–Northeast (A)
Ivy Tech Community College–Northwest (A)
Kaplan University (B)
Keiser University (A)
Lake Superior College (A)
Missouri Southern State University (A)
Mount Wachusett Community College (A)
Northeastern University (A)
Peirce College (A,B,UC)
Tompkins Cortland Community College (A)
University of Great Falls (B)
University of Massachusetts Lowell (UC)

PARALEGAL STUDIES/ ALTERNATIVE DISPUTE RESOLUTION

Kaplan University (B)

PARALEGAL STUDIES/OFFICE MANAGEMENT

Kaplan University (B)

PARALEGAL STUDIES/PERSONAL INJURY

Kaplan University (B)

PARALEGAL TECHNOLOGY

Western Piedmont Community College (A)

PARAMEDICINE COMPLETION

Western Kentucky University (A)

PARAPROFESSIONAL EDUCATION

University of Phoenix Online Campus (A)

PARKS AND RECREATION MANAGEMENT

Northern Arizona University (B,UC)

PASTORAL COUNSELING

Liberty University (M)
Regions University (M)

PASTORAL STUDIES

Southwestern College (B)

PEACE AND CONFLICT RESOLUTION (INTERNATIONAL FOCUS)

Saybrook Graduate School and Research Center (GC)

PEACE STUDIES

Prescott College (M)

PEDIATRIC NURSE PRACTITIONER

University of Missouri–Columbia (M)

PENSIONS AND EXECUTIVE COMPENSATION

The American College (UC)

PERFORMANCE CONSULTING

Roosevelt University (GC)

PERFORMANCE EXCELLENCE IN TECHNOLOGY MANAGEMENT

University of Colorado at Boulder (GC)

PERFORMANCE IMPROVEMENT

East Carolina University (GC)

PERFUSION TECHNOLOGY

Thomas Edison State College (B)

PERSONAL FINANCIAL PLANNING

City University (GC,M)
Kansas State University (M,UC)
University of Missouri–Columbia (M)

PETROLEUM ENGINEERING

University of Southern California (M)

PETROLEUM ENGINEERING (SMART OILFIELD TECHNOLOGIES)

University of Southern California (GC,M)

PHARMACEUTICAL BUSINESS

University of the Sciences in Philadelphia (M)

PHARMACEUTICAL MANAGEMENT

Drexel University (M)

PHARMACEUTICAL MANAGMENT

New Jersey Institute of Technology (GC)

PHARMACEUTICAL MANUFACTURING

Stevens Institute of Technology (M)

PHARMACEUTICAL MANUFACTURING PRACTICES

Stevens Institute of Technology (GC)

PHARMACOGENETICS ESSENTIALS

Northeastern University (GC)

PHARMACY

Auburn University (D)
University of Cincinnati (D)

PHARMACY TECHNICIAN

North Dakota State College of Science (A)
Vincennes University (UC)

PHARMACY TECHNOLOGY

Minnesota State Community and Technical College–Fergus Falls (A)

PHARMACY–PRE-PHARMACY

Darton College (A)

PHD COMMUNITY COLLEGE LEADERSHIP

Mississippi State University (D)

PHD ENGINEERING, CONCENTRATION INDUSTRIAL ENGINEERING

Mississippi State University (D)

PHILANTHROPIC AND NONPROFIT ORGANIZATIONS

Regent University (UC)

PHILOSOPHY

American Public University System (B)
Darton College (A)
Holy Apostles College and Seminary (M)
Prescott College (M)
Skidmore College (B)

Thomas Edison State College (B)
University of Illinois (B)
University of Illinois at Springfield (B)
University of Waterloo (B)

PHILOSOPHY AND RELIGION

Butler Community College (A)

PHILOSOPHY, POLITICS, AND ECONOMICS

Eastern Oregon University (B)

PHOTOGRAPHY

Academy of Art University (M,A,B)
Prescott College (M)
Thomas Edison State College (B)

PHRAMACEUTICAL SCIENCES, COSMETIC SCIENCE EMPHASIS

University of Cincinnati (M)

PHYSICAL ACTIVITY AND HEALTH

Eastern Oregon University (B)

PHYSICAL EDUCATION

Emporia State University (M)
Florida State University (M)
Jacksonville State University (M)
University of Arkansas (M)
University of South Florida (M)

PHYSICAL EDUCATION PEDAGOGY

Western Kentucky University (M)

PHYSICAL EDUCATION STUDIES

Monroe Community College (A)

PHYSICAL EDUCATION TEACHER EDUCATION

West Virginia University (M)

PHYSICAL EDUCATION– COACHING SPECIALIZATION

Ball State University (M)

PHYSICAL EDUCATION, HEALTH, AND LEISURE STUDIES

Central Washington University (M)

PHYSICAL SCIENCES (EARTH SCIENCE EMPHASIS)

Emporia State University (M)

PHYSICAL THERAPIST ASSISTANT

Clark State Community College (A)

PHYSICAL THERAPY

Darton College (A)

PHYSICAL THERAPY (IMPRINTS)

The University of Texas System (UC)

PHYSICAL THERAPY ASSISTANT

Darton College (A)

PHYSICAL THERAPY–POST-PROFESSIONAL DOCTOR OF PHYSICAL THERAPY

Rosalind Franklin University of Medicine and Science (D)

PHYSICAL THERAPY– TRANSITIONAL DOCTOR OF PHYSICAL THERAPY

MGH Institute of Health Professions (D)
University of St. Augustine for Health Sciences (D)

PHYSICAL THERAPY– TRANSITIONAL DOCTORATE OF PHYSICAL THERAPY

Utica College (D)

PHYSICIAN ASSISTANCE–MASTER OF PHYSICIAN ASSISTANCE (MPA)

Chatham University

PHYSICIAN ASSISTANT

Lock Haven University of Pennsylvania (M)

PHYSICIAN EXECUTIVE

The University of Tennessee (M)

PHYSICIANS ASSISTANT STUDIES

Drexel University (M)

PHYSICIANS EXECUTIVE MBA

Auburn University (M)

PHYSICS

Skidmore College (B)

PLASTICS ENGINEERING FUNDAMENTALS

University of Massachusetts Lowell (GC)

PLAYWRITING AND SCREENWRITING

Prescott College (M)

POLICY STUDIES

State University of New York Empire State College (M)

POLITICAL ECONOMY (3 YEAR)

Athabasca University (B)

POLITICAL ECONOMY (4 YEAR)

Athabasca University (B)

POLITICAL SCIENCE

American Public University System (M,B)
Austin Peay State University (B)
Darton College (A)
Jacksonville State University (M)
Northeastern University (B)
Prescott College (B)
Regent University (B)
Thomas Edison State College (B)
Troy University (B)
University of Windsor (B)
Virginia Polytechnic Institute and State University (M)

POLITICAL SCIENCE–CRIMINAL JUSTICE

Buena Vista University (B)

POLITICAL SCIENCE– ENVIROMENTAL POLITICS AND POLICIES

Virginia Polytechnic Institute and State University (UC)

POLITICAL SCIENCE– FOUNDATIONS OF POLITICAL ANALYSIS

Virginia Polytechnic Institute and State University (UC)

POLITICAL SCIENCE– INFORMATION POLICY AND SOCIETY

Virginia Polytechnic Institute and State University (UC)

POLITICAL SCIENCE–SECURITY STUDIES

Virginia Polytechnic Institute and State University (UC)

POLYMER SCIENCE AND ENGINEERING

Lehigh University (M)

POLYSOMNOGRAPHIC TECHNOLOGY

Oregon Institute of Technology (UC)

POST BACCALAUREATE CERTIFICATE IN HEALTH INFORMATION ADMINISTRATION

The University of Toledo (UC)

POST-BACCALAUREATE SECONDARY TEACHER

Texas Tech University (UC)

POST-MASTERS NURSING ADMINISTRATION

Fort Hays State University (UC)

POST-MASTERS NURSING EDUCATION

Fort Hays State University (UC)

POST-MBA MASTERS–GLOBAL MANAGEMENT ON-DEMAND

Thunderbird School of Global Management (M)

POSTSECONDARY EDUCATION

Troy University (M)

POSTSECONDARY STUDIES

Memorial University of Newfoundland (M)

POSTSECONDARY TEACHING

Colorado State University (UC)

POWER AND ENERGY SYSTEMS

University of Illinois (GC)

POWER ELECTRONICS

University of Colorado at Boulder (GC)

POWER ELECTRONICS AND MACHINE DRIVES (EE CONCENTRATION)

Kettering University (M)

POWER PLANT TECHNOLOGY

Bismarck State College (A,UC)

POWER SYSTEM PROTECTION AND RELAYING

University of Idaho (UC)

POWER SYSTEMS ENGINEERING

Iowa State University of Science and Technology (UC)

PRACTICAL THEOLOGY

Oral Roberts University (M)
Regent University (M)
Regions University (M)

PRACTICE OF TECHNICAL COMMUNICATIONS

New Jersey Institute of Technology (GC)

PRE-BACHELOR OF ARTS

Miami Dade College (A)

PRE-KINDERGARTEN HANDICAPPED ENDORSEMENT

University of Central Florida (GC)

PRE-MEDICINE

Darton College (A)

PRE-PHYSICIAN'S ASSISTANT

Darton College (A)

PREPARATION FOR CERTIFIED BOOKKEEPER EXAM

The University of Toledo (UC)

PREPARATION FOR CLINICAL NURSE FACULTY CERTIFICATE

California State University, San Marcos (UC)

PRIMARY HEALTH CARE AND HEALTH DISPARITIES

Oregon Health & Science University (M)

PRINCIPAL ENDORSEMENT PROGRAM

University of Wyoming (UC)

PRINCIPAL'S CERTIFICATION

Drexel University (UC)

PRINCIPALSHIP

Northern Arizona University (UC)

PRINT MEDIA

Rochester Institute of Technology (M)

PRIOR LEARNING ASSESSMENT

DePaul University (UC)

PRIVATE SECURITY

Kaplan University (UC)

PRIVATE SECURITY AND LOSS PREVENTION

Indiana State University (UC)

PROCESS ENGINEERING

University of South Florida (GC)

PROCESS PLANT TECHNOLOGY

Bismarck State College' (A,UC)

PROCUREMENT AND ACQUISITIONS MANAGEMENT

Webster University (M)

PROCUREMENT AND CONTRACT MANAGEMENT

University of Maryland University College (GC)

PRODUCT CREATION AND INNOVATIVE MANUFACTURING

Stanford University (GC)

PRODUCT DEVELOPMENT ENGINEERING

University of Southern California (M)

PRODUCTION AND INVENTORY CONTROL

California State University, Dominguez Hills (UC)

PROFESSIONAL (WEEKEND) PROGRAM

The University of Tennessee (M)

PROFESSIONAL ACCOUNTING

Strayer University (M,)

PROFESSIONAL AERONAUTICS

Embry-Riddle Aeronautical University (A,B)

PROFESSIONAL AND TECHNICAL COMMUNICATIONS

New Jersey Institute of Technology (M)

PROFESSIONAL ARTS

Saint Joseph's College of Maine (B)

PROFESSIONAL COUNSELING

Regions University (M)
Liberty University (M)

PROFESSIONAL DEVELOPMENT

Amberton University (M,B)

PROFESSIONAL DEVELOPMENT FOR TEACHERS

Kaplan University (UC)

PROFESSIONAL DOCTOR OF OCCUPATIONAL THERAPY

Chatham University (D)

PROFESSIONAL IN HUMAN RESOURCES

DePaul University (UC)

PROFESSIONAL MASTER OF ENGINEERING IN FIRE PROTECTION

University of Maryland, College Park (M)

PROFESSIONAL STUDIES

Austin Peay State University (B)
Fairfield University (B)
Saint Joseph's College of Maine (UC)
Tennessee Technological University (M,B)

PROFESSIONAL STUDIES, INFORMATION TECHNOLOGY CONCENTRATION

Middle Tennessee State University (B)

PROFESSIONAL STUDIES, ORGANIZATIONAL LEADERSHIP CONCENTRATION

Middle Tennessee State University (B)

PROFESSIONAL STUDIES, STRATEGIC LEADERSHIP CONCENTRATION

Middle Tennessee State University (M)

PROFESSIONAL TECHNOLOGY STUDIES

Pace University (B)

PROFESSIONAL WRITING

Northern Arizona University (UC)
Taylor University (UC)
University of Central Florida (GC)
Washington State University (UC)

PROFESSIONAL WRITING– MASTER OF PROFESSIONAL WRITING (MPW)

Chatham University

PROGRAM MANAGEMENT (MNM)

Regis University (GC)

PROGRAMMER ANALYST–FAST TRACK---PROGRAMMER ANALYST SHORT-TERM CERTIFICATE

Sinclair Community College (UC)

PROGRAMMING AND ANALYSIS (WWW PROGRAMMING SPECIALIZATION)

Seminole Community College (A)

PROGRAMMING AND SOFTWARE DEVELOPMENT

The University of Toledo (A)

PROGRAMMING AND SOFWARE DEVELOPMENT

The University of Toledo (UC)

PROGRAMMING ENVIRONMENT TOOLS

New Jersey Institute of Technology (GC)

PROGRAMMING IN C++

City University (UC)

PROJECT ENGINEERING AND MANAGEMENT

Montana Tech of The University of Montana (M)

PROJECT MANAGEMENT

Athabasca University (GC,M)
City University (GC,M,UC)
DeVry University Online (M)
Florida Institute of Technology (M)
Grantham University (M)
Kaplan University (UC)
Lehigh University (UC)
Missouri State University (GC)
New Jersey Institute of Technology (GC)
Northeastern University (GC)
Penn State University Park (GC,M)
Rochester Institute of Technology (GC)
Stevens Institute of Technology (GC,M)
University of Colorado at Boulder (GC)
University of Dallas (GC,M)
University of Management and Technology (GC,M,UC)
University of Maryland University College (GC)
University of Washington (UC)
University of Wisconsin–Platteville (GC)
University of Wisconsin–Platteville (M)
University of Wisconsin–Platteville (M)
University of Wisconsin–Platteville (UC)
University of Wisconsin–Platteville (UC)
Walden University (M)
Western Carolina University (M)

PROJECT MANAGEMENT CONCENTRATION

Colorado Technical University (M,B)

PROJECT MANAGEMENT CONCENTRATION (10-MONTH PROGRAM)

American InterContinental University Online (M)

PROJECT MANAGEMENT CONCENTRATION (COMPLETION PROGRAM)

American InterContinental University Online (B)

PROJECT MANAGEMENT FOR THE LIFE SCIENCES INDUSTRIES

Stevens Institute of Technology (GC)

PROJECT MANAGEMENT ONLINE

University of Illinois (GC)

PROJECT MANAGEMENT– CERTIFICATE OF ADVANCED STUDY

University of Denver (UC)

PROJECT MANAGEMENT– EXECUTIVE PROJECT MANAGEMENT (MSM)

Regis University (GC)

PROJECT MANAGEMENT– MASTER OF PROJECT MANAGEMENT

American Graduate University (M)

PROJECT MANAGEMENT, ADVANCED

Penn State University Park (GC)

PSYCHIATRIC REHABILITATION

University of Medicine and Dentistry of New Jersey (M)

PSYCHIATRIC-MENTAL HEALTH

New Mexico State University (M)

PSYCHIATRIC-MENTAL HEALTH CLINICAL NURSE SPECIALIST

The University of Toledo (GC,M)

PSYCHOLOGIE

Laurentian University (B)

PSYCHOLOGY

American Public University System (B)
Ashford University (B)
Brookdale Community College (A)

Capella University (D,M)
Chadron State College (B)
Columbia College (B)
Dallas Baptist University (B)
Darton College (A)
Drexel University (B)
Eastern Oregon University (B)
Judson College (B)
Laurentian University (B)
Liberty University (A,B)
Limestone College (B)
Lynn University (B)
Mercy College (B)
National University (B)
New York Institute of Technology (B)
Northeastern University (B)
Northern Arizona University (B)
Pacific Graduate School of Psychology (M)
Regent University (B)
Roosevelt University (B)
Saint Joseph's College of Maine (A)
Saybrook Graduate School and Research
  Center (D)
Seminole Community College (A)
Skidmore College (B)
Southern New Hampshire University (B)
Thomas Edison State College (B)
Troy University (B)
Union Institute & University (D)
University of Great Falls (B)
University of Maryland University College
  (B)
University of Massachusetts Lowell (B)
University of Phoenix Online Campus (M,B)
University of Wyoming (B)
Upper Iowa University (B)
Utah State University (B)
West Hills Community College (A)

PSYCHOLOGY (3 YEAR)

Athabasca University (B)

PSYCHOLOGY (4 YEAR)

Athabasca University (B)

PSYCHOLOGY (CHILD AND ADOLESCENT DEVELOPMENT CONCENTRATION)

Southern New Hampshire University (B)

PSYCHOLOGY IN CREATIVITY STUDIES SPECIALIZATION

Saybrook Graduate School and Research
  Center (M)

PSYCHOLOGY MENTAL HEALTH COUNSELING

Walden University (M)

PSYCHOLOGY OF THE WORKPLACE

Jamestown Community College (GC)

PSYCHOLOGY–APPLIED PSYCHOLOGY

City University (B)

PSYCHOLOGY–CLINICAL PSYCHOLOGY (LICENSURE)

Walden University (D)

PSYCHOLOGY–COUNSELING PSYCHOLOGY (LICENSURE)

Walden University (D)

PSYCHOLOGY–GENERAL

Walden University (M)

PSYCHOLOGY–GENERAL PROGRAM, EDUCATIONAL PSYCHOLOGY TRACK

Walden University (D)

PSYCHOLOGY–GENERAL PROGRAM, RESEARCH AND EVALUATION TRACK

Walden University (D)

PSYCHOLOGY–HEALTH PSYCHOLOGY

Walden University (D)

PSYCHOLOGY–INDUSTRIAL/ ORGANIZATIONAL PSYCHOLOGY

Austin Peay State University (M)

PSYCHOLOGY–ORGANIZATIONAL

Walden University (D)

PSYCHOLOGY–ORGANIZATIONAL PSYCHOLOGY AND DEVELOPMENT

Walden University (M)

PSYCHOLOGY–SCHOOL COUNSELING SPECIALIZATION

Utah State University (M)

PSYCHOLOGY–SCHOOL PSYCHOLOGY (LICENSURE)

Walden University (D)

PSYCHOLOGY, GENERAL

East Carolina University (M)

PSYCHOLOGY-SOCIOLOGY

Skidmore College (B)

PSYCHOLOGY/FAMILY STUDIES

Corban College (B)

PSYCHOLOGY/SOCIOLOGY

Carl Albert State College (A)

PUBLIC ADMINISTRATION

American Public University System (M)
Andrew Jackson University (M)
Athabasca University (UC)
Cape Breton University (UC)
DeVry University Online (M)
Florida Institute of Technology (M)
Hodges University (M)
Indiana State University (GC)
Kansas State University (GC)
Kent State University (M)
Marist College (M)
Memorial University of Newfoundland (UC)
National University (M)
Regis University (B,UC)
Strayer University (M)
Thomas Edison State College (B)
Troy University (M)
University of Alaska Southeast (M)
University of Colorado at Denver and Health
  Sciences Center (M)
University of Illinois at Springfield (M)
University of La Verne (B)
University of Management and Technology
  (M)
The University of Montana (M)
University of Nebraska at Omaha (M)
University of North Dakota (M)
University of Phoenix Online Campus (M)
The University of Texas at Arlington (M)
The University of Texas System (M)
University of Wyoming (M)
Upper Iowa University (B)
Wayland Baptist University (M)

PUBLIC ADMINISTRATION (MSA)

University of West Florida (M)

PUBLIC ADMINISTRATION–FIRE SCIENCE EMPHASIS

Upper Iowa University (B)

PUBLIC ADMINISTRATION–LAW ENFORCEMENT EMPHASIS

Upper Iowa University (B)

PUBLIC AFFAIRS

Northeastern University (B)

PUBLIC AGENCY SERVICES (BAS)

Northern Arizona University (B)

PUBLIC AND NON-PROFIT MANAGEMENT–MASTER OF PUBLIC AND NON-PROFIT MANAGEMENT

Metropolitan State University (M)

PUBLIC EXECUTIVE LEADERSHIP

Regent University (UC)

PUBLIC HEALTH

American Public University System (M,B)
Medical College of Wisconsin (M)
University of West Florida (M)
Youngstown State University (M)
West Virginia University (M)

PUBLIC HEALTH ADMINISTRATION

University of South Florida (M)

PUBLIC HEALTH GENERALIST

University of South Florida (GC)

PUBLIC HEALTH INFORMATICS

University of Illinois (M)
University of Illinois at Chicago (M)

PUBLIC HEALTH INFORMATICS CAMPUS CERTIFICATE

University of Illinois at Chicago (UC)

PUBLIC HEALTH POLICY AND PROGRAMS

University of South Florida (GC)

PUBLIC HEALTH PRACTICE

University of South Florida (M)

PUBLIC HEALTH–CAREER MASTER OF PUBLIC HEALTH PROGRAM

Emory University (M)

PUBLIC HEALTH–COMMUNITY HEALTH PROMOTION AND EDUCATION

Walden University (D)

PUBLIC HEALTH–EPIDEMIOLOGY

Walden University (D)

PUBLIC JUSTICE

State University of New York at Oswego (B)

PUBLIC LIBRARY TECHNOLOGY (PLT)

Marshall University (UC)

PUBLIC MANAGEMENT

Northern Arizona University (GC)
Park University (M)

PUBLIC MANAGEMENT AND LEADERSHIP

Walden University (M)

PUBLIC PERSONNEL ADMINISTRATION

Indiana State University (GC)

PUBLIC POLICY

Walden University (M)

PUBLIC POLICY ADMINISTRATION

Mississippi State University (M)

PUBLIC POLICY AND ADMINISTRATION–HEALTH SERVICES

Walden University (D)

PUBLIC POLICY AND ADMINISTRATION–HOMELAND SECURITY, POLICY, AND COORDINATION

Walden University (D)

PUBLIC POLICY AND ADMINISTRATION– INTERNATIONAL NONGOVERNMENTAL ORGANIZATIONS (NGOS)

Walden University (D)

PUBLIC POLICY AND ADMINISTRATION–KNOWLEDGE MANAGEMENT

Walden University (D)

PUBLIC POLICY AND ADMINISTRATION–NONPROFIT MANAGEMENT AND LEADERSHIP

Walden University (D)

PUBLIC POLICY AND ADMINISTRATION–PUBLIC MANAGEMENT AND LEADERSHIP

Walden University (D)

PUBLIC POLICY AND ADMINISTRATION–PUBLIC POLICY

Walden University (D)

PUBLIC POLICY AND ADMINISTRATION–PUBLIC SAFETY MANAGEMENT

Walden University (D)

PUBLIC POLICY AND ADMINISTRATION, GENERAL

Walden University (D)

PUBLIC RELATIONS

Montana State University–Billings (M,B)
University of Maryland University College (GC)
Webster University (M)

PUBLIC RELATIONS AND MARKETING COMMUNICATIONS–CERTIFICATE OF ADVANCED STUDY

University of Denver (UC)

PUBLIC RELATIONS AND ORGANIZATIONAL COMMUNICATION

Seminole Community College (A)

PUBLIC RELATIONS COMMUNICATIONS–PROFESSIONAL WRITING

Rochester Institute of Technology (UC)

PUBLIC SAFETY

Capella University (D,M,B)

PUBLIC SAFETY AND BUSINESS/ORGANIZATION SECURITY

Regions University (B)

PUBLIC SAFETY AND CRIMINAL JUSTICE

Regions University (B)

PUBLIC SAFETY AND HOMELAND SECURITY

Regions University (B)

PUBLIC SAFETY AND SECURITY MANAGEMENT

Western Carolina University (B)

PUBLIC SAFETY MANAGEMENT

Cardinal Stritch University (B)
Franklin University (B)
Walden University (M)

PUBLIC SCHOOL ADMINISTRATION

Oral Roberts University (D,M)

PUBLIC WORKS OPTION

The University of Tennessee (M)

PUBLISHING

Pace University (M)

PURCHASING

California State University, Dominguez Hills (UC)

QUALITY

Eastern Michigan University (M)

QUALITY ASSURANCE

California State University, Dominguez Hills (M,B,UC)
Southern Polytechnic State University (M)

QUALITY ASSURANCE AND SOFTWARE TESTING

St. Petersburg College (UC)

QUALITY ENGINEERING

Lehigh University (M)

QUALITY IMPLEMENTATION

Rochester Institute of Technology (UC)

QUALITY IMPROVEMENT AND OUTCOMES MANAGEMENT

George Mason University (GC)

QUALITY LEADERSHIP

Saint Joseph's College of Maine (M)

QUALITY MANAGEMENT

Madison Area Technical College (UC)

QUALITY MANAGEMENT CERTIFICATE

University of Wisconsin–Stout (UC)

QUALITY MANAGEMENT, BASIC

Rochester Institute of Technology (UC)

QUALITY SCHOOLS

Graceland University (M)

QUALITY SYSTEMS

Bowling Green State University (GC)

QUALITY SYSTEMS FOR PRODUCT AND PROCESS ENGINEERING

University of Colorado at Boulder (GC)

QUANTITATIVE CONSTRUCTION MANAGEMENT

University of Washington (UC)

QUANTITATIVE METHODS IN FINANCE AND RISK MANAGEMENT (STATISTICS)

Stanford University (GC)

QUANTITATIVE SOFTWARE ENGINEERING

Stevens Institute of Technology (GC,M)

RADIATION HEALTH PHYSICS

Oregon State University (D,M)

RADIATION PROTECTION

Thomas Edison State College (A,B)

RADIATION THERAPY

Thomas Edison State College (A,B)

RADIOLOGIC AND IMAGING SCIENCES

University of Southern Indiana (B)

RADIOLOGIC SCIENCES

Midwestern State University (B)
University of Central Florida (B)

RADIOLOGIC SCIENCES (EDUCATION OR ADMINISTRATION MAJOR)

Midwestern State University (M)

RADIOLOGIC SCIENCES BACHELORS COMPLETION PROGRAM (RADIOGRAPHY)

University of Missouri–Columbia (B)

RADIOLOGIC TECHNOLOGY

Minnesota State Community and Technical College–Fergus Falls (A)

RADIOLOGIC TECHNOLOGY COMPLETION PROGRAM

Presentation College (B)

RADIOLOGIC TECHNOLOGY CONTINUING EDUCATION UNITS (CEUS)

Sinclair Community College (UC)

RADIOLOGICAL SCIENCE– RADIOLOGICAL SCIENCE DEGREE COMPLETION

Oregon Institute of Technology (B)

RADIOLOGICAL SCIENCES

Saint Joseph's College of Maine (B)
Weber State University (B,UC)

RADIOLOGIST ASSISTANT

Bloomsburg University of Pennsylvania (M)

RANGELAND ECOSYSTEM SCIENCE

Colorado State University (M)

READING

Concordia University Wisconsin (M)
New Mexico State University (UC)
University of Alaska Southeast (M,UC)
Northern Arizona University (UC)

READING AND LANGUAGE

University of Massachusetts Lowell (M)

READING AND WRITING SPECIALIST P-12

University of the Cumberlands (M)

READING INSTRUCTION FOR SPECIAL EDUCATION (RISE)

Penn State University Park (GC)

READING K-12

University of Nebraska at Kearney (M)

READING SPECIALIST

The University of Texas System (UC)

READING TEACHER CERTIFICATION

University of Wisconsin–Stout (UC)

READING, ELEMENTARY EDUCATION

Utah State University (UC)

READING, LANGUAGE, AND LITERACY

The University of North Carolina at Charlotte (M)

READING, SECONDARY EDUCATION

Utah State University (UC)

REAL ESTATE

Thomas Edison State College (B)
University of Wyoming (UC)

RECEPTION SERVICES

Minot State University–Bottineau Campus (UC)

RECREATION

Emporia State University (B)

RECREATION MANAGEMENT

Minot State University–Bottineau Campus (A,UC)

RECREATION MANAGEMENT– THERAPEUTIC OPTION

Vincennes University (A)

RECREATION SERVICES

Thomas Edison State College (A,B)

REGENTS BACHELOR OF ARTS

West Virginia University (B)

REGENTS BACHELOR OF ARTS DEGREE

Marshall University (B)

REGENTS ONLINE DEGREE PROGRAM

Austin Peay State University (B)

REGISTERED EMPLOYEE BENEFITS CONSULTANT(R) (REBC(R)) DESIGNATION

The American College (UC)

REGISTERED HEALTH UNDERWRITER(R) (RHU(R)) DESIGNATION

The American College (UC)

REGULATORY AFFAIRS

Lehigh University (GC)

REGULATORY AFFAIRS FOR DRUGS, BIOLOGICS, AND MEDICAL DEVICES

Northeastern University (M)

REGULATORY AFFAIRS–MEDICAL DEVICES

University of South Florida (GC)

REGULATORY SCIENCE

University of Southern California (M)

REHABILITATION COUNSELING

Auburn University (M)
The University of Alabama (M)
Wright State University (M)
West Virginia University (M)

REHABILITATION SCIENCE

Concordia University Wisconsin (M)

REHABILITATION SCIENCES

The University of British Columbia (GC)

REHABILITATIVE SCIENCE

Clarion University of Pennsylvania (M)

RELIABILITY AND MAINTAINABILITY ENGINEERING

The University of Tennessee (GC)

RELIGION

American Public University System (B)
Liberty University (M,A,B)
Thomas Edison State College (B)

RELIGIOUS EDUCATION

Defiance College (A,B)
Global University of the Assemblies of God (B)
Newman Theological College (GC)

RELIGIOUS STUDIES

Global University of the Assemblies of God (A)
Indiana Wesleyan University (UC)
Judson College (B)
Laurentian University (B)
Prescott College (M)
Regent University (B)
Skidmore College (B)
University of Waterloo (B)

RENEWAL STUDIES

Regent University (D)

RESEARCH ADMINISTRATION

Cleveland State University (GC)

RESEARCH AND DEVELOPMENT

University of Colorado at Boulder (GC)

RESIDENTIAL DRAWING TECHNICIAN

Central Georgia Technical College (UC)

RESOURCE DEVELOPMENT (MNM)

Regis University (GC)

RESPECIALIZATION IN CLINICAL PSYCHOLOGY

Fielding Graduate University (UC)

RESPIRATORY CARE

Oregon Institute of Technology (B)
Thomas Edison State College (A,B)

RESPIRATORY CARE LEADERSHIP

Northeastern University (M)

RESPIRATORY THERAPY

Darton College (A)
J. Sargeant Reynolds Community College (A)

RESPIRATORY THERAPY BACHELORS COMPLETION PROGRAM

University of Missouri–Columbia (B)

RESTAURANT MANAGEMENT

Northern Arizona University (UC)

RESTAURANT, HOTEL, AND INSTITUTIONAL MANAGEMENT

Texas Tech University (M)

RETAIL LEADERSHIP

Drexel University (UC)

RETAIL MANAGEMENT

Strayer University (B)

RETAILING–FIVE COURSE SEQUENCE IN RETAILING

University of North Texas (UC)

RISK ANALYSIS (MANAGEMENT SCIENCE AND ENGINEERING)

Stanford University (GC)

RISK MANAGEMENT

Kaplan University (UC)

RISK MANAGEMENT AND INSURANCE

Excelsior College (B)

RISK MANAGEMENT/INSURANCE

Florida State University (M)

RURAL PUBLIC SAFETY ADMINISTRATION

University of Maine at Fort Kent (B)

SAFETY AND HEALTH TECHNOLOGY

Rochester Institute of Technology (UC)

SAFETY TECHNOLOGY

Rochester Institute of Technology (B)

SALES MANAGEMENT

Regent University (UC)

SALES MANAGEMENT CONCENTRATION

Andrew Jackson University (M)

SALES, MARKETING, AND MANAGEMENT

Northwest Technical College (A)

SCHOOL ADMINISTRATION

Indiana State University (UC)

SCHOOL ADMINISTRATION/ EDUCATIONAL LEADERSHIP

Wayne State College

SCHOOL AND CHURCH ADMINISTRATION

Shasta Bible College (M)

SCHOOL BUILDING LEADER IN EDUCATIONAL ADMINISTRATION AND SUPERVISION

St. John's University (M)
St. John's University (M)

SCHOOL COUNSELING LICENSURE

New Mexico State University (UC)

SCHOOL DISTRICT LEADER PROFESSIONAL DIPLOMA

St. John's University (GC)
St. John's University (GC)

SCHOOL FOOD SERVICE MANAGEMENT

Penn State University Park (UC)

SCHOOL LIBRARY MEDIA

Utah State University (UC)

SCHOOL LIBRARY MEDIA SERVICES

Indiana State University (GC)

SCHOOL LIBRARY MEDIA SPECIALIST

University of Washington (UC)

SCHOOL MEDIA

Syracuse University (GC)
Syracuse University (GC)

SCHOOL NURSE CAMPUS CERTIFICATE

University of Illinois at Chicago (UC)

SCHOOL SUPERINTENDENT

University of the Cumberlands (UC)

SCHOOL SUPERVISOR

University of the Cumberlands (UC)

SCHOOL SYSTEMS, SUPERINTENDENCY, AND LEADERSHIP

Webster University

SCHOOL TECHNOLOGY COORDINATION

Boise State University (GC)

SCHOOL/COMMUNITY SAFETY

Colorado State University (UC)

SCIENCE

Excelsior College (A,B)

SCIENCE AND TECHNOLOGY LEGAL STUDIES OPTION

California University of Pennsylvania (B)

SCIENCE EDUCATION

Florida State University (M)
Montana State University (M)
The University of Texas System (M)

SCIENCE IN EDUCATION

Lesley University (M)

SCIENCE OF INSTRUCTION

Drexel University (M)

SCIENCE TEACHER EDUCATION

East Carolina University (M)

SCIENCE, GENERAL NON-MAJOR

University of Waterloo (B)

SCIENCE, MATH, AND TECHNOLOGY

State University of New York Empire State College (A,B)

SCIENCES RELIGIEUSES

Laurentian University (B)

SECONDARY

University of the Cumberlands (M)

SECONDARY EDUCATION

Dickinson State University (B)
Kaplan University (M)
Montgomery County Community College (A)
Northern Arizona University (M)
Utah State University (M)

SECONDARY EDUCATION (BS ED.)

Northern Arizona University (B)

SECONDARY EDUCATION (POSTBACCALAUREATE)

Pima Community College (UC)

SECONDARY EDUCATION POSTDEGREE

Northern Arizona University (UC)

SECONDARY EDUCATION WITH CERTIFICATION EMPHASIS

Northern Arizona University (M)

SECONDARY EDUCATION– ENGLISH

Dickinson State University

SECONDARY EDUCATION–MATH

Dickinson State University (B)

SECONDARY EDUCATION– SCIENCE CONCENTRATION

The University of Alabama

SECONDARY EDUCATION– SCIENCE EMPHASIS

West Virginia University (M)

SECONDARY EDUCATION–SOCIAL STUDIES EMPHASIS

West Virginia University (M)

SECONDARY EDUCATION, ADVANCED STUDIES

California University of Pennsylvania (M)

SECONDARY MATH–ONLINE SECONDARY MATH

University of Illinois (GC)

SECONDARY TEACHING

University of Great Falls (M)

SECRETARIAL (ADMINISTRATIVE, LEGAL, MEDICAL)

University of Northwestern Ohio (A)

SECURE AND DEPENDABLE COMPUTING SYSTEMS

University of Idaho (UC)

SECURE NETWORK SYSTEMS DESIGN

Stevens Institute of Technology (GC)

SECURITY ADMINISTRATION

Southwestern College (M)

SECURITY ENGINEERING

Southern Methodist University (M)

SECURITY MANAGEMENT

American Public University System (M,B)
Southwestern College (B)

SECURITY MANAGEMENT AND HOMELAND SECURITY

University of Massachusetts Lowell (UC)

SECURITY MANAGEMENT–MASTER OF APPLIED SCIENCE IN SECURITY MANAGEMENT

University of Denver (M)

SECURITY STUDIES

University of Massachusetts Lowell (GC)
East Carolina University (GC)

SEED ANALYSIS TRAINING

Colorado State University (UC)

SEED TECHNOLOGY AND BUSINESS

Iowa State University of Science and Technology (M)

SELF DESIGNED CONCENTRATION

Green Mountain College (M)

SELF-DESIGN

Granite State College (B)

SELF-DESIGNED

St. Cloud State University (B)

SEMINARY

Briercrest Distance Learning (UC)

SENIOR EXECUTIVE

The University of Tennessee (M)

SENIOR LIVING MANAGEMENT

Rochester Institute of Technology (GC)

SERVICE SOCIAL (EN FRANÇAIS)

Laurentian University (B)

SIGNAL PROCESSING

Stanford University (GC)

SITE PLANNING

University of Washington (UC)

SIX SIGMA EBLACK BELT (20 WEEKS)

Colorado State University (UC)

SIX SIGMA EGREEN BELT (12 WEEKS)

Colorado State University (UC)

SMALL BUSINESS ADMINISTRATION

Middlesex Community College (A)

SMALL BUSINESS ENTREPRENEURSHIP

Myers University (B)

SMALL BUSINESS MANAGEMENT

Herkimer County Community College (UC)
Jefferson Community and Technical College (UC)
Middlesex Community College (UC)
University of Alaska Southeast (UC)

SNA LEVEL 3 CERTIFICATION MODULE

Penn State University Park (UC)

SOCIAL AND CRIMINAL JUSTICE

Ashford University (B)

SOCIAL DEVELOPMENT STUDIES

University of Waterloo (B)

SOCIAL PSYCHOLOGY

Park University (B)

SOCIAL SCIENCE

Ashford University (B)
California State University, Chico (B)
Central Texas College (A)
Montgomery County Community College (A)
Southern New Hampshire University (B)
Troy University (B)
University of Maryland University College (B)
University of North Dakota (B)
West Hills Community College (A)

SOCIAL SCIENCE STUDIES

University of Nevada, Las Vegas (B)

SOCIAL SCIENCES

Brookdale Community College (A)
Buena Vista University (B)
Carl Albert State College (A)
Cerro Coso Community College (A)
Colorado State University-Pueblo (B)
Edmonds Community College (A)
Rose State College (A)
Syracuse University (M)
Thomas Edison State College (B)
University of Hawaii–West Oahu (B)
University of Waterloo (B)
University of Wyoming (B)
Upper Iowa University (B)
Washington State University (B)

SOCIAL SCIENCES–APPLIED TRACK

University of Hawaii–West Oahu (B)

SOCIAL SERVICES

Thomas Edison State College (A,B)
The University of Maine at Augusta (A)

SOCIAL SERVICES ADMINISTRATION

Thomas Edison State College (B)

SOCIAL SERVICES FOR SPECIAL POPULATIONS

Thomas Edison State College (A,B)

SOCIAL STUDIES

University of Missouri–Columbia (M)

SOCIAL THEORY, SOCIAL STRUCTURE, AND CHANGE

State University of New York Empire State College (A,B)

SOCIAL WORK

Central Texas College (A)
Cleveland State University (M)
Colorado State University (M)
Darton College (A)
Florida State University (M)
Memorial University of Newfoundland (M)
Missouri State University (M)
New Mexico State University (M)
Northern Arizona University (B)
Seminole Community College (A)
The University of Alabama (M)
University of North Dakota (M)
University of Wyoming (M)
Utah State University (M)

SOCIAL WORK COMPLETION

Presentation College (B)

SOCIAL WORK–ADVANCED STANDING

Colorado State University (M)

SOCIAL WORK–NATIVE HUMAN SERVICES

Laurentian University (B)

SOCIALLY ENGAGED SPIRITUALITY

Saybrook Graduate School and Research Center (GC)

SOCIOLOGY

Adams State College (B)
American Public University System (B)
Colorado State University-Pueblo (B)
Columbia College (B)
Dallas Baptist University (B)
Darton College (A)
Fort Hays State University (B)
Laurentian University (B)
New Mexico State University (B)
New York Institute of Technology (B)
Northeastern University (B)
Seminole Community College (A)
Skidmore College (B)
Thomas Edison State College (B)
University of Colorado at Denver and Health Sciences Center (B)

SOCIOLOGY (3 YEAR)

Athabasca University (B)

SOCIOLOGY (4 YEAR)

Athabasca University (B)

SOCIOLOGY EMPHASIS

Community College of Denver (A)

SOCIOLOGY–APPLIED SOCIOLOGY

Fort Hays State University (UC)

SOCIOLOGY-ANTHROPOLOGY

Skidmore College (B)

SOCIOLOGY/CRIMINOLOGY

Colorado State University-Pueblo (B)

SOFTWARE APPLICATIONS FOR THE PROFESSIONAL

Sinclair Community College (UC)

SOFTWARE APPLICATIONS SPECIALIST

Central Texas College (UC)

SOFTWARE DEVELOPMENT

Butler Community College (A)
Virginia Polytechnic Institute and State University (GC)

SOFTWARE DEVELOPMENT AND MANAGEMENT

Rochester Institute of Technology (M)

SOFTWARE DEVELOPMENT MANAGEMENT

University of Maryland University College (GC)

SOFTWARE ENGINEERING

DePaul University (M)
Drexel University (M)
East Carolina University (M)
Florida State University (B)
Kansas State University (M)
National University (B)
North Dakota State University (GC)
Southern Methodist University (M)
Texas Tech University (M)
University of Colorado at Boulder (GC)
University of Illinois (GC)
University of Illinois at Urbana–Champaign (GC)
University of Management and Technology (M)
University of Maryland University College (GC,M)
University of Michigan–Dearborn (M)
Walden University (M)
West Virginia University (M)
Westwood Online (A)

SOFTWARE PRODUCTIVITY

University of Cincinnati (UC)

SOFTWARE SYSTEMS

Stanford University (GC)

SOFTWARE SYSTEMS, ADVANCED

Stanford University (GC)

SPACE STUDIES

American Public University System (M,B)
University of Colorado at Colorado Springs (M)
University of North Dakota (M)

SPACECRAFT DESIGN AND OPERATION PROFICIENCY

Stanford University (GC)

SPANISH

Mercy College (B)
Northern Arizona University (B)
Skidmore College (B)

SPATIAL ANALYSIS AND MANAGEMENT

Jacksonville State University (UC)

SPATIAL ANALYSIS AND MANAGEMENT CONCENTRATION

Jacksonville State University (M)

SPECIAL AND ELEMENTARY EDUCATION (BS ED.)

Northern Arizona University (B)

SPECIAL EDUCATION

Campbellsville University (M)
East Carolina University (M)
Emporia State University (M)
Florida State University (M)
Fort Hays State University (M)
Northern Arizona University (M)
Northwest Missouri State University (M)
Old Dominion University (M)
Prescott College (B)
St. Cloud State University (B)
Texas Tech University (M)
University of Alaska Southeast (UC)
University of Arkansas (M)
University of Central Florida (GC)
University of Houston–Victoria (M)
University of Nebraska–Lincoln (M,UC)
University of North Dakota (M)
University of West Florida (M)
Utah State University (M,B)
West Virginia University (M)

SPECIAL EDUCATION –GIFTED EDUCATION

University of Nebraska at Kearney (M)

SPECIAL EDUCATION (CROSS-CATEGORICAL EMPHASIS)

The University of North Carolina at Greensboro (M)

SPECIAL EDUCATION (GIFTED)

University of South Alabama (M)

SPECIAL EDUCATION—EARLY CHILDHOOD INTERVENTION SPECIALIST

The University of Toledo (M)

SPECIAL EDUCATION ADMINISTRATION

University of Nebraska–Lincoln

SPECIAL EDUCATION ALTERNATIVE LICENSURE

New Mexico State University (UC)

SPECIAL EDUCATION AND LEVEL I SPECIALIST CREDENTIAL MILD/MODERATE

National University (M)

SPECIAL EDUCATION GENERALIST LICENSURE PROGRAM

University of Colorado at Denver and Health Sciences Center (UC)

SPECIAL EDUCATION LEADERSHIP

Regent University

SPECIAL EDUCATION LEARNING AND BEHAVIOR DISORDERS P-12

University of the Cumberlands (M)

SPECIAL EDUCATION POSTDEGREE

Northern Arizona University (UC)

SPECIAL EDUCATION PROGRAM

Western Carolina University (M)

SPECIAL EDUCATION–INSTRUCTIONAL SPECIALIST I

Buena Vista University (UC)

SPECIAL EDUCATION–LEARNING AND BEHAVIOR DISORDERS

University of the Cumberlands (M)

SPECIAL EDUCATION, ADAPTED CURRICULUM

The University of North Carolina at Charlotte (UC)

SPECIAL EDUCATION, GENERAL CURRICULUM TEACHER LICENSURE

The University of North Carolina at Charlotte (UC)

SPECIAL EDUCATION, GENERIC

Texas Tech University (UC)

SPECIALIST CERTIFICATE IN AGING

University of North Texas (GC)

SPECIALIZED MINISTRIES–YOUTH AND YOUNG ADULT MINISTRY

Southwestern College (M)

SPECIALTY CONSTRUCTION

Southern Polytechnic State University (UC)

SPECIALTY NEEDS FOR PRIMARY CARE PHYSICIANS (CME ONLINE)

University of Illinois (GC)

SPEECH

Darton College (A)

SPEECH LANGUAGE AND AUDITORY PATHOLOGY

East Carolina University (M)

SPEECH LANGUAGE PATHOLOGY ASSISTANT

Williston State College (A)

SPEECH-LANGUAGE PATHOLOGY

Texas Woman's University (M)
University of Wyoming (M)

SPEECH-LANGUAGE PATHOLOGY MASTERS PREREQUISITE PROGRAM

Longwood University (GC)

SPEECH/ LANGUAGE PATHOLOGY ASSISTANT

Chemeketa Community College (UC)

SPEECH/LANGUAGE PATHOLOGY ASSISTANT

Chemeketa Community College (A)

SPIRITUAL FORMATION AND LEADERSHIP

Spring Arbor University (M)

SPORT AND FITNESS MANAGER

Troy University (B)

SPORT COACHING EDUCATION

University of Southern Mississippi (M)

SPORT MANAGEMENT

Southern New Hampshire University (GC,M)
University of Southern Mississippi (M)

SPORT MANAGEMENT STUDIES

California University of Pennsylvania (M)

SPORT MANAGEMENT STUDIES–WELLNESS AND FITNESS TRACK

California University of Pennsylvania (B)

SPORTS AND ATHLETICS ADMINISTRATION

Lynn University (M)

SPORTS AND ENTERTAINMENT MANAGEMENT

University of Dallas (GC,M)

SPORTS AND HEALTH SCIENCES

American Public University System (B)

SPORTS COACHING

United States Sports Academy (M,B,UC)

SPORTS COACHING (INTERNATIONAL CERTIFICATION)

United States Sports Academy (UC)

SPORTS FITNESS

United States Sports Academy (M)

SPORTS LEADERSHIP

Duquesne University (M)

SPORTS MANAGEMENT

American Public University System (M)
Missouri State University (GC)
United States Sports Academy (D,M,B,UC)
West Virginia University (M)

SPORTS MANAGEMENT (INTERNATIONAL CERTIFICATION)

United States Sports Academy (UC)

SPORTS MANAGEMENT–SPORTS MEDICINE EMPHASIS

United States Sports Academy (D)

SPORTS MEDICINE

United States Sports Academy (M,UC)

SPORTS NUTRITION

Simmons College (GC)

SPORTS STUDIES

United States Sports Academy (M,B)

STATISTICAL METHODS FOR PRODUCT AND PROCESS IMPROVEMENT

Rochester Institute of Technology (GC)

STATISTICAL QUALITY

Rochester Institute of Technology (GC)

STATISTICAL THEORY AND METHOD

Colorado State University (UC)

STATISTICS

Colorado State University (M)
Iowa State University of Science and Technology (M)

STRATEGIC BUSINESS MANAGEMENT (MSM)

Regis University (GC)

STRATEGIC COMMUNICATION AND LEADERSHIP

Seton Hall University (M)

STRATEGIC FORESIGHT

Regent University (GC,M)

STRATEGIC INTELLIGENCE

American Public University System (M)

STRATEGIC LEADERSHIP

Regent University (D)
Southwestern College (B)

STRATEGIC LEADERSHIP CONCENTRATION

Andrew Jackson University (M)

STRATEGIC PLANNING FOR CRITICAL INFRASTRUCTURE

University of Washington (M)

STRATEGIC TECHNOLOGY MANAGEMENT

University of Illinois (GC)
University of Illinois at Urbana–Champaign (GC)

STRUCTURAL DESIGN

Rochester Institute of Technology (UC)

STRUCTURAL ENGINEERING

University of Idaho (UC)

STRUCTURAL/GEOTECHNICAL ENGINEERING

University of Wisconsin–Platteville (GC)
University of Wisconsin–Platteville (GC)

STUDENT AFFAIRS

Regent University (M)

STUDENT AFFAIRS AND HIGHER EDUCATION

Indiana State University (M)

SUBSTANCE ABUSE AND ADDICTIONS STUDIES

University of Hawaii–West Oahu (UC)

SUBSTANCE ABUSE/ADDICTION COUNSELING

East Carolina University (GC)

SUPERINTENDENCY

Northern Arizona University (UC)

SUPERINTENDENT CERTIFICATE

The University of Texas System

SUPERINTENDENT PROFESSIONAL

Texas Tech University (UC)

SUPERINTENDENT'S LETTER OF ELIGIBILITY

California University of Pennsylvania (UC)

SUPERVISORY

Northern Arizona University (UC)

SUPERVISORY MANAGEMENT

Jefferson Community and Technical College (UC)
Mid-State Technical College (A)
Northwest Technical College (A)

SUPERVISORY MANAGEMENT/ LEADERSHIP DEVELOPMENT

Madison Area Technical College (A)

SUPPLY CHAIN AND INFORMATION SYSTEMS

Penn State University Park (GC)

SUPPLY CHAIN MANAGEMENT

Lehigh University (UC)
National University (GC)
Northeastern University (A)

SUPPLY CHAIN MANAGEMENT/ MARKET LOGISTICS

University of Dallas (GC,M)

SURGICAL TECHNOLOGY

Lock Haven University of Pennsylvania (A)
The University of Montana (A)

SURGICAL TECHNOLOGY ACCELERATED OPTION, CERTIFICATE OF GRADUATION

Vincennes University (GC)

SURVEYING

Thomas Edison State College (A,B)

SUSTAINABILITY EDUCATION

Prescott College (M)

SUSTAINABLE BUSINESS PRACTICES

Green Mountain College (M)

SUSTAINABLE COMMUNITY DEVELOPMENT

Prescott College (M,B)

SUSTAINABLE NATURAL RESOURCES

Oregon State University (GC)

SYSTEM SAFETY AND SECURITY

University of Southern California (GC,M)

SYSTEM SOFTWARE

University of Illinois at Urbana–Champaign (GC)

SYSTEMS ANALYSIS

University of Maryland University College (GC)

SYSTEMS AND ENGINEERING MANAGEMENT

Texas Tech University (M)

SYSTEMS AND ENGINEERING MANGAMENT

Texas Tech University (D)

SYSTEMS ARCHITECTURE ENGINEERING

University of Southern California (M)

SYSTEMS ARCHITECTURE ENGINEERING CERTIFICATE

University of Southern California (GC)

SYSTEMS ENGINEERING

Iowa State University of Science and Technology (GC,M)
Southern Methodist University (M)
Southern Polytechnic State University (M)
Stevens Institute of Technology (M)
University of Colorado at Colorado Springs (M)
University of Illinois at Urbana–Champaign (GC)
Virginia Polytechnic Institute and State University (M)
Walden University (M)

SYSTEMS ENGINEERING (INDUSTRIAL AND MANUFACTURING ENGINEERING CONCENTRATION)

Kettering University (M)

SYSTEMS MANAGEMENT

Florida Institute of Technology (M)

SYSTEMS SOFTWARE

University of Illinois (GC)

TAXATION

University of Tulsa (M)

TEACH AND LEARNING WITH TECHNOLOGY

Ashford University (M)

TEACHER ASSOCIATE

Haywood Community College (A)

TEACHER CERTIFICATION

Prescott College (UC)

TEACHER EDUCATION (EARLY CHILDHOOD)

Darton College (A)

TEACHER EDUCATION (MIDDLE GRADES)

Darton College (A)

TEACHER EDUCATION (SECONDARY EDUCATION)

Darton College (A)

TEACHER EDUCATION (SPECIAL EDUCATION)

Darton College (A)

TEACHER EDUCATION (TRADE AND INDUSTRIAL EDUCATION)

Darton College (A)

TEACHER EDUCATION, PARAEDUCATOR

Community College of Denver (UC)

TEACHER LEADER

Wright State University (M)

TEACHER LEADERSHIP

Roosevelt University (M)
University of Illinois at Springfield (M)
Walden University (D)

TEACHING

Ashford University (M)
Liberty University
National University (M)
State University of New York Empire State College (M)
Texas Woman's University (M)

TEACHING AND LEARNING

Lock Haven University of Pennsylvania (M)
Kaplan University (M)

TEACHING AND LEARNING WITH TECHNOLOGY

University of North Texas (M)

TEACHING AND LEARNING WITH TECHNOLOGY (GRAD AND UNDERGRAD)

Minnesota State University Moorhead (GC)

TEACHING AND LEARNING– ONLINE TEACHING AND LEARNING

California State University, East Bay (UC)
New Mexico State University (UC)

TEACHING AND LEARNING– OPTION IN ONLINE TEACHING AND LEARNING

California State University, East Bay (M)

TEACHING AND LEARNING, ADVANCED STUDIES

Middle Tennessee State University (M)

TEACHING ASSISTANT CERTIFICATE

Herkimer County Community College (UC)

TEACHING AT A DISTANCE

University of Maryland University College (GC)

TEACHING AT-RISK STUDENTS

Park University (M)

TEACHING ENGLISH TO SPEAKERS OF OTHER LANGUAGES

The New School: A University (M)

TEACHING ENGLISH AS A SECOND LANGUAGE

Northern Arizona University (M)
Oregon State University (GC)
St. Cloud State University (M)

TEACHING ENGLISH AS A SECOND LANGUAGE (TESL)

Drexel University (UC)
Oral Roberts University (M)

TEACHING ENGLISH AS A SECOND OR FOREIGN LANGUAGE

Indiana State University (GC)

TEACHING ENGLISH TO SPEAKERS OF OTHER LANGUAGES

Emporia State University (M)

TEACHING ENGLISH TO SPEAKERS OF OTHER LANGUAGES (TESOL)

University of Missouri–Columbia (M)

TEACHING IN NURSING

University of Illinois at Chicago (UC)

TEACHING IN THE VIRTUAL CLASSROOM

Fielding Graduate University (UC)

TEACHING LITERACY AND LANGUAGE–GRADES 6-12

Kaplan University (M)

TEACHING LITERACY AND LANGUAGE–GRADES K-6

Kaplan University (M)

TEACHING MATHEMATICS

University of Idaho (M)

TEACHING MATHEMATICS–GRADES 6-8

Kaplan University (M)

TEACHING MATHEMATICS–GRADES 9-12

Kaplan University (M)

TEACHING MATHEMATICS–GRADES K-5

Kaplan University (M)

TEACHING OF LANGUAGES (MATL)

University of Southern Mississippi (M)

TEACHING SCIENCE–GRADES 6-12

Kaplan University (M)

TEACHING STUDENTS WITH SPECIAL NEEDS

Kaplan University (M)

TEACHING WITH CERTIFICATION

Oral Roberts University (M)

TEACHING WITH TECHNOLOGY

Kaplan University (M)

TEACHING WITH TECHNOLOGY AND DISTANCE LEARNING CERTIFICATE

Colorado State University (UC)

TEACHING–INSTRUCTIONAL TECHNOLOGY

Northwest Missouri State University (M)

TEACHING–MASTER OF ARTS IN TEACHING

New Mexico State University (M)

TEACHING–ONLINE TEACHING

Boise State University (GC)
Cerro Coso Community College (UC)

TEACHING, LEARNING, AND CURRICULUM

Drexel University (M)

TEACHING, LEARNING, AND TEACHER EDUCATION

University of Nebraska–Lincoln (M,UC)

TECHNICAL COMMUNICATION

Southern Polytechnic State University (GC)
Texas Tech University (M)

TECHNICAL COMMUNICATION AND RHETORIC

Texas Tech University (D)

TECHNICAL COMMUNICATION, BASIC

Rochester Institute of Technology (UC)

TECHNICAL COMMUNICATIONS

Northeastern University (B)

TECHNICAL COMMUNICATIONS, ADVANCED

Rochester Institute of Technology (UC)

TECHNICAL EDUCATION AND INDUSTRY TRAINING

University of Central Florida (B)

TECHNICAL INFORMATION DESIGN

Rochester Institute of Technology (GC)

TECHNICAL MANAGEMENT

DeVry University Online (B)
Embry-Riddle Aeronautical University (A,B)
Southern New Hampshire University (B)

TECHNICAL STUDIES

Excelsior College (A)

TECHNICAL STUDIES IN INFORMATION SYSTEMS

Fairmont State University (A)

TECHNICAL WRITING CERTIFICATE

California State University, Dominguez Hills (GC)

TECHNOLOGICAL EDUCATION, ADVANCED

Bowling Green State University (B)

TECHNOLOGY

Excelsior College (A,B)

TECHNOLOGY ADMINISTRATION

Washburn University (B)

TECHNOLOGY AND INFORMATION MANAGEMENT

Upper Iowa University (B)

TECHNOLOGY APPRENTICESHIP

Vincennes University (A)

TECHNOLOGY APPRENTICESHIP–GENERAL STUDIES OPTION

Vincennes University (A)

TECHNOLOGY EDUCATION

Ball State University (M)

TECHNOLOGY FACILITATOR

East Carolina University (GC)

TECHNOLOGY FOR EDUCATION AND TRAINING

The University of South Dakota (M)
The University of South Dakota (M)

TECHNOLOGY IN EDUCATION

Lesley University (M)

TECHNOLOGY IN EDUCATION (GLOBAL)

University of Michigan–Flint (M)

TECHNOLOGY IN SCHOOLS

University of Missouri–Columbia (M)

TECHNOLOGY IN SCHOOLS (EDUCATIONAL SPECIALIST)

University of Missouri–Columbia

TECHNOLOGY INTEGRATION

Boise State University (GC)
Graceland University (M)

TECHNOLOGY LEADERSHIP

Fort Hays State University (B)

TECHNOLOGY MANAGEMENT

Bowling Green State University (D)
City University (GC)
Indiana State University (D)
Kansas State University (B)
National University (M)
Pennsylvania College of Technology (B)
St. Petersburg College (B)
Stevens Institute of Technology (GC,M)
University of Bridgeport (M)
University of Maryland University College (M)
University of Phoenix Online Campus (M)
University of Wisconsin–Stout (M)
Western Kentucky University (M,B)
Worcester Polytechnic Institute (M)

TECHNOLOGY MANAGEMENT (DEGREE COMPLETION)

Eastern Michigan University (B)

TECHNOLOGY MANAGEMENT– CERTIFICATE OF ADVANCED STUDY

University of Denver (UC)

TECHNOLOGY MANAGEMENT– MASTER OF APPLIED SCIENCE IN TECHNOLOGY MANAGEMENT

University of Denver (M)

TECHNOLOGY SYSTEMS MANAGEMENT

University of Maryland University College (GC)

TECHNOLOGY SYSTEMS– COMPUTER NETWORKING MANAGEMENT

East Carolina University (M)

TECHNOLOGY SYSTEMS–DIGITAL COMMUNICATIONS

East Carolina University (M)

TECHNOLOGY SYSTEMS– DISTRIBUTION AND LOGISTICS

East Carolina University (M)

TECHNOLOGY SYSTEMS– INFORMATION SECURITY

East Carolina University (M)

TECHNOLOGY SYSTEMS– MANUFACTURING

East Carolina University (M)

TECHNOLOGY SYSTEMS– PERFORMANCE IMPROVEMENT

East Carolina University (M)

TECHNOLOGY SYSTEMS– QUALITY SYSTEMS

East Carolina University (M)

TECHNOLOGY–BACHELOR TECHNOLOGY (BTECH)

Memorial University of Newfoundland (B)

TECHNOLOGY–HUMAN RESOURCE DEVELOPMENT

The University of Texas at Tyler (M,B)

TECHNOLOGY-BASED DISTRIBUTED LEARNING

The University of British Columbia (GC)

TECHNOLOGY-BASED LEARNING FOR SCHOOLS

The University of British Columbia (GC)

TELECOMMUNICATION MANAGEMENT

Stevens Institute of Technology (M)

TELECOMMUNICATION SYSTEMS

DePaul University (M)
DePaul University (M)

TELECOMMUNICATIONS

Columbia University (UC)
Pace University (GC,B)
Southern Methodist University (M)
Stanford University (GC)
University of Colorado at Boulder (M)

TELECOMMUNICATIONS AND NETWORK MANAGEMENT

Syracuse University (M)
Syracuse University (M)

TELECOMMUNICATIONS AND SIGNAL PROCESSING

University of Illinois (GC)

TELECOMMUNICATIONS ENGINEERING TECHNOLOGY

Rochester Institute of Technology (M)

TELECOMMUNICATIONS MANAGEMENT

Stevens Institute of Technology (GC)
University of Dallas (GC,M)
University of Management and Technology (M)
University of Maryland University College (GC,M)

TELECOMMUNICATIONS MANAGEMENT AND POLICY– CERTIFICATE OF ADVANCED STUDY

University of Denver (UC).

TELECOMMUNICATIONS NETWORKING

New Jersey Institute of Technology (GC)

TELECOMMUNICATIONS NETWORKS–CERTIFICATE OF ADVANCED STUDY

University of Denver (UC)

TELECOMMUNICATIONS SYSTEMS MANAGEMENT

Murray State University (B)

TELECOMMUNICATIONS TECHNOLOGY

Rochester Institute of Technology (B)

TELECOMMUNICATIONS TECHNOLOGY–CERTIFICATE OF ADVANCED STUDY

University of Denver (UC)

TELECOMMUNICATIONS TECHNOLOGY–VERIZON

Erie Community College (A)

TELECOMMUNICATIONS–DATA COMMUNICATIONS

Rochester Institute of Technology (UC)

TELECOMMUNICATIONS–MASTER OF APPLIED SCIENCE IN TELECOMMUNICATIONS

University of Denver (M)

TELECOMMUNICATIONS– NETWORK MANAGEMENT

Rochester Institute of Technology (UC)

TELECOMMUNICATIONS–VOICE COMMUNICATIONS

Rochester Institute of Technology (UC)

TELEVISION ARTS

Regent University (M)

TESOL

Regent University (M,UC)
University of North Texas (UC)

TEXAS TEACHER CERTIFICATION–SECONDARY EDUCATION

University of North Texas (UC)

TEXTILE AND APPAREL MARKETING

Philadelphia University (M)

TEXTILES OFF-CAMPUS PROGRAMS (TOP)

North Carolina State University (M)

TEXTILES, CLOTHING, AND DESIGN

University of Nebraska–Lincoln (M)

THE ARTS

State University of New York Empire State
 College (A,B)
Triton College (A)

THEATER

Darton College (A)
Prescott College (B)
Skidmore College (B)
Thomas Edison State College (B)

THEATER ARTS

Regent University (M)

THEOLOGICAL STUDIES

Andrews University (B)
Covenant Theological Seminary (M)
Liberty University (M)
Newman Theological College (UC)

THEOLOGY

The Catholic Distance University (M,B)
Franciscan University of Steubenville (M)
Global University of the Assemblies of God
 (UC)
Holy Apostles College and Seminary (M)
Newman Theological College

TOTAL QUALITY MANAGEMENT ENGINEERING

University of South Florida (GC)

TOURISM AND HOSPITALITY MANAGEMENT

Mount Saint Vincent University (B)

TOURISM AND TRAVEL MANAGEMENT

Chemeketa Community College (A,UC)

TOURISM PLANNING AND DEVELOPMENT

California University of Pennsylvania (M)

TOXICOLOGY AND INDUSTRIAL HYGIENE

Drexel University (UC)

TRADE & INDUSTRIAL (T&I)

The University of Texas System (UC)

TRADE AND INDUSTRIAL EDUCATION

Darton College (A)

TRAINING AND DEVELOPMENT

North Carolina State University (M)
Roosevelt University (GC,M)
Southern New Hampshire University (GC)
University of St. Francis (M)
University of Wisconsin–Stout (M)

TRAINING AND DEVELOPMENT–CERTIFICATE OF ADVANCED STUDY

University of Denver (UC)

TRAINING AT A DISTANCE

University of Maryland University College
 (GC)

TRANSFER DEGREE

Bellevue Community College (A)
Minnesota State Community and Technical
 College–Fergus Falls (A)
NorthWest Arkansas Community College (A)

TRANSFER DEGREE FOR BUSINESS STUDENTS

Bellevue Community College (A)

TRANSFER STUDIES

Anne Arundel Community College (A)

TRANSFORMATIVE LEADERSHIP

California Institute of Integral Studies (M)

TRANSFORMATIVE STUDIES

California Institute of Integral Studies (D)

TRANSLATION, FRENCH PROFESSIONAL DEVELOPMENT SEQUENCE

University of Illinois (GC)

TRANSPERSONAL PSYCHOLOGY

Naropa University (M)

TRANSPERSONAL PSYCHOLOGY WITH ECOPSYCHOLOGY CONCENTRATION

Naropa University (M)

TRANSPERSONAL STUDIES

Atlantic University (M)

TRANSPORTATION AND LOGISTICS MANAGEMENT

American Public University System (M,B)

TRANSPORTATION BUSINESS

Minnesota School of Business–Richfield (A)

TRANSPORTATION POLICY, OPERATIONS, AND LOGISTICS

George Mason University (M)

TRANSPORTATION SYSTEMS ANALYSIS

University of South Florida (GC)

TRAVEL AND TOURISM–HOSPITALITY AND EVENTS MANAGEMENT

Herkimer County Community College (A)

TRAVEL MANAGEMENT

University of Northwestern Ohio (A)

TURFGRASS MANAGEMENT

Penn State University Park (UC)

TURFGRASS MANAGEMENT, ADVANCED

Penn State University Park (UC)

TURFGRASS SCIENCE

Penn State University Park (B)

TWO-YEAR COMMUNITY COLLEGE ADMINISTRATION PROGRAM

Western Carolina University (M)

TYPEFACE DESIGN

Savannah College of Art and Design (GC)

ULTRASOUND–DEGREE COMPLETION IN ULTRASOUND, ECHOCARDIOGRAPHY OPTION

Oregon Institute of Technology (B)

ULTRASOUND–DEGREE COMPLETION IN ULTRASOUND, VASCULAR TECHNOLOGY OPTION

Oregon Institute of Technology (B)

UNIVERSITY STUDIES

Dickinson State University (B)
University of Maine (B)
University of Maine at Fort Kent (B)
The University of Tennessee at Martin (B)

UNIVERSITY TRANSFER

Clark State Community College (A)

UNIX

University of Massachusetts Lowell (UC)

URBAN FORESTRY TECHNOLOGY

Minot State University–Bottineau Campus (UC)

URBAN WATER RESOURCES DESIGN

Villanova University (GC)

USER CENTERED DESIGN

New Jersey Institute of Technology (GC)

UTAH MATHEMATICS ENDORSEMENT PROJECT

Utah State University (UC)

VACCINES–TECHNOLOGIES, TRENDS, AND BIOTERRORISM

Northeastern University (GC)

VARIOUS SUBJECTS–BIOQUALITY, ENTREPRENEUR, HUMAN RESOURCES MANAGEMENT

Central Carolina Community College (UC)

VARIOUS SUBJECTS–INCOME TAX PREPARER, LIBRARY SERVICES, MANAGER TRAINEE

Central Carolina Community College (UC)

VARIOUS SUBJECTS–MEDICAL TRANSCRIPTION, NETWORKING, NEWS WRITING

Central Carolina Community College (UC)

VARIOUS SUBJECTS–PAYROLL ACCOUNTING, PHOTO JOURNALISM, SMALL BUSINESS FINANCIAL ADVISOR I AND II

Central Carolina Community College (UC)

VETERINARY EDUCATION ONLINE

University of Illinois (GC)

VETERINARY HOSPITAL MANAGEMENT

St. Petersburg College (UC)

VETERINARY HOSPITAL MANAGER

St. Petersburg College (UC)

VETERINARY MEDICINE ONLINE

Colorado State University (UC)

VETERINARY SCIENCE–PRE-VETERINARY SCIENCE

Darton College (A)

VETERINARY TECHNOLOGY

Community College of Denver (A)
St. Petersburg College (A)

VIOLENCE PREVENTION AND RESPONSE

Saybrook Graduate School and Research Center (GC)

VIRTUAL BUSINESS

Minot State University (B)

VIRTUAL ORGANIZATIONS

Regent University (UC)

VIRTUAL REALITY IN EDUCATION AND TRAINING

East Carolina University (GC)

VISUAL COMMUNICATION

Savannah College of Art and Design (B)

VISUAL COMMUNICATION AND GRAPHICS

Southern Polytechnic State University (GC)

VISUAL COMMUNICATION CONCENTRATION

American InterContinental University Online (A)

VISUAL COMMUNICATION–DIGITAL DESIGN CONCENTRATION (COMPLETION PROGRAM)

American InterContinental University Online (B)

VISUAL COMMUNICATION–WEB DESIGN CONCENTRATION (COMPLETION PROGRAM)

American InterContinental University Online (B)

VISUAL COMMUNICATIONS

Westwood Online (B)

VISUAL IMPAIRMENT

Indiana State University (UC)
Texas Tech University (UC)

VOCATIONAL BUSINESS EDUCATION

Indiana State University (UC)

VOCATIONAL DIVERSIFIED OCCUPATIONS ENDORSEMENT

University of Nebraska at Kearney (UC)

VOCATIONAL EDUCATION–INFORMATION TECHNOLOGIES

East Carolina University (M)

VOCATIONAL REHABILITATION COUNSELING

University of Wisconsin–Stout (M)

VOCATIONAL TEACHER PREPARATION

State University of New York at Oswego (M,B)

VOLUNTEER AND COMMUNITY RESOURCE MANAGEMENT

University of North Texas (GC)

WATER RESOURCES AND ENVIRONMENTAL ENGINEERING

Villanova University (M)

WATER RESOURCES ENGINEERING

University of Idaho (UC)

WATER/WASTEWATER SPECIALIZATION

Mountain Empire Community College (A)

WEATHER FORECASTING

Penn State University Park (UC)

WEB ADMINISTRATION

University of Washington (UC)

WEB AND DESKTOP PUBLISHING

Minot State University (GC)

WEB AUTHORING

University of Alaska Southeast (UC)

WEB CONSULTANT FOR SMALL BUSINESS

University of Washington (UC)

WEB DESIGN

City University (UC)
West Valley College (A)

WEB DESIGN AND DEVELOPMENT TECHNOLOGIES–CERTIFICATE OF ADVANCED STUDY

University of Denver (UC)

WEB DESIGN AND MULTIMEDIA

Westwood Online (B)

WEB DESIGN CERTIFICATE

The University of Toledo (UC)

WEB DESIGNER

Texas State Technical College Waco (A)

WEB DEVELOPER

College of Southern Maryland (UC)
Texas State Technical College Waco (A)

WEB DEVELOPMENT

City University (GC)
Fort Hays State University (UC)

WEB FOUNDATIONS

University of Alaska Southeast (UC)

WEB LANGUAGES

City University (UC)

WEB MBA

Georgia College & State University (M)

WEB PAGE DEVELOPMENT AND DESIGN

Bismarck State College (A)

WEB PAGE DEVELOPMENT, BASIC

Bristol Community College (UC)

WEB PROGRAMMING IN E-COMMERCE

City University (GC)

WEB PROGRAMMING–VISUAL BASIC OR JAVA TRACK SHORT-TERM CERTIFICATE

Sinclair Community College (UC)

WEB PUBLISHING

Middlesex Community College (UC)

WEB SERVICES

Webster University (GC)

WEB SITE DESIGN

Webster University (UC)

WEB SITE DEVELOPMENT

Webster University (UC)

WEB SITE DEVELOPMENT CERTIFICATE

Western Wyoming Community College (UC)

WEB TECHNOLOGIES

Wake Technical Community College (A)

WEB TECHNOLOGY ESSENTIALS

University of Washington (UC)

WEB TECHNOLOGY FOCUS

University of Connecticut (B)

WEBSITE DESIGN AND DEVELOPMENT

University of Massachusetts Lowell (UC)

WEBSITE DEVELOPER

East Carolina University (GC)

WELDING ENGINEERING

The Ohio State University (M)

WELLNESS–MASTER OF ARTS IN WELLNESS (MAW)

Chatham University

WESTERN AMERICAN STUDIES

Western Wyoming Community College (UC)

WETLANDS MANAGEMENT

Prescott College (M)

WILDLIFE MANAGEMENT

Prescott College (M)

WIRELESS AND ELECTRONIC COMMUNICATIONS

Cleveland Institute of Electronics (UC)

WIRELESS AND MOBILE COMMUNICATIONS

Columbia University (UC)

WIRELESS COMMUNICATION TECHNOLOGY

University of Illinois (GC)

WIRELESS COMMUNICATION TECHNOLOGY CAMPUS CERTIFICATE

University of Illinois at Chicago (UC)

WIRELESS COMMUNICATIONS

Stevens Institute of Technology (GC)

WIRELESS COMMUNICATIONS (EE CONCENTRATION)

Kettering University (M)

WIRELESS ENGINEERING

University of South Florida (GC)

WIRELESS PERSONAL COMMUNICATION

Stanford University (GC)

WOMEN'S HEALTH

Rosalind Franklin University of Medicine and Science (GC,M)

WOMEN'S HEALTH COMPLETION PROGRAM FOR NURSE PRACTITIONERS

Drexel University (M)

WOMEN'S HEALTH NURSE PRACTITIONER

Drexel University (M)
University of Cincinnati (M)

WOMEN'S STUDIES

Laurentian University (B,UC)
Skidmore College (B)
Western Kentucky University (GC)

WOMEN'S STUDIES (3 YEAR)

Athabasca University (B)

WOMEN'S STUDIES (4 YEAR)

Athabasca University (B)

WOOD AND PAPER SCIENCE

North Carolina State University (M)

WORD PROCESSING– ADMINISTRATIVE SUPPORT

University of Northwestern Ohio (A)

WORKFORCE DEVELOPMENT EDUCATION

University of Arkansas (M)

WORKFORCE EDUCATION LEADERSHIP

Mississippi State University (M)

WORSHIP STUDIES

Liberty University (M)

WRITERS SERIES

University of Illinois (GC)

WRITING AND COMMUNICTIONS CONCENTRATION

Green Mountain College (M)

WRITING SOCIAL COMMENTARY

Penn State University Park (UC)

YOUTH DEVELOPMENT

Clemson University (M)
Kansas State University (GC,M)
University of Nebraska–Lincoln (GC)

YOUTH MINISTRY LEADERSHIP MODULE

Defiance College (UC)

NON-DEGREE-RELATED COURSE SUBJECT AREAS INDEX

Index of individual courses offered by institutions, arranged by subject. U=Undergraduate; G=Graduate; N=Noncredit

ACCOUNTING AND COMPUTER SCIENCE

Arapahoe Community College (U)
Ashford University (G)
Belmont Technical College (U)
Bismarck State College (U)
Black Hills State University (U)
Cabrillo College (U)
California State University, San Bernardino (U)
California State University, San Marcos (N,U)
Carlow University (U)
Carroll College (U)
Central Michigan University (U,G)
Chadron State College (U,G)
Chattanooga State Technical Community College (U)
Chesapeake College (U)
Clackamas Community College (U)
Clark State Community College (U)
Cleveland Institute of Electronics (N)
Cleveland State University (U)
Cloud County Community College (N,U)
Colorado State University (N,U)
Colorado Technical University (U)
Community College of Beaver County (N,U)
Darton College (U)
Daymar College (U)
Delta College (U)
Des Moines Area Community College (U)
Drake University (G)
Duquesne University (U,G)
East Central Community College (U)
Eastern Iowa Community College District (N)
Eastern Michigan University (G)
Eastern West Virginia Community and Technical College (U)
Elizabethtown College (U)
Everest College (U)
Finger Lakes Community College (U)
Flathead Valley Community College (N)
Fort Hays State University (N,U)
Gadsden State Community College (U)
Galveston College (N,U)
Hocking College (U)
Holyoke Community College (U)
Hopkinsville Community College (U)
Illinois Eastern Community Colleges, Lincoln Trail College (U)
Indiana State University (U)
Itawamba Community College (U)
Jacksonville State University (U)
James Sprunt Community College (U)
Jefferson Community and Technical College (U)
John A. Logan College (U)
Kansas State University (U)
Lewis-Clark State College (U)
Lurleen B. Wallace Community College (U)
Marlboro College (U,G)
Maryville University of Saint Louis (U)

Mesa State College (U)
Middlesex Community College (U)
Mississippi State University (U)
Mitchell Technical Institute (U)
Mount Saint Vincent University (U)
Nashville State Technical Community College (U)
New Jersey Institute of Technology (U,G)
New Mexico Junior College (U)
North Central State College (U)
Northeast Alabama Community College (U)
North Idaho College (N)
Northwestern Oklahoma State University (U)
Northwest Mississippi Community College (U)
Pamlico Community College (U)
Plymouth State University (N)
Pulaski Technical College (U)
Quinebaug Valley Community College (N)
Rose State College (U)
Saddleback College (U)
St. Louis Community College System (U)
Seminole Community College (U)
Sinclair Community College (U)
Southern New Hampshire University (U,G)
South Piedmont Community College (U)
Southwest Georgia Technical College (U)
Texas A&M University–Commerce (U)
Thomas College (U)
Three Rivers Community College (U)
Union University (U)
University of Alaska Anchorage, Kodiak College (U)
University of Cincinnati (N)
University of Idaho (G)
University of Illinois at Springfield (U)
University of Management and Technology (U,G)
University of Massachusetts Lowell (U,G)
University of New Orleans (U,G)
The University of North Carolina at Charlotte (N)
University of Southern Indiana (N)
University of South Florida (G)
University of Vermont (U)
University of West Florida (G)
University of Wisconsin–Parkside (G)
University of Wisconsin–Superior (U)
University of Wisconsin–Whitewater (U)
Upper Iowa University (N)
Viterbo University (U)
Western Piedmont Community College (U)
West Hills Community College (N)
West Liberty State College (U)
West Los Angeles College (U)
West Texas A&M University (G)
West Virginia University at Parkersburg (N)
Wharton County Junior College (U)
Williston State College (U)
Yuba College (U)

ACCOUNTING AND RELATED SERVICES

Adams State College (N)
Adelphi University (G)
Amberton University (U)
American Graduate University (G)
Anne Arundel Community College (U)
Arapahoe Community College (U)
Arizona Western College (U)
Arkansas State University–Beebe (U)
Ashford University (U,G)
Athabasca University (N,U,G)
Auburn University (G)
Bainbridge College (U)
Beaufort County Community College (N,U)
Bellevue Community College (U)
Belmont Technical College (U)
Bergen Community College (U)
Berkeley College (U)
Berkeley College-New York City Campus (U)
Berkeley College-Westchester Campus (U)
Big Bend Community College (U)
Bismarck State College (U)
Blackhawk Technical College (U)
Boise State University (U)
Brazosport College (U)
Brenau University (U,G)
Bridgewater State College (N)
Bristol Community College (N,U)
Brookdale Community College (U)
Bryant and Stratton Online (U)
Buena Vista University (U)
Butler Community College (U)
Butler County Community College (U)
Cabrillo College (U)
Caldwell Community College and Technical Institute (N,U)
California State University, Dominguez Hills (N)
California State University, San Bernardino (U)
Campbell University (U)
Cape Breton University (U)
Carl Albert State College (U)
Carroll Community College (N,U)
Cascadia Community College (U)
Casper College (U)
Cayuga County Community College (U)
Cedar Crest College (U)
Central Carolina Community College (U)
Central Georgia Technical College (U)
Central New Mexico Community College (U)
Central Texas College (U)
Central Virginia Community College (U)
Central Washington University (U,G)
Central Wyoming College (U)
Chadron State College (U,G)
Chaminade University of Honolulu (U)
Charter Oak State College (U)
Chattanooga State Technical Community College (U)

Chemeketa Community College (U)
Cincinnati State Technical and Community
  College (U)
Clackamas Community College (U)
Clatsop Community College (U)
Clemson University (N)
Cleveland State University (N,U,G)
Clinton Community College (U)
Cloud County Community College (U)
College of DuPage (U)
College of San Mateo (U)
College of Southern Maryland (U)
College of The Albemarle (N,U)
College of the Siskiyous (U)
College of the Southwest (U)
Colorado Mountain College District System
  (U)
Colorado State University (G)
Colorado Technical University (U)
Columbia College (U)
Columbus State Community College (U)
The Community College of Baltimore County
  (U)
Community College of Denver (U)
Concordia University Wisconsin (U)
Connecticut State University System (U,G)
Dakota State University (U)
Dallas Baptist University (U,G)
Danville Community College (U)
Darton College (U)
Daymar College (U)
De Anza College (U)
Delaware County Community College (U)
Des Moines Area Community College (U)
DeVry University Online (U,G)
Dickinson State University (U)
Drake University (U)
Drexel University (U,G)
East Carolina University (G)
Eastern Michigan University (N,G)
Eastern Oregon University (U)
Eastern Washington University (U)
Eastern Wyoming College (U)
East Los Angeles College (U)
East Tennessee State University (U)
Edgecombe Community College (N,U)
Edison State Community College (N,U)
Edmonds Community College (U)
EduKan (U)
Elgin Community College (U)
Elizabeth City State University (U)
Elizabethtown College (U)
Erie Community College (U)
Everest College (U)
Everett Community College (U)
Flathead Valley Community College (U)
Florida Institute of Technology (G)
Fort Hays State University (N)
Franklin Pierce University (U)
Franklin University (U)
Fullerton College (U)
Fulton-Montgomery Community College (N)
Galveston College (N,U)
Gaston College (U)
George C. Wallace Community College (U)
Governors State University (U)
Graceland University (U)
Grantham University (U,G)
Hagerstown Community College (N)
Harrisburg Area Community College (U)
Haywood Community College (U)
Herkimer County Community College (U)

Hillsborough Community College (N)
Houston Community College System (U)
Illinois Eastern Community Colleges, Olney
  Central College (U)
Illinois Eastern Community Colleges, Wabash
  Valley College (U)
Indiana State University (U)
Indiana Tech (U)
Indiana University of Pennsylvania (U)
Indiana University–Purdue University Fort
  Wayne (U)
Indiana University System (N)
Itawamba Community College (U)
Ivy Tech Community College–Northwest (U)
Jacksonville State University (U,G)
James Madison University (U)
James Sprunt Community College (U)
Jamestown Community College (N)
Jefferson Community College (U)
John A. Logan College (U)
John Tyler Community College (U)
John Wood Community College (U)
Jones College (U)
Jones County Junior College (U)
J. Sargeant Reynolds Community College (U)
Kansas City Kansas Community College (U)
Kansas State University (U)
Kaskaskia College (U)
Kean University (N,U,G)
Kellogg Community College (U)
Kirkwood Community College (U)
Lakeland College (U)
Lake Superior College (U)
Lansing Community College (U)
Lehigh Carbon Community College (U)
Lewis and Clark Community College (U)
Liberty University (U,G)
Limestone College (U)
Long Beach City College (U)
Los Angeles Harbor College (U)
Louisiana State University and Agricultural
  and Mechanical College (U)
Luzerne County Community College (U)
Manatee Community College (U)
Mansfield University of Pennsylvania (U)
Marist College (U,G)
Marshall University (U,G)
Maryville University of Saint Louis (N)
Massasoit Community College (U)
Mayville State University (U)
Mercy College (U)
Mesalands Community College (U)
Metropolitan State University (U)
Miami Dade College (U)
Middlesex Community College (U)
Middle Tennessee State University (U)
Midstate College (U)
Midway College (U)
Minnesota School of Business–Richfield (U)
Minnesota State University Moorhead (U)
Minot State University (U)
Mississippi State University (U)
Missouri Southern State University (U)
Missouri State University (U,G)
Moberly Area Community College (U)
Monroe Community College (U)
Montana State University–Billings (U)
Montgomery County Community College (U)
Mountain Empire Community College (U)
Mountain View College (U)
Mount Saint Vincent University (U)
Mt. San Antonio College (U)

Myers University (U)
Nassau Community College (U)
National University (U,G)
Naugatuck Valley Community College (N,U)
New England College of Finance (N,U)
New Jersey City University (U,G)
New York Institute of Technology (U,G)
North Arkansas College (U)
North Carolina State University (U)
North Dakota State College of Science (U)
Northeast State Technical Community College
  (U)
Northern Virginia Community College (U)
North Harris Montgomery Community
  College District (U)
North Idaho College (N,U)
Northland Community and Technical College–
  Thief River Falls (U)
North Seattle Community College (U)
NorthWest Arkansas Community College (U)
Northwestern Oklahoma State University (U)
Northwest Technical College (U)
Oakton Community College (U)
Odessa College (U)
Oklahoma State University (U)
Old Dominion University (U,G)
Orange Coast College (U)
Oregon Institute of Technology (U)
Owensboro Community and Technical College
  (U)
Pace University (U)
Palomar College (U)
Pamlico Community College (U)
Parkland College (U)
Park University (U)
Patrick Henry Community College (U)
Peirce College (U)
Peninsula College (U)
Pennsylvania College of Technology (U)
Philadelphia University (U,G)
Pittsburg State University (U)
Portland Community College (U)
Prescott College (U)
Pulaski Technical College (U)
Quinnipiac University (U,G)
Radford University (N)
Randolph Community College (N,U)
Rappahannock Community College (U)
Red Rocks Community College (U)
Reedley College (N,U)
Regent University (N,G)
Regis University (U,G)
Rend Lake College (N)
Richland Community College (U)
Riverside Community College District (U)
Roosevelt University (U)
Rose State College (U)
Ryerson University (U)
Sacred Heart University (G)
Saddleback College (U)
St. Clair County Community College (U)
Saint Joseph's College of Maine (U,G)
St. Petersburg College (U)
Sauk Valley Community College (U)
Schenectady County Community College (U)
Schiller International University (U,G)
Schoolcraft College (U)
Seattle Central Community College (U)
Seminole Community College (U)
Shippensburg University of Pennsylvania
  (U,G)
Simpson College (U)

Snead State Community College (U)
Southeastern Community College (U)
Southern New Hampshire University (U,G)
South Piedmont Community College (U)
Southwest Georgia Technical College (U)
Southwest Wisconsin Technical College (U)
Spartanburg Community College (U)
State University of New York at Oswego (G)
State University of New York College at
   Potsdam (N)
State University of New York College of
   Agriculture and Technology at Morrisville
   (U)
State University of New York Empire State
   College (U)
Strayer University (U,G)
Suffolk University (G)
Syracuse University (G)
Tacoma Community College (U)
Taylor University (N)
Tennessee Technological University (N)
Texas A&M University–Commerce (G)
Texas A&M University–Texarkana (U,G)
Texas Tech University (U)
Three Rivers Community College (U)
Thunderbird School of Global Management
   (G)
Tompkins Cortland Community College (U)
Tri-State University (U)
Triton College (U)
Troy University (U)
Tyler Junior College (N,U)
The University of Alabama (U)
University of Alaska Fairbanks (U)
University of Central Arkansas (U)
University of Central Missouri (N)
University of Cincinnati (N,U)
University of Colorado at Denver and Health
   Sciences Center (U,G)
University of Dallas (G)
University of Delaware (U)
The University of Findlay (U,G)
University of Hawaii–West Oahu (U)
University of Houston–Victoria (U,G)
University of Idaho (U)
University of Illinois at Chicago (G)
University of Illinois at Springfield (U)
University of Maine (U)
The University of Maine at Augusta (U)
University of Maryland University College
   (U,G)
University of Michigan–Flint (N,U,G)
University of Minnesota, Crookston (U)
University of Minnesota, Twin Cities Campus
   (U)
University of Missouri–Columbia (U)
The University of Montana (U)
University of Nebraska–Lincoln (U,G)
University of North Alabama (U,G)
The University of North Carolina at Chapel
   Hill (U)
The University of North Carolina at Charlotte
   (N)
University of North Dakota (U)
University of Northern Iowa (U)
University of Northwestern Ohio (U)
University of South Alabama (U)
University of Southern Mississippi (U)
The University of Tennessee at Martin (N)
The University of Texas at El Paso (U)
The University of Texas at San Antonio (U)
The University of Texas at Tyler (U)

The University of Texas System (U)
University of Toronto (N,U)
University of Vermont (N)
University of Washington (U)
University of Waterloo (U)
University of Wisconsin–La Crosse (G)
University of Wisconsin–Parkside (G)
University of Wisconsin–Platteville (U,G)
University of Wisconsin–Whitewater (G)
Upper Iowa University (N,U)
Utah State University (U)
Utah Valley State College (U)
Vance-Granville Community College (N,U)
Vincennes University (U)
Virginia Highlands Community College (U)
Virginia Polytechnic Institute and State
   University (G)
Wake Technical Community College (N,U)
Waubonsee Community College (U)
Wayland Baptist University (U,G)
Wayne State College (U,G)
Weber State University (U)
Westchester Community College (U)
Western Piedmont Community College (U)
Western Wyoming Community College (U)
West Hills Community College (N)
West Virginia University at Parkersburg (U)
Westwood Online (U)
Wichita State University (U)
Wilfrid Laurier University (U)
Wilkes Community College (U)
Wisconsin Indianhead Technical College
   (N,U)
York County Community College (U)
York Technical College (U)
York University (U)
Youngstown State University (N)

AEROSPACE, AERONAUTICAL AND ASTRONAUTICAL ENGINEERING

Auburn University (G)
Embry-Riddle Aeronautical University (U)
Georgia Institute of Technology (N,G)
Indiana State University (U)
Middle Tennessee State University (U,G)
New Mexico Institute of Mining and
   Technology (U,G)
North Dakota State University (N)
Old Dominion University (G)
Portland Community College (U)
St. Cloud State University (U)
The University of Alabama (G)
University of Colorado at Boulder (N,G)
University of Colorado at Colorado Springs
   (G)
The University of Texas at Arlington (G)
Utah Valley State College (U,G)
Virginia Polytechnic Institute and State
   University (G)

AGRICULTURAL AND DOMESTIC ANIMAL SERVICES

Central Wyoming College (N)
Kansas State University (U)
Missouri State University (U,G)
North Carolina State University (U)
Spoon River College (U)
Treasure Valley Community College (U)
University of Maryland Eastern Shore (U)

AGRICULTURAL AND FOOD PRODUCTS PROCESSING

Kansas State University (N,U,G)
North Carolina State University (U,G)
NorthWest Arkansas Community College (U)
Sampson Community College (U)
University of Arkansas (G)
University of Minnesota, Crookston (U)
University of Missouri–Columbia (U,G)
Wisconsin Indianhead Technical College
   (N,U)

AGRICULTURAL BUSINESS AND MANAGEMENT

Arkansas State University–Beebe (U)
Arkansas Tech University (U)
Athabasca University (G)
Clark State Community College (U)
Dawson Community College (U)
Dickinson State University (U)
Eastern Oregon University (U)
Iowa State University of Science and
   Technology (G)
James Sprunt Community College (U)
Kansas State University (U,G)
Mesalands Community College (U)
Middle Tennessee State University (U)
Missouri State University (U)
Murray State University (U)
North Arkansas College (U)
Nova Scotia Agricultural College (U)
Oregon State University (U)
Parkland College (U)
Sam Houston State University (U)
Southern Illinois University Carbondale (U)
State University of New York College of
   Agriculture and Technology at Morrisville
   (U)
Texas Tech University (U)
The University of British Columbia (U)
University of Idaho (U)
University of Missouri–Columbia (N,U,G)
University of Nebraska–Lincoln (U,G)
University of Northwestern Ohio (U)
University of Saskatchewan (N,U)
The University of Tennessee (U)
Wisconsin Indianhead Technical College
   (N,U)
Yuba College (U)

AGRICULTURAL MECHANIZATION

Southern Illinois University Carbondale (U)

AGRICULTURAL PRODUCTION

Colorado State University (U)
Kansas State University (U)
North Arkansas College (U)
North Carolina State University (U)
Nova Scotia Agricultural College (U)
Sampson Community College (U)
Texas A&M University–Commerce (U)
Treasure Valley Community College (U)

AGRICULTURAL PUBLIC SERVICES

Kansas State University (G)

AGRICULTURAL/BIOLOGICAL ENGINEERING AND BIOENGINEERING

New Mexico Junior College (U)
University of Idaho (U,G)
University of Missouri–Columbia (U)

AGRICULTURE

Auburn University (U)
Bismarck State College (U)
California State University, Chico (U)
Central Carolina Community College (U)
Clemson University (G)
Colorado State University (U,G)
County College of Morris (U)
Dawson Community College (U)
Iowa State University of Science and
  Technology (U)
Itawamba Community College (U)
Kansas State University (N,U,G)
Mississippi State University (G)
Murray State University (U)
North Carolina State University (U,G)
NorthWest Arkansas Community College (U)
Nova Scotia Agricultural College (N,U)
Oregon State University (U)
Rend Lake College (U)
Saybrook Graduate School and Research
  Center (G)
Southern Illinois University Carbondale (U)
State University of New York College of
  Agriculture and Technology at Morrisville
  (U)
Texas A&M University–Commerce (G)
Texas Tech University (U,G)
Three Rivers Community College (U)
The University of Arizona (U)
The University of British Columbia (U)
University of Illinois (G)
University of Minnesota, Twin Cities Campus
  (U)
University of Saskatchewan (U)
University of Wyoming (U)
Virginia Polytechnic Institute and State
  University (U)
Wisconsin Indianhead Technical College
  (N,U)

AGRICULTURE AND AGRICULTURE OPERATIONS RELATED

James Sprunt Community College (U)
Kansas State University (U,G)
Murray State University (U)
North Carolina State University (G)
Oregon State University (U)
Sampson Community College (U)
Treasure Valley Community College (U)
University of California, Riverside (N)
University of Maryland Eastern Shore (U)
University of Massachusetts Boston (N)
University of Saskatchewan (N)
Utah State University (G)
Virginia Polytechnic Institute and State
  University (U,G)
Yuba College (U)

AIR FORCE J.R.O.T.C/R.O.T.C

California State University, San Bernardino
  (U)

AIR TRANSPORTATION

Central Wyoming College (N)
Community College of Beaver County (U)
Elizabeth City State University (U)
Embry-Riddle Aeronautical University (N,G)
South Suburban College (U)
University of Nebraska at Omaha (G)
Utah Valley State College (U)
Western Michigan University (U)
West Los Angeles College (U)

ALLIED HEALTH AND MEDICAL ASSISTING SERVICES

Anne Arundel Community College (U)
Arapahoe Community College (U)
Bainbridge College (N)
Big Bend Community College (U)
Blackhawk Technical College (U)
Brenau University (U)
Bridgewater State College (N)
Butler Community College (U)
Butler County Community College (U)
Cabrillo College (U)
California State University, San Bernardino
  (U)
California State University, San Marcos (U)
Central Georgia Technical College (U)
Central Michigan University (U)
Central Oregon Community College (U)
Central Texas College (U)
Chattanooga State Technical Community
  College (U)
Chemeketa Community College (U)
Chesapeake College (U)
Cincinnati State Technical and Community
  College (U)
Clackamas Community College (U)
Clark State Community College (U)
Clemson University (N)
Cloud County Community College (U)
Columbus State Community College (U)
Danville Community College (U)
Darton College (U)
De Anza College (U)
East Central Community College (U)
East Tennessee State University (N)
Elgin Community College (U)
Everest College (U)
Everett Community College (U)
Feather River College (U)
Flathead Valley Community College (U)
Galveston College (U)
Gaston College (U)
Georgia Highlands College (U)
Hagerstown Community College (N)
Harrisburg Area Community College (U)
Hocking College (U)
Ilisagvik College (U)
Itawamba Community College (U)
James Sprunt Community College (U)
Jones College (U)
Lamar State College–Port Arthur (N)
Lock Haven University of Pennsylvania (N)
Longwood University (N)
Mesalands Community College (U)

Middle Tennessee State University (N)
Midstate College (U)
Minot State University–Bottineau Campus (U)
Montgomery Community College (N)
National University (U)
New Mexico Junior College (U)
North Central State College (U)
North Dakota State College of Science (U)
North Dakota State University (N)
North Idaho College (N,U)
Northwestern Connecticut Community College
  (U)
Northwest Technical College (U)
Odessa College (U)
Orangeburg-Calhoun Technical College (U)
Orange Coast College (U)
Pamlico Community College (U)
Peninsula College (U)
Plymouth State University (N)
Portland Community College (U)
Pulaski Technical College (U)
Quinebaug Valley Community College (N)
Randolph Community College (N,U)
Rappahannock Community College (U)
The Richard Stockton College of New Jersey
  (U,G)
Rose State College (U)
Schoolcraft College (U)
South Piedmont Community College (U)
Southwest Wisconsin Technical College (U)
Tacoma Community College (U)
Texas State University-San Marcos (U)
Three Rivers Community College (N,U)
University of Alaska Anchorage, Kodiak
  College (U)
University of California, Davis (N,U)
University of Northwestern Ohio (U)
The University of Texas System (N,G)
The University of Toledo (U)
Vincennes University (U)
Virginia Highlands Community College (U)
Wake Technical Community College (U)
Western Piedmont Community College (U)
West Los Angeles College (U)
Wharton County Junior College (U)
Youngstown State University (N)

ALLIED HEALTH DIAGNOSTIC, INTERVENTION, AND TREATMENT PROFESSIONS

Arapahoe Community College (U)
Brenau University (G)
California State University, San Bernardino
  (G)
Columbus State Community College (U)
Danville Community College (U)
Darton College (U)
Eastern Kentucky University (G)
Eastern Washington University (N)
East Tennessee State University (U)
James Madison University (N)
James Sprunt Community College (U)
Jefferson College of Health Sciences (N,U)
Jefferson Community and Technical College
  (U)
John A. Logan College (U)
Kean University (U)
Labette Community College (U)
Lamar State College–Port Arthur (N)
North Idaho College (N)
NorthWest Arkansas Community College (U)

Oregon Institute of Technology (U)
Radford University (G)
Randolph Community College (N)
Rose State College (U)
Saybrook Graduate School and Research
  Center (G)
South Piedmont Community College (U)
Tacoma Community College (U)
University of Michigan–Flint (U)
University of Minnesota, Twin Cities Campus
  (U)
University of the Sciences in Philadelphia (G)
University of West Florida (G)
Virginia Highlands Community College (U)
Washburn University (U)

ALTERNATIVE AND COMPLEMENTARY MEDICAL SUPPORT SERVICES

Arapahoe Community College (U)
Atlantic University (N,G)
DePaul University (N)
Drexel University (G)
East Tennessee State University (N)
Lamar State College–Port Arthur (N)
Rose State College (U)
Saybrook Graduate School and Research
  Center (G)
Treasure Valley Community College (U)

ALTERNATIVE AND COMPLEMENTARY MEDICINE AND MEDICAL SYSTEMS

Arapahoe Community College (U)
Atlantic University (N,G)
California State University, Dominguez Hills
  (N)
Drexel University (G)
Lamar State College–Port Arthur (N)
North Idaho College (N)
Rose State College (U)
Saybrook Graduate School and Research
  Center (G)

AMERICAN LITERATURE (UNITED STATES AND CANADIAN)

Alvin Community College (U)
Arapahoe Community College (U)
Ashford University (U)
Bellevue Community College (U)
Bellevue University (U)
Bergen Community College (U)
Berkeley College (U)
Berkeley College-New York City Campus (U)
Berkeley College-Westchester Campus (U)
Bowling Green State University (U,G)
Brenau University (U)
Brookdale Community College (U)
California State University, San Bernardino
  (U)
Campbell University (U)
Central Carolina Community College (U)
Central Texas College (U)
Charter Oak State College (U)
Chattanooga State Technical Community
  College (U)
Chemeketa Community College (U)
Chesapeake College (U)

Columbia College (U)
Columbus State Community College (U)
Community College of Beaver County (U)
Dallas Baptist University (U)
Darton College (U)
Dawson Community College (U)
Delaware County Community College (U)
Delta College (U)
Des Moines Area Community College (U)
Dickinson State University (U)
D'Youville College (U)
East Central Community College (U)
Elizabethtown College (U)
Everett Community College (U)
Galveston College (U)
Gaston College (U)
Harrisburg Area Community College (U)
Hillsborough Community College (U)
Houston Community College System (U)
Itawamba Community College (U)
Jacksonville State University (U)
James Madison University (N)
Jefferson Community College (U)
John Jay College of Criminal Justice of the
  City University of New York (U)
John Tyler Community College (U)
Jones County Junior College (U)
J. Sargeant Reynolds Community College (U)
Kansas City Kansas Community College (U)
Lamar State College–Port Arthur (N)
Lehigh Carbon Community College (U)
Limestone College (U)
Linn-Benton Community College (U)
Longwood University (U)
Manatee Community College (U)
Maranatha Baptist Bible College (U)
Mercy College (G)
Miami Dade College (U)
Middle Tennessee State University (U)
Minot State University (U)
Mississippi University for Women (U)
Monroe Community College (U)
Monterey Peninsula College (U)
Montgomery Community College (U)
Mount Allison University (U)
Myers University (U)
New England College of Finance (U)
New Mexico Junior College (U)
North Carolina State University (U)
Northeast Alabama Community College (U)
North Idaho College (N,U)
Northwest Mississippi Community College
  (U)
Oakton Community College (U)
Oklahoma State University (U)
Oregon State University (U)
Pace University (U)
Pamlico Community College (U)
Park University (U)
Peninsula College (U)
Piedmont Technical College (U)
Pulaski Technical College (U)
Rappahannock Community College (U)
Rose State College (U)
St. Cloud State University (U)
St. Louis Community College System (U)
St. Petersburg College (U)
Schoolcraft College (U)
Snead State Community College (U)
Southern Illinois University Carbondale (U)
State University of New York at New Paltz
  (U)

Tacoma Community College (U)
Taylor University (U)
Texas State University-San Marcos (U)
Texas Tech University (U)
Three Rivers Community College (U)
Tyler Junior College (U)
The University of Alabama (U)
University of Alaska Fairbanks (U)
University of Central Arkansas (U)
University of Colorado at Colorado Springs
  (U)
University of Colorado at Denver and Health
  Sciences Center (U)
University of Great Falls (U)
The University of Maine at Augusta (U)
University of Missouri–Columbia (U)
University of New Orleans (U,G)
University of South Carolina Sumter (U)
The University of Tennessee (U)
University of Washington (U)
University of Waterloo (U)
University of Wisconsin–Superior (U)
University of Wyoming (U)
Utah Valley State College (U)
Vance-Granville Community College (U)
Virginia Highlands Community College (U)
Wake Technical Community College (U)
Washburn University (U)
Waubonsee Community College (U)
Westchester Community College (U)
West Los Angeles College (U)
West Shore Community College (U)
Wharton County Junior College (U)
Wilfrid Laurier University (U)
Wilkes Community College (U)
York County Community College (U)
Youngstown State University (N)

AMERICAN SIGN LANGUAGE (ASL)

Arapahoe Community College (U)
Chattanooga State Technical Community
  College (U)
Erie Community College (U)
Hillsborough Community College (U)
John A. Logan College (U)
Missouri Southern State University (N)
Palomar College (U)
Presentation College (U)
Saddleback College (U)
University of New Orleans (U,G)

ANIMAL SCIENCES

Auburn University (N,U)
Central Wyoming College (N)
Clemson University (G)
Colorado State University (N,U)
Duquesne University (N)
James Sprunt Community College (U)
Kansas State University (U,G)
Mesalands Community College (U)
Minnesota School of Business–Richfield (U)
Murray State University (U)
North Carolina State University (U)
Nova Scotia Agricultural College (N,U)
Oklahoma State University (U)
Plymouth State University (N)
Sampson Community College (U)
Texas A&M University–Commerce (U)
Texas Tech University (G)

The University of British Columbia (U)
University of Delaware (U)
University of Maine (G)
University of Missouri–Columbia (U,G)
Virginia Polytechnic Institute and State
  University (N)
Yuba College (U)

ANTHROPOLOGY

Alvin Community College (U)
Arapahoe Community College (U)
Athabasca University (N,U)
Bellevue Community College (U)
Bemidji State University (U)
Bergen Community College (U)
Berkeley College (U)
Berkeley College-New York City Campus (U)
Berkeley College-Westchester Campus (U)
Big Bend Community College (U)
Boise State University (U)
Brenau University (U)
Bridgewater State College (U)
Brookdale Community College (U)
Broome Community College (U)
Burlington County College (U)
Cabrillo College (U)
Casper College (U)
Cayuga County Community College (U)
Cedarville University (U)
Central Texas College (U)
Central Wyoming College (U)
Cerritos College (U)
Cerro Coso Community College (U)
Chaminade University of Honolulu (U)
Chemeketa Community College (U)
Clatsop Community College (U)
College of DuPage (U)
College of San Mateo (U)
Colorado Mountain College District System
  (U)
Colorado State University (U)
Colorado State University-Pueblo (U)
Columbia College (U)
Columbia International University (N,G)
Columbus State Community College (U)
Community College of Denver (U)
Connecticut State University System (U,G)
Cumberland County College (U)
Dawson Community College (U)
De Anza College (U)
Delaware County Community College (U)
Des Moines Area Community College (U)
Eastern Kentucky University (U)
Eastern Oregon University (U)
Edison State Community College (U)
EduKan (U)
Elgin Community College (U)
Erie Community College (U)
Everett Community College (U)
Feather River College (U)
Flathead Valley Community College (U)
Governors State University (U,G)
Harrisburg Area Community College (U)
Haywood Community College (U)
Henry Ford Community College (U)
Honolulu Community College (U)
Houston Community College System (U)
Indiana University of Pennsylvania (U)
Jacksonville State University (U)
John Jay College of Criminal Justice of the
  City University of New York (U)

John Wood Community College (U)
Kansas City Kansas Community College (U)
Kellogg Community College (U)
Kirkwood Community College (U)
Lake Superior College (U)
Long Beach City College (U)
Louisiana State University and Agricultural
  and Mechanical College (U)
Manatee Community College (U)
Massasoit Community College (U)
Memorial University of Newfoundland (U)
Metropolitan State University (U)
Middlesex Community College (U)
Minnesota State University Moorhead (U)
Minot State University (U)
Missouri State University (U)
Modesto Junior College (U)
Montgomery County Community College (U)
Mount Allison University (U)
Mt. San Antonio College (U)
Murray State University (U)
Nassau Community College (U)
New York Institute of Technology (U)
North Arkansas College (U)
North Carolina State University (U)
North Idaho College (U)
North Seattle Community College (U)
Oakton Community College (U)
Oklahoma State University (U)
Orange Coast College (U)
Oregon Institute of Technology (U)
Oregon State University (U)
Pace University (U)
Palomar College (U)
Parkland College (U)
Peninsula College (U)
Portland Community College (U)
Pulaski Technical College (U)
Quinebaug Valley Community College (U)
Red Rocks Community College (U)
Regis University (G)
Rend Lake College (U)
The Richard Stockton College of New Jersey
  (U)
Riverside Community College District (U)
Rochester Institute of Technology (U)
Rockland Community College (U)
Saddleback College (U)
St. Cloud State University (U)
St. Petersburg College (U)
Sam Houston State University (U)
Schoolcraft College (U)
Seattle Central Community College (U)
Seminole Community College (U)
Southeast Arkansas College (U)
State University of New York at New Paltz
  (U)
State University of New York at Oswego
  (U,G)
State University of New York at Plattsburgh
  (U)
State University of New York College at
  Potsdam (U)
Syracuse University (G)
Tacoma Community College (U)
Texas Tech University (U)
Triton College (U)
Tunxis Community College (U)
University of Alaska Fairbanks (U)
University of Cincinnati (U)
University of Colorado at Denver and Health
  Sciences Center (U)

University of Hawaii–West Oahu (U)
University of Houston–Victoria (U,G)
University of Idaho (U)
University of Illinois (U)
University of La Verne (G)
University of Maine (G)
The University of Maine at Augusta (U)
University of Maine at Fort Kent (U)
University of Maryland University College
  (U)
University of Massachusetts Boston (U)
University of Massachusetts Dartmouth (U)
University of Missouri–Columbia (U)
The University of Montana (U,G)
University of New Orleans (U,G)
The University of North Carolina at Chapel
  Hill (U)
The University of North Carolina at
  Greensboro (U)
University of North Dakota (U)
University of North Texas (U,G)
University of Oklahoma (U)
University of Saskatchewan (U)
University of Southern Mississippi (U)
University of South Florida (U)
The University of Tennessee (U)
The University of Texas at El Paso (U)
The University of Texas at San Antonio (U)
The University of Texas at Tyler (U)
University of Vermont (U)
University of Washington (U)
University of Waterloo (U)
University of West Florida (U)
University of Wisconsin Colleges (U)
University of Wisconsin–Whitewater (U)
Utah State University (U)
Utah Valley State College (U)
Wake Technical Community College (U)
Weber State University (U)
Westchester Community College (U)
Western Michigan University (U)
Western Wyoming Community College (U)
West Valley College (U)
Wichita State University (U)
Wilfrid Laurier University (U)
Yuba College (U)

APPAREL AND TEXTILES

Academy of Art University (U,G)
Arapahoe Community College (U)
Blackhawk Technical College (N)
Drexel University (U)
Kansas State University (G)
Missouri State University (U)
Nassau Community College (U)
North Carolina State University (U)
NorthWest Arkansas Community College (U)
Orange Coast College (U)
Philadelphia University (G)
Rose State College (U)
University of Delaware (U)
University of Nebraska–Lincoln (G)
University of North Texas (U,G)
Virginia Polytechnic Institute and State
  University (U)
Western Michigan University (U)

APPLIED HORTICULTURE/ HORTICULTURAL BUSINESS SERVICES

Central Wyoming College (N)

Cincinnati State Technical and Community College (U)
Clark State Community College (U)
County College of Morris (U)
Haywood Community College (U)
Kansas State University (U)
Minot State University–Bottineau Campus (U)
Oklahoma State University (U)
Texas Tech University (U)
University of California, Riverside (N)
University of Minnesota, Twin Cities Campus (U)
University of Saskatchewan (N)
Virginia Polytechnic Institute and State University (N,U,G)
West Hills Community College (N)

APPLIED MATHEMATICS

Alvin Community College (U)
Anne Arundel Community College (U)
Arapahoe Community College (U)
Bainbridge College (U)
Bowling Green State University (U)
Butler Community College (U)
Butler County Community College (U)
California State University, San Marcos (U)
California University of Pennsylvania (U)
Central Georgia Technical College (U)
Central Texas College (U)
Central Virginia Community College (U)
Chadron State College (U)
Chemeketa Community College (U)
Clinton Community College (U)
Columbia University (N,G)
The Community College of Baltimore County (U)
County College of Morris (U)
Darton College (U)
Des Moines Area Community College (U)
Eastern Michigan University (U)
Embry-Riddle Aeronautical University (U)
Eugene Bible College (U)
Everett Community College (U)
Georgia Institute of Technology (G)
Harrisburg Area Community College (U)
Henry Ford Community College (U)
Hillsborough Community College (U)
Itawamba Community College (U)
Jacksonville State University (U)
James Madison University (N)
Linn-Benton Community College (U)
Lock Haven University of Pennsylvania (U)
Manatee Community College (U)
Midstate College (U)
Myers University (U)
North Dakota State College of Science (U)
North Dakota State University (U)
North Idaho College (N)
NorthWest Arkansas Community College (U)
Northwest Mississippi Community College (U)
Northwest Technical College (U)
Oakton Community College (U)
Pamlico Community College (U)
Pulaski Technical College (U)
Red Rocks Community College (U)
The Richard Stockton College of New Jersey (U)
Seminole Community College (U)
Snead State Community College (U)
Southeast Arkansas College (U)

South Piedmont Community College (U)
Southwest Georgia Technical College (U)
Southwest Wisconsin Technical College (U)
Spartanburg Community College (U)
Tacoma Community College (U)
Taylor University (N)
University of Alaska Fairbanks (U)
University of Idaho (G)
The University of Maine at Augusta (U)
University of Management and Technology (U)
University of New Orleans (U,G)
The University of Tennessee (U)
University of Washington (U)
University of Waterloo (U)
Utah State University (U)
Vincennes University (U)
Virginia Highlands Community College (U)
Western Wyoming Community College (U)
West Los Angeles College (U)
Wisconsin Indianhead Technical College (N,U)
York County Community College (U)
Yuba College (U)

ARCHEOLOGY

Alvin Community College (U)
Bellevue Community College (U)
Chemeketa Community College (U)
James Madison University (N)
Northwestern College (U)
Palomar College (U)
St. Petersburg College (U)
State University of New York at Oswego (U)
University of California, Los Angeles (G)
University of Massachusetts Boston (U)
University of Saskatchewan (U)
University of South Florida (U)
The University of Texas at Tyler (U)
University of Washington (U)
University of West Florida (U)

ARCHITECTURAL ENGINEERING

Boston Architectural College (N,U,G)
Georgia Institute of Technology (G)
Sinclair Community College (U)
University of New Orleans (U,G)

ARCHITECTURAL ENGINEERING TECHNOLOGY

Boston Architectural College (N,U,G)
Honolulu Community College (U)
Nashville State Technical Community College (U)
University of New Orleans (U,G)

ARCHITECTURAL TECHNOLOGY

Boston Architectural College (N,U,G)

ARCHITECTURE

Boston Architectural College (N,U,G)
James Madison University (N)
Lansing Community College (U)
Louisiana Tech University (U)
Orange Coast College (U)
Pennsylvania College of Technology (U)
Riverside Community College District (U)

Texas Tech University (G)
Triton College (U)
University of Colorado at Denver and Health Sciences Center (G)
The University of North Carolina at Charlotte (N)
Virginia Polytechnic Institute and State University (N)

ARCHITECTURE RELATED

Arapahoe Community College (U)
Boston Architectural College (N,U,G)
Central Michigan University (U)
Georgia Institute of Technology (G)
Hopkinsville Community College (U)
Lawrence Technological University (U)

AREA STUDIES

American Public University System (U)
Andrews University (U)
California Institute of Integral Studies (N,G)
Connecticut State University System (U,G)
De Anza College (U)
Delaware County Community College (U)
Naropa University (N)
Oakton Community College (U)
St. Petersburg College (U)
Taylor University (U)
Triton College (U)
The University of British Columbia (U)
University of Maine (U)
University of Maryland University College (U)
University of Nebraska–Lincoln (U)
University of North Alabama (U,G)
The University of North Carolina at Chapel Hill (U)
University of Northern Iowa (U)
University of South Florida (U)
University of Waterloo (U)
Western Michigan University (U)

AREA, ETHNIC, CULTURAL, AND GENDER STUDIES RELATED

Allen College (U)
Arapahoe Community College (U)
Berkeley College (U)
Berkeley College-New York City Campus (U)
Berkeley College-Westchester Campus (U)
Bismarck State College (U)
California State University, Chico (U)
California State University, San Bernardino (U)
Central Texas College (U)
Central Wyoming College (N,U)
Chemeketa Community College (U)
Cleveland State University (U,G)
Columbia College (U)
Delaware County Community College (U)
DeVry University Online (U)
Edgecombe Community College (N)
Elizabethtown College (U)
Everett Community College (U)
Jefferson Community and Technical College (U)
Kansas City Kansas Community College (U)
Kansas State University (U)
Mercy College (U)
Middlesex Community College (U)

Middle Tennessee State University (N,U)
Naropa University (N,U,G)
North Idaho College (U)
Oregon State University (U)
Palomar College (U)
Park University (U)
Prescott College (G)
Providence College and Theological Seminary (N,G)
State University of New York at Plattsburgh (U)
Strayer University (U)
Taylor University (U)
Tunxis Community College (U)
University of Bridgeport (U)
University of Colorado at Colorado Springs (U)
University of Connecticut (U)
University of Illinois (U)
University of Minnesota, Duluth (U)
University of Missouri–Columbia (U)
University of New Orleans (U,G)
The University of North Carolina at Chapel Hill (N)
University of South Florida (U)
The University of Toledo (U)
University of Waterloo (U)
University of Wisconsin–Whitewater (U,G)
West Los Angeles College (U)

ARMY J.R.O.T.C/R.O.T.C

Eastern Michigan University (U)
John Wood Community College (U)
Southern Illinois University Carbondale (U)

ASTRONOMY AND ASTROPHYSICS

Adelphi University (U)
Andrews University (U)
Arapahoe Community College (U)
Athabasca University (N,U)
Austin Peay State University (U)
Bellevue Community College (U)
Brenau University (U)
Butler Community College (U)
California State University, San Bernardino (U)
Cascadia Community College (U)
Casper College (U)
Central Virginia Community College (U)
Chemeketa Community College (U)
Clackamas Community College (U)
Clemson University (U)
College of San Mateo (U)
College of Southern Maryland (U)
Colorado Mountain College District System (U)
Columbia College (U)
The Community College of Baltimore County (U)
Community College of Denver (U)
Culver-Stockton College (U)
Delaware County Community College (U)
EduKan (U)
Harrisburg Area Community College (U)
Henry Ford Community College (U)
Hillsborough Community College (U)
Honolulu Community College (U)
Houston Community College System (U)
Illinois Eastern Community Colleges, Lincoln Trail College (U)

James Madison University (N)
John Wood Community College (U)
Judson College (U)
Lake Superior College (U)
Lamar State College–Port Arthur (U)
Lansing Community College (U)
Lehigh Carbon Community College (U)
Lewis and Clark Community College (U)
Limestone College (U)
Long Beach City College (U)
Michigan Technological University (N,U)
Middle Tennessee State University (U)
Missouri State University (U)
Montana State University (G)
Montgomery County Community College (U)
Mountain Empire Community College (U)
Nassau Community College (U)
Northeast State Technical Community College (U)
North Seattle Community College (U)
Northwestern College (U)
Oakton Community College (U)
Parkland College (U)
Peninsula College (U)
Riverside Community College District (U)
St. Clair County Community College (U)
St. Cloud State University (U)
St. Petersburg College (U)
Schenectady County Community College (U)
Schoolcraft College (U)
Seattle Pacific University (G)
Seminole Community College (U)
Triton College (U)
Tyler Junior College (U)
The University of Alabama (U)
University of Maine at Fort Kent (U)
University of Massachusetts Dartmouth (U)
University of Minnesota, Duluth (U)
University of Missouri–Columbia (U)
University of Nebraska at Omaha (U)
The University of North Carolina at Chapel Hill (U)
University of Oklahoma (U)
University of Oregon (U)
The University of Tennessee (U)
University of Washington (U)
University of Waterloo (U)
University of Wisconsin–Superior (U)
University of Wyoming (U)
Upper Iowa University (U)
Utah Valley State College (U)
Wake Technical Community College (U)
Wichita State University (U)
Wilfrid Laurier University (U)
Yuba College (U)

ATMOSPHERIC SCIENCES AND METEOROLOGY

Bellevue Community College (U)
Carroll Community College (U)
Central Wyoming College (U)
Clarion University of Pennsylvania (U)
Dallas Baptist University (U)
Delaware County Community College (U)
Iowa State University of Science and Technology (U,G)
Jacksonville State University (U)
Miami Dade College (U)
Millsville University of Pennsylvania (U)
Mountain Empire Community College (U)
Nassau Community College (U)

Oregon State University (U)
Seminole Community College (U)
Snead State Community College (U)
University of California, Riverside (N)
University of Missouri–Columbia (U)
University of Washington (U)
Utah Valley State College (U)

AUDIOVISUAL COMMUNICATIONS TECHNOLOGIES

Arapahoe Community College (U)
Rose State College (U)
University of Southern Indiana (N)

BEHAVIORAL SCIENCES

Anne Arundel Community College (U)
Arapahoe Community College (U)
Barclay College (U)
Big Bend Community College (U)
Boise State University (U)
Butler Community College (U)
California State University, Chico (U)
Central Georgia Technical College (U)
Central Michigan University (U,G)
Charter Oak State College (U)
Chattanooga State Technical Community College (U)
Chesapeake College (U)
Clark State Community College (U)
Cloud County Community College (U)
Columbia College (U)
Community College of Beaver County (U)
Danville Community College (U)
Des Moines Area Community College (U)
East Tennessee State University (N)
Florida Institute of Technology (N)
Galveston College (U)
Graceland University (U)
Granite State College (U)
Jacksonville State University (U)
Jefferson Community and Technical College (U)
Jefferson Community College (U)
Judson College (U)
Kansas State University (U)
Middlesex Community College (U)
Modesto Junior College (U)
Mount Saint Vincent University (U)
North Central State College (U)
Northeast Alabama Community College (U)
North Harris Montgomery Community College District (U)
North Idaho College (N)
NorthWest Arkansas Community College (U)
Northwest Mississippi Community College (U)
Northwest Technical College (U)
Oakton Community College (U)
Ouachita Technical College (U)
Owensboro Community and Technical College (U)
Palomar College (U)
Pamlico Community College (U)
St. Cloud State University (G)
Sampson Community College (U)
Seminole Community College (U)
Sinclair Community College (U)
South Piedmont Community College (U)
State University of New York College at Potsdam (U)

Tacoma Community College (U)
Taylor University (U)
Texas State University-San Marcos (U)
Union University (U)
University of Connecticut (U)
University of Maine at Fort Kent (U)
University of Management and Technology (U)
University of Massachusetts Lowell (G)
University of Missouri–Columbia (U)
University of New Orleans (U,G)
University of North Texas (N,U,G)
The University of South Dakota (U)
University of West Florida (G)
Utah Valley State College (U)
Westchester Community College (U)
West Los Angeles College (U)
Wharton County Junior College (U)
Yuba College (U)

BIBLICAL AND OTHER THEOLOGICAL LANGUAGES AND LITERATURES

Abilene Christian University (U)
Assemblies of God Theological Seminary (G)
Black Hills State University (U)
Briercrest Distance Learning (U,G)
Cincinnati Christian University (U,G)
College of Emmanuel and St. Chad (G)
Columbia International University (G)
Denver Seminary (G)
Des Moines Area Community College (U)
Earlham School of Religion (G)
Eugene Bible College (U)
Global University of the Assemblies of God (N)
God's Bible School and College (U)
Grand Rapids Theological Seminary of Cornerstone University (N,G)
Hebrew College (N,U,G)
Horizon College & Seminary (U)
Immaculata University (U)
Indiana Wesleyan University (U)
Lamar State College–Port Arthur (U)
Liberty University (U)
Life Pacific College (N)
Lincoln Christian College (N,U,G)
Master's College and Seminary (U)
New Mexico Junior College (U)
Peninsula College (U)
Providence College and Theological Seminary (N,U,G)
Southwestern Baptist Theological Seminary (G)
Taylor University (N,U)
Trinity Episcopal School for Ministry (G)
University of Missouri–Columbia (U)
University of Waterloo (U)
Western Seminary (N,G)

BIBLICAL STUDIES

Abilene Christian University (U,G)
Andover Newton Theological School (N,G)
Andrews University (U)
Arlington Baptist College (N,U)
Assemblies of God Theological Seminary (G)
Atlantic School of Theology (N,G)
Atlantic University (N,G)
Bakke Graduate University of Ministry (G)

The Baptist College of Florida (U)
Barclay College (U)
Briercrest Distance Learning (N,U,G)
Campbell University (U)
Central Carolina Community College (U)
Chattanooga State Technical Community College (U)
Cincinnati Christian University (U,G)
Clear Creek Baptist Bible College (U)
Clovis Community College (U)
College of Emmanuel and St. Chad (G)
Columbia International University (N,U,G)
Concordia College–New York (U)
Corban College (U)
Covenant Theological Seminary (N,G)
Dallas Baptist University (U)
Defiance College (U)
Denver Seminary (G)
Earlham School of Religion (G)
East Central Community College (U)
Eugene Bible College (U)
Global University of the Assemblies of God (N)
God's Bible School and College (U)
Grand Rapids Theological Seminary of Cornerstone University (N,G)
Hebrew College (N,U,G)
Hope International University (N,U,G)
Horizon College & Seminary (U)
Indiana Wesleyan University (U)
Jefferson Community and Technical College (U)
Johnson Bible College (U,G)
Judson College (U)
LeTourneau University (U)
Liberty University (U,G)
Life Pacific College (N,U)
Limestone College (U)
Lincoln Christian College (N,U,G)
Lipscomb University (U,G)
Malone College (U,G)
Maranatha Baptist Bible College (U,G)
Master's College and Seminary (U)
McMurry University (U)
Miami Dade College (U)
Montgomery Community College (N)
Northwest Christian College (U)
Northwestern College (U)
Oral Roberts University (N,U)
Park University (U)
Patrick Henry College (U)
Providence College and Theological Seminary (N,U,G)
Regent University (G)
Saint Joseph's College of Maine (N,U)
St. Petersburg College (U)
Shasta Bible College (N,U)
Snead State Community College (U)
Southwestern Baptist Theological Seminary (U,G)
Summit Pacific College (N,U)
Taylor University (N,U)
Temple Baptist Seminary (N,G)
Trinity Episcopal School for Ministry (N,G)
The University of Findlay (U)
University of Southern Mississippi (U)
University of Waterloo (U)
Viterbo University (U)
Western Seminary (N,G)

BILINGUAL, MULTILINGUAL, AND MULTICULTURAL EDUCATION

California State University, San Bernardino (U)
East Carolina University (U)
Hamline University (G)
Indiana State University (G)
Middle Tennessee State University (N)
Murray State University (G)
Northwestern Oklahoma State University (G)
Pace University (G)
Palomar College (U)
Plymouth State University (U)
Prescott College (U)
Sampson Community College (U)
Seattle Pacific University (G)
Tacoma Community College (U)
Texas Woman's University (G)
University of Alaska Fairbanks (U)

BIOCHEMISTRY, BIOPHYSICS AND MOLECULAR BIOLOGY

Arapahoe Community College (U)
Drake University (U)
Graceland University (U)
Iowa State University of Science and Technology (U,G)
Kansas State University (U)
Peninsula College (U)
State University of New York at Plattsburgh (U)
University of Colorado at Denver and Health Sciences Center (U)
University of Minnesota, Twin Cities Campus (U)
University of Southern Mississippi (G)
University of Waterloo (U)

BIOETHICS/MEDICAL ETHICS

Arapahoe Community College (U)
Cleveland State University (U,G)
Judson College (U)
Lock Haven University of Pennsylvania (U)
University of New Orleans (U)

BIOLOGICAL AND BIOMEDICAL SCIENCES RELATED

Athabasca University (U)
Cabrillo College (U)
Caldwell Community College and Technical Institute (U)
Casper College (U)
Chemeketa Community College (U)
Clark State Community College (U)
Cleveland State University (U)
Columbia College (U)
Columbus State Community College (U)
County College of Morris (U)
Danville Community College (U)
Darton College (U)
DeVry University Online (U)
D'Youville College (G)
EduKan (U)
Erie Community College (U)
Feather River College (U)
Gaston College (U)
George Mason University (G)
Immaculata University (U)

Jacksonville State University (U)
James Madison University (N)
Lewis and Clark Community College (U)
Louisiana Tech University (U)
Miami Dade College (U)
Middlesex Community College (U)
Minot State University–Bottineau Campus (U)
Pennsylvania College of Technology (U)
Quinnipiac University (U)
Schoolcraft College (U)
Snead State Community College (U)
Southern Illinois University Carbondale (U)
South Piedmont Community College (U)
University of Colorado at Colorado Springs (U)
University of New Orleans (U,G)
University of Waterloo (U)
University of West Florida (U)
University of Wyoming (U)

BIOLOGICAL AND PHYSICAL SCIENCES

Anne Arundel Community College (U)
Arkansas State University–Beebe (U)
Athabasca University (U)
Bellevue University (U)
Berkeley College (U)
Berkeley College-New York City Campus (U)
Berkeley College-Westchester Campus (U)
Boise State University (U)
Cabrillo College (U)
Caldwell Community College and Technical Institute (U)
Carl Albert State College (U)
Cascadia Community College (U)
Casper College (U)
Cayuga County Community College (U)
Central Carolina Community College (U)
Chadron State College (U)
Chemeketa Community College (U)
Chesapeake College (U)
Clark State Community College (U)
Clinton Community College (U)
Dallas Baptist University (U)
Delaware County Community College (U)
Des Moines Area Community College (U)
D'Youville College (U,G)
East Central Community College (U)
Eastern Michigan University (U)
EduKan (U)
Eugene Bible College (U)
Flathead Valley Community College (U)
Fort Hays State University (U)
Fullerton College (U)
George C. Wallace Community College (U)
Gulf Coast Community College (U)
Harrisburg Area Community College (U)
Immaculata University (U)
Indiana State University (U)
Jacksonville State University (U)
James Madison University (N)
Judson College (U)
Kansas City Kansas Community College (U)
Kansas State University (U)
Kaskaskia College (U)
Kellogg Community College (U)
Lake Superior College (U)
Lehigh University (G)
Massasoit Community College (U)
Miami Dade College (U)
Middlesex Community College (U)

Midway College (U)
Mississippi State University (U)
Missouri Southern State University (U)
Montana State University (G)
Monterey Peninsula College (U)
National University (U)
North Arkansas College (U)
North Carolina State University (U,G)
North Central State College (U)
Northeast State Technical Community College (U)
Northern State University (U)
North Seattle Community College (U)
Northwestern Connecticut Community College (U)
Northwest Mississippi Community College (U)
Northwest Technical College (U)
Oakton Community College (U)
Ouachita Technical College (U)
Pace University (U)
Pamlico Community College (U)
Patrick Henry Community College (U)
Peninsula College (U)
Quinebaug Valley Community College (U)
Quinnipiac University (U)
Sacred Heart University (U)
St. Louis Community College System (U)
St. Petersburg College (U)
Schoolcraft College (U)
Seminole Community College (U)
Snead State Community College (U)
Southern Illinois University Carbondale (U)
Syracuse University (U)
Tacoma Community College (U)
Taylor University (U)
Texas State University-San Marcos (U)
Troy University (U)
Union University (U)
The University of Alabama (U)
University of Central Oklahoma (U)
University of Great Falls (U)
University of La Verne (G)
University of Massachusetts Boston (G)
University of New Orleans (U,G)
The University of Texas at San Antonio (U)
University of Waterloo (U)
Upper Iowa University (N)
Utah Valley State College (U)
Westchester Community College (U)
Western Wyoming Community College (U)
West Virginia University at Parkersburg (U)
Wright State University (U)
York Technical College (U)

BIOLOGY

Acadia University (U)
Adams State College (G)
Alvin Community College (U)
Arapahoe Community College (U)
Arkansas State University–Beebe (U)
Arkansas State University–Mountain Home (U)
Arkansas Tech University (U)
Athabasca University (N,U)
Bellevue Community College (U)
Bismarck State College (U)
Bowling Green State University (U)
Brookdale Community College (U)
Broome Community College (U)
Burlington County College (U)

Butler County Community College (U)
Caldwell Community College and Technical Institute (U)
California State University, Dominguez Hills (U)
Carlow University (U)
Casper College (U)
Cayuga County Community College (U)
Cedarville University (U)
Central New Mexico Community College (U)
Central Virginia Community College (U)
Central Wyoming College (U)
Chattanooga State Technical Community College (U)
Chemeketa Community College (U)
Clackamas Community College (U)
Clarion University of Pennsylvania (U)
Clark State Community College (U)
Cleveland State University (U)
Clovis Community College (U)
College of DuPage (U)
College of Mount St. Joseph (U)
The College of St. Scholastica (U,G)
College of Southern Maryland (U)
College of The Albemarle (U)
College of the Southwest (U)
Colorado Mountain College District System (U)
Colorado State University (U)
Colorado State University-Pueblo (U)
The Community College of Baltimore County (U)
Community College of Denver (U)
County College of Morris (U)
Culver-Stockton College (U)
Dallas Baptist University (U)
Danville Community College (U)
Dawson Community College (U)
De Anza College (U)
Delaware County Community College (U)
Delta College (U)
Des Moines Area Community College (U)
Dodge City Community College (U)
East Carolina University (U)
Eastern Kentucky University (U)
Eastern Michigan University (U)
Eastern Oregon University (U)
Eastern Wyoming College (U)
Edison State Community College (U)
EduKan (U)
Elizabeth City State University (U)
Eugene Bible College (U)
Everett Community College (U)
Finger Lakes Community College (U)
Fullerton College (U)
Gadsden State Community College (U)
Galveston College (U)
George C. Wallace Community College (U)
Georgia Highlands College (U)
Graceland University (U)
Harford Community College (U)
Herkimer County Community College (U)
Hillsborough Community College (U)
Hopkinsville Community College (U)
Houston Community College System (U)
Immaculata University (U)
Indiana State University (U)
Indiana University–Purdue University Fort Wayne (U)
Iowa State University of Science and Technology (U)

Ivy Tech Community College–North Central (U)
Ivy Tech Community College–Wabash Valley (U)
Jacksonville State University (U,G)
James Madison University (U)
Jefferson Community and Technical College (U)
Jefferson Community College (U)
John A. Logan College (U)
John Tyler Community College (U)
J. Sargeant Reynolds Community College (U)
Kansas City Kansas Community College (U)
Lansing Community College (U)
Lehigh Carbon Community College (U)
LeTourneau University (U)
Lewis and Clark Community College (U)
Liberty University (U)
Limestone College (U)
Long Beach City College (U)
Louisiana State University and Agricultural and Mechanical College (N,U)
Lurleen B. Wallace Community College (U)
Malone College (U)
Manatee Community College (U)
Mayville State University (U)
Memorial University of Newfoundland (U)
Mercy College (U)
Mesa Community College (U)
Mesa State College (U)
Miami Dade College (U)
Middlesex Community College (U)
Minnesota School of Business–Richfield (U)
Mississippi State University (U)
Missouri Southern State University (U)
Moberly Area Community College (U)
Monroe Community College (U)
Montana State University (G)
Montana State University–Billings (U)
Montgomery County Community College (U)
Mountain Empire Community College (U)
Mt. San Antonio College (U)
Mount Wachusett Community College (U)
Nassau Community College (U)
New Mexico Junior College (U)
New York Institute of Technology (U)
North Dakota State College of Science (U)
Northeast Alabama Community College (U)
Northern Virginia Community College (U)
North Harris Montgomery Community College District (U)
North Idaho College (U)
Northland Community and Technical College–Thief River Falls (U)
NorthWest Arkansas Community College (U)
Odessa College (U)
Oral Roberts University (U)
Orange Coast College (U)
Ouachita Technical College (U)
Pace University (U)
Palomar College (U)
Pamlico Community College (U)
Parkland College (U)
Park University (U)
Pasco-Hernando Community College (U)
Patrick Henry College (U)
Pennsylvania College of Technology (U)
Piedmont Technical College (U)
Pittsburg State University (U)
Portland Community College (U)
Pulaski Technical College (U)
Queen's University at Kingston (U)

Rend Lake College (U)
Rockland Community College (U)
Rose State College (U)
St. Cloud State University (U)
St. Petersburg College (U)
Sauk Valley Community College (U)
Schenectady County Community College (U)
Schoolcraft College (U)
Snead State Community College (U)
Southeastern Community College (U)
Southern Illinois University Carbondale (U)
South Piedmont Community College (U)
South Suburban College (U)
Spoon River College (U)
State University of New York at Oswego (U)
State University of New York at Plattsburgh (U)
State University of New York College at Potsdam (U)
State University of New York Empire State College (U)
Tacoma Community College (U)
Taylor University (U)
Texas A&M University–Commerce (U)
Texas Christian University (U)
Texas State University-San Marcos (U)
Three Rivers Community College (U)
Treasure Valley Community College (U)
Triton College (U)
Tyler Junior College (U)
The University of Alabama (U)
University of Alaska Fairbanks (U)
University of Cincinnati Raymond Walters College (U)
University of Colorado at Denver and Health Sciences Center (U)
University of Delaware (U)
University of Houston–Victoria (U)
University of Idaho (U)
University of La Verne (G)
University of Maine (U)
University of Maryland University College (U)
University of Massachusetts Boston (U)
University of Minnesota, Crookston (U)
University of Minnesota, Twin Cities Campus (U)
University of Missouri–Columbia (U)
The University of Montana (U)
University of Nebraska–Lincoln (U)
University of New Orleans (U,G)
The University of North Carolina at Chapel Hill (U)
The University of North Carolina at Charlotte (G)
University of North Texas (U)
University of Pittsburgh at Bradford (U)
The University of South Dakota (U)
University of Southern Indiana (U)
University of Southern Mississippi (U,G)
University of South Florida (U)
The University of Texas at Arlington (U)
The University of Texas at San Antonio (U,G)
The University of Texas at Tyler (U)
The University of Texas System (U)
University of Waterloo (U)
University of West Florida (U)
University of Wisconsin Colleges (U)
University of Wisconsin–Superior (U)
Upper Iowa University (N,U)
Utah State University (U)
Utah Valley State College (U)

Utica College (U)
Vance-Granville Community College (U)
Wake Technical Community College (U)
Washburn University (U)
Waubonsee Community College (U)
Westchester Community College (U)
West Shore Community College (U)
West Virginia University at Parkersburg (U)
Wharton County Junior College (U)
Wilfrid Laurier University (U)
Wilkes Community College (U)
Williston State College (U)
Wright State University (U)
Yuba College (U)

BIOLOGY/BIOTECHNOLOGY LABORATORY TECHNICIAN

Charter Oak State College (U)
Clark State Community College (U)
Delta College (U)
Nashville State Technical Community College (U)
University of Minnesota, Twin Cities Campus (U)

BIOMATHEMATICS AND BIOINFORMATICS

California State University, East Bay (G)
Eastern Michigan University (G)
Wake Technical Community College (U)

BIOMEDICAL/MEDICAL ENGINEERING

California State University, East Bay (U)
Central Carolina Community College (U)
Columbia University (G)
Georgia Institute of Technology (G)
Louisiana Tech University (G)
Stanford University (N)
University of Colorado at Boulder (N,G)
University of South Florida (G)

BIOPSYCHOLOGY

State University of New York at Plattsburgh (U)
University of Minnesota, Twin Cities Campus (U)
Wilfrid Laurier University (U)

BIOTECHNOLOGY

Central Carolina Community College (U)
Eastern Michigan University (U)
Stanford University (N)

BOTANY/PLANT BIOLOGY

Bellevue Community College (U)
Butler County Community College (U)
Central Wyoming College (N)
Eastern Oregon University (U)
Indiana State University (U)
Oregon State University (U)
Palomar College (U)
St. Cloud State University (U)
Tacoma Community College (U)
Texas A&M University–Commerce (U)

University of Saskatchewan (N)
University of Wyoming (U)
West Shore Community College (U)
Wilfrid Laurier University (U)

BUILDING/CONSTRUCTION FINISHING, MANAGEMENT, AND INSPECTION

Athabasca University (N)
Bowling Green State University (G)
Central Georgia Technical College (U)
Central Michigan University (U)
Central New Mexico Community College (U)
Chattanooga State Technical Community
  College (U)
Clackamas Community College (U)
Clemson University (N)
Cleveland Institute of Electronics (N)
East Carolina University (G)
Georgia Institute of Technology (G)
James Madison University (N)
Kansas City Kansas Community College (N)
National University (U)
Pennsylvania College of Technology (U)
Pittsburg State University (U)
Quinebaug Valley Community College (N)
Red Rocks Community College (U)
Southern Polytechnic State University (U)
The University of North Carolina at Charlotte
  (N)
University of North Florida (U)
University of Washington (U,G)
Vance-Granville Community College (N)
Washtenaw Community College (U)
Weber State University (U)

BUSINESS ADMINISTRATION, MANAGEMENT AND OPERATIONS

Acadia University (U)
Adelphi University (U)
Alvin Community College (U)
Amberton University (U,G)
The American College (U,G)
American Graduate University (G)
American Public University System (U)
Andrew Jackson University (U,G)
Anne Arundel Community College (U)
Antioch University McGregor (U,G)
Arapahoe Community College (U)
Argosy University, Chicago Campus (G)
Arkansas State University–Beebe (U)
Arkansas Tech University (U)
Ashford University (U)
Athabasca University (N,U,G)
Auburn University (G)
Bainbridge College (N)
Baker College of Flint (U)
Beaufort County Community College (U)
Bellevue Community College (U)
Bellevue University (U,G)
Bemidji State University (U)
Bergen Community College (U)
Berkeley College (U)
Berkeley College-New York City Campus (U)
Berkeley College-Westchester Campus (U)
Blackhawk Technical College (U)
Black Hills State University (U)
Bloomfield College (U)
Brenau University (U,G)

Bridgewater State College (N)
Bristol Community College (N)
Brookdale Community College (U)
Bryant and Stratton Online (U)
Buena Vista University (U)
Butler County Community College (U)
Caldwell Community College and Technical
  Institute (N,U)
California State University, Monterey Bay (U)
California State University, San Bernardino
  (U)
California State University, San Marcos (U)
California University of Pennsylvania (U)
Campbell University (U)
Cape Cod Community College (U)
Capella University (G)
Cardinal Stritch University (N)
Carl Albert State College (U)
Carroll Community College (N,U)
Cascadia Community College (U)
Casper College (U)
Cayuga County Community College (U)
Central Georgia Technical College (U)
Central Michigan University (U,G)
Central New Mexico Community College (U)
Central Oregon Community College (U)
Central Texas College (U)
Central Washington University (U,G)
Chadron State College (U,G)
Chaminade University of Honolulu (U)
Charter Oak State College (U)
Chattanooga State Technical Community
  College (U)
Chemeketa Community College (U)
Cincinnati State Technical and Community
  College (U)
Clackamas Community College (U)
Clarion University of Pennsylvania (G)
Clark State Community College (U)
Clatsop Community College (U)
Clemson University (G)
Cleveland Institute of Electronics (N)
Cleveland State University (N)
Clinton Community College (U)
Clovis Community College (U)
College of DuPage (U)
College of Mount St. Joseph (U,G)
College of The Albemarle (N,U)
College of the Southwest (U)
Colorado State University (G)
Colorado State University-Pueblo (N,U)
Colorado Technical University (U,G)
Columbia College (U,G)
Columbus State Community College (U)
The Community College of Baltimore County
  (U)
Community College of Beaver County (N,U)
Community College of Denver (U)
Concordia University Wisconsin (G)
Corban College (U)
Culver-Stockton College (U)
Cumberland County College (U)
Dallas Baptist University (U,G)
Danville Community College (U)
Darton College (N,U)
Dawson Community College (U)
Daymar College (U)
De Anza College (U)
Delaware County Community College (U)
Des Moines Area Community College (U)
Dickinson State University (U)
Drake University (U,G)

Drexel University (U,G)
Duquesne University (U,G)
D'Youville College (U)
East Carolina University (U,G)
East Central Community College (U)
Eastern Michigan University (U,G)
Eastern Oklahoma State College (U)
Eastern Washington University (N)
Eastern Wyoming College (U)
East Tennessee State University (N,G)
Edgecombe Community College (N,U)
Edison State Community College (N,U)
Edmonds Community College (U)
Elizabeth City State University (U)
Elizabethtown College (U)
Embry-Riddle Aeronautical University (U,G)
Everest College (U)
Everett Community College (U)
Fayetteville State University (G)
Flathead Valley Community College (U)
Florida Institute of Technology (G)
Fontbonne University (U)
Fort Hays State University (N,U)
Franklin Pierce University (U)
Franklin University (U,G)
Fullerton College (U)
Fulton-Montgomery Community College (N)
Gadsden State Community College (U)
Galveston College (U)
George C. Wallace Community College (U)
Graceland University (U)
Granite State College (U)
Grantham University (U)
Harrisburg Area Community College (U)
Haywood Community College (U)
Herkimer County Community College (U)
Hillsborough Community College (U)
Holyoke Community College (U)
Houston Community College System (U)
Ilisagvik College (U)
Immaculata University (U)
Indiana State University (U)
Indiana Tech (U)
Indiana University–Purdue University Fort
  Wayne (G)
Iona College (U,G)
Itawamba Community College (U)
Ivy Tech Community College–Bloomington
  (U)
Ivy Tech Community College–Columbus (U)
Ivy Tech Community College–East Central
  (U)
Ivy Tech Community College–Northwest (U)
Ivy Tech Community College–Southeast (U)
Ivy Tech Community College–Southern
  Indiana (U)
Ivy Tech Community College–Southwest (U)
Ivy Tech Community College–Wabash Valley
  (U)
Ivy Tech Community College–Whitewater (U)
Jacksonville State University (U,G)
James Madison University (G)
James Sprunt Community College (U)
Jamestown Community College (N)
Jefferson College of Health Sciences (U)
Jefferson Community and Technical College
  (U)
Jefferson Community College (U)
John A. Logan College (U)
John Tyler Community College (U)
John Wood Community College (U)
Jones College (U)

J. Sargeant Reynolds Community College (U)
Judson College (U)
Kansas City Kansas Community College (U)
Kansas State University (U)
Kaplan University (N)
Kaskaskia College (U)
Kean University (N)
Kettering University (N)
Kirkwood Community College (U)
Lackawanna College (U)
Lakeland College (G)
Lamar State College–Port Arthur (N,U)
Lawrence Technological University (U,G)
Lehigh Carbon Community College (U)
Lehigh University (N,G)
Lewis and Clark Community College (U)
Lewis-Clark State College (U)
Liberty University (G)
Limestone College (U)
Linn-Benton Community College (U)
Lipscomb University (G)
Long Beach City College (U)
Longwood University (N)
Louisiana State University and Agricultural
   and Mechanical College (U)
Madison Area Technical College (U)
Malone College (U)
Manatee Community College (U)
Mansfield University of Pennsylvania (U)
Marian College of Fond du Lac (U)
Marist College (G)
Marlboro College (U,G)
Marshall University (U)
Marymount University (G)
Maryville University of Saint Louis (N)
Massasoit Community College (U)
Mayville State University (U)
McMurry University (U)
Memorial University of Newfoundland (U)
Mercy College (U,G)
Mesa Community College (U)
Metropolitan State University (U,G)
Miami Dade College (U)
Miami University–Middletown Campus (U)
Middlesex Community College (U,N,U)
Middle Tennessee State University (N,U)
Mid-State Technical College (U)
Millersville University of Pennsylvania (U,G)
Milwaukee School of Engineering (G)
Minnesota School of Business–Richfield
   (U,G)
Minot State University (G)
Mississippi State University (G)
Moberly Area Community College (U)
Montana State University–Billings (U)
Montgomery Community College (N,U)
Montgomery County Community College (U)
Mt. San Antonio College (U)
Mount Wachusett Community College (U)
Murray State University (U)
Myers University (U,G)
Nassau Community College (U)
National University (U,G)
Naugatuck Valley Community College (U)
New England College of Finance (N,U)
New Jersey City University (U)
New Jersey Institute of Technology (G)
New Mexico Junior College (U)
New Mexico State University (U)
New York Institute of Technology (U,G)
North Central State College (U)
North Dakota State College of Science (U)

Northeast Alabama Community College (U)
Northeastern Illinois University (U)
Northeast State Technical Community College
   (U)
North Harris Montgomery Community
   College District (U)
North Idaho College (N)
Northland Community and Technical College–
   Thief River Falls (U)
NorthWest Arkansas Community College (U)
Northwestern Oklahoma State University
   (U,G)
Northwest Technical College (U)
Odessa College (N)
The Ohio State University (G)
Oklahoma State University (U)
Oregon Institute of Technology (U)
Ouachita Technical College (U)
Owensboro Community and Technical College
   (U)
Pace University (U,G)
Palomar College (U)
Pamlico Community College (U)
Park University (U,G)
Pasco-Hernando Community College (U)
Patrick Henry Community College (U)
Peirce College (U)
Peninsula College (U)
Philadelphia University (U)
Piedmont Technical College (U)
Plymouth State University (N,U)
Portland Community College (U)
Prescott College (U)
Quinnipiac University (U)
Radford University (N,G)
Rappahannock Community College (U)
Reedley College (N,U)
Regent University (N,U,G)
Regis University (U)
Rend Lake College (N)
The Richard Stockton College of New Jersey
   (U)
Riverside Community College District (N,U)
Rochester Institute of Technology (U)
Rogers State University (U)
Roosevelt University (U)
Rose State College (U)
Ryerson University (U)
Sacred Heart University (U,G)
St. Clair County Community College (U)
St. John's University (U)
Saint Joseph's College of Maine (U,G)
St. Louis Community College System (N)
Saint Paul College–A Community &
   Technical College (U)
St. Petersburg College (U)
Sampson Community College (U)
Sauk Valley Community College (U)
Saybrook Graduate School and Research
   Center (N,G)
Schenectady County Community College (U)
Schiller International University (U,G)
Seminole Community College (U)
Shippensburg University of Pennsylvania (G)
Sinclair Community College (U)
Sonoma State University (N)
Southeast Arkansas College (U)
Southeastern Community College (U)
Southern New Hampshire University (U,G)
South Piedmont Community College (U)
Southwestern College (G)
Spartanburg Community College (U)

Spring Arbor University (U,G)
Stanford University (N)
State University of New York at Oswego
   (U,G)
State University of New York at Plattsburgh
   (U,G)
State University of New York College at
   Potsdam (N,U)
Syracuse University (U,G)
Tacoma Community College (N)
Taylor University (N,U)
Texas A&M University–Commerce (U)
Texas A&M University–Texarkana (U,G)
Texas Tech University (N,U)
Texas Woman's University (U,G)
Thomas College (U)
Three Rivers Community College (U)
Thunderbird School of Global Management
   (N,G)
Treasure Valley Community College (U)
Tri-State University (U)
Troy University (U)
Tunxis Community College (U)
Tyler Junior College (N,U)
United States Sports Academy (G)
University of Alaska Fairbanks (U)
University of California, Los Angeles (G)
University of Central Arkansas (N)
University of Cincinnati Raymond Walters
   College (U)
University of Colorado at Denver and Health
   Sciences Center (G)
University of Dallas (G)
University of Denver (G)
The University of Findlay (U,G)
University of Hawaii–West Oahu (U)
University of Idaho (G)
University of Illinois (U,G)
University of Illinois at Chicago (N,G)
University of Illinois at Springfield (U)
The University of Maine at Augusta (U)
University of Management and Technology
   (U,G)
University of Maryland University College
   (U,G)
University of Massachusetts Boston (U)
University of Michigan–Flint (N,G)
University of Minnesota, Crookston (U)
University of Minnesota, Twin Cities Campus
   (U)
University of Missouri–Columbia (U)
The University of Montana (G)
University of Nebraska–Lincoln (U,G)
University of New Orleans (U,G)
University of North Alabama (G)
The University of North Carolina at Chapel
   Hill (U)
The University of North Carolina at Charlotte
   (N)
The University of North Carolina at
   Greensboro (N)
University of North Dakota (U,G)
University of North Texas (N,U,G)
University of Northwestern Ohio (U)
University of Oklahoma (U)
University of St. Francis (U,G)
University of South Alabama (G)
University of South Carolina Sumter (G)
University of South Florida (N,G)
The University of Tennessee (U)
The University of Tennessee at Martin (N)
The University of Texas at San Antonio (U,G)

The University of Texas at Tyler (G)
University of Toronto (N,U)
University of Vermont (N)
The University of Virginia's College at Wise (U)
University of Washington (N)
University of West Florida (G)
University of Wisconsin–La Crosse (G)
University of Wisconsin–Parkside (G)
University of Wisconsin–Platteville (U,G)
University of Wisconsin–Stout (G)
University of Wisconsin–Superior (U)
University of Wisconsin–Whitewater (U,G)
University of Wyoming (G)
Upper Iowa University (U)
Utah State University (U,G)
Utah Valley State College (U)
Vance-Granville Community College (U)
Virginia Polytechnic Institute and State University (N)
Viterbo University (G)
Wake Technical Community College (N)
Walden University (U,G)
Washtenaw Community College (U)
Waubonsee Community College (U)
Wayland Baptist University (U,G)
Wayne State College (U,G)
Weber State University (U)
Wenatchee Valley College (N)
Western Piedmont Community College (U)
Western Wyoming Community College (U)
West Liberty State College (U)
West Los Angeles College (U)
West Shore Community College (U)
West Valley College (U)
West Virginia State University (U)
West Virginia University at Parkersburg (U)
Westwood Online (U)
Wharton County Junior College (U)
Wilkes Community College (U)
Wisconsin Indianhead Technical College (N,U)
Worcester Polytechnic Institute (G)
York County Community College (U)
York Technical College (U)
York University (U)
Youngstown State University (N)

BUSINESS OPERATIONS SUPPORT AND ASSISTANT SERVICES

Alvin Community College (N,U)
Ashford University (U,G)
Athabasca University (N)
Bainbridge College (U)
Bellevue Community College (U)
Blackhawk Technical College (N,U)
Bridgewater State College (N)
Bristol Community College (N)
Caldwell Community College and Technical Institute (N,U)
California State University, San Marcos (U)
Carroll Community College (N)
Central Carolina Community College (U)
Central Georgia Technical College (U)
Central Michigan University (U)
Central New Mexico Community College (U)
Central Texas College (U)
Central Virginia Community College (U)
Central Wyoming College (N)
Cerritos College (U)
Chemeketa Community College (U)

Cincinnati State Technical and Community College (U)
Clemson University (N)
College of The Albemarle (N)
Colorado State University-Pueblo (N)
The Community College of Baltimore County (U)
Community College of Beaver County (N)
Danville Community College (U)
Daymar College (U)
Delaware County Community College (U)
Des Moines Area Community College (U)
East Carolina University (U)
Eastern West Virginia Community and Technical College (U)
East Los Angeles College (U)
Edgecombe Community College (N)
Edison State Community College (N,U)
Feather River College (U)
Indiana State University (U)
Indiana University–Purdue University Fort Wayne (N)
Iona College (U)
Ivy Tech Community College–Bloomington (U)
Ivy Tech Community College–Central Indiana (U)
Ivy Tech Community College–Columbus (U)
Ivy Tech Community College–East Central (U)
Ivy Tech Community College–Northwest (U)
Ivy Tech Community College–Southeast (U)
Ivy Tech Community College–Southern Indiana (U)
Ivy Tech Community College–Southwest (U)
Ivy Tech Community College–Wabash Valley (U)
Ivy Tech Community College–Whitewater (U)
James Sprunt Community College (U)
Jamestown Community College (N)
J. Sargeant Reynolds Community College (U)
Kansas City Kansas Community College (U)
Kaskaskia College (U)
Kirkwood Community College (U)
Lake Superior College (U)
Lamar State College–Port Arthur (N)
Lehigh Carbon Community College (U)
Lewis and Clark Community College (U)
Lewis-Clark State College (U)
Madison Area Technical College (U)
Marlboro College (G)
Minot State University–Bottineau Campus (U)
Mitchell Technical Institute (N)
Montgomery Community College (U)
Mount Wachusett Community College (N)
Nashville State Technical Community College (N)
Naugatuck Valley Community College (U)
New England College of Finance (N,U)
North Dakota State University (N)
North Harris Montgomery Community College District (U)
Northland Community and Technical College–Thief River Falls (U)
Odessa College (U)
Orange Coast College (U)
Palomar College (U)
Plymouth State University (N)
Portland Community College (U)
Providence College and Theological Seminary (G)
Pulaski Technical College (U)

Randolph Community College (N)
Rend Lake College (N)
Saint Paul College–A Community & Technical College (U)
Sauk Valley Community College (U)
Schoolcraft College (U)
Seminole Community College (U)
Sinclair Community College (U)
Taylor University (N)
Tompkins Cortland Community College (N)
Tyler Junior College (U)
University of Cincinnati (N)
University of Minnesota, Twin Cities Campus (U)
The University of North Carolina at Charlotte (N)
University of Northwestern Ohio (U)
University of Phoenix Online Campus (U)
Utah State University (U)
Vance-Granville Community College (U)
Vincennes University (U)
Wake Technical Community College (U)
Washtenaw Community College (U)
Western Piedmont Community College (U)
Western Wyoming Community College (U)
West Los Angeles College (U)
West Virginia University at Parkersburg (N,U)
Wisconsin Indianhead Technical College (N,U)
York County Community College (U)
Youngstown State University (N)

BUSINESS, MANAGEMENT, AND MARKETING RELATED

Acadia University (U)
Adams State College (U)
Anne Arundel Community College (U)
Arapahoe Community College (U)
Arkansas State University–Beebe (U)
Ashford University (U,G)
Athabasca University (N,U,G)
Bellevue Community College (U)
Bellevue University (U,G)
Berkeley College (U)
Berkeley College-New York City Campus (U)
Berkeley College-Westchester Campus (U)
Bismarck State College (U)
Blackhawk Technical College (U)
Black Hills State University (U,G)
Bloomsburg University of Pennsylvania (U,G)
Boise State University (U)
Bowling Green State University (U)
Bradley University (U)
Brenau University (U,G)
Bridgewater State College (N)
Bristol Community College (N)
Buena Vista University (U)
Buffalo State College, State University of New York (U)
Butler Community College (U)
Butler County Community College (U)
California State University, Dominguez Hills (N)
California State University, San Bernardino (U)
Cape Breton University (N)
Capella University (G)
Carlow University (U,G)
Carroll College (U)
Carroll Community College (N,U)
Casper College (U)

Central Michigan University (U,G)
Central New Mexico Community College (U)
Central Texas College (U)
Chadron State College (U,G)
Charter Oak State College (U)
Chattanooga State Technical Community
  College (U)
Chemeketa Community College (U)
Chesapeake College (U)
Clackamas Community College (U)
Clark State Community College (U)
Clatsop Community College (U)
Clemson University (N)
College of The Albemarle (N)
Colorado State University (N,G)
Colorado Technical University (U,G)
Columbia College (U,G)
Community College of Beaver County (N,U)
Community College of Denver (U)
Concordia University Wisconsin (U)
Dallas Baptist University (U,G)
Danville Community College (U)
Darton College (N)
Delaware County Community College (U)
Des Moines Area Community College (U)
Drexel University (U,G)
Duquesne University (U)
D'Youville College (U)
East Carolina University (U,G)
Eastern Michigan University (U,G)
Eastern Washington University (N)
Eastern West Virginia Community and
  Technical College (U)
East Tennessee State University (N)
Edgecombe Community College (N,U)
Edison College (U)
Elgin Community College (U)
Elizabeth City State University (U)
Fullerton College (U)
Fulton-Montgomery Community College (N)
Galveston College (N)
Gaston College (U)
George Mason University (G)
Grand View College (U)
Granite State College (U)
Grantham University (U)
Hagerstown Community College (N)
Harrisburg Area Community College (U)
Holyoke Community College (U)
Hopkinsville Community College (U)
Indiana State University (U)
Indiana University of Pennsylvania (U,G)
Indiana University–Purdue University Fort
  Wayne (N)
Iona College (U,G)
Jacksonville State University (U,G)
James Madison University (N)
James Sprunt Community College (U)
Jamestown Community College (N)
Jefferson Community College (U)
John A. Logan College (U)
J. Sargeant Reynolds Community College (U)
Kansas City Kansas Community College (U)
Kansas State University (U)
Kean University (N)
Kettering University (N)
Lamar State College–Port Arthur (N)
Lehigh Carbon Community College (U)
LeTourneau University (G)
Liberty University (U,G)
Longwood University (U)
Lurleen B. Wallace Community College (U)

Manatee Community College (U)
Marist College (U,G)
Marlboro College (U,G)
Marymount University (G)
Mercy College (G)
Middlesex Community College (U)
Middle Tennessee State University (N)
Midstate College (U)
Millersville University of Pennsylvania (G)
Milwaukee School of Engineering (U)
Minot State University–Bottineau Campus (U)
Mitchell Technical Institute (N,U)
Monterey Peninsula College (U)
Mount Saint Vincent University (U)
Myers University (U)
Nashville State Technical Community College
  (U)
New England College of Finance (N,U)
New Jersey Institute of Technology (G)
New York Institute of Technology (U)
North Carolina State University (U)
North Dakota State College of Science (U)
North Harris Montgomery Community
  College District (U)
NorthWest Arkansas Community College (U)
Northwest Technical College (U)
Northwood University (U)
Odessa College (N,U)
Orange Coast College (U)
Oregon State University (N)
Palomar College (U)
Pamlico Community College (U)
Park University (U,G)
Peirce College (U)
Peninsula College (U)
Pittsburg State University (U)
Plymouth State University (N,G)
Portland Community College (U)
Quinebaug Valley Community College (U)
Quinnipiac University (G)
Radford University (N)
Regent University (N,U,G)
Regis University (G)
The Richard Stockton College of New Jersey
  (G)
Rose State College (U)
Saddleback College (U)
St. John's University (G)
Saint Joseph's College of Maine (G)
St. Louis Community College System (N)
Sam Houston State University (U)
Schoolcraft College (U)
Seminole Community College (U)
Sinclair Community College (U)
Sonoma State University (N)
Southeast Arkansas College (U)
Southern Illinois University Carbondale (U)
Southern New Hampshire University (U,G)
South Piedmont Community College (U)
Southwestern College (N)
Southwest Georgia Technical College (U)
State University of New York College at
  Potsdam (U)
Suffolk University (G)
Syracuse University (U)
Taylor University (N,U)
Texas A&M University–Commerce (U,G)
Thunderbird School of Global Management
  (N,G)
Tompkins Cortland Community College (N)
Union University (U)
United States Sports Academy (N,U)

The University of Alabama (U)
University of Alaska Fairbanks (U)
University of Bridgeport (U)
University of Central Arkansas (G)
University of Colorado at Denver and Health
  Sciences Center (U)
University of Delaware (N)
The University of Findlay (N)
University of Hawaii–West Oahu (U)
University of Idaho (G)
University of Illinois at Chicago (N,G)
University of Illinois at Springfield (U)
The University of Maine at Augusta (U)
University of Maine at Fort Kent (U)
University of Management and Technology
  (U)
University of Maryland University College
  (G)
University of Michigan–Flint (N)
University of Minnesota, Morris (U)
University of Minnesota, Twin Cities Campus
  (U)
University of Missouri–Columbia (N,U)
The University of Montana–Western (U)
University of Nebraska–Lincoln (G)
University of New Orleans (N,U,G)
University of North Alabama (U)
The University of North Carolina at Chapel
  Hill (N)
The University of North Carolina at Charlotte
  (N,U)
University of North Texas (U,G)
University of Pittsburgh at Bradford (U)
University of South Florida (G)
The University of Texas at Arlington (U)
The University of Texas at San Antonio (U,G)
University of the Cumberlands (G)
University of Toronto (U)
University of West Florida (N)
University of Wisconsin–Parkside (G)
University of Wisconsin–Platteville (U)
University of Wisconsin–Stout (U)
University of Wisconsin–Whitewater (U,G)
Upper Iowa University (U)
Utah Valley State College (U)
Virginia Highlands Community College (U)
Viterbo University (U)
Washburn University (U)
Webster University (G)
West Los Angeles College (U)
West Shore Community College (U)
West Virginia University at Parkersburg (U)
Wharton County Junior College (U)
Wilkes Community College (U)
Williston State College (U)
York County Community College (U)
Youngstown State University (N)

BUSINESS/COMMERCE

Acadia University (U)
Adams State College (N,U)
The American College (U,G)
American Public University System (G)
Argosy University, Chicago Campus (U,G)
Arizona Western College (U)
Ashford University (U,G)
Athabasca University (N,U)
Bainbridge College (U)
Bellevue Community College (U)
Bellevue University (U,G)
Berkeley College (U)

Berkeley College-New York City Campus (U)
Berkeley College-Westchester Campus (U)
Berklee College of Music (N,U)
Big Bend Community College (U)
Bismarck State College (U)
Black Hills State University (U)
Bowling Green State University (N,U)
Brenau University (U,G)
Bridgewater State College (N)
Bristol Community College (N,U)
Broome Community College (U)
Bryant and Stratton Online (U)
Buena Vista University (U)
Cabrillo College (U)
Caldwell Community College and Technical
   Institute (U)
California State University, San Marcos (N)
Carroll Community College (N)
Casper College (U)
Cayuga County Community College (U)
Cedar Crest College (U)
Central Carolina Community College (U)
Central Michigan University (U,G)
Central New Mexico Community College (U)
Central Washington University (U)
Cerritos College (U)
Chadron State College (U,G)
Chattanooga State Technical Community
   College (U)
Chemeketa Community College (U)
Cincinnati State Technical and Community
   College (U)
Clark State Community College (U)
Clatsop Community College (U)
Clemson University (N,U)
Cleveland Institute of Electronics (N)
Cleveland State University (N)
College of San Mateo (U)
College of Southern Maryland (U)
College of The Albemarle (N,U)
College of the Siskiyous (U)
Colorado Mountain College District System
   (U)
Colorado State University (U,G)
Colorado State University-Pueblo (U)
Colorado Technical University (U,G)
Columbia College (U)
Columbia University (N)
The Community College of Baltimore County
   (U)
Community College of Beaver County (N)
Concordia University, St. Paul (N,U,G)
County College of Morris (U)
Daemen College (U)
Dallas Baptist University (G)
Danville Community College (U)
Darton College (U)
Delaware County Community College (U)
Des Moines Area Community College (U)
DeVry University Online (U,G)
Dickinson State University (U)
Drake University (U,G)
Drexel University (U,G)
D'Youville College (G)
East Carolina University (U,G)
Eastern Michigan University (U,G)
Eastern Oregon University (U)
Eastern Washington University (N,U)
Eastern Wyoming College (U)
Edgecombe Community College (N,U)
Edison State Community College (N,U)
EduKan (U)

Elizabeth City State University (U)
Elizabethtown College (U)
Embry-Riddle Aeronautical University (U,G)
Endicott College (N,U,G)
Erie Community College (U)
Everett Community College (U)
Fairmont State University (U)
Fayetteville State University (U)
Finger Lakes Community College (U)
Flathead Valley Community College (N)
Florida Institute of Technology (G)
Franklin Pierce University (G)
Fullerton College (U)
Fulton-Montgomery Community College (N)
Gaston College (U)
Gateway Community College (U)
George C. Wallace Community College (U)
Grantham University (U)
Harrisburg Area Community College (U)
Haywood Community College (U)
Herkimer County Community College (U)
Hillsborough Community College (U)
Illinois Eastern Community Colleges, Frontier
   Community College (U)
Illinois Eastern Community Colleges, Lincoln
   Trail College (U)
Illinois Eastern Community Colleges, Olney
   Central College (U)
Illinois Eastern Community Colleges, Wabash
   Valley College (U)
Indiana State University (U)
Indiana Tech (U)
Indiana University–Purdue University Fort
   Wayne (U)
Iona College (G)
Jacksonville State University (U,G)
James Madison University (N,U)
Jamestown Community College (N)
Jefferson Community College (U)
John A. Logan College (U)
John Wood Community College (U)
Jones College (U)
Kansas City Kansas Community College (U)
Kansas State University (U)
Kellogg Community College (U)
Kirkwood Community College (N)
Lakeland College (U)
Lake Superior College (U)
Lamar State College–Port Arthur (N)
Lewis and Clark Community College (N)
Liberty University (U)
Limestone College (U)
Linn-Benton Community College (U)
Lock Haven University of Pennsylvania (N)
Los Angeles Harbor College (U)
Luzerne County Community College (U)
Malone College (U)
Manatee Community College (U)
Marlboro College (G)
Marymount University (G)
Massasoit Community College (N,U)
Mercy College (U,G)
Mesalands Community College (U)
Middlesex Community College (N,U)
Middle Tennessee State University (N)
Midwestern State University (U)
Minnesota State University Moorhead (U)
Mississippi State University (G)
Missouri Southern State University (N)
Monroe Community College (U)
Montana State University–Billings (U)

Montana Tech of The University of Montana
   (U)
Montgomery Community College (U)
Montgomery County Community College (U)
Mountain Empire Community College (U)
Murray State University (U)
Myers University (U,G)
Nassau Community College (U)
National University (U,G)
New England College of Finance (N)
New Jersey City University (U)
New Mexico State University (U)
North Carolina State University (U)
North Dakota State University (N)
Northern State University (U)
North Idaho College (N,U)
Northland Community and Technical College–
   Thief River Falls (U)
North Seattle Community College (U)
Northwestern Oklahoma State University (U)
Oakton Community College (N,U)
Odessa College (U)
The Ohio State University (U)
Orangeburg-Calhoun Technical College (U)
Oregon Institute of Technology (U)
Oregon State University (U)
Owensboro Community and Technical College
   (U)
Pace University (N,U,G)
Palomar College (U)
Pamlico Community College (U)
Park University (U)
Pasco-Hernando Community College (U)
Passaic County Community College (U)
Peirce College (U)
Peninsula College (U)
Pennsylvania College of Technology (U)
Piedmont Technical College (U)
Plymouth State University (N,G)
Pulaski Technical College (U)
Quinnipiac University (U)
Radford University (G)
Regent University (N,U,G)
Rend Lake College (N,U)
Riverside Community College District (U)
Rockland Community College (U)
Rose State College (U)
Ryerson University (U)
St. Louis Community College System (N)
St. Petersburg College (U)
Sauk Valley Community College (U)
Schiller International University (U)
Schoolcraft College (U)
Seminole Community College (U)
Snead State Community College (U)
Southeast Arkansas College (U)
Southeastern Illinois College (U)
Southern Illinois University Carbondale (U)
Southern New Hampshire University (U,G)
South Piedmont Community College (U)
Southwestern College (U)
Southwest Georgia Technical College (U)
Spartanburg Community College (U)
State University of New York College at
   Potsdam (N)
State University of New York College of
   Agriculture and Technology at Morrisville
   (U)
State University of New York Empire State
   College (G)
Strayer University (U,G)
Syracuse University (G)

Tacoma Community College (U)
Taylor University (N,U)
Texas A&M University–Commerce (U)
Texas State Technical College Waco (N)
Texas State University-San Marcos (U)
Texas Woman's University (G)
Thomas College (U,G)
Thunderbird School of Global Management (N)
Tompkins Cortland Community College (U)
Treasure Valley Community College (U)
Tri-State University (U)
Tunxis Community College (N)
Tyler Junior College (N,U)
The University of Alabama (U)
University of Alaska Fairbanks (U)
University of Bridgeport (U)
University of California, Los Angeles (G)
University of Central Oklahoma (U)
University of Cincinnati (N,U)
University of Cincinnati Raymond Walters College (U)
University of Colorado at Colorado Springs (G)
University of Colorado at Denver and Health Sciences Center (G)
The University of Findlay (U)
University of Idaho (U)
University of Illinois (N)
University of Illinois at Chicago (N,G)
University of Maine (G)
The University of Maine at Augusta (U)
University of Maine at Fort Kent (U)
University of Management and Technology (G)
University of Massachusetts Lowell (U)
University of Michigan–Flint (N,U)
University of Missouri–Columbia (U)
The University of Montana (U)
University of Nebraska–Lincoln (N)
University of North Alabama (G)
The University of North Carolina at Charlotte (N)
University of North Texas (U)
The University of Texas at San Antonio (U)
The University of Texas at Tyler (U)
University of Toronto (U)
University of Wisconsin Colleges (U)
University of Wisconsin–Platteville (U,G)
University of Wyoming (U)
Vance-Granville Community College (N)
Vincennes University (U)
Virginia Polytechnic Institute and State University (N)
Wake Technical Community College (U)
Wenatchee Valley College (N)
Westchester Community College (U)
Western Piedmont Community College (U)
Western Wyoming Community College (U)
West Los Angeles College (U)
West Valley College (U)
West Virginia University at Parkersburg (U)
Wharton County Junior College (U)
Wilfrid Laurier University (U)
Wilkes Community College (U)
Wisconsin Indianhead Technical College (N,U)
York County Community College (U)
York Technical College (U)

BUSINESS/CORPORATE COMMUNICATIONS

Abilene Christian University (U)
Acadia University (U)
Adams State College (U)
American Graduate University (G)
Arapahoe Community College (U)
Arkansas State University–Beebe (U)
Ashford University (U,G)
Athabasca University (N,U,G)
Beaufort County Community College (N)
Bellevue Community College (U)
Bellevue University (G)
Brenau University (U,G)
Bridgewater State College (U)
Bristol Community College (N)
Bryant and Stratton Online (U)
Buena Vista University (U)
Caldwell Community College and Technical Institute (N,U)
California State University, Dominguez Hills (N)
Campbell University (U)
Capella University (G)
Carroll Community College (U)
Cedarville University (U)
Central Michigan University (U,G)
Central Texas College (U)
Chadron State College (U)
Chemeketa Community College (U)
Cleveland Institute of Electronics (N)
Cleveland State University (N)
Clinton Community College (U)
College of San Mateo (U)
College of Southern Maryland (U)
College of The Albemarle (N,U)
College of the Siskiyous (U)
Colorado Mountain College District System (U)
Colorado State University (G)
Columbus State Community College (U)
The Community College of Baltimore County (U)
Community College of Beaver County (N)
Community College of Denver (U)
Dallas Baptist University (U,G)
Darton College (N)
Delaware County Community College (U)
Delta College (U)
Des Moines Area Community College (U)
Dickinson State University (U)
Drexel University (U,G)
East Carolina University (U)
Eastern Michigan University (U,G)
Eastern Washington University (N)
Edgecombe Community College (N,U)
Edison State Community College (U)
Elizabeth City State University (U)
Elizabethtown College (U)
Erie Community College (U)
Fairmont State University (U)
Finger Lakes Community College (U)
Gaston College (U)
Herkimer County Community College (U)
Indiana University–Purdue University Fort Wayne (N)
Iona College (U,G)
Jacksonville State University (G)
James Madison University (N)
James Sprunt Community College (U)
Jamestown Community College (N)

Jefferson Community College (U)
Jones College (U)
Jones County Junior College (U)
Kaplan University (N)
Kellogg Community College (U)
Lake Superior College (U)
Lehigh University (N)
Liberty University (U)
Limestone College (U)
Longwood University (N)
Marlboro College (U)
Maryville University of Saint Louis (N)
Massasoit Community College (U)
Mercy College (G)
Middlesex Community College (U)
Middle Tennessee State University (N,U)
Midwestern State University (U)
Montana State University–Billings (U)
Montgomery Community College (N)
Myers University (U)
North Arkansas College (U)
North Central State College (U)
NorthWest Arkansas Community College (U)
Northwestern Oklahoma State University (U)
Oakton Community College (U)
Oklahoma State University (U)
Old Dominion University (U)
Oregon State University (U)
Park University (U)
Pasco-Hernando Community College (N)
Pennsylvania College of Technology (U)
Plymouth State University (N,U,G)
Radford University (G)
Rappahannock Community College (U)
Regis University (G)
Rend Lake College (U)
Richland Community College (U)
Roosevelt University (U,G)
Rose State College (U)
Ryerson University (U)
St. Clair County Community College (U)
Saint Joseph's College of Maine (G)
Saint Paul College–A Community & Technical College (U)
St. Petersburg College (U)
Schiller International University (U,G)
Seminole Community College (U)
Snead State Community College (U)
Sonoma State University (N)
Southeast Arkansas College (U)
Southern New Hampshire University (U,G)
Southwest Wisconsin Technical College (U)
Spring Arbor University (G)
Taylor University (N)
Thunderbird School of Global Management (N,G)
Tompkins Cortland Community College (U)
Tyler Junior College (U)
University of Colorado at Denver and Health Sciences Center (G)
University of Denver (U)
The University of Findlay (G)
University of Illinois at Chicago (N)
The University of Maine at Augusta (U)
University of Massachusetts Lowell (U)
University of Michigan–Flint (N)
University of Minnesota, Twin Cities Campus (U)
University of New Orleans (U,G)
The University of North Carolina at Chapel Hill (N,U)

The University of North Carolina at Charlotte (N)
University of Oklahoma (U)
The University of Texas at Tyler (U)
University of Toronto (N,U)
University of Washington (U)
University of West Florida (U)
University of Wisconsin–Platteville (U,G)
Upper Iowa University (U)
Utah Valley State College (U)
Vance-Granville Community College (N)
West Virginia University at Parkersburg (N,U)
York County Community College (U)
York University (U)

BUSINESS/MANAGERIAL ECONOMICS

Adams State College (U)
American Graduate University (G)
Anne Arundel Community College (U)
Ashford University (U,G)
Athabasca University (N,U,G)
Bellevue University (U,G)
Berkeley College (U)
Berkeley College-New York City Campus (U)
Berkeley College-Westchester Campus (U)
Brenau University (U,G)
Bridgewater State College (N,U)
Buena Vista University (U)
Caldwell Community College and Technical Institute (N)
Central Michigan University (U,G)
Central New Mexico Community College (U)
Chadron State College (U,G)
Colorado State University (G)
Columbia College (G)
Community College of Beaver County (N,U)
Dallas Baptist University (U,G)
Delaware County Community College (U)
Des Moines Area Community College (U)
Drake University (U)
Drexel University (U,G)
D'Youville College (G)
East Arkansas Community College (U)
Edgecombe Community College (N)
Elizabeth City State University (U)
Embry-Riddle Aeronautical University (U)
Florida Institute of Technology (G)
Franklin Pierce University (U)
Gadsden State Community College (U)
Grand View College (U)
Grantham University (U,G)
Harrisburg Area Community College (U)
Immaculata University (U)
Jacksonville State University (U,G)
Jones College (U)
Kaplan University (N)
Kellogg Community College (U)
Labette Community College (U)
Lamar State College–Port Arthur (N)
Lewis and Clark Community College (U)
Liberty University (U)
Linn-Benton Community College (U)
Manatee Community College (U)
Marist College (G)
Marlboro College (G)
Marshall University (U)
Mercy College (G)
Middlesex Community College (U)
Middle Tennessee State University (N)
Mississippi State University (G)

Myers University (U)
New England College of Finance (N)
Old Dominion University (U)
Pamlico Community College (U)
Quinnipiac University (G)
Radford University (G)
Regis University (U,G)
Rose State College (U)
Ryerson University (U)
Saddleback College (U)
Saint Joseph's College of Maine (G)
Sampson Community College (U)
Schiller International University (U,G)
Schoolcraft College (U)
Southeast Arkansas College (U)
South Piedmont Community College (U)
Spring Arbor University (G)
Stanford University (N)
State University of New York at Oswego (U)
State University of New York College at Potsdam (U)
Syracuse University (G)
Taylor University (U)
Texas A&M University–Commerce (U,G)
Thomas College (G)
Thunderbird School of Global Management (N)
University of Colorado at Denver and Health Sciences Center (G)
The University of Findlay (N,U,G)
University of Illinois at Chicago (G)
University of Minnesota, Twin Cities Campus (U)
University of Missouri–Columbia (U)
University of Nebraska–Lincoln (G)
University of New Orleans (U,G)
The University of North Carolina at Greensboro (U)
University of South Florida (G)
University of Toronto (N,U)
University of Vermont (N,U)
University of Waterloo (U)
University of Wisconsin–Parkside (G)
Western Piedmont Community College (U)
West Liberty State College (U)
West Virginia University at Parkersburg (U)
Wilkes Community College (U)
Williston State College (U)
York University (U)
Youngstown State University (N)

CARPENTRY

Central Georgia Technical College (U)
Cleveland Institute of Electronics (N)
South Piedmont Community College (U)

CELL BIOLOGY AND ANATOMICAL SCIENCES

Cabrillo College (U)
Clark State Community College (U)
The Community College of Baltimore County (U)
County College of Morris (U)
Darton College (U)
Eastern Michigan University (U)
Edison State Community College (U)
Henry Ford Community College (U)
Hocking College (U)
John Wood Community College (U)
Lawrence Technological University (G)

Lehigh University (G)
Louisiana State University and Agricultural and Mechanical College (U)
Missouri Southern State University (U)
Palomar College (U)
Parkland College (U)
Piedmont Technical College (U)
South Piedmont Community College (U)
Texas State University-San Marcos (U)
Tyler Junior College (U)
University of Colorado at Denver and Health Sciences Center (U)
University of Minnesota, Twin Cities Campus (U)
The University of Texas at San Antonio (U)
University of Waterloo (U)

CHEMICAL ENGINEERING

Cleveland State University (G)
Columbia University (N,G)
Kansas State University (G)
Lehigh University (N,G)
Mississippi State University (G)
North Carolina State University (G)
Texas Tech University (G)
University of Delaware (U,G)
University of Idaho (U,G)
University of Illinois at Chicago (G)
University of North Dakota (U)
University of South Florida (G)

CHEMISTRY

Acadia University (U)
Anne Arundel Community College (U)
Arapahoe Community College (U)
Arkansas State University–Beebe (U)
Athabasca University (N,U)
Bellevue Community College (U)
Big Bend Community College (U)
Boise State University (U)
Brazosport College (U)
Brookdale Community College (U)
Butler Community College (U)
Butler County Community College (U)
Carlow University (U)
Cascadia Community College (U)
Casper College (U)
Central Georgia Technical College (U)
Central Virginia Community College (U)
Central Washington University (U)
Central Wyoming College (U)
Chattanooga State Technical Community College (U)
Chemeketa Community College (U)
Clackamas Community College (U)
Clarion University of Pennsylvania (U)
Clark State Community College (U)
Cleveland State University (U)
College of DuPage (U)
College of San Mateo (U)
Colorado Mountain College District System (U)
Colorado State University-Pueblo (U)
Columbia College (U)
Columbus State Community College (U)
Community College of Denver (U)
Des Moines Area Community College (U)
East Carolina University (U)
East Central Community College (U)
Eastern Michigan University (U)

Eastern Oregon University (U)
Edison State Community College (U)
EduKan (U)
Fullerton College (U)
Gadsden State Community College (U)
Galveston College (U)
Gaston College (U)
George C. Wallace Community College (U)
Graceland University (U)
Grantham University (U)
Gulf Coast Community College (U)
Honolulu Community College (U)
Houston Community College System (U)
Illinois Eastern Community Colleges, Wabash
 Valley College (U)
Indiana State University (U)
Itawamba Community College (U)
Jacksonville State University (U,G)
John Tyler Community College (U)
J. Sargeant Reynolds Community College (U)
Kansas State University (U)
Lansing Community College (U)
Lawrence Technological University (U)
Lehigh University (N,G)
Marshall University (U)
Massasoit Community College (U)
Mayville State University (U)
Miami University–Middletown Campus (U)
Millersville University of Pennsylvania (U)
Missouri State University (U)
Mt. San Antonio College (U)
North Carolina State University (U)
North Dakota State College of Science (U)
Northeast Alabama Community College (U)
Northeast State Technical Community College
 (U)
NorthWest Arkansas Community College (U)
Northwestern College (U)
Northwest Technical College (U)
Oregon State University (U)
Pace University (U)
Palomar College (U)
Pamlico Community College (U)
Parkland College (U)
Peninsula College (U)
Pennsylvania College of Technology (U)
Piedmont Technical College (U)
Portland State University (U)
Quinnipiac University (U)
Reedley College (N,U)
Rochester Institute of Technology (U)
Rockland Community College (U)
Sacred Heart University (U)
St. Clair County Community College (U)
St. Cloud State University (U)
St. Petersburg College (U)
Sam Houston State University (U)
Sinclair Community College (U)
Snead State Community College (U)
Southeastern Community College (U)
South Piedmont Community College (U)
State University of New York at Oswego (U)
Tacoma Community College (U)
Treasure Valley Community College (U)
Triton College (U)
University of Central Florida (G)
University of Colorado at Colorado Springs
 (U)
University of Delaware (U)
The University of Findlay (U)
University of Illinois at Springfield (U)
University of La Verne (G)

University of Maryland University College
 (U)
University of Nebraska–Lincoln (U)
University of New Orleans (U,G)
The University of North Carolina at Chapel
 Hill (U)
University of North Dakota (U)
University of North Texas (U,G)
University of Oklahoma (U)
University of Pittsburgh at Bradford (U)
The University of South Dakota (U)
University of Southern Mississippi (U)
University of South Florida (U,G)
The University of Tennessee (U)
University of Washington (U)
University of Waterloo (N,U)
University of Wisconsin Colleges (U)
University of Wisconsin–Stout (U)
University of Wyoming (U)
Utah State University (U)
Vincennes University (U)
Wake Technical Community College (U)
Washburn University (U)
Wayne State College (U)
Weber State University (U)
Westchester Community College (U)
Williston State College (U)
Yuba College (U)

CITY/URBAN, COMMUNITY AND REGIONAL PLANNING

Athabasca University (N)
Cleveland State University (U,G)
East Tennessee State University (G)
Middle Tennessee State University (N)
Prescott College (G)
University of Massachusetts Boston (N)
University of Missouri–Columbia (N)
University of New Orleans (U,G)
University of Southern Mississippi (G)
University of Washington (N,G)

CIVIL ENGINEERING

Auburn University (G)
Cleveland State University (U,G)
Colorado State University (G)
Columbia University (N,G)
Gadsden State Community College (U)
Georgia Institute of Technology (N,G)
Iowa State University of Science and
 Technology (G)
Kansas State University (G)
Mississippi State University (G)
North Carolina State University (G)
Southern Methodist University (G)
Stanford University (N)
Texas Tech University (G)
The University of British Columbia (U)
University of Colorado at Boulder (N,G)
University of Colorado at Denver and Health
 Sciences Center (U)
University of Delaware (U,G)
University of Idaho (U,G)
University of Illinois at Urbana–Champaign
 (G)
University of Maine (G)*
University of New Orleans (U,G)
The University of North Carolina at Charlotte
 (N)
University of North Dakota (U)

The University of Texas at San Antonio (U)
University of Washington (G)
University of Wisconsin–Platteville (G)
Virginia Polytechnic Institute and State
 University (U)

CIVIL ENGINEERING TECHNOLOGY

Auburn University (G)
Cincinnati State Technical and Community
 College (U)
Lawrence Technological University (U)
Mid-State Technical College (U)
Sinclair Community College (U)
Southern Methodist University (G)
Southern Polytechnic State University (U)
University of Maine (U)
University of South Florida (G)
The University of Texas at San Antonio (U)

CLASSICAL AND ANCIENT STUDIES

Florida State University (U)
Queen's University at Kingston (U)
University of Illinois (U)
University of Massachusetts Boston (U)
University of Missouri–Columbia (U)
University of New Orleans (U,G)
The University of North Carolina at Charlotte
 (U)
The University of North Carolina at
 Greensboro (U)

CLINICAL CHILD PSYCHOLOGY

Arapahoe Community College (U)
California State University, San Bernardino
 (U)
Cumberland County College (U)
Liberty University (U)
Middlesex Community College (U)
Rend Lake College (U)
Saybrook Graduate School and Research
 Center (G)

CLINICAL PSYCHOLOGY

Arapahoe Community College (U)
Athabasca University (N)
Capella University (G)
Delaware County Community College (U)
Jacksonville State University (U,G)
Naropa University (U)
North Dakota State University (N,U,G)
Prescott College (G)
Saybrook Graduate School and Research
 Center (G)
University of Hawaii–West Oahu (U)
Washtenaw Community College (U)

CLINICAL/MEDICAL LABORATORY SCIENCE AND ALLIED PROFESSIONS

Arapahoe Community College (U)
Central Carolina Community College (N)
Central New Mexico Community College (U)
Clinton Community College (U)
Darton College (U)

Drexel University (G)
D'Youville College (U)
Erie Community College (U)
Randolph Community College (N)
Triton College (U)
University of Illinois (G)
University of Massachusetts Lowell (G)
The University of Texas System (N,U)
Weber State University (G)

COGNITIVE PSYCHOLOGY AND PSYCHOLINGUISTICS

Arapahoe Community College (U)
California State University, San Bernardino (U)
Charter Oak State College (U)
Community College of Beaver County (U)
Iona College (U)
Modesto Junior College (U)
Treasure Valley Community College (U)
University of Southern Mississippi (G)
University of Washington (U)
Wilfrid Laurier University (U)

COGNITIVE SCIENCE

Arapahoe Community College (U)
DePaul University (G)
D'Youville College (G)
Saybrook Graduate School and Research Center (G)

COMMUNICATION AND JOURNALISM RELATED

Arapahoe Community College (U)
Athabasca University (U)
Austin Peay State University (G)
Big Bend Community College (U)
Bismarck State College (U)
Bristol Community College (N)
Buena Vista University (U)
Cabrillo College (U)
California State University, Dominguez Hills (N)
California State University, San Bernardino (U)
California State University, San Marcos (N)
Cascadia Community College (U)
Central Michigan University (G)
Cleveland State University (U)
Columbus State Community College (U)
Dallas Baptist University (U)
Drake University (U)
East Carolina University (U)
Eastern Michigan University (U)
East Tennessee State University (N)
Elizabethtown College (U)
Everett Community College (U)
Fort Hays State University (N,U)
Hopkinsville Community College (U)
Iona College (U,G)
James Madison University (N)
James Sprunt Community College (U)
Jefferson Community and Technical College (U)
Jefferson Community College (U)
Kean University (N)
Malone College (U)
Mansfield University of Pennsylvania (U)

Marshall University (U)
Metropolitan State University (U)
Middlesex Community College (U)
Mississippi State University (U)
Missouri State University (U)
Mount Wachusett Community College (U)
New Jersey Institute of Technology (G)
New Mexico Junior College (U)
The New School: A University (N,U)
North Idaho College (N)
Oakton Community College (N,U)
Odessa College (U)
Palomar College (U)
Park University (U)
Peninsula College (U)
Pittsburg State University (U,G)
Regent University (N,U,G)
Rose State College (U)
Saddleback College (U)
St. Clair County Community College (U)
St. John's University (U)
St. Louis Community College System (U)
Schoolcraft College (U)
Seminole Community College (U)
Southeastern Illinois College (U)
Southern New Hampshire University (U)
Southern Polytechnic State University (U,G)
Southwest Wisconsin Technical College (U)
State University of New York at Oswego (U)
State University of New York College at Potsdam (U)
Taylor University (N,U)
Triton College (N)
University of Alaska Fairbanks (U)
University of Central Oklahoma (U)
The University of Findlay (U)
University of Houston–Victoria (U)
University of Illinois at Springfield (U)
University of Minnesota, Twin Cities Campus (U)
University of Nebraska–Lincoln (U,G)
University of New Orleans (N)
University of Southern Indiana (N)
University of South Florida (N)
The University of Texas at Arlington (U)
University of Wisconsin Colleges (U)
University of Wisconsin–Superior (U)
University of Wisconsin–Whitewater (U,G)
Utah Valley State College (U)
Valley City State University (U)
Washtenaw Community College (U)
Webster University (G)
West Virginia State University (U)
West Virginia University at Parkersburg (U)

COMMUNICATION AND MEDIA

Abilene Christian University (U)
Andrew Jackson University (U)
Anne Arundel Community College (U)
Arapahoe Community College (U)
Arkansas State University–Beebe (U)
Ashford University (U)
Athabasca University (N,U)
Auburn University (U)
Bainbridge College (N)
Bellevue Community College (U)
Bellevue University (U)
Berkeley College (U)
Berkeley College-New York City Campus (U)
Berkeley College-Westchester Campus (U)
Bowling Green State University (U)

Bradley University (U)
Brenau University (U)
Bridgewater State College (N,U,G)
Bristol Community College (N)
Buena Vista University (U)
Buffalo State College, State University of New York (U)
Butler County Community College (U)
Caldwell Community College and Technical Institute (U)
California State University, San Bernardino (U,G)
Central New Mexico Community College (U)
Central Texas College (U)
Central Wyoming College (U)
Charter Oak State College (U)
Chattanooga State Technical Community College (U)
Chesapeake College (U)
Cincinnati State Technical and Community College (U)
Clarion University of Pennsylvania (U)
Clark State Community College (U)
Clemson University (N,U,G)
Cleveland Institute of Electronics (U)
Cleveland State University (U)
Clovis Community College (U)
College of DuPage (U)
College of Southern Maryland (U)
College of The Albemarle (N)
The Community College of Baltimore County (U)
Concordia University, St. Paul (N)
Connecticut State University System (U)
Dallas Baptist University (U)
Danville Community College (U)
Darton College (U)
Dawson Community College (U)
Des Moines Area Community College (U)
DeVry University Online (U,G)
Drake University (U)
Duquesne University (U,G)
East Carolina University (U)
Eastern Michigan University (U)
Eastern Washington University (U)
Edgecombe Community College (N)
EduKan (U)
Elizabethtown College (U)
Fontbonne University (U)
Franklin University (U)
Gaston College (U)
Governors State University (U)
Granite State College (U)
Hillsborough Community College (U)
Hocking College (U)
Holyoke Community College (U)
Illinois Eastern Community Colleges, Olney Central College (U)
Indiana University–Purdue University Fort Wayne (U)
Indiana Wesleyan University (U)
Iona College (U)
Itawamba Community College (U)
James Madison University (U)
Jamestown Community College (N)
Jefferson Community College (U)
Jones College (U)
Judson College (U)
Labette Community College (U)
Lake Superior College (U)
LeTourneau University (U)
Lewis and Clark Community College (U)

Lewis-Clark State College (U)
Liberty University (U)
Longwood University (U)
Louisiana State University and Agricultural and Mechanical College (U)
Malone College (U)
Marshall University (U)
Massasoit Community College (N)
Mesa Community College (U)
Middlesex Community College (U)
Middle Tennessee State University (U)
Midwestern State University (U)
Millersville University of Pennsylvania (U)
Minnesota School of Business–Richfield (U)
Mississippi State University (U)
Missouri Southern State University (U)
Missouri State University (G)
Monroe Community College (U)
Montana State University–Billings (U,G)
Mountain Empire Community College (U)
Mount Saint Vincent University (U)
Myers University (U)
New Mexico Junior College (U)
The New School: A University (N,U)
New York Institute of Technology (U)
North Dakota State University (U,G)
North Harris Montgomery Community College District (U)
North Idaho College (N,U)
Northland Community and Technical College–Thief River Falls (U)
North Seattle Community College (U)
NorthWest Arkansas Community College (U)
Northwestern College (U)
Northwest Missouri State University (U)
Oakton Community College (U)
Old Dominion University (U)
Oregon State University (N,U)
Owensboro Community and Technical College (U)
Pace University (U)
Palomar College (U)
Parkland College (U)
Park University (U)
Passaic County Community College (U)
Patrick Henry Community College (U)
Piedmont Technical College (U)
Plymouth State University (U)
Prescott College (U,G)
Providence College and Theological Seminary (U)
Radford University (G)
Regent University (U,G)
Regis University (U)
Riverside Community College District (U)
Ryerson University (U)
Sacred Heart University (U)
St. Cloud State University (U)
Saint Joseph's College of Maine (U)
St. Petersburg College (U)
Schoolcraft College (U)
Seminole Community College (U)
Shippensburg University of Pennsylvania (U,G)
Simpson College (U)
Sinclair Community College (U)
Southern New Hampshire University (U)
South Piedmont Community College (U)
Southwest Wisconsin Technical College (U)
State University of New York at New Paltz (U)
State University of New York at Oswego (U)

State University of New York College at Potsdam (N)
State University of New York Empire State College (U)
Syracuse University (G)
Taylor University (N)
Texas A&M University–Commerce (U)
Tompkins Cortland Community College (U)
Tunxis Community College (U)
The University of Alabama (U)
University of Colorado at Colorado Springs (U)
University of Colorado at Denver and Health Sciences Center (U)
University of Delaware (U)
University of Denver (G)
University of Illinois at Springfield (U,G)
University of La Verne (G)
The University of Maine at Augusta (U)
University of Maine at Fort Kent (U)
University of Maryland University College (U)
University of Massachusetts Boston (U)
University of Massachusetts Lowell (U)
University of Minnesota, Twin Cities Campus (U,G)
The University of Montana (U)
University of Nebraska–Lincoln (U,G)
University of North Alabama (U)
The University of North Carolina at Chapel Hill (U)
University of North Dakota (U)
University of Northern Iowa (U)
University of Oklahoma (U)
University of St. Francis (U)
University of Southern Indiana (U)
University of Southern Mississippi (G)
The University of Texas at San Antonio (U)
The University of Toledo (U)
University of Toronto (N,U)
University of Washington (U)
University of West Florida (U)
University of Wisconsin–Platteville (U,G)
University of Wisconsin–Superior (U)
University of Wisconsin–Whitewater (U)
University of Wyoming (U)
Upper Iowa University (N,U)
Utah Valley State College (U)
Virginia Polytechnic Institute and State University (U)
Washtenaw Community College (U)
Waubonsee Community College (U)
Weber State University (U)
Westchester Community College (U)
West Virginia State University (U,G)
West Virginia University at Parkersburg (N)
Wichita State University (U)
Wilfrid Laurier University (U)
Wilkes Community College (U)
Wisconsin Indianhead Technical College (N,U)
Wright State University (U,G)
York University (U)
Yuba College (U)

COMMUNICATION DISORDERS SCIENCES AND SERVICES

Athabasca University (N,U)
Auburn University (U)
Bridgewater State College (U)
East Carolina University (G)

Fontbonne University (G)
Fort Hays State University (U)
James Madison University (N)
Longwood University (U,G)
MGH Institute of Health Professions (G)
Murray State University (U,G)
Oklahoma State University (U)
Texas Woman's University (U,G)
University of Cincinnati (U,G)
University of Maine (U)
University of Nebraska–Lincoln (G)
The University of North Carolina at Greensboro (U)
University of Vermont (N,G)
Utah State University (U)
Western Carolina University (U,G)

COMMUNICATIONS TECHNOLOGIES AND SUPPORT SERVICES RELATED

Dallas Baptist University (U)
Drexel University (U)
Iona College (G)
Marlboro College (G)
North Idaho College (N)
West Virginia University at Parkersburg (N)

COMMUNICATIONS TECHNOLOGY

Arapahoe Community College (U)
Athabasca University (N,U)
California State University, San Bernardino (U,G)
Central Michigan University (G)
Dakota State University (U)
Dallas Baptist University (U)
DePaul University (G)
DeVry University Online (G)
Eastern Iowa Community College District (N)
East Tennessee State University (U)
Gaston College (U)
Grantham University (G)
Itawamba Community College (U)
James Madison University (U)
Marlboro College (G)
Maryville University of Saint Louis (N)
Mercy College (U)
Middlesex Community College (U)
Montana State University–Billings (U)
National University (U)
Pamlico Community College (U)
Quinnipiac University (U)
Regent University (U,G)
Roosevelt University (G)
South Piedmont Community College (U)
Syracuse University (U,G)
University of Illinois at Urbana–Champaign (G)
University of North Texas (G)
University of West Florida (N,U)
Wilkes Community College (U)

COMMUNITY HEALTH SERVICES

Athabasca University (N,U,G)
Brenau University (U)
California State University, Chico (U)
California State University, San Bernardino (U)

California State University, San Marcos (N)
Central Michigan University (U)
Colorado State University (N)
Dallas Baptist University (U)
Danville Community College (U)
Duquesne University (G)
Edgecombe Community College (N)
Houston Community College System (U)
Indiana State University (U)
Jacksonville State University (U)
Jefferson College of Health Sciences (U)
Kansas State University (G)
Louisiana State University and Agricultural
 and Mechanical College (U)
Mercy College (G)
Middlesex Community College (U)
Minnesota State University Moorhead (U)
Modesto Junior College (U)
New Mexico State University (U)
Old Dominion University (U)
Radford University (G)
Rappahannock Community College (U)
Ryerson University (U)
Saybrook Graduate School and Research
 Center (G)
Schoolcraft College (N)
Seminole Community College (U)
State University of New York College at
 Potsdam (U)
The University of Maine at Augusta (U)
University of South Carolina Sumter (U)
University of Southern Mississippi (U,G)
The University of Texas at Tyler (U)
Vincennes University (U)
Virginia Highlands Community College (U)
West Virginia University at Parkersburg (U)

COMMUNITY ORGANIZATION AND ADVOCACY

Athabasca University (N,U,G)
California Institute of Integral Studies (N,G)
Central Michigan University (U)
Colorado State University (N)
Duquesne University (G)
Kansas State University (G)
Mercy College (U)
Prescott College (U,G)
Saybrook Graduate School and Research
 Center (G)
University of Massachusetts Boston (U)
University of New Orleans (U)
University of North Texas (G)
University of Southern Mississippi (U)
University of Vermont (U)
University of Waterloo (U)

COMMUNITY PSYCHOLOGY

Athabasca University (N,U,G)
Central Texas College (U)
Colorado State University (N)
Delaware County Community College (U)
Jones College (U)
Kansas State University (G)
Middlesex Community College (U)
Naropa University (U)
St. Cloud State University (G)
Saybrook Graduate School and Research
 Center (G)
Texas State University-San Marcos (U)

Treasure Valley Community College (U)
University of Massachusetts Boston (U)

COMPARATIVE LITERATURE

Arapahoe Community College (U)
Ashford University (U)
Athabasca University (U)
Bellevue Community College (U)
Bellevue University (U)
California State University, San Marcos (N)
Cascadia Community College (U)
Columbus State Community College (U)
Community College of Denver (U)
Delaware County Community College (U)
Des Moines Area Community College (U)
D'Youville College (U)
East Tennessee State University (U)
Graceland University (U)
Indiana University–Purdue University Fort
 Wayne (U)
Jefferson Community College (U)
Limestone College (U)
Lock Haven University of Pennsylvania (U)
Louisiana State University and Agricultural
 and Mechanical College (U)
Mercy College (U,G)
Middlesex Community College (U)
Naropa University (U)
State University of New York at New Paltz
 (U)
Texas State University-San Marcos (U)
The University of Maine at Augusta (U)
University of Minnesota, Twin Cities Campus
 (U)
University of New Orleans (U,G)
University of Southern Mississippi (U)

COMPARATIVE PSYCHOLOGY

County College of Morris (U)
Modesto Junior College (U)
University of Central Oklahoma (U)

COMPUTER AND INFORMATION SCIENCES

Alvin Community College (N,U)
Anne Arundel Community College (U)
Arapahoe Community College (U)
Arizona Western College (U)
Arkansas State University–Beebe (U)
Arkansas Tech University (U)
Athabasca University (N,U,G)
Bainbridge College (U)
Beaufort County Community College (N,U)
Bellevue Community College (U)
Bellevue University (U)
Belmont Technical College (U)
Bowling Green State University (U)
Bradley University (U)
Brazosport College (U)
Brenau University (U,G)
Bristol Community College (N,U)
Cabrillo College (U)
Caldwell Community College and Technical
 Institute (U)
California State University, Dominguez Hills
 (N)
California State University, Monterey Bay (U)
California State University, San Marcos (N)
Capitol College (G)

Carl Albert State College (U)
Carroll Community College (U)
Casper College (U)
Cedar Crest College (U)
Central Carolina Community College (N)
Central Michigan University (G)
Central New Mexico Community College (U)
Central Oregon Community College (U)
Central Texas College (U)
Central Virginia Community College (U)
Central Wyoming College (U)
Chadron State College (U)
Charter Oak State College (U)
Chattanooga State Technical Community
 College (U)
Chemeketa Community College (U)
Cincinnati State Technical and Community
 College (U)
Clatsop Community College (U)
Clemson University (N)
Cleveland State University (U)
Clinton Community College (U)
Cloud County Community College (N)
Clovis Community College (U)
College of Mount St. Joseph (U)
The College of St. Scholastica (U)
College of The Albemarle (N,U)
Colorado State University (G)
Colorado Technical University (U)
Columbia College (U)
Columbus State Community College (U)
The Community College of Baltimore County
 (N,U)
Community College of Beaver County (N,U)
Culver-Stockton College (U)
Dakota State University (U,G)
Dallas Baptist University (U,G)
Delaware County Community College (N,U)
Delta College (U)
DePaul University (U,G)
Des Moines Area Community College (U)
DeVry University Online (U,G)
Drake University (U)
Drexel University (U,G)
Duquesne University (N,U)
D'Youville College (U)
East Carolina University (U,G)
East Central Community College (U)
Eastern Iowa Community College District (N)
Eastern West Virginia Community and
 Technical College (U)
Eastern Wyoming College (U)
East Los Angeles College (U)
East Tennessee State University (N)
Edgecombe Community College (N,U)
Edison State Community College (N,U)
EduKan (U)
Elgin Community College (U)
Everest College (U)
Everett Community College (U)
Finger Lakes Community College (U)
Fort Hays State University (U)
Franklin Pierce University (U)
Galveston College (U)
Gaston College (U)
George C. Wallace Community College (U)
Graceland University (U)
Grantham University (U)
Harford Community College (N)
Haywood Community College (U)
Henry Ford Community College (U)
Herkimer County Community College (U)

Hillsborough Community College (U)
Illinois Eastern Community Colleges, Olney Central College (U)
Immaculata University (U)
Indiana Tech (U)
Indiana Wesleyan University (U)
Jacksonville State University (U,G)
Jamestown Community College (N)
Jefferson Community and Technical College (U)
Jefferson Community College (U)
John A. Logan College (U)
John Tyler Community College (U)
John Wood Community College (N,U)
Jones College (U)
Kansas City Kansas Community College (U)
Kansas State University (U)
Kaskaskia College (U)
Kauai Community College (U)
Kean University (N)
Kellogg Community College (U)
Kirkwood Community College (N)
Knowledge Systems Institute (N)
Lake Superior College (U)
Lamar State College–Port Arthur (N,U)
Lansing Community College (U)
Lehigh Carbon Community College (U)
Lewis and Clark Community College (U)
Lewis-Clark State College (U)
Limestone College (U)
Long Beach City College (U)
Los Angeles Harbor College (U)
Madison Area Technical College (U)
Manatee Community College (U)
Mansfield University of Pennsylvania (U)
Marlboro College (U,G)
Marshall University (U,G)
Maryville University of Saint Louis (N)
Massasoit Community College (N,U)
Mercy College (U,G)
Mesalands Community College (U)
Miami Dade College (U)
Middlesex Community College (U)
Middle Tennessee State University (N)
Midstate College (U)
Mid-State Technical College (U)
Midwestern State University (U)
Milwaukee School of Engineering (U)
Mississippi State University (U)
Missouri State University (U,G)
Mitchell Technical Institute (N,U)
Montgomery Community College (N,U)
Montgomery County Community College (U)
Motlow State Community College (U)
Mountain Empire Community College (U)
Mount Saint Vincent University (U)
Mt. San Antonio College (U)
Murray State University (U)
Myers University (U)
Nashville State Technical Community College (U)
Nassau Community College (U)
National University (G)
Naugatuck Valley Community College (U)
New England College of Finance (U)
New Jersey Institute of Technology (U)
New York Institute of Technology (N)
North Dakota State College of Science (U)
North Dakota State University (N,U)
Northeast State Technical Community College (U)
Northern State University (U)

North Harris Montgomery Community College District (U)
North Idaho College (N)
Northland Community and Technical College–Thief River Falls (U)
NorthWest Arkansas Community College (U)
Northwestern Connecticut Community College (N,U)
Northwest Missouri State University (U,G)
Nova Southeastern University (G)
Oakton Community College (N,U)
Odessa College (U)
Orange Coast College (U)
Oregon Institute of Technology (U)
Ouachita Technical College (U)
Owensboro Community and Technical College (U)
Pace University (N,G)
Palomar College (U)
Pamlico Community College (U)
Parkland College (U)
Park University (U,G)
Pasco-Hernando Community College (N)
Passaic County Community College (U)
Peninsula College (U)
Pennsylvania College of Technology (U)
Pittsburg State University (U)
Plymouth State University (G)
Portland Community College (U)
Pulaski Technical College (U)
Radford University (N)
Randolph Community College (U)
Red Rocks Community College (U)
Regis University (G)
Riverside Community College District (N,U)
Sacred Heart University (U)
St. Clair County Community College (U)
St. Louis Community College System (U)
Salem State College (U)
Sampson Community College (N,U)
Sauk Valley Community College (N,U)
Schoolcraft College (U)
Seminole Community College (U)
Sinclair Community College (U)
Snead State Community College (U)
Southeastern Community College (U)
Southern Illinois University Carbondale (U)
Southern Methodist University (G)
Southern New Hampshire University (U)
Southern Polytechnic State University (G)
South Piedmont Community College (U)
South Suburban College (U)
Southwest Georgia Technical College (U)
Southwest Wisconsin Technical College (U)
State University of New York at Oswego (U)
State University of New York at Plattsburgh (U)
State University of New York College at Potsdam (N)
Syracuse University (U,G)
Tacoma Community College (N,U)
Taylor University (N,U)
Texas A&M University–Commerce (U,G)
Texas Woman's University (U,G)
Three Rivers Community College (U)
Tompkins Cortland Community College (U)
Triton College (N)
Tunxis Community College (N,U)
Tyler Junior College (N,U)
The University of Alabama (U)
University of Alaska Fairbanks (U,G)
The University of British Columbia (U)

University of California, Davis (U)
University of Central Arkansas (N)
University of Central Oklahoma (N,U)
University of Cincinnati (N)
University of Dallas (G)
University of Denver (G)
University of Great Falls (U)
University of Houston–Victoria (U,G)
University of Illinois (U,G)
University of Illinois at Urbana–Champaign (G)
The University of Maine at Augusta (U)
University of Management and Technology (U)
University of Maryland University College (U)
University of Massachusetts Boston (U)
University of Massachusetts Dartmouth (G)
University of Massachusetts Lowell (U)
University of Michigan–Dearborn (U,G)
University of New Orleans (U,G)
University of North Alabama (U)
The University of North Carolina at Chapel Hill (U)
The University of North Carolina at Charlotte (U)
University of North Florida (U)
University of North Texas (U,G)
University of Northwestern Ohio (U)
University of Pittsburgh at Bradford (U)
University of St. Francis (U)
University of Southern Indiana (N)
University of South Florida (G)
The University of Tennessee at Martin (N)
The University of Texas System (U,G)
The University of Toledo (U)
University of Washington (N)
University of Waterloo (U)
Utah Valley State College (N,U)
Vance-Granville Community College (N)
Vermont Technical College (U)
Vincennes University (U)
Virginia Highlands Community College (U)
Virginia Polytechnic Institute and State University (N)
Washtenaw Community College (U)
Waubonsee Community College (U)
Wayne State College (U)
Weber State University (U)
Webster University (U)
Westchester Community College (U)
Western Piedmont Community College (U)
West Los Angeles College (U)
West Shore Community College (U)
West Valley College (U)
West Virginia State University (U)
West Virginia University at Parkersburg (N,U)
Wharton County Junior College (U)
Wilkes Community College (U)
Wisconsin Indianhead Technical College (N,U)
Wright State University (U)
York County Community College (U)
Youngstown State University (N)

COMPUTER AND INFORMATION SCIENCES AND SUPPORT SERVICES RELATED

Alvin Community College (N)
Arapahoe Community College (U)
Athabasca University (U,G)

Bellevue Community College (U)
Bellevue University (U)
Belmont Technical College (U)
Blackhawk Technical College (U)
Boise State University (U)
Bowling Green State University (N)
Bristol Community College (N,U)
Caldwell Community College and Technical
    Institute (N)
California State University, Monterey Bay (N)
California State University, San Marcos (U)
Capitol College (G)
Cascadia Community College (U)
Central Michigan University (G)
Central Texas College (U)
Chemeketa Community College (U)
Chesapeake College (U)
Clark State Community College (U)
The Community College of Baltimore County
    (N)
Dakota State University (U,G)
Delaware County Community College (N,U)
DePaul University (G)
Des Moines Area Community College (U)
Drexel University (G)
Duquesne University (G)
East Carolina University (U)
Eastern Iowa Community College District (N)
East Tennessee State University (N)
Edgecombe Community College (N,U)
Immaculata University (U)
Iona College (U)
Jacksonville State University (U,G)
Jamestown Community College (N)
Jones College (U)
Kansas City Kansas Community College (U)
Limestone College (U)
Lock Haven University of Pennsylvania (N)
Marlboro College (G)
Marshall University (U)
Mercy College (G)
Middlesex Community College (U)
Mid-State Technical College (U)
Mountain View College (N,U)
Myers University (U)
New York Institute of Technology (N)
North Arkansas College (N)
North Dakota State College of Science (U)
North Idaho College (N)
NorthWest Arkansas Community College (U)
Northwest Missouri State University (G)
Nova Southeastern University (G)
Odessa College (U)
Pace University (U,G)
Palomar College (U)
Peirce College (U)
Portland Community College (U)
Radford University (N)
Regis University (G)
St. Louis Community College System (U)
Sampson Community College (U)
Sauk Valley Community College (U)
Seminole Community College (U)
Southern Methodist University (G)
South Piedmont Community College (U)
Southwest Virginia Community College (N)
Taylor University (N)
Texas Tech University (G)
Treasure Valley Community College (U)
Tyler Junior College (U)
The University of Alabama (G)
University of Central Arkansas (G)

University of Central Florida (U)
University of Connecticut (U)
University of Dallas (G)
University of Denver (G)
University of Maine (G)
University of Maryland Eastern Shore (U)
The University of North Carolina at
    Greensboro (N)
The University of Texas System (U)
University of Washington (N)
Wake Technical Community College (N,U)
Weber State University (U)
Webster University (G)
Westchester Community College (U)
Wilkes Community College (U)
York Technical College (N)
Yuba College (U)

COMPUTER ENGINEERING

Bristol Community College (N)
Cleveland Institute of Electronics (U)
Cleveland State University (U,G)
College of The Albemarle (N)
Delaware County Community College (N,U)
Drexel University (G)
Edison State Community College (U)
Georgia Institute of Technology (N,G)
Grantham University (U)
Jacksonville State University (G)
Kansas State University (G)
Marlboro College (G)
Marshall University (U)
Mississippi State University (G)
Myers University (U)
North Carolina State University (G)
North Dakota State University (G)
Southern Methodist University (G)
Southern Polytechnic State University (G)
University of Colorado at Boulder (N,G)
University of Idaho (U,G)
University of Michigan–Dearborn (G)
University of South Florida (G)
University of Washington (U)
University of West Florida (N)
University of Wisconsin–Platteville (G)
Virginia Polytechnic Institute and State
    University (U,G)
Western Michigan University (G)

COMPUTER ENGINEERING TECHNOLOGIES

Capitol College (G)
Drexel University (G)
Georgia Institute of Technology (G)
Grantham University (U)
Jefferson Community and Technical College
    (U)
Marlboro College (G)
Southern Methodist University (G)
University of California, Davis (N)

COMPUTER PROGRAMMING

Acadia University (U)
Alvin Community College (U)
Arapahoe Community College (U)
Arkansas State University–Beebe (U)
Athabasca University (N,U)
Bellevue Community College (U)
Bellevue University (U)

Belmont Technical College (U)
Bergen Community College (U)
Blackhawk Technical College (U)
Bowling Green State University (U)
Bristol Community College (N,U)
Bryant and Stratton Online (U)
Butler Community College (U)
Butler County Community College (U)
California State University, San Marcos (U)
Cape Breton University (N)
Carroll Community College (N,U)
Casper College (U)
Central Carolina Community College (U)
Central Georgia Technical College (U)
Central New Mexico Community College (U)
Central Texas College (U)
Cerro Coso Community College (U)
Chemeketa Community College (U)
Clemson University (N)
Cleveland Institute of Electronics (N)
Cleveland State University (U)
Clinton Community College (U)
College of DuPage (U)
College of San Mateo (U)
College of The Albemarle (N)
Columbus State Community College (U)
The Community College of Baltimore County
    (N,U)
Community College of Beaver County (U)
Dakota State University (U)
Danville Community College (U)
De Anza College (U)
Delaware County Community College (N,U)
Delta College (U)
DePaul University (U,G)
Des Moines Area Community College (U)
Eastern Iowa Community College District (N)
East Tennessee State University (N)
Edgecombe Community College (N,U)
Edison College (U)
Edison State Community College (U)
Edmonds Community College (U)
Everest College (U)
Flathead Valley Community College (N)
Galveston College (N)
Gaston College (U)
Granite State College (U)
Grantham University (U)
Hagerstown Community College (N)
Harford Community College (N)
Harrisburg Area Community College (U)
Haywood Community College (U)
Hillsborough Community College (U)
Indiana State University (U)
Iona College (U)
Itawamba Community College (U)
Jacksonville State University (U,G)
James Madison University (N)
Jones College (U)
Kean University (N)
Knowledge Systems Institute (N)
Labette Community College (U)
Lamar State College–Port Arthur (N,U)
Lansing Community College (U)
Limestone College (U)
Lock Haven University of Pennsylvania (U)
Long Beach City College (U)
Longwood University (N)
Los Angeles Harbor College (U)
Madison Area Technical College (U)
Marlboro College (U,G)
Mesa Community College (U)

Middlesex Community College (U)
Middle Tennessee State University (N)
Montgomery County Community College (U)
Mount Wachusett Community College (U)
Murray State University (U)
Myers University (U)
National University (G)
North Carolina State University (U)
North Dakota State College of Science (U)
North Dakota State University (N)
North Harris Montgomery Community
  College District (U)
North Idaho College (N)
North Seattle Community College (U)
NorthWest Arkansas Community College (U)
Nova Southeastern University (G)
Orange Coast College (U)
Pace University (U,G)
Palomar College (U)
Pamlico Community College (U)
Parkland College (U)
Park University (U)
Pasco-Hernando Community College (N,U)
Peirce College (U)
Portland Community College (N)
Red Rocks Community College (U)
Reedley College (N,U)
Regis University (U,G)
Riverside Community College District (N)
Rose State College (U)
Sauk Valley Community College (U)
Schoolcraft College (N,U)
Seminole Community College (U)
Sinclair Community College (U)
Southeast Arkansas College (U)
Southern Polytechnic State University (N,G)
South Piedmont Community College (U)
Southwest Georgia Technical College (U)
Southwest Wisconsin Technical College (U)
State University of New York College at
  Potsdam (N)
Tacoma Community College (U)
Taylor University (N)
Texas State Technical College Waco (N,U)
Tompkins Cortland Community College (U)
Treasure Valley Community College (U)
Tyler Junior College (N,U)
University of California, Davis (N,U)
University of Central Missouri (N)
University of Central Oklahoma (U)
University of Cincinnati (N)
University of Colorado at Denver and Health
  Sciences Center (U)
University of Connecticut (U)
University of Idaho (U)
University of Illinois (N)
University of Management and Technology
  (U)
University of Massachusetts Lowell (U)
University of New Orleans (U,G)
University of North Dakota (N)
University of North Florida (U)
University of South Florida (N,G)
The University of Texas at San Antonio (U)
University of Vermont (N)
University of Washington (N,U)
University of West Florida (U)
Utah State University (G)
Vance-Granville Community College (N,U)
Virginia Highlands Community College (U)
Wake Technical Community College (N)
Washtenaw Community College (U)

Waubonsee Community College (U)
Wenatchee Valley College (N)
Westchester Community College (U)
Western Piedmont Community College (U)
Westwood Online (U)
Wilkes Community College (U)
Wisconsin Indianhead Technical College
  (N,U)
York County Community College (U)
Yuba College (U)

COMPUTER SCIENCE

Acadia University (U)
Alvin Community College (U)
Anne Arundel Community College (U)
Arapahoe Community College (U)
Arkansas State University–Mountain Home
  (U)
Athabasca University (N,U,G)
Auburn University (U,G)
Azusa Pacific University (U,G)
Bellevue Community College (U)
Belmont Technical College (U)
Bergen Community College (U)
Bismarck State College (U)
Bowling Green State University (U)
Bristol Community College (N,U)
Broome Community College (U)
Buffalo State College, State University of
  New York (U)
Butler County Community College (U)
Cabrillo College (U)
California State University, Chico (G)
Capitol College (G)
Carlow University (U)
Carroll College (U,G)
Casper College (U)
Cayuga County Community College (U)
Central Carolina Community College (U)
Central Texas College (U)
Central Wyoming College (U)
Chattanooga State Technical Community
  College (U)
Chemeketa Community College (U)
Clackamas Community College (U)
Clarion University of Pennsylvania (U)
Cleveland Institute of Electronics (N)
Cleveland State University (U)
Cloud County Community College (U)
College of The Albemarle (N,U)
College of the Siskiyous (U)
College of the Southwest (U)
Colorado Mountain College District System
  (U)
Colorado State University (U,G)
Colorado Technical University (U)
Columbia University (N,U,G)
The Community College of Baltimore County
  (U)
Community College of Beaver County (N,U)
Concordia University Wisconsin (U)
Connecticut State University System (U)
County College of Morris (U)
Dakota State University (U)
Dallas Baptist University (U)
Danville Community College (U)
Delaware County Community College (N,U)
DePaul University (U,G)
Des Moines Area Community College (U)
Dickinson State University (U)
Drexel University (U,G)

East Carolina University (G)
Eastern Iowa Community College District (N)
Eastern Kentucky University (G)
Eastern Oregon University (U)
Edgecombe Community College (N)
Edison College (U)
Edison State Community College (U)
Embry-Riddle Aeronautical University (U)
Erie Community College (U)
Fayetteville State University (U)
Franklin University (U)
Fullerton College (U)
Gadsden State Community College (U)
George Mason University (U,G)
Georgia Institute of Technology (G)
Grantham University (U)
Harrisburg Area Community College (U)
Hillsborough Community College (U)
Holyoke Community College (U)
Hopkinsville Community College (U)
Houston Community College System (U)
Immaculata University (U)
Indiana State University (U)
Indiana University–Purdue University Fort
  Wayne (U)
Itawamba Community College (U)
Jacksonville State University (U,G)
James Madison University (N,G)
J. Sargeant Reynolds Community College (U)
Kansas City Kansas Community College (U)
Kansas State University (G)
Labette Community College (U)
Lakeland College (U)
Lamar State College–Port Arthur (N,U)
Lehigh Carbon Community College (U)
LeTourneau University (U)
Limestone College (U)
Long Beach City College (U)
Marlboro College (U,G)
Marymount University (G)
Memorial University of Newfoundland (U)
Mercy College (U,G)
Mesa Community College (U)
Mesalands Community College (U)
Middlesex Community College (U)
Middle Tennessee State University (N)
Midway College (U)
Minnesota School of Business–Richfield (U)
Minot State University (U)
Mississippi State University (U,G)
Missouri Southern State University (U)
Moberly Area Community College (U)
Montgomery County Community College (U)
Murray State University (U)
Myers University (U)
National University (G)
New Jersey Institute of Technology (U,G)
New Mexico Institute of Mining and
  Technology (G)
North Dakota State University (N)
Northeast Alabama Community College (U)
Nova Southeastern University (G)
Oakton Community College (U)
Odessa College (U)
Old Dominion University (U)
Pace University (U)
Palomar College (U)
Piedmont Technical College (U)
Portland Community College (U)
Quinnipiac University (U,G)
Red Rocks Community College (U)
Regis University (U,G)

Rend Lake College (U)
Riverside Community College District (U)
Rockland Community College (U)
Rose State College (U)
Sacred Heart University (U,G)
Saddleback College (U)
St. John's University (U)
St. Petersburg College (U)
Schoolcraft College (U)
Seminole Community College (U)
Shippensburg University of Pennsylvania (U)
Simpson College (U)
Snead State Community College (U)
Southeast Arkansas College (U)
Southern Methodist University (G)
Southern Polytechnic State University (U,G)
Stanford University (N)
State University of New York at New Paltz (U,G)
State University of New York at Oswego (U)
Stevens Institute of Technology (N)
Tacoma Community College (U)
Taylor University (U)
Texas A&M University–Commerce (U)
Texas State Technical College Waco (U)
Texas Tech University (G)
Three Rivers Community College (U)
Troy University (U)
Tyler Junior College (U)
Union University (U)
The University of Alabama (U)
University of Alaska Fairbanks (U)
University of California, Davis (N)
University of Central Missouri (U)
University of Colorado at Boulder (N,G)
The University of Findlay (U)
University of Great Falls (U)
University of Idaho (U,G)
University of Illinois (G)
University of Illinois at Springfield (U,G)
University of Illinois at Urbana–Champaign (G)
University of Management and Technology (U)
University of Massachusetts Boston (U)
University of Michigan–Dearborn (U,G)
University of Michigan–Flint (U)
The University of Montana (U)
University of New Hampshire (G)
University of New Orleans (U,G)
University of Pittsburgh at Bradford (U)
University of Saskatchewan (U)
The University of Texas at San Antonio (U,G)
The University of Texas at Tyler (U,G)
University of Vermont (N,U)
The University of Virginia's College at Wise (U)
University of Washington (U,G)
University of Waterloo (U)
University of West Florida (U,G)
Utah State University (G)
Virginia Polytechnic Institute and State University (U,G)
Weber State University (U)
Westchester Community College (U)
Western Michigan University (G)
Western Wyoming Community College (U)
West Los Angeles College (U)
West Valley College (U)
Wharton County Junior College (U)
Wilkes Community College (U)

Williston State College (U)
York Technical College (U)

COMPUTER SOFTWARE AND MEDIA APPLICATIONS

Adams State College (N)
Alvin Community College (U)
Arapahoe Community College (U)
Athabasca University (N,U)
Bainbridge College (N)
Beaufort County Community College (N)
Bellevue Community College (U)
Bellevue University (U)
Belmont Technical College (U)
Berkeley College (U)
Berkeley College-New York City Campus (U)
Berkeley College-Westchester Campus (U)
Bismarck State College (U)
Blackhawk Technical College (N)
Boise State University (G)
Bowling Green State University (N,U,G)
Bristol Community College (N,U)
Bryant and Stratton Online (U)
Caldwell Community College and Technical Institute (N)
California State University, East Bay (U)
California State University, Monterey Bay (U)
Cape Breton University (N)
Cape Cod Community College (U)
Capitol College (G)
Cardinal Stritch University (N)
Carroll College (G)
Carroll Community College (N)
Cascadia Community College (U)
Casper College (U)
Central Georgia Technical College (U)
Central Texas College (U)
Central Wyoming College (N)
Chemeketa Community College (U)
Cincinnati State Technical and Community College (U)
Clark State Community College (U)
Clemson University (N)
Cleveland Institute of Electronics (N)
Cleveland State University (N,U)
College of DuPage (U)
College of The Albemarle (N)
Colorado Mountain College District System (U)
Colorado State University-Pueblo (N)
Columbus State Community College (U)
The Community College of Baltimore County (N)
Community College of Beaver County (N,U)
Community College of Denver (U)
Dallas Baptist University (U,G)
Danville Community College (U)
Darton College (N,U)
Dawson Community College (U)
De Anza College (U)
Delaware County Community College (N,U)
Delta College (U)
DePaul University (G)
Des Moines Area Community College (N)
Duquesne University (G)
East Carolina University (G)
Eastern Iowa Community College District (N)
Eastern Michigan University (G)
Eastern Oklahoma State College (U)
Eastern Wyoming College (U)

East Tennessee State University (N)
Edgecombe Community College (N,U)
Edison State Community College (N,U)
Erie Community College (U)
Fairmont State University (U)
Finger Lakes Community College (N)
Flathead Valley Community College (N,U)
Florida State University (N)
Fontbonne University (U,G)
Fullerton College (U)
Fulton-Montgomery Community College (N)
Gaston College (U)
Glenville State College (U)
Granite State College (N)
Grantham University (U)
Hagerstown Community College (N)
Harrisburg Area Community College (U)
Haywood Community College (N)
Henry Ford Community College (U)
Herkimer County Community College (U)
Hillsborough Community College (U)
Ilisagvik College (U)
Illinois Eastern Community Colleges, Lincoln Trail College (U)
Immaculata University (U)
Indiana University–Purdue University Fort Wayne (N)
Indiana Wesleyan University (U)
Iona College (U)
Jacksonville State University (U,G)
James Sprunt Community College (U)
Jamestown Community College (N)
Jefferson College of Health Sciences (U)
John Wood Community College (U)
Jones College (U)
J. Sargeant Reynolds Community College (U)
Judson College (U)
Kansas City Kansas Community College (U)
Kansas State University (G)
Kaskaskia College (U)
Kean University (N)
Kellogg Community College (U)
Kirkwood Community College (N,U)
Knowledge Systems Institute (N)
Labette Community College (U)
Lake Superior College (U)
Lamar State College–Port Arthur (N,U)
Lewis and Clark Community College (N)
Limestone College (U)
Linn-Benton Community College (U)
Long Beach City College (U)
Lurleen B. Wallace Community College (U)
Luzerne County Community College (U)
Madison Area Technical College (U)
Marlboro College (U,G)
Maryville University of Saint Louis (N)
Massasoit Community College (N,U)
Mercy College (G)
Mesa Community College (U)
Middlesex Community College (N,U)
Middle Tennessee State University (N)
Midstate College (U)
Mitchell Technical Institute (N,U)
Montana Tech of The University of Montana (U)
Montgomery Community College (N,U)
Montgomery County Community College (U)
Mt. San Antonio College (N)
Mount Wachusett Community College (N,U)
Myers University (U)
National University (U,G)
New Mexico Junior College (U)

New York Institute of Technology (N)
North Arkansas College (N)
North Dakota State University (N)
North Harris Montgomery Community
  College District (U)
North Idaho College (N)
North Seattle Community College (U)
NorthWest Arkansas Community College (U)
Northwestern College (U)
Northwestern Connecticut Community College
  (N)
Northwest Mississippi Community College
  (U)
Nova Southeastern University (G)
Oakton Community College (U)
Odessa College (N)
Orange Coast College (U)
Oregon State University (N)
Ouachita Technical College (U)
Pace University (U,G)
Palomar College (U)
Pamlico Community College (U)
Parkland College (U)
Pasco-Hernando Community College (N,U)
Peirce College (U)
Peninsula College (U)
Plymouth State University (N,U)
Portland Community College (N,U)
Quinebaug Valley Community College (N)
Radford University (N)
Randolph Community College (N,U)
Red Rocks Community College (U)
Rend Lake College (N)
Richland Community College (U)
Riverside Community College District (N)
Rose State College (U)
St. Louis Community College System (U)
Saint Paul College–A Community &
  Technical College (U)
San Francisco State University (N)
Sauk Valley Community College (U)
Schenectady County Community College (U)
Schoolcraft College (N,U)
Seattle Pacific University (G)
Seminole Community College (U)
Sinclair Community College (U)
Snead State Community College (U)
Sonoma State University (N)
Southeast Arkansas College (U)
Southern Methodist University (G)
South Piedmont Community College (U)
Southwest Georgia Technical College (N,U)
Southwest Wisconsin Technical College (U)
Spartanburg Community College (U)
Spoon River College (N)
Spring Arbor University (U)
State University of New York College at
  Potsdam (N)
State University of New York College of
  Agriculture and Technology at Morrisville
  (U)
Stevens Institute of Technology (G)
Syracuse University (G)
Taylor University (N)
Texas State Technical College Waco (N,U)
Three Rivers Community College (N)
Tompkins Cortland Community College (N,U)
Tyler Junior College (N,U)
University of Alaska Fairbanks (U)
University of California, Riverside (N)
University of Central Missouri (N)
University of Cincinnati (U)

University of Cincinnati Raymond Walters
  College (U)
University of Connecticut (U)
University of Great Falls (U)
University of Illinois (N)
University of Illinois at Urbana–Champaign
  (G)
University of Lethbridge (U)
The University of Maine at Augusta (U)
University of Management and Technology
  (U)
University of Michigan–Flint (N)
University of Minnesota, Twin Cities Campus
  (U)
The University of Montana–Western (N,U)
The University of North Carolina at Charlotte
  (N)
University of North Dakota (N)
University of North Texas (U,G)
University of Southern Indiana (N)
University of South Florida (N,G)
University of Vermont (N)
University of Washington (N)
University of West Florida (U)
Utah State University (G)
Utah Valley State College (N)
Vance-Granville Community College (N)
Virginia Highlands Community College (U)
Virginia Polytechnic Institute and State
  University (N)
Wake Technical Community College (N,U)
Washtenaw Community College (U)
Wenatchee Valley College (N)
Western Michigan University (U)
Western Piedmont Community College (U)
Western Wyoming Community College (U)
West Hills Community College (N)
West Valley College (U)
West Virginia University (N)
Westwood Online (U)
Wharton County Junior College (U)
York County Community College (U)
Youngstown State University (N)

COMPUTER SYSTEMS ANALYSIS

Arapahoe Community College (U)
Athabasca University (N,U,G)
Bellevue University (U)
Bridgewater State College (N)
Bristol Community College (N,U)
Central Michigan University (G)
Central Texas College (U)
College of Southern Maryland (U)
The Community College of Baltimore County
  (U)
Dakota State University (U)
Dallas Baptist University (U,G)
Delaware County Community College (N)
DePaul University (G)
East Tennessee State University (N)
Edgecombe Community College (U)
Edison State Community College (U)
Erie Community College (U)
Grantham University (U)
Immaculata University (U)
Iona College (G)
Jacksonville State University (U,G)
Jones College (U)
Kirkwood Community College (N)
Lamar State College–Port Arthur (N)
Lawrence Technological University (U)

Limestone College (U)
Marlboro College (U,G)
Maryville University of Saint Louis (N)
Mercy College (G)
Middlesex Community College (N)
Myers University (U)
National University (G)
Nova Southeastern University (G)
Pace University (G)
Plymouth State University (N)
Quinnipiac University (U)
Red Rocks Community College (U)
Rose State College (U)
Seminole Community College (U)
Southeast Arkansas College (U)
Southern Polytechnic State University (G)
Syracuse University (G)
Texas State Technical College Waco (U)
Tyler Junior College (U)
University of California, Davis (U)
University of Dallas (G)
University of Illinois at Urbana–Champaign
  (G)
University of Management and Technology
  (U)
University of New Orleans (U,G)
University of Washington (N)
Utah State University (G)

COMPUTER SYSTEMS NETWORKING AND TELECOMMUNICATIONS

Alpena Community College (U)
Arapahoe Community College (U)
Arkansas State University–Beebe (U)
Athabasca University (U)
Bainbridge College (N)
Bellevue University (U)
Blackhawk Technical College (U)
Bowling Green State University (U)
Bristol Community College (N,U)
Bryant and Stratton Online (U)
Butler County Community College (U)
Capella University (G)
Capitol College (G)
Carl Albert State College (U)
Carroll Community College (N,U)
Cayuga County Community College (U)
Central Georgia Technical College (U)
Central Texas College (U)
Charter Oak State College (U)
Chemeketa Community College (U)
Cincinnati State Technical and Community
  College (U)
Clemson University (N)
Cleveland State University (N)
College of DuPage (U)
College of Southern Maryland (U)
College of The Albemarle (N)
The Community College of Baltimore County
  (U)
Connecticut State University System (G)
Dallas Baptist University (U,G)
Darton College (U)
De Anza College (U)
Delaware County Community College (N,U)
DePaul University (U,G)
DeVry University Online (G)
East Carolina University (G)
Eastern Iowa Community College District (N)
Eastern Michigan University (U)

East Tennessee State University (N)
Edgecombe Community College (U)
Edison State Community College (U)
Fairmont State University (N)
Fulton-Montgomery Community College (N)
Gaston College (U)
George Mason University (G)
Grantham University (U)
Hagerstown Community College (N)
Harford Community College (N)
Herkimer County Community College (U)
Illinois Eastern Community Colleges, Lincoln Trail College (U)
Indiana University–Purdue University Fort Wayne (N)
Iona College (G)
Jacksonville State University (U,G)
James Madison University (N)
Jamestown Community College (N)
Kansas City Kansas Community College (N,U)
Kirkwood Community College (N)
Labette Community College (U)
Lamar State College–Port Arthur (N,U)
Limestone College (U)
Long Beach City College (U)
Madison Area Technical College (U)
Marlboro College (U,G)
Maryville University of Saint Louis (N)
Middle Tennessee State University (N)
Murray State University (U,G)
Myers University (U)
New Jersey Institute of Technology (U,G)
North Harris Montgomery Community College District (U)
North Idaho College (N)
North Seattle Community College (U)
NorthWest Arkansas Community College (U)
Nova Southeastern University (G)
Orangeburg-Calhoun Technical College (U)
Ouachita Technical College (U)
Pace University (U,G)
Pamlico Community College (U)
Pasco-Hernando Community College (U)
Patrick Henry Community College (U)
Peirce College (U)
Plymouth State University (N)
Portland Community College (N)
Pulaski Technical College (U)
Red Rocks Community College (U)
Regis University (U,G)
Riverside Community College District (U)
Rose State College (U)
Sampson Community College (U)
Seminole Community College (U)
Sinclair Community College (U)
Sonoma State University (N)
Southeast Arkansas College (U)
Southern Methodist University (G)
Southern Polytechnic State University (G)
South Piedmont Community College (U)
Southwest Georgia Technical College (U)
Southwest Wisconsin Technical College (U)
Stanford University (N)
State University of New York at Oswego (U)
Syracuse University (U,G)
Taylor University (N)
Texas State Technical College Waco (U)
Tompkins Cortland Community College (N)
Tunxis Community College (U)
Tyler Junior College (U)
The University of Alabama (U)

University of Central Missouri (N)
University of Colorado at Boulder (N,G)
University of Dallas (G)
University of Denver (G)
University of Illinois (G)
University of Illinois at Urbana–Champaign (G)
University of Management and Technology (U)
University of Maryland University College (G)
University of Massachusetts Lowell (U)
University of Minnesota, Twin Cities Campus (U)
The University of Texas System (U)
University of West Florida (U)
University of Wisconsin–Stout (N)
Utah State University (G)
Vance-Granville Community College (N,U)
Virginia Highlands Community College (U)
Wake Technical Community College (U)
Wenatchee Valley College (N)
Westchester Community College (U)
Western Piedmont Community College (U)
Westwood Online (U)
Wharton County Junior College (U)
Youngstown State University (N)
Yuba College (U)

COMPUTER/INFORMATION TECHNOLOGY ADMINISTRATION AND MANAGEMENT

Alpena Community College (U)
Alvin Community College (U)
American Public University System (U)
Arapahoe Community College (U)
Athabasca University (N,U,G)
Auburn University (N)
Baker College of Flint (U)
Bellevue University (U)
Bloomfield College (U)
Bridgewater State College (U)
Bristol Community College (N,U)
Bryant and Stratton Online (U)
Caldwell Community College and Technical Institute (N)
California State University, Dominguez Hills (N)
Cape Breton University (N)
Capella University (G)
Capitol College (G)
Carroll Community College (U)
Central Georgia Technical College (U)
Central Washington University (U)
Cincinnati State Technical and Community College (U)
Cleveland Institute of Electronics (N)
College of Southern Maryland (N)
College of The Albemarle (N)
Colorado Technical University (U,G)
The Community College of Baltimore County (U)
Community College of Denver (U)
Dakota State University (U)
Dallas Baptist University (G)
Delaware County Community College (U)
DePaul University (G)
Drexel University (U)
Duquesne University (G)
D'Youville College (U)
East Carolina University (U,G)

Eastern Iowa Community College District (N)
Edgecombe Community College (N,U)
Edison State Community College (N,U)
Elgin Community College (U)
Fairmont State University (N)
Flathead Valley Community College (N)
Franklin Pierce University (U,G)
Galveston College (N)
Granite State College (U)
Grantham University (U)
Hillsborough Community College (U)
Houston Community College System (U)
Immaculata University (U)
Jacksonville State University (U,G)
Jefferson Community and Technical College (U)
John Jay College of Criminal Justice of the City University of New York (U)
Kettering University (N)
Lamar State College–Port Arthur (N)
Lawrence Technological University (U)
Liberty University (U)
Limestone College (U)
Madison Area Technical College (U)
Marlboro College (U,G)
Mercy College (G)
Mesa Community College (U)
Middle Tennessee State University (N)
Myers University (U)
New Jersey Institute of Technology (G)
New York Institute of Technology (N)
North Arkansas College (N,U)
North Dakota State College of Science (U)
North Idaho College (N)
Northwest Missouri State University (G)
Nova Southeastern University (G)
Orangeburg-Calhoun Technical College (U)
Orange Coast College (U)
Oregon Institute of Technology (U)
Pace University (G)
Pamlico Community College (U)
Patrick Henry Community College (U)
Peirce College (U)
Portland Community College (N)
Regis University (U,G)
Rogers State University (U)
Rose State College (U)
Ryerson University (U)
Saint Joseph's College of Maine (U)
Sauk Valley Community College (U)
Schiller International University (G)
Seminole Community College (U)
Sonoma State University (N)
Southeast Arkansas College (U)
Southern Illinois University Carbondale (U)
Southern Methodist University (G)
South Piedmont Community College (U)
Southwestern College (U)
Southwest Georgia Technical College (U)
State University of New York College of Agriculture and Technology at Morrisville (U)
State University of New York Empire State College (U)
Syracuse University (G)
Taylor University (N,U)
Tyler Junior College (U)
University of California, Davis (N)
University of Cincinnati Raymond Walters College (U)
University of Connecticut (U)
University of Denver (G)

University of Illinois (G)
University of Illinois at Urbana–Champaign (G)
University of Management and Technology (U)
University of Maryland University College (G)
University of Massachusetts Boston (U)
University of North Texas (U)
University of Southern Indiana (U)
The University of Tennessee (N)
The University of Toledo (U)
University of Toronto (N,U)
University of Vermont (N)
University of Washington (N)
Vance-Granville Community College (U)
Virginia Highlands Community College (U)
West Los Angeles College (U)
West Virginia University at Parkersburg (N,U)
York County Community College (U)

CONSTRUCTION ENGINEERING

Cleveland Institute of Electronics (N)
Seminole Community College (U)
Southern Methodist University (G)
University of South Florida (G)

CONSTRUCTION ENGINEERING TECHNOLOGY

Bowling Green State University (G)
Clemson University (N)
Delaware County Community College (U)
Indiana State University (U)
Ivy Tech Community College–Northeast (U)
James Madison University (N)
National University (U)
Orange Coast College (U)
Pennsylvania College of Technology (U)
Pittsburg State University (U)
Stanford University (N)
University of Southern Mississippi (G)
University of Washington (U,G)

CONSTRUCTION MANAGEMENT

Auburn University (N)
Central Michigan University (U)
Clemson University (U,G)
Colorado State University (U)
Columbus State Community College (U)
East Carolina University (G)
Indiana State University (U)
Texas A&M University–Commerce (G)
Washtenaw Community College (U)

CONSTRUCTION TRADES

Central Michigan University (U)
Cleveland Institute of Electronics (N)
Lock Haven University of Pennsylvania (N)

CONSTRUCTION TRADES RELATED

Alpena Community College (N,U)
Bowling Green State University (N)
Delaware County Community College (U)
James Madison University (N)

Longwood University (N)
West Virginia University at Parkersburg (N)

COSMETOLOGY AND RELATED PERSONAL GROOMING SERVICES

Central Georgia Technical College (U)
Gadsden State Community College (U)
James Madison University (N)
Pamlico Community College (U)
Southwest Wisconsin Technical College (U)

COUNSELING PSYCHOLOGY

Amberton University (G)
Athabasca University (N,U,G)
Atlantic University (N,G)
The Baptist College of Florida (U)
Briercrest Distance Learning (U)
Capella University (G)
Carlow University (G)
Central Texas College (U)
Chadron State College (G)
Cincinnati Christian University (G)
Cleveland Institute of Electronics (N)
College of the Southwest (G)
Columbus State Community College (U)
Corban College (U)
Delaware County Community College (U)
Eastern Kentucky University (G)
Immaculata University (G)
Indiana State University (G)
James Madison University (N)
Liberty University (G)
Malone College (G)
Master's College and Seminary (U)
Mercy College (G)
Mississippi State University (U,G)
Missouri State University (G)
Montana State University–Billings (G)
Naropa University (U)
National University (U,G)
North Central State College (U)
Oklahoma State University (U)
Palomar College (U)
Prescott College (U)
Providence College and Theological Seminary (N,G)
Regent University (G)
St. Cloud State University (U)
Saybrook Graduate School and Research Center (G)
Shasta Bible College (U,G)
State University of New York at Oswego (U,G)
Taylor University (U)
University of Alaska Fairbanks (G)
University of Bridgeport (U)
University of Great Falls (U,G)
University of Hawaii–West Oahu (U)
University of Houston–Victoria (G)
The University of Maine at Augusta (U)
University of Maryland Eastern Shore (G)
University of Massachusetts Boston (G)
University of Missouri–Columbia (G)
The University of North Carolina at Charlotte (N)
The University of South Dakota (G)
The University of Toledo (G)
University of Wisconsin–Superior (U)
Upper Iowa University (U)
Wayland Baptist University (G)

Wayne State College (G)
Western Michigan University (G)

CRAFTS, FOLK ART AND ARTISANRY

Big Bend Community College (U)
Blackhawk Technical College (N)
Cleveland Institute of Electronics (N)
Cleveland State University (G)
Hillsborough Community College (N)
James Madison University (N)
Lewis and Clark Community College (N)
Middle Tennessee State University (N)
Naugatuck Valley Community College (N)
The University of Tennessee at Martin (N)
West Virginia University at Parkersburg (N)

CREATIVE WRITING

Adams State College (N)
Allen College (U)
Alvin Community College (U)
Arkansas State University–Beebe (U)
Athabasca University (U)
Atlantic University (N,G)
Bellevue Community College (U)
Blackhawk Technical College (N)
Bowling Green State University (U,G)
Bridgewater State College (N)
Briercrest Distance Learning (U)
Brookdale Community College (U)
Butler County Community College (U)
Caldwell Community College and Technical Institute (N)
Cape Breton University (U)
Cardinal Stritch University (N)
Carroll Community College (N)
Casper College (U)
Central New Mexico Community College (U)
Chemeketa Community College (U)
Clark State Community College (U)
Clatsop Community College (U)
Clemson University (N)
Cleveland Institute of Electronics (N)
College of Southern Maryland (U)
College of the Siskiyous (N)
College of the Southwest (U)
Columbus State Community College (U)
Community College of Denver (U)
County College of Morris (U)
Dallas Baptist University (U)
Darton College (N)
Dawson Community College (U)
Delaware County Community College (U)
Des Moines Area Community College (U)
DeVry University Online (U)
Drake University (U)
D'Youville College (G)
Earlham School of Religion (G)
Eastern Washington University (U)
East Tennessee State University (N)
Erie Community College (U)
Feather River College (U)
Goucher College (G)
Hillsborough Community College (U)
Hocking College (U)
Holyoke Community College (U)
James Madison University (N)
Jamestown Community College (N)
Jefferson Community and Technical College (U)

Jefferson Community College (U)
John A. Logan College (U)
John Tyler Community College (U)
Jones County Junior College (U)
Judson College (U)
Kansas City Kansas Community College (N)
Kean University (N)
Lamar State College–Port Arthur (N)
Lansing Community College (U)
Lewis and Clark Community College (N)
Limestone College (U)
Linn-Benton Community College (U)
Long Beach City College (U)
Maryville University of Saint Louis (N)
Massasoit Community College (N)
Mercy College (U)
Mesa Community College (U)
Middlesex Community College (N,U)
Minnesota State University Moorhead (U)
Minot State University (U)
Missouri State University (U)
Mount Allison University (N)
Mount Saint Vincent University (N)
Mt. San Antonio College (U)
Naropa University (N,U)
National University (G)
The New School: A University (N,U)
New York Institute of Technology (U)
Northern Virginia Community College (U)
North Harris Montgomery Community
  College District (U)
North Idaho College (N)
Odessa College (N)
Oklahoma State University (U)
Oregon State University (U)
Park University (U)
Portland Community College (N)
Prescott College (U,G)
Queen's University at Kingston (U)
Reedley College (N,U)
Richland Community College (U)
Riverside Community College District (N)
Rose State College (U)
St. Clair County Community College (U)
St. Cloud State University (U)
Sam Houston State University (U)
Sinclair Community College (U)
Snead State Community College (U)
Southwest Virginia Community College (U)
Spring Arbor University (U)
State University of New York College at
  Potsdam (N)
State University of New York College of
  Agriculture and Technology at Morrisville
  (U)
Tacoma Community College (U)
Taylor University (N,U)
Texas A&M University–Commerce (U)
Texas State University-San Marcos (U)
Three Rivers Community College (U)
Treasure Valley Community College (U)
Tyler Junior College (U)
The University of Alabama (U)
University of Central Arkansas (U)
University of Colorado at Denver and Health
  Sciences Center (U)
University of Denver (G)
University of Illinois (N)
University of La Verne (G)
University of Maine (U)
The University of Maine at Augusta (U)
University of Maine at Fort Kent (U)

University of Minnesota, Morris (U)
University of Missouri–Columbia (U)
University of Nebraska at Omaha (U,G)
University of New Orleans (N,U,G)
The University of North Carolina at Chapel
  Hill (N,U)
University of North Florida (U)
The University of South Dakota (U)
University of Southern Mississippi (U)
University of South Florida (N)
The University of Tennessee (N,U)
The University of Texas at El Paso (G)
The University of Texas System (U)
University of the Pacific (U)
University of Washington (N,U)
University of Wisconsin Colleges (U)
University of Wisconsin–Whitewater (U,G)
Utah Valley State College (U)
Vincennes University (U)
Waubonsee Community College (U)
Wenatchee Valley College (N)
West Los Angeles College (U)
West Valley College (U)
Wharton County Junior College (U)
Wilkes Community College (U)
Youngstown State University (N)

CRIMINAL JUSTICE AND CORRECTIONS

Adams State College (U)
Alpena Community College (U)
American Public University System (U,G)
Andrew Jackson University (U,G)
Anne Arundel Community College (U)
Arapahoe Community College (U)
Arizona Western College (U)
Arkansas State University–Beebe (U)
Ashford University (U)
Athabasca University (N,U)
Bemidji State University (U)
Bergen Community College (U)
Berkeley College (U)
Bismarck State College (U)
Blackhawk Technical College (N,U)
Boise State University (U)
Brenau University (U)
Buena Vista University (U)
Butler Community College (U)
Cabrillo College (U)
Caldwell Community College and Technical
  Institute (N)
California State University, San Bernardino
  (U,G)
California University of Pennsylvania (U,G)
Capella University (G)
Carroll Community College (U)
Central Carolina Community College (N,U)
Central Georgia Technical College (U)
Central New Mexico Community College (U)
Central Texas College (U)
Central Washington University (U)
Cerro Coso Community College (U)
Chaminade University of Honolulu (U,G)
Chemeketa Community College (U)
Chesapeake College (U)
Clackamas Community College (U)
Clinton Community College (U)
Cloud County Community College (U)
Clovis Community College (U)
College of DuPage (U)
College of Southern Maryland (U)

College of the Southwest (U)
Colorado Technical University (U)
Columbia College (U)
The Community College of Baltimore County
  (U)
Community College of Beaver County (U)
Connecticut State University System (U)
Dallas Baptist University (U,G)
Danville Community College (U)
Darton College (U)
Dawson Community College (U)
Delaware County Community College (U)
Delta College (U)
Des Moines Area Community College (U)
East Carolina University (G)
Eastern Kentucky University (G)
Eastern Oklahoma State College (U)
Eastern Wyoming College (U)
East Tennessee State University (U)
Edison College (U)
Elizabeth City State University (U)
Erie Community College (U)
Everett Community College (U)
Fayetteville State University (U,G)
Feather River College (U)
Fort Hays State University (U)
Franklin Pierce University (U)
Gaston College (U)
Glenville State College (U)
Grand View College (U)
Granite State College (U)
Grantham University (U)
Harrisburg Area Community College (U)
Henry Ford Community College (U)
Herkimer County Community College (U)
Holyoke Community College (U)
Indiana State University (U,G)
Indiana Wesleyan University (U)
Iowa State University of Science and
  Technology (U)
Ivy Tech Community College–Bloomington
  (U)
Ivy Tech Community College–Central Indiana
  (U)
Ivy Tech Community College–East Central
  (U)
Ivy Tech Community College–Kokomo (U)
Ivy Tech Community College–Southeast (U)
Ivy Tech Community College–Southern
  Indiana (U)
Ivy Tech Community College–Southwest (U)
Ivy Tech Community College–Whitewater (U)
Jacksonville State University (U,G)
James Madison University (N)
James Sprunt Community College (U)
Jefferson Community and Technical College
  (U)
Jefferson Community College (U)
John Jay College of Criminal Justice of the
  City University of New York (U)
John Tyler Community College (U)
John Wood Community College (U)
Jones County Junior College (U)
J. Sargeant Reynolds Community College (U)
Judson College (U)
Kansas City Kansas Community College (U)
Kean University (U)
Kirkwood Community College (U)
Lehigh Carbon Community College (U)
Lewis and Clark Community College (U)
Liberty University (U)
Limestone College (U)

Linn-Benton Community College (U)
Longwood University (G)
Los Angeles Harbor College (U)
Madison Area Technical College (U)
Mansfield University of Pennsylvania (U)
Marian College of Fond du Lac (U)
Mercy College (U)
Mesa Community College (U)
Metropolitan State University (U,G)
Middlesex Community College (U)
Middle Tennessee State University (U)
Midwestern State University (U)
Minot State University (U)
Missouri Southern State University (U)
Missouri State University (G)
Monmouth University (G)
Monroe Community College (U)
Montgomery Community College (U)
Mountain Empire Community College (U)
Mount Wachusett Community College (U)
Myers University (U)
National University (U)
Naugatuck Valley Community College (U)
New Jersey City University (U)
New Mexico Junior College (U)
New Mexico State University (G)
New York Institute of Technology (U)
Northeast Alabama Community College (U)
NorthWest Arkansas Community College (U)
Northwestern Oklahoma State University (U)
Northwest Mississippi Community College (U)
Old Dominion University (U)
Orangeburg-Calhoun Technical College (U)
Ouachita Technical College (U)
Pace University (U)
Palomar College (U)
Pamlico Community College (U)
Park University (U)
Passaic County Community College (U)
Peninsula College (U)
Pittsburg State University (U)
Plymouth State University (U)
Portland State University (U)
Randolph Community College (U)
Rappahannock Community College (U)
Reedley College (U)
Rend Lake College (U)
Roger Williams University (U)
Roosevelt University (U)
Rose State College (U)
Ryerson University (U)
St. Cloud State University (U,G)
St. John's University (U)
Salem State College (U)
Sampson Community College (U)
Sauk Valley Community College (U)
Saybrook Graduate School and Research Center (G)
Schenectady County Community College (U)
Schoolcraft College (U)
Seminole Community College (U)
Shippensburg University of Pennsylvania (U,G)
Simpson College (U)
Snead State Community College (U)
Southeast Arkansas College (U)
Southern Illinois University Carbondale (U)
Southern New Hampshire University (G)
South Piedmont Community College (U)
Southwest Georgia Technical College (U)
Spring Arbor University (U,G)

State University of New York at Oswego (U)
State University of New York Empire State College (U)
Tacoma Community College (U)
Taylor University (U)
Texas A&M University–Commerce (U)
Texas A&M University–Texarkana (U)
Three Rivers Community College (U)
Tunxis Community College (N,U)
Tyler Junior College (U)
The University of Alabama (U)
University of Alaska Fairbanks (U)
University of Central Missouri (U,G)
University of Cincinnati (U)
University of Colorado at Colorado Springs (G)
University of Connecticut (U)
University of Delaware (U)
The University of Findlay (U)
University of Great Falls (U,G)
University of Hawaii–West Oahu (U)
University of Idaho (U)
The University of Maine at Augusta (U)
University of Maine at Fort Kent (N,U)
University of Maryland University College (U)
University of Massachusetts Boston (U,G)
University of Massachusetts Dartmouth (U)
University of Massachusetts Lowell (G)
University of Missouri–Columbia (N)
University of North Alabama (U)
The University of North Carolina at Chapel Hill (U)
University of Pittsburgh at Bradford (U)
The University of South Dakota (U,G)
University of Southern Mississippi (U,G)
University of South Florida (U,G)
The University of Tennessee at Martin (N)
The University of Texas at El Paso (U)
The University of Texas at Tyler (U)
University of Wisconsin–Platteville (N,G)
University of Wyoming (U)
Upper Iowa University (U)
Vance-Granville Community College (U)
Vincennes University (U)
Virginia Highlands Community College (U)
Wake Technical Community College (U)
Washburn University (G)
Waubonsee Community College (U)
Wayland Baptist University (U)
Westchester Community College (U)
Western Piedmont Community College (U)
West Los Angeles College (U)
West Shore Community College (U)
West Virginia University at Parkersburg (U)
Westwood Online (U)
Wharton County Junior College (U)
Youngstown State University (U)

CRIMINOLOGY

Adams State College (U)
Athabasca University (N,U)
Bellevue Community College (U)
Bemidji State University (U)
Berkeley College (U)
Berkeley College-New York City Campus (U)
Berkeley College-Westchester Campus (U)
Bismarck State College (U)
Brenau University (U)
Bridgewater State College (U)
Buena Vista University (U)

Butler Community College (U)
Butler County Community College (U)
Central Texas College (U)
Chadron State College (U)
Charter Oak State College (U)
Chemeketa Community College (U)
Clatsop Community College (U)
Colorado Technical University (U)
The Community College of Baltimore County (U)
Dallas Baptist University (U,G)
Danville Community College (U)
Des Moines Area Community College (U)
East Carolina University (G)
Eastern Oregon University (U)
Everett Community College (U)
Gaston College (U)
Grand View College (U)
Houston Community College System (U)
Indiana State University (U,G)
Itawamba Community College (U)
Jacksonville State University (U,G)
Jefferson Community College (U)
Kirkwood Community College (U)
Labette Community College (U)
Lewis and Clark Community College (U)
Lock Haven University of Pennsylvania (U)
Los Angeles Harbor College (U)
Louisiana State University and Agricultural and Mechanical College (U)
Memorial University of Newfoundland (G)
Middlesex Community College (U)
Montgomery County Community College (U)
Mountain Empire Community College (U)
Mount Wachusett Community College (U)
Myers University (U)
National University (G)
Neumann College (U)
New Jersey City University (G)
Northern State University (U)
Northwest Mississippi Community College (U)
Pace University (U)
Pamlico Community College (U)
Park University (U)
Plymouth State University (U)
Radford University (G)
Riverside Community College District (U)
Roger Williams University (U)
Saint Joseph's College of Maine (U)
Sauk Valley Community College (U)
Seminole Community College (U)
Snead State Community College (U)
Southeast Arkansas College (U)
Southern Illinois University Carbondale (U)
Southwest Georgia Technical College (U)
Texas State University-San Marcos (U)
Tunxis Community College (U)
University of Central Oklahoma (U)
University of Connecticut (G)
The University of Findlay (U)
University of Hawaii–West Oahu (U)
University of Massachusetts Dartmouth (U)
University of Massachusetts Lowell (G)
University of Missouri–Columbia (N)
University of Northern Iowa (U,G)
The University of South Dakota (U)
University of Southern Mississippi (U)
University of South Florida (G)
The University of Texas at Arlington (U)
The University of Texas at Tyler (U)
The University of Toledo (U)

University of Washington (U)
University of Waterloo (U)
University of Wisconsin–Platteville (G)
Upper Iowa University (U)
Vance-Granville Community College (U)
Waubonsee Community College (U)

CULINARY ARTS AND RELATED SERVICES

Blackhawk Technical College (U)
Cabrillo College (U)
Central New Mexico Community College (U)
Central Texas College (U)
Central Wyoming College (N)
Columbus State Community College (U)
County College of Morris (U)
East Tennessee State University (N)
Erie Community College (U)
Hagerstown Community College (N)
James Madison University (N)
Middle Tennessee State University (N)
Mitchell Technical Institute (U)
Naugatuck Valley Community College (U)
New York Institute of Technology (N)
Oakton Community College (N)
Schenectady County Community College (U)
Schoolcraft College (U)
Southwest Wisconsin Technical College (U)
State University of New York College at
   Potsdam (N)
University of Nebraska–Lincoln (G)
Wake Technical Community College (U)
York County Community College (U)

CURRICULUM AND INSTRUCTION

Alvin Community College (U)
Ashford University (U,G)
Athabasca University (G)
Bloomsburg University of Pennsylvania (G)
Boise State University (U,G)
Brenau University (U)
Bridgewater State College (U)
Buena Vista University (U,G)
California State University, Chico (U)
Central Michigan University (G)
Cerritos College (U)
Chadron State College (G)
Chemeketa Community College (U)
Cleveland State University (G)
The College of St. Scholastica (G)
College of the Southwest (G)
Columbia College (U)
Columbia International University (G)
Concordia University Wisconsin (G)
Connecticut State University System (U,G)
Dallas Baptist University (G)
Drexel University (G)
Duquesne University (G)
East Carolina University (U)
Eastern Kentucky University (U,G)
East Tennessee State University (U,G)
Flathead Valley Community College (U)
Indiana State University (U,G)
Jacksonville State University (U,G)
Lehigh Carbon Community College (U)
Lesley University (G)
Lewis and Clark Community College (N)
Liberty University (G)
Longwood University (U)

Louisiana State University and Agricultural
   and Mechanical College (U)
McMurry University (U)
Mississippi State University (U,G)
Missouri State University (G)
Mitchell Technical Institute (U)
Montana State University–Billings (U,G)
North Carolina State University (G)
North Dakota State University (G)
Northwestern Oklahoma State University (U)
Pace University (G)
Pittsburg State University (U,G)
Radford University (G)
Regis University (G)
Roosevelt University (U)
Saint Joseph's College of Maine (G)
Seattle Pacific University (G)
Southwest Georgia Technical College (U)
Southwest Wisconsin Technical College (U)
State University of New York at New Paltz
   (U)
State University of New York at Oswego (G)
Texas A&M University–Commerce (G)
Texas Tech University (G)
University of Alaska Fairbanks (G)
University of Arkansas (U)
University of Central Arkansas (G)
University of Central Missouri (U,G)
University of Houston–Victoria (G)
University of Illinois (G)
University of La Verne (G)
University of Massachusetts Lowell (G)
University of Missouri–Columbia (U,G)
The University of Montana (U,G)
University of Nebraska–Lincoln (U,G)
University of New Orleans (U,G)
The University of North Carolina at
   Greensboro (G)
University of North Florida (U)
University of North Texas (U,G)
University of Saskatchewan (U)
University of Southern Mississippi (G)
University of South Florida (U,G)
The University of Tennessee (U)
The University of Texas at Arlington (G)
The University of Texas at San Antonio (G)
The University of Texas at Tyler (U)
The University of Texas System (U,G)
The University of Toledo (U,G)
University of Washington (U)
University of Wisconsin–Superior (U)
University of Wisconsin–Whitewater (U)
Utah State University (G)
Virginia Polytechnic Institute and State
   University (G)

DANCE

California State University, Chico (U)
Central Wyoming College (N)
Middle Tennessee State University (N)
Naugatuck Valley Community College (N)
Orange Coast College (U)
Texas State University-San Marcos (U)
The University of North Carolina at
   Greensboro (U,G)
University of Waterloo (U)
West Virginia University at Parkersburg (N)

DATA ENTRY/MICROCOMPUTER APPLICATIONS

Arkansas State University–Beebe (U)
Athabasca University (N)
Berkeley College (U)
Berkeley College-New York City Campus (U)
Berkeley College-Westchester Campus (U)
Bristol Community College (N,U)
Butler Community College (U)
Butler County Community College (U)
Carl Albert State College (U)
Central Georgia Technical College (U)
Central Wyoming College (N,U)
Cerritos College (U)
Chemeketa Community College (U)
Clemson University (N)
Cleveland Institute of Electronics (N)
Cleveland State University (N)
College of The Albemarle (N)
Colorado State University-Pueblo (N)
De Anza College (U)
Delaware County Community College (U)
Des Moines Area Community College (U)
East Carolina University (U)
Eastern Iowa Community College District (N)
Edgecombe Community College (N,U)
Erie Community College (U)
George C. Wallace Community College (U)
Grantham University (U)
Holyoke Community College (U)
James Madison University (N)
Jefferson Community and Technical College
   (U)
John Wood Community College (U)
Kansas City Kansas Community College (U)
Kirkwood Community College (N)
Lamar State College–Port Arthur (N,U)
Lewis and Clark Community College (U)
Limestone College (U)
Marlboro College (G)
Maryville University of Saint Louis (N)
Middlesex Community College (U)
Mitchell Technical Institute (N)
Mount Saint Vincent University (U)
Myers University (U)
Naugatuck Valley Community College (N)
North Dakota State University (N,U)
North Harris Montgomery Community
   College District (U)
Oakton Community College (N,U)
Palomar College (U)
St. Louis Community College System (U)
Sampson Community College (U)
Seminole Community College (U)
Southeast Arkansas College (U)
Southwest Georgia Technical College (U)
Spartanburg Community College (U)
State University of New York College at
   Potsdam (N)
Tacoma Community College (U)
Taylor University (N)
Texas State Technical College Waco (U)
University of Minnesota, Crookston (U)
University of North Texas (U)
University of West Florida (U)
Utah State University (U)
Vance-Granville Community College (N)
Wake Technical Community College (N)
West Los Angeles College (U)

DATA PROCESSING

Adams State College (N)
Athabasca University (N,U)
Auburn University (N)
Bristol Community College (N,U)
Central Georgia Technical College (U)
Central New Mexico Community College (U)
Cincinnati State Technical and Community
 College (U)
Clemson University (N)
College of The Albemarle (N)
The Community College of Baltimore County
 (U)
Delaware County Community College (U)
Des Moines Area Community College (U)
East Carolina University (U,G)
Feather River College (U)
Jacksonville State University (U)
James Sprunt Community College (U)
John A. Logan College (U)
Jones College (U)
Kirkwood Community College (N)
Lamar State College–Port Arthur (N)
Lewis and Clark Community College (U)
Limestone College (U)
Marlboro College (G)
Maryville University of Saint Louis (N,U)
Naugatuck Valley Community College (N)
Northeast Alabama Community College (U)
Red Rocks Community College (U)
Seminole Community College (U)
Southwest Georgia Technical College (U)
State University of New York College at
 Potsdam (U)
Syracuse University (G)
Taylor University (N)
Tompkins Cortland Community College (N)
University of Illinois at Urbana–Champaign
 (G)
University of Minnesota, Crookston (U)
Utah State University (U)
Wake Technical Community College (N)
Westchester Community College (U)
Wilkes Community College (U)

DEMOGRAPHY AND POPULATION

Athabasca University (U)
Delaware County Community College (U)
University of Southern Mississippi (G)

DENTAL SUPPORT SERVICES AND ALLIED PROFESSIONS

Blackhawk Technical College (U)
Cape Cod Community College (N)
Chattanooga State Technical Community
 College (U)
Danville Community College (U)
Gulf Coast Community College (U)
John A. Logan College (U)
Middlesex Community College (U)
Missouri Southern State University (U)
Monroe Community College (U)
Montgomery County Community College (U)
Oregon Institute of Technology (U)
Peninsula College (U)
Pennsylvania College of Technology (U)
Portland Community College (U)
Tunxis Community College (U)
University of Bridgeport (U)

The University of British Columbia (U)
University of Idaho (U)
University of Southern Indiana (U)
Vermont Technical College (U)
Washtenaw Community College (U)
West Liberty State College (U)
West Los Angeles College (U)

DENTISTRY AND ORAL SCIENCES (ADVANCED/GRADUATE)

Danville Community College (U)
West Los Angeles College (U)

DESIGN AND APPLIED ARTS

Academy of Art University (U,G)
Brenau University (U)
California State University, Dominguez Hills
 (N)
Central Georgia Technical College (U)
Central Wyoming College (N)
Colorado State University (U)
Danville Community College (U)
Edison State Community College (U)
John A. Logan College (U)
Lansing Community College (U)
Minneapolis College of Art and Design
 (N,U,G)
New Mexico Junior College (U)
New York Institute of Technology (U)
Piedmont Technical College (U)
Pittsburg State University (U,G)
Red Rocks Community College (U)
San Francisco State University (N)
Tacoma Community College (U)
University of Alaska Fairbanks (U)
University of California, Los Angeles (G)
West Liberty State College (U)
West Los Angeles College (U)
Westwood Online (U)

DEVELOPMENTAL AND CHILD PSYCHOLOGY

Andrews University (U)
Anne Arundel Community College (U)
Arkansas State University–Beebe (U)
Athabasca University (N,U,G)
Bellevue Community College (U)
Bergen Community College (U)
Black Hills State University (U,G)
Brenau University (U)
Brookdale Community College (U)
Burlington County College (U)
Butler Community College (U)
Cape Breton University (U)
Cape Cod Community College (U)
Central Texas College (U)
Chadron State College (U)
Chattanooga State Technical Community
 College (U)
Chemeketa Community College (U)
Clatsop Community College (U)
Clovis Community College (U)
College of DuPage (U)
College of the Southwest (U)
Colorado Mountain College District System
 (U)
Colorado State University (U)
Columbus State Community College (U)

Community College of Beaver County (U)
Concordia University, St. Paul (U,G)
County College of Morris (U)
Danville Community College (U)
Dawson Community College (U)
De Anza College (U)
Delaware County Community College (U)
Delta College (U)
Des Moines Area Community College (U)
East Central Community College (U)
East Tennessee State University (U)
Edmonds Community College (U)
Erie Community College (U)
Fullerton College (U)
Georgia Highlands College (U)
Governors State University (U,G)
Graceland University (U)
Gulf Coast Community College (U)
Harrisburg Area Community College (U)
Herkimer County Community College (U)
Hillsborough Community College (U)
Houston Community College System (U)
Indiana State University (G)
Itawamba Community College (U)
Jacksonville State University (U,G)
Jefferson Community College (U)
John Wood Community College (U)
J. Sargeant Reynolds Community College (U)
Judson College (U)
Kansas State University (U)
Kaskaskia College (U)
Labette Community College (U)
Lehigh Carbon Community College (U)
Lewis and Clark Community College (U)
Liberty University (U)
Louisiana State University and Agricultural
 and Mechanical College (U)
Malone College (U)
Manatee Community College (U)
Marshall University (U)
Mercy College (U)
Middlesex Community College (U)
Mississippi State University (U)
Missouri Southern State University (U)
Missouri State University (U)
Monterey Peninsula College (U)
Montgomery County Community College (U)
Mountain Empire Community College (U)
Naropa University (U)
Nassau Community College (U)
National University (U)
North Dakota State College of Science (U)
North Dakota State University (U)
Northern Virginia Community College (U)
NorthWest Arkansas Community College (U)
Oakton Community College (U)
Odessa College (U)
Palomar College (U)
Parkland College (U)
Patrick Henry Community College (U)
Peninsula College (U)
Portland Community College (U)
Red Rocks Community College (U)
Richland Community College (U)
Rose State College (U)
Saddleback College (U)
Saint Joseph's College of Maine (U)
Saybrook Graduate School and Research
 Center (G)
Schoolcraft College (U)
Seattle Central Community College (U)
Seminole Community College (U)

Simmons College (N)
Sinclair Community College (U)
Southern New Hampshire University (U)
Southwest Virginia Community College (U)
State University of New York at New Paltz (U)
State University of New York at Oswego (U)
Tacoma Community College (U)
Taylor University (U)
Texas A&M University–Commerce (U)
Texas State University-San Marcos (U)
Texas Tech University (U)
Three Rivers Community College (U)
Tompkins Cortland Community College (U)
Triton College (U)
Tunxis Community College (U)
University of Arkansas (U)
University of Bridgeport (U)
University of Great Falls (U)
University of Hawaii–West Oahu (U)
University of Houston–Victoria (G)
University of La Verne (G)
University of Maine (U)
The University of Maine at Augusta (U)
University of Maine at Fort Kent (U)
University of Maryland Eastern Shore (U)
University of Minnesota, Morris (U)
University of Minnesota, Twin Cities Campus (U)
University of Missouri–Columbia (U)
University of Nebraska–Lincoln (U)
University of New Orleans (U,G)
University of North Texas (U,G)
The University of Texas at El Paso (U)
The University of Texas System (U)
The University of Toledo (U)
University of Washington (U)
University of Waterloo (U)
University of Wisconsin–Stout (U,G)
Vincennes University (U)
Waubonsee Community College (U)
Western Michigan University (G)
West Valley College (U)
Wilfrid Laurier University (U)
York Technical College (U)

DIETETICS AND CLINICAL NUTRITION SERVICES

Auburn University (N)
Big Bend Community College (U)
California State University, Dominguez Hills (N)
Central Michigan University (G)
Eastern Michigan University (U,G)
Erie Community College (U)
Kansas State University (U)
Mount Saint Vincent University (U)
South Piedmont Community College (U)
Southwest Georgia Technical College (U)
University of North Florida (G)

DRAFTING/DESIGN ENGINEERING TECHNOLOGIES

Blackhawk Technical College (N)
Butler Community College (U)
Central Georgia Technical College (U)
Chemeketa Community College (U)
Cleveland Institute of Electronics (N)
Colorado State University (G)

Columbus State Community College (U)
Danville Community College (U)
Hopkinsville Community College (U)
Indiana State University (U)
Madison Area Technical College (U)
North Dakota State College of Science (U)
Orange Coast College (U)
Sinclair Community College (U)
Triton College (U)
University of Alaska Fairbanks (U)
Wake Technical Community College (U)

DRAMATIC/THEATER ARTS AND STAGECRAFT

Arkansas State University–Mountain Home (U)
Bergen Community College (U)
Brookdale Community College (U)
California State University, San Marcos (N)
California University of Pennsylvania (U)
Central Wyoming College (N)
Chaminade University of Honolulu (U)
Columbus State Community College (U)
Eastern Michigan University (U)
Eastern Oregon University (U)
Edison State Community College (U)
Erie Community College (U)
Graceland University (U)
Jefferson Community and Technical College (U)
Jefferson Community College (U)
John A. Logan College (U)
Kaskaskia College (U)
Limestone College (U)
Louisiana State University and Agricultural and Mechanical College (U)
Metropolitan State University (U)
Middle Tennessee State University (N)
Montana State University–Billings (U)
Northern State University (U)
Northern Virginia Community College (U)
Northwest Missouri State University (U)
Oakton Community College (U)
Parkland College (U)
Queen's University at Kingston (U)
Snead State Community College (U)
State University of New York at Oswego (U)
Texas Christian University (U)
Triton College (U)
University of Alaska Fairbanks (U)
University of Arkansas (U)
University of Colorado at Denver and Health Sciences Center (U)
University of New Orleans (G)
The University of North Carolina at Chapel Hill (U)
University of Oklahoma (U)
The University of South Dakota (U)
The University of Texas at Arlington (U)
Utah Valley State College (U)
Viterbo University (U)
West Los Angeles College (U)
West Virginia University at Parkersburg (U)
Wilkes Community College (U)

ECOLOGY, EVOLUTION, AND POPULATION BIOLOGY

Arkansas State University–Beebe (U)
Bellevue Community College (U)

Boston Architectural College (N,U,G)
Burlington County College (U)
California Institute of Integral Studies (N,G)
Cascadia Community College (U)
Des Moines Area Community College (U)
Edison State Community College (U)
Judson College (U)
Louisiana State University and Agricultural and Mechanical College (U)
Oregon State University (U)
University of Minnesota, Twin Cities Campus (U)
University of Nebraska–Lincoln (U)
University of Waterloo (U)
Yuba College (U)

ECONOMICS

Abilene Christian University (U)
Acadia University (U)
Alvin Community College (U)
Anne Arundel Community College (U)
Arapahoe Community College (U)
Arkansas State University–Beebe (U)
Arkansas State University–Mountain Home (U)
Ashford University (U)
Athabasca University (N,U,G)
Bellevue Community College (U)
Bemidji State University (U)
Berkeley College (U)
Berkeley College-New York City Campus (U)
Berkeley College-Westchester Campus (U)
Big Bend Community College (U)
Bismarck State College (U)
Black Hills State University (U)
Bloomfield College (U)
Boise State University (U)
Brazosport College (U)
Brenau University (U,G)
Bridgewater State College (G)
Butler Community College (U)
Butler County Community College (U)
California State University, San Bernardino (U)
Cape Cod Community College (U)
Carl Albert State College (U)
Carroll College (U)
Carroll Community College (U)
Cascadia Community College (U)
Casper College (U)
Cayuga County Community College (U)
Central Carolina Community College (U)
Central Georgia Technical College (U)
Central Michigan University (U,G)
Central New Mexico Community College (U)
Central Texas College (U)
Central Virginia Community College (U)
Central Wyoming College (U)
Chadron State College (U,G)
Chaminade University of Honolulu (U)
Chattanooga State Technical Community College (U)
Chemeketa Community College (U)
Clarion University of Pennsylvania (U)
Clemson University (U)
Clinton Community College (U)
Cloud County Community College (U)
Clovis Community College (U)
College of DuPage (U)
The College of St. Scholastica (U)
College of Southern Maryland (U)

College of The Albemarle (U)
College of the Southwest (U)
Colorado Mountain College District System (U)
Colorado State University (U)
Colorado State University-Pueblo (U)
Columbus State Community College (U)
The Community College of Baltimore County (U)
Community College of Beaver County (U)
Community College of Denver (U)
Concordia University Wisconsin (U)
Connecticut State University System (U)
County College of Morris (U)
Cumberland County College (U)
Dallas Baptist University (U,G)
Darton College (U)
De Anza College (U)
Delaware County Community College (U)
Delta College (U)
Des Moines Area Community College (U)
DeVry University Online (U,G)
Dodge City Community College (U)
Drake University (U,G)
D'Youville College (U)
East Central Community College (U)
Eastern Oregon University (U)
Eastern West Virginia Community and Technical College (U)
Eastern Wyoming College (U)
Edison College (U)
Edison State Community College (U)
EduKan (U)
Embry-Riddle Aeronautical University (U)
Erie Community College (U)
Everett Community College (U)
Fairmont State University (U)
Finger Lakes Community College (U)
Florida State University (U)
Fontbonne University (U)
Fort Hays State University (N,U)
Franklin Pierce University (U)
Franklin University (U)
Gadsden State Community College (U)
Galveston College (U)
George C. Wallace Community College (U)
Georgia Highlands College (U)
Glenville State College (U)
Grantham University (U)
Gulf Coast Community College (U)
Harrisburg Area Community College (U)
Haywood Community College (U)
Hillsborough Community College (U)
Hocking College (U)
Holyoke Community College (U)
Houston Community College System (U)
Illinois Eastern Community Colleges, Olney Central College (U)
Indiana State University (U)
Indiana University–Purdue University Fort Wayne (U)
Iona College (U)
Iowa State University of Science and Technology (U)
Itawamba Community College (U)
Ivy Tech Community College–North Central (U)
Ivy Tech Community College–Northwest (U)
Jacksonville State University (U,G)
Jefferson Community and Technical College (U)
Jefferson Community College (U)

John Jay College of Criminal Justice of the City University of New York (U)
John Tyler Community College (U)
John Wood Community College (U)
Jones College (U)
Jones County Junior College (U)
J. Sargeant Reynolds Community College (U)
Judson College (U)
Kansas City Kansas Community College (U)
Kean University (U)
Kellogg Community College (U)
Kirkwood Community College (U)
Lake Superior College (U)
Lamar State College–Port Arthur (U)
Lehigh Carbon Community College (U)
Lewis and Clark Community College (U)
Lewis-Clark State College (U)
Liberty University (U)
Limestone College (U)
Linn-Benton Community College (U)
Long Beach City College (U)
Los Angeles Harbor College (U)
Louisiana State University and Agricultural and Mechanical College (U)
Louisiana Tech University (U)
Lurleen B. Wallace Community College (U)
Mansfield University of Pennsylvania (U)
Marist College (U)
Marlboro College (G)
Marshall University (U)
Memorial University of Newfoundland (U)
Mesa Community College (U)
Mesalands Community College (U)
Metropolitan State University (U,G)
Miami Dade College (U)
Middlesex Community College (U)
Middle Tennessee State University (U,G)
Midway College (U)
Millersville University of Pennsylvania (U)
Minot State University (U)
Missouri State University (U,G)
Montana State University–Billings (U)
Montgomery County Community College (U)
Mountain Empire Community College (U)
Mount Allison University (U)
Mount Saint Vincent University (U)
Mt. San Antonio College (U)
Mount Wachusett Community College (U)
Myers University (U)
Nassau Community College (U)
New England College of Finance (U)
New Jersey City University (U)
New Mexico Junior College (U)
New York Institute of Technology (U)
North Arkansas College (U)
North Dakota State College of Science (U)
Northeast Alabama Community College (U)
Northeast State Technical Community College (U)
Northern State University (U)
North Seattle Community College (U)
NorthWest Arkansas Community College (U)
Northwest Mississippi Community College (U)
Oakton Community College (U)
Odessa College (U)
Oklahoma State University (U)
Orangeburg-Calhoun Technical College (U)
Oregon Institute of Technology (U)
Oregon State University (U)
Pace University (U)
Palomar College (U)

Parkland College (U)
Park University (U)
Patrick Henry College (U)
Patrick Henry Community College (U)
Peninsula College (U)
Philadelphia University (U)
Pittsburg State University (U)
Portland Community College (U)
Portland State University (U)
Quinnipiac University (U,G)
Randolph Community College (U)
Reedley College (N,U)
Riverside Community College District (N,U)
Rockland Community College (U,G)
Rose State College (U)
Ryerson University (U)
Sacred Heart University (G)
St. Clair County Community College (U)
St. Cloud State University (U)
St. John's University (U,G)
St. Petersburg College (U)
Salem State College (U)
Sam Houston State University (U)
Sauk Valley Community College (U)
Schoolcraft College (U)
Seminole Community College (U)
Shippensburg University of Pennsylvania (U)
Sinclair Community College (U)
Snead State Community College (U)
Southeast Arkansas College (U)
Southeastern Community College (U)
Southern New Hampshire University (U)
South Piedmont Community College (U)
Southwestern College (U)
Southwest Georgia Technical College (U)
Southwest Wisconsin Technical College (U)
State University of New York at New Paltz (U)
State University of New York at Oswego (U,G)
State University of New York College at Potsdam (U)
Strayer University (U,G)
Taylor University (U)
Texas A&M University–Commerce (N,U,G)
Texas A&M University–Texarkana (G)
Texas Tech University (U)
Tri-State University (U)
Triton College (U)
Tyler Junior College (U)
The University of Alabama (U)
University of Alaska Fairbanks (U)
University of Bridgeport (U)
University of California, Los Angeles (G)
University of Colorado at Colorado Springs (U)
University of Colorado at Denver and Health Sciences Center (U)
University of Delaware (U)
The University of Findlay (U)
University of Hawaii–West Oahu (U)
University of Idaho (U)
University of Illinois at Chicago (G)
University of Illinois at Springfield (U)
The University of Maine at Augusta (U)
University of Maine at Fort Kent (U)
University of Management and Technology (U,G)
University of Maryland University College (U)
University of Massachusetts Boston (U)
University of Minnesota, Crookston (U)

University of Minnesota, Morris (U)
University of Minnesota, Twin Cities Campus (U)
University of Missouri–Columbia (U,G)
University of Nebraska–Lincoln (U,G)
University of New Orleans (U,G)
University of North Alabama (U)
The University of North Carolina at Chapel Hill (U)
The University of North Carolina at Greensboro (U)
University of North Dakota (U)
University of North Texas (U)
University of Oklahoma (U)
University of Oregon (U)
University of Pittsburgh at Bradford (U)
University of Saskatchewan (U)
University of Southern Indiana (U,G)
University of Southern Mississippi (G)
The University of Tennessee (U)
The University of Texas at Arlington (U)
The University of Texas at San Antonio (U,G)
The University of Texas System (U)
The University of Toledo (U)
University of Toronto (N,U)
The University of Virginia's College at Wise (U)
University of Washington (U)
University of Waterloo (U)
University of West Florida (U)
University of Wisconsin Colleges (U)
University of Wisconsin–La Crosse (G)
University of Wisconsin–Parkside (G)
University of Wisconsin–Platteville (U)
University of Wisconsin–Stout (U)
University of Wisconsin–Whitewater (U,G)
Utah State University (U)
Utica College (U)
Vance-Granville Community College (U)
Vincennes University (U)
Wake Technical Community College (U)
Waubonsee Community College (U)
Wayland Baptist University (U,G)
Wayne State College (U,G)
Westchester Community College (U)
Western Michigan University (U,G)
Western Piedmont Community College (U)
Western Wyoming Community College (U)
West Los Angeles College (U)
West Valley College (U)
Wilfrid Laurier University (U)
Wright State University (N,U,G)
York Technical College (U)
York University (U)
Youngstown State University (U)
Yuba College (U)

EDUCATION

Abilene Christian University (U,G)
Acadia University (U)
Adams State College (G)
Andrews University (G)
Antioch University McGregor (U,G)
Arapahoe Community College (U)
Argosy University, Chicago Campus (U)
Ashford University (U,G)
Auburn University (G)
Bellevue Community College (U)
Bemidji State University (G)
Bergen Community College (U)
Black Hills State University (G)

Boise State University (U)
Bradley University (U,G)
Brenau University (U,G)
Bridgewater State College (U)
Brock University (U)
Buena Vista University (U,G)
Buffalo State College, State University of New York (U)
Butler County Community College (U)
California State University, Chico (U)
California State University, Dominguez Hills (N,U)
California State University, Monterey Bay (U)
California State University, San Bernardino (U,G)
California University of Pennsylvania (U)
Cape Breton University (G)
Capella University (G)
Cardinal Stritch University (G)
Carlow University (U,G)
Casper College (U)
Cedar Crest College (U,G)
Central Carolina Community College (U)
Central Washington University (N,U,G)
Chadron State College (U,G)
Chaminade University of Honolulu (U,G)
Chattanooga State Technical Community College (U)
Chemeketa Community College (U)
Chesapeake College (U)
Cincinnati Christian University (U,G)
Clackamas Community College (U)
Clarion University of Pennsylvania (G)
Cleveland State University (U,G)
College of Mount St. Joseph (U,G)
College of Southern Maryland (N)
College of the Southwest (U)
Colorado State University (N,U,G)
Colorado State University-Pueblo (U,G)
Columbia College (U)
Columbia International University (N,G)
Community College of Beaver County (U)
Concordia College–New York (U)
Concordia University, St. Paul (U,G)
Daemen College (U)
Dallas Baptist University (U,G)
Danville Community College (U)
Darton College (U)
Drake University (U,G)
Drexel University (G)
Duquesne University (G)
D'Youville College (U,G)
East Carolina University (U,G)
East Central Community College (U)
Eastern Michigan University (N,U,G)
Eastern Washington University (N,U)
East Tennessee State University (U,G)
Elizabeth City State University (U,G)
Endicott College (U,G)
Erie Community College (U)
Eugene Bible College (U)
Fairmont State University (U,G)
Fayetteville State University (G)
Finger Lakes Community College (U)
Galveston College (U)
Georgia College & State University (G)
Goucher College (G)
Hamline University (N,G)
Harrisburg Area Community College (U)
Haywood Community College (U)
Horizon College & Seminary (U)
Indiana State University (U,G)

Indiana University–Purdue University Fort Wayne (U)
Iona College (G)
Jacksonville State University (U,G)
James Madison University (N)
Jefferson Community College (U)
John A. Logan College (U)
J. Sargeant Reynolds Community College (U)
Judson College (U)
Kansas State University (N)
Kean University (N)
Lehigh Carbon Community College (U)
Lesley University (G)
LeTourneau University (U)
Lewis-Clark State College (U)
Liberty University (U)
Lock Haven University of Pennsylvania (N,G)
Longwood University (N,U,G)
Mansfield University of Pennsylvania (U,G)
Marian College of Fond du Lac (U,G)
Marlboro College (G)
Marymount University (G)
Mayville State University (U)
Memorial University of Newfoundland (U)
Mesalands Community College (U)
Mesa State College (U)
Miami Dade College (U)
Middlesex Community College (U)
Middle Tennessee State University (U)
Midwestern State University (U)
Millersville University of Pennsylvania (U,G)
Minot State University (U)
Missouri Southern State University (U)
Missouri State University (G)
Monmouth University (U,G)
Montana State University–Billings (U,G)
Montgomery County Community College (U)
Mount Saint Vincent University (U,G)
Murray State University (U,G)
Naropa University (N,G)
National University (U,G)
North Dakota State University (U,G)
Northeast State Technical Community College (U)
Northern State University (G)
Northwestern Oklahoma State University (U)
Northwest Missouri State University (G)
Oregon State University (U,G)
Pace University (N,U,G)
Pamlico Community College (U)
Park University (G)
Pasco-Hernando Community College (N)
Peninsula College (U)
Pittsburg State University (U,G)
Plymouth State University (G)
Portland Community College (U)
Prescott College (U,G)
Pulaski Technical College (U)
Quinebaug Valley Community College (U)
Quinnipiac University (U,G)
Reedley College (U)
Regent University (N,U,G)
Roosevelt University (U,G)
Sacred Heart University (G)
St. John's University (U,G)
Saint Paul College–A Community & Technical College (U)
St. Petersburg College (U)
Salem State College (G)
Seattle Pacific University (G)
Seminole Community College (U)

Shippensburg University of Pennsylvania (U,G)
Southern Illinois University Carbondale (G)
South Piedmont Community College (U)
Southwestern College (G)
Spoon River College (U)
State University of New York at New Paltz (G)
State University of New York at Oswego (G)
State University of New York at Plattsburgh (U,G)
State University of New York Empire State College (U,G)
Stony Brook University, State University of New York (G)
Taylor University (U)
Texas A&M University–Commerce (G)
Texas Tech University (G)
Texas Woman's University (U,G)
Treasure Valley Community College (U)
Tyler Junior College (U)
Union University (U,G)
University of Alaska Fairbanks (U)
The University of British Columbia (U,G)
University of California, Davis (U)
University of Cincinnati (U)
University of Colorado at Denver and Health Sciences Center (G)
University of Delaware (U,G)
University of Houston–Victoria (U,G)
University of Illinois (U)
University of Lethbridge (G)
University of Maine (G)
University of Massachusetts Boston (G)
University of Massachusetts Dartmouth (G)
University of Massachusetts Lowell (G)
University of Minnesota, Morris (U)
University of Missouri–Columbia (N,U,G)
The University of Montana (G)
The University of Montana–Western (U)
University of Nebraska–Lincoln (G)
University of New Orleans (U,G)
University of North Alabama (U,G)
The University of North Carolina at Charlotte (U,G)
University of Northern Iowa (U,G)
University of North Florida (U)
University of North Texas (N,U,G)
University of Oklahoma (U)
University of Phoenix Online Campus (G)
University of St. Thomas (U,G)
University of Sioux Falls (G)
University of South Carolina Sumter (U)
The University of South Dakota (U,G)
University of Southern Indiana (U,G)
University of Southern Mississippi (G)
University of South Florida (U,G)
The University of Tennessee (U)
The University of Tennessee at Martin (N)
The University of Texas at El Paso (U,G)
The University of Texas System (U,G)
The University of Toledo (U,G)
University of Vermont (U)
University of Washington (U)
University of Wisconsin–Stout (U,G)
University of Wisconsin–Superior (U,G)
University of Wisconsin–Whitewater (U)
University of Wyoming (U,G)
Utah State University (G)
Valley City State University (G)
Vincennes University (U)

Virginia Polytechnic Institute and State University (N)
Viterbo University (G)
Walden University (G)
Washburn University (U,G)
Wayne State College (U,G)
Webster University (G)
Western Michigan University (U)
West Liberty State College (U)
West Texas A&M University (U)
West Virginia State University (U)
West Virginia University (N)
Wright State University (U)
Xavier University of Louisiana (U,G)

EDUCATION (SPECIFIC LEVELS AND METHODS)

Arapahoe Community College (U)
Arkansas Tech University (U)
Auburn University (G)
Bemidji State University (U)
Blackhawk Technical College (U)
Brenau University (U)
Buena Vista University (U)
Central Michigan University (G)
Chadron State College (U,G)
Cleveland State University (G)
Community College of Denver (U)
Concordia University (G)
Connecticut State University System (U,G)
Danville Community College (U)
Darton College (U)
Drexel University (G)
East Arkansas Community College (U)
Eastern Michigan University (G)
Fairmont State University (U)
Fayetteville State University (U)
Granite State College (U)
Hamline University (G)
Indiana State University (G)
Indiana University System (N)
Iona College (G)
Jacksonville State University (U)
James Madison University (N,U)
Jefferson Community and Technical College (U)
Judson College (U)
Kansas State University (N)
Kean University (U,G)
Kellogg Community College (U)
Lawrence Technological University (G)
Lehigh Carbon Community College (U)
Lesley University (G)
Liberty University (G)
Limestone College (U)
Lincoln Christian College (N,U)
Longwood University (G)
Louisiana State University and Agricultural and Mechanical College (U)
McMurry University (U)
Minot State University (U)
Mississippi State University (U)
Missouri State University (G)
North Dakota State University (G)
Northwest Christian College (U)
Oregon State University (G)
Pacific Oaks College (U,G)
Pamlico Community College (U)
Pasco-Hernando Community College (U)
Pittsburg State University (G)
Radford University (G)

Regis University (G)
Roosevelt University (U)
St. Clair County Community College (U)
St. John's University (G)
San Francisco State University (N)
Seattle Pacific University (U)
Seminole Community College (N)
South Piedmont Community College (U)
Southwest Georgia Technical College (U)
State University of New York College at Potsdam (G)
Texas A&M University–Texarkana (G)
The University of Alabama (U)
University of Alaska Fairbanks (G)
The University of Arizona (G)
University of Great Falls (G)
University of Houston–Victoria (U,G)
University of Maine at Fort Kent (U)
University of Maryland University College (G)
University of Massachusetts Lowell (U)
University of Missouri–Columbia (N)
The University of Montana–Western (U)
University of New Orleans (U,G)
University of North Dakota (U)
University of Saskatchewan (U)
University of South Alabama (U)
University of Southern Indiana (U)
University of South Florida (G)
The University of Tennessee at Martin (N)
The University of Texas at Tyler (U)
University of Vermont (G)
University of Wisconsin–Platteville (G)
University of Wisconsin–Stout (N)
Utah State University (G)
Virginia Polytechnic Institute and State University (G)
Western Piedmont Community College (U)
Western Wyoming Community College (U)
Wright State University (U)
Xavier University of Louisiana (U,G)

EDUCATION (SPECIFIC SUBJECT AREAS)

Adams State College (G)
Adelphi University (G)
Arapahoe Community College (U)
Arkansas Tech University (U,G)
Auburn University (G)
Azusa Pacific University (G)
Baltimore Hebrew University (G)
Bemidji State University (U)
Boise State University (G)
Brenau University (U)
Buena Vista University (U)
California State University, San Bernardino (U,G)
California State University, San Marcos (U,G)
Carroll College (G)
Central Michigan University (G)
Central Wyoming College (U)
Chadron State College (U,G)
Cleveland State University (G)
Community College of Denver (U)
Darton College (U)
Drexel University (G)
D'Youville College (U)
East Carolina University (U)
Eastern Michigan University (U,G)
Edgecombe Community College (U)
EduKan (U)

Elizabeth City State University (U)
Flathead Valley Community College (U)
Fort Hays State University (G)
Gaston College (U)
Glenville State College (U)
Granite State College (G)
Hamline University (N,G)
Indiana State University (G)
Iona College (G)
Jacksonville State University (U,G)
Judson College (U)
Kansas State University (N)
Kean University (U)
Kirkwood Community College (U)
Lehigh Carbon Community College (U)
Lesley University (G)
Liberty University (G)
Millersville University of Pennsylvania (U,G)
Mississippi State University (U,G)
Missouri State University (G)
Montana State University (G)
Mount Saint Vincent University (U)
National University (G)
New Mexico Institute of Mining and
  Technology (G)
North Carolina State University (U,G)
Northeastern Illinois University (G)
Oregon State University (G)
Pace University (U)
Quinnipiac University (U,G)
Randolph Community College (U)
Roosevelt University (U)
St. John's University (G)
Saint Joseph's College of Maine (U,G)
Seattle Pacific University (G)
Seminole Community College (U)
Simpson College (G)
Sioux Falls Seminary (G)
Southern Illinois University Carbondale (U)
South Piedmont Community College (U)
State University of New York at Oswego
  (U,G)
State University of New York College at
  Potsdam (U)
Texas A&M University–Texarkana (U)
Three Rivers Community College (U)
University of Arkansas (G)
University of Central Missouri (U)
University of Houston–Victoria (U,G)
University of Illinois (G)
University of Illinois at Chicago (N,G)
University of La Verne (G)
University of Maine (U)
University of Maryland University College
  (G)
University of Massachusetts Boston (G)
University of Michigan–Flint (N)
University of Minnesota, Duluth (U,G)
University of Minnesota, Morris (U)
University of Missouri–Columbia (G)
University of Nebraska at Omaha (G)
University of New Orleans (U)
University of North Dakota (U,G)
University of Saskatchewan (N,U)
University of Sioux Falls (U)
University of Southern Indiana (G)
University of South Florida (G)
The University of Texas System (U,G)
University of West Florida (N)
Utah State University (G)
Virginia Polytechnic Institute and State
  University (U,G)

Wayne State College (U,G)
West Texas A&M University (G)
Yuba College (U)

EDUCATION RELATED

Acadia University (U,G)
Arapahoe Community College (U)
Argosy University, Chicago Campus (G)
Arkansas Tech University (U,G)
Arlington Baptist College (U)
Ashford University (G)
Athabasca University (N,G)
Atlantic University (N,G)
Auburn University (G)
Barclay College (U)
Black Hills State University (U,G)
Boise State University (G)
Brenau University (U,G)
Brock University (U)
Buena Vista University (U,G)
Buffalo State College, State University of
  New York (U,G)
California State University, Dominguez Hills
  (U)
California State University, East Bay (G)
California State University, San Bernardino
  (N,U)
California State University, San Marcos (G)
Carroll Community College (U)
Casper College (U)
Central Virginia Community College (U)
Chadron State College (N,U,G)
Chemeketa Community College (U)
Clarion University of Pennsylvania (U)
Cleveland State University (N,G)
College of Southern Maryland (U)
College of The Albemarle (U)
Colorado Mountain College District System
  (U)
Colorado State University (G)
Columbia International University (G)
Concordia University Wisconsin (G)
Dakota State University (U,G)
Dallas Baptist University (U,G)
Darton College (U)
Des Moines Area Community College (U)
Drake University (U)
Drexel University (G)
Eastern Michigan University (N,G)
East Tennessee State University (U,G)
Elgin Community College (U)
Fairmont State University (U,G)
Fort Hays State University (U,G)
Fulton-Montgomery Community College (N)
Gadsden State Community College (U)
Hamline University (N,G)
Haywood Community College (U)
Hebrew College (N,U,G)
Immaculata University (G)
Indiana State University (U,G)
Indiana University System (G)
Institute for Christian Studies (G)
Jacksonville State University (U,G)
Kansas State University (N)
Lehigh Carbon Community College (U)
Lesley University (G)
Liberty University (G)
Manhattan School of Music (U,G)
Marlboro College (G)
Memorial University of Newfoundland (U,G)
Midway College (U)

Midwestern State University (G)
Mississippi State University (U)
Mount Saint Vincent University (G)
Naropa University (N)
New Mexico Junior College (U)
New Mexico State University (G)
North Arkansas College (U)
Northern Kentucky University (G)
Northwestern Oklahoma State University (G)
Nova Southeastern University (G)
The Ohio State University (G)
Oklahoma State University (U)
Old Dominion University (U,G)
Oregon State University (U,G)
Pace University (G)
Park University (U)
Pasco-Hernando Community College (N)
Portland Community College (N)
Providence College and Theological Seminary
  (N,G)
Red Rocks Community College (U)
Regent University (N)
Regis University (G)
Roosevelt University (U,G)
St. John's University (G)
Seminole Community College (U)
Shasta Bible College (U)
Southern Illinois University Carbondale (U)
South Piedmont Community College (U)
Southwestern Baptist Theological Seminary
  (G)
State University of New York at Plattsburgh
  (U,G)
Taylor University (U)
Texas A&M University–Texarkana (G)
Texas Tech University (G)
Texas Woman's University (G)
Tunxis Community College (N)
University of Alaska Fairbanks (G)
University of California, Riverside (N)
University of Central Arkansas (G)
University of Central Florida (U,G)
University of Central Oklahoma (U,G)
University of Colorado at Denver and Health
  Sciences Center (G)
University of Houston–Victoria (U,G)
University of Idaho (U)
University of Illinois at Springfield (U,G)
University of Lethbridge (G)
University of Maine at Fort Kent (U)
University of Massachusetts Lowell (N)
University of Missouri–Columbia (N,U,G)
The University of Montana (G)
University of Nebraska–Lincoln (G)
The University of North Carolina at
  Greensboro (G)
University of North Texas (G)
University of Saskatchewan (N,G)
University of South Carolina Sumter (G)
University of Southern Mississippi (U)
The University of Texas at El Paso (U)
The University of Texas at San Antonio (U)
The University of Texas System (U,G)
University of the Pacific (G)
The University of Toledo (U,G)
University of West Florida (N,G)
University of Wisconsin–Whitewater (U)
Virginia Polytechnic Institute and State
  University (G)
Wayland Baptist University (U,G)
Wilkes Community College (U)

Wright State University (N,G)
Yuba College (U)

EDUCATIONAL ADMINISTRATION AND SUPERVISION

Arapahoe Community College (U)
Argosy University, Chicago Campus (G)
Arkansas Tech University (G)
Ashford University (U,G)
Athabasca University (N,G)
Azusa Pacific University (G)
Bowling Green State University (U)
Brenau University (U,G)
Bridgewater State College (U,G)
California State University, Dominguez Hills (N,U)
California University of Pennsylvania (G)
Campbellsville University (G)
Capella University (G)
Cardinal Stritch University (G)
Chadron State College (U,G)
Charter Oak State College (U)
College of The Albemarle (N)
College of the Southwest (G)
Columbia International University (G)
Concordia University (G)
Concordia University Wisconsin (G)
Dallas Baptist University (G)
Drexel University (G)
Eastern Kentucky University (G)
Eastern Michigan University (U,G)
Elizabeth City State University (G)
Fairmont State University (G)
Fort Hays State University (U)
Hamline University (N)
Indiana State University (G)
Indiana University–Purdue University Fort Wayne (G)
Iona College (G)
Jacksonville State University (U,G)
Jefferson Community and Technical College (U)
Kansas State University (N)
Kean University (G)
Lehigh Carbon Community College (U)
Lesley University (G)
LeTourneau University (G)
Liberty University (G)
Longwood University (G)
Louisiana Tech University (U,G)
Marlboro College (G)
Mercy College (U)
Minnesota State University Moorhead (G)
Mississippi State University (G)
Missouri State University (G)
Murray State University (G)
National University (G)
New Jersey City University (G)
North Carolina State University (G)
North Dakota State University (G)
Northeastern Illinois University (G)
Northwestern Oklahoma State University (G)
The Ohio State University (G)
Oregon State University (G)
Pace University (G)
Park University (G)
Pittsburg State University (G)
Radford University (G)
Regent University (N)
Regis University (G)
Roosevelt University (G)

Saddleback College (U)
St. Cloud State University (U)
St. John's University (G)
Saint Joseph's College of Maine (G)
Saybrook Graduate School and Research Center (N,G)
Shasta Bible College (G)
Southern Illinois University Carbondale (U)
South Piedmont Community College (U)
Southwestern Baptist Theological Seminary (G)
State University of New York at Plattsburgh (G)
Stony Brook University, State University of New York (G)
Texas A&M University–Commerce (G)
Texas A&M University–Texarkana (G)
Texas Tech University (G)
Union University (G)
University of Alaska Fairbanks (U,G)
University of Central Arkansas (G)
University of Central Oklahoma (U,G)
University of Colorado at Colorado Springs (G)
University of Houston–Victoria (G)
University of Massachusetts Lowell (G)
University of Michigan–Flint (N)
University of Missouri–Columbia (G)
The University of Montana (U,G)
University of Nebraska–Lincoln (G)
University of New Orleans (U,G)
University of North Texas (N,U,G)
University of Sioux Falls (G)
University of South Alabama (G)
University of South Carolina Sumter (U,G)
University of Southern Mississippi (U,G)
University of South Florida (G)
The University of Texas at El Paso (U)
University of Wisconsin–Superior (G)
Utah State University (G)
Virginia Polytechnic Institute and State University (G)
Wayne State College (G)
Webster University (G)
Western Michigan University (U)
Xavier University of Louisiana (U,G)
Youngstown State University (G)

EDUCATIONAL ASSESSMENT, EVALUATION, AND RESEARCH

Acadia University (G)
Arapahoe Community College (U)
Ashford University (U,G)
Athabasca University (N,U,G)
Azusa Pacific University (G)
Black Hills State University (G)
Boise State University (G)
Bowling Green State University (G)
Brenau University (U,G)
Bridgewater State College (U)
Chadron State College (U,G)
Cleveland State University (G)
College of the Southwest (G)
Dallas Baptist University (G)
Drexel University (G)
East Carolina University (U,G)
Eastern Michigan University (U,G)
East Tennessee State University (G)
Fairmont State University (G)
Indiana State University (G)
Iona College (G)

Jacksonville State University (U,G)
Kansas State University (N)
Liberty University (G)
Louisiana State University and Agricultural and Mechanical College (U)
Marlboro College (G)
Middle Tennessee State University (G)
Minnesota State University Moorhead (G)
Mississippi State University (G)
Pace University (G)
Plymouth State University (G)
St. John's University (G)
Saint Joseph's College of Maine (U,G)
St. Petersburg College (U)
Southwestern Baptist Theological Seminary (G)
Texas Tech University (G)
Union University (G)
University of Central Missouri (U,G)
The University of Findlay (G)
University of Houston–Victoria (G)
University of Lethbridge (G)
University of Maryland Eastern Shore (G)
University of Michigan–Flint (N)
University of Missouri–Columbia (N,G)
University of New Orleans (U,G)
University of North Texas (U,G)
University of St. Francis (G)
University of Sioux Falls (G)
University of South Carolina Sumter (U)
University of Southern Mississippi (U,G)
University of South Florida (G)
The University of Texas at El Paso (U)
The University of Toledo (G)
Utah State University (G)
Western Michigan University (U)
West Liberty State College (U)
West Texas A&M University (G)

EDUCATIONAL PSYCHOLOGY

Arapahoe Community College (U)
Argosy University, Chicago Campus (G)
Athabasca University (N,G)
Bergen Community College (U)
Black Hills State University (U)
Bowling Green State University (U)
Brenau University (U,G)
Butler County Community College (U)
Caldwell Community College and Technical Institute (U)
Capella University (G)
Casper College (U)
Chadron State College (U,G)
Chattanooga State Technical Community College (U)
College of Southern Maryland (U)
Columbia International University (N)
Concordia University Wisconsin (G)
County College of Morris (U)
Delaware County Community College (U)
Des Moines Area Community College (U)
Dickinson State University (U)
East Carolina University (U,G)
Eastern Michigan University (G)
East Tennessee State University (U)
Elizabeth City State University (U)
Eugene Bible College (U)
Fairmont State University (G)
Harford Community College (U)
Indiana State University (G)
Indiana Wesleyan University (G)

Jacksonville State University (U,G)
Jefferson Community College (U)
Kansas State University (N)
Lehigh Carbon Community College (U)
Liberty University (U,G)
Louisiana State University and Agricultural
  and Mechanical College (U)
Mercy College (U)
Middlesex Community College (U)
Middle Tennessee State University (U)
Mississippi State University (U,G)
Mount Saint Vincent University (G)
Naropa University (N)
North Carolina State University (U)
Northern State University (U,G)
St. Petersburg College (U)
Southern Illinois University Carbondale (U)
Southwestern Baptist Theological Seminary
  (G)
State University of New York at Oswego (U)
Taylor University (U)
Texas Tech University (U)
Triton College (U)
The University of Arizona (G)
University of Central Arkansas (U)
University of Central Missouri (U,G)
University of Houston–Victoria (G)
University of Illinois (U)
University of Massachusetts Boston (G)
University of Minnesota, Twin Cities Campus
  (U)
University of Missouri–Columbia (U,G)
University of Nebraska–Lincoln (G)
University of North Texas (N,U,G)
University of Saskatchewan (G)
University of Southern Indiana (U)
University of South Florida (U)
The University of Texas at El Paso (U)
The University of Texas System (G)
University of Washington (U)
University of Waterloo (U)
University of Wisconsin–La Crosse (G)
Utah State University (G)

EDUCATIONAL/INSTRUCTIONAL MEDIA DESIGN

Acadia University (U,G)
Adams State College (G)
Arapahoe Community College (U)
Argosy University, Chicago Campus (G)
Arkansas Tech University (U,G)
Ashford University (U)
Athabasca University (N)
Azusa Pacific University (G)
Bemidji State University (G)
Black Hills State University (G)
Bloomsburg University of Pennsylvania (G)
Boise State University (U,G)
Bowling Green State University (U)
Brenau University (U)
California State University, Monterey Bay (U)
California State University, San Bernardino
  (U,G)
Capella University (G)
Chadron State College (U,G)
Charter Oak State College (U)
Concordia University (G)
Connecticut State University System (G)
Dakota State University (G)
Dallas Baptist University (G)
Danville Community College (U)

DePaul University (G)
Drexel University (G)
Duquesne University (G)
East Carolina University (G)
Eastern Michigan University (G)
East Tennessee State University (G)
Elizabeth City State University (U)
Fairmont State University (G)
Florida State University (G)
Hamline University (N,G)
Henry Ford Community College (U)
Indiana State University (G)
Iona College (G)
Jacksonville State University (U,G)
Lesley University (G)
Liberty University (G)
Malone College (U)
Maranatha Baptist Bible College (U)
Marlboro College (G)
Minnesota State University Moorhead (G)
Mississippi State University (U,G)
National University (G)
New Jersey City University (G)
New York Institute of Technology (G)
North Dakota State University (G)
Northeastern Illinois University (U)
Northwest Missouri State University (N,G)
Nova Southeastern University (G)
Pace University (G)
Palomar College (U)
Roosevelt University (U,G)
St. John's University (G)
St. Petersburg College (U)
Salem State College (G)
Sonoma State University (U)
Southern Polytechnic State University (U)
Southwestern Baptist Theological Seminary
  (G)
Southwest Georgia Technical College (U)
Southwest Wisconsin Technical College (U)
State University of New York at Plattsburgh
  (G)
Taylor University (U)
Texas A&M University–Commerce (G)
Texas A&M University–Texarkana (G)
Texas Tech University (G)
Tyler Junior College (N,U)
The University of British Columbia (U,G)
University of Central Florida (G)
The University of Findlay (G)
University of Houston–Victoria (U,G)
University of Illinois at Urbana–Champaign
  (G)
University of Maryland University College
  (G)
University of Massachusetts Boston (G)
University of Massachusetts Lowell (N)
University of Michigan–Flint (N)
University of Missouri–Columbia (G)
University of Nebraska–Lincoln (G)
University of New Orleans (G)
University of North Texas (U,G)
University of Saskatchewan (N)
University of South Alabama (G)
University of South Florida (G)
The University of Texas System (U,G)
University of West Florida (G)
University of Wyoming (G)
Utah State University (G)
Western Michigan University (U,G)
Wright State University (G)

Xavier University of Louisiana (G)
Youngstown State University (G)

ELECTRICAL AND ELECTRONIC ENGINEERING TECHNOLOGIES

Alpena Community College (U)
Arapahoe Community College (U)
Bismarck State College (N)
Boise State University (U)
Bradley University (G)
Bristol Community College (N)
Central Carolina Community College (U)
Central Georgia Technical College (U)
Clemson University (U,G)
Cleveland Institute of Electronics (U)
Cleveland State University (U)
College of The Albemarle (U)
Columbia University (U)
Drexel University (G)
Erie Community College (U)
Grantham University (U)
Indiana State University (U,G)
Miami University–Middletown Campus (U)
Moberly Area Community College (U)
Oklahoma State University (U)
Pamlico Community College (U)
St. Clair County Community College (U)
Southern Methodist University (G)
Southern Polytechnic State University (U)
Texas Tech University (G)
University of Colorado at Boulder (N,G)
University of Idaho (G)
University of Illinois at Chicago (G)
University of Massachusetts Lowell (G)
University of New Orleans (U,G)
The University of North Carolina at Charlotte
  (N)
University of North Texas (U,G)
University of South Florida (G)
University of Vermont (G)
University of Washington (G)
Virginia Polytechnic Institute and State
  University (U)

ELECTRICAL AND POWER TRANSMISSION INSTALLATION

Bristol Community College (N)
Central Wyoming College (N)
Cleveland Institute of Electronics (N)
University of Northwestern Ohio (U)

ELECTRICAL, ELECTRONICS AND COMMUNICATIONS ENGINEERING

Arkansas Tech University (U)
Boston University (G)
Bristol Community College (N)
Cleveland State University (G)
Columbia University (G)
Drexel University (G)
Grantham University (U)
Indiana State University (G)
Kansas State University (G)
Kettering University (N)
Mesa State College (U)
Michigan Technological University (G)
Mississippi State University (G)
Southern Methodist University (G)

Stanford University (N)
University of Colorado at Denver and Health
  Sciences Center (U,G)
University of Illinois at Chicago (G)
University of New Hampshire (G)
University of South Florida (G)
University of Wisconsin–Platteville (G)
Villanova University (G)

ELECTRICAL/ELECTRONICS MAINTENANCE AND REPAIR TECHNOLOGY

Bristol Community College (N)
Central Wyoming College (N)
Cleveland Institute of Electronics (N)
Orange Coast College (U)
South Piedmont Community College (U)
Utah Valley State College (U)

ELECTROMECHANICAL AND INSTRUMENTATION AND MAINTENANCE TECHNOLOGIES

Blackhawk Technical College (U)
Bristol Community College (N)
Indiana State University (G)
Miami University–Middletown Campus (U)
Orange Coast College (U)

ENGINEERING

Auburn University (N)
Capitol College (G)
Casper College (U)
Cleveland Institute of Electronics (U)
Cleveland State University (U,G)
Colorado State University (U)
Columbia University (N)
County College of Morris (U)
Drexel University (G)
Eastern Michigan University (G)
Grantham University (U)
Harrisburg Area Community College (U)
Jacksonville State University (U)
Kansas State University (G)
Kettering University (N)
Lawrence Technological University (U,G)
Memorial University of Newfoundland (U)
Mississippi State University (G)
New Jersey Institute of Technology (U)
North Carolina State University (G)
Oakton Community College (U)
Reedley College (N,U)
Schoolcraft College (U)
Stevens Institute of Technology (N)
Tacoma Community College (U)
Texas Tech University (G)
The University of Alabama (U)
The University of Arizona (G)
University of Colorado at Denver and Health
  Sciences Center (U,G)
University of Idaho (G)
University of Illinois (G)
University of Illinois at Chicago (G)
University of Illinois at Urbana–Champaign
  (G)
University of Michigan–Dearborn (G)
University of Missouri–Columbia (U)
University of Nebraska–Lincoln (U,G)
University of New Orleans (U,G)

The University of North Carolina at Charlotte
  (N,U)
University of Oklahoma (U)
University of South Carolina Sumter (U)
University of South Florida (U)
The University of Texas at San Antonio (U,G)
The University of Toledo (G)
University of Vermont (N)
University of Wisconsin–Platteville (G)
Villanova University (N)
Virginia Polytechnic Institute and State
  University (N,U)
Walden University (G)
Western Michigan University (U)

ENGINEERING DESIGN

Boston University (G)
Cleveland Institute of Electronics (N)
Edison State Community College (U)
Georgia Institute of Technology (G)
Kettering University (N)
Southern Methodist University (G)
Southern Polytechnic State University (U)
University of Colorado at Denver and Health
  Sciences Center (G)
University of South Florida (G)
University of Wisconsin–Platteville (G)

ENGINEERING MECHANICS

Columbus State Community College (U)
Michigan Technological University (N,U)
New Mexico Institute of Mining and
  Technology (G)
Rochester Institute of Technology (U)
Southern Methodist University (G)
The University of Alabama (G)
The University of Arizona (G)
University of Delaware (G)
University of Missouri–Columbia (U)
The University of Texas at Arlington (G)

ENGINEERING PHYSICS

Tacoma Community College (U)

ENGINEERING RELATED

Cleveland State University (G)
Drexel University (G)
Eastern Michigan University (G)
Kansas State University (G)
Kettering University (N)
The Ohio State University (U,G)
Southern Methodist University (G)
Tacoma Community College (U)
Texas Tech University (G)
University of Cincinnati (U,G)
University of Colorado at Denver and Health
  Sciences Center (G)
University of Illinois at Chicago (G)
The University of Texas at San Antonio (N)
The University of Toledo (G)
University of Washington (G)
University of Wisconsin–Platteville (G)
Villanova University (U)
West Virginia University (N)

ENGINEERING SCIENCE

Auburn University (G)
Casper College (U)

Drexel University (G)
Eastern Michigan University (G)
Kansas State University (G)
Southern Methodist University (G)
University of Colorado at Denver and Health
  Sciences Center (U)
University of Delaware (U)
University of Michigan–Dearborn (N,G)

ENGINEERING TECHNOLOGIES RELATED

Arapahoe Community College (U)
Bristol Community College (N)
Cincinnati State Technical and Community
  College (U)
Colorado State University (U)
Columbus State Community College (U)
Drexel University (G)
East Carolina University (G)
Eastern Michigan University (G)
Haywood Community College (U)
Miami University–Middletown Campus (U)
Michigan Technological University (N,U)
Mississippi State University (G)
New Jersey Institute of Technology (G)
Northern Kentucky University (G)
Oklahoma State University (U)
Old Dominion University (U)
Pittsburg State University (U,G)
Southern Methodist University (G)
University of Colorado at Denver and Health
  Sciences Center (G)
University of North Texas (U)
University of Southern Mississippi (U)
The University of Texas at San Antonio (G)
The University of Toledo (U)
University of West Florida (U)
Virginia Polytechnic Institute and State
  University (N)

ENGINEERING TECHNOLOGY

Cleveland State University (U)
Drexel University (G)
East Carolina University (U)
Hopkinsville Community College (U)
Southern Methodist University (G)
University of Idaho (G)
University of Illinois at Chicago (G)
Wake Technical Community College (U)

ENGINEERING-RELATED FIELDS

Auburn University (G)
Cleveland State University (U,G)
Drexel University (G)
Indiana University of Pennsylvania (G)
Kettering University (N)
Quinebaug Valley Community College (N)
Southern Methodist University (G)
University of New Orleans (U,G)

ENGINEERING-RELATED TECHNOLOGIES

Bristol Community College (N)
Cleveland State University (G)
Drexel University (G)
Indiana State University (U)
Mitchell Technical Institute (U)

Southern Methodist University (G)
University of North Texas (U)

ENGINEERING/INDUSTRIAL MANAGEMENT

Bristol Community College (N)
California State University, East Bay (U)
Cleveland Institute of Electronics (N)
Cleveland State University (G)
Columbia University (N,G)
Delta College (U)
Drexel University (G)
Eastern Michigan University (G)
Edison State Community College (U)
Florida Institute of Technology (G)
Georgia Institute of Technology (G)
Indiana University–Purdue University Fort Wayne (U)
Kansas State University (G)
Lehigh University (N)
Middle Tennessee State University (N)
Montana Tech of The University of Montana (G)
Oregon Institute of Technology (U)
Southern Methodist University (G)
Stanford University (N)
Stevens Institute of Technology (U)
University of Colorado at Boulder (N,G)
University of Colorado at Denver and Health Sciences Center (G)
University of Michigan–Dearborn (G)
University of Nebraska–Lincoln (U)
University of South Florida (G)
The University of Texas at San Antonio (G)
University of Washington (G)
University of Wisconsin–Platteville (G)
Western Michigan University (G)

ENGLISH

Abilene Christian University (U)
Acadia University (U)
Alvin Community College (U)
American Public University System (U)
Arapahoe Community College (U)
Argosy University, Chicago Campus (U)
Arizona Western College (U)
Arkansas State University–Beebe (U)
Ashford University (U)
Athabasca University (N,U)
Barclay College (U)
Beaufort County Community College (U)
Bellevue Community College (U)
Bellevue University (U)
Belmont Technical College (U)
Big Bend Community College (U)
Bismarck State College (U)
Black Hills State University (U)
Bloomfield College (U)
Bowling Green State University (U,G)
Bradley University (U)
Brenau University (U)
Brookdale Community College (U)
Buena Vista University (U)
Cabrillo College (U)
Caldwell Community College and Technical Institute (U)
California State University, Chico (U)
California State University, San Bernardino (U)
Carlow University (U)

Carroll College (U)
Cayuga County Community College (U)
Cedarville University (U)
Central Carolina Community College (U)
Central Georgia Technical College (U)
Central New Mexico Community College (U)
Central Texas College (U)
Central Virginia Community College (U)
Cerro Coso Community College (U)
Chadron State College (G)
Chaminade University of Honolulu (U)
Chattanooga State Technical Community College (U)
Chesapeake College (U)
Clark State Community College (U)
Clatsop Community College (U)
Clemson University (G)
Cleveland State University (U)
Clinton Community College (U)
Cloud County Community College (U)
College of The Albemarle (N)
Colorado State University (U)
Colorado State University-Pueblo (U)
Columbus State Community College (U)
Community College of Beaver County (U)
Community College of Denver (U)
Concordia University (U)
County College of Morris (U)
Dakota State University (U)
Dallas Baptist University (U)
Danville Community College (U)
Darton College (U)
Delaware County Community College (U)
Delta College (U)
Des Moines Area Community College (U)
Dickinson State University (U)
Dodge City Community College (U)
Drake University (U)
East Carolina University (G)
East Central Community College (U)
Eastern Michigan University (U)
Eastern Oregon University (U)
Eastern Washington University (U)
Eastern West Virginia Community and Technical College (U)
Eastern Wyoming College (U)
East Tennessee State University (U)
Edgecombe Community College (N)
Edmonds Community College (U)
Elgin Community College (U)
Elizabethtown College (U)
Embry-Riddle Aeronautical University (U)
Erie Community College (U)
Everest College (U)
Flathead Valley Community College (U)
Fort Hays State University (U)
Fullerton College (U)
Gadsden State Community College (U)
Gaston College (U)
Georgia Highlands College (U)
Glenville State College (U)
Grand View College (U)
Harford Community College (U)
Harrisburg Area Community College (U)
Haywood Community College (U)
Henry Ford Community College (U)
Herkimer County Community College (U)
Hillsborough Community College (U)
Hocking College (U)
Honolulu Community College (U)
Indiana State University (U)
Jacksonville State University (U)

James Madison University (N,U)
James Sprunt Community College (U)
Jefferson Community College (U)
John A. Logan College (U)
Jones College (N,U)
Judson College (U)
Kansas City Kansas Community College (U)
Kansas State University (U)
Kaskaskia College (U)
Lehigh Carbon Community College (U)
LeTourneau University (U)
Liberty University (G)
Limestone College (U)
Linn-Benton Community College (U)
Lipscomb University (U)
Long Beach City College (U)
Los Angeles Harbor College (U)
Louisiana State University and Agricultural and Mechanical College (U)
Louisiana Tech University (G)
Lurleen B. Wallace Community College (U)
Mansfield University of Pennsylvania (U)
Memorial University of Newfoundland (U)
Mercy College (U,G)
Mesa Community College (U)
Mesalands Community College (U)
Mesa State College (U)
Miami Dade College (U)
Middlesex Community College (U)
Middle Tennessee State University (U)
Minot State University (U)
Moberly Area Community College (U)
Montgomery Community College (N,U)
Mount Allison University (U)
Mount Saint Vincent University (U)
Naropa University (G)
National University (U)
Neumann College (U)
New England College of Finance (U)
New York Institute of Technology (U)
North Carolina State University (U)
North Dakota State College of Science (U)
Northeast State Technical Community College (U)
Northern State University (U)
North Harris Montgomery Community College District (U)
NorthWest Arkansas Community College (U)
Northwestern Oklahoma State University (U)
Northwest Mississippi Community College (U)
Oakton Community College (U)
Odessa College (U)
Oral Roberts University (U)
Oregon State University (N,U)
Owensboro Community and Technical College (U)
Pace University (U)
Palomar College (U)
Pamlico Community College (U)
Park University (U)
Passaic County Community College (U)
Pittsburg State University (U)
Plymouth State University (U)
Portland State University (U)
Prescott College (U)
Reedley College (U)
Regent University (U)
Rend Lake College (U)
Riverside Community College District (U)
Rockland Community College (U)
Rose State College (U)

Ryerson University (U)
Saddleback College (U)
St. Cloud State University (U)
St. John's University (U)
Sam Houston State University (U)
Schoolcraft College (U)
Seminole Community College (U)
Shippensburg University of Pennsylvania (U,G)
Simpson College (U)
Snead State Community College (U)
Southeast Arkansas College (U)
Southeastern Community College (U)
Southeastern Illinois College (U)
Southern Illinois University Carbondale (U)
South Piedmont Community College (U)
Southwestern College (U)
Southwest Georgia Technical College (U)
Spartanburg Community College (U)
Spoon River College (U)
State University of New York at Plattsburgh (U)
Strayer University (U)
Taylor University (U)
Texas A&M University–Commerce (U)
Texas A&M University–Texarkana (U)
Texas State University-San Marcos (U)
Texas Tech University (G)
Texas Woman's University (U)
Tompkins Cortland Community College (U)
Tunxis Community College (U)
The University of Alabama (U)
University of Alaska Fairbanks (U)
The University of British Columbia (U)
University of Central Arkansas (N)
University of Central Oklahoma (U,G)
University of Cincinnati (U)
University of Colorado at Denver and Health Sciences Center (U)
University of Delaware (U)
University of Great Falls (U)
University of Idaho (U)
University of Illinois (N,U)
The University of Maine at Augusta (U)
University of Maine at Fort Kent (U)
University of Management and Technology (U)
University of Massachusetts Boston (U)
University of Massachusetts Dartmouth (U)
University of Minnesota, Twin Cities Campus (U)
University of Missouri–Columbia (U)
University of Nebraska–Lincoln (U)
University of New Orleans (U,G)
University of North Alabama (U,G)
University of Northern Iowa (U)
University of St. Francis (U)
University of Saskatchewan (U)
University of Sioux Falls (U)
The University of South Dakota (U)
University of Southern Indiana (U)
University of Southern Mississippi (U)
University of South Florida (U,G)
The University of Tennessee (U)
The University of Texas at El Paso (U)
The University of Texas System (U)
University of the Cumberlands (G)
The University of Toledo (U)
University of Vermont (N,U)
University of Washington (N,U)
University of West Florida (U)
University of Wisconsin Colleges (N,U)

University of Wisconsin–Superior (U)
University of Wisconsin–Whitewater (U,G)
Upper Iowa University (U)
Utah State University (U,G)
Utah Valley State College (U)
Utica College (U)
Virginia Polytechnic Institute and State University (G)
Washtenaw Community College (U)
Wayne State College (U,G)
Weber State University (U)
Westchester Community College (U)
West Los Angeles College (U)
West Virginia State University (U)
Wharton County Junior College (U)
Wilfrid Laurier University (U)
Wilkes Community College (U)
Wright State University (U)
York Technical College (U)

ENGLISH AS A SECOND LANGUAGE

Acadia University (N)
Arapahoe Community College (U)
Athabasca University (N,U)
Blackhawk Technical College (N)
California State University, San Marcos (N)
Central Carolina Community College (N)
Chesapeake College (U)
College of DuPage (U)
College of the Southwest (U)
County College of Morris (U)
Drexel University (G)
Edgecombe Community College (N)
Fullerton College (U)
Hamline University (N,G)
Indiana State University (G)
James Madison University (N)
Jefferson Community and Technical College (U)
Kean University (N)
Linn-Benton Community College (N)
Middle Tennessee State University (N)
Monterey Peninsula College (U)
Mt. San Antonio College (U)
Murray State University (G)
Naugatuck Valley Community College (N)
Oregon State University (N,G)
Pamlico Community College (U)
Red Rocks Community College (U)
Regent University (N,G)
St. Cloud State University (U,G)
St. Petersburg College (U)
South Piedmont Community College (U)
Tacoma Community College (U)
Tompkins Cortland Community College (U)
University of Central Oklahoma (U,G)
University of Illinois at Chicago (N)
University of Maine (U)
University of New Orleans (U,G)
The University of North Carolina at Chapel Hill (U)
The University of North Carolina at Charlotte (U)
University of Saskatchewan (N,U)
University of South Florida (N)
The University of Texas System (U)
University of Washington (N,U)
University of Wisconsin–Whitewater (U,G)
Valley City State University (U)
Wake Technical Community College (N)

Waubonsee Community College (U)
Westchester Community College (U)
West Los Angeles College (U)
Wharton County Junior College (N)

ENGLISH AS A SECOND/FOREIGN LANGUAGE (TEACHING)

Athabasca University (N)
Ball State University (G)
Buena Vista University (G)
Dallas Baptist University (G)
Drexel University (G)
Hamline University (N,G)
Indiana State University (G)
Lehigh Carbon Community College (U)
Lincoln Christian College (U,G)
Longwood University (G)
Murray State University (G)
North Carolina State University (U)
Northwestern Connecticut Community College (U)
Oregon State University (G)
Plymouth State University (U)
Seattle Pacific University (G)
University of Maine (U)
University of Massachusetts Boston (G)
University of North Dakota (G)
University of Saskatchewan (N,U)
University of South Florida (G)
The University of Texas System (G)

ENGLISH COMPOSITION

Acadia University (U)
Adams State College (U)
Alpena Community College (U)
Alvin Community College (U)
American Public University System (U)
Andrews University (U)
Anne Arundel Community College (U)
Arapahoe Community College (U)
Argosy University, Chicago Campus (U)
Arkansas State University–Beebe (U)
Arkansas State University–Mountain Home (U)
Ashford University (U)
Athabasca University (N,U)
Barclay College (U)
Bellevue Community College (U)
Belmont Technical College (U)
Bemidji State University (U)
Bergen Community College (U)
Berkeley College (U)
Berkeley College-New York City Campus (U)
Berkeley College-Westchester Campus (U)
Big Bend Community College (U)
Bismarck State College (U)
Black Hills State University (U)
Boise State University (U)
Bowling Green State University (U)
Brazosport College (U)
Brenau University (U)
Bridgewater State College (U)
Bristol Community College (U)
Brookdale Community College (U)
Broome Community College (U)
Buena Vista University (U)
Burlington County College (U)
Butler Community College (U)
Butler County Community College (U)
Cabrillo College (U)

Caldwell Community College and Technical Institute (U)
Campbell University (U)
Cape Cod Community College (U)
Carl Albert State College (U)
Carroll Community College (U)
Cascadia Community College (U)
Casper College (U)
Central Georgia Technical College (U)
Central New Mexico Community College (U)
Central Oregon Community College (U)
Central Texas College (U)
Central Virginia Community College (U)
Central Wyoming College (N,U)
Cerritos College (U)
Chadron State College (U)
Chaminade University of Honolulu (U)
Chattanooga State Technical Community College (U)
Chemeketa Community College (U)
Clackamas Community College (U)
Clarion University of Pennsylvania (U)
Clark State Community College (U)
Clatsop Community College (U)
Clemson University (N,U)
Clinton Community College (U)
Clovis Community College (U)
College of DuPage (U)
College of San Mateo (U)
College of Southern Maryland (U)
College of The Albemarle (N,U)
College of the Siskiyous (U)
College of the Southwest (U)
Colorado Mountain College District System (U)
Colorado State University (U)
Colorado State University-Pueblo (U)
Columbus State Community College (U)
The Community College of Baltimore County (U)
Community College of Beaver County (U)
Community College of Denver (U)
Connecticut State University System (U,G)
County College of Morris (U)
Cumberland County College (U)
Daemen College (U)
Dakota State University (U)
Dallas Baptist University (U)
Danville Community College (U)
Darton College (U)
Dawson Community College (U)
De Anza College (U)
Delaware County Community College (U)
Delta College (U)
Des Moines Area Community College (U)
DeVry University Online (U)
East Arkansas Community College (U)
East Central Community College (U)
Eastern Kentucky University (U)
Eastern Michigan University (U)
Eastern Oklahoma State College (U)
Eastern Wyoming College (U)
East Tennessee State University (U)
Edgecombe Community College (U)
Edison College (U)
Edison State Community College (U)
EduKan (U)
Elgin Community College (U)
Elizabeth City State University (U)
Embry-Riddle Aeronautical University (U)
Erie Community College (U)
Everest College (U)

Everett Community College (U)
Fairmont State University (U)
Feather River College (U)
Flathead Valley Community College (U)
Fontbonne University (U)
Galveston College (U)
Gaston College (U)
George C. Wallace Community College (U)
George Mason University (U)
Georgia Highlands College (U)
Governors State University (U)
Graceland University (U)
Grand View College (U)
Grantham University (U)
Gulf Coast Community College (U)
Harford Community College (U)
Harrisburg Area Community College (U)
Haywood Community College (U)
Henry Ford Community College (U)
Hillsborough Community College (U)
Hocking College (U)
Honolulu Community College (U)
Houston Community College System (U)
Ilisagvik College (U)
Illinois Eastern Community Colleges, Lincoln Trail College (U)
Illinois Eastern Community Colleges, Olney Central College (U)
Immaculata University (U)
Indiana State University (U)
Indiana Tech (U)
Indiana University–Purdue University Fort Wayne (U)
Indiana Wesleyan University (U)
Itawamba Community College (U)
Ivy Tech Community College–Kokomo (U)
Ivy Tech Community College–North Central (U)
Ivy Tech Community College–Northwest (U)
Jacksonville State University (U)
James Madison University (N,U)
James Sprunt Community College (U)
Jamestown Community College (N)
Jefferson College of Health Sciences (U)
Jefferson Community and Technical College (U)
Jefferson Community College (U)
John A. Logan College (U)
John Tyler Community College (U)
John Wood Community College (U)
Jones College (U)
Jones County Junior College (U)
J. Sargeant Reynolds Community College (U)
Judson College (U)
Kansas City Kansas Community College (U)
Kaskaskia College (U)
Kauai Community College (U)
Kellogg Community College (U)
Kirkwood Community College (U)
Labette Community College (U)
Lake Superior College (U)
Lamar State College–Port Arthur (U)
Lansing Community College (U)
Lehigh Carbon Community College (U)
LeTourneau University (U)
Lewis-Clark State College (U)
Liberty University (U)
Limestone College (U)
Lock Haven University of Pennsylvania (U)
Long Beach City College (U)
Longwood University (N)
Los Angeles Harbor College (U)

Louisiana State University and Agricultural and Mechanical College (N,U)
Madison Area Technical College (U)
Malone College (U)
Manatee Community College (U)
Marshall University (U)
Mayville State University (U)
Mercy College (U)
Mesa Community College (U)
Metropolitan State University (U)
Miami Dade College (U)
Middlesex Community College (U)
Middle Tennessee State University (U)
Midstate College (U)
Millersville University of Pennsylvania (U,G)
Minot State University (U)
Monroe Community College (U)
Montana State University–Billings (U)
Montana Tech of The University of Montana (U)
Monterey Peninsula College (U)
Montgomery Community College (N,U)
Montgomery County Community College (U)
Mountain Empire Community College (U)
Mt. San Antonio College (U)
Mount Wachusett Community College (U)
Murray State University (U)
Myers University (U)
Nassau Community College (U)
New England Institute of Technology (U)
New Mexico Junior College (U)
New York Institute of Technology (U)
North Arkansas College (U)
North Carolina State University (U)
North Central State College (U)
North Dakota State College of Science (U)
Northeast Alabama Community College (U)
Northeast State Technical Community College (U)
Northern State University (U)
Northern Virginia Community College (U)
North Harris Montgomery Community College District (U)
North Idaho College (U)
North Seattle Community College (U)
NorthWest Arkansas Community College (N,U)
Northwestern Connecticut Community College (U)
Northwest Mississippi Community College (U)
Northwest Technical College (U)
Oakton Community College (U)
Odessa College (U)
Oklahoma State University (U)
Orangeburg-Calhoun Technical College (U)
Orange Coast College (U)
Oregon State University (U)
Ouachita Technical College (U)
Pace University (U)
Palomar College (U)
Pamlico Community College (U)
Parkland College (U)
Park University (U)
Pasco-Hernando Community College (U)
Patrick Henry College (U)
Patrick Henry Community College (U)
Peninsula College (U)
Piedmont Technical College (U)
Pima Community College (U)
Plymouth State University (U)
Portland Community College (U)

Portland State University (U)
Presentation College (U)
Pulaski Technical College (U)
Queen's University at Kingston (U)
Randolph Community College (U)
Rappahannock Community College (U)
Red Rocks Community College (U)
Reedley College (U)
Rend Lake College (U)
The Richard Stockton College of New Jersey (U)
Richland Community College (U)
Rochester Institute of Technology (U)
Rockland Community College (U)
Roosevelt University (U)
Rose State College (U)
Ryerson University (N)
Sacred Heart University (U)
St. Clair County Community College (U)
St. Cloud State University (U)
Saint Joseph's College of Maine (U)
Salem State College (U)
Sampson Community College (U)
Sauk Valley Community College (U)
Savannah College of Art and Design (U)
Schenectady County Community College (U)
Schiller International University (U)
Schoolcraft College (U)
Seattle Central Community College (U)
Seminole Community College (U)
Sinclair Community College (U)
Snead State Community College (U)
Southeast Arkansas College (U)
Southeastern Community College (U)
South Piedmont Community College (U)
South Suburban College (U)
Southwestern College (U)
Southwest Georgia Technical College (U)
Southwest Virginia Community College (U)
Spartanburg Community College (U)
Spoon River College (U)
Spring Arbor University (U)
State University of New York at New Paltz (U)
State University of New York College of Agriculture and Technology at Morrisville (U)
State University of New York Empire State College (U)
Strayer University (U)
Tacoma Community College (U)
Taylor University (N,U)
Texas A&M University–Commerce (U,G)
Texas State Technical College Waco (U)
Texas State University-San Marcos (U)
Texas Tech University (U,G)
Tompkins Cortland Community College (U)
Triton College (U)
Troy University (U)
Tunxis Community College (U)
Tyler Junior College (U)
The University of Alabama (U)
University of Alaska Fairbanks (U)
University of Arkansas (U)
The University of British Columbia (N)
University of Central Arkansas (U)
University of Central Oklahoma (U)
University of Cincinnati Raymond Walters College (U)
University of Colorado at Colorado Springs (U)

University of Colorado at Denver and Health Sciences Center (U)
University of Delaware (U)
University of Houston–Victoria (U)
University of Idaho (N,U)
University of Illinois (N,U)
University of La Verne (G)
University of Maine (U)
The University of Maine at Augusta (U)
University of Massachusetts Lowell (U)
University of Minnesota, Crookston (U)
University of Minnesota, Duluth (U)
University of Minnesota, Morris (U)
University of Missouri–Columbia (U)
The University of Montana (U)
The University of Montana–Western (U)
University of Nebraska at Omaha (U)
University of Nebraska–Lincoln (N,U)
University of New Orleans (N,U,G)
University of North Alabama (U)
The University of North Carolina at Chapel Hill (U)
University of North Dakota (U)
University of North Florida (U)
University of Oklahoma (U)
The University of South Dakota (U)
University of Southern Indiana (U)
University of Southern Mississippi (U)
University of South Florida (U)
The University of Tennessee (U)
The University of Texas at San Antonio (U)
The University of Texas System (U)
The University of Toledo (U)
University of Washington (U)
University of Waterloo (U)
University of West Florida (U)
University of Wisconsin Colleges (U)
University of Wyoming (U)
Upper Iowa University (N,U)
Utah Valley State College (U)
Valley City State University (U)
Vance-Granville Community College (U)
Vincennes University (U)
Virginia Highlands Community College (U)
Virginia Polytechnic Institute and State University (U)
Wake Technical Community College (U)
Washburn University (U)
Washington State University (U)
Washtenaw Community College (U)
Waubonsee Community College (U)
Weber State University (U)
Westchester Community College (U)
Western Michigan University (U)
Western Piedmont Community College (U)
Western Wyoming Community College (U)
West Los Angeles College (U)
West Shore Community College (U)
West Valley College (U)
West Virginia State University (U)
West Virginia University at Parkersburg (U)
Wharton County Junior College (U)
Wilfrid Laurier University (N)
Wilkes Community College (U)
Williston State College (U)
Wright State University (U)
York County Community College (U)
York Technical College (U)
Yuba College (U)

ENGLISH LANGUAGE AND LITERATURE RELATED

Acadia University (U)
Adams State College (U)
Arapahoe Community College (U)
Arkansas Tech University (U)
Ashford University (U)
Bellevue Community College (U)
Belmont Technical College (U)
Berkeley College (U)
Berkeley College-New York City Campus (U)
Berkeley College-Westchester Campus (U)
Big Bend Community College (U)
Brenau University (U)
Briercrest Distance Learning (U)
Cedarville University (U)
Central Texas College (U)
Charter Oak State College (U)
College of the Siskiyous (U)
Columbus State Community College (U)
Dakota State University (U)
Dallas Baptist University (U)
Danville Community College (U)
Des Moines Area Community College (U)
Eastern Oregon University (U)
Erie Community College (U)
Georgia Highlands College (U)
Holyoke Community College (U)
Hopkinsville Community College (U)
Itawamba Community College (U)
Jacksonville State University (U)
James Sprunt Community College (U)
Jefferson Community and Technical College (U)
Jefferson Community College (U)
John A. Logan College (U)
Jones College (U)
Lehigh Carbon Community College (U)
Limestone College (U)
Los Angeles Harbor College (U)
Louisiana State University and Agricultural and Mechanical College (U)
Mansfield University of Pennsylvania (U)
Mercy College (G)
Metropolitan State University (U)
Middlesex Community College (U)
Missouri State University (U)
Mount Allison University (U)
Nassau Community College (U)
New York Institute of Technology (U)
NorthWest Arkansas Community College (U)
Northwest Christian College (U)
Northwest Mississippi Community College (U)
Pamlico Community College (U)
Pennsylvania College of Technology (U)
Quinebaug Valley Community College (U)
Reedley College (N)
Rose State College (U)
Sacred Heart University (U)
Salem State College (U)
Schoolcraft College (U)
Southern New Hampshire University (U)
South Piedmont Community College (U)
Stony Brook University, State University of New York (G)
Syracuse University (U)
Texas State University-San Marcos (U)
Three Rivers Community College (U)
The University of Alabama (U)
University of Alaska Fairbanks (U)

University of Delaware (U)
University of Houston–Victoria (U,G)
University of Minnesota, Twin Cities Campus (U)
University of Missouri–Columbia (U)
University of Nebraska at Omaha (U)
University of New Orleans (U,G)
The University of Tennessee (U)
The University of Texas System (U)
Utah Valley State College (U)
Westchester Community College (U)
West Los Angeles College (U)
West Virginia University at Parkersburg (U)
Wharton County Junior College (U)
Wilkes Community College (U)
York University (U)
Youngstown State University (N)

ENGLISH LITERATURE (BRITISH AND COMMONWEALTH)

Arapahoe Community College (U)
Bellevue Community College (U)
Bellevue University (U)
Bowling Green State University (U,G)
Bristol Community College (U)
Central Oregon Community College (U)
Central Texas College (U)
Chadron State College (U)
Chattanooga State Technical Community College (U)
Clackamas Community College (U)
College of The Albemarle (U)
College of the Siskiyous (U)
Columbia College (U)
Columbus State Community College (U)
Community College of Beaver County (U)
Danville Community College (U)
Darton College (U)
Des Moines Area Community College (U)
D'Youville College (U)
East Arkansas Community College (U)
Eugene Bible College (U)
Galveston College (U)
Gaston College (U)
George C. Wallace Community College (U)
Harford Community College (U)
Harrisburg Area Community College (U)
Houston Community College System (U)
Itawamba Community College (U)
Jacksonville State University (U)
James Sprunt Community College (U)
Jefferson Community College (U)
John Tyler Community College (U)
Jones County Junior College (U)
Judson College (U)
Lehigh Carbon Community College (U)
Longwood University (U,G)
Louisiana State University and Agricultural and Mechanical College (U)
Malone College (U)
Mercy College (U,G)
Middlesex Community College (U)
Montgomery County Community College (U)
Mount Allison University (U)
Mount Saint Vincent University (U)
Neumann College (U)
North Central State College (U)
Northeast Alabama Community College (U)
Northwestern Oklahoma State University (U)
Oklahoma State University (U)
Orangeburg-Calhoun Technical College (U)

Pasco-Hernando Community College (U)
Patrick Henry Community College (U)
Peninsula College (U)
Piedmont Technical College (U)
Queen's University at Kingston (U)
Rose State College (U)
Snead State Community College (U)
State University of New York at New Paltz (U)
Taylor University (U)
Texas State University-San Marcos (U)
Texas Tech University (U)
Three Rivers Community College (U)
The University of Alabama (U)
University of Minnesota, Twin Cities Campus (U)
University of Missouri–Columbia (U)
University of New Orleans (U,G)
University of Saskatchewan (U)
University of Southern Indiana (U)
University of Southern Mississippi (U)
The University of Tennessee (U)
University of Waterloo (U)
University of Wyoming (U)
Utah State University (U)
Virginia Highlands Community College (U)
Wake Technical Community College (U)
Wharton County Junior College (U)
Wilfrid Laurier University (U)
Wilkes Community College (U)

ENTREPRENEURIAL AND SMALL BUSINESS OPERATIONS

Adams State College (N)
Andrew Jackson University (U,G)
Arapahoe Community College (U)
Bellevue Community College (U)
Berkeley College (U)
Berkeley College-New York City Campus (U)
Berkeley College-Westchester Campus (U)
Bridgewater State College (U)
Buena Vista University (U)
California State University, Monterey Bay (U)
Central Georgia Technical College (U)
Central Michigan University (G)
Central New Mexico Community College (U)
Central Texas College (U)
Cleveland State University (N)
Colorado State University-Pueblo (N)
Columbia College (U)
The Community College of Baltimore County (U)
Community College of Beaver County (N)
Community College of Denver (U)
Daemen College (U)
Dallas Baptist University (G)
Des Moines Area Community College (U)
DeVry University Online (G)
Dickinson State University (U)
Drexel University (G)
Eastern Michigan University (U)
East Tennessee State University (N)
Flathead Valley Community College (N)
Franklin Pierce University (G)
Fulton-Montgomery Community College (N)
Herkimer County Community College (U)
Iona College (U)
James Madison University (N)
Jamestown Community College (N)
Kansas City Kansas Community College (N)
Kellogg Community College (U)

Lamar State College–Port Arthur (N)
Marlboro College (U)
Maryville University of Saint Louis (N)
Minnesota School of Business–Richfield (U)
Missouri Southern State University (N)
Mitchell Technical Institute (N)
Mount Saint Vincent University (U)
Myers University (U)
Nassau Community College (U)
Northern Kentucky University (U)
North Idaho College (N)
Peirce College (U)
Peninsula College (U)
Rend Lake College (N)
Ryerson University (U)
Saint Joseph's College of Maine (G)
St. Petersburg College (U)
Schenectady County Community College (U)
Schoolcraft College (U)
Shippensburg University of Pennsylvania (G)
Sinclair Community College (U)
Southeast Arkansas College (U)
Southern New Hampshire University (U)
South Piedmont Community College (U)
Stanford University (N)
State University of New York at Plattsburgh (U,G)
State University of New York College at Potsdam (N,U)
Suffolk University (G)
Syracuse University (G)
Taylor University (N)
Tennessee Technological University (N)
United States Sports Academy (G)
University of Bridgeport (U)
University of Central Missouri (N)
University of Houston–Victoria (G)
University of Illinois at Urbana–Champaign (G)
University of Maryland University College (G)
University of Minnesota, Crookston (U)
University of Minnesota, Twin Cities Campus (U)
University of New Orleans (U,G)
University of South Florida (N)
Upper Iowa University (U)
Vance-Granville Community College (N)
Vincennes University (U)
Wake Technical Community College (N)
Wenatchee Valley College (N)
Youngstown State University (N)

ENVIRONMENTAL CONTROL TECHNOLOGIES

Athabasca University (N,U)
Bowling Green State University (U)
Columbus State Community College (U)
De Anza College (U)
Jacksonville State University (U,G)
Judson College (U)
New York Institute of Technology (U)
Odessa College (U)
The University of British Columbia (U)
The University of Findlay (G)
The University of Tennessee (U)

ENVIRONMENTAL DESIGN

Boston Architectural College (N,U,G)
Concordia University (U)

Sonoma State University (U)
Southern Methodist University (G)

ENVIRONMENTAL PSYCHOLOGY

Saybrook Graduate School and Research
  Center (G)
The University of Montana (U)

ENVIRONMENTAL/ ENVIRONMENTAL HEALTH ENGINEERING

Bowling Green State University (U)
Cape Breton University (U)
Clackamas Community College (U)
Cleveland State University (G)
Columbia University (N,G)
East Arkansas Community College (U)
Georgia Institute of Technology (N,G)
Harrisburg Area Community College (U)
Medical College of Wisconsin (G)
Mercy College (U)
New Mexico Institute of Mining and
  Technology (G)
Odessa College (U)
Old Dominion University (G)
Oregon State University (G)
Pennsylvania College of Technology (U)
St. Cloud State University (U)
Southern Methodist University (G)
Texas Tech University (G)
Three Rivers Community College (U)
University of Colorado at Boulder (N,G)
University of Florida (G)
University of Idaho (U,G)
University of Illinois at Springfield (G)
University of Massachusetts Boston (U)
University of South Florida (G)
The University of Texas at Arlington (G)
Worcester Polytechnic Institute (G)
York Technical College (U)

ETHNIC, CULTURAL MINORITY, AND GENDER STUDIES

American Public University System (G)
Antioch University McGregor (U)
Arapahoe Community College (U)
Athabasca University (N)
Berkeley College (U)
Berkeley College-New York City Campus (U)
Berkeley College-Westchester Campus (U)
Bowling Green State University (U)
Bridgewater State College (U)
Briercrest Distance Learning (U)
California Institute of Integral Studies (N,G)
California State University, Chico (U)
California State University, Monterey Bay (U)
California State University, San Bernardino
  (U)
Central Texas College (U)
Chemeketa Community College (U)
Colorado State University (U)
Columbus State Community College (U)
De Anza College (U)
Delaware County Community College (U)
Eastern Michigan University (U,G)
Eastern Washington University (U)
Edgecombe Community College (U)
EduKan (U)

Hebrew College (N,U,G)
Hope International University (N,G)
Kansas State University (U)
Louisiana State University and Agricultural
  and Mechanical College (U)
Master's College and Seminary (U)
Middlesex Community College (U)
Minnesota State University Moorhead (U)
Modesto Junior College (U)
Naropa University (N,U)
Northwestern College (U)
Oregon State University (U)
Pace University (U)
Palomar College (U)
Prescott College (U,G)
Queen's University at Kingston (U)
Randolph Community College (U)
The Richard Stockton College of New Jersey
  (U)
Saybrook Graduate School and Research
  Center (G)
State University of New York at Plattsburgh
  (U)
Syracuse University (U,G)
Treasure Valley Community College (U)
University of Alaska Fairbanks (U)
The University of British Columbia (U)
University of Colorado at Denver and Health
  Sciences Center (U)
University of Connecticut (U)
The University of Findlay (U)
University of Illinois (U)
University of Maine (U)
University of Massachusetts Dartmouth (U)
University of Massachusetts Lowell (U)
University of Minnesota, Twin Cities Campus
  (U)
University of Missouri–Columbia (U)
The University of North Carolina at Chapel
  Hill (N,U)
University of South Florida (U)
The University of Toledo (U)
University of Washington (U)
University of Waterloo (U)
University of Wisconsin Colleges (U)
University of Wisconsin–Whitewater (U)
University of Wyoming (U)
Virginia Polytechnic Institute and State
  University (U,G)
Western Michigan University (U)
Western Wyoming Community College (U)
Wilkes Community College (U)

EXPERIMENTAL PSYCHOLOGY

Acadia University (U)
Naropa University (U)

FAMILY AND CONSUMER ECONOMICS

California State University, San Marcos (N)
Carroll Community College (N)
Cleveland State University (N)
College of the Siskiyous (U)
Eastern Oklahoma State College (U)
East Los Angeles College (U)
Immaculata University (U)
Iowa State University of Science and
  Technology (G)
Kansas State University (N)
Longwood University (N)

North Dakota State University (G)
Oakton Community College (N)
The Ohio State University (U)
Oregon State University (N)
Palomar College (U)
Pasco-Hernando Community College (N)
Sam Houston State University (U)
Taylor University (N)
Texas Tech University (G)
Texas Woman's University (U,G)
The University of Alabama (U,G)
University of Central Oklahoma (U)
University of Idaho (U)
University of Minnesota, Twin Cities Campus
  (U)
University of Northern Iowa (U)
University of North Texas (U,G)
University of Wyoming (U)
Utah State University (U)
Wake Technical Community College (N)
Western Michigan University (U,G)
Wichita State University (U)

FAMILY AND CONSUMER SCIENCES/HUMAN SCIENCES

Bradley University (U)
Central Michigan University (U)
Chadron State College (U)
Delaware County Community College (U)
Feather River College (N)
Immaculata University (U)
Jacksonville State University (U)
James Madison University (N)
Kansas State University (N,U,G)
Kean University (N)
Liberty University (G)
Mt. San Antonio College (U)
Palomar College (U)
Saybrook Graduate School and Research
  Center (G)
Treasure Valley Community College (U)
The University of Alabama (U)
University of Central Oklahoma (U)
University of Maryland Eastern Shore (U)
University of Minnesota, Twin Cities Campus
  (U)
University of Nebraska–Lincoln (G)
Utah State University (U,G)
Wayne State College (U,G)
Western Michigan University (U)

FAMILY AND CONSUMER SCIENCES/HUMAN SCIENCES BUSINESS SERVICES

Cardinal Stritch University (N)
Jacksonville State University (U)
Palomar College (U)
Pittsburg State University (U)
The University of Alabama (U)

FAMILY AND CONSUMER SCIENCES/HUMAN SCIENCES RELATED

Central Michigan University (U)
Central Washington University (U)
Chadron State College (U)
Galveston College (N)
Jacksonville State University (U,G)

Kansas State University (N,U,G)
Mesa Community College (U)
Mount Saint Vincent University (U)
Palomar College (U)
Southeastern Illinois College (U)
The University of Alabama (U)
Western Michigan University (U)

FAMILY PSYCHOLOGY

Arapahoe Community College (U)
College of the Siskiyous (U)
Dallas Baptist University (U)
Fort Hays State University (N)
Iona College (U)
Kansas State University (N,G)
Kirkwood Community College (U)
Middlesex Community College (U)
Modesto Junior College (U)
Pacific Oaks College (G)
Peninsula College (U)
Saybrook Graduate School and Research
  Center (G)
Seminole Community College (U)
Texas State University-San Marcos (U)
University of Alaska Fairbanks (G)
University of Houston–Victoria (G)

FILM/VIDEO AND PHOTOGRAPHIC ARTS

Academy of Art University (U,G)
Arapahoe Community College (U)
Auburn University (U)
Blackhawk Technical College (N)
Bowling Green State University (U)
Burlington County College (U)
Cabrillo College (U)
California State University, Dominguez Hills
  (N)
Central Wyoming College (N)
Cleveland Institute of Electronics (N)
Cleveland State University (N)
College of San Mateo (U)
Delta College (U)
Everett Community College (U)
Feather River College (N)
Flathead Valley Community College (N,U)
Fullerton College (U)
Houston Community College System (U)
James Madison University (N)
John A. Logan College (U)
Kean University (N)
Long Beach City College (U)
Massasoit Community College (U)
Minneapolis College of Art and Design
  (N,U,G)
Missouri State University (U)
Mount Wachusett Community College (U)
Northern Virginia Community College (U)
North Idaho College (N)
North Seattle Community College (U)
Oakton Community College (U)
Oregon State University (N)
Plymouth State University (N)
Regent University (N,U)
The Richard Stockton College of New Jersey
  (U)
Sam Houston State University (U)
Seattle Central Community College (U)
Sinclair Community College (U)
University of Alaska Fairbanks (U)

The University of British Columbia (U)
University of California, Los Angeles (G)
University of Cincinnati Raymond Walters
  College (U)
University of Missouri–Columbia (U)
The University of North Carolina at Charlotte
  (N)
The University of North Carolina at
  Greensboro (U)
University of Southern Indiana (N)
The University of Toledo (U)
Wake Technical Community College (N)
Western Michigan University (U,G)
West Valley College (U)
West Virginia State University (U,G)
York University (U)

FINANCE AND FINANCIAL MANAGEMENT SERVICES

Adams State College (U)
The American College (U,G)
Andrew Jackson University (G)
Anne Arundel Community College (U)
Arapahoe Community College (U)
Athabasca University (N,U)
Bellevue University (U)
Bergen Community College (U)
Berkeley College (U)
Berkeley College-New York City Campus (U)
Berkeley College-Westchester Campus (U)
Black Hills State University (U)
Brenau University (G)
Bridgewater State College (N)
Buena Vista University (U)
Butler County Community College (U)
Caldwell Community College and Technical
  Institute (N)
California State University, Dominguez Hills
  (N)
California State University, San Bernardino
  (U)
Carroll College (U)
Carroll Community College (N)
Central Georgia Technical College (U)
Central Michigan University (G)
Central Wyoming College (N)
Chaminade University of Honolulu (U)
Charter Oak State College (U)
Chattanooga State Technical Community
  College (U)
Colorado State University (U)
Colorado Technical University (U)
Columbia University (N,G)
Columbus State Community College (U)
Concordia University Wisconsin (U)
Dallas Baptist University (U,G)
Darton College (N,U)
Delaware County Community College (U)
DePaul University (N)
Des Moines Area Community College (U)
DeVry University Online (G)
Drake University (G)
Drexel University (U,G)
Eastern Michigan University (U)
Embry-Riddle Aeronautical University (U)
Erie Community College (U)
Feather River College (N)
Florida State University (N)
Franklin Pierce University (U)
Franklin University (U)
Granite State College (U)

Grantham University (U,G)
Hillsborough Community College (U)
Indiana State University (U,G)
Indiana University of Pennsylvania (U)
Iona College (U,G)
Jacksonville State University (U,G)
Jamestown Community College (N)
Kansas State University (N,U,G)
Kaplan University (N)
Kean University (N,U)
Kent State University (G)
Labette Community College (U)
Lamar State College–Port Arthur (N)
Lehigh Carbon Community College (U)
Lewis and Clark Community College (N)
Limestone College (U)
Louisiana State University and Agricultural
  and Mechanical College (U)
Marist College (U,G)
Marlboro College (U)
Metropolitan State University (U)
Middlesex Community College (N)
Midway College (U)
Missouri State University (U,G)
Montana State University (G)
Mount Saint Vincent University (U)
Myers University (U)
New England College of Finance (N,U)
New York Institute of Technology (U)
Northern Virginia Community College (U)
Oklahoma State University (U)
Old Dominion University (U,G)
Pace University (U)
Palomar College (U)
Park University (U)
Pennsylvania College of Technology (U)
Philadelphia University (U,G)
Plymouth State University (N)
Quinnipiac University (G)
Radford University (G)
Randolph Community College (U)
Regis University (U,G)
Rockland Community College (U)
Roger Williams University (U)
Ryerson University (U)
Sacred Heart University (G)
St. Petersburg College (U)
Sam Houston State University (U)
Sampson Community College (U)
Schiller International University (G)
Shippensburg University of Pennsylvania (U)
Simpson College (U)
Southern Illinois University Carbondale (U)
Southern New Hampshire University (U)
South Piedmont Community College (U)
Spring Arbor University (U,G)
Stanford University (N)
State University of New York College at
  Potsdam (N)
State University of New York Empire State
  College (U)
Strayer University (U)
Suffolk University (G)
Syracuse University (G)
Tennessee Technological University (N)
Texas A&M University–Commerce (N,G)
The University of Alabama (U,G)
University of Dallas (U)
University of Idaho (U)
University of Illinois at Chicago (G)
The University of Maine at Augusta (U)

University of Management and Technology (U)
University of Massachusetts Lowell (G)
University of Minnesota, Twin Cities Campus (U)
University of Nebraska–Lincoln (U)
University of New Orleans (N,U,G)
University of North Alabama (U)
The University of North Carolina at Charlotte (N)
University of Oklahoma (U)
University of South Alabama (G)
University of South Florida (N)
The University of Texas at Arlington (G)
The University of Texas at Tyler (U)
University of Toronto (N,U)
University of Waterloo (U)
University of Wisconsin–La Crosse (G)
University of Wisconsin–Parkside (G)
University of Wisconsin–Platteville (U)
University of Wisconsin–Whitewater (G)
Upper Iowa University (U)
Wayland Baptist University (U)
Webster University (G)
Western Carolina University (N)
West Virginia University (N)
Wilfrid Laurier University (U)

FINE AND STUDIO ART

Academy of Art University (U,G)
Acadia University (U)
Alpena Community College (U)
Athabasca University (N,U)
Atlantic University (N,G)
Bellevue University (U)
Black Hills State University (U)
Brazosport College (U)
Burlington County College (U)
Butler Community College (U)
Caldwell Community College and Technical Institute (U)
California State University, Dominguez Hills (N)
California State University, East Bay (U)
California State University, San Marcos (N)
Campbell University (U)
Cape Cod Community College (U)
Casper College (U)
Central Texas College (U)
Central Wyoming College (N,U)
Chemeketa Community College (U)
Clovis Community College (U)
College of Southern Maryland (U)
College of The Albemarle (U)
Colorado Mountain College District System (U)
Colorado State University (U)
Community College of Beaver County (U)
Community College of Denver (U)
Concordia University, St. Paul (N)
Dakota State University (U)
Dallas Baptist University (U)
Dawson Community College (U)
Delta College (U)
Drake University (U)
Duquesne University (U)
East Carolina University (G)
Eastern Kentucky University (U)
Eastern Michigan University (U)
Eastern Washington University (U)
East Los Angeles College (U)

Edison State Community College (U)
Erie Community College (U)
Fullerton College (U)
George C. Wallace Community College (U)
Governors State University (U,G)
Haywood Community College (U)
Houston Community College System (U)
Indiana Wesleyan University (U)
James Madison University (N)
Jefferson Community and Technical College (U)
John A. Logan College (U)
John Wood Community College (U)
Judson College (U)
Kaskaskia College (U)
Kean University (N,U)
Labette Community College (U)
Lake Superior College (U)
Lewis and Clark Community College (U)
Lock Haven University of Pennsylvania (U)
Louisiana State University and Agricultural and Mechanical College (U)
Lurleen B. Wallace Community College (U)
Malone College (U)
Mercy College (U)
Middlesex Community College (N,U)
Middle Tennessee State University (N)
Minneapolis College of Art and Design (N,U,G)
Mississippi State University (U)
Moberly Area Community College (U)
Montana State University–Billings (U)
Mountain Empire Community College (U)
Naugatuck Valley Community College (U)
North Arkansas College (U)
Northeastern Illinois University (U)
Northern Virginia Community College (U)
North Idaho College (U)
NorthWest Arkansas Community College (U)
Oregon State University (N)
Pace University (U)
Palomar College (U)
Parkland College (U)
Patrick Henry Community College (U)
Pennsylvania College of Technology (U)
Piedmont Technical College (U)
Rappahannock Community College (U)
Red Rocks Community College (U)
Richland Community College (U)
Rockland Community College (U)
Sacred Heart University (U)
St. Petersburg College (U)
Savannah College of Art and Design (U,G)
Schoolcraft College (U)
Shippensburg University of Pennsylvania (U)
Sinclair Community College (U)
Snead State Community College (U)
Spoon River College (U)
Tacoma Community College (U)
Taylor University (U)
Texas Christian University (U)
Texas State University-San Marcos (U)
Tompkins Cortland Community College (U)
Tri-State University (U)
Triton College (U)
Tyler Junior College (U)
University of Alaska Fairbanks (U)
University of Central Oklahoma (U,G)
University of Colorado at Denver and Health Sciences Center (U)
The University of Findlay (U)
University of Great Falls (U)

University of Illinois (N)
University of Illinois at Springfield (U)
University of Minnesota, Twin Cities Campus (U)
University of Nebraska–Lincoln (U)
The University of North Carolina at Chapel Hill (N,U)
University of North Texas (U)
University of St. Francis (U)
University of Sioux Falls (U)
University of Southern Indiana (U)
University of South Florida (U)
The University of Texas at Arlington (U)
The University of Texas System (U)
University of West Florida (U)
University of Wisconsin–Superior (U)
Utah Valley State College (U)
Viterbo University (U)
Western Piedmont Community College (U)
West Valley College (U)
Wilfrid Laurier University (U)
Wilkes Community College (U)

FIRE PROTECTION

Arizona Western College (U)
Bellevue Community College (U)
Blackhawk Technical College (N,U)
Butler County Community College (U)
Cabrillo College (U)
Caldwell Community College and Technical Institute (U)
Central New Mexico Community College (U)
Central Texas College (U)
Chattanooga State Technical Community College (U)
Chemeketa Community College (U)
Des Moines Area Community College (U)
Gulf Coast Community College (U)
Honolulu Community College (U)
Houston Community College System (U)
Ivy Tech Community College–Northeast (U)
Ivy Tech Community College–Northwest (U)
Jacksonville State University (G)
James Madison University (N)
John Jay College of Criminal Justice of the City University of New York (U)
Kansas City Kansas Community College (U)
Middlesex Community College (U)
NorthWest Arkansas Community College (U)
Oklahoma State University (N,U)
Palomar College (U)
Pamlico Community College (U)
Passaic County Community College (U)
Portland Community College (U)
Red Rocks Community College (U)
Schenectady County Community College (U)
Seminole Community College (U)
Southeast Arkansas College (U)
State University of New York Empire State College (U)
Tyler Junior College (U)
University of Illinois (N)
University of Maryland University College (U)
University of Missouri–Columbia (N)
University of Nebraska–Lincoln (U)
The University of North Carolina at Charlotte (N)
The University of Texas at Tyler (U)
Utah Valley State College (U)
Vincennes University (U)

Wharton County Junior College (N)
Worcester Polytechnic Institute (G)

FISHING AND FISHERIES SCIENCES AND MANAGEMENT

Colorado State University (U,G)
Oregon State University (U)
University of Maryland Eastern Shore (G)
Virginia Polytechnic Institute and State University (U)
West Virginia University at Parkersburg (N)

FOOD SCIENCE AND TECHNOLOGY

Central Michigan University (G)
Central Wyoming College (N)
Delaware County Community College (U)
Eastern Michigan University (U,G)
Iowa State University of Science and Technology (U,G)
Jamestown Community College (N)
J. Sargeant Reynolds Community College (U)
Kansas State University (N,U)
Middle Tennessee State University (U)
Orange Coast College (U)
Texas Tech University (U)
University of California, Davis (U)
University of Minnesota, Twin Cities Campus (U)
University of Missouri–Columbia (U,G)
University of North Texas (U,G)
University of Vermont (N)

FOODS, NUTRITION, AND RELATED SERVICES

Acadia University (U)
Athabasca University (N,U)
Auburn University (N,G)
Bergen Community College (U)
Blackhawk Technical College (N)
Bowling Green State University (U,G)
Butler County Community College (U)
Cabrillo College (U)
Central Michigan University (G)
Central New Mexico Community College (U)
Central Texas College (U)
Central Wyoming College (N)
Charter Oak State College (U)
Chemeketa Community College (U)
Clatsop Community College (U)
Cleveland State University (N)
Colorado State University (U)
Columbus State Community College (U)
Danville Community College (U)
Des Moines Area Community College (U)
East Carolina University (G)
Eastern Michigan University (U,G)
Eastern Washington University (U)
East Los Angeles College (U)
Fairmont State University (U)
Feather River College (N)
Harrisburg Area Community College (U)
Hillsborough Community College (U)
Honolulu Community College (U)
Houston Community College System (U)
Illinois Eastern Community Colleges, Frontier Community College (U)
Immaculata University (U)

Indiana University of Pennsylvania (U,G)
Iowa State University of Science and Technology (G)
Jacksonville State University (U)
James Madison University (N)
Jefferson College of Health Sciences (U)
Jefferson Community College (U)
Kansas State University (N,U)
Lamar State College–Port Arthur (U)
Long Beach City College (U)
Louisiana Tech University (G)
Mesa Community College (U)
Middlesex Community College (U)
Montana State University (G)
Mount Saint Vincent University (U)
North Dakota State College of Science (U)
North Dakota State University (U)
NorthWest Arkansas Community College (U)
Northwest Mississippi Community College (U)
Oklahoma State University (U)
Orange Coast College (U)
Oregon State University (G)
Palomar College (U)
Portland Community College (U)
Reedley College (N,U)
Rose State College (U)
Ryerson University (U)
Sam Houston State University (U)
Southeast Arkansas College (U)
South Piedmont Community College (U)
Southwest Wisconsin Technical College (U)
Texas Tech University (U)
Treasure Valley Community College (U)
The University of Alabama (U)
University of Bridgeport (U,G)
The University of British Columbia (U)
University of Central Missouri (U)
University of Cincinnati Raymond Walters College (U)
University of Delaware (N,U,G)
University of Minnesota, Crookston (U)
University of Minnesota, Twin Cities Campus (U)
University of Missouri–Columbia (U,G)
University of Nebraska–Lincoln (U)
University of North Alabama (U)
The University of North Carolina at Chapel Hill (U)
University of Southern Mississippi (U)
University of Wyoming (U)
West Virginia University at Parkersburg (N)
Wisconsin Indianhead Technical College (N,U)
Youngstown State University (U)
Yuba College (U)

FORENSIC PSYCHOLOGY

Charter Oak State College (U)
University of Massachusetts Lowell (G)
West Virginia University (N)

FOREST ENGINEERING

University of Minnesota, Twin Cities Campus (U,G)

FORESTRY

Haywood Community College (U)
James Madison University (N)

Louisiana Tech University (U)
Mississippi State University (U)
Mount Wachusett Community College (N)
North Carolina State University (U)
The Ohio State University (U)
Oregon State University (U)
The University of British Columbia (U)
University of Missouri–Columbia (N)
Virginia Polytechnic Institute and State University (N,G)

FUNERAL SERVICE AND MORTUARY SCIENCE

Arapahoe Community College (U)
Des Moines Area Community College (U)
John Tyler Community College (U)
Kansas City Kansas Community College (U)
St. Louis Community College System (U)
St. Petersburg College (U)
University of Central Oklahoma (U,G)
Vincennes University (U)

GENETICS

Charter Oak State College (U)
Eastern Michigan University (U)
Labette Community College (U)
North Carolina State University (U)
University of Illinois at Urbana–Champaign (N,G)
University of Minnesota, Twin Cities Campus (U)

GEOGRAPHY AND CARTOGRAPHY

Alvin Community College (U)
Andrews University (U)
Anne Arundel Community College (U)
Arapahoe Community College (U)
Arkansas State University–Beebe (U)
Athabasca University (U)
Auburn University (U)
Ball State University (U)
Bellevue Community College (U)
Bemidji State University (U)
Black Hills State University (U)
Bowling Green State University (U)
Brazosport College (U)
Brenau University (U)
Bridgewater State College (U)
Bristol Community College (U)
Cabrillo College (U)
California State University, Chico (U)
Campbell University (U)
Casper College (U)
Central Texas College (U)
Central Wyoming College (U)
Chadron State College (U)
Chattanooga State Technical Community College (U)
Chemeketa Community College (U)
Cleveland State University (U)
College of Southern Maryland (U)
Colorado Mountain College District System (U)
Colorado State University (U)
Colorado State University-Pueblo (U)
Columbus State Community College (U)
The Community College of Baltimore County (U)

Community College of Denver (U)
Concordia University (U)
Connecticut State University System (U)
Danville Community College (U)
Delaware County Community College (U)
Des Moines Area Community College (U)
Dickinson State University (U)
Eastern Kentucky University (U)
Eastern Michigan University (U,G)
Eastern Oklahoma State College (U)
Eastern Oregon University (U)
Eastern Washington University (U)
East Tennessee State University (U)
EduKan (U)
Erie Community College (U)
Everett Community College (U)
Fairmont State University (U)
Fullerton College (U)
Gaston College (U)
George Mason University (U)
Governors State University (U)
Harrisburg Area Community College (U)
Houston Community College System (U)
Illinois Eastern Community Colleges, Lincoln
  Trail College (U)
Indiana State University (U)
Jacksonville State University (U,G)
James Madison University (N)
Jefferson Community College (U)
Kansas State University (U)
Kaskaskia College (U)
Labette Community College (U)
Lake Superior College (U)
Lansing Community College (U)
Lehigh Carbon Community College (U)
Limestone College (U)
Long Beach City College (U)
Louisiana State University and Agricultural
  and Mechanical College (U)
Marshall University (U)
Massasoit Community College (U)
Mesalands Community College (U)
Middlesex Community College (U)
Midway College (U)
Midwestern State University (U)
Moberly Area Community College (U)
Montana State University–Billings (U)
Montgomery County Community College (U)
Murray State University (U)
Myers University (U)
Northern Virginia Community College (U)
North Harris Montgomery Community
  College District (U)
Northwestern Connecticut Community College
  (U)
Northwest Mississippi Community College
  (U)
Northwest Missouri State University (N,U,G)
Oakton Community College (U)
Oklahoma State University (U)
Oregon State University (G)
Palomar College (U)
Park University (U)
Plymouth State University (U)
Portland Community College (U)
Queen's University at Kingston (U)
Red Rocks Community College (U)
Riverside Community College District (U)
Rockland Community College (U)
Rose State College (U)
Ryerson University (U)
Saddleback College (U)

St. Clair County Community College (U)
St. Petersburg College (U)
Salem State College (U)
Schoolcraft College (U)
Seattle Central Community College (U)
Seattle Pacific University (G)
Seminole Community College (U)
Shippensburg University of Pennsylvania (U)
Snead State Community College (U)
Southeast Arkansas College (U)
Southern Illinois University Carbondale (U)
South Piedmont Community College (U)
State University of New York at New Paltz
  (U)
State University of New York College at
  Potsdam (U)
Tacoma Community College (U)
Taylor University (U)
The University of Alabama (U)
University of Alaska Fairbanks (U)
University of Arkansas (U)
The University of British Columbia (U)
University of California, Riverside (N)
University of Central Arkansas (G)
University of Central Oklahoma (U)
University of Cincinnati (U)
University of Colorado at Colorado Springs
  (U)
University of Colorado at Denver and Health
  Sciences Center (U)
University of Idaho (U)
University of Maine at Fort Kent (U)
University of Massachusetts Dartmouth (U)
University of Missouri–Columbia (U)
University of Nebraska–Lincoln (U)
University of New Orleans (U,G)
University of North Alabama (U,G)
The University of North Carolina at Chapel
  Hill (U)
The University of North Carolina at Charlotte
  (N)
University of North Dakota (U)
University of Northern Iowa (U,G)
University of Oklahoma (U)
University of Oregon (U)
University of Saskatchewan (U)
University of Sioux Falls (U)
University of Southern Mississippi (U,G)
University of South Florida (U)
The University of Tennessee (U)
The University of Texas at San Antonio (U)
The University of Texas at Tyler (U)
The University of Toledo (U)
University of Washington (U)
University of Wisconsin Colleges (U)
University of Wyoming (U)
Virginia Polytechnic Institute and State
  University (U,G)
Weber State University (U)
Westchester Community College (U)
Western Michigan University (U)
Western Piedmont Community College (U)
West Liberty State College (U)
Wichita State University (U)
Wilfrid Laurier University (U)
York University (U)

GEOLOGICAL AND EARTH SCIENCES/GEOSCIENCES

Acadia University (U)
Alvin Community College (U)

Arapahoe Community College (U)
Arkansas State University–Beebe (U)
Athabasca University (N,U)
Bellevue Community College (U)
Bergen Community College (U)
Big Bend Community College (U)
Boise State University (U)
Bowling Green State University (U)
Bridgewater State College (U)
Cabrillo College (U)
California State University, Monterey Bay (U)
California University of Pennsylvania (U)
Cascadia Community College (U)
Central Oregon Community College (U)
Charter Oak State College (U)
Chemeketa Community College (U)
Clark State Community College (U)
Cleveland State University (U)
Colorado State University-Pueblo (U)
Community College of Denver (U)
Dallas Baptist University (U)
Eastern Michigan University (G)
Eastern Wyoming College (U)
Flathead Valley Community College (U)
Fort Hays State University (U)
Gaston College (U)
Harrisburg Area Community College (U)
Hillsborough Community College (U)
Honolulu Community College (U)
Jacksonville State University (U,G)
James Madison University (N)
Lake Superior College (U)
Lawrence Technological University (G)
Louisiana State University and Agricultural
  and Mechanical College (U)
Mesalands Community College (U)
Middle Tennessee State University (U)
Mississippi State University (U)
Montgomery County Community College (U)
Mountain Empire Community College (U)
Murray State University (U)
Nassau Community College (U)
New Mexico Junior College (U)
Northeastern Illinois University (U)
North Seattle Community College (U)
Oklahoma State University (U)
Oregon State University (U,G)
Palomar College (U)
Park University (U)
Peninsula College (U)
Pennsylvania College of Technology (U)
Portland State University (U)
Rend Lake College (U)
Rose State College (U)
Sam Houston State University (U)
Seminole Community College (U)
State University of New York at New Paltz
  (U)
State University of New York at Oswego (U)
State University of New York at Plattsburgh
  (U)
State University of New York College at
  Potsdam (U)
Tacoma Community College (U)
Treasure Valley Community College (U)
Tri-State University (U)
University of Cincinnati (U)
University of Colorado at Denver and Health
  Sciences Center (U)
University of Houston–Victoria (G)
University of Maine at Fort Kent (U)

University of Minnesota, Twin Cities Campus (U)
University of Missouri–Columbia (U)
The University of Montana–Western (U)
University of New Orleans (U,G)
The University of North Carolina at Chapel Hill (U)
The University of North Carolina at Greensboro (U)
University of North Texas (U)
University of Oklahoma (U)
University of Oregon (U)
University of Saskatchewan (U)
University of South Florida (U)
The University of Texas at San Antonio (U)
The University of Texas System (U)
University of Washington (U)
University of Waterloo (U)
University of Wisconsin Colleges (U)
Wake Technical Community College (U)
Weber State University (U)
West Shore Community College (U)
Wharton County Junior College (U)
Wilfrid Laurier University (U)
Wright State University (G)
Youngstown State University (U)

GEOLOGICAL/GEOPHYSICAL ENGINEERING

Arapahoe Community College (U)
Hillsborough Community College (U)
Rose State College (U)
University of Idaho (G)
University of New Orleans (U,G)

GERONTOLOGY

Acadia University (U)
Adams State College (N)
The American College (U)
Athabasca University (N)
Bowling Green State University (G)
Butler Community College (U)
California State University, Dominguez Hills (N)
Carroll Community College (N)
The College of St. Scholastica (U)
College of The Albemarle (N)
Des Moines Area Community College (U)
Feather River College (N)
Flathead Valley Community College (U)
Itawamba Community College (U)
Jefferson College of Health Sciences (U)
Kansas State University (G)
Kaplan University (N)
Liberty University (U)
Limestone College (U)
Massasoit Community College (N)
Middlesex Community College (N)
Mount Saint Vincent University (U)
Northeastern Illinois University (G)
The Ohio State University (N)
Randolph Community College (N)
The Richard Stockton College of New Jersey (U)
Ryerson University (U)
Sacred Heart University (G)
Saddleback College (U)
Sam Houston State University (U)
Saybrook Graduate School and Research Center (G)

Shippensburg University of Pennsylvania (U,G)
Southwest Georgia Technical College (U)
State University of New York at Oswego (G)
Texas Tech University (G)
University of Alaska Fairbanks (U)
The University of Arizona (G)
University of Colorado at Colorado Springs (U)
University of Maryland University College (U)
University of Massachusetts Boston (G)
University of Missouri–Columbia (U,G)
University of New Orleans (U,G)
University of North Alabama (U)
University of North Texas (N,G)
University of Southern California (G)
University of Southern Indiana (U)
University of Vermont (U)
University of Washington (U,G)
University of Waterloo (U)
University of Wisconsin–Stout (N)
University of Wisconsin–Superior (N)
Utica College (U)
Weber State University (U)
Western Carolina University (U,G)
West Hills Community College (N)
Wichita State University (U)

GRAPHIC COMMUNICATIONS

Academy of Art University (U,G)
Arapahoe Community College (U)
California State University, Dominguez Hills (N)
Carroll Community College (N)
Central Wyoming College (N)
Columbus State Community College (U)
Community College of Beaver County (N)
Dallas Baptist University (U)
Danville Community College (U)
De Anza College (U)
Everett Community College (U)
Murray State University (U)
North Harris Montgomery Community College District (U)
Oakton Community College (U)
Palomar College (U)
Plymouth State University (N)
Riverside Community College District (N,U)
Rose State College (U)
Texas State Technical College Waco (N)
University of North Dakota (N)

GROUND TRANSPORTATION

Arapahoe Community College (U)
Bristol Community College (N)

HEALTH AIDES/ATTENDANTS/ ORDERLIES

Arapahoe Community College (U)
James Madison University (N)
Lamar State College–Port Arthur (N)
Pamlico Community College (U)
South Piedmont Community College (N)

HEALTH AND MEDICAL ADMINISTRATIVE SERVICES

Alpena Community College (U)
American Public University System (U)

Arapahoe Community College (U)
Arkansas Tech University (U)
Athabasca University (U)
Bellevue University (U,G)
Berkeley College (U)
Berkeley College-New York City Campus (U)
Berkeley College-Westchester Campus (U)
Blackhawk Technical College (U)
Boise State University (U,G)
Bowling Green State University (U)
Brenau University (G)
Bridgewater State College (N)
Buena Vista University (U)
California State University, Chico (U)
California State University, Dominguez Hills (N)
Carroll Community College (N)
Cedar Crest College (U)
Central Georgia Technical College (U)
Central Michigan University (U,G)
Chattanooga State Technical Community College (U)
Cincinnati State Technical and Community College (U)
Cleveland State University (G)
The College of St. Scholastica (U,G)
Colorado State University-Pueblo (N)
Colorado Technical University (U,G)
Columbus State Community College (U)
Daemen College (U)
Dakota State University (U)
Darton College (U)
Des Moines Area Community College (U)
D'Youville College (G)
Edgecombe Community College (N,U)
Erie Community College (U)
Feather River College (N)
Franklin University (U)
Granite State College (U)
Iona College (U,G)
James Sprunt Community College (U)
Jamestown Community College (N)
Jefferson College of Health Sciences (U)
Kean University (U)
Lehigh Carbon Community College (U)
Linn-Benton Community College (U)
Miami Dade College (U)
Minnesota School of Business–Richfield (U)
Minot State University–Bottineau Campus (U)
Montana State University–Billings (G)
North Dakota State College of Science (U)
Northwest Technical College (U)
Oakton Community College (U)
Orange Coast College (U)
Oregon State University (N,U,G)
Pamlico Community College (U)
Park University (U)
Pulaski Technical College (U)
Quinebaug Valley Community College (N,U)
Radford University (G)
Reedley College (N,U)
Roger Williams University (U)
Saint Joseph's College of Maine (U,G)
Seminole Community College (N)
Shawnee State University (U)
Tacoma Community College (U)
Texas State University-San Marcos (N,U)
Three Rivers Community College (U)
University of Central Florida (U,G)
University of Dallas (G)
University of Idaho (U)
University of Maryland Eastern Shore (G)

University of Maryland University College (G)
University of Minnesota, Crookston (U)
University of Minnesota, Twin Cities Campus (U)
University of Missouri–Columbia (U,G)
The University of North Carolina at Charlotte (N)
The University of North Carolina at Greensboro (N)
University of North Dakota (N)
University of North Florida (U)
University of North Texas (G)
University of St. Francis (G)
University of Southern Indiana (U)
Wayland Baptist University (U,G)
Weber State University (U,G)
Youngstown State University (N)

HEALTH AND PHYSICAL EDUCATION/FITNESS

Adelphi University (U)
Anne Arundel Community College (U)
Arapahoe Community College (U)
Auburn University (U)
Austin Peay State University (U,G)
Bemidji State University (U)
Butler Community College (U)
Butler County Community College (U)
California University of Pennsylvania (U,G)
Carl Albert State College (U)
Carroll Community College (U)
Cayuga County Community College (U)
Central Carolina Community College (U)
Central Michigan University (U)
Central Oregon Community College (U)
Central Texas College (U)
Central Washington University (G)
Central Wyoming College (N,U)
Chemeketa Community College (U)
Clarion University of Pennsylvania (U)
Clatsop Community College (U)
Cleveland State University (N)
College of San Mateo (U)
College of Southern Maryland (U)
College of The Albemarle (U)
College of the Siskiyous (U)
Colorado State University (N,U)
Columbus State Community College (U)
County College of Morris (U)
Dakota State University (U)
Dallas Baptist University (U)
Danville Community College (U)
Darton College (U)
Delta College (U)
East Arkansas Community College (U)
Eastern Oregon University (U)
Eastern Washington University (N,U)
Eastern Wyoming College (U)
East Los Angeles College (U)
Elizabeth City State University (U)
Erie Community College (U)
Feather River College (U)
Fort Hays State University (U,G)
Fullerton College (U)
Gadsden State Community College (U)
Georgia Highlands College (U)
Haywood Community College (U)
Illinois Eastern Community Colleges, Frontier Community College (U)
Indiana State University (U)

Jacksonville State University (U,G)
James Madison University (N,U)
Jefferson College of Health Sciences (U)
John Jay College of Criminal Justice of the City University of New York (U)
John Wood Community College (U)
J. Sargeant Reynolds Community College (U)
Kean University (N)
Labette Community College (U)
Lehigh Carbon Community College (U)
Linn-Benton Community College (U)
Longwood University (U)
Louisiana State University and Agricultural and Mechanical College (U)
Malone College (U)
Middle Tennessee State University (U)
Millersville University of Pennsylvania (U,G)
Missouri State University (U,G)
Modesto Junior College (U)
Montana State University (G)
Mountain Empire Community College (U)
Nassau Community College (U)
Naugatuck Valley Community College (N)
North Carolina State University (U)
North Dakota State College of Science (U)
Northern State University (U)
NorthWest Arkansas Community College (U)
Northwest Mississippi Community College (U)
Oklahoma State University (U)
Pacific Union College (U)
Palomar College (U)
Parkland College (U)
Pasco-Hernando Community College (U)
Patrick Henry Community College (U)
Peninsula College (U)
Pittsburg State University (U)
Portland Community College (U)
Rappahannock Community College (U)
Rend Lake College (U)
Rose State College (N,U)
Snead State Community College (U)
Southeast Arkansas College (U)
State University of New York at Plattsburgh (U)
Texas Woman's University (U,G)
Treasure Valley Community College (U)
Triton College (U)
United States Sports Academy (N,U,G)
University of California, Los Angeles (G)
University of Great Falls (U)
University of Idaho (U)
University of Minnesota, Duluth (U)
University of Missouri–Columbia (U)
The University of Montana (U)
University of Nebraska–Lincoln (U)
University of Northern Iowa (U)
University of North Texas (U)
University of Oklahoma (U)
University of Sioux Falls (U)
University of Southern Mississippi (U,G)
The University of Texas at San Antonio (U)
The University of Texas at Tyler (U)
Utah Valley State College (U)
Valley City State University (U)
Washburn University (U)
Waubonsee Community College (U)
Westchester Community College (U)
West Los Angeles College (U)
West Virginia University at Parkersburg (U)
Youngstown State University (U)

HEALTH PROFESSIONS RELATED

Arapahoe Community College (U)
Arkansas State University–Mountain Home (U)
Athabasca University (N,U,G)
Bellevue Community College (U)
Bowling Green State University (N)
Brenau University (U,G)
Broome Community College (U)
Butler Community College (U)
Cabrillo College (U)
California University of Pennsylvania (G)
Central Michigan University (U,G)
Central Virginia Community College (U)
Central Wyoming College (N)
Chattanooga State Technical Community College (U)
Chemeketa Community College (U)
Cincinnati State Technical and Community College (U)
Clark State Community College (U)
Cleveland State University (N,G)
College of Southern Maryland (N)
Colorado Mountain College District System (U)
Columbus State Community College (U)
Daemen College (U)
Dallas Baptist University (U)
Danville Community College (U)
Darton College (U)
DeVry University Online (G)
Drake University (U,G)
Drexel University (U,G)
D'Youville College (U)
Eastern Kentucky University (U)
Everett Community College (U)
Franklin Pierce University (G)
Fulton-Montgomery Community College (N)
Galveston College (U)
George Mason University (G)
Georgia College & State University (U,G)
Hillsborough Community College (U)
Illinois Eastern Community Colleges, Lincoln Trail College (U)
Iona College (U,G)
Jacksonville State University (U,G)
James Madison University (U)
Jefferson College of Health Sciences (U)
Kansas City Kansas Community College (U)
Kaplan University (N)
Kean University (N)
Lake Superior College (U)
Lamar State College–Port Arthur (U)
Lehigh Carbon Community College (U)
Lewis and Clark Community College (N)
Lock Haven University of Pennsylvania (G)
Longwood University (N)
Louisiana Tech University (U)
Massasoit Community College (N)
Medical College of Wisconsin (G)
Mercy College (U)
Mesa Community College (U)
MGH Institute of Health Professions (G)
Miami Dade College (N)
Midwestern State University (U,G)
Mississippi State University (G)
Mitchell Technical Institute (N)
Montana Tech of The University of Montana (U,G)
Montgomery County Community College (U)
Naugatuck Valley Community College (U)

North Dakota State College of Science (U)
Oakton Community College (U)
Orange Coast College (U)
Oregon State University (G)
Pasco-Hernando Community College (N)
Passaic County Community College (U)
Peninsula College (U)
Pennsylvania College of Technology (U)
Plymouth State University (N)
Portland Community College (N,U)
Radford University (G)
The Richard Stockton College of New Jersey (U)
Riverside Community College District (N)
Rockland Community College (U)
Rose State College (U)
Ryerson University (U)
Sacred Heart University (U,G)
Sam Houston State University (U)
Schoolcraft College (U)
Seminole Community College (U)
Sinclair Community College (N)
Southeast Arkansas College (U)
Southeastern Illinois College (U)
South Piedmont Community College (U)
Spoon River College (U)
State University of New York at Plattsburgh (U)
Tacoma Community College (U)
Texas State University-San Marcos (U)
Union University (G)
The University of Alabama (U,G)
University of Alaska Fairbanks (U)
University of California, Davis (U)
University of Central Arkansas (G)
University of Cincinnati Raymond Walters College (U)
University of Colorado at Colorado Springs (U,G)
University of Connecticut (N,U,G)
University of Delaware (G)
University of Illinois (G)
University of Illinois at Chicago (G)
University of Maine at Fort Kent (U)
University of Maryland Eastern Shore (G)
University of Massachusetts Lowell (G)
University of Medicine and Dentistry of New Jersey (U,G)
University of Minnesota, Twin Cities Campus (U)
University of Missouri–Columbia (N,U)
The University of Montana (U)
University of New Hampshire (G)
University of New Orleans (U,G)
The University of North Carolina at Greensboro (U)
University of North Dakota (N)
University of St. Augustine for Health Sciences (N)
University of St. Francis (U)
University of Sioux Falls (U)
University of Southern Indiana (N,G)
University of Southern Mississippi (U)
The University of Texas at Tyler (U,G)
The University of Texas System (U,G)
University of the Sciences in Philadelphia (G)
The University of Toledo (U)
University of Wisconsin–La Crosse (U)
University of Wyoming (G)
Upper Iowa University (U)
Washtenaw Community College (U)
West Virginia State University (U)

West Virginia University (N)
West Virginia University at Parkersburg (U)
York University (U)
Youngstown State University (U,G)

HEALTH PSYCHOLOGY

Acadia University (U)
Arapahoe Community College (U)
Fullerton College (U)
Saybrook Graduate School and Research Center (G)
University of Alaska Fairbanks (U,G)
University of Maryland Eastern Shore (G)
University of Wisconsin–Superior (G)

HEALTH SERVICES/ALLIED HEALTH/HEALTH SCIENCES

Arapahoe Community College (U)
Ball State University (U)
Belmont Technical College (U)
California State University, San Marcos (N)
Central Georgia Technical College (U)
Central Michigan University (U)
Central Oregon Community College (U)
Central Wyoming College (N)
Charter Oak State College (U)
Cleveland State University (G)
Darton College (U)
Drake University (G)
Drexel University (U)
East Arkansas Community College (U)
Edison College (U)
Iona College (U,G)
Itawamba Community College (U)
Jefferson Community College (U)
John Tyler Community College (U)
Mercy College (U,G)
Mitchell Technical Institute (U)
NorthWest Arkansas Community College (U)
Oregon State University (U)
Pamlico Community College (U)
Rend Lake College (U)
Roger Williams University (U)
Rose State College (U)
Schoolcraft College (U)
South Piedmont Community College (U)
State University of New York at Oswego (U)
Texas Woman's University (U,G)
Tyler Junior College (U)
University of Connecticut (U)
University of Illinois at Chicago (G)
University of Massachusetts Lowell (G)
University of Minnesota, Twin Cities Campus (U)
University of Missouri–Columbia (N)
University of North Florida (U,G)
University of South Florida (G)
The University of Texas at San Antonio (U)
University of the Sciences in Philadelphia (G)
University of West Florida (G)
Upper Iowa University (U)
West Hills Community College (N)
West Los Angeles College (U)
West Virginia University (N)

HEALTH/MEDICAL PREPARATORY PROGRAMS

Arapahoe Community College (U)
Athabasca University (U,G)

Brenau University (U)
Caldwell Community College and Technical Institute (N)
California State University, San Marcos (N)
Chattanooga State Technical Community College (U)
Cleveland State University (G)
Community College of Denver (U)
Daemen College (U)
Darton College (U)
Edgecombe Community College (U)
Gateway Community College (U)
Gulf Coast Community College (U)
Hocking College (U)
James Madison University (N)
Jefferson College of Health Sciences (U)
Kirkwood Community College (U)
Labette Community College (U)
Lake Superior College (U)
Medical College of Wisconsin (G)
Mesa Community College (U)
Naugatuck Valley Community College (N)
Radford University (G)
Rockland Community College (U)
Rose State College (U)
Saddleback College (U)
Southern Illinois University Carbondale (U)
Southwest Wisconsin Technical College (U)
University of Minnesota, Twin Cities Campus (U)
University of Missouri–Columbia (N)
Virginia Highlands Community College (U)
West Los Angeles College (U)

HEATING, AIR CONDITIONING, VENTILATION AND REFRIGERATION MAINTENANCE TECHNOLOGY

Blackhawk Technical College (U)
Boston Architectural College (N,U,G)
Flathead Valley Community College (U)
Mitchell Technical Institute (N)
Orange Coast College (U)
South Piedmont Community College (U)
University of North Dakota (N)
Wake Technical Community College (U)

HEAVY/INDUSTRIAL EQUIPMENT MAINTENANCE TECHNOLOGIES

Bismarck State College (N)

HISTORIC PRESERVATION AND CONSERVATION

Feather River College (N)
Goucher College (N,G)

HISTORY

Acadia University (U)
Adams State College (U)
Alvin Community College (U)
American Public University System (U,G)
Andover Newton Theological School (G)
Andrews University (U)
Anne Arundel Community College (U)
Arapahoe Community College (U)
Arkansas State University–Beebe (U)
Arkansas Tech University (U)

Ashford University (U)
Assemblies of God Theological Seminary (G)
Athabasca University (N,U,G)
Azusa Pacific University (U)
Baltimore Hebrew University (G)
Bellevue Community College (U)
Bemidji State University (U)
Bergen Community College (U)
Berkeley College (U)
Berkeley College-New York City Campus (U)
Berkeley College-Westchester Campus (U)
Big Bend Community College (U)
Bismarck State College (U)
Bloomfield College (U)
Boise State University (U)
Bowling Green State University (U)
Brazosport College (U)
Brenau University (U)
Bridgewater State College (U)
Briercrest Distance Learning (N,U,G)
Bristol Community College (U)
Broome Community College (U)
Buena Vista University (U)
Buffalo State College, State University of New York (U)
Burlington County College (U)
Butler Community College (U)
Butler County Community College (U)
Cabrillo College (U)
Caldwell Community College and Technical Institute (U)
California State University, Chico (U)
California State University, Dominguez Hills (N)
Campbell University (U)
Cape Cod Community College (U)
Carl Albert State College (U)
Carroll College (U)
Carroll Community College (U)
Cascadia Community College (U)
Cayuga County Community College (U)
Cedarville University (U)
Central Carolina Community College (U)
Central Oregon Community College (U)
Central Texas College (U)
Central Virginia Community College (U)
Central Washington University (U)
Central Wyoming College (N)
Cerritos College (U)
Chadron State College (U,G)
Chaminade University of Honolulu (U)
Chattanooga State Technical Community College (U)
Chemeketa Community College (U)
Cincinnati Christian University (U,G)
Cincinnati State Technical and Community College (U)
Clark State Community College (U)
Clatsop Community College (U)
Clemson University (G)
Cleveland State University (U)
Clinton Community College (U)
Cloud County Community College (U)
Clovis Community College (U)
College of DuPage (U)
College of Southern Maryland (U)
College of The Albemarle (U)
College of the Siskiyous (U)
College of the Southwest (U)
Colorado Mountain College District System (U)
Colorado State University-Pueblo (U)

Columbia College (U)
Columbia International University (G)
Columbus State Community College (U)
The Community College of Baltimore County (U)
Community College of Beaver County (U)
Community College of Denver (U)
Concordia University (U)
Concordia University Wisconsin (U)
Corban College (U)
County College of Morris (U)
Cumberland County College (U)
Dallas Baptist University (U)
Danville Community College (U)
Darton College (U)
De Anza College (U)
Delaware County Community College (U)
Delta College (U)
Denver Seminary (G)
Des Moines Area Community College (U)
Dickinson State University (U)
Drake University (U,G)
D'Youville College (U)
East Arkansas Community College (U)
East Central Community College (U)
Eastern Kentucky University (U)
Eastern Michigan University (U)
Eastern Oklahoma State College (U)
Eastern Washington University (U)
Eastern West Virginia Community and Technical College (U)
East Los Angeles College (U)
East Tennessee State University (U)
Edgecombe Community College (U)
Elizabeth City State University (U)
Elizabethtown College (U)
Erie Community College (U)
Eugene Bible College (U)
Everett Community College (U)
Fairmont State University (U)
Fayetteville State University (G)
Feather River College (N,U)
Fort Hays State University (U)
Fullerton College (U)
Gadsden State Community College (U)
Galveston College (U)
George C. Wallace Community College (U)
Georgia Highlands College (U)
Glenville State College (U)
Graceland University (U)
Grand View College (U)
Granite State College (U)
Grantham University (U)
Gulf Coast Community College (U)
Hamline University (U)
Harrisburg Area Community College (U)
Haywood Community College (U)
Henry Ford Community College (U)
Holyoke Community College (U)
Honolulu Community College (U)
Hope International University (N,U)
Houston Community College System (U)
Illinois Eastern Community Colleges, Wabash Valley College (U)
Immaculata University (U)
Indiana State University (U)
Indiana University-Purdue University Fort Wayne (U)
Indiana Wesleyan University (U)
Itawamba Community College (U)
Ivy Tech Community College-Kokomo (U)
Ivy Tech Community College-Northwest (U)

Jacksonville State University (U)
James Madison University (N,U)
James Sprunt Community College (U)
Jefferson Community and Technical College (U)
Jefferson Community College (U)
John A. Logan College (U)
John Tyler Community College (U)
John Wood Community College (U)
Jones County Junior College (U)
J. Sargeant Reynolds Community College (U)
Judson College (U)
Kansas City Kansas Community College (U)
Kansas State University (U)
Kaskaskia College (U)
Kean University (U)
Kellogg Community College (U)
Kirkwood Community College (U)
Labette Community College (U)
Lake Superior College (U)
Lansing Community College (U)
Lehigh Carbon Community College (U)
LeTourneau University (U)
Lewis and Clark Community College (U)
Lewis-Clark State College (U)
Liberty University (U)
Limestone College (U)
Lock Haven University of Pennsylvania (U)
Long Beach City College (U)
Longwood University (U)
Louisiana State University and Agricultural and Mechanical College (U)
Louisiana Tech University (G)
Lurleen B. Wallace Community College (U)
Malone College (U)
Manatee Community College (U)
Mansfield University of Pennsylvania (U)
Marian College of Fond du Lac (U,G)
Marshall University (U)
Massasoit Community College (U)
Mercy College (U)
Mesa Community College (U)
Mesalands Community College (U)
Mesa State College (U)
Metropolitan State University (U)
Middlesex Community College (U)
Minnesota State University Moorhead (U)
Minot State University (U)
Missouri Southern State University (U)
Missouri State University (U,G)
Moberly Area Community College (U)
Modesto Junior College (U)
Montana State University–Billings (U)
Montgomery County Community College (U)
Mountain Empire Community College (U)
Mount Allison University (U)
Mount Wachusett Community College (U)
Murray State University (U)
Myers University (U)
Nassau Community College (U)
National University (U)
New England College of Finance (U)
New Mexico Junior College (U)
North Arkansas College (U)
North Carolina State University (U)
North Dakota State College of Science (U)
Northeast State Technical Community College (U)
Northern Virginia Community College (U)
North Harris Montgomery Community College District (U)
NorthWest Arkansas Community College (U)

Northwestern College (U)
Northwestern Connecticut Community College (U)
Northwest Mississippi Community College (U)
Northwest Missouri State University (U)
Oakton Community College (U)
Oklahoma State University (U)
Oral Roberts University (U)
Orangeburg-Calhoun Technical College (U)
Oregon State University (U)
Ouachita Technical College (U)
Owensboro Community and Technical College (U)
Pace University (U)
Palomar College (U)
Pamlico Community College (U)
Parkland College (U)
Park University (U)
Pasco-Hernando Community College (U)
Passaic County Community College (U)
Patrick Henry College (U)
Patrick Henry Community College (U)
Peninsula College (U)
Pennsylvania College of Technology (U)
Piedmont Technical College (U)
Pittsburg State University (U,G)
Portland Community College (U)
Portland State University (U)
Prescott College (U,G)
Pulaski Technical College (U)
Queen's University at Kingston (U)
Quinebaug Valley Community College (U)
Quinnipiac University (U)
Randolph Community College (U)
Rappahannock Community College (U)
Red Rocks Community College (U)
Regent University (U)
Regis University (U)
Rend Lake College (U)
Richland Community College (U)
Riverside Community College District (U)
Rockland Community College (U)
Roger Williams University (U)
Rose State College (U)
Ryerson University (U)
Sacred Heart University (U)
Saddleback College (U)
St. Clair County Community College (U)
St. Cloud State University (U)
St. John's University (U)
St. Louis Community College System (U)
St. Petersburg College (U)
Salem State College (U)
Sam Houston State University (U)
Sauk Valley Community College (U)
Schenectady County Community College (U)
Schiller International University (U)
Schoolcraft College (U)
Seattle Pacific University (G)
Seminole Community College (U)
Shippensburg University of Pennsylvania (U,G)
Sinclair Community College (U)
Snead State Community College (U)
Southeast Arkansas College (U)
Southeastern Community College (U)
Southeastern Illinois College (U)
Southern Illinois University Carbondale (U)
South Piedmont Community College (U)
Southwest Virginia Community College (U)
Spring Arbor University (U)

State University of New York at New Paltz (U)
State University of New York at Oswego (U)
State University of New York at Plattsburgh (U)
State University of New York Empire State College (U)
Strayer University (U)
Syracuse University (G)
Tacoma Community College (U)
Taylor University (U)
Texas A&M University–Commerce (U)
Texas A&M University–Texarkana (U)
Texas Christian University (U)
Texas State University-San Marcos (U)
Texas Tech University (U)
Texas Woman's University (U)
Three Rivers Community College (U)
Tri-State University (U)
Triton College (U)
Troy University (U)
Tunxis Community College (U)
Tyler Junior College (U)
The University of Alabama (U)
University of Alaska Fairbanks (U)
University of Arkansas (U)
University of Bridgeport (U)
The University of British Columbia (U)
University of Central Arkansas (U)
University of Central Oklahoma (U)
University of Cincinnati (U)
University of Colorado at Colorado Springs (U)
University of Colorado at Denver and Health Sciences Center (U,G)
University of Delaware (U)
The University of Findlay (U)
University of Great Falls (U)
University of Hawaii–West Oahu (U)
University of Houston–Victoria (U)
University of Idaho (U)
University of Illinois (U)
University of La Verne (G)
The University of Maine at Augusta (U)
University of Maine at Fort Kent (U)
University of Management and Technology (U)
University of Massachusetts Boston (U,G)
University of Massachusetts Dartmouth (U)
University of Minnesota, Duluth (U)
University of Minnesota, Morris (U)
University of Missouri–Columbia (U)
The University of Montana–Western (U)
University of Nebraska at Omaha (U)
University of Nebraska–Lincoln (U)
University of New Orleans (U,G)
University of North Alabama (U)
The University of North Carolina at Chapel Hill (N,U)
The University of North Carolina at Charlotte (U)
The University of North Carolina at Greensboro (U)
University of North Dakota (U)
University of North Texas (U)
University of Oklahoma (U)
University of St. Francis (U)
University of Saskatchewan (U)
University of Sioux Falls (U)
University of South Carolina Sumter (U)
The University of South Dakota (U)
University of Southern Indiana (U)

University of South Florida (U)
The University of Tennessee (U)
The University of Texas at Tyler (U)
The University of Texas System (U)
University of the Cumberlands (G)
The University of Toledo (U)
University of Washington (U)
University of Waterloo (U)
University of West Florida (U)
University of Wisconsin Colleges (U)
University of Wisconsin–Superior (U)
University of Wisconsin–Whitewater (U,G)
University of Wyoming (U)
Upper Iowa University (N,U)
Utah State University (U)
Utah Valley State College (U)
Vance-Granville Community College (U)
Vermont Technical College (U)
Vincennes University (U)
Virginia Highlands Community College (U)
Virginia Polytechnic Institute and State University (N,U)
Wake Technical Community College (U)
Washburn University (U)
Waubonsee Community College (U)
Wayland Baptist University (U)
Weber State University (U)
Westchester Community College (U)
Western Michigan University (U,G)
Western Piedmont Community College (U)
West Los Angeles College (U)
West Shore Community College (U)
West Valley College (U)
West Virginia University at Parkersburg (U)
Wharton County Junior College (U)
Wichita State University (U)
Wilfrid Laurier University (U)
Wilkes Community College (U)
Williston State College (U)
Wright State University (U)
York Technical College (U)
York University (U)
Youngstown State University (U)

HOSPITALITY ADMINISTRATION

Anne Arundel Community College (U)
Arapahoe Community College (U)
Arkansas Tech University (U)
Black Hills State University (G)
California State University, East Bay (U)
Central Michigan University (G)
Central Texas College (U)
Chemeketa Community College (U)
Colorado Mountain College District System (U)
Columbus State Community College (U)
Des Moines Area Community College (U)
East Arkansas Community College (U)
East Carolina University (U)
Eastern Michigan University (U)
Erie Community College (U)
Hocking College (U)
Indiana University of Pennsylvania (U)
Ivy Tech Community College–Northwest (U)
John A. Logan College (U)
Metropolitan State University (U)
Middlesex Community College (U)
Mount Saint Vincent University (U)
Mt. San Antonio College (U)
North Dakota State University (U)
NorthWest Arkansas Community College (U)

Orange Coast College (U)
Riverside Community College District (U)
Roosevelt University (U,G)
Ryerson University (U)
Schenectady County Community College (U)
Schiller International University (U,G)
Southwest Wisconsin Technical College (U)
Spring Arbor University (U)
State University of New York College of
   Agriculture and Technology at Morrisville
   (U)
Tompkins Cortland Community College (U)
The University of Alabama (U)
University of Delaware (N,U)
University of Maryland Eastern Shore (U)
University of New Orleans (U,G)
The University of North Carolina at Chapel
   Hill (U)
The University of North Carolina at Charlotte
   (N)
University of North Texas (U,G)
Utah Valley State College (U)
Virginia Polytechnic Institute and State
   University (U)
York County Community College (U)

HOUSING AND HUMAN ENVIRONMENTS

Chadron State College (U)
Fontbonne University (U)
Henry Ford Community College (U)
Saybrook Graduate School and Research
   Center (G)

HUMAN DEVELOPMENT, FAMILY STUDIES, AND RELATED SERVICES

Abilene Christian University (G)
American Public University System (U)
Arapahoe Community College (U)
Athabasca University (N,U,G)
Blackhawk Technical College (N)
Bowling Green State University (U)
Brenau University (U)
Butler Community College (U)
Caldwell Community College and Technical
   Institute (U)
California State University, Chico (U)
California State University, East Bay (U)
Central Michigan University (U)
Cerro Coso Community College (U)
Chadron State College (U)
Chemeketa Community College (U)
Clackamas Community College (U)
Clatsop Community College (U)
Cleveland State University (N)
Clinton Community College (U)
College of Southern Maryland (U)
College of The Albemarle (U)
Community College of Denver (U)
Concordia University, St. Paul (U,G)
Corban College (U)
Danville Community College (U)
De Anza College (U)
Delaware County Community College (U)
Des Moines Area Community College (U)
East Carolina University (U)
Edgecombe Community College (U)
Edison College (U)

Edison State Community College (U)
Elizabeth City State University (U)
Erikson Institute (N)
Everett Community College (U)
Feather River College (N)
Gaston College (U)
Granite State College (U)
Hillsborough Community College (U)
Houston Community College System (U)
Immaculata University (G)
Iowa State University of Science and
   Technology (U)
Jacksonville State University (U,G)
J. Sargeant Reynolds Community College (U)
Kansas City Kansas Community College (U)
Kansas State University (U)
Lehigh Carbon Community College (U)
Lewis-Clark State College (U)
Linn-Benton Community College (U)
Long Beach City College (U)
Louisiana Tech University (G)
Madison Area Technical College (U)
Malone College (U)
Maryville University of Saint Louis (N)
Massasoit Community College (U)
Mayville State University (U)
Miami Dade College (U)
Mississippi State University (U)
Missouri State University (U)
Moberly Area Community College (U)
Modesto Junior College (U)
Mountain Empire Community College (U)
Mount Wachusett Community College (U)
Murray State University (U)
Naropa University (N)
Naugatuck Valley Community College (U)
North Dakota State University (N,U,G)
North Idaho College (U)
North Seattle Community College (U)
Oakton Community College (U)
Orange Coast College (U)
Oregon Institute of Technology (U)
Owensboro Community and Technical College
   (U)
Pacific Oaks College (U,G)
Palomar College (U)
Peninsula College (U)
Portland Community College (U)
Prescott College (U,G)
Randolph Community College (U)
Reedley College (N)
Ryerson University (U)
Saddleback College (U)
Sampson Community College (U)
Saybrook Graduate School and Research
   Center (G)
Schenectady County Community College (U)
Seminole Community College (U)
Snead State Community College (U)
South Piedmont Community College (U)
Southwestern Baptist Theological Seminary
   (G)
Spoon River College (U)
State University of New York Empire State
   College (U)
Tacoma Community College (U)
Taylor University (N)
The University of Alabama (U)
University of Alaska Fairbanks (U,G)
University of Bridgeport (N,U)
University of Delaware (U)
University of Houston–Victoria (U)

University of Idaho (U)
University of Illinois (U)
The University of Maine at Augusta (U)
University of Missouri–Columbia (U,G)
University of Nebraska–Lincoln (U)
The University of North Carolina at
   Greensboro (U)
University of North Texas (U,G)
University of Southern Mississippi (U,G)
The University of Tennessee at Martin (N)
University of Waterloo (U)
University of Wisconsin–Stout (N)
Utah State University (G)
Vance-Granville Community College (U)
Weber State University (U)
Wilkes Community College (U)
Wisconsin Indianhead Technical College
   (N,U)
York County Community College (U)
York University (U)

HUMAN RESOURCES MANAGEMENT

Adams State College (U)
The American College (U,G)
American Public University System (U)
Andrew Jackson University (G)
Antioch University McGregor (U)
Athabasca University (N,U,G)
Bellevue University (U)
Berkeley College (U)
Berkeley College-New York City Campus (U)
Berkeley College-Westchester Campus (U)
Black Hills State University (U)
Boise State University (U,G)
Brenau University (U)
Bristol Community College (N)
Butler Community College (U)
Butler County Community College (U)
California State University, Dominguez Hills
   (N)
Capella University (G)
Central Michigan University (U,G)
Central Texas College (U)
Central Washington University (U)
Chadron State College (U,G)
Clemson University (G)
College of Southern Maryland (U)
Colorado State University (G)
Colorado Technical University (U,G)
Columbus State Community College (U)
The Community College of Baltimore County
   (U)
Dakota State University (U)
Dallas Baptist University (U,G)
Delaware County Community College (U)
DePaul University (N)
Des Moines Area Community College (U)
DeVry University Online (G)
Dickinson State University (U)
Drake University (U,G)
D'Youville College (U)
Eastern Michigan University (N,U,G)
Eastern Washington University (N,U)
Edison State Community College (N,U)
Elizabeth City State University (U)
Elizabethtown College (U)
Erie Community College (U)
Feather River College (N)
Florida Institute of Technology (G)
Florida State University (G)

Franklin University (U)
Granite State College (U)
Grantham University (U)
Herkimer County Community College (U)
Holyoke Community College (U)
Houston Community College System (U)
Illinois Eastern Community Colleges, Wabash Valley College (U)
Immaculata University (U)
Indiana State University (U,G)
Iona College (G)
Jacksonville State University (G)
James Madison University (N,U)
Jamestown Community College (N)
Jefferson College of Health Sciences (U)
Jefferson Community College (U)
John Tyler Community College (U)
Kansas City Kansas Community College (U)
Kansas State University (G)
Labette Community College (U)
Lamar State College–Port Arthur (N)
Lawrence Technological University (G)
Lehigh Carbon Community College (U)
Limestone College (U)
Longwood University (N)
Maryville University of Saint Louis (N)
Massasoit Community College (N)
Mesalands Community College (U)
Metropolitan State University (U)
Middlesex Community College (U)
Middle Tennessee State University (N,U)
Montana State University–Billings (U)
Montgomery Community College (U)
Mount Wachusett Community College (U)
Myers University (U)
National University (G)
Neumann College (U)
North Arkansas College (U)
North Harris Montgomery Community College District (U)
Oregon State University (N)
Ouachita Technical College (U)
Park University (U)
Peirce College (U)
Pittsburg State University (G)
Plymouth State University (U)
Providence College and Theological Seminary (N)
Regent University (N)
Rend Lake College (N)
Ryerson University (U)
Saint Paul College–A Community & Technical College (U)
Schiller International University (U,G)
Simpson College (U)
Southern New Hampshire University (U,G)
Southwest Wisconsin Technical College (U)
Spring Arbor University (U)
Stony Brook University, State University of New York (G)
Suffolk University (G)
Taylor University (N)
University of Alaska Fairbanks (U)
University of Connecticut (G)
The University of Findlay (U,G)
University of Hawaii–West Oahu (U)
University of Illinois (G)
The University of Maine at Augusta (U)
University of Management and Technology (U)
University of Maryland University College (U,G)

University of Michigan–Flint (G)
University of Minnesota, Twin Cities Campus (U)
University of Missouri–Columbia (N,U)
The University of Montana (U)
University of New Orleans (U,G)
The University of North Carolina at Charlotte (N)
University of North Dakota (N)
University of North Texas (G)
University of Phoenix Online Campus (U)
University of Southern Indiana (N)
The University of Texas at Tyler (U,G)
The University of Toledo (U)
University of Toronto (N,U)
University of West Florida (N)
University of Wisconsin–Platteville (U)
University of Wisconsin–Stout (N,U,G)
Upper Iowa University (U)
Utah State University (U,G)
Virginia Polytechnic Institute and State University (U)
Washburn University (N)
Waubonsee Community College (U)
Wayland Baptist University (G)
Wayne State College (U,G)
Western Carolina University (U,G)
Western Michigan University (G)
Western Piedmont Community College (U)
West Virginia University at Parkersburg (U)
York University (U)

HUMAN SERVICES

Antioch University McGregor (U)
Athabasca University (N,U,G)
Bellevue University (U)
Bismarck State College (U)
Buena Vista University (U)
Capella University (G)
Central Michigan University (U)
Chadron State College (U)
Clinton Community College (U)
College of DuPage (U)
College of The Albemarle (N)
Colorado State University (G)
Dawson Community College (U)
Des Moines Area Community College (U)
Flathead Valley Community College (U)
Herkimer County Community College (U)
Holyoke Community College (U)
Houston Community College System (U)
Indiana State University (U)
James Madison University (N)
Jamestown Community College (N)
Kellogg Community College (U)
Kirkwood Community College (U)
Lewis and Clark Community College (N)
Limestone College (U)
Louisiana State University and Agricultural and Mechanical College (G)
Mercy College (U,G)
Metropolitan State University (U)
Middlesex Community College (U)
Mount Wachusett Community College (U)
Murray State University (G)
New Mexico State University (U)
Owensboro Community and Technical College (U)
Prescott College (U,G)
Quinebaug Valley Community College (U)
Regions University (N,U,G)

Saint Joseph's College of Maine (U)
Sinclair Community College (U)
South Piedmont Community College (U)
Tacoma Community College (U)
University of Bridgeport (U)
University of Connecticut (G)
University of Great Falls (U,G)
University of Illinois at Springfield (G)
The University of Maine at Augusta (U)
University of Massachusetts Boston (N)
University of Wisconsin–Superior (U)
Upper Iowa University (U)
Vance-Granville Community College (U)
Washburn University (U)
Waubonsee Community College (U)

INDUSTRIAL AND ORGANIZATIONAL PSYCHOLOGY

Athabasca University (N,U,G)
Berkeley College (U)
Berkeley College-New York City Campus (U)
Berkeley College-Westchester Campus (U)
Capella University (G)
Central Michigan University (U)
Chadron State College (U,G)
College of the Southwest (U)
Graceland University (U)
Indiana State University (G)
Kansas State University (G)
Lehigh Carbon Community College (U)
Middle Tennessee State University (N)
Montana State University–Billings (U)
Old Dominion University (U)
Saint Joseph's College of Maine (U)
Saybrook Graduate School and Research Center (N,G)
Schiller International University (G)
State University of New York at New Paltz (U)
Texas State University-San Marcos (U)
Tunxis Community College (U)
University of Arkansas (U)
University of Colorado at Denver and Health Sciences Center (U)
University of North Dakota (U)
University of North Texas (G)
Upper Iowa University (N,U)

INDUSTRIAL ENGINEERING

Cleveland State University (G)
Kettering University (N)
New Mexico State University (G)
Southern Methodist University (G)
Texas A&M University–Commerce (U,G)
The University of Arizona (G)
University of South Florida (G)
Western Michigan University (U)

INDUSTRIAL PRODUCTION TECHNOLOGIES

Bemidji State University (U,G)
Bismarck State College (N)
Boston University (G)
California University of Pennsylvania (U)
Delta College (U)
East Carolina University (U,G)
Edison State Community College (U)
Missouri Southern State University (N)

Missouri State University (U,G)
Roger Williams University (U)
Southwestern College (U)
University of Minnesota, Crookston (U)
The University of Texas at Tyler (U)
Wayne State College (U,G)

INFORMATION SCIENCE/STUDIES

Arapahoe Community College (U)
Athabasca University (G)
Belmont Technical College (U)
Bismarck State College (U)
Bowling Green State University (U)
Brenau University (U)
Bridgewater State College (N)
Bristol Community College (N,U)
Capitol College (G)
Carlow University (U)
Cedar Crest College (U)
Central New Mexico Community College (U)
Central Virginia Community College (U)
Chadron State College (U)
Chemeketa Community College (U)
Cincinnati State Technical and Community
  College (U)
College of Southern Maryland (U)
College of The Albemarle (N)
Colorado State University (N)
Connecticut State University System (U)
Dakota State University (U,G)
Dallas Baptist University (G)
Delaware County Community College (U)
DePaul University (U,G)
Drake University (U,G)
Drexel University (G)
D'Youville College (G)
East Carolina University (U)
Fairmont State University (U)
Florida Institute of Technology (G)
Florida State University (G)
Fort Hays State University (U)
Franklin University (U)
Galveston College (U)
Gaston College (U)
Graceland University (U)
Grantham University (U)
Harrisburg Area Community College (U)
Haywood Community College (U)
Indiana University of Pennsylvania (U)
Jacksonville State University (U,G)
James Madison University (N)
Jones College (U)
J. Sargeant Reynolds Community College (U)
Kansas State University (U)
Lamar State College–Port Arthur (N)
Lawrence Technological University (G)
Limestone College (U)
Marlboro College (U)
Marymount University (G)
Maryville University of Saint Louis (N,U)
Metropolitan State University (U)
Missouri State University (N)
Myers University (U)
National University (U)
New Jersey Institute of Technology (U,G)
North Carolina State University (G)
Pace University (U,G)
Palomar College (U)
Peirce College (U)
Peninsula College (U)
Reedley College (N,U)

Regis University (U)
The Richard Stockton College of New Jersey
  (G)
Rose State College (U)
Salem State College (U)
San Francisco State University (N)
Schiller International University (U)
Shippensburg University of Pennsylvania
  (U,G)
Southern Illinois University Carbondale (U)
Southern Methodist University (G)
Southern New Hampshire University (U)
Southern Polytechnic State University (U)
State University of New York at Oswego
  (U,G)
Strayer University (U,G)
Syracuse University (U,G)
Tacoma Community College (U)
Taylor University (N,U)
Tunxis Community College (N)
Tyler Junior College (N)
University of Illinois at Chicago (G)
University of Maryland University College
  (U)
University of Massachusetts Lowell (U)
University of Minnesota, Crookston (U)
University of Missouri–Columbia (G)
The University of Montana (G)
The University of North Carolina at Charlotte
  (G)
University of North Texas (G)
University of Oregon (G)
University of South Florida (G)
The University of Texas at San Antonio (U)
The University of Texas System (U)
University of the Sciences in Philadelphia (U)
University of Toronto (U)
University of Washington (N)
University of West Florida (G)
Vance-Granville Community College (U)
Vincennes University (U)
West Valley College (U)

INSURANCE

The American College (U,G)
Central Georgia Technical College (U)
Drake University (G)
Feather River College (U)
Indiana State University (U)
John Wood Community College (N)
Mississippi State University (U)
New England College of Finance (U)
Palomar College (U)
Pasco-Hernando Community College (N)
Southeast Arkansas College (U)
Southern Illinois University Carbondale (U)
University of Central Arkansas (N)
University of Nebraska–Lincoln (U)
University of Toronto (N)
University of Waterloo (U)

INTERCULTURAL/ MULTICULTURAL AND DIVERSITY STUDIES

Anne Arundel Community College (U)
Berkeley College (U)
Berkeley College-New York City Campus (U)
Berkeley College-Westchester Campus (U)
Eugene Bible College (U)

Kansas City Kansas Community College (U)
Modesto Junior College (U)
Roosevelt University (U)
Saybrook Graduate School and Research
  Center (N)
South Piedmont Community College (U)
University of Alaska Fairbanks (G)
University of Houston–Victoria (G)
University of Missouri–Columbia (U)
West Virginia University at Parkersburg (U)

INTERIOR ARCHITECTURE

Academy of Art University (U,G)
Boston Architectural College (N,U,G)
University of Nebraska–Lincoln (G)

INTERNATIONAL AGRICULTURE

Dallas Baptist University (U)

INTERNATIONAL AND COMPARATIVE EDUCATION

Drexel University (G)

INTERNATIONAL BUSINESS

American Public University System (U)
Athabasca University (N,G)
Berkeley College (U)
Berkeley College-New York City Campus (U)
Berkeley College-Westchester Campus (U)
Black Hills State University (U)
Bradley University (U)
Brenau University (U,G)
California State University, Monterey Bay (U)
Cape Breton University (U)
Capella University (G)
Central New Mexico Community College (U)
College of Southern Maryland (U)
Dallas Baptist University (G)
Des Moines Area Community College (U)
D'Youville College (U,G)
Eastern Washington University (N)
Fullerton College (U)
Iona College (U,G)
James Madison University (N)
Jones College (U)
Lawrence Technological University (G)
Limestone College (U)
Long Beach City College (U)
Marist College (G)
Massasoit Community College (U)
Mercy College (U)
Metropolitan State University (U)
Minnesota School of Business–Richfield (U)
Monterey Peninsula College (U)
Mount Saint Vincent University (U)
Myers University (U)
North Central State College (U)
Oakton Community College (U)
Pace University (U)
Palomar College (U)
Park University (G)
Pennsylvania College of Technology (U)
Philadelphia University (G)
Regent University (N,U,G)
Regis University (G)
Sacred Heart University (U)
Saddleback College (U)
Sauk Valley Community College (U)

Schiller International University (U,G)
Shippensburg University of Pennsylvania (U,G)
Southeast Arkansas College (U)
Southern New Hampshire University (G)
Spring Arbor University (G)
State University of New York Empire State College (U)
Strayer University (U)
Suffolk University (G)
Thunderbird School of Global Management (N,G)
Tompkins Cortland Community College (U)
University of Dallas (G)
The University of Findlay (U)
University of Illinois (G)
University of Management and Technology (U)
University of Maryland University College (U,G)
University of Nebraska–Lincoln (U,G)
University of Washington (U)
University of Wisconsin–Platteville (U)
Upper Iowa University (N,U)

INTERNATIONAL RELATIONS AND AFFAIRS

American Public University System (U,G)
Athabasca University (N,U,G)
Drake University (U)
Erie Community College (U)
Jones College (U)
Miami Dade College (U)
New Jersey City University (U)
Regent University (N)
Schiller International University (U)
Southern New Hampshire University (U)
University of Massachusetts Boston (U,G)
University of Missouri–Columbia (U)
University of Vermont (U)
West Los Angeles College (U)

INTERNATIONAL/GLOBAL STUDIES

Bowling Green State University (U)
Des Moines Area Community College (U)
Drexel University (G)
D'Youville College (U)
National University (U)
Regent University (N)
Southern New Hampshire University (G)
Thunderbird School of Global Management (N)
University of Management and Technology (U)

JOURNALISM

Arapahoe Community College (U)
Arkansas Tech University (U,G)
Athabasca University (N,U)
Bergen Community College (U)
Brenau University (U)
Cabrillo College (U)
Central Carolina Community College (U)
Cerritos College (U)
Cleveland State University (N)
College of DuPage (U)
De Anza College (U)

Delaware County Community College (U)
Des Moines Area Community College (U)
Drake University (U,G)
East Carolina University (U)
Eastern Kentucky University (U)
Everett Community College (U)
Feather River College (N)
Fullerton College (U)
Henry Ford Community College (U)
Indiana University–Purdue University Fort Wayne (U)
Iona College (G)
James Madison University (N)
Jamestown Community College (N)
Jefferson Community College (U)
Kauai Community College (U)
Kirkwood Community College (U)
Linn-Benton Community College (U)
Louisiana State University and Agricultural and Mechanical College (U)
Louisiana Tech University (U)
Marshall University (U)
Maryville University of Saint Louis (N)
Massasoit Community College (N)
Middlesex Community College (U)
Middle Tennessee State University (U)
Mt. San Antonio College (U)
Mount Wachusett Community College (U)
Murray State University (U)
New York Institute of Technology (U)
Northern Virginia Community College (U)
North Seattle Community College (U)
Oakton Community College (U)
Oklahoma State University (U)
Palomar College (U)
Parkland College (U)
Peninsula College (U)
Quinnipiac University (U,G)
The Richard Stockton College of New Jersey (U)
Saddleback College (U)
Schoolcraft College (U)
Seattle Central Community College (U)
Simpson College (U)
Southern Illinois University Carbondale (U)
State University of New York at Oswego (U)
Taylor University (U)
Texas A&M University–Commerce (U)
Texas State University-San Marcos (U)
Texas Tech University (U)
The University of Alabama (U)
University of Alaska Fairbanks (U)
University of Arkansas (U)
University of Central Arkansas (N)
University of Idaho (U)
University of Maryland University College (U)
University of Minnesota, Twin Cities Campus (U)
University of Missouri–Columbia (G)
The University of Montana (U)
University of Nebraska–Lincoln (U,G)
University of New Orleans (U,G)
The University of North Carolina at Chapel Hill (U)
University of North Texas (U)
University of Oklahoma (U)
University of Southern Indiana (U)
University of South Florida (N)
The University of Toledo (U)
University of Washington (U)

University of Wisconsin Colleges (U)
University of Wisconsin–Whitewater (U,G)

LANDSCAPE ARCHITECTURE

California State University, Dominguez Hills (U)
Central Wyoming College (N)
Colorado State University (U)
James Madison University (N)
Mississippi State University (U)
Southern Illinois University Carbondale (U)
The University of British Columbia (U)
University of Massachusetts Boston (N)
University of Saskatchewan (N)

LANGUAGES (AMERICAN INDIAN/ NATIVE AMERICAN)

Central Wyoming College (U)
Palomar College (U)

LANGUAGES (CLASSICS AND CLASSICAL)

Columbia International University (N,G)
Louisiana State University and Agricultural and Mechanical College (U)
North Idaho College (N)
Patrick Henry College (U)
University of Alaska Fairbanks (U)
University of Colorado at Denver and Health Sciences Center (U)
University of Massachusetts Boston (U)
University of Minnesota, Twin Cities Campus (U)
University of Missouri–Columbia (U)
The University of North Carolina at Chapel Hill (U)
University of Waterloo (U)

LANGUAGES (EAST ASIAN)

Darton College (U)
Feather River College (N)
Naropa University (G)
Southern Illinois University Carbondale (U)
University of Toronto (N)

LANGUAGES (FOREIGN LANGUAGES RELATED)

Acadia University (U)
Blackhawk Technical College (N)
Black Hills State University (U)
Boise State University (U)
California State University, San Bernardino (U)
California State University, San Marcos (N)
Cedar Crest College (U)
Central Carolina Community College (U)
Central Wyoming College (N)
Clarion University of Pennsylvania (U)
Cleveland State University (N)
Colorado Mountain College District System (U)
Cumberland County College (U)
Darton College (U)
Dodge City Community College (U)
Eastern Washington University (N)
Flathead Valley Community College (U)

Fort Hays State University (U)
Fulton-Montgomery Community College (N)
Itawamba Community College (U)
Longwood University (N,U)
Mercy College (U)
Middlesex Community College (U)
Mount Allison University (N)
Mount Saint Vincent University (U)
Pace University (U)
Portland Community College (N)
Rend Lake College (N)
Riverside Community College District (U)
Sacred Heart University (U)
Seattle Central Community College (U)
State University of New York College at
   Potsdam (U)
Triton College (N)
University of California, Los Angeles (G)
University of Illinois (U)
University of Illinois at Springfield (U)
University of Maine (U)
University of Missouri–Columbia (N,U)
University of New Orleans (U,G)
The University of North Carolina at Chapel
   Hill (U)
University of Southern Indiana (U)
University of Toronto (N,U)
University of Waterloo (U)
University of Wisconsin–Whitewater (U)
Utah Valley State College (U)
Wake Technical Community College (N)
Wayne State College (U)
Webster University (U)
West Los Angeles College (U)

LANGUAGES (GERMANIC)

Darton College (U)
Eastern Michigan University (G)
Eastern Washington University (U)
James Madison University (N)
Jefferson Community and Technical College
   (U)
Louisiana State University and Agricultural
   and Mechanical College (U)
Marian College of Fond du Lac (U)
Northern State University (U)
Oakton Community College (U)
Oklahoma State University (U)
Queen's University at Kingston (U)
University of Arkansas (U)
University of Central Arkansas (U)
University of Illinois (U)
University of Minnesota, Twin Cities Campus
   (U)
University of Missouri–Columbia (U)
University of New Orleans (U,G)
University of South Florida (G)
The University of Tennessee (U)
University of Toronto (N)
University of Waterloo (U)
Wilfrid Laurier University (U)

LANGUAGES (IRANIAN/PERSIAN)

Palomar College (U)

LANGUAGES (MIDDLE/NEAR EASTERN AND SEMITIC)

Feather River College (N)
Hebrew College (N,U,G)

Henry Ford Community College (U)
Lincoln Christian College (N,U,G)
University of Colorado at Colorado Springs
   (U)

LANGUAGES (MODERN GREEK)

Eugene Bible College (U)
North Carolina State University (U)
Northwestern College (U)
University of Washington (U)
University of Waterloo (U)

LANGUAGES (ROMANCE LANGUAGES)

Andrews University (U)
Arapahoe Community College (U)
Boise State University (U)
Bowling Green State University (G)
Burlington County College (U)
Cabrillo College (U)
Carroll Community College (N)
Clemson University (N)
Clovis Community College (U)
College of DuPage (U)
College of San Mateo (U)
College of Southern Maryland (U)
Columbus State Community College (U)
Darton College (U)
Delta College (U)
East Arkansas Community College (U)
Hillsborough Community College (N)
Houston Community College System (U)
James Madison University (N)
Jefferson Community and Technical College
   (U)
John Jay College of Criminal Justice of the
   City University of New York (U)
Kauai Community College (U)
Kean University (N)
Lansing Community College (U)
Louisiana State University and Agricultural
   and Mechanical College (U)
Marian College of Fond du Lac (U)
Modesto Junior College (U)
Mountain Empire Community College (U)
Nassau Community College (U)
North Carolina State University (U)
Northern Virginia Community College (U)
Oakton Community College (N,U)
Oklahoma State University (U)
Oregon State University (N)
Palomar College (U)
Piedmont Technical College (U)
Pulaski Technical College (N)
St. John's University (U)
St. Louis Community College System (U)
Southern Illinois University Carbondale (U)
Southwest Virginia Community College (U)
State University of New York College at
   Potsdam (N)
Texas State University-San Marcos (U)
Texas Tech University (N,U)
Triton College (U)
Tyler Junior College (U)
The University of Alabama (U)
University of Alaska Fairbanks (U)
University of Arkansas (U)
The University of British Columbia (U)
University of California, Davis (U)
University of Central Oklahoma (U)

University of Illinois (U)
University of Massachusetts Boston (U)
University of Minnesota, Twin Cities Campus
   (U)
University of Missouri–Columbia (N,U)
University of New Orleans (U,G)
The University of North Carolina at Chapel
   Hill (U)
University of South Florida (U)
The University of Tennessee (U)
The University of Texas at Arlington (U)
The University of Texas at San Antonio (U,G)
University of Toronto (N)
University of Vermont (N,U)
University of Waterloo (U)
Virginia Polytechnic Institute and State
   University (U)
Western Michigan University (U)
West Hills Community College (N)
West Valley College (U)
Wilfrid Laurier University (U)

LANGUAGES (SLAVIC, BALTIC AND ALBANIAN)

Feather River College (N)
University of Minnesota, Twin Cities Campus
   (U)
The University of North Carolina at Chapel
   Hill (U)
University of Washington (U)
University of Waterloo (U)

LANGUAGES (SOUTH ASIAN)

Arapahoe Community College (U)
North Carolina State University (U)
University of Toronto (N)

LANGUAGES (SOUTHEAST ASIAN AND AUSTRALASIAN/PACIFIC)

Oakton Community College (U)

LEATHERWORKING AND UPHOLSTERY

Blackhawk Technical College (N)

LEGAL PROFESSIONS AND STUDIES RELATED

Arapahoe Community College (U)
California State University, Chico (U)
Chadron State College (U)
Clackamas Community College (U)
Clarion University of Pennsylvania (U)
Clemson University (N)
Cloud County Community College (U)
Colorado Technical University (U)
East Arkansas Community College (U)
Eastern Michigan University (U)
Erie Community College (U)
Everest College (U)
Iona College (G)
Itawamba Community College (U)
Kansas City Kansas Community College (U)
Kean University (N)
Lock Haven University of Pennsylvania (N)
Michigan State University College of Law
   (N,G)

Middlesex Community College (U)
Minnesota School of Business–Richfield (U)
Mount Wachusett Community College (U)
Palomar College (U)
Portland Community College (N)
Pulaski Technical College (U)
Quinebaug Valley Community College (N)
Roosevelt University (N,G)
Rose State College (U)
South Piedmont Community College (U)
South Suburban College (U)
Texas State University-San Marcos (U)
University of Alaska Fairbanks (G)
University of Central Florida (U)
University of Illinois at Springfield (G)
The University of Montana–Western (N)
University of Southern Indiana (N)
West Los Angeles College (U)

LEGAL RESEARCH AND ADVANCED PROFESSIONAL STUDIES

Arapahoe Community College (U)
California University of Pennsylvania (G)
Drake University (U)
Eastern Michigan University (U,G)
Itawamba Community College (U)
Michigan State University College of Law (N,G)
Missouri Southern State University (N)
Missouri State University (G)
Palomar College (U)
Rose State College (U)
Schiller International University (G)
Seminole Community College (U)
Strayer University (G)

LEGAL STUDIES (NON-PROFESSIONAL GENERAL, UNDERGRADUATE)

Adams State College (U)
Anne Arundel Community College (U)
Arapahoe Community College (U)
Athabasca University (U)
Berkeley College (U)
Berkeley College-New York City Campus (U)
Berkeley College-Westchester Campus (U)
Brenau University (U)
Cabrillo College (U)
California State University, Chico (U)
Carroll Community College (N,U)
Central New Mexico Community College (U)
Central Texas College (U)
Cerritos College (U)
Chadron State College (U)
College of San Mateo (U)
College of Southern Maryland (U)
College of The Albemarle (U)
Columbus State Community College (U)
The Community College of Baltimore County (U)
De Anza College (U)
Delaware County Community College (U)
Delta College (U)
DeVry University Online (U)
Eastern Michigan University (U)
Elgin Community College (U)
Embry-Riddle Aeronautical University (U)
Finger Lakes Community College (U)

Flathead Valley Community College (N)
Galveston College (N)
Gaston College (U)
Grantham University (U)
Hillsborough Community College (U)
John Jay College of Criminal Justice of the City University of New York (U)
Jones College (U)
Kellogg Community College (U)
Lansing Community College (U)
Limestone College (U)
Louisiana State University and Agricultural and Mechanical College (U)
Marist College (U)
Mercy College (U)
Metropolitan State University (U)
Michigan State University College of Law (N)
Middlesex Community College (U)
Minnesota School of Business–Richfield (U)
Mountain Empire Community College (U)
Mount Saint Vincent University (U)
Mt. San Antonio College (U)
Murray State University (U)
Myers University (U)
Nassau Community College (U)
New York Institute of Technology (U)
Northern Virginia Community College (U)
Oakton Community College (U)
Oklahoma State University (U)
Orangeburg-Calhoun Technical College (U)
Pace University (U)
Palomar College (U)
Parkland College (U)
Patrick Henry College (U)
Peirce College (U)
Philadelphia University (U)
Piedmont Technical College (U)
Randolph Community College (U)
Roger Williams University (U)
Roosevelt University (U)
Rose State College (U)
Ryerson University (U)
St. John's University (U)
Sam Houston State University (U)
Schenectady County Community College (U)
Sinclair Community College (U)
State University of New York Empire State College (U)
Strayer University (U)
Tacoma Community College (U)
Texas Tech University (U)
Tompkins Cortland Community College (U)
Tri-State University (U)
Triton College (U)
Tyler Junior College (U)
University of Alaska Fairbanks (U)
University of Arkansas (U)
University of Central Oklahoma (U)
University of Great Falls (U)
University of Minnesota, Morris (U)
The University of Toledo (U)
Upper Iowa University (U)
Utah Valley State College (U)
Washtenaw Community College (U)
Waubonsee Community College (U)
West Valley College (U)

LEGAL SUPPORT SERVICES

Adams State College (U)
Anne Arundel Community College (U)
Arapahoe Community College (U)

Blackhawk Technical College (U)
Bryant and Stratton Online (U)
Carroll Community College (N,U)
Central Georgia Technical College (U)
Cleveland State University (N)
College of Mount St. Joseph (U)
Colorado State University (N)
Columbus State Community College (U)
Duquesne University (N)
Eastern Michigan University (U)
East Tennessee State University (N)
Erie Community College (U)
Manatee Community College (U)
Michigan State University College of Law (N,G)
North Harris Montgomery Community College District (U)
Palomar College (U)
Pasco-Hernando Community College (U)
Riverside Community College District (U)
Seminole Community College (U)
Tyler Junior College (U)
The University of North Carolina at Charlotte (N)
University of North Dakota (N)
The University of Texas System (N)
Wake Technical Community College (N)
West Virginia University (N)

LIBERAL ARTS AND SCIENCES, GENERAL STUDIES AND HUMANITIES

Acadia University (U)
Alvin Community College (U)
American Public University System (U)
Arapahoe Community College (U)
Arizona Western College (U)
Ashford University (U)
Athabasca University (N)
Bainbridge College (U)
Beaufort County Community College (U)
Bellevue Community College (U)
Berkeley College (U)
Berkeley College-New York City Campus (U)
Berkeley College-Westchester Campus (U)
Bowling Green State University (U)
Brenau University (U)
Briercrest Distance Learning (U)
Caldwell Community College and Technical Institute (U)
California State University, Chico (U)
California State University, San Bernardino (U)
Central Oregon Community College (U)
Chadron State College (U)
Chattanooga State Technical Community College (U)
Chemeketa Community College (U)
Chesapeake College (U)
Clinton Community College (U)
College of DuPage (U)
College of the Siskiyous (U)
Colorado State University-Pueblo (U)
Community College of Beaver County (U)
Community College of Denver (U)
Dallas Baptist University (U,G)
Darton College (U)
Delaware County Community College (U)
DePaul University (U)
DeVry University Online (U)
Dickinson State University (U)

Drake University (U)
Eastern Michigan University (U)
East Los Angeles College (U)
East Tennessee State University (N,U,G)
Elgin Community College (U)
Everett Community College (U)
Fairmont State University (U)
Fort Hays State University (U,G)
Franklin Pierce University (U)
Gaston College (U)
Granite State College (U)
Haywood Community College (U)
Henry Ford Community College (U)
Herkimer County Community College (U)
Hocking College (U)
Honolulu Community College (U)
Illinois Eastern Community Colleges, Olney
  Central College (U)
Illinois Eastern Community Colleges, Wabash
  Valley College (U)
Indiana University of Pennsylvania (G)
Indiana University System (U)
Indiana Wesleyan University (U)
Iona College (U)
Jacksonville State University (U,G)
James Madison University (N)
Jamestown Community College (N)
John A. Logan College (U)
John Wood Community College (U)
Jones College (U)
Judson College (U)
Kansas City Kansas Community College (U)
Kean University (U)
Labette Community College (U)
Lake Superior College (U)
Lehigh Carbon Community College (U)
Lewis-Clark State College (U)
Linn-Benton Community College (U)
Lock Haven University of Pennsylvania (G)
Long Beach City College (U)
Longwood University (U)
Madison Area Technical College (U)
Malone College (U)
Mercy College (U)
Miami Dade College (U)
Middlesex Community College (U)
Middle Tennessee State University (U)
Midwestern State University (U)
Minnesota School of Business–Richfield (U)
Minot State University–Bottineau Campus (U)
Monroe Community College (U)
Montana State University–Billings (U)
Montgomery Community College (U)
Montgomery County Community College (U)
Naropa University (U,G)
Naugatuck Valley Community College (U)
The New School: A University (N,U)
Northern Kentucky University (U)
NorthWest Arkansas Community College (U)
Northwestern College (U)
Northwest Mississippi Community College
  (U)
Oral Roberts University (U)
Oregon State University (U)
Ouachita Technical College (U)
Pace University (N)
Palomar College (U)
Patrick Henry College (U)
Peninsula College (U)
Prescott College (U)
Pulaski Technical College (U)
Quinebaug Valley Community College (U)

Regions University (N,U)
Rend Lake College (U)
The Richard Stockton College of New Jersey
  (U)
Rockland Community College (U)
Rogers State University (U)
Roosevelt University (U)
Rose State College (U)
Ryerson University (U)
Sacred Heart University (U)
St. Petersburg College (U)
Seminole Community College (U)
Simpson College (U)
Sinclair Community College (U)
Skidmore College (U,G)
Southern New Hampshire University (U)
Southwestern College (U)
Stony Brook University, State University of
  New York (G)
Syracuse University (U)
Taylor University (U)
Texas State University-San Marcos (U)
Texas Tech University (U)
Tri-State University (U)
Triton College (U)
Tyler Junior College (U)
The University of Alabama (U)
University of Alaska Fairbanks (U)
University of Bridgeport (U)
University of California, Los Angeles (G)
University of Colorado at Denver and Health
  Sciences Center (U)
University of Connecticut (U)
University of Denver (G)
University of Great Falls (U)
University of Illinois (U)
University of Illinois at Springfield (U)
University of La Verne (G)
University of Maine (G)
The University of Maine at Augusta (U)
University of Maine at Fort Kent (U)
University of Massachusetts Boston (U)
University of Massachusetts Lowell (U)
University of Minnesota, Twin Cities Campus
  (U,G)
University of Missouri–Columbia (U)
The University of Montana–Western (U)
University of New Orleans (N,U,G)
The University of North Carolina at
  Greensboro (U,G)
The University of South Dakota (U)
University of Southern Mississippi (U)
University of South Florida (U)
The University of Tennessee (U)
The University of Texas at El Paso (U)
The University of Texas System (U)
The University of Toledo (U,G)
University of Waterloo (U)
University of West Florida (U)
University of Wyoming (U)
Upper Iowa University (U)
Utah State University (U)
Utica College (U)
Vance-Granville Community College (U)
Virginia Polytechnic Institute and State
  University (G)
Viterbo University (U)
Washburn University (G)
Waubonsee Community College (U)
West Shore Community College (U)
Wharton County Junior College (U)
Wright State University (U)

York University (U)
Yuba College (U)

LIBRARY ASSISTANT

Belmont Technical College (U)
College of DuPage (U)
James Madison University (N)
Palomar College (U)
Rose State College (U)
Syracuse University (G)

LIBRARY SCIENCE

Big Bend Community College (U)
Central Oregon Community College (U)
Central Wyoming College (U)
Chadron State College (U)
Clarion University of Pennsylvania (U,G)
College of DuPage (U)
Drexel University (G)
East Carolina University (G)
Eastern Kentucky University (G)
Long Beach City College (U)
Mansfield University of Pennsylvania (G)
Mayville State University (U)
Memorial University of Newfoundland (U,G)
Missouri State University (G)
Northern State University (U)
Palomar College (U)
Rose State College (U)
St. John's University (G)
Salem State College (G)
Seattle Pacific University (G)
Seminole Community College (U)
Syracuse University (G)
Tacoma Community College (U)
Texas Woman's University (G)
Union University (U)
The University of Alabama (G)
University of Alaska Fairbanks (U)
The University of Arizona (G)
University of Central Missouri (U,G)
University of Central Oklahoma (U,G)
University of Cincinnati Raymond Walters
  College (U)
University of Idaho (U,G)
University of Illinois (G)
University of Illinois at Urbana–Champaign
  (G)
University of Missouri–Columbia (G)
The University of North Carolina at
  Greensboro (G)
University of North Texas (N,U,G)
University of South Florida (U,G)
University of Vermont (U,G)
The University of Virginia's College at Wise
  (U)
University of Washington (U,G)
University of Wisconsin–Stout (G)
University of Wisconsin–Whitewater (U)
Valley City State University (U)
West Los Angeles College (U)

LIBRARY SCIENCE RELATED

Belmont Technical College (U)
Black Hills State University (U)
Bowling Green State University (U)
Cabrillo College (U)
Central Carolina Community College (U)
Central Virginia Community College (U)

Chadron State College (U)
The College of St. Scholastica (G)
Colorado Mountain College District System (U)
Des Moines Area Community College (U)
Drexel University (G)
Everett Community College (U)
Harrisburg Area Community College (U)
Indiana State University (U,G)
Louisiana State University and Agricultural and Mechanical College (U)
Miami Dade College (U)
Montana State University (G)
North Seattle Community College (U)
Oakton Community College (U)
Palomar College (U)
Pittsburg State University (G)
Rose State College (U)
Saddleback College (U)
Seminole Community College (U)
State University of New York at Plattsburgh (U)
Syracuse University (G)
Tacoma Community College (U)
Texas A&M University–Commerce (G)
The University of British Columbia (U)
University of Central Arkansas (G)
University of Central Oklahoma (U)
University of Idaho (U,G)
The University of Maine at Augusta (U)
University of Missouri–Columbia (G)
The University of Montana (U,G)
The University of Montana–Western (U)
The University of North Carolina at Greensboro (G)
University of North Texas (N,U,G)
University of Oklahoma (U)
University of Southern Mississippi (U)
University of Washington (G)
Utah State University (G)
West Valley College (U)

LINGUISTIC, COMPARATIVE, AND RELATED LANGUAGE STUDIES

Acadia University (U)
Adams State College (N)
Athabasca University (N,U)
Bainbridge College (N)
Brenau University (U)
Bridgewater State College (G)
Caldwell Community College and Technical Institute (N)
California State University, Monterey Bay (U)
Cleveland State University (U,G)
Columbia International University (G)
Daemen College (U)
Darton College (U)
EduKan (U)
Feather River College (N)
Fullerton College (U)
Hebrew College (N,U,G)
James Madison University (N,U)
James Sprunt Community College (U)
Jamestown Community College (N)
J. Sargeant Reynolds Community College (U)
Kauai Community College (U)
Lansing Community College (U)
Louisiana State University and Agricultural and Mechanical College (U)
Mesa Community College (U)
Middlesex Community College (U)

Middle Tennessee State University (N)
Millersville University of Pennsylvania (U,G)
Mountain Empire Community College (U)
Northern State University (U)
Northwest Missouri State University (U)
Oakton Community College (U)
Odessa College (N)
The Ohio State University (U)
Oregon State University (N)
Pace University (U)
Plymouth State University (U)
Reedley College (N)
Riverside Community College District (N,U)
Sacred Heart University (U)
St. Petersburg College (U)
Seattle Pacific University (U)
Snead State Community College (U)
Southwestern Baptist Theological Seminary (G)
State University of New York College at Potsdam (N)
Strayer University (U)
Tacoma Community College (U)
Triton College (U)
Tunxis Community College (U)
The University of Alabama (U)
University of Alaska Fairbanks (U)
University of Colorado at Denver and Health Sciences Center (U)
University of Denver (G)
University of Idaho (U)
University of Management and Technology (G)
University of Massachusetts Boston (U,G)
University of Minnesota, Twin Cities Campus (U)
University of Missouri–Columbia (U)
University of New Orleans (U,G)
University of North Dakota (U)
University of North Texas (U,G)
University of Oregon (U)
University of Southern Indiana (U)
University of Southern Mississippi (U,G)
The University of Texas at El Paso (U)
The University of Texas at San Antonio (U)
The University of Texas System (U)
University of Waterloo (U)
University of Wisconsin–La Crosse (U)
Virginia Polytechnic Institute and State University (U)
Weber State University (U)
Wenatchee Valley College (N)
Wright State University (U)

MANAGEMENT INFORMATION SYSTEMS

American Public University System (U)
Arapahoe Community College (U)
Athabasca University (N,U,G)
Beaufort County Community College (U)
Bellevue Community College (U)
Bellevue University (U,G)
Boston University (G)
Brenau University (U,G)
Bristol Community College (N,U)
Buena Vista University (U)
Capitol College (G)
Cardinal Stritch University (U)
Carlow University (U)
Carroll Community College (U)
Central Carolina Community College (N)

Central Michigan University (G)
Central Texas College (U)
Central Washington University (U)
Cerritos College (U)
Chadron State College (U,G)
Charter Oak State College (U)
Chemeketa Community College (U)
Cincinnati State Technical and Community College (U)
Cleveland State University (N)
College of The Albemarle (N)
Colorado State University (G)
Colorado State University-Pueblo (N)
Connecticut State University System (U,G)
Culver-Stockton College (U)
Dallas Baptist University (U,G)
Delaware County Community College (U)
Des Moines Area Community College (U)
Drake University (U)
Drexel University (G)
Duquesne University (G)
East Carolina University (U)
East Los Angeles College (U)
Edgecombe Community College (N,U)
Edison State Community College (U)
Embry-Riddle Aeronautical University (G)
Feather River College (N)
Fort Hays State University (N)
Franklin Pierce University (G)
Fullerton College (U)
Gaston College (U)
Georgia College & State University (G)
Granite State College (U)
Grantham University (U,G)
Haywood Community College (U)
Houston Community College System (U)
Indiana State University (U)
Indiana University of Pennsylvania (U)
Iona College (U,G)
Itawamba Community College (U)
Jacksonville State University (U,G)
Jones College (U)
Kansas State University (U)
Kettering University (N)
Kirkwood Community College (U)
Labette Community College (U)
Lamar State College–Port Arthur (N)
Lawrence Technological University (G)
Lewis-Clark State College (U)
Limestone College (U)
Longwood University (U)
Louisiana State University and Agricultural and Mechanical College (U)
Madison Area Technical College (U)
Manatee Community College (U)
Marlboro College (U)
Marshall University (U)
Maryville University of Saint Louis (N)
Mercy College (U,G)
Metropolitan State University (U,G)
Middle Tennessee State University (N)
Milwaukee School of Engineering (U)
Minot State University (U,G)
Missouri State University (N)
Motlow State Community College (U)
Mount Wachusett Community College (U)
Myers University (U)
Neumann College (G)
New Jersey Institute of Technology (U)
New Mexico Institute of Mining and Technology (U)
New York Institute of Technology (G)

North Arkansas College (U)
Northern Virginia Community College (U)
Nova Southeastern University (G)
Oklahoma State University (U)
Old Dominion University (U,G)
Oregon Institute of Technology (U)
Pace University (G)
Park University (U)
Patrick Henry Community College (U)
Peirce College (U)
Philadelphia University (U,G)
Piedmont Technical College (U)
Regis University (G)
Ryerson University (U)
Saddleback College (U)
St. Cloud State University (U)
St. Louis Community College System (N)
Saint Paul College–A Community &
  Technical College (U)
Schiller International University (U)
Seminole Community College (U)
Shippensburg University of Pennsylvania
  (U,G)
Southwest Wisconsin Technical College (U)
State University of New York College at
  Potsdam (U)
State University of New York Empire State
  College (U)
Stevens Institute of Technology (G)
Suffolk University (G)
Syracuse University (U,G)
Tacoma Community College (N)
Taylor University (N,U)
Texas A&M University–Commerce (U)
Texas A&M University–Texarkana (G)
Thunderbird School of Global Management
  (G)
Tunxis Community College (U)
Tyler Junior College (N)
Union University (U)
University of Colorado at Denver and Health
  Sciences Center (G)
University of Dallas (G)
The University of Findlay (N)
University of Illinois at Springfield (G)
University of Management and Technology
  (U,G)
University of Massachusetts Boston (U)
University of Massachusetts Lowell (G)
University of Michigan–Flint (N)
University of Minnesota, Crookston (U)
University of Nebraska at Omaha (U)
University of Nebraska–Lincoln (U)
University of New Orleans (U,G)
University of Oregon (G)
University of Pittsburgh at Bradford (U)
University of St. Thomas (U)
University of Southern Mississippi (U)
The University of Texas at San Antonio (G)
University of Waterloo (U)
University of Wisconsin–Parkside (G)
University of Wisconsin–Whitewater (U,G)
Upper Iowa University (N,U)
Utah Valley State College (U)
Virginia Polytechnic Institute and State
  University (G)
Waubonsee Community College (U)
Wayland Baptist University (U,G)
Webster University (G)
Westchester Community College (U)
Western Piedmont Community College (U)
West Virginia University (N)

West Virginia University at Parkersburg (U)
Wilkes Community College (U)
York County Community College (U)

MANAGEMENT SCIENCES AND QUANTITATIVE METHODS

Athabasca University (N,G)
Bellevue University (U,G)
Berkeley College (U)
Berkeley College-New York City Campus (U)
Berkeley College-Westchester Campus (U)
Boise State University (G)
Brenau University (U,G)
Bristol Community College (N)
Capitol College (G)
Cardinal Stritch University (U)
Central Michigan University (G)
Chadron State College (U,G)
Colorado State University (N,G)
Colorado Technical University (U,G)
Concordia University Wisconsin (U)
Dallas Baptist University (G)
Delaware County Community College (U)
DePaul University (N)
Des Moines Area Community College (U)
Drake University (U)
Drexel University (U,G)
Elizabeth City State University (U)
Embry-Riddle Aeronautical University (U,G)
Florida Institute of Technology (G)
Granite State College (U)
Jacksonville State University (U,G)
James Madison University (N)
Kettering University (N)
Limestone College (U)
Louisiana State University and Agricultural
  and Mechanical College (U)
Marist College (G)
Mercy College (U,G)
Mesa State College (U)
Miami Dade College (U)
Myers University (U)
National University (U)
Neumann College (G)
New Mexico Institute of Mining and
  Technology (G)
Old Dominion University (U)
Philadelphia University (U,G)
Quinnipiac University (G)
Regis University (G)
Ryerson University (U)
Saint Joseph's College of Maine (G)
Shippensburg University of Pennsylvania (U)
Southern Illinois University Carbondale (U)
Stanford University (N)
State University of New York College of
  Agriculture and Technology at Morrisville
  (U)
Stevens Institute of Technology (G)
Syracuse University (G)
Tompkins Cortland Community College (U)
University of Colorado at Denver and Health
  Sciences Center (G)
The University of Findlay (N)
University of Illinois at Urbana–Champaign
  (N,G)
University of Management and Technology
  (U)
University of Michigan–Flint (U,G)
University of New Orleans (U,G)
The University of Texas at San Antonio (G)

The University of Texas at Tyler (G)
University of Toronto (N,U)
University of Wisconsin–Parkside (G)
University of Wisconsin–Platteville (G)
University of Wisconsin–Stout (G)
Upper Iowa University (U)
Western Carolina University (N)
York University (U)

MANUFACTURING ENGINEERING

Boston University (G)
Cleveland State University (G)
East Carolina University (U)
Kettering University (N)
New Mexico State University (G)

MARKETING

Acadia University (U)
Anne Arundel Community College (U)
Arapahoe Community College (U)
Arkansas Tech University (U)
Athabasca University (N,U,G)
Bellevue Community College (U)
Bellevue University (U)
Berkeley College (U)
Berkeley College-New York City Campus (U)
Berkeley College-Westchester Campus (U)
Bismarck State College (U)
Blackhawk Technical College (U)
Black Hills State University (U)
Brenau University (U,G)
Bristol Community College (N)
Brookdale Community College (U)
Buena Vista University (U)
Burlington County College (U)
Butler Community College (U)
Butler County Community College (U)
Caldwell Community College and Technical
  Institute (U)
California State University, Monterey Bay (U)
Cape Breton University (U)
Cape Cod Community College (U)
Capella University (G)
Carroll Community College (U)
Central Carolina Community College (U)
Central Michigan University (U,G)
Central Texas College (U)
Central Virginia Community College (U)
Central Washington University (U)
Chadron State College (U,G)
Charter Oak State College (U)
Chattanooga State Technical Community
  College (U)
Clatsop Community College (U)
Clemson University (U)
Cleveland Institute of Electronics (N)
College of San Mateo (U)
College of Southern Maryland (U)
College of The Albemarle (U)
College of the Southwest (U)
Colorado State University (U,G)
Colorado State University-Pueblo (U)
Colorado Technical University (U)
Columbus State Community College (U)
The Community College of Baltimore County
  (U)
Concordia University Wisconsin (U)
Connecticut State University System (U,G)
Corban College (U)
County College of Morris (U)

Dallas Baptist University (U,G)
Danville Community College (U)
De Anza College (U)
Delaware County Community College (U)
Delta College (U)
Des Moines Area Community College (U)
DeVry University Online (U,G)
Dickinson State University (U)
Drake University (U)
Drexel University (U,G)
Eastern Kentucky University (U)
Eastern Michigan University (U,G)
East Tennessee State University (N)
Edison State Community College (U)
Elgin Community College (U)
Embry-Riddle Aeronautical University (U)
Erie Community College (U)
Everest College (U)
Finger Lakes Community College (U)
Florida Institute of Technology (G)
Fort Hays State University (U)
Franklin University (U)
Fullerton College (U)
Governors State University (U)
Graceland University (U)
Grantham University (U,G)
Hillsborough Community College (U)
Houston Community College System (U)
Illinois Eastern Community Colleges, Frontier
  Community College (U)
Indiana State University (U)
Indiana University of Pennsylvania (U)
Iona College (U,G)
Itawamba Community College (U)
Ivy Tech Community College–Northwest (U)
Jacksonville State University (U,G)
James Madison University (N)
James Sprunt Community College (U)
Jamestown Community College (N)
Jefferson Community College (U)
John A. Logan College (U)
J. Sargeant Reynolds Community College (U)
Kansas State University (U)
Kean University (U)
Kellogg Community College (U)
Lamar State College–Port Arthur (N)
Lawrence Technological University (U,G)
Lehigh Carbon Community College (U)
Lewis and Clark Community College (U)
Liberty University (U)
Limestone College (U)
Long Beach City College (U)
Louisiana State University and Agricultural
  and Mechanical College (U)
Madison Area Technical College (U)
Manatee Community College (U)
Marist College (G)
Marlboro College (U)
Marshall University (U,G)
Maryville University of Saint Louis (N)
Mercy College (U,G)
Mesalands Community College (U)
Metropolitan State University (U,G)
Miami Dade College (U)
Middlesex Community College (U)
Middle Tennessee State University (G)
Missouri State University (U,G)
Montana State University–Billings (U)
Montgomery County Community College (U)
Mountain Empire Community College (U)
Mount Saint Vincent University (U)
Mount Wachusett Community College (U)

Murray State University (G)
Myers University (U)
Nassau Community College (U)
New York Institute of Technology (U,G)
North Dakota State College of Science (U)
Northern Virginia Community College (U)
North Harris Montgomery Community
  College District (U)
Northwest Technical College (U)
Oakton Community College (U)
Oklahoma State University (U)
Old Dominion University (U,G)
Pace University (U,G)
Palomar College (U)
Parkland College (U)
Park University (U)
Peirce College (U)
Pennsylvania College of Technology (U)
Philadelphia University (U,G)
Pittsburg State University (U)
Portland Community College (U)
Quinnipiac University (U,G)
Randolph Community College (U)
Regis University (U,G)
The Richard Stockton College of New Jersey
  (U)
Riverside Community College District (U)
Rockland Community College (U)
Rose State College (U)
Ryerson University (U)
Sacred Heart University (U,G)
Saddleback College (U)
St. John's University (U)
Saint Joseph's College of Maine (U,G)
St. Louis Community College System (U)
Salem State College (U)
Sam Houston State University (U)
Schiller International University (U,G)
Schoolcraft College (U)
Seminole Community College (U)
Shippensburg University of Pennsylvania (U)
Simpson College (U)
Sinclair Community College (U)
Southeast Arkansas College (U)
Southern Illinois University Carbondale (N,U)
Southern New Hampshire University (U,G)
South Piedmont Community College (U)
Spring Arbor University (U,G)
State University of New York at Plattsburgh
  (U)
Suffolk University (G)
Syracuse University (G)
Taylor University (N,U)
Tennessee Technological University (N)
Texas A&M University–Commerce (U,G)
Texas A&M University–Texarkana (U,G)
Texas Tech University (U)
Thunderbird School of Global Management
  (N)
Tompkins Cortland Community College (U)
Tri-State University (U)
Triton College (U)
Union University (U)
United States Sports Academy (G)
University of Alaska Fairbanks (U)
University of Colorado at Denver and Health
  Sciences Center (G)
University of Dallas (G)
University of Delaware (U)
The University of Findlay (U,G)
University of Illinois (N)
University of Illinois at Chicago (N,G)

University of Maryland University College
  (G)
University of Massachusetts Boston (U)
University of Massachusetts Lowell (G)
University of Michigan–Flint (U,G)
University of Minnesota, Crookston (U)
University of Minnesota, Twin Cities Campus
  (U)
University of Missouri–Columbia (U)
University of Nebraska–Lincoln (U,G)
University of New Orleans (U,G)
University of North Alabama (U)
The University of North Carolina at Charlotte
  (N)
University of Northern Iowa (U)
University of North Texas (N,U,G)
University of Oklahoma (U)
University of Pittsburgh at Bradford (U)
University of Southern Indiana (G)
University of Southern Mississippi (U,G)
University of South Florida (G)
The University of Texas at San Antonio (U)
The University of Texas at Tyler (U)
University of Toronto (N,U)
University of Washington (U)
University of Wisconsin–Platteville (U)
University of Wisconsin–Whitewater (U,G)
Upper Iowa University (N,U)
Vance-Granville Community College (U)
Virginia Polytechnic Institute and State
  University (N,U,G)
Wake Technical Community College (U)
Wayland Baptist University (U)
Webster University (G)
Western Piedmont Community College (U)
West Los Angeles College (U)
West Shore Community College (U)
West Valley College (U)
West Virginia University at Parkersburg (U)
Wharton County Junior College (U)
Wilkes Community College (U)
Worcester Polytechnic Institute (G)
York University (U)

MASONRY

Pamlico Community College (U)

MATERIALS ENGINEERING

Boston University (G)
Delta College (U)
New Mexico Institute of Mining and
  Technology (G)
University of Idaho (G)
University of Illinois (G)
University of Illinois at Urbana–Champaign
  (G)
University of South Florida (G)
University of Washington (U,G)

MATERIALS SCIENCE

Columbia University (U,G)
Quinebaug Valley Community College (U)
University of Florida (G)
University of Illinois at Urbana–Champaign
  (G)
University of Minnesota, Twin Cities Campus
  (U)

MATHEMATICS

Alvin Community College (U)
Arapahoe Community College (U)
Argosy University, Chicago Campus (U)
Arkansas State University–Beebe (U)
Arkansas State University–Mountain Home (U)
Arkansas Tech University (U)
Ashford University (U)
Athabasca University (N,U)
Barclay College (U)
Bellevue Community College (U)
Big Bend Community College (U)
Bismarck State College (U)
Black Hills State University (U)
Boise State University (U)
Bowling Green State University (U,G)
Brazosport College (U)
Brenau University (U)
Bristol Community College (N,U)
Brookdale Community College (U)
Butler Community College (U)
Butler County Community College (U)
Cabrillo College (U)
Caldwell Community College and Technical Institute (U)
California State University, Dominguez Hills (N)
California State University, San Bernardino (U)
California State University, San Marcos (N,U)
Cape Cod Community College (U)
Carl Albert State College (U)
Carlow University (U)
Carroll Community College (U)
Cascadia Community College (U)
Casper College (U)
Cayuga County Community College (U)
Cedarville University (U)
Central Carolina Community College (U)
Central Georgia Technical College (U)
Central New Mexico Community College (U)
Central Oregon Community College (U)
Central Texas College (U)
Central Wyoming College (U)
Cerro Coso Community College (U)
Chadron State College (U,G)
Chaminade University of Honolulu (U)
Charter Oak State College (U)
Chattanooga State Technical Community College (U)
Chemeketa Community College (U)
Clackamas Community College (U)
Clatsop Community College (U)
Clemson University (N,U)
Cleveland Institute of Electronics (N)
Cloud County Community College (U)
Clovis Community College (U)
College of DuPage (U)
College of San Mateo (U)
College of Southern Maryland (U)
College of the Siskiyous (U)
Colorado State University (U,G)
Colorado State University-Pueblo (U)
Columbia College (U)
Columbus State Community College (U)
The Community College of Baltimore County (U)
Community College of Beaver County (U)
Community College of Denver (U)
County College of Morris (U)

Dakota State University (U)
Dallas Baptist University (U)
Danville Community College (U)
Darton College (U)
Delaware County Community College (U)
Delta College (U)
Des Moines Area Community College (U)
DeVry University Online (U,G)
Dodge City Community College (U)
East Arkansas Community College (U)
East Central Community College (U)
Eastern Iowa Community College District (N)
Eastern Michigan University (U,G)
East Los Angeles College (U)
Edison College (U)
Edison State Community College (U)
Edmonds Community College (U)
EduKan (U)
Elgin Community College (U)
Erie Community College (U)
Eugene Bible College (U)
Everest College (U)
Everett Community College (U)
Feather River College (U)
Fontbonne University (U)
Fullerton College (U)
Gadsden State Community College (U)
Gaston College (U)
George C. Wallace Community College (U)
Georgia Highlands College (U)
Georgia Institute of Technology (N,G)
Granite State College (U)
Grantham University (U)
Gulf Coast Community College (U)
Hamline University (G)
Harford Community College (U)
Harrisburg Area Community College (U)
Haywood Community College (U)
Henry Ford Community College (U)
Hocking College (U)
Holyoke Community College (U)
Houston Community College System (U)
Illinois Eastern Community Colleges, Lincoln Trail College (U)
Illinois Eastern Community Colleges, Olney Central College (U)
Illinois Eastern Community Colleges, Wabash Valley College (U)
Indiana State University (U)
Indiana University of Pennsylvania (U)
Indiana University–Purdue University Fort Wayne (U)
Indiana Wesleyan University (U)
Itawamba Community College (U)
Ivy Tech Community College–Bloomington (U)
Ivy Tech Community College–Central Indiana (U)
Ivy Tech Community College–Columbus (U)
Ivy Tech Community College–East Central (U)
Ivy Tech Community College–Northwest (U)
Ivy Tech Community College–Southern Indiana (U)
Ivy Tech Community College–Southwest (U)
Ivy Tech Community College–Wabash Valley (U)
Ivy Tech Community College–Whitewater (U)
Jacksonville State University (U)
James Sprunt Community College (U)
Jefferson Community and Technical College (U)

Jefferson Community College (U)
John A. Logan College (U)
John Tyler Community College (U)
John Wood Community College (U)
Jones College (N,U)
Jones County Junior College (U)
J. Sargeant Reynolds Community College (U)
Judson College (U)
Kansas City Kansas Community College (U)
Kaskaskia College (U)
Kean University (N,U)
Labette Community College (U)
Lake Superior College (U)
Lamar State College–Port Arthur (U)
Lansing Community College (U)
Lehigh Carbon Community College (U)
Lesley University (G)
Lewis and Clark Community College (U)
Limestone College (U)
Linn-Benton Community College (N,U)
Long Beach City College (U)
Longwood University (U)
Louisiana State University and Agricultural and Mechanical College (N,U)
Louisiana Tech University (U)
Lurleen B. Wallace Community College (U)
Mansfield University of Pennsylvania (U)
Marshall University (U)
Massasoit Community College (U)
Memorial University of Newfoundland (U)
Mesa Community College (U)
Mesalands Community College (U)
Mesa State College (U)
Metropolitan State University (U)
Miami Dade College (U)
Michigan Technological University (N,U)
Middlesex Community College (U)
Middle Tennessee State University (U,G)
Midway College (U)
Minnesota School of Business–Richfield (U)
Minnesota State University Moorhead (U)
Minot State University (U)
Mississippi State University (U)
Missouri Southern State University (U)
Moberly Area Community College (U)
Monroe Community College (U)
Montana State University (G)
Montana State University–Billings (U)
Montana Tech of The University of Montana (U)
Monterey Peninsula College (U)
Montgomery County Community College (U)
Motlow State Community College (U)
Mountain Empire Community College (U)
Mount Saint Vincent University (N,U)
Mount Wachusett Community College (U)
Myers University (U)
Nassau Community College (N,U)
New England Institute of Technology (U)
New Jersey City University (U)
New Mexico Institute of Mining and Technology (G)
New Mexico Junior College (U)
North Arkansas College (U)
North Carolina State University (U)
North Dakota State College of Science (U)
North Dakota State University (U)
Northeast Alabama Community College (U)
Northeast State Technical Community College (U)
Northern State University (U)

North Harris Montgomery Community College District (U)
North Idaho College (U)
Northland Community and Technical College–Thief River Falls (U)
North Seattle Community College (U)
NorthWest Arkansas Community College (N,U)
Northwestern College (U)
Northwestern Connecticut Community College (U)
Northwest Mississippi Community College (U)
Northwest Missouri State University (U)
Oakton Community College (U)
Odessa College (U)
Oral Roberts University (U)
Orangeburg-Calhoun Technical College (U)
Oregon Institute of Technology (U)
Ouachita Technical College (U)
Pace University (U)
Pacific Union College (U)
Pamlico Community College (U)
Park University (U)
Pasco-Hernando Community College (U)
Patrick Henry Community College (U)
Peninsula College (U)
Pennsylvania College of Technology (U)
Pittsburg State University (U)
Portland Community College (U)
Presentation College (U)
Pulaski Technical College (U)
Quinnipiac University (N,U)
Rappahannock Community College (U)
Red Rocks Community College (U)
Reedley College (N,U)
Regent University (U)
Rend Lake College (U)
Riverside Community College District (U)
Rockland Community College (U)
Rose State College (U)
Sacred Heart University (G)
Saddleback College (U)
St. Clair County Community College (U)
St. Cloud State University (U)
St. John's University (U)
St. Louis Community College System (U)
St. Petersburg College (U)
Schenectady County Community College (U)
Schiller International University (U)
Schoolcraft College (U)
Seattle Pacific University (G)
Seminole Community College (U)
Shippensburg University of Pennsylvania (U)
Sinclair Community College (U)
Snead State Community College (U)
Southeast Arkansas College (U)
Southeastern Community College (U)
Southeastern Illinois College (U)
Southern Illinois University Carbondale (U)
South Piedmont Community College (U)
South Suburban College (U)
Southwest Georgia Technical College (U)
Southwest Wisconsin Technical College (U)
Spartanburg Community College (U)
State University of New York at Plattsburgh (U)
State University of New York College of Agriculture and Technology at Morrisville (U)
Stevens Institute of Technology (U)
Strayer University (U,G)

Tacoma Community College (U)
Taylor University (N,U)
Texas A&M University–Commerce (U)
Texas A&M University–Texarkana (U)
Texas State Technical College Waco (U)
Texas State University-San Marcos (U,G)
Texas Tech University (G)
Three Rivers Community College (U)
Tompkins Cortland Community College (U)
Troy University (U)
The University of Alabama (U)
University of Alaska Fairbanks (U)
University of California, Los Angeles (G)
University of Central Arkansas (U)
University of Central Oklahoma (U)
University of Cincinnati (U)
University of Colorado at Colorado Springs (U)
The University of Findlay (U)
University of Great Falls (U)
University of Houston–Victoria (U,G)
University of Idaho (U,G)
University of Illinois (U,G)
University of Illinois at Springfield (U)
University of Illinois at Urbana–Champaign (G)
The University of Maine at Augusta (U)
University of Management and Technology (U)
University of Maryland University College (U)
University of Massachusetts Boston (U)
University of Michigan–Flint (U)
University of Minnesota, Crookston (U)
University of Minnesota, Morris (U)
University of Minnesota, Twin Cities Campus (U)
University of Missouri–Columbia (U)
The University of Montana (U,G)
The University of Montana–Western (U)
University of Nebraska–Lincoln (U)
University of New Orleans (N,U,G)
The University of North Carolina at Charlotte (U)
The University of North Carolina at Greensboro (U)
University of North Dakota (N,U)
University of Northern Iowa (U)
University of North Texas (U)
University of Oklahoma (U)
University of Saskatchewan (U)
The University of South Dakota (U)
University of South Florida (U)
The University of Tennessee (N,U)
The University of Texas at San Antonio (U,G)
The University of Texas at Tyler (U)
The University of Texas System (U)
University of the Cumberlands (G)
The University of Toledo (U)
University of Vermont (N)
University of Washington (U)
University of Waterloo (U)
University of West Florida (U)
University of Wisconsin Colleges (N,U)
University of Wisconsin–Platteville (U,G)
University of Wyoming (U)
Upper Iowa University (U)
Utah State University (U)
Utah Valley State College (U)
Utica College (U)
Vincennes University (U)

Virginia Polytechnic Institute and State University (U,G)
Wake Technical Community College (U)
Washtenaw Community College (U)
Waubonsee Community College (U)
Wayne State College (U,G)
Weber State University (U)
Westchester Community College (U)
Western Piedmont Community College (U)
West Los Angeles College (U)
West Shore Community College (U)
West Valley College (U)
West Virginia University at Parkersburg (U)
Wilkes Community College (U)
Williston State College (U)
Wright State University (U)
York County Community College (U)
York Technical College (U)
York University (U)
Youngstown State University (U)

MATHEMATICS AND COMPUTER SCIENCE

Alvin Community College (U)
Arapahoe Community College (U)
Athabasca University (N,U,G)
Austin Peay State University (U)
Campbell University (U)
Chadron State College (U,G)
Chemeketa Community College (U)
Chesapeake College (U)
Cleveland Institute of Electronics (N)
Columbia College (U)
Concordia University, St. Paul (N)
Danville Community College (U)
Darton College (U)
Delaware County Community College (U)
Drake University (U)
Eastern Iowa Community College District (N)
Edison State Community College (U)
Fort Hays State University (U)
Franklin University (U)
Grantham University (U)
Harrisburg Area Community College (U)
Haywood Community College (U)
Herkimer County Community College (U)
Indiana State University (U)
Iowa State University of Science and Technology (U)
Itawamba Community College (U)
Jacksonville State University (U,G)
James Madison University (N)
John A. Logan College (U)
Marshall University (U)
Middlesex Community College (U)
Pamlico Community College (U)
Peninsula College (U)
Seminole Community College (U)
Snead State Community College (U)
Southeast Arkansas College (U)
Taylor University (N)
Texas State University-San Marcos (U)
Union University (U)
University of Alaska Fairbanks (U)
University of Idaho (G)
University of Massachusetts Lowell (U)
University of New Orleans (U,G)
University of South Florida (U)
University of Wisconsin Colleges (U)
University of Wisconsin–Superior (U)
Westchester Community College (U)

West Hills Community College (N)
Yuba College (U)

MATHEMATICS AND STATISTICS RELATED

Alvin Community College (U)
Andrews University (U)
Anne Arundel Community College (U)
Arapahoe Community College (U)
Ashford University (U)
Bellevue Community College (U)
Berkeley College (U)
Berkeley College-New York City Campus (U)
Berkeley College-Westchester Campus (U)
Brenau University (U)
Bristol Community College (U)
Butler Community College (U)
Central Texas College (U)
Chadron State College (U,G)
Charter Oak State College (U)
Chattanooga State Technical Community College (U)
Chemeketa Community College (U)
Clovis Community College (U)
College of Southern Maryland (U)
College of The Albemarle (U)
Colorado Mountain College District System (U)
County College of Morris (U)
Dallas Baptist University (U)
Darton College (U)
De Anza College (U)
Delta College (U)
Des Moines Area Community College (U)
Dickinson State University (U)
East Arkansas Community College (U)
Eastern Kentucky University (U)
Eastern Michigan University (G)
Eastern Oklahoma State College (U)
Embry-Riddle Aeronautical University (U)
Grantham University (U)
Henry Ford Community College (U)
Houston Community College System (U)
Illinois Eastern Community Colleges, Wabash Valley College (U)
Indiana State University (U)
Itawamba Community College (U)
Jacksonville State University (U)
Jefferson Community College (U)
Jones College (U)
Kellogg Community College (U)
Kettering University (N)
Labette Community College (U)
Lansing Community College (U)
Lehigh Carbon Community College (U)
Lewis-Clark State College (U)
Long Beach City College (U)
Louisiana State University and Agricultural and Mechanical College (U)
Madison Area Technical College (U)
Manatee Community College (U)
Marshall University (U)
Mercy College (U)
Middlesex Community College (U)
Missouri State University (U)
Montana State University (G)
Mount Allison University (U)
Mount Wachusett Community College (U)
Murray State University (U)
Nassau Community College (U)
Neumann College (U)

New England College of Finance (U)
New Mexico Junior College (U)
Northern State University (U)
Northern Virginia Community College (U)
Odessa College (U)
Oklahoma State University (U)
Oregon State University (U)
Pace University (U)
Pamlico Community College (U)
Parkland College (U)
Passaic County Community College (U)
Peninsula College (U)
Piedmont Technical College (U)
Portland Community College (U)
Portland State University (U)
Salem State College (U)
Sam Houston State University (U)
Sauk Valley Community College (U)
Seattle Central Community College (U)
Seminole Community College (U)
Southeast Arkansas College (U)
Southern Illinois University Carbondale (U)
Southwest Virginia Community College (U)
State University of New York Empire State College (U)
Texas Tech University (U)
Treasure Valley Community College (U)
Tyler Junior College (U)
University of Alaska Fairbanks (U)
University of Arkansas (U)
University of Bridgeport (U)
University of Colorado at Denver and Health Sciences Center (U)
University of Delaware (U)
University of Great Falls (U)
University of Houston–Victoria (G)
University of Idaho (U,G)
University of Illinois (U)
University of Missouri–Columbia (U)
University of Nebraska–Lincoln (N,U)
University of New Orleans (U,G)
The University of North Carolina at Chapel Hill (U)
The University of North Carolina at Greensboro (U)
University of Southern Mississippi (U)
The University of Texas System (U)
University of Vermont (N)
University of Washington (U)
University of Waterloo (N,U)
University of West Florida (U)
University of Wisconsin Colleges (U)
Upper Iowa University (U)
Utah State University (U)
Western Piedmont Community College (U)
West Shore Community College (U)

MECHANIC AND REPAIR TECHNOLOGIES RELATED

Arkansas Tech University (U)
Bristol Community College (N)
Cleveland Institute of Electronics (N)

MECHANICAL ENGINEERING

Cleveland State University (G)
Colorado State University (G)
Columbia University (N,G)
Connecticut State University System (U,G)
Georgia Institute of Technology (N,G)
Kansas State University (G)

Kettering University (N)
Louisiana State University and Agricultural and Mechanical College (U)
Michigan Technological University (N,U,G)
New Mexico Institute of Mining and Technology (G)
New Mexico State University (G)
New York Institute of Technology (U)
Northern Virginia Community College (U)
Oakton Community College (U)
The Ohio State University (G)
Old Dominion University (G)
Rochester Institute of Technology (U)
Southern Methodist University (G)
Texas Tech University (G)
The University of Arizona (G)
University of Colorado at Boulder (N,G)
University of Colorado at Colorado Springs (U,G)
University of Colorado at Denver and Health Sciences Center (U)
University of Delaware (N,U,G)
University of Idaho (U,G)
University of Illinois (G)
University of Illinois at Urbana–Champaign (N,G)
University of Maine (U,G)
University of Michigan–Dearborn (G)
University of New Hampshire (G)
University of New Orleans (U,G)
The University of North Carolina at Charlotte (N)
University of North Dakota (U)
University of South Florida (G)
The University of Texas at Arlington (G)
The University of Texas at San Antonio (U)
University of Washington (U,G)
University of Wisconsin–Platteville (G)
Virginia Polytechnic Institute and State University (G)

MECHANICAL ENGINEERING RELATED TECHNOLOGIES

Blackhawk Technical College (U)
Boston University (G)
Bristol Community College (N)
Cincinnati State Technical and Community College (U)
Cleveland Institute of Electronics (N)
Cleveland State University (G)
Columbus State Community College (U)
Indiana State University (U)
Kansas State University (G)
Southern Methodist University (G)
University of Idaho (G)
Villanova University (G)

MECHANICS AND REPAIR

Central Wyoming College (N,U)
Cleveland Institute of Electronics (N)

MEDICAL BASIC SCIENCES

Arapahoe Community College (U)
Athabasca University (N)
Central Wyoming College (N)
Daymar College (U)
Jacksonville State University (U,G)
Minot State University–Bottineau Campus (U)
Montgomery Community College (U)

NorthWest Arkansas Community College (U)
Randolph Community College (N)
Rockland Community College (U)
Triton College (N)
The University of Montana–Western (N)

MEDICAL CLINICAL SCIENCES/ GRADUATE MEDICAL STUDIES

Arapahoe Community College (U)
Daemen College (G)
D'Youville College (G)
Nova Southeastern University (N,G)
Union University (U)
University of Illinois at Chicago (N)

MEDICAL ILLUSTRATION AND INFORMATICS

Arapahoe Community College (U)
Northwestern University (N,G)
Nova Southeastern University (G)
University of Illinois at Chicago (G)
University of Missouri–Columbia (N)

MEDIEVAL AND RENAISSANCE STUDIES

Adams State College (U)
Bellevue Community College (U)
Elizabethtown College (U)
Seattle Central Community College (U)
Taylor University (U)
The University of British Columbia (U)
University of Nebraska–Lincoln (U)
University of New Orleans (U,G)
University of Waterloo (U)
Western Michigan University (U)

MENTAL AND SOCIAL HEALTH SERVICES AND ALLIED PROFESSIONS

Arapahoe Community College (U)
Athabasca University (N,U,G)
Central Texas College (U)
Central Wyoming College (N)
College of The Albemarle (N)
Columbus State Community College (U)
Missouri State University (N)
Mount Wachusett Community College (U)
The Ohio State University (N)
Tompkins Cortland Community College (U)
The University of Maine at Augusta (U)
University of Missouri–Columbia (U,G)

METALLURGICAL ENGINEERING

Delta College (U)
The University of British Columbia (U)

MICROBIOLOGICAL SCIENCES AND IMMUNOLOGY

Acadia University (U)
Arkansas State University–Beebe (U)
Central New Mexico Community College (U)
Community College of Denver (U)
County College of Morris (U)
Delta College (U)
Gateway Community College (U)

Graceland University (U)
Harrisburg Area Community College (U)
Honolulu Community College (U)
Montana State University (G)
North Dakota State College of Science (U)
Rend Lake College (U)
St. Petersburg College (U)
Snead State Community College (U)
University of Arkansas (U)
University of Idaho (U)
University of Minnesota, Crookston (U)
The University of South Dakota (U)
University of Southern Mississippi (U)
University of Waterloo (U)
University of Wisconsin–La Crosse (G)
Weber State University (U)

MILITARY STUDIES

American Public University System (U,G)
Central Texas College (U)
Eastern Michigan University (U)
John Wood Community College (U)
Louisiana State University and Agricultural and Mechanical College (U)
Myers University (U)
University of Colorado at Colorado Springs (U)
Washburn University (U)

MILITARY TECHNOLOGIES

American Public University System (U,G)

MISSIONARY STUDIES AND MISSIOLOGY

Assemblies of God Theological Seminary (G)
Barclay College (U)
Briercrest Distance Learning (U)
Columbia International University (N,U,G)
Covenant Theological Seminary (N,G)
Dallas Baptist University (U,G)
Eugene Bible College (U)
Global University of the Assemblies of God (N)
Master's College and Seminary (U)
Northwestern College (U)
Providence College and Theological Seminary (N,G)
Regions University (N,U,G)
Taylor University (U)
Temple Baptist Seminary (N,G)
Trinity Episcopal School for Ministry (N,G)

MOVEMENT AND MIND-BODY THERAPIES

Atlantic University (N,G)
Central Wyoming College (N)
Prescott College (G)

MULTI-/INTERDISCIPLINARY STUDIES RELATED

Acadia University (U)
Berkeley College (U)
Berkeley College-New York City Campus (U)
Berkeley College-Westchester Campus (U)
California State University, San Bernardino (U)

Central Michigan University (U,G)
Central Texas College (U)
Columbia College (U)
Fairmont State University (U)
Fort Hays State University (U,G)
Glenville State College (U)
Granite State College (U)
Lehigh Carbon Community College (U)
Metropolitan State University (U)
Mississippi State University (U)
Naropa University (U,G)
North Carolina State University (U)
Roosevelt University (U)
Saint Joseph's College of Maine (U)
Taylor University (U)
University of Connecticut (U)
University of Houston–Victoria (G)
University of Minnesota, Morris (U)
University of Oregon (U)
University of Waterloo (U)
Wayne State College (U,G)

MUSEUM STUDIES

Brenau University (U)
California State University, Dominguez Hills (N)
East Tennessee State University (G)
Feather River College (N)
James Madison University (N)
Middlesex Community College (U)
University of Idaho (U)
University of La Verne (G)

MUSIC

Arapahoe Community College (U)
Arkansas State University–Beebe (U)
Arkansas Tech University (U)
Athabasca University (N,U)
Bellevue Community College (U)
Berklee College of Music (N,U)
Big Bend Community College (U)
Boise State University (U)
Bowling Green State University (U)
Brenau University (U)
Bridgewater State College (U)
Butler Community College (U)
Butler County Community College (U)
Cabrillo College (U)
Caldwell Community College and Technical Institute (U)
California State University, Dominguez Hills (N,U)
California University of Pennsylvania (U)
Casper College (U)
Central Texas College (U)
Central Virginia Community College (U)
Central Wyoming College (N,U)
Cerro Coso Community College (U)
Chaminade University of Honolulu (U)
Chattanooga State Technical Community College (U)
Chemeketa Community College (U)
Clackamas Community College (U)
Clarion University of Pennsylvania (U)
Clemson University (U)
Cleveland Institute of Music (N,U,G)
Clinton Community College (U)
College of DuPage (U)
College of Mount St. Joseph (U)
The College of St. Scholastica (U,G)

Colorado State University (U)
Dakota State University (U)
Danville Community College (U)
Darton College (U)
De Anza College (U)
Des Moines Area Community College (U)
Dodge City Community College (U)
Drake University (G)
Duquesne University (G)
East Central Community College (U)
Eastern Oregon University (U)
Eastern West Virginia Community and
  Technical College (U)
EduKan (U)
Elgin Community College (U)
Elizabeth City State University (U)
Erie Community College (U)
Eugene Bible College (U)
Everett Community College (U)
Feather River College (N)
Florida State University (U)
Fort Hays State University (U)
Fullerton College (U)
Gadsden State Community College (U)
Gulf Coast Community College (U)
Indiana State University (U)
Indiana Wesleyan University (U)
Itawamba Community College (U)
Jacksonville State University (U)
James Madison University (N)
Jefferson Community and Technical College
  (U)
John Wood Community College (U)
Judson College (U)
Kansas State University (U)
Kaskaskia College (U)
Labette Community College (U)
Lansing Community College (U)
Lehigh Carbon Community College (U)
Lewis and Clark Community College (U)
Limestone College (U)
Lock Haven University of Pennsylvania (U)
Long Beach City College (U)
Longwood University (U)
Louisiana State University and Agricultural
  and Mechanical College (U)
Lurleen B. Wallace Community College (U)
Manhattan School of Music (N,U,G)
Mansfield University of Pennsylvania (U)
Massasoit Community College (U)
Mesalands Community College (U)
Metropolitan State University (U)
Midway College (U)
Millersville University of Pennsylvania (U)
Missouri State University (U)
Mountain Empire Community College (U)
Murray State University (U)
Nassau Community College (U)
Naugatuck Valley Community College (U)
North Carolina State University (U)
Northeast Alabama Community College (U)
Northeastern Illinois University (U)
Northeast State Technical Community College
  (U)
Northern State University (U)
North Harris Montgomery Community
  College District (U)
North Seattle Community College (U)
NorthWest Arkansas Community College (U)
Northwest Mississippi Community College
  (U)
Northwest Missouri State University (U)

Oklahoma State University (U)
Orange Coast College (U)
Palomar College (U)
Parkland College (U)
Patrick Henry College (U)
Peninsula College (U)
Piedmont Technical College (U)
Plymouth State University (U)
Portland Community College (U)
Randolph Community College (U)
Red Rocks Community College (U)
Reedley College (N,U)
Rend Lake College (U)
Riverside Community College District (U)
Sacred Heart University (U)
Saddleback College (U)
St. Petersburg College (U)
Schenectady County Community College (U)
Schoolcraft College (U)
Shippensburg University of Pennsylvania (U)
Snead State Community College (U)
Southeastern Community College (U)
Southern Illinois University Carbondale (U)
Spartanburg Community College (U)
Spring Arbor University (U)
State University of New York at Plattsburgh
  (U)
State University of New York College at
  Potsdam (U)
Tacoma Community College (U)
Taylor University (U)
Texas State University-San Marcos (U)
Texas Tech University (U,G)
Treasure Valley Community College (U)
Triton College (U)
Tunxis Community College (U)
Tyler Junior College (U)
University of Alaska Fairbanks (U)
University of Bridgeport (U)
The University of British Columbia (U)
University of Central Oklahoma (U)
University of Colorado at Denver and Health
  Sciences Center (U)
University of Delaware (U)
University of Idaho (U)
University of La Verne (G)
University of Maine (U)
The University of Maine at Augusta (U)
University of Maine at Fort Kent (U)
University of Massachusetts Boston (U)
University of Massachusetts Dartmouth (U)
University of Minnesota, Twin Cities Campus
  (U)
The University of Montana (G)
University of New Orleans (U,G)
The University of North Carolina at Chapel
  Hill (N,U)
University of Northern Iowa (U)
University of North Florida (U)
University of North Texas (U)
University of Saskatchewan (U)
The University of South Dakota (U)
University of Southern Mississippi (U,G)
University of South Florida (U,G)
The University of Texas System (U)
University of the Cumberlands (G)
The University of Toledo (U)
University of Vermont (N)
University of Wisconsin Colleges (U)
University of Wisconsin–Platteville (U)
University of Wyoming (U)

Virginia Polytechnic Institute and State
  University (N,U)
Washburn University (U)
Wayland Baptist University (U)
Weber State University (U)
Western Michigan University (U)
West Los Angeles College (U)
West Shore Community College (U)
Wichita State University (U)
Williston State College (U)
Wright State University (U)
Yuba College (U)

NATURAL RESOURCES AND CONSERVATION RELATED

James Madison University (N)
Kansas State University (U)
Oregon State University (U)
Prescott College (G)
University of La Verne (G)
University of Massachusetts Boston (N,U)
University of New Orleans (U,G)

NATURAL RESOURCES CONSERVATION AND RESEARCH

Athabasca University (U)
Colorado State University (U)
Erie Community College (U)
Kansas State University (U)
Lansing Community College (U)
Oregon State University (U,G)
Prescott College (U)
Reedley College (N,U)
Virginia Polytechnic Institute and State
  University (N)

NATURAL RESOURCES MANAGEMENT AND POLICY

Athabasca University (U)
Colorado State University (G)
Kansas State University (U)
Oregon State University (U,G)
Prescott College (G)
University of Denver (G)
Virginia Polytechnic Institute and State
  University (G)

NATURAL SCIENCES

Bellevue Community College (U)
Big Bend Community College (U)
Cape Cod Community College (U)
Columbus State Community College (U)
Dallas Baptist University (U)
Danville Community College (U)
Des Moines Area Community College (U)
D'Youville College (U)
Henry Ford Community College (U)
Itawamba Community College (U)
Kansas State University (U)
Lewis-Clark State College (U)
Middlesex Community College (U)
Northwest Mississippi Community College
  (U)
Palomar College (U)
Peninsula College (U)
Pulaski Technical College (U)
Regent University (U)

University of Great Falls (U)
University of Houston–Victoria (U,G)
University of South Florida (U)
University of Wisconsin Colleges (U)
Upper Iowa University (U)
Wayne State College (U)
Western Michigan University (U)

NAVAL ARCHITECTURE AND MARINE ENGINEERING

University of New Orleans (U,G)

NEUROSCIENCE

California State University, Chico (U)
Central Wyoming College (N)
Jacksonville State University (U)
The University of Texas at San Antonio (G)

NUCLEAR AND INDUSTRIAL RADIOLOGIC TECHNOLOGIES

Bismarck State College (N,U)
Galveston College (U)
Oregon State University (G)

NUCLEAR ENGINEERING

Bismarck State College (N)
The Ohio State University (G)
University of Missouri–Columbia (U,G)

NURSING

Adelphi University (U)
Allen College (N,U,G)
Arapahoe Community College (U)
Arkansas Tech University (U)
Athabasca University (N,U,G)
Azusa Pacific University (G)
Blackhawk Technical College (U)
Bloomfield College (U)
Bloomsburg University of Pennsylvania (U)
Boise State University (U)
Bowling Green State University (U)
Bradley University (U,G)
Brenau University (U,G)
Broome Community College (U)
Butler Community College (N,U)
California State University, Chico (U,G)
California State University, San Bernardino (U)
California State University, San Marcos (N)
Cape Cod Community College (U)
Carlow University (U,G)
Cedar Crest College (U)
Central Georgia Technical College (U)
Central New Mexico Community College (U)
Central Oregon Community College (U)
Central Texas College (U)
Central Wyoming College (U)
Charter Oak State College (N)
Chesapeake College (U)
Clarion University of Pennsylvania (U,G)
Clark State Community College (U)
Clatsop Community College (U)
Cleveland State University (U,G)
The College of St. Scholastica (U,G)
College of Southern Maryland (N)
College of the Siskiyous (U)

Colorado State University-Pueblo (U)
Columbus State Community College (U)
Community College of Beaver County (U)
Community College of Denver (U)
Concordia University Wisconsin (U,G)
Connecticut State University System (U)
Culver-Stockton College (U)
Daemen College (U,G)
Danville Community College (U)
Delaware County Community College (U)
DePaul University (G)
Des Moines Area Community College (U)
Dickinson State University (U)
Drexel University (U,G)
Duquesne University (G)
D'Youville College (G)
East Carolina University (U,G)
East Central Community College (U)
Eastern Kentucky University (G)
Eastern Michigan University (U,G)
Eastern Oklahoma State College (U)
Edison State Community College (U)
Fayetteville State University (U)
Finger Lakes Community College (U)
Fort Hays State University (U,G)
Gadsden State Community College (U)
George Mason University (G)
Georgia College & State University (G)
Georgia Highlands College (U)
Glenville State College (U)
Graceland University (U)
Gulf Coast Community College (U)
Indiana State University (U,G)
Indiana University–Purdue University Fort Wayne (U,G)
Itawamba Community College (U)
Ivy Tech Community College–Northwest (U)
Jacksonville State University (U,G)
James Madison University (N)
Jefferson College of Health Sciences (N,U,G)
Jefferson Community and Technical College (U)
John Tyler Community College (U)
J. Sargeant Reynolds Community College (U)
Kent State University (U,G)
Lewis-Clark State College (U)
Long Beach City College (U)
Los Angeles Harbor College (U)
Mansfield University of Pennsylvania (U,G)
Marshall University (U)
Marymount University (U)
Memorial University of Newfoundland (U,G)
Mercy College (U)
Mesa Community College (U)
Mesa State College (U)
Metropolitan State University (U,G)
MGH Institute of Health Professions (G)
Miami Dade College (U)
Miami University–Middletown Campus (U)
Middle Tennessee State University (N,U,G)
Mid-State Technical College (U)
Midwestern State University (G)
Millersville University of Pennsylvania (U,G)
Minnesota State University Moorhead (G)
Minot State University (U)
Mississippi University for Women (U)
Missouri Southern State University (U)
Missouri State University (U,G)
Monmouth University (G)
Montana Tech of The University of Montana (U)
Montgomery County Community College (U)

Mount Wachusett Community College (U)
Murray State University (U,G)
National University (U)
Naugatuck Valley Community College (U)
Neumann College (G)
North Arkansas College (U)
Northland Community and Technical College–Thief River Falls (U)
Northwest Technical College (U)
Oakton Community College (U)
Odessa College (U)
The Ohio State University (G)
Pace University (N,U,G)
Pacific Union College (U)
Peninsula College (U)
Pennsylvania College of Technology (U)
Pittsburg State University (U,G)
Portland Community College (U)
Quinnipiac University (N,G)
Radford University (N,G)
Rend Lake College (U)
The Richard Stockton College of New Jersey (U,G)
Riverside Community College District (U)
Rockland Community College (N,U)
Rose State College (U)
Ryerson University (U)
Sacred Heart University (G)
Saddleback College (U)
St. Clair County Community College (U)
Saint Francis Medical Center College of Nursing (U,G)
Saint Joseph's College of Maine (U,G)
Samuel Merritt College (G)
Shawnee State University (U)
Snead State Community College (U)
Southeast Arkansas College (U)
South Piedmont Community College (U)
Southwestern College (U)
Southwest Wisconsin Technical College (U)
State University of New York at Plattsburgh (U)
Tacoma Community College (U)
Tennessee Technological University (N)
Texas Woman's University (U,G)
Three Rivers Community College (U)
Tompkins Cortland Community College (U)
Triton College (U)
Union University (U)
The University of Alabama (G)
The University of British Columbia (U)
University of California, Riverside (N)
University of Central Arkansas (G)
University of Central Florida (U,G)
University of Central Missouri (G)
University of Central Oklahoma (U)
University of Colorado at Colorado Springs (U,G)
University of Delaware (N,U,G)
University of Houston–Victoria (U)
University of Illinois (G)
University of Illinois at Chicago (N,G)
University of Maine (U)
The University of Maine at Augusta (U)
University of Maine at Fort Kent (U)
University of Massachusetts Boston (U,G)
University of Massachusetts Dartmouth (U,G)
University of Michigan–Flint (U)
University of Minnesota, Twin Cities Campus (U)
University of Missouri–Columbia (U,G)
The University of Montana (U)

University of Nebraska–Lincoln (U)
University of Nebraska Medical Center (N,U,G)
University of North Alabama (U)
The University of North Carolina at Chapel Hill (N)
The University of North Carolina at Charlotte (N,U,G)
The University of North Carolina at Greensboro (G)
University of North Dakota (U)
University of North Florida (U)
University of Phoenix Online Campus (G)
University of Pittsburgh at Bradford (U)
University of St. Francis (U,G)
University of Saskatchewan (U)
University of South Alabama (G)
University of South Carolina Sumter (G)
The University of South Dakota (U)
University of Southern Indiana (N,U,G)
University of Southern Mississippi (U,G)
University of South Florida (U,G)
The University of Texas at Arlington (U)
The University of Texas at El Paso (U,G)
The University of Texas at Tyler (U,G)
The University of Texas System (G)
University of Vermont (N,U,G)
University of Wyoming (U,G)
Viterbo University (U,G)
Walden University (G)
Washburn University (U)
Washtenaw Community College (U)
Waubonsee Community College (U)
Western Piedmont Community College (U)
West Liberty State College (U)
West Virginia University (N)
West Virginia University at Parkersburg (U)
Wisconsin Indianhead Technical College (N,U)
Wright State University (U,G)
York Technical College (U)
York University (U)
Youngstown State University (U)

NUTRITION SCIENCES

Acadia University (U)
Allen College (U)
Bellevue Community College (U)
Brazosport College (U)
Butler Community College (U)
Carroll Community College (U)
Cedar Crest College (U)
Central Michigan University (G)
Central Washington University (U)
Central Wyoming College (N)
Clemson University (U,G)
Cloud County Community College (U)
College of the Siskiyous (U)
Columbus State Community College (U)
Community College of Beaver County (U)
Danville Community College (U)
D'Youville College (G)
East Carolina University (G)
Eastern Michigan University (U)
Edison College (U)
Erie Community College (U)
Everett Community College (U)
Gadsden State Community College (U)
Henry Ford Community College (U)
Hillsborough Community College (U)
Illinois Eastern Community Colleges, Frontier Community College (U)

Itawamba Community College (U)
Jacksonville State University (U)
James Madison University (U)
Jones County Junior College (U)
Kansas State University (U)
Mansfield University of Pennsylvania (U)
Montgomery County Community College (U)
Mount Saint Vincent University (U)
Nassau Community College (U)
North Carolina State University (U)
North Harris Montgomery Community College District (U)
NorthWest Arkansas Community College (U)
Palomar College (U)
Pasco-Hernando Community College (U)
Peninsula College (U)
Queen's University at Kingston (U)
Quinebaug Valley Community College (U)
Rend Lake College (U)
Riverside Community College District (U)
Sam Houston State University (U)
Schenectady County Community College (U)
Seminole Community College (U)
Texas Woman's University (U,G)
Three Rivers Community College (U)
Treasure Valley Community College (U)
University of Alaska Fairbanks (U)
University of Massachusetts Boston (U)
University of Medicine and Dentistry of New Jersey (U,G)
University of North Florida (U)
University of North Texas (U)
University of South Florida (U)
The University of Toledo (U)
University of Vermont (N,U)

OCEAN ENGINEERING

Utah Valley State College (U)

OPERATIONS RESEARCH

Boston University (G)
Philadelphia University (U)
Saybrook Graduate School and Research Center (G)
Southern New Hampshire University (G)
University of Minnesota, Twin Cities Campus (U)

OPHTHALMIC AND OPTOMETRIC SUPPORT SERVICES AND ALLIED PROFESSIONS

Ferris State University (G)
Hillsborough Community College (U)
Madison Area Technical College (U)

PARKS, RECREATION AND LEISURE

Clemson University (U)
The Community College of Baltimore County (U)
Kean University (N)
Madison Area Technical College (U)
Mesa State College (U)
Prescott College (U)
Seattle Pacific University (G)
United States Sports Academy (N)
University of Missouri–Columbia (U)

The University of North Carolina at Chapel Hill (U)

PARKS, RECREATION AND LEISURE FACILITIES MANAGEMENT

Kean University (U)
North Carolina State University (U)
Prescott College (G)
United States Sports Academy (N)
University of Wisconsin–La Crosse (G)
Vincennes University (U)

PARKS, RECREATION, AND LEISURE RELATED

The Community College of Baltimore County (U)
James Madison University (N)
United States Sports Academy (N)
University of Massachusetts Boston (N)
University of Southern Mississippi (G)

PASTORAL COUNSELING AND SPECIALIZED MINISTRIES

Andover Newton Theological School (G)
Arlington Baptist College (U)
Assemblies of God Theological Seminary (G)
Briercrest Distance Learning (U)
Duquesne University (G)
Earlham School of Religion (G)
Eugene Bible College (U)
Global University of the Assemblies of God (N)
Hartford Seminary (G)
Maranatha Baptist Bible College (G)
Master's College and Seminary (U)
Providence College and Theological Seminary (N,G)
Regent University (N,G)
Regions University (N,U,G)
Saint Joseph's College of Maine (N,U)
Southwestern Baptist Theological Seminary (G)
Summit Pacific College (U)
Taylor University (U)
Temple Baptist Seminary (N,G)

PEACE STUDIES AND CONFLICT RESOLUTION

Atlantic University (N,G)
Brenau University (U)
Caldwell Community College and Technical Institute (N)
Drake University (U,G)
Earlham School of Religion (G)
Massasoit Community College (N)
Mercy College (G)
Mount Saint Vincent University (U)
Prescott College (G)
Saybrook Graduate School and Research Center (G)
Taylor University (U)
University of Massachusetts Boston (G)
The University of North Carolina at Greensboro (G)
University of Waterloo (U)

PERSONAL AND CULINARY SERVICES RELATED

California State University, Dominguez Hills (N)
Central Wyoming College (N)
Kansas City Kansas Community College (U)
Kean University (N)
Linn-Benton Community College (N)
Pace University (N)
Pasco-Hernando Community College (N)
University of Missouri–Columbia (N)
University of the Pacific (N)
Vance-Granville Community College (N)

PERSONALITY PSYCHOLOGY

Arapahoe Community College (U)
Dallas Baptist University (U)
Des Moines Area Community College (U)
Indiana State University (U)
Jefferson Community College (U)
Modesto Junior College (U)
New England College of Finance (U)
Roosevelt University (U)
University of Alaska Fairbanks (U)
University of Minnesota, Twin Cities Campus (U)
University of New Orleans (U,G)
Yuba College (U)

PETROLEUM ENGINEERING

New Mexico Institute of Mining and Technology (G)
Texas Tech University (G)

PHARMACOLOGY AND TOXICOLOGY

Arapahoe Community College (U)
Brenau University (U)
Drexel University (G)
Oregon State University (N)
Peninsula College (U)
Queen's University at Kingston (U)
University of Maryland Eastern Shore (G)
Virginia Highlands Community College (U)

PHARMACY, PHARMACEUTICAL SCIENCES, AND ADMINISTRATION

Arapahoe Community College (U)
Auburn University (G)
Charter Oak State College (N)
Cleveland State University (U)
Colorado State University-Pueblo (N)
Delaware County Community College (U)
Drake University (U,G)
Long Beach City College (U)
Oakton Community College (U)
Oregon State University (N)
Portland Community College (N)
Randolph Community College (N)
St. John's University (U)
University of Illinois (G)
University of Illinois at Chicago (N,G)
The University of North Carolina at Greensboro (N)
University of Washington (U)
Vincennes University (U)

PHILOSOPHY

Acadia University (U)
Alpena Community College (U)
American Public University System (U)
Anne Arundel Community College (U)
Arapahoe Community College (U)
Arkansas State University–Beebe (U)
Ashford University (U)
Athabasca University (N,U,G)
Bellevue Community College (U)
Belmont Technical College (U)
Bemidji State University (U)
Bergen Community College (U)
Berkeley College (U)
Berkeley College-New York City Campus (U)
Berkeley College-Westchester Campus (U)
Bismarck State College (U)
Boise State University (U)
Bowling Green State University (U)
Brenau University (U)
Butler Community College (U)
Butler County Community College (U)
Cabrillo College (U)
California State University, San Marcos (N)
California University of Pennsylvania (U)
Carlow University (U)
Carroll College (U)
Carroll Community College (U)
Central New Mexico Community College (U)
Central Texas College (U)
Central Virginia Community College (U)
Chadron State College (U)
Chaminade University of Honolulu (U)
Chattanooga State Technical Community College (U)
Chemeketa Community College (U)
Clarion University of Pennsylvania (U)
Cleveland State University (U,G)
College of San Mateo (U)
College of Southern Maryland (U)
Colorado Mountain College District System (U)
Columbus State Community College (U)
Community College of Beaver County (U)
Community College of Denver (U)
Connecticut State University System (U)
County College of Morris (U)
Dallas Baptist University (U)
Darton College (U)
Delaware County Community College (U)
Delta College (U)
Des Moines Area Community College (U)
Duquesne University (U)
East Carolina University (U)
Eastern Michigan University (U)
Eastern Oregon University (U)
Eastern Washington University (U)
East Los Angeles College (U)
Edison State Community College (U)
Erie Community College (U)
Everett Community College (U)
Feather River College (N)
Finger Lakes Community College (U)
Fontbonne University (U)
Fort Hays State University (U)
Franciscan University of Steubenville (N,U)
Gadsden State Community College (U)
Gateway Community College (U)
Harrisburg Area Community College (U)
Honolulu Community College (U)
Houston Community College System (U)

Indiana University–Purdue University Fort Wayne (U)
Institute for Christian Studies (G)
Iona College (U)
Itawamba Community College (U)
Ivy Tech Community College–North Central (U)
James Madison University (U)
Jefferson College of Health Sciences (U,G)
Jefferson Community and Technical College (U)
Jefferson Community College (U)
John Tyler Community College (U)
John Wood Community College (U)
J. Sargeant Reynolds Community College (U)
Kansas City Kansas Community College (U)
Kean University (N)
Lamar State College–Port Arthur (U)
Lehigh Carbon Community College (U)
Lewis-Clark State College (U)
Liberty University (U)
Limestone College (U)
Long Beach City College (U)
Louisiana State University and Agricultural and Mechanical College (U)
Malone College (U)
Marian College of Fond du Lac (U)
Marshall University (U)
Massasoit Community College (U)
Memorial University of Newfoundland (U)
Metropolitan State University (U)
Middlesex Community College (U)
Minot State University (U)
Modesto Junior College (U)
Montana Tech of The University of Montana (U)
Montgomery County Community College (U)
Mt. San Antonio College (U)
Murray State University (U)
Naropa University (N)
New York Institute of Technology (U)
North Carolina State University (U)
North Harris Montgomery Community College District (U)
North Idaho College (U)
North Seattle Community College (U)
NorthWest Arkansas Community College (U)
Northwestern Connecticut Community College (U)
Northwest Missouri State University (U)
Oakton Community College (U)
Old Dominion University (U)
Oregon State University (U)
Ouachita Technical College (U)
Palomar College (U)
Parkland College (U)
Patrick Henry College (U)
Peninsula College (U)
Pittsburg State University (U)
Pulaski Technical College (U)
Queen's University at Kingston (U)
Quinnipiac University (U)
Riverside Community College District (U)
Rockland Community College (U)
Rose State College (U)
Ryerson University (U)
Sacred Heart University (U)
St. Cloud State University (U)
St. Petersburg College (U)
Salem State College (U)
Sam Houston State University (U)
Schoolcraft College (U)

Shippensburg University of Pennsylvania (U)
Southeastern Illinois College (U)
Southern Illinois University Carbondale (U)
South Suburban College (U)
Southwestern College (U)
Spring Arbor University (U)
State University of New York at New Paltz (U)
Tacoma Community College (U)
Taylor University (U)
Texas State University-San Marcos (U)
Triton College (U)
Tunxis Community College (U)
The University of Alabama (U)
University of Bridgeport (U)
The University of British Columbia (U)
University of Cincinnati (U)
University of Hawaii–West Oahu (U)
University of Idaho (U)
University of Illinois (U)
University of Illinois at Springfield (U)
University of La Verne (G)
The University of Maine at Augusta (U)
University of Maine at Fort Kent (U)
University of Massachusetts Dartmouth (U)
University of Massachusetts Lowell (U)
University of Minnesota, Crookston (U)
University of Minnesota, Twin Cities Campus (U)
University of Missouri–Columbia (U,G)
The University of Montana (U,G)
The University of Montana–Western (U)
University of Nebraska–Lincoln (U)
University of New Orleans (U,G)
University of North Alabama (U)
The University of North Carolina at Chapel Hill (N,U)
The University of North Carolina at Greensboro (U)
University of North Florida (U)
University of Oklahoma (U)
University of Saskatchewan (U)
University of South Florida (U)
The University of Toledo (U,G)
University of Washington (U)
University of Waterloo (U)
University of West Florida (U)
University of Wisconsin Colleges (U)
Utah State University (U)
Utah Valley State College (U)
Virginia Highlands Community College (U)
Virginia Polytechnic Institute and State University (U)
Wake Technical Community College (U)
Washtenaw Community College (U)
Wayne State College (U)
Weber State University (U)
Webster University (U)
Westchester Community College (U)
Western Wyoming Community College (U)
West Los Angeles College (U)
West Valley College (U)
West Virginia University at Parkersburg (U)
Wilfrid Laurier University (U)
Wright State University (U)
York Technical College (U)
York University (U)
Youngstown State University (U)

PHILOSOPHY AND RELIGIOUS STUDIES RELATED

American Public University System (U)
Arlington Baptist College (U)
Ashford University (U)
Assemblies of God Theological Seminary (G)
Athabasca University (N,U)
Atlantic University (N,G)
The Baptist College of Florida (U)
Bergen Community College (U)
Berkeley College (U)
Berkeley College-New York City Campus (U)
Berkeley College-Westchester Campus (U)
Big Bend Community College (U)
Bismarck State College (U)
Bowling Green State University (U)
Brookdale Community College (U)
Butler Community College (U)
Butler County Community College (U)
Cabrillo College (U)
California Institute of Integral Studies (N,G)
California University of Pennsylvania (U)
Central Texas College (U)
Central Washington University (U)
Chadron State College (U)
Chaminade University of Honolulu (U)
Charter Oak State College (U)
Chattanooga State Technical Community College (U)
Chemeketa Community College (U)
Cleveland State University (G)
College of DuPage (U)
College of Southern Maryland (U)
Columbia College (U)
Columbus State Community College (U)
Community College of Denver (U)
Dallas Baptist University (U,G)
Darton College (U)
De Anza College (U)
Delaware County Community College (U)
Denver Seminary (G)
Des Moines Area Community College (U)
Duquesne University (U,G)
East Carolina University (U)
Eastern Kentucky University (U)
Eastern Michigan University (U)
Edison State Community College (U)
Feather River College (N)
Galveston College (U)
Global University of the Assemblies of God (N)
Hebrew College (N,U,G)
Holy Apostles College and Seminary (G)
Honolulu Community College (U)
Hopkinsville Community College (U)
Indiana Wesleyan University (U)
Institute for Christian Studies (G)
Iona College (U)
John Wood Community College (U)
Jones County Junior College (U)
Judson College (U)
Kean University (U)
Kellogg Community College (U)
Lake Superior College (U)
Lamar State College–Port Arthur (U)
Life Pacific College (U)
Louisiana State University and Agricultural and Mechanical College (U)
Manatee Community College (U)
Master's College and Seminary (U)
Miami Dade College (U)

Middlesex Community College (U)
Murray State University (U)
Naropa University (N,U)
New York Institute of Technology (U)
Northern Virginia Community College (U)
Northwestern College (U)
Oakton Community College (U)
Oregon State University (U)
Palomar College (U)
Park University (U)
Patrick Henry College (U)
Pennsylvania College of Technology (U)
Piedmont Technical College (U)
Prescott College (U,G)
Randolph Community College (U)
Regions University (N,U,G)
Regis University (U,G)
Rend Lake College (U)
Rose State College (U)
Sacred Heart University (U)
Saint Joseph's College of Maine (U)
Schoolcraft College (U)
Seattle Central Community College (U)
Southern Illinois University Carbondale (U)
Southwestern Baptist Theological Seminary (G)
Spoon River College (U)
State University of New York at Oswego (U)
Taylor University (U)
Temple Baptist Seminary (N,G)
Triton College (U)
The University of Alabama (U)
University of Arkansas (U)
University of Bridgeport (U)
University of California, Los Angeles (G)
University of Central Florida (U)
University of Cincinnati (U)
University of Colorado at Denver and Health Sciences Center (U)
University of Delaware (U)
The University of Findlay (U)
University of Great Falls (U)
University of Illinois (U)
The University of Montana (U)
University of New Orleans (U,G)
The University of North Carolina at Greensboro (U)
University of St. Francis (U)
University of Southern Mississippi (U)
University of South Florida (U)
The University of Toledo (U)
University of Waterloo (U)
Upper Iowa University (U)
Wilkes Community College (U)

PHYSICAL SCIENCE TECHNOLOGIES

Union University (U)

PHYSICAL SCIENCES

Arkansas State University–Beebe (U)
Arkansas Tech University (U)
Ashford University (U)
Athabasca University (N,U)
Barclay College (U)
Bellevue Community College (U)
Belmont Technical College (U)
Big Bend Community College (U)
Broome Community College (U)
Butler Community College (U)

Cabrillo College (U)
Caldwell Community College and Technical
   Institute (U)
Chadron State College (U)
Chemeketa Community College (U)
The Community College of Baltimore County
   (U)
Corban College (U)
Darton College (U)
Des Moines Area Community College (U)
East Central Community College (U)
EduKan (U)
Eugene Bible College (U)
Everett Community College (U)
George C. Wallace Community College (U)
Gulf Coast Community College (U)
Harrisburg Area Community College (U)
Houston Community College System (U)
Itawamba Community College (U)
Ivy Tech Community College–Northwest (U)
Jacksonville State University (U,G)
James Madison University (N)
John Wood Community College (U)
Kansas City Kansas Community College (U)
Kansas State University (U)
Labette Community College (U)
Lake Superior College (U)
Louisiana State University and Agricultural
   and Mechanical College (U)
Lurleen B. Wallace Community College (U)
Massasoit Community College (U)
Mesalands Community College (U)
Middlesex Community College (U)
Oakton Community College (U)
Pace University (U)
Pasco-Hernando Community College (U)
Passaic County Community College (U)
Peninsula College (U)
Pulaski Technical College (U)
Regent University (U)
Rockland Community College (U)
Roosevelt University (U)
Rose State College (U)
Sacred Heart University (U)
Schiller International University (U)
Schoolcraft College (U)
Seminole Community College (U)
Snead State Community College (U)
State University of New York College at
   Potsdam (U)
Taylor University (U)
Treasure Valley Community College (U)
University of Houston–Victoria (U,G)
University of La Verne (G)
The University of Maine at Augusta (U)
The University of Montana (U)
University of New Orleans (U,G)
University of North Dakota (U)
The University of South Dakota (U)
The University of Texas at San Antonio (U)
The University of Texas System (U)
University of Waterloo (U)
University of West Florida (U)
University of Wisconsin–Superior (U)
Upper Iowa University (U)
Utah State University (U)
Utah Valley State College (U)
Waubonsee Community College (U)
Wayne State College (U)
Wilkes Community College (U)

PHYSICAL SCIENCES RELATED

Ashford University (U)
Bellevue Community College (U)
Berkeley College (U)
Berkeley College-New York City Campus (U)
Berkeley College-Westchester Campus (U)
Bismarck State College (U)
Butler Community College (U)
Chadron State College (U)
Chemeketa Community College (U)
Itawamba Community College (U)
James Madison University (N)
Kansas State University (U)
Miami Dade College (U)
Mississippi State University (U)
Nassau Community College (U)
Northwest Mississippi Community College
   (U)
Portland Community College (U)
Roger Williams University (U)
Rose State College (U)
Seminole Community College (U)
Taylor University (U)
University of Houston–Victoria (U,G)
University of Maryland Eastern Shore (U)
The University of Texas System (U)
University of West Florida (U)

PHYSICS

Acadia University (U)
Arapahoe Community College (U)
Boise State University (U)
Butler Community College (U)
California State University, Dominguez Hills
   (U)
Chaminade University of Honolulu (U)
Chattanooga State Technical Community
   College (U)
Clackamas Community College (U)
Clemson University (U)
College of DuPage (U)
College of Southern Maryland (U)
Colorado Mountain College District System
   (U)
Community College of Denver (U)
Delaware County Community College (U)
D'Youville College (U)
Eastern Oregon University (U)
Edison College (U)
Edison State Community College (U)
Fort Hays State University (U)
Grantham University (U)
Indiana University of Pennsylvania (U)
Itawamba Community College (U)
Jacksonville State University (U)
James Madison University (N)
John A. Logan College (U)
John Wood Community College (U)
Lehigh Carbon Community College (U)
Louisiana State University and Agricultural
   and Mechanical College (U)
Metropolitan State University (U)
Miami University–Middletown Campus (U)
Mississippi State University (U)
Missouri Southern State University (U)
Missouri State University (U)
Montana State University (G)
Montana State University–Billings (U)
New England Institute of Technology (U)
New Jersey City University (U)

North Carolina State University (U)
Parkland College (U)
Saddleback College (U)
St. Cloud State University (U)
St. John's University (U)
Schoolcraft College (U)
Shippensburg University of Pennsylvania (U)
Snead State Community College (U)
Tacoma Community College (U)
Union University (U)
University of Cincinnati Raymond Walters
   College (U)
University of Colorado at Denver and Health
   Sciences Center (U)
University of Houston–Victoria (U,G)
University of Idaho (U)
University of Massachusetts Boston (U)
University of Massachusetts Dartmouth (U)
University of Minnesota, Crookston (U)
University of Minnesota, Twin Cities Campus
   (U)
University of Missouri–Columbia (U)
University of Nebraska–Lincoln (U)
University of New Orleans (U,G)
The University of North Carolina at Chapel
   Hill (U)
University of North Dakota (U)
University of Oregon (U)
The University of Tennessee (U)
University of Waterloo (N,U)
University of Wyoming (U)
Utah State University (U)
Virginia Highlands Community College (U)
Virginia Polytechnic Institute and State
   University (U)
Wayne State College (U)
Weber State University (U)

PHYSIOLOGICAL PSYCHOLOGY/ PSYCHOBIOLOGY

Athabasca University (U)
Chadron State College (U)
Eastern Wyoming College (U)
Mesa Community College (U)
Mount Saint Vincent University (U)
North Central State College (U)

PHYSIOLOGY, PATHOLOGY AND RELATED SCIENCES

Darton College (U)
Louisiana State University and Agricultural
   and Mechanical College (U)
New England Institute of Technology (U)
Pittsburg State University (U)
Saybrook Graduate School and Research
   Center (G)
University of Minnesota, Twin Cities Campus
   (U)
The University of South Dakota (U)
University of Waterloo (U)

PLANT SCIENCES

Athabasca University (U)
Bellevue Community College (U)
Bismarck State College (N)
Colorado State University (U)
County College of Morris (U)
James Madison University (N)

John Wood Community College (U)
Kansas State University (G)
Nova Scotia Agricultural College (N,U)
The Ohio State University (U,G)
Oregon State University (U)
Piedmont Technical College (U)
Rend Lake College (U)
Southern Illinois University Carbondale (U)
Texas Tech University (G)
University of California, Riverside (N)
University of Maine (U)
University of Missouri–Columbia (U)
University of Nebraska–Lincoln (U)
Virginia Polytechnic Institute and State
  University (N)
Yuba College (U)

POLITICAL SCIENCE AND GOVERNMENT

Acadia University (U)
Alpena Community College (U)
American Public University System (U)
Anne Arundel Community College (U)
Arapahoe Community College (U)
Arkansas State University–Beebe (U)
Arkansas Tech University (U)
Athabasca University (N,U,G)
Auburn University (U)
Ball State University (U)
Bellevue Community College (U)
Bergen Community College (U)
Berkeley College (U)
Berkeley College-New York City Campus (U)
Berkeley College-Westchester Campus (U)
Bowling Green State University (U)
Bradley University (G)
Brazosport College (U)
Brenau University (U)
Bridgewater State College (U)
Buena Vista University (U)
Buffalo State College, State University of
  New York (U)
Butler Community College (U)
Butler County Community College (U)
California State University, San Bernardino
  (U)
Campbell University (U)
Carl Albert State College (U)
Carlow University (U)
Cascadia Community College (U)
Cayuga County Community College (U)
Central Michigan University (U,G)
Central Texas College (U)
Central Virginia Community College (U)
Central Wyoming College (U)
Chaminade University of Honolulu (U)
Chattanooga State Technical Community
  College (U)
Chemeketa Community College (U)
Clatsop Community College (U)
Clinton Community College (U)
College of Mount St. Joseph (U)
College of San Mateo (U)
College of Southern Maryland (U)
College of the Siskiyous (U)
Colorado State University-Pueblo (U)
Columbia College (U)
Columbus State Community College (U)
The Community College of Baltimore County
  (U)
Community College of Denver (U)

Dallas Baptist University (U)
Danville Community College (U)
Darton College (U)
De Anza College (U)
Delta College (U)
Drake University (U,G)
D'Youville College (U)
Eastern Kentucky University (U)
Eastern Michigan University (U)
Eastern Oklahoma State College (U)
Eastern Oregon University (U)
Eastern West Virginia Community and
  Technical College (U)
Eastern Wyoming College (U)
Erie Community College (U)
Flathead Valley Community College (U)
Florida State University (U)
Fort Hays State University (U)
Fullerton College (U)
Gadsden State Community College (U)
Galveston College (U)
Gateway Community College (U)
Glenville State College (U)
Hamline University (N)
Haywood Community College (U)
Henry Ford Community College (U)
Hillsborough Community College (U)
Holyoke Community College (U)
Honolulu Community College (U)
Houston Community College System (U)
Indiana University of Pennsylvania (U,G)
Indiana University–Purdue University Fort
  Wayne (U)
Institute for Christian Studies (G)
Ivy Tech Community College–North Central
  (U)
Jacksonville State University (U,G)
James Madison University (N)
Jefferson Community and Technical College
  (U)
Jefferson Community College (U)
John A. Logan College (U)
John Jay College of Criminal Justice of the
  City University of New York (U)
John Wood Community College (U)
J. Sargeant Reynolds Community College (U)
Judson College (U)
Kansas State University (U)
Kean University (U)
Labette Community College (U)
Lake Superior College (U)
Lehigh Carbon Community College (U)
Lewis-Clark State College (U)
Limestone College (U)
Long Beach City College (U)
Los Angeles Harbor College (U)
Louisiana State University and Agricultural
  and Mechanical College (U)
Louisiana Tech University (U)
Malone College (U)
Memorial University of Newfoundland (U)
Mesa Community College (U)
Mesa State College (U)
Metropolitan State University (U)
Miami Dade College (U)
Middlesex Community College (U)
Middle Tennessee State University (U)
Midwestern State University (U)
Missouri Southern State University (U)
Missouri State University (U,G)
Mount Allison University (U)
Mount Wachusett Community College (U)

Myers University (U)
New Jersey City University (U)
New York Institute of Technology (U)
North Carolina State University (U)
Northeast State Technical Community College
  (U)
North Idaho College (U)
NorthWest Arkansas Community College (U)
Northwest Missouri State University (U)
Oakton Community College (U)
The Ohio State University (U)
Oklahoma State University (U)
Oral Roberts University (U)
Oregon State University (U)
Ouachita Technical College (U)
Pace University (U)
Palomar College (U)
Parkland College (U)
Park University (U)
Pasco-Hernando Community College (U)
Patrick Henry College (U)
Peninsula College (U)
Piedmont Technical College (U)
Pulaski Technical College (U)
Queen's University at Kingston (U)
Quinebaug Valley Community College (U)
Regent University (U,G)
Rend Lake College (U)
Riverside Community College District (U)
Rochester Institute of Technology (U)
Rockland Community College (U)
Rose State College (U)
Ryerson University (U)
Sacred Heart University (U)
Saddleback College (U)
St. Clair County Community College (U)
St. John's University (U)
St. Petersburg College (U)
Sam Houston State University (U)
Schiller International University (U)
Seminole Community College (U)
Shippensburg University of Pennsylvania
  (U,G)
Southeastern Illinois College (U)
Southern Illinois University Carbondale (U)
State University of New York at Plattsburgh
  (U)
State University of New York Empire State
  College (U,G)
Strayer University (U)
Tacoma Community College (U)
Taylor University (U)
Texas A&M University–Texarkana (U)
Texas State University-San Marcos (U)
Troy University (U)
Tyler Junior College (U)
The University of Alabama (U)
University of Alaska Fairbanks (U)
University of Bridgeport (U)
The University of British Columbia (U)
University of Central Arkansas (U)
University of Colorado at Denver and Health
  Sciences Center (U,G)
University of Delaware (U,G)
University of Hawaii–West Oahu (U)
University of Idaho (U)
University of Illinois (U)
University of Illinois at Springfield (G)
The University of Maine at Augusta (U)
University of Maine at Fort Kent (U)
University of Massachusetts Boston (U)
University of Minnesota, Morris (U)

University of Missouri–Columbia (U)
The University of Montana (U,G)
University of Nebraska at Omaha (U)
University of Nebraska–Lincoln (U,G)
University of New Orleans (U,G)
University of North Alabama (U)
The University of North Carolina at Chapel Hill (N,U)
The University of North Carolina at Charlotte (U)
University of Oklahoma (U)
University of Oregon (U)
University of Saskatchewan (U)
University of Southern Indiana (U)
The University of Tennessee (U)
The University of Texas at Arlington (U,G)
The University of Texas at El Paso (U)
The University of Texas at San Antonio (U,G)
The University of Texas at Tyler (U)
The University of Texas System (N,U,G)
The University of Toledo (U,G)
University of Washington (U,G)
University of West Florida (U,G)
University of Wisconsin Colleges (U)
University of Wisconsin–Platteville (G)
University of Wisconsin–Whitewater (U,G)
Upper Iowa University (N,U)
Utah Valley State College (U)
Vance-Granville Community College (U)
Virginia Highlands Community College (U)
Virginia Polytechnic Institute and State University (U,G)
Wake Technical Community College (U)
Washburn University (U)
Washtenaw Community College (U)
Wayland Baptist University (U)
Weber State University (U)
West Los Angeles College (U)
West Valley College (U)
Wright State University (U)
York University (U)

POLYMER/PLASTICS ENGINEERING

Lehigh University (N,G)
Quinebaug Valley Community College (U)
University of Massachusetts Lowell (G)
Wake Technical Community College (U)

PRECISION METAL WORKING

Central Wyoming College (N)
Henry Ford Community College (U)

PRECISION PRODUCTION RELATED

Bristol Community College (N)

PRECISION SYSTEMS MAINTENANCE AND REPAIR TECHNOLOGIES

James Madison University (N)
Massasoit Community College (N)

PSYCHOLOGY

Acadia University (U)
Alpena Community College (U)

Alvin Community College (U)
American Public University System (U)
Arapahoe Community College (U)
Argosy University, Chicago Campus (U,G)
Arkansas State University–Beebe (U)
Arkansas Tech University (U)
Ashford University (U)
Athabasca University (N,U,G)
Austin Peay State University (U)
Barclay College (U)
Beaufort County Community College (U)
Bellevue Community College (U)
Belmont Technical College (U)
Bemidji State University (U)
Bergen Community College (U)
Berkeley College (U)
Berkeley College-New York City Campus (U)
Berkeley College-Westchester Campus (U)
Bismarck State College (U)
Black Hills State University (U)
Bloomfield College (U)
Boise State University (U)
Bowling Green State University (U,G)
Bradley University (U)
Brazosport College (U)
Brenau University (U)
Bridgewater State College (U,G)
Bristol Community College (U)
Broome Community College (U)
Buena Vista University (U)
Butler Community College (U)
Butler County Community College (U)
Caldwell Community College and Technical Institute (U)
California State University, Chico (U)
California State University, San Bernardino (U)
California University of Pennsylvania (U)
Campbell University (U)
Cape Cod Community College (U)
Capella University (G)
Carl Albert State College (U)
Carlow University (U)
Carroll Community College (U)
Cascadia Community College (U)
Casper College (U)
Cayuga County Community College (U)
Central Georgia Technical College (U)
Central Michigan University (U)
Central New Mexico Community College (U)
Central Texas College (U)
Central Virginia Community College (U)
Central Washington University (U)
Central Wyoming College (N,U)
Chadron State College (U,G)
Chaminade University of Honolulu (U)
Charter Oak State College (U)
Chattanooga State Technical Community College (U)
Chemeketa Community College (U)
Clarion University of Pennsylvania (U)
Clark State Community College (U)
Clatsop Community College (U)
Clinton Community College (U)
Cloud County Community College (U)
College of DuPage (U)
The College of St. Scholastica (U)
College of San Mateo (U)
College of Southern Maryland (U)
College of The Albemarle (U)
College of the Siskiyous (U)
College of the Southwest (U)

Colorado Mountain College District System (U)
Colorado State University (U)
Colorado State University-Pueblo (U)
Columbia College (U)
Columbus State Community College (U)
The Community College of Baltimore County (U)
Community College of Beaver County (U)
Community College of Denver (U)
Concordia University (U)
County College of Morris (U)
Cumberland County College (U)
Dakota State University (U)
Dallas Baptist University (U)
Danville Community College (U)
Darton College (U)
Dawson Community College (U)
De Anza College (U)
Delaware County Community College (U)
Delta College (U)
Des Moines Area Community College (U)
Dickinson State University (U)
Dodge City Community College (U)
Drake University (U,G)
Drexel University (U)
East Carolina University (G)
East Central Community College (U)
Eastern Michigan University (U)
Eastern Oklahoma State College (U)
Eastern Oregon University (U)
Eastern West Virginia Community and Technical College (U)
East Los Angeles College (U)
East Tennessee State University (U)
Edgecombe Community College (U)
Edison College (U)
EduKan (U)
Elgin Community College (U)
Elizabeth City State University (U)
Embry-Riddle Aeronautical University (G)
Erie Community College (U)
Everest College (U)
Everett Community College (U)
Fayetteville State University (U)
Feather River College (N,U)
Finger Lakes Community College (U)
Flathead Valley Community College (U)
Fontbonne University (U)
Fort Hays State University (U)
Fullerton College (U)
Gadsden State Community College (U)
Galveston College (U)
Gaston College (U)
George C. Wallace Community College (U)
Georgia Highlands College (U)
Governors State University (U)
Graceland University (U)
Grand View College (U)
Grantham University (U)
Gulf Coast Community College (U)
Harford Community College (U)
Harrisburg Area Community College (U)
Haywood Community College (U)
Henry Ford Community College (U)
Herkimer County Community College (U)
Hillsborough Community College (U)
Hocking College (U)
Holyoke Community College (U)
Honolulu Community College (U)
Hope International University (N,U,G)
Horizon College & Seminary (U)

Houston Community College System (U)
Illinois Eastern Community Colleges, Lincoln Trail College (U)
Illinois Eastern Community Colleges, Olney Central College (U)
Illinois Eastern Community Colleges, Wabash Valley College (U)
Immaculata University (U)
Indiana State University (U)
Indiana Tech (U)
Indiana University of Pennsylvania (U)
Indiana University–Purdue University Fort Wayne (U)
Indiana Wesleyan University (U)
Iona College (U,G)
Itawamba Community College (U)
Ivy Tech Community College–East Central (U)
Ivy Tech Community College–North Central (U)
Ivy Tech Community College–Northwest (U)
Ivy Tech Community College–Wabash Valley (U)
Ivy Tech Community College–Whitewater (U)
Jacksonville State University (U)
James Madison University (U)
James Sprunt Community College (U)
Jefferson College of Health Sciences (U)
Jefferson Community and Technical College (U)
Jefferson Community College (U)
John A. Logan College (U)
John Jay College of Criminal Justice of the City University of New York (U)
John Tyler Community College (U)
John Wood Community College (U)
Jones County Junior College (U)
J. Sargeant Reynolds Community College (U)
Judson College (U)
Kansas City Kansas Community College (U)
Kansas State University (U,G)
Kaskaskia College (U)
Kean University (U)
Labette Community College (U)
Lake Superior College (U)
Lamar State College–Port Arthur (U)
Lansing Community College (U)
Lehigh Carbon Community College (U)
LeTourneau University (U)
Lewis and Clark Community College (U)
Lewis-Clark State College (U)
Liberty University (U,G)
Limestone College (U)
Long Beach City College (U)
Longwood University (U)
Los Angeles Harbor College (U)
Louisiana State University and Agricultural and Mechanical College (U)
Lurleen B. Wallace Community College (U)
Malone College (U)
Mansfield University of Pennsylvania (U)
Marshall University (U)
Massasoit Community College (U)
Memorial University of Newfoundland (U)
Mercy College (G)
Mesa State College (U)
Metropolitan State University (U)
Miami Dade College (U)
Miami University–Middletown Campus (U)
Middlesex Community College (U)
Midstate College (U)
Midway College (U)

Millersville University of Pennsylvania (U)
Minnesota State University Moorhead (U)
Minot State University (U)
Missouri Southern State University (U)
Missouri State University (G)
Moberly Area Community College (U)
Modesto Junior College (U)
Monroe Community College (U)
Montana State University–Billings (U)
Montana Tech of The University of Montana (U)
Monterey Peninsula College (U)
Montgomery Community College (U)
Montgomery County Community College (U)
Mountain Empire Community College (U)
Mount Allison University (U)
Mt. San Antonio College (U)
Mount Wachusett Community College (U)
Myers University (U)
Naropa University (N,U)
Nassau Community College (U)
National University (U)
Neumann College (U)
New England Institute of Technology (U)
North Arkansas College (U)
North Carolina State University (U)
North Dakota State College of Science (U)
North Dakota State University (G)
Northeast Alabama Community College (U)
Northeastern Illinois University (U)
Northeast State Technical Community College (U)
North Idaho College (U)
North Seattle Community College (U)
NorthWest Arkansas Community College (U)
Northwestern College (U)
Northwestern Connecticut Community College (U)
Northwest Mississippi Community College (U)
Northwest Missouri State University (U)
Oakton Community College (U)
Oklahoma State University (U)
Orangeburg-Calhoun Technical College (U)
Oregon Institute of Technology (U)
Oregon State University (N,U)
Ouachita Technical College (U)
Owensboro Community and Technical College (U)
Pace University (U)
Pacific Graduate School of Psychology (G)
Palomar College (U)
Pamlico Community College (U)
Parkland College (U)
Park University (U)
Pasco-Hernando Community College (U)
Passaic County Community College (U)
Patrick Henry Community College (U)
Peninsula College (U)
Piedmont Technical College (U)
Pittsburg State University (U,G)
Portland Community College (U)
Portland State University (U)
Prescott College (U,G)
Presentation College (U)
Pulaski Technical College (U)
Queen's University at Kingston (U)
Randolph Community College (U)
Rappahannock Community College (U)
Reedley College (N,U)
Regent University (U,G)
Rend Lake College (U)

The Richard Stockton College of New Jersey (U)
Richland Community College (U)
Riverside Community College District (U)
Rochester Institute of Technology (U)
Rockland Community College (U)
Roosevelt University (U)
Rose State College (U)
Ryerson University (U)
St. Clair County Community College (U)
St. Cloud State University (U)
St. Petersburg College (U)
Sam Houston State University (U)
Sauk Valley Community College (U)
Saybrook Graduate School and Research Center (N,G)
Schenectady County Community College (U)
Schiller International University (U)
Schoolcraft College (U)
Seminole Community College (U)
Shippensburg University of Pennsylvania (U,G)
Sinclair Community College (U)
Snead State Community College (U)
Southeast Arkansas College (U)
Southeastern Community College (U)
Southeastern Illinois College (U)
Southern New Hampshire University (U)
South Piedmont Community College (U)
Southwestern Baptist Theological Seminary (G)
Southwest Georgia Technical College (U)
Southwest Wisconsin Technical College (U)
Spartanburg Community College (U)
Spring Arbor University (U)
State University of New York at New Paltz (U)
State University of New York at Oswego (U,G)
State University of New York College at Potsdam (U)
Strayer University (U)
Syracuse University (G)
Tacoma Community College (U)
Taylor University (U)
Texas A&M University–Commerce (U,G)
Texas A&M University–Texarkana (U)
Texas State University-San Marcos (U)
Texas Tech University (U)
Texas Woman's University (U)
Three Rivers Community College (U)
Tompkins Cortland Community College (U)
Treasure Valley Community College (U)
Triton College (U)
Tunxis Community College (U)
Tyler Junior College (U)
Union University (U)
The University of Alabama (U)
University of Alaska Fairbanks (U,G)
The University of Arizona (U)
University of Bridgeport (U)
The University of British Columbia (U)
University of California, Los Angeles (G)
University of Central Arkansas (U)
University of Central Oklahoma (U)
University of Cincinnati (U)
University of Cincinnati Raymond Walters College (U)
University of Colorado at Colorado Springs (U)
University of Colorado at Denver and Health Sciences Center (U)

University of Great Falls (U,G)
University of Hawaii–West Oahu (U)
University of Houston–Victoria (U,G)
University of Idaho (U,G)
University of Illinois (U)
University of Illinois at Springfield (U)
University of La Verne (G)
University of Maine (U)
The University of Maine at Augusta (U)
University of Maine at Fort Kent (U)
University of Management and Technology (U,G)
University of Maryland University College (U)
University of Massachusetts Boston (U)
University of Minnesota, Crookston (U)
University of Minnesota, Duluth (U)
University of Minnesota, Morris (U)
University of Minnesota, Twin Cities Campus (U)
University of Missouri–Columbia (U)
The University of Montana (U)
The University of Montana–Western (U)
University of Nebraska at Omaha (U)
University of Nebraska–Lincoln (U)
University of New Orleans (U,G)
The University of North Carolina at Chapel Hill (U)
The University of North Carolina at Greensboro (U)
University of North Dakota (U)
University of Northern Iowa (U)
University of Saskatchewan (U)
The University of South Dakota (U)
University of Southern Indiana (U)
University of South Florida (G)
The University of Tennessee (U)
The University of Texas at San Antonio (U,G)
The University of Texas at Tyler (U)
The University of Texas System (U)
The University of Toledo (U)
University of Vermont (N,U)
University of Washington (U)
University of Waterloo (U)
University of Wisconsin Colleges (U)
University of Wisconsin–Platteville (G)
Upper Iowa University (N,U)
Utah State University (U,G)
Utah Valley State College (U)
Utica College (U)
Valley City State University (U)
Vance-Granville Community College (U)
Vincennes University (U)
Virginia Highlands Community College (U)
Wake Technical Community College (U)
Walden University (G)
Washburn University (U)
Washtenaw Community College (U)
Waubonsee Community College (U)
Wayland Baptist University (U)
Weber State University (U)
Westchester Community College (U)
Western Piedmont Community College (U)
Western Wyoming Community College (U)
West Los Angeles College (U)
West Valley College (U)
West Virginia University at Parkersburg (U)
Wharton County Junior College (U)
Wichita State University (U)
Wilfrid Laurier University (U)
Wilkes Community College (U)
Williston State College (U)

Wisconsin Indianhead Technical College (N,U)
York County Community College (U)
York Technical College (U)
Yuba College (U)

PSYCHOLOGY RELATED

Alvin Community College (U)
Ashford University (U)
Athabasca University (U)
Atlantic University (N,G)
Bellevue Community College (U)
Black Hills State University (U)
Brenau University (U)
Bristol Community College (U)
Buena Vista University (U)
California State University, Dominguez Hills (N)
California State University, San Marcos (N)
Cape Cod Community College (U)
Cedar Crest College (U)
Central Michigan University (U)
Central Texas College (U)
Chadron State College (U,G)
Charter Oak State College (U)
Chemeketa Community College (U)
Clark State Community College (U)
Community College of Beaver County (U)
Corban College (U)
Dallas Baptist University (U)
Delaware County Community College (U)
Des Moines Area Community College (U)
Drake University (U)
East Carolina University (G)
Eastern Michigan University (G)
Eastern Washington University (U)
Everett Community College (U)
Feather River College (U)
Florida Institute of Technology (N)
Gaston College (U)
Granite State College (U)
Grantham University (U)
Illinois Eastern Community Colleges, Lincoln Trail College (U)
Itawamba Community College (U)
Jacksonville State University (U)
Jamestown Community College (N)
John A. Logan College (U)
Lehigh Carbon Community College (U)
Limestone College (U)
Louisiana State University and Agricultural and Mechanical College (U)
Massasoit Community College (U)
Master's College and Seminary (U)
Mercy College (G)
Middlesex Community College (U)
Midwestern State University (U)
Modesto Junior College (U)
Mount Saint Vincent University (U)
Naropa University (N,G)
Nassau Community College (U)
North Dakota State College of Science (U)
NorthWest Arkansas Community College (U)
Owensboro Community and Technical College (U)
Palomar College (U)
Portland Community College (N)
Rose State College (U)
St. Cloud State University (G)
Saybrook Graduate School and Research Center (N,G)

Seminole Community College (U)
South Piedmont Community College (U)
Southwestern Baptist Theological Seminary (G)
State University of New York at Plattsburgh (U)
Taylor University (U)
Texas State University-San Marcos (U)
Tompkins Cortland Community College (U)
Treasure Valley Community College (U)
University of Alaska Fairbanks (G)
The University of Arizona (U)
University of Central Oklahoma (U)
University of Hawaii–West Oahu (U)
University of Idaho (G)
University of Maryland Eastern Shore (G)
University of Missouri–Columbia (U)
University of Nebraska–Lincoln (G)
The University of North Carolina at Charlotte (U)
University of North Texas (U)
University of Vermont (U)
University of Waterloo (U)
University of Wisconsin–Whitewater (G)
Upper Iowa University (U)
Wilfrid Laurier University (U)
Wilkes Community College (U)
York University (U)
Yuba College (U)

PSYCHOMETRICS AND QUANTITATIVE PSYCHOLOGY

University of Alaska Fairbanks (U)
University of New Orleans (U,G)

PSYCHOPHARMACOLOGY

Jacksonville State University (U,G)

PUBLIC ADMINISTRATION

American Public University System (U)
Andrew Jackson University (G)
Athabasca University (N,U,G)
Austin Peay State University (U)
Brenau University (U)
California State University, San Bernardino (G)
California University of Pennsylvania (G)
Central Michigan University (U,G)
Charter Oak State College (U)
Cleveland State University (U,G)
College of The Albemarle (N)
DeVry University Online (G)
Drake University (G)
Duquesne University (G)
Elizabeth City State University (U)
Feather River College (N)
Florida State University (U)
Hamline University (N)
Indiana State University (G)
Jacksonville State University (U,G)
James Madison University (N)
John Jay College of Criminal Justice of the City University of New York (U,G)
Kent State University (G)
Metropolitan State University (U,G)
Midwestern State University (U)
Mississippi State University (G)
Myers University (U)
National University (U,G)

Pace University (G)
Park University (G)
Regent University (G)
Regis University (U,G)
Roger Williams University (U)
Ryerson University (U)
Saint Joseph's College of Maine (G)
University of Central Florida (G)
University of Colorado at Colorado Springs (G)
University of Colorado at Denver and Health Sciences Center (G)
University of Delaware (G)
The University of Findlay (G)
University of Hawaii–West Oahu (U)
University of Illinois (N,G)
University of Illinois at Springfield (G)
University of La Verne (G)
University of Maine (U)
University of Maine at Fort Kent (U)
University of Management and Technology (U)
University of Maryland University College (G)
The University of Montana (U,G)
University of Nebraska at Omaha (G)
University of New Orleans (U,G)
University of North Dakota (G)
University of North Texas (G)
University of South Carolina Sumter (U)
University of South Florida (G)
The University of Texas at Tyler (G)
University of Vermont (U,G)
University of Wyoming (G)
Upper Iowa University (N,U)
Virginia Polytechnic Institute and State University (G)
Walden University (G)
Washburn University (U)
Wayland Baptist University (G)
York University (U)
Youngstown State University (G)

PUBLIC ADMINISTRATION AND SOCIAL SERVICE PROFESSIONS RELATED

American Public University System (G)
Athabasca University (N,G)
Brenau University (U)
Cardinal Stritch University (U)
Central Michigan University (U,G)
Charter Oak State College (U)
Cleveland State University (U,G)
College of The Albemarle (N)
Drake University (G)
George Mason University (G)
Hamline University (N,G)
Indiana State University (G)
Jacksonville State University (U,G)
John Jay College of Criminal Justice of the City University of New York (U)
Kent State University (G)
Mercy College (U)
Park University (G)
Regis University (G)
Roger Williams University (U)
Ryerson University (U)
Saybrook Graduate School and Research Center (N,G)
University of Central Florida (G)

University of Colorado at Denver and Health Sciences Center (G)
University of Hawaii–West Oahu (U)
University of Illinois at Chicago (N)
The University of Montana (G)
University of New Orleans (U,G)
The University of North Carolina at Charlotte (N)
The University of Toledo (U)
University of West Florida (G)
Upper Iowa University (U)
Western Michigan University (U)
York University (U)

PUBLIC HEALTH

Arapahoe Community College (U)
Athabasca University (N,U,G)
Bowling Green State University (U)
Cleveland State University (N)
Dallas Baptist University (U)
Drake University (G)
Drexel University (G)
East Tennessee State University (G)
Emory University (G)
Harrisburg Area Community College (U)
James Madison University (N)
Jefferson College of Health Sciences (U)
Kent State University (G)
Medical College of Wisconsin (G)
Mercy College (U)
Middlesex Community College (U)
Minnesota State University Moorhead (U)
Montana Tech of The University of Montana (G)
New Jersey City University (U,G)
Oregon State University (G)
Radford University (N)
Seminole Community College (U)
University of California, Davis (U)
University of Illinois (N)
University of Illinois at Chicago (N,G)
University of Minnesota, Twin Cities Campus (U,G)
The University of Montana (U)
The University of North Carolina at Greensboro (U)
University of North Florida (U)
University of South Carolina Sumter (U)
University of Southern Mississippi (G)
University of South Florida (G)
Virginia Polytechnic Institute and State University (N)
Walden University (G)
Youngstown State University (G)

PUBLIC POLICY ANALYSIS

American Public University System (U)
Athabasca University (N,U,G)
Central Michigan University (U,G)
Duquesne University (G)
Elizabeth City State University (U)
Patrick Henry College (U)
Regent University (N,G)
University of Colorado at Denver and Health Sciences Center (G)
University of Denver (U)
University of Maine at Fort Kent (U)
The University of Montana (G)
University of South Florida (G)

PUBLIC RELATIONS, ADVERTISING, AND APPLIED COMMUNICATION RELATED

Arapahoe Community College (U)
Athabasca University (N,U,G)
Berkeley College (U)
Berkeley College-New York City Campus (U)
Berkeley College-Westchester Campus (U)
Bowling Green State University (U)
Brenau University (U)
Central Michigan University (G)
Columbus State Community College (U)
Delaware County Community College (U)
Drake University (U,G)
Edison State Community College (G)
Iona College (G)
James Madison University (N)
Judson College (U)
Lamar State College–Port Arthur (N)
Linn-Benton Community College (U)
Maryville University of Saint Louis (N)
Middlesex Community College (U)
Monroe Community College (U)
Montana State University–Billings (U,G)
Mount Saint Vincent University (U)
Murray State University (U)
Myers University (U)
Northwestern Oklahoma State University (U)
Ryerson University (U)
Schoolcraft College (U)
State University of New York at New Paltz (U)
State University of New York at Oswego (U)
Taylor University (N)
The University of Alabama (U)
University of Alaska Fairbanks (U)
University of Minnesota, Twin Cities Campus (U)
University of Missouri–Columbia (G)
The University of South Dakota (U)
University of Southern Indiana (U)
University of Wisconsin–Platteville (U)
Upper Iowa University (U)
Utah Valley State College (U)
Webster University (U)
West Shore Community College (U)
Wilkes Community College (U)
Wisconsin Indianhead Technical College (N,U)
Youngstown State University (N)

PUBLISHING

Arapahoe Community College (U)
Clemson University (N)
Hagerstown Community College (N)
Maryville University of Saint Louis (N)
Middlesex Community College (U)
North Idaho College (N)
Pace University (G)
Ryerson University (U)
University of Cincinnati (N)
University of Minnesota, Twin Cities Campus (U)
University of South Florida (N)

QUALITY CONTROL AND SAFETY TECHNOLOGIES

California State University, Dominguez Hills (N)

Columbus State Community College (U)
East Carolina University (G)
Eastern Michigan University (G)
Hopkinsville Community College (U)
Ivy Tech Community College–Kokomo (U)
Jacksonville State University (U,G)
James Madison University (N)
Kansas State University (G)
Kettering University (N)
Longwood University (N)
Mitchell Technical Institute (N)
Murray State University (G)
Southern Illinois University Carbondale (U)
University of South Florida (G)
The University of Texas at Tyler (G)
University of Wisconsin–Platteville (N)
Western Piedmont Community College (U)
West Virginia University at Parkersburg (N)

RADIO, TELEVISION, AND DIGITAL COMMUNICATION

Athabasca University (N)
Cerritos College (U)
Eastern Kentucky University (U)
Feather River College (N)
James Madison University (N)
Long Beach City College (U)
Middlesex Community College (U)
Middle Tennessee State University (U)
Murray State University (U)
Oakton Community College (U)
Palomar College (U)
Saddleback College (U)
Texas A&M University–Commerce (G)
University of Alaska Fairbanks (U)
University of Missouri–Columbia (G)
University of Nebraska–Lincoln (U)
University of Southern Indiana (U)

REAL ESTATE

Arapahoe Community College (U)
Bainbridge College (N)
Ball State University (U)
Blackhawk Technical College (N)
Cabrillo College (U)
Central New Mexico Community College (U)
Central Texas College (U)
Chadron State College (U)
Clarion University of Pennsylvania (N,U)
Darton College (N)
De Anza College (U)
Feather River College (N)
Flathead Valley Community College (U)
Galveston College (N)
Harford Community College (N)
Houston Community College System (U)
James Madison University (N)
Jamestown Community College (N)
Long Beach City College (U)
Madison Area Technical College (U)
Middle Tennessee State University (N)
Mt. San Antonio College (U)
Naugatuck Valley Community College (N)
Orange Coast College (U)
Palomar College (U)
Peirce College (U)
Portland Community College (U)
Quinebaug Valley Community College (N)
Rappahannock Community College (N)
Rend Lake College (U)

Riverside Community College District (U)
Saddleback College (U)
Southeast Arkansas College (U)
Southern Illinois University Carbondale (U)
Southwest Georgia Technical College (N)
Treasure Valley Community College (N,U)
Triton College (N,U)
University of Alaska Fairbanks (U)
University of Idaho (U)
University of Maine at Fort Kent (U)
University of Nebraska–Lincoln (U)
University of New Orleans (U,G)
University of North Dakota (N)
University of Wyoming (U)
Virginia Polytechnic Institute and State University (N)
Wenatchee Valley College (N)
West Hills Community College (N)
West Los Angeles College (U)

REHABILITATION AND THERAPEUTIC PROFESSIONS

Arkansas Tech University (U)
Brenau University (G)
Clarion University of Pennsylvania (G)
Drake University (G)
East Carolina University (G)
Jefferson College of Health Sciences (U)
Montana State University–Billings (G)
Saybrook Graduate School and Research Center (G)
Southern Illinois University Carbondale (G)
Texas Woman's University (G)
The University of British Columbia (U,G)
University of Central Arkansas (G)
University of Maryland Eastern Shore (U,G)
University of Minnesota, Twin Cities Campus (U)
University of North Texas (N,U,G)
University of St. Augustine for Health Sciences (G)
Vincennes University (U)
Western Michigan University (U)

RELIGIOUS EDUCATION

Andover Newton Theological School (N,G)
Atlantic School of Theology (N,G)
Baptist Missionary Association Theological Seminary (U,G)
Briercrest Distance Learning (U,G)
Carroll College (U)
The Catholic Distance University (N,U,G)
Covenant Theological Seminary (N,G)
Dallas Baptist University (U,G)
Defiance College (U)
Denver Seminary (G)
Des Moines Area Community College (U)
Eugene Bible College (U)
Global University of the Assemblies of God (N)
Master's College and Seminary (U)
Montgomery Community College (U)
Mount Allison University (U)
Mount Saint Vincent University (U)
Naropa University (N,G)
Newman Theological College (G)
Regent University (N)
Sacred Heart University (U)
Saint Joseph's College of Maine (U)

Southwestern Baptist Theological Seminary (U,G)
Summit Pacific College (N,U)
Taylor University (U)
Temple Baptist Seminary (G)
Wayland Baptist University (U,G)
Webster University (U)
Western Seminary (N,G)

RELIGIOUS STUDIES

Andover Newton Theological School (N,G)
Andrews University (U,G)
Ashford University (U)
Assemblies of God Theological Seminary (G)
Atlantic School of Theology (N,G)
Atlantic University (N,G)
Azusa Pacific University (U)
Bakke Graduate University of Ministry (G)
Baptist Missionary Association Theological Seminary (U,G)
Bergen Community College (U)
Briercrest Distance Learning (N,U,G)
California Institute of Integral Studies (N,G)
California State University, Chico (U)
Campbellsville University (U,G)
The Catholic Distance University (N,U,G)
Central Virginia Community College (U)
Central Wyoming College (U)
Chaminade University of Honolulu (U,G)
Chattanooga State Technical Community College (U)
Chemeketa Community College (U)
Cincinnati Christian University (G)
College of DuPage (U)
College of Mount St. Joseph (U,G)
College of the Southwest (U)
Columbia International University (N,U,G)
Community College of Denver (U)
Concordia College–New York (U)
Corban College (U)
Covenant Theological Seminary (N,G)
Dallas Baptist University (U,G)
Delaware County Community College (U)
Denver Seminary (G)
Des Moines Area Community College (U)
Earlham School of Religion (G)
East Tennessee State University (G)
Erie Community College (U)
Eugene Bible College (U)
Fontbonne University (U)
Global University of the Assemblies of God (N)
Grand Rapids Theological Seminary of Cornerstone University (N,G)
Hartford Seminary (N,G)
Haywood Community College (U)
Hebrew College (N,U,G)
Henry Ford Community College (U)
Hope International University (N,U,G)
Immaculata University (U)
Itawamba Community College (U)
James Sprunt Community College (U)
John A. Logan College (U)
John Tyler Community College (U)
John Wood Community College (U)
Liberty University (U,G)
Life Pacific College (N)
Limestone College (U)
Lincoln Christian College (N,U,G)
Maranatha Baptist Bible College (G)
Master's College and Seminary (U)

McMurry University (U)
Memorial University of Newfoundland (U)
Mesa Community College (U)
Miami Dade College (U)
Midway College (U)
Missouri State University (U,G)
Mountain Empire Community College (U)
Mount Allison University (U)
Mt. San Antonio College (U)
Naropa University (N,U)
Neumann College (U)
Northwestern College (U)
Pacific Union College (U)
Pasco-Hernando Community College (U)
Patrick Henry Community College (U)
Providence College and Theological Seminary
 (G)
Pulaski Technical College (U)
Queen's University at Kingston (U)
Rappahannock Community College (U)
Regent University (N)
Regions University (N,U,G)
Regis University (U)
Rend Lake College (U)
Riverside Community College District (U)
Sacred Heart University (U)
Saint Joseph's College of Maine (N)
Shasta Bible College (U)
Snead State Community College (U)
Southeastern Illinois College (U)
Southern Illinois University Carbondale (U)
Southwestern Baptist Theological Seminary
 (U,G)
Summit Pacific College (N,U)
Taylor University (N,U)
Temple Baptist Seminary (N)
Trinity Episcopal School for Ministry (N,G)
Union University (N,U,G)
The University of Alabama (U)
University of Bridgeport (U)
The University of Findlay (U)
University of Missouri–Columbia (U)
The University of North Carolina at Chapel
 Hill (U)
University of North Dakota (U)
University of Northern Iowa (U,G)
University of Saskatchewan (U)
The University of Tennessee (U)
The University of Toledo (U)
University of Vermont (U,G)
University of Washington (U)
University of Waterloo (U)
University of West Florida (U)
Virginia Polytechnic Institute and State
 University (U)
Wake Technical Community College (U)
Wayland Baptist University (U,G)
Western Michigan University (U)
Western Seminary (N,G)
Wilfrid Laurier University (U)
Wilkes Community College (U)
Wright State University (U)
York University (U)

RELIGIOUS/SACRED MUSIC

Atlantic School of Theology (G)
Barclay College (U)
Eugene Bible College (U)
Global University of the Assemblies of God
 (N)
Naropa University (N)

Northwestern College (U)
Providence College and Theological Seminary
 (N)
Sioux Falls Seminary (G)
Southwestern Baptist Theological Seminary
 (G)
Taylor University (U)

SALES, MERCHANDISING, AND RELATED MARKETING OPERATIONS (GENERAL)

Adams State College (N)
Arapahoe Community College (U)
Athabasca University (N,U,G)
Berkeley College (U)
Berkeley College-New York City Campus (U)
Berkeley College-Westchester Campus (U)
Bismarck State College (U)
Brenau University (G)
Bristol Community College (N)
California State University, Dominguez Hills
 (N)
California State University, Monterey Bay (U)
Capella University (G)
Central Michigan University (G)
Central New Mexico Community College (U)
Cerro Coso Community College (U)
Chadron State College (U,G)
Chemeketa Community College (U)
College of DuPage (U)
Colorado Technical University (U)
Columbia College (U)
Columbus State Community College (U)
Community College of Denver (U)
Dallas Baptist University (U,G)
Delaware County Community College (U)
Drexel University (U,G)
Eastern Michigan University (U,G)
East Tennessee State University (N,U)
Elizabeth City State University (U)
Erie Community College (U)
Feather River College (N)
Fort Hays State University (N)
Grantham University (U)
Ivy Tech Community College–North Central
 (U)
Jacksonville State University (U,G)
James Madison University (N)
Jones College (U)
Kansas City Kansas Community College (U)
Lakeland College (U)
Lamar State College–Port Arthur (N)
Lansing Community College (U)
Limestone College (U)
Madison Area Technical College (U)
Massasoit Community College (N)
Middle Tennessee State University (U)
Oakton Community College (U)
Oklahoma State University (U)
Oregon State University (U)
Palomar College (U)
Park University (U)
Peirce College (U)
Quinebaug Valley Community College (N)
Quinnipiac University (G)
Reedley College (N,U)
Regis University (U)
Rend Lake College (N)
Ryerson University (U)
Saddleback College (U)
Southern Illinois University Carbondale (U)

Spartanburg Community College (U)
Syracuse University (G)
Taylor University (N)
Texas A&M University–Texarkana (U)
University of Bridgeport (U)
University of Colorado at Denver and Health
 Sciences Center (G)
University of Dallas (G)
The University of Findlay (G)
University of Maryland University College
 (U,G)
University of Southern Indiana (N)
University of Wisconsin–La Crosse (G)
University of Wisconsin–Parkside (G)
Wake Technical Community College (N)

SALES, MERCHANDISING, AND RELATED MARKETING OPERATIONS (SPECIALIZED)

Adams State College (N)
The American College (U)
Andrew Jackson University (G)
Arapahoe Community College (U)
Athabasca University (N,G)
Bellevue University (U,G)
Berkeley College (U)
Berkeley College-New York City Campus (U)
Berkeley College-Westchester Campus (U)
Blackhawk Technical College (N)
Brenau University (U,G)
Bridgewater State College (N)
Bristol Community College (N)
Caldwell Community College and Technical
 Institute (N)
California State University, Dominguez Hills
 (N)
Central Texas College (U)
Chadron State College (U,G)
Chemeketa Community College (U)
Cleveland State University (N)
College of The Albemarle (N)
Colorado State University-Pueblo (N)
Darton College (N)
Delaware County Community College (U)
Des Moines Area Community College (U)
Drexel University (G)
East Carolina University (U)
Eastern Michigan University (U)
Edgecombe Community College (N)
Feather River College (N)
Finger Lakes Community College (U)
Herkimer County Community College (U)
Jacksonville State University (U,G)
James Madison University (N)
Lamar State College–Port Arthur (N)
Madison Area Technical College (U)
Manatee Community College (U)
Massasoit Community College (N,U)
Mercy College (G)
Middle Tennessee State University (N)
Missouri State University (G)
Mt. San Antonio College (U)
Myers University (U)
Naugatuck Valley Community College (U)
Odessa College (N)
Orange Coast College (U)
Oregon State University (N)
Pasco-Hernando Community College (N)
Radford University (N)
Saddleback College (U)
Saint Joseph's College of Maine (G)

Schiller International University (G)
State University of New York at Plattsburgh (U)
State University of New York College at Potsdam (N)
Strayer University (U)
Taylor University (N)
Texas Tech University (U)
Thunderbird School of Global Management (G)
The University of Alabama (U)
University of Colorado at Denver and Health Sciences Center (G)
University of Dallas (G)
University of Michigan–Flint (N)
The University of North Carolina at Charlotte (N)
University of North Texas (U,G)
The University of Texas at San Antonio (U)
The University of Texas at Tyler (U)
University of Wisconsin–Platteville (U)
Vance-Granville Community College (N)
Vincennes University (U)
Westchester Community College (U)
Western Michigan University (U)
West Los Angeles College (U)
Wilkes Community College (U)
Wisconsin Indianhead Technical College (N,U)
Youngstown State University (N)

SCHOOL PSYCHOLOGY

Athabasca University (N)
Capella University (G)
Chadron State College (G)
Eastern Michigan University (G)
Eugene Bible College (U)
Indiana State University (G)
Jacksonville State University (U,G)
Lehigh Carbon Community College (U)
Liberty University (G)
Louisiana State University and Agricultural and Mechanical College (U)
Mesa Community College (U)
Texas Woman's University (G)
University of Houston–Victoria (G)
University of Massachusetts Boston (G)
University of Missouri–Columbia (G)
University of North Texas (N)
Utah State University (G)

SCIENCE TECHNOLOGIES RELATED

Athabasca University (N)
Columbus State Community College (U)
Delaware County Community College (U)
Drexel University (G)
Everett Community College (U)
St. John's University (U)
University of Management and Technology (U)
University of Wisconsin–Stout (G)
Virginia Polytechnic Institute and State University (U,G)

SCIENCE, TECHNOLOGY AND SOCIETY

Athabasca University (N)
Delaware County Community College (U)

DePaul University (U)
Erie Community College (U)
Everett Community College (U)
Henry Ford Community College (U)
Ilisagvik College (U)
Iona College (U)
Northwestern Connecticut Community College (U)
Oregon State University (U)
Pace University (U)
Syracuse University (U)
University of Denver (U)
University of Illinois at Urbana–Champaign (G)
University of Management and Technology (U)
The University of Montana (U)
University of the Cumberlands (G)
Western Michigan University (U)

SECURITY AND PROTECTIVE SERVICES RELATED

Arapahoe Community College (U)
Arkansas Tech University (U)
Berkeley College (U)
Berkeley College-New York City Campus (U)
Berkeley College-Westchester Campus (U)
Jacksonville State University (U,G)
John Jay College of Criminal Justice of the City University of New York (U,G)
John Wood Community College (U)
Peirce College (U)
Schoolcraft College (U)
Seminole Community College (N)
University of Connecticut (G)
University of Massachusetts Lowell (U,G)
Webster University (G)

SOCIAL AND PHILOSOPHICAL FOUNDATIONS OF EDUCATION

Arapahoe Community College (U)
Athabasca University (N)
Brenau University (U)
California State University, Monterey Bay (U)
D'Youville College (G)
Longwood University (U)
State University of New York at New Paltz (U)
University of North Texas (G)
University of South Carolina Sumter (U)
University of Southern Mississippi (G)
University of South Florida (G)
The University of Texas System (U,G)

SOCIAL PSYCHOLOGY

The American College (U)
Andrews University (U)
Anne Arundel Community College (U)
Athabasca University (N)
Beaufort County Community College (U)
Bellevue Community College (U)
Bergen Community College (U)
Brookdale Community College (U)
Cape Breton University (U)
Carlow University (U)
Carroll Community College (U)
Cayuga County Community College (U)
College of DuPage (U)

College of Mount St. Joseph (U)
College of the Southwest (U)
Colorado Mountain College District System (U)
Community College of Beaver County (U)
Dallas Baptist University (U)
Danville Community College (U)
De Anza College (U)
Delaware County Community College (U)
Des Moines Area Community College (U)
Eastern Oklahoma State College (U)
Eastern Washington University (U)
Erie Community College (U)
Gaston College (U)
Grand View College (U)
Houston Community College System (U)
Jefferson Community College (U)
John Wood Community College (U)
Kansas State University (U)
Kirkwood Community College (U)
Lansing Community College (U)
Liberty University (U)
Limestone College (U)
Long Beach City College (U)
Mercy College (U)
Middlesex Community College (U)
Missouri Southern State University (U)
Modesto Junior College (U)
Montgomery County Community College (U)
New York Institute of Technology (U)
North Harris Montgomery Community College District (U)
Northwestern Oklahoma State University (U)
Odessa College (U)
Old Dominion University (U)
Palomar College (U)
Parkland College (U)
Park University (U)
Plymouth State University (U)
Queen's University at Kingston (U)
Red Rocks Community College (U)
Regis University (U)
Richland Community College (U)
Rose State College (U)
Saint Joseph's College of Maine (U)
St. Petersburg College (U)
Saybrook Graduate School and Research Center (G)
Sinclair Community College (U)
State University of New York Empire State College (U)
Taylor University (U)
Texas State University-San Marcos (U)
Texas Tech University (U)
Tompkins Cortland Community College (U)
Triton College (U)
Union University (U)
University of Alaska Fairbanks (U)
University of Bridgeport (U)
University of Central Arkansas (U)
University of Colorado at Denver and Health Sciences Center (U)
University of Maine (U)
University of Nebraska at Omaha (U)
University of South Carolina Sumter (U)
University of Washington (U)
University of Waterloo (U)
University of Wyoming (U)
Upper Iowa University (U)
Utah State University (U)
Waubonsee Community College (U)

SOCIAL SCIENCES

Acadia University (U)
Ashford University (U)
Athabasca University (N,U,G)
Bellevue Community College (U)
Bergen Community College (U)
Bismarck State College (U)
Black Hills State University (U)
Bowling Green State University (U)
Brenau University (U)
Broome Community College (U)
Buena Vista University (U)
Butler Community College (U)
Caldwell Community College and Technical
 Institute (U)
California State University, Chico (U)
Cape Cod Community College (U)
Cayuga County Community College (U)
Cedarville University (U)
Central Texas College (U)
Central Wyoming College (U)
Chadron State College (U)
Chemeketa Community College (U)
College of DuPage (U)
College of the Siskiyous (U)
Colorado State University (U)
Community College of Beaver County (U)
Concordia University, St. Paul (N)
Dallas Baptist University (U)
Danville Community College (U)
Delaware County Community College (U)
Des Moines Area Community College (U)
Dickinson State University (U)
D'Youville College (U)
Eastern Michigan University (U)
EduKan (U)
Embry-Riddle Aeronautical University (U)
Everett Community College (U)
Galveston College (U)
Gateway Community College (U)
Granite State College (U)
Gulf Coast Community College (U)
Henry Ford Community College (U)
Hocking College (U)
Illinois Eastern Community Colleges, Olney
 Central College (U)
Indiana Tech (U)
Itawamba Community College (U)
Jacksonville State University (U,G)
James Madison University (N)
Jefferson Community College (U)
John Wood Community College (U)
Jones College (U)
Judson College (U)
Kansas City Kansas Community College (U)
Kansas State University (U)
Lehigh Carbon Community College (U)
Lewis-Clark State College (U)
Liberty University (U)
Long Beach City College (U)
Louisiana State University and Agricultural
 and Mechanical College (U)
Massasoit Community College (N)
Miami Dade College (U)
Middlesex Community College (U)
Middle Tennessee State University (U)
Monroe Community College (U)
Mount Wachusett Community College (U)
Murray State University (U)
North Dakota State College of Science (U)

Northeast State Technical Community College
 (U)
NorthWest Arkansas Community College (U)
Northwest Mississippi Community College
 (U)
Oakton Community College (U)
Oregon Institute of Technology (U)
Ouachita Technical College (U)
Pace University (U)
Palomar College (U)
Peninsula College (U)
Pittsburg State University (U)
Portland Community College (U)
Pulaski Technical College (U)
Regent University (U)
Rend Lake College (U)
Roosevelt University (U)
Rose State College (U)
Ryerson University (U)
St. Clair County Community College (U)
Schoolcraft College (U)
Southeastern Community College (U)
Southern Illinois University Carbondale (U)
Southern New Hampshire University (U)
South Piedmont Community College (U)
Southwestern College (U)
Southwest Wisconsin Technical College (U)
State University of New York at Plattsburgh
 (U)
State University of New York Empire State
 College (G)
Syracuse University (U)
Tacoma Community College (U)
Taylor University (U)
Texas State University-San Marcos (U)
Treasure Valley Community College (U)
Tri-State University (U)
Triton College (U)
Troy University (U)
The University of Alabama (U)
University of Alaska Fairbanks (U)
University of Bridgeport (U)
University of California, Los Angeles (G)
The University of Findlay (U)
University of Great Falls (U)
University of Hawaii–West Oahu (U)
University of Idaho (U)
The University of Maine at Augusta (U)
University of Maryland Eastern Shore (U)
University of Maryland University College
 (U)
University of Massachusetts Boston (U)
University of Massachusetts Dartmouth (U)
University of Nebraska at Omaha (U)
University of New Orleans (U,G)
The University of North Carolina at
 Greensboro (U)
University of North Texas (U,G)
University of St. Francis (U)
University of South Carolina Sumter (U)
University of South Florida (U)
The University of Texas System (U)
The University of Toledo (U)
University of Waterloo (U)
University of Wisconsin Colleges (U)
University of Wisconsin–Stout (G)
University of Wisconsin–Superior (U)
Upper Iowa University (U)
Utah State University (U)
Utah Valley State College (U)
Vincennes University (U)
Viterbo University (U)

Westchester Community College (U)
West Virginia University at Parkersburg (U)
York University (U)

SOCIAL SCIENCES RELATED

Anne Arundel Community College (U)
Ashford University (U)
Athabasca University (N,G)
Bellevue Community College (U)
Berkeley College (U)
Berkeley College-New York City Campus (U)
Berkeley College-Westchester Campus (U)
Bristol Community College (U)
Brookdale Community College (U)
Buena Vista University (U)
Butler Community College (U)
Cayuga County Community College (U)
Central Texas College (U)
Chadron State College (U)
Charter Oak State College (U)
Chemeketa Community College (U)
Cleveland Institute of Electronics (U)
College of DuPage (U)
Columbia College (U)
Columbus State Community College (U)
Community College of Beaver County (U)
Dallas Baptist University (U)
Delaware County Community College (U)
DePaul University (U)
Des Moines Area Community College (U)
Drake University (U)
Erie Community College (U)
Harford Community College (U)
Honolulu Community College (U)
Itawamba Community College (U)
Jones College (U)
J. Sargeant Reynolds Community College (U)
Kansas State University (N,U)
Lehigh Carbon Community College (U)
Louisiana State University and Agricultural
 and Mechanical College (U)
Malone College (U)
Mercy College (G)
Middlesex Community College (U)
Moberly Area Community College (U)
Murray State University (U)
North Arkansas College (U)
NorthWest Arkansas Community College (U)
Oregon State University (U)
Palomar College (U)
Parkland College (U)
Pasco-Hernando Community College (U)
Rockland Community College (U)
Rose State College (U)
Sacred Heart University (U)
Saddleback College (U)
St. Cloud State University (U)
Saybrook Graduate School and Research
 Center (G)
Schoolcraft College (U)
Seminole Community College (U)
Taylor University (U)
Texas State University-San Marcos (U)
The University of Alabama (U)
University of Alaska Fairbanks (U)
University of Denver (U)
University of Hawaii–West Oahu (U)
University of Idaho (U)
University of Massachusetts Lowell (U)
The University of South Dakota (U)
The University of Texas System (U)

University of Waterloo (U)
Upper Iowa University (U)
Utah State University (G)
Utah Valley State College (U)
Vermont Technical College (U)
Washburn University (N)

SOCIAL WORK

Adelphi University (N,G)
Athabasca University (N,G)
Bemidji State University (U)
Boise State University (U)
Bowling Green State University (U)
Bradley University (U)
California State University, San Bernardino (U)
California State University, San Marcos (U)
Campbellsville University (U,G)
Carlow University (U)
Cedarville University (U)
Central Texas College (U)
Chadron State College (U)
Cleveland State University (U,G)
Colorado State University (G)
Columbia College (U)
Concordia College–New York (U)
Connecticut State University System (G)
Darton College (U)
Eastern Kentucky University (U)
Eastern Washington University (N,U,G)
Fayetteville State University (G)
Governors State University (U,G)
Iona College (U)
Itawamba Community College (U)
Jacksonville State University (U,G)
Limestone College (U)
Marshall University (U,G)
Memorial University of Newfoundland (U,G)
Middle Tennessee State University (U)
Missouri State University (U,G)
Monmouth University (G)
Murray State University (U)
Naugatuck Valley Community College (U)
New York Institute of Technology (U)
Northeastern Illinois University (U)
Northwest Mississippi Community College (U)
The Ohio State University (U,G)
Shippensburg University of Pennsylvania (U,G)
Tacoma Community College (U)
Taylor University (U)
Texas A&M University–Commerce (U,G)
Three Rivers Community College (U)
University of Alaska Fairbanks (U)
University of Arkansas (U)
The University of British Columbia (U)
University of Illinois at Chicago (N,G)
University of Maine (G)
University of Michigan–Flint (U)
University of Minnesota, Twin Cities Campus (U)
University of Missouri–Columbia (U)
The University of Montana (U)
University of North Alabama (U)
University of North Dakota (U,G)
University of Northern Iowa (U,G)
University of North Texas (U)
University of South Carolina Sumter (G)
University of Southern Indiana (G)
University of Southern Mississippi (U,G)

The University of Texas at Arlington (U,G)
The University of Toledo (U)
University of Vermont (N,U,G)
University of Waterloo (U)
University of Wyoming (G)
Utah State University (U)
Vincennes University (U)
Wake Technical Community College (U)
Washburn University (U)
Waubonsee Community College (U)
Western Michigan University (U)
West Liberty State College (U)
West Virginia State University (U)
Wilfrid Laurier University (U)
York University (U)

SOCIOLOGY

Acadia University (U)
Adams State College (U)
Alpena Community College (U)
Andrews University (U)
Anne Arundel Community College (U)
Arapahoe Community College (U)
Argosy University, Chicago Campus (U)
Arkansas State University–Beebe (U)
Athabasca University (N,U,G)
Austin Peay State University (U)
Barclay College (U)
Beaufort County Community College (U)
Bellevue Community College (U)
Belmont Technical College (U)
Bemidji State University (U)
Bergen Community College (U)
Berkeley College (U)
Berkeley College-New York City Campus (U)
Berkeley College-Westchester Campus (U)
Bismarck State College (U)
Black Hills State University (U)
Bloomfield College (U)
Boise State University (U)
Bowling Green State University (U)
Bradley University (U)
Brenau University (U)
Bridgewater State College (U)
Bristol Community College (U)
Brookdale Community College (U)
Broome Community College (U)
Buena Vista University (U)
Burlington County College (U)
Butler Community College (U)
Butler County Community College (U)
Cabrillo College (U)
Caldwell Community College and Technical Institute (U)
California Institute of Integral Studies (N,G)
California State University, Chico (U)
California University of Pennsylvania (U)
Campbell University (U)
Cape Cod Community College (U)
Carlow University (U)
Cascadia Community College (U)
Casper College (U)
Cedarville University (U)
Central Carolina Community College (U)
Central New Mexico Community College (U)
Central Texas College (U)
Central Virginia Community College (U)
Central Washington University (U)
Central Wyoming College (U)
Cerritos College (U)
Chadron State College (U)

Chaminade University of Honolulu (U)
Charter Oak State College (U)
Chattanooga State Technical Community College (U)
Chemeketa Community College (U)
Cincinnati State Technical and Community College (U)
Clark State Community College (U)
Clatsop Community College (U)
Clemson University (U)
Clinton Community College (U)
Cloud County Community College (U)
Clovis Community College (U)
College of DuPage (U)
College of San Mateo (U)
College of Southern Maryland (U)
College of The Albemarle (U)
College of the Southwest (U)
Colorado Mountain College District System (U)
Colorado State University (U)
Colorado State University-Pueblo (U)
Columbia College (U)
Columbus State Community College (U)
The Community College of Baltimore County (U)
Community College of Beaver County (U)
Community College of Denver (U)
Concordia University (U)
Concordia University, St. Paul (U,G)
Connecticut State University System (U,G)
County College of Morris (U)
Cumberland County College (U)
Dakota State University (U)
Dallas Baptist University (U)
Danville Community College (U)
Darton College (U)
Dawson Community College (U)
De Anza College (U)
Delaware County Community College (U)
Delta College (U)
Des Moines Area Community College (U)
Dodge City Community College (U)
East Central Community College (U)
Eastern Kentucky University (U)
Eastern Michigan University (U)
Eastern Washington University (U)
Eastern West Virginia Community and Technical College (U)
Eastern Wyoming College (U)
Edgecombe Community College (U)
Edison College (U)
Edison State Community College (U)
EduKan (U)
Elizabeth City State University (U)
Erie Community College (U)
Eugene Bible College (U)
Everest College (U)
Everett Community College (U)
Fairmont State University (U)
Fayetteville State University (U)
Feather River College (U)
Finger Lakes Community College (U)
Flathead Valley Community College (U)
Florida State University (U)
Fort Hays State University (U)
Fullerton College (U)
Gadsden State Community College (U)
Gaston College (U)
Governors State University (U,G)
Graceland University (U)
Grand View College (U)

Grantham University (U)
Gulf Coast Community College (U)
Harrisburg Area Community College (U)
Haywood Community College (U)
Henry Ford Community College (U)
Hillsborough Community College (U)
Holyoke Community College (U)
Houston Community College System (U)
Immaculata University (U)
Indiana State University (U)
Indiana University–Purdue University Fort Wayne (U)
Iowa State University of Science and Technology (U)
Itawamba Community College (U)
Ivy Tech Community College–North Central (U)
Ivy Tech Community College–Northwest (U)
Ivy Tech Community College–Southern Indiana (U)
Jacksonville State University (U,G)
James Madison University (U)
James Sprunt Community College (U)
Jamestown Community College (N)
Jefferson College of Health Sciences (U)
Jefferson Community College (U)
John Tyler Community College (U)
John Wood Community College (U)
Jones College (U)
Jones County Junior College (U)
J. Sargeant Reynolds Community College (U)
Judson College (U)
Kansas City Kansas Community College (U)
Kansas State University (U)
Kean University (U)
Kellogg Community College (U)
Kirkwood Community College (U)
Labette Community College (U)
Lake Superior College (U)
Lansing Community College (U)
Lehigh Carbon Community College (U)
Limestone College (U)
Lock Haven University of Pennsylvania (U)
Long Beach City College (U)
Longwood University (U)
Los Angeles Harbor College (U)
Louisiana State University and Agricultural and Mechanical College (U)
Lurleen B. Wallace Community College (U)
Malone College (U)
Manatee Community College (U)
Mansfield University of Pennsylvania (U)
Marshall University (U,G)
Massasoit Community College (U)
Memorial University of Newfoundland (U)
Mercy College (U)
Mesalands Community College (U)
Middlesex Community College (U)
Middle Tennessee State University (U)
Mid-State Technical College (U)
Midwestern State University (U)
Millersville University of Pennsylvania (U)
Minnesota State University Moorhead (U)
Minot State University (U)
Missouri Southern State University (U)
Missouri State University (U)
Moberly Area Community College (U)
Modesto Junior College (U)
Montana Tech of The University of Montana (U)
Montgomery Community College (U)
Montgomery County Community College (U)

Mountain Empire Community College (U)
Mt. San Antonio College (U)
Mount Wachusett Community College (U)
Murray State University (U)
Myers University (U)
Nassau Community College (U)
New England Institute of Technology (U)
New Mexico State University (U)
New York Institute of Technology (U)
North Dakota State College of Science (U)
Northeast Alabama Community College (U)
Northern State University (U)
Northern Virginia Community College (U)
North Harris Montgomery Community College District (U)
North Idaho College (U)
NorthWest Arkansas Community College (U)
Northwestern Connecticut Community College (U)
Northwestern Oklahoma State University (U)
Northwest Mississippi Community College (U)
Oakton Community College (U)
Odessa College (U)
Oklahoma State University (U)
Old Dominion University (U)
Orangeburg-Calhoun Technical College (U)
Oregon State University (U)
Ouachita Technical College (U)
Pace University (U)
Palomar College (U)
Parkland College (U)
Pasco-Hernando Community College (U)
Passaic County Community College (U)
Patrick Henry Community College (U)
Peninsula College (U)
Piedmont Technical College (U)
Pima Community College (U)
Portland Community College (U)
Portland State University (U)
Queen's University at Kingston (U)
Quinebaug Valley Community College (U)
Randolph Community College (U)
Rappahannock Community College (U)
Red Rocks Community College (U)
Regis University (U)
Rend Lake College (U)
The Richard Stockton College of New Jersey (U)
Richland Community College (U)
Riverside Community College District (U)
Rochester Institute of Technology (U)
Roger Williams University (U)
Roosevelt University (U)
Rose State College (U)
Ryerson University (U)
Saddleback College (U)
St. Clair County Community College (U)
St. Cloud State University (U)
St. John's University (U)
Saint Joseph's College of Maine (U)
St. Louis Community College System (U)
Sam Houston State University (U)
Sampson Community College (U)
Sauk Valley Community College (U)
Schenectady County Community College (U)
Schoolcraft College (U)
Seattle Central Community College (U)
Seminole Community College (U)
Shippensburg University of Pennsylvania (U,G)
Sinclair Community College (U)

Snead State Community College (U)
Southeast Arkansas College (U)
Southeastern Community College (U)
Southern Illinois University Carbondale (U)
South Piedmont Community College (U)
Southwest Georgia Technical College (U)
Southwest Virginia Community College (U)
Southwest Wisconsin Technical College (U)
Spartanburg Community College (U)
Spring Arbor University (U)
State University of New York at New Paltz (U)
State University of New York at Oswego (U)
State University of New York at Plattsburgh (U)
State University of New York College at Potsdam (U)
State University of New York Empire State College (U)
Strayer University (U)
Syracuse University (G)
Tacoma Community College (U)
Taylor University (U)
Texas A&M University–Commerce (U)
Texas A&M University–Texarkana (U)
Texas State University-San Marcos (U)
Texas Tech University (U)
Texas Woman's University (U,G)
Three Rivers Community College (U)
Tompkins Cortland Community College (U)
Treasure Valley Community College (U)
Triton College (U)
Tunxis Community College (U)
Tyler Junior College (U)
University of Alaska Fairbanks (U)
University of Arkansas (U)
University of Bridgeport (U)
University of Central Arkansas (U)
University of Central Florida (U)
University of Central Oklahoma (U,G)
University of Cincinnati Raymond Walters College (U)
University of Colorado at Colorado Springs (U)
University of Colorado at Denver and Health Sciences Center (U)
University of Connecticut (U)
University of Delaware (U)
The University of Findlay (U)
University of Great Falls (U)
University of Hawaii–West Oahu (U)
University of Idaho (U)
University of Illinois (U)
University of Illinois at Springfield (U)
University of Maine (U)
The University of Maine at Augusta (U)
University of Maine at Fort-Kent (U)
University of Maryland Eastern Shore (U)
University of Maryland University College (U)
University of Massachusetts Boston (U,G)
University of Massachusetts Dartmouth (U)
University of Massachusetts Lowell (U)
University of Minnesota, Crookston (U)
University of Minnesota, Duluth (U)
University of Minnesota, Morris (U)
University of Missouri–Columbia (U,G)
The University of Montana (U)
University of Nebraska at Omaha (U)
University of Nebraska–Lincoln (U)
University of New Orleans (U,G)
University of North Alabama (U)

The University of North Carolina at Chapel Hill (U)

The University of North Carolina at Charlotte (U)

The University of North Carolina at Greensboro (U)

University of North Dakota (U)

University of Northern Iowa (U,G)

University of North Texas (U)

University of Oklahoma (U)

University of Saskatchewan (U)

University of Sioux Falls (U)

University of South Carolina Sumter (G)

The University of South Dakota (U)

University of Southern Mississippi (U)

University of South Florida (U)

The University of Tennessee (U)

The University of Texas at Arlington (U)

The University of Texas at Tyler (U)

The University of Texas System (U)

The University of Toledo (U)

University of Vermont (U)

University of Washington (U)

University of Waterloo (U)

University of Wisconsin Colleges (U)

University of Wisconsin–Platteville (G)

Upper Iowa University (N,U)

Utah State University (U)

Utah Valley State College (U)

Vance-Granville Community College (U)

Vincennes University (U)

Virginia Highlands Community College (U)

Virginia Polytechnic Institute and State University (U)

Wake Technical Community College (U)

Washburn University (U)

Washtenaw Community College (U)

Waubonsee Community College (U)

Wayland Baptist University (U)

Westchester Community College (U)

Western Michigan University (U)

Western Piedmont Community College (U)

West Liberty State College (U)

West Shore Community College (U)

West Valley College (U)

West Virginia University at Parkersburg (U)

Wharton County Junior College (U)

Wichita State University (U)

Wilfrid Laurier University (U)

Wilkes Community College (U)

Williston State College (U)

Wisconsin Indianhead Technical College (N,U)

York County Community College (U)

York Technical College (U)

York University (U)

Yuba College (U)

SOIL SCIENCES

Cedarville University (U)

Montana State University (G)

North Carolina State University (U)

North Central State College (U)

Oregon State University (U)

The University of British Columbia (U)

University of Missouri–Columbia (N)

University of Saskatchewan (N)

SOMATIC BODYWORK AND RELATED THERAPEUTIC SERVICES

Saybrook Graduate School and Research Center (G)

SPECIAL EDUCATION

Acadia University (U)

Arapahoe Community College (U)

Athabasca University (G)

Auburn University (G)

Ball State University (G)

Bowling Green State University (G)

Brenau University (U)

Bridgewater State College (U,G)

Buena Vista University (U)

California State University, Monterey Bay (U)

Carlow University (U,G)

Casper College (U)

Cedarville University (U)

Chadron State College (U,G)

Cleveland State University (U,G)

Dakota State University (U)

Drake University (U)

D'Youville College (U,G)

East Carolina University (G)

Eastern Kentucky University (G)

Eastern Michigan University (U)

East Tennessee State University (U)

Elizabeth City State University (U)

Fayetteville State University (U,G)

Florida State University (G)

Fort Hays State University (U,G)

Granite State College (G)

Hamline University (G)

Indiana State University (G)

Jacksonville State University (U,G)

James Madison University (N,G)

John Wood Community College (U)

Kean University (G)

Lehigh Carbon Community College (U)

Lesley University (G)

Liberty University (G)

Millersville University of Pennsylvania (U,G)

Minnesota State University Moorhead (G)

Minot State University (U,G)

Mississippi State University (U)

Missouri State University (U)

Montana State University–Billings (U)

Murray State University (G)

National University (G)

New Jersey City University (G)

North Dakota State University (G)

Northwest Missouri State University (G)

The Ohio State University (N)

Pittsburg State University (G)

Plymouth State University (G)

St. Cloud State University (U)

Seattle Pacific University (G)

South Piedmont Community College (U)

State University of New York at Plattsburgh (G)

Texas A&M University–Commerce (G)

Texas Tech University (G)

The University of Arizona (G)

University of Central Missouri (G)

University of Central Oklahoma (U)

University of Houston–Victoria (U,G)

University of Idaho (U)

University of Maine (U)

University of Maine at Fort Kent (U)

University of Massachusetts Boston (G)

University of Massachusetts Lowell (G)

University of Minnesota, Duluth (U,G)

University of Nebraska at Omaha (G)

University of Nebraska–Lincoln (G)

University of New Orleans (U,G)

The University of North Carolina at Greensboro (G)

University of North Florida (U)

University of North Texas (N,U,G)

University of South Alabama (G)

University of Southern Mississippi (U,G)

University of South Florida (G)

The University of Texas at Tyler (U,G)

University of the Cumberlands (G)

The University of Toledo (G)

University of West Florida (G)

Utah State University (U,G)

Wayne State College (G)

Western Carolina University (U)

SPEECH AND RHETORIC

Arapahoe Community College (U)

Auburn University (U)

Austin Peay State University (U)

Bainbridge College (U)

Bellevue Community College (U)

Bergen Community College (U)

Bowling Green State University (G)

Butler Community College (U)

Central New Mexico Community College (U)

Central Virginia Community College (U)

Cerro Coso Community College (U)

Charter Oak State College (U)

Chattanooga State Technical Community College (U)

Chemeketa Community College (U)

Clackamas Community College (U)

Colorado State University (U)

Columbus State Community College (U)

Community College of Denver (U)

Cumberland County College (U)

Dakota State University (U)

Dallas Baptist University (U)

Darton College (U)

Delta College (U)

Dodge City Community College (U)

East Los Angeles College (U)

EduKan (U)

Gadsden State Community College (U)

Galveston College (U)

Graceland University (U)

Grand View College (U)

Hocking College (U)

Honolulu Community College (U)

James Madison University (N)

John A. Logan College (U)

J. Sargeant Reynolds Community College (U)

Kaskaskia College (U)

Labette Community College (U)

Lansing Community College (U)

Lehigh Carbon Community College (U)

Lewis and Clark Community College (U)

Louisiana State University and Agricultural and Mechanical College (U)

Massasoit Community College (U)

Miami Dade College (U)

Moberly Area Community College (U)

Mountain Empire Community College (U)

New York Institute of Technology (U)

Northeast State Technical Community College (U)
NorthWest Arkansas Community College (U)
Northwestern College (U)
Odessa College (U)
Parkland College (U)
Pasco-Hernando Community College (U)
Piedmont Technical College (U)
Reedley College (N,U)
Rend Lake College (U)
St. Clair County Community College (U)
St. Cloud State University (U)
Schoolcraft College (U)
Shippensburg University of Pennsylvania (U)
Sinclair Community College (U)
Snead State Community College (U)
Southern Polytechnic State University (U)
Syracuse University (U)
Tacoma Community College (U)
Taylor University (U)
Three Rivers Community College (U)
Triton College (U)
University of Central Oklahoma (U)
University of La Verne (G)
University of Minnesota, Crookston (U)
University of Minnesota, Twin Cities Campus (U,G)
The University of Montana (U)
University of New Orleans (U,G)
The University of South Dakota (U,G)
University of Southern Indiana (U)
University of Vermont (G)
University of Washington (U)
University of Wisconsin–Platteville (U)
Valley City State University (U)
Vincennes University (U)
Waubonsee Community College (U)
West Los Angeles College (U)
Wharton County Junior College (U)
Wichita State University (U)

STATISTICS

Anne Arundel Community College (U)
Arkansas State University–Beebe (U)
Ashford University (U)
Athabasca University (N,U)
Belmont Technical College (U)
Berkeley College (U)
Berkeley College-New York City Campus (U)
Berkeley College-Westchester Campus (U)
Brenau University (U)
Bristol Community College (U)
Burlington County College (U)
Campbell University (U)
Cape Breton University (U)
Carroll Community College (U)
Casper College (U)
Cayuga County Community College (U)
Central Texas College (U)
Chadron State College (U,G)
Charter Oak State College (U)
Chattanooga State Technical Community College (U)
Chemeketa Community College (U)
Clatsop Community College (U)
Clemson University (G)
Clinton Community College (U)
College of Southern Maryland (U)
Colorado Mountain College District System (U)
Colorado State University (U,G)

The Community College of Baltimore County (U)
Community College of Beaver County (U)
Connecticut State University System (N,U,G)
County College of Morris (U)
Dallas Baptist University (U,G)
Darton College (U)
De Anza College (U)
Delta College (U)
Des Moines Area Community College (U)
Drexel University (G)
D'Youville College (U,G)
Eastern Michigan University (G)
East Tennessee State University (U)
Edison College (U)
Edison State Community College (U)
Elizabeth City State University (U)
Embry-Riddle Aeronautical University (U)
Erie Community College (U)
Everest College (U)
Franklin University (U)
Galveston College (U)
Graceland University (U)
Gulf Coast Community College (U)
Harrisburg Area Community College (U)
Henry Ford Community College (U)
Illinois Eastern Community Colleges, Wabash Valley College (U)
Immaculata University (G)
Itawamba Community College (U)
Jacksonville State University (U,G)
James Madison University (U)
Jefferson College of Health Sciences (U)
Jefferson Community College (U)
John Wood Community College (U)
Kansas State University (U)
Kaskaskia College (U)
Kirkwood Community College (U)
Lehigh Carbon Community College (U)
Limestone College (U)
Long Beach City College (U)
Louisiana State University and Agricultural and Mechanical College (U)
Madison Area Technical College (U)
Marist College (U)
Marshall University (U)
Massasoit Community College (U)
Memorial University of Newfoundland (U)
Mercy College (U)
Metropolitan State University (U)
Miami Dade College (U)
Miami University–Middletown Campus (U)
Middlesex Community College (U)
Mississippi State University (U)
Montana State University (G)
Montana State University–Billings (U)
Montgomery County Community College (U)
Motlow State Community College (U)
Mount Allison University (U)
Mount Wachusett Community College (U)
Nassau Community College (U)
New England College of Finance (U)
New York Institute of Technology (U)
Northern Virginia Community College (U)
Oakton Community College (U)
Oklahoma State University (U)
Oregon State University (U)
Pace University (U)
Palomar College (U)
Parkland College (U)
Park University (U)
Passaic County Community College (U)

Pennsylvania College of Technology (U)
Philadelphia University (U,G)
Piedmont Technical College (U)
Portland Community College (U)
Portland State University (U)
Presentation College (U)
Queen's University at Kingston (U)
Regis University (U)
Rockland Community College (G)
Roosevelt University (U)
St. Clair County Community College (U)
St. Cloud State University (U,G)
Sam Houston State University (U)
Schiller International University (U,G)
Seattle Central Community College (U)
Seminole Community College (U)
Simmons College (N)
Snead State Community College (U)
Southeast Arkansas College (U)
Southern Polytechnic State University (U)
Southwest Virginia Community College (U)
Southwest Wisconsin Technical College (U)
Spartanburg Community College (U)
State University of New York at Plattsburgh (U)
State University of New York Empire State College (U)
Syracuse University (U)
Texas Tech University (G)
Triton College (U)
University of Alaska Fairbanks (U)
University of Central Florida (U)
University of Colorado at Denver and Health Sciences Center (U)
The University of Findlay (U)
University of Hawaii–West Oahu (U)
University of Idaho (U,G)
University of Illinois at Chicago (G)
The University of Maine at Augusta (U)
University of Management and Technology (U)
University of Maryland Eastern Shore (U)
University of Massachusetts Boston (U,G)
University of Minnesota, Crookston (U)
University of Minnesota, Morris (U)
University of Missouri–Columbia (U)
University of Nebraska–Lincoln (U,G)
University of New Hampshire (G)
University of New Orleans (U,G)
The University of North Carolina at Chapel Hill (U)
The University of North Carolina at Charlotte (G)
The University of North Carolina at Greensboro (U)
The University of South Dakota (U)
University of Southern Mississippi (G)
The University of Texas at Tyler (U)
The University of Texas System (U)
The University of Toledo (U)
University of Vermont (N,U)
University of Washington (U)
University of Waterloo (U)
University of West Florida (U)
University of Wisconsin Colleges (U)
University of Wisconsin–Parkside (G)
University of Wisconsin–Platteville (G)
University of Wyoming (U)
Upper Iowa University (N,U)
Utah State University (U)
Vance-Granville Community College (U)
Waubonsee Community College (U)

Wisconsin Indianhead Technical College
(N,U)
Wright State University (U)
York University (U)

STUDENT COUNSELING AND PERSONNEL SERVICES

Cleveland State University (G)
College of the Siskiyous (U)
Indiana State University (G)
Jacksonville State University (U)
James Madison University (N)
Modesto Junior College (N)
University of Houston–Victoria (G)
University of Massachusetts Boston (G)
The University of North Carolina at
Greensboro (G)

SYSTEMS ENGINEERING

Boston University (G)
Bristol Community College (N)
Capitol College (G)
Colorado Technical University (U,G)
DePaul University (G)
Florida Institute of Technology (G)
Grantham University (G)
James Madison University (N)
Mid-State Technical College (U)
Southern Methodist University (G)
University of Illinois at Urbana–Champaign
(G)
University of New Orleans (U,G)
University of South Florida (G)

SYSTEMS SCIENCE AND THEORY

Capitol College (G)
Florida Institute of Technology (G)
Nova Southeastern University (G)
Syracuse University (U,G)

TAXATION

Athabasca University (N,G)
Brenau University (U,G)
Carroll Community College (U)
DeVry University Online (U,G)
Drexel University (U)
Edison College (U)
Elizabeth City State University (U)
Indiana University System (N)
James Madison University (N)
Jones College (U)
Liberty University (U)
Massasoit Community College (N)
Miami Dade College (U)
Middlesex Community College (U)
Minnesota School of Business–Richfield (U)
Missouri State University (G)
Suffolk University (G)
The University of Maine at Augusta (U)
The University of North Carolina at Charlotte
(N)
University of Toronto (U)
Western Piedmont Community College (U)

TEACHING ASSISTANTS/AIDES

Arapahoe Community College (U)
Casper College (U)

Clemson University (N)
College of the Siskiyous (U)
Community College of Denver (U)
Drexel University (G)
Haywood Community College (U)
Lewis and Clark Community College (U)
Mesalands Community College (U)
Minot State University–Bottineau Campus (U)
South Piedmont Community College (U)
University of Houston–Victoria (G)
University of Michigan–Flint (N)
The University of Texas System (G)
University of Vermont (U)
Vance-Granville Community College (U)

TECHNICAL AND BUSINESS WRITING

Arapahoe Community College (U)
Belmont Technical College (U)
Bismarck State College (U)
Black Hills State University (U)
Boise State University (U)
Bowling Green State University (U,G)
Brenau University (U)
Bridgewater State College (U)
Bristol Community College (U)
Butler County Community College (U)
Caldwell Community College and Technical
Institute (N,U)
Carroll Community College (N,U)
Central Georgia Technical College (U)
Central Texas College (U)
Central Virginia Community College (U)
Chadron State College (U)
Chattanooga State Technical Community
College (U)
Chemeketa Community College (U)
Clackamas Community College (U)
Clark State Community College (U)
Clemson University (N)
College of Southern Maryland (U)
College of The Albemarle (N)
Columbus State Community College (U)
The Community College of Baltimore County
(U)
Community College of Beaver County (U)
Community College of Denver (U)
Darton College (N)
Delta College (U)
Des Moines Area Community College (U)
DeVry University Online (U)
East Carolina University (G)
Eastern Washington University (N)
East Tennessee State University (U)
Edgecombe Community College (U)
Embry-Riddle Aeronautical University (U)
Erie Community College (U)
Feather River College (N)
Grantham University (U)
Harrisburg Area Community College (U)
Haywood Community College (U)
Henry Ford Community College (U)
Hocking College (U)
Indiana State University (U)
James Madison University (U)
Jefferson College of Health Sciences (U)
Jefferson Community and Technical College
(U)
Jefferson Community College (U)
John Jay College of Criminal Justice of the
City University of New York (U)

Jones College (U)
Judson College (U)
Kean University (N)
Lake Superior College (U)
Lamar State College–Port Arthur (N)
Lehigh Carbon Community College (U)
Limestone College (U)
Linn-Benton Community College (U)
Longwood University (N,U)
Louisiana State University and Agricultural
and Mechanical College (U)
Louisiana Tech University (U)
Marlboro College (U)
Mesa Community College (U)
Middlesex Community College (N,U)
Minnesota School of Business–Richfield (U)
Minot State University (U)
Montana Tech of The University of Montana
(U)
Montgomery Community College (U)
Montgomery County Community College (U)
Neumann College (U)
New Jersey Institute of Technology (U,G)
North Arkansas College (U)
North Carolina State University (U)
North Dakota State College of Science (U)
North Harris Montgomery Community
College District (U)
North Idaho College (N)
Northwestern Connecticut Community College
(N)
Oakton Community College (U)
Oklahoma State University (U)
Orangeburg-Calhoun Technical College (U)
Oregon Institute of Technology (U)
Oregon State University (U)
Pasco-Hernando Community College (N)
Portland Community College (U)
Schenectady County Community College (U)
Schoolcraft College (U)
Seminole Community College (U)
Sinclair Community College (U)
Southwest Georgia Technical College (U)
State University of New York College of
Agriculture and Technology at Morrisville
(U)
Syracuse University (U)
Taylor University (N)
Tennessee Technological University (N)
Texas Tech University (U,G)
University of Alaska Fairbanks (U)
University of California, Los Angeles (G)
University of Central Florida (G)
University of Central Oklahoma (U)
University of Cincinnati (N)
University of Colorado at Denver and Health
Sciences Center (U)
University of Delaware (U)
University of Great Falls (U)
University of Illinois (N)
University of Illinois at Chicago (N)
University of Maine (U)
The University of Maine at Augusta (U)
University of Management and Technology
(U)
University of Massachusetts Dartmouth (U,G)
University of Minnesota, Twin Cities Campus
(U)
University of Missouri–Columbia (U)
University of New Orleans (U,G)
University of North Texas (U)
University of Southern Mississippi (U)

The University of Tennessee (U)
The University of Texas at San Antonio (U)
The University of Toledo (U)
University of Washington (U)
University of West Florida (U)
Vance-Granville Community College (N)
Wake Technical Community College (N)
Weber State University (U)
Westchester Community College (U)
West Los Angeles College (U)
West Virginia State University (U)
West Virginia University at Parkersburg (N)
Wilkes Community College (U)
Wright State University (U,G)
York County Community College (U)
Youngstown State University (N)

TECHNOLOGY EDUCATION/ INDUSTRIAL ARTS

Adams State College (G)
Bowling Green State University (U,G)
Bristol Community College (N)
California University of Pennsylvania (U)
Chadron State College (G)
Cleveland State University (N,G)
Duquesne University (G)
East Carolina University (U,G)
Eastern Michigan University (U,G)
Fort Hays State University (U)
Indiana State University (U)
Itawamba Community College (U)
Jacksonville State University (U)
John A. Logan College (U)
Marshall University (G)
Millersville University of Pennsylvania (G)
Minnesota State University Moorhead (U)
Mississippi State University (U)
National University (G)
Nova Southeastern University (G)
Pittsburg State University (U,G)
Quinebaug Valley Community College (N)
Rogers State University (U)
Stevens Institute of Technology (N)
University of Alaska Fairbanks (U)
University of Central Missouri (U,G)
University of Massachusetts Boston (U,G)
University of Missouri–Columbia (G)
The University of Texas at San Antonio (G)
The University of Texas at Tyler (U)
University of West Florida (N)
University of Wisconsin–Stout (G)
Valley City State University (U,G)
Washburn University (U)
West Virginia University (N)
West Virginia University at Parkersburg (U)

TEXTILE SCIENCES AND ENGINEERING

North Carolina State University (U,G)
Southern Polytechnic State University (U)
Texas Tech University (G)

THEOLOGICAL AND MINISTERIAL STUDIES

Andover Newton Theological School (G)
Arlington Baptist College (N,U)
Assemblies of God Theological Seminary (G)
Atlantic School of Theology (N,G)

Azusa Pacific University (G)
Bakke Graduate University of Ministry (G)
Baptist Missionary Association Theological
  Seminary (N,U,G)
Barclay College (U)
Bradley University (U)
Briercrest Distance Learning (U,G)
The Catholic Distance University (N)
Clear Creek Baptist Bible College (U)
College of Emmanuel and St. Chad (G)
Columbia International University (N,U,G)
Corban College (U)
Covenant Theological Seminary (N,G)
Dallas Baptist University (U,G)
Danville Community College (U)
Denver Seminary (G)
Drew University (N,G)
Duquesne University (U)
Earlham School of Religion (G)
Eugene Bible College (U)
Franciscan University of Steubenville (N,U,G)
Global University of the Assemblies of God
  (N)
God's Bible School and College (U)
Grand Rapids Theological Seminary of
  Cornerstone University (N,G)
Horizon College & Seminary (U)
Institute for Christian Studies (G)
Liberty University (G)
Life Pacific College (U)
Lincoln Christian College (N,U,G)
Master's College and Seminary (U)
Naropa University (N)
Newman Theological College (U)
Northwestern College (U)
Oral Roberts University (N)
Providence College and Theological Seminary
  (N,U,G)
Regent University (U,G)
Regions University (N,U,G)
Saybrook Graduate School and Research
  Center (G)
Sioux Falls Seminary (G)
Southwestern Baptist Theological Seminary
  (U,G)
Summit Pacific College (N,U)
Taylor University (N,U)
Trinity Episcopal School for Ministry (N,G)
University of Great Falls (U)
Viterbo University (G)
Western Seminary (N,G)

THEOLOGY AND RELIGIOUS VOCATIONS RELATED

Andover Newton Theological School (G)
Assemblies of God Theological Seminary (G)
Atlantic School of Theology (N,G)
Bakke Graduate University of Ministry (G)
Baptist Missionary Association Theological
  Seminary (N,U,G)
Briercrest Distance Learning (U,G)
The Catholic Distance University (N,U,G)
Clear Creek Baptist Bible College (U)
College of Emmanuel and St. Chad (G)
Columbia International University (N,U,G)
Covenant Theological Seminary (N,G)
Duquesne University (U)
Earlham School of Religion (G)
Global University of the Assemblies of God
  (N)
God's Bible School and College (U)

Grand Rapids Theological Seminary of
  Cornerstone University (N,G)
Itawamba Community College (U)
Liberty University (U,G)
Lincoln Christian College (U)
Master's College and Seminary (U)
Naropa University (N)
Northwestern College (U)
Providence College and Theological Seminary
  (N,U,G)
Regent University (N,U,G)
St. John's University (U)
Saybrook Graduate School and Research
  Center (N)
Sioux Falls Seminary (G)
Southwestern Baptist Theological Seminary
  (G)
Taylor University (U)
Trinity Episcopal School for Ministry (N,G)
University of St. Michael's College (U,G)
Western Seminary (N,G)

TRANSPORTATION AND MATERIALS MOVING RELATED

American Public University System (G)
Clark State Community College (N)
James Madison University (N)
Riverside Community College District (U)

URBAN STUDIES/AFFAIRS

Bakke Graduate University of Ministry (G)
Cleveland State University (U,G)
Florida State University (U)
James Madison University (N)
Saybrook Graduate School and Research
  Center (G)
University of Delaware (U)
University of Massachusetts Boston (N)
University of New Orleans (U,G)
University of Washington (U)
Virginia Polytechnic Institute and State
  University (G)

VEHICLE MAINTENANCE AND REPAIR TECHNOLOGIES

Arapahoe Community College (U)
Bristol Community College (N)
Central Wyoming College (N,U)
Columbus State Community College (U)
Naugatuck Valley Community College (U)

VETERINARY BIOMEDICAL AND CLINICAL SCIENCES

Auburn University (N)
Carroll Community College (N)
Central Wyoming College (N)
Colorado State University (N)
Community College of Denver (U)
Minnesota School of Business–Richfield (U)
Plymouth State University (N)
Virginia Polytechnic Institute and State
  University (G)
West Hills Community College (N)
Yuba College (U)

VISUAL AND PERFORMING ARTS

Academy of Art University (U,G)
Arapahoe Community College (U)

Arkansas State University–Beebe (U)
Atlantic University (N,G)
Bergen Community College (U)
Berklee College of Music (N,U)
California State University, San Bernardino (U)
Central Wyoming College (N)
De Anza College (U)
Delta College (U)
East Los Angeles College (U)
Everett Community College (U)
Itawamba Community College (U)
James Madison University (N)
Jefferson Community and Technical College (U)
John A. Logan College (U)
Manhattan School of Music (N,U,G)
Marshall University (U,G)
Mesa State College (U)
Minneapolis College of Art and Design (N,U,G)
North Harris Montgomery Community College District (U)
Pace University (U)
Prescott College (U,G)
Regent University (N,U,G)
Riverside Community College District (U)
Texas Tech University (G)
Texas Woman's University (U,G)
Tompkins Cortland Community College (U)
University of California, Los Angeles (G)
The University of Findlay (U)
University of Maine (U)
University of Southern Indiana (U)
University of South Florida (G)
West Los Angeles College (U)
Wilfrid Laurier University (U)

VISUAL AND PERFORMING ARTS RELATED

Boise State University (U)
Brenau University (U)
Cabrillo College (U)
Central Virginia Community College (U)
Central Wyoming College (N)
Clarion University of Pennsylvania (U)
Columbus State Community College (U)
Drake University (U)
Goucher College (G)
Hocking College (U)
Itawamba Community College (U)
Ivy Tech Community College–North Central (U)
Minneapolis College of Art and Design (N,U,G)
Naugatuck Valley Community College (U)
North Harris Montgomery Community College District (U)
The Ohio State University (U)
Red Rocks Community College (U)
Syracuse University (U,G)
University of Oregon (U)
The University of Toledo (U)
University of Wisconsin Colleges (U)
York University (U)

WILDLIFE AND WILDLANDS SCIENCE AND MANAGEMENT

Central Wyoming College (N)
Colorado State University (U,G)
Middle Tennessee State University (N)
Oregon State University (U)

Prescott College (U,G)
University of Missouri–Columbia (N)

WOODWORKING

Blackhawk Technical College (N)
Central Wyoming College (N)
Cerritos College (U)
Cleveland Institute of Electronics (N)

WORK AND FAMILY STUDIES

Alpena Community College (N)
California State University, San Marcos (N)
Central Michigan University (U)
Kansas State University (N)
Kean University (N)
Missouri Southern State University (N)
Modesto Junior College (U)
Rend Lake College (U)
Riverside Community College District (U)
University of Minnesota, Twin Cities Campus (U)
University of Missouri–Columbia (N)
Virginia Polytechnic Institute and State University (N)

ZOOLOGY/ANIMAL BIOLOGY

Casper College (U)
Central Wyoming College (U)
Cerritos College (U)
Eastern Wyoming College (U)
Mississippi State University (U)
North Carolina State University (U)
Utah Valley State College (U)
Weber State University

GEOGRAPHICAL LISTING OF DISTANCE LEARNING PROGRAMS

In this index, the page locations of the profiles are printed in regular type and **In-Depth Descriptions** in **bold type.**

U.S. AND U.S. TERRITORIES

College of the Southwest, 119
Mesalands Community College, 183
New Mexico Institute of Mining and
Technology, 198
New Mexico Junior College, 198
New Mexico State University, 198

NEW YORK

Adelphi University, 80
Berkeley College-New York City Campus, 92
Berkeley College-Westchester Campus, 92
Broome Community College, 98
Bryant and Stratton Online, 99
Buffalo State College, State University of
New York, 99
Cayuga County Community College, 107
Clinton Community College, 116
Columbia University, 121
Concordia College–New York, 123
Daemen College, 125
D'Youville College, 133
Erie Community College, 140
Excelsior College, 141, **356**
Finger Lakes Community College, 143
Fulton-Montgomery Community College, 145
Herkimer County Community College, 152
Iona College, 158
Jamestown Community College, 163
Jefferson Community College, 164
John Jay College of Criminal Justice of the
City University of New York, 165
Manhattan School of Music, 179
Marist College, 179
Mercy College, 182
Monroe Community College, 191
Nassau Community College, 195
The New School: A University, 199, **392**
The New School: A University, 199, **394**
The New School: A University, 199, **396**
New York Institute of Technology, 199
Pace University, 210
Rochester Institute of Technology, 222, **420**
Rockland Community College, 223
St. John's University, 226
St. John's University, 226
Schenectady County Community College, 230
Skidmore College, 234, **442**
Skidmore College, 234
State University of New York at New Paltz,
240
State University of New York at Oswego,
240, **450**
State University of New York at Plattsburgh,
240
State University of New York College at
Potsdam, 241
State University of New York College of
Agriculture and Technology at Morrisville,
241
State University of New York Empire State
College, 241, **452**
Stony Brook University, State University of
New York, 242
Syracuse University, 243
Syracuse University, 243
Syracuse University, 243, **458**
Tompkins Cortland Community College, 248
Utica College, 291
Westchester Community College, 296

NORTH CAROLINA

Appalachian State University, 83
Beaufort County Community College, 90
Caldwell Community College and Technical
Institute, 101
Campbell University, 103
Central Carolina Community College, 107
College of The Albemarle, 118
Duke University, 132
East Carolina University, 133, **352**
Edgecombe Community College, 137
Elizabeth City State University, 138
Fayetteville State University, 142
Gaston College, 146
Haywood Community College, 152
James Sprunt Community College, 163
Montgomery Community College, 192
North Carolina State University, 200
Pamlico Community College, 212
Randolph Community College, 219
Sampson Community College, 228
Southeastern Community College, 235
South Piedmont Community College, 237
The University of North Carolina at Chapel
Hill, 272, **496**
The University of North Carolina at Charlotte,
273
The University of North Carolina at
Greensboro, 273
Vance-Granville Community College, 291
Wake Technical Community College, 293
Western Carolina University, 296
Western Piedmont Community College, 297
Wilkes Community College, 301

NORTH DAKOTA

Bismarck State College, 93
Dickinson State University, 130
Mayville State University, 181
Minot State University, 188
Minot State University–Bottineau Campus,
188
North Dakota State College of Science, 200
North Dakota State University, 201
University of North Dakota, 273
Valley City State University, 291
Williston State College, 301

OHIO

Antioch University McGregor, 83
Belmont Technical College, 91
Bowling Green State University, 96
Cedarville University, 107
Cincinnati Christian University, 113
Cincinnati State Technical and Community
College, 113
Clark State Community College, 114
Cleveland Institute of Electronics, 115
Cleveland Institute of Music, 115
Cleveland State University, 116
College of Mount St. Joseph, 117
Columbus State Community College, 122
Defiance College, 128
Edison State Community College, 137
Franciscan University of Steubenville, 144
Franklin University, 145, **360**
God's Bible School and College, 148
Hocking College, 153
Jefferson Community College, 164

Kent State University, 170
Malone College, 178
Miami University–Middletown Campus, 184
Myers University, 194
North Central State College, 200
The Ohio State University, 207
Shawnee State University, 232
Sinclair Community College, 233
Union Institute & University, 251
University of Cincinnati, 256
University of Cincinnati Raymond Walters
College, 256
The University of Findlay, 259
University of Northwestern Ohio, 275
The University of Toledo, 283, **506**
Wright State University, 302
Youngstown State University, 303

OKLAHOMA

Carl Albert State College, 105
Eastern Oklahoma State College, 135
Northwestern Oklahoma State University, 205
Oklahoma State University, 208
Oral Roberts University, 208
Rogers State University, 223
Rose State College, 224
University of Central Oklahoma, 256
University of Oklahoma, 275, **498**
University of Tulsa, 284, **508**

OREGON

Central Oregon Community College, 109
Chemeketa Community College, 112
Clackamas Community College, 113
Clatsop Community College, 114
Concordia University, 123
Corban College, 124, **342**
Eastern Oregon University, 135
Eugene Bible College, 140
Linn-Benton Community College, 175
Northwest Christian College, 204
Oregon Health & Science University, 209
Oregon Institute of Technology, 209
Oregon State University, 209, **404**
Portland Community College, 216
Portland State University, 217
Treasure Valley Community College, 249
University of Oregon, 275
Western Seminary, 298

PENNSYLVANIA

The American College, 81
Bloomsburg University of Pennsylvania, 94
Butler County Community College, 100
California University of Pennsylvania, 103
Carlow University, 105
Cedar Crest College, 107
Chatham University, 111
Clarion University of Pennsylvania, 114
Community College of Beaver County, 122
Delaware County Community College, 128
Drexel University, 132
Drexel University, 131, **350**
Duquesne University, 132
Elizabethtown College, 139
Gratz College, 150
Harrisburg Area Community College, 151
Immaculata University, 156
Indiana University of Pennsylvania, 157

University of Wisconsin–La Crosse, 286
University of Wisconsin–Parkside, 286
University of Wisconsin–Platteville, 287
University of Wisconsin–Platteville, 287
University of Wisconsin–Platteville, 287
University of Wisconsin–Platteville, 287
University of Wisconsin–Platteville, 288
University of Wisconsin–Stout, 288
University of Wisconsin–Superior, 288, **512**
University of Wisconsin–Whitewater, 288
Viterbo University, 293
Wisconsin Indianhead Technical College, 302

WYOMING

Casper College, 106
Central Wyoming College, 110
Eastern Wyoming College, 136
University of Wyoming, 289, **514**
Western Wyoming Community College, 298

Canada

ALBERTA

Athabasca University, 86, **312**
Newman Theological College, 198
University of Lethbridge, 263

BRITISH COLUMBIA

Summit Pacific College, 243
The University of British Columbia, 253

MANITOBA

Providence College and Theological Seminary, 217

NEW BRUNSWICK

Mount Allison University, 193

NEWFOUNDLAND AND LABRADOR

Memorial University of Newfoundland, 182

NOVA SCOTIA

Acadia University, 79
Atlantic School of Theology, 87
Cape Breton University, 104
Mount Saint Vincent University, 193
Nova Scotia Agricultural College, 206

ONTARIO

Brock University, 98
Institute for Christian Studies, 158
Laurentian University, 172
Master's College and Seminary, 181
Queen's University at Kingston, 218
Ryerson University, 224
University of St. Michael's College, 277
University of Toronto, 284
University of Waterloo, 285
University of Windsor, 286
Wilfrid Laurier University, 301
York University, 303

SASKATCHEWAN

Briercrest Distance Learning, 97
College of Emmanuel and St. Chad, 117
Horizon College & Seminary, 154
University of Saskatchewan, 277